The American People

Creating a Nation and a Society

General Editors

Gary B. Nash

University of California, Los Angeles

Julie Roy Jeffrey

Goucher College

John R. Howe
University of Minnesota

Peter J. Frederick
Heritage University

Allen F. Davis
Temple University

Allan M. Winkler
Miami University of Ohio

Charlene Mires
Villanova University

Carla Gardina Pestana
Miami University of Ohio

vango books | Read it. Get it.

New York   San Francisco   Boston   Upper Saddle River
London   Toronto   Sydney   Tokyo   Singapore   Madrid
Mexico City   Munich   Paris   Cape Town   Hong Kong   Montreal

Library of Congress Cataloging-in-Publication Data

The American people: creating a nation and a society / Gary B. Nash . . . [et al.].
    p. cm.
Includes index.
ISBN 978-0-205-64279-3 (combined)—ISBN 978-0-205-64282-3 (v. 1)—ISBN 978-0-205-64283-0 (v. 2),
1. United States—History.   I. Nash, Gary B.
E178.1.A49355 2009
973—dc22   2008026904

Editor-in-Chief: Priscilla McGeehon
Executive Editor: Michael Boezi
Executive Marketing Manager: Sue Westmoreland
Editorial Assistant: Vanessa Gennarelli
Operations Supervisor: Mary Ann Gloriande
Operations Specialist: Maura Zaldivar
Director of Media and Assessment: Brian Hyland
VangoBooks Process Coordinator: Xiaohong Zhu
Cover Preparation: Ron Walko
AV Project Manager: Mirella Signoretto
Senior Managing Editor: Ann Marie McCarthy
Project Manager: Denise Brown
Full-Service Production and Composition: Eric Arima/Elm Street Publishing Services
Manager, Rights and Permissions: Zina Arabia
Manager, Visual Research: Beth Brenzel
Manager, Cover Visual Research and Permissions: Karen Sanatar
Image Permission Coordinator: Cynthia Vincenti
Printer/Binder: Webcrafters, Inc.
Cover Printer: Phoenix Color/Hagerstown

Credits and acknowledgments borrowed from other sources and reproduced, with permission, in this textbook appear on p. C-1.

Cover Photo: Diana Ong B. 1940, Chinese/USA, "America," SuperStock.

Pearson Education Ltd., London
Pearson Education Singapore, Pte. Ltd
Pearson Education, Canada, Ltd
Pearson Education–Japan
Pearson Education Australia PTY, Limited

Pearson Education North Asia, Ltd
Pearson Educación de Mexico, S.A. de C.V.
Pearson Education Malaysia, Pte. Ltd
Pearson Education Upper Saddle River, New Jersey

10 9 8 7 6 5 4 3 2 1

Combined Edition
ISBN 13: 978-0-205-64279-3
ISBN 10:   0-205-64279-9

Examination Copy
ISBN 13: 978-0-205-64280-9
ISBN 10:   0-205-64280-2

CONTENTS

CHAPTER 18
The Rise of Smokestack America 433

CHAPTER 19
Politics and Reform 461

CHAPTER 20
Becoming a World Power 482

PART FIVE A Modernizing People, 1900–1945

CHAPTER 21
The Progressives Confront Industrial Capitalism 505

The Yoruba people of West Africa have an old saying: "However far the stream flows, it never forgets its source." Why, we wonder, do such ancient societies as the Yoruba find history so important, whereas today's American students question its relevance? This book aims to help students appreciate the usefulness of history.

History cannot make good citizens, but without history we cannot understand the choices before us and think wisely about them. Lacking a collective memory of the past, we are unaware of the human condition and the long struggles of men and women everywhere to deal with the problems of their day and to create a better society. Without historical knowledge, we deprive ourselves of knowing about the full range of approaches people have taken to political, economic, social, and cultural life; the efforts Americans have adopted to resolve human problems; and the measures they have taken to confront the obstacles in their way. With knowledge of how events beyond our national boundaries have affected our own history and how our actions have influenced other nations, we are better able to understand and deal with the challenges of contemporary globalism. In a twenty-first century marked by the increasing ethnic and racial diversity of American society, history is of central importance in preparing us to exercise our rights and responsibilities as free people in an increasingly interdependent global world.

History has a deeper, even more fundamental importance: the cultivation of the private person whose self-knowledge and self-respect provide the foundation for a life of dignity and fulfillment. Historical memory is the key to self-identity, to seeing one's place in the long stream of time, in the story of humankind.

When we study our own history, that of the American people, we see a rich and extremely complex human story that stretches back to the last ice age when nomadic hunters arrived in the Americas from Siberia. This country, whose written history began thousands of years later with a convergence of Native Americans, Europeans, and Africans, has always been a nation of diverse peoples—a magnificent mosaic of cultures, religions, and skin shades. This book explores how American society assumed its present shape and developed its present forms of government; how as a nation we have conducted our foreign affairs and managed our economy; how as individuals and in groups we have lived, worked, loved, married, raised families, voted, argued, protested, and struggled to fulfill our dreams and the noble ideals of the American experiment.

While this book covers significant public events such as presidential elections, wars and diplomatic treaties, and economic legislation, we have integrated this familiar national narrative with the smaller stories that describe and give meaning to our shared past. When, for example, national political events are discussed, we analyze their impact on social and economic life at the state and local levels. Wars are described not only as they unfolded on the battlefield and in the salons of diplomats but also on the home front, where they are history's greatest motor of social change. The interaction of ordinary Americans with extraordinary events runs as a theme throughout this book.

Above all, we have tried to show the "humanness" of our history as it is revealed in people's everyday lives. This textbook is marked by the words of ordinary Americans, the authentic human voices of those who participated in, responded to, and helped shape epic events such as war, slavery, industrialization, and reform movements.

Four Recurring Themes

Our primary goal is to provide students with a rich, balanced, and thought-provoking treatment of the American past. By this, we mean a history that treats the lives and experiences of Americans of all national origins and cultural backgrounds, at all class levels of society, and in all regions of the country. It also means a history that seeks connections among the many factors—political, economic, technological, social, religious, intellectual, and biological—that have molded and remolded American society over four centuries. And, finally, it means a history that encourages students to think about how they share an inherited and complex past filled with both notable achievements and thorny problems.

The only history befitting a democratic nation is one that inspires students to initiate a frank and informed dialogue with their past. Historians continually revise their understanding of what happened in the past. Historians reinterpret history because they find new evidence on old topics, add new voices, and are inspired by new sensibilities to ask questions about the past that did not interest earlier historians. Therefore, we hope to promote class discussions and inquiry organized around four recurring themes we see as basic to the American historical experience:

■ The peopling of America: What diverse peoples have come together to form this nation? How have their experiences shaped our larger national history? What tensions did they face in America? What contributions have they made?

- Democratic dreams: How has our political system—and how have the principles that sustain it—developed over time? What changes and continuities have helped shape American values? How has the nation coped with the needs and demands of diverse groups in the quest for a better society?
- Economic, religious, and cultural change: In what ways have economic, technological, and environmental developments affected the American people? How have religious shifts affected the nation? How have reform movements shaped the character of American life?
- America and the world: How have global events and trends shaped the United States? How has America's relationship with other nations and people evolved? What impact has America had on the rest of the world?

In writing a history that revolves around these themes, we have tried to convey two dynamics that operate in all societies. First, as we observe people continuously adjusting to new developments, such as industrialization, urbanization, and internationalism, over which they seemingly have little control, we realize that people are not paralyzed by history but are the fundamental creators of it. People retain the ability, individually and collectively, to shape the world in which they live and thus in considerable degree to control their own lives.

Second, we emphasize the connections that always exist among social, political, economic, and cultural events. Just as our individual lives are never neatly parceled into separate spheres of activity, the life of a society is made up of a complicated and often messy mixture of forces, events, and accidental occurrences. In this text, political, economic, technological, and cultural factors are intertwined like strands in a rope as ordinary and extraordinary American people seek to fulfill their dreams.

Structure of the Book

The chapters of this book are grouped into six parts that relate to major periods in American history. The title of each part suggests a major theme that helps characterize how the American people changed over time: from a colonizing to revolutionary to expanding to industrializing people, and in the last hundred years a modernizing and, most recently, a "resilient" people, adapting to challenging new forces in the world.

The authors of this book are committed to writing a text that helps student learning. They have therefore adopted a structure to enhance students' comprehension of the material covered by each chapter. Each chapter begins with an *outline* that provides an overview of the chapter's organization. Next, a personal story, called "American Stories," recalls the experience

of an ordinary or lesser-known American. The story puts a human face on history, suggesting that our past was shaped by ordinary as well as extraordinary people. Chapter 3, for example, is introduced with an account of the life of Anthony Johnson, who came to Virginia as a slave but who managed to gain his freedom along with his wife, Mary, and in the face of racial prejudice lost his hard-earned land. This brief anecdote introduces the overarching themes and major concepts of the chapter and its organizing structure.

Following the personal American story, a *brief chapter overview* links the story to the text. Each overview includes three recurring ways we seek to help students better understand, remember, and more permanently learn the significant history in the chapter; for example, in Chapter 3:

1. The overview connects Anthony and Mary Johnson's story to the *overarching themes and major concepts* of the chapter, in this case the multiracial peopling and character of American society, how enslaved Africans, Native Americans, and European immigrants interacted and coped with diversity and change, and the violent instability of late-seventeenth-century colonial economic, social, and political life.
2. These themes recall the *four recurring themes* from the Preface, in this case the multiethnic peopling of America, how diverse Americans responded to the stresses of daily life in an effort to achieve their dreams, and how the American people sought to turn their religious and political ideals into reality amidst conflicting pressures and forces.
3. Third, the overview lays out the *organizational structure* of the chapter, in this case the comparisons among six regional areas of early colonization and how each developed a different pattern of life in an effort to implement ideal goals.

We aim to facilitate the learning process for students in other ways as well. Every chapter ends with pedagogical features to reinforce and expand the narrative. A *Timeline* reviews the major events and developments covered in the chapter. A *Conclusion* briefly summarizes the main concepts and developments elaborated in the chapter, emphasizes the larger themes explored in that chapter, and serves as a bridge to the following chapter. *Questions for Review and Reflection* are intended to help students review and reflect on the major themes of the chapter and to connect them to the four major recurring themes and questions.

Features and Changes to This Edition

The new VangoBooks format is a departure from other editions of *The American People*. VangoBooks are innovative course materials designed to better meet the needs of today's students. VangoBooks are portable, present the need-to-know information, at about half the cost of a traditional textbook.

- **The prose has been streamlined to strengthen the narrative.** Though not as short as the Concise Edition of *The American People,* the text in this comprehensive version has been cut by 10 to 15%, eliminating detail which distracted from the main narrative.
- **To improve focus, graphs and maps that did not directly support the narrative have been dropped.** While the number of images has been pared down, the most important maps—with captions that encourage students to think about the significance of the material being presented—have all been retained.
- **The number of major themes explored in the book has been reduced,** so that each chapter can more effectively clarify and develop pertinent themes.
- **The distinctive and popular feature, "Recovering the Past," remains.** These RTPs, as the authors affectionately call them, introduce students to the fascinating variety of evidence—ranging from household inventories, folk tales, and diaries to tombstones, advertising, and popular music—that historians have learned to employ in reconstructing the past. Each RTP gives basic information about the source and its use by historians and then raises questions, under the heading "Reflecting on the Past," for students to consider as they study the example reproduced for their inspection.
- **A strong international context for American history also remains.** Believing that in today's global society it is particularly important for students to think across national boundaries and to understand the ways in which our history intersects with the world, we have provided an international framework. Rather than developing a separate discussion of global events, we have woven an international narrative into our analysis of the American past. We have shown the ways in which the United States has been influenced by events in other parts of the world and the connection between the history of other nations and our own. We have also drawn attention to the aspects of our history that appear to set the nation apart. Tables, charts, and maps with a global focus provide an additional dimension for this international context.

In short, this Vango edition is aimed to make the study of history more meaningful for today's students. We hope students will also appreciate the more convenient size and shape of the Vango edition and its reasonable cost.

Supplements

Instructor Supplements for Qualified College Adopters

All supplements specific to *The American People* will be offered online at Pearson's *Instructor Resource Center* (www.pearsonhighered.com/irc). As part of Pearson Education's commitment to helping you maximize your time at every stage of course preparation, we offer access to our Instructor Resource Center (IRC). Once you have registered for this instructor-only resource, you can log in to premium online products, browse and download book-specific instructor resources, and receive immediate access and instructions to installing course management content to your campus server, all from your book's Web page in our online catalog. If you already have access to CourseCompass or Supplements Central, you can log in to the IRC immediately using your existing login and password. Otherwise, visit the Instructor Resource Center welcome page at www.pearsonhighered.com/irc to register for access today.

VangoBooks.com VangoBooks.com/nash is an open-access Web site that offers educational tools and content specific to *The American People* to help your students more fully understand the course. Sample tests and quizzes with True/False, Multiple Choice, and Fill-in-the-Blank questions are correlated to chapters of the book. Students can even submit their answers for immediate online grading!

Instructor's Manual and Test Bank This guide is based on ideas generated in active learning workshops and is tied closely to the text. In addition to suggestions on how to generate lively class discussion and involve students in active learning, this supplement also offers lists of resources, including films, slides, photo collections, records, and audio. The *Test Bank* contains approximately 2,000 Multiple Choice, True/False, Short Answer, and Essay questions. All questions are keyed to specific pages in the text.

TestGen-EQ Computerized Testing System This flexible, easy-to-master computerized test bank includes all of the items in the printed test bank and allows instructors to select specific questions, edit existing questions, and add their own items to create exams. Tests can be printed in several different formats and can include figures, such as graphs and tables.

Text-specific Transparency Set A set of color transparency acetates showing maps from the text can be used in lectures.

Other supplements offered by Pearson include:

Discovering American History Through Maps and Views Transparency Set Created by Gerald Danzer of the University of Illinois at Chicago, the recipient of the AHA's James Harvey Robinson Prize for his work in the development of map transparencies, this set of 140 full-color slides—now available online—is a unique instructional tool. It contains an introduction to teaching history through maps and a detailed commentary on each transparency. The collection includes cartographic pictorial maps, views, photos, urban plans, building diagrams, and works of art. Available online at www.pearsonhighered.com/irc.

Visual Archives of American History, Updated Edition Available on two CD-ROMs and with added content, this encyclopedic collection of instructor resources contains dozens of narrated vignettes and videos as well as hundreds of photos and illustrations ready for use in PowerPoint presentations, course Web sites, or online courses.

Student Supplements for Qualified College Adopters

VangoBooks.com Visit VangoBooks.com/nash to take your understanding of the material to the next level. The site breaks down the information in the text by topic and by chapter, and features Multiple Choice, True/False, and Short Answer questions to test your knowledge. You can email your quiz results to your instructor or tutor for grading—set up a handy profile to expedite this process, so you don't have to enter the information every time. Still need more help? The site also includes access to other resources such as printable flash cards and supplemental websites.

VangoCard for American History Colorful, affordable, and packed with useful information, VangoCards make studying easier, more efficient, and more enjoyable. Course information is distilled down to the basics, helping students quickly master the fundamentals, review a subject for understanding, or prepare for an exam. Because it's laminated for durability, you can keep the VangoCard for years to come and pull it out for a quick review.

Research Navigator Guide This guidebook includes exercises and tips on how to use the Internet in your study of U.S. history. It also includes an access code for Research Navigator—the easiest way for students to start a research assignment or research paper. Research Navigator is composed of three exclusive databases of credible and reliable source material, including EBSCO's ContentSelect Academic Journal Database, the *New York Times* Search by Subject Archive, and the "Best of the Web" Link Library. This comprehensive site also includes a detailed help section.

Longman American History Atlas A full-color reference tool and visual guide to American history that includes almost 100 maps and covers the full scope of history. Atlas overhead transparencies are also available to adopters. The Longman American History Atlas is available at no extra charge when bundled with the textbook.

Mapping America: A Guide to Historical Geography, **Third Edition** Written by Ken Weatherbie of Del Mar College, this two-volume workbook contains 35 exercises correlated to the text that review basic American historical geography and ask students to interpret the role geography has played in American history. *Mapping America: A Guide to Historical Geography* is available at no additional charge to qualified college adopters when bundled with the text.

American History Firsthand Created by editors Julie Roy Jeffrey and Peter Frederick, this unique looseleaf anthology is designed to give students an up-close-and-personal view of history. The collection includes loose facsimiles of written documents, visual materials and artifacts, songs and sheet music, portraits, cartoons, film posters, and more, so that students can learn firsthand what history is and what historians do. "Placing the Sources in Context" and "Questions to Consider" accompanying each set of materials in the collection help guide students through the practice of historical analysis.

Voices of The American People This collection of primary documents reflects the rich and varied tapestry of American life and is correlated directly to the content and organization of *The American People*. It is available to qualified college adopters at no additional charge when bundled with a new book.

Sources of the African American Past, **Second Edition** Edited by Roy Finkenbine of the

University of Detroit at Mercy, this collection of primary sources covers key themes in the African American experience from the West African background to the present. Balanced between political and social history, it offers a vivid snapshot of the lives of African Americans in different historical periods and includes documents representing women and different regions of the United States. Available at a minimum cost to qualified college adopters when bundled with the text.

Women and the National Experience, **Second Edition** Edited by Ellen Skinner of Pace University, this primary source reader contains both classic and unusual documents describing the history of women in the United States. The documents provide dramatic evidence that outspoken women attained a public voice and participated in the development of national events and policies long before they could vote. Chronologically organized and balanced between social and political history, this reader offers a striking picture of the lives of women across American history. Available at a minimum cost to qualified college adopters when bundled with the text.

Reading the American West, Edited by Mitchell Roth of Sam Houston State University, this primary source reader uses letters, diary excerpts, speeches, interviews, and newspaper articles to let students experience how historians do research and how history is written. Every document is accompanied by a contextual headnote and study questions. The book is divided into chapters with extensive introductions. Available at a minimum cost to qualified college adopters when bundled with the text.

A Short Guide to Writing About History, **Sixth Edition** by Richard Marius and Melvin E. Page, this practical text teaches students how to incorporate their own ideas into their papers and to tell a story about history that interests them and their peers. Focusing on more than just the conventions of good writing, this text shows students how first to think about history, and then how to organize their thoughts into coherent essays. The *Short Guide* covers both brief essays and the document resource paper as it explores the writing and researching processes; examines different modes of historical writing, including argument; and concludes with guidelines for improving style.

Library of American Biography Series Each concise biography in this distinguished series focuses on an individual whose actions and ideas significantly influenced American history and relates the life of the subject to the issues and events of the time period. Now featuring the guiding hand of series editor Mark C. Carnes, the series is being revised and updated with today's students in mind. Each volume is offered at a lower price, and study and discussion questions have been added at the end of each new volume to encourage students to reflect on the role of the subject in the shaping of American history. Classic books in the series include Edmund S. Morgan, *The Puritan Dilemma: The Story of John Winthrop;* Harold C. Livesay, *Andrew Carnegie and the Rise of Big Business;* William T. Youngs, *Eleanor Roosevelt: A Personal and Public Life.* Many new titles have been added in recent years, including several figures from the second half of the 20th Century.

Penguin Books The partnership between Penguin Putnam USA and Longman Publishers offers your students a discount on many titles when bundled with any Longman survey. Available titles include *Narrative of the Life of Frederick Douglass* by Frederick Douglass, *Why We Can't Wait* by Martin Luther King, Jr., *Beloved* by Toni Morrison, and *Uncle Tom's Cabin* by Harriet Beecher Stowe. For a complete listing of titles, go to www.pearsonhighered /penguin.

Acknowledgments

This Vango edition of *The American People* has benefited from the helpful comments of scholars as well as the experience of instructors and students who have used previous editions of the textbook. Their comments have informed the major changes implemented here. Those whose reviews helped in the preparation of this edition include: Elizabeth Alexander, Texas Wesleyan University; Neal A. Brooks, Community College of Baltimore County; Jean Choate, Coastal Georgia Community College; Dolores Davison, Foothill College; Anthony Heideman, Front Range Community College; Mary Hoogterp, Mesa College; Michael Howe, Morgan Community College; Don Knox, Vernon College; Michael Lawson, Northland Pioneer College; Marianne McKnight, Salt Lake Community College;

Jim Piecuch, Kennesaw State University; Esther Robinson, Cy-Fair College; Scott Walker, Arizona State University; Michael White, Temple College.

Our aim has been to write a balanced and vivid history of the development of the American nation and its society. We also provide a variety of support materials to help make teaching and learning enjoyable and rewarding. The reader will be the judge of our success. We welcome your comments.

Gary B.Nash
Julie Roy Jeffrey

Read it.
Get it.

VOLUME ONE
To 1877

THE AMERICAN PEOPLE

CREATING A NATION AND A SOCIETY

The popular classic "The American People" is now available in this new, streamlined VangoBooks edition, offering a clean, smart, and efficient presentation at an affordable price.

Gary B. Nash **Julie Roy Jeffrey**
John R. Howe   **Allan M. Winkler**
Peter Frederick **Charlene Mires**
Allen F. Davis **Carla Gardina Pestana**

VOLUME 1

CHAPTERS 1–16

To order, please request
ISBN-10: 0-205-64282-9; ISBN-13: 978-0-205-64282-3

COMBINED VOLUME
CHAPTERS 1-31
IISBN-10: 0-205-64279-9
ISBN-13: 978-0-205-64279-3

VOLUME 1
CHAPTERS 1-16
ISBN-10: 0-205-64282-9
ISBN-13: 978-0-205-64282-3

VOLUME 2
CHAPTERS 16-31
ISBN-10: 0-205-64283-7
ISBN-13: 978-0-205-64283-0

CHAPTER 1

Ancient America and Africa

Portuguese troops storm Tangiers in Morocco in 1471 as part of the ongoing struggle between Christianity and Islam in the mid-fifteenth century Mediterranean world. Why would such an image have hung in a church?

(The Art Archive/Pastrana Church, Spain/Dagli Orti)

American Stories

Three Women's Lives Highlight the Convergence of Three Continents

In what historians call the "early modern period" of world history—roughly the fifteenth to the seventeenth century, when peoples from different regions of the earth came into close contact with each other—three women played key roles in the convergence and clash of societies from Europe, Africa, and the Americas. Their lives highlight some of this chapter's major themes, which developed in an era when the people of three continents began to encounter each other and the shape of the modern world began to take form.

Born in 1451, Isabella of Castile was a banner bearer for *reconquista*—the centuries-long Christian crusade to expel the Muslim rulers who had controlled Spain for centuries. When the queen of Castile married Ferdinand, the king of Aragon, in 1469, the union of their kingdoms forged a stronger Christian Spain prepared to realize a new religious and military vision. Eleven years later, after ending hostilities with Portugal, Isabella and Ferdinand began consolidating their power. By expelling Muslims and Jews, the royal couple pressed to enforce Catholic religious conformity. Their religious zeal also led them to sponsor four voyages of Christopher Columbus as a means of extending Spanish power across the Atlantic. The first was commissioned in 1492, only a few months after what the Spanish considered a "just and holy war" against infidels culminated in the surrender of Moorish Granada, the last stronghold of Islam in Christian Europe. Sympathizing with Isabella's fervent piety and desire to convert the people of distant lands to Christianity, Columbus after 1493 signed his letters "Christopher Columbus, Christ Bearer."

On the other side of the Atlantic resided an Aztec woman of influence, also called Isabella by the Spanish, who soon symbolized the mixing of her people with the Spanish. Her real name was Tecuichpotzin, which meant "little royal maiden" in Nahuatl, the Aztec language. The firstborn child of the Aztec ruler Moctezuma II and Teotlalco, his wife, she entered the world in 1509—before the Aztecs had seen a single Spaniard. But when she was 11, Tecuichpotzin witnessed the arrival of the conquistadors under Cortés. When her father was near death, he asked the conqueror to take custody of his daughter, hoping for an accommodation between the conquering Spanish and the conquered Aztecs. But Tecuichpotzin was reclaimed by her people and soon was married to her father's brother, who became the Aztec ruler in 1520. He died of smallpox within two

months, and the new emperor claimed the young girl as his wife.

But then in 1521, the Spanish besieged Tenochtitlán, the Aztec island capital in Lake Texcoco, and overturned the mighty Aztec Empire; Tecuichpotzin soon entered the life of the victorious Spanish. In 1526, her husband was tortured and hanged for plotting an insurrection against Cortés. Still only 19, she succumbed to the overtures of Cortés, agreeing to join his household and live among his Indian mistresses. Pregnant with Cortés's child, she was married off to a Spanish officer. Another marriage followed, and in all she bore seven children. These descendants of Moctezuma II subsequently became large landowners and figures of importance. Tecuichpotzin was in this way a pioneer of *mestizaje*—the mixing of races—and helped to launch the creation of a new society in Mexico.

On the west coast of Africa lived another powerful woman. Njinga was born around 1595 and named because she entered the world with the umbilical cord wrapped around her neck (which was believed to foretell a haughty character). By the time she assumed the throne of Ndongo (present-day Angola) in 1624, Queen Njinga knew that the Portuguese had converted King Affonso I of the Kongo Kingdom to Catholicism in the 1530s and that by the 1550s they had trapped her people into incessant wars in order to supply them with slaves. As soon as she became Queen, her people began to resist Portuguese rule. Leading her troops in a series of wars, her fierce battle cry was said to be heard for miles. She became a heroic figure in Angolan history.

In opening this book, the stories of Queen Isabella of Castile, Aztec princess Tecuichpotzin, and Angola's Queen Njinga set the scene for the intermingling of Europeans, Africans, and Native Americans in the New World, what Europeans called North and South America. Examining the backgrounds of the peoples of three continents and glimpsing the changes occurring with each of their many societies as the time for a historic convergence neared allows us to better understand the collision of cultures among societies rimming the Atlantic Ocean. In this chapter, we will examine the complexities of West African societies, delve into some of the communities of North and South America, and study Western Europeans of the late fifteenth century. Drawing comparisons and contrasts, we equip ourselves to see three worlds meet as a new global age began.

The Peoples of America Before Columbus

Thousands of years before the European exploratory voyages in the 1490s, the history of humankind in North America began. Thus, American history can begin with some basic questions: Who were the first inhabitants of the Americas? Where did they come from? How had the societies they formed changed over the millennia that preceded European arrival? Can their history be reconstructed from the mists of prehistoric time?

Migration to the Americas

Almost all the evidence suggesting answers to these questions comes from ancient sites of early life in North America. Archaeologists have unearthed skeletal remains, pots, tools, ornaments, and other objects to reach a tentative date for the arrival of humans in America of about 35,000 B.C.E.—about the same time that humans began to settle Japan and Scandinavia.

Nearly every Native American society has its own story about its origins in the Americas. For example, many believe that they were the first people in North America, having emerged out of the earth or from underneath the waters of a large lake.

Paleoanthropologists, scientists who study ancient peoples, generally agree that the first inhabitants of the Americas were nomadic bands from Siberia, hunting big-game animals such as bison, caribou, and reindeer. These sojourners began to migrate across a land bridge connecting northeastern Asia with Alaska. Geologists believe that this bridge, perhaps 600 miles wide, existed most recently between 25,000 and 14,000 years ago, when massive glaciers locked up much of the earth's moisture and left part of the Bering Sea floor exposed. Ice-free passage through Canada was possible only briefly at the beginning and end of this period, however. At other times, melting glaciers flooded the land bridge and blocked foot traffic. Scholars debate the exact timing, but the main migration occurred either between 11,000 and 14,000 years ago, or possibly much earlier. Some new archaeological finds suggest multiple migrations, both by sea and land, from several regions of Asia and even from Europe.

Hunters, Farmers, and Environmental Factors

Once on the North American continent, these early wanderers began trekking southward and then eastward, following vegetation and game. In time, they reached the southernmost tip of South America—some 15,000 miles from the Asian homeland to Tierra del Fuego. Moving eastward, they traversed some 6,000 miles from Siberia to the eastern edge of North America. United States history has traditionally emphasized the "westward movement" of people, but for thousands of years before Columbus's arrival, the frontier moved southward and eastward. Thus did people from the "Old World" discover and people the "New World" thousands of years before Columbus.

Archaeologists have excavated ancient sites of early life in the Americas, unearthing tools, ornaments, and skeletal remains that allow them to reconstruct the dispersion of these first Americans over an immense land mass. As centuries passed and population increased, the earliest inhabitants evolved into separate cultures, adjusting to various environments in distinct ways. By the late 1400s, the "Indians" of the Americas were enormously diverse in the size and complexity of their societies, the languages they spoke, and their forms of social organization.

Archaeologists and anthropologists have charted several phases of Native American history. The Beringian period of initial migration ended about 14,000 years ago. During the Paleo-Indian era, 14,000 to 10,000 years ago, big-game hunters flaked hard stones into spear points and chose "kill sites" where they slew herds of Pleistocene mammals. A more reliable food source allowed population growth, and settled habitations or local migration within limited territories became the norm.

Then during the Archaic era, from about 10,000 to 2,500 years ago, great geological changes and the human presence brought further changes. As the massive Ice Age glaciers slowly retreated, a warming trend turned vast grassland areas from Utah to the highlands of Central America into desert. The Pleistocene mammals suffered under more arid conditions and from over-hunting, as elsewhere. While the first wave of human intruders found a wilderness teeming with so-called megafauna: saber-toothed tigers, woolly mammoths, gigantic ground sloths, huge bison, and monstrous bears, those animals died out. The depletion of the megafauna left the hemisphere with a much restricted catalogue of animals. Humans still hunted such large animals as elk, buffalo, bear, and moose, but the extinction of the huge beasts forced them to rely on new sources of food as well, including turkeys, ducks, and guinea pigs. This change may have gradually reduced their population.

Recent archaeological evidence points to examples of environmental devastation that severely damaged the biodiversity of the Americas. In addition to over-hunting, salinization and deforestation gradually put the environment under additional stress. For example, in what is today central Arizona, the Hohokam civilization collapsed hundreds of years ago, much like that in ancient Mesopotamia, when the irrigation system became too salty to support agriculture. At New Mexico's Chaco Canyon, the fast-growing Anasazi

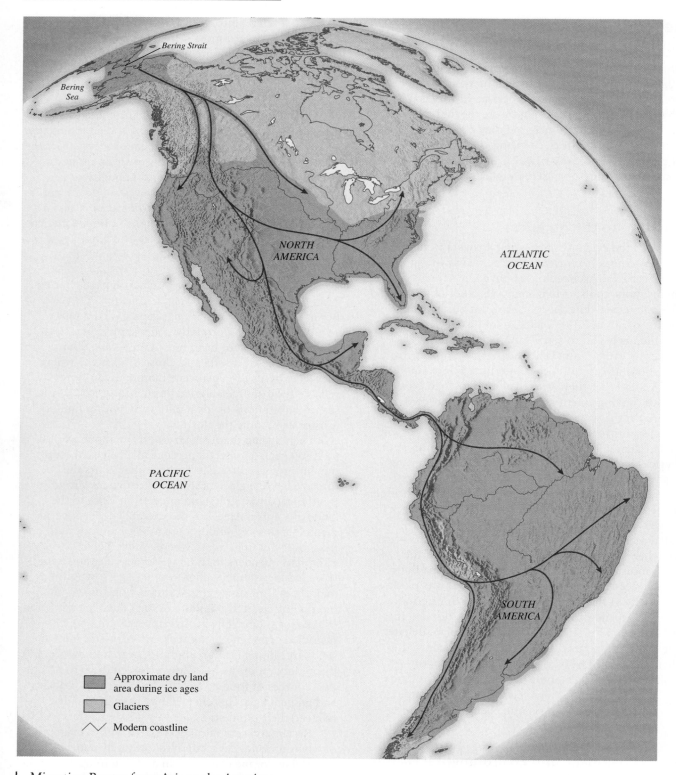

Migration Routes from Asia to the Americas

The red arrows indicate the general flow of migrating societies over thousands of years before Europeans reached the Americas. Based on fragile archaeological evidence, these migratory patterns are necessarily tentative, and new discoveries support the theory of early Stone Age arrivals by boat. Can you reconcile Native American creation myths with archaeological evidence of the first humans reaching the Americas by crossing the Bering Straits land bridge? If so, how?

denuded a magnificently forested region in their search for firewood and building materials. This resulting soil erosion impoverished the region for the Anasazi.

Human populations ably adapted as they learned to exploit new sources of food, especially plants. About 9,000 to 7,000 years ago, a technological breakthrough took place, probably independently in widely separated parts of the world, as humans learned how to plant, cultivate, and harvest. This development, which historians call the agricultural revolution, allowed humans to gain control over once-ungovernable natural forces. Agriculture slowly brought dramatic changes in human societies everywhere.

Agriculture first developed in southwestern Asia and in Africa; it spread to Europe at about the time people in the Tehuacán valley of central Mexico first planted maize and squash. Over the millennia, humans progressed from doorside planting of a few wild seeds to systematic clearing and planting of fields. As the production of domesticated plant food ended dependence on gathering wild plants and pursuing game, settled village life began to replace nomadic existence.

In the Americas, increased food supply brought about by agriculture triggered other major changes. As more ample food fueled population growth, large groups split off to form separate societies. Greater social and political complexity developed because not everyone was needed as before to secure the society's food supply. Men cleared the land and hunted game while women planted, cultivated, and harvested crops. Many societies empowered religious figures, who organized the common followers, directed their work, and exacted tribute as well as worship from them. In return, the community trusted them to ward off hostile forces. Having learned to domesticate plant life, Native Americans began the long process of transforming their relationship to the physical world.

Everywhere in the Americas, regional trading networks formed. Along trade routes carrying commodities such as salt for food preservation, obsidian rock for projectile points, and copper for jewelry also traveled technology, religious ideas, and agricultural practices. By the end of the Archaic period, about 500 B.C.E., hundreds of independent kin-based groups, like people in other parts of the world, had learned to exploit the resources of their particular area and to trade with other groups in their region. For centuries thereafter, native societies grew in size, developed more sophisticated agricultural techniques, and in some areas adopted a sedentary life.

Mesoamerican Empires

Of all the large-scale societies developing in the Americas during Europe's medieval period, the most impressive were in Mesoamerica—the middle region bridging the great land masses of South and North America. The Valley of Mexico, now dominated by Mexico City, became the center of the largest societies that emerged in the centuries before the Spanish arrived. In less than two centuries, the Aztecs built a mighty empire rivaling any known over the centuries in Europe, Asia, and Africa by subjugating smaller tribes. By the time of Columbus's first voyage in 1492, the Aztecs, with a population estimated at 10 to 20 million people, controlled most of central Mexico. They extracted tribute from conquered peoples—beans, maize, and other foodstuffs; cotton fabrics; bird feathers for war costumes; animal furs; and labor on state projects such as canals, temples, and irrigation.

Aztec society was as stratified as any in Europe, and the supreme ruler's authority was as extensive as that of any European or African monarch. Every Aztec was born into one of four classes: the nobility, including the emperor's household, priests, and military officers; free commoners with rights to land and organized in precincts with temples and schools; serfs, who like those in Europe were bound to the soil and toiled on the lands of nobles; and slaves, who had rights akin to those of slaves in ancient Rome or Greece.

Their capital in Tenochtitlán ("Place of the Prickly Pear Cactus") was one of the world's greatest cities on the eve of the Columbian voyages. A canal-ribbed city island in the great lake of Texcoco, it was connected to

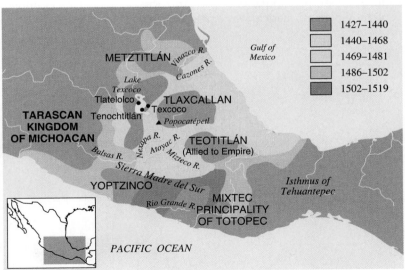

Expansion of the Aztec Empire, 1427–1519

In the century before Europeans breached the Atlantic to find the Americas, the Aztecs' rise to power brought 10 to 20 million people under their sway. Why is it significant that this was more than the entire population of Spain and Portugal at this time?

the mainland by three broad causeways and supplied with drinkable water by an impressive aqueduct; with a population of perhaps 150,000, it rivaled the medieval city–state of Venice. When they arrived in 1519, Spaniards could hardly believe the grandeur they saw. The immense capital covered about 10 square miles and boasted some 40 towers—one of them, according to the first Spaniards entering the city, higher than the cathedral of Seville, the largest in Spain. "When we saw so many cities and villages built in the water and other great towns on dry land and that straight and level causeway going towards Mexico," wrote one Spaniard in the army of Cortés, "we were amazed and said that it was like the enchantments they tell of in the legend of Amadis." Indeed, they had found their way to the most advanced civilization in the Americas, where through skilled hydraulic engineering, the Aztecs cultivated chinampas, or "floating gardens," around their capital city in which grew a wide variety of flowers and vegetables.

Regional North American Cultures

The regions north of Mesoamerica were never populated by societies of the size and complexity of the Aztecs. Some of them, particularly in what is now the American Southwest, felt the Aztec influence. Throughout the vast expanses of North America in the last epoch of pre-Columbian development—the so-called post-Archaic phase—many distinct societies evolved through a complex process of growth and environmental adaptation.

For many decades, anthropologists and historians estimated that the population of the Americas, and especially North America, was small, only about 10 percent of Europe's population at the time of Columbus's first voyage in 1492. The conventional view assumed that Native American societies peopled by nomadic hunters and gatherers could not be very large.

Recent archaeological research indicates that the sophisticated agricultural techniques of Native American societies sustained large societies. Population estimates have soared, with today's scholars estimating the pre-contact population north of the Rio Grande to be at least 4 million people, of whom perhaps half lived east of the Mississippi River and some 700,000 settled along the eastern coastal plain and in the piedmont region accessible to the early European settlers. Though estimates vary widely, the most reliable suggest that about 50 to 70 million people lived in the entire hemisphere when Europeans first arrived, contrasting with some 70 to 90 million in Europe (including Russia) around 1500, about 50 to 70 million in Africa, and 225 to 350 million in Asia. The European colonizers were not coming to a "virgin wilderness," as they often described it, but to a land inhabited for thousands of years by people whose village existence in some ways resembled that of the new arrivals.

In the southwestern region of North America, for example, Hohokam and Anasazi societies (the ancestors of the present-day Hopi and Zuñi) had developed a sedentary village life thousands of years before the Spanish arrived in the 1540s. By about 1200 C.E., these "Pueblo" people, as the Spanish later called them, planned villages composed of large, terraced, multistoried buildings and often constructed on defensive sites that would afford the Anasazi protection.

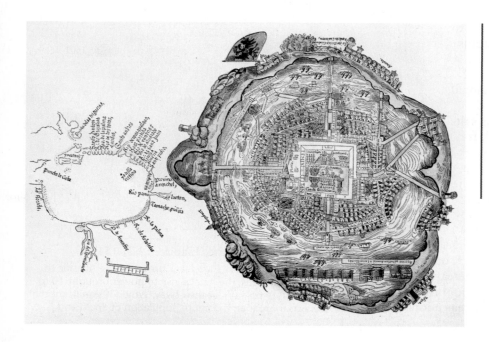

Tenochtitlán

The plan of Tenochtitlán, later Mexico City, is from the Latin edition of Cortés's "Second Letter," on his conquest of the Aztecs. Cortés's account was widely published in Europe, where the Germans, French, and English were astounded to hear of such an extraordinary Aztec metropolis with floating gardens, causeways, and monumental architecture. How would this city compare with those in Europe?

(The Granger Collection, New York)

ARCHAEOLOGICAL ARTIFACTS

The recovery of the past before extensive written records existed is the domain of archaeology. Virtually our entire knowledge of native societies in North America before the arrival of European colonizers is drawn from the work of archaeologists who have excavated the ancient living sites of the first Americans. Many Native Americans today strongly oppose this rummaging in the ancient ancestral places; they particularly oppose the unearthing of burial sites. But the modern search for knowledge about the past goes on.

Archaeological data have allowed us to overcome the stereotypical view of Native Americans as a primitive people whose culture was static for thousands of years before Europeans arrived in North America. This earlier view allowed historians to argue that the tremendous loss of Native American population and land accompanying the initial settlement and westward migration of white Americans was more or less inevitable. When two cultures, one dynamic and forward-looking and the other static and backward, confronted each other, historians have frequently maintained, the more advanced or "civilized" culture almost always prevailed.

Much of the elaborate early history of people in the Americas is unrecoverable. But many fragments of this long human history are being recaptured through archaeological research. Particularly important are studies that reveal how Indian societies were changing during the few centuries immediately preceding the European arrival in the New World. These studies allow us to interpret more accurately the seventeenth-century interaction of Native Americans and Europeans because they provide an understanding of Native American values, social and political organization, material culture, and religion as they existed when the two cultures first met.

One such investigation has been carried out over the last century at the confluence of the Mississippi and Missouri rivers near modern-day East St. Louis, Illinois. Archaeologists have found there the center of a vast Mississippi culture that began about 600 C.E., reached its peak about 300 years before Columbus's voyages, and then declined through a combination of drought, dwindling food supplies, and internal tensions. Cahokia is the name given to the urban center of a civilization that at its height dominated an area as large as New York State. At the center of Cahokia stood one of the largest earth constructions built by ancient humans anywhere on the planet. Its base covering 16 acres, this gigantic earthen temple, containing 22 million cubic feet

A reconstructed view of Cahokia, the largest town in North America before European arrival, painted by William R. Iseminger. The millions of cubic feet of earth used to construct the ceremonial and burial mounds must have required the labor of tens of thousands of workers over a long period of time. How does this relate to the population density of their communities?

William Iseminger, "Reconstruction of Central Cahokia Mounds". c. 1150 CE. Courtesy of Cahokia Mounds State Historic Site.

of hand-moved earth, rises in four terraces to a height of 100 feet, as tall as a modern 10-story office building. The central plaza, like those of the Aztecs and Mayans, was oriented exactly on a north–south axis in order to chart the movement of celestial bodies. The drawing shown on the previous page indicates some of the scores of smaller geometric burial mounds near this major temple. Notice the outlying farms, a sure sign of the settled (as opposed to nomadic) existence of the people who flourished 10 centuries ago in this region. How does this depiction of ancient Cahokia change your image of Native American life before the arrival of Europeans?

By recovering artifacts from Cahokia burial mounds, archaeologists have pieced together a picture, still tentative, of a highly elaborate civilization along the Mississippi bottomlands. Cahokian manufacturers mass-produced salt, knives, and stone hoe blades for both local consumption and export. Cahokian artisans made sophisticated pottery, ornamental jewelry, metalwork, and tools. They used copper and furs from the Lake Superior region, black obsidian stone from the Rocky Mountains, and seashells from the Gulf of Mexico, demonstrating that the people at Cahokia were involved in long-distance trade. In fact, Cahokia was a crucial crossroads of trade and water travel in the heartland of North America.

Some graves uncovered at Cahokia contain large caches of finely tooled objects while other burial mounds contain many skeletons unaccompanied by any artifacts. From this evidence archaeologists conclude that this was a more stratified society than those encountered by the first settlers along the Atlantic seaboard. Anthropologists believe that some of the Mississippi culture spread eastward before Cahokia declined, but much mystery still remains concerning the fate and cultural diffusion of these early Americans.

Reflecting on the Past What other conclusions about Cahokian culture can you draw from figures such as these? Are there archaeological sites in your area that contain evidence of Native American civilization? ▪

The largest of them, containing about 800 rooms, was at Pueblo Bonito in Chaco Canyon. By the time the Spanish arrived in the 1540s, the indigenous Pueblo people were using irrigation canals, dams, and hillside terracing to water their arid maize fields. In its agricultural techniques, skill in ceramics, use of woven textiles for clothing, and village life, Pueblo society resembled that of peasant communities in many parts of Europe and Asia. Don Juan de Oñate reported home in 1599 after reaching the Pueblo villages on the Rio Grande that the Native Americans "live very much the same as we do, in houses with two and three terraces...."

North and east of the Pueblo peoples, from the Great Plains of the midcontinent to the Atlantic tidewater region, a variety of tribes came to be loosely associated in four main language groups: Algonquian, Iroquoian, Muskhogean, and Siouan.

Among the most impressive of these societies were the mound builders of the Mississippi and Ohio valleys. When European settlers first crossed the Appalachian Mountains a century and a half after arriving on the continent, they were astounded to find hundreds of ceremonial mounds and gigantic sculptured earthworks. Believing all "Indians" to be forest primitives, they reasoned that these were the remains of an ancient civilization that had found its way to North America—perhaps Phoenicians, survivors of the sunken island of Atlantis, or the Lost Tribes of Israel spoken of in European mythology.

Archaeologists now conclude that the "Mound Builders" were the ancestors of the Creek, Choctaw, and Natchez. Their societies, evolving slowly over the centuries, had developed considerable complexity by the advent of Christianity in Europe. In southern Ohio alone about 10,000 mounds used as burial sites have been pinpointed, and archaeologists have excavated another 1,000 earth-walled enclosures, including one enormous fortification with a circumference of about $3\frac{1}{2}$ miles, enclosing 100 acres, or the equivalent of 50 modern city blocks. From the mounded tombs, archaeologists have recovered a great variety of items that have been traced to widely separated parts of the continent—evidence that the Mound Builders participated in a vast trading network linking hundreds of Native American villages across the continent.

The mound-building societies of the Ohio valley declined many centuries before Europeans reached the continent, perhaps attacked by other tribes or damaged by severe climatic changes that undermined agriculture. By about 600 C.E., another mound-building group arose in the Mississippi valley. Its center, the city of Cahokia with at least 20,000 (and possibly as many as 40,000) inhabitants, stood near present-day St. Louis. Great ceremonial plazas, flanked by a temple that rose in four terraces to a height of 100 feet, marked this first metropolis in America. This was the urban center of a far-flung Mississippian culture that encompassed hundreds of villages from Wisconsin to Louisiana and from Oklahoma to Tennessee.

An Anasazi Village

The ruins of Pueblo Bonita in Chaco Canyon, New Mexico, mark the center of Anasazi culture in the twelfth century C.E. This San Juan River basin town may have contained 1,000 people. Why would they have constructed apartment-like structures, the likes of which would not be seen elsewhere in North America until the late nineteenth century?

(© David Muench)

Before the mound-building cultures of the continental heartlands mysteriously declined, their influence was already transforming the woodland societies along the Atlantic. Numerous small tribes settled from Nova Scotia to Florida. While they never equaled the larger societies of the midcontinent in earthwork sculpture, architectural design, or development of large-scale agriculture, they added limited agriculture to their skill in using natural plants. Their food procurement strategies exploited all the resources around them.

Most of these eastern woodland tribes lived in waterside villages. In the far north were the Abenaki, Penobscot, Passamaquoddy, and others, who supplemented their diet of fish with maple sugar and a few foodstuffs. Farther south, in what was to become New England, were small tribes occupying fairly local areas, such as the Massachusetts, Wampanoag, Pequot, Narragansett, Niantic, and Mahican. The mid-Atlantic Lenape, Susquehannock, Nanticoke, Pamunkey, Shawnee, Tuscarora, Catawba, and other peoples added a few crops to the natural plants they used for food, medicine, dyes, and flavoring. Many of these peoples located their fields of maize near fishing grounds. They either migrated seasonally between inland and coastal village sites or situated themselves astride two ecological zones. In the Northeast, birch-bark canoes, light enough to be carried by a single

person, facilitated trade and communication over immense territories.

The densely populated Southeast boasted rich and complex cultures, which traced their ancestry back at least 8,000 years. Belonging to several language groups, some of them joined in loose confederacies. Called "Mississippian" societies by archaeologists, the residents of the Southeast created elaborate pottery and basket weaving and conducted long distance trade. These cultures also were influenced by Hopewell burial mound techniques, some of which involved earthmoving on a vast scale. A global warming trend that increased the annual average temperature by a few degrees for about four centuries after 900 helped agriculture flourish in this region. In some cases, as with the Natchez, highly stratified societies developed, in which chiefs and commoners were sharply divided and priests led ritual ceremonies. These people were the ancestors of the powerful Creek and Yamasee in the Georgia and Alabama regions; the Apalachee in Florida and along the Gulf of Mexico; the Choctaw, Chickasaw, and Natchez of the lower Mississippi valley; the Cherokee of the southern Appalachian Mountains; and

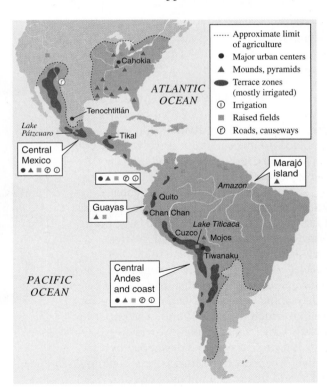

Pre-Columbian Societies of the Americas

Why do you think they were once described as nomadic hunter–gatherers? Indigenous peoples in the Americas were agriculturalists and urban dwellers in many areas and populated the land as densely as did people in many other parts of the world.

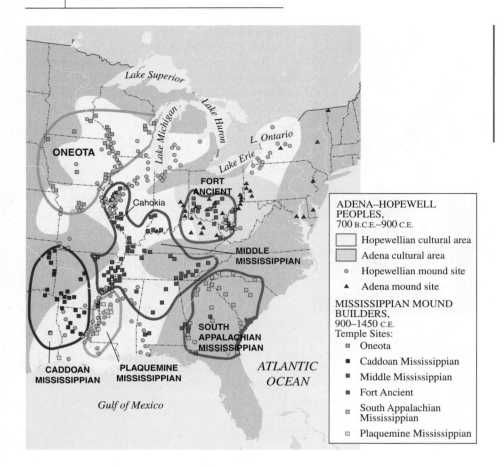

North American Mound-Building Cultures

Plows, shovels, and bulldozers have obliterated many of the earthworks created at hundreds of mound-building sites in the eastern half of North America. How do the earlier mound locations relate to the later temple sites?

several dozen smaller tribes scattered along the Atlantic coast. However, after the "Little Ice Age," which spanned several centuries after about 1300, they abandoned their mounded urban centers and devolved into less populous, less stratified, and less centralized societies.

In some important ways, the material base of Native American life differed sharply from that of Europeans. Since no large draft animals lived in the New World, Native Americans had little incentive to develop wheeled vehicles. Some technology such as that for smelting iron, which had diffused widely in the Old World, had not crossed the ocean to reach the New World. The opposite was also true: valuable New World crops, such as corn and potatoes developed by Native American agriculturists, were unknown in the Old World before Columbus.

The Iroquois

Far to the north of the declining southeastern mound-building societies, between what would become French and English zones of settlement, five tribes

A European View of Indian Women

When the Frenchman Jacques Le Moyne arrived in what is now South Carolina in 1565, he painted Indian women cultivating the soil and planting corn. Le Moyne's painting did not survive, but it was rendered as shown here by the Flemish engraver Theodor de Bry, who purchased it from Le Moyne's widow in 1588. De Bry took some liberties; for example, he put European-style hoes with metal blades into the hands of the women, whereas they tilled with large fish bones fitted to sticks. Did European women play the same role in agriculture?

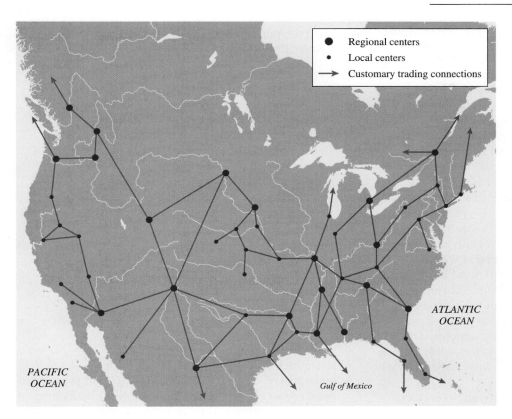

Native American Trade Networks in 1400

By recovering objects such as shell necklaces, stone tools, and decorative copper from ancient sites of Indian habitation, and by determining their place of origin, anthropologists have developed this approximate map of Native American trading networks in the century before the arrival of Europeans. What factors might explain the location of regional centers?

composed what Europeans later called the League of the Iroquois: the Mohawk, Oneida, Onondaga, Cayuga, and Seneca. The Iroquois Confederation began as a vast extension of the kinship group that characterized the northeastern woodland pattern of family settlement and embraced perhaps 10,000 people by about 1500.

Not long before Europeans began coming ashore in eastern North America, the loosely organized and strife-ridden Iroquois strengthened themselves by creating a more cohesive political confederacy. As they learned to suppress intra-Iroquois feuds, villages gained stability and population increased. The Iroquois developed political mechanisms for solving internal problems and presenting a more unified front in parlaying with their Algonquian neighbors for the use of hunting territories to the north or in admitting dependent tribes to settle in their territory. The Iroquois would be well positioned to develop a coordinated policy for dealing with the European newcomers.

In the palisaded villages of Iroquoia, some bustling with more than a thousand people, work was performed communally, and land was owned by all in common. While individuals farmed or hunted the bounty was divided among all. Similarly, several families occupied a longhouse, but the house itself, like all else in the community, was common property. "No hospitals [poorhouses] are needed among them," wrote a French Jesuit in 1657, "because there are neither mendicants nor paupers as long as there are any rich people among them. Their kindness, humanity, and courtesy not only makes them liberal with what they have, but causes them to possess hardly anything except in common. A whole village must be without corn, before any individual can be obliged to endure privation." One historian has called this "upside down capitalism," in which the success was measured not by piling up material possessions but by being able to give to others.

Out of extended kinship groups, the Iroquois organized village settlements. Like many Africans, the Iroquois had matrilineal families with family membership determined through the female rather than male line. A typical Iroquois family comprised an old woman, her daughters with their husbands and children, and her unmarried granddaughters and grandsons. Sons and grandsons remained with their kinship group until they married; then they joined the family of their wife or the family of their mother's brother. If these arrangements puzzled Europeans, whose men controlled women strictly, so did the Iroquois woman's prerogative of divorce; if she desired it, she merely set her husband's possessions outside the longhouse door.

Iroquois shared in political power in ways that Europeans found strange. Political authority in the villages derived from the matrons or senior women of the *ohwachiras*—a group of related families. These women named the men representing the clans at village and tribal councils and appointed the 49 sachems or chiefs who met periodically with the confederated Five Nations. These civil chiefs were generally middle-aged or elderly men who had gained fame as warriors but now enjoyed prestige at the council fires. The political power of the women also extended to the ruling councils, in which they caucused behind the circle of Chiefs and made sure that the tribal councils did not move too far from the will of the women who appointed them. Male chiefs were secure in their positions only as long as they could achieve a consensus with the women who had placed them in office.

The tribal economy and military affairs further demonstrated the division of power between men and women. While men did most of the hunting and fishing, the women were the community's primary agriculturists. Tending the crops, they sustained the community. When men were away on weeks-long hunting expeditions, women were left entirely in charge of village daily life. If "the forest belonged to the men," one historian explains, "the village was the woman's domain." In military affairs women played a significant role, for they supplied the moccasins and food for warring expeditions. A decision to withhold these supplies was tantamount to vetoing a military foray. Clan matrons often initiated war by calling on the Iroquois warriors to bring them enemy captives to replace fallen clan members.

In raising children, Iroquois parents were more permissive than Europeans. They did not believe in harsh physical punishment, encouraged the young to imitate adult behavior, and were tolerant of fumbling early attempts. The mother nursed and protected the infant while hardening it by baths in cold water. Weaning ordinarily began at age three or four. Childhood interest in anatomy and in sexual experimentation was accepted as normal. All this contrasted with European child-rearing techniques, which stressed accustoming the child to authority from an early age through frequent use of physical punishment, condemning early sexual curiosity, and emphasizing obedience and respect for authority.

The approach to authority in Iroquois society, as in most other native societies in North America, lacked most of the complicated machinery developed by Europeans. No laws and ordinances, sheriffs and

NATIVE POPULATION OF THE AMERICAS IN WORLD CONTEXT, 1500

Because they are from a time when censuses were rare in most parts of the world, all these population figures are estimates. Some demographers believe that 100 million people inhabited the Americas in 1500. New research and lively debate will no doubt alter these figures. **Reflecting on the Past** What is the population today of the areas listed here, and how do you account for differing distribution of the world's population?

China	100–150 million
India	75–150 million
Southwest Asia	20–30 million
Japan and rest of Asia	30–50 million
Europe (including Russia)	70–90 million
Africa	50–70 million
Americas	50–70 million

constables, judges and juries, or courts or jails—the apparatus of authority in Europe—existed in pre-contact North America. Yet the Iroquois firmly set boundaries of acceptable behavior. They prized the autonomous individual yet maintained a strict code of right and wrong. They governed behavior by imparting a sense of tradition and attachment to the group through communally performed rituals. Europeans dealt with crime through investigation, arrest, prosecution, and sentencing. But in Native American society, those who stole food, to take one example, were "shamed" and ostracized until the culprits atoned for their actions and proved ready for re-entry into village communal life.

Contrasting Worldviews

Having evolved in complete isolation from each other, European and Native American cultures exhibited a wide difference in values. Colonizing Europeans called themselves "civilized" and typically described the people they met in the Americas as "savage," "heathen," or "barbarian." Lurking behind the physical confrontation that took place when Europeans and Native Americans met were latent conflicts over humans' relationship to the environment, the meaning of property, and personal identity.

Europeans and Native Americans conceptualized their relationship to nature in starkly different ways. Regarding the earth as filled with resources for humans to exploit for their own benefit, Europeans separated the secular and sacred parts of life, and they placed their own relationship to the natural environment mostly in the secular sphere. Native Americans, however, did not distinguish between the secular and sacred. For them, every aspect of the natural world was

Native American Population
Density in North America,
ca. 1500

Historical demographers have
devised estimates of Native
American population density in
North America before the arrival
of Europeans. Estimates are
based on the "carrying capacity" of different ecological
regions: rainfall, access to fish
and animals, soil fertility, and
length of growing season are all
factors in the capacity of the
land to support human life.
How do high density areas at
that time relate to those today?

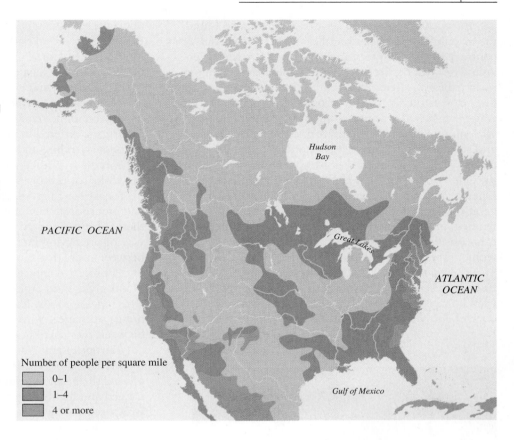

PACIFIC OCEAN

Hudson
Bay

Great Lakes

ATLANTIC
OCEAN

Gulf of Mexico

Number of people per square mile

☐ 0–1

☐ 1–4

☐ 4 or more

sacred, inhabited by a variety of "beings," each pulsat-
ing with spiritual power and all linked together to form
a sacred whole. Consequently, if one offended the land
by stripping it of its cover, the spiritual power in the
land—called "manitou" by some eastern woodland
tribes—would strike back. If one fished or hunted
beyond one's needs, the spirit forces in fish or animals
would take revenge, because humans had broken the
mutual trust and reciprocity that governed relations
between all beings—human or nonhuman. To neglect
reciprocal obligations in nature's domain was to court
sickness, hunger, injury, or death.

Europeans believed that land, as a privately held
commodity, was a resource to be exploited for human
gain. They took for granted property lines, inheritance of land, and courts to settle land disputes.
Property was the basis not only of sustenance but also
of independence, wealth, status, political rights, and
identity. The social structure directly mirrored patterns of land ownership, with a land-wealthy elite at
the apex of the social pyramid and a propertyless
mass at the bottom.

Native Americans also had concepts of property
and boundaries. But they believed that land had sacred
qualities and should be held in common. As one
German missionary explained the Native American
view in the eighteenth century, the Creator "made the
Earth and all that it contains for the common good of

mankind. Whatever liveth on the land, whatsoever
groweth out of the earth, and all that is in the rivers
and waters . . . was given jointly to all and everyone is
entitled to his share."

Communal ownership sharply limited social
stratification and increased a sense of sharing in most
Native American communities, much to the amazement of Europeans accustomed to wide disparities of
wealth. Not all Europeans were acquisitive, competitive individuals. The majority were peasant farmers
living from the soil, living in kin-centered villages with
little contact with the outside world, and exchanging
goods and labor through barter. But in Europe's cities,
a wealth-conscious, ambitious individual who valued
and sought wider choices and greater opportunities
to enhance personal status was coming to the fore.
In contrast, Native American traditions stressed the
group rather than the individual and valor rather
than wealth.

There were exceptions. The empires of the Aztec in
Central America and the Inca in South America were
highly developed, populous, and stratified. So, in
North America, were a few tribes such as the Natchez.
But on the eastern and western coasts of the continent
and in the Southwest—the regions of contact in the
sixteenth and seventeenth centuries—the European
newcomers encountered a people whose social structure and cultural values differed strikingly from theirs.

European colonizers in North America also found the matrilineal organization of many tribal societies contrary to the European male-dominated sexual hierarchy. As with the Iroquois, family membership among most tribes was determined through the female line and divorce was the woman's prerogative. In many Native American societies senior women designated the men who sat in a circle to deliberate and make decisions and stood behind them to lobby and instruct. Village chiefs were usually male, but they were often chosen by the elder women of their clans. "Our ancestors," the Oneida chief Good Peter explained, "considered it a great transgression to reject the counsel of their women, particularly the female governesses. Our ancestors considered them mistresses of the soil. . . . The women, they are the life of the nation."

The role of women in the tribal economy reinforced the sharing of power between male and female. Men hunted, fished, and cleared land, but women controlled the cultivation, harvest, and distribution of crops, supplying probably three-quarters of their family's nutritional needs. When the men were away hunting, the women directed village life. Europeans, imbued with the idea of male superiority and female subordination, perceived such sexual equality as another mark of "savagery."

In economic relations, Europeans and Native Americans differed in ways that sometimes led to misunderstanding and conflict. Over vast stretches of the continent, Native Americans had built trading networks for centuries before Europeans arrived, making it easy for them to trade with arriving Europeans and incorporate new metal and glass trade items into their culture. But trade for Indian peoples was also a way of preserving interdependence and equilibrium between individuals and communities. This principle of reciprocity displayed itself in elaborate ceremonies of gift giving and pipe smoking that preceded the exchange of goods. Europeans saw trade largely as economic exchange, with the benefit of building goodwill between two parties of relatively little importance.

European and Native people differed markedly in their religious beliefs. Europeans built their religious life around the belief in a single divinity, written scriptures, a trained and highly literate clergy, and churches with structured ceremonies. Native American societies, sharing no literary tradition, had less structured religious beliefs. Believing that human life could be affected, positively or negatively, by the mysterious power pervading everything in nature—in rocks, water, the sun, the moon, and animals—Native American people sought to maintain proper relationships with these spirits, including those of the fish, beaver, and deer they hunted. Pueblo people, for example, living in arid lands where rainfall dictated their well-being, expressed their thanks for rain by performing frequent ritual dances.

For Europeans, the Native Americans beliefs in multiple spirits was pagan and devilish. Native religious leaders used medicinal plants and sacred chants to heal the sick and facilitated the people's quests to communicate with the spiritual world. Europeans regarded these healers as especially dangerous because they spiritually misled people. Native Americans would find particularly the Protestant European insistence that the spiritual world was thinly populated ludicrous.

Mississippian Culture Shrine Figures

Carved from marble 700 to 800 years ago, these shrine figures, male and female, were found in a tomb in northwestern Georgia. The Native American carvings, known to us only as part of a South Appalachian Mississippi culture, are thought to be representations of ancestor gods. Are similar shrine figures found in African and European societies?

(Lynn Johnson/Aurora & Quanta Productions)

Africa on the Eve of Contact

Half a century before Columbus reached the Americas, a Portuguese sea captain, Antam Gonçalves, made the first European landing on the west coast of sub-Saharan Africa. If he had been able to travel the length and breadth of the immense continent, he would have encountered a rich variety of African states, peoples, and cultures that had developed over many millennia.

During the period of early contact with Europeans, Africa, like pre-Columbian America, was a diverse continent with a long history of cultural evolution.

The Spread of Islam

"The seat of Mansa Sulayman [the sultan, or ruler] was a sprawling, unwalled town set in a 'verdant and hilly' country," wrote Arab geographer Abu Abdallah Ibn Battuta in 1351, after visiting the capital of the Mali Kingdom at about the same time that the Aztecs rose to eminence in Mesoamerica. "The sultan had several enclosed palaces there . . . and covered [them] with colored patterns so that it turned out to be the most elegant of buildings." The 47-year-old Ibn Battuta, born into a family of Muslim legal scholars in Tangier, Morocco, on the southern shore of the Mediterranean Sea, was struck with Mali's splendor. "Surrounding the palaces and mosques were the residences of the citizenry, mud-walled houses roofed with domes of timber and reed." Keenly interested in their laws, Ibn Battuta wrote, "Amongst their good qualities is the small amount of injustice amongst them, for of all people

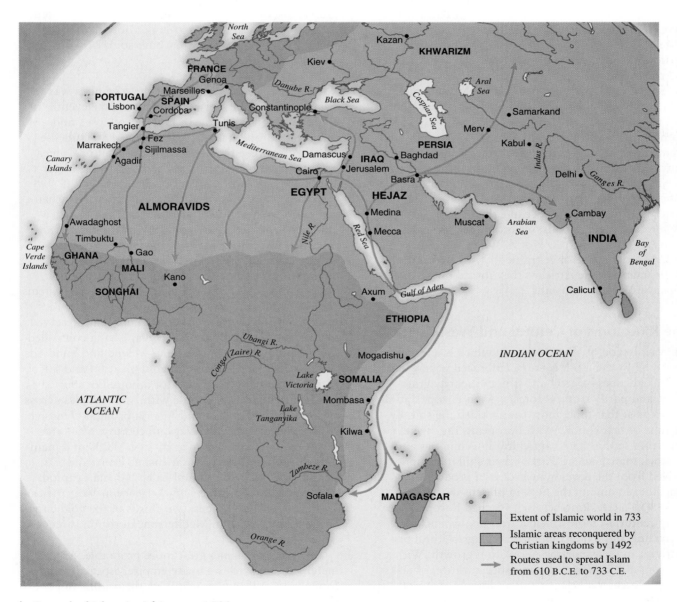

Spread of Islam in Africa, ca. 1500

This map shows the extensive reach of Islam in Africa by 1500. On most of the North African Mediterranean coast and in the powerful Mali and Songhai kingdoms, the Muslim faith predominated. Do you think enslaved Africans who had converted to Islam practiced their faith after arriving in the American colonies? How would they do so on slave plantations?

they are the furthest from it. Their sultan does not forgive anyone in any matter to do with injustice. . . . There is also the prevalence of peace in their country, the traveler is not afraid in it nor is he who lives there in fear of the thief or of the robber." With Ibn Battuta traveled the Muslim faith, or commitment to Islam (meaning "submission to Allah").

This account of Ibn Battuta, the greatest traveler of premodern times, opens a window to the trends in pre-contact Atlantic African history: the spread of Islam (meaning "submission to Allah") and the rise of great empires in West and Central Africa. This vast region was then called the Sudan, a word that comes from *al-Sudan*, Arabic for "black people." Ibn Battuta had traveled for more than 20 years through much of the Eastern Hemisphere before reaching Mali, visiting territories equivalent to some 44 present-day countries and traversing 73,000 miles.

Spreading rapidly in Arabia after Muhammad, the founder of Islam, began preaching in 610 C.E., Islam rose to global eminence after several centuries. By the tenth century, Egypt was predominantly Muslim, and Islam was spreading southward from Mediterranean North Africa across the Sahara Desert into northern Sudan, where it took hold especially in the trading centers. In time, Islam encompassed much of the Eastern Hemisphere and became the main intermediary for exchanging goods, ideas, and technologies across a huge part of the world. When Portuguese traders initiated the slave traffic in West Africa in the 1400s, many of the Africans they forced onto slave ships were devout Muslims.

The Kingdoms of Central and West Africa

The vast region of West Africa, to which Islam was spreading by the tenth century, embraced widely varied ecological zones—partly a vast desert, partly grass-lands, and partly tropical forests. As in Europe and the Americas at that time, most people tilled the soil. By the time of first contact with Europeans they were practicing sophisticated agricultural techniques and livestock management. Part of their skill in farming derived from the development of iron production, which began among the Nok in present-day Nigeria about 450 B.C.E., long before it reached Europe. Over many centuries, more efficient iron implements for cultivating and harvesting increased agricultural pro-ductivity, in turn spurring population growth. With large populations came greater specialization of tasks and thus greater efficiency and additional technical improvements. The pattern was similar to the agricul-tural revolution that occurred in the Americas, Europe, the Far East, and the Middle East.

Cultural and political development in West Africa proceeded at varying rates, largely dependent on

ecological conditions. Regions blessed by good soil, adequate rainfall, and abundance of minerals, as in coastal West Africa, engaged in interregional trade. Population growth and cultural development followed. But where deserts were inhospitable or forests impene-trable, social systems remained small and changed slowly. The Sahara Desert, once a land of flowing rivers and lush green pastures and forests, had been depopulated by climate changes that brought higher temperatures and lower rainfall. As desertification occurred between about 4000 B.C.E. and 2500 B.C.E., Sahara people moved southward in search of more fertile land, first to oases situated along a strip of grasslands, or savanna, on the desert's southern border, then farther south to the fertile rain forests of the Niger River basin. There they built some of Africa's greatest empires.

THE GHANA EMPIRE   The first of these empires was Ghana. Developing between the fifth and eleventh centuries, when the Roman Empire collapsed and medieval Europe stagnated, it occupied an immense territory between the Sahara and the Gulf of Guinea and stretched from the Atlantic Ocean to the Niger River. Though mostly a land of small villages, it became a major empire noted for its extensive urban settlement, sculpture and metalwork, long-distance commerce, and complex political and military struc-ture. Ideally positioned for trade, Ghana built its empire primarily on trade rather than military conquest. From the south came kola nuts, palm oil, copper, and gold. From the north came imported items such as ceramics, glass, oil lamps, and—absolutely essential—the salt from Saharan mines that preserved and flavored food. By the late 900s, Ghana controlled more than 100,000 square miles of land and hundreds of thousands of people. With gold plentiful and salt rare, a pound of gold traded for a pound of salt.

A thriving caravan trade with Arab peoples across the Sahara to Morocco and Algeria brought extensive Muslim influence by the eleventh century, when the king of Ghana boasted an army of 200,000 and main-tained trading contacts as far east as Cairo and Baghdad. Gold made Kumbi-Saleh, Ghana's capital, the busiest and wealthiest marketplace in West Africa. By Europe's Middle Ages, two-thirds of the gold circu-lating in the Christian Mediterranean region came from Ghana.

As trade in Ghana grew more profitable, Arab merchants came to live in the empire, especially in the capital city of Kumbi-Saleh. With the trading of goods came the exchange of ideas. Arabs brought the first system of writing and numbers to West Africa, and the Ghanaian kings adopted Arab script and appointed Arabs to government positions. As these Arabs gained influence in Ghana, they spread the Islamic faith. Most of Ghana's rulers held tightly to their traditional religion and rejected the Muslim principle of patriarchy in which royal succession would follow the father's lineage. But many Ghanaians, especially in the cities, converted to Islam. By 1050, Kumbi-Saleh boasted 12 Muslim mosques.

THE MALI EMPIRE An invasion of North African Muslim warriors beginning in the eleventh century introduced a period of religious strife that eventually destroyed the kingdom of Ghana. Rising to replace it was the Islamic kingdom of Mali, dominated by the Malinke, or Mandingo, people. Through effective agricultural production and control of the gold trade, Mali flourished. The cultivation of rice and harvesting of inland deltas for fish helped support the thriving trade for salt, gold, and copper. Under Mansa Musa, a devout Muslim who assumed the throne in 1307, Mali came to control territory three times as great as the kingdom of Ghana. Famed for his 3,500-mile pilgrimage across the Sahara and through Cairo all the way to Mecca in 1324 with an entourage of some 50,000, Mansa Musa drew the attention of Mediterranean merchants. Dispensing lavish gifts of gold as he proceeded east, he made Mali gold legendary.

Coming home, Mansa Musa brought Muslim scholars and artisans with him who were instrumental in establishing Timbuktu, at the center of the Mali Empire, as a city of great importance. Noted for its extensive wealth, Timbuktu's Islamic university developed a distinguished faculty, who instructed North African and southern European students. Traveling there in the 1330s, Ibn Battuta wrote admiringly of "the discipline of its officials and provincial governors, the excellent condition of public finance, and . . . the respect accorded to the decisions of justice and to the authority of the sovereign."

THE SONGHAI EMPIRE After Mansa Musa died in 1332, power in West Africa began to shift to the Songhai, centered on the middle Niger River. A mixture of farmers, traders, fishermen, and warriors, the Songhai declared independence from Mali in 1435. Just as Mali had grown out of a state in the empire of Ghana, the new Songhai Empire grew out of a region that had once been part of Mali. By the time Portuguese traders in the late 1400s were establishing firm commercial links with the Kongo, far to the south, the Songhai Empire was at its peak under the rule of Sonni Ali (1464–1492) and Muhammad Ture (1493–1528).

Yet Songhai, too, collapsed, as some tribes that were resentful of Muslim kings began to break away. But the most dangerous threat came from Morocco, in North Africa, whose rulers coveted Songhai's sources of salt and gold—the two critical commodities in the African trade. Equipped with guns procured in the Middle East,

Morocco's ruler conquered Timbuktu and Gao in 1591. The North Africans remained in loose control of western Sudan for more than a century, as the last great trading empire of West Africa faded. At a time when England, France, Spain, and other centralized kingdoms in Europe were emerging, the great empires of West Africa slowly devolved into smaller states. Looking back over the long centuries of the tragic Atlantic slave trade, it seems that by a melancholy quirk of history, local West African conflicts made it easier for European slave traders to persuade tribal leaders to send out warrior parties to capture tradeable slaves.

THE KINGDOMS OF KONGO AND BENIN Farther south along the Atlantic coast and in Central Africa lay the vast kingdom of Kongo. The first European to encounter these people was the Portuguese ship captain Diego Cao, who in 1482 anchored in the mouth of the mighty Kongo River. Kongo's royal capital, Mbanza, was a trade center for a kingdom of several million people and also became a center of trade relations with the Portuguese, who by the 1490s were sending Catholic missionaries to the court of King Mani-Kongo. Mani-Kongo's son was baptized Affonso I, and under Affonso's rule in the early 1500s, a flourishing trade in slaves with the Portuguese began.

Like Kongo, the kingdom of Benin developed long before seaborne Europeans reached western Africa. Benin, later so important in the English slave trade, was formed in about 1000 C.E. west of the Niger Delta. When Europeans reached Benin City hundreds of years later, they found a walled city with broad streets and hundreds of buildings. Thousands of slaves procured in the interior passed through Benin City on their way for exchange with the Portuguese, and later the English, at coastal Calabar, where one of the main slave forts stood.

African Slavery

The idea that slavery was a legitimate social condition in past societies offends modern values, and it is difficult for many Americans to understand why Africans would sell fellow Africans to European traders. But there were no people who identified themselves as Africans four centuries ago; rather, they thought of themselves as Ibos or Mandingos, or Kongolese, or residents of Mali or Songhai. Moreover, slavery was not new for Africans or any other people in the fourteenth century. It had flourished in ancient Rome and Greece, in large parts of eastern Europe, in southwestern Asia, and in the Mediterranean world in general. In times of pillage and conquest, invading people everywhere sold prisoners into slavery. Sale seemed more merciful than mass execution—and more profitable.

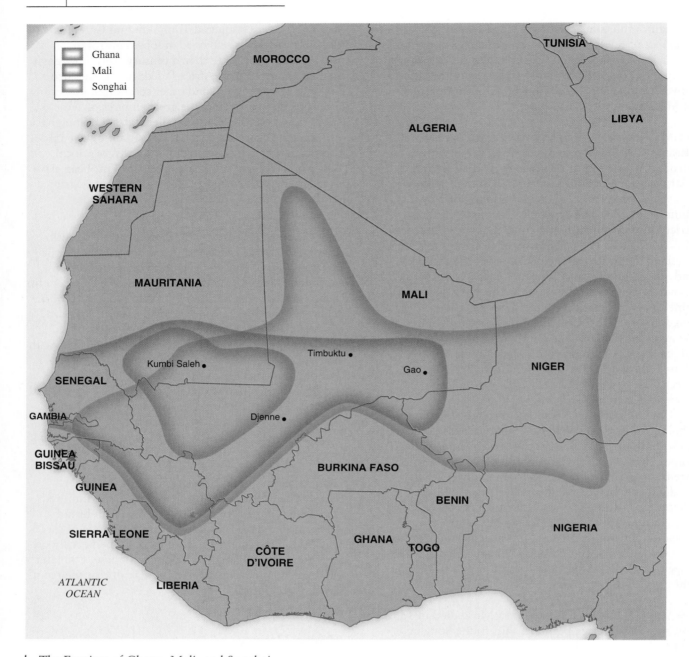

The Empires of Ghana, Mali, and Songhai

These ancient empires, each in their turn, controlled vast areas of West Africa. Ghana, which built its wealth on trade, was at its height from about 900 to 1100 C.E. Mali's devout Muslim leader, Mansa Musa, commissioned large mosques and turned Timbuktu into a center of Islamic learning. Songhai began its rise to power after the death of Mansa Musa. Why would some Europeans send their sons to Timbuktu to study? What evidence can you find that Muslim ideas contributed to European scientific and cultural knowledge?

Slavery had existed in Africa for centuries. Like other peoples, Africans accepted slavery without question as a condition of servitude and slaveholding as a mark of wealth. To own slaves was to be wealthy; to trade slaves was a way of increasing one's wealth. Olaudah Equiano—who wrote an account of his boyhood in Africa—described how his tribe traded slaves who "were only prisoners of war, or such among us as had been convicted of kidnaping, or adultery, and some other crimes which we esteemed heinous." In this way, African societies for centuries conducted an overland slave trade that carried captured people from West Africa across the vast Sahara Desert to Christian Roman Europe and the Islamic Middle East.

From the tenth to fifteenth century, about 5,000 West Africans were sold eastward as sugar workers in Egypt, as domestic servants and craftspeople throughout the Arabic world, and as soldiers in North Africa. Islam had facilitated this process by establishing secure trade routes connecting West Africa with the Mediterranean world and the lands east of it. By the time Songhai rose to prominence in West Africa, the kingdom became a major supplier of enslaved captives across the Sahara to North Africa. This trade gave Songhai's elite access to European trade goods—Venetian beads, fine cloth, and horses, the latter especially important to Songhai warriors who were waging war against neighboring peoples. Though this slave traffic was on the rise, it was still an occasional rather than a highly organized trade, and it was carried out to provide Mediterranean trading partners with soldiers, household servants, and artisans rather than gangs of field workers.

Peoples of West Africa held to a conception of slavery very different from the one that would develop in the European colonies of the Americas. "Those prisoners which were not sold or redeemed," remembered Equiano, "we kept as slaves; but how different was their condition from that of slaves in the West-Indies! With us, they do no more work than other members of the community, even their master. Their food, clothing, and lodging were nearly the same as theirs, except they were not permitted to eat with the free-born." In the African practice of slavery the enslaved served as soldiers, administrators, sometimes as royal advisers, and even occasionally as royal consorts. The status of slave was not necessarily lifelong but was revocable, and slavery did not automatically pass on to the female slave's children. African slaves might achieve high status or slaves, and freedom remained a real possibility.

The African Ethos

Many of Africa's peoples—Ashanti, Mandingo, Coromantee, Yoruba, Fon, Hausa, Ibo, Whydah, and Ga, among others—eventually became African Americans. Indeed, they would become at least two-thirds of all the immigrants who crossed the ocean to the Western Hemisphere in the three centuries after Europeans began colonizing there. They came from a rich diversity of cultures, but most of them shared certain ways of life that differentiated them from Europeans.

As in Europe, the family was the basic unit of social organization. By maintaining intimate connections between man and woman, parent and child, sister and brother, enslaved Africans developed an important defense against the cruelties of slavery. Unlike Europeans, however, where patriarchy put the father and husband at the center of family life, Africans organized themselves in a variety of kinship systems. In many African societies, as in many Native American ones, the family was matrilineal. Property rights and political inheritance descended through the mother rather than the father. When a chief died, the son of his sister inherited his position. Upon marrying, a man joined his wife's people. This matrilineal tradition carried over into slavery, as African women continued to have an influence not typical in European family

The African City of Loango

The city of Loango, at the mouth of the Kongo River on the west coast of Africa, was larger at the time of this drawing in the mid-eighteenth century than all but a few seaports in the British colonies in North America. Why would artists produce such city views of various foreign ports?

(The Granger Collection, New York)

organization. In Africa, each person was linked to others in the village, his or her identity defined by family relationships. Individualism, which would eventually become so prized in English society transplanted to North America, was an alien and distasteful concept.

Africans brought a complex religious heritage with them to the Americas. Widespread across Africa was a belief in a supreme Creator of the cosmos and in a pantheon of lesser deities associated with natural forces, such as rain, animals, and the fertility of the earth. These spiritual forces could intervene in human affairs and were, therefore, elaborately honored. West Africans, like most native North Americans, held that spirits dwelt in the trees, rocks, and rivers around them, and hence they exercised care in their treatment. Many West Africans practiced spirit possession, in which the gods spoke to men and women through priests and other religious figures.

Africans also venerated ancestors, who they believed mediated between the Creator and the living. Relatives held elaborate funeral rites to ensure the proper entrance of a deceased relative into the spiritual world. The more ancient an ancestor, the greater this person's power to affect the living; thus the "ancient ones" were revered. Deep family loyalty and regard for family lineage flowed naturally from these beliefs.

While their religious beliefs differed from those of their European slave owners, Africans shared some common ground, including a belief in an invisible "other world" inhabited by the souls of the dead who could be known through revelations interpreted by spiritually gifted people. These roughly shared foundations of religious feeling fostered the development of a hybrid African faith in the New World and shaped African Christianity. In fact, in the kingdom of Kongo and several small kingdoms close to the Niger Delta, extensive contact with the Portuguese had allowed Christianity to graft itself onto African religious beliefs by the time English colonies were planted in North America in the seventeenth century. African religious customs, funeral rites, sacred images, and charms for protection against evil spirits lost some of their power during enslavement, though how fast this happened is murky and clearly varied from place to place. But even to the present day, African religious beliefs and practices still hold at least partial sway among some African Americans.

Social organization in much of West Africa by the time Europeans arrived was as elaborate as in fifteenth-century Europe. At the top of society stood the king, supported by nobles and priests, usually elderly men. Beneath them, the great mass of people mostly cultivated the soil in innumerable villages. In urban centers, craftspeople, traders, teachers, and artists lived beneath the ruling families.

Edo Sculpture

This commemorative head, probably of a queen mother, was made by an Edo of the Benin kingdom about the time Columbus was making his first voyage across the Atlantic. The elaborate headdress and collar of beads are fashioned from copper alloy with iron inlay. Would ordinary Ibo women be dressed like this?

(Commemorative trophy head. Edo peoples, Nigeria, Late 15th–early 16th century, Copper alloy, iron inlay, H x W x D: 23.2 x 15.9 x 20 cm, Purchased with funds provided by the Smithsonian Collections Acquisition Program, 85–5–2. Photograph by Franko Khoury, National Museum of African Art, Smithsonian Institution.)

Europe on the Eve of Invading the Americas

In the ninth century, about the time that the Mound Builders of the Mississippi valley were constructing their urban center at Cahokia and the kingdom of Ghana was rising in West Africa, western Europe was an economic and cultural backwater. The center of political power and economic vitality in the Old World had shifted eastward to Christian Byzantium, which controlled Asia Minor, the Balkans, and parts of Italy. The other dynamic culture of this age, Islam, had spread through the Middle East, spilled across North Africa, and penetrated Spain and West Africa south of the Sahara.

Within a few centuries, an epic revitalization of western Europe occurred, creating the conditions that enabled its leading maritime nations vastly to extend their oceanic frontiers. By the late fifteenth century, a 400-year epoch of militant overseas European expansion was underway. Not until the second half of the twentieth century was this process of Europeanization reversed; then colonized people began to regain their autonomy and cultural identity through wars of national liberation—a process now nearing completion.

The Rebirth of Europe

The rebirth of western Europe, which began around 1000 C.E., owed much to a revival of long-distance trading from Italian ports on the Mediterranean and to the rediscovery of ancient knowledge that these contacts permitted. The once mighty cities of the Roman Empire had stagnated for centuries, but now Venice, Genoa, and other Italian ports began trading with peoples facing the Adriatic, Baltic, and North seas. These new contacts brought wealth and power to the Italian commercial cities, which gradually evolved into merchant-dominated city–states that freed themselves from the rule of feudal lords in control of the surrounding countryside. By the late 1400s, sailing ships were crossing all the sea basins of the Eastern Hemisphere—the China Sea, the Indian Ocean, the Persian Gulf, the Red and Black seas, and the Mediterranean, creating a zone of intercultural communication.

While merchants led the emerging city–states, western Europe's feudal system gradually weakened. For centuries, warrior aristocrats, not kings, had exercised the powers of the state: to tax, wage war, and administer the law. In the thirteenth and fourteenth centuries, however, kings reasserted their political authority and worked to unify their realms. They sought to curb the power of the great feudal lords who dominated entire regions and to force lesser nobles into dependence on and obedience to the crown. In England the king's consolidation of power was curbed when he accepted the Magna Carta, a basic statement of propertied men's rights. A parliament composed of elective and hereditary members eventually gained the right to meet regularly to pass money bills and therefore act as a check on the Crown. Continental nobles never shared governance with their rulers to the same extent. In France, a noble faction assassinated Henry III in 1589, and the nobles remained disruptive for nearly another century. In Spain, the final conquest of the Muslims and expulsion of the

Jews, both in 1492, strengthened the monarchy's hold, but regional cultures and leaders remained strong for some time. Concurrent with the consolidation of monarchical power in the fourteenth century, the mass of peasant people suffered greatly. Famine struck many parts of Europe after 1300 because the production of food did not keep up with population increases. Malnutrition reduced the resistance of millions when the Black Death (bubonic plague) struck with fury. It first devastated China, wiping out nearly one-third of the population, and then moved eastward following trade routes to India and the Middle East, hitting

A Chapel Made of Bone

The Black Death of the mid-fourteenth century killed nearly 40,000 people in the region of Prague. Five centuries later, a Czech woodcarver fashioned the bones of thousands of Black Death victims into a chapel where visitors are astounded to see a bone altar, bone chalices, the bone chandelier that is pictured here, and gigantic bone bells. Every bone in the human body is used in the chandelier. How does the Black Death compare with modern-day scourges such as AIDS?

(Photograph © Lubomir Stiburek)

hardest in the cities. In 1348 it reached western Europe and North Africa. Over the next quarter century, some 30 million Europeans died, a blow from which Europe did not recover demographically for centuries. This unprecedented human misery produced economic disruption, violent worker strikes, and peasant uprisings. The Black Death also promoted the unification of old realms into early modern states. The noble class with which monarchs had to contend were reduced, for the plague defied class distinction. For a time after the plague, feudal lords treated their peasants better because their labor became more valuable.

By the sixteenth century, however, great landowners in England began to "enclose" (consolidate) their estates, throwing peasant farmers off their plots and turning many of them into wage laborers. The formation of this laboring class was the crucial first step toward industrial development.

The New Monarchies and the Expansionist Impulse

In the second half of the fifteenth century, ambitious monarchs coming to power in France, England, and Spain sought social and political stability in their kingdoms by creating armies and bureaucracies strong enough to quell internal conflict and raising taxes sufficient to support their regimes. In these countries, and in Portugal as well, economic revival and the reversal of more than a century of population decline and civil disorder nourished the impulse to expand. This impulse was also fed by Renaissance culture. Ushering in a new, more secular age, the Renaissance (Rebirth) encouraged innovation (in science as well as in art and music), freedom of thought, richness of expression, and an emphasis on human abilities. Beginning in Italy and spreading northward through Europe, the Renaissance peaked dramatically in the late fifteenth century as the age of overseas exploration began.

The exploratory urge had two initial objectives: first, to circumvent overland Muslim traders by finding an eastward oceanic route to Asia; second, to tap the African gold trade at its source, avoiding Muslim intermediaries in North Africa. Since 1291, when Marco Polo returned to Venice with tales of Eastern treasures such as spices, silks, perfumes, medicines, and jewels, Europeans had bartered with the Orient via a long eastward overland route through the Muslim world. Eventually, Europe's mariners found they could voyage to Cathay (China) by both eastward and westward water routes.

Portugal seemed the least likely of the rising nation–states to lead the expansion of Europe outside its continental boundaries, yet it forged into the lead at the end of the fifteenth century. A poor country of only a million inhabitants, Portugal had gradually overcome Moorish control in the twelfth and thirteenth centuries and, in 1385, had wrenched itself free of domination by neighboring Castile. Led by Prince Henry the Navigator, for whom trade was secondary to the conquest of the Muslim world, Portugal breached the unknown. In the 1420s, Henry began dispatching Portuguese mariners to probe the unknown Atlantic "sea of darkness." Important improvements in navigational instruments, mapmaking, and ship design aided his intrepid sailors. Symbolizing the increasingly interconnected world, the compass, invented by the Chinese, was copied by Middle Eastern Arabs, then by the Portuguese.

Portuguese captains operated at sea on three ancient Ptolemaic principles: that the earth was round, that distances on its surface could be measured by degrees, and that navigators could "fix" their position at sea on a map by measuring the position of the stars. The invention in the 1450s of the quadrant, which allowed a precise measurement of star altitude necessary for determining latitude, represented a leap forward from the chart-and-compass method of navigation. Equally important was the design of a

Astrolabe

In Columbus's era, the astrolabe was the most important astronomical computer, in which the celestial sphere was projected onto the equator's plane. Once the moveable arm was set, the entire sky was visible. Why did Europeans adopt it from the Islamic world only in the twelfth century, where it had been in use for centuries?

(Courtesy of Adler Planetarium & Astronomy Museum, Chicago, Illinois)

Timeline

35,000 B.C.E.	First humans cross Bering Land Bridge to reach the Americas
12,000 B.C.E.	Beringian epoch ends
8000 B.C.E.	Paleo-Indian phase ends
500 B.C.E.	Archaic era ends
500 B.C.E.–1000 C.E.	Post-Archaic era in North America
600 C.E.–1100	Rise of mound-building center at Cahokia
632–750	Islamic conquest of North Africa spreads Muslim faith
800–1026	Kingdom of Ghana controls West Africa's trade
1000	Norse seafarers establish settlements in Newfoundland
	Kingdom of Benin develops
1000–1500	Kingdoms of Ghana, Mali, Songhai in Africa
1200s	Pueblo societies develop village life in southwestern North America
1235	Defeating the Ghanaian king, Mali becomes a West African power
1291	Marco Polo's return from East Asia to Venice quickens European trade with Eastern Hemisphere
1300s	Rise of Aztec society in Valley of Mexico
1300–1450	Italian Renaissance
1324	Mansa Musa's pilgrimage to Mecca expands Muslim influence in West Africa
1420s	Portuguese sailors explore west coast of Africa
1435	Kingdom of Songhai declares independence from kingdom of Mali
1450–1600	Northern European Renaissance
1460s–1590s	Kingdom of Songhai controls West Africa's trading societies
1469	Marriage of Castile's Isabella and Aragon's Ferdinand creates Spain
1500s	Quickening of western European trade and production of consumer goods

lateen-rigged caravel, adapted from a Moorish ship design. The triangular sails permitted ships to sail into the wind, allowing them to travel southward along the African coast—a feat the square-rigged European vessels could never perform—and return northward against prevailing winds.

By the 1430s, the ability of Prince Henry's captains to break through the limits of the world known to Europeans had carried them to Madeira, the Canary Islands, and the more distant Azores, lying off the coasts of Portugal and northwestern Africa. These were soon developed as the first European-controlled agricultural plantations, located on the continent's periphery and designed to produce cash crops such as sugar that could be marketed in Europe. Thus, the Madeiras, Canaries, and Azores became a kind of laboratory for larger European colonies much farther from their homelands.

From these islands, the Portuguese sea captains pushed farther south, navigating their way down the west coast of Africa by 1460. While carrying their Christian faith to new lands, they began a profitable trade in ivory, slaves, and especially gold. Now, they were poised to capitalize on the connection between Europe and Africa, though not yet knowing that a stupendous land mass, to become known as America, lay far across the Atlantic Ocean.

Conclusion
THE APPROACH OF A NEW GLOBAL AGE

All the forces that have made the world of the past 500 years "modern" began to come into play by the late fifteenth century. As the stories about three important women of this era demonstrate, deep transformations were underway in West Africa, in western Europe, and in the Americas. West African empires had reached new heights, some had been deeply influenced by the Islamic faith, and many had become experienced in transregional trade. Muslim scholars, merchants, and long-distance travelers were becoming the principal mediators in the interregional exchange of goods, ideas, and technical innovations.

Meanwhile the Renaissance, initiated in Italy, worked its way northward and brought new energy and ambition to a weakened, disease-ridden, and tired Europe. Advances in maritime technology also allowed Europeans to make contact with the peoples of West Africa and develop the first slave-based plantation societies in tropical islands off the West African coast. In the Americas, large empires in Mexico and—as we will see in Chapter 2, Peru—were growing more populous and consolidating their power while in North America the opposite was occurring: a decay of powerful mound-building societies and a long-range move toward decentralized tribal societies. The scene was set for the great leap of Europeans across the Atlantic, where the convergence between the peoples of Africa, the Americas, and Europe would occur.

QUESTIONS FOR REVIEW AND REFLECTION

1. To what do you attribute the remarkable diversity of cultures in the Americas in the centuries prior to contact with Europeans? What are the most marked examples of that diversity?
2. What were the major features of western African society and culture prior to contact with European traders?
3. What were the causes and major consequences of the revitalization of western Europe in the period after 1000 C.E.?
4. Africa, Europe, and the Americas at the start of the "early modern period" are often treated as dramatically different in every way, yet commonalities existed. What were the most striking of these common features?
5. Why did western Europeans expand out of their geographical confines to explore, conquer, and colonize the Americas? What factors were not present in Africa or the Americas to foster expansion into the Atlantic basin from those areas?

CHAPTER 2

Europeans and Africans Reach the Americas

"Slave deck of the *Albanoz*, Prize of the *HMS Albatross*," watercolor, by Lt. Francis Meynell (a young British naval officer) depicted a captured Spanish slave ship's deck.

(© National Maritime Museum, London)

American Stories

Old World Sojourners Mingle with New World Inhabitants

Just 15 years after conquistadors led by Hernán Cortés toppled the Aztec Empire in Mexico, Spanish horsemen, searching for Native Americans to capture as slaves, happened upon some 600 of them in northwestern Mexico. Traveling with the natives were an African and three Spaniards, all dressed in native garb. The horsemen were "thunderstruck to see me so strangely dressed and in the company of Indians," noted Álvar Núñez Cabeza de Vaca, one of the three Spaniards accompanying the natives. "They went on staring at me for a long space of time, so astonished that they could neither speak to me nor manage to ask me anything."

De Vaca, his two Spanish companions, and the African had been lost for eight years and were presumed dead. They had been part of the 1528 expedition that had tried to plant a permanent Spanish settlement in what the Spanish called La Florida. Establishing themselves near the swamplands of Tampa Bay, the Spanish adventurers encountered starvation, disease, a leadership crisis, and hostile Native Americans. Captured by the Apalachee, who enslaved them, de Vaca and his companions soon adopted Native American ways, adapted to a new environment, and convinced their captors that they possessed magical healing power. The African, already a slave of one of the captured Spaniards and known as Estevan (sometimes called Estanvanico), became an accomplished linguist, healer, guide, and negotiator. When they fled their captors, the four fugitives plunged into the wilderness and headed west. Paddling crude boats across the Gulf of Mexico, they shipwrecked on the Texas coast and took refuge among merciful Native Americans.

Such forays into a rugged and uncharted territory cast the Spanish and African adventurers into unaccustomed roles and sorely tested their ability to survive among the indigenous people, who generally opposed their intrusion into their homelands. De Vaca, a conquistador experienced in enslaving Native Americans, had become a slave himself before the flight to Texas. Estevan's status as the slave of a Spanish conquistador all but dissolved in the process of becoming a Native American slave and then a refugee from enslavement. In his journal, de Vaca described Estevan as "a black," "a Moor," and "an Arabian." But these were only words describing his skin color (dark), his religion (Islam), and his geographical homeland (Morocco). What mattered in this strange and often hostile land was not Estevan's blackness or even his slave status. What counted, in this time before the idea of racial categories, were his linguistic abilities, his fortitude, and his cleverness as a go-between. Estevan, having originated on one land bordering the Atlantic, became a new man in the process of the cultural, linguistic, and social braiding that was occurring throughout the sixteenth-century Atlantic world.

For five years, Estevan, his master Andrés Dorantes, de Vaca, and another Spaniard traveled west for about 2,500 miles. Often following friendly Native American guides, the four travelers came to be regarded as holy men, possessing the power to heal. Reaching present-day New Mexico, they found Native Americans who, according to de Vaca, described them as "four great doctors, one of them black, the other three white, who gave blessings [and] healed the sick." On one occasion, the natives gave Estevan a sacred gourd rattle. Then, in 1536, the foursome stumbled upon the Spanish expedition in northern Mexico. Three years later, after joining a new Spanish expedition, Estevan blazed a trail for Francisco Vásquez de Coronado's *entrada* (incursion) of 1540. In what would later be called Arizona, Estevan was selected to forge ahead into Zuñi country with Native American guides, in search of the fabled seven gold-filled cities of Cibola. His gift for acquiring native languages and his long experience with peoples of the vast territory north of New Spain made him the logical choice. But on this trip, Estevan met his death at the hands of Zuñi warriors, perhaps angry at his consorting with Zuñi women. *The four voyages of Christopher Columbus* from 1492 to 1504, conducted on the eve of religious conflict and reformation in Europe, brought together people like Estevan and de Vaca from three previously unconnected continents. Together, they made a new world, their lives intersecting, their cultural attributes interacting. Here was the birth of an Americas-wide cultural mosaic.

In this chapter, we follow the epoch-making voyages of Columbus, the arrival of Spanish conquistadors, their remarkable conquest of vast territories in Mesoamerica and the southern regions of North America, and the momentous effect of plants, animals, and germs as they traveled westward and eastward across the Atlantic.

We will also see how the phenomenal exploits of Hernán Cortés and Francisco Pizarro, and the discovery of immense quantities of silver, attracted the attention of other Europeans—first the French, then the Dutch and English. Latecomers in the race to exploit the treasures of the Americas while providing a place for the downtrodden settlers from Europe, the English would only appear on the scene a century after the Columbian voyages. Their presence, while escalating the rivalries among emerging European nation–states as they jumped across the Atlantic, planted the seeds of an English-dominated American nation.

Breaching the Atlantic

When Ferdinand and Isabella married in 1469 to unite Aragon and Castile, they launched this new Spanish nation into its golden age, beginning with the four voyages of Christopher Columbus to the Americas between 1492 and 1504. Meanwhile, the Portuguese extended their influence along the west coast of Africa and all the way to East Asia. In a short period, contact between peoples in different parts of the world increased markedly, shrinking the globe. The great leap across the Atlantic Ocean triggered global changes of unimaginable significance. Western Europeans were becoming the most dynamic force in the world and were on the verge of exerting a greater global influence than the people of any single region had ever done before.

The Columbian Voyages

Leading the way for Spain was an Italian sailor, Christopher Columbus. The son of a poor Genoese weaver, Columbus had married into a prominent family of Lisbon merchants, thus making important contacts at court. Celebrated for hundreds of years as a heroic discoverer and now often attacked as a ruthless exploiter of Native American peoples and lands, Columbus is best understood in the context of his own times—an age of great brutality and violence and also an age in which Catholic Spain was engaged in the final stages of expelling the Moorish people who had controlled southern Spain for centuries. Columbus's urge to explore was nourished by questions about the geographic limits of his world. He was also inspired by a desire to advance the reach of Iberian Catholicism. The Latin inscription on the tomb of monarchs Isabella and Ferdinand captures the missionary mood of the era: "Overthrowers of the Mahometan sect and repressors of heretical stubbornness."

Like many sailors, Columbus had listened to sea tales about lands to the west. He may have heard Icelandic sagas about the voyages of Leif Eriksson and several thousand Norse immigrants who had reached Newfoundland five centuries earlier. Other ideas circulated that the Atlantic Ocean stretched to India and eastern Asia. Could one reach the Indies by sailing west rather than by sailing east around Africa, as the Portuguese were attempting? Columbus hungered to know.

For nearly 10 years, Columbus unsuccessfully sought financial backing and royal sanction in Portugal for exploratory voyages. Many mocked his modest estimates of the distance westward from Europe to Japan, which he reckoned at 3,500 miles rather than contemporary estimates of 10,000 to 12,000 miles—far beyond the limit of small European ships, which could not carry enough food and water to keep sailors alive

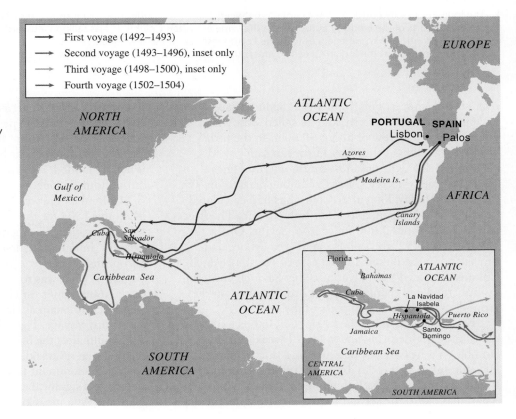

Columbus's Four Voyages

The different courses taken by Columbus on his four Atlantic crossings were prompted by his desire to explore the island-rich Caribbean Sea. He departed on his second voyage only months after reaching Seville with news about the first epic voyage. Why did he focus on the Caribbean islands?

→ First voyage (1492–1493)
→ Second voyage (1493–1496), inset only
→ Third voyage (1498–1500), inset only
→ Fourth voyage (1502–1504)

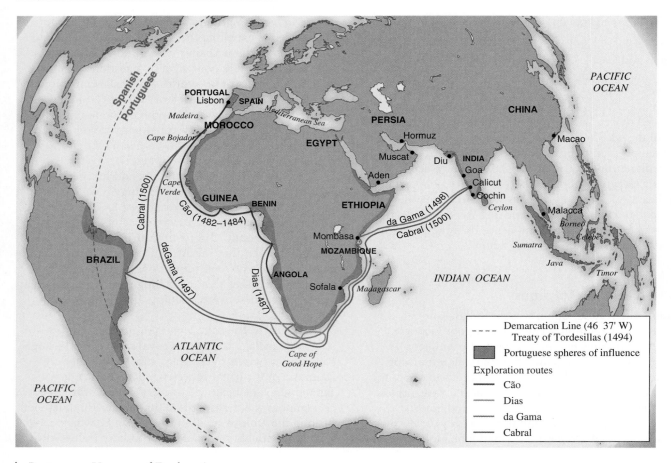

Portuguese Voyages of Exploration

The four voyages by Portuguese sea captains between 1482 and 1500 show how those who sailed southward and eastward opened up distant parts of the world to Europeans in the same era when Columbus was sailing westward to the Americas. Did Columbus share his Atlantic Ocean experiences with the Portuguese sea captains who reached the Indian Ocean? If so, how? What did Columbus learn from the Indian Ocean voyagers that helped him in his Atlantic Ocean voyages?

over such distances. Finally, in 1492, Spain's Queen Isabella commissioned him, and he sailed west with three ships and a crew of about 90 men. In the fifth week at sea—longer than any European sailors had been out of the sight of land—mutinous rumblings swept through the crews. But Columbus pressed on. On the seventieth day, long after Columbus had calculated he would reach Japan, a lookout sighted land. The fleet had traveled about 3,000 miles from Seville. On October 12, 1492, the sailors clambered ashore on a tiny island in the Bahamas (just east of Florida), which Columbus named San Salvador (Holy Savior). Grateful sailors "rendered thanks to Our Lord, kneeling on the ground, embracing it with tears of joy."

Believing he had reached Asia, Columbus explored the island-speckled Caribbean for 10 weeks. After landing on a heavily populated island that he named Hispaniola (shared today by Haiti and the Dominican Republic) and on Cuba (which he thought was the Asian mainland), he set sail for Spain with cinnamon,

coconuts, a bit of gold, and several kidnaped natives. Homeward bound, he penned a report of what he believed were his Asian discoveries: hospitable people, fertile soils, magnificent harbors, and gold-filled rivers. When he landed, his report was quickly distributed throughout Europe.

Columbus's report brought him financing between 1494 and 1504 for three much larger expeditions. The second voyage, carrying more than 1,200 Spaniards in 17 ships, initiated the first extended contact between Europeans and Native Americans. In an ominous display of what was to come, Columbus's men captured some 1,600 Taínos on Hispaniola and carried 550 of them back to Spain as slaves in 1495. Only 350 survived the stormy voyage. Here began the Atlantic slave trade that would alter the history of the world, though it began in the reverse direction of what would soon become its dominant flow. Although his discoveries seemed less significant than the Portuguese exploits in the South Atlantic, Columbus had led Spain to the threshold of a mighty empire. He died in 1506, to the end believing that he had found the water route to Asia.

While Spain began to project its power westward across the Atlantic, the Portuguese extended their influence in different directions—southward to West Africa and then eastward to Asia. In 1497, Vasco da Gama became the first European to sail around the cape of Africa; he picked up a Hindu pilot in East Africa who guided him all the way across the Indian Ocean in 1498. The Portuguese colonized the Indian Ocean region, reaching modern Indonesia and southern China by 1513. By forcing trade concessions in the islands and coastal states of the East Indies, the Portuguese unlocked the fabulous Asian treasure houses that, since Marco Polo's time, had whetted European appetites. By 1500, they had captured control of the African gold trade monopolized for centuries by North African Muslims. The gleaming metal now traveled directly to Lisbon by sea rather than by camel caravan across the Sahara to North African Muslim ports such as Tunis and Algiers.

Religious Conflict During the Era of Reconnaissance

The expansion of Spain and Portugal into new areas of the world profoundly affected patterns of economic activity in Europe. Its commercial center now shifted away from the ports of the Mediterranean to the Atlantic ports facing the New World. But this fast-growing commercial power also had a deeply religious aspect since it occurred in the midst of, and magnified, an era of religious conflict and reformation.

Shortly after Columbus's Atlantic voyages, western Europe was torn by religious schisms. At the heart of Europe's strife was a continental movement to return the church to the purity of early Christianity. Criticism of the worldliness of the Catholic church mounted during the Renaissance. Then a German monk, Martin Luther (1483–1546), broke with Rome, initiating the Protestant Reformation that changed both theology and practice. As Protestant alternatives multiplied, Catholics began to reform their Church, and the two groups began a long battle for the souls of Europeans.

Luther questioned the age-old rituals and sacraments of the Church—the Mass, confession, pilgrimages to holy places, even crusades against Muslim infidels. He believed that salvation came through an inward faith, or "grace," that God conferred on believers. Good works, Luther concluded, could not earn grace but were only evidence of grace won through faith. Insisting on "justification by faith," Luther rejected the Church's elaborate hierarchy of officials, who presided over the rituals intended to guide individuals to salvation.

In 1517, Luther openly attacked the sale of "indulgences." By purchasing indulgences, or pardons for sins, individuals had been told they could reduce their time of penance (or that of a deceased relative) in purgatory. The pope used the money raised from the sale of indulgences for the building of St. Peter's in Rome. Luther drew up 95 arguments against the sale of indulgences and other church practices. He denounced five of the seven sacraments of the Church, supporting only baptism and communion. He attacked the upper clergy for luxurious living and urged priests, who were nominally celibate but often involved in irregular sexual relations, to marry respectably. He sought to replace clerical authority with a "priesthood of all believers." He urged people to seek faith individually by reading the Bible, which he translated into German and made widely available for the first time in printed form. Most dangerously, he called on the German princes to assume control over religion in their states, directly challenging the authority of the pope in Rome and further undermining the functions of the clergy.

Printing, invented less than 70 years earlier, allowed the rapid circulation of Luther's protest. The printed word and the ability to read it were to become revolutionary weapons throughout the world. Luther's cry for reform soon inspired other northern Europeans of all classes. The basic issue dividing Catholics and Protestants thus centered on the source of religious authority. To Catholics, religious authority resided in the organized Church, headed by the pope. To Protestants, the Bible was the sole authority, and access to God's word or God's grace did not require the mediation of the Church.

Building on Luther's redefinition of Christianity, John Calvin, a Frenchman, brought new intensity and meaning to the Protestant Reformation. In 1536, at age 26, he published a ringing appeal to every Christian to form a direct, personal relationship with God. By Calvin's doctrine, God had saved a few souls at random before Creation. They were God's elect, the "saints"; the rest were damned. Human beings could not alter this predestination, but those who were good Christians must struggle to understand and accept God's saving grace if he chose to impart it. Calvin proposed reformed Christian communities structured around the elect few. To remake the corrupt world and follow God's will, "saints" must control the state, rather than the other way around. Elected bodies of ministers and dedicated laymen, called presbyteries, were to govern the church, directing the affairs of society so that all, whether saved or damned, would work for God's ends.

Calvinism, as a fine-tuned system of self-discipline and social control, was first put into practice in the 1550s in the city–state of Geneva, between France and

Switzerland. Here the brilliant and austere leader established his model Christian community. A council of 12 elders drove non-believers from the city, rigidly disciplined daily life, and stripped the churches of every appeal to the senses—images, music, incense, and colorful clerical gowns. Religious reformers from all over Europe flocked to the new holy community, and Geneva soon became the continental center of the reformist Christian movement. The city was, wrote John Knox of Scotland in 1556, "the most perfect school of Christ that ever was in the earth since the days of the apostles."

Calvin's radical program converted large numbers of people to Protestantism. Like Lutheranism, it recruited most successfully among the privileged classes of merchants, landowners, lawyers, and the nobility and among the rising middle class of master artisans and shopkeepers.

Sixteenth-century monarchs initially regarded attacks on the Catholic church with horror. But some local princes adopted the reformed faith. The most important monarch to break with Catholicism was Henry VIII of England. When Pope Clement VII refused him permission to divorce and remarry, Henry declared himself head of the Church of England. Although it retained many Catholic features, the Church of England moved further in a Protestant direction under Henry's son Edward. But when Mary, Henry's older Catholic daughter, came to the throne, she vowed to reinstate her mother's religion by suppressing Protestants. Her policy created Protestant martyrs, and many were relieved when she died in 1558, bringing Henry's younger Protestant daughter, Elizabeth, to the throne. During her long rule, the flinty Elizabeth steered England along a middle course between the radicalism of Geneva and the Catholicism of Rome.

Some of the countries most affected by the Reformation—England, Holland, and France—were slow in trying to colonize the New World, so Protestantism did not gain as early a foothold in the Americas as Catholicism, which in Spain and Portugal remained almost immune from the Protestant Reformation. Thus, Catholicism swept across the Atlantic virtually unchallenged in the colonies of Spain and Portugal during the century after Columbus's voyages.

The Spanish Conquest of America

From 1492 to 1518, Spanish and Portuguese explorers opened up vast parts of Asia and the Americas to European knowledge. Yet during this age of exploration, only modest attempts at settlement were made, mostly by the Spanish on the Caribbean

islands of Cuba, Puerto Rico, and Hispaniola. The three decades after 1518, however, became an age of conquest. In some of the bloodiest chapters in history, the Spanish nearly exterminated the native peoples of the Caribbean islands, toppled and plundered the great inland Aztec and Inca empires in Mexico and Peru, gained control of territories 10 times as large as their Spanish homeland, discovered fabulous silver mines, and built an oceanic trade. This short era of conquest had immense consequences for global history.

Portugal, meanwhile, concentrated mostly on building an eastward oceanic trade to southeastern Asia. In 1493, the pope had demarcated Spanish and Portuguese spheres of exploration in the Atlantic. Drawing a north–south line 100 leagues (about 300 miles) west of the Azores, the pope confined Portugal to the eastern side. One year later, in the Treaty of Tordesillas, Portugal obtained Spanish agreement to move the line 270 leagues farther west. These were some of the most significant lines ever drawn on a map. A large part of South America bulged east of the new demarcation line and therefore fell within the Portuguese sphere. In time, Portugal would develop this region, Brazil, into one of the most profitable areas of the Americas.

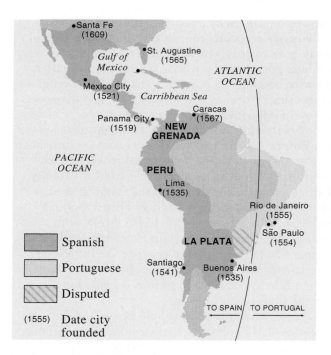

Treaty of Tordesillas

The Treaty of Tordesillas, promulgated by Pope Alexander VI, drew a line dividing all claims to land in the Americas between Portugal and Spain. Until the arrival of the Spanish and Portuguese in the Americas, never before had such small numbers of people established their dominance over such a large and populous area. Why would the pope have involved himself in this question?

Caribbean Experiments

Columbus's second Atlantic expedition in 1493 established the first Spanish colony in the New World on the island of Hispaniola (or Santo Domingo). The inhabitants, the Taíno, were the first New World indigenous people to encounter Europeans, and the encounter provided a preview of what would soon occur elsewhere in the Americas: subjugation, biological disease, and eventually immense ecological alterations to the island.

Columbus arrived with 17 ships and about 1,200 men. He was seeking gold, and when he found none, he visited Cuba before returning to Spain. Having seen that the island was teeming with as many as 3 million Taíno, the Spanish used military force to subdue them and turn them into a captive labor force. Similar conquests brought the people of Puerto Rico under Spanish control in 1508 and those of Cuba in 1511. Spanish diseases soon touched off a biological holocaust that killed most of the Native Americans on these islands within a single generation. Some Taíno women married Spanish men and produced the first mestizo society in the Americas, but by 1550, the Taíno no longer existed as a distinct people.

Spanish immigration to the Caribbean islands was underway by 1510, closely followed by the importation of enslaved Africans who were put to work on the first sugar plantations created in the Americas. Over the course of the sixteenth century, about a quarter million Spaniards—most of them young, single men—emigrated to the Americas. But the islands dotting the Caribbean did not reach their potential as cash-crop economies until much later. For now, they served as laboratories for larger experiments in Mexico and South America, launching pads from which to mount invasions of the Mesoamerican mainland, and places to build fortified ports such as San Juan, Puerto Rico, and Havana, Cuba.

The Conquistadors' Onslaught at Tenochtitlán

Within a single generation of Columbus's death in 1506, Spanish conquistadors explored, claimed, and conquered most of South America except Brazil, as well as Central America and the southern parts of North America from present-day Florida to California. Led by audacious explorers and soldiers, and usually accompanied by enslaved Africans, they established Spanish authority and Catholicism over an area that dwarfed their homeland in size and population. They were motivated by religion, pride of nation, and dreams of personal enrichment. "We came here," explained one Spanish foot soldier, "to serve God and the king, and also to get rich."

In two bold and bloody strokes, the Spanish overwhelmed the ancient civilizations of the Aztecs and Incas. In 1519, hearing of a great empire in Mexico's interior, Cortés set out from Cuba, unauthorized by its governor, with 11 ships, 550 Spanish soldiers, several hundred native Cubans, some enslaved Africans, and well-fed mounts and pack horses. Reaching the coast of Mexico at Veracruz, he marched over rugged mountains to attack Tenochtitlán (now Mexico City), the capital of Moctezuma II's Aztec Empire. Seizing towns subject to Aztec rule, Cortés enlisted Native American support against their hated overlords. Following two years of sparring with the Aztecs and their subject people, Cortés assaulted Tenochtitlán and, after a four-month siege, dramatically brought the Aztec Empire to its knees.

The Spanish use of horses and firearms provided an important advantage; so did a murderous smallpox epidemic in 1520 that felled thousands of Aztecs. Support from local peoples oppressed by Moctezuma's tyranny was also important in overthrowing the Aztec ruler. Cortés was further aided by a Nahuatl woman named Malinche, whom the Spanish would rename Doña Marina. Fluent in both Mayan and Nahuatl, the Aztec language, Malinche became Cortés's interpreter, giving him an advantage over the natives he encountered. Native peoples regarded Malinche as a traitor, and so her name passed down in the Mexican vocabulary as *malinchista*—a person betraying his or her people. In two years, the conquistadors had destroyed the empire that had dominated Mesoamerica for centuries. In the next few decades, foraying from the Valley of Mexico, the Spanish extended their dominion over the Mayan people of the Yucatán, Honduras, and Guatemala.

In the second conquest, Francisco Pizarro, marching from Panama through the jungles of Ecuador and into the towering Andes mountains of Peru with a mere 168 men, most of them not even soldiers, toppled the Inca Empire. Like the Aztecs, the populous Incas lived in a highly organized social system. But also like the Aztecs, they were riddled by smallpox and weakened by violent internal divisions. These conditions ensured Pizarro's success in capturing their capital at Cuzco in 1533, and soon other gold- and silver-rich Inca cities. Further expeditions into Chile, New Granada (Colombia), Argentina, and Bolivia in the 1530s and 1540s brought under Spanish control an empire larger than any in the Western world since the fall of Rome.

By 1550, Spain had overwhelmed the major centers of native population in the Americas. Spanish ships carried gold, silver, dyewoods, and sugar east across the Atlantic and transported African slaves, colonizers, and finished goods west. In a brief half century, Spain had exploited the advances in geographic knowledge and maritime technology of its Portuguese rivals and brought into harsh but profitable contact with each other the people of three continents.

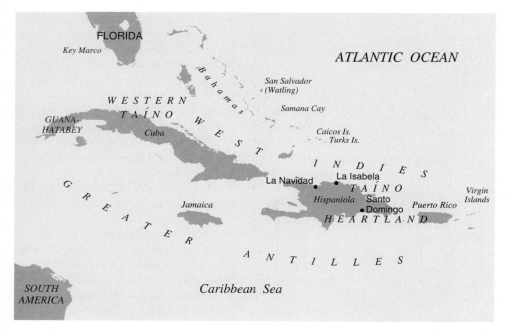

Greater Antilles in 1520

In the West Indies explored by Columbus, most of the inhabitants, as shown on this map, were Taíno. Why did Columbus think of Marco Polo's description of 7,448 islands dotting the China Sea when he found these islands?

The triracial character of the Americas was already firmly established by 1600.

For nearly a century after Columbus's voyages, Spain enjoyed almost unchallenged dominion over the fabulous hemisphere newly revealed to Europeans. Greedy buccaneers of various nations snapped at the heels of homeward-bound Spanish treasure fleets, but this was only a nuisance. France tried to contest Portuguese or Spanish control by planting small settlements in Brazil and Florida in the mid-sixteenth century, but these were quickly wiped out. England remained island-bound until the 1580s. Before the seventeenth century, only Portugal, which staked out important claims in Brazil in the 1520s, challenged Spanish domination of the Americas.

Indian Resistance

In this engraving by Theodor de Bry, who provided Europeans with some of their first images of what awaited them in the Americas, a Spanish attack on indigenous people provokes a spirited response from the heights of a spreading tree. What tactics do the native people employ? Were they likely to be effective?

(The Art Archive/Biblioteca Nazionale Marciana Venice/Dagli Orti)

The Great Dying

Spanish conquest of major areas of the Americas triggered biological disaster, setting in motion one of the most dramatic population declines in history. The population of the Americas on the eve of European arrival had grown to an estimated 50 to 70 million. In central Mexico, the highlands of Peru, and certain Caribbean islands, population density exceeded that of most of Europe. European colonizers had one extraordinary advantage: over the centuries they had built up immunities to nearly every lethal microbe that infects humans on an epidemic scale. Such biological defenses did not eliminate smallpox, measles, diphtheria, and other afflictions, but they limited their deadly power. Geographic isolation, however, had kept these diseases from the peoples of the Americas. So, too, did their lack of large domesticated animals, which were major disease carriers. Arriving Europeans therefore unknowingly encountered a huge component of the human race that was utterly defenseless against the "domesticated" infections the Europeans and their animals carried.

The results were catastrophic. In 1518, the smallpox virus erupted on Hispaniola. The Spanish priest Bartolomé de las Casas recorded that "of that immensity of people that was on this island and which we have seen with our own eyes" only about a thousand were spared among a population of between 1 and 3 million that had existed when Columbus arrived. Of some 15 million inhabitants in central Mexico before Cortés's arrival, nearly half perished within 15 years. The Valley of Mexico, where the Aztec capital of Tenochtitlán stood, had an estimated population of 1.5 to 3 million before the conquistadors arrived. Eighty years later, in 1600, only 70,000 native people could be counted.

Demographic disaster also struck the populous Inca peoples of the Peruvian Andes, speeding ahead of Pizarro's conquistadors. Smallpox "spread over the people as great destruction," an old Native American told a Spanish priest in the 1520s. "There was great havoc. Very many died of it.... And very many starved; there was death from hunger, [for] none could take care of [the sick]." Such terrifying sickness led many natives to believe that their gods had failed them, and this belief left them ready to acknowledge the greater power of the Spaniards' God.

In most areas where Europeans intruded in the hemisphere for the next three centuries, the catastrophe repeated itself. Every European participated accidentally in the spread of disease that typically eliminated, within a few generations, at least two-thirds of the native population. The first historian to appreciate the role played by disease in the Spanish conquest, writing more than a half century ago, described the role of the pathogens unleashed in the New World: these "forerunners of civilization, the companions of Christianity, the friends of the invader" were "more terrible than the conquistadors on horseback, more deadly than sword and gunpowder."

The enslavement and brutal treatment of the native people intensified the lethal effects of European diseases. Having conquered the Incas and Aztecs, the Spanish enslaved thousands of native people and assigned them work regimens that severely weakened their resistance to disease. Bartolomé de las Casas and some other priests waged lifelong campaigns to reduce the exploitation of the Native Americans, but they had only limited power to control the actions of their colonizing compatriots.

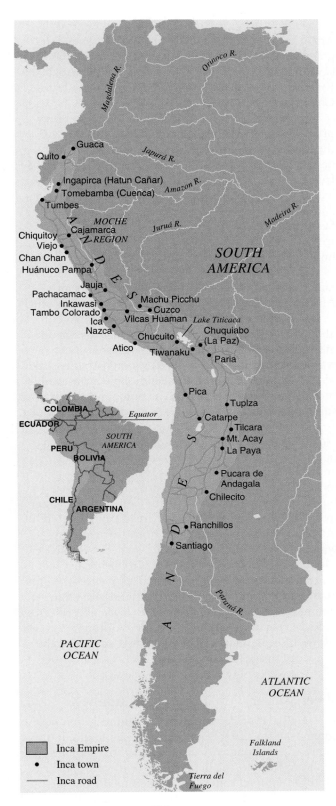

The Inca Empire in 1500

The Inca Empire in 1500 was gigantic, extending along the west coast of South America for some 2,600 miles and containing an estimated 14 million people. Why did only the Ottoman and Chinese empires in the Old World control more land than the Inca?

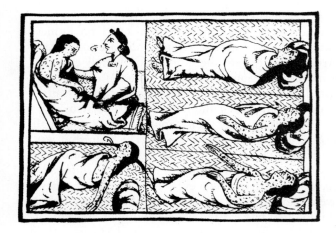

Smallpox Victims

Aztec victims of smallpox, contracted during Cortés's invasion of Tenochtitlán in the 1520s. The woodcut is from the sixteenth-century work *Historia de las Casas de Nueva Espana* by Fray Bernardo de Sahagun. According to the account of the disease, "The sores were so terrible that the victims could not lie face down, . . . nor move from one side to the other. And when they tried to move even a little, they cried out in agony." How did such epidemics affect native society?

(Firenze, Biblioteca Medicea Laurenziana (ms. Med. Palat. 220, c. 460v) Su concessione del Ministero per i Beni e le Attività Culturali Évietata ogni ulteriore riproduzione con qualsiasi mezzo.)

The Columbian Exchange

Much more than lethal microbes crossed the Atlantic with the Spaniards as they conquered the Caribbean islands and then large parts of Central and South America. With them came animal and plant life that altered ecosystems and transformed the landscape. Westward-bound Spanish ships brought wheat, rye, barley, oats, and other European grains; fruits such as cherries, peaches, pears, lemons, oranges, melons, and grapes; vegetables such as radishes, salad greens, and onions. All of these, unknown in the New World, were gradually incorporated into Native American diets.

Even more important were herd animals. Cattle, goats, horses, burros, pigs, and sheep caused the greatest transformation, flourishing as they grazed in the vast grasslands of the Americas safe from the large carnivores that attacked them in the Old World. Cattle reproduced so rapidly that feral livestock swarmed across the countryside, often increasing tenfold in three or four years. In time they ate themselves out of their favorable environment, stripping away plant life, which soon led to topsoil erosion and eventually to desertification. Pigs were even harder on the environment. Reproducing at staggering rates, they tore into the manioc tubers and sweet potatoes in the Greater Antilles where Columbus first introduced eight of them in 1493. They devoured guavas and pineapples, ravaged lizards and baby birds, and stripped the land clean. Similar swine explosions

occurred on the mainland of Mexico and Central America, where along with cattle they devastated the grasslands. Old World hoofed animals took to the savannas and meadows of the Americas "like Adam and Eve returning to Eden," as the main historian of the Columbian Exchange explains.

Spaniards brought the flora and fauna that they prized most to the Americas, but also traveling with them were unwelcome passengers. Among the most destructive were weeds, their seeds hidden in sacks of fruit and vegetable seed. Once they took root, invasive weeds including clover crowded out native flora. Rats and rabbits were pesky stowaways that reproduced as fast as pigs. They decimated native small animals, spread diseases, and added a new dimension to the human struggle for life.

The "Columbian Exchange" had its eastbound dimension but mainly this advantaged European, African, and eventually Asian recipients. Syphilis and yaws, diseases apparently unknown in Europe until about 1500, were afflictions of the Americas that created misery in the Old World as they traveled eastward, although they were never remotely on the scale of the scathing smallpox epidemics. By contrast, table foods from the Americas such as pumpkins, pineapples, squash, peanuts, and beans enriched the European diet. So did guinea pigs and turkeys. Tomatoes, known as "love apples" for their supposed stimulus to sexual potency, became a staple of European cuisine. Llamas and alpacas produced wool for warmth. Over time, the most important food transfers proved to be maize and potatoes. The potato, with its fundamental advantage over Old World grains, slowly spread from its point of introduction in northern Spain northward and eastward through Europe. From the North Sea to the Ural Mountains, farmers on the northern European plain learned that by substituting potatoes for rye—the only grain that would thrive in the short and often rainy summers—they could quadruple their yield in calories per acre. The transition to the New World potato allowed for population growth and strengthened the sinew of Europe's diet.

Silver, Sugar, and Their Consequences

The small amount of gold that Columbus brought home from the Caribbean islands raised hopes that this metal, which along with silver formed the standard of wealth in Europe, might be found in the transatlantic paradise. Though some gold was gleaned from the Caribbean islands and later from Colombia, Brazil, and Peru, it would be more than three centuries before anyone would discover gold in windfall quantities in North America.

Silver was another matter. It proved most abundant—so plenteous, in fact, that when bonanza

West Indies Slave Labor

In this 1823 lithograph by William Clark, we see West Indies gang laborers preparing the ground for sugar planting. A black overseer directs the workforce of both women and men. Has the artist romanticized slave labor in the cane fields? If so, in what ways?

strikes were made in Bolivia in 1545 and then in northern Mexico in the 1550s, much of Spain's New World enterprise focused on its extraction. For most of the sixteenth century, the Spanish Empire in America was a vast mining community. Sixteen thousand tons of silver were scooped from Spain's colonies in the Americas between 1500 and 1650.

Native people, along with some African slaves, provided the first labor supply for the mines. The Spaniards permitted the highly organized Native American societies to maintain control of their own communities but exacted from them huge labor drafts for mining. At Potosí, in Bolivia, 58,000 workers labored at elevations of up to 13,000 feet to extract the precious metal from a fabulous sugarloaf "mountain of silver." The town's population reached 120,000 by 1570, making it much larger than any in Spain at the time. Thousands of other workers toiled in the mines of Zacatecas, Taxco, and Guanajuato. By 1660, they had scooped up more than 7 million pounds of silver from the Americas, tripling the entire European supply.

The flood of bullion from the Americas to Europe triggered profound changes. It financed further conquests and settlement in Spain's American empire, spurred long-distance trading in East Asian silks and spices, and capitalized agricultural development in the New World of sugar, coffee, cacao, and indigo. The bland diet of Europeans gradually changed as items such as sugar and spices, previously luxury articles for the wealthy, became accessible to ordinary people.

The enormous increase of silver in circulation in Europe after the mid-sixteenth century also caused a "price revolution." The supply of silver increased faster than the demand for goods and services that Europeans could produce, so the value of silver coins declined. Put differently, prices rose, doubling between 1550 and 1600 in many parts of Europe and rising another 50 percent in the next half century. Farmers got more for their produce, and merchants thrived on the increased circulation of goods. Artisans, laborers, and landless agricultural workers (the vast majority of the population) suffered when wages did not keep up with rising prices. As one of the first English immigrants to America lamented, skilled artisans "live in such a low condition as is little better than beggary."

The price revolution built up the pressure to immigrate to the Americas, Europe's new frontier. While the Spaniards organized their overseas empire around the extraction of silver from the highlands of Mexico, Bolivia, and Peru, the Portuguese staked their future on sugar production in Brazil. Using cultivation techniques developed earlier on their Atlantic islands off the coast of Africa, the Portuguese colony produced sugar for export markets.

Whereas Spanish mining operations rested primarily on the backs of the native labor force, the lowland Portuguese sugar planters scattered the indigenous people and replaced them with platoons of African slaves. By 1570, this regimented workforce was producing nearly 6 million pounds of sugar annually; by the 1630s, output had risen to 32 million pounds. High in calories but low in protein, the sweet "drug food" revolutionized the tastes of Europeans and stimulated the oceanic transport of millions of African slaves across the Atlantic.

From Brazil, sugar production jumped to the Caribbean islands. Here, in the early seventeenth century, England, Holland, and France challenged Spain and Portugal. Once they secured footholds in the West Indies, Spain's enemies stood at the gates of the Hispanic New World empire. Through contraband trading with Spanish settlements, piratical attacks on

Spanish treasure fleets, and outright seizure of Spanish-controlled islands, the Dutch, French, and English in the seventeenth century gradually sapped Spain's strength.

Spain's Northern Frontier

The crown jewels of Spain's New World empire were silver-rich Mexico and Peru, with the islands and coastal fringes of the Caribbean representing lesser, yet valuable, gemstones. Distinctly third in importance were the northern borderlands of New Spain—the present-day Sun Belt of the United States. Yet the early Spanish influence in Florida, the Gulf region, Texas, New Mexico, Arizona, and California indelibly marked the history of the United States. Spanish control of the region began in the early 1500s and did not end for three centuries, when Mexico wrested independence from Spain in 1821. Far outlasting Spanish rule were the plants and animals they introduced to North America, ranging from sheep, cattle, and horses to various grasses and weeds that crowded out native plants.

Horses were of special importance. They had arrived with Columbus in 1493 but did not thrive in the tropical climate of the Greater Antilles. Once the Spanish reached the three great temperate grasslands of the Americas—the Argentine pampas, the Venezuelan llanos, and the North American Great Plains stretching all the way from southern Canada to northern Mexico—horses flourished. On the Great Plains they would reshape Native American life, so that later arriving Europeans would find mounted tribes and herds of wild horses. Spanish explorers began charting southeastern North America in the early sixteenth century. First came Juan Ponce de León's expeditions to Florida

in 1515 and 1521 and Lucas Vasquez de Ayllón's short-lived settlement at Winyah Bay in South Carolina in 1526. For the next half century, Spaniards planted small settlements along the coast as far north as the Chesapeake Bay, where their temporary encampment included enslaved Africans. The Spanish traded some with the natives, but the North American coast, especially Florida, was chiefly important to the Franciscan friars, who attempted to gather the local tribes into mission villages and convert them to Catholicism.

The Spanish made several attempts to bring the entire Gulf of Mexico region under their control. From 1539 to 1542, Hernán de Soto, a veteran of Pizarro's conquest of the Incas a few years before, led a military expedition deep into the homelands of the Creek and Choctaw. Yearning to find another Tenochtitlán or Cuzco, he explored westward from Tampa Bay across the Mississippi River to present-day Arkansas and eastern Texas. But he found only agricultural-based tribes, influenced by Mayan and Aztec people, who lived in sizable villages and built ceremonial pyramids.

De Soto's expedition could not provide what the Spanish most wanted—gold. Pillaging thickly settled native villages for furs and freshwater pearls, seizing food supplies, and enslaving Native Americans to serve as human pack animals, de Soto's men cut a brutal swath as far north as North Carolina and as far west as Arkansas. Death preceded them and intensified in their wake. De Soto never conquered the peoples he encountered; instead, the environment and tenacious Native American resistance conquered him. After seeing their leader die a miserable death, de Soto's men and enslaved Africans limped back to Mexico with what was left of their forces. Little could the English know that their Spanish enemies were paving the way for them in

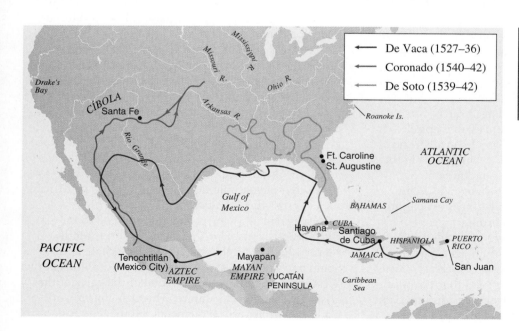

The Spanish *Entradas* in North America

What motivated the *entradas* of the Spanish conquistadors as they claimed vast territories across the lower tier of North America for the Spanish?

North America's southeastern sector by spreading lethal microbes that devastated Native American societies and broke up the great chiefdoms of the lower South.

In 1559, Spaniards again marched northward from Mexico in an attempt to establish their authority in the lower Gulf region. Everywhere they went, they enslaved Native Americans to carry provisions. In 1565, they sought to secure Florida. Building a fort at St. Augustine, they evicted their French rivals at Fort Caroline, 40 miles to the north. St. Augustine became the center of Spain's northeastern frontier, and Florida remained a Spanish possession for more than two centuries.

The Southwest became another locus of early Spanish activity in North America. Francisco Vásquez de Coronado explored the region from 1540 to 1542, leading an expedition of several hundred Spanish soldiers, a number of Africans, and a baggage train of some 1,300 hired Native Americans, servants, and slaves. Coronado never found the Seven Cities of Cíbola, reported by earlier Spanish explorers to be fabulously decorated in turquoise and gold; but he opened much of Arizona, New Mexico, and Colorado to eventual Spanish control, happened upon the Grand Canyon, and probed as far north as the Great Plains. The Southwest, like Florida and the Gulf region, had no golden cities. In New Mexico, however, Franciscan friars tried to harvest souls. A half century after Coronado's exploratory intrusions, Don Juan de Oñate led 129 soldiers, about 500 Spanish settlers, and 10 Franciscan friars up the Rio Grande in 1598 to find some 60,000 Pueblo gathered in scores of settled towns where for centuries they had been practicing agriculture. For the next 80 years, the Franciscans tried to graft Catholicism onto Pueblo culture by building churches on the edges of ancient native villages. As long as the priests were content to overlay Native American culture with a veneer of Catholicism, they encountered little resistance because the Pueblo found advantage in Spanish military protection from their Apache enemies and valued access to mission livestock and grain during years of drought. Outwardly they professed the Christian faith, while secretly adhering to their traditional religion. Meanwhile, Spanish settlers—never more than a thousand in 1680—carved out cattle ranches and built small towns.

England Looks West

By the time England awoke to the promise of the New World, Spain and Portugal were firmly entrenched there. But by the late sixteenth century, the conditions necessary to propel England overseas had ripened. During the early seventeenth century, the English, as well as the Dutch and French, began overtaking their southern European rivals. For the English, the first challenge came in the Caribbean, where between 1604 and 1640 the English planted several small colonies producing tobacco and later sugar. Few guessed that some secondary and relatively unproductive settlements then being planted on the North American mainland would in time emerge as major colonies.

England Challenges Spain

England was the slowest of the Atlantic powers to begin exploring and colonizing the New World. Although far more numerous than the Portuguese, the English in the fifteenth century had little experience with long-distance trade. They also had few contacts with cultures beyond their island aside from the French, against whom they had waged the Hundred Years' War (1337–1453). Only the voyages of John Cabot (the Genoa-born Giovanni Caboto) gave England any claim in the New World sweepstakes. But England never followed up on Cabot's voyages to Newfoundland and Nova Scotia—the first northern crossing of the Atlantic since the Vikings.

At first, England's interest in the far side of the Atlantic centered primarily on fish. This high-protein food, basic to the European diet, was the gold of the North Atlantic. Early explorers found the waters off Newfoundland and Nova Scotia teeming with fish—not only the ordinary cod but also the delectable salmon. In the 1520s, the fishermen of Portugal, Spain, and France, more than those of England, began making annual spring trips to the offshore fisheries. Not until the end of the century would the French and English drive Spanish and Portuguese fishermen from the Newfoundland banks.

Exploratory voyages along the eastern coast of North America hardly interested the English. It was for the French that Cartier and Verrazano sailed between 1524 and 1535. They sought straits so that India-bound ships could sail around the northern land mass (still thought to be a large island). The two navigators encountered many Indian tribes, charted the coastline from the St. Lawrence River to the Carolinas, and realized that the northern latitudes of North America were suitable for settlement. Since Europeans were not yet interested in settlements, their discoveries had little immediate value.

Changes in the late sixteenth century, however, propelled the English overseas. The rising production of woolen cloth, a mainstay of the English economy, had sent merchants scurrying for new markets after 1550. Their success in establishing trading companies in Russia, Scandinavia, the Middle East, and India vastly widened England's commercial orbit and raised hopes for developing still other spheres. Meanwhile, population growth and rising prices depressed the economic conditions of ordinary people and made them look across the ocean for new opportunities.

The cautious policy of Queen Elizabeth I, who ruled from 1558 to 1603, did not at first promote overseas colonies. She favored Protestantism as a vehicle of national independence rather than a missionary project. Ambitious and talented, she had to contend with Philip II, the fervently Catholic king of Spain. Regarding Elizabeth as a Protestant heretic, Philip plotted incessantly against her. The pope added to Catholic–Protestant tensions by excommunicating Elizabeth in 1571 and absolving her subjects from paying her allegiance—in effect, inciting them to overthrow her.

The smoldering conflict between Catholic Spain and Protestant England broke into open flames in 1587. Two decades before, Philip II had sent 20,000 Spanish soldiers into his Netherlands provinces to suppress Protestant revolt. Then, in 1572, he had helped arrange the massacre of thousands of French Protestants. By the 1580s, Elizabeth was providing covert aid to the Protestant Dutch revolt against Catholic rule. Philip vowed to crush the rebellion and decided as well to launch an attack on England to wipe out this growing center of Protestant power.

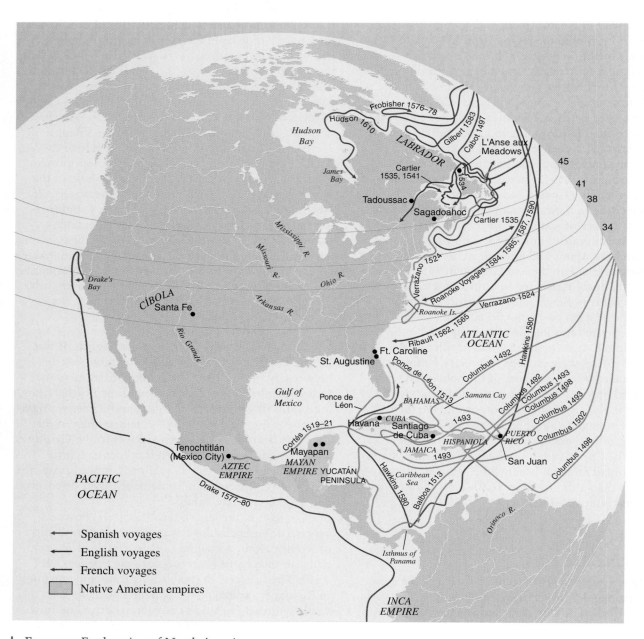

European Exploration of North America

The English and French dominated European explorations of North America in the late fifteenth and sixteenth centuries. Verrazano, an Italian sea captain, sailed in the service of the French king. Why was English and French activity directed to the north?

Elizabeth fed the flames of the international Catholic–Protestant conflict in 1585 by sending 6,000 English troops to aid the Dutch Protestants. A year later, the colorful sea dog Francis Drake, who had been raiding Spanish shipping on the coasts of Mexico and Peru, bombarded Spanish St. Augustine in Florida, looted the city, and touched off an epidemic that the Florida Indians attributed to the "English God that made them die so fast." Two years later, infuriated by Drake's piracy and support of Protestant rebels in the Netherlands, Philip dispatched a Spanish armada of 130 ships carrying 30,000 men and 2,400 artillery pieces. Sails blazing with crusaders' crosses, the fleet set forth to conquer Elizabeth's England. For two weeks in the summer of 1588, a sea battle raged off the English coast. A motley collection of smaller English ships, with Drake in the lead, defeated the armada, sinking many of the lumbering Spanish galleons and then retiring as a legendary "Protestant wind" blew the crippled armada into the North Sea.

The Spanish defeat prevented a crushing Catholic victory in Europe and brought a temporary stalemate in the religious wars. It also solidified a pride in Protestant England. Shakespeare's love of "this other Eden, this demi-paradise" spread among the people;

and with Spanish naval power checked, both the English and the Dutch found the seas more open to their rising maritime and commercial interests.

The Westward Fever

In the last decades of the sixteenth century, the idea of overseas expansion began to capture the imagination of important elements of English society. Urging them on were two Richard Hakluyts, who were cousins. In the 1580s and 1590s, they devoted themselves to advertising the advantages of colonizing across the Atlantic. For nobles at court, colonies offered new baronies, fiefdoms, and estates. For merchants, the New World promised exotic produce to sell at home and a new outlet for English cloth. For militant Protestant clergy, there awaited a continent filled with heathens to be saved from devilish savagery or Spanish Catholicism. For commoners, opportunity beckoned in the form of bounteous land, almost for the taking. The Hakluyts' pamphlets publicized the idea that the time was ripe for England to break the Iberian monopoly on the New World riches.

England first attempted colonizing, however, in Ireland. In the 1560s and 1570s, the English extended control over Ireland through brutal military conquest. The emerald island became a turbulent frontier for thousands of career-hungry younger sons of gentry families as well as landless commoners. Many of the leaders of England's initial New World colonization got their training in subjugating "savages" in Ireland. The first English attempts at overseas settlement were small, feeble, and ill-fated. Whereas the Spanish encountered unheard-of wealth and scored astounding victories over ancient and populous civilizations, the English at first met only failure in relatively thinly settled lands. Working with leftovers, England began—unsuccessfully—to mount small settlements, first in 1583 in Newfoundland. Other settlers, organized by Walter Raleigh, one of Queen Elizabeth's favorite courtiers, between 1585 and 1588 planted a small colony at Roanoke Island, off the North Carolina coast. Small and poorly financed, the colony failed to maintain peaceful relations with the local natives. By the time a relief expedition arrived in 1591, the Roanoke colonists had vanished. It was an ominous beginning for England's overseas ambitions.

Discouraged Englishmen waited another generation before trying again. Small groups of men sent out to establish a tiny colony in Guiana, off the South American coast, failed in 1604 and 1609. Another group, set down in Maine in 1607, lasted only one year. Although they would flourish in time, even the colonies founded in Virginia in 1607 and Bermuda in 1612 floundered badly for several decades.

Queen Elizabeth I

Under the leadership of Elizabeth I, here displayed in royal finery and resting her hand on the globe, England challenged and ultimately overturned Spain's domination of worldwide sea trade. Behind the placid face was a determined and sometimes ruthless ruler. What is depicted outside the window?

(Elizabeth I, Armada Portrait, c. 1588 (oil on panel) by George Gower (1540–96) (attr. to). Woburn Abbey, Bedfordshire, UK/Bridgeman Art Library, London/New York. By kind permission of the Marquess of Tavistock and Trustees of the Bedford Estate)

A Blue-Skinned Pict Male

John White, whose watercolors on Roanoke Island provided fascinating ethnographic detail of Native Americans, also painted this mythical Pict male with blue skin to accompany his Roanoke drawings. The Picts were an ancient people—the ancestors of the seventeenth-century Britons. Why might White have thought the Picts, whom he pictured as tattooed, savage, bloodthirsty people, gave insight into the state and future of Native America?

(© British Museum [1906–5–9–1 (24)/PS211689])

English merchants, sometimes supported by gentry investors, undertook these first tentative efforts, risking capital in the hope of realizing profits similar to their other overseas commercial ventures. The Spanish and Portuguese colonizing efforts were sanctioned, capitalized, and coordinated by the crown. By contrast, English colonies had their queen's blessing, but were private ventures without royal subsidies or naval protection.

English colonization could not succeed until these first merchant adventurers solicited the wealth and support of the prospering middle class. This support grew steadily in the first half of the seventeenth century, but even then investors were drawn far more to the quick profits promised in West Indian tobacco production than to the uncertainties of mixed farming, lumbering, and fishing on the North American mainland. In the 1620s and 1630s, most of the English capital invested overseas went into establishing tobacco colonies in tiny Caribbean islands, including St. Christopher (1624), Barbados (1627), Nevis (1628), Montserrat (1632), and Antigua (1632).

Apart from the considerable financing required, the vital element in launching a colony was a suitable body of colonists. The changing agricultural system, combined with population growth and the unrelenting increase in prices caused by the influx of New World silver, produced a surplus of unskilled labor, squeezed many small producers, and spread poverty and crime. By the late 1500s, wrote Richard Hakluyt, the roads were swarming with "valiant youths rusting and hurtful for lack of employment," and the prisons were "daily pestered and stuffed full of them." Pushed in response to these conditions, about 80,000 streamed out of England between 1600 and 1640, at the same time that dreams of opportunity and adventure pulled them westward. In the next 20 years, another 80,000 departed.

Religious persecution and political considerations intensified the pressure to emigrate from England in the early seventeenth century. For the first time in their history, large numbers of English people were abandoning their island homeland to carry their destinies to new frontiers. The largest number went to the West Indies, about one-third migrated to the North American mainland, and fewer went to the plantations in northern Ireland.

Anticipating North America

The early English settlers in North America were far from uninformed about the indigenous people of the New World. Beginning with Columbus's first description of the New World, published in several European cities in 1493 and 1494, reports and promotional accounts circulated among the participants in early voyages of discovery, trade, and settlement.

Colonists who read or listened to these accounts got a dual image of the native people. On the one hand, Native Americans were depicted as a gentle people who eagerly received Europeans. Columbus had written of the "great amity toward us" that he encountered in San Salvador in 1492 and had described the Arawak there as "a loving people" who "were greatly pleased and became so entirely our friends that it was a wonder to see." Verrazano, the first European to touch the eastern edge of North America, wrote optimistically about the native people in 1524. The natives, graceful of limb and tawny-colored, he related, "came toward us joyfully uttering loud cries of wonderment, and showing us the safest place to beach the boat."

This positive image of Native Americans reflected both the friendly reception that Europeans often actually received and the European vision of the New World as an earthly paradise where war-torn, impoverished, and persecuted people could build a new life. The strong desire to trade with the native people also encouraged a favorable view because only a friendly Native American could become a suitable partner in commercial exchange.

Early North American travel literature also portrayed a counterimage of a savage, hostile Indian. As early as 1502, Sebastian Cabot had paraded in England three Eskimos he had kidnaped on an Arctic voyage, describing them as flesh-eating savages and "brute beasts" who "spake such speech that no man could understand them." Many other accounts portrayed the New World natives as crafty, brutal, loathsome half-men, who lived, as Amerigo Vespucci put it, without "law, religion, rulers, immortality of the soul, and private property."

Negative images of Native Americans stemmed in part from their possession of the land necessary for settlement. For Englishmen, rooted in a tradition of the private ownership of property, this presented moral and legal, as well as practical, problems. In 1609, Anglican minister Robert Gray wondered, "By what right can we enter into the land of these savages, take their rightful inheritance from them, and plant ourselves in their places, being unwronged or unprovoked by them?" The problem could be partially solved by arguing that English settlers would offer the advantages of a more advanced culture and, most important, the Christian religion—a claim that would be repeated for generations.

A more ominous argument also justified English rights to native soil. By denying the humanity of the Native Americans, the English, like other Europeans, claimed that they had disqualified themselves from rightful ownership of the land. "Although the Lord hath given the earth to children of men," one Englishman reasoned, "the greater part of it [is] possessed and wrongfully usurped by wild beasts and unreasonable creatures, or by brutish savages, which by reason of their godless ignorance and blasphemous idolatry, are worse than those beasts which are of the most wild and savage nature."

Defining the Native Americans as "savage" and "brutish" did not give the English arriving in the New World the power to dispossess them of their soil, but it armed the settlers with a moral justification for doing so when their numbers became sufficient. Few settlers arriving in North America doubted that their technological superiority would allow them to overwhelm the indigenous people. For their part, the natives probably perceived the arriving Europeans as impractical, irreligious, aggressive, and strangely intent on accumulating things.

African Bondage

For almost four centuries after Columbus's voyages, European colonizers, in the largest forced migration in human history, transported Africans from their homelands and used their labor to produce wealth. Estimates vary widely, but at least 9.6 million Africans were brought to the Americas, and millions more perished on the long, terrible journey.

Once the transatlantic slave trade began, locales for producing desired commodities such as sugar, coffee, rice, and tobacco moved from the Old World to the Americas, building the first transoceanic European colonial empires. Europe's orientation gradually shifted from the Mediterranean Sea to the Atlantic Ocean, with African forced labor an essential part of the immense Atlantic-basin system of trade. Without African labor, the overseas colonies of European nations would never have flourished as they did.

While the economic importance of enslaved Africans can hardly be overstated, it is equally important to understand the cultural interchange that occurred. From 1519 to the early nineteenth century, African newcomers probably outnumbered Europeans two or three to one. As a result, African slavery became the context in which European life would evolve in many parts of the Americas. At the same time, the slave trade etched lines of communication for the movement of crops, agricultural techniques, diseases, and medical knowledge among Africa, Europe, and the Americas.

North America remained a fringe area for slave traders until the early eighteenth century. Yet those who came to the American colonies, about 10,000 in the seventeenth century and 350,000 in the eighteenth century, profoundly affected society there. In a prolonged period of labor scarcity, their labor and skills were indispensable to colonial economic development, while their African customs mixed continuously with those of their European masters. Moreover, the racial relations that grew out of slavery so deeply marked society that the problem of race has continued to be one of this nation's most difficult problems.

The Slave Trade

The African slave trade began as an attempt to fill a labor shortage in the Mediterranean world. As early as the eighth century, Arab and Moorish traders had driven slaves across Saharan caravan trails for delivery to Mediterranean ports. Seven centuries later, Portuguese merchants became the first European slave traders.

When Portuguese ship captains reached the west coast of Africa, they tapped into a slave-trading network that had operated in central and west Africa for many generations. For Africans, the Portuguese were

Recovering the Past

English travel accounts of New World settlements had a threefold purpose: first, to convince investors that purchasing stock issued by colonizing companies would reward them richly; second, to attract colonists through promotional descriptions of an exotic new world; and third, to serve as a Protestant weapon against colonizing Catholic countries, especially Spain. These pamphlets have furnished historians with rich ethnographic evidence of Native American lifeways in the Americas, a source of information on English attitudes toward Native Americans, and insights into how new technologies in book publishing fed the Protestant–Catholic conflict.

In 1588, Thomas Harriot (1560–1621), a minister, mathematician, and scientist trained at Oxford, published the first popular pamphlet describing and promoting English colonization. It came off the press as the English were repelling the Spanish Armada trying to destroy the English navy. In *A Briefe and True Report of the New Found Land of Virginia, directed to the Investors, Farmers and Wellwishers of the project of Colonizing and Planting there,* Harriot described what he had seen in eastern North America as a member of the second expedition to the Roanoke colony in 1585. Harriot enthusiastically described the pleasant climate and fertile land that would make farming easy, while boasting the commodities that English colonists could easily procure in Virginia—furs, pearls, iron, timber, precious metals, and more. Also on this voyage was a talented watercolorist, John White, whose many paintings depicted Native Americans living in villages, practicing agriculture, and engaging in dances, religious activities, and child rearing—a people who seemed to be ones with whom the English could settle peacefully (see figure).

Harriot's *Briefe and True Report* became a model for English colonial promotional pamphlets. In 1589, he teamed up with Théodore de Bry, a Protestant engraver who in 1570 had fled Liège, his Belgian hometown, to escape the Spanish Inquisition, and taken refuge in Strasbourg, a Protestant stronghold and a center of engraving and the book trade. Once in London, de Bry created new copperplate engravings of White's watercolor paintings for a second edition of the *Briefe and True Report.* Taking artistic liberties, de Bry made the Native Americans seem more civilized to the English (see figures). In 1590, Harriot's reissued, illustrated *Briefe Report* attracted great attention, appearing as the first volume of a series of European travel accounts gathered by de Bry and advertised as *The Grand Voyages to America.* When John Smith published his *Generall Historie of Virginia, New England, and the Summer Isles* in 1624, the first lengthy eyewitness account of early English settlement in North America, it used many of de Bry's engravings, copied from John White's watercolors.

De Bry's engravings introduced large numbers of Europeans to images of Native American life and to impressions of the first encounters of Europeans with the indigenous people. A few Europeans had seen crude woodcuts of native life in the Americas in earlier sixteenth-century travel accounts. But not until de Bry's copperplate engravings, which offered clear, precise details, did book illustration advance to the point at which a panoramic view of the European colonization of the Americas become available to the many. The great Catholic–Protestant conflict in sixteenth- and seventeenth-century Europe, being played out in the Americas, could thus be presented to a wide audience through the de Bry–illustrated travel accounts.

Just before he died in 1598, de Bry published a Latin version of Bartolomé de Las Casas's *Short Account of the Destruction of the Indies,* first published in 1541 by the Spanish Dominican friar, who had lived for nearly 40 years in

English viewers of this watercolor of a Native American town on the bank of the Pamlico River (in present-day Beaufort County, North Carolina) might see that though they called them "savages," the Eastern Woodlands natives tilled their maize fields (shown on the right), enjoyed dancing (lower right), and buried their chiefs (see tomb in lower left) in ways familiar to Europeans. At the upper right is a small, elevated watchman's hut.

(© British Museum)

John White's picture of a man and woman squatting on a mat at a meal of soaked maize. Harriot noted that "they are very sober in their eating and drinking, and consequently very long lived because they do not oppress nature." In de Bry's reinterpretation of this image, the man's and woman's posture, with legs extended, is much like that of Europeans at a picnic. Both figures have much lighter skin than in White's watercolor. The woman's face has been prettified by European standards, while the man has acquired musculature familiar to Europeans through Leonardo da Vinci paintings. De Bry has added fish, nuts, and a gourd to the scene.

(Left: British Museum [1906–5–9–1(20)/PS207965]; right: © The Mariners' Museum/Corbis)

Théodore de Bry's illustrations were based on Las Casas's accounts of actual incidents, but his imagination ran free in creating chilling images. In this engraving, a huge conquistador holds a child by the legs and prepares to dash its brains out against a rock. Another Spaniard ignites a fire to burn thirteen Native Americans hanging from a crude gallows, while other conquistadors (in the background) hunt down fleeing natives.

(From the Collections of the James Ford Bell Library, University of Minnesota, Minneapolis, Minnesota)

New Spain. Las Casas gave his life to converting the Native Americans to Catholicism and was intent on stopping the cruel Spanish treatment of them. His book was filled with details on horrific Spanish torture and killing of Native American women and children as well as adult males. Protestants had earlier republished Las Casas's exposé in French, English, and other languages, eager to offer proof of Catholic Spain's depravity in the Americas. But de Bry's illustrations for the 1598 edition published in Frankfurt showed Spanish ruthlessness with such graphic horror as to terrify the reader.

After their father's death, Jean-Théodore and Jean-Israël de Bry published another 22 illustrated volumes of voyages to the Americas, including 8 volumes with illustrations emphasizing how the Spanish Catholics brutalized the native people. Published in English, German, French, and Latin editions, the illustrated books promoted the idea of English superiority while providing Europeans with graphic material on the exotic peoples on the other side of the Atlantic.

Reflecting on the Past Look at these four illustrations and imagine that you saw them in England as you prepared to cross the Atlantic among a group of colonists. Having never lived outside the small village where you had been born, how do you see the Native Americans? How will you prepare yourself for encounters with them? How will you be able to avert the violence of the Spanish colonists? ◼

nothing more than a new trading partner, one who could provide guns, horses, copper and brass, and especially textiles. Slaveholding was deeply rooted in African societies, and was important in enhancing one's status and augmenting one's ability to produce wealth. Slaves in Africa were employed in a wide variety of occupations, often serving as soldiers, administrators, and even occasionally as royal advisers.

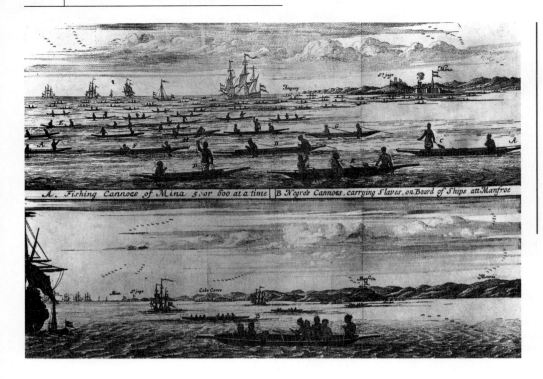

A. Fishing Cannoes of Mina 5 or 6oo at a time | B Negros Cannoes, carrying Slaves, on Board of Ships att Manfroe

Africans Being Taken to Slave Ships

This rare depiction of enslaved Africans being ferried out to European slave ships was first published in Jean Barbot's *A description of the coasts of north and south-Guinea* (1688). Why was the trade organized out of slaving stations, such as Manfroe and the others indicated on the images?

(New York Public Library, Rare Book Collection, Astor, Lenox and Tilden Foundations/Art Resource, NY)

Many Africans were relegated to slavery by judicial decree for crimes they had committed, but far more were captives in the wars between the numerous states of central and western Africa. Songhai—the largest state in Africa in the 1500s—waged several wars of territorial conquest, capturing slaves as it expanded its empire. The economy of the kingdom of Dahomey depended heavily for several centuries on commerce in slaves. One former slave, Francisco Feliz de Sousa, came to own a fleet of slave ships. But the early trade in human flesh was mainly in the hands of the Spanish and Portuguese, who carried some 100,000 enslaved Africans to the Iberian peninsula before Columbus's first voyage across the Atlantic.

More than anything else, sugar transformed the African slave trade. For centuries, sugarcane had been grown in the Mediterranean countries to sweeten the diet of the wealthy. As sugar's popularity grew, the center of production shifted to Portugal's Atlantic islands of Madeira and São Tomé, off the west coast of Africa. Here in the 1460s, a European nation for the first time established an overseas colony organized around slave labor. From Madeira, the cultivation of sugar spread to Portuguese Brazil and Spanish Santo Domingo. By the seventeenth century, with Europeans developing a taste for sugar almost as insatiable as their craving for tobacco, they vied fiercely for the tiny islands dotting the Caribbean and for control of the trading forts on the West African coast. African kingdoms, eager for European trade goods, fought each

other to supply the "black gold" demanded by white ship captains.

European nations competed for West African trading rights. In the seventeenth century, when slave traders brought about 1 million Africans to the New World, the Dutch replaced the Portuguese as the major supplier. The English, meanwhile, hardly counted in the slave trade. Only in the later seventeenth century, when they began their century-long rise to maritime greatness, did the English challenge the Dutch. By the 1690s, the English were the foremost European slave traders. Paradoxically, the nations that would later be the first to forswear chattel slavery—Holland, France, and England—raised their New World plantations on the foundation of African slave labor.

In the eighteenth century, European traders carried at least 6 million Africans to the Americas. By then, an Englishman called slavery the "strength and the sinews of this western world."

Once established on a large scale, the Atlantic slave trade dramatically altered slave recruitment in Africa. When criminals and "outsiders" were insufficient in number to satisfy the growing European demand, African kings highly desirous of European goods and others imported from Asia waged war against neighboring tribes. European guns abetted the process. By 1730, Europeans were providing some 180,000 weapons a year, spreading kidnaping and organized violence while strengthening the most militarily effective kingdoms. Again and again, coastal and interior kings invaded the hinterlands of western

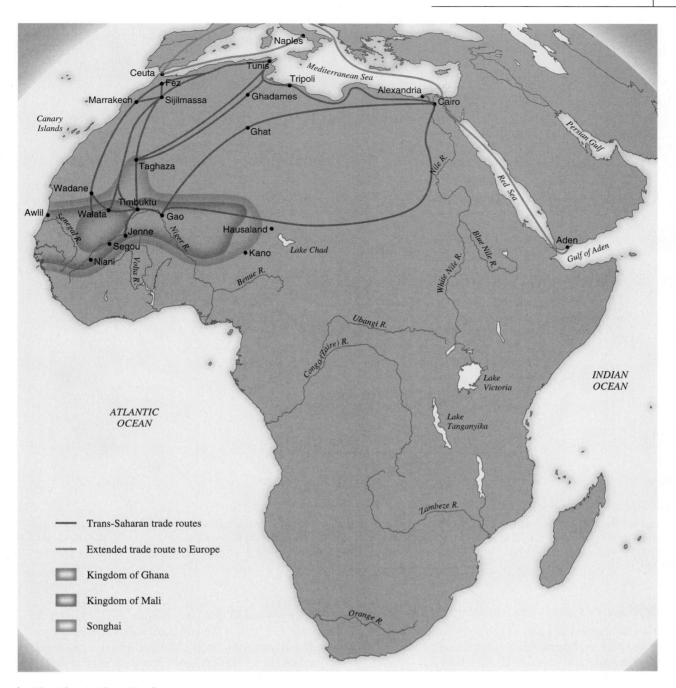

The Islamic Slave Trade

Though much less noticed than the Atlantic slave trade, the Islamic slave traffic across the Sahara Desert, Red Sea, and Indian Ocean was equally important numerically. The Islamic slave trade continued long after the Atlantic slave trade came to a halt in the late nineteenth century. Why has the Islamic slave trade received less attention than the Atlantic slave trade? Why did the Islamic slave trade continue after abolitionists succeeded in ending the Atlantic slave trade?

and central Sudan to procure slaves. Perhaps three-quarters of the slaves transported to English North America came from the part of western Africa that lies between the Senegal and Niger rivers and the Gulf of Biafra.

In this forcible recruitment of slaves, young males—most of them 10 to 24 years old—were preferred over women. The preference of New World plantation owners for male field laborers was one cause, but the trend also reflected the decision of vanquished African villagers to yield more men than women to raiding parties. Women were the chief agriculturists in their society and, in matrilineal and matrilocal kinship systems, were too valuable to be sacrificed.

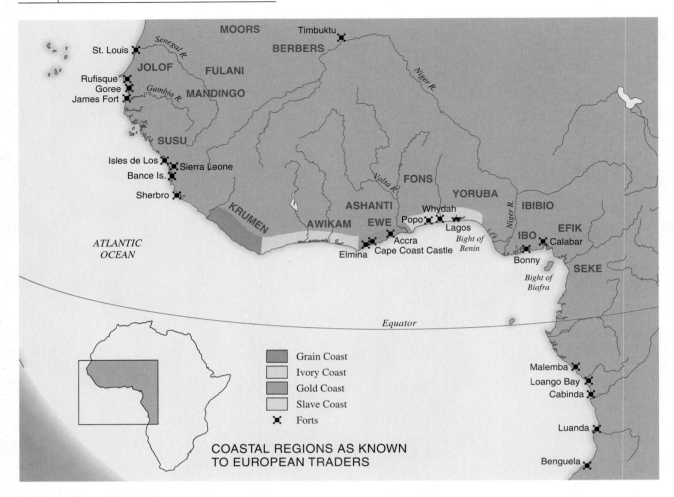

West African Slaving Forts

Europeans fought lustily for control of slaving forts on the West African coast, and many forts changed hands several times during the long period of the Atlantic slave trade. How did West Africans participating in the slave trade adjust to the languages of different European slave traders? Or did the European slave traders learn a variety of African languages in order to trade at the coastal forts?

The Middle Passage

Even the most vivid accounts of the slave trade cannot convey the pain and demoralization that accompanied the initial capture and subsequent march to slave-trading forts on the West African coast or the dreaded "middle passage" across the Atlantic. The march to the coast was bad enough: many slaves attempted suicide or died from exhaustion or hunger on these forced marches. Once they arrived at the barracoons, or fortified enclosures on the beach, the European traders often branded the African slaves with a hot iron to indicate which company had procured them. The next trauma came with the ferrying of slaves in large canoes to the ships anchored in the harbor. An English captain recounted the desperation of Africans who were about to lose touch with their ancestral homeland and embark on a vast unknown ocean. "The Negroes are so loath to leave their own country," he wrote, "that they have

often leaped out of the canoes, boat and ship, into the sea, and kept under the water till they were drowned."

Conditions aboard the slave ships were miserable, even though the traders' goal was to deliver alive as many slaves as possible to the other side of the Atlantic. Manacled slaves below decks were crowded together like corpses in coffins. One commentator described "the loathsomeness of the stench, and crying together," that took away all desire to eat. The refusal to take food was so common that ship captains devised special techniques to force food into slaves who were determined to starve themselves to death rather than reach the New World in chains. Slavers flogged their captives brutally, applied hot coals to their lips, or force-fed the slaves with a mouth wrench. Yet for all the attempts to terrify the Africans into passive commodities, the slaves rebelled on about one-tenth of slave ships crossing the Atlantic.

Timeline

1440s	Portuguese begin kidnaping Africans and trading with them for slaves on Africa's western coast
1460s	Using African labor, sugar plantations in Portuguese Madeira become major exporters
1492	Christopher Columbus lands on Caribbean islands
	Spanish expel Moors (Muslims) and Jews
1493–1504	Columbus makes three additional voyages to the Americas
1493	Spain plants first colony in Americas on Hispaniola
1494	Treaty of Tordesillas
1497–1585	French and English explore northern part of the Americas
1498	Vasco da Gama reaches India after sailing around Africa
Early 1500s	First Africans reach the Americas with Spanish
1508–1511	Spanish conquistadors subjugate native people on Puerto Rico and Cuba
1513	Portuguese explorers reach China
1517	Luther attacks Catholicism and begins Protestant Reformation
1520	First disease contracted from Spanish devastates Aztec people
1521	Cortés conquers the Aztecs
1528	Spain plants first settlement on Florida coast
1527–1536	Cabeza de Vaca *entrada* across southern region of North America
1530s	Calvin calls for religious reform
1533	Pizarro conquers the Incas
1534	Church of England established
1539–1542	De Soto expedition explores the Southeast
1540–1542	Coronado explores the Southwest
1558	Elizabeth I crowned queen of England
1585	English plant settlement on Roanoke Island
1588	English defeat the Spanish Armada
1590	Roanoke settlement fails
1603	James I succeeds Elizabeth I

The Atlantic passage usually took four to eight weeks, and one of every seven captives died en route. Many others arrived in the Americas deranged or dying. In all, the relocation of any African may have averaged about six months from the time of capture to the time of arrival at the plantation of a colonial buyer. During this protracted crisis, the slave was completely cut off from the moorings of a previous life—language, family and friends, tribal religion, familiar geography, and status in a local community. Ahead lay endless bondage.

Conclusion
CONVERGING WORLDS

The Iberian voyages of the late fifteenth and early sixteenth centuries, linking Europe and Africa with the Americas, brought together people such as the Spanish conquistador Alvar Núñez Cabeza de Vaca, the Moroccan captive Estevan, and chiefs of Creek villages in the southeastern sector of North America. Here were the beginnings of contact that ultimately joined every region of the globe and linked the destinies of widely disparate peoples living on many parts of the immense Atlantic basin. Other nations would follow but Spain was the first to erect colonial regimes. Along with the Portuguese they also initiated maritime and commercial enterprises profoundly affecting patterns of production, with the Americas destined to become the great producer of foodstuffs to be exported to Europe. Part of this fledgling global economy was the trade in human beings—Africans carried to Spain and Portugal, then to the Atlantic islands off the west coast of Africa, and finally to the Americas in one of the most tragic chapters of human history. Accompanying this, and paving the way for European settlement, was the greatest weapon possessed by Europeans—the germs that decimated the indigenous people of the Americas in the greatest biological holocaust in history.

The English immigrants who began arriving on the eastern edge of North America in the early seventeenth century came late to a New World that other Europeans had been colonizing for more than a century. The first English arrivals, immigrants to Virginia, were but a small advance wave of the large, varied, and determined fragment of English society that would flock to the western Atlantic frontier during the next few generations. Like Spanish, Portuguese, and French colonizers before them, they would establish new societies in the newfound lands in contact with the people of two other cultures—one made up of ancient inhabitants of the lands they were settling and the other composed of those brought across the Atlantic against their will. We turn now to the richly diverse founding experience of the English latecomers in the seventeenth century and their contests with French, Dutch, and Spanish contenders for control of North America.

QUESTIONS FOR REVIEW AND REFLECTION

1. How did the religious changes in Europe affect European expansion into the Americas?
2. What was the Columbian Exchange, and what impact did it have on Europe and the Americas?
3. Why was England slow to become involved in exploration and colonization? How did the late arrival of the English affect their history in the New World?
4. What were the causes and consequences of the African slave trade with the European colonies in the Americas?
5. What was the impact of the collision of cultures that occurred in the Americas in the early colonial period?

Colonizing a Continent in the Seventeenth Century

Cecil Calvert grasping a map of Maryland held by his grandfather, the second Lord Baltimore; detail of a painting by Gerard Soest, court painter to Charles II.

(Enoch Pratt Free Library, Baltimore)

American Stories

An African on the Virginia Frontier

Anthony Johnson, an African, arrived in Virginia in 1621 with only the name Antonio. Caught as a young man in the Portuguese slave-trading net, he had passed from one trader to another in the New World until he reached Virginia. There he was purchased by Richard Bennett and sent to work at Warrasquoke, Bennett's tobacco plantation on the James River. In the next year, Antonio was brought face-to-face with the world of triracial contact and conflict that would shape the remainder of his life. On March 22, 1622, the Powhatan tribes of tidewater Virginia fell on the white colonizers in a determined attempt to drive them from the land. Of the 57 people on the Bennett plantation, only Antonio and four others survived.

Antonio—his name anglicized to Anthony—labored on the Bennett plantation for some 20 years, slave in fact if not in law, for legally defined bondage had not yet fully taken hold in the Virginia colony. During this time, he married Mary, another African trapped in the labyrinth of servitude, and fathered four children. In the 1640s, Anthony and Mary Johnson gained their freedom after half a lifetime of servitude. Probably at this point they chose a surname, Johnson, to signify their new status. Already past middle age, the Johnsons began carving out a niche for themselves on Virginia's eastern shore. By 1650, they owned 250 acres, a small herd of cattle, and two black servants. In a world in which racial boundaries were not yet firmly marked, the Johnsons had entered the scramble of small planters for economic security.

By schooling themselves in the workings of the English legal process, carefully cultivating white patronage, and working industriously on the land, the Johnsons acquired property, established a family, warded off contentious neighbors, and hammered out a decent existence. But by the late 1650s, as the lines of racial slavery tightened, the customs of the country began closing in on Virginia's free blacks.

In 1664, convinced that ill winds were blowing away the chances for their family in Virginia, the Johnsons began selling their land to white neighbors. The following spring, most of the clan moved north to Maryland, where they rented land and again took up farming and cattle raising. Five years later, Anthony Johnson died, leaving his wife and four children. The growing racial prejudice of Virginia followed Johnson beyond the grave. A jury of white men in Virginia declared that because Johnson "was a Negroe and by consequence an alien," the 50 acres he had deeded to his son Richard before moving to Maryland should be awarded to a local white planter.

Johnson's children and grandchildren, born in America, could not duplicate the modest success of the African-born patriarch. Anthony's sons never rose higher than the level of tenant farmer or small freeholder. John Johnson moved farther north into Delaware in the 1680s. Members of his family married local Native Americans and became part of a triracial community that has survived to the present day. Richard Johnson stayed behind in Virginia. When he died in 1689, he had little to leave his four sons. They became tenant farmers and hired servants, laboring on plantations owned by whites. By now, slave ships were pouring Africans into Virginia and Maryland to replace white indentured servants, the backbone of the labor force for four generations. To be black had at first been a handicap. Now it became a fatal disability, an indelible mark of degradation and bondage.

Anthony and Mary Johnson's story is one of thousands detailing the experiences of seventeenth-century immigrants who arrived in North America. Their lives became intertwined with those who came from Europe trying to escape war, despotism, material want, and religious strife. Like free immigrants and indentured servants from Europe, the Johnsons coped with new environments, social situations, and mixings of people who before had lived on different continents. Mastering the North American environment involved several processes that would echo down the corridors of American history. Prominent among them were the molding of an African labor force and the gradual subjection of Native American tribes who contested white expansion. Both developments occurred in the lifetimes of Anthony and Mary Johnson and their children. Both involved a level of violence that made this frontier of European expansion a zone where some realized democratic dreams while others faced growing inequality and servitude.

This chapter reconstructs the manner of settlement and the character of immigrant life in six areas of early colonization: Chesapeake Bay, southern New England, the French and Dutch area from the St. Lawrence River to the Hudson River, the Carolinas, Pennsylvania, and the Spanish toeholds on the southern fringe of North America. The chapter shows how these regional societies changed over the course of the seventeenth century and how they experienced internal strain, a series of Native American wars, a destructive and community-shattering witchcraft craze, and reactions to England's attempts to reorganize its overseas colonies.

The Chesapeake Tobacco Coast

In 1607, a group of merchants established England's first permanent colony in North America at Jamestown, Virginia. But for the first generation, its permanence was anything but assured; even into the second and third generation of settlement along the waters flowing into the Chesapeake Bay, the English colonizers were plagued with internal discord and violent clashes with the native peoples.

Jamestown, Sot Weed, and Indentured Servants

Under a charter from James I, the Virginia Company of London operated as a joint-stock company, an early kind of corporation that sold shares of stock and used the pooled capital to outfit and supply overseas expeditions. Although the king's charter to the company began with a concern for bringing Christian religion to native people who "as yet live in darkness and miserable ignorance of the true knowledge of God," the settlers and even the leaders showed little interest in the project.

John Smith wrote "their aim was profit," but profits in the early years proved elusive. Expecting to find gold, a rewarding trade with Native Americans for beaver and deer skins, and a water route to China, the original investors and settlers got a rude shock. Dysentery, malaria, drought, and malnutrition carried off most of the first colonists. More than 900 settlers, mostly men, arrived in the colony between 1607 and 1609; only 60 survived.

Fully one-third of the first immigrants were gold-seeking adventurers with unroughened hands, a proportion of gentlemen six times as great as in the English population. Many others were unskilled servants, some with criminal backgrounds, who (according to John Smith) "never did know what a day's work was." Both types adapted poorly to wilderness conditions, and Smith got few of the carpenters, fishermen, blacksmiths, and farmers he wanted.

The colony was also hampered by the assumption that Englishmen could exploit the Native Americans as Cortés and Pizarro had done. They found instead that the some 24,000 local Powhatan were not densely settled and could not be easily subjugated. Unlike Spain, England had sent neither an army of conquistadors nor an army of priests to subdue the natives. Relations with the small groups that the able Powhatan had united into a confederacy turned bitter almost from the beginning. The Powhatan brought supplies of maize to the sick and starving Jamestown colony during the first autumn. John Smith, whose military experience in eastern Europe had schooled him in dealing with people he regarded as "barbarians,"

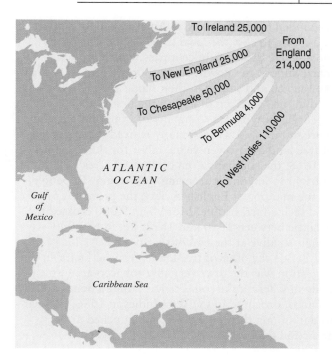

The Great English Migration, 1630–1660

This map shows that more than half of all the early English immigrants to the Americas went to the West Indies. Why would immigrants have traveled to the West Indies in such comparatively high numbers?

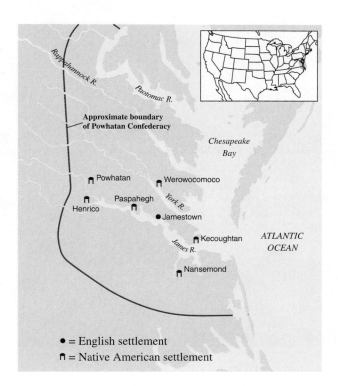

Early Chesapeake Settlement

Only the major Native American villages in the early 1600s are indicated on this map. Why would the town sites all be oriented to the rivers?

responded by raiding Native American food supplies and trying to cow the local tribes. Amid one of the most severe droughts in centuries, which reduced the maize supply, the Powhatan withdrew from trade with the English and sniped at their flanks. Many settlers died in the "starving times" of the first years.

Still, the Virginia Company of London poured in more money and settlers, many enticed with promises of free land after seven years' labor for the company. In 1618, the company even offered 50 acres of land outright to anyone journeying to Virginia. To people on the margins of English society, the promise of free land seemed irresistible. More than 9,000 crossed the Atlantic between 1610 and 1622. Yet only 2,000 remained alive at the end of that period.

Beside the offer of free land, a crucial factor in the migration was the discovery that tobacco grew splendidly in Chesapeake soil. Francis Drake's boatload of tobacco, procured in the West Indies in 1586, popularized it among the upper class and launched an addiction that continues to this day.

James I's denunciation of smoking as "loathsome to the eye, hateful to the nose, harmful to the brain, and dangerous to the lungs" failed to halt the smoking craze. "Sot weed" became Virginia's salvation. Planters shipped the first crop in 1617, and, with profits initially high, tobacco cultivation spread rapidly. By 1624, Virginia exported 200,000 pounds; in 1638, though the price had plummeted, the crop exceeded 3 million pounds. Tobacco became to Virginia in the 1620s what silver was to Mexico and Peru. In London, men joked that Virginia was built on smoke.

Because tobacco required intensive care, Virginia's planters had to find a reliable supply of cheap labor. They recruited mostly English and Irish laborers to be indentured servants, who sold years of their working lives in exchange for free passage to America. Nearly three-quarters were male, mostly between 15 and 24 years old, and nearly all came from the lower rungs of the social ladder at home.

Life for indentured servants often turned into a nightmare. Only about one in 20 realized the dream of

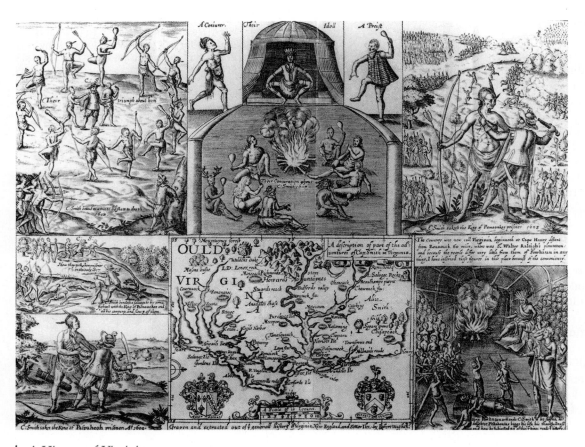

A History of Virginia

A small caption in the middle of this set of panels reads, "A description of part of the adventures of Cap: Smith in Virginia." The images were rendered by Robert Vaughan, an English engraver, and were published in *The Generall Historie of Virginia, 1624, by Captain John Smith*. In the lower right panel, an oversized Pocahontas (at the right) begs for the life of Smith, whose head is on a block, ready for dismemberment by an Indian executioner. What overall effect would this engraving have on readers of John Smith's history in England?

freedom and land. If malarial fever or dysentery did not quickly kill them, they often succumbed to brutal work routines. Even by the middle of the seventeenth century, about half died during the first few years of "seasoning." Masters bought and sold their servants as property, gambled for them, and even worked them to death. "My Master Adkins," wrote one servant in 1623, "hath sold me for £150 like a damned slave." When servants neared the end of their contract, masters found ways to add time and were backed by courts that they controlled.

Contrary to English custom, masters often put women servants to work at the hoe. Servant women also faced sexual abuse, and they paid dearly for illegitimate pregnancies. The courts fined them heavily and ordered them to serve an extra year or two to repay the time lost during pregnancy and childbirth. They also deprived mothers of their illegitimate children, indenturing them out at an early age. Many servant women accepted the purchase of their indenture by any man who suggested marriage as the best release from this hard life.

Expansion and Indian War

As tobacco production caused Virginia's population to increase, violence mounted between white colonizers and the Powhatan tribes. In 1614, the sporadic hostility of the early years ended temporarily with the arranged marriage of Chief Powhatan's daughter, the fabled Pocahontas, to planter John Rolfe. However, the profitable cultivation of tobacco continued to create an intense demand for land.

In 1617, when Powhatan retired, leadership of the Chesapeake tribes fell to Opechancanough. This proud and talented leader began preparing an all-out attack on his English enemies. The English murder of Nemattanew, a Powhatan war captain and religious prophet, triggered a fierce Native American assault in 1622 that dealt Virginia a staggering blow. More than one-quarter of the white population fell, and the casualties in cattle, crops, and buildings were equally severe.

The devastating attack bankrupted the Virginia Company. The king annulled its charter in 1624 and established a royal government, allowing the elected legislative body established in 1619, the House of Burgesses, to continue lawmaking in concert with a royal governor and his council.

The Native American assault of 1622 fortified the determination of the surviving planters to pursue a ruthless new Native American policy. John Smith noted the grim satisfaction that had followed the attack. Many, he reported, believed that "now we have just cause to destroy them by all means possible." Bolstered by instructions from London to "root out [the Native Americans] from being any longer a people," the Virginians conducted annual military expeditions against the native villages.

Ætatis suæ 21. A°. 1616.

Matoaks als Rebecka daughter to the mighty Prince Powhatan Emperour of Attanoughkomouck als virginia converted and baptized in the Christian faith, and Wife to the Wor.t M.r Tho: Rolff.

Pocahontas

Painted at the time she was presented to the court of King James I, Pocahontas appears in a red velvet jacket over a dark dress with gold buttons. She holds a fan of three ostrich feathers. We can only imagine how her elaborate shoulder collar of white lace must have felt for a 22-year-old woman accustomed to loose-fitting, comfortable clothes. Why was she painted in this attire and not that of her native culture.

(Anonymous, *Pocahontas*, c. 1595–1617, daughter of Powhatan chief. National Portrait Gallery, Smithsonian Institution/Art Resource, NY)

Population growth after 1630 and settlers' perpetual need for fresh acreage, because tobacco quickly exhausted the soil, intensified the pressure on Native American land. The tough, ambitious planters provoked war over Indian territories in 1644. The Chesapeake tribes, Virginians came to believe, were merely obstacles to be removed from the path of English settlement.

Proprietary Maryland

By the time Virginia had achieved commercial success in the 1630s, another colony on the Chesapeake took root. The founder's main aim was not profit but rather a refuge for Catholics and a New World version of England's manor-dotted countryside.

Catholic nobleman George Calvert (Lord Baltimore) designed and promoted the new colony. In 1632, Charles I, James's son, granted Baltimore 10 million acres, which Calvert named Terra Maria, or Maryland, to honor the king's Catholic wife, Henrietta Maria.

Calvert planned his colony as a haven for his coreligionists, an oppressed minority in England. Knowing that he needed more than a small band of Catholic settlers, the proprietor invited others, too. Catholics, never a majority in his colony, were quickly overwhelmed by Protestants who jumped at the offer of free land with only a modest yearly fee to the Calverts.

Lord Baltimore died in 1632, leaving his 26-year-old son, Cecilius, to carry out his plans. The charter guaranteed the proprietor control over all branches of government, but young Calvert learned that his colonists would not be satisfied with fewer liberties than they enjoyed at home or could find in other colonies. Hence, the Lords Baltimore gave up their charter-given right to initiate all colonial laws, subject only to the advice and consent of the people.

Arriving in 1634, immigrants ignored Calvert's plans for 6,000-acre manors for his relatives and 3,000-acre manors for lesser aristocrats, each to be worked by serf-like tenants. The settlers took up their free land, imported as many indentured servants as they could afford, maintained generally peaceful relations with local native tribes, grew tobacco on scattered riverfront plantations like their Virginia neighbors, and governed themselves locally as much as possible. Although Maryland grew slowly at first—in 1650, it had a population of only 600—it developed rapidly in

the second half of the seventeenth century. By 1700, its population of 33,000 was half that of Virginia.

Daily Life on the Chesapeake

Though immigrants to the Chesapeake Bay region dreamed of bettering their prospects, most found life dismal. Only a minority married and reared a family: a preponderance of men in the population prevented many from finding wives; and any marriage had to be deferred until the indenture was completed. Once made, marriages were fragile. Either husband or wife was likely to die of disease within about seven years. The vulnerability of pregnant women to malaria frequently terminated marriages, and death claimed half the children before they reached adulthood. Few children had two living parents while growing up. Grandparents were almost unknown.

In a society so numerically dominated by men, widows often remarried quickly. Such conditions produced complex families, full of stepchildren, stepparents, half-sisters, and half-brothers.

Plagued by horrendous mortality, the Chesapeake remained, for most of the seventeenth century, a land of immigrants rather than a land of settled families. Churches and schools took root very slowly. The large number of indentured servants further destabilized community life. Strangers in a household, they served their time and moved on, or died, replaced by other strangers, purchased fresh from England.

The region's architecture reflected the difficult conditions. Life was too uncertain, the tobacco economy too volatile, and the desire to invest every available shilling in field labor too great for men to build grandly. At first they lived in primitive huts and shanties, hardly more than windbreaks. Even by the early eighteenth century, most Chesapeake families lived in crude houses without interior partitions. With hardly a semblance of privacy, most ordinary Virginians and Marylanders were "pigg'd lovingly together," as one planter put it. Even prosperous planters did not begin constructing fully framed, substantial homesteads until a century after the colony was founded.

The crudity of life also showed in the household possessions of the Chesapeake colonists. Struggling farmers and tenants were likely to own only a straw mattress, a simple storage chest, and the tools for food preparation and eating—a mortar and pestle to grind corn, knives for butchering, a pot or two for cooking stews and porridges, and wooden trenchers and spoons for eating. Most ordinary settlers owned no chairs, dressers, plates, or silverware. Among middling planters, the standard of living was raised only by possession of a flock mattress, coarse earthenware for milk and butter, a few pewter plates and porringers, a frying pan or two, and a few rough tables and chairs. To be near the top of

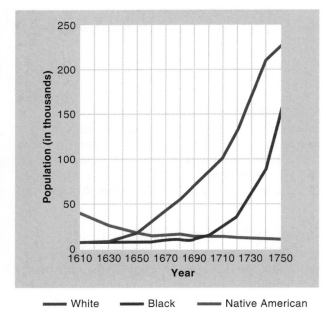

Population of the Chesapeake Colonies, 1610–1750

As indicated in this chart, it was not until the 1690s, when Chesapeake planters began turning to Africa for their labor, that the black population in the Chesapeake colonies began to rise rapidly.

Source: U.S. Bureau of the Census

Chesapeake society meant having three or four rooms, sleeping more comfortably, sitting on chairs rather than squatting on the floor, and owning such ordinary decencies as chamber pots, candlesticks, bed linen, a chest of drawers, and a desk. Four generations elapsed in the Chesapeake settlements before the frontier quality of life slowly gave way to more refined living.

Bacon's Rebellion Engulfs Virginia

The Chesapeake colonies reached an explosive point in 1675–1676 with a war fought both between the native and white populations and among the colonizers. Before it ended, hundreds of whites and Native Americans lay dead in Virginia and Maryland, Virginia's capital of Jamestown burned, and English troops were crossing the Atlantic to suppress what the king labeled an outright rejection of his authority. This tangled conflict was called Bacon's Rebellion after the headstrong, Cambridge-educated planter Nathaniel Bacon, who arrived in Virginia at age 28.

Bacon and many other ambitious young planters detested the Native American policy of Virginia's royal governor, Sir William Berkeley. In 1646, after the second

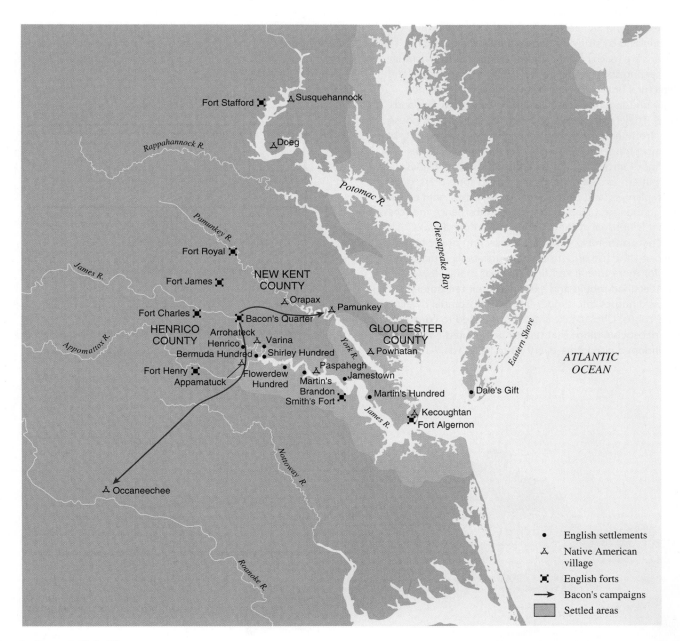

Bacon's Rebellion
In Bacon's Rebellion, Governor Berkeley fled to the Eastern Shore because it was the only part of Virginia strongly loyal to him. Berkeley raised a militia there by promising them tax exemption for 21 years. How would you explain the placement of the forts?

Recovering the Past

HOUSES

Homesteading is central to our national experience. For 300 years after the founding of the first colonies, most Americans were involved in taming and settling the land. On every frontier, families faced the tasks of clearing the fields, beginning farming operations, and building shelter for themselves and their livestock. The kinds of structures they built depended on available materials, their resources and aspirations, and their notions of a "fair" dwelling. The plan of a house and the materials used in its construction reveal much about the needs, resources, priorities, and values of the people who built it.

By examining archaeological remains of early ordinary structures and by studying houses that are still standing, historians are reaching new understandings of the social life of pioneering societies. Since the 1960s, archaeologists and architectural historians have been studying seventeenth-century housing in the Chesapeake Bay and New England regions. They have discovered a familiar sequence of house types—from temporary shanties and lean-tos to rough cabins and simple frame houses to larger and more substantial dwellings of brick and finished timber. This hovel-to-house-to-home pattern existed on every frontier, as sodbusters, gold miners, planters, and cattle raisers secured their hold on the land and then struggled to move from subsistence to success.

What is unusual in the findings of the Chesapeake researchers is the discovery that the second phase in the sequence—the use of temporary, rough-built structures—lasted for more than a century. Whereas many New Englanders had rebuilt and extended their temporary clapboard houses into timber-framed, substantial dwellings by the 1680s, Chesapeake settlers continued to construct small, rickety buildings that had to be repaired continually or abandoned altogether every 10 to 15 years.

The William Boardman house shown here, built around 1687, is an example of the "orderly, fair, and well-built" houses of late-seventeenth-century Massachusetts. Its plan shows a typical arrangement of space: the hall, used for cooking, eating, working, and socializing; the parlor; a sleeping room for the parents; and a lean-to for kitchen chores and activities such as dairying. The great central chimney warmed the main downstairs room. Upstairs were two rooms used for both storage and sleeping. As you examine the exterior of the building, note the materials that have been used and the arrangement and treatment of windows, doors, and chimney. What impression of the Boardman family might visitors have as they approached the house? What kind of privacy and comfort did the house provide for family members?

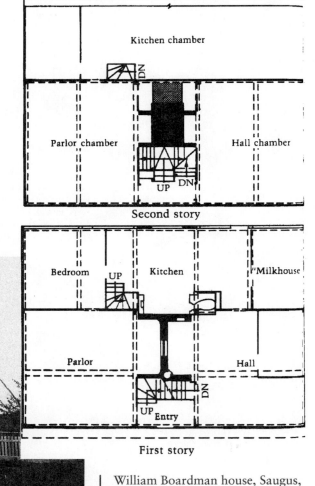

William Boardman house, Saugus, Massachusetts, ca. 1687; a floor plan of the house is shown above.

(Courtesy of the Society for the Preservation of New England Antiquities)

The smaller house shown is a typical reconstructed tobacco planter's house. It has some of the same features as the Boardman house, for both are products of an English building tradition. But there are some major differences between the two. In the Chesapeake house, the chimney is built not of brick but of mud and wood, and there is no window glass, only small shutters. The exterior is rough, unfinished planking. The placement of doors and windows and the overall dimensions indicate that this house has only one room downstairs and a loft above. The builders of this house clearly enjoyed less privacy and comfort than the Boardmans.

Historians have puzzled over this contrast between the architecture of the two regions. Part of the explanation may lie in the different climatic conditions and different immigration patterns of New England and the Chesapeake. In the southern region, disease killed thousands of settlers in the early decades. The imbalance of men and women produced a stunted and unstable family life, hardly conducive to an emphasis on constructing fine homes. In New England, good health prevailed almost from the beginning, and the family was at the heart of society. It made more sense, in this environment, to make a substantial investment in larger and more permanent houses. Some historians argue, moreover, that the Puritan work ethic impelled New Englanders to build solid homes—a compulsion unknown in the culturally backward, "lazy" South.

Archaeological evidence combined with data recovered from land, tax, and court records, however, suggests another reason for the impermanence of housing in the Chesapeake region. Living in a labor-intensive tobacco world, it is argued, planters large and small economized on everything possible in order to buy as many indentured servants and slaves as they could. Better to live in a shanty and have 10 slaves than to have a handsome dwelling and nobody to cultivate the fields. As late as 1775, the author of *American Husbandry* calculated that in setting up a tobacco plantation, five times

Reconstructed Chesapeake planter's house, typical of such simply built and unpainted structures in the seventeenth century.

(Photograph by Julie Roy Jeffrey)

as much ought to be spent on purchasing 20 black fieldhands as on the "house, offices, and tobacco-house."

Only after the Chesapeake region had emerged from its prolonged era of mortality and gender imbalance and a mixed economy of tobacco, grain, and cattle had replaced the tobacco monoculture did the rebuilding of the region begin. Excavated house sites indicate that this occurred in the period after 1720. New research reveals that the phases of home building and the social and economic history of a society were closely interwoven.

Reflecting on the Past What do houses today reveal about the resources, economic livelihood, priorities, and values of contemporary Americans? Do class and regional differences in house design continue? ■

Native uprising against the Virginians, the Powhatan tribes had been granted exclusive rights to territory beyond the limits of white settlement. Stable Native American relations suited the established planters, but became obnoxious to new settlers and ex-indentured servants who hoped for cheap frontier land.

Land hunger and dissatisfaction with declining tobacco prices, rising taxes, and lack of opportunity erupted into violence in the summer of 1675. A group of frontiersmen used an incident with a local tribe as an excuse to attack the Susquehannock, whose rich land they coveted. Governor Berkeley denounced the attack, but few supported his position. As he explained, he faced "a people where six parts of seven

at least are poor, indebted, discontented, and armed." The badly outnumbered Susquehannock prepared for war as rumors swept the colony that they were offering large sums to gain western native allies or that New England tribes would support them.

Thirsting for revenge, the Susquehannock attacked during the winter of 1675–1676 and killed 36 Virginians. That spring, Nathaniel Bacon became the rebels' leader. Joined by hundreds of runaway servants and some slaves, he attacked friendly and hostile Native Americans alike. Governor Berkeley refused to sanction these attacks and declared Bacon a rebel, sending 300 militiamen to drag him to Jamestown for trial. Bacon recruited more followers, including many substantial planters. Frontier skirmishes with Native Americans had turned into civil war. During the summer of 1676, Bacon's and Berkeley's troops maneuvered, while Bacon's men continued their forays against local tribes. Then Bacon boldly captured and razed Jamestown, forcing Berkeley to flee across Chesapeake Bay.

Virginians at all levels had chafed under Berkeley's rule. High taxes, an increase in the governor's powers at the expense of local officials, and the monopoly that Berkeley and his friends held on the Native American trade were especially unpopular. In the summer of 1676, Berkeley tried to rally public support by holding new assembly elections and extending the vote to all freemen, whether they owned property or not. But the new assembly turned on the governor, passing laws to make government more responsive to the common people. It also legalized enslaving Native Americans.

Time was on the governor's side, however. Having crushed the Native Americans, Bacon's followers began drifting home to tend their crops. Meanwhile, 1,100 royal troops were dispatched from England. By the time they arrived in January 1677, Bacon had died of swamp fever and most of his followers had dispersed. Berkeley hanged 23 rebels without benefit of trial.

Royal investigators afterward reported that Bacon's followers "seem[ed] to wish and aim at an utter extirpation of the Indians." This hatred, along with hopes of land ownership and independence, became a permanent feature of Virginia life. A generation later, in 1711, the legislature spurned the governor's plea for quieting the frontier with educational missions and regulated trade, instead voting military appropriations of £20,000 "for extirpating all Indians without distinction of Friends or Enemys." The remnants of the once populous Powhatan Confederacy lost their last struggle for the world they had known. Now they moved farther west or submitted to a life on the margins of white society as tenant farmers, day laborers, or domestic servants.

After Bacon's Rebellion, an emerging planter aristocracy annulled most of the reform laws of 1676. By making new land available, the war relieved much of the social tension among white Virginians. Equally important, Virginians with capital to invest were turning from the impoverished rural villages of England and Ireland to the villages of West Africa to supply their labor needs. White former-servants would no longer form a discontented mass at the bottom of Chesapeake society. A racial consensus, uniting whites across ranks in the common pursuit of a prosperous, slave-based economy, began to take shape.

In Virginia, the volatility of late-seventeenth-century life owed much to the region's peculiar social development. Where family formation was retarded by imbalanced gender ratios and fearsome mortality, and where geographic mobility was high, little social cohesion or attachment to community could grow. Missing in the southern colonies were the stabilizing power of mature local institutions, a vision of a larger purpose, and the presence of experienced and responsive political leaders.

The Southern Transition to Slave Labor

English colonists on the mainland of North America at first regarded Native Americans as the obvious source of labor. But European diseases ravaged native societies, and the native people, more at home in the environment than the white colonizers, were difficult to subjugate. Indentured white labor proved the best way to meet the demand for labor during most of the seventeenth century.

Within a decade of Virginia's founding, a few Africans labored in the tobacco fields alongside white servants. As late as 1671, when some 30,000 slaves toiled in English Barbados, fewer than 3,000 served in Virginia. They were outnumbered at least three to one by white indentured servants.

Only in the last quarter of the seventeenth century did the southern labor force begin to shift to a black slave majority. Three reasons explain this shift. First, the rising commercial power of England, at the expense of the Spanish and Dutch, swelled English participation in the African slave trade. Southern planters, beginning in the 1680s, could purchase slaves more readily and cheaply. Second, the supply of white servants began drying up. Third, Bacon's Rebellion, involving rebellious former servants seeking land, led white planters to seek a more pliable labor force. Consequently, by the 1730s, the number of white indentured servants dwindled to insignificance. Black hands, not white, tilled and harvested Chesapeake tobacco and Carolina rice, and slave labor became the priority in starting a plantation.

In enslaving Africans, English colonists in North America copied their European rivals in the New World and emulated their countrymen on Barbados, Jamaica, and the Leeward Islands. There, from the 1630s on, the English had used brutal repression to mold Africans into a sugar- and tobacco-producing slave labor force. Human bondage would later become the subject of intense moral debate, but in the seventeenth century, all but a few whites accepted it without question.

The System of Bondage

The first Africans brought to the American colonies were probably sold as bound servants, who served their term and then, like Anthony and Mary Johnson, gained their freedom. Once free, they could buy land, hire out their labor, and move as they pleased. Their children, like those of white indentured servants, were born free. But gradually, Chesapeake planters drew tighter lines around the activities of black servants. By the 1640s, Virginia forbade blacks, free or bound, to carry firearms. In the 1660s, marriages between white women and black men were banned as "shameful matches." By the end of the century, when incoming Africans increased from a trickle to a torrent, even the few free blacks found themselves pushed to the margins of society. Slavery, which had existed for centuries in many societies as the lowest social status, was now becoming a caste reserved for those with black skin.

In this dehumanization of Africans, the key step was instituting hereditary lifetime service. Once servitude ended only by death, other privileges quickly vanished. When a mother's slave condition legally passed on to her newborn black infant (which was not the case in slavery in Africa), slavery became self-perpetuating, passing automatically from one generation to the next.

Equiano

This portrait, painted about 1780 after Equiano had purchased his freedom, shows him as a successful Londoner with hair and clothes in the style of a fashionable Englishman. In 1792, Equiano married an English woman and had two daughters with her. He died five years later. Do you think white Londoners in the 1790s accepted mixed-race marriages calmly?

(*Portrait of a Negro Man, Olaudah Equiano*, 1780s, Robert Albert Memorial Museum, Exeter, Devon England/The Bridgeman Art Library)

Slavery became not only a system of forced labor but also a pattern of human relationships legitimated by law. By the early eighteenth century, most provincial legislatures limited black rights. Borrowed largely from England's Caribbean colonies, "Black codes" forced Africans into an ever narrower world. Slaves could not testify in court, engage in commercial activity, hold property, participate in the political process, congregate in public, travel without permission, or legally marry or be parents. Nearly stripped of human status, they became defined as chattel (a commodity), and gradually all legal restraints on the masters' treatment of them disappeared.

Eliminating rights did not eliminate slave resistance. With every African in chains a potential rebel, the rapid increase in the slave population brought anxious demands for strict control and justifications for brutality. "The planters," wrote one Englishman in Jamaica, "do not want to be told that their Negroes are human creatures." One of the great paradoxes of modern history thus occurred. Whereas many Old World immigrants imagined the Americas as a liberating and regenerating arena, the opportunity to exploit its resources led to a historic process by which masses of people were forced into a system of slavery that could be maintained only by increasing intimidation and brutality.

Massachusetts and Its Offspring

While some English settlers in the reign of James I (1603–1625) scrambled for wealth on the Chesapeake, others in England looked to the wilds of North America as a place to build a new society that would reform the corrupt world. Puritanism would powerfully affect the nation's history by nurturing a belief in America's special mission in the world. The "New England way" also represented an attempt to banish diversity on a continent where the arrival of streams of immigrants from around the globe was destined to become the primary phenomenon.

Puritanism in England

England had been officially Protestant since 1558. Some people in the late sixteenth century, however, thought the Church of England was still riddled with Catholic vestiges. They demanded the end of every taint of "the Bishop of Rome and all his detestable enormities." Wishing to purify the Church of England, they were dubbed Puritans.

Religious reformers as well as men and women hoping to find in religion an antidote to the unsettling changes sweeping over English society were attracted to the Puritan movement. The growth of turbulent cities, the increase of wandering poor, rising prices, and accelerating commercial activity made them fear for the future. They looked to religion for a guide to right living in unsettled times.

While the concept of the individual operating as freely as possible, maximizing both opportunities and personal potential, is at the core of our modern system of beliefs, many in Elizabethan England dreaded the crumbling of traditional restraints.

Puritans vowed to reverse the march of disorder by imposing a new discipline. Impressed by the model of Calvin's Geneva, they hoped the Church of England would encourage the religious conversion of the "saints" and control the sinfulness of the mass of unconverted people in society.

In 1603, when King James VI of Scotland became James I of England, the reformed-minded members of the Church of England hoped he would bring the strong discipline of the Scottish Presbyterian church to his new kingdom. James disappointed them, and the Church remained unreformed. Puritans, however, continued to occupy pulpits in many churches, control several colleges at Cambridge, and sit in Parliament. James found those who separated themselves entirely from the church, the so-called "separatists," unacceptable. He vowed to "harry them out of the land," and some small groups fled to the continent during his reign. When Charles I succeeded to the throne in 1625, he objected to the situation. Determined to strengthen the monarchy and stifle dissent, the king summoned a new Parliament in 1628 and one year later adjourned this venerable body (which was the Puritans' main instrument of reform) when it would not accede to royal demands. The king then appointed William Laud as archbishop of Canterbury, the most powerful position within the Church of England below the king himself. Laud and Charles agreed that the Puritans were the "most dangerous enemies of the state."

By 1629, as the king began ruling without Parliament, many Puritans were turning their eyes to northern Ireland, Holland, the Caribbean, and, especially, North America. They were convinced that God intended them to carry their religious and social reforms beyond the reach of persecuting authorities. A declining economy added to their discouragement about England. Many Puritans decided that they should transport a fragment of English society to some distant shore and complete the Protestant Reformation.

Puritan Predecessors in New England

Puritans were not the first European colonizers to reach northeastern North America. Since the early 1500s, fishermen from several European nations had dried their Newfoundland catches on the coast of Cape Cod and Maine, frequently encountering Algonquian-speaking natives. A short-lived attempt at settlement in Maine had been made in 1607. Seven years later, the aging Chesapeake war dog John Smith, hired to hunt whales off the North American coast, coined the term "New England."

No permanent settlement took root, however, until a group of religious separatists—actually outnumbered by non-separatists—arrived in Plymouth in 1620. Unlike the Puritans who followed, these humble Protestant farmers did not expect to convert a sinful world. Rather, they wanted to be left alone to realize their radical vision of a pure and primitive life. Instead of reforming the Church of England, they had left it, first fleeing from England to Amsterdam in 1608, then to Leyden, Holland, and, finally, in 1620, to North America. In the nineteenth century their descendents would dubbed them "Pilgrims," which is how they are known to us today.

Arriving at Cape Cod in November 1620, the Pilgrims, weakened by a stormy nine-week voyage, were ill-prepared for the harsh winter ahead. Misled by John Smith's glowing report of a warm, fertile country, they discovered instead a severe climate and a rock-bound coast. By the following spring, half the *Mayflower* passengers were dead, including 13 of the 18 married women.

The survivors, led by the staunch William Bradford, settled at Plymouth. Squabbles soon erupted with local Native Americans, whom Bradford considered "savage and brutish men." In 1622, they found themselves nearly overwhelmed by the arrival of 60 non-Pilgrims, sent out by the London Company, which had helped the Pilgrims finance their colony. For two generations, the Pilgrims tilled the soil, fished, and tried to keep intact their religious vision. But with the much larger Puritan migration that began in 1630, the Pilgrim villages nestled around Cape Cod Bay became a backwater of the thriving, populous Massachusetts Bay Colony, which absorbed them in 1691.

Errand into the Wilderness

In 11 ships, about 1,000 Puritans set out from England in 1630—the vanguard of a movement that by 1642 brought about 18,000 colonizers to New England. Led by John Winthrop, a minor member of the English gentry with a smattering of education at both Cambridge and the Inns of Court (where lawyers trained), they operated under a charter from the king to the Puritan-controlled Massachusetts Bay Company. The Puritans set about building their utopia convinced they were carrying out a divine task. "God hath sifted a nation," wrote one Puritan, "that he might send choice grain into this wilderness."

Their intention was to establish communities of pure Christians who collectively swore a covenant with God. Dreaming of homogeneous communities where the good of the group outweighed individual interests, Winthrop counseled that "We must delight in each other, make others' conditions our own, rejoice together, mourn together, labor and suffer together."

An ideology of rebellion in England, Puritanism in North America became an ideology of control, suffused with a powerful sense of mission that still remains part of American thinking. As in Plymouth and Virginia, the first winter tested the strongest souls. More than 200 of the first 700 settlers perished, and 100 others, disillusioned and sickened by the forbidding climate, soon returned to England. But Puritans kept coming, settling along the rivers that emptied into Massachusetts Bay. A few years later, they pushed south into what became Connecticut and Rhode Island, as well as northward along the rocky coast.

Motivated by their militant work ethic and sense of mission, and led by men experienced in local government, law, and exhortation, the Puritans thrived. The early leaders of Virginia were soldiers of fortune or roughneck adventurers with predatory instincts, men who had no families or had left them at home; ordinary Chesapeake settlers were mostly young men with little stake in English society who sold their labor to cross the Atlantic. But the early leaders in Massachusetts were university-trained ministers and experienced members of the lesser gentry, united by a compulsion to fulfill God's plan in New England. Most ordinary settlers came as free men and women in families. Artisans and farmers from the middle ranks of English society, they established tight-knit communities in which, from the outset, the brutal exploitation of labor rampant in the Chesapeake had little place.

Relying mostly on free labor, the Puritans built an economy based on agriculture, fishing, and timbering; for a time, they also traded beaver furs with local Native Americans. Even before leaving England, the directors of the Massachusetts Bay Company transformed their commercial charter into a rudimentary government. In North America, they laid the foundations of self-government. Free male church members annually elected a governor and deputies from each town, who formed one house of a colonial legislature, the General Court. The other house was composed of the governor's assistants, later to be called councillors. Consent of both houses was required to pass laws.

The Puritans established the first printing press in the English colonies and founded Harvard College, which opened its doors in 1636 to train clergymen. They also launched a far-sighted attempt in 1642 to create a tax-supported school system, open to all wanting an education.

In spite of these accomplishments, the Puritan colony suffered many of the tensions besetting people bent on human perfection. Surrounded by seemingly boundless land, Puritans found it difficult to stifle acquisitive instincts and to keep families confined in compact communities. "An over-eager desire after the world," wrote an early leader, "has so seized on the spirits of many as if the Lord had no farther work for his people to do, but every bird to feather his own nest." Those remaining at the nerve center in Boston agitated for broader political rights. After a few years, Governor Winthrop wondered whether the Puritans had not gone "from the snare to the pit."

Conflict erupted in 1633 when Salem's Puritan minister, Roger Williams, began to voice disturbing opinions. Contentious and charismatic, Williams argued that the Massachusetts Puritans were not truly pure because they would not completely separate from the polluted Church of England. (While Puritans still in England continued to hope for its reform, those in New England found it impolitic to admit publicly that they had in effect separated from it through their migration.) Williams also denounced mandatory worship and argued that government officials should confine themselves to civil affairs and not interfere with religious matters. "Coerced religion," he warned, "on good days produces hypocrites, on bad days rivers of blood." Today honored as the earliest spokesman for the separation of church and state, Williams in 1633 seemed to strike at the heart of the Bible commonwealth, whose leaders regarded civil and religious affairs as inseparable. Williams also questioned the king's right to grant Indian lands, which made the settlers illegal intruders.

For two years, Puritan leaders worked to quiet Williams. Convinced that he would split the colony into competing religious groups and undermine authority, the magistrates vowed to deport him to England. Warned by Winthrop, Williams fled southward through winter snow with a small band of followers to found Providence in what would become Rhode Island.

Even as they were driving Williams out, the Puritan authorities confronted another threat: a devout and magnetic woman of extraordinary talent and intellect who arrived in 1634 with her husband and seven children. Quickly gaining respect among Boston's women as a midwife, healer, and spiritual counselor, Anne Hutchinson soon began to discuss religion and suggested that the "holy spirit" was absent in the preaching of some ministers. Before long Hutchinson was leading a movement labeled *antinomianism,* which stressed God's free gift of grace while discounting the efforts the individual could make to gain salvation.

By 1636, Boston was dividing into two camps— those who followed the male clergy and those drawn to the theological views of a gifted though untrained woman without official standing. Her ideas were feared in part because they undermined the new structures put in place to contain the religious questioning that had been a hallmark of the Puritan movement in England. Hutchinson's supporters included a recently arrived elite young man, Sir Henry Vane, who had been elected governor as a result of his high status; many merchants and artisans who chafed under the price controls the magistrates imposed in 1635 to stop inflation; and women who welcomed her willingness to continue the religious dialogues they had cherished in England. Hutchinson doubly offended the leaders of the colony because she boldly stepped outside the subordinate position expected of women. "The weaker sex" set her up as a "priest" and "thronged" after her, wrote one male leader. Determined to remove this thorn from their sides, the clergy and magistrates who opposed her managed to put Hutchinson on trial in 1637. After long interrogations, they convicted her of sedition and contempt in a civil trial and banished her from the colony "as a woman not fit for our society." Six months later, the Boston church excommunicated her for preaching 82 erroneous theological opinions. In the last

month of her eighth pregnancy, Hutchinson, with a band of supporters, followed Roger Williams's route to Rhode Island in 1638.

Despite these early successes eliminating dissenting voices, the magistrates could never enforce uniformity of belief or curb the appetite for land. Growth, geographic expansion, and commerce with the outside world all eroded the ideal of integrated, self-contained communities vibrant with piety. Leaders faced the nearly impossible task of containing land-hungry immigrants in an expansive region. By 1636, groups of Puritans had swarmed not only to Rhode Island but also to Hartford and New Haven, where Thomas Hooker and John Davenport led new Puritan settlements in what became Connecticut.

New Englanders and Indians

Though the charter of the Massachusetts Bay Company spoke of converting "the natives to the knowledge and obedience of the only true God and Saviour of mankind and the Christian faith," the

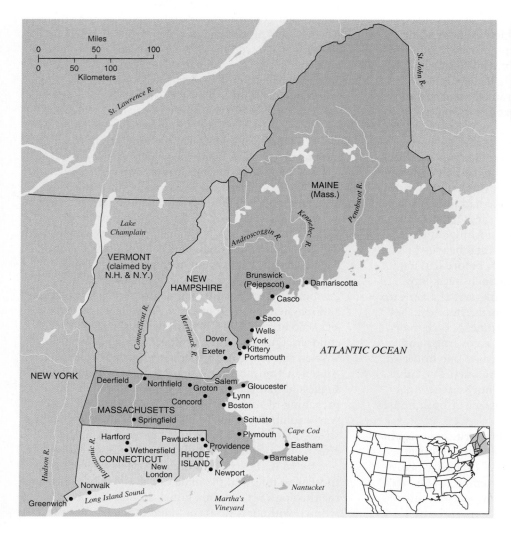

Early New England

Maine and New Hampshire became the frontier to which New England settlers migrated when their towns and farmlands became too crowded. How do settlement patterns compare to those in the Chesapeake.

instructions that Governor John Winthrop carried from England reveal other thoughts about the native inhabitants. According to Winthrop's orders, all men were to receive training in the use of firearms, a reversal of the sixteenth-century English policy of disarming the citizenry in order to quell public disorders. New England magistrates prohibited Native Americans from entering English towns and threatened to deport any colonist selling arms to a native or instructing one in their use.

Only sporadic conflict with local tribes occurred at first because disease had left much of New England vacant. In 1616, visiting English fishermen had triggered a ferocious outbreak of respiratory viruses and smallpox that wiped out three-quarters of some 125,000 Native Americans. Five years later, an Englishman exploring the area described walking through a forest where human skeletons covered the ground. The Puritans believed that God had intervened on their side, especially when smallpox returned in 1633, killing thousands more natives and allowing new settlers easy access to land. Surviving natives at first welcomed the settlers because they now had surplus land and through trade hoped to gain English protection against tribal enemies to the north.

The settlers' pressure for new land, however, soon reached into occupied areas. Land hunger mingled with the Puritan sense of mission made an explosive mix. Native Americans represented a challenge to the building of a religious commonwealth that would "shine as a beacon" back to decadent England. While the smaller, disease-ravaged tribes of eastern Massachusetts gave the settlers little trouble, unsuccessful efforts to control the stronger Pequot led to a bloody war in 1637. Their victory assured English domination over all the tribes of southern New England except the powerful Wampanoag and Narragansett of Rhode Island and removed the last obstacle to expansion into the Connecticut River valley. Missionary work, led by John Eliot, began among the remnant tribes in the 1640s. After a decade of effort, about 1,000 Native Americans had been settled in four "praying villages," learning to live according to the white settlers' ways.

The Web of Village Life

Unlike the dispersed Chesapeake tobacco planters, the Puritans established small, tightly settled villages that were vital centers of life. Most New England settlers farmed the land, while living close together in towns built around a common field used to graze livestock, bordered by a meetinghouse and eventually a tavern. These small, communal villages kept families in close touch so that each could be alert not only to its own transgressions, but also to those of its neighbors. "In a

multitude of counsellors is safety," ministers were fond of advising, and the little villages of 50 to 100 families perfectly served the need for moral surveillance, or "community watchfulness." To achieve godliness and communal unity, Puritans also prohibited single men from living by themselves, beyond patriarchal authority and group observation. Left to themselves, people would stray from the path, for, as Thomas Hooker put it, "every natural man and woman is born full of sin, as full as a toad of poison." Virginia planters counted the absence of restraint as a blessing. New England's leaders feared it as the Devil.

At the center of every Puritan village stood the meetinghouse. The community gathered twice on

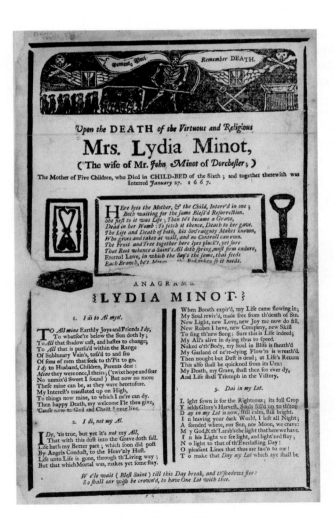

In Commemoration of Lydia Minot

Funeral testimonies like this one were cheaply printed as broadsides and were passed out to mourners. When Lydia Minot died in 1667 while giving birth to her sixth child, she was memorialized with anagrams and acrostics—popular literary exercises in the seventeenth century. What do the hourglass, coffin, and shovel, at the middle of the broadside, symbolize?

(Courtesy of the Massachusetts Historical Society)

Sundays in their plain wooden structures to hear the preaching of the town's minister. No man stood higher in the community than the minister, the spiritual leader in these small, family-based, community-oriented settlements, which viewed life as a Christian pilgrimage.

The unique Puritan mixture of strict authority and incipient democracy, of hierarchy and equality, can be seen in the way the Massachusetts town distributed land and devised local government. After receiving a grant, townsmen met to parcel out land. They awarded individual grants according to the size of a man's household, his wealth, and his usefulness to the church and town. Such a system perpetuated existing differences in wealth and status. Yet some towns wrote language into their covenants that to the modern ear has an almost socialistic ring. "From each according to his ability to each as need shall require," read one. Believing that the community's welfare transcended individual ambitions or accomplishments and that unity demanded limits on the accumulation of wealth, the founders wanted every family to have enough land to sustain it. Prosperous men were expected to use their wealth for such community projects as repairing the meetinghouse, building a school, or aiding a widowed neighbor.

Having felt the sting of centralized power in church and state, New Englanders emphasized local exercise of authority. Until 1684, only male, landowning church members could vote, and as the proportion of males who were church members declined, so did the proportion of men who could vote. These voters elected selectmen, who allocated land, passed local taxes, and settled disputes. Once a year, all townsmen gathered for the town meeting, which Thomas Jefferson later called the "wisest invention ever devised by the wit of man for the perfect exercise of self-government." At town meetings the citizens selected town officers for the next year and decided matters large and small. The appointment of many residents to minor offices—surveyors of hemp, informers about deer, purchasers of grain, town criers, measurers of salt, fence viewers, and others—bred the tradition of local government. About one of every 10 adult males in many towns was selected each year for some office, large or small.

The predominance of families also lent cohesiveness to village life. Strengthening this family orientation was a relatively healthy environment. Whereas the germs carried by English colonizers devastated neighboring Native American societies, the newcomers flourished. The low density of settlement prevented infectious diseases from spreading, and the isolation of the New England villages from the avenues of Atlantic commerce, along which diseases as well as cargo flowed, minimized biological hazards.

The result was a spectacular natural increase in the population and a life span unknown in Europe. At a time when the population of western Europe was barely growing—deaths almost equaled births—the population of New England, discounting new immigrants, doubled every 27 years. The difference was not a higher birthrate. New England women typically bore about seven children during the course of a marriage, but this barely exceeded the European norm. The crucial factor was that chances for survival after birth were far greater because of the healthier climate and better diet. In most of Europe, only half the babies born lived long enough to produce children themselves. Life expectancy for the population at large was less than 40 years. In New England, nearly 90 percent of the infants born in the seventeenth century survived to marriageable age, and life expectancy exceeded 60 years—longer than for the American population as a whole at any time until the early twentieth century. About 25,000 people immigrated to New England in the seventeenth century, but by 1700, they had produced a population of 100,000. By contrast, some 75,000 immigrants to the Chesapeake colonies had yielded a population of only about 70,000 by the end of the century.

Women played a vital role in this family-centered society. The Puritan woman was not only a wife, mother, and housekeeper; she also kept the vegetable

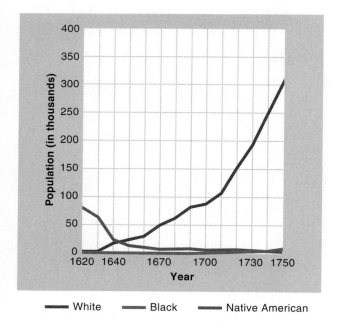

Population of the New England Colonies, 1620–1750

The fact that white population growth was far more rapid in New England than in the Chesapeake region reflected higher birthrates, a healthier environment, and a reliance on free labor.

Source: U.S. Bureau of the Census

The Mason Children

Three of Arthur and Joanna Mason's five children were captured in this 1670 painting. The nine-year-old boy on the left holds a silver-headed walking stick, signifying his status as male heir. His six-year-old sister in the middle holds a yellow fan and red and yellow ribbons. The four-year-old sister to the right holds a rose, which Puritans used as a symbol of innocence associated with childhood. Why do you think the artist portrayed these children with faces typical of older boys and girls?

(The Freake-Gibbs painter, *The Mason Children: David, Joanna, and Abigail,* 1670. Fine Arts Museum of San Francisco, Gift of Mr. and Mrs. John Rockefeller 3rd, 1979 .7.3)

garden; salted and smoked meats; preserved vegetables and dairy products; and spun yarn, wove cloth, and made clothes.

The presence of women and a stable family life strongly affected New England's regional architecture. As communities formed, the Puritans converted early economic gains into more substantial housing rather than investing in bound labor as Chesapeake colonists did. In New England, well-constructed one-room houses with sleeping lofts quickly replaced the early "wigwams, huts, and hovels." Families then added additional rooms and lean-to kitchens as soon as they could. Within a half century, New England immigrants accomplished a general rebuilding of their living structures, whereas Chesapeake residents lagged far behind.

A final binding element in Puritan communities was the stress on literacy and education, eventually to become a hallmark of American society. Placing religion at the center of their lives, Puritans emphasized the ability to read the Bible. In literacy and education, Puritans saw guarantees for preserving their central values.

Though eager to be left alone, Puritans could not escape events in England. In 1642, King Charles I pushed England into revolution by violating the country's customary constitution and continuing earlier attacks against Puritans. By 1649, the ensuing civil wars climaxed with the trial and beheading of the king. Thereafter, during the so-called Commonwealth period (1649–1660), Puritans in England could complete the

reform of religion and society at home. Meanwhile, migration to New England abruptly ceased.

The 20,000 English immigrants who had come to New England by 1642 were scattered from Maine to Long Island. Governor Winthrop of Massachusetts and William Bradford of Plymouth deplored this dispersion and condemned the "depraved appetite" for new and better land. Yet in a terrain so rock-strewn that its pastures were said to produce Yankee sheep with sharpened noses, farmers sought better plow land; population growth also propelled expansion.

King Philip's War in New England

By the 1670s, New England's population had grown to about 50,000, gradually reducing the natives' land base. By that time the Wampanoag leader was Metacomet (called King Philip by the English), the son of Massasoit, who had allied with the first Plymouth settlers in 1620. Metacomet had watched his older brother preside over the deteriorating position of his people after their father's death in 1661. Becoming chief in his turn, Metacomet faced one humiliating challenge after another, climaxing in 1671, when leaders of the Plymouth colony forced him to surrender a large stock of guns and accept his people's subjection to English law.

Metacomet began organizing a resistance movement fed by the rising anger of the young Wampanoags, who refused to imitate their parents' acquiescence to the colonizers' encroachments and abridgment of their sovereignty. For the young men, revitalization of their ancient culture through war became as important a goal as defeating the enemy. Rather than submit further, they planned a pan-Indian offensive against the intruder.

In 1675, Puritans executed three Wampanoag for murdering John Sassamon, a Christianized Native American educated at Harvard who had allegedly warned Plymouth colony of an impending native attack. The execution sparked war. That summer the Wampanoag unleashed daring hit-and-run attacks on villages in the Plymouth colony. By autumn, many New England tribes, including the powerful Narragansett, had joined Metacomet. Towns all along the frontier reeled under Native American attacks. By November, native warriors had devastated the entire upper Connecticut River valley, and by March 1676, they were less than 20 miles from Boston and Providence. As assumptions about English military superiority

faded, New England officials passed America's first draft laws. Widespread draft evasion and friction among the colonies hampered a counteroffensive.

Metacomet's onslaught faltered in the spring of 1676, sapped by food shortages, disease, and the refusal of the powerful Mohawk to join the New England tribes. Then Metacomet fell in a battle near the Wampanoag village where the war had begun. The head of this "hell-hound, fiend, serpent, caitiff and dog," as one colonial leader branded him, was displayed in Plymouth for 25 years.

At war's end, several thousand colonists and perhaps twice as many Native Americans lay dead. Of some 90 Puritan towns, 52 had been attacked and 13 completely destroyed. Some 1,200 homes lay in ruins and 8,000 cattle were lost. The estimated cost of the war exceeded the value of all personal property in New England. Not for 40 years would the frontier advance beyond the line it had reached in 1675. Native American towns were devastated even more completely, including

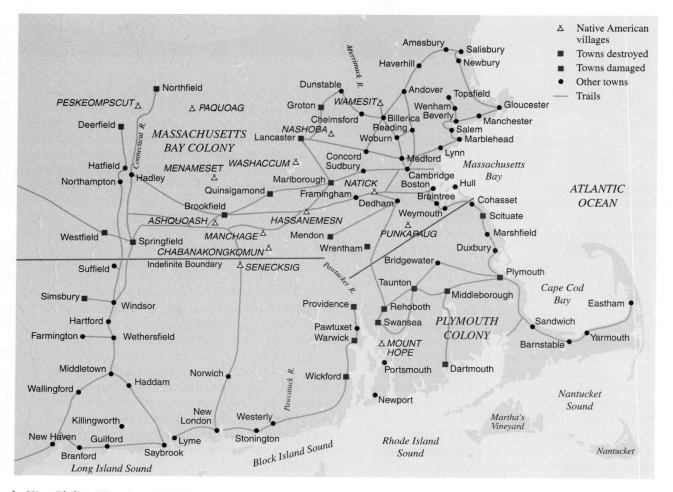

King Philip's War, 1675–1676

The home base of Metacomet, or King Philip, was within the Plymouth colony at Mount Hope. Based on this map what can you say about the geography of the conflict?

several inhabited by "praying Indians" who had converted to Christianity and allied with the whites. Almost an entire generation of young men had been annihilated. Many of the survivors, including Metacomet's wife and son, were sold into slavery in the West Indies.

Slavery in New England

The Wampanoag captives sold as slaves in the West Indies continued New England's involvement in the dirty business of slavery. New England's crops were not labor-intensive, so coerced labor never became the foundation of New England's workforce. Slavery did take root in the larger towns, though, where slaves worked as artisans and domestic servants. Northern colonial economies also became enmeshed in the Atlantic commercial network, which depended on slavery and the slave trade. New England's merchants eagerly pursued profits in the slave trade as early as the 1640s. By 1676, New England slavers were packing their holds with slaves from as far away as Madagascar, off the coast of East Africa, and transporting them 6,000 miles to the western side of the Atlantic. By 1750, half the merchant fleet of Newport, Rhode Island, reaped profits from carrying human cargo. In New York and Philadelphia, building and outfitting slave vessels proved profitable.

New England's involvement in the international slave trade deepened with the growth of its seaports as centers for distilling rum—the "hot, hellish and terrible liquor" made from West Indian sugar. Rum became one of the principal commodities traded for slaves on the African coast. As the number of slaves in the Caribbean multiplied—from about 50,000 in 1650 to 500,000 in 1750—New England's large fishing fleet found important markets for its cod. Wheat from the middle colonies and barrel staves and hoops from North Carolina also serviced the slave-based West Indies economy. In short, every North American colony participated in the slave business.

From the St. Lawrence to the Hudson

The New Englanders were not the only European settlers in the northern region, for both France and Holland created colonies there. While English settlers founded Jamestown, the French were trying again, after their failure in the 1540s, to settle Canada.

France's America

Henry IV, the first strong French king in half a century, sent Samuel de Champlain to explore deep into the territory even before the English had obtained a foothold on the Chesapeake. Champlain established a small settlement in Port Royal, Acadia (later Nova Scotia), in 1604 and another at Québec in 1608. French trading with Native Americans for furs had already begun in Newfoundland, and Champlain's settlers hoped to keep making these easy profits. But the holders of the fur monopoly in France did not encourage immigration to the colony, fearing that settlement would reduce the forests from which the furs were harvested. New France therefore remained so lightly populated that English marauders easily seized and held Québec from 1629 to 1632.

In 1609–1610, Champlain allied with the Algonquian Indians of the St. Lawrence region in attacking their Iroquois enemies to the south, earning their enmity. This drove the Iroquois to trade furs for European goods with the Dutch on the Hudson River; when the Iroquois exhausted the furs of their own territory, they turned north and west, determined to seize the forest-rich resources from the Huron, French allies in the Great Lakes region.

When the Iroquois descended on them in the 1640s, the Huron were already decimated by a decade of epidemics that spread as Jesuit priests entered their villages. In the "beaver wars" of the 1640s and 1650s, the Iroquois used Dutch guns to attack Huron parties carrying beaver pelts to the French. By midcentury, Iroquois attacks had scattered the Huron, all but ending the French fur trade and reducing the Jesuit influence to a few villages of Christianized Huron.

The bitterness bred in these years colored future colonial warfare, driving the Iroquois to ally with the English against the French. At the mid-seventeenth century, the beleaguered French colonists, who numbered only about 400, did not hinder the English efforts.

England Challenges the Dutch

By 1650, the Chesapeake and New England regions each contained about 50,000 settlers. Between them lay the mid-Atlantic area controlled by the Dutch, who planted a small colony named New Netherland at the mouth of the Hudson River in 1624. In the next four decades they extended their control to the Connecticut and Delaware river valleys. South of the Chesapeake lay a vast territory where only the Spanish, from their mission frontier in Florida, challenged the power of Native American tribes.

Although for generations they had been the Protestant bulwarks in a mostly Catholic Europe, England and Holland became bitter commercial rivals in the mid-seventeenth century. By the time the Puritans arrived in New England, the Dutch had become the mightiest carriers of seaborne commerce in western Europe. By one contemporary estimate, Holland owned 16,000 of Europe's 20,000 merchant

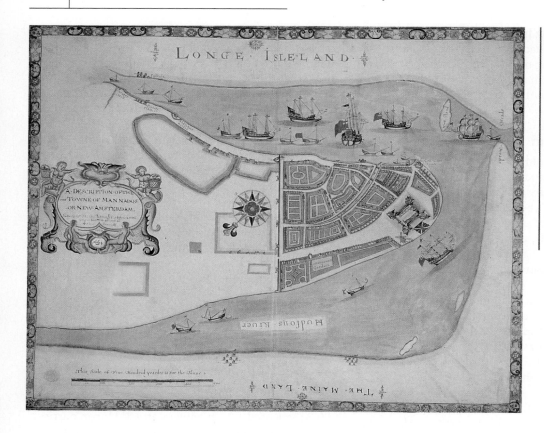

New Amsterdam in 1644
The fort at the tip of Manhattan, flying an English flag, shows prominently in this 1664 map of Dutch New Amsterdam just after it had been bloodlessly conquered by a small English fleet. The park-filled city and the Governor's garden fronting on the Hudson River were separated by a wall from the farmlands of "upper" Manhattan.

(By Permission of the British Library, Shelfmark Maps.K.Top.121.35)

ships. The Dutch had muscled in on Spanish and Portuguese transatlantic commerce, trading illegally with Iberian colonists who gladly violated their government's commercial policies to obtain cloth and slaves more cheaply. By 1650, the Dutch had temporarily overwhelmed the Portuguese in Brazil, and soon their vast trading empire reached the East Indies, Ceylon, India, and Formosa (now Taiwan). The best shipbuilders, mariners, and businessmen in western Europe, they validated the dictum of Sir Walter Raleigh that "whosoever commands the sea commands the trade; whosoever commands the trade of the world commands the riches of the world, and consequently the world itself."

In North America, the Dutch West India Company's New Netherland colony was small, profitable, and multicultural. Agents fanned out from Fort Orange (Albany) and New Amsterdam (New York City) into the Hudson, Connecticut, and Delaware river valleys, establishing a lucrative fur trade with local tribes by hooking into the sophisticated trading network of the Iroquois Confederacy, which stretched to the Great Lakes. The Iroquois welcomed the Dutch, who were few in number, did not have voracious appetites for land, and willingly exchanged desirable goods for the pelts of animals plentiful in the vast Iroquois territory. At Albany, the center of the Dutch–Iroquois trade, relations remained peaceful and profitable for several generations.

Although the Dutch never settled more than 10,000 people in their mid-Atlantic colonies, their commercial and naval powers were impressive. The Virginians learned this in 1667 when brazen Dutch raiders captured 20 tobacco ships on the James River and confiscated virtually the entire tobacco crop for that year.

By 1650, England was ready to challenge Dutch maritime supremacy. War broke out three times between 1652 and 1675, as the two Protestant nations competed to control the emerging worldwide capitalist economy. In the second and third wars, New Netherland became an easy target for the English. They captured it in 1664 and then, after it fell to the Dutch in 1673, recaptured it almost immediately. By 1675, the Dutch had been permanently dislodged from the North American mainland. But they remained mighty commercial competitors of the English around the world.

New Netherland—where from the beginning Dutch, French Huguenots, Walloons from present-day Belgium, Swedes, Portuguese, Finns, English, refugee Portuguese Jews from Brazil, and Africans had commingled in a babel of languages and religions—now became New York, so named because Charles II gave it (along with the former Dutch colonies on the Delaware River) to his brother the duke of York, later King James II. Under English rule, the Dutch colonists remained ethnically distinct for several generations, clinging to their language, their Dutch Reformed Calvinist churches, and their architecture. In time, however, English immigrants overwhelmed the Dutch, and gradual intermarriage among the Dutch, the French Huguenots (Protestants), and the English diluted ethnic loyalties. New York retained its polyglot, religiously tolerant character, and its people never allowed religious concerns or utopian plans to interfere with the pragmatic conduct of business.

Proprietary Carolina: A Restoration Reward

In 1663, three years after he was restored to his father's throne, England's Charles II granted a vast territory named Carolina to a group who supported him during his exile. Its boundaries extended from Virginia southward to central Florida and westward to the Pacific. Within this potential empire, eight London-based proprietors, including several involved in Barbados sugar plantations, gained the right to settle this vast area. The system of governance planned for Carolina had both feudal and modern features. To lure settlers, the proprietors promised religious freedom and offered land free for the asking. This generous land offer, however, included a scheme for a semimedieval government in which they, their deputies, and a few noblemen would monopolize political power. Reacting to a generation of revolutionary turbulence in England, they designed Carolina as a model of social and political stability in which a hereditary aristocracy would check boisterous small landholders.

Carolina realities bore faint resemblance to these hopes. The rugged sugar and tobacco planters who streamed in from Barbados and Virginia, where depressed economic conditions made a new beginning seem attractive, claimed their 150 acres of free land, as well as additional acreage for each family member or servant they brought. They ignored proprietary regulations about settling in compact rectangular patterns and reserving two-fifths of every county for a designated elite. In government, they also did as they pleased. Meeting in assembly for the first time in 1670, they refused to accept the proprietors' Fundamental Constitutions of 1667 and ignored orders from the proprietors' governor. Most of the settlers already knew how to run a slave society from having lived in Barbados, and they shaped local government from that experience.

The Indian Debacle

Carolina was the most elaborately planned colony in English history yet the least successful in achieving the harmony the proprietors had intended. Mindful of the violence that had plagued other settlements, they projected a well-regulated Native American trade, run exclusively by their appointed agents. By drawing the major tribes of the Southeast—the Cherokee, Creek, and Choctaw—into trade they might reap vast wealth, which the Spanish in Florida had failed to tap. But the aggressive settlers from the West Indies and the Chesapeake flouted all this.

To the consternation of the London proprietors, capturing Native Americans for sale in New England and the West Indies became the cornerstone of commerce in Carolina in the early years, plunging the colony into a series of wars. Planters and merchants selected a tribe, armed it, and rewarded it handsomely for bringing in enemy captives. Even strong tribes found that after they had used English guns to enslave their weaker neighbors, they themselves were scheduled for elimination. The colonists claimed that "thinning the barbarous Indian natives" was needed to make room for white settlement, and the "thinning" was so thorough that by the early eighteenth century the two main tribes of the coastal plain, the Westo and the Savannah, were nearly extinct.

Early Carolina Society

Carolina's fertile land and warm climate convinced many that it was a "country so delicious, pleasant, and fruitful that were it cultivated doubtless it would prove a second Paradize." In came Barbadians, Swiss, Scots, Irish, French Huguenots, English, and migrants from northern colonies. But far from creating paradise, they clashed abrasively in an atmosphere of fierce competition, ecological exploitation, brutal race relations, and stunted social institutions. Decimating the coastal Native Americans made it easier to expand the initial settlements around Charleston.

After much experimentation, planters found a profitable staple crop that would flourish in this forbidding environment: rice. Its cultivation required back-breaking labor to drain swamps, build dams and levees, and hoe, weed, cut, thresh, and husk the crop. Many early settlers had owned African slaves in Barbados, so their reliance on slavery came easily. On widely dispersed plantations, black labor came to predominate. In 1680, four-fifths of South Carolina's population was white. But by 1720, when the colony had grown to 18,000, slaves outnumbered whites two to one.

As in Virginia and Maryland, the low-lying areas of coastal Carolina were so disease-ridden that population grew slowly in the early years. "In the spring a paradise, in the summer a hell, and in the autumn a hospital," remarked one traveler. Malaria and yellow fever, especially dangerous to pregnant women, were the main killers that retarded population growth, and the scarcity of women further limited natural increase.

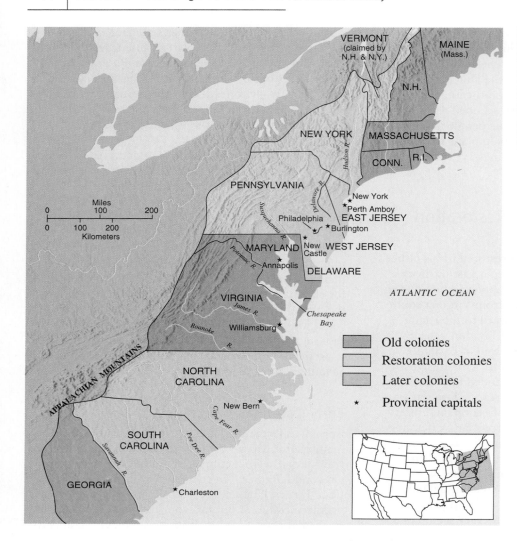

Restoration Colonies:
New York, the Jerseys,
Pennsylvania, and the
Carolinas

The Restoration era, from the
1660s to the 1680s, witnessed
the founding of numerous new
colonies. How would you explain
their locations?

Like the West Indies, the rice-growing region of Carolina was at first more a place to accumulate a fortune than to rear a family.

In healthier northern Carolina, a different kind of society emerged amid pine barrens along a sandy coast. Settled largely by small tobacco farmers from Virginia seeking free land, the Albemarle region developed a mixed economy of livestock grazing, tobacco and food production, and the extraction of naval stores—lumber, turpentine, resin, pitch, and tar.

In 1701, North and South Carolina became separate colonies, but their distinctiveness had already emerged. Slavery took root only slowly in North Carolina, which was still 85 percent white in 1720. A land of struggling white settlers, its healthier climate and settlement by families rather than by single men with servants and slaves gave it a greater potential for sustained growth. But in North as well as South Carolina, scattered settlements, ethnic and religious diversity, and a lack of shared assumptions about social and religious goals inhibited the growth of a strong colony-wide identity.

Slave Quarters on a South Carolina Plantation

This painting of Mulberry Plantation in South Carolina shows the mansion house, built in 1708, and rows of slave huts constructed in an African style. How likely was it that enslaved Africans lived in such substantial structures in the eighteenth century?

(Thomas Coram (American 1756–1811), "View of Mulberry, House and Street", ca. 1800, oil on paper. © Image Gibbes Museum of Art / Carolina Art Association, 1896.018.0001)

The Quakers' Peaceable Kingdom

Of all the utopian dreams imposed on the North American landscape in the seventeenth century, the most remarkable was the Quakers'. During the English civil war, the Society of Friends, as the Quakers called themselves, had sprung up as one of the many radical sects searching for a juster society and a purer religion. Their visionary ideas and defiance of civil authority cost them dearly in fines, brutal punishment, and imprisonment. After Charles II and Parliament stifled radical dissent in the 1660s, they, too, sent many converts across the Atlantic. More than any other colony, the society they founded in Pennsylvania foreshadowed the religious and ethnic pluralism of the future United States.

The Early Friends

Like Puritans, the Quakers regarded the Church of England as corrupt. But Quakers went much further, rejecting all Church officials and institutions and holding that every believer could find grace through the "inward light," a redemptive spark in every human soul. Rejecting predestination, Quakers offered a radical alternative to Calvinism with the idea that anyone could be saved.

Other Protestants, regarding them as dangerous fanatics, persecuted Quakers in England after their movement, led by George Fox and Margaret Fell, gathered momentum in the 1650s. The Quaker doctrine of the "light within" took precedence even over Scripture and elevated all laypeople to the position of the clergy. Practicing civil disobedience, the Quakers also threatened social hierarchy and order. They refused to observe the customary marks of deference, such as doffing one's hat to a superior, believing that God made no social distinctions. They used the familiar *thee* and *thou* instead of the formal and deferential *you*, they resisted taxes supporting the Church of England, and they refused to sign witnesses' oaths on the Bible, regarding this as profane. Most shocking, they renounced the use of force in human affairs and therefore refused to perform militia service.

Quakers also affronted traditional views when they insisted on the spiritual equality of the sexes and the right of women to participate in church matters on an equal, if usually separate, footing with men. Quaker leaders urged women to preach and to establish separate women's meetings. Among Quakers who fanned out from England to preach the doctrine of the inward light, 26 of the first 59 to cross the Atlantic were women. All but four of them were unmarried or without their husbands and therefore living, traveling, and ministering outside male authority.

Intensely committed to converting the world, Quakers ranged westward to North America and the Caribbean in the 1650s and 1660s. Nearly everywhere, they faced jeers, prison, mutilation, and deportation. Puritan Massachusetts warned them "to keep away from us and such as will come to be gone as fast as they can, the sooner the better." Hungering to serve in what they called "the Lamb's War" (the crusade of the meek), the Quakers vowed to test the Puritans' resolve and kept coming. To enforce religious conformity, the Bay Colony magistrates in 1659 hanged two Quaker men on the Boston Common and threatened to do the same to Mary Dyer, an old woman who had followed Anne Hutchinson a quarter century before. Led from the colony, Dyer returned the next year, undaunted, to meet her death at the end of a rope in 1660.

Early Quaker Designs

By the 1670s, the English Quakers were looking for a place in the New World to carry out their millennial dreams and escape repression. They found a leader in William Penn. His decision to identify with this radical and persecuted sect was surprising, for he was the son of Sir William Penn, the admiral who had captured Jamaica from Spain in 1655. In 1666, the 23-year-old Penn adopted the Quaker creed and thereafter devoted himself to the Friends' cause.

In 1674, Penn joined other Friends in establishing a North American colony, West Jersey. They had bought the land from one of the proprietors of New Jersey, itself a new English colony recently carved out of the former New Netherland. For West Jersey, Penn helped fashion a constitution extraordinarily liberal for its time that allowed virtually all free males to vote for legislators and local officials. Settlers were guaranteed freedom of religion and trial by jury. As Penn and the other trustees of the colony explained, "We lay a foundation for [later] ages to understand their liberty as men and Christians, that they may not be brought in bondage, but by their own consent; for we put the power in the people."

The last phrase, summing up the document, would have shocked anyone of property and power in England or North America at the time. Most regarded "the people" as ignorant, dangerous, and certain to bring society to a state of anarchy if allowed to rule themselves. Nowhere in the English world had ordinary citizens, especially those who did not own land, enjoyed such extensive privileges. Nowhere had a popularly elected legislature received such broad authority.

West Jersey sputtered at first. Only 1,500 immigrants arrived in the first five years, and for several decades the colony was caught up in tangled claims to the land and government. The center of Quaker hopes lay across the Delaware River, where in 1681, Charles II granted William Penn a territory almost as large as

England, paying off a large royal debt to Penn's father. Charles II also benefited by getting the pesky Quakers out of England. Thus Penn and the Quakers came into possession of the last unassigned segment of the eastern coast of North America, and one of the most fertile.

Pacifism in a Militant World: Quakers and Native Americans

On the day Penn received his royal charter for Pennsylvania, he wrote a friend, "My God that has given it to me will, I believe, bless and make it the seed of a nation." The nation that Penn envisioned was unique among colonizing schemes. Penn intended to make his colony an asylum for the persecuted and a refuge from arbitrary state power. Puritans had strived for social homogeneity and religious uniformity, excluding all not of like mind. In the Chesapeake and Carolina colonies, aggressive, unidealistic men sought to exploit their lands and bondspeople. But Penn dreamed of inviting to his forested colony people of all religions and national backgrounds, offering them peaceful coexistence. His state would neither claim authority over residents' consciences nor demand military service of them.

The Quakers began streaming into Pennsylvania in 1682, quickly absorbing earlier Dutch, Finnish, and Swedish settlers. They participated in the government by electing representatives who initiated laws. They were primarily farmers, and like colonists elsewhere, they avidly acquired land, which Penn sold at reasonable rates. Unlike other colonizers, the Quakers practiced pacifism, holding the ethic of love and nonresistance embodied in the Sermon on the Mount as literally binding on them.

Even before arriving, Penn laid the foundation for peaceful relations with the Delaware tribe inhabiting his colony. "The king of the Country where I live, hath given me a great Province," he wrote to the Delaware chiefs, "but I desire to enjoy it with your Love and Consent, that we may always live together as Neighbors and friends." In this single statement Penn dissociated himself from the entire history of European colonization in the New World and from the widely held negative view of Native Americans. Recognizing the natives as the rightful owners of the land included in his grant, Penn pledged not to sell one acre until he had first purchased it from local chiefs. He also promised to regulate strictly the Native American trade and to ban alcohol sales.

As long as the Quaker philosophy of pacifism and friendly relations with the local Native Americans held sway, interracial relations in the Delaware River valley contrasted sharply with those in other parts of North America. But ironically, the Quaker policy of toleration, liberal government, and exemption from military service attracted thousands of immigrants to the colony (especially in the eighteenth century) whose land hunger and disdain for Native Americans undermined

PENNS TREATY with the INDIANS, made 1681 without an Oath, and never broken. The foundation of Religious and Civil LIBERTY, in the U.S. of AMERICA.

Concluding a Treaty with the Indians

Edward Hicks painted *Penn's Treaty with the Indians* in the nineteenth century. It is a romanticized version of the Treaty of Shackamaxon by which the Lenape chiefs ceded the site of Philadelphia to Penn. The treaty was actually made in 1682, but Hicks was correct in implying that the Lenape held Penn in high regard for his fair treatment of them. What evidence of Quaker pacifism do you find in this painting?

(Edward Hicks, *Penn's Treaty with the Indians,* Gift of Edgar William and Bernice Chrysler Garbisch, © 2000 Board of Trustees, National Gallery of Art, Washington)

Quaker trust and friendship. Driven from their homelands by hunger and war, Germans and Scots–Irish flooded in, swelling the population to 31,000 by 1720. Neither shared Quaker idealism about racial harmony. They pressed inland and, sometimes encouraged by the land agents of Penn's heirs, encroached on the lands of the local tribes. By the mid-eighteenth century, white immigrants were spilling blood with the natives who had migrated into Pennsylvania to escape the aggression of other colonial governments.

Building the Peaceable Kingdom

Although Pennsylvania came closer to matching its founder's goals than any other European colony, Penn's dreams never completely materialized. Unpersuaded by Penn to settle in compact villages, which he believed necessary for his "holy experiment," settlers instead created open country networks without any particular centers or boundaries.

Quaker farmers prized family life and immigrated almost entirely in kinship groups. As a group they enjoyed a sense of common endeavor. Other Quaker practices, such as allowing marriage only within their society, carefully providing land for their offspring, and guarding against too great a population increase (which would cause too rapid a division of farms) by limiting the size of their families, also contributed to a distinctive identity with the sect.

Settled by religiously dedicated farming families, Pennsylvania boomed. Its countryside became a rich grainland. By 1700, the port capital of Philadelphia overtook New York City in population, and a half century later, it was the largest city in the colonies, bustling with artisans, mariners, merchants, and professionals.

The Limits of Perfectionism

Despite commercial success and peace with Native Americans, not all was harmonious in early Pennsylvania. Politics were often turbulent, in part because of Pennsylvania's weak leadership. Penn was a much-loved proprietor, but he returned to England in 1684, revisiting his colony briefly in 1700. Penn's absence created a leadership vacuum.

A more important cause of disunity resided in the Quaker attitude toward authority. In England, balking at authority was almost a daily part of Quaker life. But in Pennsylvania, the absence of persecution eliminated a crucial binding element from Quaker society. The factionalism that developed demonstrated that people never unify as well as when under attack. Free of harassment, they ceased to look inward and band together; instead they turned outward to an environment filled with opportunity. Their squabbling filled Penn with dismay. Why, he asked, were his settlers so "governmentish, so brutish, so susceptible to scurvy quarrels that break out to the disgrace of the Province?"

Meanwhile, Quaker industriousness and frugality helped produce great material success. After a generation, social radicalism and religious evangelicalism began to fade. As in other colonies, settlers discovered the door to prosperity wide open, and in they surged. Pennsylvania, it is said, was the first community since the Roman Empire to allow people of different national origins and religious persuasions to live together under the same government on terms of near equality. English, Highland Scots, French, Germans, Irish, Welsh, Swedes, Finns, and Swiss all settled in Pennsylvania. This ethnic mosaic was further complicated by a medley of religious groups, including Mennonites, Lutherans, Dutch Reformed, Quakers, Baptists, Anglicans, Presbyterians, Catholics, Jews, and a sprinkling of mystics. Their relations may not always have been friendly, but few attempts were made to discriminate against rival groups. Pennsylvanians thereby laid the foundations for the pluralism that was to become the hallmark of American society.

New Spain's Northern Frontier

Spain's outposts in Florida and New Mexico, preceding all English settlements on the eastern seaboard, fell into disarray between 1680 and the early eighteenth century just as the English colonies were sinking deep roots. Trying to secure a vast northern frontier with only small numbers of settlers, the Spanish relied on missionaries and on forced Native American labor. This reliance weakened efforts in both outposts, and New Mexico in particular.

Popé's Revolt

During the 1670s, when the Franciscans developed a new zeal to root out traditional Native American religious ceremonies, the Pueblo people turned on the Spanish intruders. In years of harsh rule, the Spanish had extracted tribute labor from the Pueblo, who at the same time suffered the ravaging impact of European diseases. Both of these punishing long-term effects contributed to Pueblo alienation, but an assault on their religion pushed the Pueblo to the edge. Launching a campaign to restrict native religious ceremonies in the 1670s, the Spanish friars seized the Pueblo kivas (underground ceremonial religious chambers), forbade native dances, and destroyed priestly masks and prayer sticks.

In August 1680, Popé, a much-persecuted religious leader from San Juan pueblo, responded by leading about two dozen Pueblo villages scattered over several hundred miles to rise up in fury. They burned Spanish ranches and government buildings, systematically destroyed churches, lay waste to fields, and killed half of the friars. As the governor in Santa Fe watched the church go up in flames, he reported his shock at the "scoffing and ridicule which the wretched and miserable Indian rebels made of the sacred things, intoning … prayers of the church with jeers."

Spanish settlers, soldiers, and friars streamed back to El Paso, abandoning their northern frontier in the Southwest for more than a decade. Only in 1694 did a new governor, the intrepid Diego de Vargas, regain Santa Fe and gradually subdue most of the Pueblo. Learning from Popé's rebellion, the Spanish declared a cultural truce, easing their demands for labor tribute and tolerating certain Pueblo rituals in return for nominal acceptance of Christianity. Periodic tension and animosity continued. The Pueblo came to terms with the Spanish because of their need for defense against their old enemies—the Navajo, Ute, and Apache.

Decline of Florida's Missions

The Franciscan missions established in Florida along the Atlantic coast and inland to the west in the Florida panhandle had firmed up New Spain's grip of the southeast corner of North America. Yet few Spanish settlers could be persuaded to settle in Florida. As the governor of Cuba put it frankly in 1673, "It is hard to get anyone to go to St. Augustine because of the horror with which Florida is painted. Only hoodlums and the mischievous go there from Cuba."

Much devastated by disease, the Florida Indians and their Franciscan spiritual shepherds were as severely pummeled as those in New Mexico in the late seventeenth century. English settlers in neighboring South Carolina were eager to use Native American allies to attack the Spanish Indian villages and sell the captives into slavery. The attacks of Carolinians in the early 1680s destroyed a number of Spanish missions.

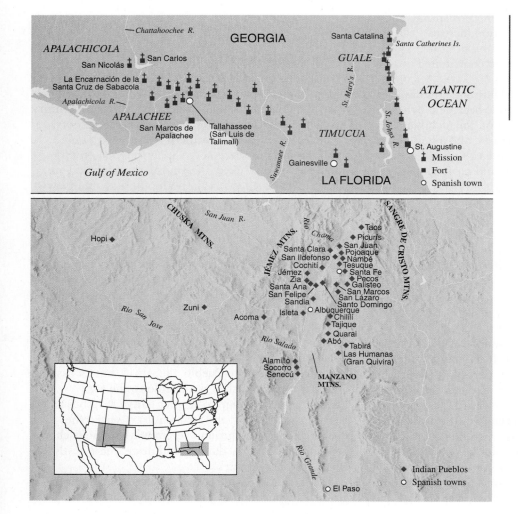

Spanish Missions in New Mexico and Florida in the Late Seventeenth Century

The extensive Spanish missionary activity in Florida and New Mexico had no English parallel. Why would the Spanish have been interested in these two areas in particular?

When England and Spain went to war in 1701—called Queen Anne's War in the colonies—the Carolinians attacked Florida. Burning mission villages to the ground, they slaughtered the Spanish friars and captured some 4,000 women and children to be sold as slaves. The Spanish mission frontier was thoroughly devastated, and only St. Augustine remained as a Spanish stronghold.

An Era of Instability

A dozen years after King Philip's War in New England and Bacon's Rebellion in Virginia, a series of insurrections and a searing witchcraft incident convulsed colonial society. The Revolution of 1688 triggered the rebellions. Known thereafter to English Protestants as the Glorious Revolution, it limited the power of the monarch and assured that only a Protestant would sit on the English throne. In the colonies, it signified a struggle for social and political dominance, as did the Salem witchcraft trials in Massachusetts.

Organizing the Empire

From the beginning of colonization, the English assumed that overseas settlements existed to promote the national interest at home. Mercantilist theory held that colonies were meant to serve as outlets for English manufactured goods, provide foodstuffs and raw materials, stimulate trade (and hence promote a larger merchant navy), and fill royal coffers by exporting commodities such as sugar and tobacco on which duties were paid. In return, colonists received English military protection and guaranteed markets.

Beginning with a small step in 1621, when the king's council forbade tobacco growers to export their crop to anywhere but England, the Crown slowly began to regulate its colonies in order to mold them into a unified empire.

In 1660, Parliament passed a comprehensive navigation act that listed colonial products (tobacco, sugar, indigo, dyewoods, and cotton) that could be shipped only to England or other English colonies. The act took dead aim at Holland's domination of Atlantic commerce, while increasing England's revenues by imposing duties on the enumerated articles. Later navigation acts closed loopholes in the 1660 law and added other enumerated articles. This regulation bore lightly on the colonists, for the laws lacked enforcement.

After 1675, international competition and war led England to impose greater imperial control. That year marked the establishment of the Lords of Trade, a committee of the king's privy council empowered to make and enforce decisions regulating the colonies. Their chief aim was to create more uniform governments in North America and the West Indies that would do the Crown's will. Although movement toward imperial centralization often sputtered, the trend was unmistakable, especially to colonists who felt the sting of royal customs agents sent to enforce the navigation acts. England was becoming the shipper of the world, and its state-regulated policy of economic nationalism was essential to commercial greatness.

The Glorious Revolution in North America

When Charles II died in 1685, his brother, the duke of York, became King James II. This set in motion a chain of events that nearly led to civil war. In contrast to the vast majority of his subjects, James II professed the Catholic faith. Nervous about the prospect of a Catholic king, the Parliament had previously tried to exclude him from the succession (in the "Exclusion Crisis of 1679–81"). Anglican England recoiled when James issued the Declaration of Indulgence, which granted liberty of worship to all. Belief that the declaration was primarily a concession to Catholics hardened when the king began creating Catholic peerages to fill the House of Lords, appointed Catholics to high government posts, and demanded that Oxford and Cambridge open their doors to Catholic students. In 1687, the king dismissed a resistant Parliament. When his wife bore a healthy son in 1688, a Catholic succession loomed.

Convinced that James aimed at absolute power, Protestant leaders in 1688 invited a Dutch prince, William of Orange, to seize the throne with his wife, Mary, who was James's Protestant daughter. James abdicated rather than fight. It was a bloodless victory for Protestantism, for parliamentary power and the limitation of kingly prerogatives, and for the merchants and gentry of England.

The response of New Englanders to these events stemmed from their previous experience with royal authority and their fear of "papists." In 1676, New England became a prime target for efforts to reorganize the empire and crack down on smuggling, which had prevailed there for two generations. Charles II annulled the Massachusetts charter in 1684, and two years later James II appointed Sir Edmund Andros, a crusty professional soldier and former governor of New York, to rule over the newly created Dominion of New England. Soon the dominion gathered under one government all the English colonies from Maine to New Jersey. Puritans now had to swallow the bitter fact that they were subjects of London bureaucrats who cared more about shaping a disciplined empire than about New England's special religious vision.

At first, New Englanders accepted Andros, though coolly. But he soon earned their hatred by invading freedoms they cherished. He imposed taxes without legislative consent, ended trial by jury, abolished the General Court of Massachusetts (which had met annually since 1630), muzzled Boston's town meetings, and challenged land titles. He also mocked the Puritans by converting a Boston meetinghouse into an Anglican chapel, held services there on Christmas Day—a gesture that to Puritans stank of popery—and insisted on religious toleration.

When news reached Boston in April 1689 that William of Orange had landed in England, Bostonians streamed into the streets. They imprisoned Andros, a suspected papist, and overwhelmed the fort in Boston harbor, which held most of the governor's small contingent of red-coated royal troops. Andros escaped, disguised in women's clothing, but was quickly recaptured. Boston's ministers, along with merchants and former magistrates, led the rebellion, but city folk of the lower orders supplied the foot soldiers. For three years, an interim government ruled Massachusetts while the Bay colonists awaited a new charter.

Although Bostonians had dramatically rejected royal authority and the "bloody devotees of Rome," no internal revolution occurred. Social conservatives such as Samuel Willard, minister of Boston's Third Church, abhorred the popular spirit he saw unloosed in Boston in the aftermath of Andros's ouster. Tensions that existed in the society, rather than manifest themselves in the political contests over authority, flowed into predictably religious channels, as the colony became gripped with a fear of witches. In New York, the Glorious Revolution was similarly bloodless at first but far more disruptive. Royal government melted away on news of James's abdication. Displacing the governor's "popishly affected dogs and rogues," German-born militia captain Jacob Leisler established an interim government and ruled with an elected Committee of Safety for 13 months until a governor appointed by King William arrived.

Leisler's government enjoyed popularity among Dutch small landowners and urban laboring people who had resented the English seizing their colony and crowding them out of the society they had built. Most of the upper Dutch echelon, however, had adjusted to English rule and many incoming English merchants had married into Dutch families.

The Glorious Revolution ignited this smoldering social conflict. Leisler shared Dutch hostility toward New York's English elite, and his sympathy for the common people, mostly Dutch, earned him the hatred of the city's oligarchy. Leisler freed imprisoned debtors, planned a town-meeting system of government for New York City, and replaced merchants with artisans in important offices. By the autumn of 1689, Leislerian mobs were attacking the property of some of New York's wealthiest merchants.

Leisler's opponents were horrified at the power of the "rabble." They believed that ordinary people had no right to challenge authority, much less exercise political power. When a new English governor arrived in 1691, the anti-Leislerians embraced him and charged Leisler and seven of his assistants with treason for assuming the government without royal instructions.

In the ensuing trial, an all-English jury convicted Leisler and Jacob Milbourne, his son-in-law and chief lieutenant, of treason and ordered them hanged. Leisler's popularity among the artisans of the city was evident when his wealthy opponents could find no carpenter in the city who would make a ladder for the scaffold. After his execution, peace gradually returned to New York, but for years provincial and city politics reflected the deep rift between Leislerians and anti-Leislerians.

The Glorious Revolution also focused dissatisfactions in several southern colonies. Because a Catholic proprietor ruled Maryland, the Protestant majority seized power in July 1689 on word of the Glorious Revolution, using it for their own purposes. They vowed to cleanse Maryland of popery and to reform a corrupt customs service, cut taxes and fees, and extend the rights of the representative assembly. The militant Protestant John Coode, formerly a fiery Anglican minister who had been involved in a brief rebellion in 1681, assumed the reins of government and held them until the arrival of Maryland's first royal governor in 1692.

The Glorious Revolution brought lasting political changes to several colonies. The Dominion of New England collapsed. Connecticut and Rhode Island regained the right to elect their own governors, but Massachusetts (now including Plymouth) and New Hampshire became royal colonies with governors appointed by the king. In Massachusetts, a new royal charter in 1691 eliminated Church membership as a voting requirement. The Maryland proprietorship was abolished (to be restored in 1715 when the Calverts became Protestant), and Catholics were barred from office. Everywhere Protestant Englishmen celebrated their liberties.

The Social Basis of Politics

The colonial insurrections associated with the Glorious Revolution revealed social and political tensions that accompanied the transplanting of English society to the North American wilderness. Colonial societies were hardly beyond the frontier stage, still fluid, unruly, competitive, and lacking the stable political systems and acknowledged leadership class thought necessary for social order.

The emerging colonial elite tried to foster stability by upholding a stratified Old World–style society in which children were subordinate to parents, women to men, servants to masters, and the poor to the rich. Hence, leaders everywhere tried to maintain social gradations and subordination. Churchgoers did not file into services to occupy the pews randomly; seats were "doomed," or assigned according to customary yardsticks of respectability—age, parentage, social position, wealth, and occupation. These social distinctions proved difficult to maintain. Regardless of previous rank, settlers rubbed elbows so frequently and faced such raw conditions together that those without pedigrees often saw little reason to defer to men of superior rank. As one early colonist noted, paying rents "would not be borne, we must all heare be independent supreame lordes of our own land." Colonists everywhere gave respect not to those who claimed it by birth but to those who earned it by deed. A native elite gradually formed, but it was not based, as in Europe, in legally defined and hereditary social rank. Planters and merchants, accumulating large estates, aped the English gentry by cultivating the arts, building fine houses, and acquiring symbols of respectability such as libraries, coaches, and racehorses. Yet their place was rarely secure. New competitors nipped constantly at their heels.

Amid such social flux, the ideal of a fixed social structure never commanded general allegiance. Ambitious men on the rise such as Nathaniel Bacon and Jacob Leisler, and their discontented followers, rose up against the constituted authorities, which they almost certainly would not have dared to do in their homelands. When they gained power during the Glorious Revolution, in every case only briefly, the leaders of these uprisings linked themselves with a tradition of English struggle against tyranny and oligarchical power. They vowed to make government more responsive to the ordinary people, who composed most of their societies.

Witchcraft in Salem

The tragic events of the Salem witch hunts arose in the period of uncertainty following the Glorious Revolution. In Massachusetts, the deposing of Governor Andros left the colony in political limbo for three years, and this allowed what might have been a brief outbreak of witchcraft in the little community of Salem to escalate into a bitter and bloody battle. The provincial government, caught in transition, reacted only belatedly.

On a winter's day in 1692, 9-year-old Betty Parris and her 11-year-old cousin Abigail Williams began to play at fortune-telling in the kitchen of a small house in Salem, Massachusetts. They enlisted the aid of Tituba, the slave of Betty's father, Samuel Parris, the minister of the small community. Possibly fearful of the

consequences of what they had done, the girls soon became seized with fits and began making wild gestures and speeches. Soon other girls and young women in the village were behaving strangely. Village elders extracted confessions that they were being tormented by Tituba and two other women, both social outcasts.

What began as play turned into a ghastly rending of a farm community capped by the deaths of 20 villagers accused of witchcraft. In the seventeenth century, people still took literally the biblical injunction "Thou shalt not suffer a witch to live." For centuries throughout western Europe, people had believed that witches followed Satan's bidding and did evil to anyone he designated. Communities had accused and sentenced women to death for witchcraft far more often than men. In Massachusetts, more than 100 people, mostly older women, had been accused of witchcraft before 1692, and more than a dozen had been hanged.

In Salem, the initial accusations against three older women quickly multiplied. Within weeks, dozens had been charged. Formal prosecution of the accused witches could not proceed because neither the new royal charter of 1691 nor the appointed royal governor had yet arrived. For three months, while charges spread, local authorities could only jail the accused without trial. When Governor William Phips arrived from England in May 1692, he ordered a special court to try the accused. By then, events had careened out of control.

All through the summer, the court listened to testimony. By September it had condemned about two dozen villagers. The authorities hanged 19 of them on barren "Witches Hill" outside the town and crushed 80-year-old Giles Corey to death under heavy stones. The trials rolled on into 1693, but by then, colonial leaders, including many of the clergy, recognized that a feverish fear of one's neighbors, rather than witchcraft itself, had possessed the little village of Salem.

Many factors contributed to the hysteria. Among them were generational differences between older Puritan colonists and the sometimes less religiously motivated younger generation, old family animosities, population growth and pressures on the available farmland, and tensions between agricultural Salem Village and the nearby commercial center called Salem Town. Refugees from a new Native American war on the Massachusetts–Maine frontier also exacerbated tensions. Probably nobody will ever fully understand the exact mingling of causes, but the fact that most of the individuals charged with witchcraft were women underscores the relatively weak position of women in colonial society. The relentless spread of witchcraft accusations suggests the anxiety of this tumultuous era of war, economic disruption, the political tension, and the erosion of the early generation's utopian vision.

Timeline

1607	Jamestown settled
1616–1621	Native American population in New England decimated by European diseases
1617	First tobacco crop shipped from Virginia
1619	First Africans arrive in Jamestown
1620	Pilgrims land at Plymouth
1622	Powhatan tribes attack Virginia settlements
1624	Dutch colonize mouth of Hudson River
1630	Puritan immigration to Massachusetts Bay
1632	Maryland grant to Lord Baltimore (George Calvert)
1633–1634	Native Americans in New England again struck by European diseases
1635	Roger Williams banished and flees to Rhode Island
1637	New England wages war against the Pequot people
1638	Anne Hutchinson exiled to Rhode Island
1640s	New England merchants enter slave trade
	Virginia forbids blacks to carry firearms
1642	English civil war ends great migration to New England
1649	Parliament executes Charles I
1643	Confederation of New England
1650–1670	Judicial and legislative decisions in Chesapeake colonies solidify racial lines
1651	Parliament passes first navigation act
1659–1661	Puritans hang three Quaker men and one Quaker woman on Boston Common
1660	Restoration of King Charles II in England
1663	Carolina charter granted to eight proprietors
1664	English capture New Netherland and rename it New York
	Royal grant of the Jersey lands to proprietors
1673–1685	French expand into Mississippi valley
1675–1677	King Philip's War in New England
1676	Bacon's Rebellion in Virginia
1680	Popé's revolt in New Mexico
1681	William Penn receives Pennsylvania grant
1684	Massachusetts charter recalled
1688	Glorious Revolution in England, followed by accession of William and Mary
1689	Overthrow of Governor Andros in New England
	Leisler's Rebellion in New York
1690s	Transition from white indentured servitude to black slave labor begins in Chesapeake region
1692	Witchcraft hysteria in Salem

Conclusion

THE ACHIEVEMENT OF NEW SOCIETIES

Nearly 200,000 immigrants who had left their European homelands reached North America in the seventeenth century. Coming from a variety of social backgrounds and spurred by different motives, they represented the rootstock of distinctive societies that would mature in the North American colonies of England, France, Holland, and Spain. For three generations, North America served as a social laboratory for religious and social visionaries, political theorists, fortune seekers, social outcasts, and, most of all, ordinary men and women seeking a better life than they had known in Europe.

By the end of the seventeenth century, 12 English colonies on the eastern edge of North America (and several others in the West Indies) had secured footholds in the hemisphere and erected the basic scaffolding of colonial life. So had Spanish and French colonies lying north, south, and west of the English. The coastal Native American tribes were reeling from disease and a series of wars that secured the English colonists' land base along 1,000 miles of coastal plain. English settlers had overcome a scarcity of labor by copying the other European colonists in the hemisphere, who had linked the west coast of Africa to the New World through the ghastly trade in human flesh. Finally, the English colonists had engaged in insurrections against what they viewed as arbitrary and tainted governments imposed by England.

The embryo of British America carried into the eighteenth century contained peculiarly mixed features. Disease, stunted family life, and the harsh work regimen imposed by the planters who commanded the labor of the vast majority ended the dreams of most who came to the southern colonies. Yet population inched upward, and the bone and sinew of a workable economy formed. In the northern colonies, to which the fewest immigrants came, life was most secure. Organized around family and community, favored by a healthier climate, and motivated by religion and social vision, the Puritan and Quaker societies thrived.

Even as settlers attained a precarious mastery in a triracial society, they were being culturally affected by the very people to whose land and labor they laid claim. Although utopian visions of life in North America still preoccupied some, most colonists had awakened to the reality that life in the New World was a mixture of unpredictable opportunity and sudden turbulence, unprecedented freedom and debilitating wars, racial intermingling and racial separation. It was a New World in much more than a geographic sense, for the people of three cultures who now inhabited it had remade it. And, while doing so, people like Anthony and Mary Johnson (whom we met at the beginning of the chapter) were remaking themselves.

QUESTIONS FOR REVIEW AND REFLECTION

1. What factors most shaped the development of the colonial Chesapeake region in the seventeenth century?
2. Early Massachusetts was organized around shared religious goals, yet it was riven by strife. How do you explain the tensions within this colony?
3. Seventeenth-century North America included a wide variety of colonial endeavors. What were the main regional divisions and distinguishing features of each area?
4. What were the causes and consequences of King Philip's War and Bacon's Rebellion? In what ways were the two conflicts similar or different?
5. What were the effects of the Glorious Revolution on the colonies and the empire?
6. Despite differences between colonial regions, it appears that prejudicial attitudes toward Africans and Native Americans were a common thread running through all colonial societies. Do you agree, and if so do you see any exceptions to this rule?

CHAPTER 4

The Maturing of Colonial Society

Joseph Beekman Smith, *Wesley Chapel on John Street, New York City—1768* (detail), completed 1817–1844 (based on earlier sketches).

(Joseph Beekman Smith, *Wesley Chapel on John Street New York City-1768*. Old John Street United Methodist Church)

American Stories

A Struggling Farmer's Wife Finds True Religious Commitment

In 1758, 37-year-old Hannah Cook Heaton stood trial for her refusal to attend her local congregationalist church. A resident of North New Haven, Connecticut, Hannah was required by Connecticut law to attend Sunday worship services—a law derived from the belief that religious uniformity was a social good. Hannah did not object to churchgoing; in fact, she was a fervent Christian. She had been a member of Isaac Stiles's church; he had performed her marriage to Theophilus Heaton, Jr., in 1743. But later in that decade, after she had been caught up in the Great Awakening, a series of religious revivals that rocked New England in the 1740s, Hannah ceased to attend Sunday worship. Thereafter, finding that her minister's preaching and church admission policies left her dissatisfied, Heaton quit the church. Stiles, she decided, had never himself undergone conversion and was therefore a "blind guide," leading his flock astray.

Hannah's decision to leave the village church was prompted by the preaching of men she believed were imbued with the spirit. Touring evangelists George Whitefield, James Davenport, and Gilbert Tennant sparked a profound conversion experience. As she later recorded in her diary, she "thought I see Jesus with the eyes of my soul." This religious transformation led her to join a small congregation headed by Benjamin Beach, a lay preacher. Uneducated and unlicensed, he was precisely the kind of man whom Harvard- and Yale-trained ministers regarded as a threat to well-ordered New England communities. Yet many like Hannah Heaton found him spiritually gifted, and so they separated themselves from the established church to meet regularly at Beach's home for worship.

Because she abandoned the established church for this community of believers, who called themselves Separatists, Hannah was pressured by both members of Stiles's church and local officials and then finally brought to trial. She remained defiant, telling the justice at her trial that "there was a day a-coming when justice would be done . . . there is a dreadful day a-coming upon them that have no Christ." Declaring that Hannah "talked sass," the justice convicted her of breaking the law and fined her twelve shillings.

To Hannah's dismay, her husband never shared her commitment. He remained a member of Stiles's church, urged Hannah to rejoin it, and, against Hannah's wishes, paid her fine in the trial of 1758. Resenting his wife's involvement with the Separatists, he hid her spectacles so she could not read her Bible or write in her diary, threw her diary in the mud, and refused to provide her with a horse to ride to religious meetings. Hannah worried about his immortal soul, disheartened that even on his deathbed she could not persuade him to repent and seek after the Lord.

Hannah Cook Heaton was in many ways a typical colonial woman, married to a farmer and the mother of numerous children. Her life would be virtually unknown to us except that she kept a diary of her spiritual experiences, in which she revealed a life that was dramatically reshaped by the Great Awakening. Her identity as a Separatist was fundamental to her life, affecting her intimate relationships. Her separatism also brought her briefly into public prominence, as one of the few members of her movement to be prosecuted in court in Connecticut in the 1750s. Her life suggests the significance of revivalism in the lives of many eighteenth-century colonists. Her religious convictions motivated her to defy various authorities in her life, including her husband, her minister, and the local magistrate.

The religious revivals that transformed Hannah Heaton's life were just one of the forces affecting colonial life during the eighteenth century. Between 1680 and 1750, a virtual population explosion occurred in the English colonies, swelling the number of settlers from 150,000 in 1680 to more than 1 million at midcentury. Such growth was rapidly closing the population gap between England and its American colonies. A high marriage rate, large families, lower mortality than in Europe, and heavy immigration accounted for the boom.

This chapter explains how population growth and economic development gradually transformed eighteenth-century British America. Regional variations of colonial society emerged: the farming society of the North, the plantation society of the South, and the urban society of the seaboard commercial towns. Although they shared some important characteristics—growing class differences and a deepening involvement with slavery except on the frontier—each region had distinctive features. Within regions, diversity increased as incoming streams of immigrants, from Germany, Ireland, France, and especially Africa added new pieces to the shifting mosaic.

Until the late seventeenth century, the Spanish, French, and English settlements in North America were largely isolated from one another. But when a long period of war erupted in Europe among these colonizing nations, North America and the Caribbean became important theaters of international conflict—a development that would reach a climax in the second half of the eighteenth century.

This chapter also explores the commercial orientation that spread from north to south, especially in the towns and their immediate hinterlands, as local economies matured and forged sturdier links within the Atlantic basin trade network. Colonists such as Hannah Heaton experienced a deep-running religious awakening that established evangelical religion as a hallmark of American society. Connected to this democratization of religion was the changing exercise of political power. From increasingly powerful legislative assemblies and local instruments of governance emerged seasoned leaders, a tradition of local autonomy, and a widespread belief in a political ideology stressing the liberties that freeborn Englishmen should enjoy. In these ways, raw settlements developed into mature provincial societies.

The North: A Land of Family Farms

Although New England strove to maintain its homogeneity by making non–English immigrants unwelcome, the mid-Atlantic colonies swarmed with waves of immigrants from the Rhineland and Ireland. About 90,000 Germans flocked in during the eighteenth century, many fleeing "God's three arrows": famine, war, and pestilence. They settled where promoters promised cheap and fertile land, low taxes, and freedom from military duty. Coming mostly in families, they turned much of the mid-Atlantic hinterland into a German-speaking region. Place names still mark their zone of settlement: including New Berlin, New York; Hanover, Pennsylvania; Hagerstown, Maryland; and Mecklenberg, North Carolina. Even more Protestant Scots–Irish arrived. Mostly poor farmers, they streamed into the same backcountry areas where Germans were settling, especially New York and Pennsylvania, and many went farther, into the mountain valleys of the Carolinas and Georgia.

Northern Agricultural Society

In the mid-eighteenth-century northern colonies, especially New England, tight-knit farming families that were organized in communities of several thousand people dotted the landscape. New Englanders staked their future on a mixed economy. They cleared forests for timber used in barrels, ships, houses, and barns. They fished offshore waters to feed both local populations and the ballooning slave population of the West Indies. And they cultivated and grazed as much of the thin-soiled rocky hills and bottomlands as they could recover from the forest.

The farmers of the middle colonies—Pennsylvania, Delaware, New Jersey, and New York—drove their wooden plows through much richer soils than New Englanders. They enjoyed the additional advantage of settling an area cleared by Native Americans who had relied more on agriculture than New England tribes. Thus favored, mid-Atlantic farm families produced modest surpluses of corn, wheat, beef, and pork. By the mid-eighteenth century, New York and Philadelphia ships were carrying these foodstuffs not only to the West Indies, always a primary market, but also to England, Spain, Portugal, and even New England. In the North, the broad ownership of land distinguished farming society from every other agricultural region of the Western world. Although differences in circumstances and ability led gradually toward greater social stratification, in most communities, few were truly rich or abjectly poor. Except for indentured servants, most men lived to purchase or inherit a farm of at least 50 acres. With their family's labor, they earned a decent existence and provided a small inheritance for their children. Settlers valued land highly, for freehold tenure ordinarily guaranteed both economic independence and political rights.

By the eighteenth century, with widespread property ownership, a rising population pressed against a limited land supply especially in New England. Family farms could not be subdivided indefinitely, for it took at least 50 acres to support a family. In Concord, Massachusetts, for example, the founders had worked farms averaging about 250 acres. A century later, in the 1730s, the average farm had shrunk by two-thirds, as farm owners struggled to provide an inheritance for the three or four sons that the average marriage produced.

Decreasing soil fertility compounded the problem of dwindling farm size. When land had been plentiful, farmers planted crops in the same field for three years and then let it lie fallow seven years or more until it regained its strength. But on the smaller farms of the eighteenth century, farmers reduced fallowing to only a year or two, reducing crop yields and forcing farmers to plow marginal land or shift to livestock production. Jared Eliot, New England's first agricultural essayist, referred to "our old land which we have worn out."

The diminishing size and productivity of family farms drove out many New Englanders. "Many of our old towns are too full of inhabitants for husbandry, many of them living on small shares of land," bemoaned one Yankee. Out-migration from Concord, one of every four adult males, was comparatively modest. Townsfolk migrated to seek land elsewhere or else opportunities as artisans or mariners in the coastal towns. As New Englanders dispersed they continued to

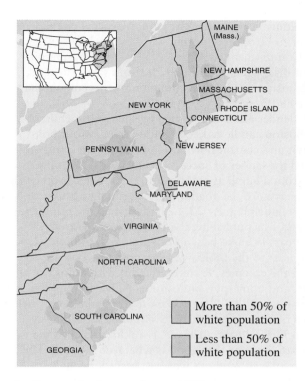

German Settlement Areas, 1775

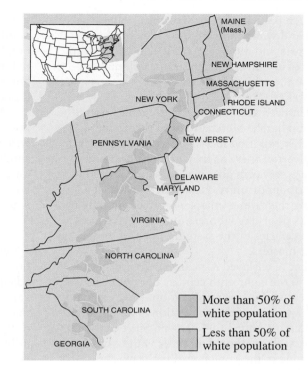

Scots–Irish Settlement Areas, 1775

Most German and Scots–Irish immigrants in the 1700s were farmers, and they quickly moved into the interior. Why did you think they did so?

alter the landscape, bringing livestock and clearing land that spread still further the ecological impact of their presence on the land.

Northern farming was less intense than in the South. The growing season was shorter, and cereal crops required incessant labor only during spring planting and autumn harvesting. This seasonal rhythm led many northern cultivators to fill out their calendars with work as clockmakers, shoemakers, carpenters, and weavers.

Unfree Labor

In the northern colonies, though the shorter growing seasons curbed the demand for labor, slaves and indentured servants made up much of the incoming human tide after 1713. The westward traffic in servants became a regular part of the commerce linking Europe and North America.

Despite official attempts to reduce the "tight packing" of indentured immigrants, shipboard conditions for both slaves and servants worsened in the eighteenth century. Crammed between decks in stifling air, they suffered from smallpox and fevers, rotten food, impure water, cold, and lice. As one Virginia observer remarked of an incoming troop of servants in 1758,

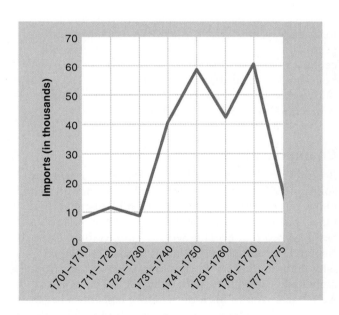

Slaves Imported to North America, 1701–1775

Overwhelmingly, Africans transported to the American colonies arrived from the 1730s to the 1770s. Rapid natural increase, as well as importation, swelled the African population to about 500,000 by the outbreak of the American Revolution.

Source: R. C. Simmons, *The American Colonies: From Settlement to Independence,* 1976.

"I never see such parcels of poor wretches, some almost naked and what had clothes was as black as chimney sweepers and almost starved." The shipboard mortality rate of about 15 percent in the colonial era made this the unhealthiest of all times to seek American shores.

Most indentured servants, especially males, found the labor system harsh. Merchants sold them, one shocked Britisher reported in 1773, "as they do their horses, and advertise them as they do their beef and oatmeal." Every servant's goal was to secure a foothold on the ladder of opportunity. However, many died before finishing their time; others won freedom only to toil for years as poor day laborers and tenant farmers. The chief beneficiaries of the system of bound white labor were the masters.

The number of enslaved Africans in the northern colonies grew in the eighteenth century but not nearly as fast as the indentured servant population. Slaves made up less than 10 percent of the population in all northern colonies and in most only 3 to 4 percent. Since in the North the typical slave labored alone or with only a few others while living in the same house as the master, slaves adapted to European ways much faster than in the South. Along with occasional Native American slaves, enslaved Africans typically worked as artisans, farmhands, or personal servants. Slavery grew fastest in the northern ports. Artisans invested profitably in slaves; ship captains purchased them for maritime labor; and an emerging urban elite of merchants, lawyers, and landlords displayed its wealth with slave coachmen and personal servants. By the beginning of the eighteenth century, more than 40 percent of New York City's households owned slaves. High labor demand outweighed reservations that slaves brought unfair competition or the threat of rebellion.

Changing Values

Boston's weather on April 29, 1695, began warm and sunny, noted the devout merchant Samuel Sewall in his diary. But by afternoon, lightning and hailstones "as big as pistol and musket bullets" pummeled the town. Sewall dined that evening with Cotton Mather, New England's prominent clergyman. Mather wondered why "more ministers' houses than others proportionately had been smitten with lightning." The words were hardly out of his mouth before hailstones began to shatter the windows. Sewall and Mather fell to their knees in prayer "after this awful Providence." They concluded that God was angry with them as leaders of a people whose piety was giving way to worldliness.

The expansive environment and the Protestant emphasis on self-discipline and hard work were breeding qualities that would become hallmarks of American culture: ambitiousness, individualism, and materialism.

One colonist remarked, "Every man expects one day or another to be upon a footing with his wealthiest neighbor." Commitment to religion, family, and community did not disappear, as Hannah Heaton's story suggests, but acquisitiveness was becoming more acceptable than it once had been.

A slender almanac, written by the twelfth child of a poor Boston candlemaker, captured the new outlook with wit and charm. Born in 1706, Benjamin Franklin climbed the ladder of success spectacularly. Running away from a harsh apprenticeship to an older brother when he was 16, he abandoned a declining Boston for a rising Philadelphia. By 23, he had learned the printer's trade and was publishing the *Pennsylvania Gazette*. Three years later, he began *Poor Richard's Almanack*, which, next to the Bible, was the most widely read book in the colonies. Franklin filled it with quips, adages, and homespun philosophy: "The sleeping fox gathers no poultry." "It costs more to maintain one vice than to raise two children." "Sloth makes all things difficult but industry all easy." Franklin preached the utilitarian doctrine that good is whatever is useful. For Franklin, the community was best served through individual self-improvement and accomplishment.

Women in the Northern Colonies

In 1662, Elnathan Chauncy, a Massachusetts schoolboy, copied into his writing book that the soul "consists of two portions, inferior and superior; the superior is masculine and eternal; the feminine inferior and mortal." Generations on both sides of the Atlantic had taught such ideas as part of a larger conception of God's design that assigned degrees of status and stations in life to all individuals. In that world, women were subordinate, taught from infancy to be modest, patient, and compliant. Regarded by men as weak of mind, they existed for and through men, subject first to their fathers and then to their husbands.

Colonial women usually accepted their narrowly circumscribed roles and few complained openly that their work was generally limited to housewifery. They silently accepted exclusion from the early public schools, laws that transferred to their husbands any property or income they brought into a marriage, and customs prohibiting them from speaking in their churches or participating in governing them (except in Quaker meetinghouses).

In her role as wife and mother, the eighteenth-century northern woman differed somewhat from her English counterpart. Whereas English women married in their midtwenties, American women typically took husbands a few years earlier, increasing their childbearing years. Hence, the average colonial family included five children (two others typically died in infancy), whereas the English family contained fewer than three.

Rebecca Jones's Sampler

Rebecca Jones, a Philadelphia teenager, spent hundreds of hours working birds, animals, and sprigs of flowers into her compartmented sampler, which also recorded the exact time of her birth. Why would young women have been expected to learn patience and artistic exactitude?

(Courtesy of the Atwater Kent Museum of Philadelphia)

Women had limited career choices and rights but broad responsibilities. The work spaces and daily routines of husband and wife overlapped and intersected far more than today. Farm women as well as men worked at planting, harvesting, and milking cows. Women also made candles and soap, butter and cheese, and smoked meat; they made cloth and sometimes marketed farm products. A merchant's wife kept shop, handled accounts when her husband voyaged abroad, and helped supervise the servants and apprentices. "Deputy husbands" and "yoke mates" were revealing terms used by New Englanders to describe eighteenth-century wives.

Despite conventional talk of inferiority, women within their families and neighborhoods nevertheless shaped the world around them. Older women modeled the behavior of young women, aided the needy, and subtly affected menfolk, who held formal authority. Women outnumbered men in church life and, like Hannah Heaton, worked within their families to promote religion, to seat and unseat ministers, and to influence morals.

Until the late eighteenth century, the "obstetrick art" was almost entirely in their hands. Midwives counseled pregnant women, delivered babies, supervised postpartum recovery, and participated in infant baptism and burial ceremonies. Mrs. Phillips, an immigrant to Boston in 1719, was a familiar figure as she hurried through the streets to attend the lying-in of about 70 women each year. In her 42-year career, she delivered more than 3,000 infants. Because colonial women were pregnant or nursing infants for about half the years between ages 20 and 40 and because childbirth was dangerous, the circle of female friends and relatives attending childbirth created strong networks of mutual assistance.

Gradually, the marriage age crept up and the number of children per family inched down.

Colonial white women were also more likely to marry than their sisters in Europe, where one in 10 never married. In the colonies, where men outnumbered women for the first century, a spinster was almost unheard of, and widows remarried with astounding speed. "A young widow with 4 or 5 children, who among the middling or inferior ranks of people in Europe would have little chance for a second husband," observed one Englishman, "is in America frequently courted as a sort of fortune." *Woman* and *wife* thus became nearly synonymous.

Another change concerned property rights. As in England, single women and widows in the colonies could make contracts, hold and convey property, represent themselves in court, and conduct business, though a woman forfeited these rights, as well as all property, when she married. In the colonies, however, legislatures and courts gave wives more control over property. They also enjoyed broader rights to act for and with their husbands in business transactions.

The Plantation South

Between 1690 and 1760, the southern white tidewater settlements changed from a frontier society with high immigration, a surplus of males, and an unstable social organization to a settled society composed mostly of native-born families. But while a mature southern culture took form from the ocean to the piedmont, after 1715 Scots–Irish and German immigrants flooded into the backcountry of Virginia, the Carolinas, and the new colony of Georgia, which was founded in 1732 as a debtors' haven and a buffer between Spanish Florida and the Carolinas. The rising slave population accounted for swifter population growth than in the North. Virginia, with a population of nearly 340,000 by 1760, remained by far the largest colony in North America.

The Carters of Virginia

Charles Carter and his wife Anne Byrd Carter are pictured here as of about 1730–1735. The Carter and Byrd families were among Virginia's wealthiest owners of land and slaves. What is the artist trying to convey in the background of the paintings?

(Top: *Portrait of Charles Carter of Cleve*, artist unidentified, ca. 1725–1730, Colonial Williamsburg Foundation; bottom: *Portrait of Mrs. Charles Carter of Cleve*, William Dering, 1735–1740, Colonial Willamsburg Foundation)

Southern Economic Change

The southern colonies developed two different coastal economies. Tobacco production in Virginia and

Maryland expanded rapidly in the seventeenth century, with exports reaching 25 million pounds annually during the 1680s. Then, two decades of war in Europe made Atlantic-basin commercial traffic more dangerous, drove up transportation costs, and dampened the demand for tobacco. Stagnation in the tobacco market lasted from the mid-1680s until about 1715.

During this period the Upper South underwent a profound social transformation. First, African slaves replaced European indentured servants so rapidly that by 1730 the unfree labor force was overwhelmingly black. Second, planters responded to the depressed tobacco market by diversifying their crops. They shifted some tobacco fields to grain, hemp, and flax; increased their herds of cattle and swine; and became more self-sufficient by developing local industries to produce iron, leather, and textiles. By the 1720s, when a profitable tobacco trade with France created a new period of prosperity, the economy was much more diverse and resilient. Third, the population structure changed rapidly. African slaves grew from about 7 percent to more than 40 percent of the region's population between 1690 and 1750, and the drastic imbalance between white men and women disappeared. Families rather than single men now predominated. The earlier frontier society of white immigrants, mostly living short, unrewarding lives as indentured servants, grew into an eighteenth-century plantation society of native-born freeholder families.

Notwithstanding the influx of Africans, slave owning was far from universal. As late as 1750, a majority of families owned no slaves at all. Perhaps one-tenth of slaveholders held more than 20 slaves. Nonetheless, the common goal was the large plantation where slaves made the earth yield up profits to support an aristocratic life for their masters.

The plantation economy of the Lower South in the eighteenth century rested on rice and indigo. Rice exports surpassed 1.5 million pounds per year by 1710 and reached 80 million pounds by the eve of the Revolution. Indigo, a smelly blue dye obtained from plants for use in textiles, became a staple crop in the 1740s after Eliza Lucas Pinckney, a wealthy South Carolina planter's wife, experimented successfully with its cultivation. Within a generation, indigo production had spread into Georgia, ranking among the leading colonial exports.

The expansion of rice production, exported to the West Indies and Europe, transformed the swampy coastal lowlands around Charleston, where planters imported thousands of slaves after 1720. By 1740, slaves composed nearly 90 percent of the region's inhabitants. White population declined as wealthy planters entrusted their estates to resident overseers. They wintered in cosmopolitan Charleston and summered in Newport, Rhode Island, their refuge from seasonal malaria along the rice coast. At midcentury, a

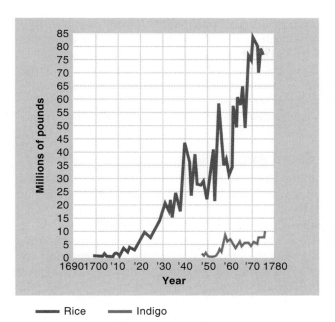

Rice and Indigo Exports from South Carolina and Georgia, 1698–1775

Just as Virginia had been built on tobacco, South Carolina and Georgia were built on rice. Much of it was sent to the West Indies to feed the huge population of enslaved Africans there.

Source: U.S. Bureau of the Census

legislative assemblies, and passed to their sons the mantle of political and social leadership. Learning how to manage and discipline slaves was as important as lessons with tutors. Bred to command, southern planters' sons developed a self-confidence and authority that propelled many of them into leadership roles during the American Revolution.

For all their airs, these southern squires were essentially agrarian businessmen. They spent their days haggling over credit, land, slaves, and tenant leases; scheduling planting and harvesting; conferring with overseers; and disciplining slaves. In the Chesapeake, tobacco cultivation (unlike that of wheat and corn) claimed the planter's year-round attention. A planter's reputation rested on the quality of his crop. To personalize their tobacco, planters stamped their hogsheads of leaf with their initials or emblem. "Question a planter on the subject," explained one observer, "and he will tell you that he cultivates such or such a kind [of tobacco], as for example, Colonel Carter's sort, John Cole's sort or [that of] some other leading crop master."

Planters' wives also shouldered many responsibilities. They superintended cloth production and the processing and preparation of food while ruling over households crowded with children, slaves, and visitors. An aristocratic veneer gave the luster of gentility to plantations from Maryland to North Carolina, but in fact these were large working farms, often so isolated from one another that the planter and his wife lived a "solitary and unsociable existence," as one phrased it.

Throughout the plantation South, the courthouse became a central male gathering place. All classes came to settle debts, dispute over land, and sue and be sued. When court was over, a multitude lingered on, drinking, gossiping, and staging horse races, cockfights, wrestling matches, footraces, and fiddling contests—all considered tests of male prowess.

The church, almost always Anglican in the South before 1750, also became a center of community gathering. A visiting northerner described the animated socializing before worship: men "giving and receiving letters of business, reading advertisements, consulting about the price of tobacco and grain, and settling either the lineage, age, or qualities of favourite horses." Then people filed into church, with lesser planters entering first and standing attentively until the wealthy gentry, "in a body," took their pews at the front. After church, socializing continued, with young people strolling together and older ones extending invitations to Sunday dinner.

shocked New England visitor described it as a society "divided into opulent and lordly planters, poor and spiritless peasants, and vile slaves." The ecological impact of these staple crop regimes was profound, as expanding colonial settlement altered the landscape.

Southern Plantation Society

Planters who acquired the best land and accumulated enough capital to invest heavily in slaves created a gentry lifestyle that set them apart from ordinary farmers. By the eighteenth century, the development of the northern colonies had produced prosperous farmers worth several thousand pounds. But such wealth paled alongside the estates of men who counted their slaves by the hundreds, their acres by the thousands, and their fortunes by the tens of thousands of pounds.

Ritual display of wealth marked southern gentry life. Racing thoroughbred horses and gambling on them recklessly, sometimes for purses of £100 (at a time when a laboring man earned £40 per year), became common sport for young gentlemen. Planters began to construct stately brick Georgian mansions, filled with imported furniture, attended by liveried black slaves, and graced by formal gardens and orchards. The emerging elite controlled the county courts, officered the local militia, ruled the parish vestries of the Anglican church, made law in their

The Backcountry

While the southern gentry matured along the tobacco and rice coasts, settlers poured into the upland backcountry. As late as 1730, only hunters and Native

American fur traders had known this vast expanse of hilly red clay and fertile limestone soils from Pennsylvania to Georgia. Over the next four decades, it attracted some 250,000 inhabitants, nearly half the southern white population.

Thousands of land-hungry German and Scots–Irish settlers spilled into the interior valleys along the eastern side of the Appalachians. They squatted on land, lived tensely with neighboring Indians in a region where boundaries were shadowy, and built a subsistence society of small farms. This "mixed medley from all countries and the off scouring of America," as one colonist described them, remained isolated from the coastal region for several generations, which helped these pioneers cling fiercely to folkways they had brought across the Atlantic.

Crude backcountry life appalled visitors from the more refined seaboard. In 1733, William Byrd described a large Virginia frontier plantation as a "poor, dirty hovel, with hardly anything in it but children that wallowed about like so many pigs." Marriage and family life were more informal in the backcountry. With vast areas unattended by ministers and with courthouses out of reach, most couples married or "took up" with each other until an itinerant clergyman on horseback appeared to bless the marriages and baptize the children. Charles Woodmason, a stiff-necked Anglican minister who tramped between settlements in the Carolina upcountry, was shocked. "Through the licentiousness of the people many hundreds live in concubinage—swopping their wives as cattle and living in a state of nature more irregularly and unchastely than the Indians."

These comments reflected the poverty of frontier life and the lack of schools, churches, and towns. Most families plunged into the backcountry with only a few crude household possessions, tools, a few chickens and swine, and the clothes on their backs. They lived in rough-hewn log cabins and planted their corn, beans, and wheat between tree stumps.

Women labored in the fields alongside their menfolk. "She is a very civil woman," noted an observer of a southern frontierswoman, "and shows nothing of ruggedness or immodesty in her carriage; yet she will carry a gun in the woods and kill deer and turkeys, shoot down wild cattle, catch and tie hogs, knock down beeves with an ax, and perform the most manful exercises as well as most men in those parts." For a generation, everyone endured a poor diet, endless work, and meager rewards.

By the 1760s, the southern backcountry had begun to emerge from the frontier stage. Small marketing towns such as Camden, South Carolina; Salisbury, North Carolina; Winchester, Virginia; and Fredericktown, Maryland, became centers of craft activity, church life, and local government. Farms began producing surpluses for shipment east. Density of settlement increased, creating a social life known for harvest festivals, log-rolling contests, horse races, wedding celebrations, dances, and prodigious drinking bouts. Class distinctions remained narrow compared with the older seaboard settlements, as many backcountry settlements acquired the look of permanence.

Enslaved Africans in the Southern Colonies

From the late seventeenth century, the slave population grew rapidly—from about 15,000 in 1690 to 80,000 in 1730 and 325,000 in 1760. By then, when they composed one-fifth of the colonial population, Africans were growing in number far more from natural increase than from importation. The generation after 1730 witnessed the largest influx of African slaves in the colonial period, averaging about 5,000 a year. In the entire period from 1700 to 1775, more than 350,000 African slaves entered the mainland North American colonies.

Most of these miserable captives were auctioned off to southern planters, but some landed in the northern cities, especially New York and Philadelphia. Merchants sold them there to artisans, farmers, and upper-class householders seeking domestic servants.

The basic struggle for Africans toiling on plantations 5,000 miles from their homes was to create strategies for living as satisfactorily as possible despite horrifying treatment. The master hoped to convert the slave into a mindless drudge who obeyed every command and worked efficiently for his profit. But attempts to cow slaves rarely succeeded completely. Masters could set the external boundaries of existence for their slaves, controlling physical location, work roles, diet, and shelter. But the authority of the master class impinged far less on how slaves established friendships, fell in love, formed kin groups, reared children, worshiped, buried their dead, and organized their leisure time.

In these aspects of daily life, slaves in the Americas drew on their African heritage to shape their existence to some degree, thus laying the foundations for an African American culture. At first, this culture had many variations because slaves came from many areas in Africa and lived under different conditions in the colonies. But common elements emerged, led by developments in the South, where about 90 percent of American slaves labored in colonial times.

Arriving in North America, Africans entered a relatively healthy environment compared with other slave-labor areas in the Western Hemisphere. In the southern colonies, where the ghastly mortality of the early decades had subsided by the time Africans were arriving in large numbers, the slave's chance for survival was much better than in the West Indies or

Brazil. This, as well as a more even gender ratio, led to a natural increase in the North American slave population unparalleled elsewhere.

Although slave codes severely restricted the lives of slaves, the possibility for family life increased as the southern colonies matured. Larger plantations employed dozens and even hundreds of slaves, with some of the men laboring in skilled crafts, and the growth of roads and market towns permitted them greater opportunities to forge relationships beyond their own plantation. By the 1740s, a growing proportion of Chesapeake slaves were American-born, had established families, and lived in plantation outbuildings where from sundown to sunup they could fashion personal lives.

In South Carolina, African slaves drew on agricultural skills practiced in Africa and made rice the keystone of the coastal economy by the early eighteenth century. Their numbers increased rapidly, from about 4,000 in 1708 to 90,000 by 1760. Working mostly on large plantations in swampy lowlands, they endured the most life-sapping conditions on the continent. But they outnumbered whites three to one by 1760 and hence could maintain more of their African culture than slaves in the Chesapeake region. Many spoke Gullah, a "pidgin" mixing several African languages. They often gave African names to their children and kept alive African religious customs.

Resistance and Rebellion

Slaves not only adapted to bondage but also resisted and rebelled in ways that constantly reminded their masters that slavery's price was eternal vigilance.

Slaveowners interpreted rebelliousness as evidence of the "barbarous, wild savage natures" of Africans, as a South Carolina law of 1712 phrased it. From the African point of view, resistance was essential to maintaining meaning and dignity in a life of degrading toil. Resisters' goals varied: to rejoin family members, to flee, to persuade masters to improve their condition, or to punish sadistic overseers.

"Saltwater" Africans, fresh from their homelands, fought slavery fiercely. "They often die before they can be conquered," said one white planter. Commonly, initial resistance took the form of fleeing—to renegade frontier settlements, to interior Native American tribes (which sometimes offered refuge), or to Spanish Florida. Rebellions, such as those in New York City in 1712 and at Stono, South Carolina, in 1739, mostly involved newly arrived slaves. There was no North American parallel, however, for the massive slave uprisings of the West Indies and Brazil.

The relatively small rebellions that did occur (or were feared) led to atrocious repression. Near Charleston in 1739, officials tortured and hanged 50 black rebels. Their decapitated heads, impaled on posts, warned other potential insurrectionists. In New York City a year later, rumors of a planned insurrection caused the hanging of 18 slaves and 4 white allies and the burning of 13 other slaves.

As slaves learned English, adjusted to work routines, and began forming families, they practiced more subtle forms of resistance. Dragging out jobs, pretending illness or ignorance, and breaking tools were ways of avoiding physical exhaustion and indirect forms of opposing slavery itself. More direct resistance included

Advertisement for a Runaway Slave

Colonial newspapers, from Boston to Charleston, were filled with ads for runaway slaves. This ad, from the *Pennsylvania Gazette* (August 26, 1762), indicates that Joe (who has renamed himself Joseph Boudron) is an accomplished linguist who speaks English, French, Spanish, and Portuguese. Read the description of the clothes worn by the runaway slave and speculate why he chose these garments.

(The Historical Society of Pennsylvania [Pennsylvania Gazette, 8/26/1762])

Philadelphia, August 24, 1762.

RUN away from the Subscriber Yesterday, a Mulattoe Man Slave, named Joe, alias Joseph Boudron, a middle-sized Man, a brisk lively Fellow, about 23 Years of Age, was born at Guadaloupe, has lived some Time in New-York, and Charles-Town, in South-Carolina, speaks good English, French, Spanish, and Portuguese: Had on when he went away, an old whitish coloured Broadcloth Coat, faced with Plush, and Metal Buttons, a Calicoe Jacket, black knit Breeches, blue Worsted Stockings, new Shoes, with large Brass Buckles, Check Shirt, an old laced Hat, and has other Things not known; he is a good Cook, and much used to the Seas, where it is thought he intends, or for New-York. Any Person that takes up said Runaway, and brings him to me, or secures him in any Goal in this Province, shall have Two Pistoles Reward, and if in any other Province, Four Pistoles, and reasonable Charges, paid by me

THOMAS BARTHOLOMEW, junior.

N. B.   All Masters of Vessels and others are desired not to carry him off, or harbour him, on any Account.

truancy, arson directed against the master's barns and houses, crop destruction, pilfering to supplement their food supply, and direct assaults on masters, overseers, and drivers. Overall, slave masters did extract labor and obedience from their slaves, but they did so only with difficulty. To push slaves too hard could be costly. One South Carolina planter drove his slaves late into the night cleaning and barreling a rice crop in 1732. When he awoke in the morning, he found his barn, with the entire harvest in it, reduced to ashes.

Black Religion and Family

The balance of power was always massively stacked against the slaves. Only the most desperate challenged the system directly. But as slaves struggled to find meaning and worth in their existence, religion and family became especially important.

Africans brought to the New World a complex religious heritage that no desolation or physical abuse could crush. Coming from cultures in which the division between sacred and secular activities was less clear than in Europe, slaves made religion central to their existence. Most slaves died strangers to Christianity until the mid-eighteenth century. Then they began to blend African religious practices with the religion of their masters, using this hybrid religion both to light the spark of resistance and to find comfort from oppression.

The religious revival that began in the 1720s in the northern colonies and spread southward thereafter made important contributions to African American religion. Evangelicalism stressed personal rebirth; it encouraged an intense emotional experience, which slaves often expressed in music and body motion. The dancing, shouting, rhythmic clapping, and singing that came to characterize slaves' religious expression represented a creative mingling of West African and Christian religions.

Besides religion, the slaves' greatest refuge from their dreadful fate lay in their families. West African social relations were centered in kinship, which included dead ancestors. Torn from their native societies, slaves placed great importance on rebuilding extended kin groups.

Most English colonies prohibited slave marriages. But in practice, slaves and masters struck a bargain. Slaves desperately wanted families, and masters found that slaves with families would work harder and be less inclined to escape or rebel.

Slaves fashioned a family life only with difficulty, however. The general practice of importing three male slaves for every two females stunted family formation. Female slaves, much in demand, married in their late teens, but males usually had to wait until their mid- to late twenties. As natural increase swelled the slave population in the eighteenth century, the gender ratio became more even.

Slave marriages could be abruptly severed by the sale of either husband or wife. This happened repeatedly, especially when a deceased planter's estate was divided among his heirs or his slaves were sold to his creditors to satisfy debts. Children usually stayed with their mothers until about age 8; then they were frequently torn from their families through sale, often to small planters needing only a hand or two. Few slaves escaped separation from family members at some time during their lives.

White male exploitation of black women represented another assault on family life. How many black women were coerced or lured with favors into sexual relations with white masters and overseers cannot be known, but the sizable mulatto (mixed-race) population at the end of the eighteenth century indicates that the number was large. Interracial liaisons, frequently forced, were widespread, especially in the Lower South. In 1732, the *South-Carolina Gazette* called racial mixing an "epidemical disease." It was a malady that had traumatic effects on slave attempts to build stable relationships.

In some interracial relationships, the coercion was subtle. In some cases, black women sought the liaison to gain advantages for themselves or their children. These unions nonetheless threatened both the slave community and the white plantation ideal. They bridged the supposedly unbridgeable gap between slave and free society and produced children who did not fit into the plantation ideal of separate racial categories.

Despite such obstacles, slaves fashioned intimate ties as husband and wife, parent and child. If monogamous relationships did not last as long as in white society, much of the explanation lies in slave life: the shorter life span of African Americans, the shattering of marriage through sale of one or both partners, and the call of freedom that impelled some slaves to run away.

Whereas slave men struggled to preserve their family role, many black women assumed a position in the family that differed from that of white women. Plantation mistresses usually worked hard in helping manage estates, but nonetheless the ideal grew that they should remain in the house guarding white virtue and setting standards for white culture. In contrast, the black woman remained indispensable to both the work of the plantation and the functioning of the slave quarters. She toiled in the fields and slave cabins alike. Paradoxically, black women's constant labor made them more equal to men than was the case of elite white women.

Above all, slavery was a set of power relationships designed to extract the maximum labor from its victims. Hence, it regularly involved cruelties that filled family life with tribulation. Still, slaves in North America toiled in less physically exhausting circumstances than slaves on sugar and coffee plantations and were better clothed, fed, and treated than Africans in the West Indies, Brazil, and other parts of the hemisphere. Therefore, they were unusually successful in establishing families. Slave family life in the American colonies brimmed with uncertainty and sorrow but was nonetheless the greatest monument to slaves' will to endure captivity and eventually gain their freedom.

Contending for a Continent

By 1750, when British colonists numbered about 1.2 million, only a small fraction of them, along with their African slaves, lived farther than 100 miles from the Atlantic Ocean. Growing rapidly, these colonies were beginning to elbow up against the French and Spanish settlements in the rich river valleys of the Ohio

and Mississippi and beyond. France posed the greatest threat to British colonists in the interior of North America, while the Spanish presented another challenge on their southern flank. On the other side of the continent, the Spanish were moving northward up the California coast until they reached the limits of Russian settlement in northern California.

France's Inland Empire

In 1661, France's Louis XIV, determined to make his country the most powerful in Europe, looked with keen interest to North America and the Caribbean. New France's timber would build the royal navy, its fish would feed the growing mass of slaves in the French West Indies, and its fur trade, if greatly expanded, would fill the royal coffers. From French Caribbean islands came precious sugar.

French North America, 1608–1763
Though thinly settled by colonists, the vast region west of the Proclamation Line claimed by France was held by a combination of forts and trading posts. How would circumstances west of the Proclamation Line have differed from those on the eastern seaboard?

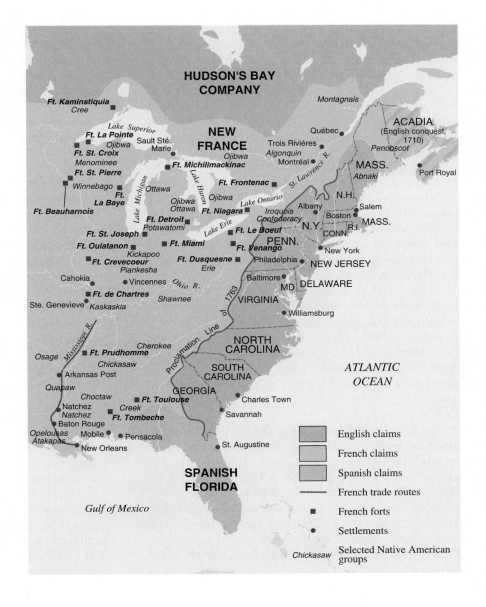

New France grew in population, economic strength, and ambition in the late seventeenth century. In 1673, Louis Joliet and Father Jacques Marquette, a Jesuit priest, explored an immense territory watered by the Mississippi and Missouri rivers. A decade later, military engineers and priests began building forts and missions in the Great Lakes region and the Mississippi valley. In 1682, René Robert de La Salle canoed down the Mississippi all the way to the Gulf of Mexico and planted a settlement in Texas at Matagorda Bay. The French solidified their claim to the North American heartland and the lower Mississippi valley when Pierre le Moyne d'Iberville established a small settlement at Biloxi in 1699 and then three years later a settlement at Mobile.

In the first half of the eighteenth century, the French developed a system of forts, trading posts, and agricultural villages throughout the heart of the continent, threatening to pin the English to the seaboard. French success in this vast region hinged partly on shrewd dealing with the Native American tribes, which retained sovereignty over the land. They did so while contending with French diseases, French arms, and French-promoted intertribal wars.

Because France's interior empire was organized primarily as a military, trading, and missionizing operation, male French settlers arrived with few French women. French men and Native American women produced mixed-race offspring—what the French called *metissage*. Such interracial marriages, called "the custom of the country," were welcomed by the natives as well as the French. Marital alliances cemented trade and military relations. French traders entered Native American kinship circles, making trade flow smoothly, while natives gained protection against their enemies and access to provisions and weapons at French trading posts.

The French presence in the continent's vast heartland, thinly dotted with small farming communities, created a shield against the expansive British. As the French population grew to about 70,000 by 1750, they demonstrated how European settlers and Native American peoples could coexist. Almost all French settlements in North America's interior were *meti (or mixed-race)* communities—a sharp contrast to the English colonies.

In 1718, French pioneers of the interior and those along the Gulf of Mexico were inundated when France settled New Orleans at great cost by transporting almost 7,000 whites and 5,000 African slaves to the mouth of the Mississippi River. Disease rapidly whittled down these numbers, and an uprising of the powerful Natchez in 1729 discouraged further French immigration. Most of the survivors settled around the little town of New Orleans and on long, narrow plantations stretching back from the Mississippi River.

While New Orleans' economy and society resembled early Charleston, South Carolina, it was run and financed by royal government and knew nothing of representative political institutions such as elections, legislative assembly, newspapers, or taxes.

French slaves were critically important to the development of Louisiana. Arriving with skills as rice growers, indigo processors, metal workers, river navigators, herbalists, and cattle keepers, Africans became the backbone of the economy. Like male slaves in the Spanish colonies, they mingled extensively with Native American women, producing mixed-race children. African women also made interracial liaisons with French immigrants, often soldiers in search of partners. By 1765 black Louisianans, outnumbering whites, served as militiamen and sometimes received freedom for military service. French law also gave slaves some protection in courts. All in all, the chance of gaining freedom in fluid French Louisiana exceeded that of any other colony in North America's Southeast, and the absorption of free blacks into white society, particularly if they were of mixed-race descent, struck a marked contrast with English practice. When the Spanish took over the colony in 1769, they guaranteed slaves the right to buy freedom with money earned in their free time. Soon a free black class emerged. When Americans acquired the colony in 1803, they suppressed freedom purchase and discouraged manumission.

A Generation of War

The growth of French strength and ambitions brought British America and New France into deadly conflict beginning in the late seventeenth century. Protestant New Englanders regarded Catholic New France as a threat to their divinely sanctioned mission. When the European wars began in 1689, precipitated by Louis XIV's territorial aggression in western and central Europe, conflict between England and France quickly extended into every overseas theater where the two powers had colonies. In North America, the battle zone included New York, New England, and eastern Canada.

In two wars, from 1689 to 1697 and 1701 to 1713, the English and French, while fighting in Europe, also sought to oust each other from the Americas. The zone of greatest importance was the Caribbean, where slaves produced huge sugar fortunes. But both home governments valued the North American settlements greatly as a source of the timber and fish that sustained the sugar-producing West Indian colonies.

The English struck three times at the centers of French power—at Port Royal, which commanded the access to the St. Lawrence River, and at Quebec, the capital of New France. In 1690, during King William's War (1689–1697), their small flotilla captured Port Royal, the hub of Acadia (which was returned to

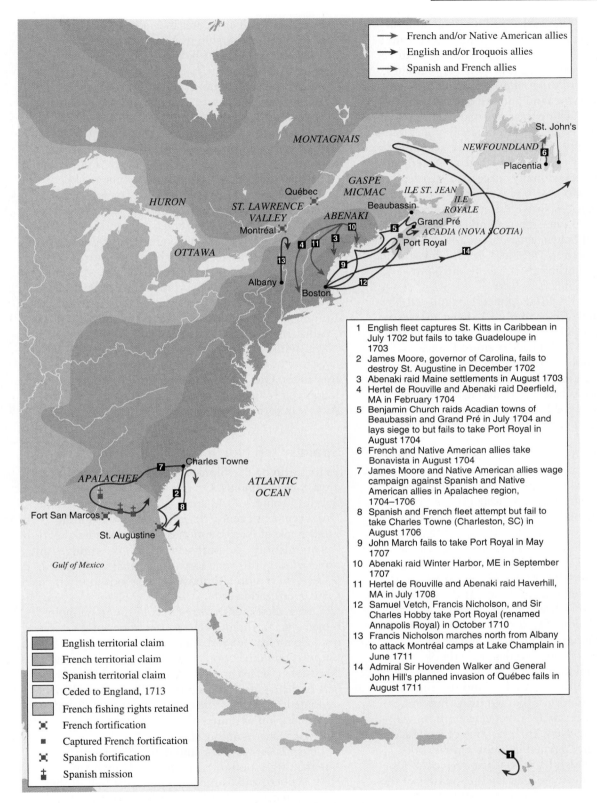

Legend (arrows):
→ French and/or Native American allies
→ English and/or Iroquois allies
→ Spanish and French allies

1 English fleet captures St. Kitts in Caribbean in July 1702 but fails to take Guadeloupe in 1703
2 James Moore, governor of Carolina, fails to destroy St. Augustine in December 1702
3 Abenaki raid Maine settlements in August 1703
4 Hertel de Rouville and Abenaki raid Deerfield, MA in February 1704
5 Benjamin Church raids Acadian towns of Beaubassin and Grand Pré in July 1704 and lays siege to but fails to take Port Royal in August 1704
6 French and Native American allies take Bonavista in August 1704
7 James Moore and Native American allies wage campaign against Spanish and Native American allies in Apalachee region, 1704–1706
8 Spanish and French fleet attempt but fail to take Charles Towne (Charleston, SC) in August 1706
9 John March fails to take Port Royal in May 1707
10 Abenaki raid Winter Harbor, ME in September 1707
11 Hertel de Rouville and Abenaki raid Haverhill, MA in July 1708
12 Samuel Vetch, Francis Nicholson, and Sir Charles Hobby take Port Royal (renamed Annapolis Royal) in October 1710
13 Francis Nicholson marches north from Albany to attack Montréal camps at Lake Champlain in June 1711
14 Admiral Sir Hovenden Walker and General John Hill's planned invasion of Québec fails in August 1711

Legend (territorial):
◼ English territorial claim
◼ French territorial claim
◼ Spanish territorial claim
◻ Ceded to England, 1713
◻ French fishing rights retained
⛫ French fortification
◼ Captured French fortification
⛫ Spanish fortification
⛪ Spanish mission

Queen Anne's War: Major Battles and Territorial Changes

Like every other Anglo-French conflict in the seventeenth and eighteenth centuries, Queen Anne's War was fought in the Caribbean as well as in North America. The sugar- and coffee-rich islands of the West Indies, teeming with enslaved Africans, made them prizes in the competition for empire.

France at the end of the war). The English assault on Quebec, however, failed disastrously. In Queen Anne's War (1701–1713), England attacked Port Royal three times before finally capturing it in 1710. A year later, when England sent a flotilla of 60 ships and 5,000 men to conquer Canada, the land and sea operations foundered before reaching their destinations.

With European-style warfare miserably unsuccessful in America, both England and France attempted to subcontract military tasks to their Native American allies. This policy occasionally succeeded, especially with the French, who gladly sent their own troops into the fray alongside Native American partners. The French and their Native American allies wiped out the frontier outpost of Schenectady, New York, in 1690; razed Wells, Maine, and Deerfield, Massachusetts, in 1703; and battered other towns along the New England frontier.

Retaliating, the English-supplied Iroquois left New France "bewildered and benumbed" after a massacre near Montreal in 1689. Assessing their own interests and too powerful to be bullied by either France or England, the Iroquois sat out the second war in the early eighteenth century. Convinced that neutrality served their purposes better than acting as mercenaries for the English, they held to the principle that "we are a free people uniting ourselves to whatever sachem [chief] we wish."

Though England had rebuffed France after a generation of war, New England suffered grievous economic and human losses. Massachusetts bore the heaviest burden. Probably one-fifth of all able-bodied males in the colony participated in the Canadian campaigns, and of these, about one-quarter never lived to tell of the terrors of New England's first major experience with international warfare. The war debt was £50,000 sterling in Massachusetts alone, a greater per capita burden than the national debt today. At the end of the second conflict, in 1713, war widows were so numerous that the Bay Colony faced its first serious poverty problem. In addition, wartime taxes and price inflation had eaten deeply into the pocketbooks of most working families.

The colonies south of New England remained on the sidelines during most of the two wars. But war at sea between European rivals affected even those who sat out the land war. New York lost one of its best grain markets when Spain, allied with France, outlawed American foodstuffs in its Caribbean colonies. The French navy plucked off nearly one-quarter of the port's fleet and disrupted Philadelphia grain merchants' access to the Caribbean.

The burdens and rewards fell unevenly on the participants, as usually happens in wartime. Some low-born men could rise spectacularly. William Phips, the twenty-sixth child in his family, had been a poor sheep farmer and ship's carpenter in Maine who eventually rose to the governorship of Massachusetts in 1691.

Other men, already rich, got richer. Andrew Belcher of Boston, who had grown wealthy on provisioning contracts, became a local titan, riding in London-built coaches, erecting a handsome mansion, and purchasing slaves.

Most men, especially those who did the fighting, gained little, and many lost everything. The least securely placed New Englanders—indentured servants, apprentices, recently arrived immigrants, unskilled laborers, fishermen, and ordinary farmers—supplied most of the voluntary or involuntary recruits, and they died in numbers that seem staggering today. In 1713, the Peace of Utrecht, which ended Queen Anne's War, capped the century-long rise of Britain—as the combined kingdoms of England and Scotland were known after 1707; it also heralded the decline of Spain in the rivalry for the sources of wealth outside Europe. Britain, the big winner, received Newfoundland, Acadia (renamed Nova Scotia), and St. Kitts and Nevis, while France recognized English sovereignty over the fur-rich Hudson Bay territory. Spain lost territory in the Old World and awarded the English the lucrative privilege of supplying its empire in the Americas with African slaves.

Spain's Frail North American Grip

Spain's grip on its colonies in North America had always been tenuous. On the East Coast, the growth of South Carolina's slave-based plantation society in the late seventeenth century stemmed partly from the English use of Native American allies to attack Spanish Indian missions and outposts and sell the captives into slavery. From this time forward, English and French traders, with more attractive trade goods to offer, held sway over Florida Indians.

After the Peace of Utrecht in 1713, Spain maintained a fragile hold on the southern tier of the continent. Spain learned how easily its thinly peopled outposts could be crippled or destroyed by chafing Native Americans and invading English. In the first half of the eighteenth century, the Spanish settlements stagnated, suffering from Spain's colonial policy that regarded them as marginal, money-losing affairs, useful only as defensive outposts.

Hispanics, mestizos, and detribalized Native Americans began to increase modestly in Texas, New Mexico, and California in the first half of the eighteenth century, but by 1745 in Florida they had only one-tenth the population of the English in South Carolina. Spanish male colonizers greatly outnumbered Spanish women, which resulted in a degree of racial intermixture similar to that in New France. Most of the immigrants became small ranchers, producing

A Chart of Mixed-Race Families

The mixing of races in Spain's New World colonies is vividly displayed in paintings of interracial families, widely produced in Mexico in the eighteenth century. In each painting shown here, the mother and father of different racial ancestries produces a child with a different racial term. In panel 5, for example, the mulatto mother and Spanish father produce a "Morisco" child. Why were paintings such as these, which spread the view that interracial mixing was the natural path of human affairs, not produced in the British colonies?

(Anonymous, *Human Races (Las Castas),* 18th century, Schalkwijk/Art Resource, NY)

estufas are always closed to us." However, California tribes had difficulty in maintaining cultural cohesion. In the 1770s, the Spanish rapidly completed their western land and sea routes from San Diego to Yerba Buena (San Francisco) to block Russian settlement south of their base in northern California. California's Spanish pioneers were Franciscan missionaries, accompanied by royal soldiers. The priests would choose a good location and then attract a few Native Americans to be baptized and resettled around the missions, which they helped build. Visiting relatives would then be induced to stay. These Native Americans lived under an increasingly harsh regimen until they were reduced to a condition of virtual slavery. The California mission, with its extensive and profitable herds and grain crops, theoretically belonged to the Native American converts, but they did not enjoy the profits. Ironically, the spiritual motives of the priests brought the same degradation as elsewhere.

Cultural and Ecological Changes Among Interior Tribes

During the first half of the eighteenth century, the inland tribes proved their capacity to adapt to the contending European colonizers in their region while maintaining political independence. Yet extensive contact with the French, Spanish, and English slowly brought ominous changes to Native American societies. European trade goods, especially iron implements, textiles, firearms and ammunition, and alcohol, altered Native American ways of life. Subsistence hunting turned into commercial hunting, restricted only by the quantity of trade goods desired. Native American males, gradually wiping out deer and beaver east of the Mississippi River, spent more time away from the villages trapping and hunting. Women were also drawn into the new economy, skinning animals and fashioning pelts into robes. Among some tribes, these commercial activities became so time-consuming that they had to procure food from other tribes.

The fur trade greatly altered Native American life. Spiritual beliefs that the destinies of humans and animals were closely linked eroded when trappers and hunters declared all-out war on the beaver and other fur-bearing animals in order to exchange pelts for attractive trade goods. Competition for furs sharpened intertribal tensions, often to the point of war. The introduction of European weaponry, which Native Americans quickly mastered, intensified these conflicts.

Political organization in the interior changed too. Earlier, most tribes had been loose confederations of villages and clans with the Creek, Cherokee, and Iroquois

livestock, corn, and wheat for export to southward Spanish provinces. New Mexico's Hispanic population of about 10,000 at midcentury held a vast region only because no European challenger appeared.

Native Americans had mixed success in resisting Spanish domination. In New Mexico, an early nineteenth-century Spanish investigator saw the key to Pueblo cultural autonomy as the underground kivas, which were "like impenetrable temples, where they gather to discuss mysteriously their misfortunes or good fortunes, their happiness or grief. The doors of these

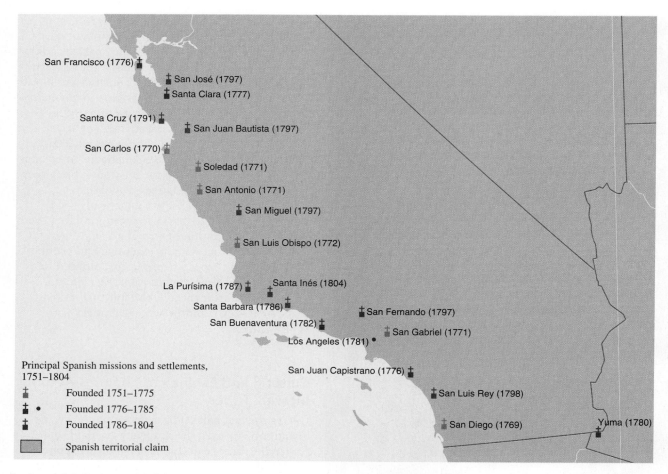

San Francisco (1776)

San José (1797)

Santa Clara (1777)

Santa Cruz (1791)

San Juan Bautista (1797)

San Carlos (1770)

Soledad (1771)

San Antonio (1771)

San Miguel (1797)

San Luis Obispo (1772)

La Purísima (1787)   Santa Inés (1804)

Santa Barbara (1786)   San Fernando (1797)

San Buenaventura (1782)   San Gabriel (1771)

Los Angeles (1781)

San Juan Capistrano (1776)

San Luis Rey (1798)

San Diego (1769)   Yuma (1780)

Principal Spanish missions and settlements, 1751–1804

Founded 1751–1775

Founded 1776–1785

Founded 1786–1804

Spanish territorial claim

Spanish Missions in California

As colonists in the British colonies on the eastern seaboard careened toward revolution, Spanish Franciscan priests were building a string of missions on the other side of the continent, hoping to convert Native Americans to Catholicism while capturing their labor. Why do you think the missions were spaced so evenly across the landscape?

peoples giving primary loyalty to the village. But trade, diplomatic contact, and war with Europeans required coordinated policies, so villagers gradually adopted more centralized leadership. For example, the basic unit of Cherokee political authority was the nearly autonomous village. But tension with Creek neighbors and intermittent hostilities with the English pressed home the need for coordinated decision making. By 1750, the Cherokee had formed an umbrella political organization that gathered together the fragmented authority of the villages and formed a more centralized confederacy. When this proved inadequate, warriors began to assume the dominant role in tribal councils, replacing the civil chiefs.

While incorporating trade goods into their material culture and adapting their economies and political structures to new situations, the interior tribes held fast to many traditions. They saw little reason to replace what they valued in their own culture. What they saw of the colonists' law and justice, religion, education, family organization, and child rearing usually convinced Native Americans that their own ways were superior. The

Native Americans' refusal to accept the superiority of white culture frustrated English missionaries, eager to win Native Americans from "savage" ways.

Overall, interior tribes suffered from contact with the British colonizers. Decade by decade, the fur trade spread epidemic diseases, intensified warfare, depleted game animals, and drew Native Americans into a market economy in which their trading partners gradually became trading masters.

The Urban World of Commerce and Ideas

Only about 5 percent of the eighteenth-century colonists lived in towns as large as 2,500, and no city boasted a population above 16,000 in 1750 or 30,000 in 1775. Yet urban societies were at the leading edge of the transition to "modern" life. There, a barter economy first gave way to a commercial economy, a social

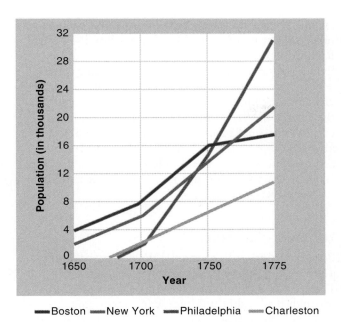

Urban Population Growth, 1650–1775
By 1755, Boston had lost its lead as British North America's largest city. Plagued by costly wars and economic difficulties, its population leveled off, whereas that of other cities grew.

Source: Gary B. Nash, *The Urban Crucible,* 1979

order based on assigned status turned into one based on achievement, rank-conscious and deferential politics changed to participatory and contentious politics, and small-scale artisanship was gradually replaced by factory production. Into the cities flowed European ideas, which radiated outward to the hinterland.

Sinews of Trade

In the half century after 1690, Boston, New York, Philadelphia, and Charleston blossomed into thriving commercial centers. Their growth accompanied the development of the agricultural interior, to which the seaports were closely linked. As the colonial population rose and spread out, minor seaports such as Salem, Newport, Providence, Annapolis, Norfolk, and Savannah gathered 5,000 or more inhabitants.

Cities were trade centers. Through them flowed colonial export staples (tobacco, rice, furs, wheat, timber products, and fish) and the imported goods that colonists needed: goods from England (glass, paper, iron implements, and cloth); wine, spices, coffee, tea, and sugar from other parts of the world; and the human cargo to fill the labor gap. The pivotal seaport figure was the merchant, often engaging in both retail and wholesale trade, usually the moneylender (for no banks yet existed), and frequently the shipbuilder, insurance agent, land developer, and coordinator of artisan production.

By the eighteenth century, the American economy was integrated into an Atlantic trading system that connected settlers to Great Britain, western Europe, Africa, the West Indies, and Newfoundland. Great Britain, like other major trading nations of western Europe, pursued mercantilist trade policies. Mercantilism's core idea was that a country must gain wealth by increasing exports, taxing imports, regulating production and trade, and exploiting colonies. These policies governed British treatment of their North American and Caribbean colonies.

The colonists could never produce enough exportable raw materials to pay for the imported goods they craved, so they had to earn credits in England by supplying the West Indies and other areas with foodstuffs and timber products. They also accumulated credit by providing shipping and distribution services. Sailing from Boston, Salem, Newport, and Providence, New Englanders became the most ambitious participants in the carrying trade.

The Artisan's World

Although merchants stood first in wealth and prestige in the colonial towns, artisans were far more numerous. About two-thirds of urban adult males (slaves excluded) labored at handicrafts. By the mid-eighteenth century, the colonial cities contained scores of specialized "leather apron men" besides the proverbial butcher, baker, and candlestick maker. Handicraft specialization increased as the cities matured, but every artisan worked with hand tools, usually in small shops.

Work patterns for artisans were irregular, dictated by weather, length of daylight, erratic delivery of raw materials, and shifting consumer demand. When ice blocked northern harbors, not only did mariners and dockworkers endure slack time but trade halted. If prolonged rain delayed the slaughter of cows in the country or made impassable the rutted roads into the city, the tanner and the shoemaker laid their tools aside. The hatter depended on the supply of beaver skins, which could stop abruptly if disease struck a Native American tribe or war disrupted the fur trade. Every urban artisan knew "broken days," slack spells, and dull seasons. Ordinary laborers dreaded winter, for it was a season when cities had "little occasion for the labor of the poor," and firewood could cost several months' wages.

Urban artisans took fierce pride in their crafts. While deferring to those above them, they saw themselves as the backbone of the community, contributing essential products and services. "Our professions rendered us useful and necessary members of our community," the Philadelphia shoemakers asserted. "Proud of that rank, we aspired to no higher." This self-esteem

Nathaniel Hurd, Boston Engraver

Not many Boston artisans became prosperous enough to have their portrait painted. But a few did, including Paul Revere and Nathaniel Hurd, the engraver shown here. Hurd came from a long line of artisans: his great-grandfather was a tailor, his grandfather a joiner, and his father a silversmith. With Hurd painted here in the open collar and rolled-up sleeves of his working outfit, how do you think this unfinished portrait relates to a more elegant portrait that showed Hurd in an embroidered silk blouse?

(John Singleton Copley, *Unfinished painting of engraver Nathaniel Hurd.* Memorial Art Gallery of the University of Rochester, Marion Stratton Gould Fund)

and desire for community recognition sometimes jostled with the upper-class view of artisans as "mere mechanicks," part of the "vulgar herd."

Striving for respectability, artisans placed a premium on achieving economic independence. Every artisan began as an apprentice, spending five or more teenage years in a master's shop, then, after fulfilling his contract, becoming a "journeyman," selling his labor to a master and frequently living in his house where he ate at his table and sometimes married his daughter. He hoped to complete within a few years the three-step climb from servitude to self-employment. After setting up his own shop, he could control his work hours and acquire the respect that came from economic independence. But in trades requiring greater organization and capital, such as distilling and ship-building, the rise from journeyman to master often proved impossible.

In good times, urban artisans did well. They expected to earn a "decent competency" and eventually to purchase a small house. But success was far from automatic, even for those following Poor Richard's advice about hard work and frugal living. An advantageous marriage, luck in avoiding illness, and an ample inheritance were often critical. In Philadelphia, about half the artisans in the first half of the eighteenth century died leaving enough personal property to have ensured a comfortable standard of living. Another quarter left more, often including slaves and indentured servants. New England's artisans did not fare so well because their economy was weaker.

Urban Social Structure

Population growth, economic development, and war altered the urban social structure between 1690 and 1765. Stately townhouses displayed fortunes built through trade, shipbuilding, war contracting, and—probably most profitable of all—urban land development. "It is almost a proverb," a Philadelphian observed in the 1760s, "that every great fortune made here within these 50 years has been by land." A merchant's estate of £2,000 sterling was impressive in the early eighteenth century. Two generations later, the wealthiest accumulated estates of £10,000 to £20,000 sterling.

The rise of Thomas Hancock, on whose fortune his less commercially astute nephew, John Hancock, would later construct a shining political career, shows how war could catapult an enterprising trader to affluence. An opportune marriage to the daughter of a prosperous merchant provided bookseller Hancock with a toehold in commerce and enough capital to invest in several vessels. By 1735, he had made enough money, much of it from smuggling tea, to build a mansion on Beacon Hill. When war broke out with Spain in 1739, Hancock obtained lucrative supply contracts for military expeditions to the Caribbean and Nova Scotia. He also invested heavily in privateers, who engaged in private warfare against enemy shipping and auctioned the enemy vessels they overpowered. When peace returned in 1748, Hancock was riding through Boston in a London-built four-horse chariot emblazoned with a heraldic shield.

Alongside urban wealth grew urban poverty. From the beginning, every city had its disabled, orphaned, and widowed who required aid. But after 1720, poverty marred the lives of many more city dwellers, including war widows with no means of support, rural migrants, and recent immigrants. Boston was hit especially hard. Its economy stagnated in the 1740s, and taxpayers groaned under the burden of paying for heavy war expenditures. Cities devised new ways of helping the needy, such as building large almshouses where the poor could be housed and fed

WEALTH DISTRIBUTION IN COLONIAL AMERICA

Percentage of wealth held by the richest 10% and the poorest 30% of the population in two cities and one rural area.

Year	Richest 10%	Poorest 30%
Boston		
1684–1699	41.2	3.3
1700–1715	54.5	2.8
1716–1725	61.7	2.0
1726–1735	65.6	1.9
1736–1745	58.6	1.8
1746–1755	55.2	1.8
1756–1765	67.5	1.4
1766–1775	61.1	2.0
Philadelphia		
1684–1699	36.4	4.5
1700–1715	41.3	4.9
1716–1725	46.8	3.9
1726–1735	53.6	3.7
1736–1745	51.3	2.6
1746–1755	70.1	1.5
1756–1765	60.3	1.1
1766–1775	69.9	1.0
Chester County, Pennsylvania		
1693	23.8	17.4
1715	25.9	13.1
1730	28.6	9.8
1748	28.7	13.1
1760	29.9	6.3
1782	33.6	4.7

Source: Gary B. Nash, *The Urban Crucible,* 1979.

more economically. But many of the indigent preferred "to starve in their homes" rather than endure the discipline and indignities of the poorhouse. Boston's poor women also resisted laboring in the linen factory that was built in 1750 to enable them to contribute to their own support through spinning and weaving. Despite the warnings of Boston's ministers that "if any would not work, neither should they eat," they refused to leave their children at home to labor in America's first textile factory.

Urban eighteenth-century tax lists reveal the increasing gap between the wealthy and the poor. The top 5 percent of taxpayers increased their share of the cities' taxable assets from about 30 to 50 percent between 1690 and 1770. The bottom half of the taxable inhabitants saw their share of the wealth shrink from about 10 to 4 percent. Except in Boston, the urban middle classes continued to gain ground. Still, the growth of princely fortunes amid increasing poverty made some urban dwellers reflect that Old World ills were reappearing in the New.

The Entrepreneurial Ethos

As the cities grew, new values took hold. In the traditional view of society, economic life was supposed to operate according to what was fair, not what was profitable. Regulated prices and wages, quality controls, supervised public markets, and other such measures seemed appropriate. Community was defined as a single body of interrelated parts, where individual rights and responsibilities formed a seamless web.

In their commercialized cities, most urban dwellers grew to regard the subordinating of private interests to the commonweal as unrealistic. Prosperity required the encouragement of acquisitive appetites rather than self-denial, for ambition would spur economic activity as more people sought more goods. The new view held that if people were allowed to pursue their material desires competitively, they would collectively form a natural, impersonal market of producers and consumers that would advantage everyone.

Hence, as the colonial port towns became imbedded in the Atlantic world of commerce, merchants began to make decisions according to the emerging commercial ethic that rejected traditional restraints on entrepreneurial activity. If wheat fetched eight shillings a bushel in the West Indies but only five in Boston, a grain merchant felt justified in sending all he could purchase from local farmers to the more distant buyer. Indifferent to individuals and local communities, the new transatlantic market responded only on supply and demand.

Tension between the new economic freedom and the older concern for the public good erupted only with food shortages or galloping inflation. Because the American colonies experienced none of the famines that ravaged Europe in this period, such crises were rare, usually occurring during war, when demand for provisions rose sharply. Such a moment struck in Boston during Queen Anne's War. Merchant Andrew Belcher contracted to ship wheat to the Caribbean, where higher prices would yield greater profit than in Boston. Ordinary neighbors, threatened with a bread shortage and angered that a townsman would put profit ahead of community needs, attacked one of Belcher's grain-laden ships and tried to seize the grain. The grand jury, composed of substantial members of the community, hinted its

Recovering the Past

HOUSEHOLD INVENTORIES

Historians use probate records to examine social changes in American society. They include wills, the legal disposition of estates, and household inventories taken by court-appointed appraisers that detail the personal possessions left at death. Inventories have been especially valuable in tracing the transformation of colonial communities.

Like tax lists, inventories can be used to show changes in a community's distribution of wealth. But they are far more detailed than tax lists, providing a snapshot of how people lived at the end of their life. Inventories list and value almost everything a person owned—household possessions, equipment, books, clothes and jewelry, cash on hand, livestock and horses, crops and stored provisions. Hence, through inventories, we can measure the quality of life at different social levels. We can also witness how people made choices about investing their savings—in capital goods of their trade such as land, ships, and equipment; in personal goods such as household furnishings and luxury items; or in real property such as land and houses.

Studied systematically (and corrected for biases, which infect this source as well as others), inventories show that by the early 1700s, ordinary householders were improving their standard of living. Finished furniture such as cupboards, beds, tables, and chairs turn up more frequently in inventories. Pewter dinnerware replaces wooden bowls and spoons, bed linen makes an appearance, and books and pictures are sometimes noted.

Among an emerging elite before the Revolution, much more fashionable articles of consumption appear. The partial inventory of Robert Oliver, a wealthy merchant and officeholder living in a Boston suburb, is reproduced here. You can get some idea of the dignified impression Oliver wished to make by looking at his furniture and dishes and by noticing that he owned a mahogany tea table, damask linen, and a bed with curtains. The inventory further suggests the spaciousness of Oliver's house and shows how he furnished each room.

It is helpful when studying inventories to categorize the goods in the following way: those that are needed to survive (basic cooking utensils, for example); those that make life easier or more comfortable (enough plates and beds for each member of the family, for example); and those that make life luxurious (slaves, silver plates, paintings, mahogany furniture, damask curtains, spices, wine, and so forth). Oliver had many luxury goods as well as items that contributed to his use of leisure time and his personal enjoyment. Which items in his inventory do you think were needed only to survive comfortably? Which were luxuries? What other conclusions can you draw about the lifestyle of rich colonial merchants like Oliver?

Beyond revealing a growing social differentiation in colonial society, the inventories help the historian understand the reaction during the Great Awakening to what many ordinary colonists regarded as sinful pride and arrogance displayed by the elite. By the 1760s, this distrust of affluence among simple folk had led to outright hostility toward men who surrounded themselves with the trappings of aristocratic life. Even the ambitious young John Adams, a striving lawyer, was shocked at what he saw at the house of a wealthy merchant in Boston. "Went over the House to view the furniture, which alone cost a thousand Pound sterling," he exclaimed. "A seat it is for a noble Man, a Prince. The Turkey Carpets, the painted Hangings, the Marble Tables, the rich Beds with crimson Damask Curtains . . . are the most magnificent of any Thing I have ever seen."

Such a description takes on its full meaning only when contrasted with what inventories tell us about life at the bottom of society. The hundreds of inventories for Bostonians dying in the decade before the American Revolution show that fully half of them died with less than £40 personal wealth and one-quarter with £20 or less. The inventories and wills of Jonathan and Daniel Chandler of Andover, Massachusetts, show the material circumstances of less favored Americans who suffered from the economic distress afflicting New England since the 1730s. Note that Daniel Chandler was a shoemaker.

Reflecting on the Past How do the possessions of these brothers compare with Oliver's partial inventory? An examination of these contrasting inventories helps explain the class tension that figured in the revolutionary experience. ■

HOUSEHOLD INVENTORY OF ROBERT OLIVER, WEALTHY MERCHANT

Dorchester Jan.ry 11.th 1763.

Inventory of what Estates Real & Personall, belonging to Coll.o Robert Oliver [Esquire] late of Dorchester Deceased, that has been Exhibited to us the Subscribers, for Apprizement. Viz.t

In the Setting Parlour Viz.tt			11 small Pictures	—.4.—
a looking Glass	£4.—.—		4 Maps	—.10.—
a Small Ditto	0.6.0		1 Prospect Glass	—.10.—
12 Metzitens pictures Glaz'd	@6/	3.12.—	2 Escutchons Glaz'd	—.4.—
8 Cartoons D.o Ditto		4.—.—	1 pair small hand Irons	—.6.—

1 Shovel & Tongs	—.8.—	
1 Tobacco Tongs	—.1.—	
1 pair Bellowes	—.2.—	
1 Tea Chest	—.2.—	
2 Small Waters	—.1.—	
1 Mehogony Tea Table	1.—.—	
8 China Cups & Saucers	—.2.—	
1 Earthen Cream Pott	—.—.1	
1 Ditto. Sugar Dish	—.—.4	
1 Black Walnut Table	1.—.—	
1 Black Ditto Smaller	0.6.—	
1 Round painted Table	0.1.—	
7 Leather Bottom Chairs @ 6/	2.2.—	
1 Arm.d Chair Common	1.3.—	
1 Black Walnut Desk	1.12.—	
1 pair Candlesticks snuffers & Stand Base Mettle	—.4.—	
6 Wine Glasses 1 Water Glass	—.1.—	
a parcell of Books	1.—.—	
a Case with Small Bottles	0.4.—	
	22.1.5	

In the Entry & Stair Case Viz.t

17 pictures	£0.10.—	
	0.10.0	

In the Kitchen Chamber Viz.t

a Bedstead & Curtains Compleat	£4.—.—	
a Bed Bolster & 2 pillows	5.—.—	
a Under Bed & 1 Chair	0.1.—	
2 Rugs & 1 Blankett @ 6/	0.18.—	
	09.19.0	

In the Dining Room Viz.t

1 pair of andirons	£0.3.—	
7 Bass Bottoms Chairs	0.7.—	
1 Large Wooden Table	0.3.—	
1 Small Ditto Oak	0.1.—	
1 Small looking Glass	0.6.—	
1 Old Desk	0.6.—	
1 Case with 2 Bottles	0.2.—	
1 Warming pan	0.12.—	
	2. 0. 0	

In the Marble Chamber Viz.t

1 Bedstead & Curtains Compleat		£8.—.—
1 feather Bed, Bolster & 2 pillows		8.—.—
1 Chest of Drawers		2.8.—
1 Buroe Table		1.—.—
6 Chairs Leather'd Bottoms	@ 6/	1.16.—
1 Small dressing Glass		—.6.—
1 Small Carpett		1.—.—
1 White Cotton Counterpin		—.18.—
1 pair Blanketts		1.12.—
1 pair holland Sheets		1.4.—
3 pair Dowlases D.o New	@ 12S/p.r	1.16.—
3 pair & 1 Ditto Coarser	@ 4/	0.14.—
3 pair Cotton & Linnen D.o	@ 3/	0.9.—
4 pair Servants Ditto	@ 2/	0.8.—
4 Coarse Table Cloths	@ 1/	0.4.—
10 Ditto Kitchen Towels	@ 1/	0.1.—
5 Diaper Table Cloths	@ 12/	3.—.—
6 Damask Table Cloths	@ 18/	5.8.—
4 N: England Diaper D.o	@ 3	0.12.—
4 pair Linnen pillow Cases	@ 2/	0.8.—
5 Coarser Ditto	@ 1/	0.5.—
6 Diaper Towels	@ 6^{d}	0.3.—
7 Damask Ditto	@ 2/	0.14.—
2 doz.n & 9 Damask Napkins	@ 24/doz.n	3.6.—
1 Gauze Tea Table Cover		0.1.—
		£43.13.0

Household Inventory of Jonathan Chandler (d. 1745)

Cash	£18p
Gun	1p
Psalmbook	8p
	£19p
Debts	£5p
Total	£14p

Household Inventory of Daniel Chandler (d. 1752), Shoemaker

Bible	
Shoe knife	
Hammer Total	£12
Last (shoe shaper)	
Various notes	

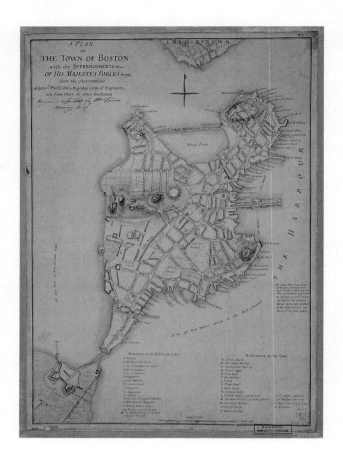

The Differing Layouts of Philadelphia and Boston

The grid pattern of Philadelphia's straight streets contrasts sharply with Boston's crooked and irregular roads and alleys. How might topography have shaped the different layouts of the two cities?

(Left: Engraving by R. Scot and S. Allardice, "Plan of the City and Suburbs of Philadelphia" 1794. Humanities and Social Sciences Library, Map Division, The New York Public Library/Art Resource, NY; right: Library of Congress Geography & Maps Division)

approval of the violent action against Belcher by refusing to indict the rioters.

The two conceptions of community and economic life continued to rub against each other for decades. Urban merchants, shopkeepers, land speculators, and ambitious artisans cleaved more and more to the new economic formulas, while many clergymen continued to preach the traditional message: "Let no man seek his own, but every man another's wealth." By the mid-eighteenth century, the pursuit of profits was winning out over the old community-oriented social compact.

The American Enlightenment

Ideas not only about economic life but also the nature of the universe and the improvement of the human condition filtered across the Atlantic. In the eighteenth century, an American version of the European intellectual movement called the Enlightenment came into focus.

In what is called the Age of Reason, European thinkers rejected the pessimistic Calvinist concept of innate human depravity, replacing it with the optimistic notion that a benevolent God had blessed humankind with the supreme gift of reason. Thinkers like John Locke, in his influential *Essay Concerning*

Human Understanding (1689), argued that God had not predetermined the content of the human mind but had instead given it the capacity to acquire knowledge. All Enlightenment thinkers prized this acquisition of knowledge, for it allowed humankind to improve its condition. As the great mathematician Isaac Newton demonstrated, systematic investigation could unlock the secrets of the physical universe. Moreover, scientific knowledge could be applied to improve society.

The scientific and intellectual advances of the seventeenth and eighteenth centuries encouraged a belief in "natural law" and fostered debate about the "natural" human rights. In Europe, French philosophers Voltaire and Denis Diderot explored the issue of equality. From 1750 to 1772, Diderot published his *Encyclopedia*, which treated such topics as equality, liberty, reason, and rights. These ideas spread in Europe and the Americas, eventually finding expression in movements for reform, democracy, and liberation—all of deep interest to those beginning to oppose slavery and the slave trade as abominations. Even as the traffic in slaves peaked, religious and humanitarian opposition to slavery arose. The idea grew in the 1750s that slavery contradicted the Christian concept of brotherhood and the Enlightenment notion of the natural equality of all humans. Abolitionist sentiment

The Quaker Benjamin Lay

Benjamin Lay was regarded as eccentric and a troublemaker, even by his fellow Quakers. Known primarily as a fervent opponent of slavery and the slave trade as early as the 1730s, he was also in the vanguard of many reform movements such as temperance and vegetarianism. The portrait shows Lay's dwarflike stature. What does the basket at bottom left symbolize?

(William Williams, *Portrait of Benjamin Lay*, 1750. National Portrait Gallery, Smithsonian Institution/Art Resource, NY)

Franklin's true genius as a figure of the Enlightenment came in his practical application of scientific knowledge. Among his inventions were the lightning rod, which reduced the age-old danger of fires when lightning struck wooden buildings; bifocal spectacles; and a stove that heated rooms more cost-effectively than the open fireplace. Franklin made his adopted city of Philadelphia a center of the American Enlightenment by helping found America's first circulating library in 1731, an artisans' debating club for "mutual improvement," and an intercolonial scientific association that in 1769 became the American Philosophical Society.

Most colonists were not educated enough to participate actively in the American Enlightenment, and only a handful read French Enlightenment authors such as Voltaire. But the efforts of men such as Franklin exposed thousands, especially in the cities, to new currents of thought. This kindled hopes that Americans, blessed by an abundant environment, might achieve the Enlightenment ideal of a perfect society.

The Great Awakening

Many of the social, economic, and political changes occurring in eighteenth-century colonial society converged in the Great Awakening, the first of many religious revivals that would sweep America during the next two centuries. Though the timing and character of the Awakening varied from region to region, this quest for spiritual renewal challenged old sources of authority and produced patterns of thought and behavior that helped fuel a revolutionary movement in the next generation.

Fading Faith

Early eighteenth-century British America remained an overwhelmingly Protestant culture. Puritanism—that is, the Congregational church—dominated all of New England except Rhode Island. Anglicanism held sway in much of New York and throughout the South except the backcountry. In the mid-Atlantic and in the back settlements, German Mennonites, Dunkers, Moravians, and Lutherans; Scots–Irish Presbyterians; and English Baptists and Quakers all mingled. Even so, two-thirds of the colonists went to no church at all, partly because in many areas, ministers and churches were simply unavailable. In the most populous colony, Virginia, only 60 parsons in 1761 served a population of 350,000—one for every 5,800 people.

Most colonial churches were voluntary ("congregated") groups, formed for reasons of conscience rather

was also fed by the growing belief that a slave master's authority "depraved the mind," as the Quaker John Woolman argued. An introspective tailor from New Jersey, in the 1750s Woolman dedicated his life to a crusade against slavery. He traveled thousands of miles on foot to convince every Quaker slaveholder of his or her wrongdoing. Only a few hundred masters freed their slaves in the mid-eighteenth century, but men such as Woolman had planted the seeds of abolitionism.

Eighteenth-century Americans began to make significant contributions to the advancement of science. Naturalists such as John Bartram of Philadelphia gathered and described American plants from all over eastern North America as part of the transatlantic attempt to classify all plant life into one universal system. Professor John Winthrop III of Harvard made an unusually accurate measurement of the earth's distance from the sun. Foremost among them was Benjamin Franklin, whose spectacular (and dangerous) experiments with electricity, the properties of which were just becoming known, earned him an international reputation.

than government compulsion. Though Catholics, Jews, and nonbelievers could not vote or hold office, the persecution of Quakers and Catholics had largely passed, and by 1720 some dissenting groups had gained the right to use long-obligatory church taxes to support their own congregations.

The clergy often administered their congregations with difficulty. Anglicans and several German sects maintained close ties to mother churches across the Atlantic. Most efforts to tighten organization and discipline failed. For example, Anglican ministers had to be ordained in England and regularly report to the bishop of London. But in his Chesapeake parish, an Anglican priest faced wealthy planters who controlled the vestry (the local church's governing body) and set his salary; the vestrymen would drive him out if he challenged them too forcefully. In Connecticut, the Saybrook Platform of 1708 created a network, or "consociation," of Congregational churches, but individual churches still preserved much of their autonomy.

Though governing their churches frustrated many clergymen, religious apathy was a more pressing problem. As early as the 1660s, New England's Congregational clergy had adopted the Half-Way Covenant in order to combat religious indifference. It allowed children of church members, if they adhered to the "forms of godliness," to join the church even if they could not demonstrate that they had undergone a conversion experience. They could not, however, vote in church affairs or take communion.

Such compromises and innovations could not halt the creeping religious apathy that many ministers observed. An educated clergy, its energies often drained by doctrinal disputes, appealed too much to the mind and not enough to the heart. As one Connecticut leader remembered it, "the spirit of God appeared to be awfully withdrawn."

The Awakeners' Message

The Great Awakening was not a unified movement; rather it was a series of revivals that swept different regions between 1720 and 1760 with varying degrees of intensity. The first stirrings came in the 1720s in New Jersey, where a Dutch Reformed minister, Theodore Frelinghuysen, excited his congregation through emotional preaching about the need to be "saved" rather than offering the usual theological abstractions. A neighboring Presbyterian, Gilbert Tennent, soon took up the Dutchman's techniques, with similar success.

From New Jersey, the Awakening spread to Pennsylvania in the 1730s, especially among Presbyterians, and then broke out in the Connecticut River valley. There its leader was Jonathan Edwards of Northampton, Massachusetts, who was later recognized as a philosophical giant. During the Northampton revival Edwards preached a powerful message that brought his trembling congregants to their knees. Fearful of remaining among the unrepentant, his Northampton neighbors were soon preparing frantically for the conversion by which they would be "born again." His *Faithful Narrative of the Surprizing Work of God* (1736), which described his town's awakening, was the first published revival narrative. This literary form would be used many times in the future to fan the flames of evangelical religion.

In 1739, these regional brushfires of evangelicalism were drawn together by a 24-year-old Anglican priest from England, George Whitefield. Inspired by John Wesley, the founder of English Methodism, Whitefield used his magnificent speaking voice in dynamic open-air preaching before huge gatherings. Whitefield barnstormed seven times along the American seaboard, beginning in 1739. In Boston, he preached to 19,000 in three days and at a farewell sermon left 25,000 writhing in fear of damnation. In his wake came American preachers whom he had inspired, mostly young men.

The appeal of the Awakeners lay both in the medium and the message. They preached that the established, college-trained clergy was too intellectual and tradition-bound. Congregations were dead, Whitefield declared, "because dead men preach to them." "The sapless discourses of such dead drones," cried another Awakener, were worthless. The fires of Protestant belief could be reignited only if individuals assumed responsibility for their own conversion.

Samson Occom

Samson Occom, a Mohegan born in Connecticut, was attracted to Christianity, like so many others who were "outsiders," by the emotional and populistic appeal of the Great Awakening preachers. On a trip to England, Occom raised £12,000 for an evangelical school for Native Americans, later to become Dartmouth College. What did the artist mean to convey by the oversize book Occom points at?

(Courtesy of the Boston Public Library, Print Department)

An important form of individual participation was "lay exhorting," which meant that anyone—young or old, female or male, black or white—could defy assigned roles and spontaneously recount a conversion experience and preach "the Lord's truth." This horrified the trained clergy and shattered their monopoly. The oral culture of common people gained new importance, their impromptu outpourings contrasting sharply with the literary culture of the gentry.

How religion, social change, and politics became interwoven in the Great Awakening can be seen by examining two regions swept by revivalism. Both Boston, the heartland of Puritanism, and interior Virginia, a land of struggling small planters and slave-rich aristocrats, experienced the Great Awakening, but in different ways and at different times.

Revivalism in the Urban North

In Boston, Whitefield-inspired revivalism blazed up amid political controversy about paper money and land banks, which pitted large merchants against local traders, artisans, and the laboring poor, who preferred the fiscally liberal land bank over the merchants' fiscally conservative silver bank.

Whitefield's arrival in Boston coincided with the currency furor. At first, Boston's elite applauded his ability to call the people to worship. It seemed that the master evangelist might restore social harmony by redirecting Bostonians from earthly matters such as the currency dispute toward concerns for their souls. But when he left Boston in 1740, others followed him who were more critical of the "unconverted" clergy and the self-indulgent accumulation of wealth. One was 25-year-old James Davenport, who appeared anything but respectable to the elite.

Finding every meetinghouse closed to him, even those whose clergy had embraced the Awakening, Davenport preached daily on the Boston Common, aroused religious ecstasy among thousands of people like Hannah Heaton, and stirred up feeling against the city's leading figures. Respectable people decided that revivalism had gotten out of hand when ordinary people began denouncing opponents of the land bank in the streets as "carnal wretches, hypocrites, fighters against God, children of the devil, [and] cursed Pharisees." A religious movement to revive the faith of backsliding Christians had overlapped with political affairs. It threatened polite culture, which stressed order and discipline from ordinary people.

Southern Revivalism

Although aftershocks continued for years, by 1744 the Great Awakening was ebbing in New England and the middle colonies. But in Virginia, where the initial religious earthquake was barely felt, tremors of enthusiasm rippled through society from the mid-1740s onward. As in Boston, the Awakeners challenged and disturbed the gentry-led social order.

Whitefield stirred some religious fervor during his early trips through Virginia. Traveling "New Light" preachers, led by the brilliant orator Samuel Davies, were soon gathering large crowds both in the backcountry and in the Anglican parishes of the older settled areas. By 1747, worried Anglican clergymen persuaded the governor to issue a proclamation restraining "strolling preachers." As in other colonies, Virginia's leaders despised traveling evangelists, who, like lay exhorters, conjured up a world without properly constituted authority. When the Hanover County court gave the fiery James Davenport a license to preach in 1750, the governor ordered the suppression of all circuit riders.

New Light Presbyterianism, challenging the gentry-dominated Anglican church's spiritual monopoly, spread in the 1750s. Then, in the 1760s, came the Baptists. Renouncing finery and ostentatious display and addressing each other as "brother" and "sister," the Baptists reached out to thousands of unchurched people. Like northern revivalists, they focused on the conversion experience. Many of their preachers were uneducated farmers and artisans who called themselves "Christ's poor" and insisted that heaven was populated more by the humble poor than by the purse-proud rich. Among the poorest of all, Virginia's 140,000 slaves in 1760, the evangelical message began to take hold.

The insurgent Baptist movement in rural Virginia became both a quest for a personal, emotionally satisfying religion among ordinary folk and a rejection of gentry values. Established Anglican pulpits denounced the Awakeners as furiously as had respectable New England divines. In both regions, social changes weakened the cultural authority of the upper class and, in the context of religious revival, produced a vision of a society drawn along more equal lines.

Legacy of the Awakening

By the time George Whitefield returned to North America for his third tour in 1745, the revival had burned out in the North. Its effects, however, were long-lasting. Notably, it promoted religious pluralism and laid the groundwork for separation of church and state. Revival and the growth of numerous denominations furthered and eventually helped to legitimize community diversity. Almost from their beginnings, Rhode Island, the Carolinas, and the middle colonies had recognized this. But uniformity had been prized elsewhere, especially in Massachusetts and Connecticut. There, the Awakening split Congregational churches into New Lights and Old Lights. Mid-Atlantic Presbyterian churches faced similar schisms. In hundreds of rural communities by the 1750s, two or three churches existed where only one had stood before. People learned that the fabric of community could be woven from threads of many hues.

This new pluralism prepared the way for another change—the separation of church and state. Once a variety of churches gained legitimacy, it was hard to justify one claiming special privileges. In the seventeenth century, Roger Williams had tried to sever church and state because he believed that ties with civil bodies would corrupt the Church. During the Awakening, groups such as the Baptists and Presbyterians in Virginia constituted their own religious bodies and broke the Anglican monopoly as *the* Church in the colony. This undermining of the church–state tie would be completed during the Revolutionary era.

New eighteenth-century colonial colleges reflected the religious pluralism. Before 1740, there existed only Congregationalist Harvard (1636) and Yale (1701) and Anglican William and Mary (1693). But between 1746 and 1769, six new colleges were added: Dartmouth, Brown, Princeton, and what are now Columbia, Rutgers, and the University of Pennsylvania. None was controlled by an established church, all had governing bodies composed of men of different faiths, and all admitted students regardless of religion. Pennsylvania had no religious affiliation whatsoever. Eager for students and funds, they made nonsectarian appeals and combined the traditional Latin and Greek curricula with natural sciences and natural philosophy.

Last, the Awakening nurtured a subtle change in values that crossed over into politics and daily life. Especially for ordinary people, the revival experience created a new feeling of self-worth. People assumed new responsibilities in religious affairs and became skeptical of dogma and authority. Many, especially the fast-growing Baptists, decried the growing materialism and deplored the new acceptance of self-interested behavior. He who was "governed by regard to his own private interest," Gilbert Tennent preached, was "an enemy to the public," for in true Christian communities, "mutual love is the band and cement." Opposing religious authority and creating new institutions to better meet their needs, thousands of colonists unknowingly rehearsed for revolution.

Political Life

"Were it not for government, the world would soon run into all manner of disorders and confusions," wrote a Massachusetts clergyman early in the eighteenth century. "Men's lives and estates and liberties would soon be prey to the covetous and the cruel," and every man would be "as a wolf" to his neighbors. Few colonists or Europeans would have disagreed. Government existed to protect life, liberty, and property.

How should political power be divided—in England, between the British government and the colonies, and within each colony? Colonists naturally drew heavily on inherited political ideas and institutions—almost entirely English ones, for it was English charters that sanctioned settlement, English governors who ruled, and English common law that governed the courts. But meeting unexpected circumstances in a new environment, colonists modified familiar political forms.

Structuring Colonial Governments

All societies consider it essential to determine the final source of political authority. In England, the notion of the God-given, supreme monarchical authority was crumbling even before the planting of the colonies. In its place arose the belief that stable government depended on blending and balancing the three pure forms of government: monarchy, aristocracy, and democracy. Unalloyed, each would degenerate into oppression. Monarchy, the rule of one, would become despotism. Aristocracy, the rule of the few, would turn into oligarchy. Democracy, the rule of the many, would descend into anarchy or mob rule. Most colonists believed that the Revolution of 1688 in England had vindicated and strengthened a carefully balanced political system.

In the colonies, political balance was achieved somewhat differently. The governor, as the king's agent (or, in proprietary colonies, the agent of the proprietor to whom the king delegated authority), represented monarchy. Bicameral legislatures arose in most of the colonies in the seventeenth century, and in most provinces they had upper houses of wealthy men appointed by the governor; as a pale equivalent of Britain's House of Lords, it formed a nascent aristocracy. The assembly, elected by white male freeholders, replicated the House of Commons and was the democratic element. Every statute required the governor's assent (except in Rhode Island and Connecticut), and all colonial laws required final approval from the king's privy council. This royal check operated imperfectly, however. A law took months to reach England and months more before word came of its final approval or rejection. In the meantime, the law took force in the colony.

Behind the formal structure of politics stood rules governing who could participate as voters and office-holders. In England, land ownership conferred political rights (women and non-Christians were uniformly excluded). Only men with property producing an annual rental income of 40 shillings or more could vote or hold office. The colonists closely followed this principle, except in Massachusetts, where until 1691 church membership was the basic requirement. As in England, the poor and propertyless were excluded,

COLONIAL FOUNDATIONS OF THE AMERICAN POLITICAL SYSTEM

1606	Virginia companies of London and Plymouth granted patents to settle lands in North America.
1619	First elected colonial legislature meets in Virginia.
1634	Under a charter granted in 1632, Maryland's proprietor is given all the authority "as any bishop of Durham" ever held—more than the king possessed in England.
1635	The council in Virginia deports Governor John Harvey for exceeding his power, thus asserting the rights of local magistrates to contest authority of royally appointed governors.
1643	The colonies of Massachusetts, Plymouth, Connecticut, and New Haven draw up articles of confederation and form the first intercolonial union, the United Colonies of New England.
1647	Under a charter granted in 1644, elected freemen from the Providence Plantations draft a constitution establishing freedom of conscience, separating church and state, and authorizing referenda by the towns on laws passed by the assembly.
1677	The Laws, Concessions, and Agreements for West New Jersey provide for a legislature elected annually by virtually all free males, secret voting, liberty of conscience, election of justices of the peace and local officeholders, and trial by jury in public so that "justice may not be done in a corner."
1689	James II deposed in England in the Glorious Revolution and royal governors, accused of abusing their authority, ousted in Massachusetts, New York, and Maryland.
1701	First colonial unicameral legislature meets in Pennsylvania under the Frame of Government of 1701.
1735	John Peter Zenger, a New York printer, acquitted of seditious libel for printing attacks on the royal governor and his faction, thus widening the freedom of the press.
1754	First congress of all the colonies meets at Albany (with seven colonies sending delegates) and agrees on a Plan of Union (which is rejected by the colonies and the English government).
1765	The Stamp Act Congress, the first intercolonial convention called outside England's authority, meets in New York.

for they lacked the "stake in society" that supposedly produced responsible voters.

In England the 40-shilling freehold requirement kept the electorate small, but in the colonies, where land was cheap, it conferred the vote on 50 to 75 percent of free adult males. However, as the proportion of landless colonists increased in the eighteenth century, the franchise contracted.

Though voting rights were broadly based, most men assumed that the wealthy and socially prominent should hold the main political positions. Balancing this elitism, however, was the notion that the entire electorate should periodically judge the performance of those entrusted with political power and reject those who were found wanting. Following the precedent of England's Glorious Revolution, in British America the people were assumed to have the right to protest openly and, in extreme cases of abuse of power, assume control and put things right. Crowd action, frequently effective, gradually achieved a kind of legitimacy.

The Crowd in Action

What gave special power to the common people when they assembled to protest oppressive authority and the trampling of traditional English liberties was the absence of a separate police force. In the countryside, where most colonists lived, only the county sheriff insulated civil leaders from angry farmers. In the towns, the sheriff had only the night watch to keep order. As late as 1757, New York's night watch was described as a "parcell of idle, drinking vigilant snorers, who never quelled any nocturnal tumult in their lives." In theory, the militia stood ready to suppress public disturbances, but crowds usually included many militiamen.

Boston's Impressment Riot of 1747 vividly illustrates the people's readiness to defend their inherited privileges and the weakness of law enforcement. It began when Commodore Charles Knowles brought his royal navy ships to Boston for provisioning—and to replenish the ranks of mariners thinned by desertion. When Knowles sent press gangs to fill the crew vacancies from Boston's waterfront population, they scooped up artisans, laborers, servants, and slaves, as well as merchant seamen from ships riding at anchor in the harbor.

But before the press gangs could hustle away their victims, a crowd of angry Bostonians seized several British officers, surrounded the governor's house, and demanded the release of their townsmen. When the sheriff and his deputies tried to intervene, the mob mauled them. The militia refused to respond. An enraged Knowles threatened to bombard the town, but

The "Paxton Boys" in Philadelphia
When frontier farmers marched on Philadelphia in 1763 to demand more protection on the frontier, a miniature civil war was narrowly averted. Philadelphians had little use for the "Paxton Boys," who had murdered 20 harmless Christian Indians in retaliation for frontier raids. Why are soldiers and mounted men commanding the public space?

(The Library Company of Philadelphia)

negotiations amid further tumult averted a showdown. Finally, Knowles released the impressed Bostonians. After the riot, a young politician named Samuel Adams defended Boston's defiance of royal authority. The people, he argued, had a "natural right" to band together against press gangs that deprived them of their liberty. He labeled local magnates who supported the governor in this incident "tools to arbitrary power."

The Growing Power of the Assemblies

While the Impressment Riot of 1747 was dramatic, a more gradual and restrained change was underway—the growing ambition and power of the legislative assemblies. For most of the seventeenth century, royal and proprietary governors had exercised greater power in relation to the elected legislatures than did England's king in relation to Parliament. Governors could dissolve the lower houses, control the election of their speakers, and in most colonies initiate legislation with their appointed councils. They had authority to appoint and dismiss judges. Governors also controlled the expenditure of public monies and had authority to grant land to individuals and groups. They lacked, however, the extensive patronage power that enabled ministers of government in England to manipulate elections and buy off opponents. By the middle of the eighteenth century, almost half of all colonies were royal colonies.

Eighteenth-century legislatures challenged the swollen powers of the colonial governors. Bit by bit, they won new rights: to initiate legislation, to elect their own speakers, to settle contested elections, to discipline members, and to nominate provincial treasurers who disbursed public funds. Most important, they won the "power of the purse"—the authority to initiate money bills, specifying how much money should be raised by taxes and how it should be spent. Thus, the elected assemblies gradually transformed themselves into governing bodies reflecting the interests of the electorate. Governors complained bitterly about the "levelling spirit" and "mutinous and disorderly behavior" of the assemblies, but they could not stop their rise.

Local Politics

Binding elected officeholders to their constituents became an important feature of the colonial political system. In England, the House of Commons claimed to represent the entire nation rather than narrow local interests, yet was filled with representatives from "rotten boroughs" (ancient places left virtually uninhabited by population shifts) and with men whose vote was controlled by the government because they had accepted offices, contracts, or gifts. American assemblies, by contrast, contained mostly representatives sent by voters who instructed them on particular issues and held them accountable.

Royal governors and colonial grandees who sat as councilors often deplored this localist, popular orientation. Sniffed one aristocratic New Yorker, the assemblies were crowded with "plain, illiterate husbandmen [small farmers], whose views seldom extended farther than the regulation of highways, the destruction of wolves, wildcats, and foxes, and the advancement of the other little interests of the particular counties which they were chosen to represent." In actuality, most lower-house members were merchants, lawyers, and substantial planters and farmers, who by the mid-eighteenth century constituted the political elite in most colonies. They took pride in upholding their constituents' interests, for they saw themselves as bulwarks against arbitrary rule, which history taught them was most frequently imposed by monarchs and their appointed agents.

Local government was usually more important to the colonists than provincial government. In New England, the town meeting decided a wide range of matters, arguing until it could express itself as a single unit. "By general agreement" and "by the free and

united consent of the whole" were phrases denoting a collective assent rather than a democratic competition among differing interests and points of view.

In the South, the county was the primary unit of government, and by the mid-eighteenth century, a landed squirearchy of third- and fourth-generation families had achieved political dominance. At court sessions, usually four times a year, deeds were read aloud and then recorded, juries impaneled and justice dispensed, elections held, licenses issued, and proclamations read aloud. On election days, gentlemen treated their neighbors (on whom they depended for votes) to "bumbo," "kill devil," and other alcoholic treats.

The Spread of Whig Ideology

Whether in local or provincial affairs, a political ideology called Whig, or "republican," had spread widely by the mid-eighteenth century. This body of thought, inherited from England, rested on the belief that concentrated power was historically the enemy of liberty and that too

Timeline	
1662	Half-Way Covenant in New England
1682	La Salle canoes down Mississippi River and claims Louisiana for France
1689–1697	King William's War
1700	Spanish establish first mission in Arizona
1701–1713	Queen Anne's War
1704	*Boston News-Letter,* first regular colonial newspaper, published
1712	First northern slave revolt erupts in New York City
1713	Peace of Utrecht
1714	Beginning of Scots–Irish and German immigration
1715–1730	Volume of slave trade doubles
1718	French settle New Orleans
1720s	Natural increase of African population begins
1732	Benjamin Franklin publishes first *Poor Richard's Almanack*
1734–1736	Great Awakening begins in Northampton, Massachusetts
1735	Zenger acquitted of seditious libel in New York
1739	Slave revolt in Stono, South Carolina
1739–1740	Whitefield's first American tour spreads Great Awakening
1740s	Slaves compose 90 percent of population on Carolina rice coast
	Indigo becomes staple crop in Lower South
1747	Impressment Riot in Boston
1750s	Quakers initiate campaign to halt slave trade and end slavery
1760	Africans compose 20 percent of colonial population
1760s–1770s	Spanish establish California mission system
1769	American Philosophical Society founded at Philadelphia

much power lodged in any person or group usually produced tyranny. The best defenses against concentrated power were balanced government, elected legislatures adept at checking executive authority, prohibition of standing armies (presumed to be controlled by tyrannical monarchs), and vigilance by the people in watching their leaders for telltale signs of corruption.

Much of this Whig ideology reached the people through some 23 newspapers circulating in the colonies by 1763. Many papers reprinted pieces from English Whig writers railing against corruption and creeping despotism. Though limited to a few pages and published only once or twice a week, the papers passed from hand to hand and were read aloud in taverns and coffeehouses, so that their contents probably reached most urban households and a substantial minority of rural farms.

The new power of the press and its importance in guarding the people's liberties against would-be tyrants (such as haughty royal governors) were dramatically illustrated in the Zenger case in New York. Young John Peter Zenger, a printer's apprentice, had been hired in 1733 by the anti-government faction of Lewis Morris to start a newspaper; *New-York Weekly Journal* would publicize the corrupt actions of Governor William Cosby.

Arrested for seditious libel, Zenger was defended brilliantly by Andrew Hamilton, a Philadelphia lawyer hired by the Morris faction to convince the jury that Zenger had been simply trying to inform the people of attacks on their liberties. Although the jury acquitted Zenger, the libel laws remained very restrictive. But the acquittal did reinforce the notion that the government was the people's servant, and it brought home the point that public criticism could keep people with political authority responsible to the people they ruled. Such ideas about liberty and corruption, raised in the context of local politics, would shortly achieve a much broader significance.

Conclusion
AMERICA IN 1750

The English colonies in North America, robust and expanding, matured rapidly between 1690 and 1750. Transatlantic commerce linked them closely to Europe, Africa, and other parts of the Americas. Churches, schools, and towns—the visible marks of the receding frontier—appeared everywhere. And everywhere, people like Hannah Heaton had been energized by the Great Awakening and were introduced to the idea of ordinary people helping to shape the future. A balanced gender ratio and stable family life had been achieved throughout the colonies. Seasoned political leaders and familiar political institutions functioned from Maine to Georgia.

Yet the sinew, bone, and muscle of American society had not yet fully knit together. The polyglot population, one-fifth of it bound in chattel slavery and its Native American component still unassimilated and uneasily situated on the frontier, was a kaleidoscopic mixture of ethnic and religious groups. While developing rapidly, its economy showed weaknesses, particularly in New England, where land resources had been strained. The social structure reflected the colonizers' emergence from a frontier stage, but the consolidation of wealth by some was matched by pockets of poverty appearing in the cities and some rural areas. Full of strength, yet marked by awkward incongruities, colonial America in 1750 approached an era of strife and momentous decisions. Much of that strife involved the growing power of France's inland empire in North America and the way that wars in Europe were becoming globe-encircling conflicts.

QUESTIONS FOR REVIEW AND REFLECTION

1. Regional variations within colonial society created different social and economic systems in areas of North America. What were the key regional divisions, and what differences characterized the societies and economies in each?
2. Why did slavery become a widespread institution in eighteenth-century colonial North America, and how did it shape society?
3. Was the Great Awakening compatible with other changes occurring in the society, or did it contradict most other trends? How do you see religious change relating to social, political, and intellectual changes?
4. Was colonial America more affected by transatlantic trends or local influences in the areas of politics, ideas, and social life?
5. What were the most important aspects of colonial society that enabled it to mature? Why do you think these particular factors most significant?

CHAPTER 5

The Strains of Empire

The Battle of Lexington, *April 19th 1775*.

(*John Warner Barber, engraved by A. Doolittle after Ralph Earle,* The Battle of Lexington, *April 19th 1775, from 'Connecticut Historical Collections,' 1832, Private Collection/Bridgeman Art Library*)

American Stories

A Shoemaker Leads a Boston Mob

In 1758, when he was 21 years old, Ebenezer MacIntosh of Boston laid down his shoemaker's awl and enlisted in the Massachusetts expedition against the French on Lake Champlain—one battle in the war that was raging between Britain and France in North America, the Caribbean, and Europe. The son of a poor Boston shoemaker who had fought against the French in a previous war, MacIntosh had known poverty all his life. Service against the French offered the hope of plunder or at least an enlistment bounty worth half a year's wages. One among thousands of colonists who fought against the "Gallic menace" in the Seven Years' War, MacIntosh contributed his mite to the climactic struggle that drove the French from North America.

But a greater role lay ahead for the Boston shoemaker. Two years after the Peace of Paris in 1763, Britain imposed a stamp tax on the American colonists. In the massive protests that followed, MacIntosh emerged as the street leader of Boston's ordinary people. In two nights of the most violent attacks on private property ever witnessed in North America, a crowd nearly destroyed the houses of two of the colony's most important officials. On August 14, they tore through the house of Andrew Oliver, a wealthy merchant and the appointed distributor of stamps for Massachusetts. Twelve days later, MacIntosh led the crowd in attacking the mansion of Thomas Hutchinson, a wealthy merchant who served as lieutenant governor and chief justice of Massachusetts. "The mob was so general," wrote the governor, "and so supported that all civil power ceased in an instant."

For several months, the Boston shoemaker's power grew. Called "General" MacIntosh and "Captain-General of the Liberty Tree," he soon sported a militia uniform of gold and blue and a hat laced with gold. Two thousand townsmen marched behind him in orderly ranks through the crooked streets of Boston on November 5 to demonstrate their solidarity in resisting the hated stamps.

Five weeks later, a crowd humiliated stamp distributor Oliver. Demanding that he announce his resignation before the assembled citizenry, they marched him across town in a driving December rain. With MacIntosh at his elbow, he finally reached the "Liberty Tree," which had become a symbol of resistance to Britain's new colonial policies. There the aristocratic Oliver ate humble pie. He concluded his resignation remarks with bitter words, hissing sardonically that he would "always think myself very happy when it shall be in my power to serve the people."

"To serve the people" was an ancient idea embedded in English political culture, but it assumed new meaning in the colonies during the epic third quarter of the eighteenth century. Few colonists in 1750 held even a faint desire to break the connection with Britain, and fewer still might have predicted the form of government that 13 states in an independent nation might fashion. Yet 2 million colonists moved haltingly toward a showdown with mighty Britain. Little-known men such as Ebenezer MacIntosh as well as his celebrated townsmen Samuel Adams, John Hancock, and John Adams were part of the struggle. Collectively, ordinary people such as MacIntosh influenced—and sometimes even dictated—the revolutionary movement in the colonies. Though we read and speak mostly of a small group of "founding fathers," the wellsprings of the American Revolution can be fully discovered only among a variety of people from different social groups, occupations, regions, and religions.

This chapter addresses the tensions in late colonial society, the imperial crisis that followed the Seven Years' War (in the colonies, often called the French and Indian War), and the tumultuous decade that led to the "shot heard round the world" fired at Concord Bridge in April 1775. It portrays the origins of a dual American Revolution. Ebenezer MacIntosh, in leading the Boston mob against Crown officers who tried to implement a new colonial policy after 1763, helped set in motion a revolutionary movement to restore ancient liberties thought by the Americans to be under deliberate attack in Britain. This movement eventually escalated into the war for American independence.

But Boston's crowd was also venting years of resentment at the accumulation of wealth and power by a few. Behind every swing of the ax, every shattered crystal goblet, and every splintered mahogany chair lay the fury of Bostonians who had seen the conservative elite try to dismantle the town meeting, had suffered economic hardship, and had lost faith that opportunity and just relations still prevailed. This sentiment, flowing from resentment of what many believed was a corrupt, self-indulgent, and elite-dominated society, produced a commitment to reshape society even while severing the colonial bond. As distinguished from the war for independence, this was the American Revolution.

The Climactic Seven Years' War

After a brief period of peace following King George's War (1744–1748), France and Britain fought the fourth, largest, and by far most significant of the wars for empire that had begun in the late seventeenth century. Known variously as the Seven Years' War, the French and Indian War, and the Great War for Empire, this global conflict in part represented a showdown for control of North America's interior between the Allegheny Mountains and the Mississippi River. In North America, the Anglo-American forces ultimately prevailed, and their victory drove the French out of New France and gave the British control of much of eastern North America. This change dramatically affected the lives of all the diverse people living in the huge region east of the Mississippi—English, German, and Scots–Irish settlers in the British colonies; French and Spanish colonizers in Canada, Florida, and interior North America; African slaves in a variety of settlements; and, perhaps most of all, the powerful Native American tribes of the interior.

War and the Management of Empire

England began constructing a more coherent administration of its far-flung colonies after the Glorious Revolution of 1688. In 1696, a professional Board of Trade replaced the old Lords of Trade; the Treasury strengthened the customs service; and Parliament created overseas vice-admiralty courts, which prosecuted smugglers who evaded the trade regulations set forth in the Navigation Acts. Parliament began playing a more active role after the reign of Queen Anne (1702–1714) and continued to do so when the weak, German-speaking King George I came to the throne. Royal governors received greater powers and more detailed instructions, as the Board of Trade demanded they enforce policies. Britain was gradually installing the machinery of imperial management tended by a corps of colonial bureaucrats.

The best test of an effectively organized state is its ability to wage war. Four times between 1689 and 1763, England matched its strength against France, its archrival in Europe, North America, and the Caribbean. These wars of empire had tremendous consequences for the home governments, their colonial subjects in the Americas, and the native North American tribes drawn into the bloody conflicts.

The Peace of Utrecht (see Chapter 4), which ended Queen Anne's War (1702–1713), brought victor's spoils of great importance to Britain. The generation of peace that followed was only a time-out, during which both England and France strengthened their war-making capacity. Britain's New World colonies made important contributions. Though known as a period of "salutary neglect" in contrast to what would come later, during this era the king and Parliament worked to increase their control over colonial affairs.

Concerned mainly with economic regulation, Parliament added new articles such as fur, copper, hemp, tar, and turpentine to the list of items produced in the colonies that had to be shipped to England before being exported elsewhere. Parliament also curtailed colonial production of articles important to England's economy: woollen cloth (1699), beaver hats (1732), and finished iron products (1750). Most important, Parliament passed the Molasses Act in 1733, an attempt to stop New England from trading with the French West Indies for molasses to convert into rum. Parliament imposed a prohibitive duty of six pence per gallon on French slave-produced molasses. The act turned many of New England's largest merchants and distillers into smugglers, for a generation schooling them, their ship captains, crews, and allied waterfront artisans in defying royal authority.

The generation of peace ended abruptly in 1739 when Britain declared war on Spain. The ostensible cause was the ear of an English sea captain, Robert Jenkins, which had been cut off eight years earlier when Spanish authorities caught him smuggling. Encouraged by his government, Jenkins publicly displayed his pickled ear in 1738 to whip up war fever. The real cause, however, was Britain's determination to continue its drive toward commercial domination of the Atlantic basin. The British Navy captured Porto Bello in Spanish Panama in 1739, but four expeditions against Spanish strongholds in 1740–1742 were disasters. Admiral Edward Vernon recruited some 3,500 colonists for these attacks, enticing them with dreams of capturing mountains of Spanish silver and gold. Most of the mainland colonists died of yellow fever, dysentery, and outright starvation, and those who limped home, including George Washington's father, Lawrence Washington, had little booty to show for their efforts. Washington did rename his Virginia plantation after Admiral Vernon, a widely admired hero.

From 1744 to 1748, the Anglo-Spanish war merged into a much larger Anglo-French conflict, called King George's War in North America and the War of Austrian Succession in Europe. Its scale far exceeded that of previous conflicts, highlighting the need for increased discipline within the empire. Colonists again contributed to the war effort. For them, except for war contractors such as Boston's Thomas Hancock, the war was costly. All New Englanders swelled with pride in June 1745 after Massachusetts volunteers, coordinating their attacks with British naval forces, captured the massive French fortress of Louisbourg on Cape Breton Island, guarding the approach to the St. Lawrence River, after a six-week siege. But the losses were

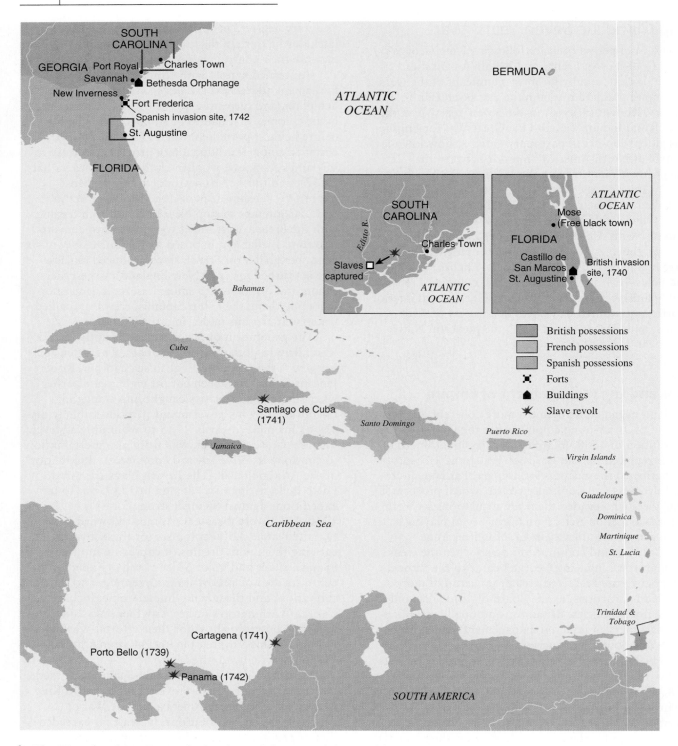

The War of Jenkins' Ear in the Southern Colonies and the Caribbean

The War of Jenkins' Ear was especially unsettling in the colonies because slave revolts broke out in New York and South Carolina during the course of the war. Why did the British suspect the Spanish enemy of having played a role in the revolts.

staggering. "One half of our militia [died] like rotten sheep," reported one Boston leader, who believed that one-fifth of all Massachusetts adult males had perished, leaving thousands of widows and orphaned children. New Englanders were bitter when at war's end in 1748,

the British government handed the prized Fort Louisbourg back to France in exchange for French withdrawal from conquests in parts of British-controlled India and an agreement to spare the British army trapped in Europe.

Outbreak of Hostilities

The return of peace in 1748 did not relieve the tension between British and French colonists in North America. The spectacular population growth of the English colonies—from 250,000 in 1700 to 1.25 million in 1750, and to 1.75 million in the next decade—ensured continued clashes. Three-quarters of the increase came in the colonies south of New York, propelling thousands of land-hungry settlers westward.

Fur traders and land speculators promoted this westward rush. First, fur traders penetrated the French-influenced region. Then, in the 1740s and 1750s, speculators (including many future revolutionary leaders) formed land companies to capitalize on the seaboard population explosion. The farther west the settlement line moved, the closer it came to the western trading empire of the French and their Native American allies.

Colonial penetration of the Ohio valley in the 1740s challenged the French where their interest was vital. While the British controlled most of the eastern coastal plain of North America, the French had nearly encircled them to the west by building a chain of trading posts and forts along the St. Lawrence River, through the Great Lakes, and southward into the Ohio and Mississippi valleys all the way to New Orleans.

Confronted by British intrusions, the French resisted. They attempted to block further encroachments west of the Alleghenies by constructing new forts in the Ohio valley and by prying some tribes loose from their new British connections. By 1753, the French were driving rival traders out of the Ohio River valley. Near present-day Pittsburgh, on May 28, 1754, the French smartly rebuffed the ambitious 21-year-old Virginia militia colonel George Washington. Virginia had dispatched Washington to drive the French away from the site where the Ohio Company, a syndicate of wealthy Virginia speculators, had built a Native American trading post. The skirmish produced only a few casualties, but it quickly escalated into a global war that rearranged the balance of power not only in North America but in Europe and the world.

The ensuing conflict, known in the colonies as the French and Indian War, would eventually drive the French from North America. Emboldened by the success in overwhelming the mighty French fortress at Louisbourg, British merchants argued that the time was ripe to destroy the French overseas trade. Convinced, the ministry ordered several thousand troops to North America in 1754; in France, 3,000 regulars embarked to meet the challenge.

With war looming, colonial governments attempted to coordinate efforts. Representatives of seven colonies met at Albany, New York, in June 1754 to plan a colonial union and rewin the allegiance of the Iroquois, whose grievances had grown sharply after a group of land speculators had tried to grab nearly a million acres of Mohawk land. Both failed. The 150 Iroquois chiefs left with 30 wagonloads of gifts but made no firm commitment to fight the French. Benjamin Franklin designed a plan for an intercolonial government to manage Native American affairs, provide for defense, and have the power to pass laws and levy taxes. But the long-standing jealousies that had thwarted previous attempts at intercolony cooperation led the colonies to reject his plan.

The opening British salvo in the war proved disastrous. Marching his newly arrived British regiments and hundreds of American recruits into the forests of western Pennsylvania, General Edward Braddock happened upon French and native forces near Fort

"Old Hendrick"

The Americans and British relied heavily on the Iroquois in attempting to vanquish the French in the Seven Years' War. "Old Hendrick," the Mohawk chief pictured here, is shown in elaborate European apparel given him by King George II in 1740 to help seal a diplomatic alliance. Chief Hendrick died at the Battle of Lake George in 1755, fighting alongside the British against the French. Which articles of his clothing are distinctly English?

(Courtesy of the John Carter Brown Library at Brown University)

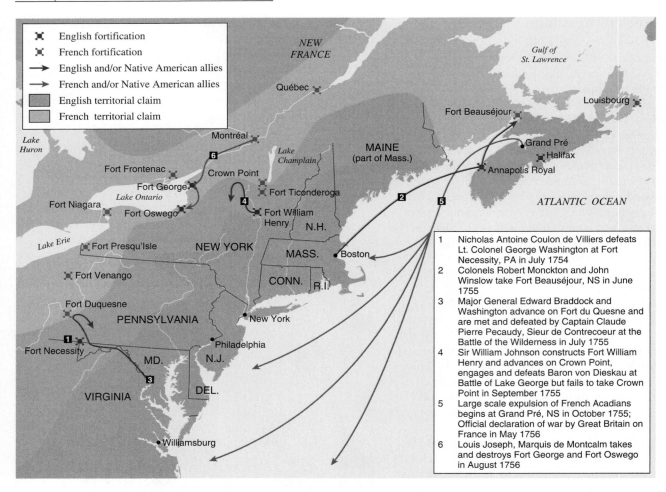

The Seven Years' War, 1754–1756

In the 1755 campaigns of the Seven Years' War, the British suffered losses except in Nova Scotia, where they captured Fort Beauséjour, which led to the deportation of the French-speaking Catholic Acadians. Why might the British have adopted this policy?

Duquesne. Despite a vastly superior force, Braddock's insistence on fighting in tidy lines resulted in defeat. Braddock perished, and two-thirds of the British and Americans were killed or wounded. Washington, his uniform pierced by four bullets, had two horses shot from beneath him. Although it had 1,000 men in reserve down the road, the Anglo-American force beat a hasty retreat.

Braddock's ignominious retreat brought almost every tribe north of the Ohio River to the French side. Throughout the summer, French-supplied Native American raiders torched the Virginia and Pennsylvania backcountry. "The roads are full of starved, naked, indigent multitudes," observed one officer. One French triumph followed another during the next two years. Never was disunity within the British colonies so glaring. With its Native American allies, French Canada, only 70,000 inhabitants strong, had badly battered 1.5 million colonists supported by the British army.

Farther north, the Anglo-American forces had more success, overpowering Fort Beauséjour, the French fort on the neck of land that connected Nova Scotia, held by the English since the Peace of Utrecht, and the French mainland. This quickly led to the expulsion of the French Acadians. They had been promised the right to practice Catholicism and keep their land if they maintained neutrality. When they refused to swear oaths of unqualified allegiance to the British king, which would revoke their religious freedom and oblige them to fight against fellow Frenchmen, the British rounded up about 6,000 Acadians, herded them aboard ships, and dispersed them among their other colonies, giving their confiscated land to New Englanders. Another 7,000 to 10,000 Acadians escaped to the French colony, and in time, about 3,000 of those deported made their way to French Louisiana. The British justified their ethnic cleansing—the first time they had relocated a civilian population by force—as a wartime security measure.

The French won most of the battles in 1756, including a victory at Fort William Henry on Lake George, where their native allies proved essential. At this point, Britain declared war on France, and the French and Indian War in North America turned into a world war with France, Austria, and Russia pitted against Britain and Prussia. The turning point in the war came after the energetic William Pitt became Britain's secretary of state in 1757. "I believe that I can save this nation and that no one else can," he boasted, abandoning Europe as the main theater of action against the French and throwing his nation's military might into the American campaign. The forces he dispatched to North America in 1757 and 1758 dwarfed all preceding commitments: about 23,000 British troops and a huge fleet with 14,000 mariners. But even forces of this magnitude, when asked to engage the enemy in the forests of North America, were not necessarily sufficient to the task without Native American support, or at least neutrality. "A doubt remains not," proclaimed one official in the colonies, "that the prosperity of our colonies on the continent will stand or fall with our interest and favour among them."

Tribal Strategies

The Iroquois knew that their interest lay in playing off one European power against the other. "To preserve the balance between us and the French," wrote a New York politician, "is the great ruling principle of modern Indian politics."

Anglo-American leaders knew that the support of the Iroquois and their tributary tribes was crucial and could be secured in only two ways: through purchase or by a demonstration of power that would convince the tribes that the British would prevail with or without their assistance.

The first stratagem failed. In 1754 colonial negotiators heaped gifts on the Iroquois at the Albany Congress but received only tantalizing half-promises of support. The second alternative fizzled with the resounding French victories in the first three years of the war. Hence, the westernmost of the Iroquois Six Nations, the Seneca, fought on the side of the French in the campaigns of 1757 and 1758, while the Delaware, a tributary tribe, harassed the Pennsylvania frontier.

In 1758, the huge British military buildup finally began to produce victories. The largest army ever assembled in North America to that point, some

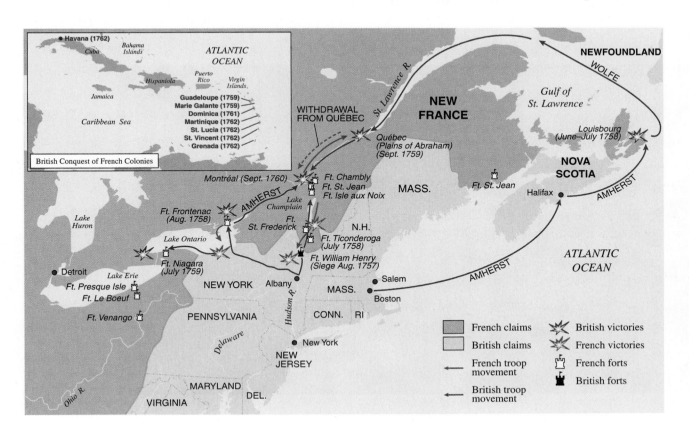

The Seven Years' War, 1757–1760

The British–American victory over France and its Native American allies in the Seven Years' War did not bring peace on the western frontier. After the war, Pontiac led the warriors of several tribes in attacks on settlers and British forts. Fought in the Caribbean and northeast North America, this war's theatre suggests what to you about the international situation?

15,000 British and American soldiers (including Bostonian Ebenezer MacIntosh), suffered terrible casualties and withdrew from the field after attempting to storm Fort Ticonderoga on Lake Champlain in June 1758. Then the tide turned. Troops under Sir Jeffrey Amherst captured Louisbourg, on Cape Breton Island, and Fort Duquesne fell to another force of 6,000. The resolute Pitt had mobilized the fighting power of the nation and put more men in the field than lived in all of New France. The colonists, in turn, had put aside intramural squabbling long enough to overwhelm the badly outnumbered French.

The victories of 1758 finally moved the Iroquois away from neutrality. Added incentive to join the Anglo-American side came when the British navy bottled up French shipping in the St. Lawrence River, cutting the Iroquois off from French trade goods. By early 1759, foreseeing a French defeat in North America, the Iroquois pledged 800 warriors for an attack on Fort Niagara, the strategic French trading depot on Lake Ontario.

Dramatic Anglo-American victories did not always guarantee Native American support. Backcountry skirmishes with the Cherokee from Virginia to South Carolina turned into a costly war from 1759 to 1761. In 1760, the Cherokee mauled a British army of 1,300 under Amherst. The following summer, a much larger Anglo-American force invaded Cherokee country, burning towns and food supplies. British control of the sea interrupted the Native Americans' supply of French arms. Beset by food shortages, lack of ammunition, and a smallpox epidemic, the Cherokee sued for peace.

Other Anglo-American victories in 1759 decided the outcome of the bloodiest war yet known in the Americas. The capture of Fort Niagara, the critical link in the system of forts that joined the French inland empire with the Atlantic, was followed by the conquest of sugar-rich Martinique in the West Indies. The culminating stroke came at Québec. Led by 32-year-old General James Wolfe, 5,000 troops scaled a rocky cliff and overcame the French on the Plains of Abraham. The capture of Montréal late in 1760 completed the shattering of French power in North America. While fighting continued for three more years in the Caribbean and in Europe, on the mainland the old dream of destroying the Gallic menace had finally come true.

Consequences of the Seven Years' War

The Treaty of Paris, ending the Seven Years' War in 1763, brought astounding changes to European and Native peoples in North America. Spain acquired New

The Taking of Québec

The storming of French Québec in 1759 was the decisive blow in England's campaign to end the French domination of Canada and the lands west of the Appalachians. The exploits of General James Wolfe made him a hero throughout England and the colonies. Why was this image produced?

(National Army Museum, London)

Orleans, the vast Louisiana territory west of the Mississippi, and Havana, and in turn surrendered Spanish Florida to the British. The interior Native American tribes, which had adeptly forced Britain and France to compete for their support, suffered a severe setback when the French disappeared and the British became their sole source of trade goods. Iroquois, Cherokee, Creek, Ojibwa, Shawnee, and scores of other interior tribes adjusted to this reality.

After making peace, the British government launched a new policy designed to separate Native Americans and colonizers by creating a racial boundary roughly following the crestline of the Appalachian Mountains from Maine to Georgia. The Proclamation of 1763 reserved all land west of the line for Native American nations. White settlers already there were told to withdraw.

This attempt to legislate racial separation failed. Even before the proclamation was issued, the Ottawa chief Pontiac, concerned that the elimination of the French threatened the old treaty and gift-giving system, had gathered together many of the northern tribes that had joined French assaults during the war. Although Pontiac's pan-Indian movement to drive the British out of the Ohio valley collapsed in 1764, it served notice that the interior tribes would fight for their lands.

London could not enforce the Proclamation of 1763. Staggering under an immense wartime debt, Britain decided to maintain only small army garrisons in America to regulate the interior. Nor could royal governors stop land speculators and settlers from privately purchasing land from trans-Appalachian tribes or simply encroaching on their land. Under such circumstances, the western frontier seethed after 1763.

Not only did the epic Anglo-American victory redraw the map of North America, but the war also had important social and economic effects on colonial society. It convinced the colonists of their growing strength, yet left them debt-ridden and short on manpower. The wartime economy spurred economic development and poured British capital into the colonies, rendering them more vulnerable to cyclic fluctuations in the British economy.

Peace ended the casualties but also brought depression. When the bulk of the British forces left North America in 1760, the economy slumped badly, especially in the coastal towns. Although even some wealthy merchants went bankrupt, the greatest hardships after 1760 fell on laboring people. Those with the smallest wages had the thinnest savings to cushion them against hard times. How quickly their security could evaporate showed in Philadelphia, where early many poor people, unable to pay their property taxes, were "disposing of

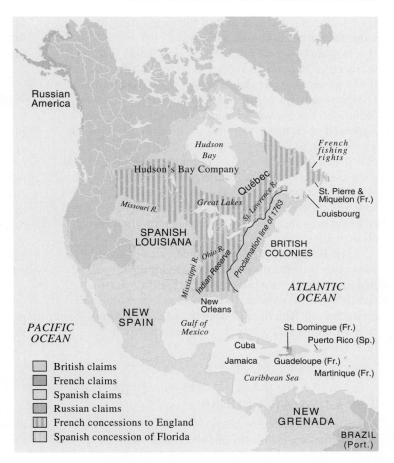

North America After 1763

At the Treaty of Paris in 1763, France surrendered huge claims west of the Mississippi River to Spain and east of the river to England. England also acquired Florida from Spain. How did this change the situation on the continent?

their huts and lots to others more wealthy than themselves." Established artisans and shopkeepers were caught between rising prices and reduced demand for their goods and services. A New York artisan found it "beyond my ability to support my family . . . [which] can scarcely appear with decency or have necessaries to subsist." His situation, he added, "is really the case with many of the inhabitants of this city."

The Seven Years' War paved the way for a far larger conflict in the next generation. The legislative assemblies, for example, which had been flexing their muscles at the expense of the governors in earlier decades, accelerated their bid for political power. During wartime, knowing that their governors must obtain military appropriations, they extracted concessions as the price for raising revenues. The war also trained a new group of military and political leaders. In carrying out military operations on a scale unknown in the colonies and in shouldering heavier political responsibilities, men such as George Washington, Samuel Adams, Benjamin Franklin, Patrick Henry, and

Christopher Gadsden acquired the experience that would serve them well in the future.

In spite of severe costs, the Seven Years' War left many colonists buoyant. New Englanders rejoiced at the final victory over the "Papist enemy of the North." Frontiersmen, fur traders, and land speculators also celebrated the French withdrawal, for the West now appeared open for exploitation. The colonists also felt a new sense of identity after the war. A French diplomat predicted at the war's end that the colonists would soon discover "that they stand no longer in need of your protection. You will call on them to contribute towards supporting the burden which they have helped to bring on you; they will answer you by shaking off all dependence."

The British thought such predictions laughable. Many royal officers who had fought alongside the Americans had little but contempt for the "martial virtue" of the colonists. "He could take a thousand grenadiers to America," boasted one officer, "and geld all the males, partly by force and partly by a little coaxing."

The Crisis with Britain

At the end of the Seven Years' War, George Grenville became the chief minister of the 25-year-old king, George III. He inherited a national debt that had billowed from £75 million to £145 million. Grenville proposed new taxes in America, asking the colonists to bear their share of running the empire. His particular concern was financing the 10,000 British regulars left in North America after 1763 to police French-speaking Canada and the Native Americans—and to remind

unruly Americans that they were still subjects. In so doing, he opened a rift between Britain and its colonies that in a dozen years would ripen into revolution.

Sugar, Currency, and Stamps

In 1764, Grenville pushed through Parliament several bills that in combination pressed hard on colonial economies. First came the Revenue Act (or Sugar Act) of 1764. While reducing the tax on imported French molasses from six to three pence per gallon, it added various colonial products to the list of commodities that could be sent only to England. It also required American shippers to post bonds guaranteeing observance of the trade regulations before loading their cargoes. Finally, it strengthened the vice-admiralty courts to prosecute violators of the trade acts.

Many colonial legislatures grumbled about the Sugar Act because a strictly enforced duty of three pence per gallon on molasses pinched more than the loosely enforced six-pence duty. New York objected that any tax by Parliament to raise revenue (rather than to control trade) violated the rights of overseas subjects who were unrepresented in Parliament.

Next came the Currency Act. In 1751, Parliament had forbidden the New England colonies to issue paper money as legal tender, and now it extended that prohibition to all the colonies. In a colonial economy chronically short of hard cash, this measure constricted trade.

The move to tighten up the machinery of empire surprised the colonists because many of the new regulations came from Parliament. For generations, colonists had viewed Parliament as a bastion of English liberty. Now Parliament began to seem like a violator of colonial rights. Colonial leaders were uncertain about

Benjamin Franklin in London

In 1774, Benjamin Franklin, shown standing silently in this oil painting, stood before members of the English Parliament in London to receive a dressing down in the "Cockpit," named for the cockfights staged there in the day of Henry VIII. Franklin was accused of releasing copies of letters from Governor Thomas Hutchinson of Massachusetts to British officials that would intensify the friction between Britain and its American colonies.

(Christian Schussele, *Benjamin Franklin Appearing Before the Privy Council,* 1867. © Huntington Library/SuperStock)

where Parliament's authority began and ended. The colonists had always implicitly accepted parliamentary power overseas because it was easier to evade distasteful trade regulations than to contest this power. But the exact limits of that authority were vague.

After Parliament passed the Sugar Act in 1764, Grenville announced his intention to extend to America the stamp duties—already imposed in Britain and Ireland—on every newspaper, pamphlet, almanac, legal document, liquor license, college diploma, pack of playing cards, and pair of dice. He gave the colonies a year to suggest alternative ways of raising revenue. The colonies objected, but none provided another plan. Knowing that colonial property taxes were comparatively slight, Grenville dismissed the petitions that poured in from the colonies and drove the bill through Parliament. The Stamp Act became effective in November 1765.

Colonial reaction ranged from disgruntled submission to mass defiance. The breadth of the reaction shocked the British government—and many Americans as well. Lieutenant Governor Hutchinson of Massachusetts believed that "there is not a family between Canada and Pensacola that has not heard the name of the Stamp Act and but very few . . . but what have some formidable apprehensions of it." In many cases, resistance involved not only discontent over tightening of the screws on the colonies but also internal resentments born out of local events. Especially in the cities, the defiance of authority and destruction of property by people from the middle and lower ranks redefined the dynamics of politics, setting the stage for a 10-year internal struggle for control among the various social elements alarmed by the new policies.

Stamp Act Riots

In late 1764, Virginia's House of Burgesses became the first legislature to react to the news of the Stamp Act. It strenuously objected to the proposed stamp tax, citing economic hardship. Virginians were already worried by a severe decline in tobacco prices and heavy war-related taxes, which mired most planters in debt. Led by 29-year-old Patrick Henry, a fiery lawyer newly elected from a frontier county, the House of Burgesses in May 1765 debated seven strongly worded resolutions. Old-guard burgesses regarded some of them as treasonable. The legislature finally adopted the four more moderate resolves, including one proclaiming that it was their "inherent" right to be taxed only by their own consent.

Many burgesses had left for home before Henry introduced his resolutions, so less than a quarter of Virginia's legislators voted for the four moderate resolves. But within a month, newspapers of other colonies published all seven resolutions, which included a defiant assertion that Virginians did not have to pay externally imposed taxes and branded as an "enemy to this, his Majesty's colony" anyone who denied Virginia's exclusive right to tax itself. Henry and the aggressive young burgesses had hurled words of defiance at Parliament for other colonies to reflect on and match.

Governor Francis Bernard of Massachusetts called the Virginia resolves an "alarm bell for the disaffected." Events in Boston in August 1765 amply confirmed his view. On August 14, Bostonians hung a rag-dressed effigy of stamp distributor Andrew Oliver from an elm tree in the south end of town. When the sheriff tried to remove it at the order of Lieutenant Governor Hutchinson, Oliver's brother-in-law, a hostile crowd intervened. In the evening, workingmen cut down Oliver's effigy, shouting boisterously as they carried it through the streets, leveled his new brick office, and reduced his luxurious mansion to a shambles. The stamp distributor promptly asked to be relieved of his commission. Twelve days later, MacIntosh led the crowd again in an all-night bout of destruction of the handsomely appointed homes of two British officials and Hutchinson, a haughty man, who was as unpopular with the common people as his great-great-grandmother, Anne Hutchinson, had been popular. Military men "who have seen towns sacked by the enemy," one observer reported, "declare they never before saw an instance of such fury."

In attacking the property of men associated with the stamp tax, the Boston crowd demonstrated not only its opposition to parliamentary policy but also its resentment of a local elite. Breaking away from the leaders of the anti-Stamp party, the "rage-intoxicated rabble" punished Hutchinson as a symbol of the uncaring elite. Characterized by young lawyer John Adams as "very ambitious and avaricious," Hutchinson was, in the popular view, chief among the "mean mercenary hirelings" of the British. The more cautious political leaders now realized that they would have to struggle to regain control of the protest movement.

Leading the resistance in Boston and elsewhere were groups calling themselves the Sons of Liberty, composed mostly of artisans, shopkeepers, and ordinary citizens. By late 1765, effigy-burning crowds all over America persuaded stamp distributors to resign. Colonists defied British authority even more directly by forcing most customs officers and court officials to open the ports and courts for business after November 1 without using the hated stamps required after that date. This often took months of pressure and sometimes mob action, but the Sons of Liberty, often led by new faces in local politics, got their way by going outside the law.

In March 1766, Parliament debated the furious reaction to the Stamp Act. Lobbied by many merchant friends of the Americans, Parliament voted to repeal it, bowing to expediency. Simultaneously it passed the

STEPS ON THE ROAD TO REVOLUTION

1763	Treaty of Paris ends Seven Years' War between England and France; France cedes Canada to England.
	Proclamation of 1763 forbids white settlement west of Appalachian Mountains.
1764	Sugar Act sets higher duties on imported sugar and lower duties on molasses and enlarges the power of vice-admiralty courts.
	Currency Act prohibits issuance of paper money by colonies.
1765	Stamp Act requires revenue-raising stamps purchased from British-appointed stamp distributors on printed documents.
	Stamp Act Congress meets in New York.
	Quartering Act requires colonies to furnish British troops with housing and certain provisions.
	Sons of Liberty formed in New York City and thereafter in many towns.
1766	Declaratory Act asserts Parliament's sovereignty over the colonies after repealing Stamp Act.
	Rent riots by New York tenant farmers.
1767	Townshend Revenue Acts impose duties on tea, glass, paper, paints, and other items.
	South Carolina Regulators organize in backcountry.
1768	British troops sent to Boston.
1770	British troops kill four and wound eight American civilians in Boston Massacre.
1771	Battle of Alamance pits frontier North Carolina Regulators against eastern militia led by royal governor.
1772	British schooner *Gaspee* burned in Rhode Island.
	Committee of Correspondence formed in Boston and thereafter in other cities.
1773	Tea Act reduces duty on tea but gives East India Company right to sell directly to Americans.
	Boston Tea Party dumps £10,000 of East India Company tea into Boston harbor.
1774	Coercive Acts close port of Boston, restrict provincial and town governments in Massachusetts, and send additional troops to Boston.
	Québec Act attaches trans-Appalachian interior north of Ohio River to government of Quebec.
	First Continental Congress meets and forms Continental Association to boycott British imports.
1775	Battles of Lexington and Concord cause 95 American and 273 British casualties; Americans take Fort Ticonderoga.
	Second Continental Congress meets and assumes many powers of an independent government.
	Dunmore's Proclamation in Virginia promises freedom to slaves and indentured servants fleeing to British ranks.
	Prohibitory Act embargoes American goods.
	George III proclaims Americans in open rebellion.
1776	Thomas Paine publishes *Common Sense*.
	British troops evacuate Boston.
	Declaration of Independence.

Declaratory Act, which asserted Parliament's power to enact laws for the colonies in "all cases whatsoever."

The crisis had passed, yet nothing was solved. The Stamp Act, one New England clergyman foresaw, "diffused a disgust through the colonies and laid the basis of an alienation which will never be healed." Stamp Act resisters had politicized their communities as never before. Scribbled John Adams in his diary: "The people have become more attentive to their liberties, . . . and more determined to defend them. . . . Our presses have groaned, our pulpits have thundered, our legislatures have resolved, our towns have voted; the crown officers have everywhere trembled, and all their little tools and creatures been afraid to speak and ashamed to be seen."

Gathering Storm Clouds

Ministerial instability in England hampered the quest for a coherent, workable American policy. George III chose ministers who commanded little respect in Parliament, which led to strife between Parliament and the king's chief ministers, and a generally chaotic political situation did nothing to aid the king's effort to overhaul the empire's administration.

To manage the colonies more effectively, the Pitt-Grafton ministry appointed by the king in 1767 obtained new laws to reorganize the customs service, establish a secretary of state for American affairs, and install in the port cities three new vice-admiralty courts. Still hard-pressed for revenue—for at home the government faced severe unemployment, tax protests, and riots over the high price of grain—the ministry pushed through Parliament the relatively small Townshend duties on paper, lead, painters' colors, and tea. A final law suspended New York's assembly until that body ceased defying the Quartering Act of 1765, which required public funds for support of British troops garrisoned in the colony since the end of the Seven Years' War. New York knuckled under in order to save its legislature.

Massachusetts led the colonial protests against the Townshend Acts. Its House of Representatives sent a circular letter written by Samuel Adams to each colony objecting to the new Townshend duties because they would be used to underwrite salaries for royal officials in America. Under instructions from England, Governor Bernard dissolved the legislature after it refused to rescind the circular letter. "The Americans have made a discovery," declared Edmund Burke before Parliament, "that we mean to oppress them; we have made a discovery that they intend to raise a rebellion. We do not know how to advance; they do not know how to retreat."

Showing more restraint than they had in resisting the Stamp Act, most colonists only grumbled and petitioned. But Bostonians protested stridently. In the summer of 1768, after customs officials seized a sloop owned by John Hancock for a violation of the trade regulations, an angry crowd mobbed them. For months the officials took refuge on a British warship in Boston harbor. Newspapers warned of new measures designed to "suck the life blood" from the people and predicted that troops would be sent to "dragoon us into passive obedience." To many, the belief grew that the British were plotting "designs for destroying our constitutional liberties."

Troops indeed came. The attack on the customs officials convinced the authorities that the Bostonians were uniquely insubordinate. The ministry dispatched two regiments from England and two more from Nova Scotia, meant to make an example of the Bostonians. Cries went up against maintaining standing armies in peacetime, but radical Bostonians who proposed force to prevent the troops from landing got little support from delegates called to a special provincial convention. On October 1, 1768, red-coated troops marched into Boston without resistance.

Thereafter, the colonists' main tactic of protest against the Townshend Acts became economic boycott. First in Boston and then in New York and Philadelphia, merchants and consumers adopted nonimportation and nonconsumption agreements, pledging neither to import nor to use British goods. These measures promised to bring the politically influential English merchants to their aid, for half of British shipping was engaged in commerce with the colonies, and one-quarter of all English exports were consumed there. When the southern colonies also adopted nonimportation agreements in 1768, it represented a new step toward intercolonial union.

Many colonial merchants, however, especially those with official connections, refused to be bound by nonimportation agreements. They had to be persuaded otherwise by street brigades, usually composed of artisans for whom nonimportation was a boon to home manufacturing. Crowd action welled up again in the seaports, as patriot bands attacked the homes and warehouses of offending merchants and "rescued" incoming contraband goods seized by customs officials.

Britain's attempts to discipline its American colonies and oblige them to share the costs of governing an empire lay in shambles by the end of the 1760s. Using troops to restore order undermined the very respect needed for colonial acceptance of parliamentary authority. Newspapers denounced new extensions of British control. Colonial governors quarreled with their legislatures. Customs officials met with determined opposition and were widely accused of arbitrary actions and excessive zeal in enforcing the Navigation Acts. The Townshend duties had failed miserably, yielding less than £21,000 by 1770 while costing British business £700,000 through the colonial nonimportation movement.

On March 5, 1770, Parliament repealed all the Townshend duties except the one on tea (which the new minister of state, Lord North, explained was retained "as a mark of the supremacy of Parliament and an efficient declaration of their right to govern the colonies"). On that same evening in Boston, British troops fired on an unruly crowd of heckling citizens. When the smoke cleared, five bloody bodies, including that of Ebenezer MacIntosh's brother-in-law, stained the snow-covered street. Bowing to furious popular reaction, Thomas Hutchinson, recently appointed governor, ordered the British troops out of town and arrested the commanding officer and the soldiers involved. They were later acquitted, with two young patriot lawyers, John Adams and Josiah Quincy, Jr., providing a brilliant defense of the soldiers.

In spite of the potential of the "Boston Massacre" for galvanizing the colonies into further resistance, opposition to British policies, including boycotts, subsided in 1770. Popular leaders such as Samuel Adams in Boston and Alexander McDougall in New York, who had made names for themselves as the standard-bearers of American liberty, had few issues left, especially when the economic depression that had helped sow discontent ended. Yet the fires of revolution had not been extinguished but merely dampened.

The Growing Rift

In June 1772, Britain created a new furor by announcing that it, rather than the provincial legislature, would henceforth pay the salaries of the royal governor and superior court judges in Massachusetts. Even though the measure saved the colony money, it looked like a scheme to impose a despotic government and thus undermine a right set forth in the colony's charter. Judges paid from London presumably would obey London.

Boston's town meeting protested loudly and created a Committee of Correspondence to win other colonies' sympathy. Crown supporters called the committee "the

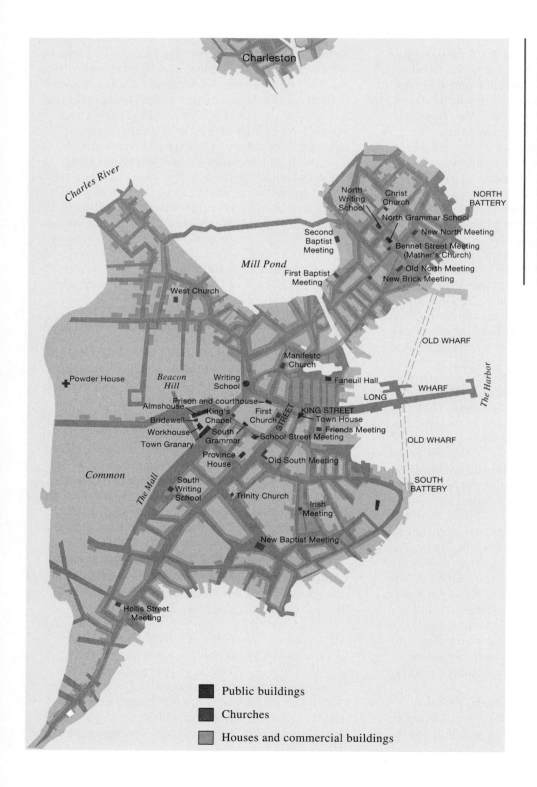

City Plan of Boston, 1772

Boston's many churches became important political meeting places in the tumultuous decade leading to the outbreak of war in 1775. Old South Meeting House, holding as many as 5,000 people, became the gathering place of "body of the people." Faneuil Hall was the usual site of town meetings, but when crowds exceeded its capacity of 1,200, meetings were adjourned and reconvened at Old South Meeting House. What does the fact that churches were the largest buildings tell you about colonial society?

Public buildings

Churches

Houses and commercial buildings

foulest, subtlest, and most venomous serpent ever issued from the egg of sedition." By the end of 1772, another 80 towns in Massachusetts had created committees. In the next year, all but three colonies established Committees of Correspondence in their legislatures.

Samuel Adams was by now the leader of the Boston radicals, for the influence of laboring men like Ebenezer MacIntosh had declined. Adams was an experienced caucus politicker and a skilled political journalist. He organized the working ranks through the taverns, clubs, and volunteer fire companies and secured the support of wealthy merchants such as John Hancock, whose ample purse financed patriotic celebrations and feasts that kept politics on everyone's mind and helped build interclass bridges. In England, the Harvard-educated Adams became known as one of the most dangerous firebrands in America.

In 1772, Rhode Islanders gave Adams a new issue. The commander of the royal ship *Gaspee* was roundly hated for hounding the fishermen and small traders of Narragansett Bay. When his ship ran aground while pursuing a suspected smuggler, Rhode Islanders burned the stranded vessel to the waterline. A Rhode Island court then convicted the *Gaspee*'s captain of illegally seizing what he was convinced was smuggled sugar and rum. London reacted with cries of high treason. Investigators found the lips of Rhode Islanders sealed. The event was tailor-made for Samuel Adams, who used it to "awaken the American colonies, which have been too long dozing upon the brink of ruin."

The final plunge into revolution began when Parliament passed the Tea Act in early 1773, allowing the practically bankrupt East India Company to ship its tea directly to North America with the colonists paying only a small tax. Americans would get inexpensive tea, the Crown a modest revenue, and the East India Company a new lease on life. American merchants who competed with the East India Company bitterly denounced the monopoly, warning that other monopolies would follow. The colonists also objected that the government was shrewdly trying to gain acceptance of Parliament's taxing power. As Americans drank the taxed tea, they would also be swallowing the right to tax them. Showing that their principles were not entirely in their pocketbooks, Americans staged mass meetings that soon forced the resignation of East India Company's agents, and vowed to stop the obnoxious tea at the water's edge.

Governor Hutchinson of Massachusetts brought the tea crisis to a climax, convinced that to yield again to popular pressure would forever cripple British sovereignty in America. The popular party led by Samuel Adams hoped to prove that colonists were not yet prepared for the "yoke of slavery" by sending the tea to England. When Hutchinson refused, 5,000 Bostonians packed Old South Meeting House on December 16, 1773, noisily passing resolutions urging the governor to grant the tea ships clearance papers to return to England with their cargoes. But Hutchinson was not swayed.

At nightfall, a band of Bostonians dressed as Native Americans boarded the tea ships, broke open the chests of tea, and flung £10,000 worth of the East India Company's property into Boston harbor. George Hewes, a 31-year-old shoemaker, recalled how he had garbed himself as a Mohawk, blackened "face and hands with coal dust in the shop of a blacksmith," and joined men of all ranks in marching stealthily to the wharves to do their work. In time, this event would be remembered as the Boston Tea Party.

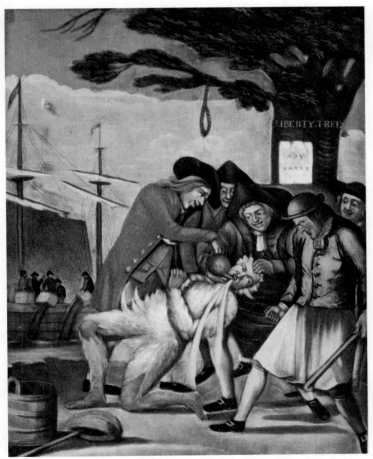

The Bostonians Paying the Excise-Man

Public sentiment against the importation of tea and other British goods often found expression in a coat of tar and feathers applied to the bare skin of the offending importer. Note the symbols in *The Bostonians Paying the Excise-Man*: the Liberty Tree with a hangman's noose and the overturned copy of the Stamp Act. What is happening in the background?

(Library of Congress)

Now the die was cast. Lord North, the king's chief minister, argued that the dispute was no longer about taxes but about whether Britain had any authority over the colonies. George III put it succinctly: "We must master them or totally leave them to themselves and treat them as aliens."

Thoroughly aroused, Parliament passed the Coercive Acts, stern laws that Bostonians promptly labeled the "Intolerable Acts." The acts closed the port of Boston to all shipping until the colony paid for the destroyed tea and barred local courts from trying British soldiers and officials for acts committed while suppressing civil disturbances. To hamstring the colony's belligerent political assemblies, Parliament amended the Massachusetts charter to transform the council from an upper legislative chamber, elected by the lower house, to a body appointed by the governor. This amendment stripped the council of its veto power over the governor's decisions.

The act also struck at local government by authorizing the governor to prohibit all town meetings except for one annual meeting to elect local officers of government. Finally, General Thomas Gage, commander in chief of British forces in America, replaced Thomas Hutchinson as governor. "This is the day, then," declared Edmund Burke in the House of Commons, "that you wish to go to war with all America, in order to conciliate that country to this."

Lord North's plan to strangle Massachusetts into submission proved popular in England. Earlier, the colonies had gained supporters in Parliament for their resistance to what many regarded as attacks on their fundamental privileges. Now this support evaporated. When the Intolerable Acts arrived in May 1774, Boston's town meeting urged all the colonies to ban trade with Britain. While this proposal met with faint support, a second call, for a meeting in Philadelphia of delegates from all colonies, received a better response. Called the Continental Congress, it began to transform a 10-year debate conducted by separate colonies into a unified American cause.

In September 1774, 55 delegates from all the colonies except Georgia converged on Carpenters' Hall in Philadelphia. The discussions centered not on how to prepare for a war that many sensed was coming but on how to resolve sectional differences that most delegates feared were irreconcilable. Overcoming prejudices was as important as the formal debates. New Englanders were eyed with suspicion especially for their reputed intolerance and self-interest. "We have numberless prejudices to remove here," wrote John Adams from Philadelphia. "We have been obliged to keep ourselves out of sight, and to feel pulses, and to sound the depths; to insinuate our sentiments, designs, and desires by means of other persons, sometimes of one province, and sometimes of another."

Portrait of a Participant in the Boston Tea Party
This portrait of George Robert Twelve Hewes was painted in 1835 when the last survivor of the Boston Tea Party was called "The Centenarian," though he was 93 years old. Why would Benjamin Bussey Thatcher's biography of this poor shoemaker published in that year, have been of interest to readers?

(Joseph G. Cole, *The Centenarian*, 1835: Portrait of George Robert Twelve Hewes. Courtesy of The Bostonian Society/Old State House)

The Continental Congress was by no means a unified body. Some delegates, led by cousins Samuel and John Adams from Massachusetts and Richard Henry Lee and Patrick Henry of Virginia, argued for outright resistance to Parliament's Coercive Acts. Moderate delegates from the middle colonies, led by Joseph Galloway of Pennsylvania and James Duane of New York, urged restraint and further attempts at reconciliation. After weeks of debate, the delegates agreed to a restrained Declaration of Rights and Resolves, which attempted to define American grievances and justify the colonists' defiance of English policies and laws by appealing to the "immutable laws of nature, the principles of the English constitution, and the several [colonial] charters and compacts." Congress had a more concrete plan of resistance. If Parliament did not rescind the Intolerable Acts by December 1, 1774, all imports and exports between the colonies and Great Britain, Ireland, and the British West Indies would be banned. To keep reluctant southern colonies in the

to obey popularly authorized boycotts, levied taxes, operated the courts, and obstructed customs officials. By the end of 1774, all but three colonies had defied their own charters by appointing provincial assemblies without royal authority. In the next year, this independently created power became evident when trade with Britain practically ceased.

The Ideology of Revolutionary Republicanism

In the tumultuous years between 1763 and 1774, the colonists had been expressing many reactions to the crisis with Britain. Mostly these took the form of newspaper articles and pamphlets written by educated lawyers, clergymen, merchants, and planters. But the middling and lower ranks of society had also expressed themselves in printed broadsides, appeals in the newspapers, and even ideologically laden popular rituals such as tarring and feathering and burning in effigy. Gradually, the colonists pieced together a political ideology, borrowed partly from English political thought, partly from the theories of the Enlightenment, and partly from their own experiences. Historians call this new ideology "revolutionary republicanism," but no single coherent ideology united all the colonists' varied interests and experiences.

A Plot Against Liberty

Many American colonists agreed with earlier English Whig writers who charged that corrupt and power-hungry men were slowly extinguishing the lamp of liberty in Britain. The so-called "country" party represented by these Whig pamphleteers proclaimed itself the guardian of the true principles of the English constitution and opposed the "court" party—the king and his appointees. From this perspective, every ministerial policy and parliamentary act in the decade after the Stamp Act appeared as a subversion of customary liberties. Most Americans regarded resistance to such blows against liberty as wholly justified.

The belief that Britain was carrying out "a deep-laid and desperate plan of imperial despotism . . . for the extinction of all civil liberty," as the Boston town meeting expressed it in 1770, spread rapidly in the next few years. By 1774, John Adams was writing of the "conspiracy against the public liberty [that] was first regularly formed and begun to be executed in 1763 and 1764." From London, America's favorite writer, Benjamin Franklin, described the "extreme corruption prevalent among all orders of men in this old rotten state." Among many Americans, especially merchants, the attack on constitutional rights blended closely with

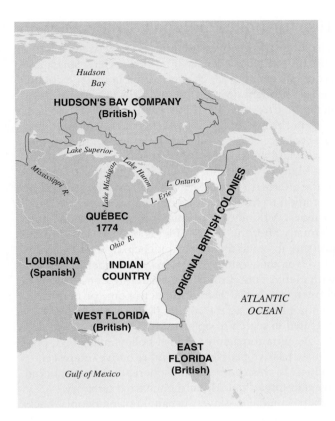

The Québec Act of 1774

The Québec Act attached the trans-Appalachian interior north of the Ohio River to the British government in Québec, and guaranteed the right of French Catholics to practice their religion freely. Why would this not have been especially offensive to New Englanders?

fold, some exceptions were made for the export of staple commodities.

By the time the Congress adjourned in late October, leaders from different colonies had transformed Boston's cause into a national movement. "Government is dissolved [and] we are in a state of nature," Patrick Henry argued dramatically. "The distinctions between Virginians, Pennsylvanians, New Yorkers, and New Englanders are no more. I am not a Virginian, but an American." Many other delegates were a long way from his conclusion; still the Congress agreed to reconvene in May 1775.

When the Second Continental Congress met, the fabric of government was badly torn in most colonies. Illegal revolutionary committees, conventions, and congresses were replacing legal governing bodies. Assuming authority in defiance of royal governors, who suspended truculent legislatures in many colonies, they often operated on instructions from mass meetings where everyone, not just those entitled to vote, gave voice. These extralegal bodies created and armed militia units, bullied merchants and shopkeepers refusing the threats to their economic interests contained in the tough new trade policies. Merchants saw a coordinated attack on their "lives, liberties, and property." If a man was not secure in his property, he could not be secure in his citizenship, for it was property that gave a man the independence to shape his identity.

Revitalizing American Society

The continuing crisis over the imperial relationship by itself inspired many colonists to resist impending tyranny. But for others, the revolutionary mentality was also fed by a belief that an opportunity was at hand to revitalize American society. They believed that the growing commercial connections with a decadent and corrupt Britain had injected poison into the American bloodstream. They worried about the luxury and vice they saw around them and came to believe that resistance would return American society to a state of civic virtue, spartan living, and godly purpose.

The colonial protest movement got much of its high-toned moralism from its fervent supporters among the colonial clergy. The concern for social improvement was especially strong in New England, where so secular a man as John Adams groaned at the "universal spirit of debauchery, dissipation, luxury, effeminacy and gaming." As in most revolutionary movements, talk of moral regeneration, of a society-wide rebirth through battle against a corrupt enemy, ennobled the cause, inspiring people in areas that had been stirred a generation before by the Great Awakening.

The Turmoil of a Rebellious People

The long struggle over colonial rights between 1763 and 1774 did not occur in a unified society. Social and economic change, which accelerated in the late colonial period, brought deep unrest and calls for reform from many quarters. By the 1760s, many colonists had lost faith in the internal social systems of the colonies, just as allegiance to England and to the British mercantile system had worn thin.

Many of the colonists who struggled for security in the aftermath of the Seven Years' War hoped that migration to frontier land would improve their fortunes. A flood of new immigrants from Ireland and Germany after the Treaty of Paris in 1763 added to the pressure to reach the trans-Appalachian river valleys. However, the western option involved much violence with Native American tribes. Therefore, most colonists chose to work out their destinies at home or in other communities along the coastal plain to which they migrated in search of opportunity.

As agitation against British policy intensified, previously passive people took a more active interest in politics. In this charged atmosphere, the constitutional struggle spread quickly into uncharted territory. Groups emerged—slaves, urban laboring people, back-country farmers, evangelicals, women—whose enunciated goals were sometimes only loosely connected to the struggle over policy. The stridency and potential power of these groups frightened many in the upper class. Losing control of the protests they had initially led, many would abandon the resistance movement.

Tarring and Feathering a Customs Official

In January 1774, after British customs officer John Malcolm bullied a small boy and then beat George Robert Twelve Hewes (who had intervened), a Boston crowd tarred and feathered Malcolm. As shown here, Bostonians force Malcolm into a cart, which was dragged through town to the hoots of the crowd. What is the origin of tarring and feathering?

(CORBIS)

Recovering the Past

POETRY

Poetry is one of the most ancient and universal of the arts. Making its effect by the rhythmic sound and imagery of its language, poetry often expresses romantic love, grief, and responses to nature. But other kinds of poetry interest historians: reflections of human experience, often expressed with deep emotion, and political verses, often written to serve propagandistic goals. For generations, American historians have drawn on poetry to recapture feelings, ideas, and group experiences. For example, Native American creation myths have often taken poetic form; the poems of Anne Bradstreet and Michael Wigglesworth in seventeenth-century Massachusetts tell us much about Puritan mentality and attitudes on topics running from marriage to death; the poetry of the American Transcendentalists tells us about nineteenth-century notions of heroism and who was admired; and Langston Hughes, Arna Bontemps, and other poets of the Harlem Renaissance have expressed through poetry the bittersweet nature of the African American experience. All this material is grist for the historian's mill.

The revolutionary generation created poetry of great interest to historians. The newspapers of several port cities published weekly "Poet's Corner" satires, drinking songs, and versed commentary on the issues of the day. Verse was widely used to provoke public discussion; in 1767 poets prompted the boycott of British goods to obtain Parliament's reversal of the hated Townshend duties.

A year later, Philadelphia's John Dickinson composed a "Liberty Song" that became the first set of verses learned in all the colonies. Boston's Sons of Liberty began using this "Liberty Song" in annual ceremonies celebrating their resistance to the Stamp Act. Soon the verses were printed in newspapers throughout the colonies and were used widely in public gatherings. Set to music and easily learned, the verses cultivated anti-British feeling and a sense of the need for intercolonial cooperation:

> *COME join Hand in Hand, brave AMERICANS all,*
> *And rouse your bold Hearts at fair LIBERTY'S Call;*
> *No tyrannous Acts shall suppress your just Claim,*
> *Or stain with Dishonor America's Name.*

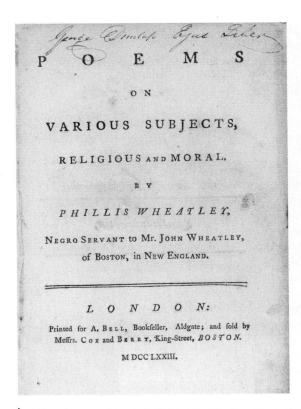

Wheatley worshiped at Old South Meeting House, which held some 5,000 people. In the 1770s, people frequently gathered there for political rallies and deliberations. This partly explains Wheatley's growing interest in the political battles raging in Boston. Wheatley's patroness in England specifically requested a drawing of Phillis for the frontispiece of this volume of poetry. Scipio Moorhead, slave of Boston's Presbyterian minister, did the drawing. Wheatley's mistress, Susannah Wheatley, called it a fine likeness.

(From the copy in the Rare Book Collection, The University of North Carolina at Chapel Hill)

Of all the poets of the revolutionary era, none has fascinated today's historians more than Phillis Wheatley, a young slave in Boston who wrote her first poem at age 14 in 1767. Within six years, she became North America's first published black poet. Boston's "Ethiopian poetess" had been brought from Africa to Boston at age 7 and purchased by a prospering tailor named John Wheatley. Soon her master and his wife discovered that she was a prodigy. After learning English so well in 16 months that she could read the most difficult passages of the Bible, she soon showed an uncanny gift for writing. Much of her writing was inspired by deep religious feelings, but she soon was caught up in the dramatic events in Boston that were bringing revolution closer and closer. In her poem entitled "To the King's Most Excellent Majesty," she saluted King George III for repealing the Stamp Act; in "On the Death of Mr. Snider [Seider], Murder'd by Richardson," she lambasted the British customs officer who murdered a teenage member of a crowd protesting the British soldiers who occupied Boston in 1768.

Wheatley was anything but radical. She had so thoroughly imbibed Christianity from her master and mistress that she wrote in one of her first poems that "Twas mercy brought me from my *Pagan* land." Many times she used poetry to implore slaves to "fly to Christ." But by 1772, she was inserting a muffled plea for an end of slavery in her odes to American rights and American resistance to British policies.

That Wheatley's poems were published in London in 1773 is remarkable. Women were not supposed to write publicly in the eighteenth century, and certainly not black women. Nonetheless, her master, supported by Boston friends and proud of his slave prodigy, shipped a sheaf of poems to a bookseller in England, who obtained the support of the Countess of Huntingdon for publishing them. They appeared under the title *Poems on Various Subjects, Religious and Moral.* Even more remarkable was that Wheatley, only 20 years old, took a ship to London to see her book come off the press. Her master and mistress financed the trip, hoping that sea air would clear her clogged lungs. There she was introduced to important reformers and public dignitaries, received a copy of Milton's *Paradise Lost* from the lord mayor of London, and met with Benjamin Franklin. She returned to Boston in 1774.

Reflecting on the Past Read the two poems that follow: Wheatley's "On the Death of Mr. Snider [Seider], Murder'd by Richardson," composed in 1770, and her poem addressed to the king's minister in charge of colonial affairs, penned two years later. As modern readers, you may find the poetry stilted, but Wheatley's style was modeled on poetic conventions of the eighteenth century. What change can you discern in Wheatley's political consciousness between 1770 and 1772? Do you consider her poem on Seider's murder by a British customs officer propagandistic? How does she relate the plight of enslaved Africans to the American colonists' struggle? More generally, how effective do you think poetry is in arousing sentiment and mobilizing political energy? Can you think of verse serving as lyrics in popular protest music today?

On the Death of Mr. Snider, Murder'd by Richardson (1770)

In heaven's eternal court it was decreed
How the first martyr for the cause should bleed
To clear the country of the hated brood
We whet his courage for the common good.
Long hid before, a vile infernal here
Prevents Achilles in his mid career
Wherev'r this fury darts his Poisonous breath
All are endanger'd to the shafts of death

To the Right Honourable William, Earl of Dartmouth, His Majesty's Principal Secretary of State for North America (1772)

HAIL, happy day, when, smiling like the morn,
Fair Freedom *rose* New-England *to adorn:*
The northern clime beneath her genial ray,
Dartmouth, congratulates thy blissful sway:
Elate with hope her race no longer mourns,
Each soul expands, each grateful bosom burns,
While in thine hand with pleasure we behold
The silken reigns, and Freedom's *charms unfold.*
No more, America, *in mournful strain*
Of wrongs, and grievance unredress'd complain,
No longer shalt thou dread the iron chain,
Which wanton Tyranny with lawless hand
Had made, and with it meant t' enslave the land.
Should you, my lord, while you peruse my song,
Wonder from whence my love of Freedom *sprung,*
Whence flow these wishes for the common good,
By feeling hearts alone best understood,
I, young in life, by seeming cruel fate
Was snatch'd from Afric's *fancy'd happy seat:*
What pangs excruciating must molest,
What sorrows labour in my parent's breast?
Steel'd was that soul and by no misery mov'd
That from a father seiz'd his babe belov'd:
Such, such my case. And can I then but pray
Others may never feel tyrannic sway? ▪

Urban People

Although the cities contained only about 5 percent of the colonial population, they were the core of revolutionary agitation. As centers of communications, government, and commerce, they led the way in protesting English policy, and they soon contained the most politicized inhabitants in America. Local politics could be rapidly transformed as the struggle against Britain meshed with calls for internal reform.

Philadelphia offers a good example of popular empowerment. Before the Seven Years' War, artisans had usually acquiesced to local leadership by merchant and lawyer politicos. But economic difficulties in the 1760s and 1770s led them to band together within their craft and community. Artisans played a central role in forging and enforcing a nonimportation agreement in 1768. They called public meetings, published newspaper appeals, organized secondary boycotts against foot-dragging merchants, and tarred and feathered their opponents. Cautious merchants complained that mere artisans had "no right to give their sentiments respecting an importation" and called the craftsmen a "rabble." But artisans, casting off their customary deference, forged ahead. By 1772, they were filling elected municipal positions and insisting on their right to participate equally with their social superiors in nominating assemblymen and other important officeholders. They also began lobbying for reform laws, calling for elected representatives to be more accountable to their constituents. Genteel Philadelphians muttered, "It is time the tradesmen were checked—they ought not to intermeddle in state affairs—they will become too powerful."

By 1774, the meddling of the Philadelphia working class in state affairs reached a bold new stage—de facto assumption of governmental powers by committees created by the people at large. Artisans had first assumed such extralegal authority in policing the nonimportation agreement in 1769. Now, responding to the Intolerable Acts, they proposed a radical slate of candidates for a committee to enforce a new economic boycott. Their ticket drubbed one nominated by conservative merchants.

The political support of the new radical leaders centered in the 31 companies of the Philadelphia militia, composed mostly of laboring men, and in the extralegal committees now controlling the city's economic life. Their leadership helped overcome the conservatism of the regularly elected Pennsylvania legislature, which was resisting the movement of the Continental Congress toward independence. The new radical leaders also demanded internal reforms: curbing the accumulation of wealth by "our great merchants . . . at the expense of the people"; abolishing the property requirement for voting; allowing militiamen to elect their officers; and imposing stiff fines, to be used for the support of the families of poor militiamen, on men who refused militia service.

Philadelphia's radicals never controlled the city. They always jostled for position with prosperous artisans and shopkeepers of more moderate views and with cautious lawyers and merchants. But mobilization among artisans, laborers, and mariners, in other cities as well as Philadelphia, became part of the chain of events that led toward independence. Whereas most of the patriot elite fought only to change imperial policy, the people of the cities also struggled for internal reforms and raised notions of how an independent American society might be reorganized.

Patriot Women

Colonial women also played a vital role in the movement toward revolution, and they drew on revolutionary arguments to define their own goals. They signed nonimportation agreements, harassed noncomplying merchants, and helped organize "fast days," on which communities prayed for deliverance from English oppression. But the women's most important role was to facilitate the boycott of English goods. The success of the nonconsumption pacts depended on substituting homespun cloth for English textiles on which colonists of all classes had always relied. From Georgia to Maine, women and children began spinning yarn and weaving cloth. "Was not every fireside, indeed a theatre of politics?" John Adams remembered after the war. Towns vied patriotically in the manufacture of cotton, linen, and woollen cloth, with the women staging open-air spinning contests to publicize their commitment.

After the Tea Act in 1773, the interjection of politics into the household economy increased as patriotic women boycotted their favorite drink. Newspapers carried recipes for tea substitutes and recommendations for herbal teas. In Wilmington, North Carolina, women paraded solemnly through the town and then made a ritual display of their patriotism by burning their imported tea.

Colonial protests and petitions against arbitrary uses of power changed women's perception of their role. The more male leaders talked about Britain's intentions to "enslave" the Americans and its callous treatment of its colonial subjects, the more American women began to rethink their own domestic situations. The language of protest reminded many American women that they too were badly treated "subjects" of their husbands, who could deal with them cruelly and exercise power over them arbitrarily.

Most American women, still bound by the social conventions of the day, were not ready to occupy such new territory. But the colonial protests had

TO THE
Delaware Pilots.

WE took the Pleasure, some Days since, of kindly admonishing you *to do your Duty*; if perchance you should meet with the *(Tea,)* SHIP POLLY, CAPTAIN AYRES; a THREE DECKER which is hourly expected,

We have now to add, that Matters ripen fast here; and that *much is expected from those Lads who meet with the Tea Ship.*----There is some Talk of A HANDSOME REWARD FOR THE PILOT WHO GIVES THE FIRST GOOD ACCOUNT OF HER.----How that may be, we cannot *for certain* determine: But ALL agree, that TAR and FEATHERS will be his Portion, who pilots her into this Harbour. And we will answer for ourselves, that, whoever is committed to us, as an Offender against the Rights of *America*, will experience the utmost Exertion of our Abilities; as

THE COMMITTEE FOR TARRING AND FEATHERING.

An Exhortation to Action

Not only Bostonians took action against the Tea Act. This Philadelphia broadside from "The Committee for Tarring and Feathering," issued several weeks before the Boston Tea Party, exhorts pilots on the Delaware River to oppose the act. What role does the broadside envision for the pilots?

(Library of Congress)

stirred up new thoughts about what seemed "arbitrary" or "despotic" in their own society. Hence, many agendas for change appeared and with them a new feeling that what had been endured in the past was no longer acceptable.

Protesting Farmers

In most of the agricultural areas of the colonies, where the majority of settlers made their livelihoods, passions over English policies awakened only slowly. After about 1740, farmers had benefited from a sharp rise in the demand for foodstuffs in England, southern Europe, and the West Indies. Rising prices and brisk markets brought a higher standard of living to thousands of rural colonists, especially south of New England. Living far from harping customs officers, impressment gangs, and occupying armies, the colonists of the interior had to be drawn gradually into the resistance movement by their urban cousins. Even in Concord, Massachusetts, only a dozen miles from the center of colonial agitation, townspeople found little to protest until the government closed the port of Boston in 1774.

Still, other parts of rural America seethed with social tension before the war. The dynamics of conflict, shaped by the social development of particular regions, eventually became part of the momentum for revolution. In three western counties of North Carolina and in the Hudson River valley of New York, for example, widespread civil disorder marked the prerevolutionary decades.

For years, the small farmers of western North Carolina had suffered exploitation by corrupt county officials appointed by the governor and a legislature dominated by eastern planter interests. Sheriffs and justices, allied with land speculators and lawyers, seized property when farmers could not pay their taxes and sold it, often at a fraction of its worth, to their cronies. The legislature rejected western petitions for lower

taxes, paper currency, and lower court fees. In the mid-1760s, frustrated at getting no satisfaction from legal forms of protest, the farmers formed associations—the so-called Regulators—that forcibly closed the courts, attacked the property of their enemies, and whipped and publicly humiliated judges and lawyers. When their leaders were arrested, the Regulators stormed the jails and released them.

In 1768 and again in 1771, Governor William Tryon led troops against the Regulators. Bloodshed was averted on the first occasion, but on the second, at the Battle of Alamance, two armies of more than 1,000 fired on each other. At least nine men died on each side before the Regulators fled the field. Six leaders were executed in the ensuing trials. Though the Regulators lost the battle, their protests became part of the larger revolutionary struggle. They railed against the self-interested behavior of a wealthy elite and asserted the necessity for people of humble rank to throw off deference and assume political responsibilities.

Rural insurgency in New York flared up in the 1750s, subsided, and then erupted again in 1766. The conditions under which land was held precipitated the violence. A few wealthy families with enormous landholdings, acquired as virtually free gifts from royal governors, controlled the Hudson River valley. The Van Rensselaer manor, for example, totaled a million acres. Hundreds of tenants with their families paid substantial annual rents for the right to farm on these lands. When tenants resisted rent increases or purchased land from Native Americans who swore that manor lords had extended the boundaries of their manors by fraud, the landlords began evicting them.

As the wealthiest men of the region, the landlords had the power of government, including control of the courts, on their side. Organizing themselves and going outside the law became the tenants' main strategy, as with the Carolina Regulators. By 1766, while New York City was absorbed in the Stamp Act furor, tenants

Timeline

1696	Parliament establishes Board of Trade
1701	Iroquois set policy of neutrality
1702–1713	Queen Anne's War
1713	Peace of Utrecht
1733	Molasses Act
1739–1742	War of Jenkins' Ear
1744–1748	King George's War
1754	Albany conference
1755	Braddock defeated by French and Indian allies
	Acadians expelled from Nova Scotia
1756–1763	Seven Years' War
1759	Wolfe defeats the French at Québec
1759–1761	Cherokee War against the English
1760s	Economic slump
1763	Treaty of Paris ends Seven Years' War
	Proclamation Line limits westward expansion
1764	Sugar and Currency acts
	Pontiac's Rebellion in Ohio valley
1765	Colonists resist Stamp Act
	Virginia House of Burgesses issues Stamp Act resolutions
1766	Declaratory Act
	Tenant rent war in New York
	Slave insurrections in South Carolina
1767	Townshend duties imposed
1768	British troops occupy Boston
1770	"Boston Massacre"
	Townshend duties repealed (except on tea)
1771	North Carolina Regulators defeated
1772	*Gaspee* incident in Rhode Island
1773	Tea Act provokes Boston Tea Party
1774	"Intolerable Acts"
	First Continental Congress meets in Philadelphia

led by William Prendergast began resisting sheriffs who tried to evict them from lands they claimed. The militant tenants threatened landlords with death and broke open jails to rescue friends. British troops from New York were used to break the tenant rebellion. Prendergast was tried and sentenced to be hanged, beheaded, and quartered. Although he was pardoned, the bitterness of the Hudson River tenants endured through the Revolution. Most of them, unlike the Carolina Regulators, fought for the British because their landlords were patriots.

Conclusion
ON THE BRINK OF REVOLUTION

The colonial Americans who lived in the third quarter of the eighteenth century participated in an era of political tension and conflict that changed the lives of nearly everyone. The Seven Years' War removed French and Spanish challengers and nurtured the colonists' sense of separate identity. Yet it left them with difficult economic adjustments, heavy debts, and growing social divisions. The colonists heralded the

Treaty of Paris in 1763 as the dawning of a new era, but it led to a reorganization of Britain's triumphant yet debt-torn empire that had profound repercussions in America.

In the prerevolutionary decade, as the colonies moved from crisis to crisis, a dual disillusionment penetrated ever deeper into the colonial consciousness. Pervasive doubt arose concerning both the colonies' role in the economic life of the empire and the sensitivity of the government in London to the colonists' needs. Meanwhile, the colonists began to perceive British policies—instituted by Parliament, the king, and his advisers—as a systematic attack on the fundamental liberties and natural rights of British colonists in North America.

The fluidity and diversity of colonial society and the differing experiences of Americans during and after the Seven Years' War evoked varying responses to the disruption that accompanied the reorganization of the empire. In the course of resisting imperial policy, many previously inactive colonists, such as the humble shoemaker Ebenezer MacIntosh, entered public life to subvert elite control of political affairs. Often occupying the most radical ground in opposing Britain, they simultaneously challenged the growing concentration of economic and political power in their own communities. What lay ahead was not only war with Britain but protracted arguments about how the American people, if they prevailed in their war for independence, should refashion their society.

QUESTIONS FOR REVIEW AND REFLECTION

1. What roles did Native Americans play in the imperial conflicts of the eighteenth century?
2. How did the Seven Years' War help pave the way for the colonies' break with Britain?
3. The British government pursued policies toward its colonies that it thought reasonable and just in the aftermath of the Treaty of Paris. Why did many colonists see these policies in an entirely different light?
4. What was the contribution of "republican ideology" to the revolutionary movement?
5. What does it mean to say that there were two American revolutions? How were the two related?

CHAPTER 6

A People in Revolution

William Mercer, *Battle of Princeton,* ca. 1786–1790. Because infantry weapons were inaccurate at long distance, lines formed in close proximity, where fire was more deadly and combat intensely personal. What must the sounds of such close-in combat been like?

(William Mercer, *Battle of Princeton,* c. 1786–1790. Atwater Kent Museum of Philadelphia, The Historical Society of Pennsylvania Collection)

American Stories

Struggling for Independence

Among the Americans wounded and captured at the Battle of Bunker Hill in the spring of 1775 was Lieutenant William Scott of Peterborough, New Hampshire. Asked by his captors how he had come to be a rebel, "Long Bill" Scott replied:

> The case was this Sir! I lived in a Country Town; I was a Shoemaker, & got [my] living by my labor. When this rebellion came on, I saw some of my neighbors get into commission, who were no better than myself....I was asked to enlist, as a private soldier. My ambition was too great for so low a rank. I offered to enlist upon having a lieutenant's commission, which was granted. I imagined my self now in a way of promotion. If I was killed in battle, there would be an end of me, but if my Captain was killed, I should rise in rank, & should still have a chance to rise higher. These Sir! were the only motives of my entering into the service. For as to the dispute between Great Britain & the colonies, I know nothing of it; neither am I capable of judging whether it is right or wrong.

Scott may have been trying to gain the sympathy of his captors, but people fought in America's Revolutionary War out of fear and ambition as well as principle. We have no way of knowing whether Long Bill Scott's motives were typical. Certainly many Americans knew more than he about the colonies' struggle with England, but many did not.

In the spring of 1775, the Revolutionary War had just begun. So had Long Bill's adventures. When the British evacuated Boston a year later, Scott was transported to Halifax, Nova Scotia. After several months' captivity, he managed to escape and make his way home to fight once more. He was recaptured in November 1776 near New York City, when his garrison fell to a surprise British assault. Again Scott escaped, this time by swimming the Hudson River at night with his sword tied around his neck and his watch pinned to his hat.

During the winter of 1777, he returned to New Hampshire to recruit his own militia company. In the fall, his unit helped defeat Burgoyne's army near Saratoga, New York, and later took part in the fighting around Newport, Rhode Island. When his light infantry company was ordered to Virginia in early 1778, Scott's health broke, and he was permitted to resign from the army. After a few months' recuperation, however, he was at it again. During the last year of the war, he served as a volunteer on a navy frigate.

For seven years, the war held Scott in its harsh grasp. His oldest son died of camp fever after six years of service. In 1777, Long Bill sold his New Hampshire farm to meet family expenses. He lost a second farm in Massachusetts shortly afterward. After his wife died, he turned their youngest children over to relatives and set off to beg a job from the government.

Long Bill's saga was still not complete. In 1792, he rescued eight people when their boat capsized in New York harbor. Three years later, General Benjamin Lincoln took Scott with him to the Ohio country, where they surveyed land that was opening for white settlement. At last he had a respectable job and even a small government pension as compensation for his nine wounds. But trouble would still not let him go. While surveying on the Black River near Sandusky, Scott and his colleagues contracted "lake fever." Though ill, he guided part of the group back to Fort Stanwix in New York, then returned for the others. It was his last heroic act. A few days after his second trip, on September 16, 1796, he died.

American independence and the Revolutionary War were not as hard on everyone as they were on Long Bill Scott, yet together they transformed the lives of countless Americans. The war lasted longer than any other of America's wars until Vietnam nearly two centuries later. And unlike the nation's twentieth-century conflicts, it was fought on American soil, among the American people, disrupting families, destroying communities, spreading disease, and making a shambles of the economy. The war had far different consequences for men than women, black slaves than their white masters, Native Americans than frontier settlers, overseas merchants than urban workers. This chapter examines each of these issues, as well as the war's military progress.

The chapter also explains how America's struggle for independence became internationalized as France, Spain, and other nations, driven by their own imperial ambitions and the realities of European power politics, joined in the conflict against England. The Treaty of Paris (1783) that ended the war not only secured American independence, but also redrew the contours of imperial ambition in North America and recast relations between England and the nations of western Europe. More than that, America's fight for independence ushered in an extended Age of Revolution that over the following half century would see a king toppled and aristocratic privilege overthrown in France, political reforms erupt throughout much of Europe, and independence movements undercut European imperialism in Haiti and Latin America.

As activity quickened under the pressure of war and revolution, the American people mounted a political revolution of profound importance, a central topic of

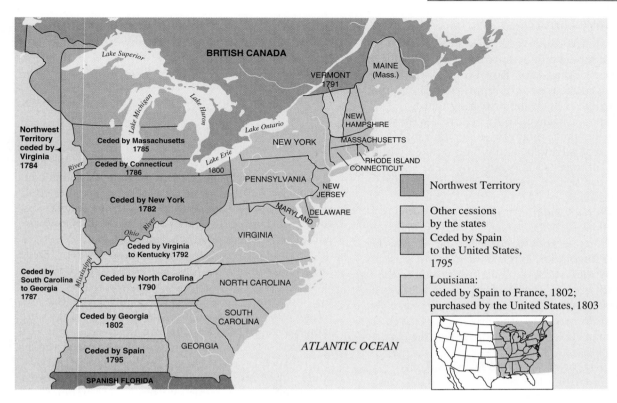

Western Land Claims Ceded by the States, 1782–1802

Seven of the original states laid claim, based on their colonial charters, to lands west of the Appalachian Mountains. Eventually the states ceded those lands to Congress, thus making ratification of the Articles of Confederation and the creation of new western states possible. Why were the western claims such a problem?

other state. Embedded in that clause was the basis for national, as distinguished from state, citizenship.

But the Articles sharply limited what Congress could do and reserved broad governing powers to the states. For example, the Congress could neither raise troops nor levy taxes but only ask the states for such support. Article 2 stipulated that each state was to "retain its sovereignty, freedom and independence," as well as "every power … which is not by this confederation expressly delegated to the United States in Congress assembled." Nor could the Congress's limited powers be easily expanded, because the Articles could be amended only by the unanimous agreement of all 13 states.

Though Congress sent the Articles to the states for approval in November 1777, they were not ratified until March 1781. Ratification required approval by all the states, and that was hard to obtain. The biggest impediment was a bitter dispute over control of lands west of the Appalachian Mountains. Some states had western claims tracing back to their colonial charters, but other states, such as Maryland and New Jersey, did not. In December 1778, the Maryland assembly announced that it would not ratify the Articles until all the western lands had been ceded to Congress. For

several years, ratification hung in the balance while politicians and land speculators jockeyed for advantage. Finally, in 1780, New York and Virginia agreed to give up their western lands. Those decisions paved the way for Maryland's ratification in early 1781. Approval of the Articles was now assured.

Meanwhile, Congress managed the war effort as best it could, using the unratified Articles as a guide. Events quickly proved its inadequacy, because Congress could do little more than pass resolutions and implore the states for support. If they refused, as they frequently did, Congress could only protest and urge cooperation. Its ability to function was further limited by the stipulation that each state's delegation cast but one vote. Disagreements within state delegations sometimes prevented them from voting at all. That could paralyze Congress, because most important decisions required a nine-state majority.

As the war dragged on, Washington repeatedly criticized Congress for its failure to support the army. Acknowledging its own ineffectiveness, Congress in 1778 temporarily granted Washington extraordinary powers, asking him to manage the war on his own. In the end, Congress survived because enough of its members realized that disaster would follow its collapse.

The War Moves South

As the war in the North bogged down in a costly stalemate, Britain adopted an alternative strategy—invasion and pacification of the South. Royal officials in the South encouraged the idea with reports that thousands of Loyalists would rally to the British standard. Moreover, if southern slaves could be lured to the British side, the balance might tip in Britain's favor. Even the threat of slave rebellion would weaken white southerners' will to resist. Persuaded by these arguments, the British shifted the war's focus to the South during its final years.

Georgia—small, isolated, and largely defenseless—was the initial target. In December 1778, Savannah, the state's major port, fell to a seaborne attack. For nearly two years, the Revolution in the state virtually ceased. Encouraged by their success, the British turned to the Carolinas, with equally impressive results. On May 12, 1780, Charleston surrendered after a month's siege. At a cost of only 225 casualties, the British captured the entire 5,400-man American garrison. It was the costliest American defeat of the war.

After securing Charleston, the British quickly extended their control north and south along the coast. At Camden, South Carolina, the British killed nearly 1,000 Americans and captured 1,000 more, temporarily destroying the southern continental army. With scarcely a pause, the British pushed on into North Carolina. There, however, British officers quickly learned the difficulty of extending their lines into the interior: distances were too large, problems of supply too great, the reliability of Loyalist troops too uncertain, and popular support for the revolutionary cause too strong.

Cornwallis's Surrender at Yorktown
Though this painting by John Trumbull captures the drama of the British surrender at Yorktown, it misrepresents one interesting fact. Asserting that he was ill, Lord Cornwallis sent a subordinate officer to yield the symbolic sword of surrender. Why do you suppose that he did so?

In October 1780, Washington sent Nathanael Greene south to lead the continental forces. It was a fortunate choice, for Greene knew the region and the kind of war that had to be fought. Determined, like Washington, to avoid large-scale encounters, Greene divided his army into small, mobile bands. Employing what today would be called guerrilla tactics, he harassed the British and their Loyalist allies at every opportunity, striking by surprise and then disappearing into the interior. Nowhere was the war more fiercely contested than through the Georgia and Carolina countryside. Neither British nor American authorities could restrain the violence. Bands of private marauders, roving the land and seizing advantage from the war's confusion, compounded the chaos.

In time, the tide began to turn. At Cowpens, South Carolina, in January 1781, American troops under General Daniel Morgan won a decisive victory, suffering fewer than 75 casualties to 329 British deaths, and taking 600 men prisoner. In March, at Guilford Court House in North Carolina, Cornwallis won, but at a cost that forced his retreat to Wilmington, near the sea.

In April 1781, convinced that British authority could not be restored in the Carolinas while the rebels continued to use Virginia as a supply and staging area, Cornwallis moved north. With a force of 7,500, he raided deep into Virginia, sending Governor Jefferson and the Virginia legislature fleeing from Charlottesville into the mountains. But again Cornwallis found the costs of victory high, and again he turned back to the coast for protection and resupply. On August 1, he reached Yorktown.

Cornwallis's position was secure as long as the British fleet controlled Chesapeake Bay, but that advantage did not last long. In 1778, the French government, still smarting from its defeat by England in the Seven Years' War and buoyed by the American victory at Saratoga in 1777, had signed an alliance with Congress, promising to send its naval forces into the war. Initially, the French concentrated their fleet in the West Indies, hoping to seize some of the British sugar islands. But on August 30, 1781, after repeated American urging, the French admiral Comte de Grasse arrived off Yorktown. Reinforced by a second French squadron from the North, de Grasse established naval superiority in Chesapeake Bay. At the same time, Washington's continentals, supplemented by French troops, marched south from Pennsylvania.

As Washington had foreseen, French entry turned the tide of war. Cut off from the sea and pinned down on a peninsula between the York and James Rivers by 17,000 French and American troops, Cornwallis's fate was sealed. On October 19, 1781, near the hamlet of Yorktown, he surrendered. While a

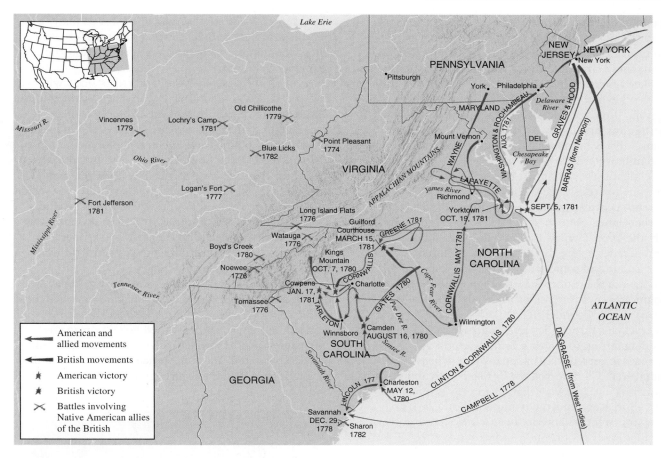

Military Operations in the South, 1778–1781

The war in the South, as in the North (see the map on p. 139), was fought along the coast and in the interior, while British and French forces battled as well in the West Indies. Important water routes shaped the course of the war from its beginning to the end. Why was this so?

military band played "The World Turned Upside Down" and hundreds of civilians looked on, nearly 7,000 British troops laid down their arms.

Learning the news in London a month later, Lord North, the king's chief minister, exclaimed, "Oh, God! It is all over." On February 27, 1782, the House of Commons cut off further support of the war. North resigned the following month. In Philadelphia, citizens poured into the streets to celebrate while Congress assembled for a solemn ceremony of thanksgiving. Though the preliminary articles of peace were not signed until November 1782, everyone knew after Yorktown that the Americans had won their independence.

Native Americans in the Revolution

The Revolutionary War drew in countless Native Americans as well as colonists and Englishmen. It could hardly have been otherwise, for the lives of all three peoples had been intertwined since the first English settlements more than a century earlier.

By 1776, the major coastal tribes had been decimated by warfare and disease, their villages displaced by white settlement. Powerful tribes, however, still dominated the interior between the Appalachians and the Mississippi River. The Iroquois Six Nations, a confederation numbering 15,000 people, controlled the area from the Hudson River to the Ohio valley. Five tribes—the Choctaw, Chickasaw, Seminole, Creek, and Cherokee, 60,000 people in all—dominated the southern interior. As the imperial crisis between England and its colonies deepened, Native and European Americans eyed each other warily across this vast "middle ground."

When the Revolutionary War began, British and American officials urged neutrality on the Indians. The Native Americans, however, were too important militarily for either side to ignore. By the spring of 1776, both were seeking Indian alliances. Recognizing their stake in the white man's conflict, Native Americans up and down the interior debated their options.

Alarmed by encroaching white settlement and eager to take advantage of the colonists' troubles with

England, a band of Cherokee, led by the warrior Dragging Canoe, launched a series of raids in July 1776 in what is now eastern Tennessee. In retaliation, Virginia and Carolina militias laid waste a group of Cherokee towns. "I hope that the Cherokees will now be driven beyond the Mississippi," declared Thomas Jefferson. "Our contest with Britain is too serious . . . to permit any possibility of [danger] . . . from the Indians." The Cherokee never again mounted a sustained military effort against the rebels. Seeing what had befallen their neighbors, the Creek stayed aloof. Their time for resistance would come in the early nineteenth century, when white settlers began to push onto their lands.

In the Ohio country, the struggle lasted longer. For several decades before the Revolution, explorers such as Daniel Boone had contested with the Shawnee and others for control of the region bordering the Ohio River. The Revolutionary War intensified these conflicts. In February 1778, George Rogers Clark led a ragtag band of Kentuckians through icy rivers and across 180 miles of forbidding terrain to attack a British outpost at Vincennes, in present-day Indiana. Though heavily outnumbered, Clark fooled the British troops and their Indian allies into believing that his force was much larger, and the British surrendered without a shot. Clark's victory tipped the balance in the war's western theater.

The Devastation of the Iroquois

To the northeast, an even more deadly scenario unfolded. At a council in Albany, New York, in August 1775, representatives of the Iroquois Six Nations listened while American commissioners urged them to remain at home and keep the hatchet buried deep. "The determination of the Six Nations," replied Little Abraham, a Mohawk leader, "[is] not to take any part; but as it is a family affair, to sit still and see you fight it out." Iroquois neutrality, however, did not last long.

In 1776, after U.S. troops raided deep into Mohawk territory west of Albany, the British urged the Iroquois to join them against the rebels. Most did so in the summer of 1777, at the urging of Joseph Brant, a Mohawk warrior who had visited England several years earlier and proclaimed England's value as an ally against American expansion. It was a fateful decision for Indians and whites alike. Over the next several years, the Iroquois and their British allies devastated large areas in central New York and Pennsylvania. An officer of the Pennsylvania militia reported somberly, "Our country is on the eve of breaking up. There is nothing to be seen but disolation, fire & smoak."

The Americans' revenge came swiftly. During the summer of 1779, American troops launched punishing raids into the Iroquois country, burning villages, killing men, women, and children, and destroying fields of corn. By war's end, the Iroquois had lost as many as one-third of their people as well as countless towns. Their domination of the northeastern interior was permanently shattered.

Not all the Eastern Woodland tribes sided with England in the Revolutionary War. The Oneida and the Tuscarora, once members of the Iroquois confederation, fought with the Americans, their decision driven by intertribal politics and effective diplomacy by emissaries of the Continental Congress. The Indians who fought for American independence, however, reaped little reward. Though the Americans spared the Oneida and Tuscarora villages, the British and their Iroquois allies destroyed them in turn. Moreover, once the war was over, tribes allied with the victorious American cause enjoyed no protection from the accelerating spread of white settlement.

Most Indians had sound reason for opposing American independence, because England provided them with trade goods, arms, and markets for their furs. England, moreover, had promised protection against colonial expansion, as the Proclamation Line of 1763 had demonstrated. Yet at the peace talks that ended the Revolutionary War, the British ignored their Indian allies.

Joseph Brant
Mohawk chief Joseph Brant (Thayendanegea) played a major role in the Iroquois's decision to enter the war on the side of Britain. Can you identify the symbols of authority in his dress?

(National Gallery of Canada)

They received neither compensation for their losses nor guarantees of their land, for the boundary of the United States was set far to the west, at the Mississippi River.

Though the Indians' struggle against white expansion would continue, their own anti-colonial war of liberation had failed. The American Revolution, declared a gathering of Indian chiefs to the Spanish governor at Saint Louis in 1784, had been "the greatest blow that could have been dealt us."

Negotiating Peace

In September 1781, formal peace negotiations began in Paris between the British commissioner, Richard Oswald, and the American emissaries, Benjamin Franklin, John Adams, and John Jay. The negotiations were complicated by the involvement in the war of several European countries seeking to weaken Great Britain. The Americans' main ally, France, had entered the war in February 1778. Eight months later, Spain declared war on England, though it declined to recognize American independence. Between 1780 and 1782, Russia, the Netherlands, and six other European countries joined in a League of Armed Neutrality aimed at protecting their maritime trade against British depredations. America's Revolutionary War had become internationalized. It could hardly have been otherwise, given England's centrality to the European balance of power and the long-standing competition among European powers for colonial dominance in North America.

Dependent on French economic and military support, Congress instructed the American commissioners to follow the advice of the French foreign minister Vergennes. But as the American commissioners soon learned, he was prepared to let the exhausting war continue in order to weaken England and tighten America's dependence on France. Even more alarming, Vergennes suggested that the new nation's boundary should be set no farther west than the crest of the Appalachian Mountains, and he hinted that the British might retain areas they controlled at the war's end. That would have left New York City and other coastal enclaves in British hands.

In the end, the American commissioners ignored their instructions and, without a word to Vergennes, arranged a provisional peace agreement with the British emissaries. It was fortunate that they did so, for Britain was prepared to be generous. In the Treaty of Paris signed in September 1783, Britain recognized American independence and agreed to set the western boundary of the United States at the Mississippi River. Britain promised as well that U.S. fishermen would have the right to fish the waters off Newfoundland and that British forces would evacuate American territory "with all convenient speed." In return, Congress would recommend that the states restore the rights and property of the Loyalists. Both sides agreed that prewar debts owed the citizens of one country by the citizens of the other would remain valid. Each of these issues would trouble Anglo-American relations in the years ahead, but for the moment it seemed a splendid outcome to a long and difficult struggle.

The Ingredients of Victory

How were the 13 weak and disunited North American states able to defeat Great Britain, the most powerful nation in the Atlantic world? Certainly Dutch loans and French military resources were crucially important. At the height of the war, France fielded a force of more than 10,000 men in North America.

More decisive, though, was the American people's determination not to submit. Repeatedly, the war effort seemed about to collapse as continental troops drifted away, state militias refused to march, and supplies failed to materialize. Yet as the war progressed, the people's estrangement from England deepened and their commitment to the "glorious cause" grew stronger.

The American victory owed much as well to Washington's organizational talents. Against massive odds, often by the sheer force of will, he held the continental army together and created a military force capable of winning selected encounters and surviving over time. Had he failed, the Americans could not possibly have won.

In the end, however, it is as accurate to say that Britain lost the war as that the United States won it. With vast economic and military resources, Britain enjoyed clear military superiority. Its troops were more numerous, better armed, and more professional. Until the closing months of the contest, Britain enjoyed naval superiority as well, enabling its forces to move up and down the coast virtually at will.

Britain, however, could not capitalize on its advantages. It had difficulty extending its command structures and supply routes across several thousand miles of ocean. As a result, decisions made in London were often based on outdated intelligence. British troops, moreover, often had to live off the land, thus reducing their mobility and increasing the resentment of Americans whose crops and animals they commandeered.

Faced with these circumstances, British leaders were often overly cautious. Burgoyne's attempt in 1777 to isolate New England by invading from Canada failed because Sir William Howe decided to attack Philadelphia rather than move northward up the Hudson River to join him. Similarly, neither Howe nor Cornwallis pressed his advantage in the central states during the middle years of the war, when more aggressive action might have crushed the continentals.

While British commanders generally failed to adapt European battlefield tactics to the realities of the

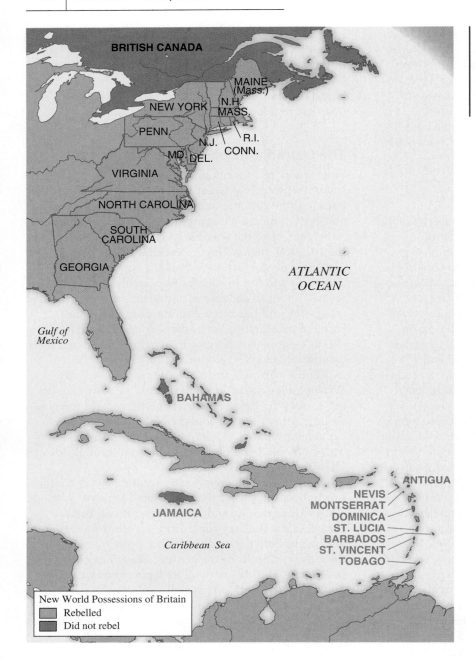

The majority of England's New World colonies did not rebel in 1776. What difference would it have made if Canada and England's Caribbean colonies had joined the 13 North American colonies in throwing off English rule?

American war, Washington and Greene were more flexible, often employing a patient strategy of harassment and strategic retreat. Guiding this strategy was a willingness, grounded in necessity, to allow England control of territory along the coast. But it was based as well on the conviction that popular support for the revolutionary cause would grow and that the cost of subduing the colonial rebellion would become greater than the British government could bear.

The American strategy proved sound. As the war dragged on and its costs escalated, Britain's will began to waver. After France and Spain entered the conflict, Britain had to worry about Europe, the Caribbean, and the Mediterranean as well as North America. Unrest in Ireland and food riots in London tied down additional English troops. As the cost in money and lives increased and prospects of victory dimmed, political support for the war eroded. With the defeat at Yorktown, it finally collapsed.

The Experience of War

In terms of the loss of life and destruction of property, the Revolutionary War pales by comparison with America's more recent wars. Yet modern comparisons are misleading, for the War of American Independence proved terrifying to the people caught up in it.

Military Recruiting

As this painting suggests, military recruiting was a community affair in the eighteenth century. What do you suppose the man with upraised arms is doing? What role might the women be playing in the recruitment process?

(William T. Ranney, *Recruiting for the Continental Army*, c. 1857–59, oil on canvas, 53³/₄ x 82¹/₄ in. Munson-Williams-Proctor Art Institute, Museum of Art, Utica, New York, [58.284])

Recruiting an Army

Estimates vary, but on the American side as many as 250,000 men may at one time or another have borne arms. That amounted to one out of every two or three adult white males. Though a majority of recruits were native born, many who fought for American freedom came from the thousands of British and European immigrants who streamed into North America during the middle decades of the eighteenth century. Of the 27 men enrolled in Captain John Wendell's New York company, for example, more than half had been born abroad, the majority in Ireland but others in Germany and the Netherlands. While the motives of these men varied, many had come to America seeking to better their lives and eagerly embraced the Revolution's democratic promise. They were the vanguard of a transatlantic migration that, over the late eighteenth and early nineteenth centuries, would tie the American revolutionaries to English reformers and French radicals during what historians have called the age of democratic revolutions.

As the war began, most state militias were not effective fighting forces. This was especially true in the South, where Nathanael Greene complained that the men "came from home with all the tender feelings of domestic life" and were not "sufficiently fortified ... to stand the shocking scenes of war, march over dead men, [or] hear without concern the groans of the wounded." The militia did serve as an efficient recruiting system, for men were already enrolled, and arrangements were in place for calling them into the field on short notice. Given its grounding in local community life, the militia also legitimated the war among the people and secured their commitment to the revolutionary cause.

During the early years of the war, when enthusiasm ran high, men of all ranks—from the rich and middle classes as well as the poor—volunteered to fight the British. But as the war went on, casualties increased, enlistment terms grew longer, military discipline became more harsh, and the army filled with conscripts. Eventually, the war was transformed, as wars often are, into a poor man's fight as wealthier men hired substitutes and communities filled their quotas with strangers lured by enlistment bonuses. Convicts, out-of-work laborers, free and unfree blacks, even British deserters filled the continental army with an array of "Tag, Rag, and Bobtail" soldiers.

For the poor and the jobless, whose ranks the war rapidly swelled, military bonuses and the promise of board and keep proved attractive. But often the bonuses failed to materialize, pay was long overdue, and soldiers frequently learned of their families' distress. As the war dragged on and desertion rose as high as 25 percent, Washington imposed harsher discipline in an effort to hold his troops in line.

Occasionally, frustration spilled over into open revolt. In 1779, Sergeant Samuel Glover and a group of soldiers from the North Carolina line, who had been unpaid for 15 months, refused to obey the commands of their superior officer "until they had justice done them." Glover was executed for insubordination.

Throughout the war, soldiers suffered from shortages of supplies. At Valley Forge during the terrible winter of 1777–1778, men went without shoes or coats. Declared one anguished soul, "I am sick, discontented, and out of humour. Poor food, hard lodging, cold weather, fatigue, nasty cloathes, nasty cookery, vomit half my time,

Recovering the Past

MILITARY MUSTER ROLLS

In almost all of America's wars, patriotism has run high and bombastic rhetoric has inspired citizens to arms. The American Revolution was no exception. But people fought for other than patriotic reasons, as the account of "Long Bill" Scott makes clear. It is always difficult to assess human motivations in something as complex as war. If we knew which Americans bore arms, however, it would help us understand why people fought and perhaps even understand what the war meant to them.

The social composition of the revolutionary army changed markedly as the war went along. At the beginning, men from all walks of life and every class fought in defense of American liberty. However, as the war lengthened and its costs increased, men who could afford to do so hired substitutes or arranged to go home, whereas men of less wealth and influence increasingly carried the burden of fighting. Many of them did so out of choice, for the army promised adventure, an escape from the tedium of daily life, a way to make a living, and even, as for "Long Bill" Scott, the chance to rise in the world. Thus thousands of poorer men hired out to defend American liberty. Such a decision was attractive to them because their opportunities were limited.

Enlistment lists of the continental army and the state militias offer one important source for studying the social history of the Revolutionary War. Although eighteenth-century records are imperfect by modern standards, recruiting officers did keep track of the men they signed up so that bounties and wages could be paid accurately. These lists usually give the recruit's name, age, occupation, place of birth, residence, and length of service.

Such lists exist for some of America's earliest wars. The muster rolls for New York City and Philadelphia during the Seven Years' War, for example, show that these two cities contributed 300 and 180 men per year, respectively, to the war effort. Most of the enlistees in that earlier war were immigrants—about 90 percent of New York's recruits and about 75 percent of Philadelphia's. Their occupations—mariner, laborer, shoemaker, weaver, tailor—indicate that they came primarily from the lowest ranks of the working class. Many were former indentured servants and many

others were servants running away from their masters to answer the recruiting sergeant's drum. In these Middle Atlantic port towns, successful, American-born artisans left the bloody work of bearing arms against the French to those beneath them on the social ladder. Enlistment lists for Boston, however, reveal that soldiers from that city were drawn from higher social classes.

A comparison of the Revolutionary War muster rolls from different towns and regions provides a view of the social composition of the revolutionary army and how it changed over time. It also offers clues to social conditions in different regions during the war and how they might have affected military recruitment.

The lists shown here of Captain Wendell's and Captain White's companies from New York and Virginia give "social facts" on 81 men. What kind of group portrait can you draw from the data? Some occupations, such as tanner, cordwainer, and chandler, may be unfamiliar, but they are defined in standard dictionaries. How many of the recruits come from middling occupations (bookkeeper, tobacconist, shopkeeper, and the like)? How many are skilled artisans? How many are unskilled laborers? What proportions are foreign and native born? Analyze the ages of the recruits. What does that tell you about the kind of fighting force that was assembled? How do the New York and Virginia companies differ in terms of these social categories and occupations? How would you explain these differences?

To extract the full meaning of the soldiers' profile, you would have to learn more about the economic and social conditions prevailing in the communities from which these men are drawn. But already you have glimpsed how social historians go beyond the history of military strategy, tactics, and battles to understand the "internal" social history of the Revolutionary War.

Reflecting on the Past How would social historians describe and analyze more recent American wars? What would a social profile of soldiers who fought in Vietnam or Iraq, including their age, region, race, class, extent of education, and other differences, suggest to a social historian of these wars? ■

NEW YORK LINE—1ST REGIMENT

Captain John H. Wendell's Company, 1776–1777

Men's Names	Age	Occupation	Place of Birth	Place of Abode
Abraham Defreest	22	Yeoman	N. York	Claverack
Benjamin Goodales	20	do [ditto]	Nobletown	do
Hendrick Carman	24	do	Rynbeck	East Camp
Nathaniel Reed	32	Carpenter	Norwalk	Westchester
Jacob Crolrin	29	do	Germany	Bever Dam
James White	25	Weaver	Ireland	Rynbveck
Joseph Battina	39	Coppersmith	Ireland	Florida
John Wyatt	38	Carpenter	Maryland	
Jacob Reyning	25	Yeoman	Amsterdam	Albany
Patrick Kannely	36	Barber	Ireland	N. York
John Russell	29	Penman	Ireland	N. York
Patrick McCue	19	Tanner	Ireland	Scholary
James J. Atkson	21	Weaver	do	Stillwater
William Burke	23	Chandler	Ireland	N. York
Wm Miller	42	Yeoman	Scotland	Claverack
Ephraim H. Blancherd	18	Yeoman	Ireland	White Creek
Francis Acklin	40	Cordwainer	Ireland	Claverack
William Orr	29	Cordwainer	Ireland	Albany
Thomas Welch	31	Labourer	N. York	Norman's Kill
Peter Gasper	24	Labourer	N. Jersey	Greenbush
Martins Rees	19	Labourer	Fishkill	Flatts
Henck Able	24	do	Albany	Flatts
Daniel Spinnie	21	do	Portsmouth	
Patrick Kelly	23	Labourer	Ireland	Claverack
Richd James Barker	12	do	America	Rynbeck
John Patrick Cronkite	11			Claverack
William Dougherty	17		Donyal, Ireland	Sch^ty

VIRGINIA LINE—6TH REGIMENT

Captain Tarpley White's Company, December 13th, 1780

Name	Age	Trade	Where Born State or Country	Where Born Town or Country	Place of Residence State or Country	Place of Residence Town or Country
Win Bails, Serjt	25	Baker	England	Burningham	Virg.	Leesburg
Arthur Harrup"	24	Carpenter	Virg.	Southampton	"	Brunswick
Charles Caffatey"	19	Planter	"	Caroline	"	Caroline
Elisha Osborn"	24	Planter	New Jersey	Trenton	"	Loudon
Benj Allday	19	"	Virg.	Henrico	"	Pawhatan
Wm Edwards Senr	25	"	"	Northumberland	"	Northumberland
James Hutcherson	17	Hatter	Jersey	Middlesex	"	P.Williams
Robert Low	31	Planter	"	Powhatan	"	Powhatan
Cannon Row	18	Planter	Virg.	Hanover	Virg.	Louisa
Wardon Pulley	18	"	"	Southampton	"	Hallifax
Richd Bond	29	Stone Mason	England	Cornwell	"	Orange
Tho Homont	17	Planter	Virg.	Loudon	"	Loudon
Tho Pope	19	Planter	"	Southampton	"	Southampton
Tho Morris	22	Planter	"	Orange	"	Orange
Littlebury Overby	24	Hatter	"	Dinwiddie	"	Brunswick
James [Pierce]	27	Planter	"	Nansemond	"	Nansemond
Joel Counsil	19	Planter	"	Southampton	"	Southampton
Elisha Walden	18	Planter	"	P.William	"	P.William
Wm Bush	19	S Carpenter	Virg.	Gloucester	Virg.	Gloucester
Daniel Horton	22	Carpenter	"	Nansemond	"	Nansemond
John Soons	25	Weaver	England	Norfolk	"	Loudon
Mara Lumkin	18	Planter	Virg.	Amelia	"	Amelia
Wm Wetherford	27	Planter	"	Goochland	"	Lunenburg
John Bird	16	Planter	"	Southampton	"	Southampton
Tho Parsmore	22	Planter	England	London	"	Fairfax
Josiah Banks	27	Planter	Virg.	Gloucester	"	Gloucester
Richd Roach	28	Planter	England	London	"	Culpeper
Joseph Holburt	33	Tailor	"	Middlesex	"	Frederickb^g
Henry Willowby	19	Planter	Virg.	Spotsylvania	"	Spotsylvania
Thos Pearson	22	Planter		Pennsylvany	"	Loudon
Jno Scarborough	19	Planter	Virg.	Brunswick	"	"
Chas Thacker	21	Planter	"	"	"	"
Nehemiah Grining	20	Planter	Virg.	Albemarle	Virg.	Albemarle
Ewing David	19	Planter	"	King W^m	"	Brunswick
Isaiah Ballance	17	Shoemaker	"	Norfolk	"	Norfolk
Wm Alexander	20	Planter	Virg.	Northumbl^d	Virg.	Northumbl^d
Wm Harden	26	Planter	"	Albemarle	"	Albemarle
John Ward	20	Sailor	England	Bristol	"	Northumbl^d
Daniel Cox	19	Planter	Virg.	Sussex	"	Sussex
George Kirk	21	Planter	"	Brunswick	"	Brunswick
John Nash	19	Planter	"	Northumbl^d	"	Northumbl^d
Wm Edward, Jr.	19	Planter	"	Northumbl^d	"	Northumbl^d
John Fry	20	Turner	"	Albemarle	"	Albemarle
Jno Grinning	25	Hatter	"	Albemarle	"	"
Daniel Howell	30	Planter	"	Loudon	"	Loudon
Milden Green	25	Planter	"	Sussex	"	Sussex
Matthias Cane	32	Planter	"	Norfolk	"	Norfolk
Wm Mayo	21	Joiner	"	Dinwiddie	"	Dinwiddie
Jas Morgan	25	Shoemaker	England	Shropshire	"	Stafford
Mathew Catson	19	Planter	Pennsylvania	York	"	Berkly
Wm B[rown]	22	Planter		"		
Richd Loyd	42	Planter	Virg.	Surry	Virg.	Surry
Abram Foress	33	Planter	"	Gloster	Virg.	Gloster
Wm White	19	Planter	"	"	"	Gloster

smoaked out of my senses. The Devil's in't, I can't Endure it. Why are we sent here to starve and freeze?"

Neither state governments nor Congress could effectively administer a war of such magnitude. Though many individuals served honorably as supply officers, others exploited the army's distress. Washington commented bitterly on the "speculators, various tribes of money makers, and stock-jobbers" whose "avarice and thirst for gain" threatened the country's ruin.

Swarms of camp followers further complicated army life. Wives and prostitutes, personal servants and slaves, con men and sutlers swarmed around the continental army camps. While often providing essential services, they slowed the army's movement and threatened its discipline.

The Casualties of Combat

The death that soldiers dispensed to each other on the battlefield was intensely personal. Because the effective range of muskets was little more than 100 yards, soldiers came virtually face-to-face with the men they killed. According to eighteenth-century practice, armies formed on the battlefield in ranks and fired in unison. After massed volleys, the lines often closed for hand-to-hand combat with knives and bayonets. Partisan warfare in the South, with its emphasis on ambush and cyclic patterns of revenge, personalized combat even more.

British officers expressed shock at the "implacable ardor" with which the Americans fought. The Americans' ferocity was attributable in part to the fact that this was a civil war. Not only did Englishmen fight Americans, but American Loyalists and Patriots fought each other as well. As many as 50,000 Americans fought for the king in some of the war's most bitter encounters. "The rage of civil discord," lamented one individual, "hath advanced among us with an astonishing rapidity. The son is armed against the father, the brother against the brother, family against family."

The passion with which American Patriots fought derived as well from their belief that the very future of human liberty depended on their success. In such a historic crusade, nothing was to be spared that might bring victory.

No one kept accurate records of how many soldiers died, but the most conservative estimate runs to over 25,000, a higher percentage of the total population than for any other American conflict except the Civil War. For Revolutionary War soldiers, death was an imminent reality.

Civilians and the War

While the experience of war varied from place to place, it touched the lives of virtually every American. Noncombatants experienced war most intensely in more densely settled areas along the coast. The British concentrated their military efforts there, taking advantage of their naval power and striking at the political and economic centers of American life. At one time or another, British troops occupied every major port city.

Urban dwellers suffered profound dislocations. About half of New York City's inhabitants fled when the British occupation began. An American officer somberly reported what he found as his troops entered New York at the war's end: "Close on the eve of an approaching winter, with an heterogeneous set of inhabitants, composed of almost ruined exiles, disbanded soldiery, mixed foreigners, disaffected Tories, and the refuse of the British army, we took possession of a ruined city."

In Philadelphia, the occupation was shorter and disruptions were less severe, but the shock of invasion was no less real. Elizabeth Drinker, living alone after local Patriots had exiled her Quaker husband, found herself the unwilling landlady of a British officer and his friends. Though the officer's presence may have protected her from the plundering that went on all around, she was constantly anxious, confiding to her journal that "I often feel afraid to go to Bed." British soldiers frequently tore down fences for their campfires and confiscated food to supplement their own tedious fare. Even Loyalists complained of the "dreadful consequences" of the British occupation.

Along the entire coastal plain, British landing parties descended without warning, seizing supplies and terrorizing inhabitants. In 1780 and 1781, the British mounted punishing attacks along the Connecticut coast, burning over 200 buildings in Fairfield and much of nearby Norwalk. The southern coast, with its broad, navigable rivers, was even more vulnerable. In December 1780, Benedict Arnold, the American traitor who by then was fighting for the British, ravaged Virginia's James River valley, uprooting tobacco, confiscating slaves, and creating panic among whites. Similar devastation befell the coastal regions of Georgia and the Carolinas. Such onslaughts sent civilians fleeing into the interior. During the first years of the war, the port cities lost nearly half their population.

At the same time, settlers in the interior fled eastward for safety as Loyalist rangers and their Indian allies fought Patriot militias in a violent, often chaotic struggle. According to one observer, after nearly five years of warfare in Tryon County in western New York, 12,000 farms had been abandoned, 700 buildings burned, thousands of bushels of grain destroyed, nearly 400 women widowed, and perhaps 2,000 children orphaned. Similar disasters unfolded up and down the backcountry from Maine to Georgia.

Wherever the armies went, they generated a swirl of refugees, who spread vivid tales of the war's devastation. The refugee traffic, together with the constant movement of soldiers between army and civilian life, brought the war home to countless people who did not experience it firsthand.

Disease, spread by the movement of people across the landscape, ravaged populations as well. During the 1770s and 1780s, a smallpox epidemic surged across the continent, wreaking its devastation from the Atlantic coast to the Pacific, and from the Southwest to Hudson's Bay in Canada. Because a crash program of inoculation launched by Washington in 1777 (the first large-scale immunization program in American history) protected much of the continental army, and because many English troops carried immunity from earlier exposure to the disease, the plague did not significantly affect the war's outcome. Still, it took a terrible toll, spread in part by returning soldiers and Britain's disease-infested prison ships. In the Chesapeake region, thousands of black Loyalists succumbed, while in the backcountry the virus raced through Indian populations, reducing their capacity to resist the rebels. Before the virus was spent, it may have killed more than 130,000 people. The pox, declared one observer gloomily, "spread its destructive and desolating power, as the fire consumes the dry grass of the field."

The Loyalists

Among the Americans suffering losses were those who remained loyal to the Crown. Though many Loyalist émigrés established successful lives in England, the Maritime Provinces of Canada, and the British West Indies, others found the uprooting an ordeal from which they never recovered. In London, a royal commission was appointed to hear Loyalist claims. Many of the several thousand Loyalists who appeared before the commission gained partial reimbursement for their losses, but it proved meager compensation for the confiscation of house and property, expulsion from familiar communities, and relocation in a distant land. The vast majority of Loyalists never appeared before the commission, and thus secured nothing.

Although we do not know how many colonists remained loyal to England, tens of thousands evacuated with British troops at the end of the war. At least as many slipped away while fighting was still underway. Additional thousands who wished the Revolution had never occurred stayed on in the new nation, struggling to rebuild their lives. The incidence of Loyalism differed from region to region. Loyalists were fewest in New England and most numerous around New York City, where British authority was most stable.

In each state, revolutionary assemblies exacted revenge against those who had rejected the revolutionary cause by depriving Loyalists of the vote, confiscating their property, and banishing them from their homes. In 1778, Georgia expelled 117 people from the state on pain of death, and declared their possessions forfeit. Probably not more than a few dozen Loyalists actually died at the hands of the revolutionary regimes, but thousands found their livelihoods destroyed, their families ostracized, and themselves subject to physical attack.

Punishing Loyalists—or people accused of Loyalism, a distinction that was often unclear in the confusion of the times—was politically popular. Most Patriots argued that such "traitors" had put themselves outside the protection of American law. Others, however, argued that republics were intended to be "governments of law and not of men" and worried that no one's rights would be safe when the rights of any were disregarded. No other wartime issue raised so starkly the nettlesome question of balancing individual liberty against the requirements of public security. That issue would return to trouble the nation in the years ahead.

Why did so many Americans remain loyal to the Crown, often at the cost of personal danger and loss? Royal appointees such as customs officers, members of the governors' councils, and Anglican clergy often remained with the king, as did groups dependent on the British presence—for example, settlers on the Carolina frontier who believed themselves mistreated by the planter elite along the coast, and ethnic minorities such as Germans who feared domination by the Anglo-American majority. Other Loyalists made their choice because they believed it futile to oppose English power and doubted that independence could be won.

Still others based their Loyalism on principle. "Every person owes obedience to the laws of the government," insisted Samuel Seabury, "and is obliged in honour and duty to support them. Because if one has a right to disregard the laws of the society to which he belongs, all have the same right; and then government is at an end." Another Loyalist worried about the kind of society independence would bring when revolutionary crowds showed no respect for the rights of dissenters such as he. "If I differ in opinion from the multitude," he asked, "must I therefore be deprived of my character, and the confidence of my fellow-citizens; when in every station of life I discharge my duty with fidelity and honour?" Such individuals claimed to be upholding reason and the rule of law against revolutionary disorder. Their defeat weakened conservatism in American society and promoted revolutionary change.

James Lafayette

James Armistead Lafayette, a Virginia slave, served as a spy against the British for the French general Lafayette. In recognition of his service, the Virginia General Assembly granted his freedom in 1786. Try to imagine how Lafayette was able to gather information on British forces.

African Americans and the War

The revolution caught up thousands of American blacks in its toils. In the northern states, free and enslaved blacks were enlisted in support of the revolutionary cause. The South's nearly 400,000 slaves were viewed by the British as a resource to be exploited and by southern whites as a source of vulnerability and danger. Sizing up the opportunities provided by the war's confusion, many southern blacks struck out for their own freedom by seeking liberty behind British lines, journeying to the north, or fleeing to mixed-race settlements in the interior. Before the war was over, the conflict generated the largest slave rebellion in American history prior to the Civil War.

Hearing their masters' talk about liberty, growing numbers of black Americans questioned their own oppression. In the North, slaves petitioned state legislatures for their freedom, while in the South pockets of insurrection appeared. In 1765, more than 100 South Carolina slaves, most of them young men in their 20s and 30s, fled their plantations. The next year, slaves paraded through the streets of Charleston chanting, "Liberty, liberty!"

In November 1775, Lord Dunmore, Virginia's royal governor, issued a proclamation offering freedom to all slaves and servants, "able and willing to bear arms," who would leave their masters and join the British forces at Norfolk. Within weeks, nearly 600 slaves responded.

Among them was Thomas Peters, an African who had been kidnapped from the Yoruba tribe in what is now Nigeria and brought to Spanish Louisiana in 1760. Peters resisted enslavement so fiercely that his master sold him into the English colonies. By 1770, he was toiling on William Campbell's plantation near Wilmington, North Carolina.

Peters's plans for his own declaration of independence may have ripened as a result of the rhetoric of liberty he heard around his master's house, for William Campbell was a leading member of Wilmington's Sons of Liberty and talked enthusiastically about inalienable rights. By mid-1775, the Cape Fear region, like many areas of the coastal South, buzzed with rumors of slave uprisings. After the British commander encouraged Negroes to "elope from their masters," the Delaware assembly dispatched patrols to disarm all blacks and imposed martial law. When 20 British ships entered the Cape Fear River in March 1776 and disembarked royal troops, Peters seized the moment to redefine himself as a man, instead of William Campbell's property, and escaped. Before long, he would fight with the British-officered Black Pioneers.

How many African Americans sought liberty behind British lines is unknown, but as many as 20 percent may have done so. Unlike their white masters, blacks saw in England the promise of freedom, not tyranny. As the war dragged on, English commanders pressed blacks into service. A regiment of black soldiers, formed from Virginia slaves who responded to Dunmore's proclamation, marched into battle, their chests covered by sashes emblazoned with the slogan "Liberty to Slaves."

Some of the blacks who joined England achieved their freedom. At the war's end, several thousand were evacuated with the British to Nova Scotia. Their reception by the white inhabitants, however, was generally hostile. By 1800, most had left Canada to help establish the free black colony of Sierra Leone in West Africa. Thomas Peters was a leader among them.

Many of the slaves who fled behind British lines never won their freedom. Under the terms of the peace treaty, hundreds were returned to their American owners. Several thousand others, their value as field hands too great to be ignored, were transported to harsher slavery on West Indian sugar plantations.

Other blacks took advantage of the war's confusion to flee. Some went north, following rumors that slavery had been abolished there. Others sought refuge among Indians in the southern interior. The Seminoles

Resettlement of Black Loyalists After the Revolution

Thousands of American blacks departed the new nation with British troops at the end of the Revolutionary War. As the map indicates, their destinations varied. How did resettlement outside the United States reshape the lives of black Loyalists?

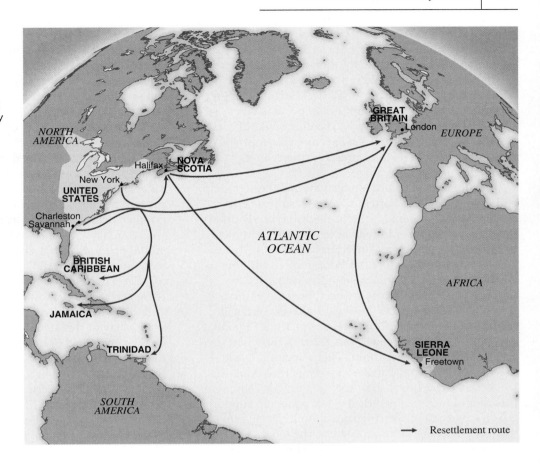

of Georgia and Florida generally welcomed black runaways and through intermarriage absorbed them into tribal society. Blacks met a more uncertain reception from the Cherokee and Creek. While some were taken in, others were returned to their white owners for bounties, and still others were held in slave-like conditions by new Indian masters.

Fewer blacks fought on America's side than on England's, in part because neither Congress nor the states were eager to see them armed. Faced with the increasing need for troops, however, Congress and each of the states except Georgia and South Carolina eventually pressed blacks into service. Of those who served the Patriot cause, many received the freedom they were promised. The patriotism of countless others, however, went unrewarded.

The Ferment of Revolutionary Politics

The Revolution altered people's lives in countless ways that reached beyond the sights and sounds of battle. No area of American life was more powerfully changed than politics and government. Who would have a voice in revolutionary politics, and who would be excluded? How vigorously would political equality be pursued, or how tenaciously would people cling to the traditional belief that citizens should defer to their political leaders? And how would the new state governments balance the need for order and the security of property against demands for democratic openness and accountability? Seldom has American politics struggled with more daunting problems than at the nation's founding.

Mobilizing the People

Under the pressure of revolutionary events, politics absorbed people's energies as never before. The politicization of American society was evident in the flood of printed material that streamed from American presses. Newspapers multiplied and pamphlets by the thousands fanned political debate. Declared one contemporary in amazement, it was

> a spectacle...without a parallel on earth....Even a large portion of that class of the community which is destined to daily labor have free and constant access to public prints, receive regular information of every occurrence, [and] attend to the course of political affairs. Never were political writings so cheap, so universally diffused, so easy of access.

Pulpits rocked with political exhortations. While religion and politics had never been sharply separated in colonial America, the Revolution drew them more tightly together. Some believed that God had designated America as the place of Christ's Second Coming and that independence foretold that glorious day. Others of a less millennial persuasion thought of America as a "New Israel," a covenanted people specially chosen by God to preserve liberty in a threatening world.

In countless sermons, Congregational, Presbyterian, and Baptist clergy exhorted the American people to repent the sins that had brought English tyranny upon them and urged them to rededicate themselves to God's purposes by fighting for American freedom. It was language that people nurtured in Puritan piety and the Great Awakening instinctively understood.

The belief that God sanctioned their revolution strengthened Americans' resolve. It also encouraged them to equate their own interests with divine intent and thus offered convenient justification for whatever they believed necessary to do. This was not the last time Americans would make that dangerous equation.

By contrast, Loyalist clergy, such as Maryland's Jonathan Boucher, urged their parishioners to support the king as head of the Anglican church. During the months preceding independence, as the local Committee of Safety interrupted worship to harass him, Boucher carried a loaded pistol into the pulpit while he preached submission to royal authority.

Belief in the momentous importance of what they were doing increased the intensity of revolutionary politics. As independence was declared, people throughout the land raised toasts to the great event: "Liberty to those who have the spirit to preserve it," and "May

Liberty expand sacred wings, and, in glorious effort, diffuse her influence o'er and o'er the globe." Inspired by the searing experience of rebellion, war, and nation building, Americans believed they held the future of human liberty in their hands. Small wonder that they took their politics so seriously.

The expanding array of crowds and committees of safety and correspondence that formed during the 1770s and 1780s provided the most dramatic evidence of the people's new political commitment. Prior to independence, crowds had taken to the streets to protest measures like the Stamp Act. After 1776, direct political action increased as people gathered to administer roughhewn justice to Loyalists and, as one individual protested, even direct "what we shall eat, drink, wear, speak, and think."

Patriots of more radical temperament defended these activities as legitimate expressions of the popular will. More conservative souls, however, worried that such behavior threatened political stability. Direct action by the people had been necessary in the struggle against England, but why such restlessness after the yoke of English tyranny had been thrown off? Even Thomas Paine expressed concern. "It is time to have done with tarring and feathering," he wrote. "I never did and never would encourage what may properly be called a mob, when any legal mode of redress can be had."

The expansion of popular politics resulted from an explosive combination of circumstances: the momentous events of revolution and war; the efforts of Patriot leaders to mobilize popular support for the struggle against England; and the determination of artisans, workingmen, farmers, and other common folk to apply the principles of liberty to the conditions of their own lives.

Tearing Down the Statue of George III

In celebration of American independence, Patriots and their slaves rushed to destroy symbols of British authority such as this statue of King George III that stood at Bowling Green in New York City. What did such actions accomplish?

A Republican Ideology

As the American people moved from colonial subordination to independence, they struggled to establish their identity as a free and separate nation. What did it mean to be no longer English, but American? "Our style and manner of thinking," observed Paine, "have undergone a revolution.... We see with other eyes, we hear with other ears, and think with other thoughts than those we formerly used." The ideology of revolutionary republicanism, pieced together from English political ideas, Enlightenment theories, and religious beliefs, constituted that revolution in thought. Many of its central tenets were broadly shared among the American people, but its larger meanings were sharply contested throughout the Revolutionary era.

In addition to the rejection of monarchy that Paine had so eloquently expressed in *Common Sense*, the American people also rejected the system of hierarchical authority on which monarchy was based, a system that promised protection by the Crown in return for obedience by the people. Under a republican system, by contrast, the people, contracting together, created public authority for their own mutual good. In that fundamental change lay much of the American Revolution's radical promise.

Basic to republican belief was the notion that governmental power, when removed from the people's close oversight, threatened to expand at the expense of liberty. Recent experience with England had made that lesson unmistakably clear. Although too much liberty could degenerate into political chaos, history seemed to demonstrate that trouble most often arose from too much, not too little, government. "It is much easier to restrain the people from running into licentiousness," went a typical refrain, "than power from swelling into tyranny and oppression."

Given the need to limit governmental power, how could political order be maintained? The revolutionary generation offered an extraordinary answer to that question. Order was not to be imposed from above through traditional agencies of central control such as monarchies, standing armies, and state churches. In a republic, political discipline had to emerge from citizens' willingness to put the public good ahead of their own private interests. In a republic, explained one pamphleteer, "each individual gives up all private interest that is not consistent with the general good." This radical principle of "public virtue" was an essential ingredient of republican belief.

By contrast, political "faction" or organized self-interest was the "mortal disease" to which popular governments throughout history had succumbed. Given the absence in republics of a strong central government capable of imposing political order, factional conflict could easily spin out of control. This fear added to the intensity of political conflict in revolutionary America by encouraging people to attribute the worst motives to their opponents.

The idea of placing responsibility for political order with the people and counting on them to act selflessly for the good of the whole alarmed countless Americans. If the attempt was made, warned one individual darkly, "the bands of society would be dissolved, the harmony of the world confused, and the order of nature subverted." A strong incentive to Loyalism lurked in such concerns.

During the first years of independence, when revolutionary enthusiasm ran high, many believed that public virtue was sufficiently widespread to support republican government. Others argued that the American people would learn public virtue by its practice. The revolutionary struggle would serve as a "furnace of affliction," refining the American character as it strengthened people's capacity for virtuous behavior. It was an extraordinarily hopeful but risk-filled undertaking.

The principle of political equality was another controversial touchstone of republicanism. It was broadly assumed that republican governments must be grounded in popular consent, that elections must be frequent, and that citizens must be vigilant in defense of their liberties. But there agreement often ended.

Some Americans took the principle of political equality literally, arguing that every citizen should have an equal voice and that public office should be open to all. This position was most forcefully articulated by tenants and small farmers in the interior, as well as by workers and artisans in the coastal cities, who had long struggled to claim a political voice. More cautious citizens emphasized that individual liberty must be balanced by political order, arguing that stable republics required leadership by men of ability and experience, an "aristocracy of talent" that could give the people direction. Merchants, planters, and large commercial farmers who were used to providing such leadership saw no need for radical changes in the existing distribution of political power.

Forming New Governments

These differences of ideology and self-interest burst through the surface of American politics during the debates over new state constitutions. Fashioning new governments would not be easy, for the American people had no experience with government making on such a scale and had to undertake it in the midst of a disruptive war. In addition, there were sharp divisions over the kinds of governments they wanted to create. One person thought it the "most difficult and dangerous business" that was to be done. Events proved those words prophetic.

Rather than create new systems of government, Connecticut and Rhode Island continued under their colonial charters, simply deleting all reference to the British Crown. The other 11 states, however, set their charters aside and started anew. By 1778, all but Massachusetts had completed the task. Two years later it had done so as well.

The task was driven by two overriding concerns: limiting the powers of government and making public officials closely accountable. The only certain way of accomplishing these goals was by establishing a fundamental law, in the form of a written constitution, that could serve as a standard for controlling governmental behavior.

In most states, provincial congresses, extralegal successors to the defunct colonial assemblies, wrote the first constitutions. But this made people increasingly uneasy. If governmental bodies wrote the documents, they could change them as well, and what would then protect liberty against the abuse of governmental power? Some way had to be found of grounding the fundamental law not in the actions of government, but directly in the people's sovereign will.

Massachusetts first perfected the new procedure. In 1779, its citizens elected a special convention for the sole purpose of writing a new constitution, which was then returned to the people for ratification. Through trial and argumentation, the revolutionary generation gradually worked out a clear understanding of what a constitution was and how it should be created. In the process, it established some of the most basic doctrines of American constitutionalism: that sovereignty resides in the people rather than government; that written constitutions embody the people's sovereign will; and that governments must function within clear constitutional limits. No principles have been more important to the preservation of American liberty.

The governments described by these new constitutions were considerably more democratic than the colonial regimes had been. Most state officials were now elected, many of them annually rather than every two or three years as before. The assemblies, moreover, were now larger and more representative than they had been prior to 1776, and many of the powers formerly exercised by colonial governors were reallocated to the assemblies.

Different Paths to the Republican Goal

Constitution making generated heated controversy, especially over how democratic the new governments should be. In Pennsylvania, a coalition of western farmers, Philadelphia artisans, and radical leaders pushed through the most democratic state constitution of all. Drafted less than three months after independence, during the most intense period of political reform, it rejected the familiar English model of two legislative houses and an independent executive. Republican governments, the radicals insisted, should be simple and easily understood. The constitution thus provided for a single, all-powerful legislative house—its members annually elected, its debates open to the public.

A truly radical assumption underlay this unitary design: that only the "common interest of society" and not "separate and jarring private interests" should be represented in public affairs. There was to

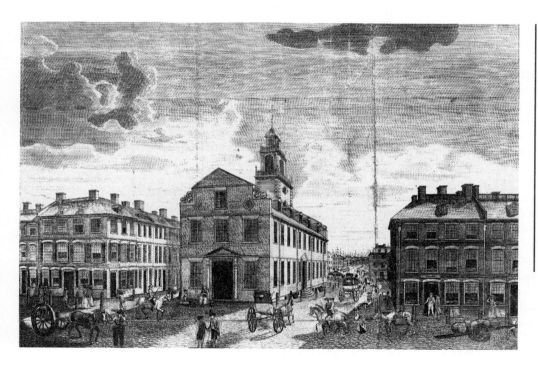

Old Massachusetts Statehouse

Massachusetts was the first state to elect a special convention to draw up a new constitution and then return that constitution to the people for approval. The new government—along with Boston's officials, courts, and the Merchants' Exchange—met in the old colonial statehouse.

(I. N. Phelps Stokes Collection, Miriam and Ira D. Wallach Division of Art, Prints and Photographs, The New York Public Library, Astor, Lenox and Tilden Foundations/Art Resource, NY)

be no governor; legislative committees would handle executive duties. Property-holding requirements for public office were abolished, and the franchise was opened to every white, taxpaying male over 21. A bill of rights guaranteed every citizen religious freedom, trial by jury, and freedom of speech.

The most radical proposal called for the partial redistribution of property. "An enormous proportion of property vested in a few individuals," declared the proposed constitution, "is dangerous to the rights, and destructive of the common happiness of mankind." Alarmed conservatives managed to fend off that threatening proposal.

Debate over the proposed constitution polarized the state. Men of wealth condemned the document's supporters as "coffee-house demagogues" seeking to introduce a "tyranny of the people." The constitution's proponents—tradesmen, farmers, and other small producers—shot back that their critics were "the rich and great men" who had no "common interest with the body of the people." In 1776, the radicals had their way, and the document was approved. For the moment, the lines of political power in Pennsylvania had been decisively redrawn.

In Massachusetts, constitution making followed a more cautious course. There the disruptions of war were less severe and the continuity of political leadership was greater. The constitution's main architect, John Adams, readily admitted that the new government must be firmly grounded in the people, yet he warned against "reckless experimentation." He thought a balance between two legislative houses and an independent executive was essential to preserving liberty.

Believing that society was inescapably divided between "democratic" and "aristocratic" forces, Adams sought to isolate each in separate legislative houses where they could guard against each other. Following Adams's advice, the Massachusetts convention provided for a popular, annually elected assembly and a senate apportioned on the basis of wealth. The constitution also provided for an independent governor empowered to veto legislation, make appointments, command the militia, and oversee state expenditures.

When the convention sent the document to the town meetings for approval on March 2, 1780, farmers and Boston artisans attacked it as "aristocratic." Despite such objections, the convention reconvened in June and declared the constitution approved. The document went into effect four months later.

Women and the Limits of Republican Citizenship

While men of the revolutionary generation battled over sharing political power, they were virtually unanimous in the belief that women should be excluded from public politics. Though women participated in revolutionary crowds and other political activities, they continued to be denied the franchise. Except on scattered occasions, women had neither voted nor held public office

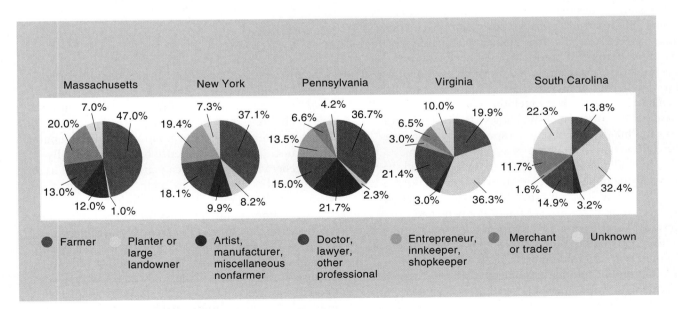

Occupational Composition of Several State Assemblies in the 1780s
Membership patterns in the revolutionary assemblies generated political conflict and differed markedly from state to state. What are the major differences between northern and southern state assemblies, and how do you explain them?

Source: Jackson T. Main, *Political Parties Before the Constitution,* 1973.

during the colonial period. Nor, with rare exceptions, did they do so in revolutionary America.

In New Jersey, the constitution of 1776 opened the franchise to "all free inhabitants" who met property and residence requirements. During the 1780s, numerous women took advantage of that opening and cast their votes, leading one disgruntled male to protest that "women, generally, are neither by nature, nor habit, nor education…fitted to perform this duty with credit to themselves, or advantage to the public." Reflecting that widely held, male belief, the New Jersey Assembly in 1807 again disenfranchised women. The author of that law, John Condict, had nearly been defeated for reelection several years earlier when women voted in conspicuous numbers for his opponent. In no other state did women even temporarily secure the vote. Not until the twentieth century would women secure the franchise, the most fundamental attribute of citizenship.

Prior to independence, most women had accepted the principle that political involvement fell outside the female sphere. Women, however, felt the urgency of the revolutionary crisis as intensely as men. "How shall I impose a silence upon myself," wondered Anne Emlen in 1777, "when the subject is so very interesting, so much engrossing conversation & what every member of the community is more or less concerned in?" With increasing frequency, women wrote and spoke to each other about public events, especially as they affected their own lives.

As the war progressed, growing numbers of women spoke out publicly. A few, such as Mercy Otis Warren and Esther DeBerdt Reed, published essays explaining women's urgent desire to contribute to the Patriot cause. In her 1780 broadside "The Sentiments of an American Woman," Reed declared that women wanted to serve like "those heroines of antiquity, who have rendered their sex illustrous," and called on women to renounce "vain ornament" as they had earlier renounced English tea. The money not spent on clothing and hair styles would be the "offering of the Ladies" to Washington's army. In Philadelphia, women responded by collecting $300,000 in continental currency from more than 1,600 individuals. Refusing Washington's proposal that the money be mixed with general funds in the national treasury, they insisted on using it to purchase materials for shirts so that each soldier might know he had received a contribution directly from the women.

Even women's traditional roles took on new political meaning. With English imports cut off and the army badly in need of clothing, spinning and weaving assumed patriotic significance. Coming together as Daughters of Liberty, women made shirts and other items of clothing. Charity Clarke, a New York teenager, acknowledged that she "felt Nationaly" as she knitted stockings for the soldiers. Though "heroines may not distinguish themselves at the head of an army," she informed an English cousin,

Mercy Otis Warren

Mercy Otis Warren, related by birth and marriage to leading Massachusetts Patriots, was one of a few women who published pamphlets and plays dealing with revolutionary politics. Why didn't more women publish such writing?

(John Singleton Copley (American, 1738-1815), "Mrs. James Warren (Mercy Otis)," ca. 1763. Oil on canvas. 49 5/8 × 39 1/2 in. (126 × 100.3 cm). Bequest of Winslow Warren. Courtesy. Museum of Fine Artrs, Boston (31.212). Reproduced with permission. © Museum of Fine Arts. Boston. All Rights Reserved.)

a "fighting army of amazons…armed with spinning wheels" would emerge in America.

The most traditional female role, the care and nurture of children, took on special political resonance during the Revolutionary era. How would the republic be sustained once independence had been won? By a rising generation of republican citizens schooled in the principles of public virtue by their "Republican Mothers," the women of the Revolution.

Most women did not press for full political equality, since the idea flew in the face of long-standing social convention, and its advocacy exposed a woman to public ridicule. Women, however, did speak out in defense of their rights. Choosing words that had resonated so powerfully during the protests against England, Abigail Adams urged her husband John not to put "unlimited power" into the hands of husbands. Remember, she warned, "all men would be tyrants if they could." John consulted Abigail on many things, but turned this admonition quickly aside.

Timeline

1775	Lexington and Concord
	Second Continental Congress
	Lord Dunmore's proclamation to slaves and servants in Virginia
	Iroquois Six Nations pledge neutrality
1776	Thomas Paine's *Common Sense*
	British evacuate Boston and seize New York City
	Declaration of Independence
	Eight states draft constitutions
	Cherokee raids and American retaliation
1777	British occupy Philadelphia
	Most Iroquois join the British
	Americans win victory at Saratoga
	Washington's army winters at Valley Forge
1778	War shifts to the South
	Savannah falls to the British
	French treaty of alliance and commerce
1779	Massachusetts state constitutional convention
	Sullivan destroys Iroquois villages in New York
1780	Massachusetts constitution ratified
	Charleston surrenders to the British
1780s	Destruction of Iroquois Confederacy
1781	Cornwallis surrenders at Yorktown
	Articles of Confederation ratified by states
1783	Peace treaty with England signed in Paris
	Massachusetts Supreme Court abolishes slavery
	King's Commission on American Loyalists begins work

While women developed new ties to the public realm during the revolutionary years, the assumption that politics was an exclusively male domain did not easily die. Indeed, republican ideology, so effectively invoked in support of American liberty against the English king and Parliament, actually sharpened political distinctions between women and men. The independent judgment required of republican citizens assumed their economic self-sufficiency, and that was denied married women by the long-established principle of *coverture,* a legal doctrine that transferred women's property to their husbands, in effect designating them economic as well as political dependents.

Republican virtue, moreover, was understood to encompass such "manly" qualities as rationality, self-discipline, and public sacrifice, qualities believed inconsistent with "feminine" attributes of emotion and self-indulgence. Finally, the desperate struggle against England strengthened patriarchal values by celebrating military heroism.

In the years ahead, new challenges to male political hegemony would emerge. When they did, women would find guidance in the universal principles enshrined in the Declaration of Independence that the women of the Revolution had helped to defend.

Conclusion
THE CRUCIBLE OF REVOLUTION

When Congress launched its struggle for national liberation in July 1776, it steered the American people into uncharted seas. The break with England and accompanying war redrew the contours of American life and changed the destinies of countless people like Long Bill Scott. Though the war ended in victory, liberty had its costs, as lives were lost, property destroyed, and local economies deranged. The conflict altered relationships between Indians and whites, for it left the Iroquois and Cherokee severely weakened and opened the floodgates of western expansion. Though women participated in revolutionary activities and achieved enhanced status as "Republican Mothers," they were still denied the vote.

By 1783, a new nation had come into being, one based not on age-encrusted principles of monarchy and aristocratic privilege but on doctrines of republican liberty. That was the greatest change of all. The political transformations that were set in motion, however, generated angry disputes whose outcome could be but dimly foreseen. How might individual liberty be reconciled with the need for public order? Who should be accorded full republican citizenship, and to whom should it be denied? How should constitutions be written and republican governments organized? Thomas Paine put the matter succinctly: "The answer to the question, can America be happy under a government of her own, is short and simple—as happy as she pleases; she hath a blank sheet to write upon." The years immediately ahead would determine whether America's republican experiment, launched with such hopefulness in 1776, would succeed.

Success would depend as well on the new nation's position in a hostile Atlantic world. Though American independence had been acknowledged, the long-established web of connections tying the United States to England and Europe remained strong. Wartime alliances had revealed that North America remained an object of imperial ambition and European power politics, while the cutoff of Atlantic trade had made clear how dependent the nation still was on overseas commerce. The new American republic, moreover, served as a model and, on occasion, an asylum for political radicals intent on reforming the corrupt systems of England and France. At the same time, many Americans regarded their republic as a beacon for the struggles of oppressed people elsewhere. In these ways as well, the meaning of American independence remained to be worked out in the years ahead.

QUESTIONS FOR REVIEW AND REFLECTION

1. Why were England and her North American colonies not able to resolve their differences peacefully?
2. Wars often produce unintended consequences for their participants. How was that the case for the American people during the Revolutionary War?
3. Loyalists and Patriots both argued that they sought to uphold the rule of law. How could that have been true?
4. Many African Americans supported the struggle for American independence, but countless others did not. Explain the difference.
5. The conflict between the United States and England quickly became internationalized. Why was this so and what difference did it make for the war's outcome?

Consolidating the Revolution

Ratification of the U.S. Constitution by the states in 1788 brought an end to the revolutionary years and ushered in a dramatically new era in the nation's history.

(John Feingersh/Stock, Boston)

American Stories

Extending the Revolution

Timothy Bloodworth of New Hanover County, North Carolina, experienced the American Revolution firsthand. A man of humble origins, Bloodworth had known poverty as a child. Lacking formal education, he had worked as an innkeeper and ferry pilot, self-styled preacher and physician, blacksmith and farmer. By the mid-1770s, he owned nine slaves and 4,200 acres of land, considerably more than most of his neighbors.

His unpretentious manner and commitment to political equality earned Bloodworth the confidence of his community. In 1758, at the age of 22, he was elected to the North Carolina assembly. Over the next three decades, he remained deeply involved in the political life of his home state.

When the colonies' troubles with England drew toward a crisis, Bloodworth spoke ardently of American rights and mobilized support for independence. In 1775, he helped form the Wilmington Committee of Safety. Filled with revolutionary fervor, he urged forward the process of republican political reform and, as commissioner of confiscated property for the district of Wilmington, pressed the attack on local Loyalists.

In 1784, shortly after the war ended, the North Carolina assembly named Bloodworth one of the state's delegates to the Confederation Congress. There he learned about the problems of governing a new nation. As Congress struggled through the middle years of the 1780s with problems of foreign trade, war debt, and control of the trans-Appalachian interior, Bloodworth shared the growing conviction that the Articles of Confederation were too weak. He supported Congress's call for a special convention to meet in Philadelphia in May 1787 for the purpose of taking action necessary "to render the constitution of the federal government adequate to the exigencies of the Union."

Like thousands of other Americans, Bloodworth eagerly awaited the convention's work. And like countless Americans, he was stunned by the result, for the proposed constitution described a government that seemed to him designed not to preserve republican liberty but to endanger it.

Once again sniffing political tyranny on the breeze, Bloodworth resigned his congressional seat and in August 1787 hurried back to North Carolina to help organize opposition to the constitution. Over the next several years, he worked tirelessly for its defeat, protesting that "we cannot consent to the adoption of a Constitution whose revenues lead to aristocratic tyranny, or monarchical despotism, and open a door wide as fancy can point, for the introduction of . . . corruption to the exclusion of public virtue." Had Americans so quickly forgotten the dangers of consolidated power?

At the very least, Bloodworth demanded the addition of a federal bill of rights to protect individual liberties. Echoing the language of revolutionary republicanism, he warned the North Carolina ratifying convention that "every possible precaution" should be taken when powers are granted, for "rulers are always disposed to abuse them."

Bloodworth also feared the sweeping authority Congress would have to make "all laws which shall be necessary and proper" for carrying into execution "all other powers vested . . . in the government of the United States." That language, he insisted, "would result in the abolition of the state governments. Its sovereignty absolutely annihilates them."

In North Carolina, the arguments of Bloodworth and his Anti-Federalist colleagues carried the day. By a vote of 184 to 84, the ratifying convention declared that a bill of rights "securing from encroachment the great Principles of civil and religious Liberty, and the unalienable rights of the People" must be approved before North Carolina would concur. The convention was true to its word. Not until November 1789, well after the new government had gotten underway and Congress had forwarded a national bill of rights to the states for approval, did North Carolina, with Timothy Bloodworth's cautious endorsement, finally enter the new union.

Just as Timothy Bloodworth knew the difficulties of achieving American independence, so he learned the problems of preserving American liberty once independence had been won. This chapter examines the threats posed to the new nation by the continuing imperial ambitions of England and France in North America; Congress's inability to pay off the foreign-held war debt; the states' failure to join together in prying open foreign ports to American commerce; and continuing restrictions on free navigation of the Mississippi River, deemed essential to the development of the nation's interior.

Chapter 7 also discusses an array of domestic issues that troubled the nation's affairs. Disputes over taxation and paper money, slavery and the separation of church and state, and democratic political reform generated turmoil in the states, in some cases leading discontented citizens openly to challenge public authority.

By 1786, Timothy Bloodworth, like countless other Americans, was caught up in an escalating debate between Federalists, who believed that the Articles of Confederation were fatally deficient and must be replaced by a stronger national government, and Anti-Federalists, who were alarmed by what they perceived to be the dangers to individual liberties posed by governmental power. That debate over the future of America's republican experiment, which constitutes the chapter's final topic, came to a head in the momentous Philadelphia convention of 1787, with its proposal for dramatic changes in the national government. With ratification of the new Constitution, the American people opened a portentous new era in their history and launched a dialogue over the very nature of American politics and government that continues to our own time.

Struggling with the Peacetime Agenda

As the war ended, daunting problems of demobilization and adjustment to the conditions of independence troubled the new nation. Whether the Confederation Congress could effectively deal with the problems of the postwar era remained unclear.

Demobilizing the Army

Demobilizing the army presented the Confederation government with immediate challenges, for when the fighting stopped, many of the troops refused to go home until Congress redressed their grievances. Trouble arose in early 1783 when officers at the continental army camp in Newburgh, New York, sent a delegation to complain about arrears in pay and other benefits that Congress had promised them during the dark days of the war. When Congress called on the army to disband, an anonymous address circulated among the officers, attacking the "coldness and severity" of Congress and hinting darkly at more direct action if grievances were not addressed.

The Resignation of General Washington, 1783

By resigning his commission in 1783 and returning to private life, Washington affirmed the supremacy of civilians over military authority. Why are women depicted in the balcony, observing the ceremony?

Several congressmen encouraged the officers' muttering, hoping the crisis would lend urgency to their own calls for a stronger central government. Most, however, found the challenge to Congress's authority alarming. Washington moved quickly to calm the situation. Promising that Congress would treat the officers justly, he urged his comrades not to tarnish the victory they had so recently won. His efforts succeeded, for the officers reaffirmed their confidence in Congress and agreed to disband.

Officers were not the only ones to take action. In June, several hundred disgruntled continental soldiers and Pennsylvania militiamen gathered in front of Philadelphia's Independence Hall, where Congress and Pennsylvania's Executive Council were meeting. When state authorities would not guarantee Congress's safety, it fled to Princeton, New Jersey. Once there, tension eased when it issued the soldiers three months' pay and furloughed them until they could be formally discharged. By early November, the crisis was over, but congressional authority had been seriously damaged.

Over the next several years, Congress shuffled between Princeton and Annapolis, Trenton and New York City, its transience visible evidence of its steadily eroding authority. A hot-air balloon, scoffed the *Boston Evening Herald*, would "exactly accommodate the itinerant genius of Congress," because it could "float along from one end of the continent to the other . . . and when occasion requires . . . suddenly pop down into any of the states they please." Never had Congress been so openly mocked.

Opening the West

The Confederation Congress was not without significant accomplishments during the postwar years. Most notable were the two great land ordinances of 1785 and 1787. The first provided for the systematic survey and sale of the region west of Pennsylvania and north of the Ohio River. The area was to be laid out in townships six miles square, which were in turn to be subdivided into lots of 640 acres

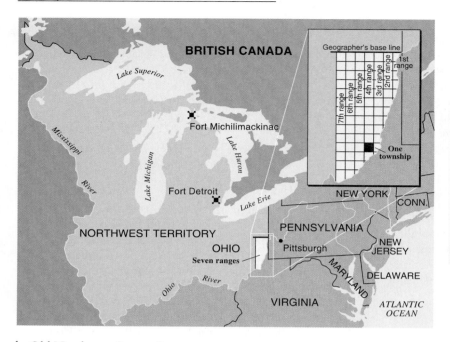

Old Northwest Survey Patterns

The Land Ordinance passed by Congress in 1785 provided for the systematic, rectangular survey of lands west of Pennsylvania and north of the Ohio River. Townships were to be divided into lots of 640 acres. The purpose of the ordinance was to promote the rapid, orderly occupation of the Old Northwest. What differences might this new survey system have made in patterns of community settlement, land use, and social life compared to the random settlement patterns along the Atlantic coast?

each. Thus began the rectangular grid pattern of land survey and settlement that to this day characterizes the Midwest and distinguishes it so markedly from the irregular settlement patterns of the older, colonial areas to the east.

Two years later, Congress passed the Northwest Ordinance. It provided for the political organization of the same interior region, first under congressionally appointed officials, then under popularly elected territorial assemblies, and ultimately as new states incorporated into the Union "on an equal footing with the original states in all respects whatsoever." The two ordinances represented a dramatic change from England's colonial administration. Rather than seeking to restrain white settlement as Parliament had attempted to do in the Proclamation Line of 1763, the central government in America's new "Empire of Liberty" sought to promote settlement's expansion. In addition, settlements in the American West would not remain colonies subordinate to an imperial power, but would be fully incorporated as new states in the expanding American nation.

Both ordinances enjoyed broad political support, for they opened land to settlers and profits to speculators. Income from land sales, moreover, promised to help reduce the national debt. While permitting slave owners living north of the Ohio River to retain their chattels, the ordinance of 1787 prohibited the

importation of new slaves into the region. This made the area more attractive to white farmers who worried about competing with slave labor and living among blacks. Southern delegates in the Congress accepted the restriction because they could look forward to slavery's expansion south of the Ohio River. During the 1780s, the country's interior seemed large enough to accommodate everyone's needs.

During the immediate postwar years, Congress operated as if Native Americans of the interior were "conquered" peoples—allies of England who had lost the war and had thus come under U.S. control. Such claims were grounded as well in notions of Indian inferiority. Most whites simply argued that the Indians must be driven out of white settlers' way. "The gradual extension of our settlements," explained George Washington, "will as certainly cause the savage as the wolf to retire; both being beasts of prey though they differ in shape."

For a few years, the conquest strategy seemed to work. During the mid-1780s, Congress imposed land treaties on the interior tribes, among them the Iroquois. Their numbers sharply reduced and their once proud confederation shattered, many Iroquois had fled into Canada. At the Treaty of Fort Stanwix in 1784, those who remained ceded most of their lands to the United States, and retreated to small reservations. By the 1790s, little remained of the once-imposing Iroquois domain but a few islands in a spreading sea of white settlement. On these "slums in the wilderness," the Iroquois struggled against disease and poverty, their traditional lifeways gone, their self-confidence broken. The Iroquois were not the only tribe to lose their land. In January 1785, representatives of the Wyandotte, Chippewa, Delaware, and Ottawa tribes relinquished claim to most of present-day Ohio.

The treaties, often exacted under the threat of force, generated widespread resentment. Two years after the Fort Stanwix negotiations, the Iroquois repudiated the treaty, asserting that they were still sovereigns of their own soil and "equally free as . . . any nation under the sun."

By the mid-1780s, tribal groups above and below the Ohio River were resisting white expansion into the interior. While the Creek resumed hostilities in Georgia, Indians north of the river strengthened their Western Confederacy and prepared to defend their homeland. As devastating Indian raids greeted settlers moving West, the entire region from the Great Lakes to the Gulf of Mexico was aflame with war. With the continental army disbanded, there was little that Congress could do.

Congress's inability to open the interior to white settlement alarmed white speculators facing the loss of their investments, farmers hoping to leave the crowded lands of the East, revolutionary soldiers eager to start afresh on the rich soil of Kentucky and Ohio that they

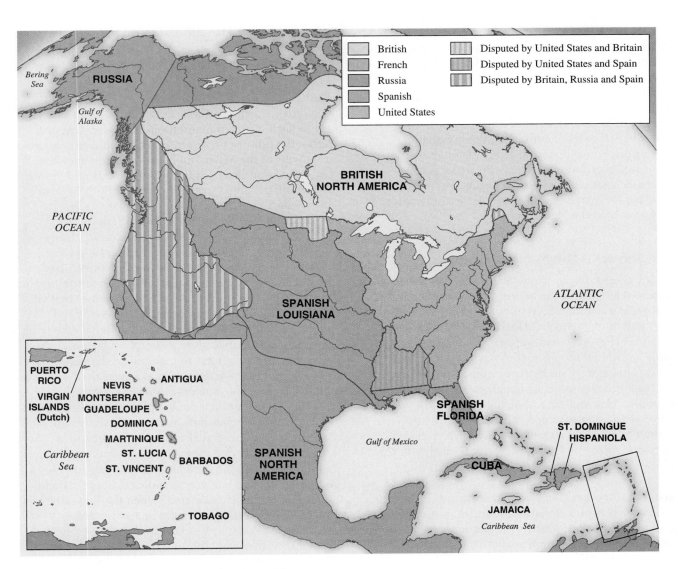

North America After the Treaty of Paris, 1783
Though victorious in its struggle for independence, the United States was surrounded to the north, west, and south by British and Spanish possessions. Russia and France continued to harbor imperial ambitions in the Americas as well. What problems and opportunities did European claims on areas of North America pose for the United States?

had been promised as payment for military service, and leaders such as Thomas Jefferson who believed that America's "empire of liberty" depended on an expanding nation of yeoman farmers.

Congress also failed to resolve problems with European nations that continued to claim areas of the trans-Appalachian west. In June 1784, Spain—still in possession of Florida, the Gulf Coast, and vast areas west of the Mississippi—closed the mouth of the Mississippi River to American shipping. The act outraged western settlers dependent on getting their produce to market by floating it downstream to New Orleans. Land speculators were alarmed that closure of the Mississippi would discourage development of the southern backcountry and reduce their profits. Rumors spread that Spanish agents were urging American frontiersmen to break away from the new nation and seek affiliation with Spain. Sensing the danger, Washington commented uneasily that settlers throughout the West were "on a pivot." "The touch of a feather," he warned, "would turn them away."

When Spain refused to reopen the Mississippi, Congress's secretary for foreign affairs, John Jay, offered to relinquish American claims to free transit of the river in return for a commercial treaty opening Spanish ports to American shipping. Though the bargain pleased merchants in the northeastern states, southern delegates in Congress were incensed at Jay's betrayal of their interests and opposed it. Stalemated, Congress could take no action at all.

Wrestling with the National Debt

Further evidence of the Confederation's weakness was Congress's inability to deal effectively with the nation's war debt. Estimated at $35 million, much was held by French and Dutch bankers. Unable to make regular payments against the loan's principal, Congress had to borrow additional money just to pay the accumulating interest. Things were no better at home. In response to the incessant demands of its creditors, the government could only delay and try to borrow more.

In 1781, Congress appointed Robert Morris, a wealthy Philadelphia merchant, as superintendent of finance and gave him broad authority to deal with the nation's troubled affairs. Morris urged the states to stop issuing paper money and persuaded Congress to demand that the states pay their requisitions in specie (gold and silver coin). In addition, he urged Congress to charter the Bank of North America and took steps to make federal bonds more attractive to investors.

Though Morris made considerable progress, the government's finances remained shaky. Lacking authority to tax, Congress depended on the states' willingness to meet their financial obligations. This arrangement, however, proved unworkable. In

October 1781, a desperate Congress requested $8 million from the states. Two and a half years later, less than $1.5 million had come in. In January 1784, Morris resigned. By 1786, federal revenue totaled $370,000 a year, not enough, one official lamented, to provide "the bare maintenance of the federal government."

Not all Americans were alarmed. Some noted approvingly that several state governments, having brought their own financial affairs under control, were beginning to assume responsibility for portions of the national debt. Others, however, saw this as additional evidence of Congress's weakening condition and wondered how long a government unable to maintain its credit could endure.

Surviving in a Hostile Atlantic World

Congress's difficulties dealing with its creditors and failure to counter Spain's closure of the Mississippi pointed to a broader problem in American foreign relations. Even after the United States had formally won independence, Britain, France, and Spain continued to harbor imperial ambitions in North America. Before the century was over, France would regain vast areas west of the Mississippi River. Meanwhile, Great Britain's Union Jack still flew over Canada and British troops still occupied strategic outposts on American soil, while Spain continued to conjure up grim memories of previous New World conquests.

The Revolutionary War had dramatically transformed America's relations with the outside world. England, once the nurturing "mother country," had become the enemy, while France, long the mortal foe of England and the colonies alike, had proven at best an uncertain friend. Given its imperial ambitions and entrenched monarchy, France feared colonial rebellions and regarded republicanism as deeply subversive. Moreover, French efforts to manipulate the peace process for its own advantage had taught the Americans a hard lesson in the dangers of power politics.

The reason for America's diplomatic troubles was clear: the country was new, weak, and republican in an Atlantic world dominated by strong, monarchical governments and divided into exclusive, warring empires. Nothing revealed the difficulties of national survival more starkly than Congress's futile efforts to rebuild America's overseas commerce. When the Revolutionary War ended, English goods once again flooded American markets. Few American goods, however, flowed the other way. John Adams learned why. In 1785, he arrived in London as the first American minister to England, carrying instructions to negotiate a commercial treaty. After endless rebuffs, he reported in frustration that England had no intention of reopening the empire's ports to American shipping. British officials testily reminded him that Americans had desired independence and must now live with its consequences.

While England remained intractable, wartime allies such as France and Spain again closed their empires to American commerce. Congressional efforts to secure authorization from the states to regulate foreign trade were unavailing because each state wanted to channel its trade for its own advantage. As a result, overseas trade languished and economic hardship deepened.

By the late 1780s, the per capita value of American exports had fallen a startling 30 percent from the 1760s. No wonder that merchants and artisans, carpenters and shopkeepers, sailors and dock workers—all dependent on shipbuilding and overseas commerce—suffered. In an Atlantic world divided into exclusive, imperial trading spheres, the United States lacked the political unity and the economic muscle to protect its essential interests.

Sources of Political Conflict

Revolutionary politics took different forms in different states, depending on the impact of the war, the extent of Loyalism, patterns of social conflict, and the disruptions of economic life. Everywhere, citizens struggled with a bewildering, often intractable array of issues.

Separating Church and State

Among the most explosive issues was deciding the proper relationship between church and state. Prior to 1776, only Rhode Island, New Jersey, Pennsylvania, and Delaware had allowed full religious liberty. In other colonies, established churches were endorsed by the government and supported by public taxes. There, civil authorities grudgingly tolerated "dissenters" such as the Methodists and Baptists. As their numbers rapidly grew, they noisily pressed their case for full religious liberty.

With independence, pressure built for severing all ties between church and state. Isaac Backus, the most outspoken of New England's Baptists, protested that "many, who are filling the nation with the cry of *liberty* and against *oppressors* are at the same time themselves violating that dearest of all rights, *liberty of conscience*." Such arguments were strengthened by the belief that throughout history alliances between government and church authorities had brought religious oppression, and that voluntary choice was the only safe basis for religious association.

In New England, Congregationalists fought to preserve their long established privileges. To separate church and state, they argued, was to risk infidelity and social disorder. Massachusetts's 1780 constitution guaranteed everyone the right to worship God "in the manner and season most agreeable to the dictates of his own conscience." But it also empowered the legislature to tax residents to support local ministers. A common religion and shared morality, avowed John Adams, were essential supports to liberty and republican government. Unsatisfied, Backus argued that official support of religious worship should be ended completely. Religious toleration, he insisted, fell far short of true religious freedom. Not until 1833 were laws linking church and state finally repealed in Massachusetts.

In Virginia, Baptists pressed their cause against the Protestant Episcopal Church, successor to the Church of England. The adoption in 1786 of Thomas Jefferson's Bill for Establishing Religious Freedom, rejecting all connections between church and state and removing all religious tests for public office, decisively settled the issue. Three years later, that statute served as a model for the First Amendment to the new federal Constitution.

But even the most ardent supporters of religious freedom were not prepared to extend it universally. The wartime alliance with Catholic France together with congressional efforts to entice Catholic settlers in Quebec to join the resistance against England had weakened long-established prejudices. Still anti-Catholic biases remained strong, especially in New England. The people of Northbridge, Massachusetts, wanted to exclude "Roman Catholics, pagons, or Mahomitents" from public office. The legal separation of church and state did not end religious discrimination, but it implanted the principle of religious freedom firmly in American law.

Slavery Under Attack

The place of slavery in a republican society also vexed the revolutionary generation. How, wondered many, could slavery be reconciled with the inalienable right to life, liberty, and the pursuit of happiness so boldly proclaimed in the Declaration of Independence?

During the several decades preceding 1776, the trade in human chattels had flourished. The 1760s had witnessed the largest importation of slaves in colonial history. The Revolutionary War, however, halted the slave trade almost completely. Though southern planters talked of replacing their lost chattels once the war ended, a combination of revolutionary principles, reduced need for field hands in the depressed Chesapeake tobacco economy, natural increase among the existing slave population, and anxiety over black rebelliousness argued for the trade's permanent extinction. By 1790, every state except South Carolina and Georgia had outlawed slave importations.

Old Methodist Church, John Street, New York

This nineteenth-century print provides a view of the Old Methodist Church on John Street, New York. Founded in 1786, it was the first Methodist church erected in America. Why did Methodists and Baptists press for religious freedom during the Revolutionary Era?

John Hill, "A Correct View of the Old Methodist Church in John Street, New York", 1824; Hand-colored aquatint, plane: 30.5 × 38.3 cm. Sheet: 31.1 × 38.5 cm. The Metropolitan Museum of Art, The Edward W.C Arnold Collection of New York Prints, Maps and Pictures, Bequest of Edward W.C Arnold, 1954 (54.90.700). Image copyright © The Metropolitan Museum of Art

Ending the slave trade had powerful implications, for it reduced the infusion of new Africans into the black population. As a result, an ever higher proportion of blacks was American born, thus speeding the cultural transformation by which Africans became African Americans.

Slavery itself came under attack during the Revolutionary era, with immense consequences for blacks and the nation's future. As the crisis with England heated up, catchwords such as *liberty* and *tyranny*, mobilized by colonists against British policies, reminded citizens that one-fifth of the colonial population was in chains. Samuel Hopkins, a New England clergyman, accosted his compatriots for "making a vain parade of being advocates for the liberties of mankind, while . . . continuing this lawless, cruel, inhuman, and abominable practice of enslaving your fellow creatures." Following independence, antislavery attacks intensified.

In Georgia and South Carolina, where blacks outnumbered whites more than two to one and where slave labor remained essential to the prosperous rice economy, slavery escaped significant challenge as whites tightened local slave codes, shuddering at the prospect of black freedom.

In Virginia and Maryland, by contrast, whites openly argued whether slavery was compatible with republicanism, and in these states significant change did occur. The weakened demand for slave labor in the depressed tobacco economy facilitated the debate. Though neither state abolished slavery, both passed laws making it easier for owners to free their slaves without continuing responsibility for their behavior. Moreover, increasing numbers of blacks purchased

Elizabeth Freeman

As the attack on slavery grew in the northern states, numerous blacks sued in state courts for their freedom. Among them was a woman named Mumbet, who argued that the "inherent liberty" cited by revolutionary leaders applied to all people, including black slaves. Why did she choose a new name once she was no longer a slave?

their own or their families' freedom, or simply ran away. By 1800, more than one of every ten blacks in the Chesapeake region was free, a dramatic increase from 30 years before. Even so, their freedom was limited, since many found themselves obligated to work for others as indentured servants.

The majority of free blacks lived and worked in towns such as Baltimore and Richmond, where they formed communities that served as centers of African American society, as well as havens for slaves escaping from the countryside. In the Chesapeake region, the conditions of life for black Americans slowly changed for the better.

The most dramatic breakthrough occurred in northern states, where slavery was either abolished or put on the road to gradual extinction. Such actions were possible because blacks were a numerical minority—in most areas, they constituted no more than four percent of the population—and slavery had neither the economic nor social importance that it did in the South. In 1780, the Pennsylvania assembly passed a law stipulating that all newborn blacks were to be free when they reached age 21. It was a cautious but decisive step. Other northern states adopted similar policies of gradual emancipation.

Northern blacks joined in the attack on slavery, eagerly petitioning state assemblies for their freedom. "Every Principle from which America has acted in the course of their unhappy difficulties with Great Britain," declared one group of Philadelphia blacks, "pleads stronger than a thousand arguments in favor of our petition."

When the first draft of the Massachusetts constitution, explicitly excluding blacks and mulattoes from the franchise, was made public, William Gordon, a white clergyman, voiced his protest. "Would it not be ridiculous . . . and unjust to exclude freemen from voting . . . though otherwise qualified, because their skins are black?" he questioned. "Why not . . . for being long-nosed, short-faced, or . . . lower than five feet nine?" In the end, Massachusetts's constitution made no mention of race and black men occasionally cast their ballots.

If civic participation by blacks was scattered and temporary in the North, it was almost totally absent in the South. With the brief exception of North Carolina, free African Americans could neither vote nor enjoy protection of their persons and property under the law. In the South, blacks remained almost entirely without political voice, other than the petitions against slavery and mistreatment that they pressed upon the state regimes.

Still, remarkable progress had been made. Prior to the Revolution, slavery had been an accepted fact of northern life. After the Revolution, it no longer was. That change made a vast difference in the lives of countless black Americans. The abolition of slavery in the North, moreover, widened the sectional divergence between North and South, with enormous consequences for the years ahead. In addition, there now existed a coherent, publicly proclaimed antislavery argument, closely linked in Americans' minds with the nation's founding. The first antislavery organizations had been created as well. Although another half century would pass before antislavery became a significant force in American politics, the groundwork for slavery's final abolition had been laid.

Politics and the Economy

The devastating economic effects of independence and the Revolutionary War plagued the American economy throughout the 1770s and 1780s. The cutoff of long-established patterns of overseas trade with England sent American commerce into a 20-year tailspin. While English men-of-war prowled the coast, American ships rocked idly at empty wharves, New England's once booming shipyards grew quiet, and communities whose livelihood depended on the sea sank into depression. Virginia tobacco planters, their British markets gone and their plantations open to seaborne attack, struggled to survive. Farmers in the middle and New England states often prospered when hungry armies were nearby, but their profits plummeted when the armies moved on.

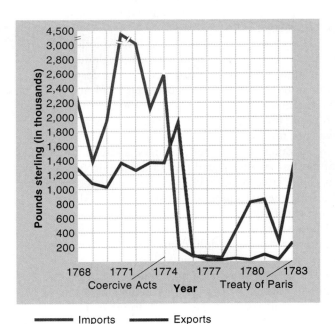

— Imports — Exports

Exports and Imports, 1768–1783

Nonimportation affected colonial commerce during the late 1760s and early 1770s, but both exports and imports plummeted in 1774 and 1775. Why? Can you explain why imports recovered somewhat beginning in 1778, while American exports remained flat?

Source: U.S. Bureau of the Census.

Not everyone suffered equally. With the wearing of homespun clothes deemed patriotic, American artisans often prospered. (The slogan "Buy American" has a long tradition.) People with the right political connections, moreover, made handsome profits from government contracts. Henry Knox, sometime merchant and commander of the continental artillery, observed that he was "exceedingly anxious to effect something in these fluctuating times, which may make . . . [me] easy for life." In the eighteenth century, as now, the boundary between private interest and public duty was often unclear.

But even as some prospered, countless others saw their affairs fall into disarray. Intractable issues such as price and wage inflation, skyrocketing taxation, and mushrooming debt set people sharply against each other. Heated debates arose over whether the states' war debts should be paid off at face value or at some reduced rate. Arguing for full value were the states' creditors—wealthy people who had loaned the states money and had bought up large amounts of government securities at deep discounts. Such people spoke earnestly of upholding the public honor and giving fair return to those who had risked their resources in the revolutionary cause. Opposed were common folk angered by speculators' profits. No one, they argued, should reap personal advantage from public distress.

The issue of taxation, seared into Americans' consciousness by their troubles with England, generated similarly heated controversy. As the costs of the war mounted, so did taxes. Between 1774 and 1778, Massachusetts levied more than £400,000 in taxes, a stunning increase over colonial days. Massachusetts was not unique.

As taxes skyrocketed, farmers, artisans, and others of modest means argued that taxes should be payable in depreciated paper money or government securities. Lacking the hard money that states required in payment, they faced foreclosure of their property. Officials responded that allowing payment in depreciated paper would deprive state governments of critically needed revenue.

Controversy swirled as well around efforts to control soaring prices. In Massachusetts, a bushel of corn that sold for less than a dollar in 1777 went for nearly $80 two years later, and in Maryland the price of wheat increased several thousandfold. Every state experimented with price controls at one time or another. Seldom were such efforts effective; always they generated controversy. In Boston a crowd of women angered by the escalating cost of food tossed a merchant suspected of monopolizing commodities into a cart and dragged him through the city's streets, while "a large concourse of men stood amazed."

Individuals not yet integrated into the market economy supported price controls. They believed that goods should carry a "just price" that was fair to buyer and seller alike. In keeping with that principle, a crowd in New Windsor, New York, seized a shipment of tea bound for Albany in 1777 and sold it for what they deemed a fair offering.

Merchants, shopkeepers, and others accustomed to a commercial economy, however, believed that supply and demand should govern economic transactions. "It is contrary to the nature of commerce," observed Benjamin Franklin, "for government to interfere in the prices of commodities." Attempts to regulate prices only created a disincentive to labor, which was "the principal part of the wealth of every country."

Disputes over paper money also divided the American people. Faced with the uncontrollable escalation of wartime expenses, Congress and the states did what colonial governments had done before and American governments have done ever since: they printed money. In the first year of the war alone, they issued more than $400 million in various kinds of paper, and that was just the beginning. Citizens' willingness to accept such money at face value disappeared as the flood of paper increased. Congressional bills of credit that in 1776 were pegged against gold at the ratio of 1.5 to 1 had slipped five years later to 147 to 1. State currencies depreciated just as alarmingly. Immense quantities of counterfeit currency produced by unscrupulous Americans out to make a profit, as well as by British agents intent on disrupting the American war effort, added to the confusion.

The social consequences of such depreciation were at times alarming. James Lovell reported nervously that "sailors with clubs" were parading the streets of Boston "instead of working for paper." With property values in disarray, it seemed at times as if the very foundations of society were coming unhinged. "The war," wrote Thomas Paine, has "thrown property into channels where before it never was." While profiteers were "heaping up wealth," the rest of society was "jogging on in their old way, with few or no advantages." The poor suffered most severely, for they were most vulnerable to losses in the purchasing power of wages and military pay. But they were not alone. Farmers and merchants, planters and artisans also faced growing debt and uncertainty.

Rarely has the American economy been in such disarray as at the nation's founding. Problems of debt, taxation, price control, and paper money seemed to exceed the capacity of politics for compromise and resolution.

Political Tumult in the States

The many issues embroiling American politics—church and state, slavery and the slave trade, taxation, debt relief, paper money, and arguments over political equality—came together with explosive force in the mid-1780s. The political crisis that resulted spurred demands for a new and more powerful national government.

The Limits of Republican Experimentation

In a pattern that would frequently recur in American history, the postwar era witnessed growing social and political conservatism. Exhausted by the war's ordeal, many Americans focused their energies on their personal lives. With the patriotic crusade against England successfully concluded, the initial surge of republican reform subsided. As a consequence, political leadership fell increasingly to men convinced that republican experimentation had gone too far, that individual liberty threatened to overbalance political order, and that the "better sort" of men, not democratic newcomers, should occupy public office.

The most dramatic change occurred in Pennsylvania, where the democratic constitution of 1776 was replaced in 1790 by a far more conservative document. The new constitution provided for a strong governor who could veto legislation and control the militia, and a conservative senate designed to balance the more democratic assembly. Gaining control even of the assembly by the mid-1780s, the conservatives proceeded to dismantle much of the radicals' program, stopped issuing paper money, and rechartered the Bank of North America. Pennsylvania's experiment in radical republicanism was over.

Shays's Rebellion

The conservative resurgence generated surprisingly little controversy in Pennsylvania. Elsewhere, however, popular opposition to hard money and high-tax policies generated vigorous protest. Nowhere was the situation more volatile than in Massachusetts. The controversy that erupted there in 1786 echoed strongly of equal rights and popular consent, staples of the rhetoric of 1776.

By the mid-1780s, increasing numbers of Massachusetts citizens found that they had to borrow money simply to pay their taxes and support their families. Those who were better off borrowed to speculate in western land and government securities. Because there were no commercial banks in the state, people borrowed from each other in a complicated, highly unstable pyramid of credit that reached from wealthy merchants along the coast to shopkeepers and farmers in the interior.

Trouble began when English goods glutted the American market, forcing prices down. In 1785, a number of English banks, heavily overcommitted in the American trade, called in their American loans. When American merchants tried in turn to collect debts due them by local storekeepers, a credit crisis surged through the state's economy.

Hardest hit were small farmers and laboring people in the countryside and small towns. Caught in a tightening financial bind, they turned to the state government for "stay laws" suspending the collection of private debts and thus easing the threat of foreclosure against their farms and shops. They also demanded new issues of paper money with which to pay both debts and taxes. The largest creditors, most of whom lived in commercial towns along the coast, fought such relief proposals because they wanted to collect what was owed them in hard money. They also feared that new paper money would quickly depreciate, further confounding economic affairs.

By 1786, Massachusetts farmers, desperate in the face of mounting debt and a lingering agricultural depression, were petitioning the Massachusetts assembly for relief in words that echoed the colonial protests of the 1760s. Their appeals, however, fell on deaf ears, for commercial and creditor interests now controlled the government. Turning aside appeals for tax relief, the government passed a law calling for full repayment of the state's Revolutionary War debt and levied a new round of taxes that would make payment possible. No matter that, as one angry citizen charged, "there was not . . . the money in possession or at command among the people" to pay what was due. Between 1784 and 1786, 29 towns defaulted on their tax obligations.

As frustrated Americans had done before and would do again when the law proved unresponsive to their needs, Massachusetts farmers took matters into their own hands. A Hampshire County convention of delegates from 50 towns condemned the state senate, court fees, and tax system. It advised against violence, but crowds soon began to form.

The county courts drew much of the farmers' wrath, because they issued the writs of foreclosure that private creditors and state officials demanded. On September 5, 1786, armed men closed the court at Worcester. When farmers threatened similar actions elsewhere, the alarmed governor dispatched 600 militiamen to protect the state Supreme Court, then meeting in Springfield.

About 500 insurgents had gathered nearby under the leadership of Daniel Shays, a popular Revolutionary War captain recently fallen on hard times. A "brave and good soldier," Shays had returned home in 1780, tired and frustrated, to await payment for his military service. Like thousands of others, he had a long wait. Meanwhile, his farming went badly, debts accumulated, and, as he later recalled, "the spector of debtor's jail . . . hovered close by." Most of the men who gathered around Shays were also debtors and veterans.

The Continental Congress, worried about a possible raid on the federal arsenal at Springfield and urged by the Massachusetts delegates to take action, authorized 1,300 troops, ostensibly for service against the Indians but actually to be ready for use against Shays and his supporters. For a few weeks, Massachusetts teetered on the brink of civil conflict.

The insurrection collapsed in eastern Massachusetts in late November, but to the west it was far from over. When several insurgent groups refused Governor James Bowdoin's order to disperse, he called out a force of 4,400 men, financed and led by worried eastern merchants. On January 26, 1787, Shays led 1,200 men toward the federal arsenal at Springfield. When they arrived, its frightened defenders opened fire, killing four of the attackers and sending the Shaysites into retreat. By the end of February, the rebellion was over. In March, the legislature pardoned all but Shays and three other leaders; in another year, they too were forgiven.

Similar challenges to public authority, fired by personal troubles and frustration over unresponsive governments, erupted in six other states. In Charles County, Maryland, a "tumultuary assemblage" rushed into the courthouse, demanding paper money and suspension of debt collection. The governor condemned the "riotous" proceedings and warned against further "violence and outrages." In South Carolina, an incensed Hezekiah Mayham, being served by the sheriff with a writ of foreclosure, forced him to eat it on the spot. Warned Judge Aedanus Burke, not even "5,000 troops, the best in America" could enforce obedience to the court under such conditions.

Across the states, politics was in turmoil. While many felt betrayed by the Revolution's promise of equal rights and were angered by the "arrogant unresponsiveness" of government, others were alarmed by the "democratic excesses" that the Revolution appeared to have unleashed. What the immediate future might hold seemed exceedingly uncertain.

Toward a New National Government

By 1786, belief was spreading among members of Congress that the nation was in crisis and the republican experiment was in danger of foundering. Explanations for the crisis and prescriptions for its resolution varied, but attention focused on the inadequacies of the Articles of Confederation. Within two years, following a deeply divisive political struggle, a new constitution had replaced the Articles, altering forever the course of American history.

The Rise of Federalism

The supporters of a stronger national government called themselves Federalists, leading their opponents to adopt the name Anti-Federalists. Led by men such as Washington, Hamilton, Madison, and John Jay, whose experiences in the continental army and Congress had strengthened their national vision, the Federalists believed that the nation's survival was at stake. Such men had never been comfortable with the more democratic impulses of the Revolution. While committed to moderate republicanism, they believed that democratic change had carried too far, property rights needed greater protection, and an "aristocracy of talent" should lead the country.

The Revolution, lamented Jay, "laid open a wide field for the operation of ambition," among men "raised from low degrees to high stations and rendered giddy by elevation." It was time, he insisted, to find better ways of protecting "the worthy against the licentious."

Federalist leaders feared the loss of their political power, but they were concerned as well about the collapse of the orderly world they believed essential to the preservation of republican liberty. In 1776, American liberty had required protection against overweening British power. Now, however, danger arose from excessive liberty that threatened to degenerate into license. "We have probably had too good an opinion of human nature," concluded Washington somberly. "Experience has taught us, that men will not adopt and carry into execution measures the best calculated for their own good, without the intervention of a coercive power." What America now needed was a "strong government, ably administered."

The Federalists regarded outbursts like Shays's uprising not as evidence of genuine social distress but as threats to social and political order. Although they were reassured by the speed with which the Shaysites had been dispatched, the episode persuaded them of the need for a stronger national government managed by the "better sort."

Congress's inability to handle the national debt, establish public credit, and restore overseas trade also troubled the Federalists. Sensitive to America's economic and military weakness, smarting from French and English arrogance, and aware of continuing Anglo-European designs on North America, Federalists called for a new national government capable of extending American trade, spurring economic recovery, and protecting the national interest. Beyond that, Federalists shared a vision of an expanding commercial republic, its people spreading across the rich lands of the interior, its merchant ships connecting America with the markets of Europe and beyond. That vision, so rich in promise, seemed clearly at risk.

The Grand Convention

The first step toward governmental reform came in September 1786, when delegates from five states who were gathered in Annapolis, Maryland, to discuss interstate commerce, issued a call for a convention to revise the Articles of Confederation. In February, the Confederation Congress cautiously endorsed the idea. Before long, it became clear that far more than a revision of the Articles was afoot.

During May 1787, delegates representing every state except Rhode Island began assembling in Philadelphia. The city bustled with excitement as they gathered, for the roster read like an honor roll of the Revolution. From Virginia came the distinguished lawyer George Mason, chief author of Virginia's trailblazing bill of rights, and the already legendary George Washington. Proponents of the convention had held their breath while Washington considered whether to attend. His presence vastly increased the prospects of success. James Madison was there as well. No one, with perhaps the single exception of Alexander Hamilton, was more committed to nationalist reform. Certainly, no one had worked harder to prepare for the convention. Poring over treatises on republican government and natural law that his friend Thomas Jefferson sent from France, Madison brought to Philadelphia a clear design for a new national government. That design, presented to the convention as the Virginia Plan, would serve as the basis for the new constitution. Nor did anyone rival the diminutive Madison's contributions to the convention's work. Tirelessly, he took the convention floor to argue the nationalist cause or buttonhole wavering delegates to strengthen their resolve. Somehow, he also found the energy to keep extensive notes of the debates in his personal shorthand. Those notes constitute our essential record of the convention's proceedings.

Two distinguished Virginians were conspicuously absent. Thomas Jefferson was in Paris as minister to France, and the old patriot Patrick Henry, an ardent champion of state supremacy, feared what the convention would do and wanted no part of it.

From Pennsylvania came the venerable Benjamin Franklin, too old to contribute significantly to the debates but still able to call quarreling members to account and re-inspire them in their work. His colleagues from Pennsylvania included the erudite Scots lawyer James Wilson, whose nationalist sympathies had been inflamed when a democratic mob, resentful of privileged lawyers and merchants, attacked his elegant Philadelphia townhouse in 1779. Robert Morris, probably the richest man in America, was there as well. Massachusetts was ably represented by Elbridge Gerry and Rufus King, while South Carolina sent John Rutledge and Charles Pinckney. Roger Sherman led Connecticut's contingent.

James Madison, Father of the U.S. Constitution
James Madison of Virginia was only 36 years old when the Philadelphia convention met. Why did he and other Federalists work so tirelessly to replace the Articles of Confederation with a new Constitution?

The New York assembly sent a deeply divided delegation. Governor George Clinton, determined to protect New York's autonomy as well as his own political power, saw to it that several Anti-Federalist skeptics made the trip to Philadelphia. They were no match for Hamilton, however.

Born in the Leeward Islands, the "bastard brat of a Scots-peddlar" and a strong-willed woman with a troubled marriage, Hamilton used his intelligence and ingratiating charm to rise rapidly in the world. Sent to New York by wealthy sponsors, he quickly established himself as a favorite of the city's mercantile community. While in his early twenties, he became Washington's wartime aide-de-camp. That relationship served Hamilton well for the next 20 years. Returning from the war, he married the wealthy Elizabeth Schuyler, thereby securing his personal fortune and strengthening his political connections. Together with Madison, Hamilton had promoted the abortive Annapolis convention. At Philadelphia, he was determined to drive his nationalist vision ahead.

Meeting in Independence Hall, where the Declaration of Independence had been proclaimed little more than a decade earlier, the convention elected Washington as its presiding officer, adopted rules of procedure, and, after spirited debate, voted to close the doors and conduct its business in secret.

Creating a New National Government

This painting by Thomas Rossiter, done in the early nineteenth century, provides an imaginative portrayal of the Philadelphia convention, with George Washington presiding and a rising sun, symbolic of the new nation, shining behind him.

(Thomas Rossiter, *Signing of the Constitution,* ca. 1860–1870. Independence National Historical Park Collection)

Drafting the Constitution

Debate focused first on the Virginia Plan, introduced on May 29 by Edmund Randolph. It outlined a potentially powerful national government and effectively set the convention's agenda. According to its provisions, there would be a bicameral Congress, with the lower house elected by the people and the upper house, or Senate, chosen by the lower house from nominees proposed by the state legislatures. The plan also called for a president who would be named by Congress, a national judiciary, and a Council of Revision, whose task was to review the constitutionality of federal laws.

The smaller states quickly objected to the Virginia Plan's call for proportional rather than equal representation of the states. On June 15, William Paterson introduced a counterproposal, the New Jersey Plan. It urged retention of the Articles of Confederation as the basic structure of government while conferring on Congress the long-sought powers to tax and regulate foreign and interstate commerce. After three days of heated debate, by a vote of seven states to three, the delegates adopted the Virginia Plan as the basis for further discussions. It was now clear that the convention would replace the Articles with a much stronger national government. The only question was how powerful the new government would be.

At times over the next four months, it seemed that the Grand Convention would collapse under the weight of its own disagreements and the oppressive summer heat. How were the conflicting interests of large and small states to be reconciled? How should the balance of power between national and state governments be struck? How could an executive be created that was strong enough to govern but not so strong as to endanger republican liberty? And what, if anything, would the convention say about slavery and the slave trade, issues on which northerners and southerners, antislavery and proslavery advocates passionately disagreed?

Hamilton presented an audaciously conservative proposal, calling for a Congress and president elected for life and a national government so powerful that the states would become little more than administrative agencies. Finding his plan under attack and his influence rapidly eroding, Hamilton withdrew from the convention in late June. He would return a month later but make few additional contributions to the convention's work.

At the other extreme stood the ardent Anti-Federalist Luther Martin of Maryland. Rude and unkempt, Martin opposed anything that threatened state sovereignty or smacked of aristocracy. Increasingly isolated by the convention's nationalist inclinations, Martin also returned home, in his case to spread the alarm.

By early July, with tempers frayed and frustration growing over the apparent deadlock, the delegates agreed to recess, ostensibly for Independence Day but

Recovering the Past

PATRIOTIC PAINTINGS

The questions that historians ask are limited only by their own imagination and the evidence left behind for them to study. In addition to written documents such as household inventories and militia rolls, and material artifacts such as tombstones and the archaeological residue of burial mounds, historians also examine paintings and other forms of visual evidence for information about the past.

While showing the development of artistic styles and techniques, paintings also provide important windows into past eras for social and cultural historians by revealing how people looked and did their work, as well as what the landscape and built environment were like. Paintings also offer insights into the values and attitudes of past times, for they are often intended not only to please the viewer's eye but also to enlighten and instruct.

So it was with Charles Willson Peale, who as a member of the Pennsylvania militia carried paint kits and canvas along with his musket as he followed George Washington during the Revolutionary War. Before the war was over, he had completed four portraits of the general.

And so it was, even more spectacularly, with the artist John Trumbull, who recorded on canvas some of the most dramatic events of the nation's founding. Slighted for promotion during the Rhode Island campaign early in the war, Trumbull resigned his commission to become a painter. After a frustrating start, he sailed for London, where he studied with the artist Benjamin West, another transplanted American. Imprisoned briefly at the urging of angry American Loyalists, Trumbull was deported to the United States. Returning to England at the war's end, he was urged by West and Thomas Jefferson to paint an ambitious series of "national history" canvases. Over the next four decades, in addition to numerous portraits, religious subjects, and landscapes, Trumbull fashioned the most famous sequence of patriotic paintings ever undertaken by an American artist.

Included were four canvases, depicting crucial military and civil turning points in the struggle for American independence, commissioned by Congress in the early nineteenth century and now hanging in the capitol rotunda in Washington, D.C.—*The Surrender of General Burgoyne at Saratoga, The Surrender of Lord Cornwallis at Yorktown, The*

John Trumbull, *The Death of General Warren at the Battle of Bunker Hill*

Declaration of Independence, and *The Resignation of General Washington* as commander of the continental army. In addition to those monumental works, Trumbull fashioned a number of heroic battle scenes, including *The Death of General Warren at the Battle of Bunker Hill,* shown here.

Though Trumbull knew Warren and others who fought at Bunker Hill, he himself had witnessed the battle from a distance. Although Trumbull was familiar with the techniques of military combat from his own months in the army, he was not primarily concerned with literal accuracy as he composed his painting. Guided by the canons of classical aesthetics popular at the time, he was more interested in the power of artistic "invention" to impart "ideal" truths through the use of brush and pigment.

Examine the painting carefully. How has the artist arranged the figures in relationship to each other? What facial expressions and postures has he given to the people depicted? In what ways do the banners, clouds, and uses of light and color contribute to the painting's overall effect? What messages about the Revolutionary War did Trumbull want viewers to carry away from the canvas?

In all his historical canvases, Trumbull was intent on promoting national pride and constructing public memory. How does this painting serve those purposes? Why was the creation of a shared public memory so important during the early years of the new republic? Might Trumbull have had future generations of Americans as well as his own contemporaries in mind as he did his work?

Art and politics have been intimately related throughout our history, for painting, theater, music, and other forms of performance art have been employed to challenge as well as celebrate political leaders and their policies.

Reflecting on the Past Think for a moment about the connections between art and politics in our own time. Why have controversies recently swirled around the National Endowments for the Arts and the Humanities? Should the government provide financial assistance for the arts? If so, should such assistance be accompanied by restrictions on the political messages such art might convey? Is art ever nonpolitical? ◼

---

actually to let Franklin, Roger Sherman of Connecticut, and several others make a final effort at compromise. All agreed that only a bold stroke could prevent a collapse.

That stroke came on July 12, as part of what has become known as the Great Compromise. The reassembled delegates settled one major point of controversy by agreeing that representation in the House of Representatives should be based on the total of each state's white population plus three-fifths of its blacks. Though African Americans were not accorded citizenship and could not vote, the southern delegates argued that they should be fully counted for this purpose. Delegates from the northern states, where relatively few blacks lived, did not want them counted at all, but the bargain was struck. As part of this compromise, the convention agreed that direct taxes would also be apportioned on the basis of population and that blacks would be counted similarly in that calculation. On July 16, the convention accepted the principle that the states should have equal votes in the Senate. Thus the interests of both large states and small were effectively accommodated.

The convention then submitted its work to a committee of detail for drafting in proper constitutional form. That group reported on August 6, and for the next month the delegates hammered out the language of the document's seven articles. On several occasions, differences seemed so great that it was uncertain whether the convention could proceed. In each instance, however, agreement was reached, and the discussion continued.

Determined to give the new government the stability that state governments lacked, the delegates created an electoral process designed to bring persons of wide experience and solid reputation into national office. An Electoral College of wise and experienced leaders, selected at the direction of state legislatures, would meet to choose the president. The process functioned exactly that way during the first several presidential elections.

Selection of the Senate would be similarly indirect, for its members were to be named by the state legislatures. (Not until 1913, with ratification of the Seventeenth Amendment, would the American people elect their senators directly.) Even the House of Representatives, the only popularly elected branch of the new government, was to be filled with people of standing and wealth, for the Federalists were confident that only such men would be able to attract the necessary votes.

The delegates' final set of compromises touched the fate of black Americans. At the insistence of southerners, the convention agreed that the slave trade would not formally end for another 20 years. As drafted, the Constitution did not contain the words *slavery* or *slave trade,* but spoke more vaguely about not prohibiting the "migration or importation of such persons as any of the states now existing shall think proper to admit." The meaning, however, was entirely clear.

Despite Gouverneur Morris's impassioned charge that slavery was a "nefarious institution" that would bring "the curse of Heaven on the states where it prevails," the delegates firmly rejected a proposal to abolish slavery, thereby tacitly acknowledging its legitimacy. More than that, they guaranteed slavery's protection, by writing in Section 2 of Article 4 that "No person held to service or labour in one state,... [and] escaping into another, shall, in consequence of any law...therein, be discharged from such service, but shall be delivered up on claim of the party to whom such service or labour may be due." Through such convoluted language, the delegates provided federal sanction for the capture and return of runaway slaves. This fugitive slave clause would return to haunt northern consciences in the years ahead. At the time, however, it seemed a small price to pay for sectional harmony and a new government. Northern accommodation to the demands of the southern delegates was eased, moreover, by knowledge that southerners in the Confederation Congress, still meeting in New York City, had agreed to prohibit new slaves from entering the Northwest Territory.

Although the Constitution's unique federal system of government called for shared responsibilities between the nation and the states, it decisively strengthened the national government. Congress would now have the authority to levy and collect taxes, regulate commerce with foreign nations and between the states, devise uniform rules for naturalization, administer national patents and copyrights, and control the federal district in which it would eventually be located. Conspicuously missing was any statement reserving to the states all powers not explicitly conferred on the central government. Such language had proved crippling in the Articles of Confederation. On the contrary, the Constitution contained a number of clauses bestowing vaguely defined grants of power on the new government. Section 8 of Article 1, for example, granted Congress the authority to "provide for the...general welfare of the United States" as well as to "make all laws...necessary and proper for carrying into execution...all...powers vested by this Constitution in the government of the United States." Later generations would call these phrases "elastic clauses" and would use them to expand the federal government's activities.

In addition, Section 10 of Article 1 contained a litany of powers now denied the states, among them issuing paper money and entering into agreements with foreign powers without the consent of Congress. A final measure of the Federalists' determination to ensure the new government's supremacy over the states, was the assertion in Article 6 that the Constitution and all laws and treaties passed under it were to be regarded as the "supreme Law of the Land."

When the convention had finished its business, 3 of the 42 remaining delegates refused to sign the document. The other 39, however, affixed their names and forwarded it to the Confederation Congress along with the request that it be sent on to the states for approval. On September 17, the Grand Convention adjourned.

Federalists Versus Anti-Federalists

Ratification presented the Federalists with a more difficult problem than they had faced at Philadelphia, for the debate now shifted to the states where sentiment was sharply divided and the political situation was more difficult to control. Recognizing the unlikelihood of gaining quick agreement by all 13 states, the Federalists stipulated that the Constitution should go into effect when any nine agreed to it. Other states could then enter the Union as they were ready. Ratification was to be decided by specially elected conventions rather than by the state assemblies. Approval by such conventions would give the new Constitution greater legitimacy by grounding it directly in the consent of the people.

In the Confederation Congress, opponents of the new Constitution charged that the Philadelphia Convention had grossly exceeded its authority. But after a few days' debate, Congress dutifully forwarded the document to the states for consideration. Word of the dramatic changes being proposed spread rapidly. In each state, Federalists and Anti-Federalists, the latter now actively opposing the Constitution, prepared to debate the new articles of government.

Opposition to the proposed Constitution was widespread and vocal. Some critics warned of the threat to state interests. Others, like Timothy Bloodworth, charged that, like all "energetic" governments, the one being proposed would be corrupted by its own power. Far from the watchful eyes of the citizenry, its officials would behave as power wielders always had, and American liberty, so recently preserved at such high cost, would again come under attack.

The Anti-Federalists were aghast at their opponents' vision of an expanding "republican empire." "The idea of...[a] republic, on an average of 1,000 miles in length, and 800 in breadth, and containing 6 millions of white inhabitants all reduced to the same standards of morals,...habits...[and] laws," exclaimed one incredulous critic, is "contrary to the whole experience of mankind." Such an extended republic would quickly fall prey to factional conflict and internal disorder. Anti-Federalists continued to believe that republican liberty could be preserved only in small, homogeneous societies, where the seeds of faction were few and public virtue guided citizens' behavior.

Nor did Anti-Federalists believe that the proposed separation of executive, legislative, and judicial

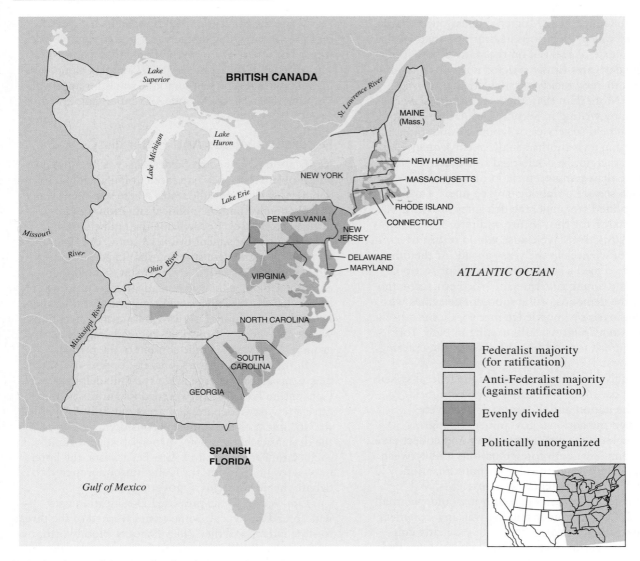

Federalist and Anti-Federalist Areas, 1787–1788

Distinct geographic patterns of Federalist and Anti-Federalist strength developed during the ratification debate. This map shows areas whose delegates to the state ratifying conventions voted for and against the Constitution. What do the patterns suggest concerning the economic and social bases of Federalist and Anti-Federalist support?

branches or the intended balance between state and national governments would prevent power's abuse. Government, they insisted, must be kept simple, for complexity only confused the people and cloaked selfish ambition.

Not all Anti-Federalists were democratic in sympathy, for southerners' appeals to local authority did not always mean support for political equality. Yet with their warnings against centralized power, many did speak fervently of democratic principles. Certainly they believed more firmly than their Federalist opponents that if government was to be safe, it must be tied closely to the people

Federalist spokesmen moved quickly to counter the Anti-Federalists' attack, for many of the criticisms

carried the sanction of the revolutionary past. Their most important effort was a series of essays penned by James Madison, Alexander Hamilton, and John Jay and published in New York under the pseudonym Publius. The *Federalist* essays, as they were called, were written to promote ratification in New York but were quickly reprinted elsewhere.

Madison, Hamilton, and Jay moved systematically through the Constitution, explaining its virtues and responding to the Anti-Federalists' charges. In the process, they described a political vision fundamentally different from that of their Anti-Federalist opponents. No difference was more dramatic than the Federalists' treatment of governmental power. Power, the Federalists argued, was not the enemy of liberty but its guarantor. Where government was not sufficiently "energetic" and "efficient," demagogues and disorganizers would find opportunity to do their nefarious work. It is far better, Hamilton wrote in *Federalist No. 26,* "to hazard the abuse of... confidence than to embarrass the government and endanger the public safety by impolitic restrictions of... authority."

The authors of the *Federalist* also countered Anti-Federalist warnings that a single, extended republic encompassing the country's economic and social diversity would lead inevitably to factional conflict and the end of republican liberty. Turning the Anti-Federalists' classic, republican argument on its head, they explained that political divisions were the inevitable accompaniment of human liberty. Wrote Madison in *Federalist No. 10:* "Liberty is to faction what air is to fire, an aliment without which it instantly expires." To suppress faction would bring the destruction of liberty itself. Politics had to heed this harsh fact of human nature and provide for peaceful compromise among conflicting groups. Out of the clash and accommodation of social and economic interests would emerge the best possible approximation of the public good.

In that argument is to be found the basic rationale for modern democratic politics, but it left Anti-Federalists sputtering in frustration. Where in the Federalists' scheme was there a place for that familiar abstraction, the public good? What would become of public virtue in a system built on the notion of competing, private interests? In such a free market of competition, Anti-Federalists warned, the wealthy and powerful would thrive, while ordinary folk would suffer.

As the ratification debate revealed, the two camps held sharply contrasting visions of the new republic. Anti-Federalists remained much closer to the original republicanism of 1776, with its suspicion of power and wealth, its emphasis on the primacy of local government, and its fears of national development. They envisioned a decentralized republic filled with citizens who were self-reliant, guided by public virtue, and whose destiny was determined primarily by the states rather than the nation. Anxious about the future, they longed to preserve the political world of an idealized past.

The Federalists, on the other hand, persuaded that America's situation had changed dramatically since 1776, embraced the idea of nationhood and looked forward with anticipation to the development of a rising "republican empire," fueled by commercial development and led by men of wealth and talent. Both Federalists and Anti-Federalists claimed to be heirs of the Revolution, yet they differed fundamentally in what they understood that heritage to be.

The Struggle over Ratification

No one knows what most Americans thought of the proposed Constitution, for no national plebiscite on it was ever taken. A majority of the people probably opposed the document, either out of indifference or alarm. Fortunately for the Federalists, they did not have to persuade most Americans but needed only to secure majorities in nine of the state ratifying conventions, a much less formidable task.

They set about it with determination. As soon as the Philadelphia Convention adjourned, its members hurried home to organize the ratification movement in their states. In Delaware and Georgia, New Jersey and Connecticut, where Federalists were confident of their strength, they pressed quickly for a vote. Where the outcome was uncertain, as in New York, Massachusetts,

Celebrating Ratification

The federal ship *Hamilton* formed the centerpiece of a grand procession in New York City celebrating the successful ratification of the new Constitution. Why was the ship used to symbolize the Constitution?

and Virginia, they delayed, hoping that word of ratification elsewhere would work to their benefit.

It took less than a year to secure approval by the necessary nine states. Delaware, Pennsylvania, and New Jersey ratified first, in December 1787. Approval came a month later in Georgia and Connecticut. Massachusetts ratified in February 1788, but only after Federalist leaders agreed to forward a set of amendments outlining a federal bill of rights along with notice of ratification.

Maryland and South Carolina were the seventh and eighth states to approve. That left New Hampshire and Virginia vying for the honor of being ninth and putting the Constitution over the top. Sensing that they lacked the necessary votes, Federalists adjourned the New Hampshire convention and worked feverishly to build support. When the convention reconvened, it took but three days to secure a Federalist majority. New Hampshire ratified on June 21.

Two massive gaps in the new Union remained—Virginia and New York. Clearly, the nation could not endure without them. In Virginia, Madison gathered support by promising that the new Congress would immediately consider a federal bill of rights. The Anti-Federalist oratory of Patrick Henry proved no match for the careful politicking of Madison and others. On June 25, the Virginia convention voted to ratify by the narrow margin of 10 votes.

The New York convention gathered on June 17 at Poughkeepsie, with the Anti-Federalist followers of Governor Clinton firmly in command. Hamilton worked for delay, hoping that news of the results in New Hampshire and Virginia would turn the tide. For several weeks, approval hung in the balance. On July 27, approval squeaked through, 30 to 27. That left two states still uncommitted. North Carolina (with Timothy Bloodworth's skeptical approval) finally ratified in November 1789. Rhode Island did not enter the Union until May 1790, more than a year after the new government had gotten underway.

The Social Geography of Ratification

Merchants and businessmen supported the Constitution most ardently. Enthusiasm also ran high among urban laborers, artisans, and shopkeepers—surprisingly so, given the Anti-Federalists' criticism of wealth and power and emphasis on democratic equality. City artisans and workers, after all, had been in the vanguard of democratic reform during the Revolution. But in the troubled circumstances of the late 1780s, they worried about their livelihoods and believed that a stronger government could better promote overseas trade and protect American artisans from foreign competition.

On July 4, 1788, a grand procession celebrating the Constitution's ratification wound through the streets of Philadelphia. Seventeen thousand strong, it graphically demonstrated the breadth of support for the Constitution. At the head of the line marched lawyers, merchants, and others of the city's elite. Close behind came representatives of virtually every trade in the city, from ship's carpenters to shoemakers, each trade with its own floats and mottoed banners. "May commerce flourish and industry be rewarded," declared the shipbuilders. "May the federal government revive our trade," exclaimed the bakers. "Home-brewed is best," insisted the maltsters. For the moment, declared the democratic-minded physician Benjamin Rush in amazement, "rank . . . forgot all its claims." Within a few years, political disputes would divide merchants and artisans once again. For the moment, however, people of all ranks joined in celebrating the new Constitution.

Outside the coastal cities, the Constitution found support among commercial farmers and southern planters eager for profit and anxious about overseas markets. But in the interior, Federalist enthusiasm waned and Anti-Federalist sentiment increased. Among ordinary farmers living outside the market economy, local loyalties and the republicanism of 1776 still held sway.

Why did the Federalists prevail when their opponents had only to tap into people's deep-seated fears of central government and appeal to their local loyalties? They won, in part, because of the widespread perception that the Articles of Confederation were inadequate and that America's experiment in republican independence was doomed unless decisive action was taken. Just

RATIFICATION OF THE CONSTITUTION

Votes of State Ratifying Conventions

State	Date	For	Against
Delaware	December 1787	30	0
Pennsylvania	December 1787	46	23
New Jersey	December 1787	38	0
Georgia	January 1788	26	0
Connecticut	January 1788	128	40
Massachusetts	February 1788	187	168
Maryland	April 1788	63	11
South Carolina	May 1788	149	73
New Hampshire	June 1788	57	47
Virginia	June 1788	89	79
New York	July 1788	30	27
North Carolina	November 1789	194	77
Rhode Island	May 1790	34	32

Timeline

1780s	Pennsylvania begins gradual abolition of slavery
	Virginia and Maryland debate abolition of slavery
1784	Treaty of Fort Stanwix with the Iroquois
	Spain closes the Mississippi River to American navigation
1785	Treaty of Hopewell with the Cherokee
	Land Ordinance for the Northwest Territory
	Jay–Gardoqui negotiations
1786	Virginia adopts Bill for Establishing Religious Freedom
	Annapolis Convention calls for revision of the Articles of Confederation
1786–1787	Shays's Rebellion
1787	Northwest Ordinance
	Constitutional Convention
	Federalist Papers published by Hamilton, Jay, and Madison
1788	Constitution ratified

as important, the Federalists succeeded because of their determination and political skill. Most of the Revolution's major leaders were Federalists. Time and again they spoke out for the Constitution, and time and again their support proved decisive. Their experience in the continental army and as members of the Continental and Confederation Congresses fired their vision of what the nation might become. They brought that vision to the ratification process and asked others to share it. Their success turned the American republic in a new and fateful direction.

Conclusion
COMPLETING THE REVOLUTION

Only five years had passed between England's acknowledgment of American independence in 1783 and ratification of the new Constitution, yet to many Americans it seemed far longer than that. At war's end, the difficulties of sustaining American liberty were abundantly evident. The experience of the 1780s added to these difficulties as the American people struggled to survive in a hostile Atlantic environment and cope with troublesome issues of church and state, slavery and the slave trade, and an economy shattered by the cutoff of overseas trade and rampant inflation. Amidst the resulting political turmoil, Americans continued to argue over how democratic their experiment in republicanism could safely be.

At the same time, the American people retained an immense reservoir of optimism about the future. Had they not defeated mighty England? Was not their Revolution destined to change the course of history

and provide a model for all mankind? Did not America's wonderfully rich interior contain the promise of limitless economic and social opportunity? Though Timothy Bloodworth continued to worry, others, filled with the enthusiasm of their new beginning, answered with a resounding "Yes." Much would depend on their new Constitution and the government soon to be created under it. As the ratification debate subsided and the Confederation Congress prepared to adjourn, the American people looked eagerly and anxiously ahead.

QUESTIONS FOR REVIEW AND REFLECTION

1. What problems did the new territory west of the Appalachian Mountains pose for the new nation, and how effectively did Congress handle those problems during the 1780s?
2. With independence, the United States had to develop its own policies for dealing with other nations. What major foreign policy problems did Congress face during the 1780s, and how effectively did it deal with them?
3. Throughout the nation's history, wars have disrupted the American economy. To what extent was this true of the Revolutionary War and what were the consequences during the 1780s?
4. The successful struggle for American independence encouraged many Americans to apply the language of rights and equality used against England to the conditions of their own lives. Identify three examples of this pressure for democratic change and explain how successful these efforts were.
5. The creation of the new Constitution in 1787–1788 has often been interpreted as a conservative reaction to the democratic tendencies of the Revolution. Is this an accurate judgment?

Creating a Nation

In December 1790, the national government moved from New York to Philadelphia, where it stayed until moving to the new capital in the District of Columbia in 1799. While in Philadelphia, the House and Senate met in Congress Hall, adjacent to the Philadelphia State House depicted here. In this image, a variety of people, including several Indians, mingle in the State House yard.

(The Historical Society of Pennsylvania (HSP), *The State House, Philadelphia,* 1800, William Birch, [Bd 61 B 531 plate 22])

American Stories

Questioning Authorities

In October 1789, David Brown arrived in Dedham, Massachusetts. Born 50 years earlier in Bethlehem, Connecticut, Brown served in the Revolutionary army. After the war, he shipped out on an American merchantman to see the world. His travels, as he reported, took him to "nineteen different... Kingdoms in Europe, and nearly all the United States." Before settling in Dedham, he visited scores of Massachusetts towns, supporting himself as a day laborer while discussing the troubled state of public affairs with local townspeople.

Once in Dedham, he made his presence felt. Though he had little formal schooling, he was a man of powerful opinions. His reading and personal experience had persuaded him that government was a conspiracy of the rich to exploit farmers, artisans, and other common folk, and he was quick to make his opinions known.

The object of his wrath was the central government recently established under the new national constitution. Though citing no evidence, he accused government leaders of engrossing the nation's western lands for themselves. "Five hundred [people] out of the union of five millions receive all the benefit of public property and live upon the ruins of the rest of the community," he fumed in one of his numerous pamphlets. Such a government, he warned, would soon lose the confidence of the people.

In the highly charged political climate of the 1790s, Brown's attacks on the new government brought a sharp response. In 1798, John Davis, the federal district attorney in Boston, issued a warrant for Brown's arrest on charges of sedition, while government-supported newspapers attacked him as a "rallying point of insurrection and disorder." Fearing arrest, Brown fled to Salem, where he was caught and charged with intent to defame the government and aid the country's enemies. Lacking $400 bail, he was clapped in prison.

In June 1799, Brown came before the U.S. Circuit Court, Justice Samuel Chase presiding. Chase's behavior was anything but judicious. Convinced that critics of the administration were enemies of the republic, Chase was determined to make Brown an example. Confused and hoping for leniency, Brown pleaded guilty to the charges against him.

Ignoring Brown's plea, Chase directed the federal prosecutor to "examine the witness... so that the degree of his guilt might be duly ascertained." Before passing sentence, Chase demanded that Brown provide the names of his accomplices and a list of subscribers to his writings. When Brown refused, protesting that he would "lose all my friends," Chase sentenced him to a fine of $480 and 18 months in jail, no matter that Brown could not pay the fine and faced the prospect of indefinite imprisonment.

In rendering judgment, Chase castigated Brown for his "disorganizing doctrines and... falsehoods, and the very alarming and dangerous excesses to which he attempted to incite the uninformed part of the community." Not all citizens, Chase thought, should be allowed to comment so brashly on public affairs. For nearly two years, Brown languished in prison. Not until the Federalist party was defeated in the election of 1800 and the Jeffersonian Republicans had taken office was he freed.

David Brown discovered how easy it was for critics of the government to get into trouble in the early republic, one of the most tumultuous eras in American political history. Though independence had been won, the struggle over political power and control of the revolutionary heritage continued. As Benjamin Rush, Philadelphia physician and revolutionary patriot explained: "The American War is over, but this is far from being the case with the American Revolution. On the contrary, nothing but the first act of the great drama is closed. It remains [for us]... to establish and perfect our new forms of government." Events would soon demonstrate how difficult, and how important to the nation's future, that task would be.

Controversy between Federalist supporters of the national government and the emerging Jeffersonian Republican opposition first erupted over domestic policies designed to stabilize the nation's finances and promote its economic development. Those policies revealed deep-seated conflicts between economic interests and raised urgent questions of how the new constitution should be interpreted. What was the proper balance of power between state and national governments? How should governing authority be allocated between the executive branch and Congress? Much depended on the answers to such troubling questions.

Within a few years, international events further roiled American politics. The French Revolution and a successful revolt by black Haitians against French colonial power in the Caribbean—the two most dramatic events in a larger web of democratic insurgencies against established authorities that reached from Europe to the Americas—inflamed congressional politics and roused the people at large. By the last years of the 1790s, the prospect of war with France and Federalist security measures such as the Alien and Sedition Acts, brought the nation to the brink of political upheaval. That prospect was narrowly avoided by the Federalists' defeat and Thomas Jefferson's election as president in 1800.

Having captured the presidency and control of Congress, the Jefferson Republicans set about the task of refashioning the government, topics addressed in Chapter 8. At home, the Jeffersonians dismantled the Federalists' war program, reduced the national debt, promoted westward expansion, and emphasized state rather than national authority. Abroad, they struggled less successfully to protect American commerce on the high seas and avoid embroilment in European war.

Adding to the political crisis was widespread anxiety over the nation's novel and still unproven "experiment" in creating a sprawling and diverse republic. The absence of fully developed political parties skilled in forging compromise among leaders at the nation's capital and organizing political energy among the people compounded the problem. As political conflict grew, it caught up countless individuals like David Brown in its toils. By the time Thomas Jefferson left the presidency in 1809, it was apparent how fragile, and yet how resilient, America's new government was proving to be.

Launching the National Republic

Once the Constitution had been ratified, its Anti-Federalist critics seemed ready to give the experiment a chance. They were determined, however, to watch closely for the first signs of danger. It was not many months before they sounded the alarm.

Beginning the New Government

On April 16, 1789, George Washington, unanimously elected president by the Electoral College, started north from Virginia to be inaugurated first president of the United States. His feelings were mixed as he set forth. "I bade adieu to Mount Vernon, to private life, and to domestic felicity," he confided to his diary, "and with a mind oppressed with more anxious and painful sensations than I have words to express, set out for New York...with the best disposition to render service to my country in obedience to its call, but with less hope of answering its expectations." He had good reason for such foreboding.

The president-elect was the object of constant adulation as he journeyed north. In villages and towns, guns boomed their salutes, church bells pealed, and local dignitaries toasted his arrival. On April 23, he was rowed on an elegant, flower-festooned barge from the New Jersey shore to New York City, where throngs of citizens and newly elected members of Congress greeted the weary traveler. That evening, bonfires illuminated the city.

Inaugural day was April 30. Shortly after noon, on a small balcony overlooking Wall Street, Washington took the oath of office. "It is done," exulted New York's chancellor, Robert Livingston. "Long live George Washington, President of the United States!" With the crowd roaring its approval and 13 guns booming in the harbor, the president bowed his way off the balcony and into Federal Hall. Late into the night, celebrations filled the air.

Though hopefulness attended the new government's beginning, the first weeks were tense, because everyone knew how important it was that the government be set on a proper republican course. "Things which appear of little importance in themselves and at the beginning," the president warned, "may have great and durable consequences."

When Washington addressed the first Congress, republican purists complained that it smacked too much of the English monarch's speech from the throne at the opening of Parliament. Congress then had to decide whether it should accord him a title. Vice President Adams proposed "His Most Benign Highness," while others offered the even gaudier suggestion "His Highness, the President of the United States, and Protector of the Rights of the Same." Howls of outrage arose from those who thought titles had no place in a republic. Good sense finally prevailing, Congress settled on the now familiar "Mr. President." The belief that such decisions might determine the new government's direction for years to come gave politics a special intensity.

The Bill of Rights

Among Congress's first tasks was consideration of the constitutional amendments that several states had made a condition of their ratification. Although Madison and other Federalists had argued that a national bill of rights was unnecessary, they were ready to keep their promise that such amendments would be considered. That would reassure the fearful, fend off calls for a second constitutional convention, and build support for the new regime. "We have in this way something to gain," Madison shrewdly observed, "and if we proceed with caution, nothing to lose."

From the variety of proposals offered by the states, Madison culled a set of specific propositions for Congress to consider. After extensive debate, Congress reached agreement in September 1789 on 12 amendments and sent them to the states for approval. By December 1791, 10 had been ratified and became the

President-Elect Washington Travels to New York

This imaginative scene of President-Elect Washington's reception in Trenton, New Jersey, during his trip from Virginia to New York City for his first inauguration depicts the popular adulation that surrounded him. What other messages can you find in the picture's details?

(Library of Congress)

national Bill of Rights. Among other things, they guaranteed freedom of speech, press, and religion; pledged the right of trial by jury and due process of law; forbade "unreasonable searches and seizures"; and protected individuals against self-incrimination in criminal cases. The Bill of Rights was the most important achievement of these early years, for it has protected citizens' democratic rights ever since.

The People Divide

During its first months, Washington's administration enjoyed almost universal support. The honeymoon, however, did not last long. By the mid-1790s, opposition groups had formed a coalition known as the Jeffersonian Republicans, while the administration's supporters rallied under the name of Federalists.

Disagreement began in January 1790, when Secretary of the Treasury Alexander Hamilton submitted to Congress the first of several major policy statements on the country's economic future. Seldom in the nation's history has a single official so dominated public affairs as did Hamilton in these early years. A man of extraordinary intelligence and ambition, Hamilton preferred to act behind the scenes, out of public view. His instincts for locating and seizing the levers of political power were unerring.

An ardent proponent of America's economic development, Hamilton, perhaps more than any of the nation's founders, foresaw the country's future strength and was determined to further its growth by promoting domestic manufacturing and overseas trade. The United States, he was fond of saying, was a "Hercules in the cradle." Competitive self-interest, whether of nations or

Alexander Hamilton

Alexander Hamilton used the office of secretary of the treasury and his personal relationship with President Washington to shape national policy during the early 1790s. What personal qualities was the portraitist attempting to convey?

(Alexander Hamilton, *The White House,* © White House Historical Association)

individuals, he thought the surest guide to behavior. He most admired ambitious entrepreneurs eager to tie their fortunes to America's rising empire, and he believed that a close alliance between them and government officials was essential to achieving American greatness.

At the same time, Hamilton's politics were profoundly conservative. He continued to be deeply impressed by the stability of the British monarchy and confident governing style of the British upper class. Hamilton distrusted the people's wisdom and feared their purposes. "The people," he asserted, "are turbulent and changing; they seldom judge or determine right."

Believing the Constitution was not "high-toned" enough, Hamilton was eager to give it proper direction. His opportunity came when Washington named him secretary of the treasury. Recognizing the potential importance of his office, he determined to build the kind of nation he envisioned.

In his first "Report on the Public Credit," Hamilton recommended funding the remaining Revolutionary War debt by enabling the government's creditors to exchange their badly depreciated securities at face value for new, interest-bearing government bonds. Second, he proposed that the federal government assume responsibility for the $21.5 million in remaining state war debts. These actions, he hoped, would stabilize the government's finances, establish its credit, build confidence in the new nation at home and abroad, and tie business and commercial interests firmly to the new administration.

Following the new Congress's first debate over slavery, debate on Hamilton's report resumed. The proposal to fund the foreign debt aroused little controversy, but Hamilton's plans for handling the government's domestic obligations generated immediate opposition. In the House of Representatives, James Madison, Hamilton's recent ally in the ratification process, protested the unfairness of funding depreciated securities at face value because speculators, some anticipating Hamilton's proposals, had acquired many of them at a fraction of their initial worth. Madison and his southern colleagues knew as well that northern businessmen held most of the securities and that funding would bring little benefit to the South.

Hamilton was not impressed. The speculators, he observed, "paid what the commodity was worth in the market, and took the risks." They should therefore "reap the benefit." If his plan served the interests of the wealthy, that was exactly as he intended, for it would further strengthen ties between wealth and national power. After considerable grumbling, Congress endorsed the funding plan.

Federal assumption of the remaining state debts aroused sharper criticism. States with the largest unpaid obligations, such as Massachusetts, thought assumption a splendid idea. But others, such as Virginia and Pennsylvania, which had already retired much of their debt, were opposed. Critics also warned that assumption would strengthen the central government at the expense of the states, since wealthy individuals would now look to it rather than the states

for a return on their investments. Moreover, with its increased need for revenue to pay off the accumulated debt, the federal government would have strong reason to exercise its newly acquired power of taxation. That was exactly as Hamilton intended.

Once again, Congress endorsed Hamilton's bill, in good measure because Madison and Jefferson supported it as part of an agreement to move the seat of government from New York to Philadelphia, and eventually to a new federal district on the Potomac River. Southerners hoped that moving the government away from northern commercial centers would enable them to align it with their own agrarian interests.

Opposition to the funding and assumption scheme, however, did not die. In December 1790, the Virginia assembly passed a series of resolutions, framed by that old Anti-Federalist Patrick Henry, warning that southern agriculture was being subordinated to the interests of northern commerce, and that the national government's powers were expanding dangerously. In response, Hamilton confided privately that "This is the first symptom of a spirit which must either be killed, or will kill the Constitution."

As the controversy grew, Hamilton introduced the second phase of his financial program, a national bank capable of handling the government's financial affairs and pooling private investment capital for economic development. He had the Bank of England and its ties to the royal government in mind, though he was careful not to say so publicly.

Opposition to the bank came almost entirely from the South where critics feared it would serve the needs of northern merchants and manufacturers far better than those of southern agrarians. Still, in February 1792, Congress approved the bank bill.

When Washington asked his cabinet whether he should sign the bill, Hamilton said yes. Following the constitutional doctrine of "implied powers"—the principle that the government had the authority to make any laws "necessary and proper" for exercising the powers specifically granted it by the Constitution—he argued that Congress could charter such a bank under its power to collect taxes and regulate trade. Secretary of State Jefferson, however, urged a veto. He saw in Hamilton's argument a blueprint for the indefinite expansion of federal authority and insisted that the government possessed only those powers specifically listed in the Constitution. Because the Constitution said nothing about chartering banks, the bill was unconstitutional and should be rejected. To Jefferson's distress, Washington took Hamilton's advice and signed the bank bill into law.

In December 1790, in his second "Report on the Public Credit," Hamilton proposed a series of excise taxes, including one on the manufacture of distilled liquor. This so-called Whiskey Tax signaled the government's intention to use its taxing authority to increase federal revenue. The power to tax and spend, Hamilton knew, was the power to govern. The Whiskey Tax became law in March 1791.

Finally, in his "Report on Manufactures" issued in December 1791, Hamilton called for tariffs (i.e., taxes) on imported European goods as a way of protecting American industries; bounties to encourage the expansion of commercial agriculture; and a network of federally sponsored internal improvements such as roads and lighthouses. These were intended to stimulate commerce and bind the nation more tightly together. Neither northern merchants nor southern agrarians, however, wanted tariffs that might reduce overseas trade and raise the cost of living, so Congress never endorsed this report.

All the while, criticism of Hamilton's policies continued to grow. In October 1791, opposition leaders in Congress established a newspaper that vigorously attacked the administration's policies. Hamilton responded with a series of anonymous articles in the administration's paper accusing Jefferson (inaccurately) of having opposed the Constitution and (also inaccurately) of fomenting opposition to the government. Alarmed, Washington pleaded for restraint. The month-long debate revealed how acrimonious politics had already become at the nation's capital.

Political conflict was now spreading beyond the circle of governing officials in Philadelphia. In northern towns and cities, artisans and other working people turned out in support of Hamilton's efforts to improve credit and stimulate economic development. With their own economic circumstances improving, they seemed undisturbed by constitutional issues or the special benefits his policies brought to a privileged few. Within a few years, many of them would move into the Jeffersonian opposition, but for the moment their support of the administration was secure.

The Whiskey Rebellion

The farmers of western Pennsylvania voiced their opposition to government policies in dramatic fashion. Their anger focused on the Whiskey Tax. Their livelihood depended on transporting surplus grain over the Appalachians to eastern markets. Shipping it in bulk was prohibitively expensive, so they distilled the grain and moved it more efficiently as whiskey. The Whiskey Tax threatened to make this trade unprofitable. The farmers also protested that people charged with tax evasion had to stand trial in federal court hundreds of miles away in Philadelphia.

Westerners also sensed control of their local affairs slipping away as the backcountry became caught up in a market economy and political system dominated by the more commercialized and populous areas to the

Washington and Hamilton Lead a Federal Army Against the Whiskey Rebels

President Washington and Treasury Secretary Hamilton led a federal army of nearly 13,000 troops into western Pennsylvania in 1794. Rebellious farmers, protesting the government's excise tax on whiskey, dispersed as the army approached. What political story is the artist trying to tell?

(Frederick Kemmelmeyer, *Washington Reviewing the Western Army at Fort Cumberland,* Maryland. The Metropolitan Museum of Art, Gift of Edgar William and Bernice Chrysler Garbisch, 1963 [63.201.2] Photograph © 1983 The Metropolitan Museum of Art)

east. In southern states such as South Carolina, the integration of coastal and interior regions went smoothly because of similar agricultural interests and a shared anxiety over the region's black majority. In the more economically diverse and racially homogenous states of the north, however, conflicts between coastal and backcountry regions sharpened.

Hamilton cared little what western farmers thought about the Whiskey Tax. The government needed revenue, and the farmers would have to bear the cost. Angered by Federalist arrogance as much as the tax, farmers quickly made their resentment known.

Trouble was brewing by the summer of 1792 as angry citizens gathered in mass meetings across western Pennsylvania. In August, a convention at Pittsburgh denounced the Whiskey Tax and vowed to prevent its collection. Like opponents of the Stamp Act in 1765 and the Shays rebels in Massachusetts, they decided that liberties would be lost if resistance did not soon begin. Alarmed, Washington issued a proclamation warning against such "unlawful" gatherings and insisting that the tax would be enforced. As collections began, the farmers took matters into their own hands.

In July 1794, when a federal marshal and a local excise inspector, John Neville, attempted to serve papers on several recalcitrant farmers near Pittsburgh, an angry crowd of 500 armed men cornered a dozen federal soldiers in Neville's home. After an exchange of gunfire, the soldiers surrendered and Neville's house was torched. Similar episodes, some of them involving the erection of liberty poles reminiscent of the Revolution, erupted across the state, while a convention of over 200 delegates debated armed resistance.

Fearing that the protests might spread through the entire backcountry from Maine to Georgia and alarmed by talk of secession in Kentucky and the western Carolinas, Washington called out federal troops to restore order. For more than a year, Hamilton had been urging the use of force against the protesters. To him, the insurrection was not evidence of an unjust policy needing change but a test of the administration's ability to govern. He eagerly volunteered to accompany the troops west.

In late August, a federal force of nearly 13,000 men marched into western Pennsylvania. At its head rode the president and secretary of the treasury. Persuaded of the danger to his safety, Washington returned to Philadelphia, but Hamilton pressed ahead. The battle for which Hamilton hoped never materialized, however, for as the federal army approached, the "Whiskey Rebels" dispersed. Of 20 prisoners taken, two were convicted of treason and sentenced to death. Later, in a calmer mood, Washington pardoned them both.

As people soon realized, the "Whiskey Rebellion" had never threatened the government's safety. "An insurrection was...proclaimed," Jefferson scoffed,

"but could never be found." Even such an ardent Federalist as Fisher Ames was uneasy at the sight of federal troops marching against American citizens. "Elective rulers," he warned, "can scarcely ever employ the physical force of a democracy without turning the moral force, or the power of public opinion, against the government." The American people would have additional reason to ponder Ames's warning in the years immediately ahead.

The Republic in a Threatening World

Because the nation was so new and the outside world so threatening, foreign policy generated extraordinary excitement during the 1790s. This was especially so after the tumultuous events of the French and Haitian Revolutions burst onto the international scene. The revolution in France and the European war that accompanied it threatened to draw America in, while across Europe, Ireland, and the Caribbean, political insurgents, invoking the Declaration of Independence and America's colonial rebellion as inspiration for their own cause, joined in what historians call the "Age of Democratic Revolution."

The Promise and Peril of the French Revolution

France's revolution began in 1789 as an effort to reform an arbitrary but weakened monarchy. Pent-up demands for social justice, however, quickly outran initial attempts at moderate reform, and in 1793, when the recently proclaimed republican regime beheaded Louis XVI, France plunged into a genuinely radical revolution. By the end of 1793, Europe was locked in a deadly struggle between revolutionary France and a counterrevolutionary coalition led by Prussia and Great Britain.

For more than a decade, the French Revolution dominated European affairs. Before it was finished, it would transform the course of Western history. The revolution also cut like a plowshare through the surface of American politics, dividing Americans against each other.

The outbreak of European war posed thorny diplomatic problems for Washington's administration. By the mid-1790s, American merchants were earning handsome profits from "neutral trade" with both England and France, while American shipbuilding was booming. In 1800, American ships carried an astonishing 92 percent of all commerce between America and Europe. The economic benefits were most evident in cities along the Atlantic coast but radiated as well into the surrounding countryside,

Urban Prosperity in the Late 1790s

This scene of bustling commercial activity in New York City in 1797 reveals the benefits that expanded neutral trade brought to the nation's major seaports. On the right of the painting is the elegant Tontine Coffee House, which served as a tavern, housed the New York Stock Exchange, and boasted of such amenities as a water closet, a bell system for communication between rooms, and an inside bath. What can you learn about urban life from the painting?

("Tontine Coffiee House", by Francis Guy, oil on canvas, c. 1797 / Collection of The New-York Historical Society, [negative number 6211, accession number 1907.32])

where cargoes of agricultural and forest goods, as well as the provisions required by ships' crews, were produced.

America's expanding commerce, however, generated problems. While England and France sought access to American goods, each was determined to prevent those goods from reaching the other, if necessary by stopping American ships and confiscating their cargoes. America's relations with England were additionally complicated by the Royal Navy's practice of impressing American sailors into service aboard its warships to meet the growing demand for seamen. Washington faced the difficult problem of protecting American citizens without getting drawn into the European conflict.

The French treaty of 1778 compounded the government's dilemma. It appeared to require that the United States aid France much as France had assisted the American states against England a decade and a half earlier. Americans sympathetic to the French cause argued that the commitment still held. Others, fearing the consequences of American involvement and the political infection that closer ties with revolutionary France might bring, insisted that the treaty had lapsed when the French king was overthrown.

The American people's intense reaction to the revolution in France further complicated the situation. At first, it seemed an extension of America's own struggle for liberty. Even the swing toward social revolution did not immediately dampen American enthusiasm. By the mid-1790s, however, especially after France's revolutionary regime launched its attack on organized Christianity, many Americans pulled back in alarm.

What connection could there possibly be between the principles of 1776 and the chaos so evident in France? The differences were indeed profound.

To Federalists, revolutionary France represented social anarchy and threatened the European order on which they believed America's commercial and diplomatic security depended. With increasing vehemence, they castigated the revolution, championed England as the defender of European civilization, and sought ways of linking England and the United States more closely together.

Many Americans, however, continued to support France. While decrying the revolution's excesses, they believed that liberty would ultimately emerge from the turmoil. Though Jefferson regretted the shedding of innocent blood, he thought it necessary if true liberty was to be achieved. John Bradford, editor of the *Kentucky Gazette*, thought similarly. "Instead of reviling the French republicans as monsters," he wrote, the "friends of royalty in this country" should admire their patience in suffering so long under their monarch.

The turmoil in France challenged American assumptions about the gendered basis of politics as well. In France, women participated in revolutionary crowds and joined in arguments over issues of political equality. When word of radical feminist activity reached North American shores, it echoed loudly in the political consciousness of many American women.

In August 1794, Philadelphia citizens gathered to celebrate the progress of French liberty. Mimicking the public festivals popular in revolutionary France, a crowd of women and men paraded down Market

Street to the French minister's residence. There, women dressed in gowns emblazoned with the French tricolor gathered around an "altar of liberty," reciting patriotic odes before finally dispersing.

Upper-class women such as Anne Willing Bingham, wife of a U.S. senator and daughter of a socially prominent Philadelphia family, opened their dinner parties and social salons to political talk, a practice that became a common part of civic life at the nation's capital. In all of these ways, women explored the boundaries of American citizenship and claimed a wider presence in the public sphere.

Democratic Revolutions in Europe and the Atlantic World

The revolution in France was but the most dramatic among an array of political insurgencies that challenged aristocratic power and promoted democratic values throughout Europe and the Atlantic world during the 1790s. As with the French revolution, they generated disputes among the American people.

Toussaint L'Ouverture

This swashbuckling portrait of the Haitian revolutionary Toussaint L'Ouverture appeared in *An Historical Account of the Black Empire of Haiti,* published in London in 1805. Is the portrayal intended to be complimentary or mocking?

(R Snark/Art Resource, NY)

Supported by invading armies from revolutionary France and inspired by the doctrine of natural rights voiced during the American and French revolutions, rebellions against long-entrenched privilege erupted from the Netherlands to the Italian peninsula.

Democratic insurgencies broke out as well in Latin America and the Caribbean. The most important occurred on the island of San Domingue, soon to be known as Haiti. Beginning in 1791, a multiracial coalition, emboldened by events in revolutionary France, rose in rebellion against French colonial rule. Conflict quickly developed between white landowners seeking to preserve their privileges while throwing off the colonial yoke, poor whites demanding access to land, mixed-race mulattoes chafing under years of discrimination, and black slaves angered by brutal repression. For more than a decade, black and white Haitians conducted a furious struggle against a combined French and British force of 30,000. England, fearing rebellion among the 300,000 slaves on Jamaica, its nearby possession, offered military support, even though France was its mortal enemy. The conflict devastated Haiti's sugar economy and caused more than 100,000 casualties among whites and blacks alike.

In 1798, the island's black majority, led by the charismatic Toussaint L'Ouverture, seized control of the rebellion, making the abolition of slavery its primary goal. Six years later, the victorious Haitian rebels established Haiti as the first black nation–state in the Americas.

While Haitian rebels celebrated the Declaration of Independence as a manifesto of universal freedom, North American whites followed events on that troubled island with a mixture of enthusiasm and dread. The Haitian revolt appeared to affirm the universal relevance of the U.S. struggle for liberty, and struck another blow against European colonialism in the New World. During the height of the Haitian insurgency, American warships ferried black troops from one part of the island to another in preparation for battle.

U.S. citizens, however, contemplated with alarm the effect on North American slaves of a successful black rebellion so close by. The Haitian achievement, moreover, cast doubt on the racial assumption that blacks were incapable of comprehending liberty's true meaning. White southerners were especially anxious. The governor of North Carolina issued a proclamation warning Haitians fleeing the island's chaos to stay away. When Haitian officials appealed in "the name of humanity" for "fraternal aid" in their liberation struggle, Congress demurred. If Haiti became an independent state, warned Pennsylvania Senator Albert Gallatin, it might become "a dangerous neighbor"

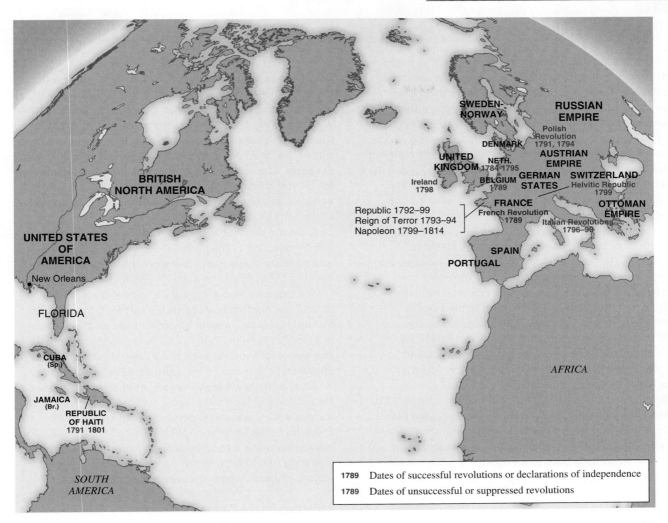

The Outbreak of Democratic Insurgencies
During the late eighteenth and early nineteenth centuries, numerous democratic insurgencies erupted in Europe and the Caribbean. What connections did these insurgencies have with the American and French revolutions?

offering asylum to runaway slaves. When the Haitian republic was proclaimed in 1804, the U.S. government withheld recognition. Not until after the American Civil War were diplomatic relations with Haiti finally established.

Though each of the democratic insurgencies that erupted during the 1790s was inspired by local experiences of injustice, they shared a common dedication to human liberty and drew upon principles articulated in revolutionary America and France. News about them circulated in the United States via newspapers, networks of personal correspondence, and an expanding human traffic of soldiers, émigrés, and political idealists who crisscrossed the Atlantic during these tumultuous years.

In the mid-1790s, Joel Barlow and numerous other Americans, motivated by curiosity and democratic principle, journeyed to France, eager to witness the

further unfolding of universal liberty. The American expatriate Thomas Paine was granted honorary French citizenship, and served briefly in France's revolutionary Convention before running afoul of the Terror. At the same time, a stream of French émigrés, fleeing the violence, sought sanctuary in the United States.

As the 1790s progressed, growing numbers of English and Irish radicals at risk from the deepening political conservatism in Britain also took passage for North America. When they arrived, many joined the Jeffersonian opposition, adding to the party's democratic commitment and anti-British stance.

The emerging transatlantic web of radical dissent was strengthened as well by a multiracial underclass of sailors, runaway slaves, and other common folk—restive men, and occasionally women, from the far corners of the Atlantic world who circulated in and out of North American ports. Their rough

Recovering the Past

Historians utilize many different kinds of sources in their quest to recover the American past. Among the most revealing are travel accounts penned by foreign visitors eager to learn about the United States and record their impressions of it. From the days of earliest explorations to our own time, travelers have been fascinated by the people, customs, institutions, and physical setting of North America. Out of this continuing interaction between America and its foreign visitors has emerged a rich and fascinating travel literature that reveals much not only about America but about the travelers who have visited it as well.

During the second quarter of the nineteenth century, a stream of perceptive European visitors—Alexis de Tocqueville, Harriet Martineau, and Francis Grund among them—toured the United States, eager to record their impressions of what Jacksonian America was like. Fifty years earlier, the American Revolution fanned similar interest in the minds of Europeans fascinated by the newly independent nation and anxious to discern its implications for them. Among the most opinionated and engaging of these earlier commentators was the Frenchman Moreau de Saint Méry.

Born on the French island of Martinique in January 1750, de Saint Méry established a successful legal practice before moving to France, where relatives introduced him to polite Parisian society. In the late 1780s, he became an ardent champion of political reform during the early days of the French Revolution. As the revolution entered its radical phase, however, he was forced to flee to the United States for safety. Arriving at Norfolk, Virginia, with his wife and two children, de Saint Méry settled in Philadelphia, where he remained from October 1794 to August 1798. While there, he mingled with civic and cultural leaders, opened a bookstore that served as a rendezvous for French émigrés who also had fled the revolution's turmoil, and published a French-language paper that reported the latest news from home. In the late summer of 1798, de Saint Méry returned safely to France.

As with all such travel accounts, de Saint Méry's commentary must be read with a critical eye, for travelers disagreed over what they thought important and worth reporting, and interpreted what they saw in very different ways. In nearly 400 pages of commentary, de Saint Méry touched on numerous aspects of American life, but none in more frank and compelling fashion than relations between the sexes. The selections that follow (somewhat rearranged for greater continuity) provide tantalizing insights into the behavior and sexual mores of American men and women in the early years of the republic.

What did de Saint Méry find most interesting about gender relations in Philadelphia? How did religion, class, and ethnicity shape men's and women's behavior? Of what forms of behavior did he approve and disapprove?

The explicit commentary of de Saint Méry is unique among the numerous accounts left by foreign travelers in the early republic, most of whom showed far more interest in America's racial makeup, political practices, and physical environment. Thus, de Saint Méry's observations may be idiosyncratic and should be approached with caution.

What other kinds of sources might enable us to evaluate the accuracy of such travel accounts? In what ways is a traveler's own nationality, gender, religion, or class likely to shape his or her impressions of the United States? Similarly, how important is it to know travelers' motives for coming, how long they stayed, which parts of the country they visited, and with whom they associated while here?

Reflecting on the Past Does the gendered world of late eighteenth-century Philadelphia, as described by de Saint Méry, seem strange or familiar, attractive or distasteful to your own sensibilities? If you were to visit another country today, how accurate do you think you could be in assessing the social behavior and cultural values of its people? To what extent would your values, perhaps like those of Moreau de Saint Méry, color your impressions? Might it be more difficult to understand some foreign cultures than others? Why?

Moreau de Saint Méry's American Journal

American men, generally speaking, are tall and thin... [and] seem to have no strength.... They are brave, but they lack drive. Indifferent toward almost everything, they sometimes behave in a manner that suggests real energy; then follow it with a "Oh-to-hell-with-it" attitude which shows that they seldom feel genuine enthusiasm.

Their dinner consists of... English roast surrounded by potatoes... baked or fried eggs, boiled or fried fish, salad which may be thinly sliced cabbage... [and] sweets to which they are excessively partial.... The entire meal is washed down with cider, weak or strong beer... [and] wine... which they keep drinking right through dessert, toward the end of which any ladies who are at the dinner leave the table and withdraw by themselves, leaving the men free to drink as much as they please .... Toasts are drunk, cigars are lighted, diners run to the corners of the room hunting night tables and vases which will enable them to hold a greater amount of liquor.... Finally the dinner table is deserted because of boredom, fatigue or drunkenness....

American women are pretty, and those of Philadelphia are prettiest of all.... Girls ordinarily mature in Philadelphia at the age of fourteen, and reach that period without unusual symptoms. ... But they soon grow pale.... After eighteen years old they lose their charms.... Their hair is scanty, their teeth bad.... In short, while charming and adorable at fifteen, they are faded at twenty-three, old at thirty-five, decrepit at forty or forty-five....

American women carefully wash their faces and hands, but not their mouths, seldom their feet and even more seldom their bodies.... They are greatly addicted to finery and have a strong desire to display themselves—a desire... inflamed by their love of adornment. They cannot, however, imitate that elegance of style possessed by Frenchwomen....

One is struck by the tall and pretty young girls one sees in the streets, going and coming from school. They wear their hair long, and skirts with closed seams. But when nubility has arrived they put up their hair with a comb, and the back of the skirt has a placket. At this time, they... become their own mistresses, and can go walking alone and have suitors....

They invariably make their own choice of a suitor, and the parents raise no objection because that's the custom of the country. The suitor comes into the house when he wishes; goes on walks with his loved one whenever he desires. On Sunday he often takes her out in a cabriolet, and brings her back in the evening without anyone wanting to know where they went.... Although in general one is conscious of widespread modesty in Philadelphia,... the disregard... of some parents for the manner in which their daughters form relationships to which they... have not given their approval is an encouragement to indiscretions....

A young woman trusts in her suitor's delicacy and charges him with maintaining for her a respect which she is not always able to command. Each day both of them are entrusted to no one but each other.... Her servant.... leaves the house as soon as night has arrived.... Her father, her mother, her entire family have gone to bed. The suitor and his mistress remain alone; and sometimes, when the servant returns, she finds them asleep and the candle out, such is the frigidity of love in this country....

When one considers the unlimited liberty which young ladies enjoy, one is astonished by their universal eagerness to be married.... When a young woman marries, she enters a wholly different existence. She is no longer a... butterfly who denies herself nothing and whose only laws are her whims and her suitor's wish. She now lives only for her husband, and to devote herself without surcease to the care of her household and her home.... The more her husband is capable of multiplying... the pleasures of matrimony... the more her health may suffer, most of all when she has a child; for sometimes while nursing it, or as soon as it is weaned, she has already conceived another....

In spite of conjugal customs which would seem to indicate a state of happiness, they do not produce the happiness which would be expected to result.... This is evidenced by the multiplicity of second marriages.... The men in particular remarry oftenest.... Divorce is obtained with scandalous ease. From this alone one can judge the extent of loose habits....

Bastards are extremely common in Philadelphia. There are two principal reasons for this. In the first place, the city is full of religious sects, but none of them give their clergymen any authority to enforce obedience. Consequently there is no way of inspiring shame in women who become mothers for no reason except the pleasure they get out of it. In the second place, once an illegitimate child is twelve months old, a mother can disembarrass herself of him by farming him out for twenty-one years. This makes it possible for her to commit the same sin for a second time. It never occurs to her that her child can never know her, and that the whole business is shameful....

There are streetwalkers... in Philadelphia. These are very young and very pretty girls, elegantly dressed, who promenade two by two, arm in arm and walking very rapidly, at an hour which indicates that they aren't just out for a stroll.... Anyone who accosts them is taken to their home... [where] they fulfill every desire for two dollars, half of which is supposed to pay for the use of the room. Quaker youths are frequent visitors in the houses of ill fame, which have multiplied in Philadelphia and are frequented at all hours. There is even a well-known gentleman who leaves his horse tied to the post outside one of these houses, so that everyone knows when he is there and exactly how long he stays....

Source: Moreau de St. Méry's American Journey, 1793–1798, trans. and ed. Kenneth Roberts and Anna M. Roberts (New York: Doubleday, 1947), 265, 281–283, 312–313.

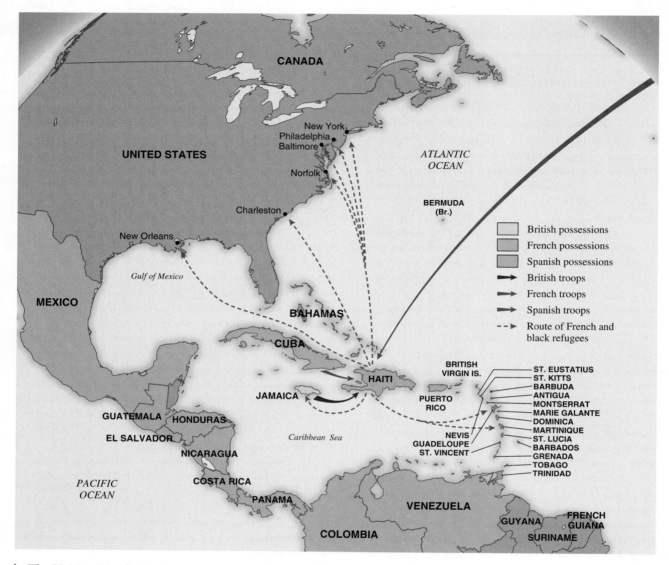

The Haitian Revolution

The Haitian Revolution was a focal point of European imperial competition in the Americas. It also resonated powerfully in the United States. Why and in what ways?

appearance, vivid tales of injustice, and readiness to challenge local authorities added to the country's political clamor.

The Democratic–Republican Societies

Political clubs, providing safe havens where dissidents could gather to read political tracts and plot political change, served as weapons of democratic reform throughout the Atlantic world during the 1790s. The Jacobin clubs in France were the best known, but similar groups appeared in the United States.

As early as 1792, ordinary citizens began to form "constitutional societies" ready to give the alarm in case of governmental encroachments on American liberty. Several dozen societies, modeled after the Sons of Liberty and Committees of Correspondence that had mobilized patriots against England 20 years earlier, formed in opposition to Hamilton's financial program. The French Revolution stoked the fires of democratic enthusiasm and spurred the societies' growth, as did the arrival in 1793 of Citizen Edmund Genêt, the new French minister to the United States.

Genêt landed at Charleston, South Carolina, to a tumultuous reception. His instructions were to court popular support and negotiate a commercial treaty with the United States. Shortly after his arrival, however, he began commissioning American privateers to attack British shipping in the Caribbean and enlisting American seamen for expeditions against Spanish Florida, clear violations of American neutrality.

As he traveled north toward Philadelphia, Genêt generated more enthusiastic receptions. His popularity, however, soon led him into trouble. In defiance of diplomatic protocol, he urged Congress to reject Washington's recently issued neutrality proclamation and side with revolutionary France. On August 2, the president demanded Genêt's recall, charging that his conduct threatened "war abroad and anarchy at home."

Though Genêt failed as a diplomat, he succeeded in fanning popular enthusiasm for revolutionary France. With his open encouragement, the Democratic Society of Pennsylvania called for the formation of similar societies in other states to join in supporting revolutionary France and promoting "freedom and equality" at home.

About 40 popular societies scattered from Maine to Georgia sprang up during the next several years. Working people—artisans and laborers in the cities, small farmers and tenants in the countryside—provided the bulk of membership. Federalist critics derided them as "the lowest orders of...draymen...broken hucksters, and trans-Atlantic traitors." That final canard referred to the growing tide of Irish immigrants, fleeing hard times and political repression at home, who combined demands for Irish independence from England with a commitment to political equality and a relish for rough-and-tumble politics.

The societies' leaders were often doctors, tradesmen, and lawyers, men of acknowledged respectability. Leaders and followers alike were united by a determination to preserve the "principles of '76" against the "royalizing" tendencies of Washington's administration. Committed to an awakened citizenry, the societies organized public celebrations, issued addresses filled with democratic principles, and fired off petitions critical of administration policies. Washington's proclamation of neutrality they labeled a "pusillanimous truckling to Britain, despotically conceived and unconstitutionally promulgated." Several of the societies openly urged the United States to enter the war on France's behalf.

West of the Appalachians, local democratic societies agitated against England's continuing occupation of frontier posts south of the Great Lakes, and berated Spain for closing the Mississippi River at New Orleans to American shipping. Everywhere they protested the Excise Tax, opposed the administration's overtures to England, and called for a press free from control by Federalist "aristocrats."

President Washington and his supporters were incensed by the societies' support of Genêt and criticism of the government. Such "nurseries of sedition," thundered one Federalist, threatened to revolutionize America as the Jacobins had revolutionized France. Such polemics indicated how inflamed public discourse had become.

Jay's Controversial Treaty

The uproar over a treaty negotiated with England further heightened political tensions at mid-decade. Alarmed by deteriorating relations between the two countries, Washington sent Chief Justice John Jay to London in the spring of 1794 to negotiate a wide range of issues carried over from the Revolutionary War. The treaty that Jay brought home in early 1795 contained British promises on a number of sensitive issues but ignored a host of other lingering problems. When its terms were made public, they triggered an explosion of protest.

The administration's pleas that the agreement headed off an open breach with England and was the best that could be obtained failed to pacify its critics. In New York City, Hamilton was stoned while defending the treaty at a mass meeting. The "rabble," sniffed one Federalist, attempted "to knock out Hamilton's brains to reduce him to an equality with themselves." Southern planters were angry because the agreement brought no compensation for their lost slaves. Westerners complained that the British were not evacuating the military posts, while merchants and sailors railed against Jay's failure to stop impressment or open the West Indies to American trade. After a long and acrimonious debate, the Senate ratified the treaty by a narrow margin.

The administration made better progress on the still volatile issue of free transit of the Mississippi River. In the Treaty of San Lorenzo, negotiated by Thomas Pinckney in 1795, Spain for the first time recognized the Mississippi River to the west and the 31st parallel to the south as U.S. boundaries and gave up all claim to U.S. territory. Spain also granted Americans free navigation of the Mississippi and the right to unload goods for transshipment at New Orleans—but only for three years. What would happen after that remained uncertain.

By mid-decade, political harmony had disappeared as divisions deepened on virtually every important issue of foreign and domestic policy. Jefferson, increasingly estranged from the administration, resigned as secretary of state, joining Madison and others in open opposition to Washington's policies.

In September 1796, in what came to be called his Farewell Address, Washington deplored the deepening political divisions, warned against entangling alliances with foreign nations, and announced that he would not accept a third term. He had long been contemplating retirement, for he was now 64 and wearied by political attacks. "As to you, sir," fumed Thomas Paine in a letter published in an opposition newspaper, "treacherous in private friendship...and a hypocrite in public life, the world will be puzzled to decide...whether you have abandoned good principles, or whether you ever had any." Few American presidents have been subjected to such public abuse.

The Political Crisis Deepens

By 1796, bitter controversy surrounded the national government. It intensified during the last half of the decade until the very stability of the country seemed threatened.

The Election of 1796

With Washington out of the picture, the presidential election quickly narrowed to Adams versus Jefferson. Both had played distinguished roles during the Revolution when they had shared the task of drafting the Declaration of Independence. They had joined forces again during the 1780s, when Adams served as first U.S. minister to Great Britain and Jefferson as minister to France. They came together a third time in Washington's administration, Adams as vice president and Jefferson as secretary of state.

Though they had earned each other's respect, they now differed sharply in their visions of the nation's future. Adams was a committed Federalist.

John Adams

John Adams, Washington's vice president, won a narrow victory over Jefferson for the presidency in 1796. His administration foundered on conflicts over foreign policy abroad and the suppression of political dissent at home.

(*Portrait of John Adams.* Adams National Historic Site/U.S. Department of the Interior, National Park Service)

He believed in a vigorous national government, was appalled by the French Revolution, and feared "excessive democracy." Jefferson, while firmly supporting the Constitution, was alarmed by Hamilton's financial program, viewed France's revolution as a logical if chaotic extension of America's struggle for freedom, and hoped to expand democracy at home. By 1796, he had become the leader of an increasingly vocal opposition, the Jeffersonian Republican party.

The election of 1796 bound Jefferson and Adams together once again, this time in a deeply strained and ill-fated alliance. Adams received 71 electoral votes and became president. Jefferson came in second with 68 and, as then specified in the Constitution, assumed the vice presidency. The narrowness of Adams's majority foreshadowed the troubles that lay ahead.

Adams later recalled his inaugural day. "A solemn scene it was indeed, and it was made more affecting by the presence of the General [Washington], whose countenance was as serene and unclouded as the day. . . . Me thought I heard him say, 'Ay! I am fairly out and you fairly in! See which of us will be the happiest.'" The answer was not long in coming.

The War Crisis with France

Adams had no sooner taken office than he confronted a deepening crisis with France, generated by French naval vessels interfering with American merchant ships in the Caribbean. That crisis would push the nation to the brink of civil conflict.

Hoping to ease relations between the two countries, Adams sent three commissioners to Paris to negotiate an accord. When they arrived, agents of the French foreign minister Talleyrand (identified only as "X," "Y," and "Z") made it clear that the success of the American mission depended on a loan to the French government and a $240,000 "gratuity" (more accurately, a bribe) for themselves. The two staunchly Federalist commissioners, John Marshall and Charles Pinckney, indignantly sailed home. The third commissioner, Elbridge Gerry, alarmed by Talleyrand's intimation that France would declare war if all three Americans left, stayed on.

When Adams reported the so-called XYZ Affair to Congress, Federalists quickly exploited the French blunder. Secretary of State Pickering urged an immediate declaration of war, while Federalist congressmen thundered against the insult to American honor and promised "millions for defense, but not one cent for tribute." Caught up in the anti-French furor and emboldened by the petitions of support that flooded in from around the country, the president lashed out at "enemies" at home and abroad. Emotions were further inflamed by the so-called Quasi War, a series of encounters between American and French ships on the high seas.

For the moment, the Republicans were in disarray. Publicly, they deplored the French government's behavior and pledged to uphold the nation's honor. But among themselves, they voiced alarm about Federalist intentions. With good reason, because the Federalists soon mounted a crash program to repel foreign invaders and root out "traitors" at home.

The Alien and Sedition Acts

In May 1798, Congress called for a naval force capable of defending the American coast against French attack. In July, it moved closer to an open breach with France by repealing the treaty of 1778 and calling for the formation of a 10,000-man army. The army's stated mission was to repel a French invasion, but this seemed an unlikely danger given France's desperate struggle in Europe. The Jeffersonians, remembering the speed with which the Federalists had deployed troops against the Whiskey Rebels only a few years earlier, feared the army would be used against them.

As criticism of the army bill mounted, Adams had second thoughts. He was still enough of an old revolutionary to worry about the dangers of standing armies. "This damned army," he burst out, "will be the ruin of the country." He was further angered when members of his party sought to put Hamilton in command of the troops. To the dismay of hard-line Federalists, Adams issued only a few of the officers' commissions that Congress had authorized. Without officers, the army could not be mobilized.

Fearful of foreign subversion and aware that French and Irish immigrants were active in the Jeffersonian opposition, the Federalist-dominated Congress acted to curb the flow of aliens into the country. In June 1798, the Naturalization Act raised the residence requirement for citizenship from 5 to 14 years, while the Alien Act authorized the president to expel aliens whom he judged "dangerous to the peace and safety of the United States." Another bill, the Alien Enemies Act, empowered the president in time of war to arrest, imprison, or banish the subjects of any hostile nation without specifying charges against them or providing opportunity for appeal. A Federalist congressman explained that there was no need "to invite hordes of Wild Irishmen, or the turbulent and disorderly of all parts of the world, to come here with a view to distract our tranquility."

The implications of these acts for basic political liberties were ominous enough, but the Federalists had not yet finished. Congress passed the Sedition Act in mid-July, making it punishable by fine and imprisonment for anyone to conspire in opposition to "any measure or measures of the government" or to aid "any insurrection, riot, unlawful assembly, or combination." Fines and imprisonment also awaited those who dared to "write, print, utter, or publish...any false, scandalous and malicious writing" bringing the government, Congress, or the president into disrepute. The Federalist moves stunned the Jeffersonians, for they threatened to smother all political opposition.

Under the terms of the Alien Act, Secretary of State Pickering launched investigations intended to force foreigners to register with the government. The act's chilling effects were immediately apparent. Noted Pickering approvingly, large numbers of aliens, especially people of French ancestry, were leaving the country. As Sedition Act prosecutions went forward, 25 people, among them David Brown of Dedham, were arrested. Fifteen were indicted, and ten were ultimately convicted, the majority of them Jeffersonian printers and editors.

Representative Matthew Lyon, a cantankerous, acid-tongued congressman from Vermont, learned the consequences of political indiscretion, even for members of Congress. Born in Ireland, Lyon had come to America as a young indentured servant, bringing with him undying enmity toward England and disrespect for privilege of every sort. A veteran of the war for American independence, he took his revolutionary principles seriously.

During a heated debate over the Sedition Act, Lyon spat in the face of Congressman Roger Griswold of Connecticut—thus earning the derisive sobriquet of the "Spitting Lion." Two weeks later, Griswold exacted revenge by caning Lyon on the House floor. Later that year, Lyon was hauled into court, fined $1,000, and sentenced to four months in prison. His crime? Reference in a personal letter to President Adams's "unbounded thirst for ridiculous pomp, foolish adulation, and selfish avarice."

The Virginia and Kentucky Resolutions

The Alien and Sedition Acts generated a firestorm of protest. On November 16, 1798, the Kentucky Assembly passed a resolution declaring that the government had violated the Bill of Rights. Faced with such an arbitrary exercise of federal power, each state had "an equal right" to judge of infractions and decide on the "mode and measure of redress." Nullification (declaring a federal law invalid within a state's borders) was the "rightful remedy" for unconstitutional laws. Similar resolutions, written by Madison and passed the following month by the Virginia assembly, asserted that when the central government threatened the people's liberties, the states were "duty bound to interpose for arresting the progress of the evil." It would not be the last time in U.S. history that state leaders would claim authority to set aside a federal law.

DIVISIVE ISSUES OF THE 1790S

Issues	Federalist Party	Jeffersonian Republican Party
Domestic Policy		
Paying the national debt	Favors—Fund remaining debt at face value.	Favors—But wants discrimination between original holders and speculators.
Assumption of remaining state debts	Favors—As way of strengthening central government.	Opposes—As unfair to Southern States and source of power for central government.
Bank of the United States	Favors—To stabilize national economy, promote economic growth, and enhance power of central government.	Opposes—As exceeding central government's constitutional authority, and adding to consolidation of central authority.
Whiskey Tax	Favors—To provide revenue for central government.	Opposes—Warns of dangers in taxing power of central government.
Whiskey Rebellion	Favors—Suppression of rebellion as challenge to central government.	Opposes—Use of federal force to suppress protest.
Alien and Sedition Acts	Favors—As necessary to protect national security.	Opposes—As infringement of constitutional rights and threat to political opposition.
Federal army	Favors—As necessary to defend against possible French invasion.	Opposes—As dangerous enhancement of federal authority and threat to political opposition.
Foreign Policy		
French Revolution	Initially endorses political reform in France, but alarmed by radicalism following 1793. Fears French influence in U.S. Cheers England as bastion of political order.	Endorses political reform in France. Continues cautious support following 1793. Suspicious of British motives.
Jay's Treaty	Supports as best agreement possible, and as promoting trade with England.	Opposes—Criticizes treaty's silence concerning impressment, return of confiscated slaves, etc.
XYZ Affair	Expresses outrage over affront to American dignity.	Also expresses outrage, though worries over domestic political fallout.
Declaration of war with France	Favors, following XYZ Affair—Badly divided when Adams opts for peace.	Opposes—As unnecessary and threatening dangerous domestic repercussions.

The Kentucky and Virginia resolutions received little support elsewhere and, as it turned out, the Alien and Sedition Acts were not enforced in the South. Still, the resolutions indicated the depth of popular opposition to the Federalist program. As the Federalists pressed ahead, the Virginia assembly called for the formation of a state arsenal at Harpers Ferry. In Philadelphia, Federalist patrols walked the streets to protect government officials from angry crowds while President Adams smuggled arms into the White House as a precaution. As 1799 began, the country seemed on the brink of upheaval.

Within a year, however, the political cycle turned once again, this time decisively against the Federalists. From Europe, the president's son, John Quincy Adams, sent assurances that Talleyrand was prepared to negotiate an honorable accord. Fearful that war with France "would convulse the attachments of the country," Adams seized the opening and determined to appoint new peace commissioners. "The end of war is peace," he explained, "and peace was offered me." He had also concluded that his only chance of reelection lay in fashioning a peace coalition from elements of both parties.

Adams's cabinet was enraged, for the Federalist war program depended for its legitimacy on continuation of the French crisis. After Secretary of State Pickering ignored the president's orders to dispatch the peace commissioners, Adams dismissed him and instructed them to depart. By year's end, the envoys secured an agreement releasing the United States from the 1778 alliance and restoring peaceful relations.

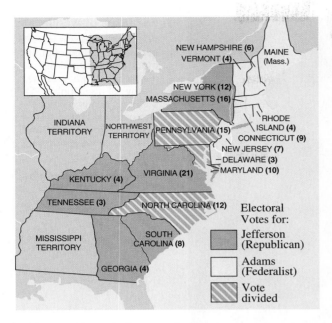

The Presidential Election of 1800

Though the federal government was little more than a decade old, the electoral vote in 1800 revealed the sectional divisions that already troubled national politics.

The "Revolution of 1800"

As the election of 1800 approached, the Federalists were in disarray, having squandered the political advantage handed them by the XYZ Affair. With peace a reality, they stood before the nation charged with exercising federal power unconstitutionally, suppressing political dissent, and threatening to use a federal army against American citizens. Adams's opponents within the Federalist Party were furious at his "betrayal." When he announced his intention to seek reelection, they plotted his defeat.

Emotions ran high as the election approached. In Philadelphia, gangs of young Federalists and Jeffersonians clashed in the streets. "A fray ensued," one observer reported, "the light horse were called in, and the city was so filled with confusion...that it was dangerous going out." In Virginia, rumors of a slave insurrection briefly interrupted the political feuding, but the scare passed and Federalists and Jeffersonians were soon at each others' throats once again. This election, Jefferson declared, will "fix the national character" by determining whether "republicanism or aristocracy" would prevail.

Election day was tense throughout the country, but passed without serious incident. As the results were tallied, it became clear that the Jeffersonians had won a decisive victory. The two Jeffersonian candidates for president, Jefferson and Aaron Burr, each had 73 electoral votes. Adams trailed with 65.

Because of the tie vote, the election was thrown into the House of Representatives, as provided in the Constitution, where a deadlock quickly developed. After a bitter struggle, the House finally elected Jefferson, 10 states to 4, on the thirty-sixth ballot. (Seeking to prevent a recurrence of such a crisis, the next Congress passed and the states then ratified the Twelfth Amendment, providing for separate Electoral College ballots for president and vice president.) The magnitude of the Federalists' defeat was even more evident in congressional elections, where they lost their majorities in both House and Senate.

The election's outcome revealed the strong sectional divisions now evident in the country's politics. The Federalists dominated New England because of regional loyalty to Adams, the area's commercial ties with England, and fears that their opponents intended to import social revolution from France. From Maryland south, political control by the Jeffersonians was almost as complete. In the middle states, the election was more closely contested.

The Federalist–Jeffersonian conflict was rooted as well in socioeconomic divisions among the American people. Federalist support was strongest among merchants, manufacturers, and commercial farmers situated within easy reach of the coast. In New York City and Philadelphia, Federalists were most numerous in wards where houses were largest and addresses most fashionable. All had supported the constitution in 1787–1788.

The Jeffersonian coalition included most of the old Anti-Federalists but was much broader than that. It found support among urban workers and artisans, many of whom had once been staunch Federalists. The coalition, moreover, was led by individuals such as Madison and Jefferson who had helped create the Constitution and set the new government on its feet. Unlike the Anti-Federalists, the Jeffersonians were ardent supporters of the Constitution, but insisted that it be implemented in ways consistent with political liberty and a strong dependence on the states.

Not all Jeffersonians were democratic in sympathy. Some continued to argue the importance of leadership by a "natural aristocracy of talent," most southern Jeffersonians found no inconsistency between black slavery and white liberty, and virtually all continued to believe that politics should remain an exclusively male domain. Still, the Jeffersonian coalition included countless individuals committed to the creation of a more democratic society. Motivated by electoral self-interest, political principle, and the determination of ordinary people to claim their rights as republican citizens,

The Death of Washington
Washington's death in 1799 generated a surge of public mourning as countless eulogies celebrated him as the "Father of his Country." The picture is rich in religious and patriotic symbols. How many can you identify, and what meanings are they intended to convey?

(Photograph Courtesy Peabody Essex Museum [AE81885])

the Jeffersonian Republicans mounted elaborate parades, organized get-out-the-vote campaigns in New York City and other urban centers, and utilized the popular press to mobilize the people. In the process they ushered in a growing tide of popular politics.

In the election of 1800, control of the federal government passed for the first time from one political party to another, not easily but peacefully and legally. The "Revolution of 1800," Jefferson claimed, was "as real a revolution in the principles of our government as that of 1776 was in its form." The years immediately ahead would reveal whether he was correct.

Restoring American Liberty

The Jeffersonians took office in 1801 determined to calm the political storms, consolidate their recent electoral victory, rescue the government from Federalist misman-agement, and set it on a proper republican course.

The New Capital

How did Washington differ from former capitals such as New York and Philadelphia? How might these differences have shaped the new government's development?

The Jeffersonians Take Control

In November 1800 the government had moved from Philadelphia to the District of Columbia located on the Potomac River. To the consternation of the arriving politicians, the new capital was little more than a swampy village of 5,000 inhabitants. Little had yet materialized of the grand design encompassing plazas and boulevards radiating outward from the Capitol that had been created by the Frenchman Pierre L'Enfant, aided by the black American mathematician and surveyor Benjamin Banneker. One wing of the capitol building containing the House of Representatives was finished, but the Senate chamber and president's mansion were uncompleted.

To rid the government of Federalist pomp, Jefferson planned a simple inauguration. Shortly before noon on March 4, he walked to the Capitol from his nearby boardinghouse. Dressed as a plain citizen, the president-elect read his short inaugural address, Chief Justice John Marshall (a fellow Virginian but staunch Federalist, recently appointed to the Supreme Court by John Adams) administered the oath of office, and a militia company fired a 16-gun salute.

Despite the modesty of the occasion, the moment was filled with significance. Mrs. Samuel Harrison Smith, Washington resident and political observer, described the moment's drama. "I have this morning witnessed one of the most interesting scenes a free people can ever witness," she wrote to a friend. "The changes of administration, which in every…age have most generally been epochs of confusion, villainy, and bloodshed, in this our happy country take place without any species of distraction or disorder." Countless Americans shared her sense of pride and relief.

In his inaugural speech, Jefferson enumerated the "essential principles" that would guide his administration: "equal and exact justice to all," support of the states as "the surest bulwarks against anti-republican tendencies," "absolute acquiescence" in the decisions of the majority, supremacy of civil over military authority, reduction of government spending, "honest payment" of the public debt, freedom of the press, and "freedom of the person under the protection of the habeas corpus." Though Jefferson never mentioned the Federalists, his litany of principles reverberated with the dark experience of the 1790s.

The president spoke also of political reconciliation. Asserting that "every difference of opinion is not a difference of principle," he affirmed that "we are all republicans—we are all federalists." Not all his followers welcomed that final flourish, for many were eager to scatter the Federalists to the political winds. Acknowledging political reality, Jefferson agreed that a "general sweep" of Federalist officeholders was necessary. By 1808, virtually all government offices were in Jeffersonian hands.

Politics and the Federal Courts

Having lost Congress and the presidency, the Federalists turned to the federal judiciary for protection against the expected Jeffersonian onslaught. In the last months of the Adams administration, the Federalist-controlled

Congress had passed a new Judiciary Act increasing the number of circuit courts, complete with judges, marshals, and clerks. Before leaving office, Adams filled many of those offices with staunch Federalists. When the new Jeffersonian-dominated Congress convened, it challenged the Federalist hold on the judiciary. In January 1802, by a strict party vote, Congress repealed the Judiciary Act.

As Federalists sputtered in anger, exultant Jeffersonians prepared to purge several highly partisan Federalist judges. In March 1803, the House of Representatives impeached District Judge John Pickering of New Hampshire. The grounds were not the "high crimes and misdemeanors" required by the Constitution, but the Federalist diatribes with which Pickering regularly assaulted defendants and juries. Impeachment, asserted a Republican congressman, is nothing more than a declaration by Congress that an individual holds "dangerous opinions," which if allowed to go into effect "will work the destruction of the Union." Such phrases echoed the language of repression used by Federalists only a few years earlier. Still, the Jeffersonian-controlled Senate convicted Pickering by a straight party vote.

Emboldened by their success, the Jeffersonians next impeached Supreme Court Justice Samuel Chase, one of the most notorious Federalist partisans, charging him with "intemperate and inflammatory political harangues." When the trial revealed that Chase had committed no impeachable offense, he was acquitted and returned triumphantly to the bench.

Chase was a sorry hero, but constitutional principles are often established in defense of less than heroic people. Had Chase's impeachment succeeded, Chief Justice Marshall would almost certainly have been next, and that would have precipitated a constitutional crisis. Sensing the danger, the Jeffersonians pulled back, content to allow time and attrition to cleanse the courts of Federalist control. The vital principle of judicial independence had been narrowly preserved.

Dismantling the Federalist War Program

The Jeffersonians quickly moved to dismantle the Federalists' war program. They ended prosecution of newspaper editors under the Sedition Act, freed its victims, and in 1802 let it lapse. While several Federalist editors felt the government's displeasure, the Jeffersonians never duplicated the Federalists' attempts to stifle political dissent. As a consequence, freedom of the press, among the bedrock principles of American liberty, was solidly affirmed. "Error of opinion may be

FEDERAL REVENUES AND EXPENDITURES, 1790–1810 (IN THOUSANDS OF DOLLARS)

What do these figures tell you about the size and functions of the federal government during these early years?

Year	Revenues		Expenditures	
1790	Customs	4,399	Military	634
	Other	19	Interest on public debt	2,349
		4,418	Other	1,426
				4,409
1800	Customs	9,081	Military	6,010
	Internal revenue	809	Interest on public debt	3,375
	Other	793	Other	1,466
		10,683		10,851
1810	Customs	8,583	Military	3,948
	Internal revenue	7	Interest on public debt	2,845
	Sale of public lands	697	Other	1,447
	Other	793		8,240
		10,080		

Note: In constant dollars, the estimated revenue of the federal government in 2001 was $2,136 trillion and its estimated expenditures were $1,856 trillion.

Source: U.S. Bureau of the Census and *Statistical Abstract of the United States, 2001.*

tolerated," Jefferson explained in his first inaugural address, "where reason is left free to combat it." The American people would struggle to reaffirm that principle in the years ahead.

Jefferson undercut the Alien Acts by dismantling the hated inspection system, and in 1802, Congress restored the requirement of 5 rather than 14 years of residence before a foreigner could become a citizen. The Federalists' provisional army was quickly disbanded; no longer would federal troops intimidate American citizens.

Jefferson was determined as well to reduce the size of the federal government, even though it had fewer than 3,000 civilian employees, only 300 of them, including the cabinet and Congress, in Washington. The "principal care of our persons and property," he declared, should be left to the states because they were more closely attuned to the needs of the people and could be held more closely accountable. The federal government should do little more than oversee foreign policy, deliver the mail, deal with Indians on federal land, and administer the public domain. Though the Jeffersonian Republicans may not have "revolutionized" the government as they claimed, they pointed it in a new direction.

Building an Agrarian Nation

The Jeffersonian Republicans did more than reverse Federalist initiatives, for they were determined to implement their own vision of an expanding, agrarian nation. That vision was mixed and inconsistent, because the Jeffersonian Party contained conflicting groups, as American political parties always have. Among them were southern planters determined to maintain a slavery-based agrarian order; lower- and middle-class southerners committed to black servitude but ardent proponents of political equality among whites; northern artisans harboring an aversion to slavery, though rarely a commitment to racial equality, and a fierce dedication to honest toil and their own economic interests; western farmers devoted to self-sufficiency on the land; and northern intellectuals committed to political democracy. In time, this diversity would splinter the Jeffersonian coalition. For the moment, however, these groups found unity not only in their common Federalist enemies, but also in a set of broadly shared principles that guided government policy through Jefferson's two administrations (1801–1809).

The Jeffersonian Vision

Political liberty, the Jeffersonians believed, could survive only under conditions of broad economic and social equality. Their strategy centered on the independent, yeoman farmer—self-reliant, industrious, and concerned for the public good. Such qualities were deemed essential to democratic citizenship.

The Jeffersonian vision was clouded, however, because industriousness generated wealth, wealth bred social inequality, and inequality threatened to destroy the very foundation of a democratic society. The solution lay in rapid territorial expansion that would provide land for the nation's citizen farmers, draw restless people out of crowded eastern cities, preserve the social equality that democratic liberty required, and delay, perhaps even prevent, the cyclical process of political growth, maturity, and decay that had been the fate of past nations.

There were other reasons for promoting expansion. Occupation of the West would secure the nation's borders against lingering threats from Britain, France, and Spain. Finally, the Jeffersonians calculated that newly created western states would strengthen their political control and ensure the Federalists' demise.

Time would reveal that the United States' ability to avoid Europe's woes by continental expansion, a basic tenet of American exceptionalism, was more limited than Jefferson imagined. Yet from the perspective of the early nineteenth century, the Jeffersonians offered a compelling and hopeful vision of the nation's future.

The Windfall Louisiana Purchase

The goal of securing agrarian democracy by territorial expansion guided Jefferson's most dramatic accomplishment, the Louisiana Purchase of 1803. It nearly doubled the nation's size.

In 1800, Spain ceded the vast trans-Mississippi region called Louisiana to France. Jefferson was disturbed at this evidence that European nations still coveted North American soil. His fears were well grounded, for in October 1802 the Spanish commander at New Orleans, which Spain had retained, closed the Mississippi River to American commerce. Spain's action raised consternation in Washington and the West.

In response, Jefferson instructed Robert Livingston, the American minister to France, to purchase a tract of land on the lower Mississippi that might serve as an American port, thus guaranteeing free transit for American shipping. By April 1803, however, the French ruler, Napoleon Bonaparte, had decided to sell all of Louisiana. Faced with the threat of renewed war with England, as well as the successful black rebellion against French rule in Haiti, Napoleon feared American designs on Louisiana and knew he could not keep American settlers out. Soon the deal was struck. For $15 million, the United States obtained nearly 830,000 square miles of new territory.

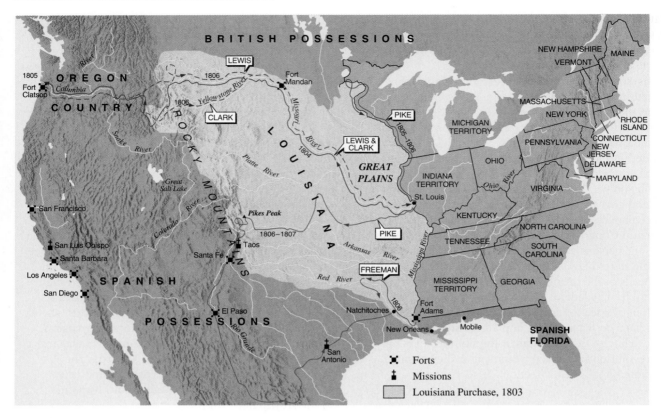

Exploring the Trans-Mississippi West, 1804–1807

During his two administrations, President Jefferson sent several exploring expeditions into the vast Louisiana Territory and beyond. Why did he send them, and what did they accomplish?

Federalists reacted to the news with alarm, fearing correctly that the states to be carved from Louisiana would be staunchly Jeffersonian. They worried as well that a rapidly expanding frontier would "decivilize" the nation.

Territorial expansion did not stop with Louisiana. In 1810, American adventurers fomented a revolt in Spanish West Florida and proclaimed an independent republic. Two years later, over vigorous Spanish objections, Congress annexed the region. In the Adams-Onís (or Transcontinental) Treaty of 1819, Spain ceded East Florida. As part of the 1819 agreement, the United States also extended its territorial claims to the Pacific Northwest.

Opening the Trans-Mississippi West

If America's expanding domain was to serve the needs of the agrarian nation, it would have to be explored and prepared for white settlement. In the summer of 1803, Jefferson dispatched an expedition led by Meriwether Lewis and William Clark to explore the far Northwest, make contact with Native Americans there, open the fur trade, and bring back scientific information about the area. For nearly two and a half years, the intrepid explorers, assisted by the Shoshoni woman Sacajawea, made their way across thousands of miles of hostile and unmapped terrain to the Pacific coast and back again to St. Louis. Lewis and Clark's journey, which some have called the greatest wilderness trip ever recorded, fanned people's interest in the Trans-Mississippi West and demonstrated the feasibility of an overland route to the Pacific.

In 1805 and 1806, Lieutenant Zebulon Pike explored the sources of the Mississippi River in northern Minnesota, then undertook an equally bold venture into the Rocky Mountains, where he surveyed the peak that still bears his name. In the following decade, the government established a string of military posts from Minnesota to Arkansas. They were intended to secure the nation's frontier, promote the fur trade, and support white settlement.

A Foreign Policy for the New Nation

While Jefferson was preoccupied with refashioning the government and extending American territory during his first term of office, his second term was dominated by foreign affairs. As Washington and John Adams had discovered and Jefferson soon learned, the Atlantic world was a dangerous place.

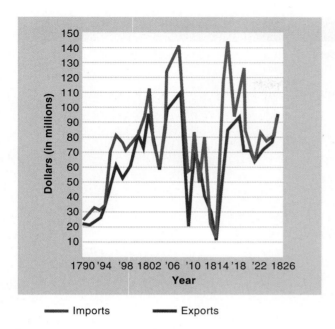

American Foreign Trade, 1790–1825
How can you explain the dramatic peaks and valleys of American overseas trade during the years 1790 to 1826?

Source: U.S. Bureau of the Census.

Jeffersonian Principles

During the early years of the nineteenth century, several goals guided the Jeffersonians' efforts to fashion a foreign policy appropriate for the expanding, agrarian nation. Chief among them were protecting American interests on the high seas, clearing the Great Lakes region of British troops, and breaking free of the country's historic dependence on Europe.

Jeffersonian foreign policy was based on the principle of "no entangling alliances" with Europe that Washington had articulated in his Farewell Address of 1796. England remained the principal enemy, but France, now that the revolution had ended in Napoleon Bonaparte's dictatorial rule, was suspect as well.

Second, Jeffersonians emphasized the importance of overseas commerce for the nation's well-being. Foreign trade would provide markets for America's agricultural produce and bring manufactured goods in return. Unlike the Federalists, the Jeffersonians hoped to keep large-scale manufacturing in Europe. They feared the concentrations of wealth and dependent working classes that domestic manufacturing would bring.

Peace was the Jeffersonians' third goal. War was objectionable not only because people died and property was destroyed, but also because it endangered liberty by inflaming politics, stifling free speech, swelling the public debt, and expanding governmental power. Jeffersonians understood the dangers lurking throughout the Atlantic world and knew that protecting the nation's interests might require the use of force.

Between 1801 and 1805, Jefferson dispatched naval vessels to defend U.S. commerce against the Barbary States (Algiers, Morocco, Tripoli, and Tunis) in the Mediterranean Sea. War, however, was to be a policy of last resort.

Struggling for Neutral Rights

After a brief interlude of peace, European war resumed in 1803. Once again Britain and France seized American shipping. Britain's naval superiority made its attacks especially serious. Its continuing refusal to stop impressment, vacate its posts south of the Great Lakes, and reopen the West Indies to American trade heightened Anglo-American tension.

In response to British seizures of U.S. shipping, Congress passed the Non-Importation Act in April 1806, banning British imports that could be produced domestically or acquired elsewhere. Tension between Britain and the United States reached the breaking point in June 1807, when the British warship *Leopard* stopped the American frigate *Chesapeake* off the Virginia coast and demanded that four crew members be handed over as British deserters. When the American commander refused, protesting that the sailors were U.S. citizens, the *Leopard* opened fire, killing 3 men and wounding 18. After the *Chesapeake* limped back into port with the story, cries of outrage rang across the land.

Knowing that the United States was not prepared to confront Britain, Jefferson proposed withdrawing American ships from the Atlantic. In December 1807, Congress passed the Embargo Act, forbidding American vessels from sailing for foreign ports. The embargo was one of Jefferson's most ill-fated decisions.

The embargo had relatively little effect on Britain, since British shipping profited from the withdrawal of American competition and British merchants found new sources of agricultural produce in Latin America. The embargo's impact at home, however, was far-reaching. U.S. exports plummeted 80 percent in a year, while imports dropped by more than half. New England was hardest hit. In ports such as Boston and Providence, ships lay idle and thousands of workers were unemployed as depression settled in.

Up and down the coast, communities openly violated the embargo. As attempts to police it failed, English goods were smuggled in across the Canadian border. Throughout the Federalist Northeast, bitterness threatened to escalate into open rebellion. When federal officials declared martial law and sent in troops in an effort to control the situation near Lake Champlain in upstate New York, local

Timeline

1789	George Washington inaugurated as first president
	Outbreak of the French Revolution
1790	Slave trade outlawed in all states except Georgia and South Carolina
	Hamilton's "Reports on the Public Credit"
1791	Bill of Rights ratified
	Whiskey Tax and national bank established
	Hamilton's "Report on Manufactures"
1792	Washington reelected
1793	Outbreak of war in Europe
	Washington's Neutrality Proclamation
	Jefferson resigns from cabinet
	Controversy over Citizen Genêt's visit
1794	Whiskey Rebellion in Pennsylvania
1795	Controversy over Jay's Treaty with England
1796	Washington's Farewell Address
	John Adams elected president
1797	XYZ Affair in France
1798	Naturalization Act
	Alien and Sedition Acts
	Virginia and Kentucky Resolutions
1798–1800	Undeclared naval war with France
1799	Trials of David Brown and Luther Baldwin
1800	Capital moves to Washington
1801	Jefferson elected president
	Judiciary Act
	New Land Act
1802	Judiciary Act repealed
1803	Louisiana Purchase
	Napoleonic wars resume
1803–1806	Lewis and Clark expedition
1804	Jefferson reelected
1805–1807	Pike explores the West
1806	Non-Importation Act
1807	Embargo Act
	Chesapeake–Leopard Affair
	Congress prohibits slave trade

citizens fired on U.S. revenue boats and recaptured confiscated goods.

In language reminiscent of the Virginia and Kentucky Resolutions, Connecticut's Federalist governor declared that states were duty-bound "to interpose their protecting shield" between the liberties of the people and oppressive acts of the general government. Faced with the embargo's ineffectiveness abroad and disastrous political consequences at home, Congress repealed the measure in 1809.

As Jefferson's presidency ended, officials found themselves in a quandary. How could American rights on the high seas be protected and the country's honor upheld without being drawn into a European war, and without further inflaming American politics? The nation would continue to struggle with that dilemma in the years immediately ahead.

Conclusion

A PERIOD OF TRIAL AND TRANSITION

The decade of the 1790s brought continuing political crises. Scarcely had the new government been formed than divisions appeared, initially among political leaders at the capital, but increasingly among the people at large. Hamilton's domestic policies generated the initial conflict. It was the French Revolution, European war, Jay's Treaty, and Federalist war program, however, that galvanized political energies and set Federalists and Jeffersonian Republicans adamantly against each other, catching up countless citizens like David Brown in the confusion. The Haitian rebellion together with other democratic insurgencies in Ireland, Europe, and the Americas further inflamed the country's politics.

In control of the federal government following the election of 1800, the Jeffersonians labored to set it on a more democratic course. At home, they fashioned domestic policies designed to redirect authority to the states and promote the country's agrarian expansion. Abroad they attempted, with more ambiguous results

and at considerable political cost, to protect American rights in a hostile Atlantic world while avoiding European entanglements.

By the time Thomas Jefferson left the presidency and James Madison took office in 1809, politics at the seat of national government and in the states had drawn more closely together, as leaders perfected such tools of democratic politics as a partisan press and political parties skilled in managing the expanding (white, male) electorate. These transitions, emerging in the midst of deep-seated controversy, would soon alter the very character of American political life.

QUESTIONS FOR REVIEW AND REFLECTION

1. Identify three foreign policy crises of the years 1790–1809, and explain why each was so controversial.
2. How did Federalists and Jeffersonians differ in their political principles? In the kind of economy they wished to have?
3. Disputes over the balance of authority between the national government and the states have been a recurring theme of American history from 1790 to our own time. Why did the issue generate such controversy during the period covered in this chapter?
4. Tension between the demands of national security and the protection of citizens' basic rights has been another recurrent theme of our history. Why did that tension become so severe during the 1790s?

CHAPTER 9

Society and Politics in the Early Republic

Detail from Thomas Coke Ruckle, *Fairview Inn or Three Mile House on Old Frederick Road* (near Baltimore), 1829. At country inns, people on the move bought supplies, exchanged goods, and secured information about the routes that lay ahead.

(T. C. Ruckle, *Fairview Inn,* 1899. Maryland Historical Society, Baltimore, Maryland)

American Stories

Creating New Lives

In May 1809, Mary and James Harrod gathered their five children, loaded a few belongings on a wagon and headed west from Spotsylvania County, Virginia, toward a new life in Kentucky. They left behind 15 years of wearying effort trying to wring a modest living from 10 acres of marginal upland, and a family cemetery holding two other children and Mary's parents.

Beyond the Appalachian Mountains, 450 difficult miles ahead, lay more hard work and uncertainty. Though central Kentucky, where the Harrods would settle, contained few Native Americans, powerful tribes from north and south of the Ohio River hunted there and fought over its control. They also opposed the growing tide of white settlers. The first years would be especially hard for James and Mary as they "opened up" the land, planted crops, and built a cabin. They would be lonesome years as well, for the Harrods would be unlikely to see even the chimney smoke of their nearest neighbors.

They were hopeful, though, as they trudged west. The land agent who had sold them their claim had promised rich, fertile soil that in time would support a good life. They were glad to leave behind Virginia's slave society with its arrogant planters and oppressed slaves, and were excited at the prospect of joining the swelling stream of migrants seeking new lives in the West. Once in Kentucky, Mary and James settled on their own plot of land and took responsibility for their lives.

In April 1795, Ben Thompson started north from Queen Anne's County, Maryland, for New York City. Ben knew little beyond farming, but he was ambitious, and when he arrived in New York he listened carefully to the ships' captains as they talked about life at sea and recruited men for their crews. Ben was lucky, for he arrived just as American overseas commerce was entering a decade of unprecedented prosperity. Sailors were in demand, pay was good, and few questions were asked. For five years, Ben sailed the seas. Having enough of travel, he returned to New York and hired out as an apprentice to a ship's carpenter.

About the same time, Phyllis Sherman left her home in Norwalk, Connecticut. She also headed for New York, where she took a job as a maid in the household of one of the city's wealthy merchants. As fate would have it, Phyllis and Ben met, fell in love, and in the spring of 1802 were married.

There is little remarkable in their stories, except that Ben and Phyllis were former slaves and were married in the African Methodist Episcopal Zion Church. Ben had cast off his slave name, Cato, as a sign of liberation, while Phyllis kept the name her master had given her. Ben was doubly fortunate, for he had purchased his freedom just as cotton production began to expand through the southern interior, creating an accelerating demand for field slaves shipped in from the Chesapeake. In another decade, he would have faced greater difficulty securing his independence. Phyllis had been freed as a child when slavery ended in Connecticut. As she grew up, she tired of living as a servant with her former owner's family and longed for the companionship of other blacks. She had heard that there were people of color in New York City, and she was correct. In 1800, it contained 6,300 African Americans, more than half of them free.

Though life in New York was better than either Ben or Phyllis had known before, it was hardly easy. They shared marginally in the city's commercial prosperity. In 1804, they watched helplessly as yellow fever carried off their daughter and many of their friends. And while they found support in newly established African American churches and the expanding black community, they had to be constantly on guard because slave ships still moved in and out of the port and slave catchers pursued southern runaways in the city's streets.

In the early republic, thousands of Americans seized opportunities to improve their lives. Some, like Ben Thompson and Phyllis Sherman, moved from the countryside to the nation's burgeoning cities, while others, such as Mary and James Harrod, joined the swelling tide of westward expansion. By their actions, they helped strengthen American values of individual initiative, social equality, and personal autonomy.

They contributed as well to a process of social transformation that historians have called the "opening" of American society. That process was powered by an accelerating movement of people across the land that disrupted families, weakened long-established communities, and created countless new settlements. The transformation was fueled as well by an expanding market economy with its relentless discipline of supply and demand, pursuit of individual profit, and contract-based relationships. In addition, a wave of religious revivalism known as the Second Great Awakening swept through American society, strengthening belief in the equality of all believers before God and the individual's responsibility for his or her own soul. This chapter examines these processes of social, economic, and religious change that would continue to transform people's lives throughout the nineteenth century.

Not all Americans benefited equally from the changes of these early nineteenth-century years. Doctrines of equality and individual autonomy resonated more powerfully in the lives of men than of women. In the South, African Americans found their lives constrained by a revitalized system of slavery, while in the North free blacks faced an increasingly racist society. West of the Appalachians, Native Americans confronted a swelling tide of white settlement. Discrepancies between the nation's values and the conditions of many Americans' lives fueled a flurry of reform movements aimed at alleviating poverty and distress and improving women's lives, other topics examined in Chapter 9.

The chapter also explores the multiple ways in which America's diverse regions became more closely knit together, as well as the political tensions that resulted. The years of the early nineteenth century also witnessed a diplomatic revolution of major importance. With the War of 1812, the American people broke free of their centuries-old dependence on Europe and turned their energies toward the settlement of the continental interior. Just as important, with the Monroe Doctrine of 1823 the United States asserted a bold, new framework for relations with other nations in the Americas as they also threw off the yoke of European colonialism.

Finally, Chapter 9 examines the collapse of the Federalist–Jeffersonian political system and the emergence of a new kind of American politics increasingly democratic in temper, organized by sophisticated political parties, and led by a new generation of political leaders eager to claim their place in shaping the nation's future.

A Nation of Regions

In the early republic, the vast majority of Americans drew their living from the land. As the nineteenth century began, 83 percent of the labor force was engaged in agriculture; that figure had hardly changed 25 years later. Yet across the nation, people occupied the land in very different ways.

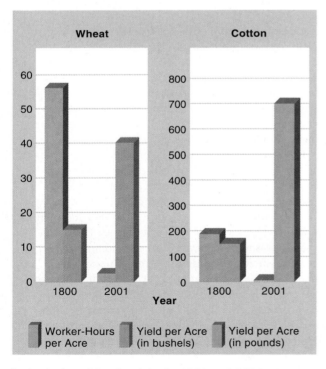

Agricultural Productivity in 1800 and 2001

Why did the ratio of worker hours to yield per acre change so dramatically during the nineteenth and twentieth centuries?

Source: U.S. Bureau of the Census.

The Northeast

In the Northeast, a region stretching from New Jersey and eastern Pennsylvania to New England, family farms dominated the landscape. On New England's rock-strewn land, farmers often abandoned field crops for the greater profits to be made from dairying and livestock. On the richer agricultural lands of New York and Pennsylvania, farmers cultivated the land intensively, planting crops year after year rather than following the time-honored practice of allowing worn-out fields to lie fallow and recover their fertility. In 1750, the mid-Atlantic landscape had looked unkempt, with wide areas still covered by timber and fallow lands lapsing into brush. Fifty years later, the countryside looked increasingly orderly, its carefully cultivated fields marked by hedges and stone walls.

Farmers in southeastern Pennsylvania and along New York's Hudson River valley produced an agricultural surplus, the produce left over after meeting their families' needs, and exchanged it in nearby towns for commodities such as tea, window glass, and tools. Across much of the rural Northeast, cash played but a small part in economic exchange. Noted an observant Frenchman, people "supply their needs in the countryside by direct reciprocal exchanges. The tailor and the bootmaker . . . do the work of their calling at the home of the farmer . . . who . . . provides the raw material for it and pays for the work in goods. . . . They write down what they give and receive on both sides, and at the end of the year . . . settle a large variety of exchanges with a very small quantity of coin."

By 1800, the average farm in longer-settled areas was no more than 100 to 150 acres, down substantially from half a century before. That was primarily a result of the continuing division of farm property from fathers to sons. Even in southeastern Pennsylvania, the

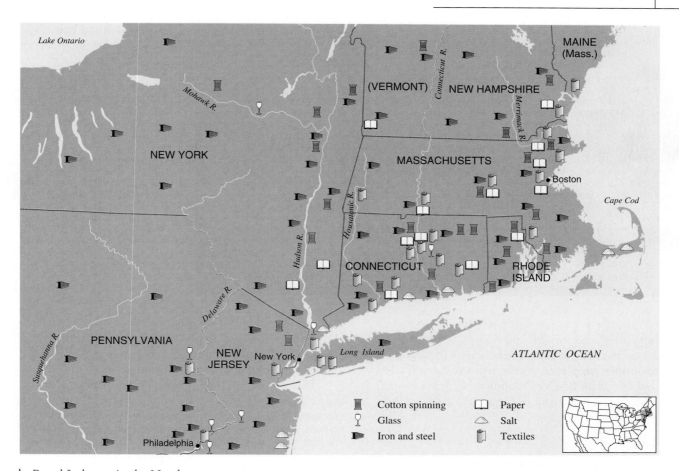

Rural Industry in the North

Prior to the expansion of urban industrialization beginning in the 1830s, American manufacturing was small in scale and was often scattered across the countryside. What circumstances would be most likely to determine the location of the different industries included on this map?

most productive agricultural region in the Northeast, opportunity was declining. Continuous cropping had robbed the soil of fertility, forcing farmers to bring more marginal land under cultivation, thus bringing a steady decline in productivity. By 1800, nearly 20 percent of male taxpayers in southeastern Pennsylvania were single, clear evidence that young men were delaying marriage until they could establish themselves financially.

Growing numbers of rural folk also worked for wages as artisans or day laborers in nearby towns, or toiled in the grain and saw mills, potash works, and iron forges that dotted the rural landscape. Farm women contributed to the family economy by helping with the livestock, preserving food, and making clothes for sale or exchange with neighbors. As the practice grew of men working for wages outside the family setting, women's unwaged domestic labor began to be regarded as less valuable.

Frustrated by the backwardness of American agriculture, leading citizens joined in creating associations, such as the Massachusetts Society for Promoting

Agriculture, that compiled agricultural libraries and endorsed "scientific" techniques. Elkanah Watson, a prosperous businessman turned gentleman farmer, was instrumental in creating the nation's first agricultural fairs in western Massachusetts. Part visionary and part huckster, Watson intended the fairs' displays of equipment and animals to educate farmers and "excite a lively spirit of competition" among them. Within a few years, rural folk by the thousands were converging on the annual Berkshire gatherings. These precursors to the county fairs that have remained a staple of rural and small town American life soon spread from Maine to Virginia and as far west as Illinois.

By 1830, the demands of the Northeast's expanding population for new farmland and a wide variety of wood products had transformed the region's once heavily forested landscape. Iron furnaces consumed firewood voraciously while the production of potash and turpentine, planking for wooden houses, and fencing further depleted forest ranges.

But more than anything, it was the demand for heating fuel during the long winter months that made

An Agricultural Fair
What does this depiction of an agricultural fair in Pennsylvania suggest of economic improvements in the early nineteenth century?

the woodcutter's axe ring. Rural households burned from 20 to 30 cords of firewood annually in highly inefficient open fireplaces. As the region's coastal cities increased in size and nearby woodlots were exhausted, fuel had to be fetched from as far as 100 miles inland.

The South

Life was different in the South, a region stretching from Maryland to Georgia along the coast, and west to the newly forming states of Alabama and Mississippi. In 1800, much of southern agriculture was in disarray.

Overseeing Enslaved Workers
In this scene from near Fredericksburg, Maryland, female slaves grub tree stumps from a field while an overseer looks on. As tobacco cultivation gave way to a more diversified economy, male slaves were often assigned to other jobs. Slave labor, provided by women as well as men, followed the spread of cotton cultivation into new lands of the southern interior.

(Benjamin Latrobe, *An Overseer Doing His Duty*. Maryland Historical Society, Baltimore)

Low prices, land exhausted by tobacco cultivation, and the loss of slaves during the Revolutionary War had left the Chesapeake's economy in shambles.

In response, southern planters experimented with wheat and other grains in hopes of boosting their sagging fortunes. Regional recovery began in earnest, however, when they turned to a new staple crop—cotton. In 1790, the South had produced 3,135 bales of cotton; by 1820, output had mushroomed to 334,378 bales. In 1805, cotton accounted for 30 percent of the nation's agricultural exports; by 1820, it exceeded half. Across the old coastal South and the newly developing states of Alabama, Mississippi, and Tennessee, cotton was becoming king.

A fortuitous combination of circumstances fueled the transformation: the growing demand of textile mills in England and the American Northeast; wonderfully productive virgin soil; a long, steamy growing season; ample slave labor; and southern planters' long experience in producing and marketing staple crops.

Eli Whitney's cotton gin speeded the process as well. The silky fibers of long-staple cotton could be easily separated from the cotton's seeds. The delicate long-staple plant, however, grew only in the hot, humid climate along the southern coast. The hardier, short-staple variety thrived in the southern interior, but its fibers clung tenaciously to the plant's sticky, green seeds. A slave could clean no more than a pound of short-staple cotton a day.

A solution began to appear in 1793 when Whitney set his mind to the problem of short-staple cotton and its seeds. His "cotton gin" was little more than a box containing a roller equipped with wire teeth designed to pull the fibers through a comb-like barrier, thus stripping them from the seeds. A hand crank activated the mechanism. With this crude device a laborer could clean up to 50 pounds of short-staple cotton a day.

The swing to cotton marked a momentous turning point in the South's—and the nation's—history. It raised the value of southern land and opened economic opportunity for countless southern whites, but also increased the demand for black field hands and breathed new life into slavery. Some of the escalating demand for slave labor was met from overseas. In 1803, Georgia and South Carolina alone imported 20,000 new slaves, as southern planters and northern suppliers rushed to meet the need before the slave trade ended in 1808. Much of the demand for agricultural labor, however, was met by the internal slave trade that moved black labor from the worn-out lands of the Chesapeake to the lush cotton fields of the southern interior.

Trans-Appalachia

West of the Appalachian Mountains, a third region of settlement was forming as the nineteenth century began. Trans-Appalachia, extending from the mountains to the Mississippi River and from the Great Lakes to the Gulf of Mexico, constituted a broad and shifting "middle ground," a zone of cultural, economic, and military interaction between Native and European Americans. In 1790, scarcely 100,000 white settlers had lived there. By 1810, their number, including Mary and James Harrod, had swollen to nearly a million. By 1820, over a million more had arrived. They came by wagon across upstate New York, through mountain passes such as the Cumberland Gap and by flatboat down the Ohio River. The human tide seemed to grow with each year. The woods are full of new settlers driven by "Genesee fever," wrote an amazed observer near Batavia in western New York in 1805. "Axes are resounding, and the trees literally falling around us as we passed." America, he exclaimed, "is breaking up and going west!"

Settlers were drawn by the promotions of speculators seeking their fortunes in the sale of western land. Between 1790 and 1820, land companies hawked vast areas of New York, Ohio, and Kentucky to prospective settlers like the Harrods. Many ventures failed, but countless others proved profitable. Settlers joined in the speculative fever, often going deeply into debt to buy extra land for resale when population increased and land values rose.

North of the Ohio River, settlement followed the grid pattern prescribed in the Land Ordinance of 1785. There, free-labor agriculture took hold and towns such as Columbus and Cincinnati emerged as service and cultural centers for the surrounding population. South of the Ohio, white settlers and their black slaves distributed themselves more randomly across the land. In Kentucky and Tennessee, free-labor agriculture was soon challenged by the spread of slavery-based cotton.

In this constantly shifting "borderland," people of different ethnicity, race, class, and regional origin mingled together. Their conflicting social and cultural values often generated tension. But as they built new communities, they fashioned new ways of life, in the process strengthening belief in America as a land of opportunity.

Given its newness and diversity, Trans-Appalachia gained a reputation for its rough and colorful ways. In towns such as Louisville along the Ohio River boatmen, gamblers, con men, and speculators gave civic life a raucous quality. Everywhere the transiency of the population and large numbers of young, unattached males kept society unsettled. No characters were more famous in popular folklore than adventurers such as Daniel Boone and the mythical riverman Mike Fink, "half man, half alligator," who could "whip his weight in grizzly bears." Nothing revealed the West's rawness more graphically than the eye-gouging, ear-biting, no-holds-barred, "rough and tumble" brawls that regularly erupted.

As settlers arrived, they began the long process of transforming the region's heavily forested land. In mountainous areas, hillsides were denuded of trees that were dragged behind wagons as brakes during jolting rides downhill. Believing, erroneously, that open lands were infertile, farmers cut girdles of bark off trees, then set them on fire or left them to die while planting crops around the decaying hulks. By this method, a family could clear

Marietta, Ohio
Located on the Ohio River, Marietta was one of the first permanent settlements west of the Appalachian Mountains. Can you explain the rectangular earthworks within which the town was established?

Five Points, New York
This rather humorous depiction of a bustling intersection in New York City in 1827 suggests the increasing crowdedness of the country's largest cities. How many different kinds of people and activities can you identify?

(*Five Points, New York,* 1827, in Valentine's Manual, 1855. Museum of the City of New York. Gift of Lou Sepersky and Leida Snow, [97.227.3])

from three to five acres a year for cultivation. "The scene is truly savage," observed an English traveler. "Immense trees stripped of their foliage, and half consumed by fire extend their sprawling limbs... now bleached by the weather." As areas of Trans-Appalachia came under the farmer's plow, forests and wildlife gave way.

The Nation's Cities

Though most Americans lived on the land or in small towns, increasing numbers dwelled in the nation's expanding cities. From 1790 to 1830, the nation's population increased by nearly 230 percent, but urban places of more than 2,500 residents grew almost twice as fast.

Patterns of urban development differed from region to region. The most dramatic growth occurred in the port cities of the Northeast. By 1830, the region contained four cities of more than 50,000. New York alone held over 100,000 people, while inland towns such as Springfield, Massachusetts, and Albany, New York, proliferated as service centers for their surrounding areas.

The cities of the Atlantic seaboard were socially diverse. In New York and Philadelphia, Irish, German, British, and African Americans, together with travelers from around the world, jostled for space on the cities' sidewalks. Sailors, often speaking strange tongues, added raucous behavior and at times an edge of danger to urban life.

Economic life still centered on the wharves where sailing ships from distant ports docked. By the 1820s, however, manufacturing was beginning to transform urban life. Philadelphia was becoming a textile manufacturing center, while New York produced shoes and

iron goods. As these enterprises expanded, artisan production gave way to factory-based wage labor.

Such changes widened the gap between richer and poorer inhabitants. Prosperous merchants rested securely at the top of the social pyramid, their households graced by fine table linens and store-bought furniture, the artifacts of an expanding consumer economy. Below them came an aspiring middle class of artisans, shopkeepers, and professional men whose families shared modestly in the general prosperity. At the bottom spread a growing underclass of common laborers, dock workers, and the unemployed, their lives a continuous struggle for survival. Whereas rich and poor had often lived close together in colonial cities, rising land values now forced the lower classes into crowded alleys and tenements, while more prosperous urban dwellers began clustering in fashionable neighborhoods.

In the Southeast, urban development centered in long-established ports such as Charleston and Savannah. As during the colonial period, they continued to serve as commercial entrepots, exporting agricultural produce and importing manufactured goods. Half their population was black, the majority of them slaves.

In Trans-Appalachia, fledgling towns such as Pittsburgh and Chicago dotted the region's rivers and lakes. Small villages in 1790, these interior cities held 30 percent of the nation's urban population by 1830. Places such as New Orleans and St. Louis reflected their multinational origins. Established as a French colony in 1718, New Orleans came under Spanish rule in 1763. When it became part of the United States in 1803, French and Spanish creole families dominated urban life. For several decades, U.S. citizens remained a minority among the white population. Of its 27,000 people, nearly 13,000 were black. Upriver from New Orleans, the smaller town of St. Louis, at different times part of French and Spanish North America, had a similarly diverse population. Enslaved blacks made up nearly one-third of the town's 1,000 residents.

Though increasing rapidly in population, America's cities were small in area. In these "walking cities," residents could easily stroll from one side of town to the other. Rapid growth, however, brought increasing congestion together with problems of public health and safety. Asa Greene, a New York physician, observed ruefully that to cross Broadway "you must button your coat tightly about you . . . settle your hat firmly on your head, look up street and down . . . to see what carts and carriages are upon you, and then run for your life."

Dust and mud plagued urban life. One alarmed citizen, finding a man embedded up to his neck in a mud hole following a violent downpour, offered to help pull him out. "No need to worry," replied the man, "I have a horse underneath me." So, at least, went a popular fable.

In the early nineteenth century, residents dumped their garbage in the streets, privies leached into open drains, and livestock roamed freely, leaving their droppings behind. Though one urban dweller thought the scavenging hogs she encountered were "disgusting," she acknowledged that without them the streets would be choked with filth. Packs of stray dogs added to the confusion.

Under such conditions, typhoid and dysentery, spread by contaminated well water, took a continuous toll. The rigors of poor diet, frequent disease, and inadequate medical care often brought life to an early end. Scarcely half of urban dwellers reached the age of 45. Unlike today, women on average died sooner than men, their bodies weakened by frequent childbirth.

Indian–White Relations in the Early Republic

Indian–white relations took a dramatic turn in the early years of the nineteenth century. In 1790, vast areas of Trans-Appalachia were still controlled by Native American tribes. North of the Ohio River, the Shawnee, Delaware, and Miami formed a western confederacy capable of mustering several thousand warriors. South of the river lived five major tribal groups: the Cherokee, Creek, Choctaw, Chickasaw, and Seminole. Together, they totaled nearly 60,000 people. By 1830, however, the balance of power throughout Trans-Appalachia had shifted decisively as white settlers, many of them bringing black slaves with them south of the Ohio River, streamed into the region.

In response, tribal groups devised various strategies of resistance and survival. Among the Cherokee, many sought peaceful accommodation, while others, like the Shawnee and the Creek, rose in armed resistance. Neither strategy was altogether successful. By 1830, the Indians faced a future of continued acculturation, military defeat, or forced migration to lands west of the Mississippi River.

Less dramatic but no less important, the social and cultural separation of Indian and white Americans sharpened during these years. As late as the 1780s, Indians still walked the streets of New York and Philadelphia, while countless Indians and whites interacted as traders or marriage partners. By 1830, racial separation had increased as Native Americans were confined on reservations or forced to move farther west.

The Goals of Indian Policy

During the years from 1790 to 1830, the federal government established policies that would govern Indian–white relations through much of the nineteenth century. Intended in part to promote the assimilation of Native Americans into white society, the policies actually speeded the transfer of Indian land to white settlers and set the stage for later, large-scale Indian removal.

With the government's initial "conquest" theory rendered obsolete by the Indians' refusal to regard themselves as a conquered people (see Chapter 7), U.S. officials shifted course by recognizing Indian rights to the land they inhabited and declaring that all future land transfers would come through treaty agreements. Explained Henry Knox, Washington's first secretary of war, the Indians, "being the prior occupants of the soil, possess the right of the soil." It should not be taken from them "unless by their free consent, or by the right of conquest in case of just war." The Indian Intercourse Act of 1790 declared that public treaties, ratified by the Congress, would henceforth be the only legal means of obtaining Indian land. Though the 1790 act promised a more humane Indian policy, the acquisition of land for white settlement remained the overarching goal.

The new, treaty-based strategy proved effective. Native American leaders frequently ceded land in return for trade goods, yearly annuity payments, and assurances that there would be no further demands. Reluctant tribal leaders could often be persuaded to cooperate by warnings about the inevitable spread of white settlement, or more tractable chieftains could be found. In these ways, vast areas of tribal land passed to white settlers.

Federal policy also attempted to regulate the fur trade, in which both Native Americans and white traders eagerly participated. The Indians, in return for their abundant furs, secured the blankets, guns, and rum that they valued highly, while white traders

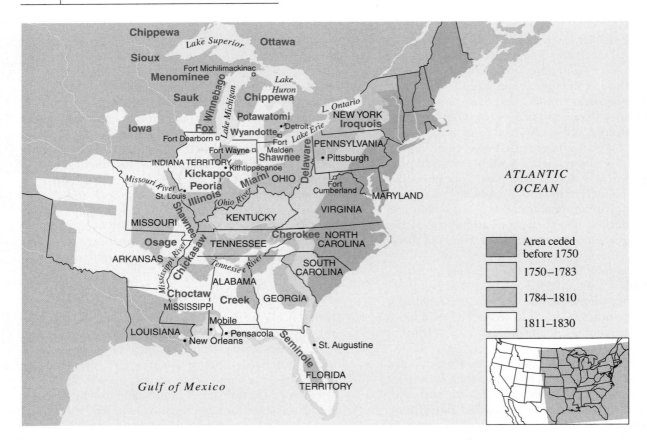

Indian Land Cessions, 1750–1830

As white settlers streamed across the nation's interior, state and federal governments wrung successive land cessions from the Indians. By 1830, only the southeastern tribes still controlled significant areas of their ancestral land east of the Mississippi River. Labels in blue indicate the major Native American tribes.

acquired desirable furs in exchange for inexpensive trade goods.

The fur trade brought handsome profits to companies such as John Jacob Astor's American Fur Company, but often worked to the Indians' disadvantage. Rum devastated Indian communities, while trade goods frequently transmitted diseases such as measles and smallpox. Indians often became dependent on the trade because it provided the only reliable supplies of coveted goods such as iron kettles and firearms. As the demand for furs and pelts increased, Native Americans frequently overtrapped their hunting grounds, forcing them to compete with other tribes for new sources of furs farther west.

In an effort to reduce trading fraud and the resulting conflict, Congress created government trading posts, or "factories," where Indians could come for fairer treatment. Often, however, Indians found themselves deeply in debt to government traders. In 1822, Congress abolished the factory system.

A third objective of federal Indian policy was to "civilize" and "Christianize" Native Americans, then assimilate them into white society. With the government's blessing, Moravians, Baptists, and other religious groups sent scores of missionaries to live among the Indians, preach the Gospel, and teach the benefits of white civilization. Among the most selfless were Quakers who labored with the Iroquois in New York. In spite of the missionaries' best efforts, however, most Indians remained aloof. The chasm between Christianity and their own religions was too wide.

Education was the other weapon of assimilation. In 1793, Congress appropriated $20,000 to promote literacy, agriculture, and vocational instruction among Indians. Federal officials encouraged missionaries to establish schools where Indian children could learn the three R's and vocational skills. But the vast majority of Indian children never attended, their parents distrusting the schools' alien environment.

Although the assimilationists cared deeply about the physical and spiritual fate of Native American people, they showed little sympathy for Indian culture, demanding that Native Americans give up their language, religion, dress, and extended family arrangements and adopt the ways of white society. Assimilation or removal were the stark alternatives posed by even the most benevolent whites.

CENSUS RETURNS

Throughout the nation's history, the American population has changed dramatically, not only in size and geographic distribution but also in birth and death rates, marriage age, and family size. In the early nineteenth century, for example, the average life expectancy of white Americans was about 45 years, and men tended to outlive women. In our own time, the average life expectancy has reached 74, and women on average live longer than men. Populations have differed as well across regions, in urban and rural settings, and among racial, ethnic, and class groups.

Changes in the demographic profile of the American population have powerful effects on the nation's economic, social, and political development. The changing size and makeup of the labor force shape economic activity, while changing proportions of older and younger Americans affect consumer habits and put different demands on health care and educational systems—as the aging of baby boomers in our own time is again making clear. When mortality rates were high, as was often the case in early American history, parents had more children in an effort to stabilize their families. As mortality declined during the nineteenth century, so too did birthrates and family size.

Demographic information can tell us a great deal about the life experiences of ordinary Americans. Indeed,

DATA FROM THE FEDERAL CENSUS OF 1820

	New York City	Charleston	Cincinnati
Free white males, 25 and under	36,122	3,780	3,419
Free white males, 26 and over	21,331	2,119	1,672
Free white males, total	57,453 (44)	5,899 (23)	5,091 (51)
Free white females, 25 and under	37,438	3,297	3,137
Free white females, 26 and over	20,070	2,033	1,152
Free white females, total	57,508 (44)	5,330 (21)	4,289 (43)
Total white population	114,961 (88)	11,229 (44)	9,380 (93)
Free colored males, 25 and under	2,201	394	120
Free colored males, 26 and over	1,993	229	99
Free colored males, total	4,194 (3)	623 (2)	219 (2)
Free colored females, 25 and under	3,342	467	132
Free colored females, 26 and over	2,832	385	82
Free colored females, total	6,174 (5)	852 (3)	214 (2)
Male slaves, 25 and under	144	3,656	0
Male slaves, 26 and over	33	2,039	0
Male slaves, total	177 (1)	5,695 (22)	0 (0)
Female slaves, 25 and under	233	4,347	0
Female slaves, 26 and over	108	2,610	0
Female slaves, total	341 (1)	6,957 (27)	0 (0)
Total black population	10,886 (8)	14,127 (55)	433 (0)
Foreigners not naturalized	5,390 (4)	425 (2)	241 (2)
Total city population	131,237	25,781	10,054
Persons engaged in agriculture	386	164	29
Persons engaged in commerce	3,142	1,138	63
Persons engaged in manufacturing	9,523	887	211

Notes: New York City did not then include Kings, Queens, or Suffolk counties. Figures in parentheses represent percentages of each city's total population.

demographic data are often the major source of information about otherwise anonymous individuals. For all these reasons, historians spend considerable time analyzing populations and the ways they change.

Two kinds of demographic data have proved most important. One consists of birth, death, and marriage records, often found in church or town registers. These records chronicle the basic demographic events in people's lives. If they are complete and continuous enough, they allow historians to trace the life course of individuals and to reconstruct patterns of family and community life.

Here we offer an example of the second kind of demographic data, a census. The material is from the federal census of 1820. Article 1, Section 2 of the Constitution called for an enumeration (or counting) of the nation's population every 10 years, "in such manner" as Congress required. The information was to be used in determining the periodic reapportionment of the House of Representatives and allocation of direct taxes to the states. The first decennial census was taken in 1790.

Compared with modern census inquiries, the first federal censuses collected limited information. The 1790s census, for example, gathered data under six headings: "Name of head of family," "Free white males, 16 years and upwards," "Free white males, under 16," "Free white females," "All other free persons," and "Slaves." As the nation grew, the

demand for additional information increased. In 1820, Congress for the first time called for the collection of economic data. In the decades following, categories of social and economic data were gradually expanded.

The table provided here contains data from three cities—New York City; Charleston, South Carolina; and Cincinnati, Ohio—located in different sections of the country. What do the data tell you about the racial, gender, and age profiles of these cities? How do they differ? Do you find significant age and gender differences between white and black populations? Between free blacks and slaves? Can you explain the differences that you find? In making your calculations, be sure to take into account both absolute numbers and proportions of the total populations.

Why were there no slaves in Cincinnati, while there were still slaves in New York? What kinds of people might have been included under the heading "Foreigners not naturalized"? The economic data included in the 1820 census was very general. What conclusions are you able to draw concerning economic activities in the three cities? Can you explain the differences?

Reflecting on the Past How would the federal census of 2000 differ from the census displayed here? Why do disputes often arise over the kinds of information that should be gathered? ■

Strategies of Survival: The Iroquois and Cherokee

Faced with the steady loss of land and tribal autonomy, Native Americans devised various strategies of resistance and survival. Among the Iroquois, a prophet named Handsome Lake led his people through a religious renewal and cultural revitalization. In 1799, following a series of visions, he preached a combination of Indian and white ways: temperance, peace, land retention, and a new religion combining elements of Christianity and traditional Iroquois belief. His vision offered renewed pride in the midst of the Iroquois' radically changed lives.

Far to the south, the Cherokee followed a different path of accommodation. As the nineteenth century began, they still controlled millions of acres in Tennessee, Georgia, and the western Carolinas. Their land base, however, was shrinking.

Southern state governments, responding to white demands for Indian land, undercut tribal autonomy. In 1801, Tennessee unilaterally brought Cherokee lands under the authority of state courts. The Cherokee, who had their own system of justice and distrusted the state courts as biased, rejected Tennessee's demands. Soon a group of full-blood leaders called for armed resistance.

Better to stand and fight, they argued, than follow the false path of accommodation. Others insisted that accommodation offered the best hope for survival.

After a bitter struggle, the accommodationists won out and brought the tribe's scattered villages under a common government, the better to protect their freedom and prevent the further loss of land. In 1808, the Cherokee National Council adopted a legal code combining elements of American and Indian law, and in 1827, it devised a written constitution patterned after those of nearby states. The Council also issued a bold declaration that the Cherokee were an independent nation with full sovereignty over their lands. In 1829, the Cherokee government made it an offense punishable by death for any member of the tribe to transfer land to white ownership without the consent of tribal authorities.

Meanwhile, the process of social and cultural accommodation, encouraged by mixed-blood leaders such as John Ross and promoted by white missionaries and government agents, went forward. As the Cherokee turned from their traditional hunting and gathering economy to settled agriculture, many moved from village settlements onto individual farmsteads. Others established sawmills, country stores, and blacksmith shops. In contrast to traditional practices of communal ownership, the concept of private property took hold.

The majority of Cherokee people continued to live a hand-to-mouth existence. But some mixed-bloods who learned how to deal with white authorities accumulated hundreds of acres of fertile land and scores of black slaves. By 1820, there were nearly 1,300 black slaves in the Cherokee nation. A tribal law of 1824 forbade intermarriage with blacks. The accelerating spread of cotton cultivation increased the demand for slave labor among the Cherokee, as it did among southern whites. Within the tribe, slave ownership became a mark of social standing.

By 1820, the strategy of peaceful accommodation had brought clear rewards. Tribal government was stronger, and the sense of Cherokee identity was reasonably secure. But success would prove the Cherokee people's undoing. As their self-confidence grew, so did the hostility of neighboring whites impatient to acquire their land. That hostility would soon erupt in a campaign to drive the Cherokee from their land forever.

Patterns of Armed Resistance: The Shawnee and Creek

Not all tribes proved so accommodating to white expansion. Faced with growing threats to their political and cultural survival, the Shawnee and Creek nations rose in armed resistance. Conflict, smoldering as the nineteenth century began, burst into flame during the War of 1812.

In the late 1780s, chieftains such as Little Turtle of the Miami and Blue Jacket of the Shawnee had led a series of devastating raids across Indiana, Ohio, and western Pennsylvania. In 1794, President Washington, determined to smash the Indians' resistance once and for all, sent a federal army into the area. It won a decisive victory over 2,000 Indian warriors in the Battle of Fallen Timbers. Shortly after, in the Treaty of Greenville, the assembled chiefs ceded the southern two-thirds of Ohio, opening the heart of the Old Northwest to white control. Subsequent treaties further reduced the Indians' land base, driving the tribes more tightly in upon each other.

By 1809, two Shawnee leaders, the brothers Tecumseh and Tenskwatawa, the latter known to whites as "the Prophet," were traveling among the region's tribes warning of their common danger and forging an alliance against the invading whites. They established headquarters at an ancient Indian town named Kithtippecanoe in northern Indiana. Soon it became a gathering point for Native Americans from across the region responding to the messages of cultural pride, land retention, and pan-Indian resistance proclaimed by the Shawnee brothers.

Between 1809 and 1811, Tecumseh carried his message south to the Creek and the Cherokee. His speeches rang with bitterness. "The white race is a wicked race,"

Tecumseh

Though Tecumseh's vision of a Pan-Indian alliance reaching from the Great Lakes to the Gulf of Mexico never materialized, he led tribes of the Northwest in militant opposition to white territorial expansion.

(The Granger Collection, New York)

he told his listeners. "Since the days when the white race first came in contact with the red men, there has been a continual series of aggressions. The hunting grounds are fast disappearing, and they are driving the red men farther and farther to the west." The only hope was "a war of extermination against the paleface." The southern tribes refused to join, but by 1811 over 1,000 fighting men had gathered at Kithtippecanoe.

Alarmed, the governor of the Indiana Territory, William Henry Harrison, surrounded the Indian stronghold with a force of 1,000 soldiers. After an all-day battle, he burned Kithtippecanoe to the ground.

The Indians, however, were not yet defeated. Aided by British troops from Canada, they mounted devastating raids across Indiana and southern Michigan. With the British, they crushed American armies at Detroit and Fort Nelson and followed up with an attack on Fort Wayne. The tide turned, however, at the Battle of the Thames near Detroit, where Harrison inflicted a grievous defeat on a combined British and Indian force. Among those slain was Tecumseh.

The American victory at the Thames signaled the end of Indian resistance in the Old Northwest. Beginning in 1815, American settlers surged once more across Ohio and Indiana, then into Illinois and Michigan. The balance of power in the Old Northwest had shifted decisively.

To the south, the Creek challenged white intruders with similar militancy. By 1800, white settlers were pushing onto Creek lands in northwestern Georgia and central Alabama. Although some Creek leaders urged accommodation, others, called Red Sticks, prepared to fight. The embers of this conflict were fanned into flame by an aggressive Tennessee militia commander named Andrew Jackson. Citing Creek atrocities against "defenseless women and children," Jackson urged President Jefferson to endorse a campaign against the "ruthless foe."

Jackson got his chance in the summer of 1813, when the Red Sticks devastated the frontier and assaulted Fort Mims on the Alabama River, killing as many as 500 men, women, and children. News of the tragedy elicited bitter cries for revenge.

At the head of 5,000 Tennessee and Kentucky militia, augmented by warriors from other tribes eager to punish their traditional Creek enemies, Jackson attacked. As he moved south, the fighting grew more ferocious. Davey Crockett, one of Jackson's soldiers, later reported that the militia volunteers shot the Red Sticks down "like dogs." The Indians gave like measure in return.

The climactic battle of the Creek War came in March 1814 at Horseshoe Bend in central Alabama. Over 800 Native Americans died, more than in any other Indian–white battle in American history. Jackson followed up his victory with a scorched-earth sweep through the remaining Red Stick towns.

After allowing the Red Stick chieftain and his followers to return home, Jackson exacted his final revenge by constructing a fort on the Hickory Ground, the Creek nation's most sacred spot. During the following months, he seized 22 million acres, nearly two-thirds of the Creek domain. Before his Indian-fighting days were over, Jackson would acquire, through treaty or conquest, nearly three-fourths of Alabama and Florida, a third of Tennessee, and a fifth of Georgia and Mississippi.

Just as Tecumseh's death had signaled the end of Indian resistance in the North, so Jackson's defeat of the Creek broke the back of Indian defenses in much of the South. With all possibility of armed resistance gone, Native Americans gave way before the swelling tide of white settlement.

Perfecting a Democratic Society

Throughout our nation's history, the American people have launched a variety of reform movements aimed at achieving social justice and bringing the conditions of daily life into conformity with democratic ideals. The first of those reform eras occurred in the early nineteenth century.

The Impulse to Reform

Reform was inspired by democratic ideals fostered during the Revolution and still fresh in Americans' minds. The Revolution also fostered a belief in the "youthfulness" of America compared to the "old" and "decadent" nations of Europe. This sense of America's uniqueness, combined with the seemingly limitless land of the interior, offered the promise of creating a nation in which ordinary citizens could create new lives if given the chance.

A surge of evangelical Christianity also inspired the reform impulse. Throughout the nation's history, religion has been a major force in American public life. This was true in the early republic, when a wave of Protestant enthusiasm known as the Second Great Awakening swept across the nation. From its beginnings in the 1790s through the first half of the nineteenth century, in settings ranging from the Cane Ridge district of backwoods Kentucky to the cities of the Northeast, Americans by the tens of thousands sought personal salvation and social belonging in the shared experience of religious revivalism.

Displayed most spectacularly at Methodist and Baptist camp meetings, the revivals reached across boundaries of class and race. Rough-hewn itinerant preachers, black as well as white, many of them theologically untrained but all of them afire with religious conviction, spread the Gospel message, in the process knitting networks of believers closely together.

Perhaps no one represented the Awakening's religious fervor and egalitarian values more vividly than Lorenzo Dow. A self-declared "holy man" claiming visionary powers and an unabashed salesman of his own religious writings, Dow traveled the country bringing a combination of Gospel message and Jeffersonian politics to frontier hamlets and eastern cities alike. During 1804 alone, he preached to as many as 800 gatherings. The following year his travels carried him over 10,000 miles. His boundless energy, communicative gifts, and common touch may well have made him the most widely known American of his time.

Though the salvation of souls was the central purpose of revival camp meetings, they ministered to other human needs as well. "The novelty of a camp especially to the women and children," noted one observer, "the dancing and singing, & the pleasure of a crowd, so tempting to the most fashionable" imparted a powerful sense of social belonging in a society undergoing rapid change.

Offering a simple message that ordinary folks could readily grasp, itinerant preachers such as Dow emphasized the equality of all believers before God, held out the promise of universal salvation, and declared each individual responsible for his or her own soul. The message's power was registered in the explosive growth of Methodist and Baptist churches. By mid-century, they

A Camp Meeting

Camp meetings were fundamental events during the Second Great Awakening. What does this depiction tell you about the kinds of people who attended and the activities that took place?

(Alexander Rider, *Camp Meeting.* © Collection of the New-York Historical Society, USA/Bridgeman Art Library)

would surpass Presbyterians and Congregationalists as the nation's largest denominations.

The Awakening also called on believers to demonstrate their faith by going into the world to lift up the downtrodden. That mandate would provide much of the energy for later reforms such as temperance and abolition (see Chapter 12). Its influence was evident as well in earlier efforts at perfecting American society.

Alleviating Poverty and Distress

In the early republic, as at other times in the nation's history, social ideals jarred awkwardly against reality. One source of tension was the contrast between affirmations of democratic equality and deepening social divisions.

As the nineteenth century began, women continued to hold far less property than men. For black slaves, ownership of anything more than the most basic personal possessions was unattainable. Though the condition of free blacks such as Ben Thompson and Phyllis Sherman was better, they, too, held little of the country's wealth.

Among white males, property was most broadly shared in rural areas of the North, where free labor and family-farm agriculture predominated, and least so in the South, where planters' control of slave labor and the best land permitted them to monopolize the lion's share of the region's wealth. The most even distribution of wealth was to be found on the edges of white settlement in Trans-Appalachia, but this was often an equality of want. As the frontier developed, differences of wealth appeared there as well.

Though America, unlike Europe, contained no permanent and destitute underclass, at least among white citizens, poverty was real and increasing. In the South, it was most evident among poor whites living in the backcountry. In the North, port cities held growing numbers of the poor. Boston artisans and shopkeepers, who together had owned 20 percent of the city's wealth prior to the Revolution, held scarcely half as much a century later.

Recurring economic recessions hit the urban poor with particular force, while winter added to hard times as shipping slowed and jobs disappeared. During the winter of 1805, New York's Mayor DeWitt Clinton, worried about the potentially disruptive behavior of 10,000 impoverished New Yorkers, asked the state legislature for help. In the winter of 1814–1815, relief agencies assisted nearly one-fifth of the city's population. Across rural New England and southeastern Pennsylvania, propertyless men and women, the "strolling poor," roamed the countryside searching for work.

Three other groups were conspicuous among the nation's poor. One consisted of old Revolutionary War veterans like Long Bill Scott, who had found poverty as well as adventure in the war. State and federal governments were peppered with petitions from grizzled veterans and their widows, describing their misery and seeking relief. Women and children suffered disproportionately. Between 1816 and 1821, they outnumbered men in New York City almshouses.

For every American who actually suffered poverty's effects, several others lived just beyond its reach. The thinness of their margin of safety became clear during the depression of 1819–1822. Triggered by a financial panic caused by the unsound practices of hundreds of newly chartered state banks, a deep depression settled over the land, generating bankruptcies and sending unemployment soaring. By the early 1820s, the depression was lifting, but it left behind broken fortunes and shattered dreams.

Alleviating poverty was one goal of the early reformers. In New York City, private and public authorities established over 100 relief agencies to assist unfortunates from orphans to poverty-stricken seamen. Across the nation, a "charitable revolution" increased benevolent institutions from 50 in 1790 to nearly 2,000 by 1820. Most of these ventures drew a distinction between the "worthy poor," respectable folk who were victims of circumstance and merited help, and the "idle poor," who were deemed to lack character and deserved their fate. No matter that a New York commission in 1823 found only 46 able-bodied adults among the 851 inmates of the city's poorhouses.

Poverty was not the only target of reform. Municipal authorities and private charities also established orphanages, insane asylums, and hospitals for the sick. Many such efforts were short-lived, but they attested to the continuing strength of revolutionary and religious ideals, and provided a foundation for the more ambitious reforms that would come later in the century.

Women's Lives

Women's lives did not change dramatically during the early nineteenth-century years. But developments occurred that set the stage for later, more significant breakthroughs.

Divorce was one area in which women achieved greater equality. When a neighbor asked John Backus, a silversmith in Great Barrington, Massachusetts, why he kicked and struck his wife, John replied that it was partly because his father had treated his mother in the same way. We do not know whether John's mother tolerated such abuse, but his wife did not. She complained of cruelty and secured a divorce. More and more women followed her example.

Securing a divorce was not easy. Most states allowed it only for adultery and South Carolina did not permit it at all. Moreover, *coverture* laws required wives to transfer their property to their husbands, making divorce a risky proposition for women. New laws enabling women to file for divorce in court rather than having to secure legislative approval made the process easier. Even so, women faced the uncomfortable task of persuading all-male juries of their husbands' infidelities.

Still, divorce was becoming more available to women. In Massachusetts during the decade after 1783, 50 percent more women than men filed for divorce, with an almost equal rate of success. Part of the explanation lay in the war's disruptions, which led some men to desert their families, thus encouraging their wives to take action. The trans-Appalachian West lured men away as well. It seems just as certain, however, that women took to heart prevailing values of individualism and equality, leading them to expect more of marriage.

Changes also occurred in women's education. Given their prospective role as "Republican Mothers," young women would have to prepare for their responsibilities as nurturers of republican citizens. Some

Young Women at School

This painting captures a ceremony at the Raleigh Female Academy in Virginia about 1816. Examine the painting closely. What kinds of people are present? What does the painting tell you about the purposes and ideals of female education?

(Jacob Marling, *The Crowning of Flora*, 1816/The Chrysler Museum of Art, Norfolk, VA, Gift of Edgar William and Bernice Chrysler Garbisch 80.118.20)

women, such as Judith Sargent Murray, demanded more of women's education. In the 1790s, Murray criticized parents who pointed their daughters exclusively toward marriage and dependence. "They should be enabled to procure for themselves the necessaries of life; independence should be placed within their grasp," she wrote. "A woman should reverence herself."

Between 1790 and 1830, a number of female academies were established, mostly in the northeastern states. Though some prescribed bookkeeping, reading, geography, and singing as proper elements of girls' education, traditionalists warned that undue intellectual activity would "unsex" women. Complained the Boston minister John Gardner, "Women of masculine minds have generally masculine manners, and a robustness of person ill calculated to inspire the tender passions." Even ardent supporters of female learning, such as Murray, conceded that education was primarily important so that women might function more effectively within the domestic sphere. Still, by 1830, literacy for white females was at an all-time high.

Women were affected by changes in American religious life. Though women had long outnumbered men in church membership, the Second Great Awakening drew them into churches in even greater numbers where they became active in fund-raising, missionary work, and charitable projects. In earlier years, when church and state had been closely allied, such activism would have seemed an open challenge to male dominance of the public sphere. When the First Amendment to the U.S. Constitution weakened the traditional connection between church and state, however, women's religious activism could be more readily accepted without seeming to threaten the gendered basis of the political order.

In important ways, however, the evangelical impulse reduced women's roles in the churches. Whereas women had previously served as religious exhorters and participated in Baptist and Methodist church governance, they now found themselves marginalized as those rapidly growing denominations, striving for social acceptance, adopted the older denominations' rigidly gendered rules. In matters of church discipline, moreover, women were more frequently charged with "disorderliness," thus departing from an earlier tradition of piety in which men and women had ministered more equally to each other's souls.

Race, Slavery, and the Limits of Reform

As we saw in Chapter 7, the Revolution initiated the end of slavery in the northern states and challenged it in the Upper South. As the new century began, however, private manumissions were declining in Maryland and Virginia, while antislavery sentiment was weakening, and more rigid categories of racial exclusiveness were appearing in the North.

In the South, the spread of cotton cultivation sent the value of slave labor soaring, just as revolutionary idealism was weakening with the passage of time. Equally important were two slave rebellions that generated alarm among southern whites. Panic-stricken refugees fleeing the successful revolt of black Haitians on the Caribbean island of Saint Domingue (see Chapter 8) spread terror through the South by fueling rumors that Haitian incendiaries would soon be landing. In response, southern legislatures tightened their "Black Codes," cut the importation of new slaves, and weeded out malcontents among their chattels.

A second shock followed in the summer of 1800, when a rebellion just outside Richmond, Virginia, was nipped in the bud. A 24-year-old slave named Gabriel devised a plan to arm 1,000 slaves for an assault on the city. Gabriel and his accomplices were American-born blacks who spoke English and worked at skilled jobs that provided a good bit of personal autonomy. They fashioned an ideology of liberation by appropriating the revolutionary tradition of Virginia's whites and applying it to the condition of their own lives.

A drenching downpour delayed the attack, giving time for several house servants (subsequently granted freedom by the Virginia Assembly) to sound the alarm. No whites died in the abortive rebellion, but scores of slaves and free blacks were arrested, and 25 suspects, including Gabriel, were hanged at the order of Governor James Monroe. The carnage alarmed and saddened Thomas Jefferson. "There is strong sentiment that there has been hanging enough," he confided to Monroe. "The other states and the world at large will forever condemn us if we...go one step beyond absolute necessity." In the midst of panic, however, the line between necessity and revenge was hard to find.

In the early nineteenth century, antislavery appeals all but disappeared from the South. Even religious groups that had once denounced slavery now grew quiet. "A majority of the (white) people of the southern states," declared a Georgia congressman in 1806, deprecated slavery as a "political evil" but did not believe it "immoral to hold human flesh in bondage." Confederate spokesmen would be saying much the same thing at the time of the Civil War. Slavery continued to exist as well in the nation's capital where black servants attended the needs of southern Congressmen and slave markets thrived in the shadow of the Capitol building.

In the Northeast, the gradual abolition of slavery soothed many consciences. With racial domination no longer enforced by law, whites invoked the doctrine of black inferiority to justify racial exclusiveness and

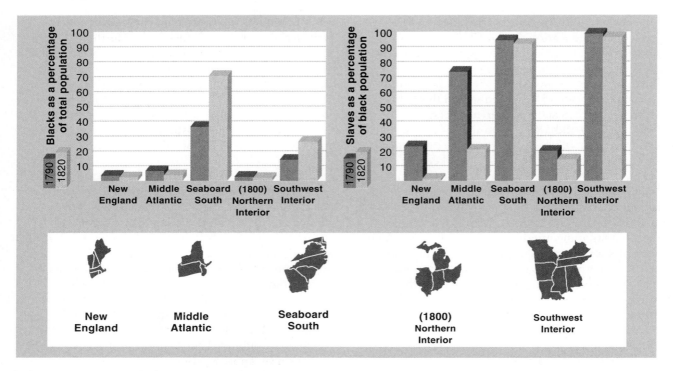

Black Americans and Slavery, 1790–1820

In 1790, regions differed significantly in the proportion of blacks in their population and in the percentage of slaves among black residents. In the ensuing decades, those differences increased. Can you explain why?

Source: U.S. Bureau of the Census.

ensure their own continued control. The belief in immutable racial differences also encouraged conciliatory attitudes toward slave owners in the South.

The hardening of racial attitudes was evident in growing sentiment for colonizing free blacks in western Africa (areas that would become Liberia and Sierra Leone). The American Colonization Society, founded in 1816, typified these attitudes. Northern members, while detesting slavery and proclaiming their benevolent intentions, were uneasy over the growing number of free blacks in their midst, while southern slave owners saw colonization as a convenient way of reducing the region's free black population and ridding themselves of troublesome bondsmen. The Society never sent many American blacks abroad, but helped to allay white anxieties.

Although some blacks were sympathetic to colonization, believing it offered the best promise of true freedom, most black spokesmen vigorously opposed it. They condemned the ideology of racial inferiority on which colonization was based and demanded their full rights as Americans. In joining together to oppose colonization, American blacks gained experience in forging a more effective political voice. That experience would prove valuable training for the abolitionist crusade that lay ahead.

Not all northern whites succumbed to the new racism. The states of Massachusetts, Rhode Island, and Pennsylvania would soon become hotbeds of a resurgent, multiracial abolition movement. Blacks, moreover, enjoyed greater liberty in the cities of the Northeast than elsewhere in the nation.

Racism reared its ugly head in the West as well. In 1823, a proslavery mob torched the Illinois capital and threatened the governor for his efforts to end de facto slavery in the state. In Cincinnati, white citizens grew anxious as the city's black population expanded—by 1829, one out of every ten residents was black—and as black leaders petitioned the Ohio legislature for repeal of the "obnoxious black laws" that required blacks to carry certificates certifying their free status. In late August, several hundred whites invaded the town's black neighborhoods. Several persons were killed in the ensuing melee. In the months that followed, over half the city's blacks fled, many seeking sanctuary in Canada.

Though the slave trade officially ended in 1808, government efforts to suppress the continuing practice were sporadic. In addition, American diplomats pressed England for the return of chattels confiscated during the Revolutionary War and War of 1812. During the early years of the republic, the revolutionary promise of equality rang hollow for many black Americans.

Forming Free Black Communities

During the half-century following independence, vibrant black communities, fed by emancipation in the Northeast and the increasing numbers of freed people in the Upper South, appeared along the Atlantic coast. In 1776, 4,000 slaves and several hundred free blacks had called the port cities home; 50 years later, 40,000 African Americans did so.

In those cities, black communities provided a measure of security and better chances of finding a marriage partner. Family formation was eased by the fact that many urban migrants were women, thus correcting a long-standing imbalance in the black population. Many blacks formed extended households that included relatives, friends, and boarders. As circumstances allowed, single-family units were formed. By 1820, most blacks in the northern cities lived in autonomous households.

As their numbers grew, African Americans created organizations independent of white control and capable of serving the needs of black communities. Schools educated children excluded from white academies, mutual-aid societies offered help to the down-and-out, and fraternal associations provided fellowship and mutual support.

Black churches quickly emerged as the cornerstones of black community life. Following the Revolution, growing numbers of free blacks joined integrated Methodist and Baptist congregations, drawn by those churches' biblical theology, enthusiastic worship, and antislavery stand. By 1790, 20 percent of Methodist church members were black. As the numbers of black communicants grew, however, they found themselves segregated in galleries, excluded from leadership roles, and even denied communion.

In 1794, a small group of black Methodists led by Richard Allen, a slave-born, itinerant preacher, organized the Bethel African American Methodist Church in Philadelphia. Originally established within American Methodism, Allen's congregation moved toward separatism by requiring that only "Africans and descendants of the African race" be admitted to membership. In 1815, it rejected oversight by the white Methodist leadership, and a year later joined a similar congregation in Baltimore to form the African Methodist Episcopal Church, the first independent black denomination in the United States. Black Baptists also formed separate churches in Boston, Philadelphia, and St. Louis.

Located in the heart of black communities, these churches nurtured African American forms of worship and provided education for black children and burial sites for families excluded from white cemeteries. Equally important, they offered secure places where the basic rituals of family and community life—marriages and births, funerals, and anniversaries—could be celebrated and where community norms could be enforced. By the 1830s, a rich cultural and institutional life had taken root in the black neighborhoods of numerous American cities. Still, white hostility remained a reality of urban life, especially during hard times when blacks competed with white laborers for scarce jobs and affordable housing.

Black life was far different in southern cities, where the vast majority remained enslaved. Of Charleston's 14,127 blacks (over half the city's population), 90 percent were slaves. That circumstance,

Black Methodist Church

"African" churches and other organizations were rare before 1800 but grew steadily in the ensuing decades. In this watercolor of a black Methodist church meeting, the Russian traveler and painter Paul Svinin offers his impression of the physical emotion often displayed by black worshipers. What do you make of his presentation?

(Pavel Petrovich Svinin, *Negro Methodists Holding a Meeting.* The Metropolitan Museum of Art, Rogers Fund, 1942. (42.95.19) Photograph © 1985 The Metropolitan Museum of Art)

together with the South's rigid "Black Codes," frustrated black community building.

In New Orleans, on the other hand, policies established during Spanish colonial control had produced the largest free black (*libre*) and mixed race (*mulatto*) population in North America. While racial hierarchies existed, *libres,* their numbers augmented by manumitted slaves and refugees fleeing revolutionary Haiti, prospered. By 1820, *libres* numbered 46 percent of the black population and constituted a uniquely prosperous black community.

Their privileges, however, were threatened by the thousands of new slaves imported to provide labor for the burgeoning sugar economy (what one historian has called the "re-Africanization" of Louisiana), alarm over black rebellion in nearby Haiti, and the introduction of a more rigid racial ideology by new white settlers.

The End of Neocolonialism

Following the election of 1808, James Madison, second in the "Virginia dynasty" of presidents, assumed office. As American ships once more ventured into the Atlantic following the embargo's collapse, and as the British Navy renewed its depredations, war fever continued to mount. Within a few years, conflict with England erupted in the War of 1812. The war brought an end to a period of neocolonialism when the United States, though formally independent, was still vulnerable to the actions of England and other European imperial powers. During the administrations of James Monroe (1817–1825), the Jeffersonian Republicans also fashioned a momentous new role for the United States within the Americas.

The War of 1812

As tensions with England grew, the loudest shouts for war came from the West and South. The election of 1810 brought to Congress a new group of leaders, firmly Jeffersonian in party loyalty but impatient with the administration's bumbling foreign policy and demanding tougher measures. These War Hawks included such future political giants as Henry Clay of Kentucky and John C. Calhoun of South Carolina.

For too long, the War Hawks cried, the United States had tolerated Britain's presence on American soil, encouragement of Indian raids, and attacks on American commerce. They talked openly of expanding the nation's boundaries north into Canada and south into Spanish Florida. Most of all, these young nationalists resented British arrogance and America's continuing humiliation. No government, they warned, could long endure unless it protected citizens' interests and upheld the nation's honor.

Responding to the growing pressure, President Madison asked Congress for a declaration of war on June 1, 1812. Opposition came entirely from the New England and Middle Atlantic states—ironically, the regions most adversely affected by Britain's European blockade—whereas the South and West voted solidly for war. Rarely had sectional alignments been more sharply drawn.

Rarely, either, had American foreign policy proven less effective. Madison decided to abandon economic for military coercion just as the British government, under domestic pressure to seek accommodation, suspended its European blockade. Three days later, unaware of Britain's action (it took three weeks for news to cross the Atlantic), Congress declared war.

The war proved a strange affair. Britain beat back several American forays into Canada and launched a series of attacks along the Gulf Coast. As it had done during the Revolutionary War, the British navy blockaded American coastal waters, while landing parties launched punishing attacks along the eastern seaboard. On August 14, 1814, a British force occupied Washington, torched the Capitol and president's mansion (soon to be called the White House after being repaired and whitewashed), and sent the president, Congress, and American troops fleeing into Virginia. Britain, however, did not press its advantage, for it was preoccupied with Napoleon's armies in Europe and wanted to end the American quarrel.

Emotions ran high among Federalist critics and Jeffersonian Republican supporters of the war. During bloody riots in Baltimore in June of 1812, several people, including an old Federalist Revolutionary War general, were badly beaten in the streets. In New England, opposition to the war veered toward outright disloyalty. In December 1814, delegates from the five New England states met at Hartford, Connecticut, to debate proposals for secession. Cooler heads prevailed, but before adjourning the Hartford Convention asserted the right of a state to "interpose" its authority against "unconstitutional" acts of the government. Now it was New England's turn to play with the nullification fire. As the war dragged on, Federalist support soared in the Northeast, while elsewhere bitterness grew over New England's disloyalty.

Before the war ended, American forces won several impressive victories, among them Commander Oliver Hazard Perry's defeat of the British fleet on Lake Erie in 1813. That victory secured American dominance on the Great Lakes and ended the threat of a British invasion from Canada. The most dramatic American triumph was Andrew Jackson's smashing victory in 1815 over an attacking British force at New Orleans, though it occurred after preliminary terms of peace had already been signed.

Increasingly concerned about Europe, the British government offered to begin peace negotiations. Madison eagerly accepted, and on Christmas Eve in 1814, at Ghent, Belgium, the two sides reached agreement. Britain agreed to evacuate the western posts, but the treaty ignored other outstanding issues, including impressment, neutral rights, and American access to Canadian fisheries. It simply declared the fighting over, called for the return of prisoners and captured territory, and provided for joint commissions to deal with unresolved disputes.

Still, the war left its mark on the American nation. Four thousand African Americans, constituting nearly 20 percent of American seamen, fought in the war, demonstrating their patriotism and challenging white racial stereotypes. At least as many served the British as spies, messengers, and guides, much as had occurred during the Revolution. A hundred or so newly liberated slaves accompanied the troops that burned the Capitol and president's house in the summer of 1814.

The war made Andrew Jackson a national hero and established him as a major political leader.

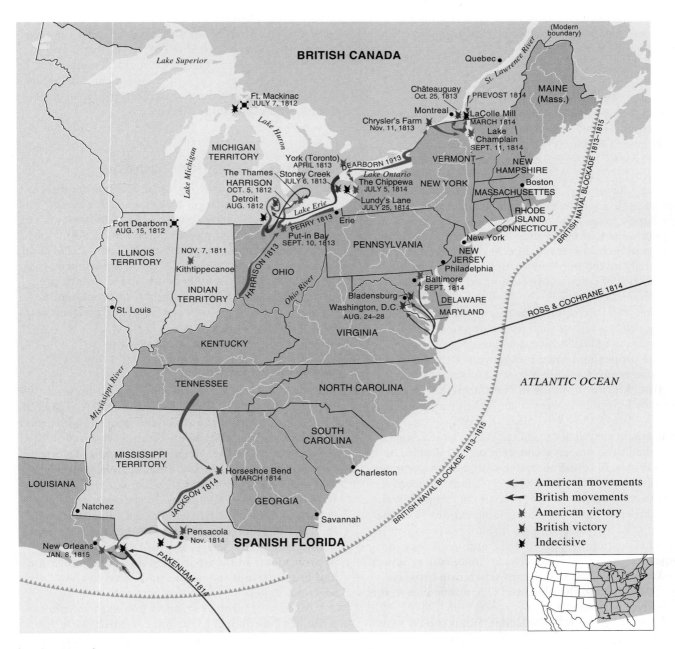

The War of 1812

The War of 1812 scarcely touched the lives of most Americans, but areas around the Great Lakes, Lake Champlain, Chesapeake Bay, and the Gulf Coast witnessed significant fighting. Why was the fighting almost entirely restricted to these areas?

The American people, moreover, regarded the contest as a "Second War of American Independence" that finally secured the nation from outside interference. That belief fed a surge of postwar nationalism.

In the years following 1815, the nation focused its energies on the task of internal development—occupying the continent, building the economy, and reforming American society. At the same time, Europe entered almost a century free of general war. In the past, European wars had involved America; in the twentieth century they would do so again. For the rest of the nineteenth century, however, that fateful link was broken. Finally, European colonialism was now shifting to Africa and Asia, and that diverted European attention from the Americas as well.

The United States and the Americas

While disengaging from Europe, the president and Congress fashioned new policies for Latin America that would guide the nation's hemispheric relations for years to come. Many Americans cheered when Spain and Portugal's Latin American colonies, holding up the American Revolution as a model of liberation, began their struggle for independence in 1808. U.S. leaders were happy to see European colonialism weakened and held out hope that newly independent nations would be open to increased trade. But they were skeptical that the racially mixed populations of Latin America, with their history of colonial oppression, could govern themselves effectively.

After initial reluctance, primarily for fear of disrupting delicate efforts then under way to secure Florida from Spain, President Monroe sent Congress a message proposing formal recognition of the Latin American republics. Congress quickly agreed.

Trouble arose, however, in November 1822, when the major European powers talked of helping Spain regain its American empire. Such prospects alarmed Great Britain as well as the United States, and in August 1823, the British foreign secretary broached the idea of Anglo-American cooperation to thwart Spain's intentions.

Secretary of State John Quincy Adams opposed the idea. Adams had joined the Jeffersonian camp several years earlier as part of the continuing exodus from the Federalist Party. Filled with the spirit of nationalism so evident following the War of 1812 and suspicious of British intentions, Adams called for independent action based on two principles: a sharp separation between the Old World and the New, and U.S. dominance in the Western Hemisphere.

Monroe agreed that the United States should issue its own policy statement. In his annual message of December 1823, he outlined a new Latin American policy. Though known as the Monroe Doctrine, Adams had devised it.

The doctrine asserted four basic principles: (1) the American continents were closed to new European colonization, (2) the political systems of the Americas were separate from those of Europe, (3) the United States would consider as dangerous to its peace and safety any attempts to extend Europe's political influence into the Western Hemisphere, and (4) the United States would neither interfere with existing colonies in the New World nor meddle in Europe's affairs. Though promulgated with Latin America primarily in mind, the Doctrine was also aimed at Russian ambitions on the northern Pacific coast.

Monroe's bold declaration had little immediate effect, for the United States possessed neither the economic nor military power to enforce it. By the end of the nineteenth century when the nation's might had increased, however, it would become clear what a fateful moment in the history of the Western Hemisphere Monroe's declaration had been.

Knitting the Nation Together

At the Philadelphia convention in 1788, Federalists and Anti-Federalists had argued whether such a diverse and sprawling republic could survive. After the vast area of Louisiana was added, those concerns increased. Given the country's primitive modes of travel, restricted forms of communication, and small central government, problems of national unity continued to bedevil the American people. Although the nation would not be securely unified until after the Civil War, progress was evident in the early republic.

Conquering Distance

It has been estimated that within half an hour of President Kennedy's assassination in Dallas, Texas, in 1963, 68 percent of the American people had learned the news. By contrast, when George Washington died in December 1799 in Alexandria, Virginia, it took five days for word to reach Philadelphia (scarcely 140 miles away) and over three weeks to penetrate west to Lexington, Kentucky. In the absence of modern technologies such as telephones, television, and the Internet, human travel was the only way of communicating across space. By the 1820s, however, improvements in transportation and communication had begun to knit the nation more effectively together.

A flurry of turnpike construction in the northeastern states contributed to the improvement. Most turnpikes consisted of little more than dirt roadways cut through the woods, with tree stumps sawed off just low enough to clear wagon axles. A trip of 25 miles often filled a day.

Still, when a turnpike between Philadelphia and Lancaster, Pennsylvania, proved profitable, dozens of others quickly followed. By 1811, New York had chartered 137 turnpike companies and the New England states 200 more. By 1830, improvement had cut travel time along these roadways in half.

In the first federal road building project, Congress in 1806 authorized construction of a National Road from Cumberland, Maryland, to the West. By 1818, it had reached Wheeling on the Ohio River and had reduced travel time between its terminals from eight days to three.

Given the difficulties of overland routes, Americans traveled by water whenever possible. During the early years of the century, the first steamboats appeared along the Atlantic coast and began to ply the waters of the Ohio and Mississippi rivers. In 1807, Robert Fulton launched his 160-ton side-wheeler *Clermont,* demonstrating the feasibility of steam travel. Four years later, the *New Orleans* made the first successful run over the falls of the Ohio River at Cincinnati, then continued down the Mississippi to New Orleans. Within a few decades, steamboats would revolutionize transportation on the nation's rivers.

Between 1790 and 1830, significant breakthroughs occurred in print communication as well. When Washington assumed the presidency, only 92 newspapers existed. Most were weeklies, and virtually all were printed in cities along the Atlantic coast. The majority had no more than 600 subscribers. By 1830, the number of newspapers had increased to over 1,000, about one-third of them dailies. Some were published in places as far inland as Pittsburgh and St. Louis.

By 1820, the ratio of newspapers to population was higher in the United States than in Great Britain.

The swelling demand for newspapers was spurred by rising literacy rates (most notably among women and lower-class men), the demand for information generated by the nation's expanding market economy, democratic belief in the importance of an informed citizenry, and the growing importance of papers as an instrument of party politics. The circulation of papers expanded people's horizons and strengthened their sense of shared experience. Only a newspaper, noted one observer, "can drop the same thought into a thousand minds at the same moment."

During these years, the American postal system expanded similarly. When Washington was inaugurated, there were only 75 post offices in the entire country. By 1820, nearly 8,500 post offices were scattered throughout the nation, while the number of letters carried by the postal system had increased ninefold. Though it cost 25 cents to send a letter 30 miles or more, a prohibitive sum for most folks when daily wages averaged only a dollar, the rate had declined by half.

Strengthening American Nationalism

If improvements in travel and communication strengthened American nationalism in the years of the early republic, so did the galvanizing experience of the Second Great Awakening. It reinforced belief in America as God's chosen nation and tied Americans together in networks of shared religious identity woven by the hundreds of itinerant ministers who

The Difficulties of Travel
Here an express coach makes its way through the forest. What does the drawing reveal of travel difficulties and improvements in the early republic?

(George Tattersal (English, 1817-1849, active U.S. (1836). Album of Western Sketches: Highways and Byeways of the Forest, a Scence on 'the Road', 1836; pen and brown ink with brush and brown wash, hightened with white gouache, over graphite pencil, on gray paper, Sheet: 21.0 × 29.8 cm (8-1/4 × 11-3/4 in). Photograph © Museum of Fine Arts, Boston. Gift of Maxim Karolik for the M. and M. Karolik Collection of American Watercolors and Drawings, 1800-1875. Museum of Fine Arts. Boston (56.400.11)

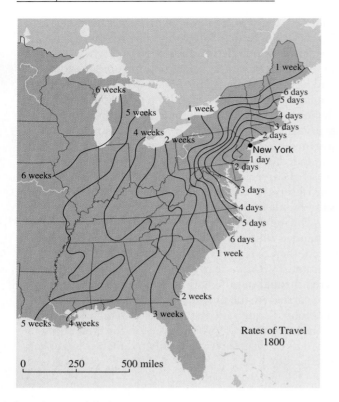

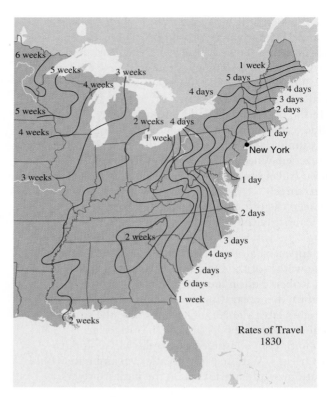

Advances in Transportation

Improvements in rates of travel were well underway by 1830. Study the two maps carefully. Did travel rates improve more dramatically between east and west or north and south? Can you explain the differences?

carried the Gospel message into communities in every part of the country. The flood of printed tracts circulated by religious organizations reinforced the sense of religious unity.

Rituals of patriotic celebration on occasions such as Washington's birthday and the Fourth of July also helped unify the country. Federalists and Jeffersonian Republicans, northerners and southerners, black and white Americans filled these occasions with their own, often conflicting meanings, yet all were eager to claim a voice in shaping the nation's heritage. Reports of these local celebrations, carried across the land via newspapers and correspondence, knitted communities together in a national conversation of patriotism.

National unity was further strengthened by several key decisions of the Supreme Court. In a series of

---

GROWTH IN COMMUNICATION, 1790–1830

Compare the rates by which the population increased on the one hand and the increases in the number of post offices, miles of post routes, and newspapers on the other. What do those comparisons reveal about the nation's development?

	1790	1810	Percent Increase, 1790–1810	1830	Percent Increase, 1810–1830
U.S. population (in thousands)	3,929	7,224	84%	12,901	79%
Post offices	75	2,300	297%	8,450	267%
Miles of post routes	1,875	36,406	185%	115,176	216%
Number of newspapers	108	390	261%	910*	133%*

*Estimated

Sources: Historical Statistics of the United States; Clarence Brigham, *Bibliography of American Newspapers, 1690–1820*; S. D. North, *History and Present Condition of the Newspaper and Periodical Press of the United States.*

trailblazing cases, the Court, led by Chief Justice John Marshall, laid down some of the most basic doctrines of American constitutional law. In *Marbury v. Madison* (1803), the Court established the principle of judicial review, the assertion that the Court had the authority to judge the constitutionality of congressional laws and executive actions. In the case of *Martin* v. *Hunter's Lessee* (1816), the Court claimed appellate jurisdiction over the decisions of state courts.

Three years later, in another landmark decision, *McCulloch* v. *Maryland*, the Court set aside claims that Congress had exceeded its authority in chartering the Second Bank of the United States in 1816. In a unanimous decision, Marshall issued a ringing endorsement of the doctrine of loose, as opposed to strict, construction of the Constitution. "Let the end [of a Congressional law] be legitimate," he declared, "let it be within the scope of the constitution, and all means which are appropriate . . . to that end, which are not prohibited, but consist with the letter and spirit of the constitution, are constitutional." The Bank's charter would thus stand.

No state, he further argued, possessed the right to tax a branch of a nationally chartered bank as Maryland had attempted to do, because "the power to tax involves the power to destroy." The principle of national supremacy lay at the very center of Marshall's finding. The doctrines elaborated in these path-breaking decisions would continue to shape the nation's history in the years ahead.

The Specter of Sectionalism

Despite the surge of national spirit following the War of 1812, Federalist talk of disunion had revealed just how fragile national unity still was. That became starkly evident in the Missouri crisis of 1819–1820.

Since 1789, politicians had labored to keep the explosive issue of slavery tucked safely beneath the surface of political life, for they understood how quickly it could jeopardize the nation. Their fears were borne out in 1819 when Missouri's application for admission to the Union raised anew the question of slavery's expansion. The Northwest Ordinance of 1787 prohibited slavery north of the Ohio River while allowing its expansion to the south. But Congress had said nothing about slavery's place in the vast Louisiana territory west of the Mississippi.

Though there were several thousand slaves in the Missouri Territory, Senator Rufus King of New York demanded that Missouri prohibit slavery before entering the Union. His proposal triggered a fierce debate over Congress's authority to regulate slavery in the Trans-Mississippi West. Southerners were adamant that the area must remain open to their slave property and

John Marshall

John Marshall, appointed chief justice of the United States by President Adams in 1801, served in that position for 34 years. Under his leadership, the Supreme Court established some of the most basic principles of American constitutional law.

(John Marshall by Chester Harding (1792-1886), Oil on canvas, 1830. U.R. 106.1830. Collection of the Boston Athenaeum.)

were determined to preserve the equal balance of slave and free states in the Senate. Already by 1819, the more rapidly growing population of the free states had given them a 105-to-81 advantage in the House of Representatives. Equality in the Senate offered the only sure protection for southern interests. Northerners, however, vowed to keep the territories west of the Mississippi open to free labor, which meant closing them to slavery.

For nearly three months, Congress debated the issue. During much of the time, free blacks, listening intently to northern antislavery speeches, filled the House gallery. "This momentous question," worried the aged Jefferson, "like a fire-bell in the night, [has] awakened and filled me with terror." Northerners were similarly alarmed. The Missouri question, declared the editor of the New York *Daily Advertiser,* "involves not only the future character of our nation, but the future weight and influence of the free states. If now lost—it is lost forever."

The House of Representatives

The House of Representatives, depicted in this 1821 painting by Samuel F. B. Morse, later inventor of the telegraph, rang with debate over the Missouri Compromise and other explosive issues.

(Samuel F. B. Morse, *The Old House of Representatives*, 1882, 86 1/2 x 130 3/4 in., oil on canvas. In the Collection of the Corcoran Gallery of Art, Washington, D.C., Museum Purchase, Gallery Fund 11.14)

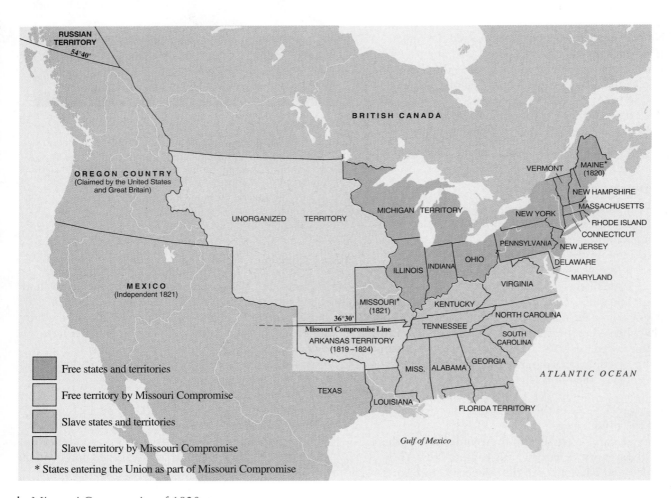

Free states and territories

Free territory by Missouri Compromise

Slave states and territories

Slave territory by Missouri Compromise

* States entering the Union as part of Missouri Compromise

Missouri Compromise of 1820

In the early nineteenth century, politicians struggled to contain the explosive issue of slavery's expansion. How was this attempted in the Missouri Compromise of 1820?

In the end, compromise prevailed. Missouri gained admission as a slave state, while Maine (formerly part of Massachusetts) came in as a counterbalancing free state. A line was drawn west from Missouri at latitude 36° 30' to the Rocky Mountains. Lands south of that line would be open to slavery; areas north of it would not.

Controversy erupted again when antislavery forces in Congress protested a clause in the Missouri constitution excluding free blacks and mulattoes from the state, arguing that the denial of citizenship to free blacks in Missouri would set a precedent for similar denials by other states. The Missouri legislature assured Congress that the offending clause would not be used to abridge the rights of any U.S. citizens, thus assuaging congressional critics and ensuring Missouri's admission to the union. In spite of such assurances, free blacks continued to be excluded from the state.

For the moment, the issue of slavery's expansion had been put to rest. It would not be long, however, before the problem would set North and South even more violently against each other.

Politics in Transition

For two decades following the election of 1800, Jeffersonian Republicans monopolized the presidency and dominated Congress, while the Federalist party languished. By the late 1820s, however, the Jeffersonian ascendancy had ended, and the Federalist–Jeffersonian party system was in disarray. As that happened, new political alignments began to appear. When they did, America was poised on the threshold of a new political era.

The Collapse of the Federalist–Jeffersonian Party System

For a while following the election of 1800, Federalists had maintained a drumfire of attack on the Jeffersonians, including the charge that Jefferson had sired several children by his slave girl Sally Hemmings. But Federalists were discredited by accusations of disloyalty during the War of 1812 and were tainted by their lingering aristocratic image. Some Federalists endorsed broad suffrage as essential to governmental legitimacy, but many did not. "There is a tendency in the majority," asserted one New York Federalist, "to tyrannize over the minority and trample down their rights." Saddled with this outlook, the Federalist Party gradually collapsed.

The Jeffersonians' political success after the War of 1812 proved their undoing. No single party could contain the nation's swelling diversity of economic and social interests, deepening sectional divisions, and ambitions of newly emerging political leaders.

In response to pressures from western and northeastern interests, as well as to nationalist sentiment stimulated by the War of 1812, Madison's administration launched a Federalist-like program of national development. In March 1816, the president signed a bill creating a second Bank of the United States (the first Bank's charter had expired in 1811), intended to stimulate economic expansion and regulate the loose currency-issuing practices of countless state-chartered banks. At Madison's urging, Congress passed America's first protective tariff, a set of duties on imported goods intended to protect America's "infant industries" from foreign competition. He also launched a federally subsidized program of road and canal building. By the early 1820s, Henry Clay and others, now calling themselves National Republicans, were proposing even more ambitious policies of tariffs and internal improvements under the name of the American System.

The administration's policies drew sharp criticism from so-called Old Republicans, southern politicians who regarded themselves as guardians of the Jeffersonian conscience and questioned whether state governments were to be "swept away." They continued to sound the alarm, even as their numbers dwindled.

The final collapse of the Federalist–Jeffersonian party system was triggered by the presidential election of 1824. For the first time since 1800, when the "Virginia dynasty" of Jefferson, Madison, and Monroe began, there was competition for the presidency from every major wing of the Jeffersonian coalition. Of the five candidates, John Quincy Adams of Massachusetts and Henry Clay of Kentucky advocated federal programs of economic development. William Crawford of Georgia and Andrew Jackson of Tennessee clung to traditional Jeffersonian principles of limited government, agrarianism, and states' rights. In between, stood John Calhoun of South Carolina, just beginning his fateful passage from nationalism to Southern nullification.

When none of the presidential candidates received an electoral majority, the election moved into the House of Representatives, as in 1800. There, an alliance of Adams and Clay supporters gave the New Englander the election, even though he trailed Jackson in electoral votes, 84 to 99. The Jacksonians' charges of a "corrupt bargain" gained credence when Adams appointed Clay secretary of state.

Adams's ill-fated administration revealed the disarray in American politics. His stirring calls for federal road and canal building, standardization of weights and measures, a national university, and government support for science and the arts quickly fell victim to sectional conflicts, political factionalism, and his own scorn for the increasingly democratic politics of the time. Within a year of his inauguration, Adams's administration had foundered. For the rest of his term, politicians jockeyed for position in the political realignment that was under way.

Women at the Republican Court

Much as aristocratic women had exerted influence at English and European courts, so elite American women forged an American style of parlor politics. Initiated at Philadelphia in the 1790s, parlor politics became an integral part of the Washington scene after 1800.

Women attended sessions of Congress, frequently circulating on the House and Senate floors and even sitting in members' seats. "The House of Representatives," observed Margaret Bayard Smith, "is a lounging place for both sexes, where acquaintance is as easily made as at public amusements." Women filled the House galleries as electoral votes were counted in the 1808 presidential election, and listened intently to debates over war in 1812.

They also utilized networks of friendship and social gatherings to lobby political appointments and promote legislation. In the process, they contributed to the new government's effectiveness while challenging long-standing boundaries separating public (male) and private (female) spheres.

If privileged women found it possible to fashion political influence at the republican court in Washington, however, most women continued to find themselves politically isolated. That was in part because of a conservative backlash against the radically feminist politics evident during the French Revolution. The claims of American women for a greater political

voice could easily be tarred with the brush of French "anarchy" by anxious American males. Also, as male-dominated political parties grew in importance and voting, still limited to men, became the defining act of political participation, politics became even more rigidly gendered.

A New Style of Politics

While women, blacks, and Native Americans continued to be excluded from the franchise, white men now flocked to the polls in unprecedented numbers. In state elections, voter turnout at times reached 80 percent of the qualifying electorate, far higher than previously.

The growing strength of democratic beliefs and decisions by state governments to abolish long-established property-owning requirements for the franchise helps explain the dramatic increase. In addition, state programs of road and canal building, bank regulation, temperance enforcement, and poor relief activated people's self-interest, thus drawing them into the political arena. And it was in the states that a new generation of political leaders such as Martin Van Buren and Henry Clay, uninhibited by the revolutionary generation's fear of political "faction" and skilled in party organization and the use of a partisan press, first perfected the techniques of mass, democratic politics. By the 1820s, voter registration drives, party conventions, and popular campaigning had become commonplace.

The election of Andrew Jackson to the presidency in 1828 represented the culmination of these democratic changes, for it brought the techniques of mass politics to presidential electioneering. When the presidential

Election Day in Philadelphia 1816

Election days were often raucous affairs in the increasingly democratic, male-dominated politics of the early republic. What purposes other than voting did election day serve?

Timeline

1790	Indian Intercourse Act
1790s	Second Great Awakening begins
1793	Invention of the cotton gin
1794	Battle of Fallen Timbers
1795	Treaty of Greenville
1800	Gabriel's Rebellion
1803	*Marbury* v. *Madison*
1806	National Road begun
1807	Fulton's steamboat *Clermont* launched
1808	James Madison elected president
	Official end of the slave trade
1811	Battle of Kithtippecanoe
1812	Madison reelected
	War declared against Great Britain
1813	Battle of the Thames
1813–1814	Creek War
1814	Treaty of Ghent
	Battle of Horseshoe Bend
1814–1815	Hartford Convention
1815	Battle of New Orleans
1816	James Monroe elected president
	Second Bank of the United States chartered
	American Colonization Society founded
	African Methodist Episcopal Church established
1819	Adams–Onís Treaty with Spain
	McCulloch v. *Maryland*
1819–1822	Bank panic and depression
1819–1820	Missouri Compromise
1822	Diplomatic recognition of Latin American republics
1823	Monroe Doctrine proclaimed
1824	John Quincy Adams elected president
1827	Cherokee adopt written constitution

election became a genuine popular referendum, American politics had changed forever.

Conclusion

THE PASSING OF AN ERA

As the early nineteenth century began, the United States still consisted of diverse, often conflicting, and loosely connected regions. Within those regions, ordinary citizens such as Mary and James Harrod, Ben Thompson, and Phyllis Sherman struggled to fashion new lives. Their efforts gave human expression to the nation's values of social equality, individual opportunity, and personal autonomy.

Those values, strengthened by the country's revolutionary heritage and the Great Awakening, inspired reforms intended to improve the conditions of American life. Though the lives of many white women were bettered, gendered restrictions continued to limit women's opportunities. The reinvigoration of chattel slavery in the South imperiled the lives of countless black slaves, while deepening racism in the North circumscribed the lives of free blacks. To the west, Native Americans, pursuing strategies of resistance and accommodation, gradually gave way in the face of expanding white settlement.

During these same years, American leaders fashioned important new relationships with the outside world. Following the War of 1812, the United States ended its neocolonial dependence on England and Europe, while the Monroe Doctrine defined a portentous new relationship with the emerging nations of Latin America.

As the country grew, American nationalism was strengthened by improvements in travel and print communication, the widely shared experience of the Great Awakening, and a series of path-breaking decisions handed down by the Supreme Court. At the same time, sectional tensions continued to simmer, breaking ominously through the surface of political life in the Missouri Crisis.

These years brought important changes to American political life as well. While most women continued to find themselves politically marginalized, sophisticated political parties, skilled in new methods of organization and communication, enlisted (white) men by the tens of thousands in electoral politics.

By the 1820s, the American people had turned from an era of founding, when the nation was new and the outcome of the republican experiment uncertain, to an era of increased national security and accelerating development, led by a new generation of political leaders.

That transition was dramatized on July 4, 1826, the fiftieth anniversary of American independence, when two of the remaining revolutionary patriarchs, John Adams and Thomas Jefferson, died within a few hours of each other. "The sterling virtues of the Revolution are silently passing away," mused George McDuffie of South Carolina during that jubilee year, "and the period is not distant when there will be no living monument to remind us of those glorious days of trial." As the anniversary celebrations ended and the revolutionary founders faded into memory, the American people pondered what the future would bring.

QUESTIONS FOR REVIEW AND REFLECTION

1. How did the nation's regions differ in the early republic? To what extent were those differences of long standing or reflect developments since the end of the Revolutionary War?
2. Why did some Indian tribes follow the path of accommodation to white expansion, while others rose in armed resistance?
3. What circumstances promoted and inhibited social reform in the early republic?
4. How and why did the United States refashion its relations with other nations in the early nineteenth century?
5. What circumstances served to unite and to divide the nation during these years?

CHAPTER 10

Economic Transformations in the Northeast and the Old Northwest

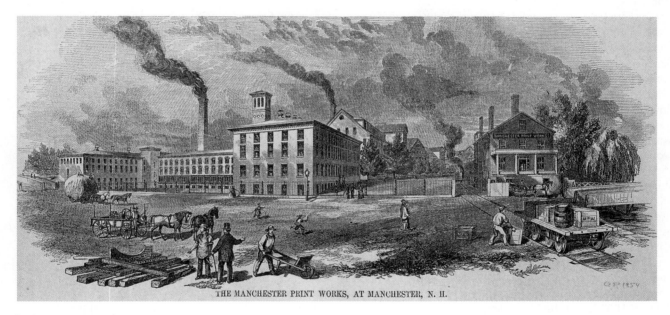

THE MANCHESTER PRINT WORKS, AT MANCHESTER, N. H.

A New Hampshire Printing Factory

Gleason's Pictorial, one of the many modestly priced publications that the introduction of steam-powered printing presses put within reach of the reading public, pictures the Manchester Print Works in New Hampshire in 1854. How has the mill complex been depicted? What signs of pollution does the picture convey? Men appear in the foreground, but more than half the workers in this calico factory were female.

(Library of Congress)

American Stories

Discovering Success in the Midst of Financial Ruin

For her first 18 years, Susan Warner was little touched by the far-reaching economic and social changes that were transforming the character of the country and her own city of New York. Whereas some New Yorkers toiled to make a living by taking in piecework and others responded to unsettling new means of producing goods by joining trade unions to agitate for wages that would enable them to "live as comfortable as others," Susan was surrounded by luxuries and privilege. Much of the year was spent in the family's townhouse in St. Mark's Place. There Susan acquired the social graces and skills appropriate for a girl of her position and background. She had dancing and singing lessons, studied Italian and French, and learned the etiquette involved in receiving visitors and making calls. When hot weather made life in New York unpleasant, the Warners escaped to the cooler airs of Canaan, where they had a summer house. Like any girl of her social class, Susan realized that her care-free existence could not last forever. With her marriage, which she confidently expected some time in the future, would come significant new responsibilities as a wife and mother but not the end of the comfortable life to which she was accustomed.

It was not marriage and motherhood that disrupted the pattern of Susan's life but financial disaster. Sheltered as she had been from the unsettling economic and social changes of the early nineteenth century, Susan discovered that she, too, was at the mercy of forces beyond her control. Her father, heretofore so successful a provider and parent, lost most of his fortune during the financial Panic of 1837. Like others experiencing a sharp economic reversal, the Warners had to make radical adjustments. The fashionable home in St. Mark's Place and the pleasures of New York were exchanged for a more modest existence on an island in the Hudson River. Susan turned "housekeeper" and learned how to do tasks once relegated to others: sewing and making butter, pudding sauces, and johnny cake.

The change of residence and Susan's attempt to master domestic skills did not halt the family's financial decline. Prized possessions, including the piano and engravings, all symbols of the life the Warners had once taken for granted, eventually went up for auction. "When at last the men and the confusion were gone," Susan's younger sister, Anna, recalled, "then we woke up to life."

Waking up to life meant facing the necessity of making money. But what could Susan do to reverse sliding family fortunes? True, some women labored as factory operatives, domestics, seamstresses, or schoolteachers, but it was doubtful Susan could even imagine herself in any of these occupations. Her Aunt Fanny, however, had a suggestion that was more congenial to the genteel young woman. Knowing that the steam-powered printing press had revolutionized the publishing world and created a mass readership, much of it female, Aunt Fanny told her niece, "Sue, I believe if you would try, you could write a story." "Whether she added 'that . . . would sell,' I am not sure," recalled Anna later, "but of course that was what she meant."

Taking Aunt Fanny's advice to heart, Susan started to write a novel that would sell. She constructed her story around the trials of a young orphan girl, Ellen Montgomery. As Ellen suffered one reverse after another, she learned the lessons that allowed her to survive and eventually triumph over adversity: piety, self-denial, discipline, and the power of a mother's love. Titled *The Wide, Wide World,* the novel was accepted for publication only after the mother of the publisher, George Putnam, read it and told her son, "If you never publish another book, you must make *The Wide, Wide World* available for your fellow men." A modest 750 copies were printed. Much to the surprise of the cautious Putnam, if not to his mother, 13 editions were published within two years. *The Wide, Wide World* became the first American novel to sell more than one million copies. It was one of the best-sellers of the century.

Long before she realized the book's success, Susan, who was now much aware of the need to make money, was working on a new story. Drawing on her own experience of economic and social reversal, Susan described the spiritual and intellectual life of a young girl thrust into poverty after an early life of luxury in New York. Titled *Queechy,* this novel was also a great success.

Though her fame as a writer made Susan Warner unusual, her books' popularity suggested how well they spoke to the concerns and interests of a broad readership. The background of social and financial uncertainty, with its sudden changes of fortune, so prominent in several of the novels, captured the reality and fears of a fluid society in the process of transformation. While one French writer was amazed that "in America a three-volume novel is devoted to the history of the moral progress of a girl of thirteen," pious heroines such as Ellen Montgomery, who struggled to master their passions and urges toward independence, were shining exemplars of the new norms for American middle-class women. Their successful efforts to mold themselves heartened readers who believed that the future of the nation depended on virtuous mothers who struggled to live up to new ideals. Susan's novels validated their efforts and spoke to the importance of the domestic sphere. "I feel strongly impelled to pour out to you my most heartful thanks," wrote one woman. None of the other leading writers of the day had been able to minister "to the highest and noblest feelings of my nature *so much as yourself.*"

Susan Warner's life and novels serve as an introduction to the focus of this chapter: the far-reaching changes that began to alter the character of the nation and its peoples. Between 1820 and 1860, as Susan Warner discovered, economic transformations in the Northeast and the Old Northwest reshaped American life. Though most Americans still lived in rural settings, economic growth and the new industrial mode of production affected them through the creation of new goods, opportunities, and markets. In cities and factory towns, the new economic order ushered in new forms of work, new class arrangements, and new forms of social strife.

After situating American economic change in an international context, another central concern of this text, and discussing the factors that fueled antebellum growth, the chapter turns to the industrial world, where so many of the new patterns of work and life appeared. Then an investigation of urbanization reveals shifting class arrangements, rising social and racial tensions, and new gender and behavioral norms that increasingly affected the new middle class. Finally, an examination of rural communities in the East and on the frontier in the Old Northwest highlights the transformation of these two sections of the country. Between 1840 and 1860, industrialization and economic growth increasingly knit them together.

Economic Growth

Between 1820 and 1860, the American economy entered a new and more complex phase as it shifted from reliance on agriculture as the major source of growth toward an industrial and technological future. Amid general national expansion, real per capita output grew an average of 2 percent annually between 1820 and 1840 and slightly less between 1840 and 1860. This doubling of per capita income over a 40-year period suggests that many Americans were enjoying a rising standard of living.

But the economy was also unstable, as the Warners discovered. Periods of boom (1822–1834, mid-1840s–1850s) alternated with periods of bust (1816–1821, 1837–1843). As never before, Americans faced dramatic and recurrent shifts in the availability of jobs and goods and in prices and wages. Particularly at risk were working-class Americans, a third of whom lost their jobs in depression years. And because regional economies were increasingly linked, problems in one area tended to affect conditions in others.

The Transatlantic Context for Growth

American economic growth was linked to and influenced by events elsewhere in the world, particularly in Great Britain. Britain was the home of the Industrial Revolution, the event that some historians believe to be among the most important of human history in terms of its impact on material life. For the first time, production of goods proceeded at a faster pace than the growth of population.

The Industrial Revolution beginning in Britain in the eighteenth century involved many technological innovations that spurred new developments and efficiencies. Among the most important developments was the discovery in the 1780s of a way to eliminate carbon and other substances from pig iron. This opened the way for cheap, durable iron machines that resulted in the increased production of goods. Another milestone, the improvement of the steam engine, originally used to pump water out of coal mines, eventually led to railroads and steamboats, thus revolutionizing transportation. Steam-powered machinery also transformed cloth production, moving it from cottages to factories. The British textile industry was the giant of the early Industrial Revolution. The use of machinery allowed the production of more and cheaper textiles. The industry became a prime market for American cotton as well as cotton from India and Brazil. British demand for raw cotton helped to cement the South's attachment to slavery.

By 1850, Great Britain was the most powerful country in the world, and its citizens were the richest. In the following decades, its factories and mines churned out most of the world's coal and more than half of its iron and textiles. Not surprisingly, Americans would look to England and English know-how as they embarked on their own course of industrialization. While American industrial development did not mimic that of the British, there were many similarities between the two countries' experiences.

Factors Fueling Economic Development

As the following table suggests, abundant natural resources and a growing population provided the raw materials, brawn, and brains for economic expansion.

SIGNIFICANT FACTORS PROMOTING ECONOMIC GROWTH, 1820–1860

Factor	Important Features	Contribution to Growth
Abundant natural resources	Acquisition of new territories (Louisiana Purchase, Florida, trans-Mississippi West); exploitation and discovery of eastern resources	Provided raw materials and energy vital to economic transformation
Substantial population growth	Increase from 9 million in 1820 to more than 30 million in 1860—due to natural increase of population and, especially after 1840, to rising immigration; importance of immigration from Ireland, Germany	Provided workers and consumers necessary for economic growth; immigration increased diversity of workforce with complex results, among them supply of capital and technological know-how
Transportation revolution	Improvement of roads; extensive canal building, 1817–1837; increasing importance of railroad construction thereafter; by 1860, 30,000 miles of tracks; steamboats facilitate travel on water	Facilitated movement of people, goods, and information; drew people into national economy market; stimulated agricultural expansion, regional crop specialization; decreased costs of shipping goods; strengthened ties between Northeast and Midwest
Capital investment	Investments by European investors and U.S. interests; importance of mercantile capital and banks, insurance companies in funneling capital to economic enterprises	Provided capital to support variety of new economic enterprises, improvements in transportation
Government support	Local, state, and national legislation; loans favoring enterprise; judicial decisions	Provided capital, privileges, and supportive climate for economic enterprises
Industrialization	New methods of producing goods, with and without involvement of machinery	Produced more numerous, cheaper goods for mass market; transformed classes and nature of work; affected distribution of wealth and individual opportunity

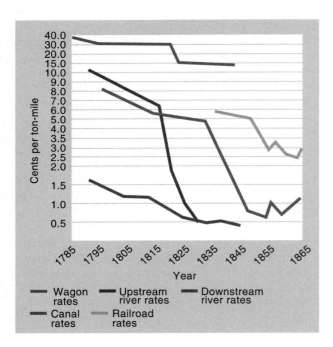

Inland Freight Rates

As this chart makes dramatically clear, the transportation revolution had a tremendous impact on the cost of shipping goods and materials to markets and factories. In what period did the cost of transporting goods by canal fall most significantly? What do you think caused the decline in upstream river rates?

Because the size of American families was gradually shrinking, European immigration played an essential role in providing the new workers, new households, and new consumers so essential to economic development as well as the capital and technological ideas that helped shape American growth.

Improved transportation made a major contribution to economic and geographic expansion. Early in the century, high freight rates discouraged production for distant markets and the exploitation of resources, while primitive transportation hindered western settlement. Canal-building projects in the 1820s and 1830s dramatically transformed this situation. The 363-mile-long Erie Canal, the last link in a chain of waterways binding New York City to the Great Lakes and the Northwest, was the most impressive of these new canals. The volume of goods and people it carried at low cost demonstrated the economic benefits of this mode of transportation and encouraged the construction of more than 3,000 miles of canals by 1840, primarily in eastern and midwestern states.

Even at the height of the canal boom, politicians, promoters, and others, impressed with Britain's success with steam-powered railways, also supported the construction of railroads. Unlike canals that might freeze during the winter, railroads could operate year-round and could be built almost anywhere. These advantages encouraged Baltimore merchants, envious of

The Transportation Revolution

This map shows the impact of the transportation revolution. Note the components of that revolution: roads, canals, and then railroad lines. What were the important regional connections opened up by transportation improvements? How would you compare northern and southern development? What were the commercial results of the new transportation networks?

New York's water link to the Northwest, to begin the Baltimore & Ohio Railroad in 1828.

Early technical problems included trains jumping their tracks and setting nearby fields ablaze. But such difficulties were quickly overcome. By 1840, there were 3,000 miles of track, more than in all the countries of Europe. At the end of the 1850s, total mileage reached 30,000. Like the canals, the new railroads strengthened the links between the Old Northwest and the East and eventually fostered shared political outlooks.

Some historians use the term *transportation revolution* in recognition of the economic impact of improved transportation. Goods, people, and information flowed more predictably, rapidly, and cheaply. In 1790, an order from Boston took two weeks to reach Philadelphia; in 1836, it took only 36 hours. Canals and railroads gave farmers, merchants, and manufacturers inexpensive, reliable access to distant markets and goods and fostered technological innovations that, in turn, spurred production. Transportation links stimulated regional specialization and expansion as farmers began to plant larger, more specialized crops for the market—grain in the Old Northwest, dairy goods and produce in New England. By 1860, American farmers were producing four to five times as much wheat, corn, cattle, and hogs as in 1810. American workers had plentiful, cheap food, and farmers had more income to spend on new consumer goods.

Railroads exerted enormous influence, especially in terms of the pattern of western settlement. As the railroads followed—or led—settlers westward, their routes could determine whether a city, town, or even homestead survived. The railroad transformed Chicago from a small settlement into a bustling commercial and transportation center. In 1850, the city contained not one mile of track, but within five years, 2,200 miles of track serving 150,000 square miles terminated in Chicago.

Capital and Government Support

Internal improvements, the exploitation of natural resources, and the cultivation of new lands all demanded capital. Between 1790 and 1861, more than $500 million in foreign capital, most of it from Great Britain, was invested in state bonds, transportation, and land. Foreign investors financed as much as one-third of all canal construction and bought about one-quarter of all railroad bonds.

American mercantile capital fueled growth as well. Members of the merchant class who had prospered in the half century after the Revolution now invested in schemes ranging from canals to textile factories. Many ventured into the production of goods and became manufacturers themselves. Other prosperous Americans also eagerly sought opportunities to put their capital to work.

Local and state government played their part by enthusiastically supporting economic growth. States often helped new ventures raise capital by passing laws of incorporation; by awarding entrepreneurs special privileges such as tax breaks or monopolistic control; by underwriting bonds for improvement projects, which increased their investment appeal; and by providing loans for internal improvements. New York, Pennsylvania, Ohio, Indiana, Illinois, and Virginia publicly financed almost 75 percent of the canal systems in their states between 1815 and 1860.

The national government also encouraged economic expansion by cooperating with states on some internal improvements, such as the National Road linking Maryland and Illinois. Federal tariff policy shielded American products, and the Second Bank of the United States provided the financial stability investors required. So widespread was the enthusiasm for growth that the line separating the public sector from the private often blurred.

The law also supported aggressive economic growth. Judicial decisions created a new understanding

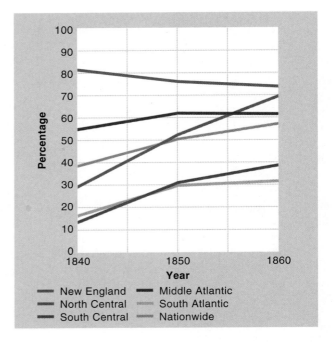

White Secondary School Enrollment, 1840–1860

Note the regional difference in school enrollment and changes over time. What area of the country made the biggest gains in school enrollment between 1840 and 1860?

Source: Albert W. Niemi, *U.S. Economic History,* 1975.

of property rights. The case of *Palmer* v. *Mulligan,* decided by the New York State Supreme Court in 1805, determined that property ownership included the right to develop property for business purposes. Land was increasingly defined as a productive asset for exploitation, not merely subsistence, as earlier judicial rulings had suggested. Developments in contract law increased predictability in the conduct of business. A series of important Supreme Court decisions between 1819 and 1824 established the basic principle that contracts were binding. In *Dartmouth College* v. *Woodward,* the Court held that a state charter could not be modified unless both parties agreed, and in *Sturges* v. *Crowninshield* it declared unconstitutional a New York law allowing debtors to repudiate their debts.

A New Mentality

Economic expansion also depended on intangible factors. When a farmer decided to specialize in apples for the New York market rather than to concentrate on raising food for his family, he was thinking in a new way. So was a merchant who invested in banks that would, in turn, finance a variety of economic enterprises. The entrepreneurial outlook—the *"universal desire,"* as one newspaper editor put it, *"to get forward"*—was shared by millions of Americans. By encouraging investment, new business and agricultural ventures, and land speculation, it played a vital role in antebellum development.

Europeans often recognized other intangible factors. As one Frenchman observed in 1834, Americans were energetic and open to change. "All here is circulation, motion, and boiling agitation. Experiment follows experiment; enterprise succeeds to enterprise." Some saw an American mechanical "genius." "In Massachusetts and Connecticut," one Frenchman insisted, "there is not a labourer who had not invented a machine or tool." He exaggerated (many American innovations drew on British precedents and were introduced by immigrants familiar with the British originals), but every invention did attract scores of imitators.

Mechanically minded Americans prided themselves on developing efficient tools and machines. The McCormick harvester, the Colt revolver, Goodyear vulcanized rubber products, and the sewing machine—all were developed, refined, and developed further. Such improvements cut labor costs and increased efficiency. By 1840, the average American cotton textile mill was about 10 percent more efficient and 3 percent more profitable than its British counterpart.

Although the shortage of labor in the United States stimulated technological innovations that replaced humans with machines, the rapid spread of education after 1800 also spurred innovation and productivity. By 1840, most whites were literate, and public schools were educating 38.4 percent of white children between ages 5 and 19. The belief that education meant economic growth fostered enthusiasm for public education, particularly in the Northeast.

The development of the Massachusetts Common School illustrates the connections many saw between education and progress. Although several states had decided to use tax monies for education by 1800, Massachusetts moved first toward mass education. In 1827, it mandated that taxes pay the whole cost of the state's public schools and in 1836 forbade factory managers to hire children who had not spent 3 of the previous 12 months in school. Still, the Massachusetts school system limped along with run-down school buildings, nonexistent curricula, and students with nothing to do.

Under the leadership of Horace Mann, the reform of state education for white children began in earnest in 1837. He and others pressed for graded schools, uniform curricula, and teacher training, and fought the local control that often blocked progress. Mann's success inspired reformers everywhere. For the first time in American history, primary education became the rule for most children outside the South between ages 5 and 19. The expansion of education created a whole new career of schoolteaching, mostly attracting young women.

Mann believed that education promoted inventiveness. Businessmen often agreed. Prominent industrialists in the 1840s were convinced that education

produced reliable workers who could handle complex machinery without undue supervision. Manufacturers valued education not merely because of its intellectual content, but also because it encouraged habits necessary for a disciplined and productive workforce.

Ambivalence Toward Change

While supporting education as a means to economic growth, many Americans, like their European counterparts, also firmly believed in its social value. They expected the public schools to mold student character. Many school activities sought to instill "virtuous habits" and "rational self-governing." Students learned facts by rote because memory work and recitation taught discipline and concentration. Nineteenth-century schoolbooks reinforced classroom goals. "It is a great sin to be idle," children read in one 1830 text, while another pointed out, "He who rises early and is industrious and temperate will acquire health and riches."

The concern with education and character suggests that while Americans welcomed economic progress, they also feared its results. Transportation improvements encouraged trade and emigration but created anxieties that as people moved far from their place of birth and familiar institutions they would forget civilized ways. Many worried that rapid change weakened the family. Schools, which taught students to be deferential, obedient, and punctual, could counter the worst by-products of change.

As the publishing revolution lowered costs and speeded the production of printed material, authors poured out tracts, stories, and manuals claiming that hard work and good character led to success. Habits like diligence, punctuality, temperance, and thrift probably did assist economic growth. Industry and perseverance often pay off. But the success of early nineteenth-century economic ventures frequently depended on the ability to take risks and to think daringly. The emphasis publicists gave to the stolid virtues and behavior suggests their desire to counter unsettling effects of change and ensure the dominance of middle-class values.

The Advance of Industrialization

As had been true for Great Britain in the eighteenth century, the advance of industrialization in the United States fueled economic growth in the decades before the Civil War. As was also the case in Britain, economic changes spilled over to transform many other aspects of life. New modes of production affected work, the workplace, and relationships between bosses and employees. The American class system was modified as a new working class dependent on wages emerged and as a new middle class took shape.

Factory production moved away from the decentralized system of artisan or family-based manufacturing using hand tools and reorganized work by breaking down the manufacture of an article into discrete steps. Manufacturers farmed out some steps to workers, both urban and rural, in shops and homes, paying them by the piece. This was the "putting-out" system. But other steps in the production process were consolidated in central shops. Eventually all the steps of production came under one roof, with hand labor gradually giving way to power-driven machinery such as "spinning jennies."

Sometimes, would-be American manufacturers sought the help of British immigrants with the practical experience and technical know-how that few Americans possessed. Thus in 1789, William Ashley and Moses Brown, Rhode Island merchants, hired 21-year-old Samuel Slater, a former apprentice in an English cotton textile mill, to devise a water-powered, yarn-spinning machine. Slater did that, but he also developed a machine capable of carding, or straightening, the cotton fibers. Within a year, Ashley and Brown's spinning mill was operating in Pawtucket, Rhode Island, with a workforce of nine children, ranging in age from 7 to 12. Ten years later, their number exceeded 100. As factory workers replaced artisans and home manufacturers, the volume of goods rose, and prices dropped dramatically. The price of a yard of cotton cloth fell from 18 cents to 2 cents over the 45 years preceding the Civil War.

The transportation improvements that gave access to large markets after 1820 also encouraged the reorganization of the production process and the use of machinery. The simple tastes and rural character of the American people suggested the wisdom of manufacturing inexpensive everyday goods such as cloth and shoes rather than luxuries for the rich.

Between 1820 and 1860, textile manufacturing became the country's leading industry. Textile mills sprang up across the New England and mid-Atlantic states, regions with swift-flowing streams to power the mills, capitalists eager to finance the ventures, children and women to tend the machines, and numerous cities and towns with ready markets for cheap textiles. Early mills were small affairs, containing only the machines for carding and spinning. The thread was then put out to home workers to be woven into cloth. The early mechanization of cloth production did not replace home manufacture but supplemented it.

Experiments were under way that would further transform the industry. In 1813, inspired by Boston merchant Francis Cabot Lowell's study of English and

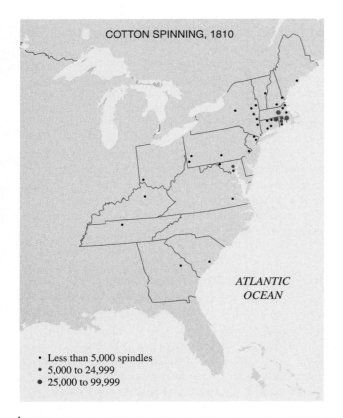

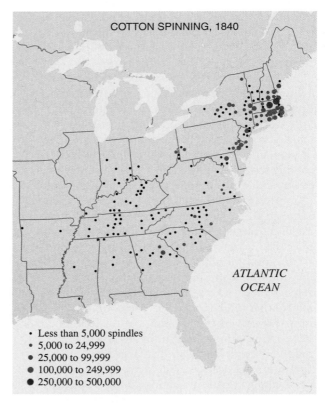

The Growth of Cotton Textile Manufacturing, 1810–1840
The concentration of textile manufacturing in New England suggests the changing economic and social trends in that region.

Scottish mechanical looms, Lowell and mechanic Paul Moody devised a power loom capable of weaving cloth. Eventually, they installed it in a mill at Waltham, Massachusetts.

Whereas mills in Rhode Island and Great Britain kept spinning and weaving as separate operations, Lowell decided to bring all the steps of cotton cloth production together under one roof. Centralization allowed the profitable mass production of inexpensive cloth and encouraged mechanical improvements and innovation. In 1823, the Boston Associates expanded their operations to East Chelmsford on the Merrimack River, a town they renamed Lowell. The Lowell system became the prototype for most New England mills although elsewhere the textile industry was more varied.

Textile mills were an important component of the increasingly industrial character of the Northeast. The majority of the South's cotton went to England, but an increasing share flowed to northeastern mills. Other manufacturing concerns, such as shoemaking, also contributed to the Northeast's economy. By 1860, fully 71 percent of all manufacturing workers lived in this region of the country. Still other important manufacturing operations reached west and south from New England. The processing of wheat, timber, and hides using power-driven machinery was common in most communities of 200 families or more. Although one-third of them were clustered in Philadelphia, paper mills were widespread. The ironworking and metalworking industry stretched from Albany, New York, south to Maryland, and west to Cincinnati.

Environmental Consequences

Economic growth had far-reaching environmental consequences. Steamboats, trains, and home heating stoves, for example, depended on wood for fuel. Armed with new steel axes, lumbermen and farmers met the increased demand for wood, and eastern forests and their wildlife rapidly disappeared. Better transportation, which facilitated western settlement, also promoted forest clearance for crops and housing. Sawmills and milldams interfered with spawning habits of fish, clogged their gills with sawdust, and even changed the flow of rivers. The process of ecological change, spurred by the desire for wood, recurred as lumber companies and entrepreneurs moved from the East to exploit the forests of the Great Lakes and the Gulf states.

As late as 1840, wood was the main source for the country's energy needs. But its high price and the discovery of anthracite coal in Pennsylvania signaled the beginning of a shift to coal as the major source of power. While the East gradually regained some of its forest cover, the heavy use of coal polluted the air as steam engines and heating stoves poured out their dirty fumes. Acrid smells and black soot became a part of urban life.

While textile mills using streams for water power presented a prettier picture than urban shops and refineries, they also affected the environment. Dams and canals supporting industrial activities contributed to soil erosion. "Industrial operations," declared the Vermont fish commissioner in 1857, are "destructive to fish that live or spawn in fresh water. . . . The thousand deleterious mineral substances, discharged into rivers from metallurgical, chemical, and manufacturing establishments, poison them by shoals."

Some Americans recognized these environmental consequences of rapid growth and change. Author James Fenimore Cooper had one of his characters in his novel *The Pioneers* condemn those who destroyed nature "without remorse and without shame." The popularity in the 1820s of a song with the lines "Woodman, / Spare that tree / Touch not a single bough" suggested sympathy for that point of view. Yet most Americans accepted the changing environment as an inevitable part of progress.

Early Manufacturing

Industrialization created a more efficient means of producing more goods at much lower cost than had been possible in the homes and small shops of an earlier day. Philadelphian Samuel Breck's diary reveals some of the new profusion and range of goods. "Went to town principally to see the Exhibition of American Manufactures at the Masonic Hall," he noted in 1833. "More than 700 articles have been sent. . . . porcelains, beautiful Canton cotton . . . soft and capacious blankets, silver plate, cabinet ware, marble mantels, splendid pianos and centre tables, chymical drugs, hardware, saddlery, and the most beautiful black broadcloth I ever saw."

Two examples illustrate how industrialization transformed American life in both simple and complex ways. Before the nineteenth century, local printing shops depended on manual labor to produce books, newspapers, and journals. The cost of reading material was high enough to make a library a sign of wealth. Many literate families of moderate means had little in their homes to read other than a family Bible and an almanac.

Between 1830 and 1850, however, adoption and improvement of British inventions revolutionized the printing and publishing industries. Like other changes in production, the transformation of publishing involved not only technological innovations but also alterations in managerial and marketing techniques. As inexpensive books and magazines proliferated, more people could afford to purchase them. This new mass market of readers made possible Susan Warner's literary success. But the implications of the changes in publishing went beyond best sellers. Cheap reading material encouraged literacy and a new sort of independence. No longer needing to rely solely on the words of the "better sort" for information, people could form their own views on the basis of what they read. At the same time, however, readers everywhere were exposed repeatedly to the mainstream norms, values, and ideas expressed in magazines and books. Even on the frontier, pioneer women could study inexpensive ladies' magazines or draw inspiration from *The Wide, Wide World*. Their husbands could follow political news, prices, or theories about scientific farming while the children learned to read from the moralistic McGuffey readers.

Meanwhile, the making of inexpensive timepieces affected the pace and rhythms of daily life. Before the 1830s, owning a clock was a luxury, making exact planning and scheduling almost impossible. But by midcentury, inexpensive mass-produced wooden clocks could be found everywhere, even in frontier "cabins where there was not a chair to sit on." Timepieces were essential for the successful operation of railroads and steamboats and imposed a new more disciplined rhythm in many workplaces. An early mill song suggested that many found the new regime oppressive. "The factory bell begins to ring / And we must all obey, / And to our old employment go / Or else be turned away."

A New England Textile Town

The process of industrialization and its impact on work and the workforce are well illustrated by Lowell, the "model" Massachusetts textile town, and Cincinnati, a bustling midwestern industrial center. Though the communities shared certain traits, they had significant differences. Lowell reveals the importance of women in the early stages of industrialization while Cincinnati shows how uneven and complex the process of industrialization could be.

Lowell was planned and built for industrial purposes in the 1820s. By 1836, it was the country's most important textile center and a center of female employment.

Lowell's planners, understanding the difficulty of luring men away from farming, realized that they might recruit unmarried women relatively cheaply for a stint in the mills. Unlike factory owners farther south, they decided not to depend on child labor. By hiring women who would work only until marriage, they hoped to avoid the depraved and depressed workforce so evident in Great Britain and to create factory communities that would become models for the world. By 1830, women composed nearly 70 percent of the Lowell textile workforce. As the first women to labor outside their homes in large numbers, they were also among the first Americans to experience the full impact of the factory system.

Working and Living in a Mill Town

At age 15, Mary Paul wrote to her father asking him "to consent to let me go to Lowell if you can." This young woman from Vermont was typical of those drawn to work in Lowell. In 1830, more than 63 percent of Lowell's population was female, and most were between ages 15 and 29.

Women workers came from New England's middling rural families and took jobs in the mills for a variety of reasons, but desperate poverty was not one of them. The decline of home manufacture deprived many women, especially daughters in farming families, of their traditional productive role. Some had already earned money at home by taking in piecework. Millwork offered them a chance for economic independence, better wages than domestic service, and an interesting environment. Few made a permanent commitment by coming to Lowell. They came to work for a few years, felt free to go home or to school for a few months, and then return to millwork. Once married—and the majority of women did marry—they left the mill workforce forever.

Millwork was regimented and exhausting. Six days a week, the workers began their 12-hour day at dawn or earlier with only a half hour for breakfast and lunch. Within the factory, the organization of space facilitated production. In the basement was the waterwheel, the source of power. Above, successive floors were completely open, each containing the machines necessary for the different steps of cloth making. Elevators moved materials from one floor to another. Under the watchful eyes of male overseers, the women tended their machines. Work spaces were noisy, poorly lit, and badly ventilated, the windows often nailed shut.

Millwork required the women to adapt to both new work and new living situations. Hoping to attract respectable and productive female workers, mill owners built company boardinghouses for them. Headed by female housekeepers, the boardinghouse maintained strict rules, including a 10 P.M. curfew, and afforded little personal privacy. The cramped quarters encouraged close ties and a sense of community. Group norms dictated acceptable behavior, clothing, and speech. Shared leisure activities included lectures, night classes, sewing and literary circles, and church.

Female Responses to Work

Although millwork offered better wages than other occupations open to women, all female workers had limited job mobility and received lower wages than men. Even those with the best female positions never earned as much as senior male employees. Economic and job discrimination characterized the early American industrial system.

Job discrimination generally went unquestioned, for most female operatives accepted gender differences as part of life. But the sense of sisterhood, so central to the Lowell work experience, supported open protest against a system that workers feared was turning them into dependent wage earners. Lowell women's critique of the new industrial order drew on both the sense of female community and the revolutionary tradition.

Trouble erupted when hard times hit Lowell in 1834. Falling prices, poor sales, and rising inventories prompted managers to announce a 15 percent wage cut. The millworkers responded, circulating petitions threatening a strike, and organizing meetings. At one lunchtime gathering, when the company agent fired an apparent ringleader, "she declared that every girl in the room should leave with her," then "made a signal, and ... they all marched out & few returned the ensuing morning." The strikers roamed the streets, appealing to other workers, and they visited other mills. In all, about a sixth of the town's workforce turned out.

Though this brief work stoppage failed to prevent the wage reduction, it demonstrated the women's concern about the impact of industrialization on the labor force. Viewing the wage reductions as an attack on their economic independence, strikers linked their protest to their fathers' and grandfathers' efforts to throw off the oppressive British bonds during the Revolution. Claiming equal status with their employers, they infused revolutionary political rhetoric with new economic overtones.

During the 1830s, wage cuts, long hours, increased workloads, and production speedups, mandated by owners' desires to protect profits, constantly reminded Lowell women and other textile workers of the possibility of "wage slavery." In Dover, New Hampshire, 800 women turned out and formed a union in 1834 to protest wage cuts. In the 1840s, women in several New England states agitated for the 10-hour day, and petitions from Lowell prompted the Massachusetts legislature to hold the first government hearing on industrial working conditions.

The Changing Character of the Workforce

Most protest efforts met with limited success. The short tenure of most female millworkers prevented permanent labor organizations. Protests mounted in hard times often failed because mill owners could easily replace striking workers. Increasingly, the arrival of impoverished Irish immigrants during the 1840s and 1850s allowed owners to replace Yankee women in the mills with a cheaper workforce. By 1860, Irish men comprised nearly half of Lowell's workforce. Lowell's reputation as a model factory town that avoided the problems of English industrial cities faded away.

The transformation of the Lowell workforces suggests the far-reaching effect of immigration on American life in the antebellum period. Immigration, of course, had been a constant part of the country's experience from the early seventeenth century. But it occurred on an unprecedented scale after 1845 with more than 2.8 million migrants arriving in the United States during the 1850s. The majority of the newcomers were young European men of working age.

This vast movement of people, which continued throughout the nineteenth century, is another example of how events in other parts of the world have influenced this country. Between 1750 and 1845, Europe experienced a population explosion. New farming and industrial practices undermined traditional means of livelihood. As one Scottish woman wrote to an American friend in 1847, "we can not mak it better [here]. All that we can duo is if you can give us any encouragement [is] to ama[grate?] to your Country."

Agricultural disaster uprooted the largest group of immigrants: the Irish. In 1845, a terrible blight attacked and destroyed the potato crop, the staple of the Irish diet. Years of famine followed. One million Irish starved to death between 1841 and 1851; another

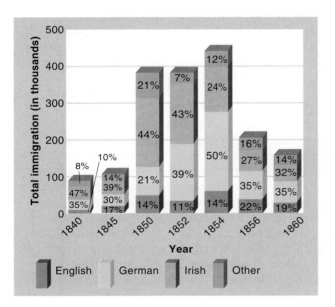

Immigration: Volume and Sources, 1840–1860

This chart captures the growing ethnic diversity of the country in the years before the Civil War. What is only implied is the element of religious diversity that immigration also introduced. Most of the Irish immigrants and half of the Germans were Roman Catholics. The presence of immigrants who differed so dramatically from Protestant Americans in background and culture contributed to the tensions of the period. Can you identify the period that witnessed the greatest influx of Roman Catholics?

Cincinnati and the Ohio River

In 1848, an unknown photographer took this picture of Cincinnati. The prominence of steamboats in the picture suggests the role that location and improvements in transportation played in the city's growth. Although the countryside is visible in the background, the rows of substantial commercial and industrial buildings make Cincinnati's status as a bustling urban center clear.

(Public Library of Cincinnati and Hamilton County, Ohio)

million and a half emigrated. Although not all came to the United States, those who did arrive almost penniless without the skills needed for good jobs. With only their raw labor to sell, employers, as one observer noted, "will engage Paddy as they would a dray horse."

German immigrants, the second-largest group of newcomers during this period (1,361,506 arrived between 1840 and 1859), were not driven to the United States by the same kind of desperate circumstances as the Irish. Some even arrived with sufficient resources to go west and buy land. Others had the training to join the urban working class as shoemakers, cabinetmakers, or tailors.

The arrival of so many non-British newcomers made American society more diverse than it had ever been. Because more than half of the Irish and German immigrants were Roman Catholics, a religion long feared and disliked by Protestants, religious differences acerbated economic and ethnic tensions.

Factories on the Frontier

Cincinnati, a small Ohio River settlement of 2,540 in 1810, grew to be the country's third-largest industrial center by 1840. With a population of 40,382, it contained a variety of industries at different stages of development. Cincinnati manufacturers of machines, machine parts, hardware, and furniture quickly

mechanized for increased volume and profits. Other trades such as carriage making and cigar making moved far more slowly toward mechanization, while artisans such as blacksmiths and riverboat builders still labored in small shops, using traditional hand tools. The new and the old ways coexisted in Cincinnati, as they did in most manufacturing communities.

No uniform work experience prevailed in Cincinnati. Some craftsmen continued to produce goods in time-honored ways. Others used their skills in new factories but focused on specialized and limited tasks. In furniture factories, for example, machines did the rough work of cutting, boring, and planing, while an array of workers carried out the other steps necessary to finish the piece. While no one worker made a chair from start to finish, all used some of their skills and earned steady wages. Though in the long run, machines threatened to replace them, these factory workers often had reason in the short run to praise the factory's opportunities.

Less fortunate was the new class of unskilled factory laborers who performed limited tasks either with or without the assistance of machinery. In the meatpacking industry, for example, workers sat at long tables. Some cleaned the ears of the hogs, others scraped the bristles, others had the unenviable task of gutting the dead animals. Whereas owners in the industry profited from efficient new operations, workers had poor pay and little job security. Without specialized skills, they were easily replaced and casually dismissed during business slowdowns.

Cincinnati's working women had a different work experience. A majority of black women labored as washerwomen, cooks, or maids. Many white women earned money as "outworkers" for the city's growing ready-to-wear clothing industry. Manufacturers purchased the cloth, cut it into basic patterns, and then contracted out the finishing work to women toiling in small workshops or at home. Like many other urban women, Cincinnati women became outworkers because husbands or fathers could not earn enough to support the family and because the work often allowed them to labor at home. Middle-class domestic ideology prescribed that home was the proper sphere for women. Many working men supported this view because they feared that female labor would undercut their wages and destroy order in the family.

Paid by the piece, female outworkers were among the most exploited of Cincinnati's workers. Long days spent sewing in darkened rooms frequently resulted in meager financial returns as well as health problems, including ruined eyes and curved spines. The successful marketing of sewing machines in the 1850s that made stitching easier increased the pool of potential workers and increased volume of work that bosses expected. As tasks were further subdivided, work also became more monotonous. As one Cincinnati citizen observed, "As many as 17 hands" contributed to a single pair of pants.

Cincinnati employers claimed that the new industrial order offered great opportunities to most of the city's male citizens. Manufacturing work encouraged the "manly virtues" so necessary to the "republican citizen." Not all Cincinnati workers agreed. The working man's plight, as Cincinnati labor leaders analyzed it, stemmed from his loss of independence. The reorganization of work meant that few could expect to progress from apprentice to journeyman to master and independent artisan. Even though a manufacturing job provided a decent livelihood for some people, the new industrial order was changing the nature of the laboring class itself. The new worker had no skills and only raw labor to sell. His dependence on wages reduced him to demeaning "wage slavery."

Workers also resented the masters' attempts to control their lives. In the new factories, owners insisted on a steady pace of work and uninterrupted production. Artisans who were used to working in spurts, stopping for a few moments of conversation or a drink, disliked the new routines. Even outside the workplace, manufacturers attacked Cincinnati's working-class culture. Crusades to abolish volunteer fire companies and to close down saloons, both attacked as nonproductive activities, suggested how little equality the Cincinnati worker enjoyed in an industrializing society.

The fact that workers' wages in Cincinnati, as in other cities, lagged behind food and housing costs compounded discontent. The working class sensed it was losing ground at the very time the city's rich were growing visibly richer. In 1817, the top tenth of the city's taxpayers owned more than half the wealth, whereas the bottom half possessed only 10 percent. In 1860, the share of the top tenth had increased to two-thirds, while the bottom half's share had shrunk to 2.4 percent. Cincinnati workers may not have known these exact percentages, but they could see growing social and economic inequality in the luxurious mansions that the city's rich were building and in the spreading blight of slums.

Like workers in Lowell and other manufacturing communities, Cincinnati's laborers, in the decades before the Civil War, formed unions, turned out for fair wages, and rallied in favor of the 10-hour day. Using language similar to the Lowell mill girls, they cloaked their protest with the mantle of the Revolution. Bosses denied workers a fair share of profits and reduced them to economic dependency. Because the republic depended on a free and independent citizenry, the male workers warned that their bosses' policies threatened to undermine the republic itself.

Only in the early 1850s did Cincinnati workers begin to suspect that their employers formed a distinct class of parasitic "nonproducers." Although most strikes still revolved around familiar issues of better hours and wages, signs appeared of the more hostile labor relations that would emerge after the Civil War.

CHANGING OCCUPATIONAL DISTRIBUTION, 1820–1860

The decline of agriculture and the increased involvement in industrial pursuits are represented in this table. In what 20-year period did agriculture decline most dramatically? In what 20-year period did manufacturing increase most?

	1820	1840	1860
Agriculture	78.8%	63.1%	52.9%
Mining	0.4	0.6	1.6
Construction	—	5.1	4.7
Manufacturing	2.7	8.8	13.8
Trade	—	6.2	8.0
Transport	1.6	1.8	2.0
Service	4.1	5.0	6.4
Other	12.4	9.4	10.6

Source: U.S. Bureau of the Census

As elsewhere, skilled workers were in the forefront of Cincinnati's labor protest and union activities. But their victories proved temporary. Depression and bad times always harmed labor organizations and canceled employers' concessions. Furthermore, Cincinnati workers did not readily unite to protest new conditions. The uneven pace of industrialization meant that these workers, unlike the Lowell mill women, had no common working experience. Moreover, growing cultural, religious, and ethnic diversity compounded differences in workplaces. By 1850, almost half the people in the city were foreign born, mostly German, whereas only 22 percent had been in 1825.

Ethnic and religious tensions simmered, often driving workers apart and concealing their common grievances. In Cincinnati, during the spring of 1855, Americans attacked barricades erected in German neighborhoods, crying out death threats. Their wrath visited the Irish as well. Such ethnic, cultural, and social hostilities weakened working class collective strength and enabled businesses to maximize productivity and profits while minimizing the cost of labor.

Urban Life

Americans experienced the impact of economic growth most dramatically in the cities. In the four decades before the Civil War, the rate of urbanization in the United States was faster than ever before or since. In 1820, about 9 percent of the American people lived in cities (defined as areas containing a population of 2,500 or more). Forty years later, almost 20 percent of them did. Older cities such as Philadelphia and New York mushroomed, while new cities such as Cincinnati, Columbus, and Chicago sprang up. Urban growth was most dramatic in the East. By 1860, more than one-third of the people living in the Northeast were urban residents, compared with only 14 percent of westerners and 7 percent of southerners. Urbanization played an important role in sustaining economic expansion. The growing number of urban dwellers represented new markets for farmers and for manufactures of shoes, clothing, furniture, and cast-iron stoves. City governments purchased cast-iron pipes for sewers and water supply, and city merchants erected cast-iron buildings.

The Process of Urbanization

Three distinct types of cities—commercial centers, mill towns, and transportation hubs—emerged during these years of rapid economic growth. Although a lack of water power limited industrial development, commercial seaports such as Boston, Philadelphia, and Baltimore expanded steadily and developed diversified

manufacturing to supplement the older functions of importing, exporting, and providing services and credit. New York replaced Philadelphia as the country's largest and most important city. The completion of the Erie Canal allowed New York merchants to gain control of much of the trade with the West. By 1840, they had also seized the largest share of the country's import and export trade.

Access to water power spurred the development of a second kind of city, exemplified by Lowell, Massachusetts; Trenton, New Jersey; and Wilmington, Delaware. Situated inland along the waterfalls and rapids that provided the power to run their mills, these cities burgeoned.

A third type of city arose between 1820 and 1840, west of the Appalachian Mountains, where one-quarter of the nation's urban growth occurred. Louisville, Cleveland, and St. Louis typified cities that served as transportation and distribution centers from the earliest days of frontier settlement. In the 1850s, Chicago's most significant business was selling lumber to prairie farmers.

Until 1840, the people eagerly crowding into cities came mostly from the American countryside. Then ships began to spill their human cargoes into eastern seaports. Immigrants who could afford it, many of them Germans or Scandinavians, left crowded port cities for the interior. Those who were penniless sought work in eastern cities. By 1860, fully 20 percent of those living in the Northeast were immigrants; in some of the largest cities, they and their children composed more than half the population. The Irish were the largest foreign group in the Northeast.

While a few cities, such as New York and Boston, provided parks where residents could escape from the sounds, noises, and smells of urban life, much about urban life was grimy and difficult, especially for those who belonged to the working class. Speculators, finding the grid pattern the cheapest and most efficient way to divide land for development, created miles of monotonous new streets and houses. Overwhelmed by rapid growth, city governments provided few of the services we consider essential today, and usually only to those who paid for them. Poor families devoted many hours to securing necessities, including water. The ability to pay for services determined not only comfort, but health.

Class Structure in the Cities

The drastic differences in the quality of urban life reflected social fluidity and the growing economic inequality that characterized many American cities. In contrast to the colonial period, the first half of the nineteenth century witnessed a dramatic rise in the concentration of wealth in the United States. The pattern was most extreme in cities.

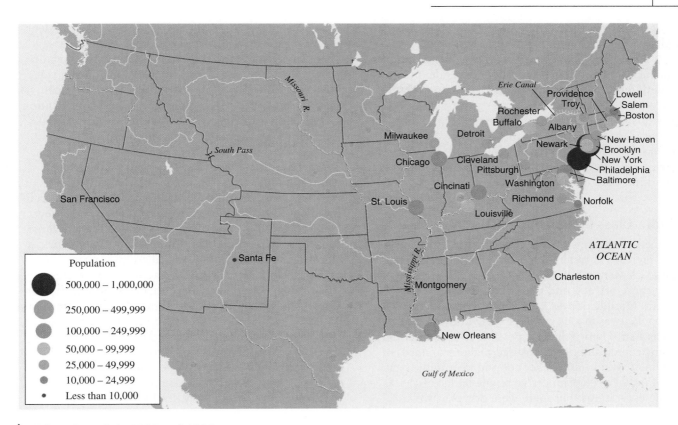

Urban Growth in 1820 and 1850

In 1820, there were few very large cities in the United States, and most of them were located along the Atlantic coast. This map shows urban growth by 1850. What are the important features of the map and what forces lie behind them?

(*Source: Statistical Abstract of the United States.*)

Because Americans believed that capitalists deserved most of their profits, the well-to-do profited handsomely from this period of growth whereas workers lost ground. Philadelphia provides one example of these economic trends. The merchants, brokers, lawyers, bankers, and manufacturers of Philadelphia's upper class gained increasing control of the city's wealth. By the late 1840s, the wealthiest 4 percent of the population held about two-thirds of the wealth. Because more wealth was being generated, the widening gap between the upper class and the working class did not cause mass suffering. But growing inequality hardened class lines and contributed to labor protests.

Between 1820 and 1860, a new working and middle class took shape in Philadelphia and elsewhere. As preindustrial ways of producing goods yielded to factory production and as the pace of economic activity quickened, some former artisans and skilled workers seized newly created opportunities. Perhaps 10 to 15 percent of Philadelphians in each decade before the Civil War improved their occupations and places of residence. Increasingly, membership in this middle class meant having a nonmanual occupation and a special place of work suited to activities depending on brainpower rather than brawn. But downward occupational mobility increased. Former artisans or journeymen became part of a new class of permanent manual workers, dependent on wages. Fed by waves of immigrants, the lower class grew at an accelerating rate. The percentage of unskilled wage earners living in poverty or on its brink increased from 17 to 24 percent between 1820 and 1860, while the proportion of artisans, once the heart of the laboring class, shrank from 56 to 47 percent.

The Urban Working Class

As with so much else in urban life, housing patterns reflected social and economic divisions. Behind the substantial houses fronting the main streets, in unpaved alleys and even in backyards, were rickety shacks and two-room houses surrounded by uncollected garbage, privy runoffs, and fetid decay. Here lived the poorest residents who rented their slum dwellings, moved often, and found it difficult to create close-knit neighborhoods and support networks.

Slums were not merely the abodes of poverty but places where working-class family life was in the midst of transformation. Men, no longer confident of their ability to support their families even when they were employed, sensed a loss of authority and power at home. The shortage of money colored family relations. Some men thought their wives too independent or careless with money. When one woman failed to explain clearly what she had done with the grocery money, her angry husband "said if she did not give him a full account ... he would kill her or something like that." The squabble ended in murder. This family was an extreme case, but family violence was not uncommon in working-class quarters.

Middle-Class Life and Ideals

Members of the new middle class profited from the dramatic increase in wealth in antebellum America. They lived in pleasantly furnished houses, enjoying more peace, more privacy, and more comfort than the less affluent. Franklin stoves gave warmth in winter, and iron cookstoves made cooking easier. Conveniences such as Astral lamps made it possible to read after dark. Bathing stands and bowls ensured higher standards of cleanliness. Rugs muffled sounds and kept in the heat.

Material circumstances were one badge of middle-class status, but there were others as well.

The acceptance of certain norms and values also identified a person as a member of the new middle class. Genteel behavior and the careful observance of elaborate rules of etiquette (for example, a gentleman was expected to back out of a parlor after making a call upon a lady), the appropriate clothes and conversation, an elegantly furnished parlor—all served to establish the standing of a middle-class family.

New expectations about the roles of men and women, prompted partly by economic change, also shaped middle-class life. In the colonial period, all members of the family worked to contribute to its economic well-being. But improved transportation, new products, and the rise of factory production and large businesses changed the family economy. Falling prices for processed and manufactured goods such as soap, candles, clothing, and even bread made it unnecessary for women, except on the frontier, to continue making these items at home. Although middle-class women and children still worked in their homes, they often neither produced vital goods nor earned money. Even the rhythm of their lives, oriented to housework, separated them from their husbands who, through commerce or market farming, were increasingly involved in a bustling money economy. By 1820, the notion that

WEALTH DISTRIBUTION IN THREE EASTERN CITIES IN THE 1840S

Americans and foreign visitors often commented on the rough equality they believed characterized American life. What do these wealth distribution figures, although incomplete, suggest?

Level of Wealth	Percentage of Population	Approximate Noncorporate Wealth Owned	Percentage Noncorporate Wealth
Brooklyn in 1841			
$50,000 or more	1	$10,087,000	42
$15,000 to $50,000	2	$14,000,000	17
$4,500 to $15,000	9	$15,730,000	24
$1,000 to $4,500	15	$12,804,000	12
$100 to $1,000	7	$11,000,000	4
Under $100	66	—	—
New York City in 1845			
$50,000 or more	1	$85,804,000	40
$20,000 to $50,000	3	$55,000,000	26
Boston in 1848			
$90,000 or more	1	$47,778,500	37
$35,000 to $90,000	3	$34,781,800	27
$4,000 to $35,000	15	$40,636,400	32
Under $4,000	81	$16,000,000	4

Source: Edward Pessen, *Riches, Class, and Power Before the Civil War*, 1973.

the sexes occupied separate spheres emerged. Men's sphere was the public world, whereas women's was the domestic.

Men were charged with the task of financial support, a responsibility that (as Susan Warner's family experience suggested) was a heavy one in a changing economy. Women's duties included working at home—not as producer but as housekeeper. This role had both pleasure and frustration built into it. Susan Warner's celebration of domestic life in her novels suggested the satisfactions derived from a cozy household. Yet it was sometimes impossible to achieve the new standards of cleanliness, order, and beauty. Catharine Beecher's "Words of Comfort for a Discouraged Housekeeper" listed just a few of the problems—an inconvenient house, sick children, poor domestics—that undermined efforts to create a perfect, harmonious home.

Although women were expected to become "systematic, neat and thorough" housekeepers, whatever the personal costs might be, they were also given more elevated responsibilities as moral and cultural guardians of their own families and, by extension, of society as a whole. Believing that women were innately pious, virtuous, unselfish, and modest (all characteristics that men lacked), publicists built on the argument developed during the Revolutionary era. By training future citizens and workers to be obedient, moral, patriotic, and hardworking, mothers ensured the welfare of the republic. Just as important, they preserved important values in a time of rapid change. Because men had none of women's virtues and were daily caught up in the fast-paced world of business, wives were responsible for helping husbands cope with temptations and tensions. In the words of one preacher, a wife was the "guardian angel" who warned her husband "against dangers, comforts him under trial; and by . . . pious, assiduous, and attractive deportment, constantly endeavors to render him more virtuous, more useful, more honourable, and more happy."

This view, characterizing women as morally superior to and different from men, had important consequences for female life. Although the concept of domesticity seemed to confine women to their homes, it actually prompted women to take on activities in the outside world. If women were the guardians of morality, why should they not carry out their tasks in the public sphere? "Woman," said Sarah Hale, editor of the popular magazine *Godey's Lady's Book*, was "God's appointed agent of *morality*." Such reasoning lay behind the tremendous growth of voluntary female associations in the early decades of the nineteenth century. Female associations provided companionship and activities suited to women's supposedly "moral character." Initially, most involved religious and charitable activities like distributing Bibles or establishing Sunday schools. By the 1830s, as we shall see in Chapter 12, women added more controversial moral concerns such as the abolition of slavery to their missionary and benevolent efforts and often clashed with men and with social conventions about "woman's place."

The notion of separate spheres established norms for middle-class men and women but were far more flexible than they appeared. Men played a much greater part in the household and in child rearing and women a more active role in the public world than gender proscriptions would suggest. Obviously, men were not always aggressive and rational nor were all women pious, cheerful, and loving. But these ideas influenced how men and women thought of themselves. It helped promote "male" and "female" behavior by encouraging particular choices, and it helped many men and women make psychological sense of their lives.

New norms, effectively spread by the publishing industry, also influenced rural and urban working women. The insistence on marriage and service to family discouraged married women from entering the workforce, and made those who had to work feel guilty. Many took in poorly paid piecework so that they could remain at home. Though the new feminine ideal may have suited urban middle-class women, it created difficult tensions for working-class women.

As family roles were reformulated, so too were views of childhood. Working-class children still worked or scavenged for goods to sell or use at home, but middle-class children were no longer expected to contribute economically to the family. Middle-class parents now came to see childhood as a special stage of life, a period of preparation for adulthood. In a child's early years, mothers were to impart important values, including the necessity of behaving in accordance with gender prescriptions. Harsh punishments lost favor. As Catharine Beecher explained, "Affection can govern the human with a sway more powerful than the authority of reason or [even] the voices of conscience." Schooling also prepared a child for the future, and urban middle-class parents supported the public school movement.

Children's fiction, which poured off the printing presses, also socialized children. Stories pictured modest, obedient, and dutiful youngsters happily making the correct choices. The consequences of failing to observe new norms were made abundantly clear. *The Child at Home* (1833) depicted a young girl whose ailing mother died when the daughter refused to bring her a glass of water.

The growing publishing industry played a key role in popularizing new ideas about family roles and appropriate family behavior. Novels, magazines, etiquette and child rearing manuals, and schoolbooks all carried the message from northern and midwestern centers of publishing to the South, to the West, and to the frontier. Probably few Americans lived up to the

Two Children

This daguerreotype shows two children posed on an uphol-stered bench. Each child holds a book. While we do not know the identity of these children or even whether they were related, the image reveals new middle-class norms. The fact that the children are holding books suggests the impor-tance now attached to primary education. Note the groomed hair styles and clothing. Neat appearance and cleanliness were also important middle-class values. The fact that the children are the subject of this picture hints at the importance attached to children in the middle-class family.

(The Library of Congress, LC-USZ6–1988 DLC)

new standards established for the model parent or child, but the standards increasingly influenced them.

New notions of family life, especially the belief that children required loving attention and training for adulthood, promoted a desire for smaller families and the widespread use of contraception for the first time in American history. The declining birthrate was evident first in the Northeast, particularly in cities and among the middle class. Contraceptive methods included abor-tion, which was legal in many states until 1860. This medical procedure terminated perhaps as many as one-third of all pregnancies. Other birth control meth-ods included coitus interruptus and abstinence. The success of these methods that relied on self control sug-gests that many men and women may have internalized the view of women as naturally affectionate but pas-sionless and sexually restrained.

Mounting Urban Tensions

The social and economic changes transforming American cities and festering ethnic and racial tensions in the half century before the Civil War produced unprecedented urban violence. Mob actions sometimes lasted for days because there was no force strong enough to quell group disorder. American cities were slow to establish modern police forces. Traditional

constables and night watches did not try to stop crimes, discover offenses, or "prevent a tumult."

An unsavory riot in Philadelphia in August 1834 revealed not only racial and social antagonisms but the inability of the city's police force to control the mob. Starting off with the destruction of a merry-go-round patronized by both blacks and whites, the riot turned into an orgy of destruction, looting, and intimidation of black residents. In the several days of violence, at least one black person was killed, and numerous others injured. As one shocked eyewitness reported, "The mob exhibited more than fiendish brutality, beating and mutilating some of the old, confiding and unoffending blacks with a savageness surpassing anything we could have believed men capable of."

This racial explanation overlooked the range of causes underlying the rampage of fury and destruction. The rioters were young and generally of low social standing. Many were Irish; some had criminal records. A number of those arrested, however, were from a "class of mechanics of whom better things are expected," and middle-class onlookers egged the mob on. The rioters revealed that in the event of an "attack by the city police, they confidently counted" on the assistance of these bystanders.

The mob's composition hints at some of the rea-sons for participation. Many of the rioters were newly arrived Irish immigrants at the bottom of the economic ladder who competed with blacks for jobs. Subsequent violence against blacks suggested that economic rivalry was an important component of the riot. But if blacks threatened the dream of advancement of some whites, this was not the complaint of the skilled workers. These men were more likely to have believed them-selves injured by a changing economic system that undermined the small-scale mode of production. Dreams of a better life seemed increasingly illusory as declining wages pushed them closer to unskilled work-ers than to the middle class. Like other rioters, they were living in one of the poorest and most crowded parts of the city. Their immediate scapegoats were blacks, but the intangible villain was the economic system itself.

Urban expansion also figured as a factor in the racial violence. Most of the rioters lived either in the riot area or nearby. Racial tensions generated by squalid surroundings and social proximity go far to explain the outbreak of violence. The same area would later become the scene of race riots and election trouble and became infamous for harboring criminals and juvenile gangs. The absence of middle- or upper-class participants did not mean that these groups were untroubled during times of growth and change, but their material circumstances cushioned them from some of the more unsettling forces.

Recovering the Past

FAMILY PAINTINGS

Although paintings are often admired and studied for artistic reasons alone, their value as historical documents should not be overlooked. In an age before the camera, paintings, sketches, and even pictures done in needlework captured Americans at different moments of life and memorialized their significant rituals. Paintings of American families in their homes, for example, reveal both an idealized conception of family life and the details of its reality. In addition, the paintings provide us with a sense of what the houses of the middle and upper classes (who could afford to commission art) were like.

Artists trained in the European tradition of realism painted family scenes and portraits, but so did many painters who lacked formal academic training, the so-called primitive artists. Their art was abstract in the sense that the artists tended to emphasize what they knew or felt rather than what they actually saw.

Some primitive artists were women who had received some drawing instruction at school. They often worked primarily for their own pleasure. Other artists were artisans, perhaps house or sign painters, who painted pictures in their leisure time. Some traveling house decorators made a living by making paintings and wall decorations. Many primitive paintings are unsigned, and even when we know the painter's identity, we rarely know more than a name and perhaps a date. Primitive artists flourished in the first three-quarters of the nineteenth century, eventually supplanted by the camera and inexpensive prints.

We see here a painting of the Sargent family done by an unknown artist around 1800. Though not an exact representation of reality, it does convey what the artist and the buyer considered important. Like any piece of historical evidence, this painting must be approached critically and carefully. Our questions focus on four areas: (1) the individual family members and their treatment, (2) the objects associated with each, (3) the implied or apparent relationship between family members, and (4) the domestic environment. The painting gives us an idealized version of what both the painter and the subjects felt ought to be as well as what actually was. First, study the family itself. Describe what you see. How many family members are there, and what is each one doing? What seems to be the relationship between husband and wife? Why do you think Mr. Sargent is painted with his hat on? Who seems to dominate the painting, and how is this dominance conveyed (positioning, attitude or facial expression, eye contact, clothing)? What can you conclude about different "spheres" and roles for men and women?

Anonymous, The Sargent Family, 1800
(Sargent Family, gift of Edgar William and Bernice Chrysler Garbisch, Image © 2003 Board of Trustees, National Gallery of Art, Washington)

255

H. Knight, *The Family at Home,* 1836

(Private collection)

Why do you think the artist painted two empty chairs and included a ball and a dog in this scene of family life? What do these choices suggest about attitudes toward children and their upbringing? What seems to be the role of the children in the family? What does the painting suggest about how this family wished to be viewed? How do your conclusions relate to information discussed in this chapter?

Take a look at the room in which the Sargents are gathered. Make an inventory of the objects and furnishings in it. The room seems quite barren in comparison with present-day interiors. Why? Why do you think the chairs are placed near the window and door? What kind of scene does the window frame?

The *Family at Home,* painted by H. Knight in 1836, is a more detailed painting showing a larger family gathering almost 40 years later. Similar questions can be asked about this painting, particularly in relationship to the different treatment of boys and girls and the positioning and objects associated with each gender. There are many clues about the different socialization of male and female children. The family's living room can be contrasted with the Sargent family's room to reveal some of the changes brought about by industrialization.

Reflecting on the Past How do these nineteenth-century homes and gender roles differ from those in colonial New England and the Chesapeake? ◼

Philadelphia, like other eastern cities, was beginning to create a police force, but only continued disorder would convince residents and city officials there (and in other large cities) to support an expanded, quasi-military, preventive, and uniformed police. By 1855, most sizable eastern cities had such forces.

Finally, the character of the free black community itself was a factor in producing those gruesome August events. Not only was the community large and visible, but it also had created its own institutions and its own elite. The mob vented its rage against black affluence by targeting the solid brick houses of middle-class

African Americans in Philadelphia

This cartoon was one of a series titled "Life in Philadelphia." Philadelphia had a large, free African American community that often became the target for racial animosity. In what ways has the cartoonist presented a negative picture of the man and woman in the cartoon? Notice the exaggerated racial features of the two figures and the overelaborate clothing of the dandified man passing his card to the woman coming up from the basement. The verbal message reinforced the visual one. The man asks, "Is Miss Dinah at home?" The woman replies, "Yes sir but she bery potickly engaged in washing de dishes." He replies, "Ah! I'm sorry I cant have the honour to pay my devours to her. Give her my card."

(The Print & Picture Collection, The Free Library of Philadelphia)

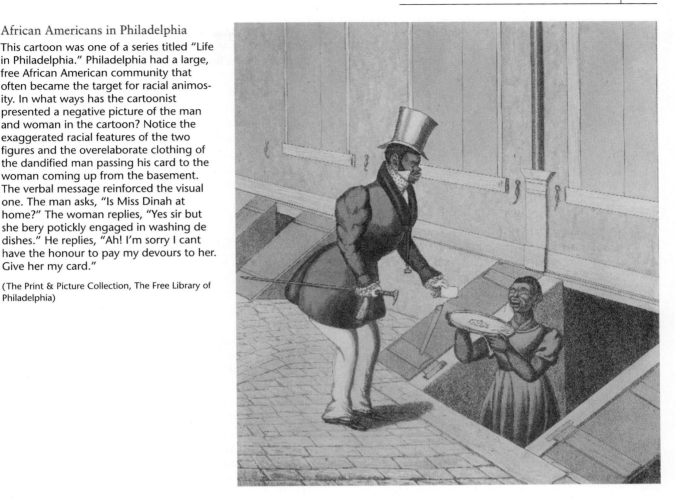

blacks and robbing them of silver and watches. Black wealth threatened the notion of the proper social order held by many white Philadelphians and seemed unspeakable when whites could not afford life's basic necessities or lacked jobs.

The Black Underclass

Between 1800 and 1860, the number of free blacks in the United States grew dramatically, from 108,435 in 1800 to 488,070 in 1860. Most of these lived in northeastern cities, although Baltimore had the largest free African American population of all, and New Orleans also had a sizable free black community. While African Americans constituted a minority of urban residents, whites noted the increased numbers, often with negative feelings. As one African American woman confessed, white prejudice based on "dislike to the color of the skin" had "often embittered" her feelings.

Events in Philadelphia showed how hazardous life for free blacks could be. Although a small elite group of blacks emerged in Philadelphia and in other cities as well, most African Americans did not enjoy the rewards of economic expansion and industrial progress. Black

men, often with little or no education, held transient and frequently dangerous jobs. Black women, many heading their households because the men were away working or had died, held jobs before and after marriage. In Philadelphia in 1849, almost half of the black women washed clothes for a living. Others took boarders into their homes, thus adding to their domestic chores.

Northern whites, like southerners, believed in black inferiority and depravity and feared black competition. Although northern states had passed gradual abolition acts between 1780 and 1803 and the national government had banned slaves from entering new states to be formed out of the Northwest Territory, nowhere did any government extend equal rights and citizenship or economic opportunities to free blacks in their midst.

For a time in the early nineteenth century, some blacks living in the North were permitted to vote, but they soon lost that right. Beginning in the 1830s, in part because of the influx of fugitive slaves and manumitted blacks without property or jobs, Pennsylvania, Connecticut, and New Jersey disenfranchised blacks. Only the New England states (except for Connecticut), which had tiny black populations, preserved the right to vote regardless of color. By 1840, fully 93 percent of the northern free black population lived in states where law or custom prevented them from voting.

Other black civil rights were also restricted. In five northern states, blacks could not testify against whites or serve on juries. In most states, the two races were thoroughly segregated. Blacks increasingly endured separate and inferior facilities in railway cars, steamboats, hospitals, prisons, and other asylums. In some states, they could enter public buildings only as personal servants of white men. They sat in "Negro pews" in churches and took communion only after whites had left the church. Although most Protestant religious denominations in the antebellum period split into northern and southern branches over the issue of slavery, most northern churches were not disposed to welcome blacks as full members.

As the Philadelphia riot revealed, whites were driving blacks from their jobs. In 1839, *The Colored American* blamed the Irish. "These impoverished and destitute beings ... are crowding themselves into every place of business ... and driving the poor colored American citizen out." Increasingly after 1837, these "white niggers" became coachmen, stevedores, barbers, cooks, and house servants—all occupations blacks had once held.

Educational opportunities for blacks were also severely limited. Only a few school systems admitted blacks, in separate facilities. The case of Prudence Crandall illustrates the lengths to which northern whites would go to maintain racial segregation. In 1833, Crandall, a Quaker schoolmistress in Canterbury, Connecticut, announced that she would admit "young colored ladies and Misses" to her school. The outraged townspeople, fearful that New England would become the "Liberia of America," tried all sorts of persuasion and intimidation to stop Crandall.

Nonetheless, Crandall opened the school. Hostile citizens harassed and insulted students and teachers, refused to sell them provisions, and denied them medical care and admission to churches. Ministers preached against Crandall's efforts, and local residents dumped manure in the school's well, set the school on fire, and knocked in walls with a battering ram. Crandall was arrested, and after two trials—in which free blacks were declared to have no citizenship rights—she finally gave up and moved to Illinois.

Crandall likely did not find the Old Northwest much more hospitable. The fast-growing western states were intensely committed to white supremacy and black exclusion. In Ohio, the response to talk of freeing the slaves was to pass "Black laws" excluding them from the state. In 1829 in Cincinnati, where evidence of freedom papers and $500 bond were demanded of blacks who wished to live in the city, white rioters ran nearly 2,000 blacks out of town.

As an Indiana newspaper editor observed in 1854, informal customs made life dangerous for blacks. They were "constantly subject to insults and annoyance in traveling and the daily avocations of life; [and] are practically excluded from all social privileges, and even from the Christian communion." An Indiana senator proclaimed in 1850 that a black could "never live together equally" with whites because "the same power that has given him a black skin, with less weight or volume of brain, has given us a white skin with greater volume of brain and intellect." A neighboring politician, Abraham Lincoln of Illinois, would not have disagreed with this assessment.

Rural Communities

Although the percentage of American workers involved in farming fell from 71 to 53 percent between 1830 and 1860, agriculture persisted as the country's most significant economic activity. The small family farm still characterized eastern and western agriculture, and farm products still made up most of the nation's exports.

Even though farming remained the dominant way of life, agriculture changed in the antebellum period. Vast new tracts of land came under cultivation in the West. Railroads, canals, and better roads pulled rural Americans into the orbit of the wider world. Some crops were shipped to regional markets; others, such as grain, hides, and pork, stimulated industrial processing. Manufactured goods, ranging from cloth to better tools, flowed in return to farm families. Like city dwellers, farmers and their families read books, magazines, and papers that exposed them to new ideas. Commercial farming encouraged different ways of thinking and acting and lessened the isolation so typical before 1820.

Farming in the East

Antebellum economic changes created new rural patterns in the Northeast. Marginal lands in New England, New York, and Pennsylvania, cultivated as more fertile lands ran out, yielded discouraging returns. Gradually, after 1830, farmers abandoned these farms, forest reclaimed farmland, and the New England hill country began a slow decline.

Those farmers who did not migrate west had to transform production. Unable to compete with western grain, they embraced new agricultural opportunities created by better transportation and growing urban markets. The extension of railroad lines into rural areas, for example, allowed farmers as far away as Vermont to ship cooled milk to the city. Other farmers used the new railroads to ship fruit and vegetables to the cities. By 1837, a Boston housewife could buy a wide variety of fresh vegetables and fruits, ranging from cauliflower to raspberries, at the central market. Cookbooks began to include recipes calling for fresh ingredients.

As northern farmers adopted new crops, they began to regard farming as a scientific endeavor. After 1800, northern farmers started using manure as fertilizer; by the 1820s, some farmers were rotating their crops and planting new grasses and clover to restore fertility to the soil. These techniques recovered worn-out wheat and tobacco lands in Maryland and Delaware for livestock farming. While farmers in the Delaware River valley were leaders in adopting new methods, interest in scientific farming was widespread. New journals informed readers of modern farming practices, and many states established agricultural agencies. Although wasteful farming practices did not disappear, they became less characteristic of the Northeast. Improved farming methods contributed to increased agricultural output and helped reverse a 200-year decline in farm productivity in some of the oldest areas of settlement. A "scientific" farmer in 1850 could often produce two to four times as much per acre as in 1820. Experimentation and the exchange of information also led to the development of thousands of special varieties of plants for local conditions by 1860.

Rural attitudes also changed. Cash transactions replaced the exchange of goods. Country stores became more reluctant to accept wood, rye, corn, oats, and butter as payment for goods instead of cash. As some farmers adopted the "get-ahead" ethic and entered the market economy, those who were content with just getting along fell behind. Wealth inequality increased throughout the rural Northeast.

Frontier Families

Many people who left the North during these years headed for the expanding frontier. After the War of 1812, Americans flooded into the Old Northwest. Early communities dotted the Ohio River, the link to the South. Concentrating on corn and pork, settlers sent their products down the Ohio and Mississippi rivers to southern buyers. In 1820, less than one-fifth of the American population lived west of the Appalachians; by 1860, almost half did, and Ohio and Illinois had become two of the nation's most populous states.

By 1830, Ohio, Indiana, and southern Illinois were heavily settled, but Michigan, northern Illinois, Wisconsin, and parts of Iowa and Missouri were still frontier. During the next decade, land sales and settlement boomed in the Old Northwest. Changes in federal land policy, which reduced both prices and the minimum acreage a settler had to buy, helped stimulate migration. Eastern capital also contributed to the boom with loans, mortgages, and speculative buying. Speculators frequently bought up large tracts of land from the government and then subdivided them and sold parcels off to settlers.

Internal improvement schemes after 1830 also contributed to new settlement patterns and tied the Old Northwest firmly to the East. Wheat for the eastern market rather than corn and hogs for the southern market became increasingly important with the transportation links eastward. Between 1840 and 1860, Illinois, southern Wisconsin, and eastern Iowa turned into the country's most rapidly growing grain regions. In the 1850s, these three states accounted for 70 percent of the increase in national wheat production.

Although the Old Northwest passed rapidly through the frontier stage between 1830 and 1860, its farming families faced severe challenges. Catharine Skinner, who moved from New York to Indiana with her husband when she was 24, described her rigorous existence. "We are poor and live in the woods where deers roam plentifully and the wolf is occasionally heard," she wrote to her sister in 1849. "We are employed in honest business and trying to do the best we can; we have got 80 acres of land in the woods of Indiana, a very level country; we have got two acres cleared and fenced and four more pirty well under way; we have got about five acres of wheat in the ground; we raised corn enough for our use and to fat our pork … we have a cow so that we have milk and butter and plenty of corn bread but wheat is hard to be got in account of our not having mony."

The Skinners were typical. Western farms were small, for there were limits to what a family with hand tools could manage. A family with two healthy men could care for about 50 acres. In wooded areas, it took several years to get even that much land under cultivation, for only a few acres could be cleared in a year. Even on the prairies, the typical settler needed five years to get his farm in full operation.

Catharine Skinner mentioned the shortage of money and described her family as "poor." Although money was in short supply in the Northwest, she probably overstated her family's poverty. It took capital to begin farming—a minimum initial investment of perhaps $100 for 80 acres of government land, $300 for basic farming equipment, and another $100 or $150 for livestock. To buy an already "improved" farm cost more, and free bidding at government auctions could drive the price of unimproved federal land far above the minimum price. Once farmers moved onto the prairies of Indiana and Illinois, they needed an initial investment of about $1,000 because they had to buy materials for fencing, housing, and expensive steel plows. If farmers invested in the new horse-drawn reapers, they could cultivate more land, but all their costs also increased.

Opportunities in the Old Northwest

It was possible to begin farming with less, however. Some farmers borrowed from relatives, banks, or insurance companies. Others rented land from farmers who had bought more acres than they could manage. Tenants who furnished their own seeds and animals could expect to keep about one-third of the yield.

Within a few years, some saved enough to buy their own farms. Even those without any capital could work as hired hands. Labor was scarce, so they earned good wages. In Indiana, German settler Jacob Schramm hired men "to help with heavy labors of lumbering and field work, ditch-digging, and so on." Five to 10 years of frugal living and steady work for men like those hired by Schramm would bring the sum needed to get started.

Probably about one-quarter of the western farm population consisted of young men laboring as tenants or hired hands. Although they stood on the bottom rung of the agricultural ladder, their chances of moving up and joining the rural middle class were favorable. Widespread ownership of land characterized western rural communities. Lucinda Easteen knew as much when she told her younger sister to come to Illinois, where "you can have a home of your own, but never give your hand or heart to a lazy man."

Rural communities, unlike the cities, had no growing class of propertyless wage earners, but inequalities nevertheless existed in the Old Northwest. In Butler County, Ohio, for example, 16 percent of people leaving wills in the 1830s held half the wealth. By 1860, the wealthiest 8 percent held half the wealth. Although rural wealth was not as concentrated as urban, a few residents benefited more from rapid economic development than others.

Nevertheless, the Northwest offered many American families the chance to become independent producers and to enjoy a "pleasing competence." The rigors of frontier life faded with time. As Catharine Skinner wrote to her sister from her new Illinois home

Timeline

1805	*Palmer* v. *Mulligan*
1816	Second Bank of the United States chartered
1817	New York Stock Exchange established
1819	*Dartmouth College* v. *Woodward*
1820	Land Act of 1820
	The expression "woman's sphere" becomes current
1823	City of Lowell, Massachusetts, founded by Boston Associates
1824	*Sturges* v. *Crowninshield*
1824–1850	Construction of canals in the Northeast
1825–1856	Construction of canals linking the Ohio, the Mississippi, and the Great Lakes
1828	Baltimore & Ohio Railroad begins operation
1830	Preemption Act facilitates western land acquisition by squatters
1830s	Boom in the Old Northwest
	Increasing discrimination against free blacks
	Public education movement spreads
1833	Philadelphia establishes small police force
1834	Philadelphia race riots
	Lowell work stoppage
	Cyrus McCormick patents his reaper
1837	Horace Mann becomes secretary of Massachusetts Board of Education
1837–1844	Financial panic and depression
1840	Agitation for 10-hour day
1840s–1850s	Rising tide of immigration
	Expansion of railroad system
1850s	Rise of urban police forces
1857	Financial panic

in 1850, "We here have meetings instead of hearing the hunters gun and the woo[d]man's ax on the sabbath."

Commercial farming brought new patterns of family life. As one Illinois farmer told his wife and daughter, "Store away your looms, wheels, [and] warping bars . . . all of your utensils for weaving cloth up in the loft. The boys and I can make enough by increasing our herds." Many farm families had money to spend on new goods. As early as 1836, the *Dubuque Visitor* was advertising the availability of ready-made clothing and "Calicoes, Ginghams, Muslins, Cambricks, Laces and Ribbands." The next year the *Iowa News* told of the arrival of "Ready Made Clothing from New York."

Agriculture and the Environment

Shifting agricultural patterns in the East and expanding settlement into the Old Northwest contributed to the changing character of the American landscape. As naturalist John Audubon mused in 1826, "A century hence," the rivers, swamps, and mountains "will not be here as I see them. Nature will have been robbed of many brilliant charms, the rivers will be tormented and turned astray from their primitive course, the hills will be levelled with the swamps, and perhaps the swamps will have become a mount surmounted by a fortress of a thousand guns." His sense of the consequences of the movement of peoples and the exploitation of land was shared by one French visitor who remarked that Americans would never be satisfied until they had subdued nature.

More than the subjugation of nature was involved, however. When eastern farmers changed their agricultural practices as they became involved in the market economy, their decisions left an imprint on the land. Selling wood and potash stimulated clearing of forests, as did the desire for new tools, plow castings, threshing machines, and wagon boxes, which were produced in furnaces fueled by charcoal. As forests disappeared, so, too, did their wildlife. Even using mineral manures such as gypsum or lime or organic fertilizers such as guano to revitalize worn-out soil and increase crop yields meant the depletion of land elsewhere.

When farmers moved into the Old Northwest, they used new steel plows, like the one developed in 1837 by Illinois blacksmith John Deere. Unlike older eastern plows, the new ones could cut through the dense, tough prairie cover. Deep plowing and the intensive cultivation of large cash crops had immediate benefits. But these practices could result in robbing the soil of necessary minerals such as phosphorus, carbon, and nitrogen. When farmers built new timber houses as frontier conditions receded, they helped fuel the destruction of the country's forests.

Conclusion
THE CHARACTER OF PROGRESS

Between 1820 and 1860, the United States experienced tremendous growth and economic development. Transportation improvements facilitated the movement of people, goods, and ideas. Larger markets stimulated both agricultural and industrial production. There were more goods and ample food for the American people. Cities and towns were established and thrived. Visitors constantly remarked on the amazing bustle and rapid pace of American life. The United States was, in the words of one Frenchman, "one gigantic workshop, over the entrance of which there is the blazing inscription 'NO ADMISSION HERE, EXCEPT ON BUSINESS.'"

Although the wonders of American development dazzled foreigners and Americans alike, economic growth had its costs, as Susan Warner's novel made clear. Expansion was cyclic, and financial panics and depression punctuated the era. Industrial profits were based partly on low wages to workers. Time-honored routes to economic independence disappeared, and a large class of unskilled, impoverished workers appeared in U.S. cities. Growing inequality characterized urban and rural life, prompting some labor activists to criticize new economic and social arrangements. But workers, still largely unorganized, did not speak with one voice. Ethnic, racial, and religious diversity divided Americans in new and troubling ways.

Yet a basic optimism and sense of pride also characterized the age. To observers, however, it frequently seemed as if the East and the Old Northwest were responsible for the country's achievements. During these decades, many noted that the paths between the East, Northwest, and South seemed to diverge. The rise of King Cotton in the South, where slave rather than free labor formed the foundation of the economy, created a new kind of tension in American life, as the next chapter will show.

QUESTIONS FOR REVIEW AND REFLECTION

1. List what you consider the most significant factors underlying American economic growth and explain why you think the factors you have chosen were so important.
2. Explain the ways in which Great Britain contributed to American economic development. How was American industry both similar to and different from British industry?
3. Compare and contrast industrialism in Lowell and Cincinnati.
4. How did economic changes transform the American class system and the relationship between classes?
5. What were the benefits and drawbacks of the economic and technological changes discussed in this chapter? Consider daily life, work, the division of wealth, gender roles, and community relations.

CHAPTER 11

Slavery and the Old South

The Young Frederick Douglass

Shown here in a photograph from about 1855, Douglass understood as well as any American the profound human, social, and political complexities and consequences of slavery. What qualities do you see in his face? Do they match the Douglass whose words and actions are described in this chapter?

(Schomburg Center for Research in Black Culture/Art Resource, NY)

American Stories

A Young Slave Discovers the Path to Freedom

As a young slave, Frederick Douglass was sent by his master to live in Baltimore. When he first met his mistress, Sophia Auld, he was "astonished at her goodness" as she began to teach him to read. Her husband, however, ordered her to stop. Maryland law forbade teaching slaves to read. A literate slave, he said, was "unmanageable," "utterly unfit . . . to be a slave." From this episode Douglass learned that "what he most dreaded, that I most desired . . . and the argument which he so warmly urged, against my learning to read, only served to inspire me with a desire and determination to learn."

In the seven years he lived with the Aulds, young Frederick used "various stratagems" to teach himself to read and write. In the narrative of his early life, written after his dramatic escape to the North, Douglass acknowledged that his master's "bitter opposition" had helped him achieve his freedom as much as did Mrs. Auld's "kindly aid."

Most slaves did not, like Douglass, escape. But all were as tied to their masters as Douglass was to the Aulds. Nor could whites in antebellum America escape the influence of slavery. Otherwise decent people were often compelled by the "peculiar institution" to act inhumanely. After her husband's interference, Sophia Auld, Douglass observed, was transformed into a demon by the "fatal poison of irresponsible power." Her formerly tender heart turned to "stone" when she ceased teaching him. "Slavery proved as injurious to her," Douglass wrote, "as it did to me."

A slavebreaker, Mr. Covey, to whom Douglass was sent in 1833 to have his will broken, also paid the cost of slavery. Covey succeeded for a time, Douglass sadly reported, in breaking his "body, soul, and spirit" by brutal work and discipline. But one hot August day in 1833, the two men fought a long, grueling battle. Douglass won. Victory, he said, "rekindled the few expiring embers of freedom, and revived within me a sense of my own manhood." Although it would be four more years before his escape north, the young man never again felt like a slave. The key to Douglass's resistance to Covey's power was not just his strong will, or even the magical root he carried, but rather his knowledge of how to challenge and jeopardize Covey's reputation and livelihood as a slavebreaker. The oppressed survive by knowing their oppressors.

As Mrs. Auld and Covey discovered, as long as some people were not free, no one was free. Douglass observed, "You cannot outlaw one part of the people without endangering the rights and liberties of all people. You cannot put a chain on the ankle of the bondsman without finding the other end of it about your own necks." After quarreling with a house servant, one plantation mistress complained that she "exercises dominion over me—or tries to do it. One would have thought . . . that I was the Servant, she the mistress." Many whites lived in constant fear of a slave revolt. A Louisiana planter recalled that he had "known times here when there was not a single planter who had a calm night's rest; they then never lay down to sleep without a brace of loaded pistols at their sides." In slave folktales, the clever Brer Rabbit usually outwitted the more powerful Brer Fox or Brer Wolf, thus reversing the roles of oppressed and oppressor.

Slavery in America was both an intricate web of human relationships and a labor system. Two large themes permeate this chapter. First, after tracing the economic development of the Old South in a global context, in which slavery, cotton, and world economic developments played vital roles, this chapter will emphasize the diverse dreams, daily lives, and relationships of masters and slaves who, like Douglass and the Aulds, lived, loved, learned, worked, and struggled with one another in the years before the Civil War.

Perhaps no issue in American history has generated as many interpretations or as much emotional controversy as slavery. Three interpretive schools developed over the years, each adding to our knowledge of "the peculiar institution." The first saw slavery as a relatively humane institution in which plantation owners took care of helpless, childlike slaves. The second depicted slavery as a harsh and cruel system of exploitation. The third, and most recent, interpretation described slavery from the perspective of the slaves, who did indeed suffer brutal treatment yet nevertheless survived with integrity, agency, and self-esteem supported by community and culture.

The first and second interpretive schools emphasized workaday interactions among powerful masters and seemingly passive, victimized slaves, while the third focused on the creative energies, agency, and vibrancy of life in the slave quarters from sundown to sunup. In a unique structure, this chapter follows these masters and slaves through their day, from morning in the Big House through hot afternoon in the fields to the slave cabins at night. Although slavery was the crucial institution in defining the Old South, diverse social groups and global trade patterns contributed to the tremendous economic growth of the South from 1820 to 1860. We will look first at these socioeconomic aspects of antebellum southern life and then follow whites and blacks through a southern day from morning to noon to night.

Building a Diverse Cotton Kingdom

Many myths obscure our understanding of the antebellum South. It was not a monolithic society filled only with large cotton plantations worked by hundreds of slaves. The realities were much more complex. Large-plantation agriculture was dominant, but most southern whites were not even slaveholders. Most southern farmers lived not in huge, white-columned mansions but in dark, two-room cabins. Cotton was the key cash crop in the South, but more acreage was planted in corn. Some masters were kindly, but many were not; some slaves were contented, but most were not.

There were many Souths, encompassing several geographic regions, each with different economic bases and social structures reflecting differing cultural values. The older Upper South of Virginia, Maryland, North Carolina, and Kentucky grew different staple crops from those grown in the newer Lower or "Black Belt" South, from South Carolina to eastern Texas. Within each state, moreover, the economies of flat coastal or river areas differed from inland upcountry forests and pine barrens in the Appalachian highlands. Southern cities, few in number—New Orleans, Savannah, Charleston, and Richmond—differed dramatically from rural areas.

Although the South was diverse, agriculture dominated industry and commerce. In 1859, a Virginia planter complained about a neighbor who was considering abandoning his farm to become a merchant. "To me it seems to be a wild idea," the planter wrote in his diary. Southerners placed a high value on agricultural labor. Slavery was primarily a labor system intended to produce wealth for landowners. A paternalistic institution, with masters and slaves owing mutual obligations, slavery increasingly became a capitalistic enterprise intended to maximize profits tied into a growing international system of trade.

The Expansion of Slavery in a Global Economy

In the 20 years preceding the Civil War, the South's agricultural economy grew slightly faster than the North's. If the South had become an independent nation in 1860, it would have ranked as one of the wealthiest countries in the world in per capita income.

The world was deeply involved in the tremendous economic growth of the South in the early nineteenth century. The expansion of cotton, the basis of the growth, depended on five factors: technology, land, labor, demand, and a global system of trade. The technological breakthrough was the cotton gin, invented by Eli Whitney in 1793, which allowed farmers to separate the cotton fibers from the sticky seeds in the hardier "short staple" cotton plant. The gin wedded the southern economy to cotton production, increased the need for more land and labor, and stimulated slavery's southwestward expansion into Alabama and Mississippi and, with the Louisiana

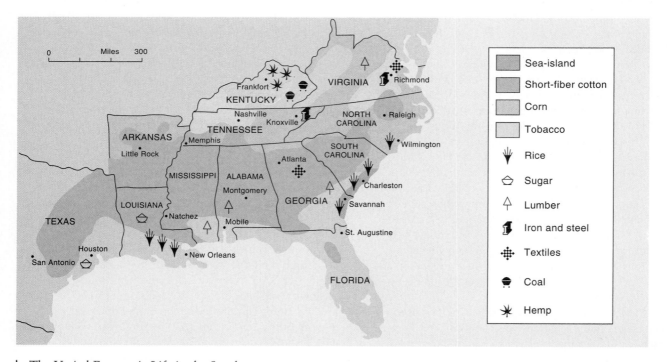

The Varied Economic Life in the South

What surprises you about the economic activity on this map? Can you trace the short-fiber cotton–growing "Black Belt"? What seems to be the second largest crop?

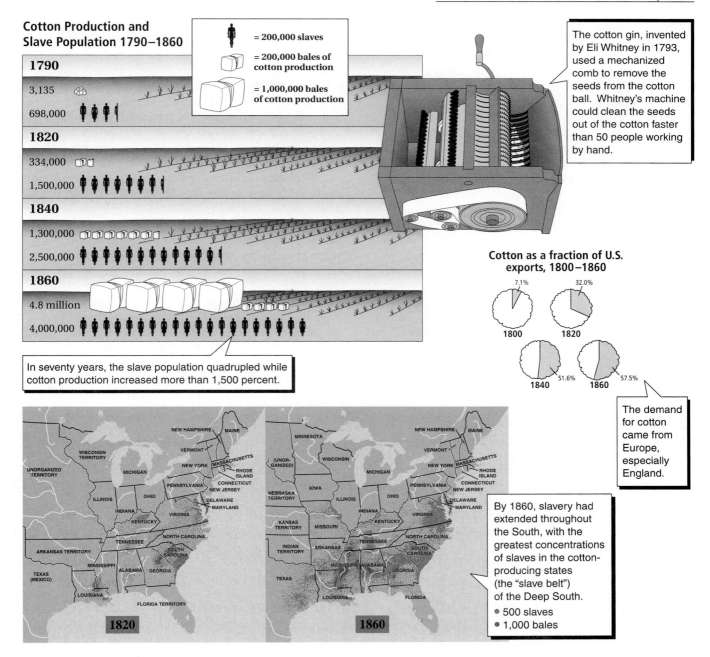

Cotton Production and Slave Population 1790–1860

= 200,000 slaves
= 200,000 bales of cotton production
= 1,000,000 bales of cotton production

1790
3,135
698,000

1820
334,000
1,500,000

1840
1,300,000
2,500,000

1860
4.8 million
4,000,000

The cotton gin, invented by Eli Whitney in 1793, used a mechanized comb to remove the seeds from the cotton ball. Whitney's machine could clean the seeds out of the cotton faster than 50 people working by hand.

In seventy years, the slave population quadrupled while cotton production increased more than 1,500 percent.

Cotton as a fraction of U.S. exports, 1800–1860

7.1%
1800

32.0%
1820

51.6%
1840

57.5%
1860

The demand for cotton came from Europe, especially England.

By 1860, slavery had extended throughout the South, with the greatest concentrations of slaves in the cotton-producing states (the "slave belt") of the Deep South.
● 500 slaves
● 1,000 bales

1820

1860

Southern Cotton Production and Concentration of Slavery, 1820 & 1860

By 1860, which states have the densest concentration of cotton production? Where are the most slaves? How do you explain any differences? How do you explain the large numbers of slaves still in Virginia and South Carolina? Can you identify (and circle) the "Black Belt"?

Purchase, into Louisiana, Arkansas, and eastern Texas. This expansion and growth brought the South into a global economy of trade.

For several centuries, British, Dutch, French, and Spanish merchants had been developing a worldwide system of trade, exchanging European manufactured goods for gold and silver from Latin America; silk, spices, and tea from China and India; and tobacco, coffee, sugar, and lumber from the Caribbean and

North America. This international web of trade in turn motivated further technological developments, speeding the coming of the Industrial Revolution.

Starting in England in the late eighteenth century, the industrial factory system, made possible by an agricultural revolution providing surplus food and labor to cities, gradually replaced "putting out" various textile production tasks to cottages. Inventions of the spinning jenny, the flying shuttle, and the steam engine, which mechanized textile manufacturing, put textile production under one roof. At the same time, European working classes were demanding inexpensive, lightweight clothing to replace heavy linen and woolen clothes. As British textile manufacturers sought to supply this demand, they eagerly bought all the cotton they could from the American South. Compared to the importation of only 22 million pounds of cotton in the pre–cotton gin year of 1787, by 1840, England imported 366 million pounds! To meet this huge demand, southern farmers rushed westward to the fresh, fertile lands of the Gulf states. Large-plantation owners, who alone could afford to purchase the gins, slaves, and vast lands needed to grow cotton, spread the plantation system southwestward. Despite the abolition of slavery in the North and some talk of emancipation in the South, slavery became more deeply entrenched in southern life. Thoughts of ending slavery were dispelled by one word: cotton.

Although more acreage was planted in corn, cotton was the largest cash crop and for that reason was called "king." In 1820, the South became the world's largest producer of cotton, and from 1815 to 1860 cotton represented more than half of all American exports. Cotton spurred economic growth not only in England but also throughout the United States. New England textile mills bought it, northern merchants profitably shipped, insured, and marketed it, and northern bankers acquired capital from cotton sales. The supply of American cotton to Sheffield and Leeds in England, Brussels, and other European cities, as well as to Lowell and Lawrence, Massachusetts, grew at an astonishing rate. Cotton production soared from 461,000 bales in 1817 to 4.8 million bales in 1860, a more than tenfold jump.

Slavery in Latin America

Europeans depended on the slave-based economy in Latin America as well as in the American South. Africans were enslaved not only in Virginia and the Carolinas but also in Jamaica, Barbados, and Cuba in the West Indies, in Spanish Mexico and Central America, and throughout South America, including Portuguese Brazil, which at 1 million in 1800 had the largest slave population in all the Americas.

Slavery emerged in Latin America out of economic necessity to provide labor where the indigenous population of Indians, decimated by both disease and intermarriage, could not be replaced. Sugar was to Latin America as cotton was to the southern United States, doubling in output at the beginning of the nineteenth century to meet growing European demands. In the Caribbean islands and in the Bahia region of Brazil, slaves were indispensable to the sugarcane industry, providing refined sugar for a growing global market

that included rum and other liquor distilleries. By 1840, Cuba was the world's largest producer of cane sugar.

Enslaved Africans also worked in Peruvian and Chilean vineyards and in cacao, coca, cotton, and tobacco fields throughout Latin America. They toiled in Mexican, Colombian, Peruvian, Venezuelan, and Brazilian gold, silver, and copper mines; as cowboys, tradesmen, dockworkers, and muleteers; and as servants to royal and religious officials. Women were generally expected to perform the same physical labor as men.

Working conditions in Bolivian mines or Brazilian sugar fields were as harsh as in American cotton fields, and perhaps even worse. Slaves labored in gangs yet were held accountable as individuals. As market demands for sugar increased in the nineteenth century, sugar growers pressured slaves to increase their productivity, which rose from 1,500 to 2,500 pounds per year. Since slaves had to produce sugar valued at more than the price of their purchase, they were literally worked to debilitation and death, the average working life in the fields falling from 15 to 7 years and the death rate increasing from 6 to 10 percent. Whippings were used to enforce obedience. Strict supervision and control were maintained to prevent Africans from mixing with Indians and Europeans and from fleeing to communities of escaped slaves in nearby jungles, called maroons.

Perhaps the most distinctive aspect of Latin American slavery was the heavy preponderance of enslaved African men and the absence of women and families compared to the United States. By the nineteenth century, the gender ratio was three men to every two women, with a 2:1 ratio on the sugar estates of Brazil and Cuba; as late as 1875, only one in six Brazilian slaves was recorded as married. The death rate in Latin America was appalling, the result of hard work, tropical epidemic diseases, malnutrition, and an extremely high infant-mortality rate. With low birthrates and lower life expectancy (age 23 in Brazil, 35 in the United States), the slave population in Latin America actually dropped in the nineteenth century. While Brazil's slave population only climbed to 1,510,000, the United States' numbers reached over 4 million by 1860.

Unlike in the United States, where natural births increased the slave population, Latin Americans used the African slave trade to replenish lost labor. Between 1810 and 1870, after the 1807 abolition of the slave trade by Great Britain and the United States, nearly 2 million Africans were taken to the Americas, 60 percent to Brazil and 32 percent to Cuba and Puerto Rico, as compared to 2.7 percent smuggled illegally to the American South. The last American countries to abolish slavery were Cuba (1880) and Brazil (1888). Although slow to abolish slavery officially, intermarriages among Europeans, Indians, and Africans in Latin America led to an increase in the population of free people of color, who by mid-century vastly outnumbered slaves (80 percent in Brazil)—strikingly different from the United States, where free blacks comprised only 12 percent.

Latin American slaves obtained their freedom by various means: through racial intermarriage, as payment for special favors and other contracts, in wills upon a master's death, and by purchasing their own freedom by extra work and hiring out. Relative autonomy and incentives such as presents, privileges, extra rations, holidays, and their own gardens to supplement diet deficiencies were given to many Latin American slaves. One slaveholder manual said, "the slave who owns neither flees nor causes disorder." Thus, although conditions in Latin America were often even harsher than in the American South, rights of slaves were more fluid, shifting with changing economic and demographic conditions.

White and Black Migrations in the South

Conditions changed in the United States, too. Seeking profits from the British and from the worldwide demand for cotton, southerners migrated southwestward between 1830 and 1860, pushing the southeastern Indians and Mexicans in Texas out of the way. Like northern grain farmers, southern farmers followed parallel migration paths westward. By the 1830s, the center of cotton production had shifted from the Carolinas and Georgia to Alabama and Mississippi. This process continued in the 1850s as southerners forged into Arkansas, Louisiana, and eastern Texas. Usually, a father and his sons would go first, find land and clear it, plant some corn and cotton, and build a cabin, before returning east to pack up the household and bring wife and daughters to the new home.

Not only were these migrating southern families pulled by the prospect of fresh land and cheap labor, but they were also pushed westward by deteriorating economic conditions. A long depression in the Upper South beginning in the 1820s affected tobacco and cotton prices, as years of constant use had exhausted formerly fertile lands. In a society that valued land ownership, farm families had several choices. One was to move west; another was to stay and diversify. Farmers of the Upper South therefore shifted to grains, mainly corn and wheat, which required less slave labor, and to selling slaves.

The internal slave trade from the Upper South "down the river" to the Old Southwest became a multimillion-dollar "industry." Between 1830 and 1860, an estimated 300,000 Virginia slaves were

A Slave Coffle

This engraving of a group of slaves in chains depicts the stark inhumanity of the slave trade. Note the white man (in the right corner) raising the whip to hurry the slaves along. In front of him are a woman and child, and another woman stares at him in moral disbelief. What is your response to this engraving?

(Library of Congress)

transported south for sale. One of the busiest routes was from Alexandria, Virginia, almost within view of the nation's capital, to a huge depot near the large, rich plantations of Natchez, Mississippi. Although most southern states occasionally attempted to control the traffic in slaves, these efforts were poorly enforced. Besides, the reason for outlawing the slave trade was generally not humanitarian, but rather reflected fear of a rapid increase in the slave population. Deep South states banned the importation of slaves after the Nat Turner revolt in Virginia in 1831, resuming only in the profitable 1850s.

Congress formally ended external slave imports on January 1, 1808, the earliest date permitted by the Constitution and the same year that Great Britain ended its slave trade. Enforcement by the United States was weak, and Africans continued to be smuggled to North America until the end of the Civil War. The increase in the slave population was not the result of this illegal trade, however, but of natural reproduction, often encouraged by slave owners eager for more human property and higher profits.

Southern Dependence on Slavery

The increase in the number of slaves, from 1.5 million in 1820 to 4 million in 1860, marked southern economic growth and its dependence on both cotton and slavery. A Tennessee senator said that slavery was "sacred," the basis of civilization, and an English traveler noted that it would be easier to attack popery in Rome or Islam in Constantinople than slavery in the American South.

Although most slaves worked on plantations and medium-sized farms, they were found in all segments of the southern economy. In 1850, some 75 percent of all slaves were engaged in agricultural labor: 55 percent growing cotton, 10 percent tobacco, and 10 percent rice, sugar, and hemp. Of the remaining one-fourth, about 15 percent were domestic servants, while others worked in mining, lumbering, construction, dock and steamship labor, and iron and tobacco factories.

The Tredegar Iron Company of Richmond, which manufactured boilers and steam engines, axes and saws, and cannon and shot, decided in 1847 to shift from white labor "almost exclusively" to slave laborers, who were cheaper and not likely to organize. This strategy foreshadowed the many future companies that exploited black labor while putting an economic squeeze on organized white workers who, along with southern white artisans, were threatened by black slave competition.

Whether in factories, mines, or cotton fields, slavery was profitable as a source of labor and capital investment. The "crop value per slave" increased from about $15 in 1800 to $125 in 1860. In 1859, the average plantation slave produced $78 in cotton earnings for his master annually while costing only about $32 to be fed, clothed, and housed. Enslaved women were likely to bear from two to six children, increasing their value. Slaves were therefore a good investment. In 1844, a "prime field hand" sold for $600. A cotton boom beginning in 1849 raised this price to $1,800 by 1860. A slave owner could prosper by buying slaves, working them for several years, and selling them for a profit.

The economic growth of the South was impressive, but the dependence on a cotton and slave economy was limiting. Generally, agricultural growth spurs the rise of cities and industry, but not in the Old South. In 1860, the South had 35 percent of the U.S. population but only 15 percent of its manufacturing. Just before the Civil War, one southerner in 14 was a city dweller, compared with one of every three northerners.

Some southerners were aware of the dangers of the single focus on cotton. De Bow's *Review,* an important journal published in New Orleans, called for more economic independence in the South through agricultural diversification, industrialization, and an improved transportation system. De Bow urged using slave labor in factories. But the planter class disagreed. As long as money could be made through an agricultural slave system that also valued honor and regulated race and gender relationships, plantation owners saw no reason to risk capital in new ventures.

Paternalism and Honor in the Planter Class

The aversion to industrialism in the South stemmed from the fact that most southerners, inheriting traditions of medieval chivalry, Protestantism, and their Celtic Scots–Irish cultural heritage, espoused a lifestyle of refined paternalism based on a rigid sense of social-class hierarchy and obligations. Wealthy planters, emulating the aristocratic English landowning class, claimed a privileged status as social "betters" and insisted on being treated with deference by those below them. This was especially important for those living in elegant mansions in isolated areas surrounded by black slaves and envious poor whites, circumstances that led to a violent undercurrent throughout the South.

The head of the plantation had to care for his "inferiors," much like a kindly father. This meant providing the necessities of life to slaves (and white overseers) and expecting faithful obedience, loyalty, and hard work in return. The plantation wife was an essential part of this culture. Placed on a pedestal and expected to uphold genteel values of sexual purity, spiritual piety, and submissive patience, she managed the household and extended gracious hospitality to social equals. She also had to put up with a double sexual standard and the hyper-masculinity of plantation life, which made it all the more important that she reflect ladylike virtues and be fiercely protected.

This masculine code, which valued activities such as politics, war, hunting, and gambling, carried with it a rigid code of honor. Southern men enjoyed leisure activities of the hunt, cards, cockfighting, and horse racing. They were sensitive to lapses of appropriate, chivalrous behavior and to insults to their honor. Such slights led to duels, regulated by strict rules. One southern visitor said that the "smallest breach of courtesy" was "sufficient grounds for a challenge." Although duels were eventually outlawed in most states, the laws were routinely ignored.

Slavery, Class, and Yeoman Farmers

Slavery clearly served social as well as economic purposes. Although the proportion of southern white families that owned slaves slowly declined from 40 to 25 percent, the ideal of slave ownership permeated all classes and determined southern society's patriarchal and hierarchical character. At the top stood the paternalistic planter aristocracy, much of it new wealth, elbowing its way among old established families like the Byrds and Carters of Virginia. Some 10,000

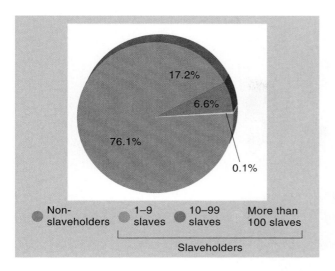

White Class Structure in the South, 1860

In a pyramidal class structure, the richest southerners were those few with the largest number of slaves. As the chart shows, three-fourths of antebellum southerners held no slaves at all. Why did each socioeconomic class support slavery?

families owned 50 or more slaves in 1860; about 3,000 of these owned over 100. A slightly larger group of small planters held from 10 to 50 slaves. But the largest group, 70 percent of all slaveholders in 1860, comprised 270,000 middle-level, yeoman farm families with fewer than 10 slaves. The typical slaveholder worked a small family farm of about 100 acres with fewer than 10 slaves. The typical slave, however, was more likely to be one of 20 or more on a large farm or small plantation.

William Airs, a South Carolina low-country farmer, owned nine slaves and worked 130 acres of cotton in 1850. A decade later, with one more slave, he bought more land and produced 54 bushels of rice in addition to cotton. In 1841, a young, landless North Carolinian, John Flintoff, dreamed of wealth and prestige as a planter. Beginning as an overseer managing an uncle's farm, he bought a "negro boy 7 years old," and after several years of struggle, he was able to buy 124 acres and a few more blacks. By 1860, he had a modest farm with several slaves growing corn, wheat, and tobacco. Although Flintoff never realized his grandest dreams, his son went to college, and his wife, he reported proudly, "has lived a Lady." Economic, social, and political standing for middle-level farmers like Airs and Flintoff depended on owning slaves.

Middling white southerners supported slavery not only for economic reasons but also because it gave them feelings of superiority over blacks and of kinship, if not quite equality, with other whites. Although a few white southerners believed in emancipation, most did not. An Alabama farmer told a

northern visitor in the 1850s that if the slaves got their freedom, "they'd all think themselves just as good as we.... How would you like to hev a nigger feelin' just as good as a white man?"

Yeoman farmers also stoutly defended their way of life as "self-working farmers" with "households of faith." Their land and household was indispensably important to their livelihood, self-esteem, and political rights in a region dominated by the privileged elite. Fiercely proud of their independence and jealously protective of their modest properties, the yeoman farmers struggled for a share of political power against the planters and stoutly defended states' rights. They believed in an evangelical Christianity that endorsed the divine sanctity of both the male-headed family and of slavery. Acknowledging spiritual equality (slaves, one woman said, may have "souls as well as white people"), they practiced a small measure of equality in their daily lives working alongside their slaves in the fields.

The Nonslaveholding South

Below Airs, Flintoff, and other yeoman farmers lived the majority of white southerners who owned no slaves at all. Some 30 to 50 percent were landless, and of those who owned land, 60–70 percent had less than 100 acres. This nonslaveholding class, 75 percent of all southerners, was scattered throughout the South. Newton Knight, for example, worked a harsh piece of land cut out of the pines of southern Mississippi. He and his wife lived in a crude log cabin, scratching out their livelihood by growing corn and sweet potatoes and raising chickens and hogs. A staunch Baptist given to fits of violence, Knight had once killed a black.

Living throughout the South but especially upcountry in the Appalachian highlands, whites like Knight worked poorer lands than yeomen and planters. Far from commercial centers, they were largely self-sufficient, raising almost all their food and trading hogs, eggs, small game, or homemade items for cash and necessary manufactured items such as kettles and rifles. With the indispensable help of their wives and children, they maintained a subsistence household economy, making soap, shoes, candles, whiskey, coarse textiles, and ax handles. Their drab, isolated life in two-room log cabins was brightened when neighbors and families gathered at corn huskings and quilting parties, logrolling and wrestling matches, and political stump and revivalist Baptist or Methodist camp meetings.

Despite numerical majorities, these farmers were politically marginalized. Resenting the tradition of political deference to "betters," they were unable to challenge planters for political power. Most fought with the Confederacy during the Civil War; a few silently harbored Unionist views.

The Life of Yeoman Farm Families

What do the pictures tell you about the daily lives of women and men in southern non-plantation rural cultures? How self-sufficient do they seem to be? How isolated are they? What social purposes did the quilting party fulfill (other than revealing a uniquely female American form of useful art)? Note that men were also at the party, talking (politics, perhaps) by the stove, bouncing a baby, carrying food, and courting a young woman by the quilt.

(Above: Abby Aldrich Rockefeller Folk Art Museum, Willamsburg, VA; Right: North Wind Picture Archives)

Other nonslaveholders were herdsmen raising hogs and other livestock, fed on corn or allowed to roam in the woods. These whites supplied bacon and pork to local slaveholders (who thought hog growing beneath their dignity) and drove herds to stockyards in Nashville, Louisville, and Savannah. The South raised two-thirds of the nation's hogs. In 1860, the value of southern livestock was $500 million, twice that of cotton. Even so, hog herdsmen were low on the southern social ladder.

Below them were the poorest whites of the South, about 10 percent of the population. Often sneeringly called "dirt eaters" and "crackers," they eked out a living in isolated, inhospitable areas growing vegetables, hunting small game, and raising a few pigs. Some made corn whiskey, and many hired out as farmhands for an average wage of $14 per month. Because of poor diet and bad living conditions, these poor whites often suffered from hookworm and malaria. This, along with the natural debilitation of heat and poverty, gave them a reputation as lazy, shiftless, and illiterate. An English visitor described them as "the most degraded race of human beings claiming an Anglo-Saxon origin that can be found on the face of the earth."

Poor whites stayed poor partly because the slave system allowed the planter class to accumulate a disproportionate amount of land and political power. Entry into the planter class was difficult, raising class

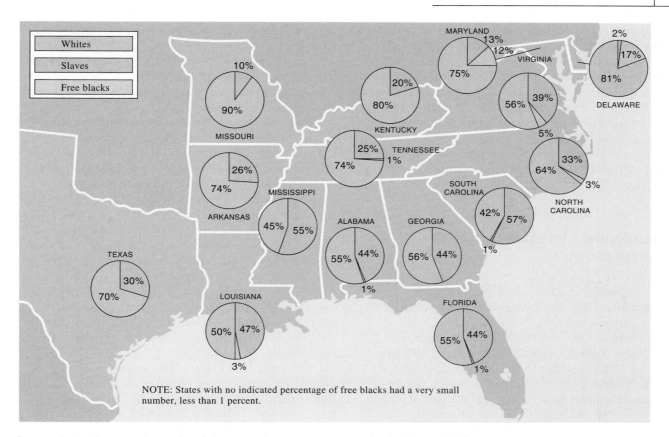

Population Patterns in the South: White, Slaves, and Free Blacks, by State, 1860

Where were most free blacks, and how would you explain their location? How do you explain the tiny percentage of free blacks in South Carolina, Florida, and Louisiana? Which two states had the largest percentage of slaves, and how do you think that affected the regulation of race relations? Given the data on this map, where would you predict the strongest sentiments among whites for states' rights and secession from the Union? Why?

tensions. Because large planters dominated southern life and owned the most slaves, slavery and the relations between slaves and masters is best understood by looking at plantation life during a typical day from morning to night.

Morning: Master and Mistress in the Big House

It is early morning in the South. Imagine four scenes. In the first, William Waller of Virginia is preparing to leave with 20 choice slaves on a long trip to the slave market in Natchez, Mississippi. Waller is making this "intolerable" journey to sell some of his slaves in order to ease his heavy debts. Although he "loaths the vocation of slave trading," he must recover some money to see his family "freed" from his "bondage" of indebtedness. To ease his conscience, he intends to supervise the sale personally, thus securing the best possible deal not only for himself but also for his departing slaves.

On another plantation, owned by the wealthy James Hammond of South Carolina, the horn blows an hour before daylight to awaken slaves for field work. Hammond rises soon after, aware that to run an efficient plantation he must "draw the rein tighter and tighter" to hold his slaves "in complete check." In general, he says, "15 to 20 lashes will be sufficient flogging" for most offenses, but "in extreme cases" the punishment "must not exceed 100 lashes in one day."

On an Alabama plantation, Hugh Lawson is up early, writing a sorrowful letter telling about the death of a "devotedly attached and faithful" slave, Jim. "I feel desolate," Hugh writes, "my most devoted friend is gone." As Lawson pens his letter, a female slave, already awake, "walked across a frosty field in the early morning" to the big house to build a fire for her mistress. As the mistress wakes up, she says to the slave, a grown woman taking care of two families, "Well, how's my little nigger today?"

In a fourth household, a middling farm in upcountry Georgia, Charles Brock awakens at dawn to join his two sons and four slaves digging up stumps and plowing fields of grains and sweet potatoes, while Brock's wife and a female slave tend the cows.

As these diverse scenes suggest, slavery thoroughly permeated the lives of southern slaveholders. For slaves, morning was a time for getting up early for work. But for white slaveholders, morning involved contact with slaves in many ways: as burdens of figuring profit and loss, as objects to be kept obedient and orderly, as intimates and fellow workers, and as ever-present reminders of fear, hate, and uncertainty.

The Burdens of Slaveholding and the Plantation Mistress

Robert Francis Withers Allston (1801–1864) was a major rice planter in a low, swampy, mosquito-infested tidal area of South Carolina. It was a perfect spot for growing rice, but so unhealthy that few whites wanted to live there. The death rate among slaves was appallingly high. Robert was the fifth generation of Allstons to live in this inhospitable land. By 1860, he owned seven plantations along the Peedee River, totaling some 4,000 acres, and another 9,500 acres of pasture and timberland. He held nearly 600 slaves, 236 of whom worked at the home plantation, Chicora Wood. Although the total value of Allston's land and slaves was approximately $300,000, he had large mortgages and debts.

Allston was an enlightened, talented, public-spirited man. Educated at West Point and trained for the law, he both practiced agriculture and served South Carolina many years as state senator and governor. His political creed of "virtue and purity," he wrote in 1838, was based on "the principles of Thomas Jefferson." The core of his conviction was a "plain, honest, commonsense reading of the Constitution," which for Allston meant the constitutionality of slavery and the illegitimacy of abolitionism and the United States Bank. Allston also reflected Jefferson's humane side. Active in the Episcopal Church, he advocated the liberalization of South Carolina's poor laws; an improved system of public education open to rich and poor; humanitarian care of disabled people; and the improvement of conditions for the Catawba Indians.

In 1832, Allston married Adele Petigru. Although Adele was equally enlightened, she fully participated in the management of the plantation, especially when Robert was away on political business. In a letter to her husband in 1850, Adele demonstrated her diverse interests by reporting on family affairs and the children's learning, sickness among the slaves, the status of spring plowing, the building of a canal and causeway, the bottling of wine, and current politics. After Robert's death during the Civil War, she would assume control of the Allston plantations. Except during the worst periods of mosquitoes and heat, both Allstons were fully engaged in plantation operations, managing thousands of slaves and acres of rice. Although growing rice rather than cotton, the Allstons were typical of large planters.

Robert's letters frequently expressed the burdens—and ironies—of owning slaves. Although careful to distribute enough cloth, blankets, and shoes to his slaves and to give them rest, the sickness and death of slaves, especially young fieldworkers, headed his list of concerns. "I lost in one year 28 negroes," he complained. He tried to keep slave families together, but sold slaves when necessary. In a letter to his son Benjamin, he expressed concern over the bad example set by a slave driver who was "abandon'd by his hands" because he had not worked with them the previous Sunday. Allston also urged Benjamin to keep up the "patrol duty," both to guard against runaway slaves and to restrain "vagabond whites," thus showing the planter class's need to control lower-class whites as well as black slaves.

Other planters likewise saw slavery as both a duty and a burden. Many insisted that they worked harder than their slaves to feed and clothe them. R. L. Dabney of Virginia exclaimed, "there could be no greater curse inflicted on us than to be compelled to manage a parcel of Negroes." Curse or not, Dabney and other planters profited from their burdens, a point they seldom admitted.

Plantation wives experienced other kinds of burdens. "The mistress of a plantation," wrote one, "was the most complete slave on it." Another complained, "It is the slaves who own me. Morning, noon, and night, I'm obliged to look after them," burdens that Adele Allston would have understood. In accord with the southern code of honor, plantation mistresses were expected to tame their husbands' excess cruelty and beautify their parlors. They also suffered under a double standard of morality. Expected themselves to act as chaste ladies, their husbands had nearly unrestricted sexual access to slave women. "God forgive us, but ours is a monstrous system," Mary Boykin Chesnut wrote in her diary. "Any lady is ready to tell you who is the father of all the mulatto children in everybody's household but her own. Those, she seems to think, drop from the clouds." But plantation wives had their own double standard: a former slave woman said of her mistress, "though a warm-hearted woman, [she] was a violent advocate of slavery. I have...puzzled how to reconcile this with her otherwise Christian character."

Chesnut called the sexual dynamics of slavery "the sorest spot." There were others. Together with female slaves, plantation mistresses had to tend to the food, clothing, health, and welfare of not just their husbands and children, but the slaves, too. A Tennessee planter's son remembered his mother and grandmother as "the busiest women I ever saw." The plantation mistress, then, served many roles: as a potential humanizing influence on men; as a tough, resourceful, responsible manager of numerous plantation affairs; as a perpetuator of the system; and sometimes as a victim herself.

Justifying Slavery

The behavior of Douglass's mistress discussed at the beginning of this chapter suggests that slavery led otherwise good people to act inhumanely. Increasingly attacked as immoral, slaveholders felt compelled to justify the institution, not only to opponents of the system, but perhaps also to themselves. Until the 1830s, they explained away slavery as a "necessary evil." But after abolitionist attacks in that decade, they shifted to justifying slavery in five arguments as "a positive good."

A biblical justification was based on the curse that had fallen on the son of Ham, one of Noah's children, and on Old and New Testament admonitions to servants to obey their masters. In a historical justification, southerners claimed that slavery had always existed and all the great ancient civilizations—Egypt, Greece, Rome—were built on it. A leading southern magazine, De Bow's *Review,* said in 1851 that "civilization itself...depend[s] upon the continued servitude of blacks in America."

The legal justification rested on the U.S. Constitution's refusal to forbid slavery and on three passages clearly implying its legality: the "three-fifths" clause, the protection of the overseas slave trade for 20 years, and the mandate for returning fugitive slaves.

A fourth justification for slavery was pseudo-scientific. Until the 1830s, most white southerners believed that blacks were degraded not by nature but by African climate and their slave condition. With the rise of the "positive good" defense, however, southerners began to argue that blacks had been created separately as an inherently inferior race, and therefore the destiny of the inferior Africans was to work for the superior Caucasians. At best, the slave system would domesticate "uncivilized" blacks. As Allston put it, "The educated master is the negro's best friend upon earth."

A sociological defense of slavery was implicit in Allston's paternalistic statement. George Fitzhugh, a leading advocate of this view, argued, "the Negro is but a grown child and must be governed as a child," and so needed the paternal guidance, restraint, and protection of a white master. Many southerners would have agreed with Allston's claim that emancipation was unthinkable because it would lead to "giving up our beautiful country to the ravages of the black race and amalgamation with savages." Fitzhugh compared the treatment of southern slaves favorably with that of free laborers working in northern factories. These "wage slaves," he argued, worked as hard as slaves, yet with their paltry wages they had to feed, clothe, and shelter themselves. Since southern masters took care of these necessities, freeing slaves would be a heartless burden to both blacks and whites.

Southern apologists for slavery faced the difficult intellectual task of justifying a system that ran against the main ideological directions of nineteenth-century American society: the expansion of individual liberty, mobility, economic opportunity, and democratic political participation. The southern defense of slavery had also to take into account the 75 percent of white families who owned no slaves but envied those who did. To deflect potential for class antagonisms among whites, wealthy planters developed a justification of slavery that emphasized white superiority regardless of class.

The underlying but rarely admitted motive behind all these justifications was that slavery was profitable, as it was in Latin America. As the southern defense of slavery intensified in the 1840s and 1850s, it aroused greater opposition from northerners and from slaves themselves. Perhaps slavery's worst cruelty was not physical but psychological: to be enslaved and barred from participation in a nation that espoused freedom and equality of opportunity.

Noon: Slaves in House and Fields

It is two o'clock on a hot July afternoon on the plantation. The midday lunch break is over, and the slaves are returning to work in the fields. Lunch was the usual cornmeal and pork. The slaves now work listlessly, their low stamina resulting from a deficient diet and suffocating heat and humidity. Douglass remembered that "we worked all weathers....It was never too hot, or too cold." Mary Reynolds, a Louisiana slave, recalled that she hated most having to pick cotton "when the frost was on the bolls," which made her hands "git sore and crack open and bleed."

Daily Toil

The daily work schedule for most slaves, whether in the fields or the "Big House," was long and demanding. Awakened before daybreak, they worked on an average day 14 hours in the summer and 10 hours in the winter; during harvest, an 18-hour workday was not uncommon. Depending on the size of the workforce and the crop, the slaves were organized either in gangs or according to tasks. Gangs, usually of 20 to 25, worked the cotton rows under the watchful eye and quick whip of a driver. Ben Simpson, a Georgia slave, remembered vividly his master's "great, long whip platted out of rawhide" that struck any slave who would "fall behind or give out."

Under the task system, which slaves preferred and negotiated for cleverly, each slave had a specific task to complete daily. It gave slaves incentive to work hard enough to finish early, but their work was scrutinized constantly. An overseer's weekly report to Robert Allston in 1860 noted that he had "flogged for hoeing corn bad Fanny 12 lashes, Sylvia 12, Monday 12, Phoebee 12, Susanna 12, Salina 12, Celia 12, Iris 12." Black slave drivers were no less demanding. One reported to his master, "I gave Julyann eight or ten licks for misplacing her hoe."

An average slave was expected to pick 130 to 150 pounds of cotton per day; work on sugar and rice plantations was even harder. Sugar demanded constant cultivation, digging ditches in snake-infested fields. At harvest time, cutting, stripping, and carrying the cane to the sugar house for boiling was exhausting, as was cutting and hauling huge quantities of firewood. Working in the low-country rice fields was worse: slaves spent long hours standing in water up to their knees.

House slaves, mostly women, had relatively easier assignments, though they were usually called on to help with the harvest. Their usual work was in or near the Big House as maids, cooks, seamstresses, laundresses, coachmen, drivers, gardeners, and "mammies." Slaves did most of the skilled artisan work on the plantation as carpenters, stonemasons, blacksmiths, weavers, and millers. House slaves ate and dressed better than those in the fields. But there were disadvantages: close supervision, duty day and night, and conflicts with whites that could range from being given unpleasant jobs to insults, spontaneous angry whippings, and sexual assault. The most feared punishment, however, other than sale to the Deep South, was to be sent to the fields.

Slave Health and Punishments

Although slave owners had an interest in keeping their workforce healthy, slaves led sickly lives. Home was a crude, one-room log cabin with a dirt floor and a fireplace. Cracks and holes allowed mosquitoes easy entry, disturbing sleep. Typical furnishings included a table, some stools or boxes to sit on, an iron pot and wooden dishes, and perhaps a bed. Cabins were crowded, usually housing more than one family. Clothing, issued once or twice a year, was shabby and uncomfortable.

Studies on the adequacy of slave diet disagree. But compared with Latin American slaves, North American slaves were fed relatively well. Once a week, each slave got an average ration of a peck of cornmeal, three to four pounds of salt pork or bacon, some molasses, and perhaps some sweet potatoes. The mainstay was corn. While a few slaves were able to grow vegetables and to fish or hunt, most rarely enjoyed fresh meat, dairy products, fruits, or vegetables. The limitations of their diet led to theft of food and the practice of eating dirt, which caused worms. Deficient slave diet also resulted in skin disorders, cracked lips, sore eyes, vitamin deficiency diseases, and even mental illness.

Enslaved women especially suffered weaknesses caused by vitamin deficiency, hard work, and disease, as well as those associated with childbirth. Women were expected to do the same tasks in the fields as the men, in addition to cooking, sewing, child care, and traditional female jobs in the quarters when the fieldwork was finished. "Pregnant women," the usual rule stated, "should not plough or lift" and had a three-week recovery period following birth. But these guidelines were often violated. Mortality of slave children under age 5 was twice as high as for white children.

Life expectancy for North American slaves in 1850 was 21.4 years as compared to 25.5 for whites. In part because of poor diet and the climate, slaves were highly susceptible to epidemics. Despite some resistance as a result of the sickle-cell trait, many slaves died from malaria, yellow fever, cholera, and other diseases spread by mosquitoes or bad water. Slaves everywhere suffered and died from intestinal ailments in the summer and respiratory diseases in the winter. An average of 20 percent (and sometimes more than 50 percent) of the slaves on a given plantation would be sick at one time, and no overseer's report was complete without recording sicknesses and days of lost labor.

The relatively frequent incidence of whippings and other physical punishments aggravated the poor physical condition of the slaves. Many slaveholders offered rewards—a garden plot, an extra holiday, hiring out, and passes—as inducements for faithful labor, and they withheld these privileges as punishment. But southern court records, newspapers, plantation diaries, and slave memoirs reveal that sadistic punishments were frequent and harsh. William Wells Brown reported that on his plantation the whip was used "very frequently and freely" for inadequate or uncompleted work, stealing, running away, and insolence and lying. Another slave described a good owner as one who did not "whip too much" and a bad owner as one who "whipped till he'd bloodied you and blistered you." Whippings ranged from 10 to 100 strokes of the lash. Other punishments included confinement in stocks and jails during leisure hours, chains, muzzling, salting lash wounds, branding, burning, castration, and mauling by dogs.

Nothing testifies better to the physical brutality of slavery than the advertisements for runaways printed in antebellum newspapers. In searching for the best way to describe the physical characteristics of a missing slave, slave owners unwittingly condemned their own behavior. A Mississippi runaway was described as having "large raised scars...in the small of his back and on his abdomen nearly as large as a person's finger." Another fugitive, Betty, was described as recently "burnt...with a hot iron on the left side of her face." "I tried to make the letter M," her master admitted in his diary.

Slave Law and the Family

Complicating master–slave relationships was the status of slaves as both human beings and property, a legal and psychological ambiguity the South never resolved. On the one hand, slaves had names, personalities, families, and wills of their own, making them fellow humans. On the other hand, they were items of property, purchased to perform specific profit-making tasks. A Kentucky court put the problem in 1836, "Although the law of this state considers slaves as property,...it recognizes their personal existence."

This ambiguity led to confusion in the laws governing treatment of slaves. Until the early 1830s, some southern abolitionist activity persisted, primarily in the Upper South, and slaves had slight hopes of being freed. But they also suffered careless, often brutal treatment. This confusion changed with the convergence in 1831 of Nat Turner's revolt and William Lloyd Garrison's attack on slavery in the

Liberator (see Chapter 12). After 1831, the South tightened up the slave system. Laws prohibited manumission, and slaves' hopes of freedom other than by revolt or escape vanished. At the same time, laws protecting them from overly severe treatment were strengthened.

But laws were rarely enforced, and treatment varied with individual slaveholders, depending on their mood and other circumstances. Most planters, like Robert Allston, encouraged their slaves to marry and tried to keep families intact, in part as a way to keep black males more docile and less inclined to run away. But some masters failed to respect slave marriages or broke them up because of financial problems, which was permitted by southern law. As a North Carolina Supreme Court justice said in 1853, "Our law required no solemnity or form in regard to the marriage of slaves."

Adding to the pain of forced breakup of the slave family was the sexual abuse of enslaved women. Although the frequency of such abuse is unknown, the presence of thousands of mulattoes in the antebellum era points to the practice. White men in the South took advantage of slave women by offering gifts for sexual "favors," by threatening those who refused sex with physical punishment or the sale of a child or loved one, by purchasing concubines, and by outright rape. As Frederick Douglass put it, "The slave woman is at the mercy of the fathers, sons or brothers of her master."

To obtain cheap additional slaves for the workforce, slaveholders encouraged young slave women to

The breakup of families and friendships was an ever-present fear for slaves, who could be sold for economic reasons or for uncooperative behavior. Study this painting of a slave market by an unidentified artist, and describe what you see. Note the varied colors and conditions of the African Americans (the light-skinned young woman in the center, the mulatto male in the left foreground staring longingly at her, and the dark-skinned woman clutching her children to the right). Note also the diversity of the whites (the suave merchant reclining in a chair on the porch, nattily attired slave auctioneers and buyers, and the gaudily dressed man cracking the whip over the mother clutching her child). Analyze the painting in terms of race, class, and gender. What conclusions about slavery do you draw from this one complex image?

(*Slave Market*, ca. 1850–1860, Carnegie Museum of Art, Pittsburgh; Gift of Mrs. W. Fitch Ingersoll)

bear children, whether married or not. If verbal prodding and inducements such as less work and more rations did not work, masters would force mates on slave women. "Massa" Hawkins, for example, chose Rufus to live with an unwilling 16-year-old Rose Williams. Years later, she recalled how she first repulsed him: "I puts de feet 'gainst him and give him a shove and out he go on de floor." When Rufus persisted, Rose took a poker and "lets him have it over de head." Hawkins then threatened Rose with a "whippin' at de stake" or sale away "from my folks." This was too much for her. "What am I's to do? So I 'cides to do as de massa wish and so I yields."

Slaves, however, usually chose their own mates on the basis of mutual attraction during a courtship complicated by threats of white interference. As among poor whites, premarital intercourse was frequent, but promiscuous behavior was rare. Most couples maintained affectionate, lasting relationships. This, too, led to numerous sorrows. Members of slave families, powerless to intervene, had to witness the flogging or physical abuse of loved ones. William Wells Brown remembered that "cold chills ran over me and I wept aloud" when he saw his mother whipped. For this reason, some slaves preferred to marry a spouse from another plantation.

Although motherhood was the key event in an enslaved woman's life, bearing children and the double burden of work and family responsibilities challenged her resourcefulness. Some masters provided time off for nursing mothers, but the more common practice was for them to work in the fields with their newborn infants lying nearby, wrapped in cloth for protection from the sun. Women developed support networks, looking after one another's children; meeting to sew, quilt, cook, or do laundry; and attending births, caring for the sick and dying, and praying together.

The worst trauma for slaves was the separation of families, a haunting fear rarely absent from slave consciousness. Although many slaveholders had both moral and economic reasons to maintain families, inevitably they found themselves destroying them. One study of 30 years of data from the Deep South shows that masters dissolved one-third of all slave marriages. Even then, the slaves tried to maintain contact with loved ones sold elsewhere. "My Dear Wife for you and my Children my pen cannot Express the Griffe I feel to be parted from you all," wrote Abream Scriven.

There was a sound basis, in fact, for the abolitionists' contention that slavery was a harsh, brutal system. However, two points need to be emphasized. First, although slavery led otherwise decent human beings to commit inhumane acts, many slaveholders throughout the South were not cruel; they did what they could for their slaves, out of both economic self-

Announcement of a slave sale in Charleston, 1860. What do you learn about the economics and morality of slavery from this poster?

(Five Slave Narratives: A Compendium)

interest and Christian morality. Second, whether under kind or cruel masters, the slaves endured with personal dignity, occasional joy, and communal strength. If daytime in the fields describes slavery at its worst, nighttime in the quarters, as examined from the black perspective, reveals noble survival powers and the capacity to mold an African American community culture even under slavery.

Night: Slaves in Their Quarters

It is near sundown, and the workday is almost over. Some slaves begin singing the gentle spiritual "Steal Away to Jesus," and others join in. To the unwary overseer or master, the song suggests happy slaves, looking forward to heaven. To the blacks, however, the song is a signal that, as ex-slave Wash Wilson put it, they are to "steal away to Jesus" because "dere gwine be a 'ligious meetin' dat night." At night, away from whites and daily work, Wilson said, "sometimes us sing and pray all night."

In the quarters, slaves preserved much of their African heritage and created an elaborate black community that helped them make sense out of and cope with their lives. In family life, religion, song, dance, the playing of musical instruments, and the telling of stories, the slaves both sought release from suffering and created a vibrant community and culture.

Black Christianity

As suggested by the scene Wash Wilson described, Christian worship, mixed with elements of Islamic and African religious practices, was an essential part of life in the slave quarters. The revivals of the early nineteenth century led to an enormous growth of Christianity among black Americans. Although black religious gatherings were usually forbidden unless white observers were present or white preachers led them, black Baptist and Methodist religious services grew among slaves and free blacks alike. Black preachers in independent churches and in "hush arbors" behind the slave quarters steered a careful path to maintain their freedom and avoid white interference.

The vast majority of southern black slaves attended plantation churches set up by their masters. Robert Allston built a prayer house for his slaves, reporting with pride that they were "attentive... and greatly improved in intelligence and morals." For the slaveholders, religion was a form of social control. Churches were rigidly segregated with blacks sitting in the back or in roped off sections. Sermons emphasized the importance of work, obedience, and respect for the master's property. "All that preacher talked about," one slave remembered, "was for us slaves to obey our master and not to lie and steal."

There were limits, however, to white control. Although some slaves accommodated to the master's brand of Christianity and patiently waited for heavenly deliverance, others rebelled and sought earthly liberty. Not far from Allston's plantation, several slaves were discovered (and imprisoned) for singing "We'll soon be free / We'll fight for liberty / When de Lord will call us home." Douglass organized an illegal Sabbath school, "the sweetest engagement with which I was ever blessed," where he and others risked whippings while learning about Christianity and how to read. In religious schools and meetings like these, the slaves created an "invisible" church. On Sunday morning, they duti-

Describe what you see in this painting by John Antrobus of a slave burial ceremony. Where are they? What time of day? What are they doing? How free do they seem to be, and why do you think so?

(John Antrobus, *A Plantation Burial,* 1860. The Historic New Orleans Collection, accession no. 1960.46)

fully sat through the "white fo'ks service in de morning" while waiting for the "real meetin'" and "real preachin'" later that night.

Long into the night, they would sing, dance, shout, and pray in the call-and-response pattern characteristic of black religion to this day. "Ya' see," Sarah of Alabama explained, "niggers lack ta shout a whole lot an' wid de white fo'ks al'round 'em, dey couldn't shout jes' lack dey want to." But at night they could, taking care to deaden the sound to keep the whites away. African-influenced dance, forbidden by Methodists, was transformed into the "ecstatic shout," praising the Lord. These nightly religious ceremonies relieved the day's burdens and expressed communal religious values when, as a former slave proudly recalled, "the darkies really did have they freedom of spirit."

Although many of the expressive forms were African, the messages reiterated over again in the invisible slave church were the Judeo-Christian themes of suffering and deliverance from bondage. "We prayed a lot to be free," Anderson Edwards said, but the freedom the slaves sought was a complex blend of a peaceful soul and an earthly escape from slavery.

The Power of Song

Spirituals, expressing two moods of grief and praise, were born in these gatherings in the woods behind the slave quarters at night. First, singers mourned with "trebbled spirit" being stolen from Africa, their families "sold apart." But second, they celebrated "a better day a-coming. / Will you go along with me? / There's a better day a-coming. / Go sound the jubilee."

Music was a crucial form of expression on both secular and religious occasions. Slaves were adept at creating a song, as one woman recalled, "on de spurn of de moment." Jeanette Robinson Murphy described a process of spontaneous creation that, whether in rural gospels or urban jazz, describes black music to this day. "We'd all be at the 'prayer house' de Lord's day," she said, when all of a sudden in the midst of a white preacher's sermon, "de Lord would come a-shinin' thoo dem pages and revive dis ole nigger's heart." She continued, "I'd jump up dar and den and holler and shout and sing and pat, and dey would all cotch de words and I'd sing it to some ole shout song I'd heard 'em sing from Africa, and dey'd all take it up and keep at it, and keep a-addin' to it, and den it would be a spiritual."

Spirituals reiterated one basic Judeo-Christian theme: a chosen people, the children of God, were held in bondage but would be delivered: "To the Promised Land I'm Bound to Go." What they meant by deliverance often had a double meaning: freedom in heaven and freedom in the North. Where, exactly, was the desired destination of "Oh Canaan, sweet Canaan / I am bound for the land of Canaan"? Was it heaven? Freedom "anyplace else but here"? Was it a literal reference to the terminus of the Underground Railroad in Canada? For different slaves, and at different times for the same person, it meant all of these.

Slave songs did not always contain double or hidden meanings. Sometimes slaves gathered simply for music, to play fiddles, drums, and other instruments fashioned on West African models. Slave musicians were invited to perform at white ceremonies and parties, but most played for the slave community. Weddings, funerals, holiday celebrations, family reunions, and a successful harvest were all occasions for a communal gathering, usually with music.

So, too, was news of external events that affected their lives—a crisis in the master's situation, a change in the slave code, a Civil War battle, or emancipation. "The songs of the slave," Douglass wrote, "represent the sorrows of his heart": broken families, burdens of work, trouble, toil, and homelessness. But they also expressed joy, triumph, and deliverance. Each expression of sorrow usually ended in an outburst of eventual liberation and justice. The deep sorrow of "sometimes I feel like a motherless chile" was transformed later in the song into "Gonna spread my wings an' / Fly, fly, fly."

The Enduring Family

Family life was also central to life in the slave quarters. Although sexual abuse and family separation were all too real, so also was the hope for family continuity. Naming practices, for example, show that children were connected to large extended families.

The benefits of family cohesion are universal: love, protection, education, moral guidance, cultural transmission, status, role models, and support. All these existed in the slave quarters, where parents passed on to their children the family story, language patterns and words, recipes, folktales, musical traditions, and models of strength and beauty. Thus they preserved cultural traditions, which enhanced the identity and self-esteem of parents and children alike. Parents also taught their children how to cope with slavery and survive. As young ones neared the age for full-time fieldwork, their parents instructed them in the best ways to pick cotton or corn, how to avoid the overseer's whip, whom to trust and learn from, and ways of fooling the master.

Opportunities existed on many plantations for parents to perform extra work for money to buy sugar or clothing; to hunt and fish, thereby adding protein to their family's diet; or to tend a small garden to grow vegetables. In such small ways, they improved the welfare of their families. J. W. C. Pennington

Recovering the Past

FOLKTALES

A frequent activity of family life in the slave quarters was telling stories. The folktale was an especially useful and indirect way in which older slaves could express defiance toward their masters, impart wisdom and ways of survival to the young, and have a little entertainment. Folktales, cleverly indirect, reveal to historians a great deal about the enslaved Africans' view of their experience and aspirations.

Although the tales took many forms, perhaps the best known are the "Brer [brother] Rabbit" animal stories. The trickster rabbit, who existed originally in West African folklore (and in Brazilian African fables as an Amazonian tortoise), was weak and careless, often looked down on by the other animals. Like the slaves, he seemed a victim. But he was also boastful, outwardly happy, and full of mischief. He knew how to use cleverness and cunning to outwit stronger foes, usually by knowing them better than they knew him, a psychological necessity for all who are oppressed.

In one story, the powerful Brer Tiger took all the water and food for himself during a time of famine, leaving the weaker animals miserable. Brer Rabbit, however, turned things around. He played on Brer Tiger's fears that he would be blown away by a "big wind," which was secretly manufactured by the rabbit with the help of other creatures. The tiger was so afraid of the wind (perhaps the winds of revolt?) that he begged Brer Rabbit to tie him "tightly" to a tree to keep from being blown away. Brer Rabbit, although initially resistant in order to make Brer Tiger beg harder, was finally happy to oblige, after which all the creatures of the forest were able to share the cool water and juicy pears that the tiger had denied them.

In another folktale, Brer Rabbit fell into a well but then got out by tricking Brer Wolf into thinking it was better to be in the cool bottom of the well than outside where it was hot. As the wolf lowered himself down in one bucket, Brer Rabbit rose up in the other, laughingly saying as he passed Brer Wolf, "Dis am life; some go up and some go down." In these stories, the weaker animal usually switched roles with the more powerful adversary.

The accompanying story excerpt is from perhaps the most famous animal tale, "The Wonderful Tar Baby Story," written in 1881 by a southern white writer, Joel Chandler Harris, as told by a fictional old black plantation storyteller, Uncle Remus. In this way Harris sought to "preserve the legends themselves in their original simplicity" and capture the "genuine flavor of the old plantation." Therefore, he used dialect, which is best understood if you read the tale out loud as if you were an Uncle Remus reading to a group of children.

We enter the story as a wily but thwarted Brer Fox has decided on a plan to catch the lazy but happy go lucky Brer Rabbit, who has been stealing cabbages from a local garden, skillfully avoiding Brer Fox.

Reflecting on the Past When you have finished the story, ask yourself what you learned about slavery from it? Why a "tar baby"? Did violence work for Brer Rabbit or did it only make things worse? What finally worked? How do you interpret the ending? Brer Rabbit returned to the briar patch, a place where he was "bred en bawn." Is the briar patch, with all its thorns, scratches, and roots, a symbol of Africa or slavery? Or what?

Think about the stories you heard as a child or now find yourself telling others. How do they express the values and dreams, strengths and flaws of the American people? The same question applies to the songs we sing, the art we make, the rhythms we move to, and the jokes we tell: What do they tell us about ourselves and our values? Answering these questions deepens our knowledge of history.

The Wonderful Tar Baby Story

"Didn't the fox never catch the rabbit, Uncle Remus?" asked the little boy the next evening.

"He come mighty nigh it, honey, sho's you born—Brer Fox did. One day atter Brer Rabbit fool 'im wid dat calamus root, Brer Fox went ter wuk en got 'im some tar, en mix it wid some turkentime, en fix up a contrapshun w'at he call a Tar-Baby, en he tuck dish yer Tar-Baby . . . in de big road, en den he lay off in de bushes fer to see what de news wuz gwine ter be. En he didn't hatter wait long, nudder, kaze bimeby here come Brer Rabbit pacin' down de road—lippity-clippity, clippity-lippity—dez ez sassy ez a jay-bird. Brer Fox, he lay low. Brer Rabbit come prancin' 'long twel he spy de Tar-Baby, en den he fotch up on his behime legs like he wuz 'stonished. De Tar Baby, she sot dar, she did, en Brer Fox, he lay low.

"'Mawnin'!' sez Brer Rabbit, sezee—'nice wedder dis mawnin',' sezee.

"Tar-Baby ain't sayin' nuthin', en Brer Fox he lay low.

. . . "'Is you deaf?' sez Brer Rabbit, sezee. 'Kaze if you is, I kin holler louder,' sezee. "Tar-Baby stay still, en Brer Fox, he lay low.

"'You er stuck up, dat's w'at you is,' says Brer Rabbit, sezee, 'en I'm gwine ter kyore you, dat's w'at I'm a gwine ter do,' sezee.

"Brer Fox, he sorter chuckle in his stummick, he did, but Tar-Baby ain't sayin' nothin'.

"'I'm gwine ter larn you how ter talk ter 'spectubble folks ef hit's de las' ack,' sez Brer Rabbit, sezee. 'Ef you don't take off dat hat en tell me howdy, I'm gwine ter bus' you wide open,' sezee. "Tar-Baby stay still, en Brer Fox, he lay low.

"Brer Rabbit keep on axin' 'im, en de Tar-Baby, she keep on sayin' nothin', twel present'y Brer Rabbit draw back wid his fis', he did, en blip he tuck 'er side er de head. Right dar's whar he broke his merlasses jug. His fis' stuck, en he can't pull loose. De tar hilt 'im. But Tar-Baby, she stay still, en Brer Fox, he lay low.

"'Ef you don't lemme loose, I'll knock you agin,' sez Brer Rabbit, sezee, en wid dat he fotch 'er a wipe wid de udder han', en dat stuck. Tar-Baby, she ain'y sayin' nuthin', en Brer Fox, he lay low.

"'Tu'n me loose, fo' I kick de natal stuffin' outen you,' sez Brer Rabbit, sezee, but de Tar-Baby, she ain't sayin' nuthin'. She des hilt on, en de Brer Rabbit lose de use er his feet in de same way. Brer Fox, he lay low. Den Brer Rabbit squall out dat ef de Tar-Baby don't tu'n 'im loose he butt 'er cranksided. En den he butted, en his head got stuck. Den Brer Fox, he sa'ntered fort', lookin' dez ez innercent ez wunner yo' mammy's mockin'-birds.

"'Howdy, Brer Rabbit,' sez Brer Fox, sezee. 'You look sorter stuck up dis mawnin',' sezee, en den he rolled on de groun', en laft en laft twel he couldn't laff no mo'. 'I speck you'll take dinner wid me dis time, Brer Rabbit. . . .' sez Brer Fox, sezee."

Here Uncle Remus paused, and drew a two-pound yam out of the ashes.

"Did the fox eat the rabbit?" asked the little boy to whom the story had been told.

"Dat's all de fur de tale goes," replied the old man . . . "I hear Miss Sally callin'. You better run 'long."

"Uncle Remus," said the little boy one evening, when he had found the old man with little or nothing to do, "did the fox kill and eat the rabbit when he caught him with the Tar-Baby?"

"Law, honey, ain't I tell you 'bout dat?" replied the old darkey, chuckling slyly. "I'clar ter grashus I ought er tole you dat, but old man Nod wuz ridin' on my eyeleds. . . .

"W'at I tell you w'en I fus' begin? I tole you Brer Rabbit wuz a monstus soon creetur; leas'ways dat's w'at I laid out fer ter tell you. . . . 'Fo' you begins fer ter wipe yo' eyes 'bout Brer Rabbit, you wait en see whar'bouts Brer Rabbit gwineter fetch up at. But dat's needer yer ner dar.

"W'en Brer Fox fine Brer Rabbit mixt up wid de Tar-Baby, he feel mighty good, en he roll on de groun' en laff. Bimeby he up'n say, sezee:

"'Well, I speck I got you dis time, Brer Rabbit,' sezee; 'maybe I ain't, but I speck I is. You been runnin' roun' here sassin' atter me a mighty long time, but I speck you done come ter de een' er de row. You bin cuttin' up yo' capers en bouncin' 'roun' in dis neighborhood ontwel you come ter b'leeve yo'se'f de boss er de whole gang,'. . . sez Brer Fox, sezee. 'Who ax you fer ter come en strike up a 'quaintance wid dish yer Tar-Baby? En who stuck you up dar whar you iz? Nobody in de roun' worril. You des tuck en jam yo'se'f on dat Tar-Baby widout waitin' fer enny invite,' sez Brer Fox, sezee, 'en dar you is, en dar youll stay twel I fixes up a bresh-pile and fires her up, kaze rm gwineter bobby-cue you dis day, sho,' sez Brer Fox, sezee.

"Den Brer Rabbit talk mighty 'umble.

"'I don't keer w'at you do wid me, Brer Fox,' sezee, 'so you don't fling me in dat brier-patch. Roas' me, Brer Fox' sezee, 'but don't fling me in dat brierpatch,' sezee.

"'Hit's so much trouble fer ter kindle a fier,' sez Brer Fox, sezee, 'dat I speck I'll hatter hang you,' sezee.

"'Hang me des ez high as you please, Brer Fox,' sez Brer Rabbit, sezee, 'but do fer de Lord's sake don't fling me in dat brier-patch,' sezee.

"'I ain't got no string,' sez Brer Fox, sezee, 'en now I speck I'll hatter drown you,' sezee.

"'Drown me des ez deep ez you please, Brer Fox,' sez Brer Rabbit, sezee, 'but do don't fling me in dat brier-patch,' sezee.

"'Dey ain't no water nigh,' sez Brer Fox, sezee, 'en now I speck I'll hatter skin you,' sezee.

"'Skin me, Brer Fox,' sez Brer Rabbit, sezee, 'snatch out my eyeballs, t'ar out my years by de roots, en cut off my legs,' sezee, 'but do please, Brer Fox, don't ffing me in dat brier-patch,' sezee.

"Co'se Brer Fox wanter hurt Brer Rabbit bad ez he kin, so he cotch 'im by de behime legs en slung 'im right in de middle er de brier-patch. Dar wuz a considerbul flutter whar Brer Rabbit struck de bushes, en Brer Fox sorter hang 'roun' fer ter see w'at wuz gwineter happen. Bimeby he hear somebody call 'im, en way up de hill he see Brer Rabbit settin' cross-legged on a chinkapin log koamin' de pitch outen his har wid a chip. Den Brer Fox know dat he bin swop off mighty bad. Brer Rabbit wuz bleedzed fer ter fling back some er his sass, en he holler out:

"'Bred en bawn in a brier-patch, Brer Fox—bred en bawn in a brier-patch!' en wid dat he skip out des ez lively ez a cricket in de embers."

proudly recalled helping his "father at night in making straw hats and willow-baskets, by which means we supplied our family with little articles of food, clothing and luxury."

Nor were slaves totally at the mercy of abusive masters and overseers. Mary Prince used sass to tell her Antigua mistress "not to use me so" and told her Bermuda master that because "he was a very indecent man,...I would not live longer with him." Sometimes, one family member would intervene to prevent the abuse of another. Harriet Jacobs fended off her master's advances partly by her cleverness and sass ("I openly...expressed my contempt for him"), and partly by threats to use her freed grandmother's considerable influence in the community against him. When family intervention, appeals for mercy, or threats did not work, some slaves resorted to force. In 1800, a slave named Ben shot dead a white man for living with Ben's wife, and another slave killed an overseer in 1859 for raping his wife. Female slaves were especially forceful. When Cherry Loguen was attacked by a knife-wielding rapist, she knocked him out with a large branch. When an Arkansas overseer abused one slave mother, her son reported that she "jumped on him and like to tore him up."

The love and affection that slaves had for each other was sometimes a liability. Many slaves, women especially, were reluctant to run away because they did not want to leave their families. Those who fled were easily caught because, as an overseer told a northern visitor, they "almost always kept in the neighborhood, because they did not like to go where they could not sometimes get back and see their families."

As these episodes suggest, violence, sexual abuse, and separation constantly threatened slave families. Yet slave parents continued to serve as protectors, providers, comforters, transmitters of culture, and role models for their children.

Slave Families in Their Quarters

In these photographs of the quarters at "night," men, women, and children, despite separation, sale, and sexual abuse by whites, created a vibrant black community and provided love, support, and self-esteem to family members. How many generations do you see in the 1862 photograph (top) of a Hilton Head, South Carolina, family, and what activities are going on in the bottom picture? What do you observe about gender roles in these two photographs?

(Top: Library of Congress; Bottom: Collection of the New-York Historical Society [PR-002–347.20])

Resistance and Freedom

Songs, folktales (as seen in this chapter's "Recovering the Past" feature), and other forms of cultural expression enabled slaves to articulate their resistance to slavery. For example, in the song "Ole Jim," on Jim's "journey" to the "kingdom," he invited others to "go 'long" with him, taunting his owner: "O blow, blow, Ole Massa, blow de cotton horn / Ole Jim'll neber wuck no mo' in de cotton an' de corn." From refusal to work, it was a short step to outright revolt. In another song, "Samson," slaves clearly stated their determination to abolish the house of bondage: "An' if I had-'n my way / I'd tear the buildin' down! /... And now I got my way / And I'll tear this buildin' down." Every defiant song, story, or event, like Douglass's fight with Covey, was an act of agency and resistance in gaining a measure of freedom

Forms of Black Protest

Slaves protested the oppressive demands of continuous forced labor both individually and collectively. Various individual acts of "day-to-day" resistance included breaking tools, self-mutilation, feigning illness and other forms of getting out of work, stealing food, defending fellow slaves from punishment, and even occasionally burning buildings and poisoning masters.

Slave women, aware of their childbearing value, were adept at missing work on account of "disorders and irregularities." They established networks of support while winnowing and pounding rice or shucking corn, sharing miseries but also encouraging each other in private acts of sass and subtle defiance such as ruining the master's meals and faking sickness or painful menstrual cramps.

Overseers also suffered from these acts of disobedience, for their job depended on productivity, which in turn depended on the goodwill of the slave workers. Slaves adeptly played on the frequent struggles between overseer and master.

Many slaveholders resorted to using black drivers rather than overseers, but this created other problems. Slave drivers were "men between," charged with the tricky job of getting the master's work done without alienating fellow slaves or compromising their own loyalties. Although some drivers were as brutal as white overseers, many became leaders and role models for other slaves. A common practice of the drivers was to appear to punish without really doing so. Solomon Northrup reported that he "learned to handle the whip with marvelous dexterity and precision, throwing the lash within a hair's breadth of the back, the ear, the nose, without, however, touching either of them."

Another form of resistance was to run away. The typical runaway was a young male who ran off alone and hid out in a nearby wood or swamp. He left to avoid a whipping or because he had just been whipped, to protest excessive work demands, and to experience moments of freedom away from the restraints and discipline of the plantation. Many runaways would sneak back to the quarters for food, and after a few days, if not tracked down by hounds, they would return, perhaps to be whipped, but also perhaps with some concessions for better treatment. Some left again and again. Remus and his wife Patty ran away from their Alabama master three times, each time caught and jailed.

Many runaways hid out for months and years in communities of escaped slaves known as *maroons,* especially in Florida, where Seminole Indians befriended them. In these maroons, blacks and Natives intermarried and shared a common hostility to whites, though sometimes Creek and other southeastern Indians were hired to track down runaways. Black Seminoles in Florida, and later in the Indian Territory of Oklahoma, successfully evaded American troops for years, some eventually escaping to the Texas-Mexican borderlands.

Slaves were ingenious in their means of escape: forging passes, posing as master and servant, disguising one's sex, sneaking aboard ships, and pretending loyalty until taken by the master on a trip to the North. One man even had himself mailed to the North in a large box. The Underground Railroad, organized by abolitionists, was a series of safe houses and stations where runaways could rest, eat, and spend the night before continuing. Harriet Tubman, who led some 300 slaves out of the South on 19 separate trips, was the railroad's most famous "conductor." It is difficult to know exactly how many slaves actually escaped to the North and Canada, but the numbers were not large. One estimate suggests that in 1850, about 1,000 slaves (out of more than 3 million) attempted to run away, and most of them were returned. Nightly patrols by whites reduced the chances for any slave to escape and probably deterred many slaves from even trying.

Other ways in which slaves sought their freedom as individuals included petitioning Congress and state legislatures, bringing suit against their masters that they were being held in bondage illegally, and persuading masters to provide for emancipation in their wills. Many toiled to purchase their own freedom by hiring out to do extra work at night and on holidays.

Slave Revolts

The ultimate act of resistance was rebellion. Countless slaves committed individual acts of revolt. But they also considered collective action. In hundreds of conspiracies slaves planned group escape, often with the massacre of whites. Most of these conspiracies never led to action, either because circumstances changed or the slaves lost the will to follow through or, more often, because some fellow slave—perhaps planted by the master—betrayed the plot. Such spies thwarted the elaborate conspiracies of Gabriel in Virginia in 1800 and Denmark Vesey in South Carolina in 1822. Both men were skilled, knowledgeable leaders who planned their revolts in hopes that larger events would support them—a possible war with France in 1800 and the Missouri

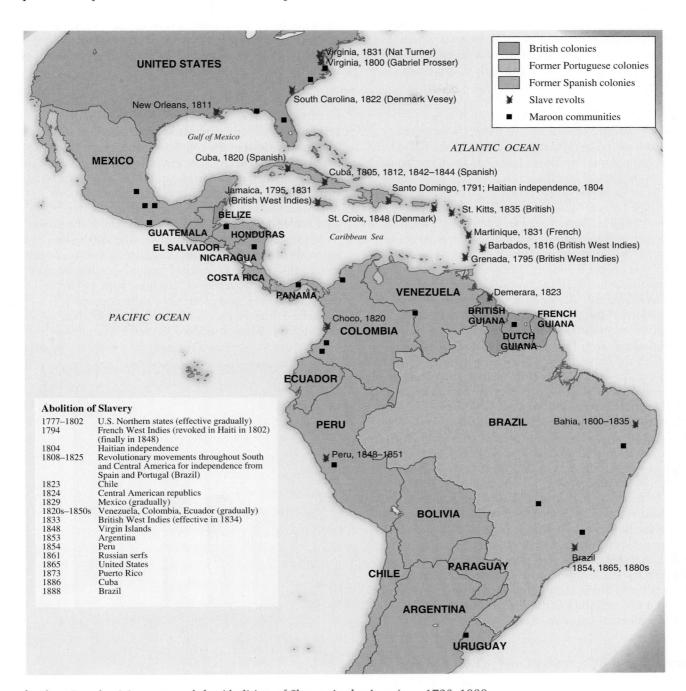

Slave Revolts, Maroons, and the Abolition of Slavery in the Americas, 1790–1888

Throughout the Americas, enslaved Africans found many ways to protest their enslavement, including revolt, escape, and petitioning the abolition of slavery altogether. Maroons were communities of successful runaway slaves who fled to densely forested and largely inaccessible areas where they often intermarried with Native groups. Some carried on a kind of guerrilla warfare with Europeans who tried to track them down. What patterns (of either place or time) do you see in the outbreaks of this partial mapping of slave revolts? What relationships do you see between slave revolts and abolition, and between abolition and national independence movements?

debates in 1820. Both conspiracies were thwarted before revolts could begin, and both resulted in severe reprisals by whites, including mass executions of leaders and the random killing of innocent blacks. The severity of these responses indicated southern whites' enormous fear of slave revolt.

Only a few organized revolts ever actually took place, especially compared to Latin America where slaves revolted far more frequently. In Brazil, continued dependence on the African slave trade to replenish workers, weaker military control, easier escape to rugged interior areas, the larger proportion of blacks to whites, and the disproportionate ratio of males to females explained these frequent revolts. Compared with the near 1:1 gender ratio of slaves in the United States, Latin American slaves had little family or female restraint on violent revolts.

The most famous slave revolt in North America, led by Nat Turner, occurred in Southampton County, Virginia, in 1831. Turner was an intelligent, skilled, unmarried, religious slave who had experienced many visions of "white spirits and black spirits engaged in battle." He believed himself "ordained for some great purpose in the hands of the Almighty." He and his followers intended, Turner said, "to carry terror and devastation" throughout the country. On a hot, August night, they crept into the home of Turner's master—a "kind master" with "the greatest confidence in me"—and killed the entire family. Before the insurrection was finally put down, 55 white men, women, and children had been murdered and twice as many blacks killed in the aftermath. Turner hid for two weeks before he was apprehended and executed, but not before dictating a chilling confession to a white lawyer. The Nat Turner revolt was a crucial moment for southern whites. A Virginia legislator suspected that there was "a Nat Turner . . . in every family."

The fact that Turner was an intelligent and trusted slave and yet led such a terrible revolt suggests again how difficult it is to generalize about slavery and slave behavior. Slaves, like masters, had diverse personalities and changeable moods, and their behavior could not be predicted easily. Sometimes humble and deferential, at other times obstinate and rebellious, slaves made the best of a bad situation and did what they needed to do to survive with a measure of self-worth.

Free Blacks: Becoming One's Own Master

Frederick Douglass said of the slave, "Give him a bad master, and he aspires to a good master; give him a good master, and he wishes to become his own master." In 1838, Douglass forged a free black's papers as a seaman and sailed from Baltimore to become his own master in the North, where he found "great insecurity and loneliness." Apart from the immediate difficulties of finding

food, shelter, and work, he realized that he was a fugitive in a land "whose inhabitants are legalized kidnappers" who could at any moment seize and return him to the South. Douglass thus joined the 12 percent of the African American population who were not slaves.

Between 1820 and 1860, the number of free blacks in the United States doubled, from 233,500 to 488,000. This rise resulted from natural increase, successful escapes, "passing" as whites, purchasing of freedom, and manumission.

More than half the free blacks lived in the South, most (85 percent in 1860) in the Upper South. They were found scattered on impoverished rural farmlands and in small towns, feared by whites as an inducement to slave unrest. One-third of the southern free African American population lived in cities or towns. In part because it took a long time to buy freedom, they tended to be older, more literate, and lighter-skinned than other African Americans. In 1860, more than 40 percent of free blacks were mulattoes (compared with 10 percent of the slaves).

Most free African Americans in the antebellum South were poor farmhands, day laborers, or woodcutters. In the cities, they worked in factories and lived in appalling poverty. A few skilled jobs, such as barbering, shoemaking, and plastering, were reserved for black men, but they were barred from more than 50 other trades. Women worked as cooks, laundresses,

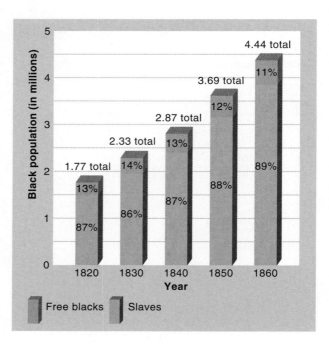

Growth of Black Population: Slave and Free, 1820–1860

Although the number of free African Americans doubled in size between 1820 and 1860, their proportion relative to the total black population actually decreased. Does this mean that southern whites were more or less likely to end slavery voluntarily?

and domestics. The 15 percent of free African Americans who lived in the Lower South were divided into two distinct castes. Most were poor. But in New Orleans, Charleston, and other southern cities, a small, mixed-blood, free black elite emerged, closely connected to white society and distant from poor blacks. A handful even owned land and slaves.

Most free blacks had no such privileges. Legally, they could not vote, bear arms, buy liquor, assemble, speak in public, form societies, or testify against whites in court. Socially, urban whites sought to restrain free blacks from mixing with whites in working-class grogshops, gambling halls, and brothels, as well as to confine them to certain sections of the city or (increasingly by the 1850s) to compel them to leave altogether. Those who stayed had trouble finding work, were required to carry papers, and had to have their actions supervised by a white guardian. Southern whites especially feared contact between free blacks and slaves. A Baltimore black paper said in 1826 that "though we are not slaves, we are not free."

Nevertheless, the African American persistence for freedom and a decent life was stronger than white efforts to impede it. In Charleston, Baltimore, Richmond, New Orleans, and other southern cities blacks developed vibrant African American communities, with churches, schools, and benevolent societies flourishing in the midst of white hostility.

The key institution was the African American church, "the Alpha and Omega of all things," Martin Delaney wrote to Douglass. Welcoming freedom from white control, independent urban black churches grew enormously in the two decades before the Civil War. The African Methodist Episcopal (AME) Church in Baltimore doubled its membership between 1836 and 1856. By 1860, Baltimore had 15 African American churches representing five different denominations, and in Virginia 14 new black Baptist churches were founded between 1841 and 1860. These institutions gave spiritual solace, set community standards, and offered a host of educational, insurance, self-help, and recreational opportunities.

Nor were African American Catholics left out. Baltimore and New Orleans had strong black Catholic communities made up of Creoles, converts, former slaves, and refugees from Haiti. The first ordained black priests were three Georgians born of a mulatto slave mother and an Irish immigrant father educated at Holy Cross. Since it would be three decades before another black priest was ordained, black sisterhoods took on special importance. The Sisters of the Holy Family and other Catholic black women started schools and ministered to the aged and infirm in community religious work reaching westward to Louisville and St. Louis.

African American churches were centers of vital urban black community activities and springboards for activist black preachers seeking larger changes in American society. The Reverend J. C. Pennington, an escaped slave, attended lectures at Yale Divinity School (though he was denied the right to enroll or borrow books). Licensed to preach in 1838, he headed prominent black churches in New Haven, Hartford, and New York City. Pennington started several schools, was an abolitionist leader of the National Negro Convention movement, and founded a black missionary society focused on Africa. Religious leaders like Pennington (and Maria Stewart, who crusaded for both abolitionism and equal rights for blacks and women) not only stimulated the growth of African American churches but also prepared the way for civil war and expanded rights.

A young AME minister, Henry M. Turner, proudly proclaimed in the 1850s, "We, as a race, have a chance to be Somebody, and if we are ever going to be a people, now is the time." As free blacks

Timeline

1787	Constitution adopted with proslavery provisions
1793	Eli Whitney invents cotton gin
1808	External slave trade prohibited by Congress
1820	South becomes world's largest cotton producer
1822	Denmark Vesey's conspiracy in Charleston
1830s	Southern justification of slavery changes from a necessary evil to a positive good
1831	Nat Turner's slave revolt in Virginia
1845	*Narrative of the Life of Frederick Douglass* published
1850s	Cotton boom: production and prices peak
1860	4 million slaves in the United States

became more of a "people" demanding their rights, they faced a crisis in the 1850s. The worsening conflict between the North and South over slavery in the territories heightened many white southerners' concerns with the presence of free blacks in their midst and prompted greater pressures to either deport or enslave them. Some black leaders, not surprisingly, began to look more favorably on migration elsewhere. That quest was interrupted, however, by the outbreak of the Civil War. In a bitter speech as a free man in 1852, Douglass had said that "to the American slave," the Fourth of July celebration was an "empty and heartless...hollow mockery...of liberty and equality...a thin veil to cover up crimes which would disgrace a nation of savages." But the news of civil war in 1861 rekindled in Douglass, the "expiring embers of freedom."

Conclusion

DOUGLASS'S DREAM OF FREEDOM

When Frederick Douglass forged a free black sailor's pass and escaped to the North, in a real sense he wrote himself into freedom. The *Narrative of the Life of Frederick Douglass,* "written by himself" in 1845, was a way for Douglass both to expose the many evils of slavery and to create his own identity, even choosing his own name. Ironically, Douglass had learned to value reading and writing from his Baltimore masters, the Aulds. This reminds us again of the intricate and subtle ways in which the lives of slaves and masters were tied together in the antebellum South and of the challenges of bringing diverse peoples together in forming the American nation. Our understanding of the complexities of slavery is enhanced as we consider the variations of life in the

Big House in the morning, in the fields during the afternoons, in the slave quarters at night, and in the degrees of freedom blacks achieved through resistance, revolt, and free status.

In a poignant moment in his *Narrative,* Douglass described his boyhood dreams of freedom as he looked out at the boats on the waters of Chesapeake Bay. Contrasting his own enslavement with the boats he saw as "freedom's swift-winged angels," Douglass vowed to escape: "This very bay shall yet bear me into freedom.... There is a better day coming." As conflicts between slaves and masters simmered in the antebellum South, many northern Americans were concerned with various undemocratic and immoral aspects in their society, slavery among them, and sought ways of shaping a more democratic and just America. We turn to these other dreams in the next chapter.

QUESTIONS FOR REVIEW AND REFLECTION

1. How much variety—social and economic—existed in the Old South? In what ways—social and economic—was the South dependent on slavery and cotton, and what were the consequences of this dependency?
2. Compare and contrast North American with Latin American slavery.
3. Show your understanding of the morning, noon, and night structure of this chapter by explaining it to a friend not in the course. How does this structure reflect three different interpretations of slavery?
4. Can you name five or six ways in which slaves resisted their enslavement and achieved a measure of autonomy, agency, and self-esteem? Can you identify in any way with these methods of resistance?
5. What does the author of this chapter think was the worst thing about slavery? What do you think? What does the institution of slavery suggest about American values and how they have changed over time?

CHAPTER 12

Shaping a Democratic America in the Antebellum Age

This 1839 painting of a camp meeting captures the religious fervor that many Americans turned to in the face of social and economic upheavals. Describe the scene. What do you see? Are there any gender differences? How would a revival like this lead to social reform?

(J. Maze Burbank, Jr., *Religious Camp Meeting*, c. 1839. Courtesy of The Whaling Museum)

American Stories

Experiencing the Costs of a Commitment

On November 19, 1836, as the second term of President Andrew Jackson neared its end, two young white reformers, Marius Robinson and Emily Rakestraw, were married near Cincinnati, Ohio. Two months later, Marius went on the road to speak against slavery and organize abolitionist societies in Ohio. Emily stayed in Cincinnati to teach in a school for free blacks. During their 10-month separation, they exchanged affectionate letters that told of their love and work.

Writing to Emily after midnight from Ohio, Marius complained of the "desolation of loneliness" he felt without her. Emily responded that she felt "about our separation just as you do" and confessed that her "womanish nature" did not enjoy self-denial. In their letters, each imagined the "form and features" of the other and chided the other for not writing more often. Each voiced concern for the other's burdens. Each expressed support, doubted his or her own abilities ("a miserable comforter I am"), and agreed that in their separation, as Marius put it, "we must look alone to God."

With such love for each other, what prompted this painful separation? Emily wrote of their duty "to labor long in this cause so near and dear to us both," together if possible, but apart if so decreed by God. Marius, who had been converted by revivalist Charles G. Finney and his abolitionist disciple Theodore Weld, described the reason for their separation: "God and humanity bleeding and suffering demand our services apart." Driven by a strong religious commitment to serve others, Marius and Emily dedicated themselves to several social causes: abolition of slavery, equal rights and education for free blacks, temperance, and women's rights.

Their commitments cost more than separation. When Emily went to Cincinnati to work with other young reformers, her parents disapproved. When she married Marius, who already had a reputation as a "rebel," her parents disowned her. Emily wrote with sadness that her sisters and friends also "love me less . . . than they did in by-gone days." Marius responded that he wished he could "dry your tears." Emily's family eventually accepted their marriage, but there were other troubles. Teaching at the school in Cincinnati was demanding, and Emily could not get rid of a persistent cough. Furthermore, the white citizens of the city treated the school and its teachers with contempt. Earlier in the year, Marius had escaped an angry mob by disguising himself and mingling with the crowd that came to sack the offices of a reformist journal edited by James G. Birney. Emily, meanwhile, tirelessly persisted in the work

of "our school" while worrying about the safety of her husband.

She had good reason for concern, for Marius's letters were full of reports of mob attacks, disrupted meetings, stonings, and narrow escapes. At two lectures near Granville, Ohio, he was "mobbed thrice, once most rousingly," by crowds of "the veriest savages I ever saw," armed with clubs and intense hatred for those speaking against slavery. In June, he was dragged from his Quaker host's home, beaten, and tarred and feathered. Never quite recovering his health, Marius spent six months in bed, weak and dispirited. For nearly 10 years after that, the Robinsons lived quietly on an Ohio farm, only slightly involved in abolitionist activity. Despite the joyous birth of two daughters, they felt lonely, restless, and guilt-ridden, "tired of days blank of benevolent effort and almost of benevolent desires."

The work of Emily and Marius Robinson represents one response by the American people to the rapid social and economic changes of the antebellum era described in Chapters 10 and 11. In September 1835, a year before the Robinsons' marriage, the *Niles Register* described some 500 recent incidents of mob violence and social upheaval. "Society seems everywhere unhinged, and the demon of 'blood and slaughter' has been let loose upon us. . . . [The] character of our countrymen seems suddenly changed." How did Americans adapt to these changes? In a world that seemed everywhere "unhinged" and out of control, in which old rules and patterns no longer provided guidance, how did people maintain some sense of control over their lives? How did they seek to shape their altered world? How could they both adopt the benefits of change and reduce the accompanying disruptions?

One way was to embrace the changes fully. Thus, some Americans became entrepreneurs in new industries; invested in banks, canals, and railroads; bought more land and slaves; and invented new machines. Others went west or to the new textile mills, enrolled in Common Schools, joined trade unions, specialized their labor in both the workplace and the home, and celebrated modernization's practical benefits. Marius Robinson eventually went into life insurance, though he and Emily never fully abandoned their democratic idealism.

But many Americans were uncomfortable with the character of the new era. Some worried about the unrestrained power and selfish materialism symbolized by the slave master's control over his slaves. Others feared that institutions like the U.S. Bank represented a "monied aristocracy" capable of undermining the country's honest producers. Seeking positions of leadership and authority, these critics of the new order tried to shape a nation that retained the benefits of economic change without sacrificing basic American principles of liberty, democracy, equality of opportunity, and community virtue. This chapter examines four ways in which the American people responded to change by attempting to influence their country's development along more democratic lines: religious revivalism, party politics, perfectionist utopian communities, and specific social reforms.

Religious Revival and Reform

When the Frenchman Alexis de Tocqueville visited the United States in 1831 and 1832, he observed that he could find "no country in the whole world in which the Christian religion retains a greater influence over the souls of men than in America." Tocqueville was describing a new and powerful religious enthusiasm among American Protestants. Religious rebirth gave some Americans a mooring in a fast-changing world, while others were inspired to refashion their society, working through new political parties to shape an agenda for the nation or through reform associations targeting a particular social evil. Although not all evangelicals agreed about politics or what to reform, they saw that religion led to change.

Finney and the Second Great Awakening

From the late 1790s until the late 1830s, a wave of religious revivals swept through the United States. While there were many links between Protestant denominations in the United States and in Great Britain, the popular character of American revivalism gave it a distinctive stamp. As British religion became more conservative, American Protestantism became more democratic.

The turn-of-the-century frontier camp meeting revivals and the New England revivals sparked by Lyman Beecher took on a new emphasis and location after 1830. Led by the spellbinding Charles G. Finney, revivalism shifted to upstate New York and the Old Northwest, two areas undergoing profound economic and social changes.

Rochester, New York, was typical. Like Lowell and Cincinnati, by the 1830s it was booming. Located on the recently completed Erie Canal, it was changed by the canal from a sleepy village of 300 in 1815 to a bustling commercial and milling city of nearly 20,000 by 1830. As in other cities, economic growth distanced the relationship between masters and workers, weakening the masters' control. Saloons and unions sprang up in workingmen's neighborhoods, and workers became more transient, following opportunities westward.

In 1830, prompted partly by concerns about poverty and absenteeism, both caused presumably by alcohol, prominent Rochester citizens invited Charles Finney to the city. He led what became one of the most successful revivals of the Second Great Awakening. Finney preached nearly every night and three times on Sundays, first converting the city's business elite, often through their wives, and then converting many workers. For six months, Rochester experienced a citywide prayer meeting in which one conversion led to another.

The Rochester revival was part of a wave of religious enthusiasm in America that contributed to the tremendous growth of Methodists, Baptists, and other evangelical denominations in the first half of the nineteenth century. By 1844, Methodism became the country's largest denomination with over a million members. Revivalist preachers emphasized emotion over doctrine, softening Calvinist tenets like predestination that said that individual salvation came from God rather than human effort and faith.

Jonathan Edwards had believed that revivals were God's miracles, but Finney understood that the human "agency" of the minister was crucial in causing a revival. "We must have exciting, powerful preaching," he said, "or the devil will have the people." He even published a do-it-yourself manual for revivalists. But few could match his powerful preaching style that relied upon both logic and emotions to trigger conversions. When he threw an imaginary brick at the Devil, people ducked.

American Catholics also caught the revival fervor in the 1830s. Scattered in small but growing numbers in the East and the Ohio River valley, urban Catholic leaders recognized that survival as a small, often despised religion depended on constant reinvigoration and evangelism. Focusing on the parish mission, energetic retreats and revivals gathered Catholics from miles around to preserve a religious heritage seriously threatened by life in Protestant America.

Many revivalists, especially in the South, sought personal conversion that brought with it the promise of salvation. Finney, however, insisted that conversion and salvation were not the end of religious experience but the beginning. He believed that humans were not passive objects of God's predestined plan, but moral free agents who could choose good over evil and thereby eradicate sin. Finney encouraged not only individual reformation but also the commitment by

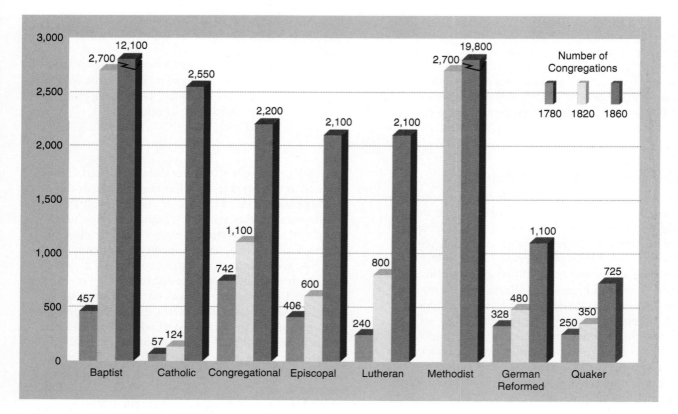

Denominational Growth, 1780–1860

As this bar graph makes clear, the early nineteenth century was a time of explosive religious growth. What were the decades that saw the greatest growth? Which denominations expanded most quickly and which most slowly? When, and why then?

converted Christians to seek social reform, a message he imparted to Marius Robinson and other ordinary Americans, as we will see.

The Transcendentalists

Ralph Waldo Emerson, a Concord, Massachusetts, Unitarian, would have agreed, saying, "What is man born for but to be a Reformer?" Emerson's essays influenced a group of New England writers and reformers called Transcendentalists, men and women who believed that intuitive truth transcended sense experience. Casting off the European intellectual tradition, Emerson urged Americans to look inward and to nature for self-knowledge, self-reliance, and the spark of divinity burning within. "To acquaint a man with himself," he wrote, would inspire a "reverence" for self and others, which would then lead outward to social reform.

Inspired by self-reflection, the Transcendentalists asked troublesome questions about the quality of American life. They challenged not only slavery, an obvious evil, but also the obsessive, competitive pace of economic life, the overriding materialism, and the

restrictive conformity of social life. Emerson's brilliant friend, Margaret Fuller, questioned the absence of women's voices and founded and edited *The Dial*, an influential Transcendentalist journal. Fuller broke new ground by writing not just about women's rights but also about literature, prison reform, and the moral quality of American life. New York *Tribune* editor Horace Greeley called her "the most remarkable woman in America."

Although not considered Transcendentalists, Nathaniel Hawthorne and Herman Melville, two giants of mid-century American literature, also wrote of these concerns in their fiction. Like Emerson, they celebrated virtue over self-interest and emotion over reason. Hawthorne's great subject was the "truth of the human heart." In his greatest novel, *The Scarlet Letter* (1850), Hawthorne sympathetically told the story of a courageous Puritan woman's adultery and her eventual loving triumph over the narrowness of both cold intellect and intolerant conformity. Melville's epic novel *Moby Dick* (1851) was on one level a rousing story of whaling on the high seas in pursuit of the great white whale, and on another an allegory of good and evil, bravery and weakness, innocence and experience. Like Emerson and Fuller, Hawthorne and Melville mirrored the tensions of the age as they explored issues of freedom and control.

When Emerson wrote, "Whoso would be a man, must be a nonconformist," he described his friend Henry David Thoreau. No one thought more deeply about the virtuous natural life than Thoreau. On July 4, 1845, he went to live in a small hut by Walden Pond, near Concord, to confront the "essential facts of life"—to discover who he was and how to live well. When Thoreau left Walden two years later, he protested against slavery and the Mexican War by refusing to pay his taxes. He went to jail briefly and wrote an essay, "Civil Disobedience" (1849), and a book, *Walden* (1854), both classic statements of what one person can do to protest unjust laws and wars and live a life of principle.

Although Transcendentalism touched only a few elite New Englanders, perhaps 40 percent of Americans were affected by evangelical Protestantism. But political values and loyalties as well as religious ones affected many people's understanding of the appropriate role of government in shaping change.

The Political Response to Change

As politics became more a popular than an elite interest, it was not surprising that religious commitments spilled over into it. At the heart of American politics, as with revivalism, was concern for the continued health of the democratic experiment and how to meet the needs and demands of diverse groups in the quest for a better society. In the 1850s, a Maine newspaper warned that the preservation of the nation's freedom depended on the "positive duty of every citizen of a Republic to vote."

Before the 1820s, politics in both the United States and Europe was primarily an activity for social and economic elites. In Europe, conservatives feared the political involvement of the lower classes and both Great Britain and France resisted popular pressures to gain universal male suffrage. In the United States, however, the power of revolutionary era ideas and the relative weakness of the country's upper classes led to a gradual extension of the franchise, albeit only to white men. The spirited presidential campaigns of Andrew Jackson helped create the distinctive style of American politics in seeking to better society for the democratic masses.

Changing Political Culture

Styling himself as the people's candidate in 1828, Andrew Jackson derided the administration of John Quincy Adams as corrupt and aristocratic and promised

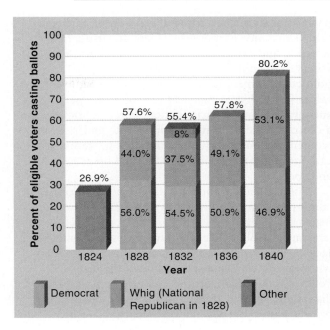

More Americans Vote for President

The single-party system (Jeffersonian Democratic Republican) that existed in 1824 collapsed with the personal rivalries and ideological differences of the 1820s and 1830s. It was replaced by the emergence of a two-party system and a huge increase in (white male) voter participation. How do you explain this tremendous growth? Who benefited? What percentages vote now?

a more democratic political system. He told voters that he intended to "purify" and "reform the Government," purging all "who have been appointed from political considerations or against the will of the people." Most Americans believed the campaign rhetoric. Four times more men voted in the election of 1828 than in 1824. They gave Jackson a resounding 56 percent of their ballots. No other president in the century would equal that percentage of popular support.

Despite campaign rhetoric and his image as a democratic hero, Jackson was not personally very democratic, nor did the era he symbolized involve any significant redistribution of wealth. Jackson owned slaves, defended slavery, and condoned mob attacks on abolitionists like Marius Robinson. He disliked Native Americans and ordered the forcible removal of the southeastern tribal nations to west of the Mississippi River in blatant disregard of treaty rights and a Supreme Court decision. Belying promises of widening opportunity, the rich got richer during the Jacksonian era, and most farming and urban laboring families struggled.

But the nation's political life had changed in important ways. The old system of politics, based on elite coalitions bound by ties of family and friendship and dependent on voters deferring to their "betters," largely disappeared. In its place emerged a competitive party system oriented toward heavy voter participation. The major parties grew adept at raising money, selecting and promoting candidates, and bringing voters to the polls. A new "democratic" style of political life emerged as parties sponsored conventions, rallies (much like evangelical revivals), and parades to encourage political participation. Party politics became a central concern for many adult white males. Even women, although excluded from voting, were often caught up in party politics and turned up at rallies and speeches.

Political parties appealed to popular emotions, ethnic prejudices, and religious views. Party newspapers regularly indulged in scurrilous attacks on rivals. The language of politics became contentious and militaristic. Jackson's rhetoric described an opponent as an "enemy" who waged "war against the cause of the people." Politicians talked of elections as battles and of their disciplined "rank and file." Strong party identification became part of the new national political culture.

Jackson's Path to the White House

Andrew Jackson's early career gave few hints of his future political importance. Orphaned at 14, young Jackson grew up in poverty and was often in trouble. As a law student, he was "a most roaring, rollicking, game-cocking, horse-racing, card-playing, mischievous fellow." Still, he passed the bar and set out to seek his fortune in frontier Nashville, where he built up a successful law practice and went on to become state attorney general, a substantial landowner, and a prominent citizen.

Jackson's national reputation stemmed mainly from his military exploits, primarily against Native Americans. As major general of the Tennessee militia, he proved able and popular, winning the nickname of "Old Hickory" for his toughness. His victory over the Creek nation in the South in 1813 and 1814 brought notoriety and an appointment as major general in the U.S. Army. Victory at New Orleans over the English in 1815 made him a national hero. Aggressive military forays into Spanish Florida in 1818 increased both his popularity and his interest in the presidency.

Jackson won both the popular and the electoral votes in 1824 but lost in the House of Representatives to John Quincy Adams, who gained the support of Henry Clay. Vowing to avenge this "corrupt bargain," Jackson built a political organization based initially in the West and South. A loose coalition promoting Jackson's candidacy began to call itself the Democratic party, attracting politicians from all sections of the country, including Martin Van Buren of New York. Jackson masterfully waffled on controversial issues, concealing his dislike of banks and paper money and advocating a "middle and just course" on the tariff.

He promised only to cleanse government of corruption and privileged interests.

The Jackson–Adams campaign in 1828 degenerated into a nasty but entertaining contest. The Democrats whipped up enthusiasm with barbecues, mass rallies, and parades and distributed buttons and hats with "old hickory" leaves attached. Few people discussed issues, and both sides made slanderous personal attacks. Supporters of Adams and Clay, who called themselves National Republicans, branded Jackson "an adulterer, a gambler, a cockfighter, a brawler, a drunkard, and a murderer," and maligned his wife Rachel as immoral.

The Jacksonians charged Adams with buying Clay's support in 1824 and described him as a "stingy, undemocratic" aristocrat determined to destroy the people's liberties. Worse yet, they said, Adams was an elitist intellectual. Campaign slogans contrasted the hero of New Orleans, "a man who can fight," to a wimpy Adams, "a man who can write."

Jackson's supporters in Washington worked to ensure his election by devising a tariff bill to win necessary support in key states. Under the leadership of Van Buren, who hoped to replace John C. Calhoun as Jackson's heir apparent, Democrats in Congress passed what opponents called the "Tariff of Abominations." It arbitrarily raised rates to protect New England textiles, Pennsylvania iron, and some agricultural goods, leading an opponent to sneer that the tariff "referred to manufactures of no . . . kind but the manufacture of a President of the United States."

The efforts of Jackson and his party paid off as he won an astonishing 647,286 ballots, about 56 percent of the total. Organization, money, effective publicity, and a popular style of campaigning had brought the 60-year-old Jackson to the presidency. His inauguration, however, horrified many. Washington was packed for the ceremonies. He was all but mobbed by admirers hoping to shake his hand after taking the oath of office. At the White House reception, the crowd got completely out of hand. As Justice Joseph Story observed, a throng of "the most vulgar and gross" people poured into the White House, overturning furniture in a rush for food and punch. As Jackson escaped through a side door, many guests dove out windows in pursuit of wine and ice cream on the lawn. The inauguration, to Story, meant the "reign of King Mob." But another observer called it a "proud day for the people." Their contrasting views captured the essence of the Jackson era.

Old Hickory's Vigorous Presidency

Although Jackson adopted vague positions on important issues during the campaign, as president he needed to confront many of them. Two key principles, drawn from Jefferson, guided him: the limited power of the national government and the obligation of government to defend ordinary people against the "monied aristocracy." Seeing himself as the people's most authentic representative (only the president was elected by all the people), Jackson intended to be a vigorous executive. More than any predecessor, he used presidential power in the name of the people. Jackson asserted power most forcefully by the veto. His six predecessors had cast only nine vetoes, but Jackson vetoed 12 bills during his two terms, often because they conflicted with his political agenda and not just because he thought them unconstitutional.

As president, Jackson promised to correct what he called an undemocratic and corrupt system of government office-holding. Too often, he said, "unfaithful or incompetent" men clung to government jobs for years. Jackson proposed to throw these "scoundrels" out and establish a system of rotation of office. But his rhetoric was more extreme than his actions. In the first year and a half of his presidency, he removed only 919 officeholders of a total of 10,093, mostly for corruption or incompetence, replacing them with Democratic appointees. Still, Jackson's rhetoric helped create a new democratic political culture that would last for most of the nineteenth century.

His policy on internal improvements—roads, canals, and other forms of transportation—was less far-seeing. Like most Americans, Jackson recognized their economic importance and wished "to see roads and canals extended to every part of the country." But Jackson opposed infringing on states' rights. When proposals for federal support for internal improvements seemed to rob local and state authorities of their proper function, he opposed them. In 1830, he vetoed the Maysville Road bill, which proposed federal funding for a road in Henry Clay's Kentucky. But projects of national significance, such as river improvements and lighthouses, were different. During his presidency, Jackson supported an annual average of $1.3 million in internal improvements.

In a period of rapid economic change, tariffs stirred heated debate. New England and the mid-Atlantic states, centers of manufacturing, favored protective tariffs. The South had long opposed them because they made it more expensive to buy manufactured goods from the North or abroad. Feelings ran particularly high in South Carolina, where leaders mistakenly believed that the tariff was the prime reason for a statewide depression. In addition, some worried that the federal government might eventually interfere with slavery, a frightening prospect in a state where slaves outnumbered whites.

Vice President Calhoun, a brilliant political thinker and opponent of the tariff, provided a theory to check federal power and to protect minority rights. "We are not a nation," he once remarked, "but a Union, a confederacy of equal and sovereign states."

In 1828, the same year as the hateful tariff, Calhoun anonymously published *Exposition and Protest*, presenting nullification as a means by which southern states could protect themselves from harmful national action by declaring legislation null and void.

Two years later, Calhoun's doctrine was aired in a Senate debate over public land policy. South Carolina's Robert Hayne urged western states to use nullification in the name of liberty to oppose the policy. New England's Daniel Webster responded. The federal government, he said, was no mere agent of the state legislatures, but was "made for the people, made by the people, and answerable to the people." Aware that nullification could mean a "once glorious Union…drenched…in fraternal blood," Webster proclaimed in powerful closing words that the appropriate motto for the nation was not "Liberty first and Union afterwards, but Liberty and Union, now and forever, one and inseparable!"

The drama was repeated a month later in a dinner toast, when President Jackson declared his position. Despite his support of states' rights, Jackson did not believe that any state had the right to reject the will of the majority or to destroy the Union. The President rose for a toast, held high his glass, and said, "Our Union—it must be preserved." Challenged, Vice President Calhoun followed: "The Union—next to our liberty most dear." The split between them widened over personal as well as ideological issues, and in 1832 Calhoun resigned.

The national government and South Carolina soon collided over the tariff and nullification. In 1832, hewing to Jackson's "middle course," Congress modified the tariff of 1828 by retaining high duties on some goods but lowering other rates to an earlier level. A South Carolina convention later that year adopted an Ordinance of Nullification, voiding the tariffs of 1828 and 1832 in the state. The legislature funded a volunteer army and threatened secession if the federal government tried to force the state to comply. Jackson responded forcefully. To the "ambitious malcontents" in South Carolina, he proclaimed emphatically that "the laws of the United States must be executed….The Union will be preserved and treason and rebellion promptly put down."

Jackson's proclamation stimulated an outburst of national patriotism, isolating South Carolina. Jackson asked Congress for legislation to enforce tariff duties (the Force Bill of 1833), and new tariff revisions. Engineered by Clay and supported by Calhoun, these revisions called for gradual reductions. South Carolina quickly repealed its nullification of the tariff laws but saved face by nullifying the Force Bill, which Jackson smartly ignored. The crisis was over. Left unresolved, however, were the constitutional issues it raised. Was the Union permanent? Was secession a valid way to protect minority rights? Such questions would trouble Americans until the civil war.

JACKSON.
New Orleans Jan! 8º 1815.

Andrew Jackson

This representation of Andrew Jackson was from his 1832 campaign for reelection. Study the depiction of Jackson carefully. What clothing is he wearing? What are the objects surrounding the oval portrait? Why is the eagle in the picture? What message and appeal does the image convey?

(Library of Congress, cph 3b37026)

Jackson's Native American Policy

Jackson threatened force on South Carolina, but he used it on southeastern Native Americans. His policy of forcible relocation westward and on reservations defined white practice toward Native Americans for the rest of the century.

In the early nineteenth century, the vast lands of the five "civilized nations" of the Southeast (Cherokee, Choctaw, Chickasaw, Seminole, and Creek) had been seriously eroded by land-hungry whites supported by military campaigns led by professional Native American fighters such as Jackson. The Creek lost 22 million acres in Georgia and Alabama after Jackson defeated them in 1814. Cessions to the government and private sales accounted for even bigger losses: Cherokee holdings of more than 50 million acres in 1802 dwindled to only 9 million 20 years later.

A Supreme Court decision in 1823 declaring that American Indians could occupy but not hold title to land in the United States bolstered the trend. Seeing

that their survival was threatened, Indian nations acted. By 1825, the Creek, Cherokee, and Chickasaw restricted land sales to government agents. The Cherokee, having already adopted such elements of white culture as Christianity, constitutionalism, and slaveholding, established a police force to prevent local leaders from selling off tribal lands. Indian determination to resist whites confronted white resolve to gain more land. Jackson's election in 1828 boosted efforts to relocate the Native Americans west of the Mississippi.

Almost immediately, Jackson recommended to Congress removal of the southeastern tribes. Appealing at first to sympathy, Jackson argued that because the Native Americans were "surrounded by the whites with their arts of civilization," they were inevitably doomed to "weakness and decay." Removal was justified, Jackson claimed, by both "humanity and national honor." He also insisted that state laws should prevail over the claims of either Native Americans or the federal government (contradicting his tariff policy).

The crisis came to a head in Georgia in 1829, when the Georgia legislature declared the Cherokee tribal council illegal and claimed jurisdiction over both the tribe and its lands. The Cherokee were forbidden to bring suits or testify against whites in the Georgia courts. The Cherokee protested to the Supreme Court. In two landmark cases in 1831 and 1832 (*Cherokee Nation v. Georgia* and *Worcester v. Georgia*), Chief Justice Marshall held that the Georgia law was "repugnant to the Constitution" with "no force" over the Cherokee, and that by inviolable treaty rights Native Americans were considered "domestic dependent nations" of the U.S. federal government, a kind of quasi sovereignty.

Legal victory, however, did not suppress white land hunger. With Jackson's blessing, Georgians defied Marshall's decision. By 1835, harassment, intimidation, and bribery had persuaded a minority of chiefs to sign a removal treaty. That year, Jackson informed the Cherokee, "You cannot remain where you are. Circumstances...render it impossible that you can flourish in the midst of a civilized community." A native chief, Speckled Snake, responded with clever sarcasm, pointing out that "our great father" says he "loved his red children" but ended every speech by telling them to move ever westward, this time beyond the Mississippi. "Brothers, will not our great father come there also?"

Many Cherokee refused to leave and the nation split into two factions. Chief John Ross protested to Congress that the treaty was illegitimate. "We are stripped of every attribute of freedom....Our property may be plundered...our lives may be taken away." His words did no good. In 1837 and 1838, the

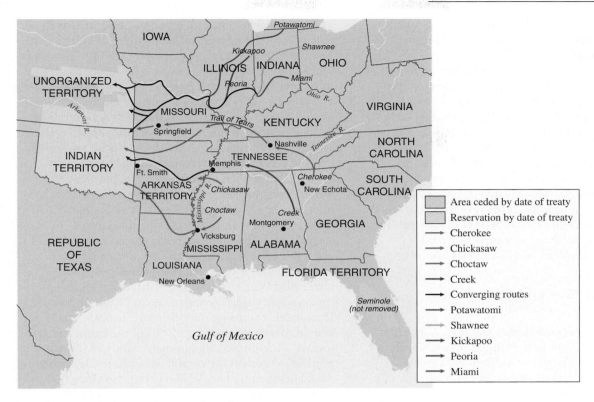

Indian Removals: Southeast and Midwest

This map shows the westward routes of Native Americans removed from the Southeast to the new Indian Territory in Oklahoma and from the Midwest (Old Northwest Territory) to present-day Kansas. Why Kansas and Oklahoma? Who already lived there? What were the consequences of removal?

The Trail of Tears

Their attempts at preserving their lands having failed, the Cherokee finally succumbed to white intimidation and their own internal divisions and were forced to travel the "Trail of Tears" to Oklahoma in 1838. About 4,000 died along the way. Describe as much as you can about this painting. What do you see? What emotions are aroused?

(Robert Lindneaux, *Trail of Tears*. Woolaroc Museum, Bartlesville, Oklahoma)

U.S. Army gathered the terrified Indians in stockades before herding them west to the "Indian Territory" in present-day Oklahoma.

About a quarter of the 15,000 who were removed died on a trek the Cherokee remember bitterly as the "trail of tears." Between 1821 and 1840 the Miami, Shawnee, and other tribes of the Old Northwest were also forced westward to Kansas and Oklahoma. Despite resistance from some tribes, most notably the Seminole, most nations were removed west of the Mississippi. Although the Removal Act of 1830 had promised to protect and forever guarantee Native American lands in the West, within a generation those promises, like others before and since, would be broken. Indian removal left the eastern United States open for the enormous economic expansion described in Chapter 10.

Jackson's Bank War and "Van Ruin's" Depression

As the (white) people's advocate, Jackson could not ignore the Second Bank of the United States, which in 1816 had received a charter for 20 years. The bank generated intense feelings. Although the bank was not as irresponsible as Jackson thought, he called it a "monster" that threatened the people's liberties.

Guided since 1823 by the aristocratic Nicholas Biddle, the Philadelphia bank and its 29 branches generally played a responsible economic role in an expansionary period. As the nation's largest commercial bank, the "B.U.S." accepted federal deposits, made commercial loans, bought and sold government bonds, and shifted funds around the country as needed. It also influenced state banking activity by restraining state banks from making unwise loans by insisting that they back their notes with specie (gold or silver coin). Most businessmen and nationalist politicians such as Webster and Clay, who were on the bank's payroll, favored it.

Other Americans, led by the president, distrusted the bank. Speculators in western lands resented its control over state banking and wanted cheap, inflated money to finance new projects and expansion. Some state bankers resented its power over their actions. Southern and western farmers regarded it as immoral because it dealt with paper rather than landed property. Others simply thought it was unconstitutional.

Jackson had long opposed the B.U.S. He hated banks in general because of a personal near–financial disaster and because he and his advisers considered the B.U.S. the chief example of a special privilege monopoly that hurt the common people—farmers, artisans, and debtors. Jackson called the bank an "irresponsible" threat to the republic. Its power and financial resources, he thought, made it a "vast electioneering engine."

Aware of Jackson's hostility, Clay and Webster persuaded Biddle to ask Congress for a new charter in 1832, four years ahead of schedule. They reasoned that in an election year, Jackson would not risk a veto. The bill to recharter the bank swept through Congress. Jackson took up the challenge. "The bank...is trying to kill me," he told Van Buren, "but I will kill it."

Jackson determined not only to veto the bill but also to carry his case to the public. His veto message, condemning the bank as undemocratic, un-American, and unconstitutional, was meant to stir up voters. He presented the bank as a dangerous monopoly that gave special privileges to the rich and harmed "the humble members of society." He also pointed to the high percentage of foreign investors in the bank. Jackson's veto message turned the issue into a struggle between the people and the aristocracy.

The bank furor helped clarify party differences. In the election of 1832, the National Republicans, now called Whigs, nominated Henry Clay, and spent thousands of dollars trying to defeat "King Andrew." Democratic campaign rhetoric pitted Jackson, the people, and democracy against Clay, the bank, and aristocracy. Jackson won handsomely, with 124,000 more popular votes than the combined total for Clay and an Anti-Mason candidate, William Wirt. "He may be President for life if he chooses," Wirt said of Jackson.

Seeing the election as a victory for his bank policy, Jackson closed in on Biddle, even though the bank's charter had four years to run. He decided to weaken the bank by transferring $10 million in government funds to state banks. Although two treasury secretaries balked at the request as financially unsound, Jackson persisted until he found one, Roger Taney, willing to do it.

Jackson's war with Biddle and the bank had serious financial consequences. A wave of speculation in western lands and ambitious new state internal improvement schemes in the mid-1830s produced inflated land prices and a flood of paper money. Even Jackson was concerned, and he tried to curtail irresponsible economic activity. In 1836 he announced that the government would accept only gold and silver in payment for public lands. Panicky investors rushed to change paper notes into specie, and banks started calling in loans. The result was the Panic of 1837. Jackson was blamed for this rapid monetary expansion followed by sudden deflation, but international trade problems with Britain and China probably contributed more to the panic and to the ensuing seven years of depression.

Whatever the primary cause, Jackson left his successor, Martin Van Buren (elected in 1836 over a trio of Whig opponents), with an economic crisis. "Martin Van Ruin," as he came to be called, had barely taken the oath of office in 1837 when banks and businesses began to collapse. His presidency was marked by a severe depression. By the fall of 1837, one-third of America's workers were unemployed, and thousands of others had only part-time work. Those who kept their jobs saw wages fall by 30 to 50 percent within two years as the price of necessities, such as flour and coal, nearly doubled. As the winter of 1837 neared, an observer estimated that 200,000 New Yorkers were "in utter hopeless distress with no means of surviving the winter but those provided by charity." People took to the streets, but as one worker said, most laborers called "not for the bread and fuel of charity, but for Work!"

But soup kitchens and bread lines grew faster than jobs. Laboring families were defenseless, for the depression destroyed the trade union movement begun a decade earlier—a demise hastened by employers who imposed longer hours, cut wages and piece rates, and divided workers into competing ethnicities. Violence against Irish strikebreakers broke out in Philadelphia in 1842 after textile employers lowered wages below subsistence. "How is it," a Philadelphia mechanic asked, that in a country as rich as the United States so many people were "pinched for the common necessaries of life …[and] bowed down with gloom and despair?" Van Buren's responses were sympathetic but limited. An executive order in 1840 declaring a 10-hour workday for federal employees affected few workers.

The Second American Party System

By the mid-1830s, a new two-party system and a lively national political culture had emerged in the United States. The parties had taken shape amid the conflicts of Jackson's presidency and the religious and ethnic fervor of the Second Great Awakening; thus, they reflected political, regional, religious, and ethnic differences.

The Democrats had the better claim as "the party of the common man" and were found in the South, West, and eastern cities. In the Jeffersonian tradition, the Democrats espoused liberty and local rule. They wanted freedom from legislated morality, religious tyranny, special privilege, and too much government. For them, the best society was one in which all Americans were free to follow individual interests. Democrats appealed to those such as Irish Catholics and other non-Anglicans who had suffered discrimination under established churches in the late colonial era. Democrats were less moralistic than Whigs on matters such as drinking and slavery. Their religions generally taught the inevitability of sin and evil, which meant separating politics from moral issues.

THE SECOND AMERICAN PARTY SYSTEM

By the 1830s, two political parties, "Democrats" and "Whigs," reflecting two traditions going back to Jefferson and Hamilton in the 1790s, emerged in American politics. How do you explain their differences?

	Democrats	Whigs
Leaders	Andrew Jackson	Henry Clay
	John C. Calhoun	Daniel Webster
	Martin Van Buren	John Quincy Adams
	Thomas Hart Benton	William Henry Harrison
Political tradition	Republican party (Jefferson, Madison)	Federalist party (Hamilton, John Adams)

Major Political Beliefs		
	State and local autonomy	National power
	Opposition to monopoly and privilege	Support for U.S. Bank, high tariff
	Low land prices and tariffs	Internal improvements
	Freedom from government interference	Broad government role in reforming America

Primary Sources of Support		
Region	South and West	New England, mid-Atlantic, Upper Midwest
Class	Middle-class and small farmers, northeastern urban laborers and artisans	Big southern planters and wealthy businessmen, pockets of middling farmers in Midwest and South, artisans
Ethnicity	Scots–Irish, Irish, French, German, and Canadian immigrants	English, New England old stock
Religion	Catholics, frontier Baptists and Methodists, free thinkers	Presbyterians, Congregationalists, Quakers, moralists, reformers

Whigs represented greater wealth than Democrats and were strongest in New England, the middle Atlantic, and the Upper Midwest. Appealing to businessmen, bankers, manufacturers, and a few wealthy southern cotton planters, Whigs generally endorsed Clay's American System: a national bank, tariff protectionism, internal improvements, and other government action to promote economic development. For many Whigs, religious and moral values also shaped political goals. They did not think Americans needed more freedom, but rather had to learn to use freedoms they already had. Old-stock Yankee Congregationalists and Presbyterians, as well as Quakers and reform-minded evangelicals were usually Whigs. They believed that government action could change moral behavior and eradicate sin. Whigs supported reforms like temperance, antislavery, public education, and strict observance of the Sabbath.

Party identification played an increasingly large part in the lives of American men. Gaudy new electioneering styles were designed to recruit new voters into the political process and ensure loyalty. Politics offered excitement, camaraderie, and a way to shape the changing world.

The election of 1840 illustrated the new political culture. Democrats unenthusiastically renominated Van Buren. Passing over Henry Clay, the Whigs nominated William Henry Harrison, the aging hero of the Battle of Tippecanoe of 1811. The Whig reversed conventional images by labeling Van Buren an aristocratic dandy and their man as a humble candidate. The Whig campaign featured every form of popularized appeal: songs, cartoons, barbecues, and torchlight parades, and posed Harrison (who lived in a mansion) in front of a rural log cabin dispensing jugs of hard cider to grateful voters. Harrison reminded voters of General Jackson, and they swept him into office, with 234 electoral votes to Van Buren's 60. In one of the largest turnouts in American history, over 80 percent of eligible voters marched to the polls. A Democratic party leader admitted, "We taught them how to conquer us."

Harrison died after one month in office. During the campaign, one man had complained that he was tired of all the hoopla over "the Old Hero. Nothing but politics…mass-meetings are held in every groggery." The implied criticism of the role that alcohol played in party politics highlights the moral and religious perspective many Americans, especially Whigs, brought to politics.

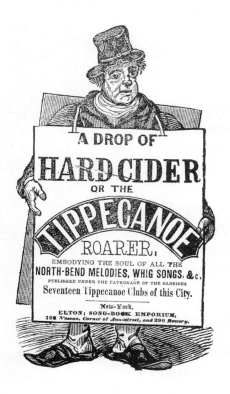

FEDERAL BANK WHIG MOTTO.

"WE STOOP TO CONQUER."

FEDERAL-ABOLITION-WHIG TRAP.

TO CATCH VOTERS IN.

Appealing to the Voters

In the cartoon depiction from the election of 1840 (left), the Whigs played to popular political appeals. How? In the log cabin cartoon (above), what dangers await this unwary voter by the promise of hard cider? "Just let him get a taste," the text said, "and they come down at once upon him, hard and heavy, swig after swig…" Which party do you think used this cartoon? Why?

(Left: Cincinnati Historical Society Library; Above: Library of Congress)

Perfectionist Reform and Utopianism

"Be ye therefore perfect even as your Father in heaven is perfect," commanded the Bible. Mid-nineteenth-century reformers, inspired by the Finney revivals, took the challenge seriously. Some believed that a perfect millennium—1,000 years of Christian peace, harmony, and brotherhood—would usher in the Second Coming of Christ.

This perfectionist thrust in religion fit America's sense of itself as chosen by God to reform the world. The impulse to reform in the 1830s had many deep-rooted causes: the Puritan idea of American mission; the secular examples of founding fathers such as Benjamin Franklin to do good; romantic beliefs in the natural goodness of human nature; the social activist tendencies in Whig political ideology; anxiety over socioeconomic change and shifting class relationships; the desire of young people to choose careers of principled service; and perhaps above all, the influence of revivalism.

The International Character and Dilemmas of Reform

Not all the forces leading to reform came from within. During the early decades of the nineteenth century, the Atlantic Ocean was a highway for reform ideas and reformers. Many of the conditions that troubled Americans, often spawned by industrialization, also troubled Europeans. Societies for temperance and to reform prostitutes were organized in England, Germany, and Ireland as well as the United States. French and British liberals agitated to end the slave trade as did their American counterparts.

A steady stream of men and women traveled from one side of the Atlantic to the other, raising money, publicizing their ideas, studying what had been done outside their own country, setting up social experiments, and exchanging ideas. Abolitionists Frederick Douglass and William Lloyd Garrison visited England to gain support for their struggle against slavery, while English abolitionists toured the northern states to assist abolitionists. Scottish cotton mill owner Robert Owen, after creating a model factory town in Scotland, came to the United States to set one up in Indiana. Owen's *The Book of the Moral World* (1820) inspired many cooperative efforts while the work of female antislavery societies in Britain and Scotland served as models for American women. Letters among reformers from different countries exchanged protest strategies, strengthened commitments, and inspired action.

Throughout the Atlantic world, reformers faced difficult dilemmas about how best to effect change. Is it more effective to appeal to people's minds and hearts in order to change flawed institutions or to change institutions first, assuming that altered behavior will then change attitudes? Taking the first path, the reformer relies on education, the moral suasion of sermons, tracts, arguments, and personal testimony. Following the second, the reformer acts politically and institutionally, seeking to pass laws, win elections, form unions, boycott goods, and create or abolish institutions.

Reformers must also decide whether to attempt to bring about limited, piecemeal, practical change on a single issue or seek idealistic perfection in eliminating all social evils. Should they use or recommend force, even violence, and enter into coalitions with less principled potential allies? Reformers invariably disagree on appropriate ideology and tactics, so they end up quarreling with one another. As Marius and Emily Robinson understood, promoting change had its costs as reformers suffered internal squabbles, social pressures, economic recriminations, and physical harm.

Utopian Communities

To redeem a flawed society, Thoreau tried to lead an ideal solitary life. Others sought to create miniature utopian societies—alternatives to a world of factories, foreigners, immorality, and materialism. Many also rejected middle-class ideals of marriage and the family.

In 1831, as President Jackson and the nullifiers squared off, as Nat Turner planned his revolt, and as the citizens of Rochester sought ways to control their workers' drinking habits, a young man in Putney, Vermont, heard Charles Finney preach. John Humphrey Noyes was an instant, if unorthodox, convert.

Noyes believed that final conversion led to perfection and complete release from sin. But his earthly happiness was soon sorely tested when a woman he loved rejected both his doctrine and his marriage offer. Despondent, he wrote to a friend, "when the will of God is done on earth as it is in heaven there will be no marriage." All men and women belonged equally to each other, he argued, while others called his doctrines "free love" and socialism. Noyes recovered from his unhappy love affair and married a loyal follower. When she bore four stillborn babies within six years, Noyes again revised his unconventional ideas about sex.

In 1848, Noyes and 51 devoted followers founded a "perfectionist" community at Oneida, New York. Sexual life at the commune was subject to many regulations, including male continence except under carefully prescribed conditions. Only certain spiritually advanced males (usually Noyes) could father children. Other controversial practices included communal child rearing, sexual equality in work, the removal of competition from both work and play, and a program of "mutual criticism" at community meetings presided over by "Father" Noyes. Although many found the Oneida rejection of middle-class marriage norms immoral, wise economic policies led to an impressive prosperity. Rather than the agricultural emphasis that typified most communes, Noyes opted for modern manufacturing, first producing steel animal traps and later silverware.

Noyes greatly admired the Shakers, who also believed in perfectionism and communal property in order to create the millennial kingdom of heaven. But unlike the Oneidans, Shakers condemned sexuality and demanded absolute chastity, so that only conversions could bring in new members. Founded by an Englishwoman, Mother Ann Lee, Shaker conversions grew during the Second Great Awakening and peaked around 6,000 souls by the 1850s, with communities from Maine to Kentucky. Shakers believed that God had a dual personality, male and female, and that Ann Lee was the female counterpart to the masculine Jesus. Shaker worship featured frenetic dancing intended to release (or "shake") sin out through the fingertips. Shaker communities were known for their communal ownership of property, equality of women and men, simplicity, and beautifully crafted furniture.

Over 100 utopian communities like Oneida and the Shaker colonies were founded. Some were religiously motivated; others were secular. Most were small, lasting only a few months or years before collapsing, while a few, such as the Amana Society of Iowa, exist to this day. While Pietistic German-speaking immigrants founded the earliest American communities to preserve their language, spirituality, and ascetic lifestyle, secular utopians focused on responding more directly to the social misery and wretched working conditions accompanying industrialization. Evil, they assumed, came from bad environments, not from individual sin.

The Scottish industrialist Owen was the best known of the secular communalists. Witnessing the miserable lives of cotton mill workers in Scotland, he envisioned a society of small towns with good schools, healthy work, and no poverty or immorality. In 1824, he established a model "harmonist" community at New Harmony, Indiana. But little harmony prevailed, and it failed within three years.

Brook Farm, founded by Concord friends of Emerson, tried to integrate "intellectual and manual labor." Residents would hoe in the fields and shovel manure for a few hours each day and then recite poetry. Although the colony lasted less than three years, it produced some notable literature in Margaret Fuller's journal, *The Dial*. Nathaniel Hawthorne briefly lived at Brook Farm and wrote a novel, *The Blithedale Romance* (1852), criticizing the utopians' naive optimism.

The utopian communities all failed for similar reasons. Most Americans seemed unwilling to share either their property or their spouses. Nor did celibacy arouse much enthusiasm. Other recurring problems included unstable leadership, financial bickering, local hostility toward sexual experimentation and other unorthodox practices, the indiscriminate admission of members, and waning enthusiasm. Emerson pinned failure on an inability to combat individualism. As he said of Brook Farm, "It met every test but life itself."

Millerites and Mormons

If utopian communities failed to bring about the peaceful millennium, an alternative hope was to leap directly to the Second Coming of Christ. William Miller, a shy farmer from upstate New York, figured out the exact time: 1843, probably in March. A sect gathered around him to prepare for Christ's return and the Day of Judgment. Excitement and fear grew as the day came closer. Some people gave away all their belongings, put on robes, and flocked to high hills and rooftops. When 1843 passed without the end of the world, Miller recalculated. Each new disappointment diminished his followers, and he died discredited in 1848. But a small Millerite sect, the Seventh-Day Adventists, abandoned predicting the date of the Second Coming, living rather with the expectation that it will be "right soon." They continue to this day.

Other groups that emerged from the same religiously active area of upstate New York were more successful. As Palmyra, New York, was being swept by Finney revivalism, young Joseph Smith, a recent convert, claimed to be visited by the angel Moroni, who led him to golden tablets buried near his home. On these were inscribed *The Book of Mormon,* which described the one true church and a "lost tribe of Israel" missing for centuries. The book also predicted the appearance of an American prophet who would establish a new and pure kingdom of Christ in America. Smith published his book in 1830 and soon founded the Church of Jesus Christ of Latter-Day Saints (the Mormons). His visionary leadership attracted thousands of ordinary people trying to escape what they viewed as social disorder, religious impurity, and commercial degradation in the 1830s.

Smith and a steadily growing band of converts migrated first to Ohio, next to Missouri, and then back to Illinois. The frequent migrations were one consequence of encountering ridicule, persecution, and violence. Hostility stemmed in part from their missionary work and support for Indians and in part from rumors of unorthodox sexual practices. But despite persecution and dissension over Smith's strong leadership style, the Mormons prospered. Converts from England and northern Europe added substantially

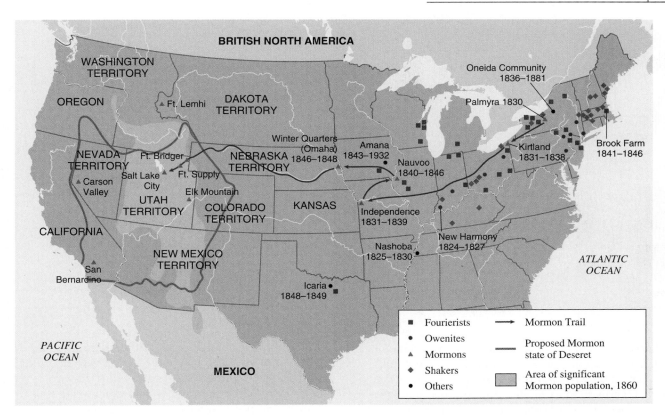

Utopian Communities Before 1860

The Mormons migrated to the trans-Mississippi West to realize their vision of a better society, but most communitarians did not go far from "civilization" to establish their experiments. Why did they not flee more settled and ordinary communities? Why did they avoid the South? Where were the most utopias (and revivals)? Why?

to their numbers. By the mid-1840s, Nauvoo, Illinois, with a thriving population of nearly 15,000, was the showplace of Mormonism.

Smith petitioned Congress for separate territorial status and ran for the presidency in 1844. This was too much for the citizens of nearby towns, who arrested and imprisoned him for breaking local laws, then broke into a weakly guarded jail and murdered him. Under the brilliant leadership of Smith's successor, Brigham Young, the Mormons headed westward in 1846 in their continuing search for the "land of promise."

Reforming Specific Social Evils

The Mormons and the utopian communitarians had as their common goal, in Young's words, "the spread of righteousness upon the earth." Most people, however, preferred to focus on remedying a specific social ill.

"We are all a little wild here," Emerson wrote in 1840, "with numberless projects of social reform." Reformers created and joined all kinds of social reform societies. Their ranks were swelled by thousands of women, stirred to action by the religious revivals and

freed from domestic burdens by delayed marriage and smaller families. In hundreds of voluntary societies, people like Emily and Marius Robinson tackled such issues as slavery, drinking, diet and health, sexuality, treatment of the mentally ill and other social outcasts, and the rights of workers and women.

Temperance

On New Year's Eve in 1831, a Finney disciple, Theodore Dwight Weld, delivered a four-hour temperance lecture in Rochester. Graphically, he described the awful fate of those who refused to stop drinking and urged his audience not only to stop their own tippling but that of others too. Several were converted on the spot. The next day, the largest providers of whiskey in Rochester rolled their barrels onto sidewalks and smashed them, as Christians cheered.

Nineteenth-century Americans drank heavily. It was said that "a house could not be raised, a field of wheat cut down, nor could there be a log rolling, a husking, a quilting, a wedding, or a funeral without the aid of alcohol." With drinking came poverty, crime, illness, insanity, battered and broken families, and corrupt politics.

Temperance propaganda

This piece of temperance propaganda is from a journal entitled *Cold Water Magazine*. Why that title? From the whole picture, what are the effects of drinking?

(The Library Company of Philadelphia [Pert 8, 51767.0, v. 1])

Early efforts at curbing alcohol emphasized moderation. Local societies agreed to limit what they drank. Some agreed only to imbibe beer and wine; others met in local taverns to toast moderation. Influenced by the revivals, the movement soon achieved clearer goals and better organization. The American Temperance Society, founded in 1826, aimed at the "teetotal" pledge, vowing to avoid all alcohol including communion wine. Within a few years thousands of local and state societies had formed.

Temperance advocates copied revival techniques. Fiery lecturers expounded on the evil consequences of drink and urged group pressure on the weak-willed. A deluge of graphic and sometimes gory and exaggerated temperance tracts poured out. "Some are killed instantly," one claimed, "some die a lingering, gradual death; some commit suicide in fits of intoxication; and some are actually burnt up" by breathing lighted candles.

By 1840, disagreements over goals and methods split the temperance movement into many separate organizations. In the "Van Ruin" depression, many out-of-work laborers, moved more by practical concerns than religious fervor, joined the crusade. The Washington Temperance Society, founded in a Baltimore tavern in 1840, was enormously popular with unemployed young workers and grew to an estimated 600,000 members in three years. The Washingtonians, arguing that alcoholism was a disease rather than moral failure, changed the shape of the temperance movement. They replaced revivalist techniques with those of the new party politics by organizing parades, picnics, and melodramas to encourage people to take the pledge.

Tactics in the 1840s shifted away from moral suasion to political action. Temperance societies lobbied for local option laws, which allowed communities to prohibit the sale, manufacture, and consumption of alcohol. The first such law in the nation was passed in Maine in 1851. Fifteen other states followed with similar laws before the Civil War. Despite weak enforcement, per capita drinking fell dramatically in the 1850s. Interrupted by the Civil War, the movement reached its ultimate objective with passage of the Eighteenth Amendment in 1919.

The temperance crusade reveals the many practical motivations for Americans to join reform societies. For some, as in Rochester, temperance provided an opportunity for the Protestant middle classes to exert some control over laborers, immigrants, and Catholics. Perfectionists saw abstinence as a way of practicing self-control. For many women, the temperance effort represented a way to control abusive husbands. For many young men, especially after the onset of the depression of 1837, a temperance society provided entertainment, fellowship, and contacts to help their careers. In temperance societies as in political parties, Americans found jobs, purpose, support, spouses, and relief from the uncertainties of a changing world.

Health and Sexuality

It was a short step from the physical and psychological ravages of drink to other potentially harmful effects on the body. Reformers were quick to attack excessive eating and stimulants, and, above all, too much sex. Many endorsed a variety of special diets and exercise programs for maintaining good health. Some promoted cure-all panaceas, including hydropathy (bathing and water purges to treat urogenital infections), hypnotism, phrenology (the study of bumps on the head), and "spiritualist" séances.

Sylvester Graham, inventor of the graham cracker, combined all these enthusiasms. In 1834, he delivered a series of lectures on chastity, later published as an advice book. To those "troubled" by sexual desire, he recommended "cold baths" and "open air exercise." Women were advised to "have intercourse only for procreation," and one doctor argued that women ought not to be educated because blood needed for the womb would be diverted to the head, thus breeding "puny men." Many females, however, developed ways of regulating sexuality for their own purposes.

Authors of antebellum "health" manuals advocated abstinence from sexual activity for men as well as women. "Sexual purity" advocates urged restraint, warning men not to "spend their seed" in unnatural acts. The body, they argued, was a closed energy system in which each organ had particular and limited functions to perform. Semen must be saved for reproductive purposes and should not be wasted in masturbation or intercourse only for pleasure. Such waste would cause enervation, disease, insanity, and death. Some argued further that the "expenditure" of sperm meant a loss of energy from the economy.

Humanizing the Asylum

Struggling to restore order to American society, some reformers preferred to work not to influence individuals but to change such institutions as asylums, almshouses, prisons, schools, and factories. Dealing with social outcasts presented special challenges. Colonial families and communities had looked after orphans, paupers, the insane, and even criminals. Beginning early in the nineteenth century, states built various institutions to house social victims. In these prisons and almshouses, the sane and insane, children and hardened adult criminals were thrown together in terrible conditions. In 1843, Dorothea Dix, a frail New Englander, reported to a horrified Massachusetts legislature that the state's imprisoned insane people lived in the "extremest state of degradation and misery," confined in "cages, closets, stalls, pens! Chained, naked, beaten with rods, and lashed into obedience!" Dix recommended special asylums where the insane could be "humanly and properly controlled" by trained attendants.

Idealistic reformers like Dix believed that asylums could reform society's outcasts. Convinced that bad institutions corrupted basically good human beings, they reasoned that reformed institutions could rehabilitate them. In 1853, Charles Loring Brace started a Children's Aid Society in New York City that was a model of change through effective education and self-help. Reformers like Dix and Brace, as well as Samuel Gridley Howe and Thomas Gallaudet, who founded institutions for the care and education of the blind and deaf, achieved remarkable results.

But all too often, results were disappointing. Prison reformers believed that a penitentiary with the right architectural design could bring a hardened criminal "back to virtue." Some preferred the rectangular prison at Auburn, New York, with its tiny cells and common workrooms; others praised Pennsylvania's star-shaped penitentiaries, each inmate in solitary confinement. Prison reformers assumed that "penitents" in isolated cells, studying the Bible and reflecting on their wrongdoing, would eventually decide to become good citizens. In fact, many criminals went mad or committed suicide. Institutions built by well-intentioned reformers became dumping places for society's outcasts, as they are today.

Working-Class Reform

Efforts to improve the institutional conditions of American life were not all top-down movements initiated and led by middle-class reformers. For working-class Americans, as in England, the institution most in need of transformation was the factory. Workers, many of them involved in other issues such as temperance, peace, and abolitionism, tried to improve their own lives.

Between 1828 and 1832, dozens of workingmen's parties arose. They advocated free, tax-supported schools; free public lands in the West; equal rights for the poor; and elimination of monopolistic privilege. Trade union activity began in Philadelphia in 1827 as skilled workers organized journeymen carpenters, plasterers, printers, weavers, tailors, and other tradesmen. That same year, 15 unions combined into a citywide federation, a process followed in other cities. The National Trades Union, founded in 1834, was the first attempt at a national labor organization.

Trade unions fared better than workingmen's parties, as Jacksonian Democrats siphoned off workers' votes. Union programs set more practical goals, including shorter hours, wages that would keep pace with rising prices, and ways (such as the closed shop) of warding off the competitive threat of cheap labor. In addition, both workers and middle-class supporters called for the abolition of imprisonment for debt and of compulsory militia duty (both of which often cost workers their jobs), free public education, improved living conditions, and the right to organize.

Fired by revolutionary tradition, rising political influence, and a union membership of near 300,000, workers struck some 168 times between 1834 and 1836. Over two-thirds of the strikes were over wages (see Chapter 10); the others were for shorter hours. Identifying with the "blood of our fathers" shed on the battlefields of the American Revolution, Boston tradesmen struck in 1835 for a 10-hour workday. They failed, and the Panic of 1837 ushered in a depression that dashed their hopes and efforts further. The 10-hour workday movement reemerged in the 1850s, promising a strengthened labor movement later in the century.

Antislavery and Its Tensions

As American workers struggled for better wages and hours in 1834, Emily and Marius Robinson arrived in Cincinnati to fight for the abolition of slavery along with others attracted by the newly founded Lane Seminary, a school to train abolitionist leaders. Financed by two wealthy New York brothers, Arthur and Lewis Tappan, Lane became a center of reform. When nervous local residents persuaded president Lyman Beecher to crack down, 75 "Lane rebels" fled to Oberlin in northern Ohio, turning Oberlin College into the first institution in the United States open both to women and men, blacks and whites. The goal of abolishing slavery often seemed as distant and unrealizable as the millennium itself. Yet by focusing on this—and other—specific evils in American society, reformers sought to bring the millennial era of peace, justice, and harmony closer.

The antislavery movement revealed more clearly than any other the passions and difficulties of the effort to improve, if not perfect, a flawed world. On January 1, 1831, eight months before Nat Turner's revolt, William Lloyd Garrison published the first issue of *The Liberator,* soon to become the leading antislavery journal in the United States. "I am in earnest," he wrote. "I will not equivocate—*and I will be heard.*" After organizing the New England Anti-Slavery Society with a group of blacks and whites in a church basement in Boston, in 1833 Garrison and 62 others established the American Anti-Slavery Society, which called for an immediate end to slavery.

Until then, most antislavery whites had advocated gradual emancipation by individual slave owners. Many joined the American Colonization Society, founded in 1816, which sent a few ex-slaves to Liberia. But these efforts proved inadequate, the main goal being to rid the country of free blacks. Rejected by African Americans, colonization lost much of its support. American opponents of slavery then turned to outright abolition. They were buoyed by antislavery victories elsewhere in the world, especially in newly independent Latin American nations and by the success of English activists in ending slavery in the British West Indies in 1833.

Garrison and others in the American Anti-Slavery Society viewed slavery as a sin and called for immediate emancipation in uncompromising language. As Garrison declared, "I do not wish to think, or speak, or write, with moderation." There could be "no Union with slaveholders," he argued, condemning the Constitution that perpetuated slavery as "an agreement with Hell." Inspired by *The Liberator* and antislavery lecturers such as Garrison and the African American activist Maria Stewart, dozens of local male and female abolitionist societies dedicated to the immediate emancipation of the slaves arose, mostly in the Northeast and the old Northwest. The African-American Female Intelligence Society, founded by free black women in Boston in 1831, was the first antislavery organization dedicated to immediate emancipation. Many others, however, still favored a gradual approach.

Abolitionists differed over tactics as well as goals. Their primary method was to convince slaveholders that slavery was a sin and slaveholders immoral. These whites, black abolitionist David Walker declared, were guilty of hypocrisy in using Christianity to justify whippings. "See how they treat us in open violation of the Bible." By 1837 abolitionists had flooded the nation with over a million pieces of antislavery literature. Slave owners were described as "manstealers," men who, as Garrison wrote, led lives of "unbridled lust . . . of infinite self-conceit, of unequalled oppression, of more than savage cruelty." In 1839, Weld published

An Abolitionist Message

This image of an imploring slave was one of the favorite abolitionist devices. Sometimes the caption asked, "Am I not a Man and a Brother?" In this case, the caption has been changed to encourage antislavery supporters to make weekly donations to the Massachusetts Anti-Slavery Society. What does the biblical text suggest? How do the objects portrayed reinforce the message?

Recovering the Past

SLAVE NARRATIVES

In the 1840s and 1850s, abolitionists eagerly sought out and published book-length accounts of slavery written by runaway slaves themselves. These chilling stories of captivity and successful escapes, in the voices of former slaves, were instrumental in influencing public opinion to end slavery. Over 100 book-length "slave narratives" were published, selections from two of which are included here.

These narratives were derived from three American autobiographical traditions: spiritual confessionals by Puritans; the rags-to-riches individualistic success story of Benjamin Franklin; and Native American captivity narratives. The last tradition, popular reading in the early nineteenth century, described the three-part process of white captives (usually women) being taken from their villages by Indians, then suffering the trials and coping adaptations of living in a Native American village, and finally returning home. Some women refused to be "redeemed," preferring to stay, often with an Indian husband.

The African American slave narratives followed a similar three-stage pattern, beginning with either a childhood in a West African village or the relative innocence of childhood on a southern plantation. Aimed at northern white readers, these stories, in vivid detail, described the brutal oppressions of slave captivity, dwelling on the horrors of the slave ships, slave auctions and the breakup of families, and the daily beatings, punishments, and harsh rigors of life on the plantation. But the narratives also described a creative and self-empowering will to survive: cunning strategies for avoiding work, sassing one's owner, connecting with loved ones, and learning how to read and write.

The narratives usually concluded with the story of escape and adopting a new identity in freedom. As William L. Andrews put it in *To Tell a Free Story,* for blacks to write their story was "in some ways uniquely self-liberating, the final, climactic act in the drama of their lifelong quests for freedom." Other themes included poignant appeals to white readers to agitate for the abolition of slavery; contrasts between the slaveholder's use of religion to justify slavery and the spiritually based Christianity of the slaves themselves; and the supportive strength of the slave community and the white and black underground network in facilitating a successful runaway.

Although not the first, the prototypical slave narrative was that of Frederick Douglass, whose story is told in Chapter 11. Douglass grew up witnessing the horrors of slavery on a Maryland plantation and in Baltimore, learned to read and write, successfully defied the cruel Mr. Covey's efforts to break his will, and finally escaped to fight for abolitionism. Similar stories were told by William Wells Brown, Olaudah Equiano, Mary Prince, Solomon Northup, Sojourner Truth, and many others; all provided gory details of whippings, the wrenching loss of loved ones, and eventual escape to freedom.

The two short selections here—from James W. C. Pennington's *Fugitive Blacksmith* (1849) and Harriet Jacobs's

Incidents in the Life of a Slave Girl (1861)—focus on the initial process of planning an escape. Jacobs wrote under the pseudonym Linda Brent. As background to this passage, she discovers that her two children are to be taken to her master's plantation to be "broke in." As you read, look for restraints on running away, anticipated difficulties, sources of support, and the intelligent cleverness of the runaways.

Reflecting on the Past What role does religion play in their efforts? What about issues of family, trust, safety, and self-reliance? What do you learn about slavery in these brief descriptions of the first moments of self-emancipation? Can you imagine the impact they had on northern readers, and why abolitionists avidly used the narratives as part of their attack on slavery?

Pennington's "he Flight"—from Fugitive Blacksmith

It was the Sabbath: the holy day which God in his infinite wisdom gave for the rest of both man and beast. In the state of Maryland, the slaves generally have the Sabbath, except in those districts where the evil weed, tobacco, is cultivated; and then, when it is the season for setting the plant, they are liable to be robbed of this only rest.

... It was a bright day, and all was quiet. Most of the slaves were resting about their quarters; others had leave to visit their friends on other plantations, and were absent. The evening previous I had arranged my little bundle of clothing, and had secreted it at some distance from the house. I had spent most of the forenoon in my workshop, engaged in deep and solemn thought.

It is impossible for me now to recollect all the perplexing thoughts that passed through my mind during that forenoon; it was a day of heartaching to me. But I distinctly remember the two great difficulties that stood in the way of my flight: I had a father and mother whom I dearly loved,—I had also six sisters and four brothers on the plantation. The question was, shall I hide my purpose from them? moreover, how will my flight affect them when I am gone? Will they not be suspected? Will not the whole family be sold off as a disaffected family, as is generally the case when one of its members flies? But a still more trying question was, how can I expect to succeed, I have no knowledge of distance or direction. I know that Pennsylvania is a free state, but I know not where its soil begins, or where that of Maryland ends? Indeed, at this time there was no safety in Pennsylvania, New Jersey, or New York, for a fugitive, except in lurking-places, or under the care of judicious friends, who could be entrusted not only with liberty, but also with life itself.

With such difficulties before my mind... I had resolved to let no one into my secret; but the other difficulty was now to be met.... The consequences of a failure would be most serious. Within my recollection no one had attempted to escape from my master; but I had many cases in my mind's eye, of slaves of other planters who had failed, and who had been made examples of the most cruel treatment, by flogging and selling to the far South, where they were never to see their friends more. I was not without serious apprehension that such would be my fate. The bare possibility was impressively solemn; but the hour was now come, and the man must act and be free, or remain a slave for ever.... The emotions of that moment I cannot fully depict. Hope, fear, dread, terror, love, sorrow, and deep melancholy were mingled in my mind together; my mental state was one of most painful distraction. When I looked at my numerous family—a beloved father and mother, eleven brothers and sisters, &c.; but when I looked at slavery as such; when I looked at it in its mildest form, with all its annoyances; and above all, when I remembered that one of the chief annoyances of slavery, in the most mild form, is the liability of being at any moment sold into the worst form; it seemed that no consideration, not even that of life itself, could tempt me to give up the thought of flight. And then when I considered the difficulties of the way—the reward that would be offered—the human blood-hounds that would be set upon my track—the weariness—the hunger—the gloomy thought, of not only losing all one's friends in one day, but of having to seek and to make new friends in a strange world. But, as I have said, the hour was come, and the man must act, or for ever be a slave.

Harriet Jacobs—from Incidents in the Life of a Slave Girl

I was meditating upon some means of escape for myself and my children. My friends had made every effort that ingenuity could devise to effect our purchase, but all their plans had proved abortive. Dr. Flint was suspicious, and determined not to loosen his grasp upon us. I could have made my escape alone; but it was more for my helpless children than for myself that I longed for freedom. Though the boon would have been precious to me, above all price, I would not have taken it at the expense of leaving them in slavery. Every trial I endured, every sacrifice I made for their sakes, drew them closer to my heart, and gave me fresh courage to beat back the dark waves that rolled and rolled over me in a seemingly endless night of storms....

My plan was to conceal myself at the house of a friend, and remain there a few weeks till the search was over. My hope was that the doctor would get discouraged, and, for fear of losing my value, and also of subsequently finding my children among the missing, he would consent to sell us; and I knew somebody would buy us. I had done all in my power to make my children comfortable during the time I expected to be separated from them....

Mr. Flint was hard pushed for house servants, and rather than lose me he had restrained his malice. I did my work faithfully, though not, of course, with a willing mind. They were evidently afraid I should leave them. Mr. Flint wished that I should sleep in the great house instead of the servants' quarters.... I did as I was ordered.

But now that I was certain my children were to be put in their power, in order to give them a stronger hold on me, I resolved to leave them that night. I remembered the grief this step would bring upon my dear old grandmother; and nothing less than the freedom of my children would have induced me to disregard her advice. I went about my evening work with trembling steps. Mr. Flint twice called from his chamber door to inquire why the house was not locked up. I replied that I had not done my work. "You have had time enough to do it," said he. "Take care how you answer me!"

I shut all the windows, locked all the doors, and went up to the third story, to wait till midnight. How long those hours seemed, and how fervently I prayed that God would not forsake me in this hour of utmost need! I was about to risk every thing on the throw of a die; and if I failed, O what would become of me and my poor children? They would be made to suffer for my fault.

At half past twelve I stole softly down stairs. I stopped on the second floor, thinking I heard a noise. I felt my way down into the parlor, and looked out of the window. The night was so intensely dark that I could see nothing. I raised the window very softly and jumped out. Large drops of rain were falling, and the darkness bewildered me. I dropped on my knees, and breathed a short prayer to God for guidance and protection. I groped my way to the road, and rushed towards the town with almost lightning speed. I arrived at my grandmother's house, but dared not see her. She would say, "Linda, you are killing me;" and I knew that would unnerve me. [She therefore stayed with another woman.]

... My grandmother's house was searched from top to bottom. As my trunk was empty, they concluded I had taken my clothes with me. Before ten o'clock every vessel northward bound was thoroughly examined, and the law against harboring fugitives was read to all on board. At night a watch was set over the town. Knowing how distressed my grandmother would be, I wanted to send her a message; but it could not be done. Every one who went in or out of her house was closely watched. The doctor said he would take my children, unless she became responsible for them; which of course she willingly did. The next day was spent in searching. Before night, the following advertisement was posted at every corner, and in every public place for miles round:—

$300 Reward! Ran away from the subscriber, an intelligent, bright, mulatto girl, named Linda, 21 years of age. Five feet four inches high. Dark eyes, and black hair inclined to curl; but it can be made straight. Has a decayed spot on a front tooth. She can read and write, and in all probability will try to get to the Free States. All persons are forbidden, under penalty of law, to harbor or employ said slave. $150 will be given to whoever takes her in the state, and $300 if taken out of the state and delivered to me, or lodged in jail.

Dr. Flint

Note: James Pennington successfully escaped to New York, where he became a Presbyterian minister and later performed Frederick Douglass's marriage rites. Harriet Jacobs hid for seven years in a cramped, tiny attic in her grandmother's house before finally escaping in disguise by ship; she eventually was reunited with her children. ■

American Slavery as It Is, which described in the goriest possible detail the inhumane treatment of slaves.

Other abolitionists preferred more direct political and economic methods. Some brought antislavery petitions before Congress and formed third parties. Boycotting goods made by slave labor was another tactic. Still another approach, although rare, was to call for slave rebellion, as did two northern blacks, Walker in an 1829 pamphlet and Henry Highland Garnet in a speech at a convention of black Americans in 1843. Walker's powerful essay, "David Walker's Appeal," called on slaves to cease their submissiveness and rise up and throw off the yoke of slavery. "Now I ask you," Walker wrote, "had you not rather be killed than to be a slave to a tyrant, who takes the life of your mother, wife, and dear little children?" It was Walker, however, who was mysteriously found dead on a Boston street a year after the publication of his pamphlet. Garnet's call for rebellion ended with the ringing cry: "*Rather die freemen, than live to be slaves.* Remember that you are THREE MILLIONS!"

Abolitionists' tactical disagreements helped splinter the movement. Garrison's unyielding personal style and support of even less popular causes such as women's rights offended many abolitionists. In 1840, at its annual meeting in New York, the American Anti-Slavery Society split. Several delegates walked out when a woman, Abby Kelley, was elected to a previously all-male committee. Those who supported multiple issues and moral suasion stayed with Garrison; others left to pursue political action and the Liberty party.

Class differences and race further divided abolitionists. Northern workers, though fearful of the potential job competition with blacks implicit in emancipation, nevertheless saw their "wage slavery" as similar to chattel slavery. Strains between northern labor leaders and middle-class abolitionists (who minimized workingmen's concerns) were similar to those between white and black antislavery forces. Whites such as Wendell Phillips decried slavery as a moral blot on American society; blacks such as Douglass were more concerned with the effects of slavery and discrimination on blacks themselves. Moreover, white abolitionists tended to see slavery and freedom as absolute opposites: a person was either a slave or free. African Americans knew that there were degrees of freedom and that northern blacks had less of it.

Black abolitionists themselves experienced prejudice, not just from ordinary northern citizens but also from white abolitionists. Many antislavery businessmen refused to hire blacks. The antislavery societies usually provided less than full membership rights for blacks, assigning them menial tasks, and perpetuated black stereotypes in their literature. A white abolitionist, a black wrote, was described as one who hated "slavery which is 1,000 to 1,500 miles away," but who hated even more "a man who wears a black skin."

Conflict between Garrison and Douglass reflected these tensions. The famous runaway was one of the most effective orators in the movement. But after a while, rather than simply describing his life as a slave, Douglass began skillfully to analyze abolitionist policies. Garrison warned him that if he sounded too smart, audiences would never believe he had been a slave; other whites told him to stick to the facts and let them take care of the philosophy. Douglass gradually moved away from Garrison's views, endorsing political action and sometimes even slave rebellion. Garrison's response was to denounce his independence as "ungrateful. . . and malevolent in spirit." In 1847, Douglass started his own journal, the *North Star,* later called *Frederick Douglass's Paper.* In it, he expressed his appreciation for the help of that "noble band of white laborers" but declared that it was time for those who "suffered the wrong" to lead the way in advocating liberty.

Moving beyond Garrison, a few black nationalists, such as the fiery Martin Delany, totally rejected white American society and advocated emigration to Africa. Most blacks, however, were practical and agreed with Douglass to work to end slavery and discrimination in the United States. David Ruggles in New York and William Still in Philadelphia led black vigilance groups that helped fugitive slaves escape to Canada or to safe northern black settlements. Black ministers and leaders such as Douglass, Garnet, Maria Stewart, William Wells Brown, and Sojourner Truth lectured and wrote journals and slave narratives on the evils of slavery. They also organized a National Negro Convention movement, which began holding annual meetings in 1830, meeting not only to condemn slavery but also to discuss issues of discrimination facing northern free blacks.

Flood Tide of Abolitionism

Black and white abolitionists, however, usually worked together well. The first subscribers to Garrison's *Liberator* were nearly all African American, and an estimated 80 percent of the readers of Douglass's paper were white. Weld and Garrison often stayed in the homes of black abolitionists when they traveled. In addition, black and white "stations" cooperated on the Underground Railroad, passing fugitives from one hiding place to the next.

The two races worked together to fight discrimination as well as slavery. When David Ruggles was dragged from the "white car" of a New Bedford, Massachusetts, railway in 1841, Garrison, Douglass, and 40 other protesters organized the first successful integrated "sit-in" in American history. Blacks and whites also worked harmoniously in protesting segregated schools; after several years of legal challenges in Massachusetts, in 1855 they forced it to become the first state to outlaw segregated public education. It would take 99 years before the U.S. Supreme Court began desegregating schools throughout the country.

White and black abolitionists were united perhaps most closely by defending themselves against attacks by people who regarded them as dangerous fanatics bent on disrupting society. As abolitionists organized to rid the nation of slavery, many southerners and northerners increasingly sought to rid the nation of abolitionists. Mob attacks, like the one on Marius Robinson in Ohio, occurred frequently in the mid-1830s. Abolitionists were stoned, dragged through streets, ousted from their jobs and homes, and reviled by northern mobs. Weld, known as "the most mobbed man in the United States," could hardly finish a speech without disruption. Douglass endured similar attacks. Garrison was saved from a Boston mob only by being put in jail. In 1837, Elijah Lovejoy, an Illinois antislavery editor, was murdered.

Antiabolitionists were as fervid as the abolitionists. "I warn the abolitionists, ignorant and infatuated barbarians as they are," growled one South Carolinian, "that if chance shall throw any of them into our hands, they may expect a felon's death." One widely circulated book in 1836 described opponents of slavery, led by the "gloomy, wild, and malignant" Garrison, as "crack-brained enthusiasts" and "female fanatics." President Jackson denounced abolitionists in his annual message in 1835 as "incendiaries" who

deserved to have their "unconstitutional and wicked" activities broken up by mobs, and he urged Congress to ban antislavery literature from the U.S. mails. A year later, southern Democratic congressmen passed a "gag rule" to stop the flood of abolitionist petitions in Congress.

By the 1840s, the antislavery movement had gained significant strength. Many northerners, including workers otherwise unsympathetic to ending slavery, decried mob violence, supported free speech, and denounced the South and its northern defenders as undemocratic. The gag rule, interference with the mails, and the killing of Lovejoy seemed proof of the growing influence of an evil slave power. Former president John Quincy Adams, now a congressman, devoted himself to repeal of the gag rule, which he finally achieved in 1844, keeping the matter alive until the question of slavery in the territories became the dominant national political issue of the 1850s (see Chapter 14). Meanwhile, black and white abolitionists struggled on using many different tactics without yet knowing that the only one that would eventually work would be civil war.

Women's Rights

In a religious reflection in 1832, Maria Stewart asked who would rid "people of color" of their burdens: "Shall it be a woman?" she wondered. Stewart, Ann Lee, Dorothea Dix, and many other women came to reform through religious conviction. Activism in the movements for abolitionism, care of society's outcasts, black rights, and other reforms led many women to

Stopping a Debate on Abolition

It was dangerous to be an abolitionist. In this 1860 Winslow Homer engraving for *Harper's Weekly*, Homer shows Frederick Douglass being forced from a Boston temple platform by pro-southern demonstrators, who interrupted the meeting called to debate "How can American slavery be Abolished?" With opposition like this in Boston, the heart of abolitionist sentiment, how *could* slavery be abolished?

(Expulsion of the Negroes and Abolitionists from Tremont Temple, Boston, Massachusetts, on December 3, 1860, 1860, Winslow Homer. The Museum of Fine Arts, Houston; The Mavis P. Wilson Kelsey Collection of Winslow Homer Graphics)

realize the need to struggle for their own rights, beginning with the right to speak in public.

In 1836, Abby Kelley, a young Quaker teacher in Massachusetts, began circulating antislavery petitions. Two years later, Kelley braved the threats of an angry crowd in Philadelphia by delivering a fiery abolitionist speech to a convention of antislavery women so eloquently that Weld told her that if she did not join the movement full-time, "God will smite you." Before the convention was over, incensed by both abolitionism and women speaking in public, a mob burned the hall to the ground. The opposition to her work led Kelley to observe that American women "have good cause to be grateful to the slave," for in "striving to strike his iron off, we found most surely, that we were manacled *ourselves*."

Dress Reform

One of the reforms proposed during the antebellum period was the reform of women's clothing. How would you describe the bloomer costume pictured here? What advantages did it offer compared to women's usual attire? Are there class implications to this costume? What reasons might a person have to oppose dress reform?

(Library of Congress)

Kelley left teaching to devote all her efforts to antislavery and women's rights. When she married, she retained her own name and went on lecture tours of the West while her husband stayed home to care for their daughter. Other young women were also defining unconventional new relationships while illustrating the profound difficulty of both fulfilling traditional roles and speaking out for change. Angelina and Sarah Grimké, outspoken Quaker sisters from Philadelphia who had grown up in slaveholding South Carolina, went to New England in 1837 to lecture for abolitionism. Criticized for speaking to audiences containing both men and women, Angelina defended women's rights to speak in public. After the tour, Angelina married Theodore Weld and stopped her public lectures to show that she could also be a good wife and mother. But she and Sarah, who moved in with her, undertook most of the research and writing for Weld's book attacking American slavery.

Young white couples like these, while pursuing reform, also experimented with equal relationships in an age that assigned distinctly unequal roles to husbands and wives. On the one hand, women were told that their sphere was the home, upholding piety and virtue. On the other hand, they were assured that their ethical influence would be "felt around the globe." Not surprisingly, many women joined movements to cleanse America of its sins, as well as to improve their own condition.

To achieve greater personal autonomy, antebellum American women, like their English sisters, pursued several paths depending on their class and cultural situation. In 1834, Lowell textile workers went on strike against wage reductions while looking to marriage as an escape from millwork. In what has been called "domestic feminism," Catharine Beecher argued that by accepting marriage and the home as woman's sphere and by doing domestic duties women could best achieve power and autonomy. They also could exert control over their own bodies by persuading their husbands to practice abstinence, coitus interruptus, and other forms of birth control.

Other women found an outlet for their role as moral guardians by attacking the sexual double standard. In 1834, a group of Presbyterian women formed the New York Female Moral Reform Society. Inspired by revivalism, they visited brothels, opened a refuge house to convert prostitutes, and even publicly identified brothel patrons. Within five years, there were 445 auxiliaries of the society.

Lowell mill workers and New York moral reformers generally accepted the duties—and opportunities—of female domesticity. Other women did not, preferring to gain control over their lives by working directly for more legally protected rights, campaigning for married women's control of their property and custody of their children. The more active women were in fighting for their rights the more hostility they encountered, especially from conservative clergymen quoting the Bible to justify female inferiority and servility. Sarah Grimké was criticized once too often. She struck back in 1837 with *Letters on the Condition of Women and the Equality of the Sexes*, stating that "whatever is right for man to do, is right for woman." Arguing that men ought to be satisfied with 6,000 years of dominion based on a false interpretation of the Creation story, Grimké concluded that she sought "no favors for my sex. I surrender not our claim to equality. All I ask of our brethren is, that they will take their feet from off our necks and permit us to stand upright on that ground which God designed us to occupy."

Grimké's strong message was soon translated into an active movement for women's rights. Illustrative of its international character, the American movement was

Timeline

1826	American Temperance Society founded
1828	Jackson defeats Adams for the presidency
	Tariff of Abominations
	Calhoun publishes *Exposition and Protest*
1830	Webster–Hayne debate and Jackson–Calhoun toast
	Joseph Smith, *The Book of Mormon*
	Indian Removal Act
1830–1831	Charles Finney's religious revivals
1831	Garrison begins publishing *The Liberator*
1832	Jackson vetoes U.S. Bank charter and reelected
	Worcester v. *Georgia*
1832–1833	Nullification crisis and Force Bill
1832–1836	Removal of funds from U.S. Bank to state banks
1833	American Anti-Slavery Society founded
1834	New York Female Moral Reform Society founded
	Whig party established
1835–1836	Countless incidents of mob violence
1836	"Gag rule" against antislavery petitions
1837	Financial panic, depression to follow
	Sarah Grimké, *Letters on the Condition of Women and the Equality of the Sexes*
1837–1838	Cherokee "Trail of Tears"
1840	William Henry Harrison elected president
	American Anti-Slavery Society splits
	World Anti-Slavery Convention
1840–1841	Transcendentalists found Brook Farm
1843	Dorothea Dix's report on treatment of the insane
1844	Joseph Smith murdered in Nauvoo, Illinois
1846–1848	Mormon migration to the Great Basin in Utah
1847	First issue of Frederick Douglass's *North Star*
1848	Oneida community founded
	First women's rights convention at Seneca Falls, New York
1855	Massachusetts bans segregated public schools

born in London. At the World Anti-Slavery Convention in 1840, attended by many American abolitionists, male delegates refused to let women participate. Two of the women, Elizabeth Cady Stanton and Lucretia Mott, had to sit behind curtains and were forbidden to speak. When they returned home, they resolved to "form a society to advocate the rights of women." In 1848, in Seneca Falls, New York, their intentions, though delayed, were fulfilled in one of the most significant protest gatherings of the antebellum era.

In preparing for the meeting, Mott and Stanton drew up a list of women's grievances. Modeling their "Declaration of Sentiments" on the Declaration of Independence, the women at Seneca Falls proclaimed it a self-evident truth that "all men and women are created equal" and that men had usurped women's freedom and dignity. The remedy was expressed in 11 resolutions calling for equal opportunities in education and work, equality before the law, and the right to appear on public platforms. The most controversial resolution called for women's "sacred right to the elective franchise." The convention approved all the resolutions.

Throughout the 1850s, led by Stanton and Susan B. Anthony, women continued to meet in annual conventions, working by resolution, persuasion, and petition campaign to achieve equal political, legal, and property rights with men. The right to vote, however, was considered the cornerstone of the movement. It remained so for 72 years of struggle until 1920 with the passage of the Nineteenth Amendment. The Seneca Falls convention was crucial in beginning the campaign for gender equity as well as sowing the seeds of other forms of liberation that continue to this day.

Conclusion
PERFECTING AMERICA

Responding to profound socioeconomic developments in American society, and inspired by religious revivalism, advocates for temperance, antislavery, women's rights, and other reforms carried on very different crusades than those waged by Jackson against Native Americans, nullificationists, and the U.S. Bank. In fact, Jacksonian politics and antebellum reform were often at odds. Most reformers were anti-Jackson Whigs. Jackson and most Democrats disliked the moral fervor of reformers.

Yet both sides shared more than either side would admit. Reformers and political parties both mirrored new tensions in a changing, growing society. Both had an abiding faith in democratic dreams of a better America. Both believed in the idea of progress, yet feared that sinister forces jeopardized that progress. Whether ridding the nation of alcohol or the national bank, slavery or political opponents, both forces saw these responsibilities in terms of patriotic duty. Whether inspired by religious revivalism or party loyalty, both believed that by stamping out evil forces, they could shape a better America. Whether politicians like Jackson and Clay, religious community leaders like Noyes and Ann Lee, or reformers like Garrison, the Grimkés, and Emily and Marius Robinson, antebellum Americans sought to remake their country politically and morally as it underwent social and economic change.

As the United States neared mid-century, slavery emerged as the most divisive issue. Against much opposition, the reformers had made slavery a matter of national political debate by the 1840s. Although both major political parties tried to evade the question, westward expansion would soon make avoidance impossible. Would new states be slave or free? The question increasingly aroused the deepest passions of the American people. For the pioneer family, who formed the driving force behind the westward movement, however, questions involving their dreams seemed more immediate. We turn to this family and that movement in the next chapter.

QUESTIONS FOR REVIEW AND REFLECTION

1. How does the story of Marius Robinson and Emily Rakestraw introduce the major themes and structure of the chapter?
2. What social, economic, and political forces motivated Americans to seek ways of controlling their lives? How did they try to shape both their own lives and also America?
3. What were the major issues of Jackson's presidential administration? Do you think he was primarily a unifier or a divider? Did he advance or set back the development of American democracy? Explain your response.
4. What were the key differences between Democrats and Whigs? Who supported each party and why? Which would you have supported, and why?
5. What was the role of religion in antebellum American life? How did revivalism affect social change? Do you agree that this was the proper function of religion?
6. What were the three (or four) major antebellum reform movements? What motivations, values, challenges, and resources were common to each of them? Would you have been a reformer? Why or why not?

CHAPTER 13

Moving West

A Vision of the Westward Movement

This 1872 painting by John Gast—with its large, goddesslike figure trailing telegraph lines, its parade of settlers, and its depiction of technological progress—captures the confidence of white Americans that the acquisition of the West was a positive and inevitable event. What picture does this painting give of the emigration to the West? What emigrants moving into the West are omitted?

(John Gast, *Westward, Ho! (American Progress).* Museum of the American West Collection, Autry National Center)

American Stories

The Surprises of a Missionary Life

It was July 4, 1836, but nothing in her 28 years had prepared Narcissa Whitman for the sights and sounds that marked this particular holiday. Earlier in the day, Narcissa and the party with which she was traveling had crossed over the South Pass of the Rocky Mountains, a memorable milestone for the nation's birthday. Now evening had come, and the caravan had set up camp for the night. Suddenly, wild cries and the sound of gunshots and galloping horses broke the silence. Fourteen or fifteen men, most dressed as Native Americans, advanced toward the camp. Frightened by the threatening appearance of the horsemen, the noise, and the bullets whizzing over her head, Narcissa may well have wondered if her journey and even her life were to end. But as the horsemen approached, the anxious travelers could make out a white flag tied to one of the riders' rifles. These were not foes but friends who had ridden out from the annual fur traders' rendezvous to greet the caravan.

Two days later Narcissa reached the rendezvous site, where hundreds of Indians as well as 200 whites, mostly traders and trappers, were gathered to exchange furs, tell stories, drink, and enjoy themselves. Some of the mounted Native Americans, "carrying their war weapons, wearing their war emblems and implements of music," put on a special display. The exhibition was a novelty for Narcissa as was her presence for the Native Americans. Narcissa found herself the center of attention "in the midst of [a] gazing throng" of curious Indians. The experience was not unpleasant, and Narcissa's impression of the natives was favorable: "They all like us and that we have come to live with them."

Narcissa Whitman was one of the first white women to cross the Rocky Mountains and live in Oregon Territory in the 1830s. While many more Americans would follow her, only a few would share her reasons for coming west. They would come to farm, dig for gold, speculate in land, open a store, or practice law. However, Narcissa and her husband, Dr. Marcus Whitman, did not go west to better their lives but to carry God's word to the Native Americans. Inspired by the revivals of the Second Great Awakening and convinced that all non-Christians were headed toward eternal damnation, Narcissa and her husband came to settle among the Native Americans in Oregon Territory and to convert them to Christianity and the American way of life.

This dream of becoming a missionary was one Narcissa had nourished since her early teens. But once the Whitmans had established their mission station in the Walla Walla valley, Narcissa slowly discovered that missionary work was nothing like her youthful fantasies.

Although the Cayuse Indians listened to the missionaries and even adopted some Christian practices, they never lived up to the Whitmans' high standards. None had the conversion experiences that the Whitmans judged necessary for admittance to the Presbyterian church nor were they quick to abandon Native American customs. They continued to consult their medicine men and refused to settle permanently next to the mission station. Cayuse women seemed little interested in the middle-class domestic skills Narcissa wished to teach them. Narcissa's positive impression of Native Americans disappeared. The Cayuse, she wrote, were "insolent, proud, domineering, arrogant, and ferocious."

There were other disappointments and personal tragedies as well. Marcus was often away from the mission on medical business, and Narcissa was lonely and sometimes frightened when he was absent. Her beloved daughter fell into the river and drowned. Often sick and unhappy, Narcissa did not conceive again.

As time passed, however, Narcissa's dismay and depression over her lack of success faded as hopeful signs of new possibilities other than Indian missionary work appeared. As she wrote to her mother in 1840, "a tide of immigration appears to be moving this way rapidly." In the following years, more and more American families made their way past the mission station, headed for the Willamette valley. In one wagon train was a family of children who had been orphaned during their journey. The Whitmans took them in and adopted all seven children. Narcissa threw herself into caring for them and found herself too busy to work actively with the Cayuse.

The Native Americans were dismayed at the numbers of whites coming into the territory, but the Whitmans, convinced that the future of the West lay with the emigrants, welcomed them. The day of the Indians had passed. As a "hunted, despised and unprotected" people, the Whitmans believed that the Native Americans were headed toward "entire extinction." But in an unexpected turn of events, some of the Cayuse protested against this vision, turned against the Whitmans, and killed them both. Such violent actions did nothing to hold back the swarm of Americans heading west.

Narcissa Whitman and her husband, Marcus, were among thousands of Americans who played a part in the nation's expansion into the trans-Mississippi West. While the religious faith that drove them west differentiated them from many crossing the western plains and prairies, the Whitmans' cultural beliefs about the inferiority of the Native Americans and the necessity of American settlement were widely shared. Shared too was the conviction that American values and way of life were superior to those of the Native Americans and Mexicans who occupied the land.

This chapter describes the public and private events between 1830 and 1865 that created a nation that stretched from the Atlantic to the Pacific ocean. The story of the expansion that resulted in the country as we know it today has long constituted one of the great themes in American history. Here, we will consider how and when Americans moved into the trans-Mississippi West, by what means the United States acquired the vast territories that in 1840 belonged to other nations, and the meaning of "Manifest Destiny," the slogan used to defend the conquest of the continent west of the Mississippi River. Then we explore the nature of life on the western farms; in western mining communities where Latin American, Chinese, and European adventurers mingled with American fortune seekers; and in western cities. Finally, the chapter examines responses of Native Americans and Mexican Americans to expansion and illuminates the ways different cultural traditions intersected in the West.

Probing the Trans-Mississippi West

Until the 1840s, most Americans lived east of the Mississippi in a nation with fluid and changing boundaries. By 1860, however, some 4.3 million Americans had moved beyond the great river into the trans-Mississippi West, and the United States had acquired fixed boundaries with Canada and Mexico and reached the western edge of the continent.

The International Context for American Expansionism

When the Whitmans arrived in Oregon Territory, they stayed at a bustling British fur trading post with hundreds of workers, French Canadians, English, Scots, and many from mixed European–Indian backgrounds. The establishment symbolized the international setting within which American expansionism occurred. The shifting interests and fortunes of several European nations helped shape the character and timing of westward emigration even though individual settlers might not recognize the global forces affecting their experiences.

In 1815, except for Louisiana Territory, Spain held title to most of the trans-Mississippi West. For hundreds of years, Spaniards had marched north from Mexico to explore, settle, and spread Spanish culture to native peoples. Eventually, Spanish holdings included present-day Texas, Arizona, New Mexico, Nevada, Utah, western Colorado, California, and parts of Wyoming, Kansas, and Oklahoma. Spanish rulers tried to exclude foreigners from these frontier areas but increasingly found this policy difficult to enforce. The area was vast, and Spain itself was experiencing internal difficulties that weakened its hold on its New World colonies. In 1820, the conservative Spanish monarch faced liberal revolt at home. Its ideas sparked liberation movements in the New World.

In 1821, Mexico declared its independence and acquired Spain's territories in the trans-Mississippi West with a population that included 75,000 Spanish-speaking inhabitants and numerous Native American tribes. While maintaining control of this distant region and its peoples would have been difficult under any circumstances, Mexico was not successful in forming a strong or a stable government until the 1860s. It was in a weak position to resist the avid American appetite for expansion.

North of California lay Oregon country, a vaguely defined area extending to Alaska. Russia, Spain, and Great Britain, all had claims to Oregon, but negotiations with Russia and Spain in 1819 and 1824 left just the United States and Britain in contention for the territory. Joint British–American occupation, agreed on in 1818 and 1827, delayed settling the boundary question. With only a handful of Americans in the territory, Oregon's future would depend partly on how Britain, the world's richest and most powerful country, defined its interests there as Americans began to stream into Oregon in the 1840s.

Early Interest in the West

Some Americans penetrated the trans-Mississippi West long before the great migrations of the 1840s and 1850s. The fur business attracted American trappers and traders to Oregon by 1811 and a decade later to the Rockies. Many of these men married Native American women and established valuable connections with tribes involved in trapping. Along with their wives, they occupied a cultural middle ground characterized by elements from both American and native ways of life. Some ultimately became guides for Americans who emigrated later to the West.

Like the Whitmans, Methodist missionaries established early outposts in Oregon territory to teach native tribes Christian and American practices. Roman Catholic priests, sent from Europe, also worked among

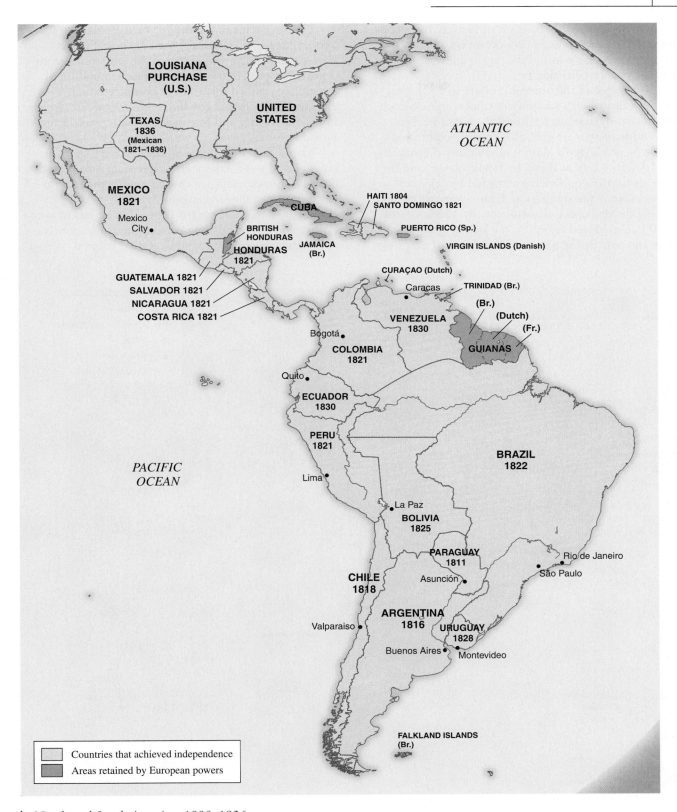

North and South America, 1800–1836

Events in Europe had a dramatic impact on the Americas. The popularization of the ideas of the French Revolution and Napoleon's defeat of the Spanish king in 1808 contributed to ending Spanish rule in the Americas. Note how rapidly countries claimed their independence in the Southern Hemisphere and Latin America. How did the changing political landscape of the Americas affect the power and influence of the United States in the region?

the native peoples. More tolerant of Native American culture than their Protestant counterparts, the Catholics had greater initial success in converting native peoples to Christianity.

The collapse of the Spanish Empire in 1821 provided Americans with a variety of opportunities. Each year American caravans followed the Santa Fe Trail, loaded with weapons, tools, and brightly colored calicoes for New Mexico's 40,000 inhabitants. Eventually, some "Anglos" settled there. In Texas, cheap land for cotton rather than commerce attracted settlers and squatters just as the small local Tejano population was adjusting to Mexico's independence. By 1835, almost 30,000 had migrated to Texas, the largest group of Americans outside the nation's boundaries at that time.

On the Pacific, a handful of New England traders carrying sea-otter skins to China anchored in the harbors of Spanish California in the early nineteenth century. By the 1830s, as the near extermination of the animals ruined this trade, a commerce that exchanged California cowhides and tallow for clothes, boots, hardware, and furniture manufactured in the East developed.

Tribes driven from the South and the Old Northwest by the American government into present-day Oklahoma and Kansas were among the earliest easterners to settle in the trans-Mississippi West. Ironically, some of these tribes acted as agents of white civilization by introducing cotton, the plantation system, black slavery, and schools. Other tribes triggered

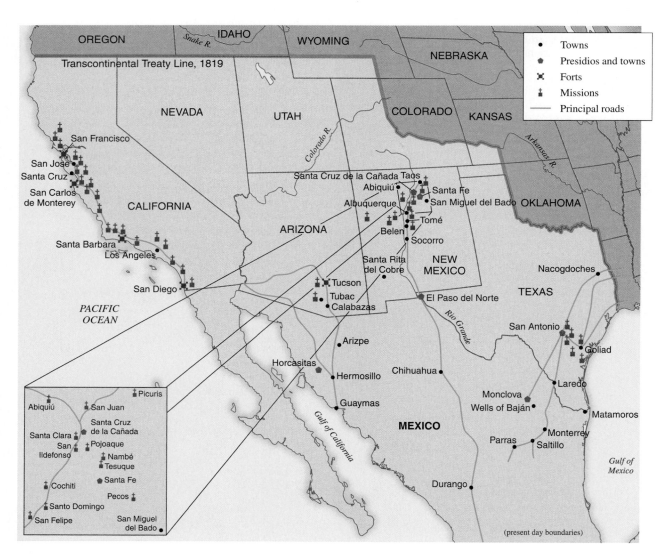

Mexico in 1821

Mexico won its independence from Spain in 1821 and inherited vast Spanish territories north of the Rio Grande. This map suggests the modest development of these northern holdings and their distance from the center of Mexico. How might the geographical realities represented in this map have affected the attitudes of American and Mexican diplomats and ordinary people?

conflicts that weakened the western tribes with whom they came into contact. These disruptions foreshadowed white incursions later in the century.

The fact that much of the trans-Mississippi West lay outside U.S. boundaries and that the government had guaranteed Indian tribes permanent possession of some western territories failed to deter American economic or missionary activities. By the 1840s, a growing volume of published works like Lansford Hastings's *Emigrants' Guide to Oregon and California* (1845) provided both practical information and a rationale for emigration. American settlement would bring "genuine Republicanism and unsophisticated Democracy" to the West, replacing "ignorance, superstition, and despotism."

Hastings's confidence that the future of the West lay with the United States was speedily realized. During the 1840s the United States, by war and diplomacy, acquired Mexico's possessions in the Southwest and on the Pacific and title to the Oregon country up to the 49th parallel. With the Gadsden Purchase in 1853, the country obtained another chunk of Mexican territory.

Manifest Destiny

Florid rhetoric accompanied territorial growth, and Americans used the slogan "Manifest Destiny" to justify expansion. The phrase, coined in 1845, suggested that the country's superior institutions and culture gave Americans a God-given right, even an obligation, to spread their civilization across the entire continent. This sense of uniqueness and mission shows the continuing legacy of early Puritan utopianism and Revolutionary republicanism. By the 1840s, the successful absorption of the Louisiana Territory, rapid population growth, and advances in transportation, communication, and industry bolstered the belief in national superiority. Publicists of Manifest Destiny proclaimed that the nation not only could but must absorb new territories.

Winning the Trans-Mississippi West

Manifest Destiny justified expansion, but events in Texas triggered the government's determination to move west of the Mississippi River. The Texas question originated in the years when Spain held the sparsely populated and underdeveloped Southwest. Primarily a buffer zone for Mexico, the area had scattered Spanish settlements, distant from one another and thousands of miles from Mexico City. Vulnerable as this weak defensive perimeter of the Spanish Empire was, the United States had recognized its legal status with the Adams-Onís Treaty of 1819, which, in return for Florida, specifically conceded Texas to Spain.

Annexing Texas, 1845

By the time the treaty was ratified in 1821, Mexico was independent but hardly able to defend its borderlands or to develop powerful bonds of national identity. Mexicans soon had reason to wonder whether Americans would honor the terms of the treaty. As American politicians like Henry Clay began to cry out for "reannexation" of Texas, Mexican fears about American intentions grew.

In 1823, the Mexican government resolved to strengthen border areas by increasing population. In return for token payments and pledges to adopt Roman Catholicism and Mexican citizenship, settlers were promised land. Stephen F. Austin was among the first Americans to take up this offer. Most settlers were southerners, and some brought slaves. By the end of the decade, some 15,000 white Americans, 1,000 slaves, and just 5,000 Tejanos lived in Texas.

Mexican officials soon had second thoughts. Although Austin converted to Roman Catholicism, few settlers honored their bargain. Some were malcontents who disliked Mexican laws and customs and the limitations on their opportunities. In late 1826, a small group declared the Republic of Fredonia. Although Stephen Austin helped to crush the uprising, American newspapers praised the rebels as "apostles of democracy."

Mexican anxiety rose. Secretary of Foreign Relations Lucas Aláman branded American settlers advance agents of the United States. In 1829, the Mexican government determined to curb American influence by abolishing slavery in Texas. In 1830, it forbade further American emigration. But little changed. American slave owners evaded the mandate to abolish slavery while emigrants still crossed the border into Texas.

Tensions escalated, and in October 1835, a skirmish between the colonial militia and Mexican forces opened hostilities. Sam Houston, onetime governor of Tennessee and army officer, became commander in chief of the Texas forces. Although Texans called the war with Mexico a revolution, it was in fact as one Vermont soldier observed, "a rebellion."

The new Mexican dictator and general Antonio López de Santa Anna hurried north to crush the rebellion with an army of 6,000 conscripts, many of them Mayan Indians who spoke no Spanish and were exhausted by the long march. Supply lines were spread thin. Nevertheless, Santa Anna and his men won initial engagements. They took the Alamo in San Antonio, defended by 187 Americans, all of whom were killed, and then the fortress of Goliad, where more than 300 Americans lost their lives.

As he pursued Houston and the Texans toward the San Jacinto River, carelessness proved Santa Anna's undoing. Although anticipating an American attack, the Mexican general and his men settled down to their usual siesta on April 21, 1836, without posting an adequate guard. As the Mexicans dozed, the Americans attacked. With cries of "Remember the Alamo! Remember Goliad!" the Texans overcame the army, captured its commander in his slippers, and won the war within 20 minutes. American casualties were minimal, but 630 Mexicans lay dead.

Vanquished and threatened with lynching, Santa Anna signed treaties recognizing Texan independence. When news of the disaster reached Mexico City, however, the Mexican Congress repudiated an "agreement carried out under the threat of death" and maintained that Texas was still part of Mexico.

The new republic, financially unstable with questionable diplomatic status, sought admission to the Union. Jackson, whose Texas agent reported that the republic's "future security must depend more upon the weakness and imbecility of her enemy than upon her own strength," was reluctant to act quickly. With 13 free and 13 slave states, many northerners violently opposed annexing another slave state. Petitions poured into Congress in 1837 opposing annexation, and John Quincy Adams repeatedly denounced it. Soon the explosive idea was dropped.

For the next few years, the Lone Star Republic led a precarious existence. Mexico refused to recognize it, but could send only an occasional raiding party across the border. Texans suffered an ignominious defeat in an ill-conceived attempt to capture Santa Fe in 1841. Diplomatic maneuvering in European capitals for financial aid and recognition was only moderately successful. Financial ties with the United States, however, increased.

Texas became headline news again in 1844. As one Alabama expansionist declared, "I predict [it] will agitate the country more than all the other public questions ever have." He was right. The annexation issue exploded after President John Tyler (who assumed office after Harrison's sudden death) reopened it as a means of ensuring his reelection. Powerful sectional, national, and political tensions sprang to life, demonstrating the divisiveness of the slavery-expansion question. Southern Democrats claimed that the South's future hinged on the annexation of Texas.

Other wings of the Democratic party capitalized more successfully on the issue, however. Stephen Douglas of Illinois, among others, vigorously supported annexation, not because it would expand slavery (a topic he avoided), but because it would spread American civilization. Such arguments, classic examples of the basic tenets of Manifest Destiny, put the question into a national context of expanding American freedom. So powerfully did he and others link Texas to Manifest Destiny while avoiding sectional issues that their candidate, James Polk of Tennessee, secured the Democratic nomination in 1844. Polk called for both "the reannexation of Texas at the earliest practicable period" and the occupation of the Oregon Territory.

Afraid of the addition of another slave state, Whigs tended to oppose annexation. They accused Democrats of exploiting Manifest Destiny, more as a means of securing office than of bringing freedom to Texas. As the Whigs had feared, Polk rode the issue to win a close election in 1844.

But by the time he took the oath of office in March 1845, Tyler had resolved the question of annexation. In his last months of office, he pushed through Congress a joint resolution admitting Texas to the Union. Unlike a treaty, which required the approval of two-thirds of the Senate, a joint resolution needed only majority support. Nine years after its revolution, Texas finally joined the Union with the right to divide into five states if it chose to do so.

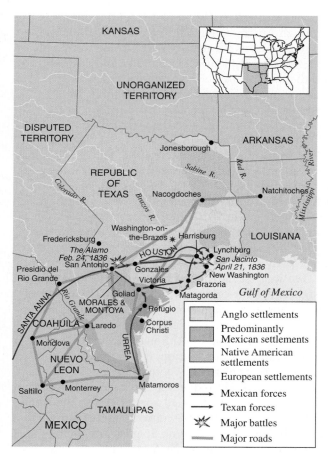

U.S. Territorial Expansion by 1860

This map reveals the different stages of American expansion west. How would you contrast the expansion of the United States after the Revolution to the nineteenth century territorial acquisitions?

War with Mexico, 1846–1848

Learning of Texas's annexation, Mexico promptly severed diplomatic ties with the United States. It was easy for Mexicans to interpret the events from the 1820s on as an American plot to steal Texas. During the war for Texas independence, American newspapers, especially those in the South, enthusiastically supported the rebels, while southern money and volunteers had aided the Texans. Now, in his 1845 inaugural address, President Polk asserted "that our system may easily be extended to the utmost bounds of our territorial limits, and that as it shall be extended the bonds of our Union, so far from being weakened will become stronger." Did those territorial limits extend deeper into Mexico?

Polk, like many other Americans, failed to appreciate how the annexation of Texas humiliated Mexico and increased pressures on its government to respond belligerently. Because Mexico was weak, the president anticipated acquiescence to his grandiose demands: a Texas boundary at the Rio Grande rather than the Nueces River 150 miles to the north, as well as California and New Mexico.

As a precaution, Polk ordered General Zachary Taylor to move "on or near the Rio Grande." By October 1845, Taylor and 3,500 American troops had reached the Nueces River. The presence of the army did not mean that Polk actually expected war. Rather, he hoped that military might, coupled with secret diplomacy, would bring the desired concessions. In November, the president sent his agent, John L. Slidell, to Mexico City with instructions to secure the Rio Grande border and to buy Upper California and New Mexico. When the Mexican government refused to receive Slidell, Polk angrily decided to force Mexico into accepting American terms. He ordered Taylor south to the Rio Grande. To the Mexicans, this constituted an act of war. Democratic newspapers and expansionists enthusiastically hailed Polk's provocative decision; Whigs opposed it.

In late April, the Mexican government declared a state of defensive war. Two days later, a skirmish between Mexican and American troops resulted in 16 American casualties. When Polk heard the news, he quickly drafted a war message for Congress. Despite the fact that the skirmish had occurred partly on contested ground and partly on Mexican territory, Polk claimed that Mexico had "passed the boundary of the United States . . . invaded our territory and shed American blood upon American soil." "War exists," he claimed, "by act of Mexico."

Although Congress declared war, the conflict bitterly divided Americans. Many Whigs, including

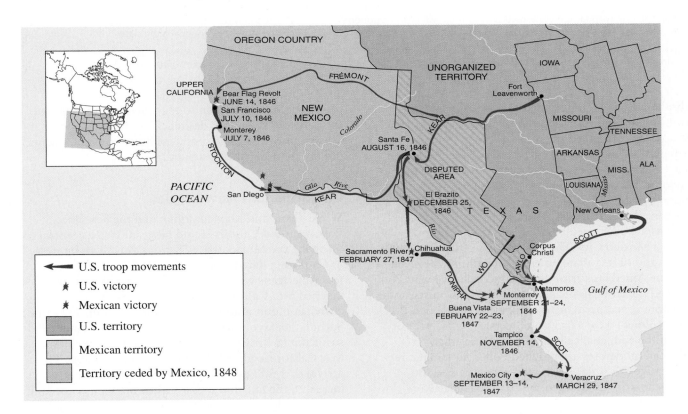

The Texas Revolution, 1836

This map shows the significance of American settlement in Texas and the major military engagements of the war. What clues does the map contain about the reasons for Texans' military success?

The Battle of Buena Vista

In February 1847, American forces, depleted by the departure of 9,000 troops for the Veracruz campaign, met Santa Anna's much larger army several miles north of the hacienda of Buena Vista. The Americans, largely inexperienced volunteers, dug themselves into the valley's gullies and ravines. After bitter conflict, the Americans won the day with far fewer casualties than their Mexican opponents. This victory secured northeastern Mexico for the Americans and helped make General Zachary Taylor into a popular hero and potential political candidate.

(Frances Flora Bond Palmer, *Battle of Buena Vista. View of the Battle-Ground of "The Angostura" fought near Buena Vista, Mexico February 23rd. 1847. [Looking S. West]* Toned lithograph (hand-colored), 1847, 19$^1/_4$ x 29$^1/_2$ inches. Amon Carter Museum, Fort Worth, Texas 1971.48)

Abraham Lincoln, questioned the accuracy of Polk's truthfulness, and their opposition grew louder as time passed. Lincoln called the war one "of conquest brought into existence to catch votes." The American Peace Society revealed sordid examples of army misbehavior in Mexico, and Frederick Douglass accused the country of "cupidity and love of dominion." Many workers also criticized the war.

Debate continued as American troops swept toward Mexico City. The government refused to admit defeat and or negotiate an end to hostilities. Yet even as some Americans criticized the inconclusive war, Polk enjoyed the enthusiastic support of expansionists, some of whom urged permanent occupation of Mexico. Most soldiers were eager volunteers.

In the end, chance helped end the conflict. Mexican moderates approached Polk's diplomatic representative, Nicholas Trist, who accompanied the American army in Mexico. In Trist's baggage were detailed though out-of-date instructions outlining Polk's requirements: the Rio Grande boundary, Upper California, and New Mexico. Although the president had lost confidence in Trist, Trist remained in Mexico

to negotiate a conclusion to the war. Having obtained less territory than Polk desired, Trist returned to Washington where the president fired him, denouncing him as an "unqualified scoundrel."

California and New Mexico

While Texas and Mexico dominated the headlines, Polk regarded California and New Mexico as central to resolving the Mexico crisis. Serious American interest in California dated from the late 1830s. Before then, few Americans were living in California. Many had married into California families and taken Mexican citizenship. But gradual recognition of California's fine harbors, its favorable position for the China trade, and suspicion of British designs there fed the conviction that California must belong to the United States. The arrival of 1,500 overland emigrants in the 1840s increased the likelihood that California would not long remain a Mexican outpost.

In 1845, Polk appointed Thomas Larkin, a successful American merchant in Monterey, as his confidential agent. "If the people [of California] should desire to unite their destiny with ours," wrote Polk's secretary of state, James Buchanan, to Larkin, "they would be received as brethren." Polk's efforts to buy California suggested the fragility of American claims to the region. But Santa Anna, having lost Texas, was in no position to sell.

New Mexico was also on Polk's list. Profitable economic ties with the United States dating back to the 1820s stimulated American territorial ambitions. As part of the oldest and largest Mexican community in North America, however, most New Mexicans had little desire for annexation. The unsuccessful attempt by the Texans to capture Santa Fe in 1841 and border clashes in the two following years did not enhance the attractiveness of Anglo neighbors. By standing awkwardly in the path of westward expansion and further isolated from Mexico by the annexation of Texas in 1846, New Mexico's future was uncertain.

In June 1846, shortly after the declaration of war with Mexico, American troops led by Colonel Stephen W. Kearney left Fort Leavenworth, Kansas, for New Mexico with orders to occupy Mexico's northern provinces and to protect the lucrative Santa Fe trade. Two months later, the army took Santa Fe without a shot, although one eyewitness noticed "surly" countenances and a "wail of grief." New Mexico's upper class, having already made strategic alliances with Americans, readily accepted the new rulers. However, ordinary Mexicans and Pueblo Indians did not take conquest so lightly. After Kearney departed for California, resistance flared first in New Mexico and then in California. Kearney was wounded, and the first appointed American governor of New Mexico killed. In the end, superior American military strength won the day. By January 1847, both California and New Mexico were firmly in American hands.

The Treaty of Guadalupe Hidalgo, 1848

Negotiated by Trist and signed on February 2, 1848, the Treaty of Guadalupe Hidalgo resolved the original issues favorably for the United States. The Rio Grande became the boundary between Mexico and the United States, and the Southwest and California passed into American hands. At a cost of 13,000 American lives, mostly due to disease, the United States gained 75,000 Spanish-speaking inhabitants, 150,000 Native Americans, and 529,017 square miles, almost a third of prewar Mexico. It paid Mexico $15 million (and another $10 million in 1853 for the Gadsden Purchase), agreed to honor American claims against Mexico, and guaranteed the civil, political, and property rights of former Mexican citizens. Although sporadic violence would continue for years in the Southwest as Mexicans protested the outcome, the war was over, and the Americans had won.

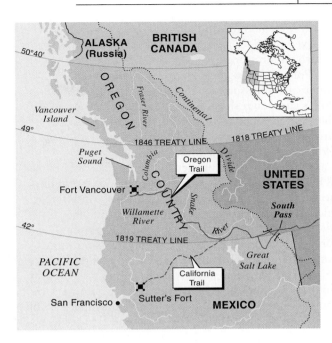

The Mexican-American War
How does this map reveal or explain the character and consequences of the war?

The Oregon Question, 1844–1846

In the Pacific Northwest, the power of Great Britain suggested the wisdom of diplomacy. Glossing over the disputed nature of American claims to the Oregon Territory, Polk declared on his inauguration that "our title to the country of Oregon is 'clear and unquestionable.'" The British did not agree. Nor did a French newspaper that remarked, "The message of the President of the United States respecting the Oregon question, is not of a tenour to indicate that Mr. Polk is animated by a spirit of conciliation. He dwells much upon his moderation, but he shows it so little, and his tone is such, that should a similar tone be assumed by the British Government, the affair must inevitably terminate in a war."

Though Europeans considered the president's speech belligerent, Polk correctly noted that Americans were emigrating to the disputed territories, especially south of the Columbia River. Between 1842 and 1845, the number of Americans in Oregon grew from 400 to more than 5,000. By 1843, these settlers had written a constitution and soon after elected a legislature. At the same time, declining British interest in the area set the stage for an eventual compromise. The near destruction of the beaver had weakened the fur trade, and the riches produced in Britain by the Industrial Revolution made colonies appear less important than they had been in the eighteenth century. Britain had already granted Canada self-rule. Attractive commercial opportunities were opening up in other parts of the world such as India and China, while New Zealand, annexed in 1840, and Australia became magnets for British emigration.

Polk's flamboyant posture and the expansive American claims made mediation difficult, however. Polk's campaign slogan claimed a boundary of 54°40′. But Polk was not willing to go to war with Great Britain and privately considered a boundary at the 49th parallel, which would extend the existing Canadian–American border to the Pacific, reasonable. When Polk offered his compromise to Great Britain, however, his tone antagonized the British. In his year-end address to Congress in 1845, the president increased diplomatic tensions by again claiming Oregon and giving the required one year's notice of American intention to cancel the joint occupation.

Despite slogans, most Americans did not want military hostilities over Oregon. As war with Mexico loomed, the task of resolving the disagreement became more urgent. The British, too, were eager to settle, and in June 1846 they agreed to the 49th-parallel boundary if Vancouver Island remained British. Polk ended the crisis just weeks before the declaration of war with Mexico; he escaped some of the responsibility

for retreating from slogans by sharing it with the Senate, who approved the compromise.

As these events show, Manifest Destiny was an idea that supported and justified expansionist policies. It reflected Americans' basic belief that expansion was necessary and right. As early as 1816, American geography books pictured the nation's western boundary at the Pacific and included Texas. Popular literature typically described Native Americans as a dying race and Mexicans as "injurious neighbor[s]." Only whites could make the wilderness flower. Thus, as lands east of the Mississippi filled up, Americans automatically called on familiar ideas to justify westward expansion.

Going West and East

Americans lost little time in moving into the new territories. Between 1841 and 1867, thousands of Americans headed west. By 1860, California alone had 380,000 settlers. At the same time, thousands of Chinese headed south and east to destinations such as Australia, Hawaii, and North and South America to escape the unrest caused by the opium wars in the

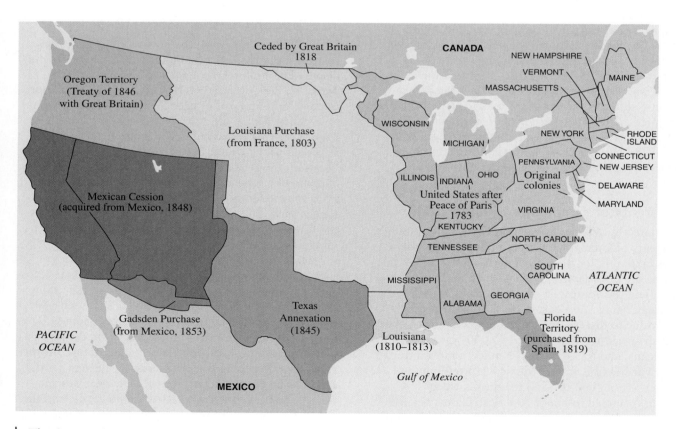

The Oregon Country

What does this map reveal about the claims to Oregon voiced during the election of 1844? How do the claims correspond to the eventual boundaries established with Great Britain? The major trails that brought American settlers to the West suggest the population movements that lay behind the Oregon controversy.

1840s with Great Britain, internal unrest, and poor economic conditions. Sixty-three thousand had come to the United States by 1870. Most were in California, the land of the "Gold Mountain."

One Chinese folk song depicted the "perilous journey" to the United States "sailing [in] a boat with bamboo poles across the sea." The Chinese, of course, had little choice on their travel route to the American West, but American migrants did. Some chose the expensive sea route from Atlantic or Gulf Coast ports around South America to the West Coast or across Panama and then by sea to the coast. Most American emigrants, however, chose land routes. In 1843, the first large party succeeded in crossing the plains and mountains to Oregon. More followed. Between 1841 and 1867, some 350,000 traveled the overland trails to California or Oregon, while others trekked part of the way to intermediate points such as Colorado and Utah.

The Emigrants

Most of the emigrants heading for the Far West, where slavery was prohibited, were white and American born. They came from the Midwest and the Upper South. A few free blacks made the trip as well. Pioneer Margaret Frink remembered seeing a "Negro woman . . . tramping along through the heat and dust, carrying a cast iron black stove on her head, with her provisions and a blanket piled on top . . . bravely pushing on for California." Emigrants from the Deep South usually selected Arkansas or Texas as their destination, and many took their slaves with them. By 1840, more than 11,000 slaves toiled in Texas and 20,000 in Arkansas.

The many pioneers who kept journals during the five- to six-month overland trip captured the human dimension of emigrating. Their journals, usually their only contribution to the historical record, focused on day-to-day events and expressed some of the thoughts and emotions experienced on the long journey west. One migrant, Lodisa Frizzell, described her feelings at parting in 1852:

> Who is there that does not recollect their first night when started on a long journey, the well known voices of our friends still ring in our ears, the parting kiss feels still warm upon our lips, and that last separating word farewell! sinks deeply into the heart! It may be the last we ever hear from some or all of them, and to those who start . . . there can be no more solemn scene of parting only at death.

Except for the Gold Rush, migration was a family experience, usually involving men and women in their late 20s to early 40s. A sizable number of them had recently married. For most, migration was the latest in a series of moves, often as children or as newlyweds. But this time, vast distances seemed to mean a final separation from home.

Migrants' Motives

While emigrant expectations varied, many believed that the West would offer rich opportunities. Thousands sought gold but others hoped to succeed as merchants, lawyers, or doctors. Would-be speculators intended to acquire large blocks of land and then sell them at a handsome profit to settlers. Some hoped the western climate would restore their physical health although others were concerned about the religious and cultural health of new communities. Stirred by tales of the "deplorable morals" on the frontier, minister David and Catherine Blaine willingly left the comforts of home to evangelize and educate westerners in frontier Seattle. Still others, like the Mormons, made the long trek to Utah to establish a society conforming to their religious beliefs.

Most migrants dreamed of bettering their life by farming. As one settler explained, "The motive that induced us to part with pleasant associates and dear friends of our childhood days, was to obtain from the government of the United States a grant of land that 'Uncle Sam' had promised." Federal and state land policies made the acquisition of land increasingly alluring. During the 1830s and 1840s, pre-emption acts allowed "squatters" to settle public lands before the government offered them for sale and then to purchase these lands at the minimum price once they came on the market. At the same time, the amount of land a family had to buy shrank to 40 acres. In 1862, the Homestead Act went further by offering 160 acres of government land free to citizens or future citizens over 21 who lived on the property, improved it, and paid a small registration fee. Oregon's land policy, which predated the Homestead Act, was even more generous. It awarded a single man 320 acres of free land and a married man 640 acres, provided he occupied his claim for four years and made improvements.

Unlike earlier migrations west, the trip to the Far West involved considerable expense. The relatively comfortable sea route around Cape Horn cost an estimated $600 per person. For the same sum, four people could travel overland. And if the emigrants sold their wagons and oxen at the journey's end, the final expenses might amount to only $220. Such sums put the trip out of reach of the very poor. American migration to the Far West (with the exception of group migration to Utah) was a movement of the middle class.

Like many Americans, Chinese migrants also dreamed of bettering their condition. Most were married men with limited opportunities in their homeland.

Recovering the Past

PERSONAL DIARIES

Nineteenth-century journals kept by hundreds of ordinary men and women traveling west on the overland trails constitute a rich source for exploring the nature of the westward experience. They are also an example of how private sources can be used to deepen our understanding of the past. Diaries, journals, and letters all provide us with a personal perspective on major happenings. These sources tend to focus on the concrete, so they convey the texture of daily life in the nineteenth century, daily routines and amusements, clothing, habits, and interactions with family and friends. They also provide evidence of the varied concerns, attitudes, and prejudices of the writers, thus providing a test of commonly accepted generalizations about individual and group behavior.

Like any historical source, personal documents must be used carefully. It is important to note the writer's age, gender, class, and regional identification. Although this information may not be available, some of the writer's background can be deduced from what he or she has written. It is also important to consider for what purpose and for whom the document was composed. This information will help explain the tone or character of the source and what has been included or left out. It is, of course, important to avoid generalizing too much from one or even several similar sources. Only after reading many diaries, letters, and journals is it possible to make valid generalizations about life in the past.

Here we present excerpts from two travel journals of the 1850s. Few of the writers considered their journals strictly private. Often they were intended as a family record or as information for friends back home. Therefore, material of a personal nature has often been excluded. Nineteenth-century Americans referred to certain topics, such as pregnancy, only indirectly or not at all.

One excerpt comes from Mary Bailey's 1852 journal. Mary was 22 years old when she crossed the plains to California with her 32-year-old doctor husband. Originally a New Englander, Mary had lived in Ohio for six years before moving west. The Baileys were reasonably prosperous and were able to restock necessary supplies on the road west. The other writer, Robert Robe, was 30 years old when he crossed along the same route a year earlier than the Baileys, headed for Oregon. Robert was a native of Ohio and a Presbyterian minister.

As you read these excerpts, notice what each journal reveals about the trip west. What kinds of challenges did the emigrants face on their journey? Do these correspond to the picture you may have formed from novels, television, and movies? What kinds of work needed to be done, and who did it? Can you see any indication of a division of work based on gender? What kinds of interactions appear to have occurred between men and women on the trip? What does the pattern tell us about nineteenth-century society? How does the painting of the "emigrant train" reinforce the journal accounts of men's and women's roles?

Reflecting on the Past Even these short excerpts suggest that men and women, as they traveled west, may have had different concerns and different perspectives on the journey. In what ways do the two accounts differ, and in what ways are they similar?

(Benjamin Franklin Reinhart, "An Evening Halt - Emigrants Moving to the West in 1840," c.1867, oil on canvas, 40 × 70 inches, 59.21. In the Collection of The Corcoran Gallery. Courtesy of Corcoran Gallery of Art, Washington, D.C. Gift of Mr. and Mrs. Lansdell K. Christie.)

Journal of Mary Stuart Bailey

Wednesday, April 13, 1852 Left our hitherto happy home in Sylvania amid the tears of parting kisses of dear friends, many of whom were endeared to me by their kindness shown to me when I was a stranger in a strange land, when sickness and death visited our small family & removed our darling, our only child in a moment, as it were. Such kindness I can never forget....

Friday, 21st [May] Rained last night. Slept in the tent for the first time. I was Yankee enough to protect myself by pinning up blankets over my head. I am quite at home in my tent.

12:00 Have traveled in the rain all day & we are stuck in the mud. I sit in the wagon writing while the men are at work doubling the teams to draw us out....

Sunday, 23rd. Walked to the top of the hill where I could be quiet & commune with nature and nature's God. This afternoon I was annoyed by something very unpleasant & shed many tears and felt very unhappy....

Thursday, 4th [June] Very cold this morning after the shower.... We stopped on the banks of the Platte to take dinner. I am sitting on the banks of the Platte with my feet almost in the water. Have been writing to my Mother. How I wish I had some of my own relations with me....

Sunday, 4th [July] Started at 3 o'clock to find feed or know where it was. Had to go 4 or 5 miles off the road. Found water & good grass. Camped on the sand with sage roots for fuel. It is wintery, cold & somewhat inclined to rain, not pleasant. Rather a dreary Independence Day. We speak of our friends at home. We think they are thinking of us....

Monday, 12th. Stayed in camp another day to get our horse better. He is much improved. It is cold enough. Washed in the morning & had the sick headache in the afternoon....

Thursday, 12th [August] Very warm. Slept until we stopped to take breakfast. Mr. Patterson starts as soon as light & stops in the heat of the day to rest the animals. We do not have much time to do anything except 4 or 5 hours in the middle of the day....

Friday, 17th [September] Have been confined ever since Monday with ague in my face which is very much swollen. Have suffered very much. We are now in Carson Valley. Plenty of trees but the country is very barren.

Saturday, 18th. Very pleasant, delightful weather. Feel much better today. We are not stirring this afternoon. We have heard to a great deal of suffering, people being thrown out on the desert to die & being picked up & brought to the hospital....

Source: From *Ho for California! Women's Overland Diaries*, Sandra L. Myers, ed., Reprinted with the permission of the Henry E. Huntington Library.

Journal of Robert Robe

[May] 19, [1851] A fine day. The first spent in travelling on the plains of the Platte river.

20. Continue our journey up the Platte valley which I would judge to be here some 12 miles wide on this side of the river. The only game seen here are the antelope and wolf beside some wild fowl.

21. A rainy morning started early passed an old Pawnee village in ruins. The houses are constructed by placing timbers in forks and upon these without placing upright poles then rushes bound with [illegible] and finally earth. Chimney in center. Day became more & more rainy and wound up with a storm which beggared description.

22. Bluff approach the river—travelling less monotonous river finely skirted with timber.

23. Roads very muddy in afternoon. Today our wagon severed itself from our former companions & joined a company of Californians.

24. Before starting a trader direct from Ft. Kearney arrived at our camp. He informs us it is yet 25 miles thither. Travelling is by no means dangerous a waggon of provisions passing with only three guards. In the afternoon passed the entrance of the Independence Weston & St. Jo. roads. Emigrants became more numerous.

25. Passed Fort Kearney this morning and after a short drive encamped. Having conversed with some of the soldiers I find they consider life very monotonous.

26. Roads heavy—short drive—a storm.

27. High Bluffs on the opposite side of river approach and present a beautiful appearance. At night a fearful storm.

28. Roads heavy nothing singular.

29. Have arrived in the region abounding in Buffalo. At noon a considerable herd came in sight. The first any of us had ever seen. Thus now for the chase—the horsemen proved too swift in pursuit and frightened them into the Bluffs without capturing any—the footmen pursued however and killed three pretty good success for the first.

30. Nothing remarkable today.

31. Game being abundant we resolved to rest our stock and hunt today— Started in the morning on foot. Saw probably 1,000 Buffalo. Shot at several and killed one. Where ever we found them wolves were prowling around as if to guard them. Their real object is however no doubt to seize the calves as their prey. Saw a town of Prairie dogs, they are nearly as large as a gray squirrel. They bark fiercely when at a little distance but on near approach flee to their holes. Wherever they are we see numerous owls. After a very extensive ramble and having seen a variety of game we returned at sunset with most voracious appetites.

June 1. The Bluffs became beautifully undulating losing their precipitous aspect and the country further back is beautifully rolling prairie.

2. In the evening camped beside our old friends Miller and Dovey. They had met with a great loss this morning their 3 horses having taken fright at a drove of buffalo and ran entirely away. Some of our company killed more buffalo this evening & a company went in the night with teams to bring them in.

Source: "Robert Robe's Diary while Crossing the Plains in 1851" from *Washington Historic Quarterly*, Volume 19, Number 1, January 1928.

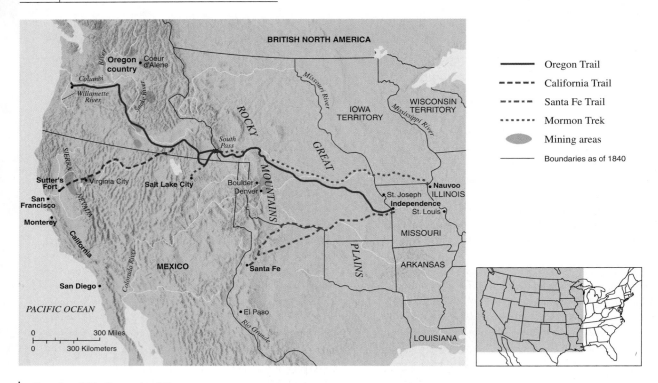

Overland Trails to the West
The various trails over which thousands of Americans traveled during the 1840s, 1850s, and 1860s are depicted on this map. What natural obstacles do the map's geographic features suggest the travelers faced and at what point during their trip did travelers encounter them?

Labor circulars assured them that Americans "want the Chinaman to come.... Money is in great plenty and to spare in America." Emigrants to Hawaii and the United States reinforced this message when they returned with money in their pockets. In the 1860s, Chinese laborers could earn $30 a month working for the railroad, far more than the $3 to $5 they could expect if they stayed home.

The Overland Trails

The trip for American emigrants began in the late spring at starting points in Iowa and Missouri. By mid-May the grass was usually up for the stock, and the emigrant trains set out. Making only 15 miles a day, emigrants first followed the valley of the Platte River up to South Pass in the Rockies. This part of the trip seemed novel, even enjoyable. Until the 1850s, conflict with Native Americans was rare. The traditional division of labor persisted: Men did "outdoor" work such as driving and repairing wagons, and women handled domestic chores. Young children stayed out of the way in wagons, while older brothers and sisters walked alongside and lent a hand. Wagon trains might stop to observe the Sabbath, allowing for rest and laundry.

Later, difficulties multiplied. Cholera often took a heavy toll. Deserts and mountains replaced rolling prairies. Emigrants had to cross the final mountain ranges—the Sierras and the Cascades—before the first snowfall, so they pushed on relentlessly. Animals weakened by constant travel, poor feed, and bad water sickened, collapsed, and often died. Families had to lighten wagons by throwing out prized possessions. Food supplies dwindled, and the familiar division of responsibilities often collapsed. Women found themselves loading and driving wagons, even helping to drag them over rocky mountain trails. Their husbands worked frantically with the animals and the wagons as the time of the first snowfall drew closer. Tempers frayed. Family harmony often collapsed. Mary Power, who with her husband and three children crossed in 1853, revealed exasperation and depression in her journal: "I felt my courage must fail me, for there we were in a strange land, almost without anything to eat, [with] a team that was not able to pull an empty wagon."

Finally, five or six months after setting out, emigrants arrived, exhausted and often penniless, in Oregon or California. As one wrote at the end of her journey in 1854, its "care, fatigue, tediousness, perplexities and dangers of various kinds, can not be excelled."

A Mormon Wagon Train

What does this view of a Mormon wagon train in the 1850s suggest about the terrain that emigrant families encountered as they went west? The Mormon migrations were the most organized of the migrations into the trans-Mississippi West, although not all Mormons were lucky enough to travel by wagon. Some emigrants to Utah pushed handcarts across the plains to their destination.

Living in the West

Whether elated or depressed when they reached their destinations, emigrants had no choice but to start anew. As they did so, they naturally drew on their experiences back East. "Pioneers though we are, and proud of it, we are not content with the wilds... with the idleness of the land, the rudely construct[ed] log cabin," one Oregon settler explained.

Farming in the West

Pioneer farmers faced the urgent task of establishing homesteads and beginning farming. First, they had to locate a suitable claim, then clear land, and construct a shelter. Only then could they plant crops. As they labored "to get the land subdued and the wilde nature out of it," they repeated a familiar process. Felling timber, pulling out native plants, and establishing familiar crops began a transformation of the landscape with some unanticipated results. Seed brought from home also introduced flourishing weeds, like the Canadian thistle that gradually displaced native grass and rendered land useless for grazing. But so urgent was the goal of taming nature that few emigrants had the time or inclination to wonder about the ecological transformation they set in motion.

Early challenges ranged from working without familiar tools and implements to assuming unaccustomed duties. Men often found themselves assisting wives in unfamiliar domestic chores while women helped with the heavy outdoor work. After months of intense interaction with other travelers, families often felt lonely and thought longingly of friends and family back home. Cultural biases usually precluded close friendships with nearby Native Americans.

One pioneer remembered that "in those days anyone residing within twenty miles was considered a neighbor." But the isolation usually ended within a few years as new emigrants arrived and old settlers sought better claims. As rural communities grew, settlers began to replicate the organizations they had known at home. The determination to reestablish continuity by setting up familiar institutions was most apparent in law and politics. In Oregon, pioneers initiated a political system based on eastern models before territorial status was resolved. Before permanent schools or churches existed, men resumed familiar political rituals of electioneering, voting, and talking politics. They went to court to ensure law and order.

Instituting common schools and churches was more difficult and less urgent than beginning political life. Few settlers initially thought education important enough to tax themselves for permanent public schools. Schools operated sporadically and only for students paying at least part of the fees. While confirmed believers attended early church services, they often discovered that there were too few members of individual denominations to support separate churches. Nor were converts plentiful, for many settlers had lost the habit of regular churchgoing. David Blaine learned the "unwelcome lesson" that "separation from gospel influences" had left many "quite indifferent to gospel truth."

The chronic shortage of cash on the frontier hampered the growth of both schools and churches. Until farmers could send their goods to market, they had little cash to spare. Geographic mobility also contributed to institutional instability. Up to three-quarters of the population of a frontier county might vanish within a 10-year period. Some farmed in as many as four locations before finding a satisfactory claim. Institutions relying on continuing personal and financial support suffered accordingly.

Yet newspapers, journals, and books, which circulated early on the frontier, reinforced familiar norms and determination. As more settlers arrived, support for educational, religious, and cultural institutions that defined acceptable behavior and enforced conventional standards grew. Only 16 years after crossing the plains, one woman explained, "We have a telegraph line from the East, a daily rail road train, daily mail and I am beginning to feel quite civilized. And here ended my pioneer experience."

Although the belief in special economic and social opportunities in the west encouraged emigration, the dream was often illusory. Western society rapidly acquired a social and economic structure similar to that of the East. Frontier newspapers referred to leading settlers as the "better" sort, and workers for hire and tenant farmers appeared. Widespread geographic mobility also suggests that many failed to capitalize on the benefits of homesteading. Those who left communities were generally less successful than the core of stable residents, who became economic and social leaders. But they hoped that fortune would finally smile at their next stop. Said one wife when her husband announced another relocation: "I seemed to have heard all this before."

Mining Western Resources

In 1848 news of the discovery of gold in California swept the country and prompted thousands to abandon their ordinary lives in hopes of a fortune. Within a year, California's population ballooned from 14,000 to almost 100,000. By 1852, that figure more than doubled.

Chinese and American Miners

This photograph captures some of the international character of the mining fields. American miners stand on the left and Chinese laborers on the right. How would you compare the two groups of men? Are there any signs of the racial animosity that was one of the realities of mining life?

(Courtesy of the California History Room, California State Library, Sacramento, California)

Unlike farming pioneers, the "forty-niners" were mostly young unmarried men (in 1850, more than half the people in California were in their 20s). Of those pouring into California in 1849, about 80 percent came from the United States, 13 percent from Mexico and South America; the rest were Europeans and Asians. California was thus one of the most diverse places in the country. Few, however, were interested in settling the West. Instead they dreamed of returning home rich.

California was the first and most dramatic of the western mining discoveries. In 1858, 25,000 to 30,000 emigrants, many from California, hurried to British Columbia. The next year gold strikes in Colorado set off another rush. Precious metals lured prospectors to the Pacific Northwest early in the decade, to Montana and Idaho a few years later, and in the mid-1870s to the Black Hills of North Dakota.

Unlike isolated farming settlements, mining communities sprang up almost overnight after a strike. Ramshackle mining camps soon housed hundreds or even thousands of miners and the merchants, saloonkeepers, cooks, druggists, gamblers, and prostitutes who served them. Usually, about half the residents of any mining camp were there to prospect the miners rather than the mines.

Given the motivation, character, and ethnic diversity of the boomtowns and the feeble attempts to set up local government in what were perceived as temporary communities, mining life was often disorderly. Racial antagonism between American miners and foreigners led to ugly riots and lynchings. Miners had few qualms about eliminating Indians and others who got in the way. Fistfights, drunkenness, and murder occurred often enough to become part of the lore of the gold rush. Wrote one woman, "In the short space of twenty four days, we have had murders, fearful accidents, bloody deaths, a mob, whippings, a hanging, an attempt at suicide, and a fatal duel."

Mining camps were usually not this violent but they tolerated behavior unacceptable farther east. Miners were trying to get rich, not to re-create eastern communities. Married men, knowing the raucous character of mining communities, hesitated to bring wives and families west.

Although a lucky few struck it rich or made enough money to return home with their pride intact, many made only enough to keep going. Wrote one, "it is hard for a man to leave . . . with nothing. . . . I have no pile yet, but you can bet your life I will never come home until I have something more than when I started." Easily mined silver and gold deposits soon ran out. Although Chinese miners proved adept at finding what early miners overlooked, the remaining rich deposits lay deeply embedded in rock or gravel. Extraction required cooperative efforts, capital, technological experience, and expensive machinery. Eventually, mining became a corporate industrial concern. As early as 1852, the changing nature of mining in California had transformed most of the miners into wage workers.

Probably 5 percent of early gold rush emigrants to California were women and children. Many of the women also anticipated getting "rich in a hurry." Because there were so few of them, the cooking, nursing, laundry, and hotel services women provided had a high value. When Luzena Wilson arrived in Sacramento, a miner offered to pay her $10 for a biscuit. That night, Luzena dreamt she saw "crowds of bearded miners striking gold from the earth with every blow of the pick, each one seeming to leave a share for me." Yet it was wearying work. As Mary Ballou thought it over, she decided, "I would not advise any Lady to come out here and suffer to toil and fatigue I have suffered for the sake of a little gold." As men's profits shrank, so, too, did those of the women who served them.

Prostitutes were among the first women to arrive. Rejecting the hard labor of "respectable" women, they hoped that the favorable gender ratio would make their profession especially profitable. Prostitutes may have constituted as much as 20 percent of California's female population in 1850, and they probably vastly outnumbered other women in early mining camps. During boom days, they made good money and sometimes won a recognized place in society. But prostitution was a risky business in such a disorderly environment.

The Mexicans, South Americans, Chinese, and small numbers of blacks seeking their fortunes in California soon discovered that despite their contributions to California's growth they faced racial antagonism and discrimination. At first, American miners hoped to expel foreigners of color from the goldfields by declaring mining illegal for all foreigners. The attempt failed, but a high tax on foreign miners drove thousands of Mexicans and Chinese from the mines. As business stagnated in mining towns, however, white miners reduced the levy. By 1870, when the tax was declared unconstitutional, the Chinese, who had paid 85 percent of it, had "contributed" $5 million to California for the right to prospect. While not affected by legislation against foreigners, black Americans also faced bleak prospects. They were deprived of the vote, forbidden to testify in civil or criminal cases involving whites, and excluded from the bounties of the homestead law.

For the Native American tribes of the interior, the mining rushes were disasters. Accustomed to foraging for food, they found fish and game increasingly scarce as miners diverted streams, hunted game, or drove it from mining areas altogether. When Native Americans responded by raiding mining camps, miners erupted with fury. They stalked and killed native men and women, sometimes collecting bounties offered by some mining communities for their scalps. Indian women were raped; children were kidnapped and offered as apprentices. As one miner pointed out, "Indians seven or eight years old are worth $100 . . . [and] it is a damn poor Indian that's not worth $50." Without legal recourse because of their skin color, Native Americans could not withstand the onslaught of white society. Subjected not only to violence but to white disease, they died by the thousands. In 1849, there had been about 150,000 Native Americans in California. In just over 20 years, their numbers had tumbled to fewer than 30,000.

Although the mining experience was never as brutal for whites as for people of color, white men and women's fantasies of dazzling riches rarely came true. The ghost towns of the West testify to the typical pattern: boom, bust, decay, death. The empty streets and rotting buildings symbolized dashed hopes and disappointed dreams. Eroded soil, deforested mountains, diverted waterways, and silt, all the result of mining operations, were other physical manifestations of the underside of the dream of striking it rich.

After the Rush

This picture of the near–ghost town of Ophir City, Nevada, taken in the 1870s, points to the way the mining frontier left its mark on the landscape and suggests the unstable nature of such a frontier.

(Photo by W.H. Jackson, The Denver Public Library, Western History Collection)

It was difficult, however, to recognize some of the negative consequences of the discovery of gold, for it had many positive effects on the West as a whole. Between 1848 and 1883, California mines supplied two-thirds of the country's gold. Gold transformed San Francisco from a sleepy town into a bustling metropolis. It fueled the agricultural and commercial development of California and Oregon, as miners provided a market for goods and services. Gold built harbors, railroads, and irrigation systems not just in California and Oregon but all over the West. Though few people made large fortunes, both the region and the nation profited from gold.

Establishing God's Kingdom

In the decades before 1860, many emigrants going west stopped to rest and buy supplies in Salt Lake City, the heart of the Mormon state of Deseret. There they encountered a society both familiar and shockingly different. Visitors admired the attractively laid-out town, but they also gossiped about polygamy and searched for signs of rebellion in the faces of Mormon women. They were amazed that so few seemed interested in escaping from plural marriage, which outsiders equated with slavery.

Violence and chance both played a part in the Mormon migration to the Great Basin area. Two years after Joseph Smith's murder in 1844, angry mobs chased the last of the "Saints" out of Nauvoo,

Illinois. As they struggled to temporary camps in Iowa, Smith's successor, Brigham Young, realized the wisdom of situating the kingdom of God somewhere in the West, far from the United States. The Mexican-American War unexpectedly furthered Mormon plans. By raising Mormon troops for Kearney's army, Young acquired sorely needed capital. The battalion's advance pay bought wagonloads of supplies for starving and sick Mormons strung out along the trail between Missouri and Iowa and helped finance the impending great migration.

Young selected the Great Basin area, technically part of Mexico, for his future kingdom. It was arid and remote, 1,000 miles from its nearest "civilized" neighbors. But Mormon leaders concluded that if irrigated, the area might prove as fertile as the fields and vineyards of ancient Israel. In April 1847, Young led an exploratory expedition west. Reaching Salt Lake in late July, Young declared, "This is the place" and announced a generous land policy. After Young left, the expeditionary group followed his directions to construct irrigation ditches and begin planting.

Young's organizational talents and his followers' cooperative abilities were fully tested. By September 1847, fully 566 wagons and 1,500 of the Saints had made the arduous trek to Salt Lake City; more came the next year. Church leaders planned and directed everything. By 1850, the Mormon settlement had over 11,000 settlers. Missionary efforts in the United States, Great Britain, and Scandinavia drew thousands of converts to the Great Basin. The Church emigration society and a loan fund facilitated the journey for many who could never have otherwise undertaken the trip. By the end of the decade, more than 30,000 Saints lived in Utah, not only in Salt Lake City but also in more than 90 village colonies. Despite the early hardships, the Mormons thrived.

Most Mormons were farmers; many came from New England and the Midwest and shared many of the customs, attitudes, and political structures as other Americans. But "Gentile" outsiders recognized profound differences. The heart of Mormon society was not the individual farmer but the cooperative village. Years of persecution had promoted a strong group identity and acceptance of Church guidance. With Church leaders making essential decisions, farming became a collective enterprise. All farmers received land and access to community water. During Sunday services, the local bishop might give farming instructions to his congregation along with his sermon. Furthermore, church and state were not separate. Despite familiar government forms, Church leaders occupied all important political posts. Brigham Young's Governing Quorum included the high priests of the Church, who made both religious and political decisions.

When it became clear that Utah would become a territory, Mormon leaders devised a constitution dividing religious and political power. But the change was cosmetic. As one Gentile pointed out, "This intimate connection of church and state seems to pervade everything that is done. The supreme power in both being lodged in the hands of the same individuals, it is difficult to separate their two official characters, and to determine whether in any one instance they act as spiritual or merely temporal officers."

Although the Treaty of Guadalupe Hidalgo officially incorporated Utah into the United States, it hardly affected political and religious arrangements. Brigham Young became territorial governor. Local bishops continued as spiritual leaders and civil magistrates. Mormons had come to Utah to establish a kingdom, not a republic. Their motives dictated the unique politico-religious nature of the Utah experience.

Other aspects of the Mormon frontier were distinctive. Mormon policy toward the Native American tribes was remarkably enlightened. After 1850, Mormons concentrated on converting rather than killing Native Americans. Mormon missionaries learned Bannock, Ute, Navajo, and Hopi languages to bring the faith to these tribes. They also encouraged Native Americans to ranch and farm.

Although most Gentiles could accept some of the peculiarities of the Mormon settlement, few could tolerate polygamy. Smith and other Church leaders had

San Francisco in 1853

This view of San Francisco reveals the rapid transformation of the city. Brick buildings (several stories high, with elaborate cornices), board sidewalks, kerosene street lamps, and the inevitable grid street pattern give San Francisco the appearance of an eastern city rather than a raw western community, though it was only four years after the gold rush. How far from the San Francisco harbor are these buildings?

(Courtesy of The Bancroft Library, University of California, Berkeley)

secretly practiced polygamy in the early 1840s, but Young only publicly revealed the doctrine in 1852, when the Saints were safely in Utah. Smith believed that the highest or "celestial" form of marriage brought special rewards in the afterlife. Because wives and children contributed to these rewards, polygamy was a means of sanctification. From a practical standpoint, polygamy also served to incorporate into Mormon society single female converts who had left their families to come to Utah.

Although most Mormons accepted the doctrine and its religious justification, some found it hard to follow. One woman called it a "great trial of feelings." Actually, relatively few families were polygamous. During the 40-year period in which Mormons practiced plural marriage, only 10 to 20 percent of

Mormon families were polygamous. Few men had more than two wives. Because of the expense of maintaining several families and the personal strains involved, usually only the most successful and visible Mormon leaders practiced polygamy.

Polygamous family life hardly resembled outsiders' fantasies of sexual excess. Since jealousy among wives could destroy the institution of plural marriage, Mormon leaders minimized the role of romantic love and sexual attraction in courtship and marriage. Instead, they encouraged marriages founded on mutual attachment, with sex for procreation rather than pleasure.

To the shock of outsiders, Mormon women considered themselves not slaves but highly regarded members of the community. Whether plural wives or not, they saw polygamy as the cutting edge of their society and defended it to outsiders. Polygamy was preferable to monogamy, which left the single woman without the economic and social protection of family life and forced some of them into prostitution. Furthermore, although polygamy was often difficult, it offered surprising rewards. Without the constant presence of husbands, many plurals wives enjoyed unusual independence. Many treated visiting husbands as revered friends, deriving emotional satisfaction from their children, not their spouses. Occasionally, plural wives lived together and became close friends.

The Mormon settlement succeeded in terms of numbers, its unity, and growing economic prosperity. Long-term threats loomed, however, once the region became part of the United States. Attacks on Young's power and heated verbal denunciations of polygamy proliferated. Efforts began in Congress to outlaw polygamy. In the years before the Civil War, Mormons withstood these assaults on their way of life. But as Utah became more connected to the rest of the country, pressures on plural marriage would increase.

Cities in the West

Many emigrants went west not to farm or pan for gold but to live in cities such as San Francisco, Denver, and Portland. There they pursued business and professional opportunities or perhaps speculated in real estate. Bustling commercial life offered residents a wide range of both occupations and services.

Cities were integral to frontier life. Some, like St. Joseph, Missouri, which catered to the emigrant trade, preceded agricultural settlement. Others, like Portland, became destinations or market and supply centers for emigrant farmers. San Francisco and Denver were "instant cities," transformed when the discovery of precious metals attracted thousands of miners to and through them. Once the strike ran out, many miners returned to these cities to make a new start.

In San Francisco, a Chinese community took shape as Chinese laborers abandoned mining and railroad work. In 1860, almost 3,000 Chinese lived in Chinatown; 10 years later, that number grew to 12,022.

Young, single men seeking their fortunes made up a disproportionate share of urban populations. Frontier Portland had more than three men for every woman. Predictably, urban life was often noisy and rowdy, and occasionally violent. Some women tried to reform the atmosphere by attempting to close stores on Sunday or to prohibit drinking. Others, of course, enjoyed all the attention that came with the presence of so many young men. Eventually, the gender ratio became balanced, but as late as 1880, fully 18 of the 24 largest western cities had more men than women.

Western cities soon lost their distinctiveness. The history of Portland suggests the common pattern of development. In 1845, it was only a clearing in the forest. By the early 1850s, Portland had become a small trading center with a few rough log structures and muddy tracks for streets. As farmers poured into Oregon, the city emerged as a regional commercial center. More permanent structures were built, giving it an "eastern" appearance.

The belief that western cities offered special opportunities initially drew many young men to Portland and other urban areas. Success was greatest, however, for those arriving with assets. By the 1860s, when the city's population had reached 2,874, Portland's Social Club symbolized the emergence of an elite. Portland's businessmen, lawyers, and editors controlled an increasing share of the community's wealth and set its social standards, showing how rapidly and far Portland had traveled from its raw beginnings.

Cultures in Conflict

Looking at westward expansion through the eyes of white emigrants provides only one view of the migration experience. In such a diverse region, many other views existed.

Some heading to the American West came from southern China. Mostly men, they planned to work for a few years and then return home. Initially, California welcomed them. One San Francisco merchant reported in 1855 that the Chinese were "received like guests" and treated "with politeness. From far and near we came and were pleased." However, such tolerance vanished as more Chinese arrived and took jobs in mining camps, on the railroads, and elsewhere. Increasingly perceived by whites as racial threats, called "nagurs" with an appearance supposedly "but a slight removal from the African race," Chinese workers faced many forms of harassment. In 1880, California legislators expressed white hostility by passing a law that made illegal any marriage between a white person and a "negro, mulatto, or Mongolian."

Confronting the Plains Tribes

Some whites likened the Chinese to the Native Americans, another group that would see the western experience differently from white emigrants. An entry from an Oregon Trail journal hints at what one such perspective might be. On May 7, 1864, Mary Warner, a bride of only a few months, described a frightening event. That day, a "fine-looking" Indian had visited the wagon train and tried to buy her. Mary's husband, probably uncertain how to handle the situation, played along, agreeing to trade his wife for two ponies. The Indian generously offered three. "Then," wrote Mary, "he took hold of my shawl to make me understand to get out [of the wagon]. About this time I got frightened and really was so hysterical [that] I began to cry." Everyone laughed at her, she reported, though surely the Indian found the whole incident no more amusing than she had.

An Indian Child

This dark image, made in about 1851, provides a rare glimpse of one of California's Native American children. What do the boy's clothes suggest about the impact of white society on Native American culture during the gold rush? Generally, the gold rush was a disaster for Native American tribes in California, where violence against Native Americans was all too common.

(Oakland Museum of California, Gift of Anonymous Donor)

This ordinary encounter on the overland trail only begins to point to the social and cultural differences separating white Americans moving west and the native peoples they encountered. Confident of their values and rights, emigrants little regarded those who had lived in the West for centuries and had no compunction in seizing their lands. Like the Whitmans, many predicted that the Native American race would die out, a just reward for tribal "degeneracy."

During the 1840s, white Americans for the first time came into extensive contact with the powerful Plains tribes, whose culture differed from that of the more familiar eastern woodland tribes. Probably a quarter million Native Americans occupied the area from the Rocky Mountains to the Missouri River and from the Platte River to New Mexico. Nearest the Missouri and Iowa frontier lived "border" tribes—the Pawnee, Omaha, Oto, Ponca, and Kansa. These groups, unlike other Plains tribes, lived in villages and raised crops, supplementing their diet with buffalo meat during the summer months. On the Central Plains lived the Brulé and Oglala Sioux, Cheyenne, Shoshone, and Arapaho, aggressive tribes who followed the buffalo and often raided the border tribes. In the Southwest were the Comanche, Ute, Navajo, and some Apache bands; the Kiowa, Wichita, Apache, and southern Comanche claimed northern and western Texas as their hunting grounds. Many of the southwestern tribes had adopted aspects of Spanish culture and European domestic animals such as cattle, sheep, and horses.

Although differences existed, most of the Plains tribes had adopted a nomadic way of life after the introduction of Spanish horses in the sixteenth century increased their seasonal mobility from 50 to 500 miles. Horses allowed Native American braves to hunt the buffalo with such success that tribes (with the exclusion of the border groups) came to depend on the beasts for food, clothing, fuel, teepee dwellings, and trading purposes. Because women were responsible for processing buffalo products, some men had more than one wife to tan skins for trading.

Mobility also increased tribal contact and conflict. War was central to the Plains tribes. No male achieved full tribal status until he had proved himself in battle. But tribal warfare was not like the warfare of white men. Native Americans sought not to exterminate their enemies or to claim territory but rather to steal horses and to demonstrate prowess. They considered it braver to touch an enemy than to kill or scalp him. Moreover, because individual tribes were loosely organized, chiefs had only limited authority. As Chief Low Horn, a Blackfoot, explained, chiefs "could not restrain their young men . . . their young men were wild, and ambitious, in their turn to be braves and chiefs. They wanted by some brave act to win the favor of their young women, and bring scalps and horses to show their prowess."

This pattern of conflict on the Great Plains discouraged political unity. But even so, armed with guns, mounted on fast ponies, and skilled in warfare and raiding, the Plains tribes posed a fearsome obstacle to white expansion. They had signed no treaties with the United States and had few friendly feelings toward whites. Their contact with white society had brought gains through trade in skins, but the trade had also introduced alcohol and destructive epidemics of smallpox and scarlet fever.

In the early 1840s, relations between Native Americans and whites were peaceful. But the intrusion of whites set off an environmental cycle that eventually caused conflict. Native American tribes depended on the buffalo but respected this source of life. The Teton Sioux performed rituals to ensure a continuing supply of the animals, while hunters often ritualistically apologized to the Great Unseen Buffalo for slaughtering what the tribe needed. The grasses that nourished the buffalo also sustained the Indians' own ponies and the animals that supported horse traders such as the Cheyenne.

Whites, however, put their stock to graze on the grass that was so central to Native American life and adopted the "most exciting sport," the buffalo hunt. As the great herds began to shrink, Native American tribes turned against one another for hunting grounds and food. The powerful Sioux swooped down into the hunting grounds of their enemies. In an 1846 petition to President Polk, the Sioux explained that "for several years past the Emigrants going over the Mountains from the United States, have been the cause that Buffalo have in great measure left our hunting grounds, thereby causing us to go into the Country of Our Enemies to hunt, exposing our lives daily for the necessary subsistence of our wives and Children and getting killed on several occasions." Despite their plight, the Sioux had "all along treated the Emigrants in the most friendly manner, giving them free passage through our hunting grounds."

The Sioux requested compensation for white damages. When the president denied their request, they tried to extract taxes from those passing over their lands. Emigrants were outraged. Frontier newspapers printed letters denouncing the Sioux, demanding

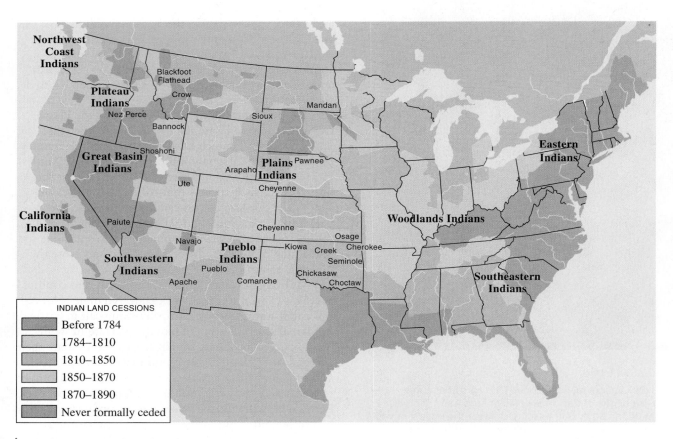

Native American Land Cessions in 1840

This map of Native American tribes and groupings reveals locations in 1840, but it presents too static a picture of tribal territories. Some of the Native American groups in the West had been forced across the Mississippi by events in the Midwest. What does the map show about the pace of Native American land cessions in the nineteenth century, especially in the trans-Mississippi West?

adequate protection for travelers and some chastening of the "savages." However, little was done to relieve the suffering of the tribes bearing the brunt of Sioux aggression, the dismay of the Sioux at the white invasion, or the fears of the emigrants themselves.

The discovery of gold in California, which lured more than 20,000 across the Great Plains in 1849 alone, became the catalyst for federal action. The vast numbers of gold seekers and their animals wrought such devastation in the Platte valley that it rapidly became a wasteland for the Indians. The dreaded cholera that whites carried with them spread to the Indians, killing thousands. To meet the crisis, government officials devised a two-pronged plan. The government would construct a chain of forts to protect emigrants and, simultaneously, call the tribes to a general conference. Officials expected that in return for generous presents, Native Americans would end tribal warfare and limit their movements to prescribed areas. They instructed tribes to select chiefs to speak for them at the conference.

The Fort Laramie Council, 1851

In 1851, the tribal council convened at Fort Laramie. As many as 10,000 Native Americans, hopeful of ending the destruction of their way of life and eager for the promised presents, gathered at the fort. Tribal animosities simmered, however. Skirmishes occurred on the way to the fort, and the border tribes, fearful of the Sioux, declined to participate. The Comanche, Kiowa, and Apache also refused to come, because their enemies, the Sioux and the Crow, were to be there.

At the conference, whites told the gathered tribes that times had changed. In the past, "you had plenty of buffalo and game... and your Great Father well knows that war has always been your favorite amusement and pursuit. He then left the question of peace and war to yourselves. Now, since the settling of the districts West... by the white men, your condition has changed." Tribes would receive compensation for the destruction of grass, timber, and buffalo and annual payments of goods and services. In return they must abandon their rights of free movement. The government drew tribal boundaries, and chiefs promised to stay within them. In most cases, some tribal lands were sold. The Fort Laramie Treaty, the first agreement between the Plains tribes and the U.S. government, expressed the conviction of whites that Indians must remain apart in clearly defined areas.

But this system of isolation was not achieved at Fort Laramie. During the conference, signs appeared that it would be difficult to resolve Native American–white affairs. Sioux Chief Black Hawk told whites, "You have split the country and I do not like it." His powerful tribe refused to be restricted to lands north of the Platte, for south of the river lay their recently conquered lands. "These lands once belonged to the Kiowas and the Crows," one Sioux explained, "but we whipped those nations out of them and in this we did what the white men do when they want the lands of the Indians." The words suggested that Native Americans, despite agreements, would not willingly abandon their traditional way of life for confinement. In the following years, it would become evident that Americans and Sioux had conflicting interests south of the Platte. Elsewhere in the trans-Mississippi West, other tribes, like the fierce Navajo of New Mexico, also resisted white attempts to confine them.

Overwhelming the Mexican Settlers

In the Southwest, in Texas, and in California, Americans encountered a Spanish-speaking population and Hispanic culture. Americans regarded Mexicans whom they often outnumbered as lazy, ignorant, and cunning, the "dregs of society." Although Anglo–Mexican interaction differed from place to place, few Anglos heeded the Treaty of Guadalupe Hidalgo's assurances that Mexicans would have citizens' rights and the "free enjoyment of their liberty and property." Most Spanish-speaking people lived in New Mexico, and, of all former Mexican citizens, they probably fared the best. Most were of mixed blood, living marginally as ranch hands for rich landowners or as farmers and herdsmen in small villages dominated by a *patron*, or headman. As the century wore on, Americans produced legal titles and took over lands long occupied by peasant farmers and stock raisers. But despite economic reversals, New Mexicans survived, carrying their rural culture well into the twentieth century.

Light-skinned, upper-class landowners fared better. Even before the conquest, rich New Mexicans had protected their future by establishing contacts with American businessmen and by sending their sons east to American schools. When the United States annexed New Mexico, this substantial and powerful class contracted strategic marriage and business alliances with the Anglo men slowly trickling into the territory. Only rarely did they worry about their poorer countrymen. Class interests outweighed ethnic or cultural considerations.

In Texas, the Spanish-speaking residents, only 10 percent of the population in 1840, shrank to a mere 6 percent by 1860. Although the upper class also intermarried with Americans, they lost most of their power as Germans, Irish, French, and Americans poured into the state. Poor, dark-skinned Hispanics clustered in low-paying and largely unskilled jobs.

In California, the discovery of gold radically changed the situation for the Californios. In 1848, there were 7,000 Californios and about twice as many

Timeline

1803–1806	Lewis and Clark expedition
1818	Treaty on joint U.S.–British occupation of Oregon
1819	Spain cedes Spanish territory in United States and sets transcontinental boundary of Louisiana Purchase, excluding Texas
1821	Mexican independence
	Opening of Santa Fe Trail
	Stephen Austin leads American settlement of Texas
1821–1840	Native American removals
1830	Mexico abolishes slavery in Texas
1836	Battles of the Alamo and San Jacinto
	Texas declares independence
1840s	Emigrant crossings of overland trails
1844	James Polk elected president
1845	"Manifest Destiny" coined
	United States annexes Texas and sends troops to the Rio Grande
	Americans attempt to buy Upper California and New Mexico
1846	Mexico declares defensive war
	United States declares war and takes Santa Fe
	Resolution of Oregon question
1847	Attacks on Veracruz and Mexico City
	Mormon migration to Utah begins
1848	Treaty of Guadalupe Hidalgo
1849	California gold rush begins
1850	California admitted to the Union
1851	Fort Laramie Treaty
1853	Gadsden Purchase
1862	Homestead Act

Anglos. By 1860, the Anglo population had ballooned to 360,000. Hispanic Americans were hard pressed to cope with the rapid influx of outsiders. At first, Californios and several thousand Mexicans from Sonora joined Anglos and others in the gold fields. But competition fed antagonism and finally open conflict. Posters warned foreigners out of the gold fields. In Anglo eyes, one Hispanic was much like another, even if one claimed to be a Californio with political rights and another a Sonoran. Taxes and terrorism ultimately succeeded in forcing most Spanish speakers out of the mines and established the racial contours of the new California.

Other changes were even more disastrous. In 1851, Congress passed the Gwin Land Law, supposedly validating Spanish and Mexican land titles. But it violated the Treaty of Guadalupe Hidalgo because it forced

California landowners to defend what was already theirs and encouraged squatters to settle on land in the hopes that the Californios' titles would prove false. It took an average of 17 years to establish clear title to land. Landowners found themselves paying American lawyers large fees, often in land, and borrowing at high interest rates to cover court proceedings. A victory at court often turned into a defeat when legal expenses forced owners to sell their lands to pay debts.

Working-class Hispanic Americans, laboring for Anglo farmers or for mining and later railroad companies, earned less money and did more unpleasant jobs than Anglo workers. By 1870, the average Hispanic American worker's property was worth only about a third of its value of 20 years earlier.

Various forms of resistance to American expansion emerged. Some, like Tiburcio Vásquez in southern

California, became *bandidos*. As he explained, the American presence provoked a "spirit of hatred and revenge...I believed we were unjustly and wrongfully deprived of the social rights that belonged to us." Others, like the members of Las Gorras Blancas in New Mexico, ripped up railroad ties and cut the barbed-wire fences of Anglo ranchers and farmers, while the religiously oriented Penitentes tried to work through the ballot box. Ordinary men, women, and children resisted efforts to convert them to Protestantism and held onto familiar customs and beliefs while learning some of the skills they hoped would enable them to flourish in a changing culture.

Conclusion
FRUITS OF MANIFEST DESTINY

Like Narcissa Whitman and her husband, many nineteenth-century Americans decided that they had a unique right to settle the West and make it flower. They were not much concerned with the fate of those who had lived for centuries on the land. The process of acquiring the western half of the continent was so swift that there seemed little point in worrying about the losers. The tale of western expansion loomed large in the imagination of the American people for many years. Some western settlers became folk heroes. The Whitmans were remembered by the founding of Whitman College in Walla Walla, Washington. All white Americans could be thankful for the special opportunities and the new chance that the West seemed to hold out. Certainly, the nation did gain vast natural wealth in the trans-Mississippi West. But only a small fraction of the hopeful emigrants heading for the frontier realized their dreams of success. And the move west and east had a dark side, as the acquisition of new territories fueled the controversy over the future of slavery.

QUESTIONS FOR REVIEW AND REFLECTION

1. Explain how and why the westward movement entangled the United States in the affairs of foreign powers.
2. Compare and contrast the acquisition of Texas and the Southwest with the annexation of Oregon.
3. What racial and ethnic tensions emerged in the West because of American expansionism?
4. What factors caused problems and tensions between Native Americans and whites?
5. What important American beliefs and values were involved in the westward movement? How did they shape the westward experience?

CHAPTER 14

The Union in Peril

George Caleb Bingham's *Stump Speaking* (1856) captures the democratic energy of politics at mid-century. But does it capture the passions? How democratic *was* America in the 1850s, and how well did the democratic process work? Note the Lincoln-like figure sitting to the right.

(Private Collection/Bridgeman Art Library)

American Stories

Four Men Respond to the Union in Peril

The autumn of 1860 was a time of ominous expectations. The election was held on November 6 in an atmosphere of crisis. Abraham Lincoln, taking coffee and sandwiches prepared by the "ladies of Springfield," waited in Springfield, Illinois, as the telegraph brought in the returns. By 1 A.M., victory was certain. He reported later, "I went home, but not to get much sleep, for I then felt, as I never had before, the responsibility that was upon me." Indeed, he and the American people faced the most serious crisis since the founding of the Republic.

Lincoln won a four-party election with only 39 percent of the popular vote. He appealed almost exclusively to northern voters in a blatantly sectional campaign, defeating his three opponents by carrying every free state except New Jersey. Only Illinois senator Stephen Douglas campaigned actively in every section of the country. For his efforts, he received the second-highest number of votes. Douglas's appeal, especially in the closing days of the campaign, was "on behalf of the Union," which he feared—correctly—was in imminent danger of splitting apart.

That fall, other Americans sensed the crisis and faced their own fears and responsibilities. A month before the election, South Carolina plantation owner Robert Allston wrote his oldest son, Benjamin, that "disastrous consequences" would follow from a Lincoln victory. Although his letter mentioned the possibility of secession, he dealt mostly with plantation concerns: a new horse, the mood of the slaves, ordering supplies from the city, instructions for making trousers on a sewing machine. After Lincoln's election, Allston corresponded with a southern colleague about the need for an "effective military organization" to resist "Northern and Federal aggression." In his shift from sewing machines to military ones, Robert Allston prepared for what he called the "impending crisis."

Frederick Douglass greeted the election of 1860 with characteristic optimism. This was an opportunity to "educate...the people in their moral and political duties," he said, adding, "slaveholders know that the day of their power is over when a Republican President is elected." But no sooner had Lincoln's victory been determined than Douglass's hopes turned sour. He noted that Republican leaders, who were trying to keep border states from seceding, sounded more anti-abolitionist than antislavery. They vowed not to touch slavery in areas where it already existed (including the District of Columbia), to enforce the hated Fugitive Slave Act, and to put down slave rebellions. In fact, Douglass bitterly contested, slavery would "be as safe, and safer" with Lincoln than with a Democrat.

Iowa farmer Michael Luark was not so sure. Born in Virginia, he was a typically mobile nineteenth-century American. Growing up in Indiana, he followed the mining booms of the 1850s to Colorado and California, then returned to the Midwest to farm. Luark sought a good living and resented the furor over slavery. He could not, however, avoid the issue. Writing in his diary on the last day of 1860, Luark looked ahead to 1861 with a deep sense of fear. "Startling" political changes would occur, he predicted, perhaps even the "Dissolution of the Union and Civil War with all its train of horrors." He blamed abolitionist agitators, perhaps reflecting his Virginia origins. On New Year's Day, he expressed his fears that Lincoln would let the "most ultra sectional and Abolition" men disturb the "vexed Slavery question" even further, as Frederick Douglass wanted. But if this happened, Luark warned, "then farewell to our beloved Union of States."

Within four months of this diary entry, the guns of the Confederate States of America fired on a federal fort in South Carolina. The Civil War had begun.

The firing on Fort Sumter made real Luark's fears, Douglass's hopes and dreams, and Lincoln's and Allston's preparations for responsibility. America's shaky democratic political system faced its worst crisis. The explanation of the peril and dissolution of the Union forms the theme of this chapter.

Such calamitous events as Civil War had numerous causes, large and small. The reactions of Allston, Douglass, and Luark to Lincoln's election suggest some of them: moral duties, sectional politics, growing apprehensions over emotional agitators, and a concern for freedom and independence on the part of blacks, white southerners, and western farmers. But as Douglass understood, by 1860, it was clear that "slavery is the real issue, the single bone of contention between all parties and sections."

This chapter analyzes how the momentous issue of slavery disrupted not only individual democratic dreams but also the political system and eventually the Union itself. We will look at how four major developments between 1848 and 1861 contributed to the Civil War: first, a sectional dispute over the extension of slavery into the western territories; second, the breakdown of the political party system; third, growing cultural differences in the views and lifestyles of southerners and northerners; and fourth, intensifying emotional and ideological polarization between the two regions over losing their way of life and sacred republican rights at the hands of the other. A preview of civil war, bringing all four causes together, occurred in Kansas in 1855–1856. Eventually, emotional events, mistrust, and irreconcilable differences made conflict inevitable. Lincoln's election was the spark that touched off the conflagration of civil war, with all its "train of horrors."

Slavery in the Territories

As Narcissa Whitman sadly discovered with the Cayuse Indians in eastern Washington (see Chapter 13), white migration westward was often downright dangerous. But it was especially damaging to the lives and cultural integrity of Native Americans and Mexicans, whose lands stood in the way. Moreover, the westward movement imperiled freedom and eventually the Union by causing a collision between Yankees and slaveholders.

The North and the South had mostly contained their differences over slavery for 60 years after the Constitutional Convention. Compromise in 1787 had resolved questions of the slave trade and how to count slaves for congressional representation. Although slavery threatened the uneasy sectional harmony in 1820 ("like a fire bell in the night," Jefferson had said), the Missouri Compromise had established a workable balance of free and slave states and had defined a geographic line (36°30') to determine future decisions. In 1833, compromise had defused South Carolina's attempt at nullification, and the gag rule in 1836 had kept abolitionist petitions out of Congress.

Each apparent resolution, however, raised the level of conflict between North and South and postponed ultimate settlement of the slavery question. One reason why these compromises temporarily worked was the two-party system, with Whigs and Democrats in both North and South serving as an "antidote," as Van Buren put it, to sectional allegiance. The parties differed over cultural and economic issues, but slavery was largely kept out of political campaigns and congressional debates. This changed in the late 1840s.

Free Soil or Constitutional Protection?

After war with Mexico broke out in 1846, Pennsylvania congressman David Wilmot proposed a bill declaring that "neither slavery nor involuntary servitude shall ever exist" in any territories acquired from Mexico. Legislators debated the Wilmot Proviso not as Whigs and Democrats but as northerners and southerners.

A Boston newspaper prophetically observed that Wilmot's resolution "brought to a head the great question which is about to divide the American people." When the war ended, several solutions were presented to deal with slavery in the territories. First was the "free soil" idea of preventing any extensions of slavery. Two precedents suggested that Congress could do this. One was the Northwest Ordinance, which had barred slaves from the Upper Midwest; the other was the Missouri Compromise.

Free-Soilers had mixed motives. For some, slavery was a moral evil to be destroyed. But for many northern white farmers looking westward, the threat of economic competition with an expanding system of large-scale slave labor was even more serious. Nor did they wish to compete with free blacks. As Wilmot put it, his proviso was intended to preserve lands for the "sons of toil, of my own race and own color." Other northerners supported the proviso as a means of restraining the growing political power and "insufferable arrogance" of the "spirit and demands of the Slave Power."

An opposing position to the Free-Soilers was the argument of South Carolina Senator John C. Calhoun in 1847. Congress not only lacked the constitutional right to exclude slavery from the territories, he argued, but also had a duty to protect it. Therefore, the Wilmot Proviso was unconstitutional. So were the Missouri Compromise and other federal acts that prevented slaveholders from taking their slave property into the territories.

Economic and political considerations stood behind Calhoun's position. Many southerners hungered for new cotton lands in the West and Southwest, even in Central America and the Caribbean. Southerners feared that northerners wanted to trample their right to protect their institutions against abolitionism. Southern leaders saw the Wilmot Proviso touching basic republican principles. One congressman called it "treason to the Constitution," and Senator Robert Toombs of Georgia warned that if it passed, he would favor disunion.

Popular Sovereignty and the Election of 1848

With such divisive potential, it was natural that many Americans sought a compromise solution to keep slavery out of politics. Polk's secretary of state, James Buchanan of Pennsylvania, proposed extending the Missouri Compromise line to the Pacific Ocean, thereby avoiding thorny questions about the morality of slavery and the constitutionality of congressional authority. So would "popular sovereignty," the proposal of Michigan senator Lewis Cass to leave decisions over slavery to territorial legislatures. This idea appealed to the American democratic belief in local self-government but left many details unanswered. At what point in the progress toward statehood could a territorial legislature decide about slavery?

Cass left such concerns ambiguous. Democrats, liking popular sovereignty because it could mean all things to all people, nominated him for president in 1848. Cass denounced abolitionists and the Wilmot Proviso but otherwise avoided the issue of slavery. Democrats printed two campaign biographies of Cass, one for the South and one for the North.

The Whigs found an even better way to hold the party together. Rejecting Henry Clay, they nominated the Mexican-American War hero General Zachary Taylor, a Louisiana slaveholder. Taylor compared himself to Washington as a "no party" man above politics. This was about all he stood for. Southern Whigs supported Taylor because they thought he

Recovering the Past

SENATE SPEECHES

The history of ordinary Americans is recovered in letters, diaries, and folktales. But in times of political conflict, as in the years before the Civil War, historians turn to more conventional sources such as congressional speeches. Recorded in the *Congressional Globe,* these speeches are a revealing means of recovering the substance, tone, and drama of political debate.

The mid-nineteenth century was an era of giants in the U.S. Senate: Daniel Webster, Henry Clay, John C. Calhoun, William Seward, and Stephen Douglas. When Congress debated a major issue, such as nullification or the extension of slavery, large crowds packed the Senate galleries. These spectacular oratorical encounters provided mass entertainment and political instruction. Such was the case with the Senate speeches over the Compromise of 1850. The three principal figures early in the debates were Clay (Kentucky), Calhoun (South Carolina), and Webster (Massachusetts), each of whom delivered memorable speeches to crown brilliant careers.

Born within five years of each other, each man began his political career in the House of Representatives in the War of 1812 era. Each served a term as secretary of state; and each served in the Senate for an average of 16 years. Clay and Webster were leaders of the Whig party, and Calhoun was a leader of the Democrats. All three were failing candidates for president between 1824 and 1844. All three clashed with and spent most of their careers in the political shadow of Andrew Jackson.

Forty years of political and ideological conflict with each other not only sharpened their oratorical skills but also led to mutual respect. Webster said of Calhoun that he was "the ablest man in the Senate. He could have demolished Newton, Calvin, or even John Locke as a logician." Calhoun said of Clay, "He is a bad man, but by god, I love him." And "Old Man Eloquent" himself, John Quincy Adams, said of Webster that he was "the most consummate orator of modern times."

Therefore, it was a momentous event when they each prepared speeches and met for one last encounter in 1850. Clay was over 70 years old and in failing health, but he sought to keep the Union together by defending his compromise proposals in a four-hour speech spread over two days in February. The Senate galleries were so packed that listeners were pushed into hallways and even into the rotunda of the Capitol. Copies of his speech were in such demand that over 100,000 were printed.

A month later, on March 7, Webster rose to join Clay in defending the compromise, three days after a seriously ill Calhoun had "tottered into the Senate" on the arm of a friend to hear James Mason of Virginia read his rejection of the compromise. Within a month, Calhoun was dead. Clay and Webster followed him to the grave two years later.

Reflecting on the Past As you read these brief excerpts from each speech, try to imagine yourself sitting in the gallery overlooking the Senate floor absorbing the drama. What oratorical devices does each speaker use? How do they differ? To what extent does each man reflect his region, especially on the fugitive slave issue? To what extent do they appeal to an indivisible Union? On whom do they put the burden of resolving the conflicts? Which speaker is most persuasive to you? Why?

Henry Clay

February 5–6, 1850

I have seen many periods of great anxiety, of peril, and of danger in this country, and I have never before risen to address any assemblage so oppressed, so appalled, and so anxious. . . .

Mr. President, it is passion, passion-party, party, and intemperance—that is all I dread in the adjustment of the great questions which unhappily at this time divide our distracted country. Sir, at this moment we have in the legislative bodies of this Capitol and in the States, twenty old furnaces in full blast, emitting heat, and passion, and intemperance, and diffusing them throughout the whole extent of this broad land. Two months ago all was calm in comparison to the present moment. All now is uproar, confusion, and menace to the existence of the Union, and to the happiness and safety of this people. . . .

Sir, when I came to consider this subject, there were two or three general purposes which it seemed to me to be most desirable, if possible, to accomplish. The one was, to settle all the controverted questions arising out of the subject of slavery. . . . I therefore turned my attention to every subject connected with this institution of slavery, and out of which controverted questions had sprung, to see if it were possible or practicable to accommodate and adjust the whole of them. . . .

We are told now, and it is rung throughout this entire country, that the Union is threatened with subversion and destruction. Well, the first question which naturally rises is, supposing the Union to be dissolved,—having all the causes of grievance which are complained of,—How far will a dissolution furnish a remedy for those grievances? If the Union is to be dissolved for any existing causes, it will be dissolved because slavery is interdicted or not allowed to be introduced into the ceded territories; because slavery is threatened to be abolished in the District of Columbia, and because fugitive slaves are not returned, as in my *opinion they ought to be, and restored to their masters. These, I believe, will be the causes; if there be any causes, which can lead to the direful event to which I have referred. . . .*

Mr. President, I am directly opposed to any purpose of secession, of separation. I am for staying within the Union, and defying any portion of this Union to expel or drive me out of the Union.

John C. Calhoun

March 4, 1850
Having now, Senators, explained what it is that endangers the Union, and traced it to its cause, and explained its nature and character, the question again recurs—How can the Union be saved? To this I answer, there is but one way by which it can be— and that is—by adopting such measures as will satisfy the States belonging to the Southern section, that they can remain in the Union consistently with their honor and their safety. . . .

But will the North agree to this? It is for her to answer the question. But, I will say, she cannot refuse, if she has half the love of the Union which she professes to have, or without justly exposing herself to the charge that her love of power and aggrandizement is far greater than her love of the Union. At all events, the responsibility of saving the Union rests on the North, and not on the South. . . .

Daniel Webster

March 7, 1850
Mr. President: I wish to speak to-day, not as a Massachusetts man, nor as a Northern man, but as an American, and a member of the Senate of the United States. . . .
I speak to-day for the preservation of the Union. "Hear me for my cause." I speak to-day, out of a solicitous and anxious heart, for the restoration to the country of that quiet and that harmony which make the blessing of this Union so rich, and so dear to us all. . . . I shall bestow a little attention, Sir, upon these various grievances existing on the one side and on the other. I begin with complaints of the South . . . and especially to one which has in my opinion just foundation; and that is, that there has been found at the North, among individuals and among legislators, a disinclination to perform fully their constitutional duties in regard to the return of persons bound to service who

have escaped into the free States. In that respect, the South, in my judgment, is right, and the North is wrong. Every member of every Northern legislature is bound by oath, like every other officer in the country, to support the Constitution of the United States; and the article of the Constitution which says to these States they shall deliver up fugitives from service is as binding in honor and conscience as any other article. . . .
Where is the line to be drawn? What States are to secede? What is to remain American? What am I to be? An American no longer? Am I to become a sectional man, a local man, a separatist, with no country in common with the gentlemen who sit around me here, or who fill the other house of Congress? Heaven forbid! Where is the flag of the republic to remain? Where is the eagle still to tower? or is he to cower, and shrink, and fall to the ground?

might understand the burdens of slaveholding, and northern Whigs were pleased that he took no stand on the Wilmot Proviso.

The evasions of the two major parties disappointed Calhoun, who tried to create a new, unified southern party. His "Address to the People of the Southern States" threatened secession and called for a united stand against further attempts to interfere with the southern right to extend slavery. Although only 48 of 121 southern representatives signed the address, Calhoun's argument raised the specter of secession and disunion.

Warnings also came from the North. A New York Democratic faction bolted to support Van Buren for

president. At first, the split had more to do with state politics than moral principles, but it soon involved the question of slavery in the territories. Disaffected "conscience" Whigs from Massachusetts also explored a third-party alternative. These groups met in Buffalo, New York, to form the Free-Soil party and nominated Van Buren. The platform of the new party, an uneasy mixture of ardent abolitionists and opponents of free blacks moving into western lands, pledged to fight for "free soil, free speech, free labor and free men."

Taylor won easily, largely because defections from Cass to the Free-Soilers cost the Democrats New York and Pennsylvania. Although weakened, the

Describe what you see in this 1848 painting by Richard Caton Woodville, titled *War News from Mexico*. What do you suppose the men are hearing about the war in Mexico and how are they reacting? Do you think this "American Hotel" is in the North or South? How would the war news be heard in each place? How do you think the black man and little girl are responding to the news? Why would the Mexican War and its outcomes interest them?

(Richard Caton Woodville, "War News from Mexico," Oil on canvas, .686 × .627 (27 × 24-3/4). The Manovgian Foundation on loan to the National Gallery of Art, Washington, Dc. © Board of Trustees, National Gallery of Art, Washington.)

two-party system survived. Purely sectional parties had failed. The Free-Soilers took only 10 percent of the popular vote.

The Compromise of 1850

Taylor won the election by avoiding slavery questions. But as president, he had to deal with them. When he was inaugurated in 1849, four issues faced the nation. First, the rush of some 80,000 gold miners to California qualified it for statehood. But California's entry as a free state would upset the slave–free state balance in the Senate. The unresolved status of the Mexican cession in the Southwest posed a second problem. The longer the area remained unorganized, the louder local inhabitants called for an application of either the Wilmot Proviso or the Calhoun doctrine. The Texas–New Mexico boundary

was also disputed, with Texas claiming everything east of Santa Fe. Northerners feared that Texas might split into five or six slave states. A third problem, especially for abolitionists, was the existence of slavery and a huge slave market in the nation's capital. Fourth, southerners resented the lax federal enforcement of the Fugitive Slave Act of 1793. They called for a stronger act that would end protection for runaways fleeing to Canada.

Taylor was a political novice (he had never voted in a presidential election before 1848), and tackled these problems somewhat evasively. He succeeded only in alienating nearly everyone.

Early in 1850, the old compromiser Henry Clay sought to regain control of the Whig party by proposing solutions to the divisive issues before the nation. With Webster's support, Clay introduced a series of resolutions in an omnibus package intended to settle these issues once and for all. The stormy debates, great speeches, and political maneuvering that followed constituted a crucial and dramatic moment in American history. After 70 stirring speeches on behalf of the compromise, the Senate defeated Clay's Omnibus Bill. Tired and disheartened, the 73-year-old Clay left Washington and died two years later. Into the gap stepped Senator Stephen Douglas of Illinois, who saw that Clay's resolutions had a better chance of passing if voted on individually. Under Douglas's leadership, and with the support of President Millard Fillmore, who succeeded to the presidency upon Taylor's sudden death, a series of bills was finally passed.

The Compromise of 1850 put Clay's resolutions, slightly altered, into law. First, California entered the Union as a free state, ending the balance of free and slave states. Second, territorial governments were organized in New Mexico and Utah, letting local people decide whether to permit slavery. The Texas–New Mexico border was settled, denying Texas the disputed area. In return, the federal government gave Texas $10 million to pay debts owed to Mexico. Third, the slave trade, but not slavery, was abolished in the District of Columbia.

The fourth and most controversial part of the compromise was the Fugitive Slave Act, containing many provisions that offended northerners. One denied alleged fugitives a jury trial, leaving special cases for decision by commissioners (who were paid $5 for setting a fugitive free but $10 for returning a fugitive). An especially repugnant provision compelled northern citizens to help catch runaways.

Consequences of Compromise

The Compromise of 1850 was the last attempt to keep slavery out of politics. Voting on the different bills followed sectional lines on some issues and party lines on others. Douglas felt pleased with his "final settlement" of the slavery question.

But the compromise only delayed more serious sectional conflict, and it added two new ingredients to American politics. First, political realignment along sectional lines tightened. Second, although repudiated by most ordinary citizens, the ideas of secessionism, disunion, and a "higher law" than the Constitution entered political discussions. People wondered whether the question of slavery in the territories could be compromised away next time.

Henry Clay argues for the compromise package of 1850 in this painting by R. Whitechurch, titled *The United States Senate, 1850*. Clay warned that failure to adopt his bill would lead to "furious" and "bloody" civil war. Was he right?

(Library of Congress, LC-USZ62–689)

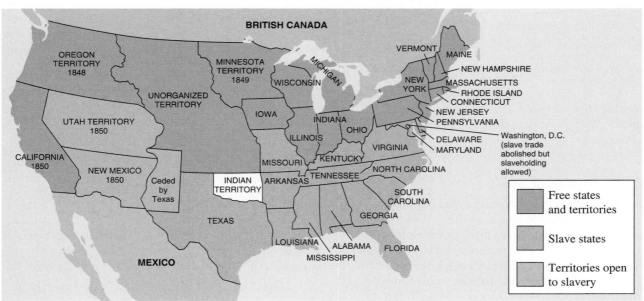

The Compromise of 1850

In February 1850, Henry Clay told Congress that he asked "Him who holds the destinies of nations and individuals in His hands . . . to calm the violence and rage of party." What followed were Senate debates that led eventually to the passage of the Compromise of 1850. Can you find three of the four major parts of the bill on the map? What was the fourth? Was violence and party rage calmed?

Others were immediately upset. The new fugitive slave law angered many northerners because it brought the evils of slavery right into their midst. Owners of runaway slaves hired agents (labeled "kidnappers" in the North) to hunt down fugitives. In a few dramatic episodes, notably in Boston, literary and religious intellectuals led mass protests to resist slave hunters. When Webster supported the law, New England abolitionists denounced him as "indescribably base and wicked." Ralph Waldo Emerson said he would not obey the "filthy law."

Frederick Douglass would not obey it either. As a runaway slave, he faced arrest and re-enslavement until friends overcame his objections and purchased his freedom. Douglass still risked harm by his strong defiance of the Fugitive Slave Act. Arguing the "rightfulness of forcible resistance," he urged free blacks to arm themselves. "The only way to make the Fugitive Slave Law a dead letter," he said in Pittsburgh in 1853, "is to make a half dozen or more dead kidnappers." Douglass raised money for black fugitives, hid runaways in his home, and helped hundreds escape to Canada.

Other northerners, both white and black, stepped up work for the Underground Railroad and helped runaway slaves evade capture. Several states passed "personal liberty laws" that prohibited using state officials and institutions in the recovery of fugitives. But most northerners complied. Of some 200 blacks

arrested in the first six years of the law, only 15 were rescued and only 3 of these by force. In two celebrated cases in the early 1850s, angry mobs of abolitionists in Boston failed to prevent the forcible return of blacks to the South, which aroused more antislavery emotions among northerners than the abolitionists had been able to do with their tracts and speeches. One man wrote of the trial of Anthony Burns that sent him back to the South: "We went to bed one night old fashioned, conservative Compromise Union Whigs and waked up stark mad abolitionists."

Longtime abolitionists escalated their rhetoric in both spoken and written word. Douglass's Independence Day speech in 1852, wondering "What, to the American slave, is your 4th of July?" said that the day revealed to the slave that American claims of national greatness were vain and empty; the "shouts of liberty and equality" were "fraud, deception, impiety, and hypocrisy."

At a women's rights convention in 1851 in Akron, Ohio, the ex-slave Sojourner Truth delivered one of the decade's boldest statements. Clergymen attending the convention heckled female speakers. Truth stood to speak in words still debated by historians. She pointed to her many years of childbearing and hard, backbreaking work as a slave, crying out a refrain, "And ar'n't I a woman?" She taunted the ministers, saying that Jesus came "from God and a woman: Man had nothing to do with Him." Referring to Eve, she concluded, "If the

As a group of runaways makes its way north in this painting by Theodor Kaufmann entitled *On to Liberty* (1867), the peril of the journey, even if successful, is reflected in this broadside published by a Boston abolitionist, which alerted the city's black community in 1851 to the dangers posed by the Fugitive Slave Act. What were the difficult decisions and daily realities of runaway slaves?

(Left: Theodor Kaufmann, *On to Liberty*, 1867. The Metropolitan Museum of Art, Gift of Erving and Joyce Wolfe, 1982. (1982.443.3) Photograph © 1982 The Metropolitan Museum of Art; right: Harold Washington Library Center, Special Collections & Preservation Division, Chicago Public Library)

first woman God ever made was strong enough to turn the world upside down all alone, these women together ought to be able to turn it back, and get it right side up again! And now they is asking to do it, the men better let them." She silenced the hecklers.

As Truth spoke, another American woman, Harriet Beecher Stowe, was finishing a novel, *Uncle Tom's Cabin,* which went far toward turning the world upside down. As politicians hoped the American people would forget slavery, Stowe's novel brought it to the attention of thousands. She gave readers an absorbing indictment of slavery's horrors. Published initially as magazine serials, each month's chapter ended at a nail-biting dramatic moment as readers cheered Eliza's daring escape across the ice floes on the Ohio River, cried over Uncle Tom's humanity and Little Eva's death, suffered under the lash of Simon Legree, and rejoiced in the reuniting of black family members.

Although it outraged the South when published in full in 1852, *Uncle Tom's Cabin* became one of the all time best-sellers in American history. In the first year, more than 300,000 copies were printed, and Stowe's novel was eventually published in 20 languages. When President Lincoln met Stowe in 1863, he is reported to have said to her: "So you're the little woman who wrote the book that made this great war!"

Political Disintegration

The response to *Uncle Tom's Cabin* and the Fugitive Slave Act indicated that politicians had congratulated themselves too soon for saving the Republic in 1850. Political developments, not all dealing with slavery, were already weakening the ability of political parties—and ultimately the nation—to withstand the passions slavery aroused.

Weakened Party Politics in the Early 1850s

As we see in modern elections, political parties seek to persuade voters that their party stands for moral values and economic policies crucially different from those of the opposition. Between 1850 and 1854 these differences blurred, undermining party loyalty.

Both parties scrambled to convince voters that they had favored the Compromise of 1850. In addition, several states rewrote their constitutions and remodeled their laws. These changes reduced the number of patronage jobs that politicians could dispense and regularized the process for securing banking, railroad, and other corporate charters, ending the role formerly played by the legislature and undermining the importance of parties in citizens' lives. For almost a quarter of a century Whigs and Democrats had disagreed over the tariff, the National Bank, and internal improvements. But in the more prosperous times of the early 1850s, party distinctions over economic policies seemed less important.

Political battles were fought over local social issues rather than national economic ones. Thus, Georgia voters in 1851 pitted "the jealousies of the poor who owned no slaves, against the rich slaveholder." In Indiana, where a Congressman observed that people "hate the Negro with a perfect if not a supreme hatred," legislators rewrote the state constitution in 1851, depriving blacks of the rights to vote, attend white schools, or make contracts, paving the way to make it a crime for blacks to settle in Indiana. In Massachusetts, temperance reform and the length of the working day were hot issues. As political alliances

CHANGING POLITICAL PARTY SYSTEMS AND LEADERS

It is characteristic of American politics that when the two major parties fail to respond to the pressing issues of the day, new parties are born and major party realignment occurs. This happened in the 1850s over the issue of slavery and its extension into the territories, which resulted in the collapse of the Whigs and the emergence of the Republicans. Note that the "Republican" party begins in one political tradition and ends up in the other. Is political realignment happening again in American politics? What do the two parties stand for today?

First Party System: 1790s–1820s

Republican	Federalist
Jefferson	Hamilton
Madison	John Adams
Monroe	

Transition: 1824 and 1828

Democrat-Republican	National Republican
Jackson	J.Q. Adams

Second Party System: 1830s–1850s

Democrat	Whig
Jackson	Clay
Van Buren	Webster
Calhoun	W.H. Harrison
Polk	

Third Party System: 1856–1890s

Democrat	Republican
Douglas	Lincoln
Pierce	Seward
Buchanan	Grant

developed around local issues and personalities, a Baltimore businessman observed, "The two old parties are fast melting away."

The election of 1852 illustrated this decline. The Whigs nominated General Winfield Scott, another Mexican-American War hero, who they hoped would repeat Taylor's success four years earlier. Still, it took 52 ballots to nominate Scott over the moderate Fillmore. Democrats had their own problems. After 49 ballots, the party turned to a lackluster compromise candidate, Franklin Pierce of New Hampshire.

The two parties offered little choice and downplayed issues so as not to widen intra-party divisions. Voter interest diminished. "Genl. Apathy is the strongest candidate out here," was a typical report from Ohio, while the Baltimore *Sun* remarked, "there is no issue that much interests the people." Democratic leaders resorted to bribes and drinks to buy the support of thousands of new Catholic immigrants from Ireland and Germany, who could be naturalized and were eligible to vote after only three years. Pierce won easily, 254 to 42 electoral votes.

The Kansas–Nebraska Act

The Whig party's final disintegration came on a February day in 1854 when southern Whigs, choosing to be more southern than Whig, supported Stephen Douglas's Nebraska bill. The Illinois senator had many reasons for introducing a bill organizing the Nebraska Territory (which included Kansas). As an ardent nationalist, he was interested in the continuing development of the West. He wanted the eastern terminus for a transcontinental railroad in Chicago rather than in rival St. Louis. This meant organizing the lands west of Iowa and Missouri.

Politics also played a role. Douglas hoped to recapture the party leadership he had held in passing the Compromise of 1850 and aspired to the presidency. Although he had replaced Cass as the great advocate of popular sovereignty, thus winning favor among northern Democrats, he needed southern Democratic support. Many southerners, especially neighboring Missouri slaveholders, opposed organizing the Nebraska Territory unless open to slavery. But the Nebraska Territory lay north of the Missouri Compromise line prohibiting slavery.

Douglas's bill, introduced early in 1854, recommended using popular sovereignty in organizing the Kansas and Nebraska territories. Douglas reasoned that the climate and soil of the prairies in Kansas and Nebraska would never support slavery-based agriculture, and that the people would choose to be a free state. Therefore, he could win the votes he needed for the railroad without also getting slavery. By stating that the states created out of the Nebraska Territory would enter the Union "with or without slavery, as their constitution may prescribe," his bill in effect cancelled the Missouri Compromise.

Douglas miscalculated. Northerners from his own party immediately attacked him and his bill as a "criminal betrayal of precious rights" and as part of a plot promoting his own presidential ambitions. Whigs and abolitionists were even more outraged. Frederick Douglass branded the act a "hateful" attempt to extend slavery, the result of the "audacious villainy of the slave power."

But the more Stephen Douglas was attacked, the harder he fought. What began as a railroad measure ended in reopening the question of slavery in the territories, which Douglas thought settled in 1850. What began as a way of avoiding conflict ended in violence over whether Kansas would be slave or free. What began as a way of strengthening party lines ended up destroying the Whig party, planting deep divisions in the Democrats, and creating two new parties.

Expansionist "Young America" in the Larger World

The Democratic party was weakened in the early 1850s not only by the Kansas–Nebraska Act but also by an expansive energy that led Americans to adventures far beyond Kansas. As republican revolutions erupted in 1848 in Europe (Austria-Hungary, France, Germany), Americans hailed them as evidence that republicanism was the wave of the future. "Young America" was the label assumed by patriots eager to spread Americanism abroad; however, these ardent republican nationalists ironically also abetted the spread of slavery.

Pierce's platform in 1852 reflected this nationalism, declaring that the war with Mexico had been "just and necessary." Many Democrats took the victory over Mexico as a mandate to continue adding territory. A Philadelphia newspaper in 1853 described the United States as a nation bound on the "East by sunrise, West by sunset, North by the Arctic Expedition, and South as far as we darn please."

Many of the president's diplomatic appointees were southerners interested in adding new cotton-growing lands to the Union, especially from Latin America where newly independent nations were wracked by internal disputes over the distribution of land. Pierce's ambassador to Mexico, South Carolinian James Gadsden, was instructed to negotiate with Mexican president Santa Anna for the acquisition of large parts of northern Mexico. Gadsden did not get all he wanted, but he did manage to purchase a strip of southwestern desert for a transcontinental railroad linking the Deep South with the Pacific Coast.

Failure to acquire more territory from Mexico legally did not discourage expansionist Americans

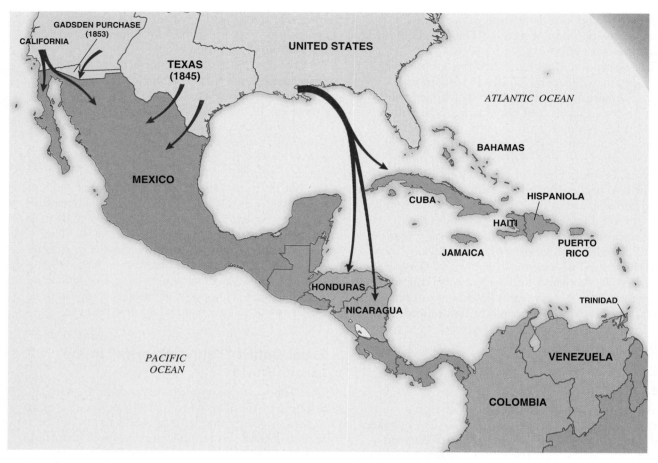

Expansionist "Young America" in the 1850s: Attempted Raids into Latin America

Note the flurry of expansionist American raids and forays southward into Mexico and the Caribbean between the mid-1840s and mid-1850s. What major events and motives caused the expansionist interest? Why was Cuba a key target? Why Mexico? Are there similar events today?

from pursuing illegal means. During the 1850s, Texans and Californians staged dozens of raids ("filibusters") into Mexico. The most daring such adventurer was William Walker, a tiny Tennessean with a zest for danger and power. In 1853, he invaded Mexican Baja California with fewer than 300 men and declared himself president of the Republic of Sonora. Arrested and tried in the United States, he was acquitted in eight minutes. Two years later, he invaded Nicaragua, where he proclaimed himself an elected dictator and legalized slavery. When the Nicaraguans regained control, the U.S. Navy rescued Walker. After a triumphant tour in the South, he tried twice more to conquer Nicaragua. Walker came to a fitting end in 1860 when, invading Honduras this time, he was captured and shot by a firing squad.

Undaunted by failures in the Southwest, the Pierce administration looked to the acquisition of Cuba. Many Americans thought this Spanish colony was destined for U.S. annexation and would be an ideal place for expanding the slave-based economy. Some argued that Cuba belonged to the United States because it was

physically connected by alluvial deposits from the Mississippi River. "What God has joined together let no man put asunder," one said. In the 1840s, the Polk administration had vainly offered Spain $10 million for Cuba. Unsuccessful efforts were then made to foment a revolution among Cuban sugar planters, who were expected to request annexation by the United States, which might then carve it into several slave states.

Although Pierce did not support these illegal efforts to acquire Cuba, he wanted the island. His Secretary of State, William Marcy, instructed the minister to Spain to offer $130 million for Cuba, upping the price. If that failed, Marcy suggested stronger measures. In 1854, the secretary arranged for the American ministers to France and England to meet in Belgium, where they issued the Ostend Manifesto to pressure Spain to sell Cuba to the United States.

The manifesto argued that Cuba "belongs naturally" to the United States for trade and commerce and that they were "one people with one destiny." Moreover, southern slaveholders feared that a slave rebellion would "Africanize" Cuba, like Haiti, and suggested all kinds of "horrors to the white race" in the nearby southern United States. American acquisition of Cuba was necessary, therefore, to "preserve our rectitude and self-respect." If Spain refused to sell, the ministers at Ostend threatened a Cuban revolution with American support. If that failed, "we should be justified in wresting it from Spain."

Even Marcy was shocked when he received the document and he quickly repudiated the manifesto. Democrats supported the Ostend Manifesto in order to further the expansion of slavery, but the outraged reaction of northerners further divided and weakened their party.

Immigration, Know-Nothings, and Republicans

The increasing immigration of Irish and German Catholics alarmed many native-born Americans and damaged an already enfeebled Whig party. To the average hardworking Protestant American, foreigners spoke unfamiliar languages, wore funny clothes, drank alcohol freely, and bred crime and pauperism. Moreover, they seemed content with a lower standard of living by working for lower wages and thus threatened to take jobs away from American workers.

Worst of all from the Protestant perspective, Irish and German immigrants spearheaded an unprecedented growth of American Catholicism. By the 1850s, there were nearly 3 million Catholics in the United States, not only in eastern cities but expanding westward into the Ohio valley and along old French-Canadian trade routes into the Great Lakes region. The most disturbing developments were Catholic success in converting Protestants and the opening of Catholic schools.

Many Protestants charged that Catholic immigrants corrupted American politics. Most Catholics did indeed prefer the Democratic party, which was less inclined than Whigs to interfere with religion, schooling, drinking, and other aspects of personal behavior. It was mostly former Whigs, therefore, who in 1854 founded the American party to oppose the new immigrants. Members wanted a longer period of naturalization to guarantee the "vital principles of Republican Government" and pledged never to vote for Irish Catholics, whose highest loyalty was supposedly to the pope in Rome. They also agreed to keep information about their order secret, answering questions by saying, "I know nothing."

The "Know-Nothing" party appealed to the middle and lower classes—to workers worried about their jobs and to farmers and small-town Americans nervous about change. A New Yorker said in 1854, "Roman Catholicism is feared more than American slavery." It was widely believed that Catholics slavishly obeyed the orders of their priests, who represented a Church associated with European despotism. In the 1854 and 1855 elections, the Know-Nothings gave anti-Catholicism a national, political focus for the first time.

Describe this cartoon from the mid-1850s (above). What stereotypes of Irish and Germans are shown? Are they stealing the ballot box, and what is going on in the background? The Know-Nothing flag (right) makes starkly clear that party's view on the reasons for concern. Who are the "Native Americans"? Can you imagine what Indian Americans might have thought of this banner?

(Photo: Courtesy of the Milwaukee County Historical Society)

To other northerners, however, the "slave power" seemed a more serious threat than the alleged schemes of the pope. No sooner had debates over Nebraska ended than the nucleus of another new party appeared: the Republicans. Drawn almost entirely from "conscience" Whigs and disaffected Free-Soil Democrats, the Republicans combined four elements.

Moral fervor led the first group, headed by senators Seward (New York), Charles Sumner (Massachusetts), and Salmon P. Chase (Ohio), to demand prohibiting slavery in the territories, freeing slaves in the District of Columbia, repealing the Fugitive Slave Act, and banning the internal slave trade. There were, however, limits to most Republicans' idealism. A more moderate and larger group, typified by Abraham Lincoln of Illinois, opposed slavery in the western territories, but would not interfere with it where it already existed. Many in this group also opposed equal rights for northern free blacks.

Many Republicans were anti-Catholic as well as antislavery. A third element of the party wanted to cleanse America of intemperance, impiety, parochial schooling, and other forms of immorality—including voting for Democrats, who catered to the "grog shops, foreign vote, and Catholic brethren" and combined the "forces of Jesuitism and Slavery."

The fourth element of the Republican party, a legacy of Hamilton and Clay, included those who wanted the federal government to promote economic development and the dignity of free labor, believing that both led to progress. At the heart of the new party and the future of America were hardworking, middle-class, mobile, free white laborers—farmers, small businessmen, and independent artisans. Lincoln's hometown paper, the Springfield *Republican,* said in 1856 that Republican strength came from "those who work with their hands, who live and act independently, who hold the stakes of home and family, of farm and workshop, of education and freedom."

These strengths were tested in a three-party race in 1856. The Know-Nothing (American) party nominated ex-President Fillmore. The Republicans chose John C. Frémont, an ardent Missouri Free-Soiler known mainly as a western explorer with military success against Mexicans in California. The Democrats nominated Pennsylvanian James Buchanan, a "northern man with southern principles." Frémont carried several free states, while Fillmore took only Maryland. Benefiting from a divided opposition, Buchanan won with only 45 percent of the popular vote.

After 1856, the Know-Nothings died out, partly because Republican leaders cleverly redirected anti-immigrant fears—and voters—to their party, and partly because Know-Nothing secrecy, hatred, and occasional violent attacks on Catholics damaged their image. Still, they represented a powerful current in American

politics that would return each time socioeconomic changes seemed to threaten the nation. It became convenient to label certain people "un-American" or "illegal" immigrants, and try to root them out. The Know-Nothing party disappeared but American hostilities to new immigrants did not.

Kansas and the Two Cultures

The slavery issue also would not go away. As Democrats sought to expand slavery westward across the plains and south into Cuba, Republicans wanted to halt the advance of slavery itself. In 1854, Lincoln worried that slavery "deprives our republican example of its just influence in the world." The specific cause of his concern was the likelihood that slavery might be extended into Kansas as a result of the passage that year of Stephen Douglas's Kansas–Nebraska Act.

Competing for Kansas

During the congressional debates over the Nebraska bill, Seward accepted the challenge of slave-state senators to "engage in competition for the virgin soil of Kansas." Soon after Congress passed the Kansas–Nebraska Act in 1854, the Massachusetts Emigrant Aid Society was founded to recruit free-soil settlers for Kansas. By the summer of 1855, about 1,200 New England colonists had migrated to Kansas.

One migrant was Julia Louisa Lovejoy, a Vermont minister's wife. As a riverboat carried her into a slave state for the first time, she wrote of the dilapidated plantation homes on the monotonous Missouri shore as the "blighting mildew of slavery." By the time she and her husband arrived in the Kansas Territory, Julia had concluded that the slaveholding "morals" of Missourians moving into Kansas were of an *undescribably repulsive and undesirable character.* To her, northerners came to bring the "energetic Yankee" virtues of morality and economic enterprise to drunken, unclean slaveholders.

Perhaps she had in mind David Atchison, Democratic senator from Missouri. Atchison believed that Congress must protect slavery in the territories, allowing Missouri slaveholders into Kansas. In 1853, he pledged "to extend the institutions of Missouri over the Territory at whatever sacrifice of blood or treasure." New England migrants, he said, were "abolition tyrants," and recommended to fellow Missourians if need be, "to kill every God-damned abolitionist in the district."

Under Atchison's inflammatory leadership, secret societies sprang up in the Missouri counties adjacent to Kansas dedicated to combating the Free-Soilers. One editor exclaimed that northerners came to Kansas "for the express purpose of stealing, running off and hiding runaway negroes from Missouri [and] taking to their own bed...a stinking negro wench." New Englanders, he said, were immoral, uncivilized, and hypocritical. Rumors of 20,000 Massachusetts migrants spurred Missourians to action. Thousands poured across the border late in 1854 to vote on permitting slavery in the territory. Twice as many ballots were cast as the number of registered voters.

These proslavery forces overreacted. The permanent population of Kansas consisted primarily of migrants from Missouri and elsewhere more concerned with land titles than slavery; they opposed any blacks—slave or free—moving into their state. As one clergyman put it, "I kem to Kansas to live in a free state and I don't want niggers a-trampin' over my grave."

In March 1855, a second election was held to select a territorial legislature. The pattern of border crossings, intimidation, and illegal voting was repeated. Atchison himself, drinking "considerable whiskey," led an armed band across the state line to vote and frighten away would-be free-soil voters. Not surprisingly, swollen numbers of illegal voters elected a proslavery territorial legislature to meet in Lecompton. Free-Soilers held their own convention and created a second government in Topeka and Lawrence.

The struggle shifted to Washington. Although President Pierce could have nullified the illegal election, he did nothing. Congress sent an investigating committee, which further inflamed passions. Throughout 1855, the call to arms grew more strident as proslavery forces vowed to bring weapons to "send the scoundrels" from the North "back to whence they came, or...to hell, it matters not which." In South Carolina, Robert Allston wrote his son Benjamin that he was "raising men and money...to fight the battle of our rights...on the field of Kansas."

Both sides saw Kansas as a holy battleground. An Alabama colonel sold his slaves to raise money to hire an army of 300 men to fight for slavery in Kansas, promising free land to his recruits. A Baptist minister blessed their departure from Montgomery, promised them God's favor, and gave each man a Bible. Northern Christians responded in kind. At Yale University, the noted minister Henry Ward Beecher presented 25 Bibles and 25 Sharps rifles to young men who would go fight for the Lord in Kansas. "There are times," he said, "when self-defense is a religious duty." Beecher said that rifles would be of greater use than Bibles. Missourians dubbed them "Beecher's Bibles" and vowed, as one newspaper put it, "Blood for Blood!"

"Bleeding Kansas"

As civil war threatened in Kansas, Brooklyn poet Walt Whitman heralded American democracy in his epic poem *Leaves of Grass* (1855). Whitman identified himself as the embodiment of average Americans "of every hue and caste...of every rank and religion." His poems embraced urban mechanics, southern woodcutters, runaway slaves, mining camp prostitutes, and a long list of others in his poetic celebration of "the word Democratic, the word En-Masse." But Whitman's faith in the American masses faltered in the mid-1850s. He worried that a knife plunged into the "breast" of the Union would bring on the "red blood of civil war."

Blood indeed flowed in Kansas. In May 1856, supported by a pro-southern federal marshal, a mob entered Lawrence, smashed the offices and presses of a Free-Soil newspaper, fired several cannonballs into the Free State Hotel, and destroyed homes and shops. Three nights later, believing he was doing God's will, John Brown led a small New England band, including four of his sons, to a proslavery settlement near Pottawatomie Creek and hacked five men to death with swords.

Violence also entered the halls of Congress. That same week, abolitionist Senator Charles Sumner lashed out at the "incredible atrocities of the Assassins and... Thugs" from the South. He accused proslavery Senate leaders, especially Andrew Butler of South Carolina, of cavorting with the "harlot, Slavery." Two days later, a nephew, Congressman Preston Brooks, avenged Butler's honor by beating Sumner senseless with a cane as he sat at his Senate desk.

The sack of Lawrence, the Pottawatomie massacre, and the caning of Sumner set off a minor civil war in "Bleeding Kansas" that lasted throughout the summer. Crops were burned, homes were destroyed, fights broke out in saloons and streets, and night raiders tortured and murdered their enemies. For Charles Lines, who just wanted to farm his land in peace, it was impossible to remain neutral. Lines hoped his Lawrence neighbors would avoid further "trouble." But when proslavery forces tortured a mild-mannered neighbor to death, Lines joined the battle. "Blood," he wrote, "must end in the triumph of the right."

Even before the bleeding of Kansas began, the New York *Tribune* warned, "We are two peoples. We are a people for Freedom and a people for Slavery. Between the two, conflict is inevitable." As the rhetoric and violence in Kansas demonstrated, competing visions of two separate cultures for the future destiny of the United States were at stake. Despite many similarities, the gap between North and South widened with the hostilities in Kansas.

Northern Views and Visions

As Julia Lovejoy suggested, the North saw itself as a prosperous land of bustling commerce and expanding, independent agriculture. Northern farmers and workers were self-made free men and women who believed in individualism and democracy. The "free labor system" of the North, as both Seward and Lincoln often said, offered equality of opportunity and upward mobility. Both generated more wealth. Although the North contained many growing cities, northerners revered the values of the small towns that spread from New England across the Upper Midwest. These values included a respect for the rights of the people, tempered by the rule of law; individual enterprise, balanced by a concern for one's neighbors; and a fierce morality rooted in Protestantism. Northerners would regulate morality—by persuasion if possible, by legislation if necessary—to purge irreligion, illiteracy, and intemperance from American society.

Northerners valued the kind of republican government that guaranteed the rights of free men, enabling them to achieve economic progress. This belief supported government action to promote free labor, industrial growth, immigration, foreign trade (protected by tariffs), and the extension of railroads and free farm homesteads westward across the continent. Energetic mobility, both westward and upward, would dissolve state, regional, and class loyalties and increase the sense of nationhood. A strong Union could achieve national and even international greatness. These were the conditions befitting a chosen people who would, as Seward put it, spread

Describe the socioeconomic contrasts in these two pictures. How many differences can you identify? Are there any similarities? Chicago (top) was a rapidly growing, bustling northern city in the 1850s; situated on the Great Lakes and a developing railroad hub, Chicago became the distribution center for industrial and agricultural goods throughout the Midwest. The vital unit of southern commerce was, by contrast, the individual plantation (bottom), with steamboats and flatboats carrying cotton and sugar to port cities for trade with Europe. Are there examples today in America of cultural contrasts like these?

(Top: Corbis; Bottom: Library of Congress)

American institutions around the world and "renovate the condition of mankind." These were the principles of the Republican party.

Only free men could achieve economic progress and moral society. In northerners' eyes, therefore, the worst sin was the loss of one's freedom. Slavery was the root of all evil. It was, Seward said, "incompatible with all . . . the elements of the security, welfare, and greatness of nations." The South was the antithesis of everything that northerners saw as good. Southerners were unfree, backward, economically stagnant, uneducated, lawless, immoral, and in conflict with the values and ideals of the nineteenth century. Julia Lovejoy's denunciation of slaveholding Missourians was mild. Other Yankee migrants saw southerners as "wild beasts" who guzzled whiskey, ate dirt, swore, raped slave women, and fought or dueled at the slightest excuse. In the slang of the day, they were "Pukes."

The Southern Perspective

Southerners were a diverse people who, like northerners, shared certain broad values, generally those of the planter class. If in the North the values of economic enterprise were most important, southerners revered social values most. They admired the English gentry and saw themselves as courteous, refined, hospitable, and chivalrous—and saw "Yankees" as rude, aggressive, and materialistic. In a society where one person in three was a black slave, racial distinctions and paternalistic relationships were crucial in maintaining order and white supremacy. Fear of slave revolt was ever-present. The South had five times as many military schools as the North. Northerners educated the many for economic utility; southerners educated the few for character. In short, the white South saw itself as an ordered society guided by the planters' genteel code.

Southerners agreed with northerners that sovereignty in a republic rested in the people, who created a government of laws to protect life, liberty, and property. But unlike northerners, southerners believed that self-government was best preserved in local political units such as the states. Believing themselves true revolutionary patriots, they were ready to fight to resist any tyrannical encroachment on their liberty, as they had in 1776. Like northerners, southerners cherished the Union. But they preferred the loose confederacy of the Jeffersonian past, not Seward's centralized nationalism.

To southerners, Yankees were in too much of a hurry—to make money, to reform others' behavior, to put dreamy theories (like racial equality) into practice. Two images dominated the South's view of northerners: either they were stingy, hypocritical, moralizing Puritans, or they were grubby, slum-dwelling,

Catholic immigrants: "a conglomeration of greasy mechanics, filthy operatives, small-fisted farmers, and moon-struck theorists."

Each side saw the other threatening its freedom and degrading a proper republican society. Each saw the other imposing barriers to its vision for America's future, which included the economic systems described in Chapters 10 and 11. As hostilities rose, the views each section had of the other grew steadily more rigid and conspiratorial. Northerners saw the South as a "slave power," determined to foist the slave system on free labor throughout the land. Southerners saw the North as full of "black Republicanism," determined to destroy their way of life.

Polarization and the Road to War

The struggle over Kansas solidified the image of the Republicans as a northern party and threatened to split the Democrats in half. Further events, mostly over the question of slavery in the territories, eventually split the nation itself in half: the *Dred Scott* decision of the Supreme Court (1857), the constitutional crisis in Kansas (1857), the Lincoln–Douglas debates in Illinois (1858), John Brown's raid in Virginia (1859), and Lincoln's election (1860). These incidents further polarized the negative images each culture held of the other, accelerating the nation down the road to civil war.

The *Dred Scott* Case and Kansas

The events of 1857 reinforced the arguments of those who believed in a slave power conspiracy. Two days after Buchanan's inauguration, the Supreme Court finally ruled in *Dred Scott* v. *Sanford*. Back in 1846, Dred and Harriet Scott had filed suit in Missouri for their freedom. They argued that their master had taken them into northern territories where the Missouri Compromise prohibited slavery, and therefore they should be freed.

When the Court, with its southern majority, issued a 7–2 decision, it made three rulings. First, because blacks were, as Chief Justice Roger Taney put it, "beings of an inferior order [who] had no rights which white men were bound to respect," Dred Scott was not a citizen and had no right to sue in federal courts. The second ruling stated that the Missouri Compromise was unconstitutional because Congress had no power to ban slavery in a territory. Third, the court decided that taking the Scotts into free states did not affect their status.

The implications of these decisions went far beyond the Scotts' personal freedom. The arguments about black citizenship infuriated many northerners. Frederick Douglass called the ruling "a most scandalous and devilish perversion of the Constitution." Many citizens worried about the few rights free blacks still held while others feared that slavery might be made legal in the North. People suspecting a conspiracy were not calmed when Buchanan endorsed the *Dred Scott* decision as a final settlement of the right of citizens to take their "property of any kind, including slaves, into the common Territories...and to have it protected there under the Federal Constitution." Far from settling the issue of slavery in the territories, as Buchanan had hoped, *Dred Scott* threw it back into American politics and worsened sectional hostilities.

Dred Scott and Buchanan's endorsement fed northern suspicions of a slave power conspiracy to impose slavery everywhere. Events in Kansas, which still had two governments, heightened these fears. In the summer of 1857, Kansas had yet another election, with so many irregularities that only 2,000 out of a possible 24,000 votes counted. A proslavery slate of delegates was elected to a constitutional convention meeting at Lecompton as a preparation for statehood. The convention barred free blacks from the state, guaranteed the property rights of the few slaveholders in Kansas, and asked voters to decide in a referendum whether to permit more slaves.

The proslavery Lecompton constitution, clearly unrepresentative of the wishes of the majority of the people of Kansas, was sent to Congress for approval with Buchanan's support. Stephen Douglas challenged the president's power and jeopardized his standing with southern Democrats by opposing it. Facing reelection to the Senate from Illinois in 1858, Douglas needed to hold the support of the northern wing of his party. Congress sent the Lecompton constitution back to the people of Kansas for another referendum. This time they defeated it, which meant that Kansas remained a territory rather than becoming a slave state. While Kansas was left in an uncertain status, the larger political effect of the struggle was to split the Democratic party almost beyond repair.

No sooner had Douglas settled the Lecompton question than he faced reelection in Illinois. Douglas's opposition to the Lecompton constitution had restored his prestige in the North as an opponent of the slave power. This cut some ground out from under Republicans' claim that only they could stop the spread of southern power. Party leaders from the West, however, had a candidate who understood the importance of distinguishing Republican moral and political views from those of the Democrats.

Lincoln and the Illinois Debates

Although relatively unknown nationally and out of elective office for several years, by 1858 Abraham Lincoln of Illinois challenged William Seward for leadership of the Republican party. Lincoln's character was shaped on the midwestern frontier, where he had educated himself, developed mild abolitionist views, and dreamed of America's greatness.

Douglas was clearly the leading Democrat, so the 1858 election in Illinois gave a preview of the presidential election of 1860. The other Douglass, Frederick, observed that "the slave power idea was the ideological glue of the Republican party." Lincoln's handling of this idea would be crucial in distinguishing him from Stephen Douglas. The Illinois campaign featured seven debates between Lincoln and Douglas in different Illinois cities. Addressing a national as well as a local audience, the debaters confronted the heated racial issues before the nation.

Lincoln set a solemn tone when he accepted the Republican senatorial nomination in Chicago. The American nation, he said, was in a "crisis" and building toward a worse one. "A House divided against itself cannot stand. I believe this government cannot endure, permanently half *slave* and half *free*." Lincoln said he did not expect the Union "to be dissolved" or "the house to fall," but rather that "it will become *all* one thing, or *all* the other." Then he rehearsed the history of the South's growing influence over national policy since the Kansas–Nebraska Act, which he blamed on Douglas. Lincoln stated his firm opposition to the *Dred Scott* decision, which he believed part of a conspiracy involving Pierce, Buchanan, Taney, and Douglas. He and others like him opposing this conspiracy wished to place slavery on a "course of ultimate extinction."

Debating Douglas, Lincoln reiterated these controversial themes. Although far from a radical abolitionist, in these debates Lincoln skillfully staked out a moral position on race and slavery not just in advance of Douglas but well ahead of his time.

Lincoln was also very much a part of his time. He believed in white superiority, opposed granting specific equal civil rights to free blacks, and said that differences between whites and blacks would "forever forbid the two races from living together on terms of social and political equality." He proposed "Separation" and colonization in Liberia or Central America as the best solution. But Lincoln differed from most contemporaries in his deep commitment to the equality and dignity of all human beings. Countering Douglas's racial slurs, Lincoln said that he believed not only that blacks were "entitled to all the natural rights...in the Declaration of Independence" but also that they had many economic rights as well, such as "the right to put into his mouth the bread that his own hands have earned." In these rights, blacks were "my equal and the equal of Judge Douglas, and the equal of every living man."

Lincoln hated slavery. "I contemplate slavery as a moral, social, and political evil." Douglas was more equivocal and dodged the issue, pointing out that slavery would not exist if favorable local legislation did not support it. But Douglas's moral indifference to slavery was clear: he did not care whether a territorial legislature voted it "up or down." Republicans did care, Lincoln answered, saying that by stopping the expansion of slavery, the course toward "ultimate extinction" had begun. Although barred by the Constitution from interfering with slavery where it already existed, Lincoln said that Republicans believed slavery wrong, and "we propose a...policy that shall deal with it as a wrong."

What Lincoln meant by "policy" was not yet clear, not even to himself. However, he did succeed in affirming that Republicans were the only moral and political force capable of stopping the slave power. It seems ironic now (though not then), that Douglas won the election. Elsewhere in 1858, however, Democrats did poorly, losing 18 congressional seats.

John Brown's Raid

Unlike Lincoln, John Brown was prepared to act decisively against slavery. On October 16, 1859, he and a band of 22 men attacked a federal arsenal at Harpers Ferry, Virginia (now West Virginia). He hoped to provoke a general uprising of slaves throughout the Upper South or at least provide the arms for slaves to make their way to freedom. Federal troops overcame him, killing half his men, including two sons. Brown was captured, tried, and hanged, ending a lifetime of failures.

In death, however, Brown was not a failure. His daring if foolhardy raid and his dignified behavior during his trial and speedy execution unleashed powerful passions. Many northerners responded to Brown's death with an outpouring of sympathy. Thoreau compared him to Christ, calling Brown an "angel of light." Abolitionist William Lloyd Garrison, a pacifist, wished "success to every slave insurrection" in the South. Ministers called slave revolt a "divine weapon" and glorified Brown's treason as "holy." Brown's raid, Frederick Douglass pointed out, showed that slavery was a "system of brute force" that would be ended only when "met with its own weapons."

Southerners were filled with "dread and terror" over the possibility of a wave of slave revolts led by hundreds of imaginary John Browns and Nat Turners, and concluded that northerners would stop at nothing to free the slaves. This suspicion further eroded freedom of thought and expression. A North Carolinian described a "spirit of terror, mobs, arrests, and violence" in his state. Twelve families in Berea, Kentucky, were evicted from the state for their

What images are in this modern mural of John Brown? What opposing forces? How violent is the mural? What do you make of the angry sky? (God's wrath?) What do you think about John Brown?

(Kansas State Historical Society, Copy and Reuse Restrictions apply.)

mild abolitionist sentiments. A Texas minister who criticized the treatment of slaves in a sermon got 70 lashes.

But with Brown's raid and southern sympathizers being tarred and feathered in Massachusetts, southerners became more convinced of a "black Republican" plot in the North "arrayed against the slaveholders." In this atmosphere of mistrust, southern Unionists lost their influence, and power passed to those favoring secession. Senator Robert Toombs of Georgia warned fellow southerners late in 1859, "Never permit this Federal government to pass into the traitorous hands of the black Republican party."

The Election of 1860

When the Democratic convention met in Charleston, South Carolina, a secessionist hotbed, it sat for a record 10 days and went through 59 ballots without being able to name a candidate. Reconvening in Baltimore, the Democrats acknowledged their irreparable division by choosing two candidates at two separate conventions: Douglas for northern Democrats and John C. Breckinridge, Buchanan's vice president, for the proslavery South. The Constitutional Union party, made up of border-state and southern Whigs, claimed

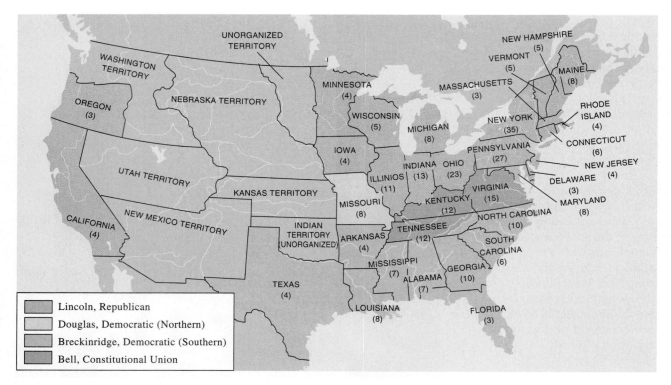

UNORGANIZED TERRITORY

WASHINGTON TERRITORY

OREGON (3)

NEBRASKA TERRITORY

MINNESOTA (4)

NEW HAMPSHIRE (5)

VERMONT (5)

MAINE (8)

WISCONSIN (5)

MASSACHUSETTS (3)

MICHIGAN (8)

NEW YORK (35)

RHODE ISLAND (4)

UTAH TERRITORY

IOWA (4)

PENNSYLVANIA (27)

CONNECTICUT (6)

NEW JERSEY (4)

KANSAS TERRITORY

ILLINIOS (11)

INDIANA (13)

OHIO (23)

DELAWARE (3)

MARYLAND (8)

NEW MEXICO TERRITORY

MISSOURI (8)

KENTUCKY (12)

VIRGINIA (15)

CALIFORNIA (4)

INDIAN TERRITORY (UNORGANIZED)

ARKANSAS (4)

TENNESSEE (12)

NORTH CAROLINA (10)

SOUTH CAROLINA (6)

TEXAS (4)

MISSISSIPPI (7)

ALABAMA (7)

GEORGIA (10)

LOUISIANA (8)

FLORIDA (3)

- Lincoln, Republican
- Douglas, Democratic (Northern)
- Breckinridge, Democratic (Southern)
- Bell, Constitutional Union

The Presidential Election of 1860

Lincoln won the election with only 40% of the popular vote. Note the states he carried. How did he win? How do you explain each candidate's success? Why didn't Douglas do better? Who would you have voted for?

the middle ground and nominated John Bell, a slave-holder from Tennessee who favored compromise.

With Democrats split and a new party in contention, the Republican strategy aimed at adding Pennsylvania, Illinois, and Indiana to the states carried in 1856. Seward, the leading candidate, had been tempering his antislavery views to appear more electable. So had Lincoln, who seemed more likely than Seward to carry those key states. After shrewd maneuvers emphasizing his "availability" as a moderate, Lincoln was nominated.

The Republican platform exuded moderation, opposing only slavery's extension. Mostly it spoke of tariff protection, subsidized internal improvements, free labor, and a homestead bill. Republicans, like southern Democrats, defended their view of what republican values meant for America's future, which did not include the equal rights envisioned by Frederick Douglass. An English traveler in 1860 observed that in America "we see, in effect, two nations—one white and another black—growing up together within the same political circle, but never mingling on a principle of equality."

The Republican moderate strategy worked as planned. Lincoln was elected by sweeping the entire Northeast and Midwest. Although he got less than 40 percent of the popular vote nationwide, his triumph in the North was decisive. Even a united Democratic party could not have defeated him. With victory assured,

Lincoln finished his sandwich and coffee on election night in Springfield and prepared for his awesome new responsibilities. They came even before his inauguration.

The Divided House Falls

The Republicans overestimated Unionist sentiment in the South. A year earlier, some southern congressmen had walked out in protest when the House chose an antislavery speaker. Recalling this, Republican leader Carl Schurz said that the southerners had taken a drink and come back. Now, he predicted, they would walk out, take two drinks, and come back again. He was wrong.

Secession and Uncertainty

On December 20, 1860, South Carolina seceded from the Union, declaring the "experiment" of putting people with "different pursuits and institutions" under one government a failure. By February 1, the other six Deep South states—Mississippi, Florida, Alabama, Georgia, Louisiana, and Texas—also left. A week later, delegates meeting in Montgomery, Alabama, created the Confederate States of America and elected Jefferson Davis, a Mississippi senator and cotton planter, its provisional president. The divided house had fallen, as

THE CAUSES OF THE CIVIL WAR

Starting with the seven items at the top of this chart, how would you explain the primary cause of the Civil War? Which four or five of the following "specific issues and events" would you use to support your argument? Can you make a distinction between underlying causes and immediate sparks of the Civil War?

Date	Issues and Events	Deeper, Underlying Causes of Civil War
1600s–1860s	Slavery in the South	Major underlying pervasive cause
1700s–1860s	Development of two distinct socioeconomic systems and cultures	Further reinforced slavery as fundamental socioeconomic, cultural, moral issue
1787–1860s	States' rights, nullification doctrine	Ongoing political issue, less fundamental as cause
1820	Missouri Compromise (36°30')	Background for conflict over slavery in territories
1828–1833	South Carolina tariff nullification crisis	Background for secession leadership in South Carolina
1831–1860s	Antislavery movements, southern justification	Thirty years of emotional preparation for conflict
1846–1848	War with Mexico (Wilmot Proviso, Calhoun, popular sovereignty)	Options for issue of slavery in territories

Date	Issues and Events	Specific Impact on the Road to War
1850	Compromise of 1850	Temporary and unsatisfactory "settlement" of divisive issue
1851–1854	Fugitive slaves returned and rescued in North; personal liberty laws passed in North; Harriet Beecher Stowe's Uncle Tom's Cabin	Heightened northern emotional reactions against the South and slavery
1852–1856	Breakdown of Whig party and national Democratic party; creation of a new party system with sectional basis	Made national politics an arena where sectional and cultural differences over slavery were fought
1854	Ostend Manifesto and other expansionist efforts in Central America	Reinforced image of Democratic party as favoring slavery
	Formation of Republican party	Major party identified as opposing the extension of slavery
	Kansas-Nebraska Act	Reopened "settled" issue of slavery in the territories
1856	"Bleeding Kansas"; Senator Sumner physically attacked in Senate	Foretaste of Civil War (200 killed, $2 million in property lost) inflamed emotions and polarized North and South
1857	Dred Scott decision; proslavery Lecompton constitution in Kansas	Made North fear a "slave power conspiracy," supported by President Buchanan and the Supreme Court
1858	Lincoln–Douglas debates in Illinois; Democrats lose 18 seats in Congress	Set stage for election of 1860
1859	John Brown's raid and reactions in North and South	Made South fear a "black Republican" plot against slavery; further polarization and irrationality
1860	Democratic party splits in half; Lincoln elected president; South Carolina secedes from Union	Final breakdown of national parties and election of "northern" president; no more compromises
1861	Six more southern states secede by February 1; Confederate Constitution adopted February 4; Lincoln inaugurated March 4; Fort Sumter attacked April 12	Civil War begins

Lincoln had predicted. But it was not yet certain whether the house could be put back together or whether there would be civil war.

The government in Washington had three options. First was compromise, but the emotions of the time ruled that out. Second, as suggested by New York *Tribune* editor Horace Greeley, Washington might let the seven states "go in peace," taking care not to lose the border states. Northern businessmen, fearing the loss of profitable economic ties with the South, were opposed, as were those who believed in an indissoluble Union. The third option was to compel secessionist states to return, which probably meant war.

Republican hopes that southern Unionism would assert itself and make none of these options necessary seemed possible when no more states seceded. The nation waited, wondering what outgoing President Buchanan would do, what Congress would do, and what Virginia and the border states would do. Buchanan did nothing. Congress made some feeble efforts to pass compromise legislation, waiting in vain for the support of the president-elect. Virginia and the border states, like the entire nation, waited for Lincoln.

Frederick Douglass waited, too, guardedly. He wanted the "complete and universal *abolition* of the whole slave system," as well as equal suffrage and other rights for free blacks. His hopes that Lincoln Republicans had the will to do this were dashed, especially when the voters of New York soundly defeated a referendum for black suffrage. Douglass saw northern politicians "granting the most demoralizing concessions to the Slave Power." In his despair, he began to explore emigration to Haiti, an idea he had long opposed. To achieve full freedom and citizenship in the United States for all blacks, Douglass said in January 1861, he would "welcome...a dissolution of the Union." Opposing all compromises, Douglass hoped that with Lincoln's inauguration in March it would "be decided, and decided forever, which of the two, Freedom or Slavery, shall give law to this Republic."

Lincoln and Fort Sumter

As Douglass penned these thoughts, Lincoln began a long, slow train ride from Springfield, Illinois, to Washington, writing and rewriting his inaugural address. Lincoln's quietness in the period between his election and his inauguration led many to judge him weak and indecisive. He was not. Lincoln firmly opposed secession and any compromises with the principle of stopping the extension of slavery. He would neither conciliate secessionist southern states nor force their return.

Lincoln believed in his constitutional responsibility to uphold the laws of the land. The focus of his attention was a federal fort in the harbor of Charleston, South Carolina. Major Robert Anderson, the commander of Fort Sumter, was running out of provisions and had requested new supplies from Washington. Lincoln would enforce the laws and protect federal property at Fort Sumter.

As the new president delivered his inaugural address on March 4, he faced a tense and divided nation. Asserting his unequivocal intention to enforce the laws of the land, Lincoln argued that the Union was "perpetual" and indissoluble. He reminded the nation that the "only substantial dispute" was that "one section of our country believes slavery is *right,* and ought to be extended, while the other believes it is *wrong,* and ought not to be extended." Still appealing to Unionist strength among southern moderates, Lincoln said he would make no attempts to interfere with existing slavery and would respect the law to return fugitive slaves. Nearing the end of his address, Lincoln put the burden of initiating a civil war on the "dissatisfied fellow-countrymen" who had seceded. As if foreseeing the horrible events that might follow, he closed his speech eloquently:

> I am loath to close. We are not enemies, but friends. We must not be enemies. Though passion may have strained, it must not break our bonds of affection. The mystic chords of memory, stretching from every battlefield, and patriot grave, to every living heart and hearthstone, all over this broad land, will yet swell the chorus of the Union, when again touched, as surely they will be, by the better angels of our nature.

Frederick Douglass was not impressed with Lincoln's "honied phrases" and accused him of "weakness, timidity and conciliation." Also unmoved, Robert Allston wrote his son from Charleston, where he was watching the crisis over Fort Sumter, that the Confederacy's "advantage" was in having a "much better president than they have."

On April 6, Lincoln notified the governor of South Carolina that he was sending "provisions only" to Fort Sumter. No effort would be made "to throw in men, arms, or ammunition" unless the fort was attacked. On April 10, Jefferson Davis directed General P. G. T. Beauregard to demand the surrender of Fort Sumter and to reduce the fort if Major Anderson refused.

On April 12, as Lincoln's relief expedition neared Charleston, Beauregard's batteries began shelling Fort Sumter, and the Civil War began. Frederick Douglass was about to leave for Haiti when he heard the news. He immediately changed his plans, announcing his readiness to support the Union by organizing freed slaves "into a liberating army" to "make war upon...the savage barbarism of slavery." The Allstons had changed places, and it was Benjamin who described the events in Charleston harbor to his father. On April 14, he reported exuberantly the "glorious and astonishing news that Sumter has fallen." With it fell America's divided house.

Timeline

1833–1840s	Intensification of abolitionist attacks on slavery
1846	Wilmot Proviso
1848	Free-Soil party founded
1850	Compromise of 1850, including Fugitive Slave Act
1850–1854	"Young America" expansionist movement
1852	Harriet Beecher Stowe publishes *Uncle Tom's Cabin*
1854	Ostend Manifesto
	Kansas–Nebraska Act nullifies Missouri Compromise
	Republican and Know-Nothing parties formed
1855	Walt Whitman publishes *Leaves of Grass*
1855–1856	Thousands pour into "Bleeding" Kansas
1856	John Brown's massacre in Kansas
	Sumner–Brooks incident in Senate
	James Buchanan elected president
1857	*Dred Scott* decision legalizes slavery in territories
	Lecompton constitution in Kansas
1858	Lincoln–Douglas debates
1859	John Brown's raid at Harpers Ferry
1860	Democratic party splits
	Abraham Lincoln elected president
1860–1861	Seven southern states secede
1861	Confederate States of America founded
	Attack on Fort Sumter begins Civil War

Conclusion

THE "IRREPRESSIBLE CONFLICT"

Lincoln had been right. The nation could no longer endure half-slave and half-free. The collision between North and South, William Seward said, was not an "accidental, unnecessary" event but an "irrepressible conflict between opposing and enduring forces." Those forces had been at work for many decades, but they developed with increasing intensity after 1848 in the conflict over the extension of slavery into the territories. Although economic, cultural, political, constitutional, and emotional forces all contributed to the developing opposition between North and South, slavery was the fundamental, enduring force that underlay all others, causing what Walt Whitman called the "red blood of civil war." Abraham Lincoln, Frederick Douglass, the Allston family, Michael Luark, and the American people all faced a radically altered national scene. All wondered whether the American democratic system would be able to withstand this challenge.

QUESTIONS FOR REVIEW AND REFLECTION

1. What options existed for dealing with slavery in the territories, and what compromises did Congress propose? How well did they work?
2. How did political party alignments change in the 1850s and how did that affect the path to civil war?
3. Examine how southerners and northerners viewed each other, especially in Kansas. How did cultural stereotypes and emotional attitudes contribute to the outbreak of civil war?
4. Can you explain four basic, underlying causes of the American Civil War? Which *one* cause do you think was most significant, and what specific events would you use to support your choice?
5. To what extent was the American democratic political system flexible enough to handle the issues of the 1850s? Could the Civil War have been avoided, or was it inevitable?

CHAPTER 15

The Union Severed

This image, printed on an envelope, shows a design for a Confederate 50-cent piece. Who do you think the man on the right is? Who is the man on the left and what is he pointing at the man wearing the top hat? In the background, you can see a group of men hard at work and standing before them a man wielding a whip. What is the overall message of this design?

(Collection of the New-York Historical Society, [PR-022–3–91–38])

American Stories

A War That Touched Lives

In his remarks to Congress in 1862, Abraham Lincoln reminded congressmen that "We cannot escape history. We of this Congress and this administration will be remembered in spite of ourselves. No personal significance, or insignificance, can spare... us. The fiery trial through which we pass, will light us down, in honor or dishonor, to the latest generation." Lincoln's conviction that Americans would long remember him and other major actors of the Civil War was correct. Jefferson Davis, Robert E. Lee, Ulysses S. Grant—these are the men whose characters, actions, and decisions have been the subject of continuing discussion and analysis, whose statues and memorials dot the American countryside and grace urban squares. Whether seen as heroes or villains, great men have dominated the story of the Civil War.

Yet from the earliest days, the war touched the lives of even the most uncelebrated Americans. From Indianapolis, 20-year-old Arthur Carpenter wrote to his parents in Massachusetts begging for permission to enlist in the volunteer army: "I have always longed for the time to come when I could enter the army and be a military man, and when this war broke out, I thought the time had come, but you would not permit me to enter the service... now I make one more appeal to you." The pleas worked, and Carpenter enlisted, spending most of the war fighting in Kentucky and Tennessee.

In that same year, in Tennessee, George and Ethie Eagleton faced anguishing decisions. Though not an abolitionist, George, a 30-year-old Presbyterian preacher, was unsympathetic to slavery and opposed to secession. But when his native state left the Union, George felt compelled to follow and enlisted in the 44th Tennessee Infantry. Ethie, his 26-year-old wife, despaired over the war, George's decision, and her own forlorn situation.

Mr. Eagleton's school dismissed—and what for? O my God, must I write it? He has enlisted in the service of his country—to war—the most unrighteous war that ever was brought on any nation that ever lived. Pres. Lincoln has done what no other Pres. ever dared to do—he has divided these once peaceful and happy United States. And Oh! the dreadful dark cloud that is now hanging over our country—'tis enough to sicken the heart of any one.... Mr. E. is gone.... What will become of me, left here without a home and relatives, a babe just nine months old and no George.

Both Carpenter and the Eagletons survived the war, but the conflict transformed each of their lives. Carpenter had difficulty settling down. Filled with bitter memories of the war years in Tennessee, the Eagletons moved to Arkansas. Ordinary people such as Carpenter and the Eagletons are historically anonymous. Yet their actions on the battlefield and behind the lines helped to shape the course of events, as their leaders realized, even if today we tend to remember only the famous and influential.

For thousands of Americans, from Lincoln and Davis to Carpenter and the Eagletons, war was both a profoundly personal and a major national event. Its impact reached far beyond the four years of hostilities. The war that was fought to conserve two political, social, and economic visions ended by changing familiar ways of life in both North and South. War was a transforming force, both destructive and creative in its effect on the structure and social dynamics of society and on the lives of ordinary people. This theme underlies this chapter's analysis of the war's three stages: the initial months of preparation, the years of military stalemate between 1861 and 1865, and, finally, resolution.

Organizing for War

The Confederate bombardment of Fort Sumter on April 12, 1861, and the surrender of Union troops ended the uncertainty of the secession winter. The North's response to Fort Sumter was a virtual declaration of war as President Lincoln called for state militia volunteers to crush southern "insurrection." His action pushed several slave states (Virginia, North Carolina, Tennessee, and Arkansas) off the fence into the southern camp. Other states (Maryland, Kentucky, and Missouri) agonizingly debated which way to go. The "War Between the States" was now a reality.

Many Americans were dismayed. Southerners like George Eagleton reluctantly followed Tennessee out of the Union. When he enlisted, he complained of the "disgraceful cowardice of many who were last winter for secession and war... but are now refusing self and means for the prosecution of war." Robert E. Lee of Virginia also hesitated but finally decided that he could not "raise [a] hand against... relatives... children... home." Whites living in the southern uplands (where blacks were few and slaveholders were heartily disliked), yeoman farmers in the Deep South (who owned no slaves), and many border state residents opposed secession and war. Many would eventually join the Union forces.

In the North, large numbers supported neither the Republican party nor Lincoln. Irish immigrants fearing the competition of free black labor and southern residents of Illinois, Indiana, and Ohio harbored misgivings. Northern Democrats initially blamed Lincoln and the Republicans almost as much as southern secessionists for the nation's crisis.

Nevertheless, the days following Fort Sumter and Lincoln's call for troops saw an outpouring of support on both sides, fueled in part by relief at decisive action, in part by patriotism and love of adventure, and in part by unemployment. Northern blacks and even some southern freedmen proclaimed themselves "ready to go forth and do battle," while whites like Carpenter flocked to enlist. In some places, workers were so eager to join up that trade unions collapsed. Women set to work making uniforms during these days "of terrible excitement."

Lincoln's call for 75,000 state militiamen for only 90 days of service, and a similar enlistment term for Confederate soldiers, supported the notion that the war would be short. The conviction that the conflict would rapidly come to a glorious conclusion produced a throng of volunteers that overwhelmed officials. Northern authorities turned aside offers from blacks to serve. Both sides sent thousands of white would-be soldiers home.

The Balance of Resources

While Americans have often viewed the Civil War as a uniquely American event, it was, in fact, just one of several military conflicts during the nineteenth century that sought national independence. In Europe, Italian and German patriots struggled to create new nations out of individual states. Southern nationalists differed from their European counterparts in proclaiming their independence by withdrawing from an already unified state. Likening their struggle to that of the Revolutionary generation, southerners claimed to have "enlisted in The Holy Cause of Liberty and Independence." While they legitimized secession by appealing to freedom, however, southerners were also preserving freedom's antithesis, slavery.

The outcome of the southern bid for autonomy was much in doubt. Although statistics of population and industrial development suggested a northern victory, Great Britain with similar advantages in 1775 had lost that war. Many northern assets would become effective only with time.

The North's white population greatly exceeded the South's, giving the appearance of a military advantage. Yet early in the war, the armies were more evenly matched. Almost 187,000 Union troops bore arms in July 1861, while just over 112,000 men marched under Confederate colors. Southerners believed that their army would prove to be superior fighters. Many northerners feared so, too. And slaves could carry on vital work behind the lines, freeing most adult white males to serve the Confederacy.

The Union also enjoyed impressive economic advantages. The North had 1 million workers in 110,000 manufacturing establishments while the South claimed only 110,000 southern workers in 18,000 manufacturing concerns. But northern industrial resources had to be mobilized. That would take time, especially because the government did not intend to direct production. A depleted northern treasury made the government's first task the raising of funds to pay for military necessities.

The South depended on imported northern and European manufactured goods. If Lincoln cut off that trade, the South would have to create its industry almost from scratch. Its railroad system was organized to move cotton, not armies and supplies. Yet the agricultural South had important resources of food, draft animals, and, of course, cotton, which southerners believed would secure British and French support. By waging a defensive war, the South could tap regional loyalty and enjoy protected lines. Because much of the South raised cotton and tobacco rather than food crops, Union armies could not live off the land, and extended supply lines were always vulnerable. The Union had to conquer and occupy; the South merely had to survive until its enemy gave up.

The Border States

Uncertainty and divided loyalties led border states, except for Unionist Delaware, to adopt a wait-and-see attitude. Their decisions would be of critical importance. For the Confederacy, the states of the Upper South offered natural borders along the Ohio River, access to its river traffic, and vital resources, wealth, and population. The major railroad link to the West ran through Maryland and western Virginia. Virginia boasted the South's largest ironworks, and Tennessee provided its principal source of grain. Missouri opened the road to the West and controlled Mississippi River traffic. For the North, every border state remaining loyal represented a psychological triumph for the idea of union as well as offering obvious economic and strategic advantages. Maryland, precariously balanced between the pro-Confederate southern and Eastern Shore counties and Unionist western and northern areas, and with pro-southern enthusiasts abounding in Baltimore, vividly demonstrated the significance of border state loyalty.

On April 19, the 6th Massachusetts Regiment, heading for Washington, marched through Baltimore and was attacked by a mob of some 10,000 southern

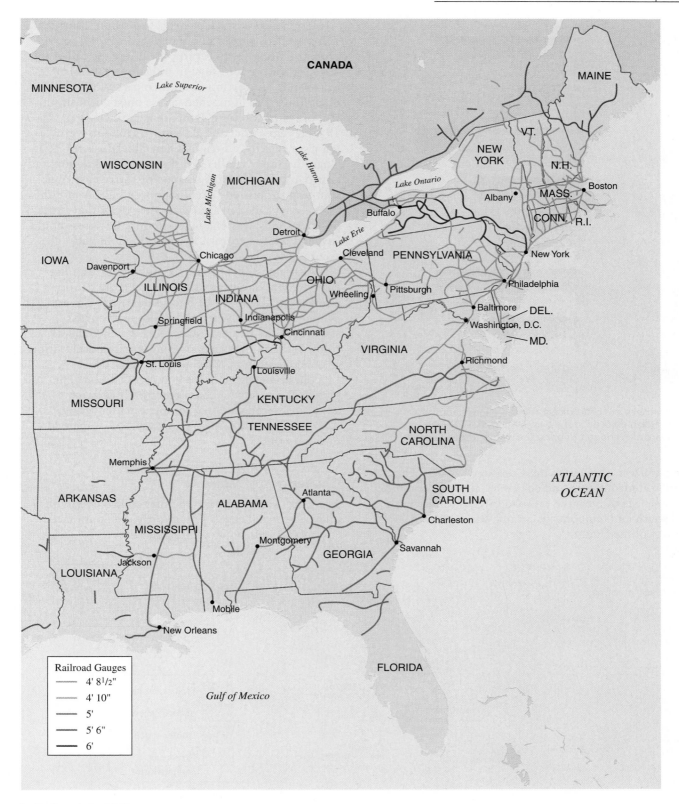

Railroads in 1860

This map shows the railroads at the beginning of the Civil War. What does it reveal about the differences in the transportation systems in the North and the South? In what ways was the war effort of each side helped or hindered by the rail system? In what ways did the configuration of southern transportation benefit the South?

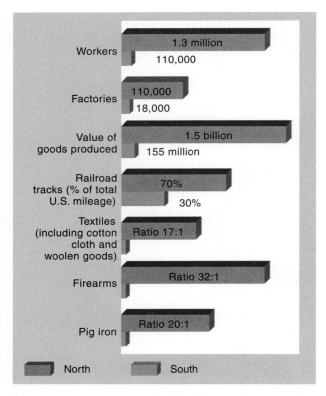

Workers — 1.3 million / 110,000

Factories — 110,000 / 18,000

Value of goods produced — 1.5 billion / 155 million

Railroad tracks (% of total U.S. mileage) — 70% / 30%

Textiles (including cotton cloth and woolen goods) — Ratio 17:1

Firearms — Ratio 32:1

Pig iron — Ratio 20:1

North — South

What does this chart reveal about the long-range advantages the North enjoyed in the war? Why weren't these advantages enough to bring the war to a speedy end?

sympathizers, some carrying Confederate flags. The bloody confrontation and confusion allowed would-be secessionists to burn the railroad bridges to the north and south and temporarily cut off Washington from the rest of the Union.

Lincoln took stern measures to secure Maryland. The president agreed temporarily to route troops around Baltimore. In return, the governor called the state legislature into session in Unionist western Maryland. This action and Lincoln's swift violation of civil liberties dampened secessionist enthusiasm. Hundreds of southern sympathizers, including 19 state legislators and Baltimore's mayor, were imprisoned without trial. When Chief Justice Roger B. Taney challenged the president's action and issued a writ of habeas corpus for the release of a southern supporter, Lincoln ignored him. A month later, Taney ruled in *Ex Parte Merryman* that if the public's safety was endangered, only Congress could suspend habeas corpus. By then, Lincoln had secured Maryland.

Although Lincoln's quick and harsh response ensured Maryland's loyalty, he was more cautious elsewhere. Above all, he had to deal with slavery prudently, for hasty action would push border states into the Confederacy. Thus, when General John C. Frémont issued an unauthorized declaration of emancipation in Missouri in August 1861, Lincoln revoked the order and recalled him. The president expected a chain reaction if certain key states seceded. After complex maneuvering, Kentucky and Missouri, like Maryland, remained in the Union.

Challenges of War

The tense weeks after Fort Sumter spilled over with unexpected challenges. Both North and South faced enormous organizational problems.

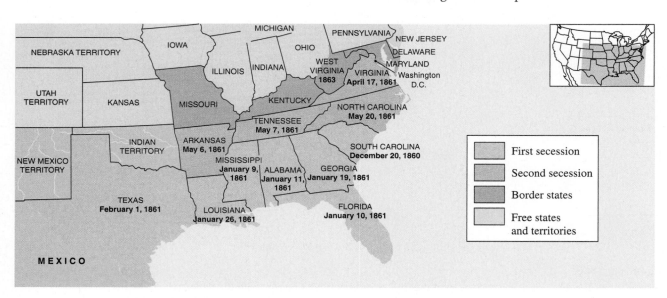

Secession of the Southern States

What does the map show about the process of secession and the forces that prompted southern states to leave the Union? Describe the geographic importance of the border states. What does the map suggest about the location of Washington and the reason for many of Lincoln's early actions?

Southerners had to create a nation-state and devise everything from a constitution to a flag. An important question hovered behind the frantic organizational efforts. Could the new political entity create bonds of nationhood and inspire the patriotism that would be necessary if the conflict was long and difficult?

In February 1861, the original seceding states began the work of creating a nation. The first task was to establish a provisional framework and to choose a provisional president and vice president. The delegates swiftly wrote a constitution much like the federal constitution but emphasizing the "sovereign and independent character" of the states and explicitly recognizing slavery. The provisional president, Jefferson Davis of Mississippi, tried to assemble a balanced cabinet of moderates. His appointees took on the daunting challenge of creating government departments. When an army captain came to the treasury with a warrant from Davis for blankets, he found only one clerk. After reading the warrant, the clerk offered the captain a few dollars of his own, explaining, "This, Captain, is all the money that I will certify as being in the Confederate Treasury at this moment."

Despite such challenges, the new Confederate government enjoyed enthusiastic civilian support and a growing sense of nationalism. Ordinary people spoke proudly of the South as "our nation" and described themselves as the "southern people." Georgia's governor insisted that "poor and rich, have a common interest, a common destiny." Southern Protestant ministers encouraged a sense of collective identity, reminding southerners that they were God's chosen people and the conflict a sacred one.

While Lincoln inherited the federal government, he lacked administrative experience and faced his own organizational problems. Military officers and government clerks defected daily to the South. The treasury was empty. Floods of office seekers thronged the White House looking for rewards. Knowing few of the "prominent men of the day" Lincoln appointed important Republicans from different factions of the party to cabinet posts whether they agreed with him or not. Several scorned him as a bumbling backwoods politician. Treasury Secretary Salmon P. Chase actually hoped to replace Lincoln as president in four years' time. Soon after the inauguration, Secretary of State William Seward sent Lincoln a memo condescendingly offering to oversee the formulation of presidential policy.

Lincoln and Davis

Lincoln soon demonstrated his leadership skills. His reply to Seward made it clear that he intended to run his own administration. After Sumter, he acted swiftly, calling up state militias, expanding the navy, and suspending habeas corpus. Because Congress was not in session, he ordered a naval blockade of the South and approved the expenditure of funds for military purposes on his own authority. As Lincoln told legislators later, "The dogmas of the quiet past are inadequate to the stormy present. . . . As our case is new, so must we think anew, and act anew . . . and then we shall save our country." This willingness to "think anew" was a valuable personal asset, even though some regarded the expansion of presidential power as despotic.

By coincidence, Lincoln and his rival, Jefferson Davis, were born only 100 miles apart in Kentucky. However, the course of their lives diverged radically. Lincoln's father migrated north to farm in Indiana and Illinois. With a rudimentary formal education, Lincoln was largely self-taught. Davis's family had moved south to Mississippi and become cotton planters. Davis grew up in comfortable circumstances, went to West Point, fought in the Mexican-American War, and was elected to the U.S. Senate before becoming secretary of war under Franklin Pierce.

Although Davis had not been eager to accept the presidency, he loyally responded to the call of the provisional congress in 1861 and worked tirelessly as chief executive. As his wife observed, "the President hardly takes time to eat his meals and works late at night." Some, however, criticized his endless busyness as an inability to delegate work. Others found him reserved, humorless, and too sensitive to criticism. But, like Lincoln, Davis found it necessary to "think anew." He reassured southerners in his inaugural address that his goal was "to preserve the Government of our fathers in spirit." Yet under the pressure of events, he moved toward creating a new kind of South.

Clashing on the Battlefield, 1861–1862

The Civil War was the most destructive conflict in American history. Much of the bloodshed resulted from changing military technology, especially the increasing range of rifles, from 100 to 500 yards. The greater reach of the rifles, partly the result of using the new French minié bullet, meant that it was impossible to position the artillery close enough to enemy lines to support an infantry charge. Attacking infantry soldiers faced a final, often fatal, dash of 500 yards in the face of deadly enemy fire.

As it became clear that infantry charges produced horrible carnage, military leaders increasingly valued strong defensive positions. Although Confederate soldiers at first criticized General Lee as "King of Spades," the epithet evolved into one of affection as it became obvious that earthworks saved lives. Union commanders followed suit.

War in the East

The war's brutal character only gradually revealed itself. The Union's commanding general, 70-year-old Winfield Scott, at first favored a cautious, long-term strategy, the Anaconda Plan. Scott proposed weakening the South gradually through blockades on land and sea until the northern army was strong enough for the kill. The public, however, hungered for quick victory. So did Lincoln. The longer the war lasted, the more embittered the South and the North would both become, making reunion ever more difficult. So 35,000 partially trained men led by General Irwin McDowell left Washington in sweltering July weather, heading for Richmond.

On July 21, 1861, only 25 miles from the capital at Manassas Creek (also called Bull Run), inexperienced northern troops confronted 25,000 raw Confederate soldiers commanded by Brigadier General P. G. T. Beauregard, McDowell's West Point classmate. Although sightseers, journalists, and politicians gaily accompanied the Union troops, Bull Run was no picnic. The battle was inconclusive until the arrival of 2,300 fresh Confederate troops, brought by trains, decided the day. Terrified and bewildered Union soldiers and sightseers fled toward Washington. Defeated though the Union forces were, inexperienced and disorganized Confederate troops could not turn the rout into a quick, decisive victory. In many ways, the Battle of Bull Run was prophetic. Victory would be neither quick nor easy. Both armies were unprofessional, with questionable short-term enlistments. Each army faced severe logistical problems involved in moving and supplying the largest military forces ever put in the field.

South Carolinian Robert Allston viewed the battlefield at Bull Run and decided it had been a "glorious tho bloody" day. For the Union, the loss was sobering. Lincoln began his search for a winning commander by replacing McDowell with 34-year-old General George McClellan. Formerly an army engineer, McClellan began the process of transforming the Army of the Potomac into a fighting force. Short-term militias went home. In the fall of 1861, McClellan became general in chief of the Union armies.

McClellan had considerable organizational ability but no desire to be a daring battlefield leader. Convinced that the North must combine military victory with persuading the South to rejoin the Union, he sought to avoid embittering loss of life and property—to win "by maneuvering rather than fighting."

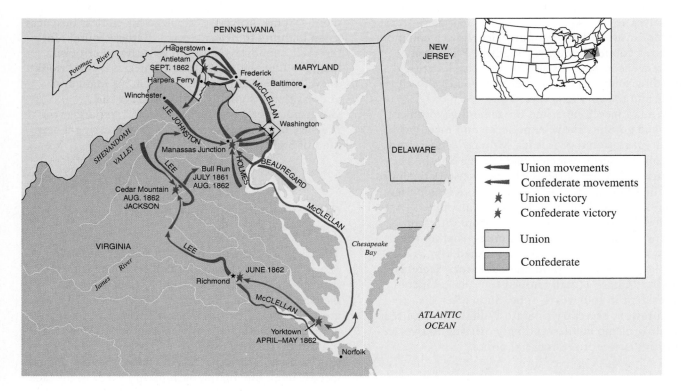

Eastern Theater of the Civil War, 1861–1862

Using this map, describe the military actions in the East during the early years of the war. What were the areas that saw hostilities? What strategies was each side pursuing?

In March 1862, pushed by an impatient Lincoln, McClellan finally led his army of 130,000 toward Richmond, now the Confederate capital. But just as it seemed that victory was within grasp, Lee drove the Union forces back. The Peninsula campaign was abandoned. For the Union, the campaign was a frustrating failure. For Lee, the success in repelling the invasion was one step in the process that was making him and the Army of Northern Virginia into a symbol of the spirit of the new nation.

Other Union defeats followed in 1862 as commanders came and went. In September, the South took the offensive with a bold invasion of Maryland. But after a costly defeat at Antietam, in which more than 5,000 soldiers were slaughtered and another 17,000 wounded on the grisliest day of the war, Lee withdrew to Virginia. The war in the East was stalemated.

War in the West

The early struggle in the East focused on Richmond, the Confederacy's capital and one of the South's most important railroad, industrial, and munitions centers. But the East was only one of three theaters. Between the Appalachians and the Mississippi lay the western theater where both George Eagleton and Arthur Carpenter served. Beyond was the trans-Mississippi West—Louisiana, Arkansas, Missouri, Texas, and the Great Plains. There Native American tribes joined the conflict on both sides.

In the Western theater, the Mississippi River, with its vital river trade and great port of New Orleans, was a major strategic objective. Union forces sought to dominate Kentucky and eastern Tennessee, the avenues to the South and West, and to win control of the Mississippi in order to split the South in two.

It was in this theater that Ulysses S. Grant rose to prominence. Enlisting as a colonel in an Illinois militia regiment shortly after Sumter, Grant was soon a brigadier general. Despite very modest military credentials, Grant proved to be a military genius, able to see beyond individual battles to larger goals. In 1862, he realized that the Tennessee and Cumberland rivers offered pathways for the successful invasion of Tennessee. A premature Confederate invasion of Kentucky allowed Grant to bring his forces into that state without arousing sharp local opposition. Assisted by gunboats, Grant was largely responsible for the capture of Fort Henry and Fort Donelson, key points on the rivers, in February 1862. His successes there raised fears among Confederate leaders that southern mountaineers, loyal to the Union, would rush to Grant's support.

Despite Grant's grasp of strategy, his army was nearly destroyed by a surprise Confederate attack at Shiloh Church in Tennessee. The North won, but at

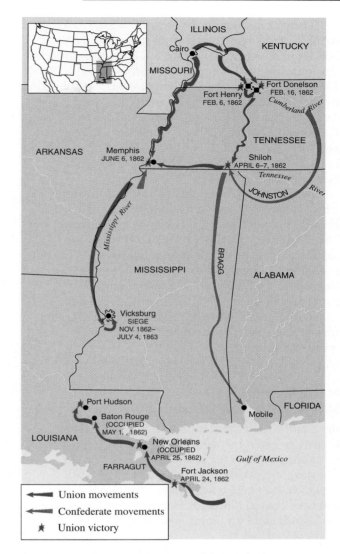

Trans-Mississippi Campaign of the Civil War
What course of action were Union forces operating in the Mississippi valley pursuing? What was the ultimate goal?

enormous cost. In that two-day engagement, the Union suffered more than 13,000 casualties, while 10,000 Confederates lay dead or wounded. More American men fell in this battle than in the American Revolution, the War of 1812, and the Mexican-American War combined. Because neither army offered sufficient care on the battlefield, untreated wounds caused many fatalities. A day after the battle ended, nine-tenths of the wounded still lay in the rain, many dying of exposure or drowning. Those who survived the downpour had infected wounds by the time they received medical attention.

Though more successful than efforts in the East, such devastating Union campaigns failed to bring decisive results. Western plans were never coordinated with eastern military activities. Victories there did not force the South to its knees.

The war in the trans-Mississippi West was a sporadic, far-flung struggle. California was the prize that lured both armies into the Southwest. Confederate Texan troops held Albuquerque and Santa Fe briefly in 1862, but a mixed force, including volunteer soldiers from the Colorado mining fields and Mexican Americans, drove them out. Union recruits from California arrived after the Confederates were gone and spent the remainder of the Civil War years fighting the Apache and the Navajo, brutally crushing both Native American nations.

Farther east was another prize, the Missouri River, which flowed into the Mississippi River, bordered Illinois, and affected military campaigns in Kentucky and Tennessee. Initially, Confederate troops were successful here, as they had been in New Mexico. But in March 1862, at Pea Ridge in northern Arkansas, Union forces whipped a Confederate army that included a brigade of Native Americans from the Five Civilized Nations. Missouri entered the Union camp for the first time in the war, but fierce guerrilla warfare continued.

Naval Warfare

At the beginning of the war, Lincoln decided to strangle the South with a naval blockade. But success was elusive. In 1861, the navy intercepted only about one blockade runner in ten and in 1862, one in eight. The navy increased the likelihood of an effective blockade, however, when Union expeditions gained southern coastal footholds like the South Carolina sea islands and Port Royal Sound, where the first slaves were freed.

The Union's major naval triumph in the early war years was the capture of the South's biggest port, New Orleans, in 1862. The success of this amphibious effort stimulated other joint attempts to cut the South in two.

Recognizing that they could not match the Union fleet, Confederates concentrated on developing new weapons such as torpedoes and ironclad vessels. The *Merrimac* was one key to southern naval strategy. Originally a U.S. warship that had sunk when the federal navy abandoned the Norfolk Navy Yard early in the war, the Confederates raised the vessel and covered it with heavy iron armor. Rechristened the *Virginia,* the ship steamed out of Norfolk in March 1862, heading directly for the Union ships blocking the harbor. Using its 1,500-pound ram and guns, the *Virginia* drove one-third of the vessels aground and destroyed the squadron's largest ships. But the next day, the *Virginia* confronted the *Monitor,* a newly completed Union iron vessel. They dueled inconclusively, and the *Virginia* withdrew. It was burned during the evacuation of Norfolk that May. Southern attempts to buy ironclad ships abroad faded and, with them, southern hopes of escaping the northern noose.

Still, Confederate attacks on northern commerce brought some success. Southern raiders, many of them built in Britain, wreaked havoc on northern shipping. In its two-year career, the *Alabama* destroyed 69 Union merchant vessels valued at more than $6 million. But such blows did not seriously damage the North's war effort.

Thus the first two years brought victories to both sides, but the war remained deadlocked. The South was far from defeated; the North was equally far from giving up. Costs in manpower and supplies far exceeded what either side had expected.

Cotton Diplomacy

Both sides in the Civil War realized Europe's critical importance to the eventual outcome of the struggle. Diplomatic recognition would give the Confederacy international credibility, and European loans and assistance might bring victory—just as French and Dutch aid had helped the American colonies win their independence. If the European powers refused to recognize the South, the fiction of the Union was kept alive. Such a refusal undermined both long-term Confederate survival and the critical process of knitting the Confederacy together as one nation. European powers, of course, consulted their own interests. Neither England nor France wished to back a loser. Nor did they wish to upset Europe's delicate balance of power by hasty intervention in American affairs. One by one, therefore, the European states declared a policy of neutrality.

Southerners were sure that cotton would be their trump card. English and French textile mills needed cotton, and southerners believed that their owners would eventually force their governments to recognize the Confederacy and end the North's blockade. But a glut of cotton in 1860 and 1861 left foreign mill owners oversupplied. As stockpiles dwindled, European industrialists found cotton in India and Egypt. The faith that cotton was "king" proved false.

Union secretary of state Seward's goal was to prevent diplomatic recognition of the Confederacy. The North had its own economic ties with Europe, so the Union was not as disadvantaged as southerners thought. Seward threatened Great Britain with war if it interfered. Some called his boldness reckless, but it succeeded. Although Britain allowed the construction of Confederate raiders in its ports, neither it nor other Europeans intervened in American affairs in 1861 or 1862. Unless the military situation changed dramatically, the Europeans would sit on the sidelines.

Common Problems, Novel Solutions

As the conflict dragged on into 1863, unanticipated problems arose. In response, Union and Confederate leaders devised novel approaches to solve them.

The challenge of the long conflict was partly monetary. Both treasuries had been empty initially, and the war proved extraordinarily expensive. Neither side considered imposing direct taxes, which would have alienated support, but both initiated taxation on a small scale. Ultimately, taxes financed 21 percent of the North's war expenses but only 1 percent of southern expenses. Both treasuries also tried borrowing. Northerners purchased over $2 billion worth of bonds, but southerners proved reluctant to buy their government's securities. As in the American Revolution, printing paper money provided the unwelcome solution. In August 1861, the Confederacy circulated $100 million in crudely engraved bills. Millions more followed the next year. Five months later, the Union issued $150 million in paper money, soon nicknamed "greenbacks." The result of this paper money policy was inflation. Inflation was particularly troublesome in the Confederacy, but rising prices contributed to urban discontent, north and south.

Both sides confronted manpower problems as initial enthusiasm for the war evaporated and the swarm of volunteers disappeared. Soldiering, with its impersonal carnage and diseases along with the boredom of camp life, was nothing like the militia parades familiar to most American males. Many in the service longed to go home. Rather than filling military quotas from within, rich northern communities began offering bounties of $800 to $1,000 to outsiders who would join up.

Arthur Carpenter's letters give a good picture of life in the ranks and a young man's growing disillusionment with the war. As Carpenter's regiment moved into Kentucky and Tennessee in the winter of 1862, his spirits sank. "Soldiering in Kentucky and Tennessee," he complained, "is not so pretty as it was in Indianapolis.... We have been half starved, half frozen, and half drowned. The mud in Kentucky is awful." Soldiering often meant marching with 50 or 60 pounds of equipment and insufficient food, water, or supplies. One blanket was not enough in the winter. In the summer, stifling woolen uniforms attracted lice and other vermin. Poor food, bugs, inadequate sanitation, and exposure invited disease. Carpenter marched through Tennessee suffering from diarrhea and then fever. His regiment left him behind in a convalescent barracks in Louisville, which he fled as soon as he could.

Confederate soldiers, less well supplied than their northern counterparts, complained similarly. In 1862, a Virginia captain described what General Lee called the best army "the world ever saw":

> During our forced marches and hard fights, the soldiers have been compelled to throw away their knapsacks and there is scarcely a private in the army who has a change of clothing of any kind. Hundreds of men are perfectly barefooted and there is no telling when they can be supplied with shoes.

Such circumstances often led to desertion. An estimated one of every seven Union soldiers and one of every nine Confederates deserted.

As manpower problems became critical, both governments resorted to the draft. Despite sacrosanct

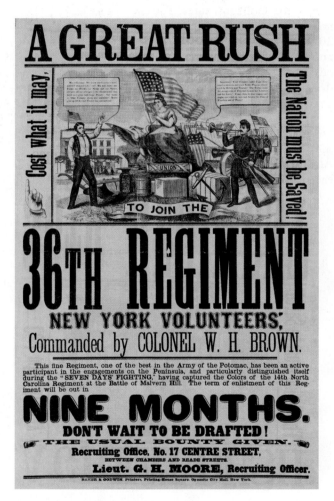

How many different strategies does this poster use to persuade men to join the 36th Regiment of New York Volunteers? The central picture shows a soldier on the right who calls out, "Americans! Your country calls. Your cherished institutions and your Noble Flag are threatened by rebels and traitors." The man on the left replies, "We will come. We know our country's needs and will respond to the call." Who does the female figure in the center represent?

(Collection of the New-York Historical Society [PR-055–3–149])

states' rights, the Confederate Congress passed the first conscription act in American history in March 1862. Four months later, the Union Congress followed. Both laws encouraged soldiers to reenlist and sought volunteers rather than forcing men to serve. Ultimately, over 30 percent of the Confederate army and 6 percent of Union forces were draftees. The South relied more heavily on the draft because the North's manpower pool was larger and growing as foreigners of military age poured into northern states. Some came specifically to claim bounties and fight. Immigrants constituted at least 20 percent of the Union army.

Although necessary, draft laws were very unpopular. The first Confederate conscription declared all able-bodied men between 18 and 35 eligible for military service but allowed numerous exemptions and the purchase of substitutes. The exemption from military service granted to every planter with more than 20 slaves fed class tension and encouraged disloyalty and desertion, particularly among mountaineers. The advice one woman shouted after her husband as he was dragged off to the army was hardly unique. "You desert again, quick as you kin. . . . Desert, Jake!"

Northern legislation was neither more popular nor fair. The 1863 draft allowed the hiring of substitutes, and $300 bought an exemption from military service. Already suffering from inflation, workers resented the ease with which moneyed citizens could avoid army duty.

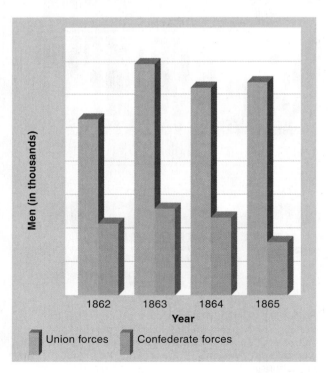

What does this chart demonstrate about the manpower problem and the impact of the draft laws in the South and the North? What manpower resources did the North have that the South lacked?

In July 1863, resentment boiled over in New York City in the largest civil disturbance of the nineteenth century, a three-day riot sparked by the process of conscripting several thousand men. Events spun out of control as a mob (mainly Irish workmen) burned draft records, torched the armory, plundered the houses of the rich, and looted jewelry stores. Blacks, hated as economic competitors and the cause of the war, became special targets. Mobs beat and lynched blacks and burned the Colored Orphan Asylum. More than 100 people died. There was much truth in the accusation that the war on both sides was a rich man's war but a poor man's fight.

Political Dissension, 1862

As the war continued, rumbles of dissension grew louder. In February, 1862, the *Richmond Examiner* summarized many southerners' frustration. "The Confederacy has had everything that was required for success but one, and that one thing it was and is supposed to possess more than anything else, namely Talent." Criticism of Confederate leaders mounted. Jefferson Davis's vice president, Alexander Stephens of Georgia, became one of the administration's bitterest accusers. Without a party system, southern dissatisfaction with Davis's handling of the war tended to be factional, petty, and personal. No party mechanism channeled or curbed irresponsible criticism. Detractors rarely offered alternative policies. Without a party leader's traditional weapons and rewards, Davis had no mechanism to generate enthusiasm for his war policies.

Although Lincoln has since become a folk hero, at the time of the Civil War, many northerners derided his performance. Peace Democrats, called Copperheads, claimed that Lincoln betrayed the Constitution and that working-class Americans bore the brunt of his conscription policy. Immigrant workers in eastern cities and those who lived in the southern parts of the Midwest had little sympathy for abolitionism or blacks, and they supported the antiwar stance of the Copperheads. Even pro-war Democrats found Lincoln arbitrary and tyrannical and worried that extreme Republicans would push Lincoln into making the war a crusade for the abolition of slavery. Some Republicans judged Lincoln indecisive and inept.

Republicans gradually divided into two factions. The moderates favored a cautious approach toward winning the war, fearing the possible consequences of emancipating the slaves, confiscating Confederate property, or arming blacks. The radicals, however, urged Lincoln to make emancipation a wartime objective. They sought a victory that would revolutionize southern social and racial arrangements. The reduction of the congressional Republican majority in the fall elections of 1862 made it imperative that Lincoln heed both factions as well as Democratic opposition.

The Tide Turns, 1863–1865

Hard political realities and Lincoln's sense of the public's mood help explain why he delayed action on emancipation until 1863. Many northerners supported a war for the Union, not for emancipation. Most whites regarded blacks as inferior and feared that emancipation would bring former slaves north to steal white jobs and political rights. Northern race riots dramatized white attitudes.

The Emancipation Proclamation, 1863

If the president moved too fast on emancipation, he risked losing the allegiance of northern racists, offending the border states, and increasing the Democrats' chances for political victory. But if Lincoln did not move at all, he would alienate abolitionists and lose the support of radical Republicans, which he could ill afford.

So Lincoln proceeded cautiously. At first, he hoped the border states might take the initiative. In the early spring of 1862, he urged Congress to pass a joint resolution offering federal compensation to states beginning a "gradual abolishment of slavery." Border-state opposition killed the idea. Abolitionists and northern blacks, however, greeted Lincoln's proposal with a "thrill of joy."

That summer, Lincoln told his cabinet he intended to emancipate the slaves. Secretary of State Seward urged delaying until the North won a decisive military victory. Otherwise, he warned, Lincoln would appear to be urging racial insurrection behind the Confederate lines to compensate for northern military bungling. Lincoln followed Seward's advice, using that summer and fall to prepare the North for the shift in the war's purpose. To counteract white fears of free blacks, he promoted schemes for establishing free black colonies in Haiti and Panama. When Horace Greeley, the influential abolitionist editor of the New York *Tribune,* printed an open letter to Lincoln attacking him for failing to act on slavery, Lincoln prepared the groundwork for emancipation by linking it to military necessity. His primary goal, he wrote, was to save the Union:

> If I could save the Union without freeing any slave, I would do it; and if I could save it by freeing all the slaves, I would do it; and if I could do it by freeing some and leaving others alone, I would also do that. What I do about Slavery and the colored race, I do because I believe it helps to save this Union.

If Lincoln attacked slavery, then, it would only be because emancipation would save white lives, preserve the democratic process, and restore the Union.

In September 1862, the Union success at Antietam provided the opportunity for a preliminary emancipation proclamation. It stated that unless rebellious states (or parts of states in rebellion) returned to the Union by January 1, 1863, the president would declare their slaves "forever free." Although supposedly aimed at bringing the southern states back into the Union, Lincoln never expected the South to lay down arms. Rather, he was preparing northerners to accept the eventuality of emancipation on the grounds of necessity. Frederick Douglass greeted the president's action with a "shout for joy." But not all northerners shared Douglass's elation. The September proclamation probably harmed Republicans in the fall elections.

Although the elections of 1862 weakened the Republicans' grasp on the national government, they did not destroy it. Still, cautious cabinet members begged Lincoln to forget about emancipation. His refusal demonstrated his vision and humanity. So did his efforts to reduce racial fears. "Is it dreaded that the freed people will swarm forth and cover the whole land?" he asked. "Are they not already in the land? Will liberation make them any more numerous? Equally distributed among the whites of the whole country, and there would be but one colored to seven whites. Could the one, in any way, greatly disturb the other?"

Finally, on New Year's Day 1863, Lincoln issued the final Emancipation Proclamation. It was an "act of justice, warranted by the Constitution upon military necessity." Thus, what began as a war to save the Union became a struggle that, if victorious, would free the slaves. Yet the proclamation had no immediate impact on slavery. It affected only slaves living in the unconquered portions of the Confederacy and said nothing about slaves in the border states and in parts of the South already in northern hands. These limitations led Elizabeth Cady Stanton and Susan B. Anthony to establish the women's Loyal National League to lobby Congress to emancipate all southern slaves.

Yet the Emancipation Proclamation had a tremendous symbolic importance. On New Year's Day, blacks gathered outside the White House to cheer the president and tell him that if he would "come out of that palace, they would hug him to death." They realized that the proclamation had transformed the nature of the war as the government committed itself to freeing slaves. Jubilant blacks could only believe that the president's action heralded a new era for their race. More immediately, the proclamation sanctioned the policy of accepting blacks as soldiers. Blacks also hoped that the news would reach southern slaves, encouraging them either to flee to Union lines or to subvert the southern war effort by refusing to work for their masters.

Diplomatic concerns also lay behind the Emancipation Proclamation. Lincoln and his advisers anticipated that the commitment to abolish slavery would favorably impress foreign powers. European

This depiction of African Americans celebrating the Emancipation Proclamation appeared in the French publication *Le Monde Illustre*. How has the artist provided a triumphant and sympathetic picture of rejoicing freedpeople? What does this picture, published in France, suggest about the diplomatic importance to the Union cause of the Emancipation Proclamation?

statesmen did not abandon their cautious stance toward the Union. However, important segments of the British public who opposed slavery now came to regard any attempt to help the South as immoral. Foreigners could better understand and sympathize with a war to free the slaves than they could with a war to save the Union. In diplomacy, where image is so important, Lincoln had created a more attractive picture of the North. The Emancipation Proclamation became the North's symbolic call for human freedom.

Unanticipated Consequences of War

The Emancipation Proclamation was but another example of the war's surprising consequences. In the final two years of the war, both North and South experimented on the battlefields and behind the lines in desperate efforts for victory.

One of the Union's experiments involved using black troops for combat duty. Blacks had offered themselves as soldiers in 1861 but had been rejected. They were serving as cooks, laborers, teamsters, and carpenters in the army, however, and composed as much as a quarter of the navy. But as white casualties mounted, so did pressure for black service on the battlefield. The Union government allowed states to escape draft quotas if they enlisted enough volunteers, and they allowed them to count southern black enlistees on their state rosters. Northern governors grew increasingly interested in black military service.

Anticipating blacks' postwar interests, Frederick Douglass pressed for military service. "Once let the black man get upon his person the brass letter, U.S., let him get an eagle on his button, and a musket on his shoulder and bullets in his pocket," Douglass believed that "there is no power on earth that can deny that he has earned the right to citizenship." By the war's end, 186,000 blacks (10 percent of the army) had served the Union cause, 134,111 of them escapees from slave states.

But the black experience in the army highlighted some of the obstacles to racial acceptance. Black soldiers, usually led by white officers, were second-class soldiers for most of the war, receiving lower pay, poorer food, often more menial work, and fewer benefits than whites. Even whites working to equalize black and white pay often considered blacks inferior.

The army's racial experiment had mixed results. But the faithful and courageous service of black troops helped modify some of the most demeaning white racial stereotypes of blacks. The black soldiers, many former slaves, who conquered the South felt a sense of pride and dignity. Wrote one, "We march through these fine thoroughfares where once the slave was forbid being out after nine P.M. . . . Negro soldiers!—with banners floating."

As the conflict continued, basic assumptions weakened about how it should be waged. One wartime casualty was the courtly idea that war involved only armies. Early in the war, many officers tried to protect civilians and their property. Northern concern for rebel property soon vanished. On the few occasions when they came North, southern troops lived off the land. War touched all of society, not just the battlefield participants.

This photograph was taken in the summer of 1862 in Cumberland Landing, Virginia. Sitting in front of the cabin are about 20 men and women who had fled to Union lines and freedom. The flight of slaves, called contrabands, had the potential of seriously undermining the southern war effort and southern morale, but their presence also posed difficulties for Union commanders and northern leaders who were often not sure what to do with them. What might be some of the reasons why there were more women than men in this picture?

(Library of Congress [LC-B811–0383])

Changing Military Strategies, 1863–1865

In the early war years, southern strategy combined defense with selective offensive maneuvers, an approach that seemed to succeed, at least in the eastern theater, until summer 1863. But occasional victories over the invading northern army, such as at Fredericksburg in December 1862, did not change the course of the war. Realizing this, Lee concluded, "There is nothing to be gained by this army remaining quietly on the defensive." Without victories in the North, he believed, it could not prevail. He was willing to take risks to gain peace and national recognition.

In the summer of 1863, Lee led the Confederate army of northern Virginia into Maryland and southern Pennsylvania. His goal was a victory that would threaten both Philadelphia and Washington; he even dreamed of capturing a northern city. Such feats would surely bring diplomatic recognition and possibly force the North to sue for peace.

At Gettysburg on a hot and humid July 1, Lee confronted a Union army led by General George Meade. During three days of fighting, the fatal obsession with the infantry charge returned as Lee ordered costly infantry assaults that probably lost him the battle. On July 3, Lee sent three divisions, about 15,000 men in all, against the Union center. The assault, known as Pickett's Charge, was gallant but futile. At 700 yards, the Union artillery opened fire. One southern officer described the scene: "Pickett's division just seemed to melt away in the blue musketry smoke which now covered the hill. Nothing but stragglers came back."

Despite the carnage, Lee procured the food and fodder he needed and captured thousands of prisoners. Gettysburg was a defeat, but neither Lee, nor his men, nor southern civilians regarded it as conclusive. Fighting would continue for another year and a half. In 1864, one high army officer revealed his continuing belief in the struggle's outcome. "Our hearts are full of hope," he wrote. "Oh! I do pray that we may be established as an independent people,...[and] recognized as God's Peculiar People!" While many remained hopeful, Lee's heavy Gettysburg losses spelled the end of further southern offensives.

Gettysburg was a Union victory, but Lincoln was dissatisfied with General Meade, who had failed to finish off Lee's retreating army. His disappointment faded with news of a great victory on July 4 at Vicksburg in the western theater. The capture of the city completed the Union campaign to gain control of the Mississippi River and to divide the South. Ulysses S. Grant, who was responsible for the victory, demonstrated the boldness and flexibility that Lincoln had been looking for in a commander.

By the summer of 1863, the military situation finally looked promising for the North. The Union controlled much of Arkansas, Louisiana, Mississippi, Missouri, Kentucky, and Tennessee. In March 1864, Lincoln appointed Grant general in charge of all Union armies. Grant planned for victory within a year. "The art of war is simple enough," he reasoned. "Find out where your enemy is. Get at him as soon as you can. Strike at him as hard as you can, and keep moving on."

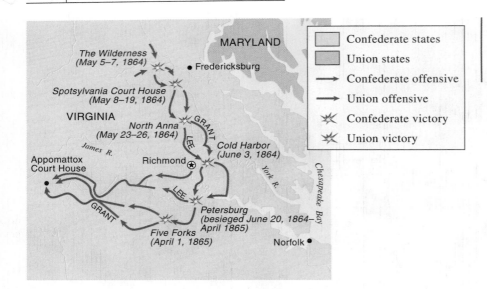

The Last Year of Conflict

This map shows the major campaigns in the East during the final year of the conflict. How would you describe Grant's offensive in the spring of 1864?

As an outsider to the prewar military establishment, Grant had no difficulty in rejecting conventional military wisdom. "If men make war in slavish observance of rules, they will fail," he asserted. He sought not one decisive engagement but rather a campaign of annihilation, using the North's superior resources to grind down the South. Although Grant's plan entailed large casualties on both sides, he justified it by arguing that "now the carnage was to be limited to a single year."

A campaign of annihilation involved the destruction not only of enemy armies but also of enemy resources. Although the idea of cutting the enemy off from needed supplies was implicit in the naval blockade, economic or "total" warfare was a relatively new and shocking idea. Grant, however, "regarded it

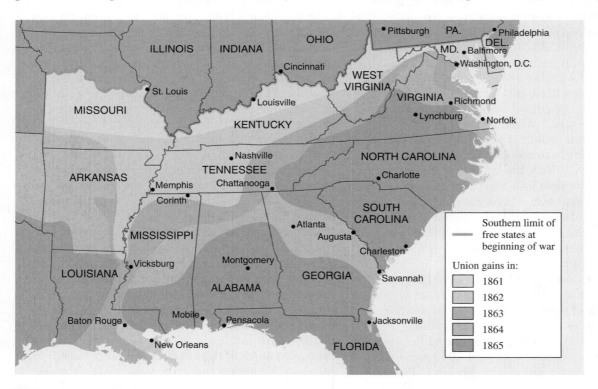

The Progress of War, 1861–1865

In this map you can see the very slow progression of the North's effort to conquer the South. For much of the war, the South controlled large areas of contiguous territory. This control of the southern homeland helped southerners to feel that it was possible for them to win the war. At what point in time might the realities depicted in this map have made southerners decide their cause was lost?

as humane to both sides to protect the persons of those found at their homes, but to consume everything that could be used to support or supply armies." Following this policy, he set out after Lee's army in Virginia. General William Tecumseh Sherman, who pursued General Joseph Johnston from Tennessee toward Atlanta, further refined this plan.

The war, Sherman believed, must also be waged on the minds of civilians to make them "fear and dread" their foes. His campaign to seize Atlanta and his march to Savannah spread destruction and terror. Ordered to forage "liberally" on the land, his army left desolation in its wake. This havoc, with its goal of total victory, demonstrated once more how conflict produced the unexpected. The war that both North and South had hoped would be quick and relatively painless was ending after four long years with great cost to both sides. Furthermore, the bitter warfare of that final year threatened Lincoln's hopes for reconciliation.

Changes Wrought by War

As bold new tactics emerged both on and off the battlefield, both governments took steps that changed their societies in surprising ways. Of the two, the South, which had left the Union to conserve a traditional way of life, experienced the more radical transformation.

A New South

The expansion of the central government's power in the South, starting with the passage of the 1862 Conscription Act, continued in the last years of the war. States' rights had inspired secession, but victory necessitated central direction and control. Many southerners denounced Davis as a despot for his recognition that the central government must take the lead. Despite the accusations, the Confederate Congress cooperated with him and established important precedents, including serious interference with property rights. For example, government impressment of slaves for war work in 1863 affected the very form of private property that had originally driven the South from the Union.

The Conscription Act of 1862 did not solve the Confederate army's manpower problems. By 1864, the southern armies were one-third the size of the Union forces. Hence, in February 1864, an expanded conscription measure subjected all white males between ages 17 and 50 to the draft. By 1865, the necessities of war had led to the unthinkable: arming slaves as soldiers. Black companies were recruited but the war was over before any blacks could fight for the Confederacy.

In a message sent to Congress in November 1864, Davis speculated on some of the issues involved in

My only support—both boys gone to the war. I wonder if they would take me?

On the Home Front

Appearing on a printed envelope, this image reveals several aspects of female experience during wartime. Why is this woman doing laundry? What is being suggested about the changes in her life that have occurred as a result of the war? What feelings does she express? This woman's speculation about the possibilities of doing humble work in the military alerts us to the fact that washerwomen accompanied the armies wherever they went.

(Collection of the New-York Historical Society [PR-022-3-88-5])

arming slaves. "Should a slave who had served his country" be retained in servitude, he wondered, "or should his emancipation be held out to him as a reward for faithful service, or should it be granted at once on the promise of such service...?" The South had begun the war to preserve slavery but ended it contemplating emancipation.

Southern agriculture also changed under the pressure of war. Earlier, the South had imported food from the North, concentrating on producing cotton and tobacco for market. Now, more and more land was turned over to food crops. Some farmers voluntarily shifted crops, but others responded only to state laws reducing the acreage permitted for cotton and tobacco cultivation. These measures never succeeded in raising enough food to feed southerners adequately but helped dramatically cut cotton production.

The South had always relied on imported manufactured goods. Even though some blockade runners evaded the Union ships, the noose tightened after 1862. The Confederacy could not, in any case, rely on blockade runners to arm and equip the army. Thus, war triggered the expansion of military-related industries in the South. Here, too, the government played a crucial role. The war and navy offices directed industrial development, awarding contracts to private manufacturing firms such as Richmond's Tredegar Iron Works and operating other factories themselves. The number of southern industrial workers rose dramatically. At the end of the war, the soldiers were better supplied with arms and munitions than with food.

Although the war did not transform the southern class structure, relations between the classes began to change. The pressures of the struggle undermined the solidarity of whites, based on racism and supposed political unanimity. Draft resistance and desertion reflected the growing alienation from a war perceived as serving only the interests of plantation owners. More and more yeoman families suffered grinding poverty as the men went off to war and government officials and armies requisitioned needed resources.

The North

Although changes in the South were more noticeable, the Union's government and economy also responded to the demands of war. Like Davis, Lincoln was accused of being a dictator. Although he rarely tried to control Congress, veto its legislation, or direct government departments, Lincoln exercised executive power freely. He violated the writ of habeas corpus by suspending the civil rights of more than 13,000 northerners, who languished in prison without trials; curbed the freedom of the press because of supposedly disloyal and inflammatory articles; established conscription; issued the Emancipation Proclamation; and removed army generals. Lincoln argued that this vast extension of presidential power was temporarily justified because, as president, he was responsible for defending and preserving the Constitution.

Many of the wartime changes in government proved more permanent than Lincoln imagined. Wartime financial necessities helped revolutionize the country's banking system. Ever since Andrew Jackson's destruction of the Bank of the United States, state banks had served American financial needs. Treasury Secretary Chase found this banking system inadequate and proposed to replace it. In 1863 and 1864, Congress reestablished a federal banking system by passing legislation establishing a national currency issued by federally chartered banks and backed by government bonds.

The necessity of feeding soldiers and civilians encouraged the expansion of northern agriculture and increased investment in farm machinery. Because so many men were off soldiering, farmers were short of labor. Mechanical reapers performed the work of four to six men, and farmers began to buy them. During the war, McCormick sold 165,000 of his machines. Northern farming, especially in the Midwest, was well on the way to becoming mechanized. Farmers even accumulated a surplus for export.

The war also selectively stimulated manufacturing. Although it is easy to imagine that northern industry as a whole expanded during the Civil War, in fact, the war retarded overall economic growth. War consumed rather than generated wealth. Between 1860 and 1870, the annual rate of increase in real manufacturing value added was only 2.3 percent, in contrast with 7.8 percent for the years between 1840 and 1860 and 6 percent for the period from 1870 to 1900. However, war industries, especially those with advantages of scale, expanded and made large profits. Each year, the Union army required 1.5 million uniforms and 3 million pairs of shoes; the woollen and leather industries grew accordingly. Meatpackers and producers of iron, steel, and pocket watches all profited from wartime opportunities.

On the Home Front, 1861–1865

Events on the battlefield were intimately connected to life behind the lines. As both northern and southern leaders realized, civilian morale was crucial to the war's outcome. If civilians lost faith, they would lack the will to continue the conflict.

The war stimulated religious efforts to generate enthusiasm and loyalty on the home front. On both sides, Protestant clergymen threw themselves behind the war effort. As northern preacher Henry Ward Beecher proclaimed, "God hates lukewarm patriotism as much as lukewarm religion, and we hate it too." Southern ministers gave similar messages and urged southerners to reform their lives, for victory depended on moral change. In North and South, every defeat was a cause for soul searching. Fast days and revivals provided a spiritual dimension to the conflict and helped people deal with discouragement and death.

In numerous ways, the war transformed northern and southern society. The very fact of conflict established a new perspective for most civilians. War news vied with local events for attention. They read newspapers and national weekly magazines with a new eagerness. The use of the mails increased dramatically as they corresponded with faraway relatives and friends. Wrote one North Carolina woman, "I never liked to write letters before, but it is a pleasure as well as a relief now." Distant events became almost as real and vivid as those at home. The war helped make Americans less parochial, integrating them into the larger world.

For some Americans, such as John D. Rockefeller and Andrew Carnegie, war brought army contracts and unanticipated riches. The New York *Herald* reported that New York City had never been "so gay,...so crowded, so prosperous," as it was in March 1864. Residents of Cincinnati noted people who "became suddenly immensely wealthy, and in their fine equipages, with liveried servants, rolled in magnificence along the city streets." In the South, blockade runners made fortunes slipping luxury goods past Union ships.

For the majority of Americans, however, war meant deprivation. The war effort gobbled up a large part of each side's resources, and ultimately ordinary people suffered. To be sure, the demand for workers ended unemployment and changed employment patterns. Large numbers of women and blacks entered the workforce, a phenomenon that would be repeated in all future American wars. But whereas work was easy to get and wages appeared to increase, real income actually declined. Inflation, especially destructive in the South, was largely to blame. By 1864, eggs sold in Richmond for $6 a dozen; butter brought $25 a pound. Strikes and union organizing pointed to working-class discontent.

Low wages compounded the problem of declining income and particularly harmed women workers. Often forced into the labor market because husbands earned only small army stipends, army wives and other women took what pay they could get. As more women entered the workforce, employers cut costs by slashing wages. In 1861, the Union government paid Philadelphia seamstresses 17 cents per shirt. At the height of inflation, three years later, the government reduced the piecework rate to 15 cents. Private employers paid even less, about 8 cents a shirt. Working women in the South fared no better. War may have brought prosperity to a few Americans in the North and South, but for most it meant trying to survive on an inadequate income.

Economic dislocation caused by the war reduced the standard of living for civilians. Shortages and hardships were severe in the South, which bore the brunt of the fighting. Most white southerners did without food,

manufactured goods, and medicine during the war. Farming families without slaves to help with fieldwork fared poorly. As one Georgia woman explained, "I can't manage a farm well enough [alone] to make a suporte." Conditions were most dismal in cities, where carts brought in vital supplies, because trains were reserved for military use. Hunger was rampant. Food riots erupted in Richmond and other cities; crowds of hungry whites broke into stores to steal food. The very cleanliness of southern cities pointed to urban hunger. As one Richmond resident noted, everything was so "cleanly consumed that no garbage or filth can accumulate."

Thousands of southerners who fled as Union armies advanced suddenly found themselves homeless. "The country for miles around is filled with refugees," noted an army officer in 1862. "Every house is crowded and hundreds are living in churches, in barns and tents." Caught up in the effort of mere survival, refugees worried about what had happened to homes and possessions left behind and whether anything would remain when they returned. Life was probably just as agonizing for those who chose to stay put when Union troops arrived. Virginia Gray, an Arkansas woman, wrote in her diary of her fear of the "Feds" and the turmoil they caused when they suddenly appeared and then disappeared.

White flight also disrupted slave life. Even the arrival of Union forces could prove a mixed blessing. One slave described the upsetting behavior of the Yankees at his plantation in Arkansas: "Them folks stood round there all day. Killed hogs...killed cows.... Took all kinds of sugar and preserves....Tore all the feathers out of the mattresses looking for money. Then they put Old Miss and her daughter in the kitchen to cooking." So frightened was this slave's mother that she hid in her bed, only to be roused by the lieutenant, who told her, "We ain't a-going to do you no hurt....We are freeing you." But the next day, the Yanks were gone and

The Impact of the War in the South

The dislocations caused by the war were many. These southerners, forced to leave their home by invading troops, have packed what few belongings they could transport and stand ready to evacuate their homestead. How many children can you find in the picture? What does the fact that the woman in the foreground is smoking a pipe suggest about the social class of this group?

(Library of Congress)

the Confederates back. During Sherman's march through Georgia in 1864, his troops stole not only from whites but from slaves as well. Indeed some soldiers flogged blacks who tried to stop the looting.

Wartime Race Relations

The journal kept by Emily Harris in South Carolina conveys some of the character of life behind the lines. She revealed not only the predictable story of shortages, hardships, and the psychological burdens of those at home but also the subtle social changes the war stimulated. Emily and her husband, David, lived on a 500-acre farm with their seven young children and 10 slaves. When David went to war, Emily had to manage the farm, even though David worried that she would be "much at a loss with the . . . farm and the negroes."

Emily's early entries establish two themes that persist for the years she kept her diary. She worried about how David would survive the "privation and hardships" of army life and was also anxious about her own "load of responsibilities." Her December 1862 entry provides a poignant picture of a wife's thoughts. "All going well as far as I can judge but tonight it is raining and cold and a soldier's wife cannot be happy in bad weather and during a battle." The dozens of tasks she had to do depressed her. "I shall never get used to being left as the head of affairs," she wrote in January 1863. "I am not an independent woman nor ever shall be." As time passed and the war went badly, the dismal news and mounting list of casualties heightened her concern about David's safety.

Her relations with her slaves compounded Emily's problems. As so many southerners discovered, war transformed the master–slave relationship. Because Emily was not the master David had been, her slaves gradually claimed unaccustomed liberties. At Christmas in 1864, several left the farm without her permission; others stayed away longer than she allowed. "Old Will" boldly requested his freedom. Worse yet, she discovered that her slaves had helped three Yankees who had escaped from prison camp.

The master–slave relationship was crumbling, and Emily reported in her journal the consequences for whites. "It seems people are getting afraid of negroes." Although not admitting to fear, she revealed that she could no longer control the blacks, who were increasingly unwilling to play a subservient role.

Understanding what was at stake, slaves, in their own way, often worked for their freedom. Said one later, "Us slaves worked den when we felt like it, which wasn't often." Emily's journal entry for February 22 confessed a "painful necessity." "I am reduced," she said, "to the use of a stick but the negroes are becoming so impudent and disrespectful that I cannot bear

it." A mere two weeks later she added, "The Negroes are all expecting to be set free very soon and it causes them to be very troublesom."

Similar scenes occurred throughout the South. Insubordination, refusal to work, and refusal to accept punishment marked the behavior of black slaves, especially those who worked as field hands. Thousands of blacks (probably 20 percent of all slaves), many of them women who had been exploited as workers and as sexual objects, fled toward Union lines after the early months of the war. Their flight pointed to the changing nature of race relations and the harm slaves could do to the southern cause. Reflected one slaveowner, "The 'faithful slave' is about played out."

Women and the War

If Emily Harris's journal reveals that she was sometimes overwhelmed by her responsibilities and shocked by the changes in dealings with her slaves, it also illustrates how the war affected women's lives. Nineteenth-century ideology promoted women's domestic role and minimized their economic importance. But the war made it impossible for many women to live according to conventional norms. So many men on both sides had gone off to fight that, just like many of their grandmothers during the American Revolution, women had to find jobs and carry on farming operations. During the war years, southern women who had no slaves to help with the farmwork and northern farm wives who labored without the assistance of husbands or sons carried new physical and emotional burdens. For southern women, who faced shortages and even displacement, sanity sometimes seemed at stake. Emily Harris felt she was going crazy. Others found their patriotism waning and urged their men to come home.

Women supported the war effort by participating in numerous war-related activities. In both North and South, they entered government service in large numbers. In the North, hundreds of women became military nurses. Under the supervision of Drs. Emily and Elizabeth Blackwell; Dorothea Dix, superintendent of army nurses; and Clara Barton, northern women nursed the wounded and dying for low pay or even for none at all. They also attempted to improve hospital conditions by attacking red tape and bureaucracy. The diary of a volunteer, Harriet Whetten, revealed the activist attitude of many others:

> I have never seen such a dirty disorganized place as the Hospital. The neglect of cleanliness is inexcusable. All sorts of filth, standing water, and the embalming house near the Hospital. . . . No time had to be lost. Miss Gill and I set the contrabands at work making beds & cleaning.

Recovering the Past

PHOTOGRAPHY

The invention of photography in 1839 expanded the visual and imaginative world of nineteenth-century Americans. For the first time, Americans could visually record events in their own lives and see images of people and incidents from far away. Photographs, of course, also expand the boundaries of the historian's world. As photographic techniques became simpler, more and more visual information about the nineteenth century was captured. Historians can use photographs to discover what nineteenth-century Americans wore, how they celebrated weddings and funerals, and what their families, houses, and cities looked like. Pictures of election campaigns, parades, strikes, and wars show the texture of public life. But historians can also study photographs, as they do paintings, to glean information about attitudes and norms. The choice of subjects, the way people and objects are arranged and grouped, and the relationships between people in photographs are all clues to the social and cultural values of nineteenth-century Americans.

Some knowledge of the early history of photography helps place the visual evidence in the proper perspective. The earliest type of photograph, the daguerreotype, was not a print but the negative itself on a sheet of silver-plated copper. The first daguerreotype required between 15 and 30 minutes for the proper exposure. This accounts for the stiff and formal quality of many of these photographs. Glass ambrotypes (negatives on glass) and tintypes (negatives on gray iron bases), developed after the daguerreotype, were easier and cheaper to produce. But both techniques produced only one picture and required what to us would seem an interminable time for exposure.

A major breakthrough came in the 1850s with the development of the wet-plate process. In this process, the photographer coated a glass negative with a sensitive solution, exposed the negative (took the picture), and then quickly developed it. The new procedure required a relatively short exposure time of perhaps five seconds outdoors and one minute inside. Action shots, however, were still not feasible. The entire process tied the photographer to the darkroom. Traveling photographers carried their darkrooms with them. The advantage of the wet-plate process was that it was possible to make many paper prints from one negative, opening new commercial vistas for professional photographers.

Mathew Brady, a fashionable Washington photographer, realized that the camera was the "eye of history" and asked Lincoln for permission to record the war with his camera. He and his team of photographers left about 8,000 glass negatives, currently stored in the Library of Congress and the National Archives, as their record of the Civil War. Shown here are two photographs, one of three Confederate soldiers captured at Gettysburg, the other of the battlefield of Cold Harbor in Virginia.

In the first photograph, study and describe the three soldiers. How are they posed? What kind of clothes are they wearing? What about their equipment? What seems to be their physical condition?

The second picture was taken in April 1865, about a year after the battle at Cold Harbor. In the background, you can see two Union soldiers digging graves. In the foreground

Mathew Brady, Confederate Captives, Gettysburg

(National Archives)

Mathew Brady, Burial Party
at Cold Harbor

(Chicago Historical Society, ICHi-07868)

are the grisly remains of the battle. What do you think is the intent of the photograph? The choice of subject matter shows clearly that photography reveals attitudes as well as facts. What attitude toward war and death is conveyed in this picture? Why is the burial taking place a full year after the battle? What does this tell us about the nature of civil warfare? Notice that the soldiers ordered to undertake this ghastly chore are black, as was customary. What might this scene suggest about the experience of black soldiers in the Union army?

Reflecting on the Past Using the photograph of Confederate captives as evidence, what might you

conclude about the southern soldier—his equipment, uniforms, shoes? How well fed do the men in the picture appear? What attitudes are conveyed through their facial expressions and poses? What kind of mood was the northern photographer trying to create? What might a northern viewer conclude about the South's war effort after looking at this picture?

These photographs just begin to suggest what can be discovered from old photographs. Your local historical society and library probably have photograph collections available to you. In addition, at home or in a relative's attic, you may find visual records of your family and its history. ■

Although men largely staffed southern military hospitals, Confederate women also cared for the sick and wounded in their homes and in makeshift hospitals behind the battle lines. Grim though the work was, many women felt that they were participating in the real world for the first time in their lives.

Women moved outside the domestic sphere in other forms of volunteer war work. Some women gained administrative experience in soldiers' aid societies and in the U.S. Sanitary Commission, which raised $50 million by the war's end for medical supplies, nurses' salaries, and other wartime necessities.

Others made bandages and clothes, put together packages for soldiers at the front, and helped army wives and disabled soldiers find jobs.

Many of the changes women experienced during the war years ended when peace returned. Jobs in industry and government disappeared when the men came to reclaim them. Women turned over the operation of farms to returning husbands. But for women whose men came home maimed or not at all, the work had not ended. Nor had the discrimination. Trying to pick up the threads of their former lives, they found it impossible to forget what they had done to help the war effort. At least some of them were sure they had equaled their men in courage and commitment.

The Election of 1864

In the North, the election of 1864 brought some of the transformations of wartime into the political arena. The Democrats, seeking to regain power by capitalizing on war weariness, nominated General George McClellan for president. The party proclaimed the war a failure and demanded an armistice with the South. During the campaign, Democrats accused Lincoln of arbitrarily expanding executive power and denounced sweeping economic measures such as the banking bills. Arguing that the president had transformed the war from one for Union into one for emancipation, they tried to inflame racial passions by insinuating that if the Republicans won, a fusion of blacks and whites would result.

Although Lincoln gained the Republican renomination because of his tight control over party machinery and patronage, his party did not unite behind him. Lincoln seemed to please no one. His veto of the radical reconstruction plan for the South, the Wade–Davis bill, led to cries of "usurpation." The Emancipation Proclamation did not sit well with conservatives. Union defeats during the summer encouraged those who wanted to make peace with the South. In August 1864, a gloomy Lincoln told his cabinet that he expected to lose the election. As late as September, some Republicans actually hoped to reconvene the convention and select another candidate.

Sherman's capture of Atlanta in September 1864 and the march through Georgia to Savannah helped swing voters to Lincoln. In the end, Republicans had no desire to see the Democrats oust their party. Lincoln won 55 percent of the popular vote and swept the electoral college.

Why the North Won

In the months after Lincoln's reelection, the war drew to an agonizing conclusion. Sherman moved north from Atlanta to North Carolina, while Grant pummeled Lee's forces in Virginia. The losses Grant sustained in Virginia were staggering: 18,000 in the Battle of the Wilderness, more than 8,000 at Spotsylvania, and another 12,000 at Cold Harbor. New recruits stepped forward to replace the dead. On April 9, 1865, Grant accepted Lee's surrender at Appomattox. Southern soldiers and officers were allowed to return home with their personal equipment after promising to remain there peaceably. The war was finally over.

Technically, the war was won on the battlefield and at sea. But Grant's military strategy succeeded because the Union's manpower and economic resources could survive staggering losses of men and equipment while the Confederacy's could not. As Union armies pushed back the borders of the Confederacy, the South lost control of territories essential for its war effort. Finally, naval strategy eventually paid off because the North could build enough ships to make its blockade work. In 1861, fully 90 percent of the blockade runners were slipping through the naval cordon. By the war's end, only half made it.

The South had taken tremendous steps toward meeting war needs. But despite the impressive growth of manufacturing and the increasing acreage devoted to foodstuffs, the southern army and the southern people were poorly fed and poorly clothed. As one civilian realized, "The question of bread and meat . . . is beginning to be regarded as a more serious one even than that of War." Women working alone or with disgruntled slaves on farms could not produce enough food. Worn-out farm equipment was not replaced. The government's impressment of slaves and animals cut production. The half million blacks who fled to Union lines also played their part in pulling the South down in defeat.

New industries could not meet the extraordinary demands of wartime, and advancing Union forces destroyed many of them. A Confederate officer in northern Virginia observed, "Many of our soldiers are thinly clothed and without shoes and in addition to this, very few of the infantry have tents. With this freezing weather, their sufferings are indescribable." Skimpy rations, only one-third of a pound of meat for each soldier a day by 1864, weakened the Confederate force, whose trail was "traceable by the deposit of dysenteric stool" it left behind. By that time, the Union armies were so well supplied that soldiers often threw away heavy blankets and coats as they advanced.

The South's woefully inadequate transportation system also contributed to defeat. Primitive roads deteriorated and became all but impassable without repairs. The railroad system, geared to the needs of cotton, not war, was inefficient. When tracks wore out or were destroyed, they were not replaced. Rails were too heavy for blockade runners to bother with, and as the Confederate railroad coordinator observed in 1865, "Not a single bar of railroad iron has been rolled in the Confederacy since the war, nor can we hope to do better." Thus, food intended for the army rotted awaiting shipment. Supplies were tied up in bottlenecks and soldiers went hungry. Food riots in southern cities pointed to the hunger, anger, and growing demoralization of civilians.

Ironically, measures the Confederacy took to strengthen its ability to win the war, as one Texan later observed, "weakened and paralyzed it." Conscription, impressment, and taxes all contributed to resentment and sometimes open resistance. They fueled class tensions already strained by the poverty that war brought to many yeoman farmers and led some of them to assist the invaders or to join the Union army. The proposal to use slaves as soldiers called into question the war's purpose. The many southern governors who refused to contribute men, money, and supplies on the scale Davis requested implicitly condoned disloyalty to the cause.

It is natural to compare Lincoln and Davis as war leaders. There is no doubt that Lincoln's humanity, his awareness of the terrible costs of war, his determination to save the Union, and his eloquence set him apart as one of this country's most extraordinary presidents. Yet the men's personal characteristics were probably less important than the differences between the political and social systems of the two regions. Without the support of a party behind him, Davis failed to engender enthusiasm or loyalty. Even though the Republicans rarely united behind Lincoln, they uniformly wanted to keep the Democrats from office. Despite all the squabbles, Republicans tended to support Lincoln's policies in Congress and back in their home districts. Commanding considerable resources of patronage, Lincoln was able to line up federal, state, and local officials behind his party and administration.

Just as the northern political system provided Lincoln with more flexibility and support, its social system also proved more able to meet the war's extraordinary demands. Although both societies adopted innovations in an effort to secure victory, northerners were more cooperative, disciplined, and aggressive in meeting the organizational and production challenges of wartime. In the southern states, old attitudes, habits, and values impeded the war effort. Southern governors, wedded to states' rights, refused to cooperate with the Confederate government. North Carolina, the center of the southern textile industry, actually kept back most uniforms for its own regiments. At the war's end, 92,000 uniforms and thousands of blankets, shoes, and tents still lay in its warehouses. When Sherman approached Atlanta, Georgia's governor would not turn over the 10,000 men in the state army to Confederate commanders. Even slaveholders, whose property had been the cause for secession, resisted the impressment of their slaves for war work.

In the end, the Confederacy collapsed, exhausted and bleeding. Hungry soldiers received letters from their families revealing desperate situations at home. They worried and then slipped away. By December 1864, the Confederate desertion rate had passed 50 percent. Replacements could not be found. Farmers hid livestock and produce from tax collectors. Many southerners felt their cause was lost and resigned themselves to defeat. But some fought on till the end. One northerner described them as they surrendered at Appomattox:

> Before us in proud humiliation stood the embodiment of manhood: men whom neither toils and sufferings, nor the fact of death, nor disaster, nor hopelessness could bend from their resolve; standing before us now, thin, worn, and famished, but erect, and with eyes looking level into ours, waking memories that bound us together as no other bond.

The Costs of War

The long war was over, but the memories of that event would fester for years to come. About 3 million American men, one-third of all free males between ages 15 and 59, had served in the army. Each would remember his own personal history of the war. For George Eagleton, who had worked in army field hospitals, the history was one of "Death and destruction! Blood! Blood! Agony! Death! Gaping flesh wounds, broken bones, amputations, bullet and bomb fragment extractions." Of all wars Americans have fought, none has been more deadly. The death rate during this war was more than five times the death rate during World War II. About 360,000 Union soldiers and another 258,000 Confederate soldiers died, about one-third of them because their wounds were either improperly treated or not treated at all. Disease claimed more lives than combat. Despite the efforts of men such as Eagleton and the women army nurses, hospitals could not handle the scores of wounded and dying. "Glory is not for the private soldier, such as die in the hospitals," reflected one Tennessee soldier, "being eat up with the deadly gangrene, and being imperfectly waited on."

Thousands of men would be reminded of the human costs of war by the injuries they carried with them to the grave, by the missing limbs that marked them as Civil War veterans. About 275,000 on each side were maimed. Another 410,000 (195,000 northerners and 215,000 southerners) would remember wretchedly overcrowded and unsanitary prison camps. The lucky ones would recall only the dullness and boredom. The worst memory was of those who rotted in prison camps, such as Andersonville in Georgia, where 31,000 Union soldiers were confined. At the war's end, more than 12,000 graves were counted there.

Some Americans found it hard to throw off wartime experiences and adjust to peace. As Arthur Carpenter's letters suggest, he gradually grew accustomed to army life. War provided him with a sense of purpose. When it was over, he felt aimless. A full year after the war's end, he wrote, "Camp life agrees with me better than any other." Many others

had difficulty returning to civilian routines and finding a new focus for life. Even those who adjusted successfully discovered that they looked at life from a different perspective. The experience of fighting, of mixing with all sorts of people from many places, and of traveling far from home had lifted former soldiers out of their familiar local world and widened their vision. Fighting the war made the concept of national union real.

Unanswered Questions

What, then, had the war accomplished? On the one hand, death and destruction. Physically, the war devastated the South. Historians have estimated a 43 percent decline in southern wealth during the war years, exclusive of the value of slaves. Great cities like Atlanta, Columbia, and Richmond lay in ruins. Fields lay weed-choked and uncultivated. Tools were worn out. One-third or more of the South's stock of mules, horses, and swine had disappeared. Two-thirds of the railroads had been destroyed. Thousands were hungry,

homeless, and bitter about their four years of what now appeared a useless sacrifice. More than 4 million slaves, a vast financial investment, were free.

On the other hand, the war had resolved the question of union and ended the debate over the relationship of the states to the federal government. During the war, Republicans seized the opportunity to pass legislation that would foster national union and economic growth: the Pacific Railroad Act of 1862, which set aside huge tracts of public land to finance the transcontinental railroad; the Homestead Act of 1862, which was to provide yeoman farmers cheaper and easier access to the public domain; the Morrill Act of 1862, which established support for agricultural (land-grant) colleges; and the banking acts of 1863 and 1864.

The war had also resolved the issue of slavery, the thorny problem that had so long plagued American life. Yet uncertainties outnumbered certainties. What would happen to the former slaves? When blacks had fled to Union lines during the war, commanders had not known what to do with them. Now the problem

Timeline

1861	Lincoln calls up state militia and suspends habeas corpus
	First Battle of Bull Run
	Union blockades the South
1862	Battles at Shiloh, Bull Run, and Antietam
	Monitor and *Virginia* battle
	First black regiment authorized by Union
	Union issues greenbacks
	South institutes military draft
	Pacific Railroad Act
	Homestead Act
	Morrill Land-Grant College Act
1863	Lincoln issues Emancipation Proclamation
	Congress adopts military draft
	Battles of Gettysburg and Vicksburg
	Union Banking Act
	Southern tax laws and impressment act
	New York draft riots
	Southern food riots
1864	Sherman's march through Georgia
	Lincoln reelected
	Union Banking Act
1865	Lee surrenders at Appomattox
	Lincoln assassinated; Andrew Johnson becomes president

became even more pressing. Were blacks to have the same civil and political rights as whites? In the Union army, they had been second-class soldiers. The behavior of Union forces toward liberated blacks in the South showed how deep the stain of racism went. One white soldier, caught stealing a quilt by a former slave, shouted, "I'm fighting for $14 a month and the Union"—not to end slavery. Would blacks be given land, the means for economic independence? What would be their relations with their former owners?

What, indeed, would be the status of the conquered South in the nation? Should it be punished for the rebellion? Some people thought so. Should southerners keep their property? Some people thought not. There were clues to Lincoln's intentions. As early as December 1863, the president had announced a generous plan of reconciliation. He was willing to recognize the government of former Confederate states established by a group of citizens equal to 10 percent of those voting in 1860, as long as the group swore to support the Constitution and to accept the abolition of slavery. He began to restore state governments in three former Confederate states on that basis. But not all northerners agreed with his leniency, and the debate continued.

In his 1865 inaugural address, Lincoln urged Americans to harbor "malice towards none...and charity for all." "Let us strive," he urged, "to finish the work we are in; to bind up the nation's wounds...to do all which may achieve a just and lasting peace." Privately, the president said the same thing. Generosity and goodwill would pave the way for reconciliation. On April 14, he pressed the point home to his cabinet. His wish was to avoid persecution and bloodshed. That same evening, only five days after the surrender at Appomattox, the president attended a play at Ford's Theatre. There, as one horrified eyewitness reported,

a pistol was heard and a man ... dressed in a black suit of clothes leaped onto the stage apparently from the President's box. He held in his right hand a dagger whose blade appeared about 10 inches long.... Every one leaped to his feet, and the cry of "the President is assassinated" was heard—Getting where I could see into the President's box, I saw Mrs. Lincoln...in apparent anguish.

John Wilkes Booth, a southern sympathizer, had killed the president.

Conclusion
AN UNCERTAIN FUTURE

As the war ended, many Americans grieved for the man whose decisions had so marked their lives for five years. "Strong men have wept tonight & the nation will mourn tomorrow," wrote one eyewitness to the assassination. Many more wept for friends and relations who had not survived the war, but whose actions had in one way or another contributed to its outcome. The lucky ones, like Arthur Carpenter and George and Ethie Eagleton, now faced the necessity of putting their lives back together and moving forward into an uncertain future. Perhaps not all Americans realized how drastically the war had altered their lives, their prospects, and their nation. It was only as time passed that the war's impact became clear to them. And it was only with time that they recognized how many problems the war had left unsolved. It is to these years of Reconstruction that we turn next.

QUESTIONS FOR REVIEW AND REFLECTION

1. Assess the strengths and weaknesses of the North and South at the beginning of the war. What northern strengths actually led to northern victory and what Confederate weaknesses explain southern defeat?
2. Describe the military campaigns in each region of the country over the course of the war.
3. What were the most important transformations in the Union and Confederacy during the war and why, in your opinion, were these changes so significant?
4. Compare and contrast Lincoln and Davis as war leaders and the two governments over which they presided.
5. What role did race play during the war?
6. Consider the Civil War as a struggle between differing beliefs and values and assess the importance of northern victory for this struggle. In what ways did the war's outcome realize or fail to realize the founding principles of this nation?

Read it.
Get it.

VOLUME TWO
Since 1865

THE AMERICAN PEOPLE

CREATING A NATION AND A SOCIETY

*T*he popular classic
*"The American People"
is now available in this
new, streamlined
VangoBooks edition,
offering a clean,
smart, and efficient
presentation at an
affordable price.*

Gary B. Nash   **Julie Roy Jeffrey**
John R. Howe   Allan M. Winkler
Peter Frederick   Charlene Mires
Allen F. Davis   Carla Gardina Pestana

VOLUME 2

CHAPTERS 16–31

To order, please request
ISBN-10: 0-205-64283-7; ISBN-13: 978-0-205-64283-0

COMBINED VOLUME
CHAPTERS 1-31
IISBN-10: 0-205-64279-9
ISBN-13: 978-0-205-64279-3

VOLUME 1
CHAPTERS 1-16
ISBN-10: 0-205-64282-9
ISBN-13: 978-0-205-64282-3

VOLUME 2
CHAPTERS 16-31
ISBN-10: 0-205-64283-7
ISBN-13: 978-0-205-64283-0

CHAPTER 16

The Union Reconstructed

In a scene like the one depicted in this Winslow Homer painting titled *A Visit from the Old Mistress*, imagine Adele Allston returning to her plantation to reunite with former slaves. What sort of new relationships might they form in a world that had been profoundly changed by the wrenching Civil War?

(Winslow Homer, A Visit from the Old Mistress, 1876, National Museum of American Art/Art Resource, NY)

American Stories

Blacks and Whites Redefine Their Dreams and Relationships

In April 1864, a year before Lincoln's assassination, Robert Allston died, leaving his wife, Adele, and his daughter, Elizabeth, to manage their many rice plantations. Elizabeth felt a "sense of terrible desolation and sorrow" as the Civil War raged around her. With Union troops moving through coastal South Carolina in the winter of 1864–1865, Elizabeth's sorrow turned to "terror" as Union soldiers arrived and searched for liquor, firearms, and valuables. The women fled. Later, Yankee troops encouraged the Allston slaves to take furniture, food, and other goods from the Big House. Before they left, the liberating Union soldiers gave the keys to the crop barns to the semifree slaves.

After the war, Adele Allston swore allegiance to the United States and secured a written order for the newly freed African Americans to relinquish those keys. She and Elizabeth returned in the summer of 1865 to reclaim the plantations and reassert white authority. She was assured that although the blacks had guns, "no outrage has been committed against the whites except in the matter of property." But property was the issue. Possession of the keys to the barns, Elizabeth wrote, would be the "test case" of whether former masters or former slaves would control land, labor, and its fruits, as well as the subtle aspects of interpersonal relations.

Nervously, Adele and Elizabeth confronted ex-slaves at their old home. To their surprise, a pleasant reunion took place as the Allston women greeted the blacks by name, inquired after their children, and caught up on their lives. A trusted black foreman handed over the keys to the barns. This harmonious scene was repeated elsewhere.

But at one plantation, the Allstons met defiant and armed African Americans, who ominously lined both sides of the road as the carriage arrived. An old black driver, Uncle Jacob, was unsure whether to yield the keys to the barns full of rice and corn, put there by slave labor. Mrs. Allston insisted. As Uncle Jacob hesitated, an angry young man shouted out: "If you give up the key, blood'll flow." Uncle Jacob slowly slipped the keys back into his pocket.

The African Americans sang freedom songs and brandished hoes, pitchforks, and guns to discourage anyone from going to town for help. Two blacks, however, slipped away to find some Union officers. The Allston women spent the night safely, if restlessly, in their house. Early the next morning, they were awakened by a knock at the unlocked front door. There stood Uncle Jacob. Silently, he gave back the keys.

The story of the keys reveals most of the essential human ingredients of the Reconstruction era. Defeated southern whites were determined to resume control of both land and labor. The law and federal enforcement generally supported the property owners. The Allston women were friendly to the blacks in a maternal way and insisted on restoring prewar deference in black–white relations. Adele and Elizabeth, in short, both feared and cared about their former slaves.

The African American freedpeople likewise revealed mixed feelings toward their former owners: anger, loyalty, love, resentment, and pride. They paid respect to the Allstons but not to their property and crops. They wanted not revenge but rather economic independence and freedom.

Northern officials played a most revealing role. Union soldiers, literally and symbolically, gave the keys of freedom to the freed men and women, but did not stay around long enough to guarantee that freedom. Despite initially encouraging blacks to plunder the master's house and seize the crops, in the crucial encounter after the war, northern officials had disappeared. Understanding the limits of northern help, Uncle Jacob handed the keys to land and liberty back to his former owner. The blacks realized that if they wanted to ensure their freedom, they had to do it themselves.

This chapter describes what happened to the conflicting goals and dreams of three groups as they sought to redefine new social, economic, and political relationships during the postwar Reconstruction era. It also shows how America sought to reestablish stable democratic governments. Amid vast devastation and bitter race and class divisions, Civil War survivors sought to put their lives back together. Victorious but variously motivated northern officials, defeated but defiant southern planters, and impoverished but hopeful African Americans could not all fulfill their conflicting goals and dreams, yet each had to try. Reconstruction would be divisive, leaving a mixed legacy of human gains and losses.

The Bittersweet Aftermath of War

"There are sad changes in store for both races," the daughter of a Georgia planter wrote in the summer of 1865. To understand the bittersweet nature of Reconstruction, we must look at the state of the nation after the assassination of President Lincoln.

The United States in 1865

Constitutionally, the "Union" faced a crisis in April 1865. What was the status of the 11 former Confederate states? The North had denied the South's constitutional right to secede but needed four years of civil war and over 600,000 deaths to win the point. Lincoln's official position had been that the southern states had never left the Union and were only "out of their proper relation" with the United States. The president, therefore, as commander in chief, had the authority to decide how to set relations right again. Lincoln's congressional opponents retorted that the rebellious states had broken their constitutional ties, were now like "conquered provinces," and that Congress should resolve the constitutional issues and direct Reconstruction.

Politically, differences between Congress and the White House mirrored a wider struggle between the two branches of the national government. During war, as has usually been the case, the executive branch assumed broad powers to mobilize resources and ensure domestic security. Many believed that Lincoln had far exceeded his constitutional authority and that his successor, Andrew Johnson, was worse. Would Congress reassert its authority?

In April 1865, the Republican party ruled nearly unchecked. Republicans claimed huge achievements in winning the war, preserving the Union, and freeing the slaves. They had enacted sweeping economic programs on behalf of free labor, economic growth, and the creation of land-grant colleges to teach agricultural and mechanical skills. But the still-young party remained an uneasy grouping of former Whigs, Unionist Democrats, and antislavery idealists.

The Democrats were in shambles. Republicans depicted southern Democrats as traitorous rebels and northern Democrats as weak-willed, disloyal, and opposed to economic progress. Nevertheless, in the election of 1864, needing to show that the war was a bipartisan effort, the Republicans had named a Tennessee Unionist Democrat, Andrew Johnson, as Lincoln's vice president. Now the tactless Johnson headed the government.

Economically, the United States in the spring of 1865 presented stark contrasts. Northern cities and railroads hummed with productive activity; southern cities and railroads lay in ruins. Northern banks flourished; southern financial institutions were bankrupt. Mechanized northern farms were more productive than ever; southern farms and plantations, especially those along Sherman's march, resembled a "howling waste."

Socially, the widespread devastation in the South affected southern attitudes. A later southern writer, Wilbur Cash, explained, "If this war had smashed the Southern world, it had left the essential Southern mind and will...entirely unshaken." Many white southerners were determined to resist Reconstruction and restore their former life and institutions; others, the minority who had remained quietly loyal to the Union, sought reconciliation.

In this context, nearly 4 million newly freed blacks faced the challenges of freedom. After initial joy and celebration in jubilee songs, freedmen and freedwomen

---

The United States in 1865: Crises at the End of the Civil War

Given the enormous casualties, costs, and crises of the immediate aftermath of the Civil War, what attitudes, goals, dreams, and behaviors would you predict for the three major groups?

Military Casualties

360,000 Union soldiers dead
260,000 Confederate soldiers dead
620,000 Total dead
375,000 Seriously wounded and maimed
995,000 Casualties nationwide in a total male population of 15 million (nearly 1 in 15)

Physical and Economic Crises

The South devastated; its railroads, industry, and some major cities in ruins; its fields and livestock wasted

Constitutional Crisis

Eleven former Confederate states not a part of the Union, their status unclear and future status uncertain

Political Crisis

Republican party (entirely of the North) dominant in Congress; a former Democratic slaveholder from Tennessee, Andrew Johnson, in the presidency

Social Crisis

Nearly 4 million black freedpeople throughout the South facing challenges of survival and freedom, along with thousands of hungry, demobilized Confederate soldiers and displaced white families

Psychological Crisis

Incalculable stores of resentment, bitterness, anger, and despair, North and South, white and black

Conflicting Goals During Reconstruction

Examine these conflicting goals, which, at a human level, were the challenge of Reconstruction. How could each group possibly fulfill its goals when so many of them conflict with those of other groups? You may find yourself referring back to this chart throughout the chapter. How can each group fulfill its goals?

Victorious Northern ("Radical") Republicans

- Justify the war by remaking southern society in the image of the North
- Inflict political but not physical or economic punishment on Confederate leaders
- Continue programs of economic progress begun during the war: high tariffs, railroad subsidies, national banking
- Maintain the Republican party in power
- Help the freedpeople make the transition to full freedom by providing them with the tools of citizenship (suffrage) and equal economic opportunity

Northern Moderates (Republicans and Democrats)

- Quickly establish peace and order, reconciliation between North and South
- Bestow on the southern states leniency, amnesty, and merciful readmission to the Union
- Perpetuate land ownership, free labor, market competition, and other capitalist ventures
- Promote local self-determination of economic and social issues; limit interference by the national government
- Provide limited support for black suffrage

Old Southern Planter Aristocracy (Former Confederates)

- Ensure protection from black uprising and prevent excessive freedom for former slaves
- Secure amnesty, pardon, and restoration of confiscated lands
- Restore traditional plantation-based, market-crop economy with blacks as cheap labor force
- Restore traditional political leaders in the states
- Restore traditional paternalistic race relations as basis of social order

New "Other South": Yeoman Farmers and Former Whigs (Unionists)

- Quickly establish peace and order, reconciliation between North and South
- Achieve recognition of loyalty and economic value of yeoman farmers
- Create greater diversity in southern economy: capital investments in railroads, factories, and the diversification of agriculture
- Displace the planter aristocracy with new leaders drawn from new economic interests
- Limit the rights and powers of freedpeople; extend suffrage only to the educated few

Black Freedpeople

- Secure physical protection from abuse and terror by local whites
- Achieve economic independence through land ownership (40 acres and a mule) and equal access to trades
- Receive educational opportunity and foster the development of family and cultural bonds
- Obtain equal civil rights and protection under the law
- Commence political participation through the right to vote

---

quickly realized their continuing dependence on former owners. A Mississippian woman said:

> I used to think if I could be free I should be the happiest of anybody in the world. But when my master come to me, and says—Lizzie, you is free! it seems like I was in a kind of daze. And when I would wake up in the morning I would think to myself, Is I free? Hasn't I got to get up before day light and go into the field of work?

For Lizzie, and 4 million other blacks, everything—and nothing—had changed.

Hopes Among the Freedpeople

Throughout the South in the summer of 1865, optimism surged through the old slave quarters as Richmond blacks chanted: "Slavery chain done broke at last! Gonna praise God till I die!" But the slavery chain broke slowly, link by link. After Union troops swept through an area, "we'd begin celebratin'," one man said, but Confederate soldiers would follow, or master and overseer would return, and "tell us to go back to work." The freedmen and freedwomen learned, therefore, not to rejoice too quickly or openly.

This 1867 engraving shows two southern women and their children soon after the Civil War. In what ways are they similar and in what ways different? Is there a basis for bonds of sisterhood? What separates them, if anything? From *Frank Leslie's Illustrated Newspaper,* February 23, 1867.

(The Granger Collection, New York)

Gradually, though, African Americans began to test the reality of freedom. Typically, their first step was to leave the plantation, if only for a few hours or days. "If I stay here I'll never know I am free," said a South Carolina woman, who went to work as a cook in a nearby town. Some freedpeople cut their ties entirely—returning to an earlier master, or, more often, going into towns and cities to find jobs, schools, churches, and association with other blacks, safe from whippings and retaliation.

Many blacks left the plantation in search of a spouse, parent, or child sold away years before. Advertisements detailing these sorrowful searches filled African American newspapers. For those who found a spouse and for those who had been living together in slave marriages, freedom meant getting married legally in mass ceremonies in the first months of emancipation. In addition to its moral importance, legal marriage

established the legitimacy of children and meant access to land titles and other economic opportunities. Marriage brought special burdens for black women who assumed the double role of housekeeper and breadwinner. Their determination to create a traditional family life and care for their children resulted in the withdrawal of many women from plantation field labor.

Freedpeople also demonstrated their new status by choosing surnames. Names connoting independence, such as Washington, were common. Revealing mixed feelings toward their former masters, some would adopt their master's name, while others would pick "any big name 'ceptin' their master's." Emancipation changed black manners around whites as well. Masks fell, and expressions of deference—tipping a hat, stepping aside, calling whites "master" or "ma'am"—diminished. For blacks, these changes were necessary expressions of selfhood, proving that race relations had changed; whites, however, saw such behaviors as "insolence" and "insubordination."

Education and land were priorities. A Mississippi farmer vowed to "give my children a chance to go to school, for I consider education next best ting to liberty." A traveler through the South counted "at least five hundred" schools "taught by colored people." Other than the passion for education, the primary goal for most freedpeople was land. "All I want is to git to own fo' or five acres ob land, dat I can build me a little house on and call my home," a Mississippi black said. Through educational and economic independence, freedpeople like Lizzie would make sure that emancipation was real.

During the war, some Union generals had put liberated slaves in charge of confiscated and abandoned lands. In the Sea Islands of South Carolina and Georgia, African Americans had been working 40-acre plots of land and harvesting their own crops for several years, and some even held title to these lands. Northern philanthropists had organized others to grow cotton for the Treasury Department to prove the superiority of free labor. In Mississippi, thousands of former slaves worked 40-acre tracts on leased lands ironically once owned by Jefferson Davis. In this highly successful experiment, they made profits sufficient to repay the government for initial costs, then lost the land to Davis's brother.

Many freedpeople expected a new economic order as fair payment for their years of involuntary work. "Gib us our own land," said one, "and we take care ourselves; but widout land, de ole massas can hire us or starve us, as dey please." Freedmen expected the "forty acres and a mule" that had been promised (although one man was willing to settle for less, desiring only one acre—"Ef you make it de acre dat Marsa's house sets on"). Once they obtained land, education, and family unification, some looked forward to equal civil rights and the vote—along with protection from vengeful defeated Confederates.

The White South's Fearful Response

White southerners had equally strong dreams and expectations. Middle-class (yeoman) farmers and poor whites stood beside rich planters in bread lines, all hoping to regain land and livelihood. Suffering from "extreme want and destitution," as a Cherokee County, Georgia, resident put it, southern whites responded to the immediate postwar crises with feelings of outrage, loss, and injustice. "My pa paid his own money for our niggers," one man said, "and

Describe what you see in these two scenes from 1865, one an early photograph of a group of newly freed former slaves leaving the cotton fields after a day of labor, the other a painting titled *The Armed Slave*. What has changed and not changed from slavery times? What is the meaning of the painting? Note the position of gun and bayonet. Could you create a story about these two images?

(Top: © Collection of The New-York Historical Society; Bottom: William Spang, *The Armed Slave*. The Civil War Library and Museum, Philadelphia)

The Promise of Land: 40 Acres

Note the progression in various documents in this chapter from promised lands (this page), to lands restored to whites (p. 392), to work contracts (p. 397), to semiautonomous tenant farms (p. 398). Freedom came by degrees to freedpeople. To what extent was this progress?

To All Whom It May Concern
Edisto Island, August 15th, 1865
George Owens, having selected for settlement forty acres of Land, on Theodore Belab's Place, pursuant to Special Field Orders, No. 15, Headquarters Military Division of the Mississippi, Savannah, Ga., Jan. 16, 1865; he has permission to hold and occupy the said Tract, subject to such regulations as may be established by proper authority; and all persons are prohibited from interfering with him in his possession of the same.
By command of R. SAXTON
       Brev't Maj. Gen.,
       Ass't Comm.
       S.C., Ga., and Fla.

The Black Codes, widespread violence against freedpeople, and President Johnson's veto of the civil rights bill gave rise to the sardonic title "(?)Slavery Is Dead(?)" in this Thomas Nast cartoon. Describe the two scenes and the two images of justice. What is Nast saying?

(Courtesy of The Newberry Library, Chicago)

that's not all they've robbed us of. They have taken our horses and cattle and sheep and everything." Others mourned the loss of former faithful slaves: "My dear black mammy has left us," a Florida woman wrote, "I feel lost.... Whatever will I do without my Mammy?"

A dominant emotion was fear. The entire structure of southern society was shaken, and the semblance of racial peace and order that slavery had provided was shattered. Having lost control of all that was familiar, whites feared everything—from losing their cheap labor to having blacks sit next to them on trains to having to do housework. Eliza Andrews complained that it seemed to her a "waste of time for people who are capable of doing something better to spend their time sweeping and dusting while scores of lazy negroes that are fit for nothing else are lying around idle."

Ironically, given the rape of black women during slavery, southern whites' worst fears were of rape and revenge. African American "impudence," some thought, would lead to legal intermarriage and "Africanization," the destruction of the purity

of the white race. Black Union soldiers seemed especially ominous. But these fears were exaggerated, as demobilization of black soldiers came quickly, and rape and violence against whites was extremely rare.

Believing their world turned upside down, the former planter aristocracy sought to set it right again. To reestablish white dominance, southern legislatures passed "Black Codes" in the first year after the war. Many of the codes granted freedpeople rights that were highly qualified. Complicated passages explained under exactly what circumstances blacks could testify against whites or own property (mostly they could not). Forbidden were racial intermarriage, bearing arms, possessing alcoholic beverages, sitting on trains (except in baggage compartments), being on city streets at night, and congregating in large groups.

Many of the qualified rights guaranteed by the Black Codes were only passed to induce the federal government to withdraw its remaining troops from the South. This was a crucial issue, for in many places marauding groups of whites were terrorizing defenseless blacks. In one small district in Kentucky, for example, a government agent reported in 1865:

> Twenty-three cases of severe and inhuman beating and whipping of men; four of beating and shooting; two of robbing and shooting; three of robbing; five men shot and killed; two shot and wounded; four beaten to death; one beaten and roasted; three women assaulted and ravished; four women beaten; two women tied up and whipped until insensible....

Freedpeople clearly needed protection and the right to testify in court against whites.

Key provisions of the Black Codes regulated freedpeople's economic status. "Vagrancy" laws provided that any blacks not "lawfully employed" (by a white employer) could be arrested, jailed, fined, or hired out to a man who would assume responsibility for their debts and behavior. The codes regulated black laborers' work contracts with white landowners, including severe penalties for leaving before the yearly contract was fulfilled and rules for proper behavior, attitude, and manners. A Kentucky newspaper was blunt: "The tune...will not be 'forty acres and a mule,' but... 'work nigger or starve.'"

National Reconstruction Politics

The Black Codes directly challenged the national government in 1865. Would it use its power to uphold the codes, white property rights, and racial intimidation, or to defend the liberties of freedpeople? Although the primary drama of Reconstruction pitted white landowners against black freedmen over land, labor, and liberties in the South, these local struggles were affected by Reconstruction and race relations policy set by politicians in Washington. That drama extends to today.

Presidential Reconstruction by Proclamation

After initially demanding that the defeated Confederates be punished for "treason," President Johnson soon adopted a more lenient policy. On May 29, 1865, he issued two proclamations setting forth his Reconstruction program. Like Lincoln's, it rested on the claim that the southern states had never left the Union.

Johnson's first proclamation continued Lincoln's policies by offering "amnesty and pardon, with restoration of all rights of property" to most former Confederates who would swear allegiance to the Constitution and the Union. Johnson revealed his Jacksonian hostility to "aristocratic" planters by

Promised Land Restored to Whites

Richard H. Jenkins, an applicant for the restoration of his plantation on Wadmalaw Island, S.C., called "Rackett Hall," the same having been unoccupied during the past year and up to the 1st of Jan. 1866, except by one freedman who planted no crop, and being held by the Bureau of Refugees, Freedmen and Abandoned Lands, having conformed to the requirements of Circular No. 15 of said Bureau, dated Washington, D.C., Sept. 12, 1865, the aforesaid property is hereby restored to his possession.

. . . The Undersigned, Richard H. Jenkins, does hereby solemnly promise and engage, that he will secure to the Refugees and Freedmen now resident on his Wadmalaw Island Estate, the crops of the past year, harvested or unharvested; also, that the said Refugees and Freedmen shall be allowed to remain at their present houses or other homes on the island, so long as the responsible Refugees and Freedmen (embracing parents, guardians, and other natural protectors) shall enter into contracts, by leases or for wages, in terms satisfactory to the Supervising Board.

Also, that the undersigned will take the proper steps to enter into contracts with the above described responsible Refugees and Freedmen, the latter being required on their part to enter into said contracts on or before the 15th day of February, 1866, or surrender their right to remain on the said estate, it being understood that if they are unwilling to contract after the expiration of said period, the Supervising Board is to aid in getting them homes and employment elsewhere.

exempting ex-Confederate government leaders and rebels with taxable property valued over $20,000. They could, however, apply for individual pardons, which Johnson granted to nearly all applicants.

In his second proclamation, Johnson accepted the reconstructed government of North Carolina and prescribed the steps by which other southern states could reestablish state governments. First, the president would appoint a provisional governor, who would call a state convention representing those "who are loyal to the United States," including persons who took the oath of allegiance or were otherwise pardoned. The convention must ratify the Thirteenth Amendment, which abolished slavery; void secession; repudiate Confederate debts; and elect new state officials and members of Congress.

Under Johnson's plan, all southern states completed Reconstruction and sent representatives to Congress, which convened in December 1865. Defiant southern voters elected dozens of former officers and legislators of the Confederacy, including a few not yet pardoned. Some state conventions hedged on ratifying the Thirteenth Amendment, and some asserted former owners' right to compensation for lost slave property. No state convention provided for black suffrage, and most did nothing to guarantee civil rights, schooling, or economic protection for the freedmen. Eight months after Appomattox, the southern states were back in the Union, freedpeople were working for former masters, and the new president was firmly in charge. Reconstruction seemed to be over.

Congressional Reconstruction by Amendment

Late in 1865, northern leaders painfully saw that almost none of their postwar goals were being fulfilled and that the Republicans were likely to lose their political power. Would Democrats and the South gain by postwar elections what they had lost by civil war?

A song popular in the North in 1866 posed the question, "Who shall rule this American Nation?"—those who would betray their country and "murder the innocent freedmen" or those "loyal millions" who had shed their "blood in battle"? The answer was obvious. Congressional Republicans, led by

Congressman Thaddeus Stevens of Pennsylvania and Senator Charles Sumner of Massachusetts, decided to set their own policies for Reconstruction. Although labeled "radicals," the vast majority of Republicans were moderates on the economic and political rights of African Americans.

Rejecting Johnson's position that the South had already been reconstructed, Congress exercised its constitutional authority to decide on its own membership. It refused to seat the new senators and representatives from the old Confederate states. It also established the Joint Committee on Reconstruction to investigate conditions in the South, which reported widespread white resistance, disorder, and the appalling treatment of freedpeople.

Congress passed a civil rights bill in 1866 to protect the fragile rights of African Americans and extended for two more years the Freedmen's Bureau, an agency providing emergency assistance at the end of the war. Johnson vetoed both bills and called his congressional opponents "traitors." His actions drove moderates into the radical camp, and Congress passed both bills over his veto—both, however, watered down by weakening the power of enforcement. Southern courts regularly disallowed black testimony against

RECONSTRUCTION AMENDMENTS

Constitutional Seeds of Dreams Deferred for 100 Years (or More)

What three fundamental rights were guaranteed by these three amendments? What patterns do you see? How well were the dreams of the freedmen and women fulfilled?

Substance	Outcome of Ratification Process	Final Implementation and Enforcement
Thirteenth Amendment—Passed by Congress January 1865		
Prohibited slavery in the United States	Ratified by 27 states, including 8 southern states, by December 1865	Immediate, although economic freedom came by degrees
Fourteenth Amendment—Passed by Congress June 1866		
(1) Defined equal national citizenship; (2) reduced state representation in Congress proportional to number of disfranchised voters; (3) denied former Confederates the right to hold office; (4) Confederate debts and lost property claims voided and illegal	Rejected by 12 southern and border states by February 1867; Congress made readmission depend on ratification; ratified in July 1868	Civil Rights Act of 1964
Fifteenth Amendment—Passed by Congress February 1869		
Prohibited denial of vote because of race, color, or previous servitude (but not sex)	Ratification by Virginia, Texas, Mississippi, and Georgia required for readmission; ratified in March 1870	Voting Rights Act of 1965

Note: See exact wording in U.S. Constitution in the Appendix.

whites, acquitted whites of violence, and sentenced blacks to compulsory labor.

In such a climate, southern racial violence erupted. In a typical outbreak, in May 1866, white mobs in Memphis, encouraged by local police and a newspaper that urged the mob to "go ahead and kill the last damned one of the nigger race," rampaged for over 40 hours, killing, beating, robbing, and raping virtually helpless black residents and burning houses, schools, and churches. Forty-eight people, all but two of them black, died. The local Union army commander took his time restoring order, arguing that his troops "hated Negroes too." A congressional inquiry concluded that Memphis blacks had "no protection from the law whatever."

A month later, Congress sent to the states for ratification the Fourteenth Amendment, the single most significant act of the Reconstruction era. The first section of the amendment promised permanent constitutional protection of the civil rights of blacks by defining them as citizens. States were prohibited from depriving "any person of life, liberty, or property, without due process of law," and citizens were guaranteed the "equal protection of the laws." Section 2 granted black male suffrage in the South, inserting the word "male" into the Constitution for the first time, and said states denying the black vote would have their representation reduced. Other sections of the amendment barred leaders of the Confederacy from national or state offices (except by act of Congress), repudiated the Confederate debt, and denied claims of compensation to former slave owners. Johnson urged the southern states to reject the Fourteenth Amendment, and 10 immediately did so.

The Fourteenth Amendment was the central issue of the 1866 midterm election. Johnson barnstormed the country asking voters to throw out the "radical" Republicans and trading insults with hecklers. Democrats north and south appealed openly to racial prejudice in charging that the Fourteenth Amendment would "Africanize" America, threatening both the marketplace and the bedroom. Republicans responded by attacking Johnson personally, waving the "bloody shirt" to remind voters of Democrats' treason during the civil war. Self-interest and local issues moved voters more than fiery speeches, and Republicans won an overwhelming victory. The mandate was clear: presidential Reconstruction had not worked, and Congress could present its own.

Early in 1867, Congress passed three Reconstruction acts. The southern states were divided into five military districts, whose commanders had broad powers to maintain order and protect civil and property rights. Congress also defined a new process for readmitting a state. Qualified voters—including blacks and excluding unreconstructed rebels—would elect delegates to state constitutional conventions that would write new constitutions guaranteeing black suffrage. After the new voters of the states had ratified these constitutions, elections would be held to choose governors and state legislatures. When a state ratified the Fourteenth Amendment, its representatives to Congress would be accepted, completing readmission to the Union.

The President Impeached

Congress also restricted presidential powers and established legislative dominance over the executive branch. The Tenure of Office Act, designed to prevent Johnson from firing the outspoken Secretary of War Edwin Stanton, limited the president's appointment powers. Other measures trimmed his powers as commander in chief.

Johnson responded exactly as congressional Republicans had anticipated. He vetoed the Reconstruction acts, hindered the work of Freedmen's Bureau agents, limited the activities of military commanders in the South, and removed cabinet officers and other officials sympathetic to Congress. The House Judiciary Committee charged the president with "usurpations of power" and of acting in the "interests of the great criminals" who had led the rebellion. But moderate House Republicans defeated the impeachment resolutions.

In August 1867, Johnson dismissed Stanton and asked for Senate consent. When the Senate refused, the president ordered Stanton to surrender his office, which he refused, barricading himself inside. The House quickly approved impeachment resolutions, charging the president with "high crimes and misdemeanors." The three-month trial in the Senate early in 1868 was similar to the trial of President Bill Clinton 130 years later in that evidence was skimpy that Johnson, like Clinton, had committed any constitutional crime justifying his removal. With seven moderate Republicans joining Democrats against conviction, the effort to find the president guilty fell one vote short of the required two-thirds majority. Not until the late twentieth century (Nixon and Clinton) would an American president face removal from office through impeachment.

Moderate Republicans were fearful that by removing Johnson, they might get Ohio senator Benjamin Wade, a leading radical Republican, as president. Wade had endorsed woman suffrage, rights for labor unions, and civil rights for African Americans. As moderate Republicans gained strength in 1868 through their support of the eventual presidential election winner, Ulysses S. Grant, radicalism lost most of its power within Republican ranks.

What Congressional Moderation Meant for Rebels, Blacks, and Women

Congress's political battle against the president was not matched by a principled resolve on behalf of the freedpeople. State and local elections of 1867 showed that voters preferred moderate Reconstruction policies. It is important to look not only at what Congress did during Reconstruction but also at what it did not do.

With the exception of Jefferson Davis, Congress did not imprison rebel Confederate leaders, and only one person, the commander of the infamous Andersonville prison camp, was executed. Congress did not insist on a long probation before southern states could be readmitted to the Union. It did not reorganize southern local governments. It did not mandate a national program of education for freedpeople. It did not confiscate and redistribute land to the freedmen. It did not, except indirectly and with great reluctance, provide economic help to black citizens.

Congress did, however, grant citizenship and suffrage to freedmen, but not to freedwomen. But Northerners were no more prepared than southerners to make all African Americans fully equal citizens. Between 1865 and 1869, voters in seven northern states turned down referendums proposing black (male) suffrage. Such proposals gained support in the North only after the election of 1868, when General Grant, the supposedly invincible military hero, barely won the popular vote in several states. Republicans needed black votes, so in 1870, Congressional Republicans, who had twice rejected a constitutional suffrage amendment, finally passed the Fifteenth Amendment, forbidding all states to deny the vote "on account of race, color, or previous condition of servitude." A Pittsburgh black preacher observed, "the Republican party had done the Negro good, but they were doing themselves good at the same time."

One casualty of the Fourteenth and Fifteenth Amendments was the goodwill of women who had worked for their suffrage for two decades. They had hoped that male legislators would recognize their wartime service in support of the Union and were shocked that black males got the vote but not loyal white (or black) women. Elizabeth Cady Stanton and Susan B. Anthony, veteran suffragists and opponents of slavery, opposed the Amendments, breaking with abolitionist allies such as Frederick Douglass, who had long supported woman suffrage yet declared that this was "the Negro's hour." Anthony vowed to "cut off this right arm of mine before I will ever work for or demand the ballot for the Negro and not the woman."

Disappointment over the suffrage issue helped split the women's movement in 1869. Anthony and Stanton continued their fight for a national amendment for woman suffrage and a long list of property, educational, and sexual rights, while other women focused on securing the vote state by state. Abandoned by radical and moderate men alike, women had few champions in Congress and their efforts were put off for half a century.

Congress compromised the rights of African Americans as well as women. It gave blacks the vote but not land, the opposite of what they preferred. Almost alone, Thaddeus Stevens argued that "forty acres...and a hut would be more valuable...than the...right to vote." But Congress never seriously considered his plan to divide the land of the "chief rebels" into 40-acre plots for freedmen. Congress did pass the Southern Homestead Act of 1866, making public lands available to blacks and loyal whites in five southern states. But the land was poor and inaccessible; no tools or seed were provided; and most blacks were bound by contracts that prevented them from making claims before the deadline. Only about 4,000 African American families even applied for the Homestead Act lands, and fewer than 20 percent of them saw their claims completed. White claimants did little better.

The Lives of Freedpeople

Union army major George Reynolds boasted late in 1865 that in the area of Mississippi under his command, he had "kept the negroes at work, and in a good state of discipline." Clinton Fisk, a well-meaning white who helped found a black college in Tennessee, told freedmen in 1866 that they could be "as free and as happy" working again for their "old master...as any where else in the world." Such pronouncements reminded blacks of white preachers' exhortations during slavery to work hard and obey their masters. Ironically, Fisk and Reynolds were agents of the Freedmen's Bureau, the agency intended to aid the black transition from slavery to freedom.

The Freedmen's Bureau

Never in American history has one small agency—underfinanced, understaffed, and undersupported—been given a harder task than the Bureau of Freedmen, Refugees and Abandoned Lands. Controlling less than 1 percent of southern lands, the Bureau's name is telling; its fate epitomizes Reconstruction.

The Freedmen's Bureau performed many essential services. It issued emergency food rations, clothed and sheltered homeless victims of the war, and established medical and hospital facilities. It provided funds to relocate thousands of freedpeople. It helped blacks search for relatives and get legally married. It represented African Americans in local civil courts to ensure that they got fair trials. Working with northern missionary aid societies and southern black churches, the

Bureau became responsible for an extensive education program, and by 1870 there were almost 250,000 pupils in 4,329 agency schools.

The Bureau's largest task was to promote African Americans' economic well-being. This included settling blacks on abandoned lands and getting them started with tools, seed, and draft animals, as well as arranging work contracts with white landowners. But the Freedmen's Bureau, determined not to instill a new dependency, more often than not supported the needs of white landowners to find cheap labor than of blacks to become independent farmers.

Although a few agents were idealistic northerners eager to help freedpeople adjust to freedom, most were Union army officers more concerned with social order than social transformation. Working in a postwar climate of resentment and violence, Freedmen's Bureau agents were overworked, underpaid, spread too thin (at its peak only 900 agents were scattered across 11 states), and constantly harassed by local whites. Even the best-intentioned agents would have agreed with General Howard's belief in the nineteenth-century American values of self-help, minimal government interference in the marketplace, the sanctity of private property, contractual obligations, and white superiority.

On a typical day, overburdened agents would visit local courts and schools, file reports, supervise the signing of work contracts, and handle numerous complaints, most involving contract violations between whites and blacks or property and domestic disputes among blacks. A Georgia agent wrote that he was "*tired out* and *broke down. . . .* Every day for 6 months, day after day, I have had from 5 to 20 complaints, *generally trivial* and of no moment." To find work for freedmen, agents often sided with white landowners by telling blacks to obey orders, trust employers, and accept disadvantageous contracts. One agent sent a man who had complained of a severe beating back to work with the advice, "Don't be sassy [and] don't be lazy when you've got work to do."

Despite numerous constraints, the agents accomplished much. In little more than two years, the Freedmen's Bureau issued 20 million rations (nearly one-third to poor whites); reunited families and resettled some 30,000 displaced war refugees; treated some 450,000 people for illness and injury; built 40 hospitals and more than 4,000 schools; provided books, tools, and even some land, to the freedmen; and occasionally protected their civil rights. The great African American historian and leading black intellectual W. E. B. Du Bois wrote, "In a time of perfect calm, amid willing neighbors and streaming wealth," it "would have been a herculean task" for the Bureau to fulfill its many purposes. But in the midst of hunger, hate, sorrow, suspicion, and cruelty, "the work of . . . social regeneration was in large part foredoomed to failure."

But Du Bois also recognized that in laying the foundation for black labor, future land ownership, a public school system, and recognition before courts of law, the Freedmen's Bureau was "successful beyond the dreams of thoughtful men."

Economic Freedom by Degrees

Despite the best efforts of the Freedmen's Bureau, the failure of Congress to provide the promised 40 acres and a mule forced freedpeople into a new economic dependency on former masters. Blacks made some progress, however, in degrees of economic autonomy and were partly responsible, along with international economic developments, in forcing the white planter class into making major changes in southern agriculture.

First, a land-intensive system replaced the labor intensity of slavery. Land ownership was concentrated into fewer and even larger holdings than before the war. From South Carolina to Louisiana, the wealthiest tenth of the population owned about 60 percent of the real estate in the 1870s. Second, these large planters increasingly concentrated on one crop, usually cotton, and were tied into the international market. This resulted in a steady drop in food production. Third, one-crop farming created a new credit—and dependency—system whereby most farmers, black and white, rented land, seed, farm implements, provisions, and housing from local merchants.

This new system took a few years to develop after emancipation. At first, most African Americans signed contracts with white landowners and worked fields in gangs very much as during slavery. Supervised by superintendents who still used the lash, all members of the family had to toil from sunrise to sunset for meager wages and a monthly allotment of bacon and meal. Many freedpeople resented this new semiservitude, refused to sign the contracts, and sought independence working the land themselves. A South Carolina freedman said, "If I can't own de land, I'll hire or lease land, but I won't contract."

Many blacks, therefore, broke contracts, ran away, haggled over wages, engaged in work slowdowns, burned barns, and sought other means of negotiation to get away from the contract system. In the Sea Islands and rice-growing regions of coastal South Carolina and Georgia, resistance was especially strong. The freedmen "refuse work at any price," a bureau agent reported, and the women "wish to stay in the house or the garden all the time." Insisting on "no more outdoor work," they also wanted to send their children to school rather than to the fields and apprenticeships.

Blacks' insistence on autonomy and land of their own forced a change from the contract system to tenancy and sharecropping. Families would hitch mules to

A Freedman's Work Contract

As you read this rather typical work contract defining the first economic relationship between whites and blacks in the early months of the postwar period, note the regulation of social behavior and deportment, as well as work and "pay" arrangements. How different is this from slavery? As a freedman or freedwoman, would you have signed such an agreement? Why or why not? What options would you have had?

State of South Carolina
Darlington District
Articles of Agreement

This Agreement entered into between Mrs. Adele Allston Exect of the one part, and the Freedmen and Women of The Upper Quarters plantation of the other part Witnesseth:

That the latter agree, for the remainder of the present year, to reside upon and devote their labor to the cultivation of the Plantation of the former. And they further agree, that they will in all respects, conform to such reasonable and necessary plantation rules and regulations as Mrs. Allston's Agent may prescribe; that they will not keep any gun, pistol, or other offensive weapon, or leave the plantation without permission from their employer; that in all things connected with their duties as laborers on said plantation, they will yield prompt obedience to all orders from Mrs. Allston or his *[sic]* agent; that they will be orderly and quiet in their conduct, avoiding drunkeness and other gross vices; that they will not misuse any of the Plantation Tools, or Agricultural Implements, or any Animals entrusted to their care, or any Boats, Flats, Carts or Wagons; that they will give up at the expiration of this Contract, all Tools & c., belonging to the Plantation, and in case any property, of any description belonging to the Plantation shall be willfully or through negligence destroyed or injured, the value of the Articles so destroyed, shall be deducted from the portion of the Crops which the person or persons, so offending, shall be entitled to receive under this Contract.

Any deviations from the condition of the foregoing Contract may, upon sufficient proof, be punished with dismissal from the Plantation, or in such other manner as may be determined by the Provost Court; and the person or persons so dismissed, shall forfeit the whole, or a part of his, her or their portion of the crop, as the Court may decide.

In consideration of the foregoing Services duly performed, Mrs. Allston agrees, after deducting Seventy five bushels of Corn for each work Animal, exclusively used in cultivating the Crops for the present year; to turn over to the said Freedmen and Women, one half of the remaining Corn, Peas, Potatoes, made this season. He *[sic]* further agrees to furnish the usual rations until the Contract is performed.

All Cotton Seed Produced on the Plantation is to be reserved for the use of the Plantation. The Freedmen, Women and Children are to be treated in a manner consistent with their freedom. Necessary medical attention will be furnished as heretofore.

Any deviation from the conditions of this Contract upon the part of the said Mrs. Allston or her Agent or Agents shall be punished in such manner as may be determined by a Provost Court, or a Military Commission. This agreement to continue till the first day of January 1866.

Witness our hand at The Upper Quarters this 28th day of July 1865.

their old slave cabin and drag it to their plot, as far from the Big House as possible. Sharecroppers received seed, fertilizer, implements, food, and clothing. In return, the landlord (or a local merchant) told them what and how much to grow, and he took a share—usually half—of the harvest. The croppers' half usually went to pay for goods bought on credit from the landlord. Thus, sharecroppers remained tied to the land.

Tenant farmers had only slightly more independence. Before a harvest, they promised to sell their crop to a local merchant in return for renting land, tools, and other necessities. From the merchant's store they also had to buy goods on credit (at higher prices than whites paid) against the harvest. At "settling up" time, income from sale of the crop was compared to accumulated debts. It was possible, especially after an unusually bountiful season, to come out ahead and eventually to own one's own land. But tenants rarely did; in debt at the end of each year, they had to pledge the next year's crop. With world cotton prices low, big landowners generated profits through large-scale operations, and their tenants rarely made much money. If tenants were able to pay their debts, landowners frequently altered loan agreements. Thus, debt peonage replaced slavery, ensuring a continuing cheap labor supply to grow cotton and other staples.

Despite this bleak picture, painstaking, industrious work by African Americans helped many to accumulate a measure of income, personal property, and autonomy, especially in the household economy of producing eggs, butter, meat, food crops, and other staples. Debt did not necessarily mean a lack of subsistence living. In Virginia the declining tobacco crop forced white planters to sell off small parcels of land to blacks. Throughout the

Sharecroppers and tenant farmers, though more autonomous than contract gang laborers, remained dependent on the landlord for their survival. Yet how different is this from the photograph at the top of p. 390? What are the differences, and how do you explain the change?

(Brown Brothers)

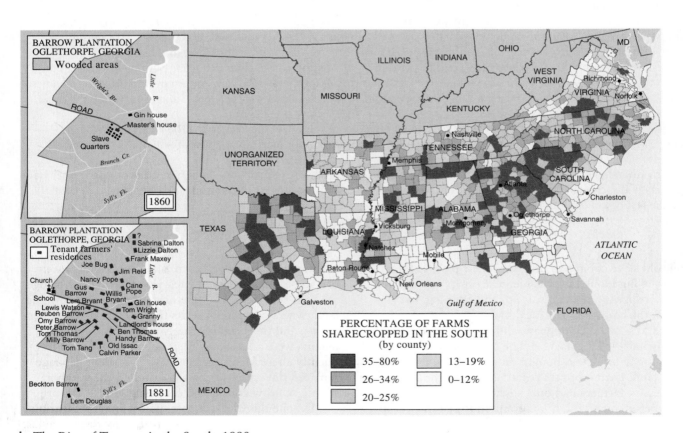

The Rise of Tenancy in the South, 1880

Although no longer slaves and after resisting labor contracts and the gang system of field labor, the freedpeople (as well as many poor whites) became tenant farmers, working on shares in the New South. The former slaves on the Barrow plantation in Georgia, for example, moved their households to individual 25-to 30-acre tenant farms, which they rented from the Barrow family in annual contracts requiring payment in cotton and other cash crops. Where was the highest percentage of tenant farms, and how do you explain it? How would you explain the low-percentage areas? What do you notice about how circumstances have changed—and not changed—on the Barrow plantation?

South, a few African Americans became independent landowners—about 3–4 percent by 1880, but closer to 25 percent by 1900.

White Farmers

Changes in southern agriculture affected yeoman and poor white farmers as well, and planters worried about a coalition between poor black and white farmers. As a white Georgia farmer said in 1865, "We should tuk the land, as we did the niggers, and split it, and giv part to the niggers and part to me and t'other Union fellers." But confiscation and redistribution of land was no more likely for white farmers than for blacks. Whites, too, had to concentrate on growing staples, pledging their crops against high-interest credit, and facing perpetual indebtedness. In the upcountry piedmont area of Georgia, for example, the number of whites working their own land dropped from nine in ten before the Civil War to seven in ten by 1880, while cotton production doubled.

Reliance on cotton meant fewer food crops and therefore greater dependence on merchants for provisions. In 1884, Jephta Dickson of Jackson County, Georgia, purchased more than $50 worth of flour, meal, meat, syrup, peas, and corn from a local store; 25 years earlier he had been almost completely self-sufficient. Fencing laws seriously curtailed the livelihood of poor whites raising pigs and hogs, and restrictions on hunting and fishing reduced the ability of poor whites and blacks alike to supplement incomes and diets.

In the worn-out flatlands and barren mountainous regions of the South, poor whites' antebellum poverty, health, and isolation worsened after the war. A Freedmen's Bureau agent in South Carolina described the poor whites in his area as "gaunt and ragged, ungainly, stooping and clumsy in build." They lived a marginal existence, hunting, fishing, and growing corn and potato crops that, as a North Carolinian put it, "come up puny, grow puny, and mature puny." Many poor white farmers, in fact, were even less productive than black sharecroppers. Some became farmhands at $6 a month (with board). Others fled to low-paying jobs in cotton mills, where they would not have to compete against blacks.

The cultural life of poor southern whites reflected both their lowly position and their pride. Their emotional religion centered on camp meeting religious revivals where, in backwoods clearings, men and women praised God, told tall tales of superhuman feats, and exchanged folk remedies for poor health. Their ballads and folklore told of debt, chain gangs, and deeds of drinking prowess. Their quilt making and house construction reflected a marginal culture in which everything was saved and reused.

In part because their lives were so hard, poor whites clung to their belief in white superiority. Many joined the Ku Klux Klan (founded by six Confederate veterans) and other southern white terrorist groups that emerged between 1866 and 1868. A federal officer reported, "The poorer classes of white people...have a most intense hatred of the Negro." Actually populated by a cross-section of southern white classes, the Klan expressed its hatred in midnight raids on teachers in black schools, laborers who disputed their landlords' discipline, Republican voters, and any black whose "impudence" caused him not to "bow and scrape to a white man, as was done formerly."

Black Self-Help Institutions

Victimized by Klan intimidation and violence, African Americans found their hopes and dreams thwarted. A Texan, Felix Haywood, recalled: "We thought we was goin' to be richer than white folks, 'cause we was stronger and knowed how to work....But it didn't turn out that way. We soon found out that freedom could make folks proud but it didn't make 'em rich." It was clear to many black leaders, therefore, that because white institutions could not fulfill the promises of emancipation, blacks would have to do it themselves.

Traditions of black community self-help survived in the organized churches and schools of the antebellum free Negro communities and in the "invisible" cultural institutions of the slave quarters. After the Civil War, the membership in African American churches exploded. The Negro Baptist Church grew from 150,000 members in 1850 to 500,000 in 1870, while the membership of the African Methodist Episcopal Church increased fourfold in the postwar decade, from 100,000 to more than 400,000 members. Similar growth occurred in the Reformed Zion Union Apostolic and other churches.

African American ministers continued to exert community leadership. Many led efforts to oppose discrimination, some by entering politics: more than one-fifth of the black officeholders in South Carolina were ministers. As preachers, however, they focused on sin, salvation, and revivalist enthusiasm. An English visitor in 1867–1868 noted the intensity of black "devoutness." As one woman explained: "We make noise 'bout ebery ting....I want ter go ter Heaben in de good ole way."

The freedpeople's desire for education was as strong as for religion. A school official in Virginia said that the freedmen were "down right crazy to learn"; another said that blacks were "determined to be self-taught." At first, most teachers were northern "schoolmarms." One Yankee teacher, Esther Douglass, found "120 dirty, half naked, perfectly wild black children" in her schoolroom near Savannah. After eight months she reported, "their progress was wonderful"; they

Along with land of their own and equal civil rights, what freedpeople wanted most was education. What do you see in the faces (and dress) of these school children? Why was education so important? What obstacles were in the way?

(Valentine Museum, Richmond, Virginia)

could read, sing hymns, and repeat Bible verses. Such glowing reports waned as white (and black) teachers grew frustrated with crowded facilities, limited resources, white opposition, and high absenteeism caused by fieldwork. In Georgia, for example, only 5 percent of black children went to school for part of any one year between 1865 and 1870, as opposed to 20 percent of white children.

Blacks increasingly preferred their own teachers, and assumed more responsibility for the costs of schooling. By 1868, 43 percent of Freedmen's Bureau teachers were black, and in Louisiana and Kentucky blacks contributed more to education than the Bureau itself. Moreover, black teachers were consistently positive. Charlotte Forten, who taught in the Sea Islands, noted that even after a half day's "hard toil" in the fields, her older pupils were "as bright and as anxious to learn as ever." Despite the taunting insults of "the haughty Anglo-Saxon race," she said, blacks showed "a desire for knowledge, and a capability for attaining it." To train teachers such as Forten, northern philanthropists founded Fisk, Howard, Atlanta, and other black universities in the South between 1865 and 1867.

By 1870 there was a 20 percent gain in black adult literacy, a figure that, against difficult odds, would

continue to grow for all ages to the end of the century, when more than 1.5 million black children attended schools with 28,560 black teachers. African American schools, like churches, became community centers. They published newspapers, provided training in trades and farming, and promoted political participation and land ownership with increasingly scientific methods of farming. These efforts made black schools objects of local white hostility. A Virginia freedman told a congressional committee that in his county, anyone starting a school would be killed. In 1869, in Tennessee alone, 37 black schools were burned to the ground.

White opposition to black education and land ownership stimulated African American nationalism and separatism. In the late 1860s, Benjamin "Pap" Singleton, a former Tennessee slave, urged freedpeople to abandon politics and migrate westward. He organized a land company, purchased public property in Kansas, and in the early 1870s took several groups from Tennessee and Kentucky to establish separate black towns in the prairie state. In following years, thousands of "exodusters" from the Lower South bought some 10,000 infertile acres in Kansas. But natural and human obstacles to self-sufficiency often proved insurmountable. By the 1880s, despairing of ever finding economic independence in the United States, Singleton and other nationalists advocated emigration to Canada and Liberia. Other black leaders such as Frederick Douglass continued to press for full citizenship rights within the United States.

Reconstruction in the Southern States

Douglass's confidence in the power of the ballot seemed warranted in the enthusiastic early months under the Reconstruction Acts of 1867. With President Johnson neutralized, the Republican congressional program finally prevailed. Local Republicans, taking advantage of the inability or refusal of many southern whites to vote, overwhelmingly elected their delegates to state constitutional conventions in the fall of 1867. Guardedly optimistic and sensing the "sacred importance" of their work, black and white Republicans began creating new state governments.

Republican Rule

Contrary to early twentieth-century pro-southern historians, the southern state governments under Republican rule were not dominated by illiterate black majorities intent on "Africanizing" the South. Nor were these governments unusually corrupt or extravagant, nor did they use massive numbers of federal troops to enforce their will. By 1869, only 1,100 federal soldiers remained in Virginia, and most federal troops in Texas were guarding the frontier against Mexico and hostile Native Americans. Lacking strong military backing, the new state governments would face increasingly violent harassment.

Diverse coalitions made up the new governments elected under congressional Reconstruction. These "black and tan" governments (as opponents called them) were actually predominantly white, except for the lower house of the South Carolina legislature. Many of the new leaders were local people interested more in economic growth and sectional reconciliation than in radical social reforms. A second group consisted of northern Republican capitalists who headed south to invest in land, railroads, and new industries. Others included Union veterans, missionaries, and teachers inspired to work in Freedmen's Bureau schools. Such people were unfairly labeled "carpetbaggers."

Moderate African Americans made up a third group in the Republican state governments. A large percentage of black officeholders were well-educated preachers, teachers, and soldiers from the North. Others were self-educated southern black tradesmen and landowners. In South Carolina, of some 255 black state and federal officials elected between 1868 and 1876, only 15 percent owned no property. This class composition meant that black leaders often supported policies that largely ignored the land redistribution needs of the black masses. African American leaders reminded whites that they too were southerners, seeking only, as an 1865 petition put it, that "the same laws which govern white men shall govern black men…in equity and justice."

The primary accomplishment of Republican rule in the South was to eliminate undemocratic features from prewar state constitutions. All returning states provided universal male suffrage and loosened requirements for holding office. Laws were enacted ending imprisonment for debt, shortening the list of crimes punishable by death, relieving poverty, and caring for

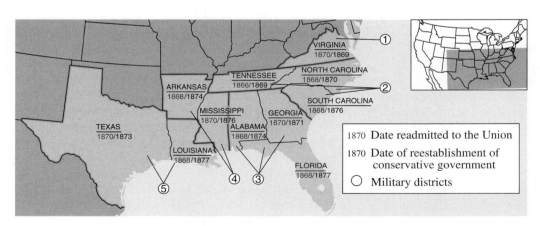

The Return of Conservative Democratic Control in Southern States During Reconstruction

Note that the duration of Republican governments in power to implement even moderate Reconstruction programs varied from state to state. In North Carolina and Georgia, for example, Republican rule was very brief, while in Virginia it never took place at all. "Redemption," the return of conservative control, took longest in three Deep South states. How would you explain these variations among the southern states?

the disabled. Many southern states passed laws granting property rights to married women.

Republican governments also reconstructed the South financially by overhauling tax systems and approving generous railroad and other capital investment bonds. Harbors, roads, and bridges were rebuilt; hospitals and asylums were established; and the South's first public school system was created. Although these schools were largely segregated, for the first time, rich and poor, black and white alike had access to education. By the 1880s, school attendance increased from 5 percent to more than 40 percent for blacks and from 20 percent to more than 60 percent for whites.

These modernizing achievements came in the face of strong opposition. A convention of Louisiana planters labeled the Republican leaders the "lowest and most corrupt body of men ever assembled in the South." There was some corruption, mostly in land sales, railway bonds, and construction contracts. But this was similar to corruption in postwar northern politics.

Despite—or perhaps because of—the modest black role in southern state governments, which Du Bois described as "negro honesty, knowledge, and efficiency," Republican rule was short-lived. It lasted longest in the Deep South, where the black population was equal to or greater than the white. In Virginia, Republicans ruled hardly at all. In South Carolina, African American leaders' unwillingness to use their power to help black laborers contributed to their loss of political control. In Alabama a flood of northern capital created a new industrial and merchant class to rival the old planter aristocracy. And in Louisiana, class divisions among blacks and white paramilitary violence, which led to the killing of 60 blacks at Colfax in 1873, without judicial consequences, seriously weakened the Republican regime.

Violence and "Redemption"

The primary reason for the return of Democrats to power in southern states was the widespread use of violence. A Mississippi paper said, "We must render this either a white man's government, or convert the land into a Negro man's cemetery." The Ku Klux Klan was only one of several secret terrorist organizations that forcibly drove black and white Republicans from office. Although violence was pervasive throughout the South, North Carolina and Mississippi typified the pattern.

After losing a close election in North Carolina in 1868, conservatives waged a concentrated campaign of terror in several areas of strong Unionist support. If the Democrats could win these counties in 1870, they would most likely win statewide. Before the election, several prominent Republicans were killed, including a white state senator, whose throat was cut, and a leading black Union League organizer, who was hanged in the courthouse square with a sign pinned to his breast: "Bewar, ye guilty, both white and black." Scores of citizens were flogged, fired from their jobs, or driven in the middle of the night from burning homes and barns. Courts consistently refused to prosecute anyone for these crimes, which local papers blamed on "disgusting negroes and white Radicals." The violence worked. In the election of 1870, some 12,000 fewer Republicans voted in the two crucial counties than had voted two years earlier, and the Democrats swept back into power.

In Mississippi's state election in 1875, Democrats used similar tactics, including death threats, in what became known as the "Mississippi Plan." Local Democratic clubs formed armed militias, marching defiantly through black areas, breaking up Republican meetings, and provoking riots to justify killing hundreds. Armed men posted during voter registration intimidated Republicans. At the election itself, voters were either "helped" by gun-toting whites to cast a Democratic ballot, or chased away by clubs. Counties that had given Republican majorities in the thousands managed a total of less than a dozen votes in 1875.

Congress and President Grant did not totally ignore southern violence. Three Force Acts, passed in 1870 and 1871, had given the president strong powers to protect voters from force or fraud, but were rarely used. A Ku Klux Klan Act had declared secret organizations using disguise and coercion to deprive others of equal protection of the laws illegal, and Congress created a joint committee to investigate Klan violence. Its 1872 report had filled 13 huge volumes with horrifying testimony. Grant sent messages to Congress proclaiming the right to vote, and dispatched troops to South Carolina, but not to Mississippi, to stop violence against black Republicans.

Calling their victory "redemption," conservative Democrats resumed control of each state government. Reconstruction ended by a combination of persistent white southern resistance, violence and coercion, and a failure of northern will. As Albion Tourgée wrote, in his Reconstruction-era novel, "The spirit of the dead Confederacy was stronger than the mandate of the nation to which it had succumbed in battle."

Northern Republicans lost interest in defending African Americans, and realized that they could keep political power without black votes. In 1875, Grant's advisers told him that Republicans might lose an important Ohio election unless he rejected appeals by Mississippi blacks for troops to guarantee free elections. He did so, saying that he and the nation "had tired of these annual autumnal outbreaks." The success of the Democrats' Mississippi Plan in 1875, repeated a year later in South Carolina and Louisiana, indicated that congressional reports and acts and presidential proclamations did little to stop the reign of

Recovering the Past

NOVELS

We read novels and other forms of fiction for pleasure, that is, for the enjoyment of plot, character development, style, symbolism, and timeless themes. "Classic" novels such as *Moby Dick, Huckleberry Finn, The Great Gatsby, The Invisible Man,* and *Beloved* explore enduring questions of good and evil, of innocence and knowledge, of noble dreams fulfilled and shattered. We enjoy novels because we often find ourselves identifying with one of the major characters. Through that person's struggles, triumphs, relationships, and search for identity, we gain insights about our own.

Even though they may be historically untrue, we can also read novels as social history, for they reveal much about the attitudes, dreams, fears, and ordinary, everyday experiences of human beings in a particular period. They show how people responded to the major events of that era. The novelist, like the historian, is a product of time and place and has an interpretive point of view. Consider the two novels about Reconstruction quoted here. Neither is reputed for great literary merit, yet both reveal much about the impassioned attitudes of the post–Civil War era. *A Fool's Errand* was written by Albion Tourgée, a northerner, while *The Clansman* was written by Thomas Dixon, Jr., a southerner.

Tourgée was a young northern teacher and lawyer who fought with the Union army and moved to North Carolina after the war to begin a legal career. He became a judge and was an active Republican, supporting black suffrage and helping to shape the new state constitution. Because he boldly criticized the Ku Klux Klan for its campaign of terror against blacks, his life was threatened many times. When he left North Carolina in 1879, he published an autobiographical novel about his experiences as a judge challenging Klan violence against the freedpeople.

The "fool's errand" in the novel is that of the northern veteran Comfort Servosse, who, like Tourgée, seeks to fulfill humane goals on behalf of both blacks and whites in post–Civil War North Carolina. His efforts are thwarted, however, by threats, intimidation, a campaign of violent "outrages" against Republican leaders in the county, and a lack of support from Congress. Historians have verified the accuracy of many of the events in Tourgée's novel. While exposing the brutality of the Klan, Tourgée features loyal southern Unionists, respectable planters ashamed of Klan violence, and even guilt-ridden, poor white Klansmen who try to protect or warn intended victims.

In the year of Tourgée's death, 1905, another North Carolinian published a novel with a very different account of Reconstruction. Thomas Dixon, Jr., was a lawyer, North Carolina state legislator, Baptist minister, pro-Klan lecturer, and novelist. *The Clansman,* subtitled *A Historical Romance of the Ku Klux Klan,* reflects turn-of-the-century attitudes most white southerners still had about Republican rule during Reconstruction. According to Dixon, once the "Great Heart" Lincoln was gone, a power-crazed, vindictive, radical Congress, led by scheming Austin Stoneman (Thaddeus Stevens), sought to impose corrupt carpetbagger and brutal black rule on a helpless South. Only through the inspired leadership and redemptive role of the Ku Klux Klan was the South saved from the horrors of rape and revenge.

Dixon dedicated *The Clansman* to his uncle, who was a Grand Titan of the Klan in North Carolina during the time when two crucial counties were being transformed from Republican to Democratic through intimidation and terror. No such violence shows up in Dixon's novel. When the novel was made the basis of D. W. Griffith's film classic *Birth of a Nation* in 1915, the novel's attitudes were firmly imprinted on the twentieth-century American mind.

Both novels convey Reconstruction attitudes toward the freedpeople. Both create clearly defined heroes and villains. Both include exciting chase scenes, narrow escapes, daring rescues, and tragic deaths. Both include romantic subplots. Yet the two novels are strikingly different.

Reflecting on the Past Even in these brief excerpts, what differences of style and attitude do you see in the descriptions of Uncle Jerry and Old Aleck? What emotional responses do you have to these passages? How do you think turn-of-the-twentieth-century Americans might have responded?

A FOOL'S ERRAND
ALBION TOURGÉE (1879)

When the second Christmas came, Metta wrote again to her sister:

"The feeling is terribly bitter against Comfort on account of his course towards the colored people. There is quite a village of them on the lower end of the plantation. They have a church, a sabbath school, and are to have next year a school. You can not imagine how kind they have been to us, and how much they are attached to Comfort....I got Comfort to go with me to one of their prayer-meetings a few nights ago. I had heard a great deal about them, but had never attended one before. It was strangely weird. There were, perhaps, fifty present, mostly middle-aged men and women. They were singing in a soft, low monotone, interspersed with prolonged exclamatory notes, a sort of rude hymn, which I was surprised to know was one of their old songs in slave times. How the chorus came to be endured in those days I can not imagine. It was

'Free! free! free, my Lord, free!
An' we walks de hebben-ly way!'

"A few looked around as we came in and seated our-selves; and Uncle Jerry, the saint of the settlement, came forward on his staves, and said, in his soft voice,

"'Ev'nin', Kunnel! Sarvant, Missus! Will you walk up, an' hev seats in front?'

"We told him we had just looked in, and might go in a short time; so we would stay in the back part of the audience.

"Uncle Jerry can not read nor write; but he is a man of strange intelligence and power. Unable to do work of any account, he is the faithful friend, monitor, and director of others. He has a house and piece of land, all paid for, a good horse and cow, and, with the aid of his wife and two boys, made a fine crop this season. He is one of the most promising colored men in the settlement: so Comfort says, at least. Everybody seems to have great respect for his character. I don't know how many people I have heard speak of his religion. Mr. Savage used to say he had rather hear him pray than any other man on earth. He was much prized by his master, even after he was disabled, on account of his faithfulness and character."

THE CLANSMAN   THOMAS DIXON, JR. (1905)

At noon Ben and Phil strolled to the polling-place to watch the progress of the first election under Negro rule. The Square was jammed with shouting, jostling, perspiring negroes, men, women, and children. The day was warm, and the African odour was supreme even in the open air. . . .

The negroes, under the drill of the League and the Freedmen's Bureau, protected by the bayonet, were voting to enfranchise themselves, disfranchise their former masters, ratify a new constitution, and elect a legislature to do their will. Old Aleck was a candidate for the House, chief poll-holder, and seemed to be in charge of the movements of the voters outside the booth as well as inside. He appeared to be omnipresent, and his self-importance was a sight Phil had never dreamed. He could not keep his eyes off him. . . .

[Aleck] was a born African orator, undoubtedly descended from a long line of savage spell-binders, whose eloquence in the palaver houses of the jungle had made them native leaders. His thin spindle-shanks supported an oblong, protruding stomach, resembling an elderly mon-key's, which seemed so heavy it swayed his back to carry it.

The animal vivacity of his small eyes and the flexibility of his eyebrows, which he worked up and down rapidly with every change of countenance, expressed his eager desires. . . .

He was already mellow with liquor, and was dressed in an old army uniform and cap, with two horse-pistols buck-led around his waist. On a strap hanging from his shoulder were strung a half-dozen tin canteens filled with whiskey.

---

terror against black and white Republicans throughout the South. Despite hundreds of arrests, all-white juries refused to find whites guilty of crimes against blacks. The U.S. Supreme Court backed them in two 1874 decisions throwing out cases against whites convicted of preventing blacks from voting and declaring key parts of the Force Acts unconstitutional. Officially the Klan's power ended, but the attitudes (and tactics) of Klansmen would continue long into the next century.

Shifting National Priorities

The American people in the North, like their leaders, were tired of battles over freedpeople. Frustrated with the difficulties of trying to transform an unwilling South, the easiest course was to give citizenship and the vote to African Americans, leaving them to fend for themselves. Americans of increasing ethnic diversity were primarily interested in starting families, finding work, and making money. Slovakian immigrants fired furnaces in Pittsburgh; Chinese men pounded in rail-road ties for the Central Pacific over the Sierra Nevada mountains and across the Nevada desert; Yankee women taught in one-room schoolhouses in Vermont for $23 a month; Mexican *vaqueros* drove Texas cattle herds to Kansas; and Scandinavian families battled heat, locusts, and exorbitant railroad rates on Dakota farmsteads.

American priorities had shifted at both the individual and national levels. Failing to effect a smooth transition from slavery to freedom for freedpeople, northern leaders focused their efforts on accelerating and solidifying their programs of economic growth and industrial and territorial expansion.

As North Carolina Klansmen convened in dark forests in North Carolina in 1869, the Central Pacific and Union Pacific railroads met in Utah, linking the Atlantic and Pacific. As southern cotton production revived, northern iron and steel manufacturing and western settlement of the mining, cattle, and agricultural

How "free" is this voter? In this cartoon, titled "Of course he wants to vote the Democratic Ticket," one of the two pistol-wielding men is saying: "You're as free as air, ain't you? Say you are, or I'll blow your black head off!" Note that another freedman is being led down the street to the polling place. Do you think he will also vote Democratic or for the party of Lincoln?

(CORBIS)

" The negroes of the South are free—free as air," says the parliamentary Watterson. This is what the *State*, a well-known Democratic organ of Tennessee, says, in huge capitals, on the subject : ' Let it be known before the election that the farmers have agreed to spot every leading Radical negro in the county, and rest him as an enemy for all time to come. The rotten ring must and shall be broken at any and all costs. The Democrats have determined to withdraw all employment from their enemies. Let this fact be known."

frontiers surged. As black farmers haggled over work contracts with landowners in Georgia, white workers organized the National Labor Union in Baltimore. As Elizabeth and Adele Allston demanded the keys to their crop barns in the summer of 1865, the Boston Labor Reform Association demanded that "our…education, morals, dwellings, and the whole Social System" needed to be "reconstructed." If the South would not be reconstructed, labor relations might be.

The years between 1865 and 1875 featured not only the rise (and fall) of Republican governments in the South but also a spectacular surge of working-class organizations. Stimulated by the Civil War to improve working conditions in northern factories, trade unions and labor reform associations flourished, culminating in the founding of the National Labor Union in 1866. By 1873, an estimated 300,000 to 500,000 American workers enrolled in some 1,500 trade unions, the largest such increase in the nineteenth century. This growth inevitably stirred class tensions. In 1876, hundreds of freedmen in the rice region along the Combahee River in South Carolina went on strike to protest a 40-cent-per-day wage cut, clashing with local sheriffs and white Democratic rifle clubs. A year later, also fighting wage cuts, thousands of northern railroad workers went out in a nationwide wave of strikes, clashing with police and the National Guard.

As economic relations in America changed, so did the Republican party, changing from a party of moral reform to material interest. In the ongoing struggle in American political values between "virtue and commerce," self-interest was again winning. Abandoning

the Freedmen's Bureau as an inappropriate federal expense, Republican politicians had no difficulty handing out huge grants of money and land to the railroads. As freedpeople were told to fend for themselves, the Union Pacific was given subsidies of between $16,000 and $48,000 for each mile of track it laid. As Susan B. Anthony and other suffragists tramped through the snows of upstate New York petitioning for the right to vote, Boss Tweed and other urban bosses defrauded New York taxpayers of millions of dollars. As Native Americans in the Great Plains struggled to preserve the sacred Black Hills from gold prospectors protected by U.S. soldiers, government officials in the East "mined" public treasuries.

By 1869, the year financier Jay Gould almost cornered the gold market, the nation was increasingly defined by its sordid, materialistic "go-getters." Henry Adams, descendant of two presidents, was living in Washington, D.C., at the time. As he explained in his 1907 autobiography *The Education of Henry Adams,* he had had high expectations in 1869 that Grant, like George Washington, would restore moral order and peace. But when Grant announced his cabinet, a group of army cronies and rich friends to whom he owed favors, Adams felt betrayed, charging that Grant's administration "outraged every rule of decency."

Honest himself, Grant showed poor judgment of others. The scandals of his administration touched his relatives, his cabinet, and two vice presidents. Outright graft, loose prosecution, and generally negligent administration flourished in a half dozen

The election of 1872 showed that the public was uninterested in reform. "Liberal" Republicans, disgusted with Grant, formed a third party calling for lower tariffs and fewer grants to railroads, civil service reform, and the removal of federal troops from the South. Their candidate, Horace Greeley, editor of the New York *Tribune,* was also nominated by the Democrats, whom he had spent much of his earlier career condemning. Despite his wretched record, Grant easily won a second term.

The End of Reconstruction

Soon after Grant's second inauguration, a financial panic, caused by railroad mismanagement and the collapse of some eastern banks, started a terrible depression that lasted throughout the mid-1870s. In these hard times, economic issues dominated politics, further diverting attention from southern blacks. As Democrats took control of the House of Representatives in 1874 and looked toward winning the White House in 1876, politicians talked about the latest Grant scandals, the currency, and tariffs, but no one said much about freedpeople. In 1875, Congress passed a civil rights bill but it was not enforced, and in 1883 the Supreme Court declared it unconstitutional. Congressional Reconstruction, long dormant, was over.

The election of 1876, closest in American history until 2000, sealed the end. Republicans nominated a former governor of Ohio, Rutherford B. Hayes, partly because of his reputation for honesty, partly because he had been a Union officer (a necessity for post–Civil War candidates), and partly because, as Henry Adams put it, he was "obnoxious to no one." The Democrats chose Governor Samuel J. Tilden of New York, a civil service reformer who had broken the corrupt Tweed ring.

Like Al Gore in 2000, Tilden won a popular-vote majority and appeared to have enough electoral votes (184 to 165) for victory—except for 20 disputed votes, all but one in three Deep South states (one of them Florida) where Republicans still controlled the voting apparatus despite Democratic intimidation. To settle the dispute, Congress created a commission of eight Republicans and seven Democrats who voted along party lines to give Hayes all 20 votes and a narrow electoral-college victory, 185 to 184.

Outraged Democrats protested the outcome and threatened to prevent Hayes's inauguration. There was talk of a new civil war. But unlike the 1850s, a North–South compromise emerged. Northern investors wanted the government to subsidize a New Orleans-to-California railroad. Southerners wanted northern dollars but not northern political influence—no social agencies, no federal enforcement of the Fourteenth and Fifteenth Amendments, and no military occupation, not even the symbolic presence left in 1876.

Under a caption quoting a Democratic party newspaper, "This is a white man's government," this Thomas Nast cartoon from 1868 shows three white groups (stereotyped as apelike northern Irish workers, unrepentant former Confederates, and rich northern capitalist Democrats) joining hands to bring Republican Reconstruction to an end almost before it began. They stand on the back of a black Union soldier still clutching the flag and reaching in vain for a ballot box. What is each standing figure holding in his hands? What else do you see here? What's in the background? No single image better captures the story of the end of Reconstruction.

(*Harper's Weekly,* September 5, 1868/The Granger Collection, New York)

departments. The Whiskey Ring affair, for example, cost the public millions of dollars in lost tax revenues siphoned off to government officials. Gould's gold scam received the unwitting aid of Grant's Treasury Department and the knowing help of the president's brother-in-law.

Nor was Congress pure. Crédit Mobilier, a dummy corporation supposedly building the transcontinental railroad, received generous bonds and contracts in exchange for giving congressmen gifts of money, stocks, and railroad lands. An Ohio congressman described the House of Representatives in 1873 as an "auction room where more valuable considerations were disposed of under the speaker's hammer than any place on earth."

Timeline

1865	Civil War ends
	Lincoln assassinated; Andrew Johnson becomes president
	Johnson proposes general amnesty and Reconstruction plan
	Racial confusion, widespread hunger, and demobilization
	Thirteenth Amendment ratified
	Freedmen's Bureau established
1865–1866	Black Codes
	Repossession of land by whites; freedpeople work contracts
1866	Freedmen's Bureau renewed and Civil Rights Act passed over Johnson's veto
	Ku Klux Klan formed
1867	Reconstruction Acts passed over Johnson's veto
	Impeachment controversy
	Freedmen's Bureau ends
1868	Fourteenth Amendment ratified
	Ulysses Grant elected president
1868–1870	Ten states readmitted under congressional plan
1869	Georgia and Virginia reestablish Democratic party control
1870	Fifteenth Amendment ratified
1870s–1880s	Black "exodusters" migrate to Kansas
1870–1871	North Carolina and Georgia reestablish Democratic control
1872	Grant reelected president; scandals follow
1874	Alabama and Arkansas reestablish Democratic control
1875	Civil Rights Act passed
	"Mississippi Plan" reestablishes Democratic control
1876	Hayes–Tilden election
1876–1877	South Carolina, Louisiana, and Florida reestablish Democratic control
1877	Compromise of 1877; Rutherford B. Hayes assumes presidency and ends Reconstruction
1880s	Tenancy and sharecropping prevail in the South
	Disfranchisement and segregation of southern blacks begins

As the inauguration approached, these forces of mutual self-interest concluded the "compromise of 1877" in which Hayes was declared president. After his inauguration, he ordered the last federal troops out of the South, sending them west to fight Native Americans; appointed a former Confederate general to his cabinet; supported federal aid for economic and railroad development in the South; and most significantly, promised to let southerners handle race relations themselves. On a goodwill trip to the South, he told blacks that "your rights and interests would be safer if...let alone by the general government." The message was clear: Hayes would not enforce the Fourteenth and Fifteenth Amendments, initiating a pattern of governmental inaction and abandonment of African Americans that lasted to the 1960s. But the immediate crisis was averted, officially ending Reconstruction.

Conclusion
A MIXED LEGACY

In the 12 years between Appomattox and Hayes's inauguration, victorious northern Republicans, defeated white southerners, and hopeful black freedpeople each dreamed of goals the others mostly refused to give. Yet each got something. The compromise of 1877 cemented the reunion of South and North, providing new opportunities for economic development in both regions. The Republican party achieved its economic goals and generally held the White House, though not always Congress, until 1932. As ex-Confederate states came back into the Union, southerners retained their grip on southern lands and black labor, though not without struggle and significant changes. The Allstons' freedmen, for example, refused to sign work contracts, even when offered various favors, and in 1869 Adele Allston had to sell much of her lands—to whites.

In 1880, Frederick Douglass wrote: "Our Reconstruction measures were radically defective.... To the freedmen was given the machinery of liberty, but there was denied to them the steam to put it in motion.... The old master class...retained the power to starve them to death, and wherever this power is held there is the power of slavery." The wonder, Douglass said, was "not that freedmen have made so little progress, but, rather, that they have made so much; not that they have been standing still, but that they have been able to stand at all."

Freedpeople had made strong gains in education and in economic and family survival. Despite sharecropping and tenancy, black laborers organized themselves to achieve a measure of autonomy and opportunity in their lives. Finally, the three Reconstruction amendments, despite flagrant violation over the next 100 years, held out the promise that the dreams of equal citizenship and democratic political participation would yet be realized.

QUESTIONS FOR REVIEW AND REFLECTION

1. At the end of the Civil War, what were the goals and dreams of defeated southern whites, victorious northerners, and emancipated freedpeople? Can you name three for each group?
2. How did each group pursue its goals and dreams, what resources did each have, and how did they conflict with each other between 1865 and 1877?
3. What differences existed *within* each of the three major groups?
4. What was the relationship between northern presidential and congressional politics and southern daily life and race relations during Reconstruction?
5. What is your assessment of how well American democratic politics and values served the dreams of diverse American peoples in the postwar era?

CHAPTER 17

Rural America: The West and the New South

Ranching in the West
Here a lone cowboy herds cattle. Although novels and movies often romanticize cowboys, their job was far from glamorous or financially rewarding. How would you describe the landscape in this photograph? How does it suggest some of the realities of herding cattle?

(Brown Brothers)

American Stories

Realizing Dreams: Life on the Great Plains

In 1873, Milton Leeper, his wife, Hattie, and their baby, Anna, climbed into a wagon piled high with their possessions and set out to homestead in Boone County, Nebraska. Once on the claim, the Leepers dreamed confidently of their future. Hattie wrote to her sister in Iowa, "I like our place the best of any around here. When we get a fine house and 100 acres under cultivation," she added, "I wouldn't trade with any one." But Milton had broken only 13 acres when disaster struck. Hordes of grasshoppers appeared, and the Leepers fled their claim and took refuge in the nearby town of Fremont.

There they stayed for two years. Milton first worked at a store and then hired out to other farmers. Hattie sewed, kept a boarder, and cared for chickens and a milk cow. The family lived on the brink of poverty but never gave up hope. "Times are hard and we have had bad luck," Hattie acknowledged, but "I am going to hold that claim . . . there will [be] one gal that won't be out of a home." In 1876, the Leepers triumphantly returned to their claim with the modest sum of $27 to help them start over.

The grasshoppers were gone, there was enough rain, and preaching was only half a mile away. The Leepers, like others, began to prosper. Two more daughters were born and cared for in the comfortable sod house—"homely" on the outside but plastered and cozy within. As Hattie explained, the homesteaders lived "just as civilized as they would in Chicago."

Their luck did not last. Hattie, pregnant again, fell ill and died in childbirth along with her infant son. Heartbroken, Milton buried his wife and child and left the claim. The last frontier had momentarily defeated him, although he would try farming in at least four other locations before his death in 1905.

The same year that the Leepers established their Boone County homestead, another family tried their luck in a Danish settlement about 200 miles west of Omaha. Rasmus and Ane Ebbesen and their eight-year-old son, Peter, had arrived in the United States from Denmark in 1868, lured by the promise of an "abundance" of free land "for all willing to cultivate it." By 1870, they had made it as far west as Council Bluffs, Iowa. There they stopped to earn the capital that would be necessary to begin farming. Rasmus dug ditches for the railroad, Ane worked as a cleaning woman in a local boarding-house, and young Peter brought drinking water to thirsty laborers who were digging ditches for the town gas works.

Like the Leepers, the Ebbesens eagerly settled on their homestead and began to cultivate the soil. Peter later recalled that the problems that the family had anticipated never materialized. Even the rumors that the Sioux, "flying demons" in the eyes of settlers, were on the rampage proved false. The real problems the family faced were unexpected: rattlesnakes, prairie fires, and an invasion of grasshoppers. The grasshoppers were just as devastating to the Ebbesen farm as they had been to the Leeper homestead. But unlike the Leepers, the Ebbesens stayed on the claim. Although the family "barely had enough" to eat, they survived the three years of grasshopper infestation.

In the following years, the Ebbesens thrived. Rasmus had almost all the original 80 acres under cultivation and purchased an additional 80 acres from the railroad. A succession of sod houses rose on the land and finally even a two-story frame house, paid for with money Peter earned teaching school. By the time they were in their 50s, they could look with pride at their "luxurient and promising crop." But once more natural disaster struck: a "violent hailstorm . . . which completely devastated the whole lot."

The Ebbesens were lucky, however. A banker offered to buy them out, although the amount was $1,000 less than what the family calculated as the farm's "real worth." But it was enough for the purchase of a "modest" house in town. Later, there was even a "dwelling of two stories and nine rooms . . . with adjacent park."

The stories of the Leepers and the Ebbesens, though different in their details and endings, hint at some of the problems confronting rural Americans in the last quarter of the nineteenth century. As a mature industrial economy transformed agriculture and shifted the balance of economic power permanently away from America's farmlands to the country's cities and factories, many farmers found it impossible to realize the traditional dream of rural independence and prosperity. Even bountiful harvests no longer guaranteed success. "We were told two years ago to go to work and raise a big crop; that was all we needed," said one farmer. "We went to work and plowed and planted; the rains fell, the sun shone, nature smiled, and we raised the big crop they told us to; and what came of it? Eight cent corn, ten cent oats, two cent beef and no price at all for butter and eggs—that's what came of it." Native Americans also discovered that changes in rural life threatened their values and dreams. As the Sioux leader Red Cloud told railroad surveyors in Wyoming, "We do not want you here. You are scaring away the buffalo."

This chapter explores several of this book's basic themes as it analyzes the agricultural transformation of the late nineteenth century. Highlighting the ways in which rural Americans—red, white, yellow, and black—joined the industrial world, it asks how diverse groups responded to new economic and social conditions. The rise of large-scale agriculture in the West, the exploitation of its natural resources, and the development of the Great Plains form a backdrop for discussing the impact of white settlement on western tribes and assessing how well native peoples were able to preserve their culture and traditions. In an analysis of the South, the efforts of whites to create a "New South" contrast with the underlying realities of race and cotton. Although the chapter shows that most black southerners faced discrimination and economic peonage during this period, it also describes new black protest tactics and ideologies. Finally, the chapter highlights the ways in which agricultural problems of the late nineteenth century, which would persist during the twentieth century, led American farmers to become reformers.

Modernizing Agriculture

Between 1865 and 1900, the nation's farms more than doubled in number as Americans flocked west of the Mississippi. Farmers raised specialized crops with modern machinery and sped them to market over an expanding railroad system. And they became capitalists, and, as one farmer observed, had to "understand farming as a business."

While small family farms still typified American agriculture, vast mechanized operations devoted to one crop appeared, especially west of the Mississippi River. The bonanza farms, established in the late 1870s on the northern plains, symbolized the trend to large-scale agriculture. Thousands of acres in size, these wheat farms required large capital investments; corporations owned many of them. Like factories, they depended on machinery, hired hundreds of workers, and relied on efficient managers. Although bonanza farms were not typical, they dramatized the agricultural changes that were occurring everywhere on a smaller scale.

Despite their success in adapting farming to modern conditions, farmers were slipping from their dominant position in the workforce. In 1860, they represented almost 60 percent of the labor force; by 1900, less than 37 percent of employed Americans farmed. At the same time, farmers' contribution to the nation's wealth declined from one-third to one-quarter.

American Agriculture and the World

The expansion of American agriculture was tied to changing global patterns and demands. During the nineteenth century, the population of Europe exploded. While some Europeans still cultivated the land, increasing numbers abandoned farming for industrial work. In Britain, farmers, only 10 percent of the total workforce, could not produce enough to feed the nation. Like other European countries, Great Britain imported substantial food supplies for its citizens. The growing demand prompted American farmers along with their counterparts in Eastern Europe, Australia, and New Zealand to expand their operations for the European market.

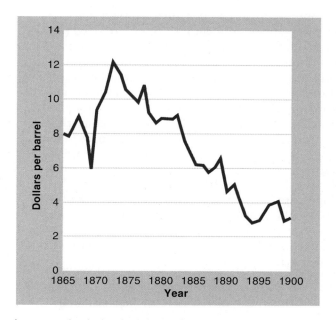

Price of Wholesale Wheat Flour, 1865–1900

The plummeting price of wheat flour was just one indication of the difficulties farmers faced in the late nineteenth century. How much lower was the price of wheat flour in 1900 than in 1865?

Source: U.S. Bureau of the Census.

In efforts to improve crop yields and livestock, American farmers both benefited from and contributed to trends in agriculture elsewhere in the world. German scientists facilitated agricultural expansion after 1850 by developing better seeds, livestock, and chemical fertilizers. The American land-grant university system, established during the Civil War, provided farmers with access to research into and development of better strains of crops and animals and more effective farming methods. For their part, American farmers led the way in using farm machinery such as the horse-drawn harvester, showing agriculturalists in other parts of the world how to raise bigger harvests.

The move toward global integration depended on improved transportation at home and abroad. Reliable, cheap transportation in the United States allowed farmers to specialize: wheat on the Great Plains, corn in the Midwest. Eastern farmers turned to vegetable, fruit, and dairy farming—or sold out. Cotton, tobacco, wheat, and rice dominated in the South, and grain, fruits, and vegetables prevailed in the Far West. The development of steamships and an ever-expanding European network of railroads ensured that American goods and products could move swiftly, efficiently, and cheaply across land and sea to distant markets.

As farmers specialized for national and international markets, their success depended increasingly on outside forces and demands. Bankers and investors, many of them European, provided the capital to improve transportation and expand operations; intermediaries stored and sometimes sold produce; and railroads and steamships carried it to market. A prosperous economy at home and abroad put money into laborers' pockets for food purchases. But when several European countries banned American pork imports between 1879 and 1883, fearing trichinosis, American stock raisers suffered. As Russian, Argentinean, and Canadian farmers turned to wheat cultivation, increased competition in the world market affected the United States' chief cash crop. Moreover, the worldwide deflation of prices for crops such as wheat and corn affected all who raised these crops for the international market, including American farmers.

The Character of American Agriculture

Technological innovation played a major role in facilitating American agricultural expansion. Harvesters, binders, and other new machines, pulled by work animals, diminished much of the drudgery of farming life, making the production of crops easier, more efficient, and cheaper. Moreover, they allowed a farmer to cultivate far more land than was possible with hand tools. But machinery was expensive, and many American farmers borrowed to buy it. In the decade of the 1880s, mortgage indebtedness grew two and a half times as fast as agricultural wealth.

Only gradually did farmers realize the perils of their new situation in the world. Productivity rose 40 percent between 1869 and 1899. But the harvests for crops such as wheat were so large that the domestic market could not absorb them. Foreign competition and deflation further affected steadily declining prices. In 1867, corn sold for 78 cents a bushel; by 1889, it had tumbled to 23 cents. Wheat similarly plummeted from about $2 a bushel in 1867 to only 70 cents a bushel in 1889. Cotton profits also spiraled downward.

Falling prices did not automatically hurt all farmers. Because the supply of money rose more slowly than productivity, all prices declined—by more than half

between the end of the Civil War and 1900 (for a discussion of the money issue, see Chapter 19). Farmers were receiving less for their crops but also paying less for their purchases. But deflation may have encouraged overproduction. To make the same amount of money, many farmers believed they had to raise larger and larger crops. As they did, prices fell even lower. Furthermore, deflation increased the real value of debts. In 1888, it took 174 bushels of wheat to pay the interest on a $2,000 mortgage at 8 percent. By 1895, it took 320 bushels. Falling prices thus affected most negatively farmers in newly settled areas who borrowed heavily to finance their new operations.

The West

In 1893, the young American historian Frederick Jackson Turner addressed historians gathered at Chicago's World's Fair, and his remarks must have startled some of his listeners. The age of the American frontier had ended, Turner declared, pointing to recent census data that suggested the disappearance of vacant land in the West. Although Turner overstated his case (for even in the twentieth century much of the West remained uninhabited), his analysis reflected rapid expansion into the trans-Mississippi West after the Civil War. Between 1870 and 1900, acreage devoted to farming tripled west of the Mississippi, while from 1880 to 1900, the western population grew at a faster rate than that of the nation as a whole.

The Frontier Thesis in National and Global Context

Turner considered the end of the frontier a milestone in the nation's history. The frontier had played a central role, he argued, in shaping the American character and American institutions. Over the course of American history, the struggle to tame the wilderness had changed settlers from Europeans into Americans and created a rugged individualism that "promoted democracy." Turner's thesis, emphasizing the unique nature of the American experience and linking it to the frontier, won many supporters. His interpretation complemented long-held ideas about the exceptional nature of American society and character. It accorded with what many saw as a long struggle to conquer what Turner called the "wilderness."

But the American westward movement was less unusual than Turner suggested. The settlement of the trans-Mississippi West was part of a global pattern that redistributed European populations into new areas of the world. Paralleling their American counterparts, farmers, miners, and ranchers were claiming land in Argentina, Brazil, New Zealand, Australia, Canada, and South Africa. Like Americans, they argued that native occupants had failed to make the land productive, and they used their technological superiority to wrest the land from those they considered backward and inferior. Around the world, many native peoples were facing domination by settler societies or retreating as far away from "civilization" as they could.

Turner's frontier scheme gave the place of honor to the frontier farmer who transformed and civilized the wilderness. Before the Civil War, however, real farmers avoided settling many parts of the West, especially the Great Plains, an area from 200 to 700 miles wide, extending from Canada to Texas. Much of this region, especially beyond the ninety-eighth meridian, had little rain. The absence of trees seemed to symbolize the plains' unsuitability for agriculture.

The Cattleman's West, 1860–1890

While the region of the Great Plains initially discouraged farmers, its grasses provided the foundation for the cattle kingdom. Cattle raising dated back to Spanish mission days, but the commercial cattle frontier was the unanticipated result of the Union's success in separating Texas from Confederate cattle markets. By war's end, millions of longhorns roamed the Texas range. The postwar burst of railroad construction provided the means of turning cattle into dollars. In the late 1860s and 1870s, cowboys herded thousands of longhorns north to towns such as Abilene, Kansas, where they were loaded on trains for Chicago and Kansas City packinghouses.

Ranchers on the Great Plains bought some of the cattle and bred them with Hereford and Angus cows to create cattle acclimatized to severe winters. In the late 1870s and early 1880s, huge ranches arose from eastern Colorado to the Dakotas. Such ventures, many owned by outside investors, paid handsomely. Cattle on the public domain cost owners little but commanded good prices. The cowboys (one-third of them Mexican and black) who herded the steers made meager wages, just enough for a fling at the trail's end.

By the mid-1880s, the first phase of the cattle frontier was ending as farmers moved onto the plains, buying and fencing public lands once used for grazing. But the arrival of farmers was only one factor in the changing cattle frontier. Ranchers overstocked their herds in the mid-1880s. Hungry cattle ate everything in sight, then weakened as grass became scarce. Memorable blizzards followed the very hot summer of 1886. By spring, 90 percent of the cattle were dead. Frantic owners dumped their surviving cattle on the market, getting $8 or less per animal.

Ranchers who survived the disaster adopted new techniques. Experimenting with new breeds, they began to fence in their herds and to feed them grain during the winter. Since consumers were hungering for tender beef, these new methods suited the market. Ranching, like farming, was becoming a modern business.

Farmers on the Great Plains, 1865–1890s

Views of the agricultural possibilities of the Great Plains brightened after the Civil War, with railroads playing a key role in publicizing the region's potential. Now that rail lines crossed the continent, they needed customers, settlers, and freight to make a profit. Along with town boosters and land speculators, also hoping to capitalize on their investments, railroads joined in extravagant promotional campaigns. "This is the sole remaining section of paradise in the western world," promised one newspaper. "All the wild romances of the gorgeous orient dwindle into nothing when compared to the everyday realities of Dakota's progress." Propaganda reached beyond the United States to Scandinavia, Germany, and elsewhere. Dismissing the fear that the plains lacked adequate rainfall, promotional material assured readers that "All that is needed is to plow, plant, and attend to the crops properly; the rains are abundant." Above-average rainfall in the 1880s strengthened the case.

During the first boom period of settlement, from 1879 to the early 1890s, tens of thousands of eager families began farming on the Great Plains. The majority came from Illinois, Iowa, and Missouri. Like the Ebbesens, many others were immigrants, making the Great Plains the second most important destination for foreign immigration. The largest numbers came from Germany, the British Isles, and Canada, but Scandinavians, Czechs, and Poles also arrived. Unlike many migrating to American cities for work, they came with their families and intended to stay.

Some claimed land under the Homestead Act, which granted 160 acres to any family head or adult who lived on the claim for five years or paid $1.25 an acre after six months of residence. Because homestead land was frequently less desirable, however, most settlers bought land from railroads or land companies. Starting up costs were thus higher than the Homestead Act would suggest. Although western land was cheap compared with eastern farmland, a farmer was lucky to buy a good quarter section for under $500. Machinery added another $700. Although some farmers thought leasing rather than buying land made economic sense, many rented only because they lacked capital. In 1880, some 20 percent of the Plains farmers were tenants, and this percentage rose over time.

Late-nineteenth-century industrial innovations helped settlers overcome some the natural obstacles.

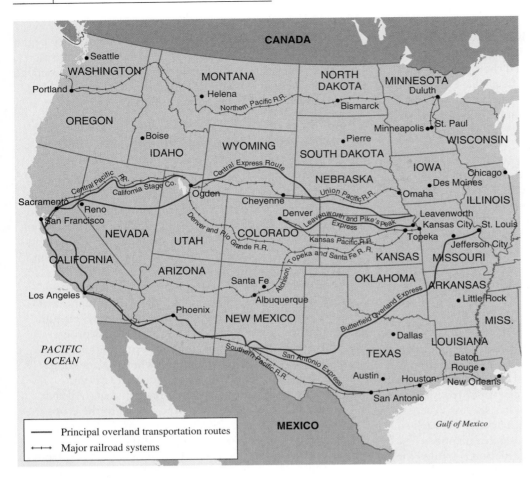

Routes West

On this map, you can trace the various overland routes to the West. How many railroad lines ran across the West? Notice how the railroads contributed to urban growth as trains made their way west. The transcontinental railroads also provided the basis for the economic and demographic expansion and helped to tie East and West together.

The shortage of timber for fencing and housing had encouraged early emigrants to go elsewhere. But in the 1870s, Joseph Glidden developed barbed wire as a cheap alternative to timber fencing. Other innovations met other challenges. Twine binders, which speeded up grain harvesting, reduced the threat of losing crops to the unpredictable weather. And mail-order steel wind-mills for pumping water from deep underground wells relieved some of the water shortages by the 1890s.

Industrial innovations, however, could not resolve all of the problems confronting Great Plains settlers. Miriam Peckham, a Kansas homesteader, wrote:

> I tell you Auntie no one can depend on farming for a living in this country. Henry is very industrious and this year had in over thirty acres of small grain, 8 acres of corn and about an acre of pota-toes. We have sold our small grain...and it come to $100; now deduct $27.00 for cutting, $16.00 for threshing, $19.00 for hired help, say nothing of boarding our help, none of the trouble of drawing

> 25 miles to market and 25 cts on each head for ferriage over the river and where is your profit. I sometimes think this a God forsaken country, the [grass]hopper hurt our corn and we have 1/2 a crop and utterly destroyed our garden. If one wants trials, let them come to Kansas.

This letter highlights the uncertainties of frontier life: high costs, market fluctuations, pests, and natural disasters. Since many plains pioneers took up their homesteads with only a few dollars in their pockets, survival often depended on how well families managed to do during the crucial first years.

The first boom on the Great Plains halted abruptly in the late 1880s and early 1890s. Falling prices cut prof-its. Then, the unusual rainfall that had lured farmers into the semiarid region near the 100th meridian vanished. A devastating drought followed. One farmer reported in 1890 that he had earned $41.48 from his wheat crop, yet his expenses for seed and threshing amounted to $56.00. The destitute survived on boiled

The Wheat Harvest

This 1880 photo highlights the role of machine and animal power rather than human power during the wheat harvest. With more land under cultivation, there was a strong impetus to develop larger and/or more efficient harvesting machines.

(CORBIS)

weeds, a few potatoes, and a little bread and butter. Many lost their farms to creditors. Some stayed on as tenants. Homesteaders like the Leepers gave up. By 1900, two-thirds of homesteaded farms had failed. In western Kansas, the population declined by half between 1888 and 1892 and eastward-bound wagons bore a sad epitaph: "In God We Trusted: In Kansas We Busted."

Both ranching and agriculture had a long-term impact on the region's environment. Ranchers disrupted a complex natural balance when they killed off antelope, elk, wolves, and wildlife. As cattle on overstocked ranges devoured perennial grasses, less nutritious grasses sprang up and, in turn, sometimes disappeared altogether. Lands once a lush home for large herds of cattle turned into deserts of sagebrush, weeds, and dust. Farmers who bought steel windmills to pump water from deep underground depleted the water table level. When they removed sod to build their houses and plowed, they removed the earth's protective covering. Heavy winds, common on the prairies, could lift exposed topsoil and carry it miles away. Deep plowing, essential for dry farming techniques introduced after the drought of the 1880s, worsened the situation. The dust bowl of the 1930s was the eventual outcome of such human interventions.

Cornucopia on the Pacific

When gold was discovered in California, Americans rushed west to find it. But as one father told his son, "Plant your lands; these be your best gold fields." He was right; with the completion of a national railroad system, farming became California's greatest asset. But California

Domestic Work in the West

This photograph shows some of the hard physical labor involved in homesteading. How many steps were involved in doing the family laundry? The clothing of these women, probably settlers in North Dakota, identifies them as immigrants. Their presence reminds us that the West was the home of diverse peoples including Asians, European newcomers, Native Americans, black migrants, and Hispanics whose families had lived in the West for generations.

(The Fred Hulstrand History in Pictures Collection, NDSU, Fargo, ND)

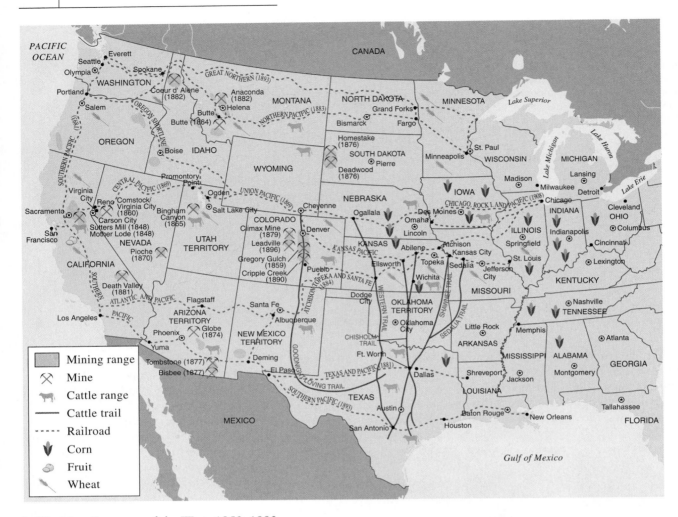

The New Economy of the West, 1850–1893
Describe the areas where corn was an important crop. What states were important wheat producers? Where were the most important mining centers? What areas of the West were involved in ranching?

farming resembled neither the traditional picture of rural life nor the dreams of homesteaders; instead it depended upon railroads, and vast farms using machinery and irrigation to cultivate the land.

Little of California's land was homesteaded or developed as modest family farms. When California entered the Union, speculators acquired much of the property held by Mexican ranchers and sold it at prices beyond the reach of many small farmers. Those small farmers and ranchers who managed to acquire holdings found it hard to compete with large, mechanized operators using cheap migrant laborers, usually Mexican or Chinese. One wheat farm in the San Joaquin Valley was so vast that workers started plowing in the morning at one end of the 17-mile field, ate lunch at its halfway point, and camped at its end that night.

The value of much of California's agricultural land, especially the southern half of the Central Valley, depended on water. By the 1870s, water, land, and

railroad companies, using the labor and expertise of Chinese workers, were taking on the huge costs of building dams, headgates, and canals. They passed on the costs of construction to settlers now eager to acquire hitherto barren lands along with water rights. By 1890, over a quarter of California's farms were irrigated. The irrigation ditches symbolized the importance of technology and a managerial attitude toward the land that characterized late-nineteenth-century agriculture, particularly in California.

Although grain was initially California's most valuable crop, it faced stiff competition from farmers on the plains and in other parts of the world. Some argued that land capable of raising luscious fruits "in a climate surpassing that of Italy, is too valuable for the cultivation of simple cereals." But high railroad rates and lack of refrigeration limited the volume of fresh fruit and vegetables sent to market. As railroad managers in the 1880s realized the potential profit of California

AGRICULTURAL PRODUCTIVITY, 1800–1900

The astonishing gains in the productivity of wheat farmers point to the use of reapers that cut and bound the wheat and thrashers that knocked the grain off the stalks. The combine integrated both operations and also cleared and bagged the grain.

Crop and Productivity Indicator	1800	1840	1880	1900
Wheat				
Worker-hours/acre	56	35	30	15
Yield/acre (bushels)	15	15	13	14
Worker-hours/100 bushels	373	233	152	108
Corn				
Worker-hours/acre	86	69	46	38
Yield/acre (bushels)	25	25	26	26
Worker-hours/100 bushels	344	276	180	147
Cotton				
Worker-hours/acre	185	135	119	112
Yield/acre (bushels)	147	147	179	191
Worker-hours/bale	601	439	318	280

Source: U.S. Bureau of the Census.

produce, they cut rates and introduced refrigerated railroad cars. In June 1888, fresh apricots and cherries successfully survived the trip from California to New York. Fruit and vegetable production rose, benefiting from the agricultural expertise of Chinese laborers, tenant farmers, and Chinese entrepreneurs. So important were their contributions that some have argued that Chinese know-how was mainly responsible for the shift to produce farming. Before long, California fruit was sold as far away as London.

The Mining West

Mining hastened rapid western growth and development. The first and best-known mining rush occurred in 1848 when gold was discovered in California, but others followed as precious metals—silver, iron, copper, coal, lead, zinc, and tin—lured thousands west to Colorado, Montana, Idaho, and Nevada as well as to states such as Minnesota. Mining discoveries were transformative events, for they attracted people and businesses west, often to places far away from agricultural settlements. Hastily built mining communities might be eyesores, but they had bustling urban characters. If and when the strike was over, however, residents abandoned the mining camps and towns as fast as they had rushed into them. The pattern of boom and bust characterized much of mining life.

Cripple Creek, Colorado

This photograph shows the houses and mining buildings at "The Summit," a mining camp at Cripple Creek, Colorado, in the 1880s. How does this picture suggest the impact of mining on the environment? What would it be like to live and work at The Summit?

(Photo by W. E. Hook, Denver Public Library, Western History Collection)

Mining in the West

The map depicts the major areas for mining between 1848 and 1900 as well as some of the important western cities and towns. In what ways did mining stimulate urban growth in the West? What relationships between mining and regional development do you see suggested here?

The reality of late-nineteenth-century mining was nothing like the popular stereotype of the independent miner panning for gold. Retrieving minerals from rock was difficult, expensive, and dangerous, and required a large workforce, industrial tools, and railroad links. Miners worked far below the earth's surface in poorly ventilated tunnels, with no means for removing human or animal waste. Temperatures could reach as high as 120 degrees. Accidents were part of a job that depended on blasting equipment and industrial machinery. In 1884, a Montana miner drilled into an unexploded dynamite charge and lost his eyes and ear. He received no compensation, for the court decided that the accident "was the result of an unforeseen and unavoidable accident incident to the risk of mining." As the next chapter will show, in time, western miners became one of the most radical groups of industrial workers.

Exploiting Natural Resources

Mining was a big business with high costs and a basic dynamic that encouraged rapid and thorough exploitation of the earth's resources. The decimation of the nation's forests went hand in hand with large-scale mining and the railroads' construction. Both railroads and mining depended on wood—railroads for wooden ties, mines for shaft timber and ore reduction. In California, the California State Board of Agriculture estimated in the late 1860s that one-third of the state's forests had already disappeared.

When lumber companies cut down timber, they affected the flow of streams and destroyed the habitat supporting birds and animals. Like the activities of farmers and ranchers, companies that stripped the earth of its forest cover were also contributing to soil erosion. The idea that the public lands belonging to the federal government ought to be rapidly developed supported such exploitation of the nation's natural resources. Often, in return for royalties, the government leased parts of the public domain to companies that hoped to extract valuable minerals, not to own the land permanently. In other cases, companies bought land, but not always legally. In 1878, Congress passed the Timber and Stone Act, which initially applied to Nevada, Oregon, Washington, and California. This legislation allowed the sale of 160-acre parcels of the public domain considered "unfit for cultivation" and "valuable chiefly for timber." Timber companies quickly took advantage of the new law by hiring men willing to register for claims and then to turn them over to timber interests. By the century's end, over 3.5 million acres of the public domain had been acquired under the legislation, and most of it was in corporate hands.

The rapacious and rapid exploitation of resources combined with the increasing pace of industrialization made some Americans uneasy. Many believed that forests stimulated rainfall and that their destruction would adversely affect the climate. Others, like John Muir, lamented the destruction of the country's great natural beauty.

In 1868, Muir came upon the Great Valley of California, "all one sheet of plant gold, hazy and vanishing in the distance…one smooth, continuous bed of honey-bloom." He soon realized, however, that a "wild, restless agriculture" and "flocks of hoofed locusts, sweeping over the ground like a fire" would destroy such loveliness. Muir became a preservation champion. He played a part in the creation of Yosemite National Park in 1890, participated in a successful effort to allow President Benjamin Harrison to classify certain parts of the public domain as forest reserves (the Forest Reserve Act of 1891), and in 1892 established the Sierra Club. At the same time, conservation ideas were also emerging. Gifford Pinchot, who became a leading advocate of these ideas, was less interested in the preservation of the nation's wilderness areas than in careful management of its natural resources. "Conservation," he explained, "means the wise use of the earth and its resources for the lasting good of man." Both perspectives, however, were more popular in the East than in the West, where the seeming abundance of natural resources and the profit motive diminished support.

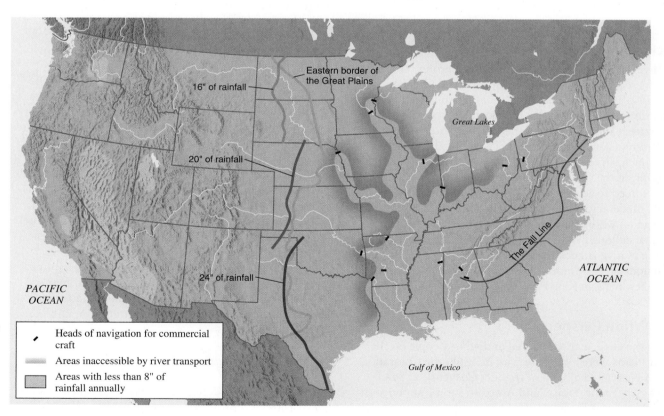

The Natural Environment of the West

Study the patterns of rainfall and the natural features of the West, including rivers and mountain ranges. What do these patterns suggest about native vegetation and the prospects for farming? What is revealed about the role of water and irrigation in the West? What difficulties facing the settlers are revealed?

Resolving the Native American Question

Black Elk, an Oglala Sioux, listened to a story his grandfather had told his father:

> A long time ago…there was once a Lakota [Sioux] holy man, called Drinks Water, who dreamed what was to be…long before the coming of the Wasichus [white men]. He dreamed…that a strange race had woven a spider's web all around the Lakotas. And he said: "When this happens, you shall live in square gray houses, in a barren land, and beside those square gray houses you shall starve."

Black Elk saw this strange dream come true.

As farmers settled the West and became entangled in a national economy, they clashed with the Native American tribes who lived on the land. In California, disease and violence killed 90 percent of the Native American population within 30 years of the gold rush. Elsewhere, the struggle among Native Americans, white settlers, the U.S. Army, and government officials and reformers was prolonged and bitter. Some tribes moved onto government reservations with little protest. But most—including the Nez Percé in the Northwest, the Apache in the Southwest, and the Plains Indians—resisted stubbornly.

Background to the Plains Wars

The lives of most Plains Indians revolved around the buffalo. Increased emigration to California and Oregon in the 1840s and 1850s disrupted tribal pursuits and animal migration patterns. Initially, the federal government tried to persuade the Plains tribes to stay away from white wagon trains and white settlers. The effort did not meet with much success.

During the Civil War, some of the eastern tribes forced to relocate in Oklahoma supported the Confederacy. Others sided with the Union. But after the war, all were branded as "traitors." The federal government callously nullified earlier pledges and treaties, leaving Native Americans defenseless against further incursions on their lands. As settlers pushed into Kansas, the tribes living in Kansas were shunted into Oklahoma.

The White Perspective

When the Civil War ended, red and white people on the Great Plains were already at war. In 1864, the Colorado militia massacred a band of friendly Cheyenne at Sand Creek. Cheyenne, Sioux, and Arapaho soon responded in kind. The Great Plains wars had begun.

Although not all whites condoned this butchery, the congressional commission authorized to make peace viewed Native Americans' future narrowly. The commissioners, including the commander of the army in the West, Civil War hero William T. Sherman, believed that the West belonged to an "industrious, thrifty, and enlightened population" of whites. Native Americans must relocate to western South Dakota or Oklahoma to learn white ways with annuities, food, and clothes to ease their transition to "civilized" life.

At two major conferences in 1867 and 1868, chiefs listened to these drastic proposals to end traditional native life. Some agreed; others, like one Kiowa chief, insisted, "I don't want to settle. I love to roam over the prairies." In any case, the agreements were not binding because no chief had authority to speak for his tribe. For its part, the U.S. Senate delayed approving the treaties. Supplies promised to Indians who settled in the arid reserved areas never materialized, and wildlife proved too sparse to support them. These Indians soon drifted back to their former hunting grounds.

Sherman warned, "All who cling to their old hunting ground are hostile and will remain so till killed off." When persuasion failed, the U.S. Army went to war. "The more we can kill this year," Sherman remarked, "the less will have to be killed the next war." In 1867, he ordered General Philip Sheridan to deal with the tribes. Sheridan introduced winter campaigning, aimed at seeking out Indians who divided into small groups during the winter and exterminating them.

Completion of the transcontinental railroad in 1869 added yet another pressure for "solving" the Indian question. Transcontinental railroads wanted rights-of-way through tribal lands and needed white settlers to make their operations profitable. Few whites considered Native Americans to have any right to lands they wanted.

In his 1872 annual report, the commissioner for Indian affairs, Francis Amasa Walker, addressed two fundamental questions: how to prevent Indians from blocking white migration to the Great Plains, and what to do with them over the long run. Walker suggested buying off the "savages" with promises of food and gifts, luring them onto reservations, and there imposing a "rigid reformatory discipline," necessary because Indians were "unused to manual labor." Though Walker wanted to save the Indians from destruction, he offered only one grim choice: "yield or perish."

The Tribal View

Native Americans defied such attacks on their ancient way of life and protested the wholesale violation of treaties. Black Elk remembered that, in 1863, when he was only three, his father had his leg broken in a fierce battle against the white men. "When I was older," he recalled,

Weekly and monthly magazines constitute a rich primary source for the historian, offering a vivid picture of the issues of the day and useful insights into popular tastes and values. With advances in the publishing industry and an increasingly literate population, the number of these journals soared in the years following the Civil War. In 1865, only 700 periodicals were published. Twenty years later, there were 3,300. As the *National Magazine* grumbled, "Magazines, magazines, magazines! The newsstands are already groaning under the heavy load, and there are still more coming."

Some of these magazines were aimed at the mass market. *Frank Leslie's Illustrated Newspaper,* established in 1855, was one of the most successful. At its height, circulation reached 100,000. Making skillful use of pictures (sometimes as large as

Harper's Weekly delivered powerful messages about the Native Americans in its choice of illustrations.

INDIAN SCOUTS CELEBRATING THE VICTORY OVER BLACK KETTLE.

THE SCALPED HUNTER.

two by three feet and folded into the magazine), the weekly covered important news of the day as well as music, drama, sports, and books. Although Leslie relied more heavily on graphics and sensationalism than do modern news weeklies, his publication was a forerunner of *Newsweek* and *Time.*

Another kind of magazine was aimed primarily at middle- and upper-class readers. Editors such as the oft-quoted Edwin Lawrence Godkin of *The Nation,* with a circulation of about 30,000, hoped to influence those in positions of authority and power by providing a forum for the discussion of reform issues. In contrast, *Scribner's* revealed a more conservative, middle-of-the-road point of view. Both magazines, however, exuded a confident, progressive tone that was characteristic of middle-class Americans.

Harper's Weekly was one of the most important magazines designed primarily for middle- and upper-class readers. Established in 1857, this publication continued in print until 1916. The success of *Harper's Weekly,* which called itself a "family newspaper," rested on a combination of its moderate point of view and an exciting use of illustrations and cartoons touching on contemporary events. The popular cartoons of Thomas Nast appeared in this magazine. In large part because of the use of graphics, the circulation of *Harper's Weekly* reached a peak of 160,000 in 1872.

Illustrated here is a page from the January 16, 1869, issue of *Harper's Weekly.* The layout immediately suggests the importance of graphics. Most of the page is taken up with the three pictures. The top and bottom pictures are wood engravings based on drawings by Theodore R. Davis, one of *Harper's* best-known illustrator-reporters. The center picture was derived from a photograph.

The story featured on this page concerns a victory of General George Custer in the war against the Cheyenne tribe that the U.S. Army was waging that winter. Davis had been a correspondent in the West covering Custer's actions in 1867. But when news of Custer's victory arrived, Davis was back in New York. He thus drew on his imagination for the two scenes reproduced on the next page. What kind of characterization of Native Americans does Davis give in the picture at the top of the page? What view of American soldiers does he suggest? At the bottom of the page, you can see soldiers slaughtering "worthless" horses while Cheyenne teepees burn in the background. Would the average viewer have any sympathy for the plight of the Cheyenne after looking at this picture? This "victory," in fact, involved the slaughter not only of horses but also of all males over age 8.

The editors' decision to insert a picture that had nothing to do with the incident being reported was obviously significant. As you can see, the subject in the center illustration is a white hunter who had been killed and scalped by Indians. By considering the choice of graphics and text, you can begin to discover how magazines provide insight, not only into the events of the day but also into the ways magazines shaped the values and perspectives of nineteenth-century men and women.

Reflecting on the Past What kind of special relationship were the editors suggesting by placing the picture of one dead white hunter in the center of a page that primarily covered a specific conflict between the Indians and the U.S. Army? How might the reader respond to the group of pictures as a whole? How do you? How does the text contribute to the overall view of the Indian–white relationship that the pictures suggest? ■

I learned what the fighting was about.... Up on the Madison Fork the Wasichus had found much of the yellow metal that they worship and that makes them crazy, and they wanted to have a road up through our country to the place where the yellow metal was; but my people did not want the road. It would scare the bison and make them go away, and also it would let the other Wasichus come in like a river. They told us that they wanted only to use a little land, as much as a wagon would take between the wheels; but our people knew better.

Black Elk's father and many others soon realized that fighting was the only "way to keep our country." But "wherever we went, the soldiers came to kill us."

Broken promises fired Indian resistance. In 1875, the federal government allowed gold prospectors into the Black Hills, part of the Sioux reservation and one of their sacred places. Chiefs Sitting Bull, Crazy Horse,

and Rain-in-the-Face led the angry Sioux on the warpath. At the Battle of Little Big Horn in 1876, they vanquished General George Custer. But their bravery and skill could not permanently withstand the power of the well-supplied, well-armed, and determined U.S. Army. Elsewhere, the pattern of resistance and ultimate defeat was repeated. In Texas, General Sherman vanquished Native American tribes, and in the Pacific Northwest, Nez Percé Chief Joseph surrendered in 1877.

The wholesale destruction of the buffalo that were central to Indian life was an important element in white victory. Plains Indians could be wasteful of buffalo in areas where the animals were abundant, but white miners and hunters wiped out the herds. Sportsmen shot the beasts from train windows. Railroad crews ate the meat. Ranchers' cattle competed for grass. And demand for buffalo bones for fertilizer and hides for robes and shoes encouraged the decimation.

An Indian School

These girls, attending an Indian school, are neatly dressed in identical dresses and aprons, with hair pulled into buns rather than braided. What does this picture reveal about the objective of this education for young Indian girls?

(Bettmann/CORBIS)

The slaughter of 13 million animals by 1883 appears disgraceful today. Certainly, Indians considered white men demented. "They just killed and killed because they like to do that," said one, whereas when "we hunted the bison…[we] killed only what we needed." But the destruction of the herds pleased whites who were determined to curb the movements of Native Americans.

The 1887 Dawes Act

Changing federal policy was aimed at ending Native American power and culture. In 1871, Congress abandoned the practice, in effect since the 1790s, of treating the tribes as sovereign nations. Other measures supported the effort to attempt to undermine tribal integrity and leaders. Federal authorities extended government jurisdiction to the reservations and warned tribes not to gather for religious ceremonies.

The Dawes Severalty Act of 1887 pulled together the strands of federal Indian policy and set its course for the rest of the century. Believing that tribal bonds kept Indians in savagery, reformers intended to destroy them. Rather than allotting reservation lands to tribal groups, the act allowed the president to distribute these lands to individuals. The lure of private property, the framers of the bill reasoned, would undermine communal norms and tribal identity and encourage the adoption of settled

agricultural life. Those who accepted an allotment would become citizens and presumably abandon their tribal identity. But another force was at work as speculators' support for the legislation suggested. Even if each Indian family head claimed a typical share of 160 acres, millions of "surplus" acres would remain for white settlers to purchase. Within 20 years of the Dawes Act, 60 percent of Indian lands had been sold, with the federal government holding the profits "in trust" for its "civilizing" mission.

The Ghost Dance: An Indian Renewal Ritual

By the 1890s, this grim reality prepared many Native Americans for the message of the Paiute prophet, Wovoka. Predicting the destruction of the white race through natural disasters, Wovoka promised that Indians who performed the Ghost Dance would survive and gain new strength as their ancestors and wild game returned to life. Wovoka's prophecies spread rapidly. Believers expressed their hope for change through new rituals of ghost or spirit dancing, hypnosis, and meditation.

American settlers were uneasy even though the prophet did not encourage harming whites. Indian agents tried to prevent the ghost dances and filed hysterical reports. One agent determined that the Sioux medicine man Sitting Bull, a strenuous opponent of American expansion, was a leading

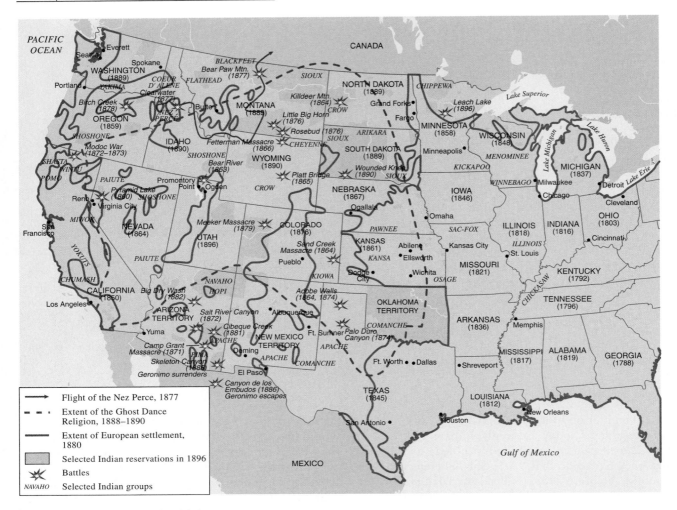

Native Americans, 1850–1896
What does this map reveal about the character of white settlement in 1880? Can you see any relationship between that pattern and the location of reservations? How widespread was the Ghost Dance movement?

troublemaker and decided to arrest him. In the confusion, Indian police killed Sitting Bull. Bands of Sioux fled the reservation with the army in swift pursuit. In late December 1890, the army caught up with them at Wounded Knee Creek. Although the Sioux had raised a flag of truce and started turning over weapons, a scuffle led to a bloody massacre. Using the most up-to-date machine guns and Hotchkiss cannons, the army killed more than 200 men, women, and children. An eyewitness described the desolate scene a few days later. "Among the fragments of burned tents...we saw the frozen bodies lying close together or piled one upon another."

With such measures, white Americans defeated the western tribes. Once independent, proud, and strong, Native Americans suffered dependency, poverty, and social and cultural disorganization on the reservations, in grim Indian schools, and in city slums. The country's original inhabitants had no place in the American nation.

The New South

The trans-Mississippi West was transformed as native peoples were subdued, the Great Plains were settled, and commercial agriculture helped knit the region into the larger world. Mining camps turned into industrial centers. Western cities grew at a fast pace; by 1900, nearly 40 percent of westerners lived in cities. The large number of itinerant workers who worked in mines, forests, and fields provided a flexible workforce that supported economic growth.

In contrast to this pattern, the southern economy sputtered. Of all the nation's agricultural regions, the

South was the poorest. In 1880, southerners' yearly earnings were only half the national average. The agricultural labor force was neither efficient, nor mobile, nor prosperous enough to invest in needed improvements. The dream some southerners harbored of creating an agricultural South to rival the industrial North never came true. The region remained dependent on the North, its industrial workers poorly paid, caught in dead-end jobs with little hope of advancement.

Postwar Southerners Face the Future

After the painful war and Reconstruction, compelling arguments for regional self-sufficiency rang out. Advocates for a "New South" argued that southern backwardness did not stem from the war itself as so many southerners wished to believe but from southern conditions, especially a cotton-based economy. Defeat only made clearer the reality that power and wealth came from factories, machines, and cities.

In hundreds of speeches, editorials, pamphlets, articles, and books, spokesmen for the New South tried to persuade fellow southerners to replace genteel prewar ideals with the ethic of hard work. Because the South was short of capital, New South advocates also held attractive investment opportunities to northern bankers and manufacturers. Several southern state governments offered tax exemptions and the cheap labor of leased convicts. Texas and Florida awarded the railroads land grants, and cities including Atlanta and Louisville mounted huge industrial exhibitions. Middle-class southerners increasingly accepted new entrepreneurial values.

During the late nineteenth century, northern money flowed south as dollars replaced the moral fervor and political involvement of the Civil War and Reconstruction. In the 1880s, northerners increased their investment in the cotton industry sevenfold and financed the expansion of the southern railroad system. Northern capital fueled southern urban expansion. By 1900, some 15 percent of all southerners lived in cities, compared to 7 percent in 1860. (The national averages for these years were 40 and 20 percent, respectively.)

Birmingham, Alabama, symbolized the New South. In 1870, the site was a cornfield. The next year, two northern real estate speculators arrived, attracted by the area's rich iron deposits. Despite cholera and the depression of the 1870s, Birmingham rapidly became the center of the southern iron and steel industry. By 1890, a total of 38,414 people lived in the city. Coke ovens, blast furnaces, rolling mills, iron foundries, and machine shops belched. Mills and factories poured out millions of dollars' worth of finished goods, and eight railroad lines carried them away.

Other southern cities also flourished. Memphis prospered from its lumber industry and the manufacturing of cottonseed products while Richmond became the country's tobacco capital even as its flour mills and iron and steel foundries continued to produce wealth. Augusta, Georgia, led the emerging textile industry that blossomed in Georgia, the Carolinas, and Alabama.

The Other Side of Progress

New South leaders—a small group of merchants, industrialists, and planters—bragged about their iron and textile industries and paraded statistics to prove the success of modernization. The South, one writer boasted, was "throbbing with industrial and railroad activity." But progress was slow, and older values persisted. Even New South spokesmen romanticized the recent past, impeding full acceptance of a new economic order. While southern industry grew in absolute terms, it declined in relative terms. Whereas in 1860 the South had 17 percent of the country's manufacturing concerns, by 1904, it had only 15 percent.

Moreover, the South failed to reap many of industrialization's possible benefits. The South remained an economic vassal of the North. Southern businessmen grew in number, but with the exception of the American Tobacco Company, no great southern corporations arose. Instead, southerners worked for northern companies and corporations, which absorbed southern businesses or dominated them financially. Profits and critical decision-making power flowed north. In many cases southern mills and factories were allowed to handle only the early stages of processing; Northern factories finished the goods.

Individual workers in the new industries may have preferred factory life to sharecropping, but their rewards were meager. The presence of thousands of women and children in factories highlighted husbands' and fathers' inability to earn a "family wage." As usual, women and children were paid less than men. Justifying these policies, one Augusta factory president claimed that the employment of children was "a matter of charity with us; some of them would starve if they were not given employment.... Ours are not overworked. The work we give children is very light." Actually, many children at his factory were doing the same work as adults, but for children's pay.

In general, workers earned less and toiled longer in the South than elsewhere. Per capita income was the same in 1900 as it had been in 1860—half the national average. In North Carolina in the 1890s, workers were paid an average of 50 cents a day with a 70-hour week.

Black workers, 6 percent of the southern manufacturing force by 1890 (with the exception of textile mills that excluded them), usually had the worst jobs and the lowest pay.

Cotton Still King

Although New South advocates envisioned the South's transformation from a rural to an industrial society, they always recognized the need for agricultural change. "It's time for an agricultural revolution," proclaimed Henry Grady, the New South's most vocal spokesman. Overdependence on "King Cotton" hobbled southern agriculture by making farmers the victims of faraway market forces and an oppressive credit system. Subdivide old cotton plantations into small diversified farms, Grady urged, that would raise choice produce for urban markets and yield "simply wonderful profits."

A new agricultural South with new class and economic arrangements did emerge, but not the one Grady envisioned. Despite the breakup of some plantations, large landowners were resourceful in keeping their property and dealing with postwar

The South Carolina Cotton Fields

What evidence does this photograph, taken in the 1870s, provide for understanding the character of black life after the Civil War and the limitations of the New South's effort to transform southern life?

(Photography Collection, Robert N. Dennis Collection of Stereoscopic Views, The New York Public Library/Art Resource, NY)

conditions, as Chapter 16 showed. As they adopted new agricultural arrangements, former slaves sank into peonage.

White farmers on small and medium-size holdings fared only slightly better than black tenants and sharecroppers. Immediately after the war, high cotton prices tempted them to raise as much cotton as they could. Then prices began a disastrous decline, from 11 cents a pound in 1875 to less than 5 cents in 1894. Yeoman farmers became entangled in debt. Each year, farmers bought supplies on credit from merchants so they could plant the next year's crop and support their families until harvest. In return, merchants demanded their exclusive business and acquired a lien (claim) on their crops. But when farmers sold their crops at declining prices, they usually discovered that they had not earned enough to settle with the merchant, who had charged dearly for store goods and whose annual interest rates might exceed 100 percent. Each year, thousands of farmers fell further behind. By 1900, more than half of the South's white farmers and three-quarters of its black farmers were tenants. Tenancy increased all over rural America, but nowhere faster than in the Deep South.

These patterns had baneful results for individual southerners and for the South as a whole. Caught in a cycle of debt and poverty, few farmers could think of improving techniques or diversifying crops. Desperate to pay debts, they concentrated on cotton despite falling prices. Landowners pressured tenants to raise a market crop. Far from diversifying, farmers increasingly limited their crops. By 1880, the South was not growing enough food to feed its people adequately.

The Nadir of Black Life

Grady and other New South advocates visualized a strong, prosperous, and industrialized South, a region that could deal with the troublesome race issue without interference. Grady had few regrets over the end of slavery, which he thought had contributed to southern economic backwardness. Realizing that black labor would be crucial to the transformation he sought, he advocated racial cooperation. But racial cooperation did not mean equality. Grady assumed that blacks were racially inferior and supported an informal system of segregation. "The negro is entitled to his freedom, his franchise, to full and equal legal rights," Grady wrote in 1883. But "social equality he can never have."

By the time of Grady's death in 1889, a much harsher perspective on southern race relations had emerged. In 1891, at a national assembly of women's clubs in Washington, D.C., Frances Watkins Harper, a black speaker, writer, and former abolitionist, appealed to the white women at the meeting not to abandon black suffrage. "I deem it a privilege to present the negro," she said, "not as a mere dependent asking for Northern sympathy or Southern compassion, but as a member of the body politic who has a claim upon the nation for justice, simple justice." Women, of all people, should not seek to achieve their own right to vote at the expense of the vote for black men, she explained. "Instead of taking the ballot from his hands, teach him how to use it, and add his quota to the progress, strength, and durability of the nation."

The decision by congressional leaders in 1890 to shelve a proposed act for protecting black civil rights and the defeat of the Blair bill providing federal assistance for educational institutions left black Americans vulnerable, as Harper realized. The traditional sponsor of the rights of freedpeople, the Republican party, left blacks to fend for themselves as a minority in the white South. The courts also abandoned blacks. In 1878, the Supreme Court declared unconstitutional a Louisiana statute banning discrimination in transportation. In 1882, the Court voided the Ku Klux Klan Act of 1871, which had been passed to break the power of the Klan. In 1883, the provisions of the Civil Rights Act of 1875, which assured blacks of equal rights in public places, were declared unconstitutional on the grounds that the federal government did not have the right to involve itself in racial relations between individuals.

Northern leaders did not oppose these actions. In fact, northerners increasingly promulgated negative stereotypes in magazines, newspapers, cartoons, advertisements, "coon songs," serious art and theater, and the minstrel shows that dominated northern entertainment. The *Atlantic Monthly* in 1890 anticipated a strong current in magazine literature when it expressed doubts that this "lowly variety of man" could ever be brought up to the intellectual and moral standards of whites. Other magazines openly opposed suffrage as wasted on people too "ignorant, weak, lazy and incompetent" to make good use of it. *Forum* magazine suggested that "American Negroes" had "too much liberty." When this freedom was combined with natural "race traits" of stealing and hankering after white women, the *Forum* advised in 1893, black crime increased. Only lynching and burning would deter the "barbarous" rapist and other "sadly degenerated" Negroes corrupted since the Civil War by independence and too much education.

Encouraged by northern public opinion, and with the blessing of Congress and the Supreme Court, southern citizens and legislatures sought to make blacks permanently second-class members of southern society. In the political sphere, white southerners amended state constitutions to disfranchise black voters. By various legal devices—the poll tax, literacy tests, "good character" and "understanding" clauses administered by white voter registrars, and all-white primary elections—blacks lost the right to vote. The most ingenious method was the "grandfather clause," which specified that only citizens whose grandfathers were registered to vote on January 1, 1867, could cast their ballots. This virtually excluded blacks. Although the Supreme Court outlawed blatantly discriminatory laws such as grandfather clauses, a series of other constitutional changes such as those just mentioned, beginning in Mississippi in 1890 and spreading to all 11 former Confederate states by 1910, effectively excluded the black vote. The results were dramatic. Louisiana, for example, contained 130,334 registered black voters in 1896. Eight years later, there were only 1,342.

In a second tactic in the 1890s, state and local laws legalized informal segregation in public facilities. Beginning with railroads and schools, "Jim Crow" laws were extended to libraries, restaurants, hospitals, prisons, parks and playgrounds, cemeteries, toilets, drinking fountains, and nearly every other place where blacks and whites might mingle. The Supreme Court upheld these laws in 1896 in *Plessy* v. *Ferguson* by declaring that "separate but equal" facilities did not violate the equal protection clause of the Fourteenth Amendment because separation did not necessarily mean the inferiority of a group. The Court's decision opened the way for as many forms of legal segregation as southern lawmakers could devise.

Political and social discrimination made it ever more possible to keep blacks permanently confined to agricultural and unskilled labor. In 1900, nearly 84 percent of black workers nationwide engaged in some form of agricultural labor as farmhands, overseers, sharecroppers, or tenant or independent farmers or in service jobs, primarily domestic service and laundry work. These had been the primary slave occupations. The remaining 16 percent worked in forests, sawmills, mines, and, with northward migration, northern cities. As whites systematically excluded blacks from trades, the percentage of blacks laboring in these jobs dropped to under 10 percent, although at the end of the Civil War, at least half the skilled craftsmen in the South had been black. The factory work that blacks had been doing was also reduced, largely to separate poor blacks and whites and to undercut unionization. The exclusion of blacks from industry prevented them from acquiring the skills and habits that would enable them to rise into the middle class as would many European immigrants and their children by the mid-twentieth century.

Blacks did not accept their declining position passively. In the mid-1880s, they enthusiastically joined the mass worker organization the Knights of Labor (discussed in Chapter 18), first in cities such as Richmond and Atlanta and then in rural areas. But southern whites feared that the Knights' policies of racial and economic cooperation might lead to social equality. The Charleston *News and Courier* warned darkly about "mongrels and hybrids." As blacks continued to join it, whites fled the organization. White violence finished it off.

Lynching and other forms of violence against blacks increased. Lynching was a way to show both black men and white women the dire consequences of stepping out of line. On February 21, 1891, the *New York Times* reported that in Texarkana, Arkansas, a mob apprehended Ed Coy, a 32-year-old black man who was charged with the rape of a white woman. He was tied to a stake and then burned alive. As Coy proclaimed his innocence to a large crowd, his alleged victim somewhat hesitatingly put the torch to his oil-soaked body. The *Times* report concluded that only by the "terrible death such as fire…can inflict" could other blacks "be deterred from the commission of like crimes." Ed Coy was one of more than 1,400 black men lynched or burned alive during the 1890s. About one-third were charged with sex crimes. The rest were accused of a variety of "crimes" related to not knowing their place; this included marrying or insulting a white woman, testifying in court against whites, or having a "bad reputation."

Diverging Black Responses

White discrimination and exploitation nourished new protest tactics and ideologies among blacks. For years, Frederick Douglass had been proclaiming that blacks should remain loyal Americans and trust the Republican party. But on his deathbed in 1895, his last words were allegedly, "Agitate! Agitate! Agitate!"

Agitation had its costs. In Memphis, Tennessee, Ida B. Wells, the first female editor of an important newspaper, launched an antilynching campaign in 1892. So hostile was the response from the white community that Wells carried a gun to protect herself. When white citizens finally destroyed the press and threatened her partner, Wells left Memphis to pursue her activism elsewhere.

Calls for black separatism within white America rang out. Insisting that blacks must join together to fight the rising tide of discrimination, T. Thomas Fortune in 1891 organized the Afro-American League. The League, a precursor of the NAACP, encouraged independent black voting, opposed segregation and lynching, and urged the establishment of black institutions such as banks to support black businesses. As a sympathetic journalist explained, "The solution of the problem is in our own hands….The Negro must preserve his identity." In the 1890s, black leaders lobbied to make the Oklahoma Territory, recently opened to white settlement, an all-black state. Blacks founded 25 towns there as well as many towns in other states and even in Mexico. But these attempts, like earlier ones, were short-lived, for they were crippled by limited funds and by the hostility of white neighbors.

There were more radical voices, too. Bishop Henry McNeal Turner, a former Union soldier and prominent black leader, despaired of ever securing equal rights for American blacks. He described the Constitution as "a dirty rag, a cheat, a libel" and said that it ought to be "spit upon by every Negro in the land." In 1894, he organized the International Migration Society to return blacks to Africa, arguing that "this country owes us forty billions of dollars" to help. He succeeded in sending two boatloads of emigrants to Liberia, but this colonization effort worked no more successfully than those earlier in the century.

As Frederick Douglass had long argued, no matter how important African roots might be, blacks had been in the Americas for generations and would have to win justice and equal rights here. W. E. B. Du Bois, the first black to receive a Ph.D. from Harvard, agreed. Yet in 1900, he attended the first Pan-African Conference in London, where he argued that blacks must lead the struggle for liberation both in Africa and in the United States. It was at this conference that Du Bois first made his prophetic comment that "the problem of the Twentieth Century" would be "the problem of the color line."

Despite these vigorous voices of militant anger and nationalistic fervor, most black Americans continued to follow the slow, moderate, self-help program of Booker T. Washington, the best-known black leader in America. Born a slave, Washington had risen through hard and faithful work to become the founder (in 1881) and principal of Tuskegee Institute in Alabama, which he personally and dramatically built into the nation's largest and best-known industrial training school. At Tuskegee, young blacks received a highly disciplined education in scientific agricultural techniques and vocational skilled trades. Washington believed that economic self-help and the familiar Puritan virtues of hard work, frugality, cleanliness, and moderation would lead to success for African Americans despite the realities of racism. He spent much of his time traveling through the North to secure philanthropic gifts to support Tuskegee. In time, he became a favorite of the American entrepreneurial elite whose capitalist assumptions he shared.

In 1895, Washington was asked to deliver a speech at the Cotton States and International Exposition in Atlanta, celebrating three decades of industrial and agricultural progress since the Civil War. He took advantage of that invitation, a rare honor for a former slave, to make a significant statement about the position of blacks in the South. Without a hint of protest, Washington decided "to say something that would cement the friendship of the races." He therefore proclaimed black loyalty to the economic development of the South while accepting the lowly status of southern blacks. "It is at the bottom of life we must begin, and not at the top," he declared. "In all things that are purely social we can be as separate as the fingers, yet one as the hand in all things essential to mutual progress." Although Washington worked actively behind the scenes for black civil rights, in Atlanta, he publicly renounced black interest in either the vote or civil rights as well as social equality with whites. Whites throughout the country enthusiastically acclaimed Washington's address, but many blacks called his "Atlanta Compromise" a serious setback in the struggle for black rights.

Washington has often been charged with conceding too quickly that political rights should follow rather than precede economic well-being. In 1903, Du Bois confronted Washington directly in *The Souls of Black Folk*, arguing instead for the "manly assertion" of a program of equal civil rights, suffrage, and higher education in the ideals of liberal learning. A trip through the Black Belt of Dougherty County, Georgia, showed Du Bois the "forlorn and forsaken" condition of southern blacks. The young sociologist saw that most blacks were confined to dependent agricultural labor, "fighting a hard battle with debt" year after year. Although "here and there a man has raised his head above these murky waters…a pall of debt hangs over the beautiful land." Beneath all others was the cotton picker, who, with his wife and children, would have to work from sunup to sundown to pick 100 pounds of cotton to make 50 cents. The lives of most blacks were still tied to the land of the South. If they were to improve their lives, rural blacks would have to organize.

Farm Protest

During the post–Civil War period, many farmers, black and white, began to realize that only through collective action could they improve rural life. Not all were dissatisfied; midwestern farmers and those near city markets adjusted to changing economic conditions. Southern and western farmers, however, faced new problems that led to the first mass organization of farmers in American history.

The Grange in the 1860s and 1870s

The earliest effort to organize white farmers came in 1867 when Oliver Kelley founded the Order of the Patrons of Husbandry. Originally a social and cultural organization, it soon was protesting the powerlessness of the "immense helpless mob" of farmers, victims of "human vampires." The depression of the 1870s (discussed in Chapter 18)

sharpened discontent. By 1875, an estimated 800,000 had joined Kelley's organization, now known as the National Grange.

The Grangers recognized some, but not all, of the complex changes that had created rural problems. Some of their "reforms" attempted to bypass intermediaries by establishing buying and selling cooperatives. Although many cooperatives failed, they indicated that farmers realized the need for unified action. Midwestern farmers also accused grain elevator operators of cheating them, and they pointed to the railroads, America's first big business, as the worst offenders. As Chapter 18 will show, cutthroat competition among railroad companies generally brought lower rates. But even though charges dropped nationwide, railroads often set high rates in rural areas, and their rebates to large shippers discriminated against small operators.

Farmers recognized that confronting the mighty railroads demanded cooperation with others, like western businessmen whose interests railroads also hurt, and political action. Between 1869 and 1874, businessmen and farmers successfully pressed Illinois, Iowa, Wisconsin, and Minnesota to pass so-called Granger laws (an inaccurate name, for the Grangers did not deserve complete credit for them) establishing maximum rates that railroads and grain elevators could charge. Other states set up railroad commissions to regulate railroad rates, or outlawed railroad pools, rebates, passes, and other practices that seemed to represent "unjust discrimination and distortion."

Railroad companies and grain elevators quickly challenged the new laws. In 1877, the Supreme Court upheld them in *Munn* v. *Illinois*. Even so, it soon became apparent that state commissions might regulate local rates but not long-haul rates. While Granger laws did not control the railroads and raised questions difficult to resolve on the local level, they established an important principle. The Supreme Court had made it clear that state legislatures could regulate businesses of a public nature such as the railroads. When the Court reversed its ruling in *Wabash* v. *Illinois* in 1886, pressure increased on Congress to continue the struggle.

The Interstate Commerce Act of 1887

In 1887, Congress responded to farmers, railroad managers who wished to curb the fierce competition that threatened to bankrupt their companies, and shippers who objected to transportation rates by passing the Interstate Commerce Act. That legislation required that railroad rates be "reasonable and just," that rate schedules be made public, and that practices such as rebates be discontinued. The act also set up the first federal regulatory agency, the Interstate Commerce Commission (ICC) with power to investigate and prosecute lawbreakers but with only limited authority to control commerce conducted between states.

Like state railroad commissions, the ICC found it difficult to define a reasonable rate. Moreover, thousands of cases overwhelmed the tiny staff in the early months of operation. In the long run, the lack of enforcement power was most serious. The ICC's only recourse was to bring offenders into the federal courts for lengthy legal proceedings. Few railroads worried about defying it. When they appeared in court four or five years later, they often won their cases from judges suspicious of new federal authority. Between 1887 and 1906, a total of 16 cases made their way to the Supreme Court, which decided 15 of them in the railroads' favor.

The Southern Farmers' Alliance in the 1880s and 1890s

The Grange declined in the late 1870s as the nation recovered from depression. But farm protest did not die. Depression struck farmers once again in the late 1880s and worsened in the early 1890s. Official statistics told the familiar, dismal story of falling grain prices on the plains and prairies. The national currency shortage, which usually reached critical proportions at harvest time, helped drive agricultural prices ever lower. Debt and shipping costs, however, climbed. It sometimes cost a farmer as much as one bushel of corn to send another bushel to market. Distraught farmers again tried organization, education, and cooperation.

The Southern Farmers' Alliance became one of the most important reform organizations of the 1880s. Its ambitious organizational drive sent lecturers across the South and onto the Plains where they proposed programs that would meet their objective of "Equal rights to all, special privileges to none." Among the Alliance's efforts were experiments with cooperatives to free farmers from the clutches of supply merchants, banks, and other credit agencies. While cooperatives often failed, the Alliance also supported legislative efforts to regulate powerful monopolies and corporations that, they believed, gouged farmers. Many Alliance members believed that increasing the money supply was critical to improving the position of farmers and supported a national banking system empowered to issue paper money. Finally, the Alliance called for a variety of measures to improve the quality of rural life. Better rural public schools, state agricultural colleges, and improvements in the status of women were all on its agenda.

By 1890, rural discontent swept more than a million farmers into the Alliance. Included in this burst of organization growth were black as well as white farmers. Organized in 1888, the Colored Farmers' Alliance recognized that farmers of both races shared common economic problems and therefore must cooperate. But many southern cotton farmers, depending on black labor, disagreed. In 1891, black cotton pickers on plantations near Memphis went on strike. Revealing the racial tensions simmering just below the surface, white posses chased the strikers and lynched 15 of them.

The Ocala Platform, 1890

In December 1890, the National Alliance gathered in Ocala, Florida, to develop a platform. Most delegates believed that the federal government had failed to address the farmers' problems. They attacked both parties as too subservient to the "will of corporation and money power."

Much of the Alliance's program was radical in the context of late-nineteenth-century political life. It called for the direct election of U.S. senators and supported lowering the tariff (a topic much debated in Congress) with the dangerous-sounding justification that prices must be reduced for the sake of the "poor of our land." The money plank boldly envisioned a new banking system controlled by the federal government. The platform also called for the government to take an active economic role by increasing the amount of money in circulation in the form of treasury notes and silver. More money would cause inflation and help debtors pay off loans.

The platform also called for subtreasuries (federal warehouses) in agricultural regions where farmers could store their produce at low interest rates until market prices favored selling. To tide farmers over, the federal government would lend farmers up to 80 percent of the current local price for their produce. Other demands included a graduated income tax and the regulation of transportation and communication networks—or, if regulation failed, their nationalization.

Even though a minority of farmers belonged to the Alliance, many Americans feared it. The New York *Sun* reported that the Alliance had caused a "panic" in the two major parties.

Although the Alliance was not formally in politics, it supported sympathetic candidates in the fall elections of 1890. A surprising number of them won. Alliance victories in the West hurt the Republican party enough to cause President Harrison to refer to "our election disaster." Before long, many Alliance members were pressing for an independent political party. Legislators elected with Alliance support did not necessarily bring action on issues of interest to farmers, or even respect. On the national level, no one had much interest in the Ocala platform. But among rural spokesmen, the first to realize the necessity of forming an independent third party was Georgia's Tom Watson, who also knew that success in the South would depend on unity between white and black farmers.

Timeline

1860s	Cattle drives from Texas begin
1865–1867	Sioux wars on the Great Plains
1867	National Grange founded
1869	Transcontinental railroad completed
1869–1874	Granger laws
1873	Financial panic triggers economic depression
1874	Barbed wire patented
1875	Black Hills gold rush incites Sioux war
1876	Custer's last stand at Little Big Horn
1877	*Munn* v. *Illinois*
	Bonanza farms in the Great Plains
1878	Timber and Stone Act
1880s	Attempts to create a "New South"
1881	Tuskegee Institute founded
1883–1885	Depression
1884	Southern Farmers' Alliance founded
1886	Severe winter ends cattle boom
	Wabash v. *Illinois*
1887	Dawes Severalty Act
	Interstate Commerce Act
	Farm prices plummet
1888	Colored Farmers' Alliance founded
1890	Afro-American League founded
	Sioux ghost dance movement
	Massacre at Wounded Knee
	Ocala platform
	Yosemite National Park established
1890s	Black disfranchisement in the South
	Jim Crow laws passed in the South
	Declining farm prices
1891	Forest Reserve Act
1892	Sierra Club founded
1895	Booker T. Washington's "Atlanta Compromise" address
1896	*Plessy* v. *Ferguson*

Conclusion

FARMING IN THE INDUSTRIAL AGE

The late nineteenth century brought turbulence to rural America. The "Indian problem," which had plagued Americans for 200 years, was tragically solved for a while, but not without resistance and bloodshed. Few whites found these events troubling. Most were caught up in the challenge of responding to a fast-changing world. Believing themselves to be the backbone of the nation, white farmers brought Native American lands into cultivation, modernized their farms, and raised bumper crops. But success and a comfortable competency eluded many of them. Some, like Milton Leeper, never gave up hope or farming. Many were caught in a cycle of poverty and debt. Others fled to towns and cities as did the Ebbesen family. Once there, many joined the industrial workforce, described in the next chapter. Some turned to collective action and politics. Their actions demonstrate that they did not merely react to events but attempted to shape them.

QUESTIONS FOR REVIEW AND REFLECTION

1. Compare and contrast farming on the Great Plains with farming in California.
2. How did technology affect agriculture and mining in the West?
3. Describe the differing viewpoints of Native Americans and whites and the differing cultural values lying behind these viewpoints.
4. What were the reasons that the New South did not achieve its goals?
5. Compare and contrast the treatment of Native Americans and African Americans in this period. Are there any similarities?
6. In what ways did agricultural life in the West and South create conditions that did not mesh with the ideals of American life?

CHAPTER 18

The Rise of Smokestack America

This anxious scene of a strike hints at the tensions between workers and owners during the industrial era.

(Robert Koehler (1850–1917), *The Strike*, 1886. Oil on canvas. Deutsches Historisches Museum, Berlin, Germany/Bridgeman Art Library)

American Stories

Telling His Story: O'Donnell and the Senators

By 1883, Thomas O'Donnell, an Irish immigrant, had lived in the United States for more than a decade. He was 30 years old, married, with two young children. His third child had died in 1882, and O'Donnell was still in debt for the funeral. Money was scarce, for O'Donnell was a textile worker in Fall River, Massachusetts, and not well educated. "I went to work when I was young," he explained, "and have been working ever since." However, O'Donnell worked only sporadically at the mill. New machines needed "a good deal of small help," and the mill owners preferred to hire man-and-boy teams. Because O'Donnell's children were very young, he often saw others preferred for day work. Once, when he was passed over, he asked the boss "what am I to do; I have got two little boys at home . . . how am I to get something for them to eat; I can't get a turn when I come here. . . . I says, 'Have I got to starve; ain't I to have any work?'"

O'Donnell and his family were barely getting by, even though he worked with pick and shovel when he could. He estimated that he had earned only $133 the previous year. Rent came to $72. The family spent $2 for a little coal but depended for heat on driftwood that O'Donnell picked up on the beach. Clams were a major part of the family diet, but on some days there was nothing to eat at all.

The children "got along very nicely all summer," but by November they were beginning to "feel quite sickly." It was hardly surprising. "One has one shoe on, a very poor one, and a slipper, that was picked up somewhere. The other has two odd shoes on, with the heel out." His wife was healthy, but not ready for winter. She had two dresses, one saved for church, and an "undershirt that she got given to her, and . . . an old wrapper, which is about a mile too big for her; somebody gave it to her."

O'Donnell was describing his family's marginal existence to a Senate committee gathering testimony in Boston in 1883 on the relations between labor and capital. As the senators heard the tale, they asked him why he did not go west. "It would not cost you over $1,500," said one senator. The gap between the worlds of the senator and the worker could not have been more dramatic. O'Donnell replied, "Well, I never saw over a $20 bill . . . if some one would give me $1,500 I will go." Asked by the senator if he had friends who could provide him with the funds, O'Donnell sadly replied no.

The senators, of course, were far better acquainted with the world of comfort and leisure than with the poverty of families like the O'Donnells. From their vantage point, the fruits of industrial progress were clear. As the United States became a world industrial leader in the years after the Civil War, its factories poured forth an abundance of ever-cheaper goods ranging from steel rails and farm reapers to mass-produced parlor sets. These were years of tremendous growth and broad economic and social change. Manufacturing replaced agriculture as the leading source of economic growth between 1860 and 1900. By 1890, a majority of the American workforce held nonagricultural jobs; more than a third lived in cities. A rural nation of farmers was becoming a nation of industrial workers and city dwellers.

As O'Donnell's appearance before the Senate committee illustrates, industrial and technological advances profoundly changed the nature of American life. For O'Donnell and others like him, the benefits of this transformation were hard to see. Although no nation-wide studies of poverty existed, estimates suggest that perhaps half of the American population was too poor to take advantage of the new goods of the age. Eventually, the disparity between the reality of life for humble families like the O'Donnells and American ideals would give rise to attempts to improve conditions for working-class Americans, but it is unlikely that O'Donnell ever profited from such efforts.

This chapter examines the maturing of the American industrial economy, a phenomenon that affected all facets of American life, from the rhythms of daily life and work to the allocation of wealth. Focusing on the years between 1865 and 1900, it describes the rise of heavy industry and the factors that contributed to it, including the mass production of machine-made goods, a new organization of the workplace, and the emergence of big business. It then examines the cities housing the diverse peoples that provided the workers and consumers driving American industry. The chapter's central theme grows out of O'Donnell's story: As the United States built up its railroads, cities, and factories, its production and profit orientation resulted in unequal distribution of wealth and power. New inequalities did not go unquestioned, however, as workers used strikes and other forms of resistance to assert their dignity and power and to demand more generous compensation for the labor they performed. The ineffectiveness of these efforts highlights the obstacles confronting those protesting the status quo.

The Character of Industrial Progress

When Americans went to war in 1861, agriculture was the country's leading source of economic growth. Forty years later, manufacturing had taken its place. Big business became the characteristic form of economic organization. Able to raise the capital to build huge factories, acquire expensive, modern, and efficient machinery, and hire hundreds of workers, big industrial firms poured out a bounty of goods. Indeed, the production of manufactured goods outpaced population growth.

Dramatically rising industrial productivity was linked to the changing character of the industrial sector. Pre–Civil War manufacturers concentrated either on producing textiles, clothing, and leather products for consumers or on processing agricultural and natural resources such as grain, logs, and lumber. The rapid growth of heavy industry after the war was based on manufacturing steel, iron, and machinery that fueled further industrial development rather than solely furnishing consumers.

Industrialization helped to shape and transform regional character. From New England to the Midwest stretched the country's industrial heartland. New England remained a center of light industry, while the Midwest still processed natural resources.

Now, however, the production of iron, steel, and transportation equipment joined older manufacturing operations there. In the Far West, manufacturers concentrated on processing the region's natural resources, but heavy industry made strides as well. In the South, the textile industry put down roots by the 1890s.

The Contribution of Technology

As the following example of the steel industry suggests, an accelerating pace of technological change also contributed to the industrial transformation of the late nineteenth century by allowing more efficient production that, in turn, generated new needs and further innovation. Before the Civil War, skilled workers used a slow, expensive process to produce an iron so soft that train rails wore out within a few years. The need for a harder metal stimulated the development of the Bessemer converter that transformed iron into steel by forcing air through the liquid iron, thus reducing the carbon. The new process facilitated the rapid expansion of the steel industry and had the added advantage of reducing the need for highly paid skilled workers.

The Homestead Steel Works

The Homestead Steel Works, pictured here in about 1890, was located near Pittsburgh, Pennsylvania. The vast scale of the enterprise suggests the ways in which technological innovation stimulated the expansion of the steel industry in the late nineteenth century. Although the two small figures in the foreground humanize the picture, what does this picture suggest about the character of work in the steel mills?

(Courtesy of Rivers of Steel Archives)

While neither an inventor nor an engineer, entrepreneur Andrew Carnegie grasped both the importance of technological innovations and the benefits of new ways of organizing the industry. Carnegie's company and others as well acquired access to raw materials and markets and brought all stages of steel manufacturing, from smelting to rolling, into one mill. Output soared, and prices fell. When Andrew Carnegie introduced the Bessemer process in his plant in the mid-1870s, the price of steel dropped from $100 a ton to $12 a ton by 1900.

In turn, the production of a cheaper, stronger, more durable material than iron created new goods, new demands, and new markets, and stimulated further technological change. Bessemer furnaces were geared toward making steel rails. Experimentation with the open-hearth process, using very high temperatures, yielded steel usable by bridge and ship builders, engineers, architects, and even designers of subways. Steel use increased dramatically.

New power sources also facilitated American industry's shift to mass production. In 1869, about half of the nation's industrial power came from water. Then the opening of new anthracite deposits made coal cheaper, and American industry rapidly converted to steam. By 1900, steam engines generated 80 percent of the nation's industrial energy supply. But soon electricity began to replace steam as a power source. Its development owed much to Thomas Edison, who had decided in 1878 to solve the problem of electric lighting. Rather than relying on individual creativity, Edison believed that professional collaboration fostered successful innovation. His research lab had a range of specialists and facilities that included an advanced library, a chemical lab, and eventually a glassblowing lab. From these beginnings came the electric light, the generator, and eventually the electric machine.

Railroads: Pioneers of Big Business

As this discussion makes clear, no one cause triggered the transformation of the American economy; rather a range of factors contributed to it. Among them was the completion of an effective and speedy national transportation and communications network. The network owed much to the largess of both federal and state governments that granted railroads lands from the public domain. The first transcontinental railroad was finished in 1869. Four additional transcontinental lines and miles of feeder and branch roads were laid down in the 1870s and 1880s with telegraph lines running alongside them. Transportation and communications worked together to create a national market that supported mass production and mass marketing.

Railroads also pioneered new management techniques that helped their own operations and those of other big businesses to be more productive and efficient. Railroads were large and complicated organizations that could not be run in the same way as smaller businesses. In 1854, the Erie Railroad hired engineer and inventor Daniel McCallum to discover how to make managers and the many employees more accountable. The system he worked out divided responsibilities, separated management from operations, and ensured a regular flow of information. His organizational model transformed railroads and proved useful for other businesses as they grew in scale.

Despite the generosity of government, railroads required unprecedented amounts of capital to finance construction. These high costs and heavy indebtedness encouraged aggressive business practices that led to instability in the industry. Slashing wages as a way of economizing often resulted in powerful worker unrest. Fierce competition led some companies to offer customers lower rates or secret rebates (cheaper fares in exchange for all of a company's traffic) to secure their business. Such practices instigated rate wars. Customers might benefit from declining freight rates, but they could end in bankruptcy for the railroad. In an attempt to bring some order to the railroad business in the 1870s, railroad leaders set up "pools"—informal agreements that set uniform rates or divided up the traffic. Yet these deals never completely succeeded. Too often, companies broke them, especially during business downturns.

Growth in Other Industries

By the last quarter of the century, the textile, metal, and machinery industries equaled the railroads in size. By 1900, more than 1,000 American factories had giant labor forces ranging between 500 and 1,000 workers. The huge size of such "workforce," as elsewhere combined with the subdivision of work contributed to the pattern of increasing production.

Business expansion was accomplished in one of two ways (or a combination of both). Some owners, like steel magnate Andrew Carnegie, integrated their businesses vertically—adding operations either before or after the production process. Even though he had introduced the most up-to-date innovations in his steel mills, Carnegie acquired his own sources of pig iron, coal, and coke—"backward" integration—to avoid dependence on suppliers. When Carnegie gained control of steamships and railroads to transport his finished products, he was integrating "forward." Companies that integrated vertically frequently achieved economies of scale through more efficient management techniques.

Other companies copied the railroads and integrated horizontally by combining similar businesses. They did not intend to control the various stages of production but rather to gain a monopoly of the market to eliminate competition and to stabilize prices. John D. Rockefeller used horizontal integration to control the oil market. Rockefeller bought or drove out competitors of his Standard Oil of New Jersey. Although the company never achieved a complete monopoly, by 1898 it was refining 84 percent of the nation's oil. While horizontal integration sometimes brought economies and greater profits, monopolistic control over prices did boost earnings.

In the oil business, Rockefeller observed, "the day of individual competition . . . is past and gone." As giant businesses competed intensely, often cutting wages and prices, they absorbed or eliminated smaller and weaker producers. Business ownership became increasingly concentrated. In 1870, some 808 American iron and steel firms competed in the marketplace. By 1900, fewer than 70 were left.

As businesses grew, like the railroads, they recognized the many advantages of legal incorporation. A corporation could raise money to finance large-scale operations by selling stock. Its legal identity meant that it survived the death of original and subsequent shareholders while the principle of limited liability protected the personal assets of both shareholders and investors. Such characteristics made investing in corporations more attractive.

Financing Postwar Growth

The economic transformation sketched here demanded huge amounts of capital along with the willingness to accept financial risks. The creation of the railroad system alone cost more than $1 billion by 1859; after the war another $10 billion went to complete the national railroad network. Foreign investors contributed a third of it. Americans too began to devote an increasing percentage of the national income to investment.

Although savings and commercial banks continued to invest depositors' capital, investment banking houses such as Morgan & Co. played a new and vital role in transferring resources to economic enterprises. These banks acquired blocks of corporate bonds (which offered set interest rates and eventually the repayment of principal) at a discount for interested investors and also sold stocks (which paid dividends only if the company made a profit). Because stocks were riskier investments than bonds, buyers were cautious at first. But when John Pierpont Morgan, a respected investment banker, began to market stocks, they became more popular. The market for industrial securities expanded rapidly in the 1880s and 1890s.

Although some Americans distrusted the financial markets, they were integral to the economic expansion of the late nineteenth century.

American Industry and the World

The industrialization of the late nineteenth century represented the second stage of the great transformation that began in Great Britain in the eighteenth century. By reorganizing production, often through the use of machinery, early manufacturers were able to turn out more and cheaper goods than at any time in human history. Innovation created the textile, mining, and metal industries and stimulated changes in transportation and communications. From Britain, industrialization spread to other countries in Europe as well as to the United States.

The second stage of the Industrial Revolution was marked by the application of science and technology to manufacturing and by the creation of new ways to mass-produce goods. The United States was the leader in developing techniques of mass production, while Germany excelled in using science and technology to reshape production. Technological innovations transformed German industry. As in the United States, giant firms turned out goods (especially heavy machinery and chemicals) for ever-lower prices. Along

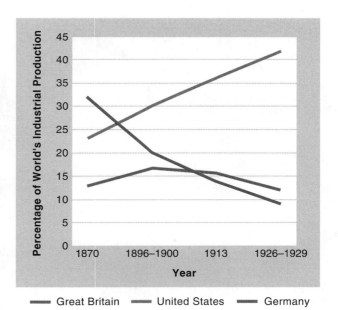

— Great Britain — United States — Germany

World's Industrial Output

This graph shows the changing pattern of industrial production among the world's most significant manufacturing nations. In which period did American industry make its greatest gains? What lies behind these rapid gains? What economic impact does the graph suggest that World War I (1914–1918) had on the three countries? How might the patterns of the 1920s shape the three countries' experiences during the 1930s?

with Great Britain, Germany and the United States produced two-thirds of the world's manufactured products between 1870 and 1930.

Great Britain, the world's most powerful nation during the nineteenth century, had long been its economic leader. But now the balance of power began to shift as German and American businesses developed large new enterprises, introduced new ways of organizing and efficiently managing them, invested heavily in equipment, and promoted research. Great Britain lost ground, preferring traditional ways of organizing businesses rather than the new corporate structure. British manufacturing continued to be centered in older industries such as textiles, while British investors channeled their capital away from domestic industries toward investment opportunities abroad. American railroads and subways were constructed partly with the assistance of British investors.

The full impact of the changed position of the United States in the world triggered by its industrial might became fully apparent only in the twentieth century. But the importance of connections with other nations was obvious. Standard Oil sent two-thirds of the kerosene it refined to overseas markets. Firms manufacturing sewing machines, office machines such as typewriters, and farm machinery dominated the world market. Singer Sewing Machine had a factory in Scotland in the 1880s and two decades later manufactured more than 400,000 machines in Moscow, employing 2,500 workers and 300 managers. American locomotives were exported to South America, parts of Africa and Europe, the Middle East, and Asia. The Baldwin Locomotive Works of Philadelphia produced as many engines as any other locomotive company in the world.

These connections between American business and other nations meant that events elsewhere in the world could affect the American economy. Furthermore, they suggested the intricate ties binding American business to other parts of the world. American industrial production contributed to the economic development of other countries around the globe, while American business also competed with foreign producers. John D. Rockefeller told a congressional committee that Standard Oil "spared no expense in forcing its products into the markets of the world among people civilized and uncivilized," and that the company was "holding its market against the competition of Russia and all the many countries which are producers of oil and competitors against American oil."

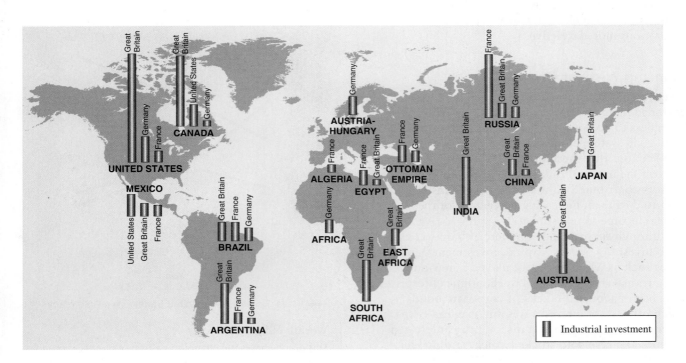

European and American Industrial Investment, 1900

Here we can see the broad impact that industrialized countries had on the rest of the world. Although industrialization was initially centered in western Europe and the United States, its influence was global. Industrial countries sought new markets, new sources of raw material, and new places for investment and development. In what places was the United States most interested? Where did individual European countries invest heavily? How would you compare the global impact of the United States to that of major European countries?

An Erratic Global Economy

Affected by national and worldwide economic trends, the transformation of the American economy was neither smooth nor steady. Two depressions, from 1873 to 1879 and from 1893 to 1897, surpassed the severity of economic downturns before the Civil War. Collapsing land values, unsound banking practices, and changes in the supply of money had caused antebellum depressions. The depressions of the late nineteenth century, when the economy was larger and more interdependent, were industrial, intense, and accompanied by widespread unemployment, a phenomenon new to American life. They were also related to economic declines in European industrial nations.

The business cycle had a recurring rhythm. The global pattern of falling prices encouraged fierce business competition that led to overproduction and the flooding of the market with goods. When the market was saturated, sales and profits declined, and the economy spiraled downward. Owners laid off workers (who lived solely on their wages for their livelihood). As workers economized and bought less food, farm prices plummeted. Farmers, like wage workers, cut purchases. Business stagnated. Finally, the railroads were hurt. Eventually, the cycle bottomed out, but millions of workers lost employment, thousands of businesses went bankrupt, and many Americans suffered.

Urban Expansion in the Industrial Age

As postwar manufacturers shifted from water to steam power, industries located in urban locations offered workers, specialized services, local markets, and railroad links to raw materials and distant markets. Industry, rather than commerce or finance, fueled urban expansion between 1870 and 1900, and cities of all sizes grew. New York and Philadelphia doubled and tripled their populations. Smaller cities, especially those in the industrial Midwest and the South, shared the growth; far western cities grew most rapidly of all. In 1870, some 25 percent of Americans lived in cities; by 1900, fully 40 percent of them did.

A Growing Population

The American population grew about 2 percent a year, but cities expanded more rapidly. Births contributed only modestly to urban explosion. Urban families tended to have fewer children than rural ones, and the host of urban health hazards meant that the death rate for infants was twice as high in cities as in the countryside. In the 1880s, half the children born in Chicago did not live to celebrate their fifth birthdays.

The real cause of rapid urban growth was the spectacular ability of the cities to attract newcomers from the nation's small towns and farms and abroad. In America's farmlands, machines were replacing human hands and freeing young people from agricultural life. The appeal of the city lay in the promise of employment. Although urban jobs were often dirty, dangerous, and exhausting, so was farm work. Furthermore, by 1890 industrial workers were earning hundreds of dollars more a year than farm laborers even though living costs were higher in urban areas. Additionally, the "gilded metropolis" offered a host of "marvels" absent from rural life. Shops, theaters, restaurants, department stores, baseball games, and the crowds amazed and amused young people coming from towns and farms.

Southern blacks, often single and young, also joined the migratory stream into the cities. In the West and North, blacks formed only a tiny part of the population, but in southern cities they were more numerous. About 44 percent of late-nineteenth-century Atlanta's residents were black, and so were 38 percent of Nashville's.

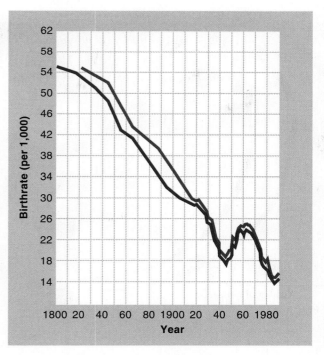

—— Total Birthrate   —— White Birthrate

Falling Birthrates

This chart shows the falling birthrate over the course of almost 200 years. By 1860, the average size of an American family was 5.3 members as compared to 5.8 in 1800. In what 20-year period during the nineteenth century did the largest decline in birthrates occur?

While the American birthrate was falling, it was higher than in Europe. By 1860, natural increase and immigration combined to make the American population as a whole larger than the British population. It was not long before the United States was also larger than Germany and France.

The New Immigration, 1880–1900

Sadie Frowne was born in a small village in Poland, where her mother ran a small grocery store and her father farmed. After her father died, times were hard, and mother and daughter came by steerage to New York, where they had relatives. Although she was only 13 years old, Sadie went to work, first as a domestic servant and then in a sweatshop. Her mother found a job in an underwear factory. Mother and daughter were part of a mass migration from Europe that sent 40 million people to the United States between 1815 and 1915 and another 20 million to Canada and Latin America. Like the Frownes, three-quarters of the newcomers arriving in the United States in the last quarter century stayed in the Northeast. Many of the rest settled in cities across the nation, where they soon outnumbered native-born whites.

Until 1880, three-quarters of the immigrants, so-called "old immigrants," hailed from the British Isles, Germany, and Scandinavia. Irish and Germans were the largest groups. Then the pattern slowly changed.

By 1890, "old immigrants" composed only 60 percent of the total number of newcomers. "New immigrants" such as the Frownes from southern and eastern Europe made up most of the rest. Italian Catholics and eastern European Jews (many of them Orthodox) were most numerous, followed by Slavs (Russians and Poles).

A variety of forces prompted the tide of migration. Better and cheaper transportation made the trip possible. Trains reached far into eastern and southern Europe. Even steerage passengers on transatlantic vessels could now expect a bed and communal washroom. The modernization of European economies also stimulated immigration. New agricultural techniques led landlords to consolidate their land, evicting longtime tenants. Some moved to European cities, others to Canada or South America. The largest group went to the United States. Artisans, their skills made obsolete by machinery, also pulled up stakes. But dissatisfaction with life at home also played a part. Especially in Russia, government persecutions and the expansion of military drafts drove millions of Jews and other minorities to emigrate.

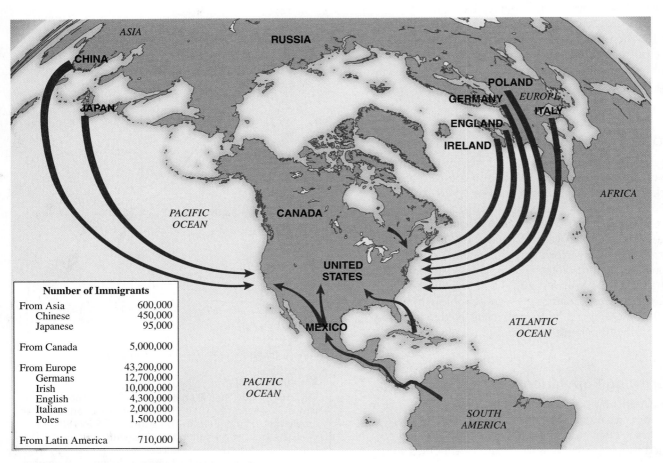

Number of Immigrants	
From Asia	600,000
Chinese	450,000
Japanese	95,000
From Canada	5,000,000
From Europe	43,200,000
Germans	12,700,000
Irish	10,000,000
English	4,300,000
Italians	2,000,000
Poles	1,500,000
From Latin America	710,000

Migration to the United States, 1860–1910

This map makes clear the many parts of the world that sent population to the United States. Many of those who came were dislodged by economic changes in their home countries. What were the most important short-term consequences of these migratory streams? What have been the most important long-term consequences?

Opportunity in "golden" America was the lure. State commissioners of immigration and American railroad and steamship companies wooed potential immigrants. Friends and relatives wrote optimistic letters promising help in finding work. American industrial cities were great places for "blast frnises and Rolen milles," explained one unskilled worker. Often letters included money for the passage or pictures of friends in alluringly fashionable clothes.

Like rural and small-town Americans, Europeans came primarily to work. Most were young, single men with few skills. Jews, however, came most often in family groups, and women predominated among the Irish. When times were good and American industry needed unskilled laborers, migration was heavy. In bad times, numbers fell off. Many immigrants hoped to earn enough money in America to realize their ambitions at home, and as many as a third eventually went back.

Although the greatest influx of Mexicans would come in the twentieth century, Mexican laborers also migrated to the United States. Like Europe, Mexico was in the throes of modernization. Overpopulation and new land policies uprooted many inhabitants, while the construction of a railroad from the Texas border 900 miles into Mexico in 1895 facilitated migration. Many Mexicans ended up in the Southwest and West, often working on railroads and in mines.

RECIPIENTS OF EUROPEAN MIGRATION, 1846–1932

While most migration from Europe was headed toward the United States, immigrants flocked to South America, Canada, and Australia and New Zealand as well. In Argentina, Italian immigrants made up a larger percentage of the population than they did in the United States and thus influenced Argentinean culture more profoundly than they affected American culture. What does this table suggest about the push–pull factors in the process of migration?

(Estimates in millions)

United States	34.2
Argentina and Uruguay	7.1
Canada	5.2
Brazil	4.4
Australia and New Zealand	3.5
Cuba	.9

Overpopulation, turmoil, unemployment, and crop failures brought Asians, mostly from south China, to the "Land of the Golden Mountains." Although only 264,000 Chinese came to the United

Life in the Old Country
Here we see a village street in Russia in the late nineteenth century. What is the condition of the street? What signs of utilities are there? How are the children clothed? What might immigrants who came from this village think about the urban conditions they encountered in the United States?

(Keystone-Mast Collection, URL/California Museum of Photography, University of California, Riverside)

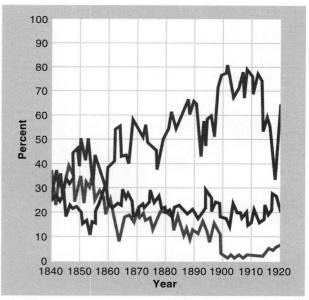

Unskilled laborers, domestics, and farmhands • Skilled workers • Farmers

Working-Class Immigration, 1840–1920
The large numbers of unskilled workers coming to the United States were responding to the need for unskilled labor during the second Industrial Revolution.

Source: U.S. Bureau of the Census.

States between 1860 and 1900, they constituted a significant minority on the West Coast. Most were unskilled male contract laborers, away from wives and families for years. They held some of the worst jobs in the West. They worked in mining and agriculture and on railroad and levee construction, and labored in factory and laundry work. To serve them, contractors brought in Chinese women to serve as prostitutes. Virtually enslaved, few of these women could pay off the costs of their passage or escape from brothel life.

The importance of migration from Europe, Mexico, and Asia can hardly be overestimated. Immigrants contributed to the country's rapid urbanization and provided much of the labor needed to accomplish the economic transformation of the late nineteenth century. Their presence also helped transform American society. The American population became far more heterogeneous in terms of ethnicity and religion than any other industrial nation. Since most immigrants were workers, they altered the character of the laboring class. Differences between immigrant groups and between immigrants and American workers weakened immigrants' ability to respond to employers with one voice. The presence of those who spoke little or no English and

had values and experiences very different from those of native-born Americans challenged American ideals, beliefs, and practices.

The Industrial City, 1880–1900

The late-nineteenth-century industrial city had new physical and social arrangements. Slums, nothing new, grew disturbingly, but grand mansions, handsome business and industrial buildings, grandiose civic monuments, parks, and acres of substantial middle-class homes also characterized urban life.

By the last quarter of the nineteenth century, the jumbled arrangements of the antebellum city based upon the necessity of walking to work disappeared. First the slow, horse-drawn "omnibus," then faster and bigger horse railways, and finally cable cars, trolleys, and subways extended city boundaries and allowed people who could afford to pay the fares to live far from their work. Distinctive central districts became places for professional employment and shopping. Surrounding the business center were areas of light manufacturing and wholesale activity with housing for workers. Beyond these working-class neighborhoods stretched middle-class residential areas and then the suburbs, with "pure air, peacefulness," and "natural scenery."

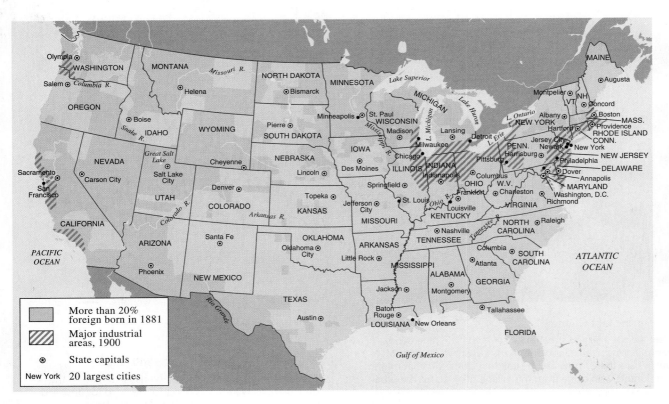

Foreign Immigration, 1880–1920

What areas does this map show that immigrants favored? Which did they avoid and why?

Scattered throughout the city were pockets of industrial activity surrounded by crowded working-class housing.

This new pattern, still characteristic of American cities today, reversed the early nineteenth-century urban form, in which the most desirable housing was in the heart of the city. Now it was on the perimeter. New living arrangements were also more segregated by race and class than those in the preindustrial walking city.

Lower East Side, New York

Here is a picture of life on Hester Street on New York's Lower East Side. Study the photograph to see what it reveals about living conditions in New York City. What indications are there of commercial activity? Why are there so many women on the street and so few men? What is suggested about children? What does the picture suggest about city services to this poor neighborhood? What are the major contrasts between this part of New York and the downtown scene shown on p. 444?

(New York City Views, Milstein Division of U.S. History, Local History & Genealogy, The New York Public Library/Art Resource, NY)

Neighborhoods and Neighborhood Life

Working-class neighborhoods clustered near the center of most industrial cities. Here lived newcomers from the American countryside and, because most immigrants settled in cities, crowds of foreigners as well. Although such districts often had an ethnic flavor, they were not ghettos. Immigrants and native-born Americans often lived in the same neighborhoods, on the same streets, and even in the same houses.

Working-class districts were often what would be called slums today, and it was not until the turn of the century that the public health movement began to improve living conditions there. Neighborhoods were crowded and unsanitary with inadequate public services. Many workers lived in houses once occupied by middle- and upper-class residents, now divided and subdivided to accommodate more people than originally intended. Others squeezed into tenements, built to accommodate as many families as possible. Outdoor privies, shared by several families, were the rule. Water came from outdoor hydrants, and women had to carry it inside. Such indoor fixtures as existed frequently emptied waste directly into unpaved alleys. Refuse piles stank in the summer and froze in the winter. Even when people kept their own living quarters clean, their outside environment was unsanitary. It was no surprise that urban death rates were so high.

Working-class housing, however, was far from uniform. Skilled workers might rent comfortable quarters, and a few even owned their own homes. Unskilled and semiskilled workers were not so fortunate. Yet despite the often drab circumstances, families succeeded in creating a sense of community. A wide range of institutions and associations came to life. Religious and ethnic associations helped immigrants feel at home. Jews gathered in their synagogues, Hebrew schools, and Hebrew- and Yiddish-speaking literary groups. Germans had their family saloons and educational and singing societies. Such organizations provided companionship, a social network, spiritual consolation, and a bridge between life in the "old country" and life in America. Yet they also separated those involved in them from native-born Americans and other ethnic groups.

African Americans faced the worst living conditions in the city, confined to segregated black neighborhoods in the North and back alleys and small streets in the South. But they too were sustained by a rich religious and associational life. Rapidly growing black churches like the African Methodist Episcopal Church retained the emotional exuberance of slave

New York City

Downtown New York City in 1890 hosted a mixture of horse-drawn vehicles and the new "horseless carriages." The nonresidential nature of the central business district gave a special character to the late-nineteenth-century city. What sorts of people appear in the picture? What signs of their social class does the picture provide?

(Brown Brothers)

religion. Black members of mainline Protestant denominations established separate branches that provided fellowship and support. The emergence of a small black middle class of ministers, businessmen, doctors, and lawyers furnished leaders for urban black communities.

Beyond working-class neighborhoods and pockets of black housing lay streets of middle-class houses. Here lived the urban lower middle class: clerks, shopkeepers, bookkeepers, salespeople, and small tradespeople. Their salaries allowed them to buy or rent houses with some privacy and comfort. Separate spaces for cooking and laundry work kept hot and often odorous housekeeping tasks away from other living areas. Many houses boasted up-to-date gas lighting and bathrooms. Outside, the neighborhoods were cleaner and more attractive than in the inner city. Residents could pay for garbage collection, gaslights, and other improvements.

On the fringes of the city were the districts peopled by the substantial middle class and the rich, who made their money in business, commerce, and the professions or inherited family fortunes. Public transportation sped them to and from their offices. Their houses were comfortable and inviting. Robert Work, a modestly successful cap and hat merchant, lived with his family in West Philadelphia and commuted more than four miles to work. The 1880 census revealed that the household contained two servants, two boarders, Robert's wife, and their son, who was in school. The Works' house had running hot and cold water, indoor bathrooms, central heating, and other modern conveniences. Elaborately carved furniture, rugs, draperies, and lace curtains probably graced the downstairs, where the family entertained and gathered for meals. Upstairs, comfortable bedrooms provided a maximum of privacy for family members. The live-in servants, who did most

of the housework, shared little of this space or privacy, and were probably restricted to the kitchen, the pantry, and bedrooms in the attic.

The Social Geography of the Cities

In industrial cities of this era, people were sorted by class, income, occupation, and race. Physical distances between upper- and middle-class neighborhoods and working-class neighborhoods eliminated or distorted firsthand knowledge of each other and bred social disapproval. While middle-class newspapers criticized "crowds of idlers, who, day and night, infect Main Street," often the "idlers" were men who could not find employment. A working-class woman's response to visitors who were attacking the use of alcohol captures the critical view from the bottom of society. "When the rich stopped drinking, it would be time to speak to the poor about it."

The Life of the Middle Class

The sharp comments made by different classes of Americans suggest the economic and social polarization that late-nineteenth-century industrialization spawned. For middle-class Americans, there was much to value in the new age. Between 1865 and 1890, average middle-class income rose about 30 percent. By 1900, fully 36 percent of urban families owned their homes.

More leisure time and greater access to consumer goods signaled industrialism's power to transform the lives of middle-class Americans. Plentiful immigrant servant girls relieved urban middle-class wives of many housekeeping chores, and smaller families lightened the burdens of motherhood. New department stores began to appear in the central business districts

Middle-Class Comfort

This photograph of a middle-class house in River Forest, Illinois, suggests the comfort available to those who could afford it and the ways suburban life shielded the middle class from the squalor and ugliness of industrial life. What does the exterior of the house suggest about what the inside might be like? How are the porch and garden treated? Why was the porch so large?

(Culver Pictures)

in the 1870s, feeding the desire for material possessions and revolutionizing retailing. Shopping for home furnishings and clothes became integral to many middle-class women's lives.

New Freedoms for Middle-Class Women

As many middle-class women acquired leisure time and enhanced purchasing power, they also won new freedoms. Several states granted women more property rights in marriage, adding to their growing sense of independence. Casting off confining crinolines, they now wore a shirtwaist blouse and ankle-length skirt that was more comfortable for working, school, and sports.

Using their new freedom, women joined organizations of all kinds—literary societies, charity groups, reform clubs. There they gained organizational experience, awareness of their talents, and contact with people and problems outside their traditional family roles. The depression of 1893 stimulated many women to investigate slum and factory conditions, and some began even earlier. Jane Addams, who told her college classmates in 1881 to lead lives "filled with good works and honest toil," went on to found Hull House, a famous social settlement.

After the Civil War, educational opportunities for women expanded. New women's colleges offered programs similar to those at competitive men's

colleges, while midwestern and western state schools dropped prohibitions against women. In 1890, some 13 percent of all college graduates were women; by 1900, nearly 20 percent were. Higher education prepared middle-class women for conventional female roles as well as for work and public service. A few courageous graduates overcame many barriers to enter the professions. By the early twentieth century, the number of women professionals (including teachers) was increasing at three times the rate for men.

Job opportunities for educated middle-class women, however, were generally limited to the social services and teaching, a highly demanding but poorly paying field that grew as urban schools expanded under the pressure of a burgeoning population. By the 1890s, the willingness of middle-class women to work for low pay opened up new forms of employment in office work, nursing, and department stores. But moving up to high-status jobs proved difficult, even for middle-class women.

One reason for the greater independence of American women was that they were having fewer babies. This was especially true of educated women. In 1900, nearly one married woman in five was childless. Advances in birth control technology (the modern diaphragm was developed in 1880) helped make new patterns possible. Decreasing family size and an increase in the divorce rate (1 out of 12 marriages in 1905) fueled male fears. Arguments against the new woman intensified as many men reaffirmed Victorian stereotypes of "woman's sphere." One male orator in 1896 inveighed against the new woman's public role because "a woman's brain involves emotions rather than intellect." Male campaigns against prostitution and for sex hygiene, as well as efforts to reinforce traditional sex roles, reflected deep fears that female passions might weaken male vigor.

Male Mobility and the Success Ethic

As middle-class women's lives were changing, so were men's. Expansion of the postwar economy and changes in the structure of American business opened up many new job opportunities for middle-class men. The growing complexity of census classifications reveals some of these new jobs. Where the census taker had once noted only the occupation of "clerk," now were listed "accountant," "salesman," and "shipping clerk." As the lower ranks of the white-collar world became more specialized, the number of middle-class jobs increased.

Because these new careers required more education, the educational system expanded. Public high schools increased from 160 in 1870 to 6,000 in 1900. By that year, most states and territories had compulsory school attendance laws. Enrollment in colleges and universities nearly doubled, from 53,000 in 1870 to 101,000 in 1900. Universities gained a new stature in American life. Land-grant state universities (made possible by the Morrill Act of 1862) expanded, and philanthropists established research universities such as Stanford, Johns Hopkins, and the University of Chicago.

These developments led to greater specialization and professionalism. Before the Civil War, a Swedish pioneer in Wisconsin described a young mason who "laid aside the trowel, got himself some medical books, and assumed the title of doctor." But by the 1890s, with government licensing and the rise of professional schools, the word *career* began to take on its modern meaning. No longer were tradespeople likely to read up on medicine and become doctors. Organizations such as the American Medical Association and the American Bar Association were regulating and professionalizing membership.

The need for lawyers, bankers, architects, and insurance agents to serve business and industry expanded career opportunities. As large companies formed and became bureaucratized, business required many more managerial positions. As the public sector expanded, new careers in social services and government opened up as well. Young professional experts with graduate training in the social sciences filled many of them. The professional disciplines of history, economics, sociology, psychology, and political science all date from the last 20 years of the nineteenth century.

The social ethic of the age stressed that economic rewards were available to anyone who fervently sought them. Many people argued that, unlike in Europe, where family background and social class determined social rank, in America, few barriers held back those of good character and diligent work habits. It was endlessly pointed out that while John D. Rockefeller had raised turkeys as a boy and Andrew Carnegie's mother had been a washerwoman, both men had risen spectacularly through their own efforts. Horatio Alger's rags-to-riches novels, read by millions, reinforced the message. In his popular novel, *Ragged Dick,* the hero begins as a ragged shoeshine boy living on the streets. An unexpected gift of a new suit of clothes helps to raise Dick's aspirations to "learn the business and grow up 'spectable." As he begins the process of becoming respectable, good fortune intervenes again. Dick rescues a child who tumbles into the icy waters of the harbor. Her father completes the hero's transformation from Ragged Dick to Richard Hunter, Esq., by offering him a job as a clerk in his counting house. Although moralists pointed to virtuous habits as crucial in Alger's heroes, success often depended as much on luck as on pluck.

Unlimited and equal opportunity for upward advancement in America has never been as easy as the "bootstraps" ethic maintains. But the persistence of the success myth owes something to the fact that many

Americans, particularly those who began well, did rise rapidly. Native-born, middle-class whites tended to have the skills, resources, and connections that opened up the most desirable jobs. The typical big businessman was a white, Anglo-Saxon Protestant from a middle- or upper-class family whose father was most likely in business, banking, or commerce.

Industrial Work and the Laboring Class

David Lawlor, an Irish immigrant who came to the United States in 1872, might have agreed with the message of the Alger stories. As a child, he worked in the Fall River textile mills and read Horatio Alger in his free time. Like Alger's heroes, he went to night school and rose in the business world, eventually becoming an advertising executive.

But Lawlor's success was exceptional. Most working-class Americans labored long hours on dangerous factory floors, in cramped sweatshops, or in steamy basement kitchens for meager wages. As industrialization transformed the nature of work and the composition of the workforce, traditional opportunities for mobility and even for a secure livelihood slipped from the grasp of many working-class Americans.

The Impact of Ethnic Diversity

Immigrants made up a sizable portion of the urban working class in the late nineteenth century. They formed 20 percent of the labor force and more than 40 percent of laborers in the manufacturing and extractive industries. In cities, where they tended to settle, they accounted for more than half the working-class population.

Industrial work, urban life, labor protest, and local politics were influenced by the fact that more than half the urban industrial class was foreign, unskilled, perhaps illiterate, and often possessed only a limited command of the English language. Eager for the unskilled positions rapidly being created as mechanization and mass production took hold, immigrants often shared little with native-born workers or even with one another. Because of immigration, American working-class society was a mosaic of nationalities, cultures, religions, and interests.

The ethnic diversity of the industrial workforce helps explain its occupational patterns. Generally occupation was related to ethnic background and experience. At the top of the working-class hierarchy, native-born Protestant whites held a disproportionate share of well-paying skilled jobs. They were the aristocrats of the working class. Their jobs demanded expertise and training, as had been true of skilled industrial workers in the pre–Civil War period. But their occupations bore the mark of late-nineteenth-century industrialism. They were machinists, iron puddlers and rollers, engineers, foremen, mechanics, and printers.

Skilled northern European immigrants filled most of the middle-rank positions. Often they had held similar jobs in their homeland. The Germans found work as tailors, bakers, brewers, and shoemakers, while Cornish and Irish miners secured skilled jobs in midwestern and western mines. The Jews, who had tailoring experience in their homelands, became the backbone of the garment industry (where they faced little competition from American male workers, who considered it unmanly to work on women's clothes).

But most of the "new immigrants" from southern and central Europe had no urban industrial experience. They labored in the unskilled, dirty jobs near the bottom of the occupational ladder. They relined blast furnaces in steel mills, carried raw materials or finished products from place to place, or cleaned up after skilled workers. Often, they were carmen or day laborers on the docks, ditchdiggers, or construction workers. Hiring was often on a daily basis, arranged through intermediaries such as the Italian padrone. Unskilled work provided little in the way of either job stability or income.

At the bottom, blacks occupied the most marginal positions as janitors, servants, porters, and laborers. Racial discrimination generally excluded them from industrial jobs, even though their occupational background differed little from that of rural white immigrants. There were always plenty of whites eager to work, so it was not necessary to hire blacks except occasionally as scabs during a labor strike. "It is an exceptional case where you find any colored labor in the factories, except as porters," observed one white. "Neither colored female…nor male laborer is engaged in the mechanical arts."

The Changing Nature of Work

The rise of big business, characterized by mechanization and mass production, changed the size and shape of the workforce and the nature of work itself. More and more Americans became wage earners. The number of manufacturing workers doubled between 1880 and 1900, with the fastest expansion in the unskilled and semiskilled ranks.

But the need for skilled workers remained. New positions, as in steam fitting and structural ironwork, appeared as industries expanded and changed. Increasingly, older skills became obsolete, however. And all skilled workers faced the possibility that technical advances would eliminate their favored jobs or that employers would hire unskilled helpers to take over parts of their jobs. In industries as different as shoemaking, cigar making, and iron puddling, new methods of production and organization undermined the position of skilled workers.

INCREASE IN SIZE OF INDUSTRIES, 1860–1900

This table highlights the dramatic changes in the workplace over a 40-year period. Think about what the figures suggest about the experience of work. What industries typically had the largest workforces in 1900? What industries had the most dramatic increases in the size of their workforces between 1860 and 1900?

Industry	Average Number of Workers per Establishment	
	1860	1900
Cotton goods	112	287
Glass	81	149
Iron and steel	65	333
Hosiery and knit goods	46	91
Silk and silk goods	39	135
Woollen goods	33	67
Carpets and rugs	31	213
Tobacco	30	67
Slaughtering and meatpacking	20	61
Paper and wood pulp	15	65
Shipbuilding	15	42
Agricultural implements	8	65
Leather	5	40
Malt liquors	5	26

Source: U.S. Bureau of the Census.

Work Settings and Experiences

The workplace could be a dock or cluttered factory yard, a multistoried textile mill, a huge, barnlike steel mill with all the latest machinery, or a mine tunnel hundreds of feet underground. A majority of American manufacturing workers now labored in factories, and the numbers of those working in large plants dominated by the unceasing rhythms of machinery increased steadily.

Some Americans, however, still toiled in small shops and sweatshops tucked away in basements, lofts, or immigrant apartments. Even in these smaller settings, the pressure to produce was relentless, for volume, not hours, determined pay. When contractors cut wages, workers had to speed up to earn the same pay.

The organization of work divided workers. Those paid by the piece competed against the speed, agility, and output of other workers. In large factories, workers separated into small work groups and mingled only rarely with the rest of the workforce. The clustering of ethnic groups in certain types of work also undermined working-class solidarity.

A Garment Factory

Many young Jewish women worked in the garment industry. You see an example of their working conditions here. How would you describe these women's workplace? How safe is it? How comfortable is it? What might it be like to work here in the summer? Who are the men in the background?

(Brown Brothers)

All workers had a very long working day in common. Although the factory day had fallen from the 12 hours expected before the Civil War, people still spent more than half their waking hours on the job—usually 10 hours a day, six days a week. Different occupations had specific demands. Bakers worked 65 hours a week; canners worked 77. Sweatshop workers might labor far into the night, long after factory workers had gone home.

Work was usually unhealthy, dangerous, and comfortless. Although a few states passed laws to regulate work conditions, enforcement was spotty. Few owners observed regulations about toilets, drinking facilities, or washing areas. Nor did they concern themselves with the health or safety of their employees. Women, bent over sewing machines, developed digestive illnesses and curved spines. Poorly ventilated mines stank of human waste and spoiled garbage, with temperatures sometimes rising above 120 degrees. Miners worked with dynamite and all too often died in cave-ins caused by inadequate timber supports in the mine shafts. When new drilling machinery was introduced into western mines, it produced tiny stone particles that caused lung disease.

Accident rates in the United States far exceeded those of Europe's industrial nations. Each year, 35,000 workers died from industrial mishaps. Iron and steel mills were the big killers, although the railroads alone accounted for 6,000 fatalities a year during the 1890s. Nationwide, nearly one-quarter of the men reaching age 20 in 1880 would not live to see 44 (compared with 7 percent today). American business owners had

little legal responsibility—and some felt none—for employees' safety or health. The law placed the burden of avoiding accidents on the workers, who were expected to quit if they thought conditions were unsafe.

Industrial workers labored at jobs that were also increasingly specialized and monotonous. The size of many firms allowed a kind of specialization that was impossible in a small enterprise. Even skilled workers did not produce a complete product, and the range of their skills was narrowing. "A man never learns the machinist's trade now," one New Yorker grumbled. "The different branches of the trade are divided and subdivided so that one man may make just a particular part of a machine and may not know anything whatever about another part of the same machine." Cabinetmakers found themselves not crafting cabinets but putting together and finishing pieces made by others. In such circumstances, many skilled workers complained that they were being reduced to drudges and wage slaves. This discontent with the nature of work contributed to working-class unrest.

Still, industrial work provided some personal benefits. New arrangements helped humanize the workplace. Workers who obtained jobs through family and friends labored alongside them. In most industries, the foreman controlled day-to-day activities. He chose workers from the crowds at the gate, fired those who proved unsatisfactory, selected appropriate materials and equipment, and determined the order and pace of production. Because the foreman was himself a member of the working class who had climbed his way up, he might sympathize with subordinates. Yet the foreman could also be authoritarian and harsh, especially if the workers he supervised were unskilled or belonged to another ethnic group.

The Worker's Share in Industrial Progress

The huge fortunes accumulated by famous industrialists such as Andrew Carnegie and John D. Rockefeller during the late nineteenth century dramatized the pattern of wealth concentration that had begun in the early period of industrialization. In 1890, the top 1 percent of American families possessed more than a quarter of the wealth, whereas the share held by the top 10 percent was about 73 percent. Economic growth still benefited people who influenced its path, and they claimed the lion's share of the rewards.

But what of the workers who tended the machines that lay at the base of industrial wealth? Working-class Americans made up the largest segment of the labor force (more than 50 percent), so their experience reveals important facets of the American social and economic systems and American values.

Statistics of increasing production, of ever more goods, tell part of the story. Figures on real wages also reveal something important. Industry still needed skilled workers and paid them well. Average real wages rose more than 50 percent between 1860 and 1900. Skilled manufacturing workers, about one-tenth of the nonagricultural working class in the late nineteenth century, saw their wages rise by about 74 percent. But wages for the unskilled increased by only 31 percent. The differential was substantial and widened as the century drew to a close.

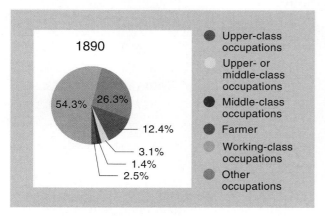

Labor Force Distribution, 1890

Whereas a majority of Americans in the twentieth century defined themselves as middle class, in the nineteenth century, most Americans held working-class jobs. Approximately what percentage of workers held middle- or upper-class jobs?

Source: U.S. Bureau of the Census.

Taken as a whole, the working class accrued substantial benefits in the late nineteenth century, even if its share of the total wealth did not increase. American workers had more material comforts than their European counterparts. But the general picture conceals the realities of working-class economic life. A U.S. Bureau of Labor study of working-class families in 1889 revealed great disparities of income: a young girl in a silk mill made $130 a year; a laborer earned $384 a year; a carpenter took home $686. The carpenter's family lived in a four-room house. Their breakfast usually included meat or eggs, hotcakes, butter, cake, and coffee. The silk worker and the laborer, by contrast, ate bread and butter as the main portion of two of their three daily meals. Their yearly income fell far short of the $600 to $800 that was necessary for a family to survive in any comfort.

For workers without steady employment, rising real wages were meaningless. Workers, especially those who were unskilled, often found work only sporadically. When times were slow or conditions depressed, as they were between 1873 and 1879 and 1893 and 1897, employers, especially in small firms, laid off both skilled and unskilled workers and reduced wages. Even in a good year like 1890, one out of every five men outside agriculture had been unemployed at least a month. One-quarter lost four months or more.

Unemployment insurance did not exist, so workers had no cushion against losing their jobs. One woman grimly recalled, "If the factory shuts down without warning, as it did last year for six weeks, we have a growing expense with nothing to counterbalance." Older workers who had no social security or those who had accidents on the job but no disability insurance had severely reduced incomes. Occasionally, kindhearted employers offered assistance in hard times, but it was rarely enough. The Lawrence Manufacturing Company compensated one of its workers $50 for the loss of a hand and awarded another $66.71 for a severed arm.

Although nineteenth-century ideology pictured men as breadwinners, many working-class married men could not earn enough to support their families. A working-class family's standard of living thus often depended on its number of workers. Today, two-income families are common. But in the nineteenth century, married women did not usually take outside employment, although they contributed to family income by taking in sewing, laundry, and boarders. In 1890, only 3.3 percent of married women worked in the paid labor force.

The Family Economy

If married women did not work for pay outside their homes, their children did. The laborer whose annual earnings amounted to only $384 depended on his

TWO NINETEENTH-CENTURY BUDGETS

What do these two monthly family budgets reveal about different standards of living and different consumption choices? What do you consider the most significant differences between the lives of these two families? In 2001 dollars, the laborer took home $448 a month while the accountant earned about $1,259 a month. The laborer spent about $530 on his monthly expenses while the accountant's budgeted expenses came to about $817.

	Monthly budget of a laborer, his wife, and one child in 1891; his income is $23.67	Monthly budget of a married bank accountant with no children in 1892; his income is about $66.50
Food	$6.51	$13.22
Rent	9.02	9.88
Furniture	3.61	0.30
Taxes and insurance	3.32	7.11
Utilities	2.94	4.99
Sundries	1.09	2.10
Liquor and tobacco	0.66	0.42
Medicine	0.29	0.27
Clothes	0.21	0.19
Dry goods	0.16	2.45
Postage	0.10	—
Transportation	0.08	1.71
Reading material	—	0.53
	$27.99	$43.17

Source: Chart from *The Changing Face of Inequality* by Oliver Zunz © University of Chicago Press. Reprinted with permission.

NUMBER OF WOMEN EMPLOYED IN SELECTED INDUSTRIES, 1870–1910

This chart shows the growth of women workers in several key industries. Although far fewer women had paid jobs than men, they were never absent from the workplace.

Year	Industry					
	Chemical	Electrical	Paper	Printing	Food	Metal
1870	403	—	6,242	4,397	2,460	5,217
1880	862	—	14,126	9,322	4,503	7,668
1890	2,140	—	22,444	24,640	10,169	15,232
1900	3,427	—	27,261	32,938	19,713	21,335
1910	15,198	12,093	33,419	47,640	48,099	56,208

Source: U.S. Department of Labor, Women's Bureau, *Women's Occupations Through Seven Decades,* Bulletin no. 218 (Washington, D.C.: Government Printing Office, 1947), 95, 120, 121, 123, 130, 133.

13-year-old son, not his wife, to go out and earn an extra $196, critical to the family's welfare. Sending children into the labor market was an essential survival strategy for many working-class Americans. In 1880, one-fifth of the nation's children between ages 10 and 14 held jobs.

Child labor was closely linked to a father's income, which in turn depended on skill, ethnic background, and occupation. Immigrant families more frequently sent their young children out to work (and also had more children) than native-born families. Middle-class reformers who sentimentalized childhood disapproved of parents who put their children to work. As one investigator of working-class life reported, "Father never attended school, and thinks his children will have sufficient schooling before they reach their tenth year, thinks no advantage will be gained from longer attendance at school, so children will be put to work as soon as able." Reformers believed that such fathers condemned their children to future destitution by denying them education. Actually, sending children to work was a means of coping with the immediate threat of poverty, financing the education of one of the children, or paying off the mortgage.

Many more young people over age 14 were working for wages than was the case for children. Half of all Philadelphia's students had quit school by that age. Daughters as well as sons were expected to take positions, although young women from immigrant families were more likely to work than young American women. As *Arthur's Home Magazine* for women pointed out, a girl's earnings would help "to relieve her hard-working father of the burden of her support, to supply home with comforts and refinements, to educate a younger brother." By 1900, nearly 20 percent of American women were in the labor force.

Employed women earned far less than men. An experienced female factory worker might be paid between $5 and $6 a week, whereas an unskilled male laborer could make about $8. Discrimination, present from women's earliest days in the workforce, persisted. Still, factory jobs were desirable because they often paid better than other kinds of work open to women.

By the 1890s, new forms of employment in office work, nursing, and clerking in department stores offered some young women attractive opportunities. In San Francisco, the number of clerical jobs doubled between 1852 and 1880. But most women faced limited employment options, and ethnic taboos and cultural traditions helped shape choices. About a quarter of working women secured factory jobs. Italian and Jewish women (whose cultural backgrounds virtually forbade their going into domestic service) clustered in the garment industry, and Poles and Slavs went into textiles, food processing, and meatpacking. In some industries, such as textiles and tobacco, women composed an important segment of the workforce. But about 40 percent of them, especially those from Irish, Scandinavian, and black families, took jobs as maids, cooks, laundresses, and nurses.

Domestic service was arduous, with few machines to lighten the labor. A Minneapolis housemaid described an exhausting routine. "I used to get up at four o'clock every morning and work till ten P.M. every day of the week. Mondays and Tuesdays, when the washing and ironing was to be done,

I used to get up at two o'clock and wash or iron until breakfast time." Nor could domestics count on much sympathy from their employers. "Do not think it necessary to give a hired girl as good a room as that used by members of the family," said one lady of the house. "She should sleep near the kitchen and not go up the front stairs or through the front hall to reach her room." Live-in servants received room and board plus $2 to $5 a week. The fact that so many women took domestic work despite the job's disadvantages speaks clearly of their limited opportunities.

The dismal situation facing working women drove some, such as Rose Haggerty, into prostitution. Burdened with a widowed and sickly mother and four young brothers and sisters, Rose was only 14 years old when she started work at a New York paper-bag factory. Her fortunes improved when a friend helped her buy a sewing machine. Rose then sewed shirts at home, often working as long as 14 hours a day, to support her family. Suddenly, the piecework rate for shirts was slashed, and, desperate, Rose contemplated suicide. But when a sailor offered her money for spending the night with him, she realized she had an alternative. Prostitution meant food, rent, and heat for her family. "Let God Almighty judge who's to blame most," the 20-year-old Rose reflected, "I that was driven, or them that drove me to the pass I'm in."

Prostitution appears to have increased in the late nineteenth century, although there is no way of knowing the actual numbers of women involved. Probably most single women accepted the respectable jobs open to them. They tolerated discrimination and low wages because their families depended on their contributions. They also knew that when they married, they would probably leave the paid workforce forever.

Marriage hardly ended women's work, however. Like colonial families, late-nineteenth-century working-class families operated as cooperative economic units. The unpaid domestic labor of working-class wives was critical to family survival. With husbands away for 10 to 11 hours a day, women bore the burden of child care and the domestic chores. Because working-class families could not afford labor-saving conveniences, housework was time-consuming and arduous. Without an icebox, a working-class woman spent part of each day shopping for food (more expensive in small quantities). Doing laundry entailed carrying water from outside pumps, heating it on the stove, washing the clothes, rinsing them with fresh water, and hanging them up to dry. Ironing was a hot and unpleasant job in small and stuffy quarters. Keeping an apartment or house clean when the atmosphere was grimy and unpaved roads were littered with refuse and horse dung was a challenge.

CONGRESSIONAL HEARINGS

Students of history can discover fascinating materials on nineteenth-century life by exploring the published records of the American political system. Privately published from 1833 to 1873, the *Congressional Globe* details the proceedings of the Senate and the House, revealing the nature of congressional deliberations in an era when debate, such as that over the Compromise of 1850 in the Senate, was the focus of the national political process. After 1873, the government published these proceedings in the *Congressional Record*. The *Record* is not a literal transcription of debate, for members can edit their remarks, insert speeches, and add supporting materials. Still, it gives a good sense of the proceedings of both the Senate and the House.

Much of the serious work of government, past and present, takes place in congressional committees. One foreign observer called Congress "not so much a legislative assembly as a huge panel from which committees are selected." The committee system is almost as old as the constitutional system itself and is rooted in the Constitution's granting of lawmaking power to Congress. From the start, Congress divided into assorted committees to gather information, enabling members to evaluate legislative proposals intelligently.

Two kinds of committees existed in the House and Senate. Standing committees had permanent responsibility for reviewing legislative proposals on a host of financial, judicial, foreign, and other affairs. By 1892, the Senate had 44 standing committees and the House had 50. Select committees were temporary, often charged with investigating specific problems. In the late nineteenth century, congressional committees investigated such problems as Ku Klux Klan terrorism, the sweatshop system, tenement house conditions, and relations between labor and capital. In each case, extensive hearings were held.

Congressional hearings have become increasingly important sources of historical evidence in recent years. They show the Senate and the House of Representatives in action as they seek to translate popular sentiment into law.

But they also reveal public attitudes as they record the voices of Americans testifying in committee halls. Because one function of legislative hearings is to enable diverse groups to express their frustrations and desires, they often contain the testimony of witnesses drawn from many different social and economic backgrounds. Included here is the partial testimony of a Massachusetts laborer who appeared before the Senate Committee on Education and Labor in 1883. Because working-class witnesses like this man usually left no other record of their experiences or thoughts, committee reports and hearings provide valuable insight into the lives and attitudes of ordinary people.

Hearings also reveal the attitudes and social values of committee members. Hence, caution is needed in the use of hearings. Witnesses often have vested interests and are frequently coached and cautious in what they communicate on the stand. Rather than seeking to illuminate issues, committee members often speak and explore questions for other—usually political—reasons.

Despite these limitations, committee hearings are rich sources of information. In this excerpt, what can you learn about the life of the witness testifying before the committee? In what way do the values of the committee members conflict with those of the witness? Why is the chairman so harsh toward the witness? Is he entirely unsympathetic? Why do you think the questioner overemphasizes the relationship between moral beliefs and economic realities? What kind of social tensions does the passage reveal?

Reflecting on the Past Have you observed any recent hearings of congressional investigating committees on television? Are moral behavior and hunger still topics of concern for Americans? How is the interaction between modern "haves" and "have-nots" similar to and different from the interaction between this laborer and the committee members in 1883? Do ethical beliefs and economic realities still separate social classes?

Hearings on the Relations Between Labor and Capital

Q. You get a dollar a day, wages?—A. That is the average pay that men receive. The rents, especially in Somerville, are so high that it is almost impossible for the working men to live in a house.

Q. What rent do you pay?—A. For the last year I have been paying $10 a month, and most of the men out there have to pay about that amount for a house—$10 a month for rooms.

Q. For a full house, or for rooms only?—A. For rooms in a house.

Q. How many rooms?—A. Four or five.

Q. How much of your time have you been out of work, or idle, for the last full year, say?—A. I have not been out of work more than three weeks altogether, because I have been making a dollar or two peddling or doing something, when I was out of work, in the currying line.

Q. Making about the same that you made at your trade?—A. Well, I have made at my trade a little more than that, but that is the average.

Q. Are you a common drunkard?—A. No, sir.

Q. Do you smoke a great deal?—A. Well, yes, sir; I smoke as much as any man.

The CHAIRMAN. I want to know how much you have got together in the course of a year, and what you have spent your money for, so that folks can see whether you have had pay enough to get rich on.

The WITNESS. A good idea.

The CHAIRMAN. That is precisely the sort of idea that people ought to know. How much money do you think you have earned during this last year; has it averaged a dollar a day for three hundred days?

The WITNESS. I have averaged more than that; I have averaged $350 or $400. I will say, for the year.

Q. You pay $10 a month rent; that makes $120 a year?—A. Yes, sir.

The CHAIRMAN. I have asked you these questions in this abrupt way because I want to find out whether you have spent much for practices that might have been dispensed with. You say you smoke?

The WITNESS. Yes, sir.

Q. How much a week do you spend for that?—A. I get 20 cents worth of tobacco a week.

Q. That is $10.40 a year?—A. Yes, sir.

Q. And you say you are not a common drunkard?—A. No, sir.

Q. Do you imagine that you have spent as much more for any form of beer, or ale, or anything of that kind, that you could have got along without?—A. No, sir.

Q. How much do you think has gone in that way?—A. About $1 or $2.

Q. During the whole year?—A. Yes, sir.

Q. That would make $11.40 or $12.40—we will call it $12—gone for wickedness. Now, what else, besides your living, besides the support of your wife and children?—A. Well, I don't know as there is anything else.

Q. Can you not think of anything else that was wrong?—A. No, sir.

Q. Twelve dollars have gone for sin and iniquity; and $120 for rent; that makes $132?—A. Yes.

Q. How many children have you?—A. Two.

Q. Your family consists of yourself, your wife, and two children?—A. Yes.

Q. One hundred and thirty-two dollars from $400 leaves you $268, does it not?—A. Yes, sir.

Q. And with that amount you have furnished your family?—A. Yes, sir.

Q. You have been as economical as you could, I suppose?—A. Yes.

Q. How much money have you left?—A. Sixty dollars in debt.

Q. How did you do that?—A. I don't know, sir.

Q. Can you not think of something more that you have wasted?—A. No, sir.

Q. Have you been as careful as you could?—A. Yes, sir.

Q. And you have come out at the end of the year $60 in debt?—A. Yes, sir.

Q. Have you been extravagant in your family expenses?—A. No, sir; a man can't be very extravagant on that much money. . . .

Q. And there are four of you in the family?—A. Yes, sir.

Q. How many pounds of beefsteak have you had in your family, that you bought for your own home consumption within this year that we have been speaking of?—A. I don't think there has been five pounds of beefsteak.

Q. You have had a little pork steak?—A. We had a half a pound of pork steak yesterday; I don't know when we had any before.

Q. What other kinds of meat have you had within a year?—A. Well, we have had corn beef twice I think that I can remember this year—on Sunday, for dinner.

Q. Twice is all that you can remember within a year?—A. Yes—and some cabbage.

Q. What have you eaten?—A. Well, bread mostly, when we could get it; we sometimes couldn't make out to get that, and have had to go without a meal.

Q. Has there been any day in the year that you have had to go without anything to eat?—A. Yes, sir, several days.

Q. More than one day at a time?—A. No.

Q. How about the children and your wife—did they go without anything to eat too?—A. My wife went out this morning and went to a neighbor's and got a loaf of bread and fetched it home, and when she got home the children were crying for something to eat.

Q. Have the children had anything to eat to-day except that, do you think?—A. They had that loaf of bread—I don't know what they have had since then, if they have had anything.

Q. Did you leave any money at home?—A. No, sir.

Q. If that loaf is gone, is there anything in the house?—A. No, sir; unless my wife goes out and gets something; and I don't know who would mind the children while she goes out.

As managers of family resources, married women bore important responsibilities. What American families had once produced for themselves now had to be bought. It was up to the working-class wife to scour secondhand shops to find cheap clothes for her family. Domestic economies were vital to survival. Women also supplemented family income by taking in work. Jewish and Italian women frequently did piecework and sewing at home. Other families kept boarders. Immigrant families in particular often made ends meet by taking single, young countrymen into their homes. Having boarders meant providing meals and clean laundry, juggling different work schedules, and sacrificing privacy. But the advantages of extra income far outweighed the disadvantages for many working-class families.

Black women's working lives reflected the obstacles African Americans faced in late-nineteenth-century cities. Although only about 7 percent of married white women worked outside the home, African American women did so both before and after marriage. In southern cities in 1880, about three-quarters of single black women and one-third of married black women worked outside the home. Because industrial employers would not hire African American women, most of them were domestics or laundresses. The high percentage of married black women in the labor force reflected the marginal wages their husbands earned. But it may also be explained in part by the lesson learned during slavery that children could thrive without the constant attention of their mothers.

Capital Versus Labor

Class conflict characterized late-nineteenth-century industrial life. Although workers welcomed the progress that factories made possible, many rejected their employers' values, which emphasized individual gain at the expense of collective good. While owners reaped most of the profits, workers believed they were turning into wage slaves and that the process threatened to undermine the republic itself.

On-the-Job Protests

Workers and employers struggled over control of the workplace. Many workers staunchly resisted unsatisfactory working conditions and the tendency of bosses to treat them "like any other piece of machinery, to be made to do the maximum amount of work with the minimum expenditure of fuel." Skilled workers, such as iron puddlers and glassblowers, had indispensable knowledge about the production process as well as practical experience and were in a key position to direct on-the-job actions. Sometimes they attempted to make critical work decisions. Detroit printers, for example, tried to retain the right to distribute headlines and white space (the "fat") rather than letting their bosses hand out the fat as a special reward and means of increasing competition among workers. Others hoped to humanize work. Cigar makers clung to their custom of having one worker read to others as they performed their tedious chores.

Workers sought to regulate the pace of production. Too many goods meant an inhuman pace of work and even overproduction, layoffs, and lowered prices paid for piecework. So an experienced worker might whisper to a new hand, "See here, young fellow, you're working too fast. You'll spoil our job for us if you don't go slower."

A newspaper account of a glassblowers' strike in 1884 illustrates the clash between capital and labor. With an eye toward bigger profits, the boss tried to increase output. "He knew if the limit was taken off, the men could work ten or twelve hours every day in the week; that in their thirst for the mighty dollar they would kill themselves with labor; they would 'black sheep' their fellows by doing the labor of two men." But his employees resisted his proposal, refusing to drive themselves to exhaustion for a few dollars more. "They thundered out no. They even offered to take a reduction that would average ten percent all around, but they said, 'We will keep the forty-eight box limit.' Threats and curses would not move them." For these workers, a decent pace of work and a respectable wage were more important than promises of extra money.

In attempting to protect themselves and the dignity of their labor, workers devised ways of combating employer attempts to speed up the production process. Denouncing fellow workers who refused to honor production codes as "hogs," "runners," "chasers," and "job wreckers," they ostracized and even injured them. As the banner of the Detroit Coopers' Union proudly proclaimed at a parade in 1880: "Each for himself is the bosses' plea / [but] Union for all will make you free."

Absenteeism, drunkenness at work, and general inefficiency were other widespread worker practices that contained elements of protest. In three industrial firms in the late nineteenth century, one-quarter of the workers stayed home at least one day a week. Some of these lost days were due to layoffs, but not all. The efforts of employers to impose stiff fines on absent workers suggested their frustration with uncooperative workers.

To a surprising extent, workers made the final protest by quitting their jobs altogether. Most employers responded by penalizing workers who left without giving sufficient notice—but to little avail. A Massachusetts labor study in 1878 found that although two-thirds of the workers surveyed had been in the same occupation for more than 10 years, only 15 percent of them were in the same job. A similar rate of turnover occurred in the industrial workforce in the early twentieth century. Workers unmistakably and clearly voted with their feet.

Strike Activity After 1876

The most direct and strenuous attempts to change conditions in the workplace came in the form of thousands of strikes punctuating the late nineteenth century. In 1877, railroad workers staged the first and most violent nationwide industrial strike of the nineteenth century. The immediate cause of the disturbance was the railroad owners' decision to reduce wages. But the rapid spread of the strike from Baltimore to Pittsburgh and then to cities as distant as San Francisco, Chicago, and Omaha, as well as the violence of the strikers, who destroyed railroad property and kept trains idle, indicated more fundamental discontent.

An erratic economy, high unemployment rates, and the lack of job security all contributed to the conflagration. More than 100 people died before federal troops ended the strike. The frenzied response of the propertied class, which saw the strike as the beginning of revolution and favored the intervention of the military, forecast the pattern of later conflicts. Time and time again, middle- and upper-class Americans would turn to the power of the state to crush labor activism.

A wave of confrontations followed the strike of 1877. Between 1881 and 1905, a total of 36,757 strikes erupted, involving more than 6 million workers—three times the strike activity in France.

These numbers indicate the involvement of more than the "poorest part" of the working class. Many investigations of this era found evidence of widespread working-class discontent. When Samuel M. Hotchkiss, commissioner of the Connecticut Bureau of Labor Statistics, informally surveyed the state's workers in 1887, he was shocked by the "feeling of bitterness," the "distrust of employers," and the "discontent and unrest." These sentiments exploded into strikes, sabotage, and violence, most often linked to demands for higher wages and shorter hours.

Nineteenth-century strike activity underwent important changes, however, as the consciousness of American workers expanded. In the period of early industrialization, discontented laborers rioted in their neighborhoods rather than at their workplaces. Between 1845 and the Civil War, however, strikes at the workplace began to replace neighborhood riots. Although workers showed their anger against their employers by turning out and often calling for higher wages, they had only a murky sense that the strike could be a weapon to force employers to improve working conditions.

As industrialization transformed work and an increasing percentage of the workforce entered factories, collective actions at the workplace spread. Local and national unions played a more important role in organizing protest, conducting 60 percent of the strikes between 1881 and 1905. As working-class leaders realized more clearly the importance of collective action and perceived that transportation had knit the nation together, they worked to coordinate local and national efforts. By 1891, more than one-tenth of the strikes called by

Labor Unrest

This depiction of working-class unrest appeared in *Harper's Weekly* in 1894. Why does the artist give a prominent place to the National Guardsmen and the destruction wrought during the trouble? Contrast the individualized guardsmen with the faceless mob in the background and draw some general conclusions about the artist's choices and intent.

(The Granger Collection, New York)

unionized workers were sympathy strikes. Coordination among strikers employed by different companies improved as workers made similar wage demands. Finally, pay among the most highly unionized workers became less of an issue. Workers sought more humane conditions. Some attempted to end subcontracting and the degradation of skills. Others, such as the glassblowers, struggled to enforce work rules. Indeed, by the early 1890s, more than one-fifth of strikes involved the rules governing the workplace.

Labor Organizing, 1865–1900

Civil War experience colored postwar labor organizing. As one working-class song pointed out, workers had borne the brunt of that struggle. "You gave your son to the war / The rich man loaned his gold / And the rich man's son is happy to-day, / And yours is under the mold." Workers who had fought to save the Union argued that wartime sacrifices justified efforts for justice and equality in the workplace.

Labor leaders quickly realized the need for national as well as local organizations to protect the laboring class against "despotic employers." In 1866, several craft unions and reform groups formed the National Labor Union (NLU). Claiming 300,000 members by the early 1870s, the organization supported a range of causes including temperance, women's rights, and the establishment of cooperatives to bring the "wealth of the land" into "the hands of those who produce it."

The call for an eight-hour day reveals some of the basic assumptions of the organized labor movement. Few workers saw employers as a hostile class or wanted to destroy the economic system. But they did believe bosses were often dangerous tyrants whose demands for their time threatened to turn citizens into slaves. The eight-hour day would curb the power of owners and allow workers the time to cultivate the qualities necessary for republican citizenship.

Many of the NLU's specific goals survived, although the organization did not. An unsuccessful attempt to create a political party and the depression of 1873 decimated the NLU. Survival and job searches took precedence over union causes.

The Knights of Labor and the AFL

As the depression wound down, a new mass organization, the Noble and Holy Order of the Knights of Labor, rose to prominence. Founded as a secret society in 1869, the order became public and national when Terence V. Powderly was elected Grand Master Workman in 1879. The Knights of Labor insisted that workers deserved "the full enjoyment of the wealth they create." Convinced that the industrial system denied workers their fair share as producers of wealth,

the Knights of Labor proposed a cooperative system of production paralleling the existing system. Cooperative efforts would provide workers with the economic independence necessary for citizenship, and an eight-hour day would allow them time for moral, intellectual, and political pursuits.

The Knights of Labor was open to all American "producers," defined as all contributing members of society—skilled and unskilled, black and white, men and women, even merchants and manufacturers. Only the idle and the corrupt (gamblers, saloonkeepers, speculators, bankers, lawyers) were excluded. Many shopkeepers joined, advertising themselves as a "friend of the workingman." This inclusive membership policy provided the organization with the potential power of great numbers. The organization grew in spurts, attracting miners between 1874 and 1879, skilled urban tradespeople between 1879 and 1885, and unskilled workers thereafter.

Although Powderly frowned on strikes, the organization reaped the benefit of grassroots strike activity. Local struggles proliferated after 1883. In 1884, unorganized workers of the Union Pacific Railroad walked off the job when management announced a wage cut. Within two days, the company caved in, and the men joined the Knights. The next year, a successful strike against the Missouri Pacific Railroad brought in another wave of members. Then, in 1886, the Haymarket Riot in Chicago caused such a growth in labor militancy that in that single year the membership of the Knights of Labor ballooned from 100,000 to 700,000.

The "riot" at Haymarket was, in fact, a peaceful protest meeting connected with a lockout at the McCormick Reaper Works. When the Chicago police arrived to disperse the crowd, a bomb exploded. Seven policemen died. Although no one knows who planted the bomb, eight anarchists were tried and convicted. Three were executed, one committed suicide, and the others served prison terms.

Alarmed by the Haymarket Riot, employers determined to destroy the Knights of Labor, but internal weaknesses also contributed to the organization's decline. A strike against Jay Gould's southwestern railroad system in 1886 collapsed. Consumer and producer cooperatives fizzled; the policy of accepting both black and white workers led to discord in the South. The two major political parties co-opted labor politicians. Furthermore, national leaders of the organization also failed. Powderly could neither unify his diverse following nor control militants opposing him. By 1890, membership plummeted to 100,000, although the Knights continued to play a role well into the 1890s.

The American Federation of Labor (AFL), founded in 1886, became the nation's dominant union in the 1890s. The history of the Knights pointed up the problems of a national union admitting all who worked for wages, but officially rejecting strikes as a tactic. The leader of the AFL, Samuel Gompers, had a different notion of effective worker organization. He was convinced that skilled workers should put their specific occupational interests first, so that they could control the supply of skilled labor and keep wages up.

Gompers organized the AFL as a federation of skilled trades—cigar makers, iron molders, ironworkers, carpenters, and others—each one autonomous, yet linked through an executive council to work together for prolabor national legislation and mutual support during boycott and strike actions. He repudiated dreams of a cooperative commonwealth or of ending the wage system, instead focusing on immediate "bread and butter" issues—higher wages, shorter hours, industrial safety, and the right to organize. Although Gompers rejected direct political action as a means of obtaining labor's goals, he believed in the value of the strike. A shrewd organizer, he knew from bitter experience the importance of dues high enough to sustain a strike fund through a long, tough fight.

Under Gompers's leadership, the AFL grew from 140,000 in 1886 to nearly 1 million by 1900. Although his notion of a labor organization was elitist, he steered his union through a series of crises, fending off challenges from socialists on his left and corporate opposition to strikes on his right. But there was no room in his organization for the unskilled or for blacks. The AFL did make a brief, halfhearted attempt to unionize women in 1892, but men resented women as coworkers and preferred them to stay in the home. The AFL agreed. In 1900, the International Ladies' Garment Workers Union (ILGWU) was established. Although women were its backbone, men dominated the leadership.

Working-Class Setbacks

Despite the growth of working-class organizations, workers lost many battles. Some of the more spectacular clashes reveal why working-class activism often failed and why so many workers lived precariously.

In 1892, silver miners in Coeur d'Alene, Idaho, struck when their employers installed machine drills in the mines, reduced skilled workers to shovelmen, and cut wages. The owners, supported by state militiamen and the federal government, successfully broke the strike by using scabs, but not without fighting. Several hundred union men were eventually tried and found guilty of a wide variety of charges. Out of the defeat emerged the Western Federation of Miners (WFM), whose chief goal was an eight-hour law for miners.

The Coeur d'Alene struggle set the pattern for many subsequent strikes. Mine owners fought strikes by shutting off credit to union men, hiring strikebreakers and armed guards, and infiltrating unions with spies. Violence was frequent, usually ending with the arrival of state militia, arrests or intimidation, legal action, and blacklisting. Despite this, the WFM won as many strikes as it lost.

The Homestead and Pullman Strikes of 1892 and 1894

Labor's worst setback came in 1892 at the Homestead steel mills near Pittsburgh. Carnegie had purchased the Homestead plant and put Henry Clay Frick in charge. Together, they wanted to break the union that threatened to extend its organization of the steel industry. After three months of stalemated negotiations over a new wage contract, Frick issued an ultimatum. Workers must accept wage cuts or be replaced. Frick barricaded the entire plant and hired 300 armed Pinkerton guards. As they arrived on July 6, they and armed steelworkers fought a daylong gun battle. Several men on both sides were killed, and the Pinkertons retreated. Then, at Frick's request, the governor of Pennsylvania sent 8,000 troops to crush the strike and the union. Two and a half weeks later, a New York anarchist tried to assassinate Frick.

The Homestead strike dramatized the lengths to which both labor and capital would go. Eugene Debs, an ardent organizer of railroad workers, wrote, "If the year 1892 taught the workingmen any lesson worthy of heed, it was that the capitalist class, like a devilfish, had grasped them with its tentacles and was dragging them down to fathomless depths of degradation."

Debs saw 1893 as the year in which organized labor would "escape the prehensile clutch of these monsters." Instead, 1893 brought a serious depression and more setbacks for labor. Undaunted, Debs combined several of the separate railroad brotherhoods into a united American Railway Union (ARU). Within a year, more than 150,000 railroadmen joined the ARU, and Debs won a strike against the Great Northern Railroad, which had attempted to slash wages.

Debs faced his toughest crisis at the Pullman Palace Car Company in Chicago. The company maintained a model company town near Chicago—naturally, called Pullman—where management controlled all aspects of workers' lives. Late in 1893, as the depression worsened, the Pullman Company cut wages by one-third and laid off many workers, without reducing rents or prices in its stores. Desperate Pullman workers joined the ARU in the spring of 1894 and struck.

In late June, after Pullman refused to submit the dispute to arbitration, Debs led the ARU into a sympathy strike supporting the striking Pullman workers. Remembering the ill-fated railroad strike of 1877, Debs advised his lieutenants to "use no violence" and "stop no trains." Rather, he sought to boycott trains handling

Pullman cars throughout the West. As the boycott spread, the General Managers Association (GMA), which ran the 24 railroads centered in Chicago, came to Pullman's support. Hiring 2,500 strikebreakers, the GMA appealed to the state and federal governments for military and judicial support in stopping the strike.

Governor Richard Altgeld of Illinois, sympathizing with the workers and believing that local law enforcement was sufficient, opposed using federal troops. But U.S. attorney general Richard Olney, a former railroad lawyer, obtained a court injunction on July 2 to end the strike as a "conspiracy in restraint of trade." Two days later, President Cleveland ordered federal troops to crush the strikers. Violence escalated rapidly. Local and federal officials hired armed guards, and the railroads paid them to help the troops. Within two days, strikers and guards were fighting bitterly. As troops poured into Chicago, the violence worsened, leaving scores of workers dead.

Debs knew he needed wider labor support. "We must all stand together or go down in hopeless defeat," he warned other unions. When Gompers refused support, the strike collapsed. Debs and several other leaders were found guilty of contempt of court. His arrest and the defeat of the Pullman strike killed the American Railway Union. In 1895, in *In re Debs*, the Supreme Court upheld the legality of using an injunction to stop a strike, giving management a powerful weapon against unions. Most unions survived the difficult days of the 1890s, but the labor movement emerged as a distinct underdog in its conflicts with organized capital.

Although in smaller communities strikes against outside owners might win local middle-class support, most labor conflicts encountered the widespread middle- and upper-class conviction that unions were un-American. Many people claimed to accept the idea of worker organizations, but argued unions should not participate in making economic or work decisions. Most employers violently resisted union demands as infringements of their right to manage their business. The sharp competition of the late nineteenth century, combined with a pattern of falling prices, stiffened employers' resistance to workers' demands. State and local governments and the courts frequently supported them.

The severe depressions of the 1870s and 1890s further undermined working-class activism. Workers could not focus on union issues when survival itself was in question. Many unions collapsed during hard times.

A fundamental problem was the reluctance of most workers to organize even in favorable times. In 1870, less than one-tenth of the industrial workforce belonged to unions, about the same as on the eve of the Civil War. Thirty years later, despite the expansion of the workforce, only 8.4 percent (mostly skilled workers) were union members. Why were workers so slow to join unions? Many native-born American workers still clung to the tradition of individualism or dreamed of entering the middle class. In addition, diverse work settings and ethnic and religious differences made it difficult for workers to recognize common bonds. Some Americans blamed immigrants for both low wages and failed worker actions. Those foreigners, planning to return to their homeland, had limited interest in changing conditions in the United States—and because their goal was to work, they took jobs as scabs. Much of the violence that accompanied working-class actions erupted when owners brought in strikebreakers.

Tensions between workers was evident in the anti-Chinese campaign of the 1870s and 1880s. White workers in the West began to blame the Chinese for economic hardships. In 1877, a meeting of San Francisco workers supporting the eight-hour day exploded into a rampage against the Chinese. In following years, angry mobs killed Chinese workers in Tacoma, Seattle, Denver, and Rock Springs, Wyoming. Local hostility was expressed at the national level when, in 1882, Congress passed the Chinese Exclusion Act with the support of the Knights of Labor, prohibiting the immigration of Chinese workers for a 10-year period. It was extended in 1892 and made permanent in 1902.

Yet many immigrants, especially skilled ones, supported unions and cooperated with native-born Americans. Often ethnic bonds tied members to one another and to the community. For example, in the 1860s and 1870s, as the Molders' Union in Troy, New York, battled with manufacturers, its Irish membership won sympathy and support from the Irish-dominated police force, the Roman Catholic Church, fraternal orders, and public officials.

The importance of workers' organizations lay not so much in their success as in the implicit criticism they offered of American society. Workers lashed out at an economic order that robbed them of their dignity and humanity. As producers of wealth, they protested that so little of it was theirs. As members of the working class, they rejected the middle-class belief in individualism and social mobility.

The Balance Sheet

Industrial expansion raised living standards for the increasing numbers of Americans, especially those in the middle and upper class. They were able to purchase dozens of products, manufactured, packaged, and promoted in an explosion of technological inventions and shrewd marketing techniques. They had comfortable living quarters in attractive urban districts. The men of the family had more professional and business opportunities than ever before.

Skilled workers also enjoyed many benefits produced by industrialization. But most laboring people found it impossible to earn much of a share in the new material bounty. Newly arrived immigrants especially suffered from low pay and economic uncertainty. Long hours on the job and the necessity of walking to and from work left workers with little free time. Family budgets could include, at best, only small amounts for recreation. Even a ticket to a baseball game was a luxury.

Although few Americans worried about it, many experienced some of the adverse environmental effects of industrialization. By the late nineteenth century, industrial processes were polluting urban air, eastern lakes and rivers, and creating acid soil. In Birmingham, Alabama, for example, the production of iron and steel befouled the air with smoke, soot, and ashes. Coal tar, a by-product of the process, was dumped, making the soil infertile.

Despite modern disapproval of these consequences of industrialization, the intellectual rationale stressed growth, development, and the rapid exploitation of the country's resources—not conservation. And our view of the harshness of working-class life partly grows out of contemporary standards of what is acceptable today. Because so few working-class men or women recorded their thoughts and reactions, it is hard to know just what they expected or how they viewed their experiences. But culture and background influenced their perspectives. The family tenement, one Polish immigrant remarked, "seemed quite advanced when compared with our home" in Poland. A Lithuanian agreed. "Even though the toilet was in the hall, and the

Timeline	
1843–1884	"Old immigration"
1844	Telegraph invented
1850s	Steam power widely used in manufacturing
1859	Value of U.S. industrial production exceeds value of agricultural production
1866	National Labor Union founded
1869	Transcontinental railroad completed
	Knights of Labor organized
1870	Standard Oil of Ohio formed
1870s–1880s	Consolidation of continental railroad network
1873	Bethlehem Steel begins using Bessemer process
1873–1879	Depression
1876	Alexander G. Bell invents telephone
	Thomas Edison establishes his "invention factory" at Menlo Park, New Jersey
1877	Railroad workers hold first nationwide industrial strike
1879	Thomas Edison invents incandescent light
1882	Chinese Exclusion Act
1885–1914	"New immigration"
1886	American Federation of Labor founded
	Haymarket Riot in Chicago
1887	Interstate Commerce Act
1890	Sherman Anti-Trust Act
1892	Standard Oil of New Jersey formed
	Coeur d'Alene strike
	Homestead steelworkers strike
1893	Chicago World's Fair
1893–1897	Depression
1894	Pullman railroad workers strike
1900	International Ladies' Garment Workers Union founded
	Corporations responsible for two-thirds of U.S. manufacturing

whole floor used it, yet it was a toilet. There was no such thing in Lithuania." A 10-hour job in the steel mill might be an improvement over dawn-to-dusk farmwork that brought no wages.

Studies of several cities show that nineteenth-century workers moved up the occupational ladder. One worker in five in Los Angeles and Atlanta during the 1890s, for example, managed to climb into the middle class. While most immigrant workers were stuck in ill-paid, insecure jobs, their children ended up doing better. The son of an unskilled laborer might move on to become a semiskilled or skilled worker as new immigrants took the jobs at the bottom. Second-generation Irish made progress, especially in the West and the Midwest. Even in Boston, 40 percent of the children of Irish immigrants obtained white-collar jobs.

Mobility, like occupation, was related to background. Native-born whites, Jews, and Germans rose more swiftly and fell less often than Irish, Italians, or Poles. Cultural attitudes, family size, education, and group leadership all contributed to different ethnic mobility patterns. Jews, for example, valued education and sacrificed to keep children in school. By 1915, Jews represented 85 percent of the free City College student body in New York City, 20 percent of New York University's student body, and one-sixth of those studying at Columbia University. With an education, they moved upward. The Slavs, however, who valued a steady income over mobility and education, took their children out of school and sent them to work at an early age. They believed that this course of action not only helped the family but gave the child a head start in securing reliable, stable employment. The southern Italian proverb "Do not make your child better than you are" suggests the value Italians placed on family rather than individual success. Differing attitudes and values led to different aspirations and career patterns.

Two groups enjoyed little mobility: African Americans and Hispanic Americans. African Americans were largely excluded from the industrial occupational structure and were restricted to unskilled jobs. Unlike immigrant industrial workers, they did not have the opportunity to move to better jobs as new, unskilled workers took the positions at the bottom. A study in Los Angeles suggests that Hispanic residents made minimal gains. Their experiences elsewhere may have been much the same.

Although immigrants' occupational mobility was limited, other kinds of rewards often compensated for the lack of success at the workplace. Home ownership for groups such as the Irish, who in their homeland had rarely owned their own homes, was an achievement that also could bring in extra income from boarders and provide some cushion against the uncertainties of industrial life and old age. Adept politicians, the Irish came to dominate big-city government in the late nineteenth century,

filling many city jobs, particularly in the police force. The Irish were also successful in the construction industry and dominated the hierarchy of the Catholic church. Likewise, participation in social clubs and fraternal orders compensated in part for lack of advancement at work. Ethnic associations, parades, and holidays provided a sense of identity and security that offset the limitations of the job world.

Moreover, a few rags-to-riches stories always encouraged those who struggled. For example, the family of John Kearney in Poughkeepsie, New York, achieved modest success. After 20 years as a laborer, John started his own business as a junk dealer and even bought a simple house. His sons started off in better jobs than their father. One became a grocery store clerk and then later a baker, a policeman, and, finally, at age 40, an inspector at the waterworks. Another was an iron molder, and the third son was a post office worker and eventually the superintendent of city streets. If this success paled next to that of industrial giants such as Andrew Carnegie and John D. Rockefeller, it was still enough to keep the American dream alive.

Conclusion
THE COMPLEXITY OF INDUSTRIAL CAPITALISM

The rapid growth of the late nineteenth century made the United States one of the world's industrial giants. Many factors contributed to the "wonderful accomplishments" of the age. They ranged from sympathetic government policies to the rise of big business and the emergence of a cheap industrial workforce. But it was also a turbulent period. Many Americans benefited only marginally from the new wealth. Some of them protested by joining unions, walking out on strike, or initiating on-the-job actions. Most lived their lives more quietly and never had the opportunity that Thomas O'Donnell did of telling their story to others. But middle-class Americans began to wonder about the O'Donnells of the country. It is to their concerns, worries, and aspirations that we now turn.

QUESTIONS FOR REVIEW AND REFLECTION

1. What factors explain the United States' rise to industrial and economic prominence in the late nineteenth century?
2. In what ways did American cities change in this period?
3. Explain which groups were able to realize the American dream of success and which were not and why.
4. Compare and contrast the experiences of middle-class and working-class women.
5. What factors undermined the working-class efforts at collective action and which promoted them? In your opinion, which were the most important factors underlying the failures of the working class?

CHAPTER 19

Politics and Reform

Gilded Age Election: 1892 painting by John Klir "The Lost Bet"

Although this 1892 painting by John Klir shows the outcome of a "Lost Bet" in the election that year, note the ethnic, racial, and class diversity of the street crowds, momentarily united in the enjoyment of watching the humiliated loser pulling his victorious opponent (and a wagon full of American flags). What kind of diversity do you see in the painting? Will a more diverse America hold together?

(Library of Congress [LC-USZC4–2113])

American Stories

A Utopian Novelist Warns of Two Americas

At the start of his best-seller *Looking Backward* (1888), Edward Bellamy likened the American society of his day to a huge stagecoach. Dragging the coach along sandy roads and over steep hills were the "masses of humanity." While they strained desperately "under the pitiless lashing of hunger" to pull the coach, at the top sat the favored few, riding in breezy comfort yet fearful that they might fall from their seats and have to pull the coach themselves.

Bellamy's famous coach allegory began a utopian novel in which the class divisions and pitiless competition of the nineteenth century were replaced by a classless, caring, cooperative new society. Economic anxieties and hardships were supplanted by satisfying labor and leisure. In place of the coach, all citizens in the year 2000 walked together and shopped in equal comfort and security under a huge umbrella (not unlike modern malls) over the sidewalks of the city.

The novel opens in 1887. The hero, a wealthy Bostonian, falls asleep worrying about the effect local labor struggles might have on his upcoming wedding. When he wakes up, it is the year 2000. Utopia has been achieved peacefully through the development of one gigantic trust, owned and operated by the national government. All citizens between ages 21 and 45 work in an industrial army with equal pay and work difficulty. Retirement after 45 is devoted to hobbies, reading, culture, and the minimal leadership necessary in a society without crime, corruption, poverty, or war.

Bellamy's book was popular with educated middle-class Americans, who were attracted by his vision of a society in which humans were both morally good and materially well off—and in which core values of the 1880s survived intact, including individual incentive, private property, and rags-to-riches presidents. He filled the novel with futuristic technological wonders, such as television and credit cards, a double-dream surprise ending, and a love story. Women in 2000 married for love and were relieved of housework by labor-saving gadgets. Although they worked in the industrial army (in "lighter occupations"), their primary role was still to supervise domestic affairs, nurture the young, and beautify culture.

Like most middle-class Americans of his day, Bellamy disapproved of European socialism. Although some features of his utopia were socialistic, he called his system "nationalism." This appealed to a new generation of Americans who had put aside Civil War antagonisms to embrace the greatness of a growing, if economically divided, nation. In the early 1890s, with Americans buying nearly 10,000 copies of *Looking Backward* every week, more than 160 Nationalist clubs were formed to crusade for the adoption of Bellamy's ideas.

The inequalities of wealth described in Bellamy's coach scene reflected a political life in which many participated, but only a few benefited. The wealthiest 10 percent, who rode high on the coach, dominated national politics, while untutored bosses held sway in governing cities. Except for token expressions of support, national political leaders ignored the cries of factory workers, immigrants, farmers, African Americans, Native Americans, and other victims of the vast transformation of American industrial, urban, and agrarian life in the late nineteenth century. But as the century closed, middle-class Americans like Bellamy, as well as labor, agrarian, and ethnic leaders, proposed various reforms. Their concern was never more appropriate than during the depression of the mid-1890s, a real-life social upheaval that mirrored the worst features and fears of Bellamy's fictional coach.

In this chapter, we will examine American democratic politics at the national and local level from the end of Reconstruction to the 1890s, a period that bolstered the rich and neglected the corrosive human problems of urban industrial life. Then we will look at the growing social and political involvement of educated middle-class reformers who, despite their distaste for mass politics, were inspired by a religious social gospel to work for social change both locally and nationally. We will conclude with an account of the pivotal importance of the 1890s, and how the Populist revolt, the depression of 1893–1897, and the election of 1896 shook many comfortable citizens out of their apathy and began the reshaping of American politics.

Politics in the Gilded Age

Co-authoring a satirical book in 1873, Mark Twain coined the expression "Gilded Age" to describe Grant's corrupt presidency. The phrase, with its suggestion of shallow glitter, characterized social and political life in the last quarter of the nineteenth century. Politics was marred by corruption, and politicians ignored basic issues for the mass entertainment of pomp, parades, and penny beer. Yet voter participation in national elections between 1876 and 1896 hovered at an all-time high of 73 to 82 percent.

Behind the glitter, two gradual changes occurred that would greatly affect twentieth-century politics. First was the development of a professional bureaucracy of elite specialists in congressional committees and executive offices. These experts emerged as a counterfoil to the perceived dangers of majority rule represented by high voter participation, especially by the millions of new immigrant "newcomers alien to our traditions," as a New Englander put it. Second, after a period of close elections and party stalemate, new issues and concerns fostered a political realignment in the 1890s.

Politics, Parties, Patronage, and Presidents

American government in the 1870s and 1880s clearly supported the interests of riders atop Bellamy's coach. Few nineteenth-century Americans would have agreed that the national government should tackle problems of poverty, unemployment, and trusts. They mistrusted organized power and believed that all would benefit from an expansive economic life free of government interference.

The Gilded Age, Henry Adams observed, was the most "thoroughly ordinary" period ever in American politics. "One might search the whole list of Congress, Judiciary, and Executive during the twenty-five years 1870–95 and find little but damaged reputation." Few eras of American government were so corrupt, and Adams was especially sensitive to the low quality of democratic politics compared to the presidencies of his grandfather John Quincy Adams and great-grandfather John Adams.

During the weak Johnson and Grant presidencies, Congress emerged as the dominant branch of government with power centered in the committee system. Senators James G. Blaine (R-Maine) and Roscoe Conkling (R-New York) typified the moral quality of legislative leadership. Despite lying about having been paid off by favors to railroads, Blaine was probably the most popular Republican politician of the era. Charming, intelligent, witty, and able, he served twice as secretary of state and was a serious contender for the presidency in every election from 1876 to 1892. His intra-party foe, Conkling, dispensed lucrative jobs at the New York customhouse and spent most of his career rewarding the party faithful with government jobs. In more than two decades in Congress, he never drafted a bill.

Legislation was not Congress's primary purpose. In 1879, a disgusted student of legislative politics, Woodrow Wilson, wrote: "No leaders, no principles; no principles, no parties." A British observer, Lord Bryce, concluding that American politics was mainly about the "desire for office and for office as a means of gain," compared the two parties to two bottles of liquor, they bore different labels, yet "each was empty."

Yet these characterizations were not entirely accurate. There were differences, as party professionals solidified their popular base to achieve political ends. Republican votes came from northeastern Yankee industrial interests and Scandinavian Lutherans across the Upper Midwest. Democrats depended on southern whites, northern workers, and urban immigrants. Like today, party affiliation reflected not just economic but also cultural, social, and religious issues. Because the Republican party was willing to mobilize the power of the state to reshape society, people who wanted to regulate moral and economic life were attracted to it. White southerners and various immigrant groups preferred the Democratic party because it opposed government efforts to regulate morals. Said one Chicago Democrat, "A Republican is a man who wants you t' go t' church every Sunday. A Democrat says if a man wants t' have a glass of beer on Sunday he can have it."

In the 1860s, Civil War and Reconstruction issues generated party differences. But after 1876, the two parties were evenly matched, and they avoided controversial stands on national issues. In three of the five presidential elections between 1876 and 1892, a mere 1 percent of the vote separated the two major candidates. In 1880, James Garfield won by only 7,018 votes; in 1884, Grover Cleveland squeaked past Blaine by a popular-vote margin of 48.5 to 48.2 percent. In two elections (1876 and 1888), the electoral-vote winner had fewer popular votes. Only twice, each time for only two years, did one party control the White House and both houses of Congress. Although all the presidents in the era except Cleveland were Republicans, the Democrats controlled the House of Representatives in 8 of 10 sessions of Congress between 1875 and 1895.

Gilded Age presidents were undistinguished and played a minor role in national life. None of them—Hayes (1877–1881), Garfield (1881), Chester A. Arthur (1881–1885), Cleveland (1885–1889 and 1893–1897), and Benjamin Harrison (1889–1893)—served two consecutive terms. None was strongly identified with any particular issue. None has been highly regarded by historians. The only Democrat in the group, Cleveland, differed little from the Republicans. Upon his election in 1884, financier Jay Gould sent him a telegram stating that "the vast business interests of the country will be entirely safe in your hands."

National Issues

Four issues were important at the national level in the Gilded Age: the tariff, currency, civil service, and government regulation of railroads (see Chapter 18). In confronting these issues, legislators tried to serve both their own self-interest and the national interest of an efficient, productive, growing economy.

The federal government depended on tariffs and excise taxes (primarily on tobacco and liquor), along with land sales, for most of its revenue. Republicans stood for a high tariff to protect American business, wage earners, and farmers from foreign competition.

PRESIDENTIAL ELECTIONS, 1872–1892

A British observer of American politics, James Bryce, said in 1888 that "the American usually votes with his party, right or wrong, and the fact that there is little distinction of view between the parties makes it easier to stick to your old friends." To what extent does this chart show that American voters stuck to their party? How close were the elections? What was the usual percent difference? In which two elections did the popular-vote winner, as in 2000, lose the election? Are parties today more like or unlike those from the late nineteenth century?

Year	Candidate	Party	Popular Vote	Electoral Vote
1872	ULYSSES S. GRANT	Republican	3,596,745 (56%)	286
	Horace Greeley*	Democrat	2,843,446 (44%)	0*
1876	Samuel J. Tilden	Democrat	4,284,020 (51%)	184
	RUTHERFORD B. HAYES	Republican	4,036,572 (48%)	185
1880	JAMES A. GARFIELD	Republican	4,449,053 (48.5%)	214
	Winfield S. Hancock	Democrat	4,442,035 (48.1%)	155
	James B. Weaver	Greenback-Labor	308,578	0
1884	GROVER CLEVELAND	Democrat	4,911,017 (48.5%)	219
	James G. Blaine	Republican	4,848,334 (48.2%)	182
	Minor parties		325,739 (03.3%)	0
1888	Grover Cleveland	Democrat	5,540,050 (48.6%)	168
	BENJAMIN HARRISON	Republican	5,444,337 (47.9%)	233
	Minor parties		396,441 (03.5%)	0
1892	GROVER CLEVELAND	Democrat	5,554,414 (46%)	277
	Benjamin Harrison	Republican	5,190,802 (43%)	145
	James B. Weaver	Populist	1,027,329 (9%)	22

*Greeley died before the Electoral College met.

Note: Winners' names are in capital letters.

Democrats demanded a low tariff because "the government is best which governs least." But in passing tariffs politicians accommodated local interests. An Indiana senator explained, "I am a protectionist for every interest which I am sent here by my constituents to protect." Tariff revisions, containing a jumble of mostly higher but some lower rates, were bewilderingly complex as legislators catered to these many special interests.

The currency question was even more complicated. During the Civil War, the federal government had circulated paper money (greenbacks) that could not be exchanged for gold or silver (specie). In the late 1860s and 1870s, politicians debated whether the United States should return to a metallic standard, which would allow paper money to be exchanged for specie. "Hard-money" advocates supported either withdrawing all paper money from circulation or making it convertible to specie. They opposed increasing the volume of money, fearing inflation. "Soft money" Greenbackers argued that there was not enough currency in circulation for an expanding economy and urged increasing the supply of paper money in order to raise farm prices and cut interest rates.

Hard-money interests had more clout. In 1873, Congress demonetized silver, gradually retiring greenbacks from circulation and putting the nation firmly on the gold standard. But as large supplies of silver were mined in the West, pressure resumed for increasing the money supply by coining silver. Soft-money advocates pushed for the unlimited coinage of silver in addition to gold. In an 1878 compromise, the Treasury was required to buy between $2 million and $4 million of silver each month and to coin it as silver dollars. Despite this increase in the money supply, prices fell, prompting disappointing soft money supporters to push for more silver.

The issue of civil service reform, Henry Adams observed, was a "subject almost as dangerous in political conversation in Washington as slavery itself in the old days before the war." The worst feature of the

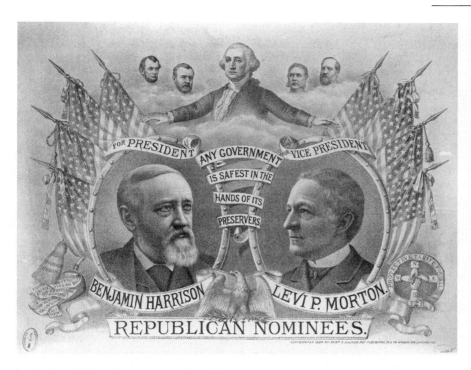

Political Advertisements of the 1880s

Although the tariff protectionist Harrison defeated Cleveland in 1888 (the results were reversed in 1892), all Gilded Age presidents were essentially "preservers" rather than innovators. None had approached the greatness of Washington, Lincoln, and the other presidents hovering over Harrison and Morton in this illustration. In a second image from 1888, titled *The Presidential B.B. Club,* politics and business are merged in a tobacco advertisement, which shows Cleveland the fielder tagging out Harrison the batter—true enough for the election of 1892 but not for 1888, which Harrison won. Why baseball? What other images (and people) do you see in these two campaign visuals?

(Left: Library of Congress [LC-USZ62–7177]; right: From the collection of David J. and Janice L. Frent)

spoils system was that parties financed themselves by assessing holders of patronage jobs often as much as 1 percent of their annual salaries. Reformers, mostly middle-class, native-born, white Protestants, demanded competitive examinations to create an honest and professional civil service—but also one that would bar immigrants and their urban political machine bosses from the spoils of office.

Most Americans expected their presidents to reward the faithful with government jobs, but Garfield's assassination by a crazed office seeker created a public backlash. "My God! Chet Arthur in the White House!" a loyal Republican exclaimed, knowing the new president was closely identified with corrupt machine politics. But Arthur surprised doubters by being a capable and dignified president, responsive to growing demands for civil service reform. Congress passed the Pendleton Act of 1883, mandating merit examinations for about one-tenth of federal offices. Gradually, more bureaucrats fell under its coverage, but parties became no more honest. As campaign contributions from government employees dried up, parties turned to huge corporate contributions, which in 1888 helped elect Benjamin Harrison.

The Lure of Local Politics

The fact that the major parties did not disagree substantially on issues such as money and civil service does not mean that nineteenth-century Americans found politics dull. Far more eligible voters turned out in the late nineteenth century than at any time since. The 78.5 percent average turnout to vote for president in the 1880s is a sharp contrast with the near 50 percent of eligible Americans who vote in recent elections.

American men were drawn to the polls in part by the hoopla of party parades, buttons, and banners, but also by local issues. Midwestern farmers turned out to vote for state representatives who favored curbing the power of the railroads. But emotional social issues of race, religion, nationality, alcohol, and education often overrode economic self-interest. Southern whites, stripping the vote away from blacks, supported laws that established segregated railroad cars and other public facilities. Iowa, Illinois, and Ohio farmers voted for temperance and compulsory attendance education laws, while Irish and German Catholics in New York and Milwaukee supported aid to parochial schools and opposed local temperance laws.

Urban immigrants played a large role in stimulating political participation. As traditional native-born elites left local government for more-lucrative and higher-status business careers, urban bosses stepped in. Their control rested on their ability to deliver the immigrant vote, which they secured by operating informal welfare systems. Bosses handed out jobs and money for rent and fuel, and provided personal touches like giving turkeys to poor families at Thanksgiving, bailing drunks out of jail, and attending Jewish weddings, Catholic confirmations, and Italian funerals. As New York Tammany Hall boss, George Washington Plunkitt, explained, "I think that there's got to be in every ward somebody that any bloke can come to—no matter what he's done—and get help."

Party leaders also won votes by making politics exciting. The parades, rallies, buttons, songs, and oratory of late-nineteenth-century campaigns generated excitement as party leaders used hoopla to win votes. In the election of 1884, for example, emotions ran high over the moral lapses of the opposing candidates—Blaine's corruption and Cleveland's illegitimate child. Democrats chanted in election eve rallies: "Blaine! Blaine! James G. Blaine! / Continental liar from the state of Maine!" while Republicans responded: "Ma! Ma! Where's my pa? / Gone to the White House, Ha! Ha! Ha!" Cleveland won in part because a Republican clergyman called the Democrats the party of "rum, Romanism, and rebellion," ensuring Cleveland an outpouring of Catholic support in crucial New York.

Prohibition also provoked spirited local contests. Many Americans considered drinking a serious social problem. Annual consumption of brewery beer had risen from 2.7 gallons per capita in 1850 to 17.9 gallons in 1880. In one city, saloons outnumbered churches 31 to 1. Such statistics shocked those who believed that drinking would destroy character, corrupt politics, and cause poverty, crime, and unrestrained sexuality. Because they were often the targets of violent, drunken men, women especially supported temperance and increasingly sought to ban drinking by making it illegal.

The battle in San Jose, California, where reformers put a referendum to ban the sale of liquor on the ballot, illustrates the strong passions of the temperance issue. Women erected a tent where they held daily temperance meetings heckled by men and even some clergymen. On election eve, large crowds gathered at both the tent and at a pro-liquor rally. The next morning, women roamed the streets urging men to adopt the referendum, while their children marched to saloons, singing, "Father, dear father, come home with me now." By afternoon, the mood grew uglier as women were harassed and threatened by drunken men. The proposal lost by a vote of 1,430 to 918.

Emotional conflicts boiled in the 1880s at the state level over education as well as drinking. In Iowa, Illinois, and Wisconsin, Protestant Republicans sponsored laws mandating that children attend "some public or private day school" where instruction was in English. These laws, not the last move for English-only education, aimed to undermine parochial schools, which taught in the language of the immigrants. In Iowa, where a state prohibition law passed, the Republican slogan was "A schoolhouse on every hill, and no saloon in the valley." Republicans bragged that "Iowa will go Democratic when hell goes Methodist," and indeed they won. But in Wisconsin, a law for compulsory school attendance was so strongly anti-Catholic that it backfired. Many voters, disillusioned with Republican moralism, shifted to the Democrats.

Party leaders sometimes used local and ethnic issues to achieve sordid economic goals. In New Mexico, for example, the Santa Fe ring, a small group of Anglo-Protestant Republican bankers, lawyers, and politicians, had long exploited local anti-Mexican feelings to grab lands. The ring controlled judges and legislators. When desperate Mexican-American tenant farmers turned to sometimes violent protest in the 1880s, the ring used the situation to dispossess Mexican Americans, Native Americans, and poor white squatters from enormous tracts of land.

Middle-Class Reform

Most middle-class white Americans were unmoved by race issues and avoided reformist politics. But urban corruption, poverty, and labor violence frightened many out of their aversion to politics.

Frances Willard and the Women's Christian Temperance Union (WCTU) is an example. As president of the WCTU from 1879 until 1898, Willard headed the largest women's organization in the country. Most WCTU members were churchgoing, white, Protestant women who believed drunkenness caused poverty and family violence. But after 1886, the WCTU reversed its position, attributing drunkenness to unemployment, bad labor conditions, and poverty. Willard joined the Knights of Labor in 1887 and by the 1890s had influenced the WCTU to extend its programs to alleviate the problems of working men, women, and children.

The Gospel of Wealth and Social Darwinism

Willard called herself a Christian socialist because she believed in applying the ethical principles of Jesus to economic life. For her and many other educated, middle-class reformers, Christianity called for a cooperative social order that would reduce inequalities of wealth. But for most Gilded Age Americans, Christianity supported the competitive individualistic ethic. Philadelphia Baptist preacher Russell Conwell's famous sermon "Acres of Diamonds," delivered 6,000 times to an estimated 13 million listeners, praised riches as a sure sign of "godliness" and stressed the power of money to "do good."

Industrialist Andrew Carnegie expressed the ethic most clearly. In an article titled "The Gospel of Wealth" (1889), Carnegie celebrated competition for producing better goods at lower prices. The concentration of wealth in a few hands, he concluded, was "not only beneficial but essential to the future of the race." The fittest would bring order and efficiency out of the chaos of rapid industrialization. Carnegie's defense of the new economic order in his book *Triumphant Democracy* (1886) found many supporters. Partly this was because Carnegie insisted that the rich must spend some of their wealth to benefit their "poorer brethren." Carnegie built hundreds of libraries to help the poor get an uplifting education.

Carnegie's ideas reflected an ideology known as social Darwinism, based on the work of the English naturalist Charles Darwin. In his *Origin of Species,* published in 1859, Darwin concluded that plant and animal species evolved through natural selection. In the struggle for existence, some species managed to adapt to their environment and survived; others failed to adapt and perished. Herbert Spencer, an English social philosopher, applied this "survival of the fittest" notion to human society. Progress, Spencer said, resulted from relentless competition in which the weak were eliminated and the strong climbed to the top, as in Bellamy's coach. Spencer warned against any interference in the economic world by tampering with the natural laws of selection: "The whole effort of nature is to get rid of such as are unfit, to clear the world of them, and make room for better."

Spencer's leading American followers, many of whom like Carnegie and Yale economist William Graham Sumner, gathered in 1882 to celebrate him at a lavish banquet in New York City, insisted that poverty resulted from the struggle for existence. It was "absurd," Sumner wrote, to pass laws permitting society's "worst members" to survive, or to "sit down with a slate and pencil to plan out a new social world."

The scientific vocabulary of social Darwinism injected scientific rationality into what often seemed a baffling economic order. Sumner and Spencer argued that underlying social laws, like those in the natural world, dictated economic affairs. Social Darwinists also believed in the superiority of the Anglo-Saxon race, which they maintained had reached the highest stage of evolution. Their theories were used to justify race supremacy and imperialism (see Chapter 20) as well as the monopolistic efforts of American businessmen.

The Gap Between Rich and Poor

Describe the two living spaces in these two photographs. Note the contrasts between them, one the bedroom in Alexander Stewart's Fifth Avenue mansion, representing society's "fittest" element, the other an immigrant tenement on New York's Lower East Side. How might the inhabitants of these two dwellings differ in their social and political views?

(Left: Brown Brothers; right: International Museum of Photography/George Eastman House)

"The growth of a large business," John D. Rockefeller, Jr., told a YMCA class in Cleveland, happens by "sacrificing" less fit companies. This was, he said, "merely the working out of a law of nature and a law of God."

Reform Darwinism and Pragmatism

Others questioned social Darwinism. Brooks Adams wrote that social philosophers such as Spencer and Sumner were "hired by the comfortable classes to prove that everything was all right." Fading aristocrats such as the Adams family, increasingly displaced by the new rich industrial elite, may have felt a touch of envy. With roots in antebellum abolitionism, women's rights, and other crusades for social justice, men and women intellectual reformers directly challenged the gloomy social Darwinian notion that nothing could be done to alleviate poverty. Franklin Sanborn, for example, an inspector of charities in Massachusetts, founded the American Social Science Association in 1865 to "treat wisely the great social problems of the day." An early advocate of doing social scientific research on society's problems, Sanborn was known as the "leading social worker of his day."

Reformer Henry George, an amateur social scientist, observed that wherever the highest degree of "material progress" had been realized, "we find the deepest poverty." George's book *Progress and Poverty* (1879) dramatically showed the contradictions of American life. With Bellamy's *Looking Backward,* it was the most influential book of the age, selling 2 million copies by 1905. George admitted that economic growth had produced wonders, but he pointed out the social costs and the loss of Christian values. His remedy was to break up land-holding monopolists who profited from the increasing value of their land, which they rented to those who actually did the work. He proposed a "single tax" on the unearned increases in land value.

George's solution may seem simplistic, but his religious tone and optimistic faith in the capacity of humans to effect change appealed to many middle-class intellectuals. Some went further. Sociologist Lester Frank Ward and economist Richard T. Ely both found examples of cooperation in nature and demonstrated that competition and laissez-faire had proved both wasteful and inhumane. Reform Darwinists urged an economic order marked by cooperation and regulation.

Two pragmatists, John Dewey and William James, established a philosophical basis for reform. While Dewey applied principles of democracy to education, James argued the importance of human will in effecting the course of human events. "What is the 'cash value' of a thought, idea, or belief?" James asked. "The ultimate test for us of what a truth means," he suggested, was in the "consequences" of a particular idea and what kind of moral "conduct it dictates."

James and young social scientists including Ward and Ely gathered statistics documenting social wrongs and rejecting social determinism. They argued that the application of intelligence and human agency could change the "survival of the fittest" into the "fitting of as many as possible to survive." Their position encouraged educators, economists, and reformers of every stripe, giving them an intellectual justification to struggle against misery and inequalities of wealth.

Settlements and Social Gospel

Jane Addams saw the gap between progress and poverty in the streets of Chicago in the winter of 1893. "The stream of laboring people goes past you," she wrote, and "your heart sinks with a sudden sense of futility." Born in rural Illinois, Addams founded Hull House in Chicago in 1889 "to aid in the solution of the social and industrial problems...in a great city." Also in 1889, Wellesley literature professor Vida Scudder and six other Smith College graduates formed an organization of college women to work in settlement houses.

Middle-class activists like Addams and Scudder worried in particular about the degradation of life and labor in America's cities, factories, and farms. Most of them drew upon the ethical teachings of Jesus, as well as those of social prophets such as Tolstoy, Hugo, Emerson, and Bellamy for inspiration in solving social problems. They preferred a society marked by cooperation rather than competition—where, as they liked to say, people were guided by the "golden rule rather than the rule of gold." They sought to apply the ethics of Jesus to industrial and urban life in order to bring about the kingdom of heaven on earth. Some preferred to put their reformist goals in more secular terms, and worked within existing institutions. As middle-class intellectuals and professionals, they stressed a practical, educational approach to social problems. They sought change by crusading for tenement-house and factory-conditions legislation, mediating labor disputes, and living among the poor.

The settlement house movement typified 1890s middle-class reformers' blend of idealism and practicality. The primary purpose of settlement houses was to help immigrant families, especially women, adapt Old World rural styles of childbearing, child care, and housekeeping to American urban life. They launched day nurseries, kindergartens, and boarding rooms for immigrant working women; they offered classes in sewing, cooking, nutrition, health care, and English; and they tried to keep young people out of saloons by organizing sports clubs and coffeehouses.

A second purpose of the settlement house movement was to give college-educated women meaningful work at a time when they faced professional barriers and to allow them to preserve the strong feelings of

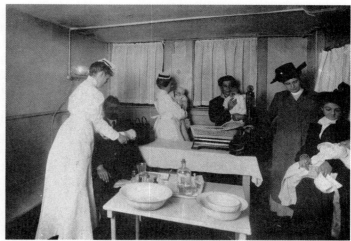

Lessons and Services of the Settlement House

What is being taught to immigrant women in this typical settlement house poster? The public health clinic is in Vida Scudder's Denison House in Boston. Settlement house work, Scudder wrote, fulfilled "a biting curiosity about the way the Other Half lived, and a strange hunger for fellowship with them." Do you see evidence of cross-cultural, cross-class bonding and fellowship?

(Left: U.S. Government Education Bureau of the National Geographic Image Collection; right: Schlesinger Library, Radcliffe Institute, Harvard University)

sisterhood and service they had experienced at college. A third goal was to gather data exposing social misery in order to spur legislative action—developing city building codes for tenements, abolishing child labor, and improving factory safety. Hull House, Addams said, was intended in part "to investigate and improve the conditions in the industrial districts of Chicago." The settlement house movement, with its dual emphasis on the scientific gathering of facts and spiritual commitment, thus blending academic study and Christian beliefs, nourished the new discipline of sociology, first taught in divinity schools.

By contrast, Dwight Moody preached a traditional evangelical Christianity in American cities, leading hundreds of urban revivals in the 1870s. Mastering the art of the folksy sermon filled with Bible and family stories and an easy path from sin to salvation, the Moody revivals appealed to lower-class, rural folk who were drawn to the city by their hopes and pushed there by economic disappointment. Supported by businessmen who believed that religion would make workers and immigrants more docile, the revivalists battled sin through individual conversion. Moody's revivals helped to nearly double Protestant church membership in the last two decades of the century. Although some urban workers drifted into secular faiths such as socialism, most remained conventionally religious.

Other Protestant ministers embraced the Social Gospel movement of the 1890s, which tied salvation to social betterment. Like the settlement house workers, these religious leaders sought to make Christianity relevant to urban problems. Congregational minister Washington Gladden advocated collective bargaining

and corporate profit sharing. A young Baptist minister in the notorious Hell's Kitchen area of New York City, Walter Rauschenbusch raised an even louder voice. Often called on to conduct funeral services for children killed by the airless, diseased tenements and sweatshops, Rauschenbusch scathingly attacked capitalism and church ignorance of socioeconomic issues. His progressive ideas for social justice and a welfare state were later published in two landmark books: *Christianity and the Social Crisis* (1907) and *Christianizing the Social Order* (1912).

Perhaps the most influential book promoting social Christianity was a best-selling novel *In His Steps,* published in 1897 by Charles Sheldon. The novel portrayed the dramatic changes made possible by a few community leaders who resolved to base all their actions on a single question: "What would Jesus do?" For a minister, this meant seeking to "bridge the chasm between the church and labor." For the idle rich, it meant settlement house work and reforming prostitutes. For landlords and factory owners, it meant improving the living and working conditions of tenants and laborers. Although filled with naive sentimentality characteristic of much of the Social Gospel, *In His Steps* prepared thousands of influential, middle-class Americans for progressive civic leadership.

Reforming the City

No late-nineteenth-century institution needed reforming more than urban government, called by the president of Cornell "the worst in Christendom—the most expensive, the most inefficient, and the most corrupt."

A Philadelphia committee pointed to years of "inefficiency, waste, badly paved and filthy streets, unwholesome and offensive water, and slovenly and costly management." New York and Chicago, where cholera and typhoid epidemics resulted from raw sewage poured into lakes and rivers, were even worse.

Creating a "city beautiful" through environmental remedies was one approach to cleaning up dirty cities. Urban planners put in water mains and sewers and landscape architects built city parks (like Central Park in New York) and planted trees along broadened boulevards lined by elegant homes and public buildings—libraries, museums, theaters, and music halls. But the transformation of urban space rarely reached the squalid sections of the city inhabited by recent immigrants and rural transplants found packed into tenements along filthy streets filled with garbage.

Rapid urban growth swamped city leaders with new demands for service. Flush toilets, thirsty horses pulling street railways, and industrial users of water exhausted the capacity of municipal waterworks built for an earlier age. As city governments struggled, they raised taxes and incurred vast debts, which bred graft and gave rise to the boss. Urban bosses awarded utility franchises and construction contracts to local businesses in return for kickbacks, while new immigrant voters received jobs and welfare in return for their votes. Bosses tipped off friendly real estate agents about projected city improvements and received favors from the owners of saloons, brothels, and gambling

clubs in return for help with police protection, bail, and influence with judges. These institutions were vital to the urban economy and played an important role in easing the immigrants' way into American life. For many young women, prostitution meant economic survival. For men, the saloon offered friendship, cheap meals, and job leads.

Bossism deeply offended native-born, ethnocentric urban reformers. Many "goo-goos" (as bosses called advocates of "good government") not only opposed graft and vice but also the different cultural values of immigrants. As one said, immigrants "follow blindly leaders of their own race, are not moved by discussion, and exercise no judgment of their own"—and so were "not fit for the suffrage." Therefore, they advocated the "Americanization" of immigrants in public schools, opposed parochial schooling, and formed clubs and voters' leagues to educate new and old citizens about the failings of municipal government. They delighted in exposing electoral irregularities and large-scale graft, which often led to strident calls for replacing an Irish Catholic mayor with an Anglo-Saxon Protestant.

Ethnic politics colored every reform issue. Anglo-Saxon men favored prohibition partly to remove Irish saloon-owner influence from politics and supported woman suffrage partly to gain a middle-class political advantage against male immigrant voters. Most urban reformers disdained the "city proletariat mob." They proposed replacing bosses with expert city managers,

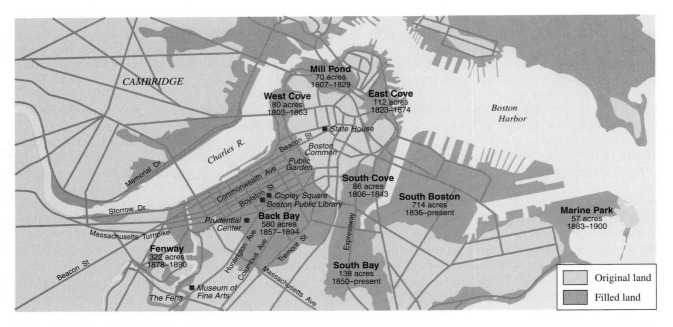

The City Beautiful: Enlarging Boston

As part of the "city beautiful" movement, Boston filled in more than 500 acres of tidal flats and swampy lowlands with gravel, thus adding the fashionable Back Bay along tree-lined Commonwealth Avenue. What is the effect of beautifying cities on different classes and ethnicities? Who benefits? Who uses Central Park in New York City? Who uses the parks in your city or town?

Favors from a Party Boss

Reformers wanted to eliminate the rule of urban party bosses. What in this *Puck* magazine cartoon would they criticize and want to change? What good did bosses do? Did the good outweigh the bad? What is local politics like now in your city?

(Courtesy of The Newberry Library, Chicago)

who would bring honest professionalism to city government. They hoped to make government cheaper and thereby lower taxes. One effect of their emphasis on cost efficiency was to cut services to the poor. Another was to disfranchise working-class and ethnic groups, whose political participation depended on the boss system.

Not all urban reformers were so elitist. Samuel Jones, for example, both opposed bossism and passionately advocated political participation by urban immigrants. He himself had begun as a poor Welsh immigrant in the Pennsylvania oil fields but worked his way up to the ownership of several oil fields and a factory in Toledo, Ohio. In 1894, Jones decided to "apply the Golden Rule as a rule of conduct" in his factory, with an eight-hour workday, a $2 minimum daily wage (50 to 75 cents higher than the local average for 10 hours), cooperative insurance, and an annual 5 percent Christmas dividend. Plastering the Golden Rule on factory walls, he hired social outcasts, offered employees cheap hot lunches (for 15 cents) and recreational facilities, and established Golden Rule Hall, where social visionaries could speak.

In 1897, Jones was elected to the first of four terms as mayor of Toledo. A maverick Republican who antagonized prominent citizens, Jones was adored by ordinary people with his advocacy of municipal ownership of utilities; public-works jobs and housing for the unemployed; more civic parks and playgrounds with free pools, skating rinks, and sleigh rides; and free vocational education and kindergartens. A pacifist, he took away policemen's weapons. In police court, Jones regularly dismissed most cases of petty theft and drunkenness on grounds that the accused were victims of social injustice, and he often released prostitutes after fining every man in the room 10 cents—and himself a dollar—for condoning prostitution. Crime in notoriously sinful Toledo fell during his term. When "Golden Rule" Jones died in 1904, nearly 55,000 people, "tears streaming down their faces," filed past his coffin.

The Struggle for Woman Suffrage

Women served, in Jane Addams's phrase, as "urban housekeepers" in the settlement house and good-government movements. Their work reflected the tensions many women felt between their public and private lives, between their obligations to self, family, and society. This tension was seldom expressed openly. A few women, however, began to vent the frustrations of middle-class domestic life. In her novel *The Awakening* (1899), Kate Chopin told the story of a young woman who, in discovering her own sexuality and life's possibilities beyond being a "mother-woman," defied conventional expectations of a woman's role. Her sexual affair and eventual suicide prompted a St. Louis newspaper to label the novel "poison."

Some middle-class women—Addams and Scudder, for example—avoided marriage, preferring the nurturing relationships found in the female settlement house community. "Married life looks to me . . . terribly impoverished for women," a Smith graduate observed, adding, "most of my deeper friendships have been with women." A few women boldly advocated free love or, less openly, formed lesbian relationships. Although most preferred traditional marriages and chose not to work outside the home, the generation of women that came of age in the 1890s married less—and later—than at any other time until today.

Many women reconciled the conflicting pressures between their private and public lives, and deflected male criticism, by seeing their work as maternal. Addams called Hull House the "great mother breast of our common humanity." Frances Willard told Susan B. Anthony in 1898 that "government is only housekeeping on the broadest scale," a job men had botched, requiring women's saving participation. A leading labor organizer was "Mother" Jones, and the fiery feminist anarchist Emma Goldman titled her monthly journal *Mother Earth*. By using nurturant language to describe their work, women furthered the very arguments used against them. Many remained economically dependent on men, and all women still lacked the essential rights of citizenship. How could they be municipal housekeepers if they could not yet even vote?

After the Seneca Falls Convention in 1848, women's civil and political rights advanced very slowly. Although several western states gave women the right to vote in municipal and school board elections, before 1890 only the territory of Wyoming (1869) granted full political equality. Colorado, Utah, and Idaho enfranchised women in the 1890s, but no other states granted suffrage until 1910. This slow pace resulted in part from male opposition led by an odd combination of ministers and saloon interests, as well as men threatened by women voting. "Equal suffrage," said a Texas senator, "is a repudiation of manhood."

In the 1890s, leading suffragists reexamined their situation. The two wings of the women's rights movement, split since 1869, combined in 1890 as the National American Woman Suffrage Association (NAWSA). Although Elizabeth Cady Stanton and Susan B. Anthony continued to head the association, both were in their seventies and leadership passed to younger, more moderate women. At a NAWSA convention in 1896, a resolution critical of Stanton's *Woman's Bible,* a devastating attack on the religious argument against woman suffrage, marked the shift. The new leaders also dropped other issues to focus only on suffrage.

Changing leadership also meant new strategies for getting the vote. Since 1848, suffragists had argued primarily from the principle of "our republican idea, individual citizenship," as Stanton put it in 1892. But younger leaders shifted to three expedient arguments. The first was that women needed the vote to pass self-protection laws to guard against rape and unsafe industrial work. The second argument, Addams's notion of urban housekeeping, pointed out that political enfranchisement would further women's role in cleaning up immoral cities and corrupt politics.

The third expedient argument reflected urban middle-class reformers' prejudice against non-Protestant immigrants. Machine bosses saw to it that immigrant men got to vote, sometimes several times in a day. Suffragists argued that educated, native-born American women should get the vote to counteract the undesirable influence of illiterate male immigrants. In a speech in Iowa in 1894, Carrie Chapman Catt, who would succeed Anthony as president of NAWSA in 1900, argued that the "Government is menaced with great danger . . . in the votes possessed by the males in the slums of the cities," a danger that could be averted only by giving the vote instead to women. Woman suffrage was finally achieved in 1920. But anti-immigrant attitudes would continue for another century.

Politics in the Pivotal 1890s

Americans mistakenly think of the last decade of the nineteenth century as the "gay nineties," symbolized by mustached baseball players and sporty Gibson girls riding bicycles. The 1890s was indeed a decade of baseball and bicycles but it was also a decade of disturbing gaps between rich and poor. The nineties featured enormous wealth but also dark tenements, grinding work, desperate unemployment, and debilitating poverty. The early 1890s saw Populism and protesting farmers; Wounded Knee and the "second great removal" of Native Americans; segregation, disfranchisement, and lynchings for blacks; and devastating labor defeats at Coeur d'Alene, Homestead, and Pullman.

Anticipated by Bellamy, the 1890s were years of contrasts and crises. Supreme Court justice John Harlan saw a "deep feeling of unrest" everywhere among people worrying that the nation was in "real danger . . . from aggregations of capital in the hands of a few." Populist "Sockless" Jerry Simpson simply saw a struggle between "the robbers and the robbed."

The pivotal nature of the 1890s hinged on this feeling of polarizing unrest and upheaval as the nation underwent the traumas of change from a rural to an urban society. The new immigration from Europe, the internal migrations of African Americans and white farmers, and the depression of 1893 all widened socioeconomic gaps, accelerating demands for reform. The federal bureaucracy slowly began to adapt to the needs of governing a complex specialized society, and Congress purposefully, if ineffectively, moved to confront national problems.

Republican Legislation in the Early 1890s

As the English and Germans were enacting national health, housing, and social insurance laws, Republicans, who gained control of the American

From the Depths

The conflicts between rich and poor and threat of social upheaval are dramatically illustrated in this turn-of-the-century work titled *From the Depths*. Can you tell a story about what is happening in the picture, and what is likely to happen next?

(Culver Pictures)

Congress in 1888, inched forward with legislation in five areas: trusts, the tariff, the money question, rights for African Americans, and pensions for Civil War veterans. The last was easiest, as a bill providing generous support for Union veterans and their dependents sailed through Congress.

The Sherman Anti-Trust Act in 1890 declared illegal "every contract, combination . . . or conspiracy in restraint of trade or commerce." Although the Act was vague and not really intended to break up big corporations, it was an initial attempt to restrain large business combinations. In *United States* v. *E. C. Knight* (1895), the Supreme Court ruled that the American Sugar Refining Company, which controlled more than 90 percent of the nation's sugar-refining capacity, was not in violation of the Sherman Act.

A tariff bill introduced in 1890 by Ohio Republican William McKinley stirred more controversy. McKinley's bill raised tariffs higher than ever. Despite heated opposition from agrarian interests,

whose products were generally not protected, McKinley's bill passed the House and, after nearly 500 amendments, also the Senate.

Silver was trickier. Recognizing the appeal of free silver to agrarian debtors and organized farmers, Republican leaders feared their party might be hurt by the issue. Senator John Sherman (R-Ohio) proposed a compromise that momentarily satisfied almost everyone. The Sherman Silver Purchase Act ordered the Treasury to buy 4.5 million ounces of silver monthly and to issue treasury notes for it. Silverites were pleased by the proposed increase in the money supply. Opponents felt they had averted the worst—free coinage of silver. The gold standard still stood.

Republicans were also prepared to confront violations of the voting rights of southern blacks in 1890. As usual, political considerations trumped moral ones. Since 1877, the South had become a Democratic stronghold, where party victories could be traced to fraud and intimidation of black Republican voters. Republican legislation, then, was intended to improve party fortunes in the South. A bill proposed by Massachusetts senator Henry Cabot Lodge sought to ensure African American voter registration and fair elections. A storm of Democratic disapproval arose. Former president Cleveland called it a "dark blow at the freedom of the ballot," and the Mobile *Daily Register* claimed that the "Force Bill" "would deluge the South in blood." Senate Democrats delayed action with a filibuster.

To pass the McKinley Tariff, Republican leaders bargained away Lodge's bill, ending major-party efforts to protect African American voting rights in the South until the 1960s. In a second setback for blacks, the Senate, fearful of giving the federal government a role in education, defeated a bill to provide federal aid to black schools in the South that received a disproportionately small share of local and state funds. "The plain truth is," said the New York *Herald*, "the North has got tired of the negro," foreshadowing a similar retreat from civil rights legislation 100 years later.

Labeled the "billion-dollar Congress," the legislative efforts of the summer of 1890, impressive by nineteenth-century standards, fell far short of solving the nation's problems. Trusts grew more rapidly after the Sherman Act than before. Union veterans were pleased with their pensions, but southerners complained that Confederate veterans were left out. Tariff protection was seen as a benefit primarily for eastern manufacturers. Farm prices continued to slide, and gold and silver advocates were only momentarily silenced. African American rights were put off to another time. Polarizing inequalities of wealth remained. Voters abandoned the GOP in droves in the 1890 congressional elections. Two years later, Cleveland won a presidential rematch with Harrison, claiming that government should do more in "support of the people."

Formation of the People's Party, 1892

Farmers knew all too well in 1890 that government did not support them; as Kansas orator Mary E. Lease said, "What you farmers need to do is to raise less corn, and more Hell." In February 1892, the People's, or Populist, party was established with Leonidas Polk as its presidential candidate. "The time has arrived," Polk thundered, "for the great West, the great South, and the great Northwest, to link their hands and hearts together and march to the ballot box and take possession of the government...and run it in the interest of the people." But by July, at the party convention in Omaha, Polk had died and the party nominated James B. Weaver, a Union army veteran from Iowa, for president and a former Confederate soldier for vice president.

The platform preamble, written by Ignatius Donnelly, a Minnesota farmer–politician, blazed with the urgent spirit of the agrarian protest movement, proclaiming that in the midst of political and corporate corruption "the people are demoralized....The fruits of the toil of millions are boldly stolen to build up colossal fortunes...we breed two great classes—paupers and millionaires." To heal that divide and end "oppression, injustice, and poverty," Donnelly advocated restoring government "to the hands of 'the plain people.'"

The Omaha demands expanded the Ocala platform of 1890. They included more direct democracy (popular election of senators, direct primaries, the initiative and referendum, and the secret ballot), and several pro-labor planks (the eight-hour workday, immigration restriction, and condemnation of the use of Pinkerton agents to break strikes). The Populists also endorsed a graduated income tax, free and unlimited coinage of silver at a ratio of 16 to 1, and government ownership of railroads, telephone, and telegraph. "The time has come," the platform said, "when the railroad corporations will either own the people or the people must own the railroads."

Although attempting to widen political debate by promoting a new vision of government activism to resolve farmers' problems, the Populists faced huge obstacles, not least weaning the South from the Democrats and encouraging southern whites to work with blacks. But the new party pressed ahead. Weaver campaigned actively in the South, where he faced egg- and rock-throwing Democrats spreading racial fears. Surprisingly, Weaver won more than 1 million popular votes (the first third-party candidate to do so), and carried four states and parts of two others for a total of 22 electoral votes.

The Populists' support was substantial but regional, coming from western miners and mine owners who favored the demand for silver coinage and from rural Americans from the Great Plains. But the People's party failed to break the Democratic stranglehold on the South. Populists did not appeal to city workers of the Northeast who were suspicious of the party's anti-urban tone and its desire for higher agricultural prices (which meant higher food prices). Perhaps most damaging, the Populists made few inroads among Midwestern farmers, who were relatively more prosperous than farmers elsewhere and saw little value in the Omaha platform. Although the Populists were not yet finished, most discontented farmers in 1892 voted for Cleveland and the Democrats.

The Depression of 1893

Though winning the election, Cleveland soon faced a difficult test. Shortly after taking office, one of the worst depressions ever to grip the American economy began, lasting from 1893 to 1897. Its severity heightened by global economic interdependence, the depression started in Europe and spread to the United States as overseas buyers cut back on their purchases of American products. Shrinking markets abroad soon crippled American manufacturing. Foreign investors, worried about the stability of American currency, dumped some $300 million of their securities in the United States. As gold left the country to pay for these securities, the nation's money supply declined. At the same time, falling prices hurt farmers, who discovered that it cost more to raise their crops and livestock than they could make in the market. Workers fared no better: wages fell faster than the price of food and rent.

The collapse in 1893 was also caused by an overextension of the domestic economy, especially in railroad construction and crops. Farmers, troubled by falling prices, planted more, hoping the market would pick up. But economic confidence gave way to financial panic. When Wall Street crashed early in 1893, investors frantically sold their shares and many people rushed to exchange paper notes for gold, further reducing gold reserves. Banks called in loans, which by the end of the year led to 16,000 business bankruptcies and 500 bank failures. The capital crunch and diminished buying power of Americans forced massive factory closings. Within a year, an estimated 3 million Americans—20 percent of the workforce—lost jobs. People fearfully watched tramps wandering from city to city looking for work, "with thousands of homeless and starving men in the streets" of Chicago.

As in Bellamy's coach image, the misery of the many was not shared by the few, which increased discontent. While unemployed men foraged in garbage dumps for food, the wealthy gave lavish parties, sometimes costing as much as $100,000. While poor families shivered in poorly heated tenements, the very rich built million-dollar summer resorts at Newport, Rhode Island, or grand mansions on New York's Fifth Avenue. While Lithuanian immigrants walked or rode packed

A City of Contrasts in 1893

Describe the contrasts in these two images of boating on the lagoons near the Palace of Electricity at the Chicago World's Columbian Exposition (above) and slum children playing in the streets less than a mile away (left). What is your response?

(Above: Bettman/CORBIS; left, Library of Congress)

streetcars to work, wealthy men luxuriated on huge pleasure yachts.

Nowhere were these inequalities more apparent than in Chicago during the World's Columbian Exposition, which opened on May 1, 1893, five days before a plummeting stock market began the depression. The Chicago World's Fair showcased, as President Cleveland said in an opening-day speech, the "stupendous results of American enterprise." When he pressed an ivory telegraph key, he started electric current that unfurled flags, spouted water through gigantic fountains, lit 10,000 electric lights, and powered huge steam engines. For six months, some 27 million visitors strolled around the White City, admiring its wide lagoons, its neoclassical white plaster buildings, and its exhibit halls filled with inventions. Built at a cost of $31 million, the fair celebrated the marvelous mechanical accomplishments of

American enterprise and of the "city beautiful" movement to make cities more livable.

But as fairgoers sipped pink champagne, in immigrant wards less than a mile away people drank contaminated water, crowded into packed tenements, looked in vain for jobs, and frequented saloons and brothels. "If Christ came to Chicago," British journalist W. T. Stead wrote in 1894, this would be "one of the last precincts into which we should care to take Him." Stead's book depicted the "ugly sight" of corruption, poverty, and wasted lives in a city with 200 millionaires and 200,000 unemployed men.

Despite the magnitude of despair during the depression, national politicians and leaders were reluctant to respond. Mass demonstrations forced city authorities to provide soup kitchens and places for the homeless to sleep. When an army of unemployed led by Jacob Coxey marched on Washington in the spring of

1894 to press for public work relief, its leaders were arrested for walking on the Capitol grass. Later that summer, President Cleveland sent federal troops to Chicago to crush the Pullman strike.

The president blamed the depression on the Silver Purchase Act, and convinced Congress to repeal it. But repeal only worsened the financial crisis, highlighted the silver panacea, and hurt conservative Democrats. With workers, farmers, and wealthy silver miners alienated, voters abandoned the Democrats in the midterm elections of 1894, giving both Populists and Republicans high hopes for 1896.

The Crucial Election of 1896

The 1896 presidential campaign, waged during the depression and featuring a battle over the currency, was one of the most critical in American history. Although Cleveland was in disgrace for ignoring depression woes, few leaders in either major party thought the federal government was responsible for alleviating the suffering of the people. But unemployed Polish meatpackers in Chicago, Slavic workers in Pennsylvania blast furnaces, Italian immigrant women in New Haven tenements, and white and black tenant farmers in Georgia all wondered where relief might be found. Would either major party respond to the pressing human needs of the depression? Would the People's party set a new national agenda for politics? These questions were largely resolved in the election of 1896.

As the election approached, Populist leaders, influenced by silver mine owners, became convinced that they must make a single-issue commitment to the free and unlimited coinage of silver at the ratio of 16 to 1. In the throes of the depression, silver took on enormous importance as the symbol of the many grievances of downtrodden Americans. Popular literature captured the rural, moral dimensions of the silver movement. L. Frank Baum's *Wonderful Wizard of Oz* (1900) was a free-silver moral allegory of rural values (Kansas, Auntie Em, the uneducated but wise scarecrow, and the good-hearted tin woodsman) and Populist attitudes and policies (the wicked witch of the East, and the magical silver shoes in harmony with the yellow brick road, in "Oz"—ounces).

The Republicans nominated William McKinley. Twice governor of Ohio, McKinley was identified with the high protective tariff that bore his name. Citing the familiar argument that prosperity depended on the gold standard and protection, Republicans blamed the depression on Cleveland's attempt to lower the tariff.

The excitement of the Democratic convention in July contrasted with the staid, smoothly organized Republican gathering. With Cleveland repudiated, state after state elected delegates pledged to silver. Gold Democrats, however, had enough power to wage a close battle for the platform plank on money. Leading the silver forces was an ardent young silverite, William Jennings Bryan, a 36-year-old former congressman from Nebraska. Few saw him as presidential material, but Bryan arranged to give the closing argument for a silver plank himself. His dramatic speech, one of the most famous in American political history, swept the convention for silver and ensured his nomination. As he concluded his attack on the "goldbugs" and defense of the "holy...cause of liberty," Bryan said:

> Having behind us the producing masses of this nation...and toilers everywhere, we will answer their demand for a gold standard by saying to them: "You shall not press down upon the brow of labor this crown of thorns, you shall not crucify mankind upon a cross of gold."

Bryan stretched out his arms as if on a cross, and the convention exploded in applause.

Populist strategy lay in shambles when the Democrats named a silver candidate. Some party leaders favored fusion with the Democratic ticket but anti-fusionists were outraged. Unwisely, the Populists also nominated Bryan, with Georgia Populist Tom Watson for vice president. Running on competing silver slates damaged Bryan's chances.

During the campaign, McKinley stayed home in Canton, Ohio, where some 750,000 admirers came to visit him, brought by low excursion rates offered by the railroads. The Republicans made an unprecedented effort to reach voters through an expensive media campaign, heavily financed by major corporations. Party leaders distributed more than 200 million pamphlets in 14 languages to voters advertising McKinley as the "advance agent of prosperity." To unemployed workers, McKinley promised a "full dinner pail." On the money issue he declared that "our currency today is...as good as gold." Free silver, he warned, would cause inflation and more economic disaster. Recovery depended not on money, but on tariff reform to stimulate industry and provide jobs.

Bryan took his case directly to the people. Three million Americans in 27 states heard him speak as he traveled more than 18,000 miles, giving as many as 30 speeches a day. Bryan's message was simple: prosperity required free coinage of silver and government should attend to the needs of the producing classes rather than the vested interests. But the rhetoric favored rural toilers. "The great cities rest upon our broad and fertile prairies," he said in the "Cross of Gold" speech. Urban workers were not inspired by this rhetoric, nor were immigrants by Bryan's prairie moralizing. To influential easterners, the brash young Nebraskan represented a threat. A Brooklyn minister

Recovering the Past

POLITICAL CAMPAIGN ARTIFACTS: BUTTONS AND POSTERS

Throughout American history, presidential political campaigns have produced, in addition to the streams of speeches, sound bites, and words, mountains of material objects: buttons, badges, banners, bumper stickers, yard signs, posters, and other campaign paraphernalia to persuade voters to support one candidate or another.

The election of 1896 was no exception, producing a plethora of political campaign artifacts on behalf of William McKinley and William Jennings Bryan. The fervor of that pivotal political contest led to the production of thousands of lapel pins, buttons, ribbons, bandanas, shirts, teacups, paper and soap dolls, posters, and other articles intended to influence American voters. Although some of it seems silly, symbolic imagery was important. The examination of just two kinds of material objects —buttons and posters— reveals a great deal about the issues, values, symbolism, and style of the election of 1896.

Reflecting on the Past Examine the buttons pictured here (as well as the "goldbug" and other stickpins). What issues are voters reminded of? How many different ways is the message, reinforced by recurring symbols, repeated on these buttons? Now compare the buttons and pins with the two posters. Do not worry that you cannot read most of the words; focus instead on the visual imagery and such words as you can make out. How do the posters reinforce key symbols, slogans, and substantive issues associated with each candidate? What visual images do the posters add? What audience do you think these campaign artifacts had in mind? What do you conclude about the 1896 campaign on the basis of these material items? Do these artifacts suggest that voters were more or less involved with political issues and party identification than they are today? What artifacts, images, and symbols would best reflect an early twenty-first-century presidential campaign, and what would future historians learn from them? ■

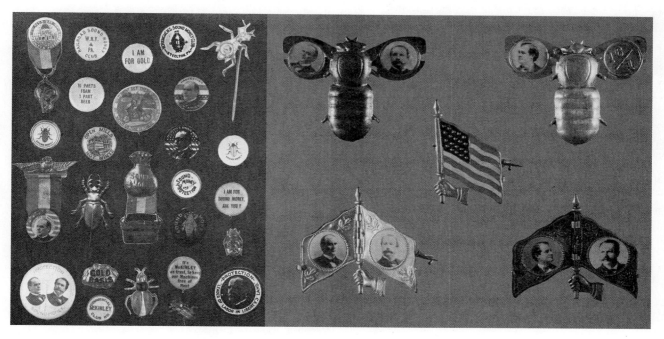

Artifacts from the McKinley and Bryan campaigns

(Left: Courtesy Michael Kelly; right: © David J. and Janice L. Frent Collection/Corbis)

Campaign poster showing William McKinley and his running mate, Garret Hobart.

(Library of Congress [LC-USZC4–3162])

Campaign poster showing William Jennings Bryan, his wife and children, and the text of the "Cross of Gold" speech.

(The Granger Collection, New York)

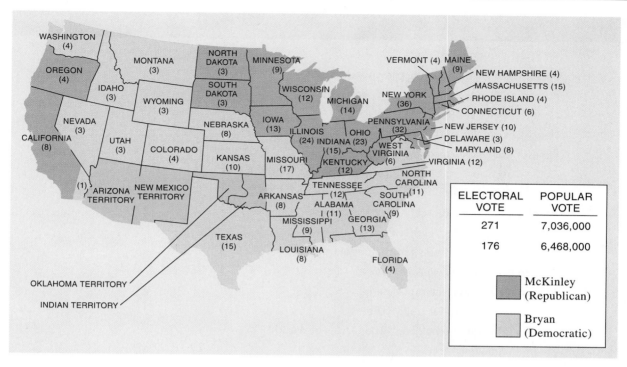

The Presidential Election of 1896

What do you notice about the sectional basis of the voting in McKinley's victory? Why did sections vote the way they did? In his cabled congratulations, Bryan, ever the "democrat," said: "We have submitted the issues to the American people and their will is law." Does the map and the constitutional role of the electoral college validate Bryan's belief that the people's will is law?

declared that the Democratic platform was "made in Hell," and Theodore Roosevelt wrote, "This silver craze surpasses belief. Bryan's election would be a great calamity."

Voters turned out in record numbers. In key states such as Illinois, Indiana, and Ohio, 95 percent of those eligible to vote went to the polls. McKinley won 271 electoral votes to Bryan's 176, the largest margin of victory in a quarter century. Millionaire Mark Hanna jubilantly wired McKinley: "God's in his heaven, all's right with the world."

Although Bryan won more than 6 million votes (47 percent of the total), more than any previous Democratic winner, he failed to carry the Midwest or urban middle and working classes, who had little confidence that free silver would stimulate economic growth. McKinley's promise of a "full dinner pail" was more convincing. Northern laborers feared that inflation would drive up prices and rents faster than wages. Catholic immigrants distrusted Populist Protestantism. In the Great Lakes states, prosperous farmers felt less discontent than farmers elsewhere. Chance also played a part in Bryan's defeat. Bad wheat harvests in India, Australia, and Argentina drove up world grain prices, and many of the complaints of American farmers evaporated.

The New Shape of American Politics

The landslide Republican victory broke the stalemate in post–Civil War American politics. Republicans dropped their identification with the politics of piety and strengthened their image as the party of prosperity and national greatness, which gave them a party dominance that lasted until the 1930s. The Democrats, under Bryan's leadership until 1912, put on the mantle of Populist moralism but were largely reduced to a sectional party, reflecting narrow southern views on money and race. The 1896 election demonstrated that the Northeast and the Great Lakes states had acquired so many immigrants that they now controlled the nation's political destiny. The Populists disappeared, yet within the next 25 years, many Populist issues (direct election of senators, graduated income tax, woman suffrage) were adopted by the two major parties and became law.

Another result of the election of 1896 was a change in the patterns of political participation. Because the Republicans were so dominant in the Northeast and Midwest, and Democrats so powerful in the South, parties had less reason to mobilize large numbers of voters and voters had little motivation to cast a ballot. Many black voters in the South, moreover, were disfranchised, and middle-class

Timeline

1873	Congress demonetizes silver
1875	Specie Resumption Act retires greenback dollars
1877	Rutherford B. Hayes becomes president
1878	Congress permits partial coining of silver
1879	Henry George, *Progress and Poverty*
1880	James A. Garfield elected president
1881	Garfield assassinated; Chester A. Arthur succeeds to presidency
1882	Chinese Exclusion Act
1883	Pendleton Civil Service Act
1884	Grover Cleveland elected president
1887	College Settlement House Association founded
1888	Edward Bellamy, *Looking Backward*
	Benjamin Harrison elected president
1889	Jane Addams establishes Hull House
	Andrew Carnegie promulgates "The Gospel of Wealth"
1890	Sherman Anti-Trust Act
	Sherman Silver Purchase Act
	McKinley Tariff
	Elections bill protecting black voting rights defeated
1890s	Wyoming, Colorado, Utah, and Idaho grant woman suffrage
1892	Cleveland elected president for the second time
	Populist party wins more than 1 million votes
	Homestead steel strike
1893	World's Columbian Exposition, Chicago
1893–1897	Financial panic and depression
1894	Pullman strike
	Coxey's march on Washington
1896	Charles Sheldon, *In His Steps*
	Populist party fuses with Democrats
	William McKinley elected president
1897	"Golden Rule" Jones elected mayor of Toledo, Ohio
	Economic recovery begins

good-government reformers were not as effective as party bosses in turning out urban voters. The tremendous rate of political participation that had characterized the nineteenth century since the Jackson era gradually declined. In the twentieth century, political involvement among poorer Americans declined considerably, a phenomenon unique among western democracies.

McKinley had promised that Republican rule meant prosperity, and as soon as he took office, the economy recovered. Discoveries of gold in the Yukon and the Alaskan Klondike increased the money supply, ending the silver mania. Industrial production returned to full capacity. Touring the Midwest in 1898, McKinley spoke to cheering crowds about the hopeful shift from "industrial depression to industrial activity."

McKinley's election marked not only the return of economic health but also the emergence of the executive as the dominant focus of the American political system. Just as McKinley's campaign saw the extravagant corporate contributions that have marked recent presidential campaigns, his conduct as president foreshadowed the presidency in our time. McKinley rejected traditional views of the president as the passive executor of laws, instead playing an active role in dealing with Congress and the press. His frequent trips away from Washington showed an increasing regard for gathering public opinion in the interests of advancing federal and national power. As we shall see in Chapter 20, McKinley began the transformation of the presidency into a potent force in world affairs as well.

Conclusion
LOOKING FORWARD

This chapter began with Edward Bellamy's imaginary look backward from the year 2000 at the grim economic realities and unresponsive politics of American life in the late nineteenth century. McKinley's triumph in 1896 indicated that in a decade marked by depression, Populist revolt, and cries for action to close the inequalities of wealth—represented by Bellamy's coach—the established order remained intact. Calls for change did not necessarily lead to change. But in the areas of personal action and the philosophical bases for social change, intellectual middle-class reformers such as Edward Bellamy, Frances Willard, Jane Addams, and "Golden Rule" Jones showed the way to progressive reforms in the next century. More Americans were able to look forward to the kind of cooperative, caring, and cleaner world envisioned in Bellamy's utopian novel.

As 1900 approached, people took a predictably intense interest in what the new century would be like. Henry Adams envisioned an ominous future, predicting the explosive and ultimately destructive energy of unrestrained industrial development, symbolized by the "dynamo" and other engines of American and European power. Such forces, he warned, would overwhelm the gentler, moral forces represented by art, woman, and religious symbols. Others were more optimistic, preferring to place their confidence in America's self-image as an exemplary democratic nation. Surely the new century, most thought, would see not only the continued perfection of these values and institutions but also the spread of the American model around the globe. Such confidence resulted in foreign expansion by the American people even before the old century had ended. We turn to that next.

QUESTIONS FOR REVIEW AND REFLECTION

1. How would you characterize the politics of the Gilded Age? How does it compare to present-day politics?
2. What political issues concerned the American people in the late nineteenth century, and do you think they were the appropriate ones?
3. What role did middle-class reformers, especially women, play in dealing with social and political problems in the Gilded Age? How did religion influence reform?
4. Why was the election of 1896 such a crucial and pivotal one in the development of American political parties? How were the policies and areas of support of the two major parties similar to and different from those of the present?
5. Was the American democratic system responsive to the needs of the American people in the Gilded Age? Was it even "democratic"? How well did politics reflect national ideals and values? Does it still?

CHAPTER 20

Becoming a World Power

Dewey at Manila Bay, May 1, 1898 (painting by Rufus Zogbaum): American Expansionism Triumphant. What artistic elements make this a heroic painting?

(CORBIS)

American Stories

Private Grayson Kills a Soldier in the Philippines

In January 1899, the U.S. Senate was locked in a dramatic debate over whether to ratify the Treaty of Paris concluding the recent war with Spain over Cuban independence. At the same time, American soldiers uneasily faced Filipino rebels across a neutral zone around the outskirts of Manila, the capital of the Philippines. Until recent weeks, the Americans and Filipinos had been allies, together defeating the Spanish to liberate the Philippines. The American fleet under Admiral George Dewey had destroyed the Spanish naval squadron in Manila Bay on May 1, 1898. Three weeks later, an American ship brought from exile the native Filipino insurrectionary leader, Emilio Aguinaldo, to lead rebel forces on land, while U.S. gunboats patrolled the seas.

At first, the Filipinos looked on the Americans as liberators. Although the intentions of the United States were never clear, as in a later intervention in Iraq, Aguinaldo believed that, as in Cuba, the Americans had no territorial ambitions. They would simply drive the Spanish out and then leave. In June, therefore, Aguinaldo declared the independence of the Philippines and began setting up a constitutional government. American officials pointedly ignored the independence ceremonies. When the war ended in August, American troops denied Aguinaldo's Filipino soldiers an opportunity to liberate their own capital city and shunted them off to the suburbs. The armistice agreement recognized American rights to the "harbor, city, and bay of Manila," while the proposed Treaty of Paris gave the United States the entire Philippine Islands archipelago.

Tension mounted in the streets of Manila and along 14 miles of trenches separating American and Filipino soldiers. Taunts, obscenities, and racial epithets were shouted across the neutral zone. Barroom skirmishes and knifings filled the nights; American soldiers searched houses without warrants and looted stores. Their behavior was not unlike that of English soldiers in Boston in the 1770s.

On the night of February 4, 1899, Privates William Grayson and David Miller of Company B, 1st Nebraska Volunteers, were on patrol in Santa Mesa, a Manila suburb surrounded on three sides by insurgent trenches. The Americans had orders to shoot any Filipino soldiers in the neutral area. As the two Americans cautiously worked their way to a bridge over the San Juan River, they heard a Filipino signal whistle, answered by another. The two froze as four Filipinos emerged from the darkness on the road ahead. "Halt!" Grayson shouted. The native lieutenant in charge answered, "Halto!"—either mockingly or because he had similar orders. Standing less than 15 feet apart, the two men repeated their commands. After a moment's hesitation, Grayson fired, killing his opponent. The other Filipinos jumped out at them, and Grayson and Miller shot two more. Then they turned and ran back to their own lines shouting warnings of attack. A full-scale battle followed.

The next day, Commodore Dewey cabled Washington that the "insurgents have inaugurated general engagement" and promised a hasty suppression of the insurrection. The outbreak of hostilities ended the Senate debates. On February 6, the Senate ratified the Treaty of Paris, thus formally annexing the Philippines and sparking a war between the United States and Aguinaldo's Filipino nationalist revolutionaries, who represented a small but growing percentage of the population.

In a guerrilla war similar to those that Americans would fight later in Vietnam, Afghanistan, and Iraq, Filipino nationalists tried to undermine the American will by hit-and-run attacks. American soldiers remained in heavily garrisoned cities and undertook search-and-destroy missions to root out rebels and pacify the countryside. The Filipino-American War lasted until July 1902, three years longer than the Spanish-American War that caused it and involving far more troops, casualties, and monetary and moral costs.

How did all this happen? What brought Private Grayson to "shoot my first nigger," as he put it, halfway around the world? For the first time in history, regular American soldiers found themselves fighting outside North America. The "champion of oppressed nations," as Aguinaldo said, had turned into an oppressor nation itself, imposing the American way of life and American institutions on faraway peoples against their will. It would not be the last time.

The war in the Philippines marked a critical transformation of America's role in the world. As the United States sought to exert a wider influence, global events influenced America. Within a few years at the turn of the century, the United States acquired an empire, however small by European standards, and established itself as a world power. In this chapter, we will review the historical dilemmas of America's role in the world. In an increasingly global context, we will examine the U.S. motivations for expansionism in the 1890s and how they were manifested in Cuba, the Philippines, and elsewhere. Finally, we will look at how the fundamental patterns of American foreign policy to this day were established for Latin America, eastern Asia and the Middle East, and Europe. We will see that the tension between idealism and self-interest that has permeated America's domestic history has also guided its foreign policy.

Steps Toward Empire

The circumstances that brought Privates Grayson and Miller from Nebraska to the Philippines originated deep in American history. As early as the seventeenth-century Puritan migration, Americans worried about how to do good in a sinful world. John Winthrop sought to set up a "city on a hill" in the New World, a model community of righteous living for the rest of the world to imitate. "Let the eyes of the world be upon us," Winthrop had said. That wish, reaffirmed during the American Revolution, became a permanent goal of American policy toward the outside world.

America as a Model Society

Nineteenth-century Americans, like the Russians, French, English, and Chinese, continued to believe in their nation's special mission in the world. But only the United States claimed a mission of spreading democratic governments. The Monroe Doctrine in 1823, pointing out the differences between autocratic Europe and America, warned Europe's monarchies to keep out of the New World and not to interfere with emerging Latin American independence movements. In succeeding decades, distinguished European visitors came to observe the "great social revolution" in the United States. They found representative democratic political and legal institutions, a Protestant religious commitment to human perfectibility, unlimited energy, and an ability to apply unregulated economic activity and inventive genius to produce more things for more people.

In an evil world, Americans, then as now, believed that they stood as a transforming force for good. But how could a nation committed to isolationism and to avoiding entanglements with European nations do the transforming? One way was to encourage other countries to observe and imitate the American example. Other nations, however, were often attracted to competing models of modernization, such as socialism, or preferred their own religious traditions, such as Islam. These differences often led to a more aggressive American foreign policy, as seen in the aftermath of 9/11.

Americans have rarely just focused on perfecting the good example at home and waiting for others to copy it, which requires patience and passivity, two traits not characteristic of the American people. Leaders of the United States have therefore actively and sometimes forcefully sought to impose their ideas and institutions on others. These international crusades, as in recent years in the Caribbean, Central America, Afghanistan, and Iraq, have been motivated by a mixture of noble idealism and crass self-interest. Hence, the effort to spread the American model to an imperfect world has been both a blessing and a burden—for others as well as for the American people.

Early Expansionism

Persistent expansionism marked the first century of American independence. Jefferson's purchase of Louisiana in 1803, the taking of Indian lands during the War of 1812, and the midcentury pursuit of "Manifest Destiny" spread the United States across North America. In the 1850s, Americans began to look beyond their own continent as Commodore Perry in 1853 "opened" Japan, and southerners sought more cotton lands in the Caribbean.

After the Civil War, Secretary of State William Seward spoke of an America that would hold a "commanding sway in the world," destined to exert commercial domination in the Pacific. He purchased Alaska from Russia in 1867 for $7.2 million and acquired a coaling station in the Midway Islands near Hawaii, where missionaries and merchants were already active. He advocated annexing Cuba and other Caribbean islands, tried to negotiate a treaty for an American-built canal through Panama, and dreamed of "possession" of the entire North and Central American continent and ultimately "control of the world."

In 1870, foreshadowing the Philippines debates 30 years later, supporters of President Grant, arguing the strategic and economic importance of the Caribbean, tried to persuade the Senate to annex Santo Domingo on the island of Hispaniola. Opponents responded that annexation violated American principles of self-determination and government by consent. They also claimed that brown-skinned Caribbean peoples were unassimilable, and that expansionism would involve foreign entanglements, a large and expensive navy, bigger government, and higher taxes. The Senate rejected annexation.

Although reluctant to add territory outright, Americans eagerly sought commercial dominance in Latin America and Asia. But American talk of building a canal across Nicaragua produced only Nicaraguan suspicions. In 1881, secretary of state James G. Blaine sought to convene a conference of American nations to promote hemispheric peace and trade. Latin Americans may have wondered what Blaine intended, for in 1881 he intervened in three separate border disputes in Central and South America, in each case at the cost of goodwill. After an incident and threat of war with Chile in 1889, Blaine's efforts resulted in the first Pan-American Conference to improve economic ties among the nations of the Americas.

American influence spread to the Pacific. In the mid-1870s, American sugar-growing interests in the Hawaiian Islands put whites in positions of influence over the monarchy. In 1875, they obtained a treaty admitting Hawaiian sugar duty-free to the United

Waging War in the Philippines

When the United States went to war against Spain in 1898, partly to help the Cubans win their independence from harsh Spanish rule, no one could have imagined the ironic outcome. Within a year, Americans would themselves impose imperial rule over the Philippines, marching through and burning villages (as the Twentieth Kansas Volunteers are doing here) and waging war against civilians in a faraway Asian land. How did that happen? Has it happened since?

(Above: Courtesy of The Newberry Library, Chicago; right: Keystone-Mast Collection [24039], URL/California Museum of Photography, University of California at Riverside)

States, and in 1887, the United States won exclusive rights to build a naval base at Pearl Harbor. Native Hawaiians resented the influence of American sugar interests, especially as they brought in Japanese to replace native people in the sugarcane fields, with some 200,000 arriving between 1885 and 1924.

In 1891, the nationalistic queen Liliuokalani assumed the throne and pursued a policy of "Hawaii for the Hawaiians." Two years later, in what one journalist called a revolution "of sugar, by sugar, for sugar," white planters staged a coup with the help of U.S. gunboats and marines, imprisoned the queen, and sought formal annexation by the U.S. Senate. But when Grover Cleveland, who opposed expansion, returned to the presidency for his second term, he stopped the move. The sugar growers waited patiently for a more desirable time for annexation, which came during the war in 1898.

American Expansionism in Global Context

American forays into the Pacific and Latin America brought the United States increasingly into contact and conflict with European nations. The nineteenth century was marked by European imperial expansionism

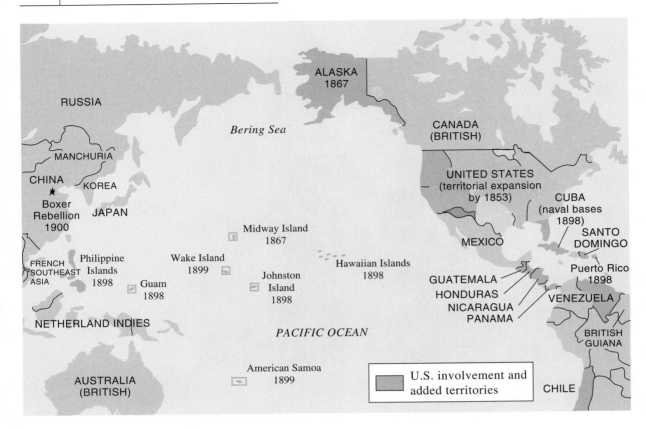

U.S. Territorial Expansion to 1900

U.S. territorial expansion to 1860 is represented in miniature in the U.S. portion of this map. What obvious differences are apparent between earlier expansion and areas of U.S. involvement and acquisitions after 1860 (in green)? How was each new territory acquired? What patterns and problems do you see with this expansion?

throughout much of the world. In southern and southeastern Asia, the British were in India, Burma, and Malaya; the French in Cambodia, Vietnam, and Laos; the Dutch in Singapore and the East Indies; and the Spanish in the Philippines. These and other colonial powers divided China—its Manchu dynasty weakened by the opium trade, internal conflicts, and European pressure—into spheres of economic influence. A Chinese newspaper editorial complained that other nations "all want to satisfy their ambitions to nibble at China and swallow it." The Russians wrested away Manchuria, and Japan took Korea after intervention in a Korean peasant rebellion in 1894. China was forced to cede Taiwan and southern Manchuria to Japanese influence and control.

In Africa, Europeans scrambled to gain control of both coastal and interior areas, with England, France, Germany, Portugal, and Belgium grabbing the most land and exploiting African peoples. Only two independent African nations existed in the late nineteenth century: Liberia, founded in 1822 by Americans to resettle free blacks, and the fragmented kingdom of Ethiopia, which thrashed the Italians when they invaded in 1896. With nearly all of Africa colonized,

the only way imperial powers could acquire more land was to fight one another. Thus, in 1899, war broke out in southern Africa between the British and the Boers, descendants of Dutch settlers—a war waged with a savagery Europeans usually reserved for indigenous peoples. The English destroyed Boer farms and drove civilians into camps where an estimated 20,000 women and children perished from starvation and malnutrition. The British won, but at a horrific cost.

Africa was not then of interest to the United States, but in the Pacific and the Caribbean, it was inevitable that the United States, a late arrival to imperialism, would collide with European rivals. Moving outward from Hawaii closer to the markets of eastern Asia, the United States acquired a naval and coaling station in the Samoan Islands in 1878. American and German naval forces almost fought each other there in 1889—before a typhoon ended the crisis by nearly wiping out both navies. Troubles in the Pacific also occurred in the late 1880s over the American seizure of several Canadian ships in fur seal and fishing disputes in the Bering Sea, settled only by the threat of British naval action and an international arbitration ruling ordering the United States to pay damages.

Closer to home, the United States sought to replace Great Britain as the most influential nation in Central America and northern South America. In 1895, a boundary dispute between Venezuela and British Guyana threatened to bring British intervention against the Venezuelans. President Cleveland, needing a popular political issue during the depression, asked Secretary of State Richard Olney to send a stern message to Great Britain. Invoking the Monroe Doctrine, Olney's note (stronger than Cleveland intended) called the United States "practically sovereign on this continent" and demanded international arbitration to settle the dispute. The British ignored the note, and war loomed. Both sides realized that war would be an "absurdity," and the boundary dispute was settled.

Despite these expansionist blusters, the United States in 1895 had neither the means nor a consistent policy for enlarging its role in the world. The diplomatic service was small and unprofessional. No U.S. embassy official in Beijing spoke Chinese. The U.S. Army, with about 28,000 men, was smaller than Bulgaria's. The navy, dismantled after the Civil War and only partly rebuilt, still had many obsolete ships and ranked no higher than tenth in the world. By 1898, things would change.

Expansionism in the 1890s

In 1893, the historian Frederick Jackson Turner wrote that for three centuries "the dominant fact in American life has been expansion." The "extension of American influence to outlying islands and adjoining countries," he thought, indicated still more expansionism. Turner struck a responsive chord in a country that had always been restless and optimistic. With the western frontier declared closed, Americans would surely look for new frontiers, for mobility and markets as well as for morality and missionary activity. The motivations for the expansionist impulse of the late 1890s resembled those that had prompted Europeans to settle the New World in the first place: greed, glory, and God. We will examine expansionism as a reflection of profits, patriotism, piety, and politics.

Profits: Searching for Overseas Markets

Senator Albert Beveridge of Indiana bragged in 1898 that "American factories are making more than the American people can use; American soil is producing more than they can consume. Fate has written our policy for us; the trade of the world must and shall be ours." Americans such as Beveridge revived older dreams of an American commercial empire in the Caribbean Sea and the Pacific Ocean. American businessmen saw huge profits beckoning in heavily

populated Latin America and Asia, and they wanted to get their share of these markets, as well as access to the sugar, coffee, fruits, oil, and minerals that were abundant in these lands.

Understanding that commercial expansion required a stronger navy and coaling stations and colonies, business interests began to shape diplomatic and military strategy. But not all businessmen in the 1890s liked commercial expansion or a vigorous foreign policy. Some preferred traditional trade with Canada and Europe rather than risky new ventures in Asia and Latin America. Some thought it more important to recover from the depression than annex distant islands.

But the drop in domestic consumption during the depression also encouraged businesses to expand into new markets. The tremendous growth of American production in the post–Civil War years made expansionism more attractive than drowning in overproduction, cutting prices, and firing workers. The National Association of Manufacturers led the way, proclaiming in 1896 that "the trade centers of Central and South America are natural markets for American products."

Despite the 1890s depression, products spewed from American factories at a staggering rate. The

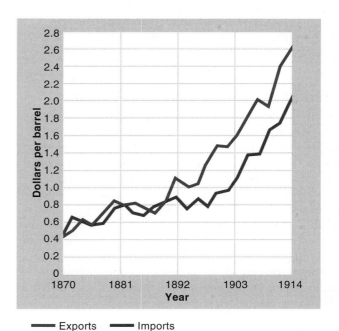

American Foreign Trade, 1870–1914

After a rather gradual increase in trade through the boom-and-bust cycles of the 1870s and 1880s and an actual dip during the depression of 1893–1895, American foreign trade saw spectacular increases during the Republican era of Presidents McKinley, Roosevelt, and Taft. What is the relationship between foreign trade and imperial expansion?

Source: U.S. Bureau of the Census.

United States moved from fourth place in the world in manufacturing in 1870 to first place in 1900, doubling the number of factories and tripling the value of farm output. Manufactured goods, led by steel products, agricultural machinery, sewing machines, cash registers, and telephones, grew nearly fivefold between 1895 and 1914. The total value of American exports tripled, from $434 million in 1866 to nearly $1.5 billion in 1900. By 1914, exports had risen to $2.5 billion, a 67 percent increase over 1900. The increased trade continued to go mainly to Europe rather than Asia (less than 5 percent). But interest in Asian markets grew, especially as agricultural output continued to increase and prices stayed low.

Investments followed a similar pattern. American direct investments abroad increased from about $634 million to $2.6 billion between 1897 and 1914. Although the greatest activity was in Britain, Canada, and Mexico, attention increased on actual and potential investment in Latin America and Eastern Asia. Central American investment grew from $21 million in 1897 to $93 million by 1914, mainly in mines, railroads, and banana and coffee plantations. At the turn of the century came the formation and growth of America's largest multinational corporations, including Dupont, Alcoa, American Tobacco, and the United Fruit Company. Although slow to respond to investment and market opportunities abroad, these companies soon supported an aggressive foreign policy.

Patriotism: Asserting National Power

In 1898, a State Department memorandum stated that "we can no longer afford to disregard international rivalries now that we ourselves have become a competitor in the world-wide struggle for trade." The national state, then, should support commercial interests.

More Americans, however, saw expansion in terms of national glory and greatness. In the late 1890s, a group centered around Assistant Secretary of the Navy Theodore Roosevelt and Massachusetts senator Henry Cabot Lodge emerged as highly influential leaders of a changing American foreign policy. These intensely nationalistic young men shifted to what Lodge called the "large policy." Roosevelt agreed that economic interests should take second place to questions of what he called "national honor."

Naval strategist Alfred Thayer Mahan greatly influenced the new foreign policy elite. Mahan's books argued that in a world of Darwinian struggle for survival, national power depended on naval supremacy, control of sea lanes, and vigorous development of domestic resources and foreign markets. He advocated colonies in both the Caribbean and the Pacific, linked by a canal built and controlled by the United States. In

a world of constant "strife" where "everywhere nation is arrayed against nation," he said, it was imperative that Americans "look outward."

Piety: The Missionary Impulse

As Mahan's statements suggest, a strong sense of God-given duty and the missionary ideal of doing good for others also motivated expansionism—and sometimes rationalized the exploitation and oppression of weaker peoples. As a missionary put it in 1885, "The Christian nations are subduing the world in order to make mankind free." Richard Olney agreed, saying in 1898, "the mission of this country is . . . to forego no fitting opportunity to further the progress of civilization," as defined by American values and geo-political interests.

Josiah Strong, a Congregationalist minister, was perhaps the most ardent advocate of American missionary expansionism. He argued that in the struggle for survival among nations, the United States had emerged as the center of Anglo-Saxonism and was "divinely commissioned" to spread political liberty, Protestant Christianity, and civilized values over the earth. "This powerful race," he wrote, "will move down upon Mexico, down upon Central and South America, out upon the islands of the sea, over upon Africa and beyond." Indiana senator Albert Beveridge agreed, saying in 1899 that God had prepared English-speaking Anglo-Saxons to become "the master organizers of the world to establish and administer governments among savages and senile peoples."

Missionaries carried these ideas to non-Christian lands around the world, especially China. The number of American Protestant missionaries in China increased from 436 in 1874 to 5,462 in 1914, and the estimated number of Christian converts in China jumped from 5,000 in 1870 to nearly 100,000 in 1900. Although this was much less than missionaries hoped, this tiny fraction of the Chinese population included young reformist intellectuals who, absorbing Western ideas, in 1912 helped overthrow the Manchu dynasty. Economic relations between China and the United States increased roughly at the same rate as missionary activity.

Politics: Manipulating Public Opinion

Public opinion and national politics also played a role. The psychological tensions and economic hardships of the depression in the 1890s jarred national self-confidence. Foreign adventures then, as now, provided a distraction from domestic turmoil and promised to restore patriotic pride—and maybe even win votes.

This process was helped by the growth of a highly competitive popular penny press, which brought international issues before a mass readership. When New York City newspapers, notably William Randolph

Hearst's *Journal* and Joseph Pulitzer's *World,* competed in stirring up public support for the Cuban rebels against Spain, politicians dared not ignore the outcry. Daily reports of Spanish atrocities in 1896 and 1897 kept public moral outrage constantly a part of political discourse. When Democrat William Jennings Bryan entered the fray by raising a regiment of Nebraska volunteers for war, the McKinley administration kept him far from battle and therefore far from the headlines.

Politics, then, joined profits, patriotism, and piety in motivating the expansionism of the 1890s. These four impulses interacted to produce the Spanish-American War, the annexation of the Philippine Islands and subsequent war, and the energetic foreign policy of President Theodore Roosevelt.

War in Cuba and the Philippines

Lying 90 miles off Florida, Cuba had been the object of intense American interest for a half century. Spain could not halt the continuing struggle of the Cuban people for a measure of autonomy and relief from exploitive labor in the sugar plantations, even after slavery itself ended. Cuban uprisings and pressure for complete independence raised tensions between Spain and the United States.

The Road to War

When the Cuban revolt flared up anew in 1895, the Madrid government again failed to implement reforms. Instead, it sent General Valeriano Weyler y Nicolau,

dubbed "the butcher" by the American press, with 50,000 troops to quell the disturbance. When Weyler began herding rural Cubans into "reconcentration" camps, Americans were outraged. An outpouring of sympathy swept the nation, especially as sensationalist reports of horrible suffering and the deaths of thousands in the camps ("butchered without mercy") filled American newspapers.

The Cuban struggle appealed to a country convinced of its role as protector of the weak and defender of the right of self-determination. One editorial deplored Spanish "injustice, oppression, extortion, and demoralization," while describing the Cubans as heroic freedom fighters "inspired by our glorious example of beneficent free institutions and successful self-government." Motivated in part by genuine humanitarian concern and a sense of admiration for heroic Cuban freedom fighters, many Americans held rallies to raise money and food for famine relief, and called for land reform and even armed intervention. But neither Cleveland nor McKinley wanted war.

Self-interest also played a role. Since the 1850s, Americans had noted the profitable resources and strategic location of the island. American companies had invested extensively in Cuban sugar plantations. Appeals for reform had much to do with ensuring a stable environment for further investments and trade ($27 million in 1897), as well as for protecting the sugar fields against the ravages of civil war.

The election of 1896 only temporarily diverted attention from Cuba. A new government in Madrid recalled Weyler and made halfhearted concessions.

The *Maine* Blows Up in Havana Harbor

The artist has captured here the horror of the sinking of the *Maine,* with scenes before and after the explosion. What emotions do these images evoke in you? What do you think caused the explosion and how might both diplomats and historians use different explanations?

(Chicago Historical Society [ICHi-08428])

But conditions worsened in the reconcentration camps, and the American press kept harping on the plight of the Cuban people. McKinley, eager not to upset recovery from the depression, skillfully resisted war pressures. But he could not control Spanish misrule or Cuban aspirations for freedom.

Events early in 1898 sparked the outbreak of hostilities. Rioting in Havana intensified both Spanish repression and American outrage. A letter from the Spanish minister to the United States, Dupuy de Lôme, calling McKinley a "weak," hypocritical politician, was intercepted and made public. Americans fumed.

A second event was more serious. When the rioting broke out, the U.S. battleship *Maine* was sent to Havana harbor to protect American citizens. On February 15, a tremendous explosion blew up the *Maine,* killing 262 men. Advocates of American intervention blamed the Spanish. Newspapers trumpeted slogans such as "Remember the *Maine!* To hell with Spain!"

Assistant Secretary of the Navy Theodore Roosevelt had been preparing for war for many years. He said that he believed the *Maine* had been sunk "by an act of dirty treachery on the part of the Spaniards" and would "give anything if President McKinley would order the fleet to Havana tomorrow." When the president did not, Roosevelt privately declared that McKinley had "no more backbone than a chocolate éclair" and continued readying the navy for action. Although a board of inquiry at the time concluded that an external submarine mine caused the disaster, later studies showed that a faulty boiler or some other internal defect set off the explosion, possibilities even Roosevelt later conceded.

After the sinking of the *Maine,* Roosevelt took advantage of the secretary of the navy's absence from the office one day to cable Commodore George Dewey, commander of the U.S. Pacific fleet at Hong Kong. Roosevelt ordered Dewey to fill his ships with coal and, "in the event" of a declaration of war with Spain, to sail to the Philippines and make sure "the Spanish squadron does not leave the Asiatic coast." "The Secretary is away and I am having immense fun running the Navy," Roosevelt wrote in his diary that night.

Roosevelt's act was consistent with policies he had been urging on his more cautious superior for more than a year. As early as 1895, the navy had contingency plans for attacking the Philippines. Influenced by Mahan, Roosevelt wanted to enlarge the navy. He also believed that the United States should construct an interoceanic canal, acquire the Danish West Indies (the Virgin Islands), annex Hawaii, and oust Spain from Cuba. As Roosevelt told McKinley late in 1897, he was putting the navy in "the best possible shape" for the day "when war began."

The public outcry over the *Maine* drowned out McKinley's efforts to avoid war. With the issues politicized, McKinley pressured the Madrid government to make further concessions. Spain did, though refusing to grant full independence to Cuba, and the president finally acted. On April 11, 1898, he sent an ambiguous message to Congress that seemed to call for war. Two weeks later, Congress authorized using troops against Spain and recognized Cuban independence, actions amounting to a declaration of war. In a significant additional resolution, the Teller Amendment, Congress stated that the United States had no intention of annexing Cuba. A Cuban revolutionary general cautiously observed, "I expect nothing from the Americans. We should trust everything to our efforts. It is better to rise or fall without help than to contract debts of gratitude with such a powerful neighbor."

"A Splendid Little War": Various Views

The outbreak of war between Spain and the United States did not go unnoticed in Europe. Kaiser Wilhelm II of Germany sarcastically offered to join with other European monarchs to help Spain resist the efforts of "the American-British Society for International Theft and Warmongering . . . to snatch Cuba from Spain." But Spain was left to face the United States alone, fully expecting a defeat. When war broke out, a Spanish rear admiral said that the ruptured relations with the United States "would surely be fatal."

Indeed, the war was short and relatively easy for the Americans, and "fatal" for the Spanish, who at the war's conclusion were left with "only two major combat vessels." The Americans won naval battles, at Guam and Puerto Rico for example, virtually without gunfire. At the two major engagements, Manila Bay and Santiago Bay in Cuba, only two Americans died, one from heat prostration while stoking coal. Only 385 men died from Spanish bullets, but more than 5,000 succumbed to tropical diseases. As the four-month war neared its end in August, Secretary of State John Hay wrote Roosevelt that "it has been a splendid little war; begun with the highest motives, carried on with magnificent intelligence and spirit."

The Spanish-American War seemed splendid in other ways, as letters from American soldiers suggest. One young man wrote that his comrades were all "in good spirits" because oranges and coconuts were plentiful and "every trooper has his canteen full of lemonade all the time." Another wrote his brother that he was having "a lot of fun chasing Spaniards."

But the war was not much fun for other soldiers. One said, "Words are inadequate to express the feeling of pain and sickness when one has the fever. For about a week every bone in my body ached and I did not care much whether I lived or not." Another described a man shot in the head as "a mass of blood." Nor was the war splendid for African American soldiers, who

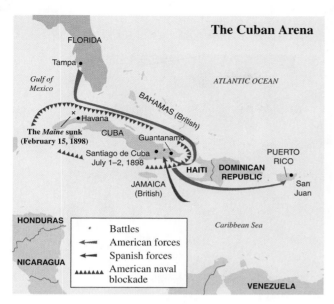

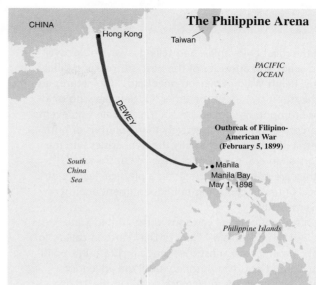

The Spanish-American War
Refer to the map on page 486 to see how far apart these two war zones were. How could the United States more easily manage a widely separated two-ocean empire? What did it need to do? What costs to a two-ocean war? Or any extension of conflict to more than one place?

fought in segregated units and noted stark differences between their rude treatment in the American South yet warm, grateful greetings in Cuba and Puerto Rico.

For Colonel Roosevelt, who resigned from the navy to lead a cavalry unit as soon as war was declared, the war was excitement and political opportunity. After a close brush with death in Cuba, Roosevelt declared with delight that he felt "the wolf rise in the heart" during "the power of joy in battle." But ironically, he needed help from African American soldiers to achieve his goals. His celebrated charge up Kettle Hill near Santiago was made possible by black troops first clearing the hill and then protecting his flank. The "charge" made three-inch headlines and propelled him toward the New York governor's mansion. "I would rather have led that charge," he said later, "than served three terms in the U.S. Senate." More than anyone, Roosevelt used the war to advance not only his political career but also the glory of national expansionism.

The Philippines Debates and War

Roosevelt's ordering Admiral Dewey to Manila initiated a chain of events that led to the annexation of the Philippines. The most crucial battle of the Spanish-American War occurred on May 1, 1898, when Dewey destroyed the Spanish fleet in Manila Bay and cabled McKinley for additional troops. Although the president admitted later that he was uncertain "within two thousand miles" where "those darned islands were," he sent twice as many troops as Dewey had asked for and

immediately began shaping American public opinion to accept the "political, commercial [and] humanitarian" reasons for annexing the Philippines. The Treaty of Paris gave the United States all 7,000 islands in the archipelago in exchange for a $20 million payment to Spain.

The treaty went to the Senate for ratification during the winter of 1898–1899. Senators hurled arguments across the floor of the Senate as American soldiers hurled racial taunts across the neutral zone at Aguinaldo's insurgents near Manila. Private Grayson's encounter, as we have seen, led to the passage of the treaty in a close Senate vote—and began the Filipino-American War and debates over what to do with the Philippines.

The entire nation joined the argument. At stake were two very different views of America's vision of itself in the world. After several months listening to public opinion, McKinley finally recommended annexation. Many Democrats supported the president out of fear of being labeled disloyal. At a time when openly racist thought flourished in the United States, fellow Republicans confirmed McKinley's arguments for annexation, adding even more insulting ones. Filipinos were described as childlike, dirty, and backward, and were compared to blacks and Native Americans. "The country won't be pacified," a Kansas veteran of the Sioux wars told a reporter, "until the niggers are killed off like the Indians." Roosevelt called Aguinaldo a "renegade Pawnee" and said that the Filipinos had no right "to administer the country which they happen to be occupying."

A small but prominent and vocal Anti-Imperialist League vigorously opposed war and annexation. These

Recovering the Past

POLITICAL CARTOONS

One of the most enjoyable—and telling—ways of recovering the values and attitudes of the past is through political cartoons. Ralph Waldo Emerson once said, "Caricatures are often the truest history of the times." A deft drawing of a popular or unpopular politician can freeze ideas and events in time, conveying more effectively than columns of print the central issues—and especially the hypocrisies and misbehaviors of an era. Cartoonists are often at their best when they are critical, exaggerating a physical feature of a political figure or capturing public sentiment against the government.

The history of political cartoons in the United States goes back to Benjamin Franklin's "Join or Die" cartoon calling for colonial cooperation against the French in 1754. But political cartoons did not gain notoriety until the advent of Thomas Nast's cartoons in *Harper's Weekly* in the 1870s. Nast drew scathing cartoons exposing the corruption of William "Boss" Tweed's Tammany Hall, depicting Tweed and his men as vultures and smiling deceivers. "Stop them damn pictures," Tweed ordered. "I don't care so much what the papers write about me. My constituents can't read. But, damn it, they can see pictures." Tweed pressured Nast with an offer of $100,000 to "study art" in Europe. The $5,000-a-year artist negotiated up to a half million dollars before refusing the offer. "I made up my mind not long ago to put some of those fellows behind bars," Nast said, "and I'm going to put them there." His cartoons helped drive Tweed out of office.

The emergence of the United States as a world power and the rise of Theodore Roosevelt gave cartoonists plenty to draw about. At the same time, the rise of cheap newspapers such as William Randolph Hearst's *Journal* and Joseph Pulitzer's *World* provided a rich opportunity for cartoonists, whose clever images attracted more readers. When the Spanish-American War broke out, newspapers whipped up public sentiment with lurid fake pictures of fierce Spaniards violating American women and killing helpless Cubans. Hearst used these tactics to increase his paper's daily circulation to 1 million copies.

By the time of the debates over Philippine annexation, many cartoonists took an anti-imperialist stance, pointing out American hypocrisy. Within a year, cartoonists shifted from depicting "The Spanish Brute Adds Mutilation to Murder" (1898) to "Liberty Halts American Butchery in the Philippines" (1899), both included here. Note the similarities and differences. Although Uncle Sam is not nearly as

"The Spanish Brute Adds Mutilation to Murder," by Grant Hamilton in *Judge*, July 9, 1898.

(Culver Pictures)

menacing a killer as the figure of Spain as an ugly gorilla, both cartoons share similarities of an aggressive stance, blood-covered swords, and a trail of bodies behind.

Theodore Roosevelt's rise to the presidency and his broad grin, eyeglasses, and walrus mustache gave cartoonists a perfect target for caricature, as did his energetic style and such distinctive aspects as the "big stick" symbol and his "rough rider" image. The Roosevelt cartoons "Panama or Bust" (1903) and "For President!" (1904), filled with symbols and images, were both printed in American daily newspapers.

Reflecting on the Past What symbols and images do you see in these cartoons? How many can you identify, and how are they used? Who is the female figure, and what does she represent? How would you explain the change of bloodied sword bearer within one year? What is the attitude of the Roosevelt cartoonists toward the president? Can you identify the significance of each symbol? Check some recent newspapers: Who is criticized in political cartoons today, and how do cartoonists reveal their attitudes and political positions? ■

"Liberty Halts American Butchery in the Philippines," from *Life,* 1899.

L. C. Gregg in the Atlanta Constitution.

FOR PRESIDENT!

"Panama or Bust," from the *New York Times,* 1903 (above); "For President!" by L. C. Gregg, in the *Atlanta Constitution,* 1904 (right).

dignitaries included former presidents Harrison and Cleveland, Andrew Carnegie, Jane Addams, and Mark Twain. In arguments heard more recently about Iraq, anti-imperialists argued that taking over other countries contradicted American ideals. First, the annexation of territory without postwar planning (or steps toward statehood) was unwise and unprecedented. Second, to occupy and govern a foreign people without their consent violated American ideals. Third, social reforms needed at home demanded American energies and money. "Before we attempt to teach house-keeping to the world," one writer put it, we needed "to set our own house in order."

Not all anti-imperialist arguments were so noble. They, too, alleged that Filipinos were nonwhite, Catholic, inferior in size and intelligence, and therefore unassimilable. Annexation would lead to miscegenation and contamination of Anglo-Saxon blood, said South Carolina senator Ben Tillman, who opposed "incorporating any more colored men into the body politic." A practical argument suggested that once in possession of the Philippines, the United States would have to defend them and acquire more territories—in turn leading to higher taxes and bigger government, and requiring that American troops fight distant Asian wars.

The last argument became fact when Private Grayson's encounter started the Filipino-American War. Before it ended in 1902, some 126,500 American troops served in the Philippines, 4,234 died there, and

Two Views of War's Results

Compare the photograph with the cartoon from 1898–1899. The photo shows American soldiers standing guard over captured Filipino guerrillas in 1899. The cartoon, by Charles L. (Bart) Batholomew of the *Minneapolis Journal* (July 2, 1898), presents a happier, if stereotyped, view of three new Americans, including one labeled "Philippines" on the skirt to the right. Or are they happier? What is the cartoonist's message? What similarities and differences do you see in these two visual images?

(Photo: Library of Congress)

2,800 more were wounded. The cost was $400 million. Filipino casualties were much higher. In addition to 18,000 killed in combat, an estimated 200,000 Filipinos died of famine and disease as American soldiers burned villages and destroyed crops and live-stock. General Jacob H. Smith told his troops that "the more you kill and burn, the better you will please me." Insurgent ineptness, Aguinaldo's inability to extend the fight across ethnic boundaries, and atrocities on both sides increased the frustrations of a lengthening war. The American "water cure" and other tortures were especially brutal.

As U.S. treatment of the Filipinos became more like Spanish treatment of the Cubans, the hypocrisy of American behavior became even more evident. This was especially true for black soldiers. Many identified with the dark-skinned insurgents, whom they saw as tied to the land, burdened by debt, and pressed by poverty like themselves. "I feel sorry for these people," a sergeant in the Twenty-Fourth Infantry wrote. "You have no idea the way these people are treated by the Americans here."

The war starkly exposed the hypocrisies of shoul-dering "the white man's burden." Aguinaldo wrote that America's "vague verbal offers of friendship and aid" were "drowned . . . out with the boom of cannons and the rattle of Gatling guns." On reading a report that 8,000 Filipinos had been killed in the first year of the war, Carnegie wrote a letter, dripping with sarcasm, con-gratulating McKinley for "civilizing the Filipinos. . . . About 8,000 of them have been completely civilized and sent to Heaven. I hope you like it." An anti-imperialist poet and New York legislator, Ernest Howard Crosby, wrote a sarcastic parody of Kipling's poem, which he titled "The Real 'White Man's Burden'":

> Take up the White Man's burden.
> Send forth your sturdy kin,
> And load them down with Bibles
> And cannon-balls and gin.
> Throw in a few diseases
> To spread the tropic climes,
> For there the healthy niggers
> Are quite behind the times.
> They need our labor question too.
> And politics and fraud—
> We've made a pretty mess at home,
> Let's make a mess abroad.

Another writer penned a devastating one-liner: "Dewey took Manila with the loss of one man—and all our institutions."

The anti-imperialists failed either to prevent annex-ation or to interfere with the war effort. They were out of tune with the period of exuberant expansionist national pride, prosperity, and promise.

Expansionism Triumphant

By 1900, Americans had ample reason to be patriotic. Within a year, the United States had acquired several island territories in the Pacific and Caribbean. But several questions arose over what to do with the new territories. Were they colonies? Would they be granted statehood, or become something else? Did Hawaiians, Puerto Ricans, and Filipinos have the same rights as American citizens on the mainland? Were they protected by the U.S. Constitution?

Although slightly different governing systems were worked out for each new territory, the solution in each case was to define its status as somewhere between a colony and a candidate for statehood. The indigenous people were usually allowed to elect their own legislature, but had governors and other judicial and administrative officials appointed by the American president. The first full governor of the Philippines, McKinley appointee William Howard Taft, effectively moved the Filipinos toward self-government, which came finally in 1946.

The question of constitutional rights was resolved by deciding that Hawaiians and Puerto Ricans, for example, would be treated differently from Texans and Oregonians. In the "insular cases" of 1901, the Supreme Court ruled that these people would achieve citizenship and constitutional rights only when Congress said they were ready. To the question, "Does the Constitution follow the flag?" Secretary of State Elihu Root answered, "Ye-es . . . the Constitution fol-lows the flag—but doesn't quite catch up with it."

In the election of 1900, Bryan was again the Democratic nominee and tried to make imperialism the "paramount issue" of the campaign. He failed, in part because the country strongly favored annexing the Philippines. In the closing weeks of the campaign, Bryan shied away from imperialism and focused on domestic issues—trusts, the labor question, and free silver.

That did Bryan no good either. Prosperity returned with the discovery of gold in Alaska. The McKinley forces rightly claimed that four years of Republican rule had brought more money, jobs, thriving factories, and manufactured goods, as well as tremendous growth in American prestige abroad. As one politician put it, noting the end of the Populist revolt with the war fervor over Cuba, "The blare of the bugle drowned out the voice of the reformer."

He was more right than he knew. Within one year, expansionist Theodore Roosevelt rose from assistant secretary of the navy to colonel of the Rough Riders to governor of New York. For some Republican politicos, who thought he was too vigorous and independent, this quick rise as McKinley's potential rival came too fast. One way to slow down Roosevelt's progress was to make him vice president, which they did in 1900. But six months into McKinley's second term, an

Republican Campaign Poster

What is the persuasive political point of this 1900 campaign poster to reelect William McKinley? What was life like under the Democrats in 1896 and what has changed? Why would voters want to vote again for McKinley?

(David J. and Janice L. Frent Collection/CORBIS)

anarchist killed him, the third presidential assassination in less than 40 years. "Now look," exclaimed party boss Mark Hanna, who had opposed putting Roosevelt on the ticket, "that damned cowboy is President of the United States!"

Theodore Roosevelt's Energetic Diplomacy

At a White House dinner party in 1905, a guest told a story about visiting the Roosevelt home when "Teedie" was a baby. "You were in your bassinet, making a good deal of fuss and noise," the guest reported, "and your father lifted you out and asked me to hold you." Secretary of State Elihu Root looked up and asked, "Was he hard to hold?" Whether true or not, the story reveals much about President Roosevelt's principles and policies on foreign affairs. As president from 1901 to 1909, and as the most dominating American personality for the 15 years between 1897 and 1912, Roosevelt

made much fuss and noise about the activist role the United States should play in the world, and he often seemed "hard to hold." Yet Roosevelt's energetic foreign policy in Latin America, eastern Asia, and Europe paved the way for the vital role as a world power that the United States would play for the next century.

Foreign Policy as Darwinian Struggle

Roosevelt advocated both individual physical fitness and collective national strength. An undersized boy, he had pursued a rigorous bodybuilding program, and as a young man on his North Dakota ranch, he learned to value the "strenuous life." Reading Darwin taught him that life was a constant struggle for survival. As president, his ideal was a "nation of men, not weaklings." Although he believed in Anglo-Saxon superiority, he admired—and feared—Japanese military prowess. Powerful nations, like individuals, Roosevelt believed, had a duty to cultivate vigor, strength, courage, and moral commitment to civilized values. In practical terms, this meant developing natural resources, building large navies, and being prepared to fight.

Although famous for saying "speak softly and carry a big stick," Roosevelt often not only wielded a large stick but spoke loudly as well. In a speech in 1897, he used the word *war* 62 times, saying, "no triumph of peace is quite so great as the supreme triumphs of war." But despite his bluster, Roosevelt was usually restrained in exercising force. He won the Nobel Peace Prize in 1906 for helping end the Russo-Japanese War. The big stick and the loud talk were meant to preserve order and peace.

Roosevelt divided the world into "civilized" and "uncivilized" nations. Civilized nations had a responsibility to "police" the uncivilized, not only maintaining order but also spreading "superior" values and institutions. Taking on the "white man's burden," civilized nations (usually Anglo-Saxon, English-speaking) sometimes had to wage war on the uncivilized—justly so, he argued, because the victors bestowed the blessings of their culture and racial superiority on the vanquished. But a war between two civilized nations (for example, Germany and Great Britain) would be foolish. Above all, Roosevelt believed in the balance of power. Strong, advanced nations had a duty to use their power to preserve order and peace. With a booming economy and growing population of 75 million, the United States could no longer "avoid responsibilities" to exercise a greater role in world affairs.

Roosevelt developed a highly personal style of diplomacy. Bypassing the State Department, he preferred face-to-face contact and personal exchanges with foreign diplomats and heads of state. He made foreign policy while horseback riding with the German ambassador and while discussing history with a French minister. A British emissary observed that Roosevelt had a "powerful personality" and a commanding knowledge of the world. Ministries from London to Tokyo respected him.

When threats failed to accomplish his goals, Roosevelt used direct personal intervention. "In a crisis the duty of a leader is to lead," he said, noting that Congress was too slow. When he wanted Panama, Roosevelt bragged later, "I took the Canal Zone" rather than submitting a long "dignified State Paper" for congressional debate. And while Congress debated, he gloated, the building of the canal began. Roosevelt's energetic executive activism in foreign affairs, for better or worse, influenced presidents from Woodrow Wilson to George W. Bush.

Taking the Panama Canal

To justify the intervention of 2,600 American troops in Honduras and Nicaragua in 1906, Philander Knox, later a secretary of state, said that "because of the

Monroe Doctrine" the United States is "held responsible for the order of Central America." The closeness of the Panama Canal, he said, "makes the preservation of peace in that neighborhood particularly necessary." The canal was not yet finished when Knox spoke, but it had already become a cornerstone of U.S. policy.

After resolving an 1850 treaty with Great Britain to jointly build a canal linking the Atlantic and Pacific, the United States had two problems. The first was where to build it. American engineers rejected a long route through Nicaragua in favor of a shorter, more rugged path across Panama, where a French firm had already begun work. This raised the second problem: Panama was a province of Colombia, which rejected the terms the United States offered. The refusal angered Roosevelt, who called the Colombians "Dagoes" who tried to "hold us up" like highway robbers.

Aware of Roosevelt's fury, encouraged by hints of American support, and eager for the economic benefits that a canal would bring, Panamanian nationalists in 1903 staged a revolution led by several rich families and Philippe Bunau-Varilla of the French canal company. With the help of an American warship to deter Colombian intervention, and the buying off of some Colombian officers, a bloodless revolution occurred on November 3. The next day Panama declared its independence and three days later the United States recognized it. Two weeks later, a treaty established the American right to build and operate a canal through Panama and to exercise "titular sovereignty" over the 10-mile-wide Canal Zone. Panamanians protested in vain. Roosevelt later claimed that the diplomatic and engineering achievement, completed in 1914, would "rank...with the Louisiana Purchase and the acquisition of Texas."

Policing the Caribbean

When Roosevelt took office in 1901, American policy toward Latin America was that although no nation had a right "to get territorial possessions," all nations had equal commercial rights. But as American investments poured into Central America and the Caribbean, the policy changed to one of asserting U.S. dominance in all the Americas, and especially the Caribbean.

This change was demonstrated in 1902 when Germany and Great Britain blockaded Venezuela's ports to force the government to pay defaulted debts. Roosevelt was especially worried that German influence would replace the British. He insisted that the European powers accept arbitration and threatened to "move Dewey's ships" to the Venezuelan coast. The crisis passed, largely for other reasons, but Roosevelt's threat of force made clear the presence and self-interest of the United States in the Caribbean.

The United States kept liberated Cuba under a military governor, Leonard Wood, until 1902, when the Cubans elected a congress and president. The United States honored Cuban independence, as it had promised to do, but in the Platt Amendment, which Cubans reluctantly added to their constitution in 1901, the United States obtained many economic rights in Cuba, a naval base at Guantanamo Bay (and later a prison), and the right to intervene if Cuban sovereignty were ever threatened. Cuban newspapers assailed this violation of their recent independence.

American policy intended to make Cuba a model of how a newly independent nation could achieve orderly self-government with only minimal guidance. Cuban self-government, however, was shaky. When in 1906 a political crisis threatened to spiral into civil war, Roosevelt expressed his fury with "that infernal little Cuban republic." He sent warships to patrol the coastline and special commissioners and troops "to restore order and peace and public confidence." As he left office in 1909, Roosevelt proudly proclaimed, "we have done our best to put Cuba on the road to stable and orderly government." The road was paved with sugar, as U.S. trade with Cuba increased from $27 million to $43 million in the decade following 1898. Along with economic development, which mostly benefited American companies, American involvement in Cuban affairs would continue for over a century.

The pattern was repeated throughout the Caribbean. The Dominican Republic, for example, suffered from unstable governments and great poverty. In 1904, as a revolt erupted, European creditors pressured the Dominican government for payment of $40 million in defaulted bonds. Sending its warships to discourage European intervention, the United States took over the collection of customs in the republic. Two years later, the United States intervened in Guatemala and Nicaragua, where American bankers controlled nearly 50 percent of all trade, the first of several twentieth-century interventions in those countries.

In a policy known as the Roosevelt Corollary to the Monroe Doctrine, the president announced in his annual message to Congress in 1904 that civilized nations should "insist on the proper policing of the world." The goal of the United States, he said, was to have "stable, orderly and prosperous neighbors." A country that paid its debts and kept order "need fear no interference." But "chronic wrong-doing" would require the United States to intervene as an "international police power." Whereas the Monroe Doctrine had warned European nations not to intervene in the Western Hemisphere, the Roosevelt Corollary justified American intervention. Starting with a desire to protect property, loans, and investments, the United States wound up supporting the regimes of despotic elites who owned most of the land, suppressed the poor, and blocked reforms.

After 1904, the Roosevelt Corollary was invoked in several Caribbean countries. Intervention usually meant the landing of U.S. Marines to counter a threat to American property. Occupying capital cities and major seaports, Marines, bankers, and customs

TR as Caribbean Policeman

The "big stick" became a memorable image in American diplomacy as Teddy Roosevelt sought to make the United States a "policeman" not only of the Caribbean basin but also of the whole world. What image does Roosevelt convey, and how are the people of the world responding to him?

(Puck, 1901)

officials remained for several years. Roosevelt's successors, William Howard Taft and Woodrow Wilson, pursued the same interventionist policy. So would more recent presidents: Ronald Reagan (Grenada and Nicaragua), George H. W. Bush (Panama), and Bill Clinton and George W. Bush (Haiti).

Opening Doors to China and Closing Doors to America

Throughout the nineteenth century, American relations with China were restricted to a small but profitable trade. Britain, in competition with France, Germany, and Russia, took advantage of the crumbling Manchu dynasty to force treaties on China, creating "treaty ports" and granting exclusive trading privileges in various parts of

the country. After 1898, the United States, with dreams of exploiting the seemingly unlimited markets of China, wanted to join the competition and enlarge its share. Those with moral interests, however, including many missionaries, reminded Americans of their revolutionary tradition against European imperialism. They opposed U.S. commercial exploitation of a weak nation and supported China's political integrity as imperial powers partitioned the country.

Although some admired China's ancient culture, the dominant American attitude viewed the Chinese as heathen, exotic, and backward. Workingmen's riots against the competition of Chinese workers in the 1870s and 1880s and the Chinese Exclusion Act of 1882 barring immigration reflected this negative stereotype. The Chinese, in turn, regarded the

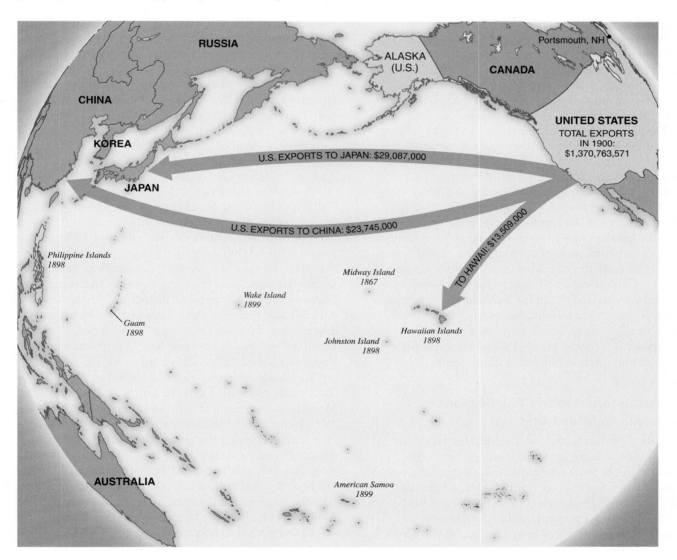

U. S. Involvement in the Pacific and Eastern Asia, 1898–1909

By 1898, the United States expanded far into eastern Asia and the Pacific. Which motivations do you think were most important for U.S. expansionism at the turn of the twentieth century: profits, patriotism, piety, or politics? What major events followed the acquisition of territories in the Pacific and the development of greater trade with eastern Asia? Where in the world is America still a strong presence? Can a nation expand too far?

United States with a mixture of admiration, curiosity, resentment, suspicion, and disdain.

The annexation of Hawaii and the Philippines in 1898 convinced Secretary of State Hay that the United States should announce a China policy. The Open Door notes of 1899–1900 became the cornerstone of U.S. policy in eastern Asia for more than half a century. The first note demanded an open door for American trade by declaring the principle of equal access to commercial rights in China by all nations. The second note, addressing Russian movement into Manchuria, called on all countries to respect the "territorial and administrative integrity" of China. This second principle announced a larger American role in Asia, offering China protection and preserving an East Asian balance of power.

An early test of this new role came during the Boxer Rebellion in 1900. The Boxers were a society of young traditionalist Chinese in revolt against both the Manchu dynasty and the growing Western influence and presence in China. During the summer of 1900, Boxers killed some 242 missionaries and other foreigners and besieged the western quarter of Beijing. An international military force of 19,000 troops, including some 3,000 Americans, ended the siege.

Despite an exclusionist immigration policy and laws inhibiting Chinese in America from becoming naturalized citizens, the idea that the United States had a unique guardian relationship with China persisted into the twentieth century. When Yale-educated Yung Wing had his American citizenship revoked for visiting his homeland in 1898, he bemoaned "how far this Republic has departed from its high ideal." But Chinese students and workers kept coming to the United States, entering illegally through Mexico and British Columbia. In 1905, Chinese nationalists at home boycotted American goods and called for a change in immigration policy. Roosevelt, contemptuous of what he called "backward" Chinese, bristled and sent troops to the Philippines as a threat. He also asked Congress for a modified immigration bill, but nothing came of it.

Balancing Japan in the Pacific from California to Manchuria

Population pressures, war, and a quest for economic opportunities caused Japanese immigration to the United States to increase dramatically around the turn of the century. Some came from Hawaii, where they had "worked like machines" in the sugarcane fields, many dying from overwork and white diseases. Pursuing "huge dreams of fortune…across the ocean," some 200,000 Japanese went directly to the West Coast of the United States to work on railroads and in West Coast canneries, mines, and logging camps.

Others worked on farms in the valleys of California, Oregon, and Washington, many successfully rising to own their own lands and turning marginal farmlands into productive agricultural businesses. Japanese-owned farms increased from 4,698 acres in 1900 to 194,742 by 1910, when they produced 70 percent of the California strawberry crop. Kinji Ushijima, for example, developed 10,000 acres of potato lands worth $500,000 in the fertile deltas between Stockton and Sacramento. By 1912, known then as George Shima, the "Potato King," he was praised by the *San Francisco Chronicle*. But when Shima moved to Berkeley, local newspapers and protesting professors complained of the "Yellow Peril in College Town." Shima refused to move.

Threatened by this competitive success, native white Californians discriminated against Japanese immigrants and limited their ability to own or lease land. They were barred from factory jobs and shunted off to agricultural labor in California fields and orchards. In 1906, the San Francisco school board, claiming that Japanese children were "crowding the whites out of the schools," segregated them into separate schools. Californians passed an anti-Japanese resolution and asked Roosevelt to persuade Japan to stop the emigration. Denouncing anti-Japanese rioting in San Francisco, Roosevelt favored restriction rather than exclusion. In the "Gentlemen's Agreement" notes of 1907–1908, the Japanese agreed to limit the migration of unskilled workers to the United States in return for the repeal of some anti-Japanese laws. But tensions continued.

It was one thing to check Japanese power in California but quite another to stop it in eastern Asia, where Roosevelt was determined to maintain the balance of power. The Boxer Rebellion of 1900 left Russia with 50,000 troops in Manchuria, making it the strongest regional power. Roosevelt's admiration for the Japanese as a "fighting" people and valuable factor in the "civilization of the future" contrasted with his low regard for the Russians, whom he described as "treacherous" and "incompetent." As Japan moved into Korea and Russia into Manchuria, Roosevelt hoped that each would check the other.

Roosevelt welcomed news in 1904 that Japan had successfully mounted a surprise attack on Port Arthur in Manchuria, beginning the Russo-Japanese War. He was "well pleased with the Japanese victory," he told his son, "for Japan is playing our game," but as Japanese victories continued, he worried that Japan might play the game too well, shutting the United States out of Asian markets. Roosevelt tilted toward Russia. When the Japanese expressed an interest in ending the war, the American president was pleased to exert his influence.

Roosevelt's goal was to achieve peace and leave a balanced situation. Nothing better symbolized the new American presence in the world than the 1905 negotiation and signing of a peace treaty in Portsmouth, New Hampshire, ending a war between Russia and Japan halfway around the globe in Manchuria. The Treaty of

Portsmouth left Japan dominant in Manchuria (and Korea) with the United States as the major balance to Japan's power. In the Root-Takahira Agreement of 1908, in return for recognizing these developments, Roosevelt got Japan's promise to honor U.S. control in the Philippines and to make no further encroachments into China.

The agreement barely papered over Japanese-American tensions. Some Japanese blamed Roosevelt for the fact that the Treaty of Portsmouth had not given them indemnities from Russia. American insensitivity on the immigration issue left bad feelings. In Manchuria, the U.S. consul general aggressively pushed an anti-Japanese program of financing capital investment projects in banking and railroads. This policy, known as "dollar diplomacy" under Roosevelt's successor, William Howard Taft, like the pursuit of markets, was larger in prospect than results. Nevertheless, the United States was in Japan's way, and rumors of war circulated.

It was clearly a moment for Roosevelt's "big stick." In 1907, he told Secretary of State Root that he was "more concerned over the Japanese situation than almost any other. Thank Heaven we have the navy in good shape." Although the naval buildup had begun over a decade earlier, under Roosevelt the U.S. Navy developed into a formidable force. In 1907, to make it clear that "the Pacific was as much our home waters as the Atlantic," Roosevelt sent his new, modernized "Great White Fleet" on a goodwill world tour. Pointedly, the first stop was Yokohama, Japan. Although American sailors were greeted warmly, the act may have stimulated a naval buildup in Japan, which came back to haunt the United States at Pearl Harbor in 1941. But for the time being, the balance of power in eastern Asia was preserved.

Preventing War in Europe

The United States had stretched the Monroe Doctrine to justify sending Marines and engineers to Latin America and the navy and dollars to eastern Asia. Treaties, agreements, and the protection of territories and interests entangled the United States with foreign nations from Panama and Nicaragua to the Philippines and Japan. Toward European nations, however, traditional neutrality continued.

Roosevelt believed that the most serious threats to world peace and civilized order lay in the relationships among Germany, Great Britain, and France, especially as these nations collided with one another over colonies in Asia and Africa and engaged in a naval arms race. Roosevelt established two fundamental policies toward Europe that would define the U.S. role throughout the century. The first was to make friendship with Great Britain the cornerstone of U.S. policy. The second was

to prevent a general war in Europe. Toward this end, Roosevelt depended on his personal negotiating skills with the leaders of major European nations.

The Venezuelan crisis of 1895 shocked the United States and Britain into an awareness of their mutual interests. Both nations, sharing language and cultural traditions, appreciated the neutrality of the other in their respective colonial wars in the Philippines and South Africa. Roosevelt supported British imperialism because he favored the dominance of the "English-speaking race" and believed that Britain was "fighting the battle of civilization." Both nations, moreover, were worried about growing German power. To protect itself from the German navy, Britain brought its fleet closer to home, concluded a mutual protection treaty with Japan, and trusted the United States to police the Caribbean.

Roosevelt was unashamedly pro-British. He knew, as he wrote to Lodge in 1901, that the United States had "not the least particle of danger to fear" from Britain and that German ambitions and militarism represented the major threat to peace in Europe. As Roosevelt left the presidency in 1909, one of his final acts was to proclaim the special friendship between the United States and Great Britain.

German Kaiser Wilhelm II underestimated the Anglo-American friendship and thought that Roosevelt was really pro-German. Roosevelt cultivated the Kaiser's illusion, flattering him while cleverly rejecting his overtures for diplomatic advantages. During the Moroccan crisis in 1905 and 1906, when Germany and France threatened to go to war over the control of Morocco and the western Mediterranean, Roosevelt arranged a conference in Algeciras, Spain, to head off conflict. The treaty signed in 1906 peacefully settled the Moroccan issue favorably for the French. When the German emperor tried to promote a German-Chinese-American agreement to balance the Anglo-Japanese Treaty in Asia, Roosevelt rebuffed him. Touring Europe in 1910, the former president was warmly entertained by Wilhelm, who continued to misunderstand him. Roosevelt, meanwhile, kept urging his English friends to counter the German naval buildup in order to maintain peace in Europe.

In 1911, Roosevelt wrote that there would be nothing worse than that "Germany should ever overthrow England and establish the supremacy in Europe she aims at." Roosevelt's European policy therefore included cementing friendship with Britain and, while maintaining official neutrality, using diplomacy to prevent European hostilities. The relationship between Great Britain and Germany, however, continued to deteriorate, and by 1914, when World War I broke out, no American was more eager to fight on the British side against the Germans than Colonel Roosevelt of the Rough Riders.

GLOBAL IMPERIAL ACTIVITIES, 1893–1904

Reflecting on the Past Note the growing role of the United States and the global nature of imperialism. Can you locate on a map or globe the many places mentioned in this chart? What implications do you draw about the race and ethnicity of the "where" and the "who"? What larger conclusions do you make about this era of history? Who benefited? Who did not?

Year	Where	Who	What
1893	Hawaii	United States	U.S.-backed annexationists overthrow Hawaiian queen.
1893	Laos	France	Laos becomes a French protectorate.
1893	French Guyana; Ivory Coast	France	France establishes two colonies on two continents.
1894–1895	China	Japan	Japan starts and wins war with China. Japan acquires Taiwan and gets an indemnity for war costs.
1895	South Africa	Britain	British annex Tongaland.
1895	Venezuela	United States; Britain	Tensions over boundary dispute with British Guyana.
1896	Ethiopia	Italy	Italy invades Ethiopia and is defeated by the Ethiopian army.
1896	Rhodesia (Zimbabwe)	Britain	A revolt begins in Rhodesia and is suppressed.
1896–1897	Madagascar	France	French claim Madagascar and depose the queen.
1896–1898	Sudan	Britain	British reconquer Sudan.
1897–1898	Hawaii	United States	United States annexes Hawaii.
1897	China	Germany	Germans occupy Shandong Province.
1898–1899	Philippines	Spain; United States	Annexed by United States after Spanish-American War.
1898–1902	Guam; Puerto Rico; Cuba	Spain; United States	Islands become U.S. territories or protectorates after Spanish-American War.
1899	China	United States	United States establishes Open Door policy.
1899–1902	South Africa; Philippines	Britain; Boers; United States; Philippines	Wars pass control of indigenous peoples to British and Americans.
1899	Ghana	Britain	Ashanti rebellion suppressed.
1900–1901	China	United States; Japan; Britain; Germany; and others	Boxer Rebellion suppressed.
1902	Venezuela	United States; Britain; Germany	Blockade ports and compete with one another over Venezuelan debt crisis.
1903	Colombia/Panama	United States	United States backs Panamanian revolutionaries for independence from Colombia.
1904	Manchuria	Japan; Russia	Japan attacks Port Arthur, starting the Russo-Japanese War.

Timeline

1823	Monroe Doctrine
1853	Trade opens with Japan
1867	Alaska purchased from Russia
1870	Failure to annex Santo Domingo (Hispaniola)
1875	Sugar reciprocity treaty with Hawaii
1882	Chinese Exclusion Act
1887	United States acquires naval base at Pearl Harbor
1889	First Pan-American Conference
1890	Alfred Mahan publishes *Influence of Sea Power upon History*
1893	Hawaiian coup by American sugar growers
1895	Cuban revolt against Spanish
1898	Sinking of the *Maine*
	Dewey takes Manila Bay and Spanish-American War
	Teller Amendment
	Annexation of Hawaiian Islands
	Treaty of Paris; annexation of the Philippines
1899	Senate ratifies Treaty of Paris
1899–1900	Open Door notes and Boxer Rebellion in China
1899–1902	Filipino-American War
1900	William McKinley reelected president
1901	Supreme Court cases on new territories
	McKinley assassinated; Theodore Roosevelt becomes president
1902	U.S. military occupation of Cuba ends
	Platt Amendment
1903	Panamanian revolt and independence
	Hay–Bunau–Varilla Treaty establishes American canal zone
1904	Roosevelt Corollary to the Monroe Doctrine
1904–1905	Russo-Japanese War ended by treaty signed at Portsmouth, New Hampshire
1904–1906	United States intervenes in Nicaragua, Guatemala, and Cuba
1906	Roosevelt receives Nobel Peace Prize
1907–1908	Gentleman's Agreement and Root-Takahira Agreements with Japan
1909	U.S. Navy ("Great White Fleet") sails around the world
1914	Opening of the Panama Canal
	World War I begins

Conclusion

THE RESPONSIBILITIES OF POWER

The realities of power in the 1890s brought increasing international responsibilities. Roosevelt said in 1910 that because of "strength and geographical situation," the United States had itself become "more and more, the balance of power of the whole world." This ominous responsibility was also an opportunity to extend American economic, political, moral, and military influence around the globe even while insulting new and would-be immigrants at home.

As president in the first decade of the twentieth century, Roosevelt (admired by President George W. Bush) established aggressive American policies toward the rest of the world that would last to this day. The United States dominated and policed Central America and the Caribbean Sea to maintain order and protect its investments and other economic interests. In eastern Asia, Americans marched through Hay's Open Door with treaties, troops, navies, missionaries, and dollars to protect the Philippines, develop markets and investments, and try to preserve the balance of power in Eastern Asia (and more recently, the Middle East). In Europe, the United States sought to remain neutral in European affairs and at the same time to cement Anglo-American friendship to prevent "civilized" nations from going to war.

How well these policies worked would unfold in the next 100 years. America's fundamental ambivalence has persisted whether to be an isolationist example to others or an active, interventionist savior. As questionable actions around the world—Private Grayson's and others' in the Filipino-American War, for example—painfully demonstrated, it was increasingly difficult for the United States to be both responsible and good, both powerful and loved. The American people experienced, therefore, both the benefits and burdens of their increasing international role, as they have to this day.

QUESTIONS FOR REVIEW AND REFLECTION

1. What is the fundamental dilemma of American foreign policy inherited from the Puritans, and to what extent do you think it fits historical events?

2. What are the four P's (or the three G's) that explain the motivations for American expansionism in the 1890s, and which do you think is most important?

3. Compare and contrast the causes and consequences of the Spanish-American and Filipino-American wars. What are the major differences between these two conflicts?

4. Give three or four justifications for annexing the Philippine Islands and three or four reasons opposing annexation. Which set of arguments do you think is most compelling?

5. Outline the major principles, with examples, of President Roosevelt's foreign policy in the Caribbean, eastern Asia, and Europe. How well have these policies worked in the 100 years since Roosevelt's time?

6. Do you think that U.S. foreign policy has been primarily as an interventionist savior of other nations or as an interfering expansionist into the affairs of other nations? Or some of both? Give examples.

CHAPTER 21

The Progressives Confront Industrial Capitalism

John Sloan, *Women Drying Their Hair*, 1912

Sloan (1871–1951) was one of the leading members of the "ash can school," a group of artists who experimented with new techniques and painted ordinary scenes of urban life, such as that shown here. His paintings offended many because he flouted genteel codes of propriety and decorum, and he showed working-class women in ways that were just as shocking as progressive-era reports on child labor and prostitution. Why was this painting shocking to Americans in 1912?

(John Sloan (1871–1951) "Sunday, Women Drying Their Hair", 1912, Oil on canvas, 26-1/8 in. × 32-1/8 in (66.36 cm × 81.65 cm). 1938.67, Museum Purchase. Addison Gallery of American Art, Phillips Academy, Andover, Massachusetts. © ARS, NY)

American Stories

A Professional Woman Joins the Progressive Crusade

Frances Kellor, a young woman who grew up in Ohio and Michigan, received her law degree in 1897 from Cornell University and became one of the small but growing group of professionally trained women in the United States. Deciding that she was more interested in solving the nation's social problems than in practicing law, she moved to Chicago, studied sociology, and trained herself as a social reformer. Kellor believed passionately that poverty and inequality could be eliminated in America. She also had the progressive faith that if Americans could only hear the truth about the millions of people living in urban slums, they would rise up and make changes. She was one of the experts who provided the evidence to document what was wrong in industrial America.

Like many progressives, Kellor believed that environment was more important than heredity in determining ability, prosperity, and happiness. Better schools and better housing, she thought, would produce better citizens. While a small group of progressives advocated the sterilization of criminals and the mentally defective, Kellor argued that even criminals were victims of their environment. Kellor demonstrated that poor health and deprived childhoods explained the only differences between criminals and college students. If it were impossible to define a criminal type, then it must be possible to reduce crime by improving the environment.

Kellor was an efficient professional. Like the majority of the professional women of her generation, she never married but devoted her life to social research and social reform. She lived for a time at Hull House in Chicago and at the College Settlement in New York, centers not only of social research and reform but also of lively community. For many young people, the settlement, with its sense of commitment and its exciting conversation around the dinner table, provided an alternative to the nuclear family or the single apartment.

While staying at the College Settlement, Kellor researched and wrote a muckraking study of employment agencies, published in 1904 as *Out of Work.* She revealed how employment agencies exploited immigrants, blacks, and other recent arrivals in the city. Kellor's book, like the writing of most progressives, spilled over with moral outrage. But Kellor went beyond moralism to suggest corrective legislation at the state and national levels. She became one of the leaders of the movement to Americanize the immigrants pouring into the country in unprecedented numbers. Between 1899 and 1920, more than 8 million people came to the United States, most from southern and eastern Europe. Many Americans

feared that this flood of immigrants threatened the very basis of American democracy. Kellor and her coworkers represented the side of progressivism that sought state and federal laws to protect the new arrivals from exploitation and to establish agencies and facilities to educate and Americanize them. Another group of progressives, often allied with organized labor, tried to pass laws to restrict immigration. Kellor did not entirely escape the ethnocentrism that was a part of her generation's worldview, and like most progressives she tried to teach middle-class values to the new arrivals, but she did believe that all immigrants could be made into useful citizens.

Convinced of the need for a national movement to promote reform legislation, Kellor helped found the National Committee for Immigrants in America, which tried to promote a national policy "to make all these people Americans," and a federal bureau to organize the campaign. Eventually, she helped establish the Division of Immigrant Education within the Department of Labor. But a political movement led by Theodore Roosevelt excited her most. More than almost any other individual, Kellor had been responsible for alerting Roosevelt to the problems immigrants faced in American cities. When Roosevelt formed the new Progressive party in 1912, she was one of the many social workers and social researchers who joined him. She campaigned for Roosevelt and directed the Progressive Service Organization, intended to educate voters in all areas of social justice and welfare after the election. After Roosevelt's defeat and the collapse of the Progressive party in 1914, Kellor continued to work for Americanization. She spent the rest of her life promoting justice, order, and efficiency as well as trying to find ways of resolving industrial and international disputes.

While no one person can represent all facets of a complex movement, Frances Kellor's life illustrates two important aspects of progressivism, the first nationwide reform movement of the modern era: first, a commitment to promote social justice, ensure equal opportunity, and preserve democracy; second, a search for order and efficiency in a world complicated by rapid industrialization, immigration, and spectacular urban growth. Like many progressive leaders, Kellor was a part of a global movement to confront these problems, and she was influenced by writers and reformers in England and Germany as well as those in the United States. Progressivism reached its height in the years between 1900 and 1914. Like most American reform movements, the progressive movement did not plot to overthrow the government; rather, it sought to use government to promote American ideals and to ensure survival of the American way of life.

This chapter traces the most important aspects of progressivism. It examines the social justice movement, which sought to promote reform among the poor and to improve life for those who had fallen victim to an urban and industrial civilization. It surveys life among workers, a group the reformers sometimes helped but often misunderstood. Then it traces the reform movements in the cities and states, where officials and experts tried to reduce chaos and promote order and democracy. Finally, it examines progressivism at the national level during the administrations of Theodore Roosevelt and Woodrow Wilson, the first thoroughly modern presidents.

The Social Justice Movement

Historians write of a "progressive movement," but actually there were a number of movements, some of them contradictory, but all focusing on problems created by a rapidly expanding urban and industrial world. Some reformers, often from the middle class, sought to humanize the modern city. They hoped to improve housing and schools and to provide a better life for the poor and recent immigrants. Others were concerned with the conditions of work and the rights of labor. Still others pressed for changes in the political system to make it more responsive to popular interests, including women. Progressivism had roots in the 1890s, when many reformers were shocked by the devastation caused by the depression of 1893, and they were influenced by Henry George's *Progress and Poverty* (1879) and Edward Bellamy's *Looking Backward* (1888). They were appalled by a British pamphlet titled *The Bitter Cry of Outcast London*, which revealed the horrors of the slums of East London. They were also influenced by the British and American Social Gospel movement, which sought to build the kingdom of God on earth by eliminating poverty and promoting equality (see Chapter 19).

The Progressive Movement in Global Context

Most progressives saw their movement in a global context with a particular focus on an Atlantic world. Many had studied at European universities. They attended conferences on urban and industrial problems at the Paris Exposition of 1900, and they belonged to organizations such as the International Association for Labor Legislation, which tried to promote legislation to aid workers. They read the latest sociological studies from Britain, France, and Germany. Many were introduced to the problems of the modern industrial city by walking through the streets of East London or the slums of Berlin. Others were inspired by visiting Toynbee Hall, the pioneer social settlement in London, and by observing the municipal housing and government-owned streetcar lines in Glasgow, Scotland, and Dresden, Germany. At the same time, European reformers visited American cities and took part in American conferences.

The United States lagged behind much of the industrialized world in passing social legislation, perhaps because it lacked the strong labor and socialist movements present in most European countries. Many European countries, along with Australia, New Zealand, and Brazil, passed laws regulating hours and wages and creating pensions for the elderly. Germany enacted sickness, accident, and disability insurance in the 1880s. Great Britain had workers' compensation by the late 1890s, and old age, sickness, and unemployment insurance by 1911, all paid for with public funds. But American cities, unlike those in Europe, were filled with immigrants from a dozen countries who had cultural adjustments and a language barrier to overcome. The American federal system meant that most reform battles had to be fought first at the local and state levels before they could reach the national scene. A unique mix of religion, politics, and moral outrage imparted a particular character to the progressive movement in the United States.

The Progressive Worldview

Intellectually, the progressives were deeply influenced by Darwinism. They believed that the world was in flux, and they rebelled against the fixed and the formal in every field. One of the philosophers of the movement, John Dewey, wrote that ideas could become instruments for change. In his philosophy of pragmatism, William James tried to explain all ideas in terms of their consequences. Most progressives were convinced that environment was much more important than heredity in forming character. Thus, if one could build better schools and houses, one could make better people and a more perfect society. Yet even the more advanced reformers thought in racial and ethnic categories. They believed that some groups could be molded and changed more easily than others. Thus, progressivism did not usually mean progress for blacks.

In many ways, progressivism was the first modern reform movement. It sought to bring order and efficiency to a world that had been transformed by rapid

DOCUMENTARY PHOTOGRAPHS

Photographs are a revealing way of recovering the past visually. When looking at a photograph, especially an old one, it is easy to assume that it is an accurate representation of the past. However, much like novelists and historians, photographers have a point of view. They take their pictures for a reason—often to prove a point. As one photographer remarked, "Photographs don't lie, but liars take photographs."

To document the need for reform in the cities, progressives collected statistics, made surveys, described settlement house life, and even wrote novels. But they discovered that the photograph was often more effective than words. Jacob Riis, the Danish-born author of *How the Other Half Lives* (1890), a devastating exposure of conditions in New York City tenement house slums, was also a pioneer in urban photography. Others had taken pictures of dank alleys and street urchins before, but Riis was the first to photograph slum conditions with the express purpose of promoting reform. At first he hired photographers, but then he bought a camera and taught himself how to use it. He even tried a new German flash powder to illuminate dark alleys and tenement rooms to record the horror of slum life.

Riis made many of his photographs into lantern slides and used them to illustrate his lectures on the need for housing reform. Although he was a creative and innovative photographer, his pictures were often far from objective. His equipment was awkward, his film slow. He had to set up and prepare carefully before snapping the shutter. His views of tenement ghetto streets and poor children now seem like clichés, but they were designed to make Americans angry and to arouse them to reform.

Another important progressive photographer was Lewis Hine. Although trained as a sociologist, he taught himself photography. Hine used his camera to illustrate his lectures at the Ethical Culture School in New York. In 1908, he was hired as a full-time investigator by the National Child Labor Committee. His haunting photographs of children in factories helped convince many Americans of the need to abolish child labor. Hine's children were appealing human beings. He showed them eating, running, working, and staring wistfully out factory windows. His photographs avoided the pathos that Riis was so fond of recording, but just as surely they documented the need for reform.

Another technique that the reform photographer used was the before-and-after shot. The two photographs shown on the following page of a one-room apartment in Philadelphia early in the century illustrate how progressive reformers tried to teach immigrants to imitate middle-class manners. The "before" photograph shows a room cluttered with washtubs, laundry, cooking utensils, clothes, tools, even an old Christmas decoration. In the "after" picture,

Lewis Hine, *Carolina Cotton Mill*, 1908.

(Lewis Hine, *Carolina Cotton Mill*, 1908. George Eastman House)

much of the clutter has been cleaned up. A window has been installed to let in light and fresh air. The wallpaper, presumably a haven for hidden bugs and germs, has been torn off. The cooking utensils and laundry have been put away. The woodwork has been stained, and some ceremonial objects have been gathered on a shelf.

What else can you find that has been changed? How well do you think the message of the photographic combinations like this one worked? Would the immigrant family be happy with the new look and condition of their room? Could anyone live in one room and keep it so neat?

Reflecting on the Past As you look at these, or any photographs, ask yourself: What is the photographer's purpose and point of view? Why was this particular angle chosen for the picture? And why center on these particular people or objects? What does the photographer reveal about his or her purpose? What does the photographer reveal unintentionally? How have digital cameras changed photography? On what subjects do reform-minded photographers train their cameras today? ▪

The reality of one-room tenement apartments (above) contrasted with the tidiness that reformers saw as the ideal (right).

(Urban Archives, Temple University, Philadelphia, PA)

growth and new technology. Yet elements of nostalgia infected the movement as reformers tried to preserve the handicrafts of a preindustrial age and to promote small-town and farm values in the city. The progressive leaders were almost always middle class, and they consciously tried to teach middle-class values to the immigrants and the working class. Often, the progressives seemed more interested in control than in reform; frequently, their efforts smacked of paternalism.

The progressives were part of a statistics-minded generation. They conducted surveys, gathered facts, wrote reports, and usually believed that their reports would lead to change. The haunting photographs of young workers taken by Lewis Hine, the stark and beautiful city paintings by John Sloan, and the realist

novels of Theodore Dreiser and William Dean Howells reflect the progressives' drive to document and record.

The progressives were optimistic about human nature, and they believed that change was possible. In retrospect, they may seem naive or bigoted, but they wrestled with many social questions, some of them old but fraught with new urgency in an industrialized society. What is the proper relation of government to society? In a world of large corporations, huge cities, and massive transportation systems, how much should the government regulate and control? How much responsibility does society have to care for the poor and needy? The progressives could not agree on the answers, but they struggled with the questions.

The Muckrakers

Writers who exposed corruption and other social evils were labeled "muckrakers" by Theodore Roosevelt. Not all muckrakers were reformers—some wrote just for the money—but reformers learned from their techniques of exposé. In part, the muckrakers were a product of a journalistic revolution in the 1890s. Older magazines often had elite audiences and few illustrations. The new magazines had slick formats, more advertising, and wide sales. Competing for readers, editors eagerly published articles telling the public what was wrong in America.

Lincoln Steffens, a young California journalist, wrote articles exposing the connections between respectable businessmen and corrupt politicians. When published as a book in 1904, *The Shame of the Cities* became a battle cry for people determined to clean up city government. Ida Tarbell, a teacher turned journalist, revealed the ruthlessness of John D. Rockefeller's Standard Oil Company. David Graham Phillips uncovered the alliance of politics and business in *The Treason of the Senate* (1906). Robert Hunter, a young settlement worker, shocked Americans in 1904 with his book *Poverty*. In his compelling novel *The Octopus*, Frank Norris dramatized the railroads' stranglehold on farmers, while Upton Sinclair's novel *The Jungle* (1906) described the horrors of the Chicago meatpacking industry.

Child Labor

Nothing disturbed social justice progressives more than the sight of children, sometimes as young as 8 or 10, working long hours in dangerous and depressing factories. The crusade against child labor was a typical social justice reform effort. Its origins lay in the moral indignation of middle-class reformers. But reform went beyond moral outrage as reformers gathered statistics, took photographs documenting abuse of children, and used the evidence to push for local, state, and federal legislation.

Florence Kelley was one of the most important leaders in the crusade against child labor. Kelley had grown up in an upper-class Philadelphia family and graduated from Cornell in 1882. Like Addams and Kellor she was a member of the first generation of college women in the United States. When the University of Pennsylvania refused her admission as a graduate student because she was a woman, she went to the University of Zurich in Switzerland. Her European experience was crucial in transforming her from upper-class dilettante to committed reformer. She married a Polish-Russian scholar and became a socialist. The marriage failed, and some years later, Kelley moved to Chicago with her children, became a Hull House resident, and poured her considerable energies into the campaign against child labor. A friend described her as "explosive, hot-tempered, determined . . . a smoking volcano that at any moment would burst into flames." When she could find no attorney in Chicago to argue child labor cases against prominent corporations, she went to law school, passed the bar exam, and argued the cases herself.

Kelley and other child labor reformers pressured the Illinois state legislature into passing an anti–child labor law. A few years later, however, the state supreme court ruled it unconstitutional, convincing reformers that national action was necessary. Edgar Gardner Murphy, an Alabama clergyman, suggested the formation of the National Child Labor Committee. Based in New York, this new organization drew up a model state child labor law, encouraged state and city campaigns, and coordinated the movement around the country.

Although two-thirds of the states passed some form of child labor law between 1905 and 1907, many had loopholes that exempted large numbers of children, including newsboys and youngsters who worked in the theater. A national bill was defeated in 1906, but in 1912 the child labor reformers convinced Congress to establish a children's bureau in the Department of Labor. Despite these efforts, compulsory school attendance laws did more to reduce the number of children who worked than federal and state laws, which proved difficult to pass and even more difficult to enforce.

Like other progressive reform efforts, the battle against child labor was only partly successful. Too many businesses, both small and large, were profiting from employing children at low wages. Too many politicians and judges were reluctant to regulate the work of children or adults because work seemed such an individual and personal matter. And some parents, who often desperately needed the money their children earned in the factories, opposed the reformers and even broke the law to allow their children to work.

The reformers also worried over the young people who got into trouble with the law, often for pranks that in rural areas would have seemed harmless. They feared for young people tried by adult courts and thrown into jail with hardened criminals. Reformers organized juvenile courts, in which judges had the authority to put delinquent youths on probation, take them from their families and make them wards of the state, or assign them to an institution. A uniquely American invention, the juvenile court often helped prevent young delinquents from adopting a life of crime. Yet juvenile offenders frequently were deprived of all rights of due process, a fact that the Supreme Court finally recognized in 1967, when it ruled that children were entitled to procedural rights when accused of a crime.

Working Women and Woman Suffrage

Closely connected with the anti–child labor movement was the effort to limit the hours of women's work. Florence Kelley and the National Consumers League led the campaign. The most important court case on women's work came before the U.S. Supreme Court in 1908. Kelley's friend Josephine Goldmark wrote the brief for *Muller* v. *Oregon,* and Goldmark's brother-in-law, Louis Brandeis, argued the case. The Court upheld the Oregon law limiting the workday of women in factories and laundries to 10 hours largely because Goldmark's sociological argument detailed the danger and disease that these women workers faced. Most states fell into line with the Supreme Court decision and passed protective legislation for women, though many companies found ways to circumvent the laws. Even the work permitted by the law seemed too long to some women who had to come home to child care and housekeeping.

By contending that "women are fundamentally weaker than men in all that makes for endurance: in muscular strength, in nervous energy, in the powers of persistent attention and application," reformers won some protection for women workers. But for the next half century, their arguments that women were weaker than men were used to reinforce gender segregation.

In addition to working for protective legislation for working women, the social justice progressives also campaigned for woman suffrage. The early battles for the right of women to vote were fought at the state level, with greatest success in the West. Wyoming (1869), Utah (1870), Colorado (1893), Idaho (1896), Washington (1910), California (1911), Arizona and Oregon (1912), and Montana and Nevada (1914) gave women the right to vote in at least some elections. But this did not mean that western states were more enlightened on gender issues. In the East and Midwest, both with large immigrant populations, suffrage and

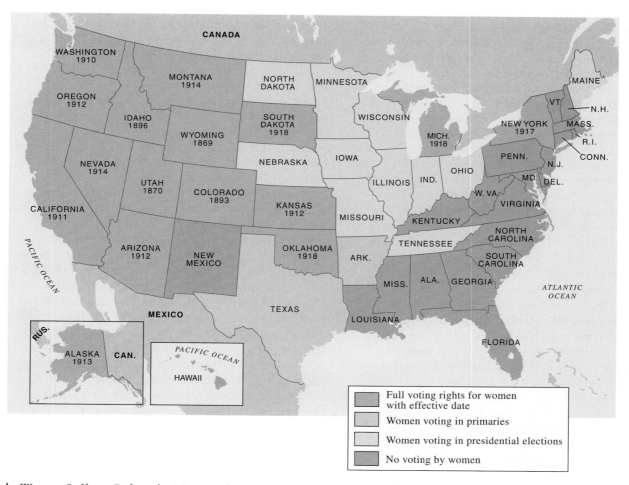

Woman Suffrage Before the Nineteenth Amendment

Western states led the battle for women's right to vote, but key victories in New York (1917) and Michigan (1918), and a carefully organized campaign in all parts of the country, finally led to the ratification of the Nineteenth Amendment. Why was this success considered a triumph of progressive reform?

prohibition were often tied closely together. Many men believed that women, if given the vote, would support prohibition.

The campaign to win the vote for women was a global movement, and suffrage leaders in the United States were in touch with women in other countries. They often met their international counterparts at meetings of the International Woman Suffrage Alliance. The United States lagged behind New Zealand, Finland, Norway, and several other countries in granting female suffrage. Women in Great Britain were allowed to vote in 1918, but not until 1938 could they vote on an equal basis with men.

The political process that eventually led to woman suffrage in the United States was slowed by the difficulty of amending the Constitution and the need to fight the battle one state at a time. But the progressives pressed on. Some suffrage advocates argued that middle-class women would offset the votes of ignorant and corrupt immigrant men, but many progressives supported votes for all women. Jane Addams argued that urban women not only could vote intelligently but also needed the vote to protect, clothe, and feed their families. Women in an urban age, she suggested, needed to be municipal housekeepers. Through suffrage, they would ensure that elected officials provided adequate services—pure water, uncontaminated food, proper sanitation, and police protection. The progressive insistence that all women needed the vote helped ensure the victory for woman suffrage that would come after World War I.

Much more controversial than either votes for women or protective legislation was the movement for birth control. Even the most advanced progressives could not imagine themselves teaching immigrant women how to prevent conception, especially because the Comstock Law of 1873 made it illegal to promote or even write about contraceptive devices.

Margaret Sanger, a nurse who had watched poor women suffer from too many births and even die from dangerous, illegal abortions, was one of the founders of the modern American birth control movement. Middle-class Americans had limited family size in the nineteenth century through abstinence, withdrawal, and abortion, as well as through the use of primitive birth control devices, but much ignorance and misinformation remained. Sanger obtained the latest medical and scientific European studies and in 1914 explained in her magazine, *The Woman Rebel,* and in a pamphlet, *Family Limitation,* that women could separate sex from procreation. She was promptly indicted for violation of the postal code and fled to Europe to avoid arrest.

Birth control remained controversial, and in most states illegal, for many years. Yet Sanger helped bring the topic of sexuality and contraception into the open. When she returned to the United States in 1921, she founded the American Birth Control League, which became the Planned Parenthood Federation in 1942.

Reforming Home and School

Reformers believed that better housing and education could transform the lives of the poor and create a better world. Books such as Jacob Riis's *How the Other Half Lives* (1890) horrified them with its vivid language and haunting photographs of misery in New York's slums.

In the first decade of the twentieth century, the progressives took a new approach toward housing problems. They combined their vision of what needed to be done to improve society with their practical ability to organize public opinion and get laws passed. They collected statistics, conducted surveys, organized committees, and constructed exhibits to demonstrate the effect of urban overcrowding. Then they worked to pass tenement house laws in several cities. These laws created fire codes and regulated the number of windows and bathrooms and the size of apartments, but the laws were often evaded or modified. In 1910, the progressives organized the National Housing Association, and some of them looked ahead to federal laws and even to government-subsidized housing. American housing reformers were inspired by model working-class dwellings in London, municipal housing in Glasgow, and various experiments in government-constructed housing in France, Belgium, and Germany, but they realized that in the United States, they had to start with local regulation.

Ironically, many middle-class women reformers who tried to teach working-class families how to live in their tenement flats had never organized their own homes. Often they lived in settlement houses, where they ate in a dining hall and never had to worry about cleaning, cooking, or doing laundry. Some of them, however, began to realize that the domestic tasks expected of women of all classes kept many of them from taking their full place in society. Charlotte Perkins Gilman, author of *Women and Economics* (1898), dismantled the traditional view of "woman's sphere" and sketched an alternative. Suggesting that entrepreneurs ought to build apartment houses designed to allow women to combine motherhood with careers, she advocated shared kitchen facilities and a common dining room, a laundry run by efficient workers, and a roof-garden day nursery with a professional teacher.

Gilman, who criticized private homes as "bloated buildings, filled with a thousand superfluities," was joined by a few radicals in promoting new living arrangements. However, most continued to view the home as sacred space where the mother ruled supreme and created an atmosphere of domestic tranquility.

Next to better housing, the progressives stressed better schools as a way to produce better citizens. Public school systems were often rigid and corrupt. Far from producing citizens who would help transform society, the schools' emphasis on repetitious rote learning seemed to reinforce conservative habits.

Progressive education, like many other aspects of progressivism, opposed the rigid and the formal in favor of flexibility and change. John Dewey was the key philosopher of progressive education. In his laboratory school at the University of Chicago, he experimented with new methods. He replaced the school desks, which were bolted down and always faced the front, with seats that could be moved into circles and arranged in groups. The movable seat, in fact, became one of the symbols of the progressive education movement.

Dewey insisted that the schools be child-centered, not subject-oriented. Teachers should teach children rather than teach history or mathematics. He did not mean that history and math should not be taught but that those subjects should be related to the students' experience. Students should learn by doing. They should not just learn about democracy; the school itself should operate like a democracy.

Dewey also maintained that schools should become instruments for social reform. But like most progressives, Dewey was never quite clear whether he wanted schools to help students adjust to the existing society or to turn out graduates who would change the world. Although he wavered on that point, the spirit of progressive education, like the spirit of progressivism in general, was optimistic. Dewey's progressive education, which sought to educate all Americans, stood in sharp contrast to European models, in which educating the intellectual and social elite took precedence over schooling the masses.

Crusades Against Saloons, Theaters, and Prostitution

Progressives often displayed moral outrage when it came to the behavior of the working class. American attitudes toward prostitution and prohibition surprised and confused foreign observers, especially many Europeans. Most social justice progressives opposed the sale of alcohol. Some came from Protestant homes in which consumption of liquor was considered a sin, but most advocated prohibition because they saw

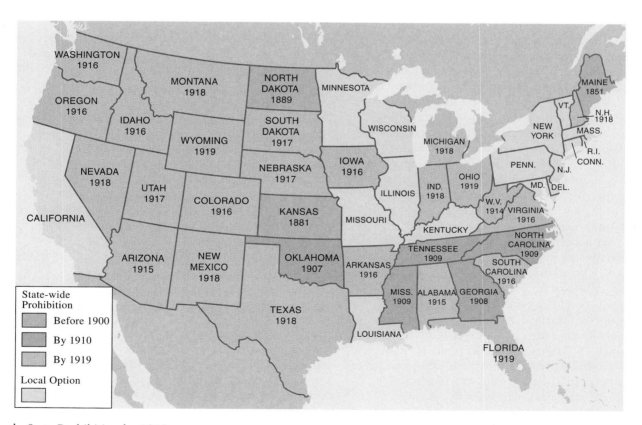

State Prohibition by 1919

Temperance reform had achieved considerable success even before the adoption of the Eighteenth Amendment in 1919. What regional patterns do you observe in the spread of state prohibition laws? What might explain these patterns?

eliminating the sale of alcohol as part of the process of reforming cities and conserving human resources.

Americans did drink great quantities of beer, wine, and hard liquor, and the amount they consumed rose rapidly after 1900, peaking between 1911 and 1915. An earlier temperance movement had achieved some success in the 1840s and 1850s, but only three states still had prohibition laws in force. The modern antiliquor movement was spearheaded in the 1880s and 1890s by the Women's Christian Temperance Union and after 1900 by the Anti-Saloon League and a coalition of religious leaders and social reformers. During the progressive era, temperance forces had considerable success in influencing legislation. Seven states passed temperance laws between 1906 and 1912.

Reformers were appalled to see young children going into saloons to bring home a pail of beer for the family and horrified by tales of alcoholic fathers beating wives and children. But most often progressives focused on the saloon, which they not only viewed as a place for drinking but also linked to drug traffic, prostitution, and political corruption.

Although they never quite understood the role that alcohol played in the social life of many ethnic groups, Jane Addams and other settlement workers appreciated the saloon's importance as a neighborhood social center. Addams started a coffeehouse at Hull House in an attempt to lure people away from saloons. Although the progressives never found an adequate substitute for the saloon, they set to work to pass local and state prohibition laws. Joining forces with diverse groups to push for change, they achieved victory when, on December 22, 1917, Congress sent to the states for ratification a constitutional amendment prohibiting the sale, manufacture, and import of intoxicating liquor within the United States. The spirit of sacrifice for World War I facilitated rapid ratification of the amendment.

In addition to the saloon, progressives saw the urban dance hall and the movie theater as threats to the morals and well-being of young people, especially young women. The motion picture, invented in 1889, developed as an important form of entertainment during the first decade of the twentieth century. At first, the "nickelodeons," as the early movie theaters were called, appealed mainly to a lower-class and largely ethnic audience. Not until World War I, when D. W. Griffith produced long feature films, did the movies begin to attract a middle-class audience. The most popular of these early films was Griffith's *Birth of a Nation* (1915), a blatantly racist and distorted epic of black debauchery during Reconstruction. Many early films were imported from France, Italy, and Germany; because they were silent, it was easy to use subtitles in any language. But one did not need to know the language, or even be able to read, to enjoy the action. That was part of the attraction of the early films. Some films stressed slapstick humor or romance and adventure; others bordered on pornography. The reformers objected not only to the plots and content of the films but also to the location of the theaters (near saloons and burlesque houses) and to their dark interiors. But for young immigrant women, who made up the bulk of the audience at most urban movie theaters, the films provided rare exciting moments in their lives.

Saloons, dance halls, and movie theaters all seemed dangerous to progressives interested in improving life in the city, because all appeared to be somehow connected with the worst evil of all, prostitution. Campaigns against prostitution had been waged since the early nineteenth century, but they were nothing compared with the progressives' crusade to wipe out what they called the "social evil." All major cities and many smaller ones appointed vice commissions and made elaborate studies of prostitution.

The progressive crusade against prostitution attracted many kinds of people, for often contradictory reasons. Racists and immigration restrictionists maintained that inferior people—blacks and recent immigrants, especially those from southern and eastern Europe—became prostitutes and pimps. Most progressives, however, stressed environmental causes. They viewed prostitution, along with child labor and poor housing, as evils that education and reform could eliminate.

Despite their efforts, the progressives failed to end prostitution and did virtually nothing to address its roots in poverty. They wiped out a few red-light districts, closed a number of brothels, and managed to push a bill through Congress (the Mann Act of 1910) that prohibited the interstate transport of women for immoral purposes. Perhaps more important, they persuaded several states to raise the age of consent for women and in 20 states they made the Wassermann test for syphilis mandatory for both men and women before a marriage license could be issued.

The Worker in the Progressive Era

Progressive reformers sympathized with industrial workers who struggled to earn a living for themselves and their families. But often they had little understanding of what it was really like to sell one's strength by the hour. For example, they supported labor's right to organize at a time when labor had few friends, yet they often opposed the strike as a weapon against management. And neither organized labor nor the reformers, individually or in shaky partnership, had power over industry in the years before World War I.

The Changing Nature of Industrial Labor

Many workers—whether from eastern Europe, rural Vermont, or Michigan—confronted a bewildering world based on order and routine. Unlike farm or craft work, factory life was dominated by the clock, the bell tower, and the boss. Workers resisted the mindless routine and relentless pace of factory work, and they subtly sabotaged employers' efforts to control the workplace. They stayed home on holidays when they were supposed to work, took unauthorized breaks, and set their own informal productivity schedules. Often they were fired or quit. In the woollen industry, for example, the annual turnover of workers between 1907 and 1910 was more than 100 percent. In New York needleworker shops in 1912 and 1913, the turnover rate was more than 250 percent. Overall in American industry, one-third of the workers stayed at their jobs less than a year.

The nature of work continued to change in the early twentieth century as industrialists extended late-nineteenth-century efforts to make their factories and workforces more efficient, productive, and profitable. In some industries, new machines revolutionized work and eliminated highly paid, skilled jobs. Power-driven machines, better-organized operations, and finally the moving assembly line, perfected by Henry Ford, transformed the nature of work and turned many laborers into unskilled tenders of machines.

Principles of scientific management, which set new rules for organizing work, were also important. The key figure was Frederick Taylor, the son of a prominent Philadelphia family. After Taylor had a nervous breakdown while at a private school, his physicians prescribed manual labor as a cure, and he went to work as a laborer at the Midvale Steel Company in Philadelphia. Working his way up rapidly while studying engineering at night, he became chief engineer at the factory in the 1880s. Later he used this experience to develop his four principles of scientific management: centralized planning, systematic analysis of each job, detailed instructions to and close supervision of each worker, and an incentive wage system to encourage laborers to work harder and faster.

Taylor studied all kinds of workers and timed the various components of their jobs with a stopwatch in order to determine the fastest way of performing a task. Many owners enthusiastically adopted Taylor's concepts of scientific management, seeing an opportunity to increase their profits and shift control of the workplace from the skilled workers to the managers. Not surprisingly, many workers resented the emphasis on higher productivity and tighter control.

Samuel Gompers, head of the American Federation of Labor (AFL) was quick to recognize that Taylorism would reduce workers to "mere machines." Under Gompers, the AFL prospered during the progressive

Climbing into the Promised Land

Immigrants from eastern and southern Europe came to the United States in great numbers from 1890 to 1914. Many of them were detained at Ellis Island in New York. There usually was a long wait, embarrassing questions to answer, forms to fill out, a complicated bureaucracy to get past. There was also a medical exam to endure. Some immigrants failed the exam and were rejected and sent back to Europe. Still they came with hope and determination. Lewis Hine titled this photo *Climbing into Ellis Island, 1908.* Did the United States live up to the hopes of most immigrants? What emotions, thoughts, and concerns can you read on the faces of these immigrants?

(Lewis Hine, *Climbing into the Promised Land, Ellis Island, 1908.* © Brooklyn Museum of Art, New York, USA, Gift of Mr. and Mrs. Walter Rosenblum/Bridgeman Art Library.)

era. Between 1897 and 1904, union membership grew from 447,000 to more than 2 million, with three out of every four union members claimed by the AFL. By 1914, the AFL alone had more than 2 million members. Gompers's "pure and simple unionism" was most successful among coal miners, railroad workers, and the building trades. As we saw in Chapter 18, Gompers ignored the growing army of unskilled and immigrant workers and concentrated on raising the wages and improving the working conditions of the skilled artisans who were members of unions affiliated with the AFL.

For a time, Gompers's strategy seemed to work. Several industries negotiated with the AFL as a way of avoiding disruptive strikes. But cooperation was short-lived. Labor unions were defeated in a number of disastrous strikes, and the National Association of Manufacturers (NAM) launched an aggressive counterattack. NAM and other employer associations provided strikebreakers, used industrial spies, and blacklisted union members to prevent them from obtaining other jobs.

The Supreme Court came down squarely on management's side, ruling in the Danbury Hatters case (*Loewe* v. *Lawler*, 1908) that the boycott of an industry by a labor union violated the Sherman Anti-Trust Act. The boycott had been a valuable tool for striking workers, enabling them to picket and pressure companies doing business with their employers during a strike.

Working women and their problems aroused more sympathy among progressive reformers than the plight of working men. The number of women working outside the home increased steadily during the progressive era, from more than 5 million in 1900 to nearly 8.5 million in 1920. But few belonged to unions.

Many upper-class women reformers tried to help working women in a variety of ways. The settlement houses organized day-care centers, clubs, and classes, and many reformers tried to pass protective legislation. Tension and misunderstanding often cropped up between reformers and the working women, but one organization in which there was genuine cooperation was the Women's Trade Union League. Founded in 1903, the league was organized by Mary Kenney and William English Walling, a socialist and reformer, but it also drew local leaders from the working class, such as Rose Schneiderman, a Jewish immigrant cap maker, and Leonora O'Reilly, a collar maker. The league established branches in most large eastern and midwestern cities and served for more than a decade as an important force in organizing women into unions. The league forced the AFL to pay more attention to women, helped during strikes, and publicized the plight of working women.

Garment Workers and the Triangle Fire

Thousands of young women, most of them Jewish and Italian, were employed in the garment industry in New York City. Most were between ages 16 and 25; some lived with their families, and others lived alone or with a roommate. They worked a 56-hour, six-day week and made about $6 a week for their efforts. New York was the center of the garment industry, with more than 600 shirtwaist (blouse) and dress factories employing more than 30,000 workers.

Like other industries, garment manufacturing changed in the first decade of the twentieth century. Once conducted in thousands of dark and dingy tenement rooms, operations became centralized in large loft buildings in lower Manhattan. These buildings were an improvement over the tenements, but many were overcrowded, and they had few fire escapes or safety features. The owners applied scientific management techniques to heighten productivity and thereby increase their profits. But conditions for the workers were miserable. Most of the women had to rent their sewing machines and pay for the electricity they used. They were penalized for making mistakes or talking too loudly. They were usually supervised by a male contractor who badgered and sometimes sexually harassed them.

In 1909, some of the women went on strike to protest working conditions. The International Ladies' Garment Workers Union (ILGWU) and the Women's Trade Union League supported them. But strikers were beaten and sometimes arrested. At a mass meeting in New York on November 22, 1909, Clara Lemlich, a young shirtwaist worker who had been injured on the picket line, rose and in an emotional speech in Yiddish demanded a general strike. The entire audience pledged agreement. The next day, all over the city, the shirtwaist workers went on strike.

"The uprising of the twenty thousand," as the strike was called, startled the nation. One young worker wrote in her diary, "It is a good thing, that strike is. It makes you feel like a grown-up person." The Jews learned a little Italian and the Italians a little Yiddish so that they could communicate. Many social reformers, ministers, priests, and rabbis urged the strikers on. Mary Dreier, an upper-class reformer and president of the New York branch of the Women's Trade Union League, was arrested for marching with the strikers. A young state legislator, Fiorello La Guardia, later a congressman and mayor of New York, was one of many public officials to aid the strikers.

The shirtwaist workers won recognition for their union and some improvements in the factories, but their victory was limited. The young women went back to work amid still oppressive and unsafe conditions. On Saturday, March 25, 1911, a fire broke out on the eighth floor of the 10-story loft building housing the Triangle Shirtwaist Company near Washington Square in New York. There had been several small fires in the factory in previous weeks, so no one thought much about another one. But this fire was different. Within minutes, the top three floors of the factory were ablaze. The owners had locked most of the exit doors. The elevators broke down. There were no fire escapes. Forty-six women jumped to their deaths, some of them in groups of three and four holding hands. More than 100 died in the flames.

Shocked by the Triangle fire, the state legislature appointed a commission to investigate working conditions in the state. One investigator for the commission was a young social worker named Frances Perkins, who in the 1930s would become secretary of labor. She led the politicians through the dark lofts, filthy tenements, and unsafe factories around the state to show them the conditions under which young women worked. The result was state legislation limiting the work of women to 54 hours a week, prohibiting labor by children under age 14, and improving safety regulations in factories. One supporter of the bills in Albany was a young state senator named Franklin Delano Roosevelt.

The investigative commission was a favorite progressive tactic. The federal Industrial Relations Commission, created in 1912 to study the causes of industrial unrest and violence, conducted one of the most important investigations, a study of the labor–management conflict at the Colorado Fuel and Iron Industry near Ludlow, Colorado. In the fall of 1913, miners at the company, which was largely owned by the Rockefeller family, went on strike demanding an eight-hour workday, better safety precautions, and the removal of armed guards. When the company refused to negotiate with the striking workers, the strike turned violent. In the spring of 1914, strikebreakers and national guardsmen armed with machine guns fired on the workers, killing 11 children and 2 women in an incident that became known as the Ludlow Massacre.

The Industrial Relations Commission called John D. Rockefeller, Jr., to testify and implied that he was personally guilty of the murders. The commission decided in its report that violent class conflict could be avoided only by limiting the use of armed guards and detectives, by restricting monopoly, by protecting the right of the workers to organize, and, most dramatically, by redistributing wealth through taxation. The commission's report, not surprisingly, fell on deaf ears. Most progressives, like most Americans, denied the commission's conclusion that class conflict was inevitable.

Radical Labor

Not everyone accepted the progressives' faith in investigations and protective labor legislation. Nor did everyone approve of Samuel Gompers's conservative tactics or his emphasis on getting higher wages for skilled workers. In 1905 in Chicago, about 200 radicals met to organize the Industrial Workers of the World (IWW) as an alternative to the AFL. Like the Knights of Labor in the 1880s, the IWW welcomed all workers regardless of skill, gender, or race.

Eugene Debs attended the organizational meeting. He had become a socialist after the Pullman strike of 1894 and emerged by 1905 as one of the outstanding radical leaders in the country. Also attending were "Big Bill" Haywood of the Western Federation of Miners and the legendary Mary Harris "Mother" Jones, who dressed like a society matron but attacked labor leaders "who sit on velvet chairs in conferences with labor's oppressors." Now in her sixties, "Mother" Jones had been a dressmaker, a Populist, and a member of the

Knights of Labor. During the 1890s, she had marched with miners' wives on the picket line in western Pennsylvania.

The IWW remained a small organization, troubled by internal squabbles and disagreements. Haywood dominated the movement, which played an important role in organizing the militant strikes of textile workers in Lawrence, Massachusetts, in 1912 and the following year in Paterson, New Jersey, and Akron, Ohio. The IWW had its greatest success organizing itinerant lumbermen and migratory workers in the Northwest. But in other places, especially in times of high unemployment, the Wobblies (as they were called) helped unskilled workers vent their anger against their employers.

Most American workers did not feel, as European workers did, that they were involved in a perpetual class struggle with their capitalist employers, but that did not mean that they were docile and passive. Many American workers struggled with their managers over control of the workplace, and workers occasionally went on strike for better wages and working conditions. Immigrants often did not join in these actions. Some immigrant workers, intent on earning enough money to go back home, had no time to join the conflict. Most of those who stayed in the United States held fast to the dream of a better job or moving up into the middle class. They avoided organized labor militancy. They knew that even if they failed, their sons and daughters would profit from the American way. The AFL, not the IWW, became the dominant American labor movement.

Reform in the Cities and States

Reform movements of the progressive era usually started at the local level, then moved to the state, and finally to the nation's capital. Progressivism in the cities and states had roots in the depression and discontent of the 1890s. Reformers called for more democracy, more power for the people, and legislation regulating railroads and other businesses. Yet often the professional and business classes were the movement's leaders. They intended to bring order out of chaos and to modernize the city and the state during a time of rapid growth.

Municipal Reformers

American cities grew rapidly in the last part of the nineteenth and the first part of the twentieth century. New York, which had a population of 1.2 million in 1880, grew to 3.4 million by 1900 and 5.6 million in 1920. Chicago expanded even more dramatically, from 500,000 in 1880 to 1.7 million in 1900 and 2.7 million in 1920. Los Angeles was a town of 11,000 in 1880 but multiplied 10 times by 1900, and then increased another 5 times, to more than a half million, by 1920.

The spectacular and continuing growth of the cities caused problems and created a need for housing, transportation, and municipal services. But many observers worried most about the kinds of people who were moving into the cities. Immigration produced the greatest surge. Fully 40 percent of New York's population and 36 percent of Chicago's was foreign born in 1910; if one included the children of the immigrants, the percentage approached 80 percent in some cities. To many Protestant Americans, the new immigrants seemed to threaten the American way of life and the very tenets of democracy.

The presence of large immigrant populations was the most important difference between American and European cities, and it made attempts to reform the city different in the United States. Twentieth-century reformers, mostly middle-class citizens like those in the nineteenth century, wanted to regulate and control the sprawling metropolis, restore democracy, reduce corruption, and limit the power of the political bosses and their immigrant allies. When these reformers talked of restoring power to the people, they usually meant ensuring control for people like themselves. The chief aim of municipal reform was to make the city more organized and efficient for the business and professional classes.

Municipal reform movements varied from city to city, but everywhere the reformers tried to limit the power of the city political bosses, whom they saw as corrupt and antidemocratic. In Boston, the reformers tried to strengthen the power of the mayor, break the hold of the city council, and eliminate council corruption. They succeeded in removing all party designations from city election ballots, and they extended the term of the mayor from two to four years. But to their chagrin, in the election of 1910, John Fitzgerald, grandfather of John F. Kennedy and foe of reform, defeated their candidate.

The most dramatic innovation in municipal reform was the replacement of both mayor and council with a nonpartisan commission of administrators. This scheme began quite accidentally when a hurricane devastated Galveston, Texas, in September 1900. More than 6,000 people died in the worst natural disaster in the nation's history. The existing government was helpless to deal with the crisis, so the state legislature appointed five commissioners to run the city during the emergency.

The idea spread to Houston, Dallas, and Austin and to cities in other states. It proved most popular in small to medium-sized cities in the Midwest and the Pacific Northwest. By World War I, more than 400 cities had adopted the commission form. Dayton, Ohio, went one step further: after a disastrous flood in 1913, the city hired a manager to run the city and to report to the elected council. Appointed, not elected, the city manager was more a businessman or technician than a politician. Government by experts

A Traffic Jam in Chicago in 1909

Cities grew so rapidly that they often ceased to work. This 1909 photograph shows Dearborn Street looking south from Randolph Street in Chicago. Horse-drawn vehicles, streetcars, pedestrians, and even a few early autos clogged the intersection and created the urban inefficiency that angered municipal reformers. How have urban centers changed today? Have we solved the problem of urban transportation and crowding?

(Chicago Historical Society, [ICHi-04151])

was the perfect symbol of what most municipal reformers had in mind.

The commission and the expert manager did not replace the mayor in most large cities. One of the most flamboyant and successful of the progressive mayors was Tom Johnson of Cleveland. Johnson had made a fortune by investing in utility and railroad franchises before he was 40. But Henry George's *Progress and Poverty* so influenced him that he began a second career as a reformer. Elected mayor of Cleveland in 1901, he reduced transit fares and built parks and municipal bathhouses throughout the city. Johnson also broke the connection between the police and prostitution by promising the madams and brothel owners that he would not bother them if they would be orderly and not steal from their customers or pay off the police.

His most controversial move, however, was advocating city ownership of the street railroads and utilities. Like many American urban reformers, Johnson admired the municipally owned transportation systems in European cities. "Only through municipal ownership," he argued, "can the gulf which divides the community into a small dominant class on one side and the unorganized people on the other be bridged." Johnson was defeated in 1909 in part because he alienated many powerful business interests, but one of his lieutenants, Newton D. Baker, was elected mayor in 1911 and carried on many of his programs. Cleveland was one of many cities that began to regulate municipal utilities or take them over from the private owners.

In Cleveland, both Tom Johnson and Newton Baker promoted the arts, music, and adult education. They also supervised construction of a civic center, library, and museum. In Cleveland and other cities, such "city beautiful" projects were influenced at least in part by the great, classical White City constructed for the Chicago World's Fair of 1893, but even more by grand European boulevards such as the Champs-Élysées in Paris. The city beautiful leaders tried to make their cities more attractive and meaningful for the middle and upper classes. The museums and the libraries were closed on Sundays, the only day the working class could possibly visit them.

Social justice progressives were more concerned with neighborhood parks and playgrounds than with ceremonial boulevards and grand buildings. In Chicago, Hull House established the first public playground. In New York, Jacob Riis, the housing reformer, and Lillian Wald of the Henry Street Settlement campaigned for small parks and for the opening of schoolyards on weekends. Some progressives looked back nostalgically to their rural childhoods and desperately tried to get urban children out of the city in the summertime to attend rural camps. But they also tried to make the city more livable as well as more beautiful.

Most progressives had an ambivalent attitude toward the city. They feared it, and they loved it. Some saw the great urban areas filled with immigrants as a threat to American democracy, but one of Tom Johnson's young assistants, Frederic C. Howe, who had traveled and studied in Europe, wrote a book titled *The City: The Hope of Democracy* (1905). Hope or threat, the progressives realized that the United States had become an urban nation and that the problems of the city had to be faced.

Reform in the States

The progressive movements in the states had many roots and took many forms, but because of the American federal system, the states took on an importance that confused observers from other parts of the world. In some states, especially in the West, progressive attempts to regulate railroads and utilities were simply an extension of Populism. In other states, the reform drive emerged from municipal reform efforts. Most states passed laws during the progressive era designed to extend democracy and give more authority to the people. Initiative and referendum laws allowed citizens to originate legislation and to overturn laws passed by the legislature, and recall laws gave the people a way to remove elected officials.

Much progressive state legislation promoted order and efficiency, but many states passed social justice measures as well. Maryland enacted the first workers' compensation law in 1902, paying employees for days missed because of job-related injuries. By 1917, 37 states (almost all outside the South) had passed workers' compensation laws and 28 states had set maximum hours for women working in industry. Illinois approved a law aiding mothers with dependent children. Several states passed anti–child labor bills, and Oregon's 10-hour law restricting women's labor became a model for other states.

The states with the most successful reform movements elected strong and aggressive governors: Charles Evans Hughes in New York, Hoke Smith in Georgia, Hiram Johnson in California, Woodrow Wilson in New Jersey, and Robert La Follette in Wisconsin. After Wilson, La Follette was the most famous and in many ways the model progressive governor. Of small-town origin and an 1879 graduate of the University of Wisconsin, he began his career as a railroad lawyer and became a reformer only after the depression of 1893. Taking advantage of the general mood of discontent, he won the governorship in 1901. Ironically, he owed his victory to his attack on the railroads. But La Follette was a shrewd politician. He used professors from the University of Wisconsin (in the capital)

LANDMARK SOCIAL LEGISLATION IN THE STATES

1902   Maryland passed the first state worker's compensation law.

1903   Oregon adopted a law limiting women's work to ten hours a day in factories (upheld by the United States Supreme Court in *Muller* v. *Oregon*, 1908).

1911   Illinois enacted the first state law providing public assistance to mothers with dependent children.

1912   Massachusetts passed the first minimum-wage law. A commission fixed wage rates for women and children. This and other similar state laws were overturned by the United States Supreme Court in *Atkins* v. *Children's Hospital*, 1923.

to prepare reports and do statistical studies. Then he worked with the legislature to pass a state primary law and an act regulating the railroads. "Go back to the first principles of democracy; go back to the people" was his battle cry. Journalists helped popularize Wisconsin as the "laboratory of democracy." La Follette won national recognition and was elected to the Senate in 1906.

The progressive movement did improve government and made it more responsible to the people in Wisconsin and other states. For example, the railroads were brought under the control of a railroad commission. But by 1910, the railroads no longer complained about the new taxes and restrictions. They had discovered that it was to their advantage to make their operations more efficient, and often they were able to convince the commission that they should raise rates or abandon the operation of unprofitable lines.

Progressivism in the states, like progressivism everywhere, had mixed results. But the spirit of reform that swept the country was real, and progressive movements on the local level did eventually have

an impact on Washington, especially during the administrations of Theodore Roosevelt and Woodrow Wilson.

Theodore Roosevelt and the Square Deal

President William McKinley was shot in Buffalo, New York, on September 6, 1901, by Leon Czolgosz, an anarchist. McKinley died eight days later, making Theodore Roosevelt, at age 42, the youngest man ever to become president.

No one knew what to expect from Roosevelt. Some politicians thought he was too radical; a few social justice progressives remembered his suggestion that the soldiers should fire on the strikers during the 1894 Pullman strike. Nonetheless, under his leadership, progressivism reshaped the national political agenda. Although early progressive reformers had attacked problems that they saw in their own communities, they gradually understood that some problems could not be

TR's Bully Pulpit

Theodore Roosevelt was a dynamic public speaker who used his position to influence public opinion. Despite his high-pitched voice, he could be heard at the back of the crowd in the days before microphones. Note the row of reporters decked out in their summer straw hats writing their stories as the president speaks. How have presidential speeches and the role of reporters changed since Roosevelt's time?

(Brown Brothers)

solved at the state or local level. The emergence of a national industrial economy had spawned conditions that demanded national solutions.

Progressives at the national level turned their attention to the workings of the economic system. They scrutinized the operation and organization of railroads and other large corporations. They examined threats to the natural environment. They reviewed the quality of the products of American industry. As they fashioned legislation to remedy the flaws in the economic system, they vastly expanded the power of the national government.

A Strong and Controversial President

Roosevelt came to the presidency with considerable experience. He had run unsuccessfully for mayor of New York, served a term in the New York state assembly, spent four years as a U.S. civil service commissioner, and served two years as the police commissioner of New York City. His exploits in the Spanish-American War brought him to the public's attention, but he had also been an effective assistant secretary of the navy and a reform governor of New York. While police commissioner and governor, he had been influenced by a number of progressives. He had supported conservation, an eight-hour workday, and other progressive measures in New York. But no one was sure how he would act as president. He came from an upper-class family, had traveled widely in Europe, and had associated with the important and the powerful all over the world. He had written a number of books and was one of the most intellectual and cosmopolitan presidents since Thomas Jefferson. But there was no guarantee that he would be a progressive in office.

Roosevelt loved being president. He called the office a "bully pulpit," and he enjoyed talking to the people and the press. His appealing personality and sense of humor made him a good subject for the new mass-market newspapers and magazines. The American people called him "Teddy" and named a stuffed bear after him. Sometimes his exuberance got a little out of hand. On one occasion, he took a foreign diplomat on a nude swim in the Potomac River. You have to understand, another observer remarked, that "the president is really only six years old."

Roosevelt was much more than an exuberant six-year-old. He was the strongest president since Lincoln. By revitalizing the executive branch, reorganizing the army command structure, and modernizing the consular service, he made many aspects of the federal government more efficient. He established the Bureau of Corporations, appointed independent commissions staffed with experts, and enlisted talented and well-trained men to work for the government. "TR," as he became known, called a White House conference on the care of dependent children, and in 1905, he even summoned college presidents and football coaches to the White House to discuss ways to limit violence in football. Although he angered many social justice progressives who felt he did not go far enough, he was the first president to listen to the pleas of the progressives and to invite them to the White House. Learning from experts such as Frances Kellor, he gradually became more concerned with social justice. In 1904, running on a platform of a "Square Deal" for the American people, he was reelected by an overwhelming margin.

Dealing with the Trusts

One of Roosevelt's first actions as president was to attempt to control large industrial corporations. He took office in the middle of an unprecedented wave of business consolidation. Between 1897 and 1904, some 4,227 companies combined to form 257 large corporations. U.S. Steel, the first billion-dollar corporation, was formed in 1901 by joining Carnegie Steel with its eight main competitors. The new company controlled two-thirds of the market, and financier J. P. Morgan made $7 million on the deal.

The Sherman Anti-Trust Act of 1890 had been virtually useless in controlling the trusts, and muckrakers and progressives called for new regulation. Some even demanded a return to the age of small business. Roosevelt opposed neither bigness nor the right of businessmen to make money. "We draw the line against misconduct, not against wealth," he said.

To the shock of much of the business community, he directed his attorney general to file suit to dissolve the Northern Securities Company, a giant railroad monopoly put together by James J. Hill and J. P. Morgan. Morgan came to the White House to tell Roosevelt, "If we have done anything wrong, send your man to my man and they can fix it up." A furious Roosevelt let Morgan and other businessmen know that they could not deal with the president of the United States as just another tycoon. The government won its case and proceeded to prosecute some of the largest corporations, including Standard Oil of New Jersey and the American Tobacco Company.

Roosevelt's antitrust policy did not end the power of the giant corporations or even alter their methods of doing business, nor did it force down the price of kerosene, cigars, or railroad tickets. But it did breathe some life into the Sherman Anti-Trust Act and increased the role of the federal government as regulator. It also caused large firms such as U.S. Steel to diversify to avoid antitrust suits.

Roosevelt sought to strengthen the regulatory powers of the federal government in other ways. He steered the Elkins Act through Congress in 1903 and the Hepburn Act in 1906, which together increased the power of the Interstate Commerce Commission (ICC).

The first act eliminated the use of rebates by railroads, a method that many large corporations had used to get favored treatment. The second act broadened the power of the ICC and gave it the right to investigate and enforce rates. Opponents in Congress weakened both bills, however, and the legislation neither ended abuses nor satisfied the farmers and small-business owners who had always been the railroads' chief critics.

Roosevelt firmly believed in corporate capitalism. He detested socialism and felt much more comfortable around business executives than labor leaders. Yet he saw his role as mediator and regulator. His view of the power of the presidency was illustrated in 1902 during the anthracite coal strike. Led by John Mitchell of the United Mine Workers, the coal miners went on strike to protest low wages, long hours, and unsafe working conditions. In 1901, a total of 513 coal miners had died in industrial accidents. The mine owners refused to talk to the miners. They hired strikebreakers and used private security forces to threaten and intimidate the workers.

Roosevelt had no particular sympathy for labor, but in the fall of 1902, schools began closing for lack of coal, and it looked as if many citizens would suffer through the winter. Coal, which usually sold for $5 a ton, rose to $14. Roosevelt called the owners and representatives of the union to the White House, even though the mine owners protested that they would not deal with "outlaws." Finally, the president appointed a commission that included representatives of the union as well as the community. Within weeks, the miners went back to work with a 10 percent raise, back pay, and a nine-hour day. But the agreement failed to recognize the union, and neither side was entirely happy with the agreement.

Meat Inspection and Pure Food and Drugs

Roosevelt's first major legislative reform began almost accidentally in 1904 when Upton Sinclair, a 26-year-old muckraking journalist, started research on the Chicago stockyards. In his 1906 novel about the meat industry, *The Jungle*, Sinclair documented exploitation but his description of contaminated meat drew more attention. He described spoiled hams treated with formaldehyde and sausages made from rotten meat scraps, rats, and other refuse. Hoping to convert his readers to socialism, Sinclair instead turned their stomachs and caused a public outcry for better regulation of the meatpacking industry.

Roosevelt, who read the book, ordered a study of the meatpacking industry and then used the report to pressure Congress and the meatpackers to accept a bill introduced by Albert Beveridge, the progressive senator from Indiana. In the end, the Meat Inspection Act of 1906 was a compromise. It enforced some federal inspection and mandated sanitary conditions in all companies selling meat in interstate commerce. The meatpackers defeated a provision that would have required the dating of all meat. Some of the large companies supported the compromise because it gave them an advantage in their battle with the smaller firms. But the act was a beginning and an example of how muckrakers, social justice progressives, and public outcry eventually led to reform legislation. Passage of the act also shows how Roosevelt used the public mood and manipulated the political process to achieve his goals. Many of the progressive reformers were disappointed with the final result, but Roosevelt was always willing to settle for half a loaf rather than none at all. Ironically, the Meat Inspection Act restored the public's confidence in the meat industry and helped the industry increase its profits.

Taking advantage of the publicity that circulated around *The Jungle*, a group of reformers, writers, and government officials supported legislation to regulate the sale of food and drugs. Americans consumed an enormous quantity of patent medicines, which they purchased through the mail, from traveling salesmen, and from local stores. Many packaged and canned foods contained dangerous chemicals and impurities. One popular remedy, Hosteter's Stomach Bitters, was revealed on analysis to contain 44 percent alcohol. Coca-Cola, a popular soft drink, contained a small amount of cocaine, and many medicines were laced with opium. Many people, including women and children, became alcoholics or drug addicts in their quest to feel better. The Pure Food and Drug Act, which Congress passed on the same day in 1906 as the Meat Inspection Act, was not a perfect bill, but it corrected some of the worst abuses, including eliminating the cocaine from Coca-Cola.

Conservation

Roosevelt, an outdoorsman and amateur naturalist, considered his conservation program his most important domestic achievement. Using his executive authority, he more than tripled the land set aside for national forests, bringing the total to more than 150 million acres.

Because he had traveled widely in the West, Roosevelt understood, as few easterners did, the problems created by limited water in the western states. In 1902, with his enthusiastic support, Congress passed the Newlands Act, named for its chief sponsor, Congressman Francis Newlands of Nevada. The National Reclamation Act (as it was officially called) set aside the proceeds from the sale of public land in 16 western states to pay for the construction of irrigation projects in those states. Although it tended to help big farmers more than small producers, the Newlands Act federalized irrigation for the first time.

More important were Roosevelt's efforts to raise public consciousness about the need to save the nation's natural resources. He appointed a National Conservation Commission charged with making an inventory of the natural resources in the entire country. To chair the commission, Roosevelt appointed Gifford Pinchot, probably the most important conservation advocate in the country.

Pinchot's conservation policies pleased many in the timber and cattle industries; at the same time, they angered those who simply wanted to exploit the land. But his policies were denounced by the followers of John Muir, who believed passionately in preserving the land in a wilderness state. Muir had founded the Sierra Club in 1862 and had led a successful campaign to create Yosemite National Park in California. With his shaggy gray beard, rough blue work clothes, and black slouch hat, Muir seemed like an eccentric to many, but thousands agreed with him when he argued that preserving the American wilderness was a spiritual and psychological necessity for overcivilized and overstimulated urban dwellers. Muir was one of the leaders in a "back to nature" movement at the turn of the century. Many middle-class Americans took up hiking, camping,

and other outdoor activities, and children joined the Boy Scouts (founded in 1910) and the Camp Fire Girls (1912). The "back to nature movement" was not strictly American. The Boy Scouts were patterned after the British Boy Scouts, and hiking and mountain climbing were popular activities in many countries early in the twentieth century.

The conflicting philosophies of conservationist Pinchot and preservationist Muir were most dramatically demonstrated by the controversy over Hetch-Hetchy, a remote valley deep within Yosemite National Park. It was a pristine wilderness area, and Muir and his followers wanted to keep it that way. But in 1901, the mayor of San Francisco decided the valley would make a perfect place for a dam and reservoir to supply his growing city with water for decades to come. Muir argued that wilderness soon would be scarcer than water and more important for the moral strength of the nation. Pinchot, on the other hand, maintained that it was foolish to pander to the aesthetic enjoyment of a tiny group of people when the comfort and welfare of the great majority were at stake.

In the end, the conservationists won out over the preservationists. Roosevelt and Congress sided with

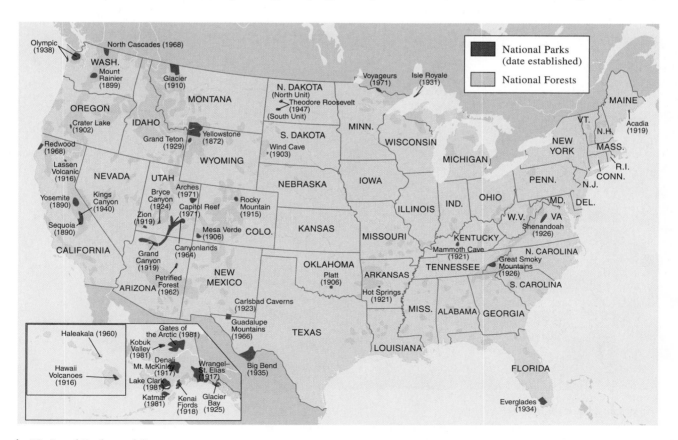

National Parks and Forests

Yellowstone, Yosemite, and a few other national parks were established before Theodore Roosevelt became president, but his passionate interest in conservation led to a movement to set aside and preserve thousands of acres of the public domain. What legacy did this create for future generations?

Pinchot and eventually the dam was built, turning the valley into a lake. But the debate over how to use the nation's land and water would continue throughout the twentieth century.

Progressivism for Whites Only

Like most of his generation, Roosevelt thought in stereotyped racial terms. He called Native Americans "savages" and once remarked that blacks were "wholly unfit for the suffrage." He believed that blacks, Asians, and Native Americans were inferior, and he feared that massive migrations from southern and eastern Europe threatened the United States. This kind of racism was supported by scientific theories accepted by many experts in the universities. Supporters of eugenics, who believed that selective breeding would improve the human race, advocated the forced sterilization of criminals, mental patients, and other undesirable types. Roosevelt was influenced by these theories, but he was first of all a politician, so he made gestures of goodwill

to most groups. He even invited Booker T. Washington to the White House in 1901, though many southerners viciously attacked the president for this breach of etiquette. Roosevelt also appointed several qualified blacks to minor federal posts, notably Dr. William D. Crum to head the Charleston, South Carolina, customs house in 1905.

At other times, however, Roosevelt seemed insensitive to the needs and feelings of black Americans. This was especially true in his handling of the Brownsville, Texas, riot of 1906. Members of a black army unit stationed there, angered by discrimination against them, rioted one hot August night. Exactly what happened no one was sure, but one white man was killed and several were wounded. Waiting until after the midterm elections of 1906, Roosevelt ordered all 167 members of three companies dishonorably discharged. It was an unjust punishment for an unproven crime, and 66 years later, the secretary of the army granted honorable discharges to the men, although most of them were by that time dead.

An American History Class

Tuskegee Institute followed Booker T. Washington's philosophy of black advancement through accommodation to the white status quo. Here students study white American history, but most of their time was spent on more practical subjects. This photo was taken in 1902 by Frances Benjamin Johnson, a pioneer woman photographer. How have classrooms changed in the last hundred years? How have they stayed the same?

(Library of Congress)

The progressive era coincided with the years of greatest segregation in the South, and in southern states, progressivism meant keeping blacks outside the political process. Even the most advanced progressives seldom included blacks in their reform schemes. Like most social settlements, Hull House was segregated, although Jane Addams (more than most progressives) struggled to overcome the racist attitudes of her day. She helped found a settlement that served a black neighborhood in Chicago, and she spoke out repeatedly against lynching. Addams also supported the founding of the National Association for the Advancement of Colored People (NAACP) in 1909, the most important organization of the progressive era aimed at promoting equality and justice for blacks.

The founding of the NAACP is the story of cooperation between a group of white social justice progressives and a number of courageous black leaders. Even in the age of segregation and lynching, blacks in all parts of the country—through churches, clubs, and schools—sought to promote a better life for themselves. The most important black leader who argued for equality and opportunity for his people was W. E. B. Du Bois. He differed dramatically from Booker T. Washington on the proper position of blacks in American life (see Chapter 17). Whereas Washington advocated vocational education, Du Bois argued for the best education possible for the most talented tenth of the black population. Whereas Washington preached compromise and accommodation to the dominant white society, Du Bois increasingly urged aggressive action to ensure equality.

Denouncing Washington for accepting the "alleged inferiority of the Negro," Du Bois called a meeting of young and militant blacks in 1905. They met in Canada, not far from Niagara Falls, and issued an angry statement. "We want to pull down nothing but we don't propose to be pulled down," the platform announced. "We believe in taking what we can get but we don't believe in being satisfied with it and in permitting anybody for a moment to imagine we're satisfied." The Niagara movement, as it came to be called, was small, but it was soon augmented by a group of white liberals concerned with violence against blacks and race riots in Atlanta and even in Springfield, Illinois, the home of Abraham Lincoln. Jane Addams joined the new organization, as did Oswald Garrison Villard, grandson of abolitionist William Lloyd Garrison.

In 1910, the Niagara movement combined with the NAACP, and Du Bois became editor of its journal, *The Crisis*. He toned down his rhetoric, but he tried to promote equality for all blacks. The NAACP was a typical progressive organization, seeking to work within the American system to promote reform. But to Roosevelt and many others who called themselves progressives, the NAACP seemed dangerously radical.

William Howard Taft

After two terms as president, Roosevelt decided to step down. But he soon regretted his decision. Only 50 years old, he was at the peak of his popularity and power. Because the U.S. system of government provides little creative function for former presidents, Roosevelt decided to travel and to go big-game hunting in Africa.

William Howard Taft, Roosevelt's personal choice for the Republican nomination and winner over Democratic candidate William Jennings Bryan in 1908, was a distinguished lawyer, federal judge, and public servant. Born in Cincinnati, Taft had been the first civil governor of the Philippines and Roosevelt's secretary of war. In some ways, he seemed more progressive than Roosevelt. His administration instituted more suits against monopolies in one term than Roosevelt had in two. He supported the eight-hour workday and legislation to make mining safer, and he urged the passage of the Mann–Elkins Act in 1910, which strengthened the ICC by giving it more power to set railroad rates and extending its jurisdiction over telephone and telegraph companies. Taft and Congress also authorized the first tax on corporate profits. He also encouraged the process that eventually led to the passage of the federal income tax, which was authorized under the Sixteenth Amendment, ratified in 1913.

But Taft soon ran into difficulties. His biggest problem was his style. He was a huge man, weighing more than 300 pounds. (Rumors circulated that he had to have a special, oversize bathtub installed in the White House.) Easily ridiculed, the president wrote ponderous prose and spoke uninspiringly. He also lacked Roosevelt's political skills and angered many of the progressives in the Republican party, especially the midwestern insurgents led by Senator Robert La Follette of Wisconsin. Many progressives were annoyed when he signed the Payne–Aldrich Tariff, which midwesterners thought left rates on cotton and wool cloth and other items too high and played into the hands of the eastern industrial interests.

Even Roosevelt was infuriated when his successor reversed many of his conservation policies and fired chief forester Gifford Pinchot. Roosevelt broke with Taft and let it be known that he was willing to run again for president. This set up one of the most exciting and significant elections in American history.

The Election of 1912

Woodrow Wilson won the Democratic nomination for president in 1912. The son and grandson of Presbyterian ministers, Wilson grew up in a comfortable and intellectual southern household and early on seemed more interested in politics than in religion. He graduated from Princeton University in 1879, studied law at the University of Virginia, and practiced law briefly before entering graduate school at the Johns Hopkins University in Baltimore. His book, *Congressional Government* (1885), established his reputation as a shrewd analyst of American politics. Less flamboyant than Roosevelt, he was an excellent public speaker, possessing the power to convince people with his words. In 1902 Wilson was elected president of Princeton University, and during the next few years he established a national reputation as an educational leader. Wilson never lost interest in politics, however, so when offered a chance by the Democratic machine to run for governor of New Jersey, he took it eagerly. In his two years as governor, he showed courage as he quickly alienated some of the conservatives who had helped elect him. Building a coalition of reformers, he worked with them to pass a direct primary law and a workers' compensation law. He also created a commission to regulate transportation and public utility companies. By 1912, Wilson not only was an expert on government and politics but had also acquired the reputation of a progressive.

Roosevelt, who had been speaking out on a variety of issues since 1910, competed with Taft for the Republican nomination, but Taft, as the incumbent president and party leader, was able to win it. Roosevelt then startled the nation by walking out of the convention and forming a new political party, the Progressive party. The new party would not have been formed without Roosevelt, but it was always more than Roosevelt. It appealed to progressives from all over the country who had become frustrated with the conservative leadership in both major parties.

Many social workers and social justice progressives supported the Progressive party because of its platform, which contained provisions they had been advocating for years. The Progressives supported an eight-hour workday, a six-day workweek, the abolition of child labor under age 16, and a federal system of accident, old age, and unemployment insurance. Unlike the Democrats, the Progressives also endorsed woman suffrage.

Most supporters of the Progressives in 1912 did not realistically think they could win, but they were convinced that they could organize a new political movement that would replace the Republican party, just as the Republicans had replaced the Whigs after 1856. To this end, Progressive leaders led by Frances Kellor set up the Progressive Service, designed to apply the principles of social research to educating voters between elections.

The Progressive party convention in Chicago seemed to many observers more like a religious revival meeting or a social work conference than a political gathering. The delegates sang "Onward Christian Soldiers," "The Battle Hymn of the Republic," and "Roosevelt, Oh

Roosevelt" (to the tune of "Maryland, My Maryland"). They waved their bandannas, and when Jane Addams rose to second Roosevelt's nomination, a large group of women marched around the auditorium with a banner that read "Votes for Women."

Behind the unified facade lurked many disagreements. Roosevelt had become more progressive on many issues since leaving the presidency. He even attacked the financiers "to whom the acquisition of untold millions is the supreme goal of life, and who are too often utterly indifferent as to how these millions are obtained." But he was not as committed to social reform as some of the delegates. Perhaps the most divisive issue was the controversy over seating black delegates from several southern states. A number of social justice progressives fought hard to include a plank in the platform supporting equality for blacks and for seating the black delegation. Roosevelt, however, thought he had a realistic chance to carry several southern states, and he was not convinced that black equality was an important progressive issue. In the end, no blacks sat with the southern delegates, and the platform made no mention of black equality.

The political campaign in 1912 became a contest primarily between Roosevelt and Wilson; Taft, the Republican candidate and incumbent, was ignored by most reporters who covered the campaign. On one level, the campaign became a debate over political philosophy. What is the proper relationship of government to society in a modern industrial age? Roosevelt spoke of a "New Nationalism." In a modern industrial society, he argued, large corporations were "inevitable and necessary." What was needed was not the breakup of the trusts but a strong president and increased power in the hands of the federal government to regulate business and industry and to ensure the rights of labor, women and children, and other groups. The government should be the "steward of the public welfare." He argued for using Hamiltonian means to ensure Jeffersonian ends, for using strong central government to guarantee the rights of the people.

Wilson responded with a program he called the "New Freedom." Drawing on the ideas of Louis Brandeis, he emphasized the need for the Jeffersonian tradition of limited government with open competition. He spoke of the "curse of bigness" and argued against too much federal power.

The level of debate during the campaign was impressive, making this one of the few elections in American history in which important ideas were actually discussed. It also marked a watershed for political thought for liberals who rejected Jefferson's distrust of a strong central government. It is easy to exaggerate the differences between Roosevelt and Wilson. Certainly, in the end, the things that Roosevelt and Wilson could agree on were more important than the

PRESIDENTIAL ELECTIONS OF THE PROGRESSIVE ERA

Year	Candidate	Party	Popular Vote	Electoral Vote
1900	WILLIAM MCKINLEY	Republican	7,218,039 (51.7%)	292
	William Jennings Bryan	Democratic, Populist	6,358,345 (45.5%)	155
1904	THEODORE ROOSEVELT	Republican	7,628,834 (56.4%)	336
	Alton B. Parker	Democratic	5,084,401 (37.6%)	140
	Eugene V. Debs	Socialist	402,460 (3.0%)	0
1908	WILLIAM H. TAFT	Republican	7,679,006 (51.6%)	321
	William Jennings Bryan	Democratic	6,409,106 (43.1%)	162
	Eugene V. Debs	Socialist	420,820 (2.8%)	0
1912	WOODROW WILSON	Democratic	6,296,547 (41.9%)	435
	Theodore Roosevelt	Progressive	4,118,571 (27.4%)	88
	William H. Taft	Republican	3,486,720 (23.2%)	8
	Eugene V. Debs	Socialist	897,011 (6.0%)	0
1916	WOODROW WILSON	Democratic	9,129,606 (49.4%)	277
	Charles E. Hughes	Republican	8,538,221 (46.2%)	254
	Allan L. Benson	Socialist	585,113 (3.2%)	0

Note: Winners' names appear in capital letters.

issues that divided them. Both Roosevelt and Wilson urged reform within the American system. Both defended corporate capitalism, and both opposed socialism and radical labor organizations such as the IWW. Both wanted to promote more democracy and to strengthen conservative labor unions. And both were very different in style and substance from the fourth candidate, Eugene Debs, who ran on the Socialist party ticket in 1912.

In 1912, Debs was the most important socialist leader in the country. Socialism has always been a minority movement in the United States, but it reached its greatest success in the United States in the first decade of the twentieth century. Thirty-three cities, including Milwaukee, Wisconsin; Reading, Pennsylvania; Butte, Montana; Jackson, Michigan; and Berkeley, California, chose socialist mayors. Socialists Victor Berger from Wisconsin and Meyer London from New York were elected to Congress. The most important socialist periodical, *Appeal to Reason,* published in Girard, Kansas, increased its circulation from about 30,000 in 1900 to nearly 300,000 in 1906. Socialism appealed to a diverse group. In the cities, some who called themselves socialists merely favored municipal ownership of street railways. Some reformers, such as Florence Kelley and William English Walling, joined the party because of their frustration with the slow progress of reform. The party also attracted many recent immigrants, who brought with them a European sense of class and loyalty to socialism.

A tremendously appealing figure and a great orator, Debs had run for president in 1900, 1904, and 1908, but in 1912 he reached much wider audiences in more parts of the country. His message differed radically from that of Wilson or Roosevelt. Unlike the progressives, socialists argued for fundamental change in the American system. Debs polled almost 900,000 votes in 1912 (6 percent of the popular vote), the best showing ever for a socialist in the United States. Wilson received 6.3 million votes; Roosevelt, a little more than 4 million; and Taft, 3.5 million. Wilson garnered 435 electoral votes; Roosevelt, 88; and Taft, only 8.

Woodrow Wilson and the New Freedom

Wilson was elected largely because Roosevelt and the Progressive party split the Republican vote. But once elected, Wilson became a vigorous and aggressive chief executive who set out to translate his ideas about progressive government into legislation. Wilson was the first southerner elected president since the Civil War, but Wilson, like Roosevelt, had to work within his party, and that restricted how progressive he could be. But he was also constrained by his own background and inclinations. Still, like Roosevelt, Wilson became more progressive during his presidency.

Tariff and Banking Reform

Wilson was not as charismatic as Roosevelt. He had a more difficult time relating to people in small groups, but he was an excellent public speaker who dominated through the force of his intellect. He probably had an exaggerated belief in his ability to persuade and a tendency to trust his own intuition too much. His ability to push his legislative program through Congress during his first two years in office was matched only by Franklin Roosevelt during the first months of the New Deal and by Lyndon Johnson in 1965.

Within a month of his inauguration, Wilson went before a joint session of Congress to outline his legislative program. He recommended reducing the tariff to eliminate favoritism, freeing the banking system from Wall Street control, and restoring competition in industry. By appearing in person before Congress, he broke a precedent established by Thomas Jefferson.

The first item on Wilson's agenda was tariff reform. The Underwood Tariff, passed in 1913, was not a free-trade bill, but it did reduce tariff rates on hundreds of items for the first time in many years. Attached to the Underwood bill was a provision for a small and slightly graduated income tax, which had been made possible by the passage of the Sixteenth Amendment. It imposed a modest rate of 1 percent on income over $4,000 (thus exempting a large portion of the population), with a surtax rising to 6 percent on high incomes. The income tax was enacted to replace the money lost from lowering the tariff. Wilson seemed to have no interest in using it to redistribute wealth in America.

The next item on Wilson's agenda was reform of the banking system. A financial panic in 1907 had revealed the need for a central bank, but few people could agree on the exact nature of the reforms. A congressional committee, led by Arsène Pujo of Louisiana, had revealed a massive consolidation of banks and trust companies and a system of interlocking directorates and informal arrangements that concentrated resources and power in the hands of a few firms, such as the J. P. Morgan Company. The progressive faction of the Democratic party, armed with the Pujo Committee's findings, argued for a banking system and a currency controlled by the federal government. But talk of banking reform raised the specter among conservative Democrats and the business community of socialism, populism, and the monetary ideas of William Jennings Bryan.

The bill that passed Congress was a compromise. In creating the Federal Reserve System, it was the first reorganization of the banking system since the Civil War. The bill provided for 12 Federal Reserve banks and a Federal Reserve Board appointed by the president. The bill also created a flexible currency, based on Federal Reserve notes, that could be expanded or contracted as the situation required. The Federal Reserve System was not without its flaws, as later developments would show, and it did not end the power of the large eastern banks; but it was an improvement, and it appealed to the part of the progressive movement that sought order and efficiency.

Despite these reform measures, Wilson was not very progressive in some of his actions during his first two years in office. In the spring of 1914, he failed to support a bill that would have provided long-term rural

Opposing Woman Suffrage

Many men opposed suffrage for women because they feared the vote would change gender roles and destroy women's feminine ways. They also believed that women with the vote would support prohibition and other dangerous reforms. They often argued that women had no place in the masculine and corrupt world of politics. Many women also opposed suffrage because they believed their husbands and fathers or because they feared change. Would you have supported the vote for women if you had been alive in 1920? How have women's votes changed America?

(Library of Congress [LC-USZ62–25338])

Key Progressive Legislation

National Reclamations Act (Newlands Act), 1902
Used proceeds from sale of public lands in the western states to finance construction and maintenance of irrigation projects.

Elkins Act, 1903
Strengthened the Interstate Commerce Commission Act primarily by eliminating rebates to selected corporations.

Hepburn Act, 1906
Strengthened the Interstate Commerce Commission by giving it power to fix rates and broadening its jurisdiction to include express companies, oil pipelines, terminals, and bridges.

Meat Inspection Act, 1906
Provided for federal inspection of all companies selling meat in interstate commerce.

Pure Food and Drug Act, 1906
Prohibited the manufacture, sale, or transportation of adulterated or fraudulently labeled foods or drugs in interstate commerce.

Mann–Elkins Act, 1910
Put telephone, telegraph, cable, and wireless companies under the jurisdiction of the Interstate Commerce Commission.

Mann Act, 1910
Prohibited interstate transportation of women for immoral purposes.

Sixteenth Amendment to the Constitution, 1913 (proposed in 1909)
Gave Congress the power to impose a federal tax on income from all sources. An inheritance tax was added in 1916.

Federal Child Labor Law (Keatings–Owen Act), 1916
Barred products of child labor from interstate commerce; declared unconstitutional in 1918. Another act passed in 1919 was declared unconstitutional in 1920. In 1924 a child labor amendment to the Constitution was submitted to the states, but was never ratified.

Adamson Act, 1916
Provided for an eight-hour day and time and a half for overtime on interstate railroads.

Federal Farm Loan Act, 1916
Provided farmers with long-term credit.

Eighteenth Amendment to the Constitution, 1919 (proposed in 1917)
Prohibited the manufacture, sale, or transportation of intoxicating beverages; repealed by the Twenty-First Amendment in 1933.

Nineteenth Amendment to the Constitution, 1920 (proposed in 1919)
Provided that the right of citizens of the United States to vote should not be denied or abridged by the United States or any state on account of sex.

credit financed by the federal government. He opposed a woman suffrage amendment, arguing that the states should decide who could vote. He also failed to support an anti–child labor bill after it had passed the House. Most distressing to some progressives, he ordered the segregation of blacks in several federal departments. When southern Democrats, suddenly in control in many departments, began dismissing black federal officeholders, especially those "who boss white girls," Wilson did nothing. When the NAACP complained that the shops, offices, restrooms, and lunchrooms of the post office and treasury departments and the Bureau of Engraving were segregated, Wilson replied, "I sincerely believe it to be in [the blacks'] best interest." When the president endorsed the blatantly racist movie *Birth of a Nation*, others doubted that he believed in justice for the African American people. "Have you a 'new freedom' for white Americans and a new slavery for your African-American fellow citizens?" Boston journalist William Monroe Trotter asked.

Timeline

1901	McKinley assassinated; Theodore Roosevelt becomes president
	Robert La Follette elected governor of Wisconsin
	Tom Johnson elected mayor of Cleveland
	Model tenement house bill passed in New York
	U.S. Steel formed
1902	Anthracite coal strike
1903	Women's Trade Union League founded
	Elkins Act
1904	Roosevelt reelected
	Lincoln Steffens writes *The Shame of the Cities*
1905	Frederic C. Howe writes *The City: The Hope of Democracy*
	Industrial Workers of the World (IWW) formed
1906	Upton Sinclair writes *The Jungle*
	Hepburn Act
	Meat Inspection Act
	Pure Food and Drug Act
1907	Financial panic
1908	*Muller* v. *Oregon*
	Danbury Hatters case (*Loewe* v. *Lawler*)
	William Howard Taft elected president
1909	National Association for the Advancement of Colored People (NAACP) founded
1910	Ballinger–Pinchot controversy
	Mann Act
1911	Frederick Taylor writes *The Principles of Scientific Management*
	Triangle Shirtwaist Company fire
1912	Progressive party founded by Theodore Roosevelt
	Woodrow Wilson elected president
	Children's Bureau established
	Industrial Relations Commission founded
1913	Sixteenth Amendment (income tax) ratified
	Underwood Tariff
	Federal Reserve System established
	Seventeenth Amendment (direct election of senators) passed
1914	Clayton Act
	Federal Trade Commission Act
	AFL has more than 2 million members
	Ludlow Massacre in Colorado

Moving Closer to a New Nationalism

How to control the great corporations in America was a question Wilson and Roosevelt had debated extensively during the 1912 campaign. Wilson's solution was the Clayton Act, submitted to Congress in 1914. The bill prohibited a number of unfair trading practices, outlawed the interlocking directorate, and made it illegal for corporations to purchase stock in other corporations if doing so tended to reduce competition. But the law was vague and hard to enforce, and the courts interpreted it to mean that labor unions remained subject to court injunctions during strikes.

More important than the Clayton Act was the creation of the Federal Trade Commission (FTC). Powerful enough to move directly against corporations accused of restricting competition, the FTC was the idea of Louis Brandeis. Wilson accepted it even though it seemed closer to the philosophy of New Nationalism than to Wilson's New Freedom.

The Federal Trade Commission and the Clayton Act did not end monopoly, and the courts in the next two decades did not increase the government's power to regulate business. The success of Wilson's reform agenda appeared minimal in 1914, but the outbreak of war in Europe and the need to win the election of 1916 would influence him in becoming more progressive in the next years (see Chapter 22).

Neither Wilson nor Roosevelt satisfied the demands of the advanced progressives. These two progressive presidents spent most of their efforts on trying to regulate economic power rather than promoting social justice. Yet the most important legacy of these two powerful politicians was their attempts to strengthen the office of president and the executive branch of the federal government. The nineteenth-century American presidents after Lincoln had been relatively weak, and much of the federal power had resided with Congress. The progressive presidents reasserted presidential authority, modernized the executive branch, and began the creation of the federal bureaucracy, which has had a major impact on the lives of Americans.

Both Wilson and Roosevelt used the presidency as a bully pulpit to make pronouncements, create news, and influence policy. Roosevelt strengthened the Interstate Commerce Commission and Wilson created the Federal Trade Commission, both of which were the forerunners of many other federal regulatory bodies. By breaking precedent and delivering his annual message in person before a joint session of Congress, Wilson symbolized the new power of the presidency.

The nature of politics was changed by more than just the increased power of the executive branch. The new bureaus, committees, and commissions brought to Washington a new kind of expert, trained in the universities, at the state and local level, and in voluntary organizations. Julia Lathrop, a coworker of Jane Addams at Hull House, was one such expert. Appointed by President Taft in 1912 to become chief of the newly created Children's Bureau, she was the first woman ever appointed to such a position. She used her post not only to work for better child labor laws but also to train a new generation of women experts who would take their positions in state, federal, and private agencies in the 1920s and 1930s. Other experts emerged in Washington during the progressive era to influence policy in subtle and important ways. The expert, the commission, the statistical survey, and the increased power of the executive branch were all legacies of the progressive era.

Conclusion
THE LIMITS OF PROGRESSIVISM

The progressive era was a time when many Americans set out to promote reform because they saw poverty, despair, and disorder in a country transformed by immigration, urbanism, and industrialism. But unlike the socialists, the progressives saw nothing fundamentally wrong with the American system. Progressivism, part of a global movement to regulate and control rampaging industrialism, was largely a middle-class effort that sought to help the poor, the immigrants, and the working class. Yet the poor were rarely consulted about policy, and many groups, especially African Americans, were almost entirely left out of reform plans. Progressives had an optimistic view of human nature and an exaggerated faith in statistics, commissions, and committees. They talked of the need for more democracy, but they often succeeded in promoting bureaucracy and a government run by experts. They saw a need to regulate business, promote efficiency, and spread social justice, but these were often contradictory goals. In the end, their regulatory laws tended to aid business and strengthen corporate capitalism, while social justice and equal opportunity remained difficult to achieve. By contrast, most of the industrialized nations of western Europe, especially Germany, Denmark, and Great Britain, passed legislation during this period providing for old-age pensions and health and unemployment insurance.

Progressivism was a broad, diverse, and sometimes contradictory movement that had its roots in the 1890s and reached its height in the early twentieth century. It began with many local movements and voluntary efforts to deal with the problems created by urban industrialism and then moved to the state and finally the national level, where it enlisted government to regulate the private sector and to promote reform. Women played important roles in organizing reform, and many became experts at gathering statistics and writing reports. Eventually, they began to fill positions in the new agencies in the state capitals and in Washington. Frances Kellor was one of those professional women who devoted her life to reform and to helping immigrants. Neither Theodore Roosevelt nor Woodrow Wilson was an advanced progressive, but during both their administrations, progressivism achieved some success. Both presidents strengthened the power of the presidency, and both promoted the idea that the federal government had the responsibility to regulate and control and to promote social justice. Progressivism would be altered by World War I, but it survived, with its strengths and weaknesses, to affect American society through most of the twentieth century.

QUESTIONS FOR REVIEW AND REFLECTION

1. What contributions did women make to the progressive movement?
2. Why did the United States lag behind several European countries, Australia, New Zealand, and Brazil in passing social legislation?
3. Was Prohibition a progressive measure?
4. How did progressivism differ from socialism?
5. What was the long-range legacy of the progressive movement?

CHAPTER 22

The Great War

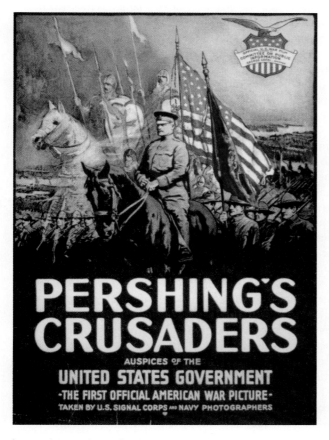

Pershing's Crusaders

This official 1917 U.S. government publication compares American soldiers to medieval knights. It makes explicit the American belief that by entering World War I they were joining not only a war but also a crusade to make the world safe for democracy. They were not just supporting the Allied cause, but they had a special mission to rescue the old world and to spread the American way of life. How do you suppose Europeans reacted to this American sense of mission and superiority?

(Library of Congress, LC-USZC4–1539)

American Stories

A Young Man Enlists in the Great Adventure

On April 7, 1917, the day after the United States officially declared war on Germany, Edmund P. Arpin, Jr., a young man of 22 from Grand Rapids, Wisconsin, decided to enlist in the army. The war seemed to provide a solution for his aimless drifting. It was not patriotism that led him to join the army but his craving for adventure and excitement. A month later, he was at Fort Sheridan, Illinois, along with hundreds of other eager young men, preparing to become an army officer. He felt a certain pride and sense of purpose, and especially a feeling of comradeship with the other men, but the war was a long way off.

Arpin finally arrived with his unit in Liverpool on December 23, 1917, aboard the *Leviathan,* a German luxury liner that the United States had interned when war was declared and then pressed into service as a troop transport. In England, he discovered that American troops were not greeted as saviors. Hostility against the Americans simmered partly because of the previous unit's drunken brawls. Despite the efforts of the U.S. government to protect its soldiers from the sins of Europe, drinking seems to have been a preoccupation of the soldiers in Arpin's outfit. Arpin also learned something about French wine and women, but he spent most of the endless waiting time learning to play contract bridge.

Arpin saw some of the horror of war when he went to the front with a French regiment as an observer, but his own unit did not engage in combat until October 1918, when the war was almost over. He took part in the bloody Meuse-Argonne offensive, which helped end the war. But he discovered that war was not the heroic struggle of carefully planned campaigns that newspapers and books described. War was filled with misfired weapons, mix-ups, and erroneous attacks. Wounded in the leg in an assault on an unnamed hill and awarded a Distinguished Service Cross for his bravery, Arpin later learned that the order to attack had been recalled, but word had not reached him in time.

When the armistice came, Arpin was recovering in a field hospital. He was disappointed that the war had ended so soon, but he was well enough to go to Paris to take part in the victory celebration and to explore some of the famous Paris restaurants and nightclubs. In many ways, the highlight of his war experiences was not a battle or his medal but his adventure after the war was over. With a friend, he went absent without leave and set out to explore Germany. They avoided the military police, traveled on a train illegally, and had many narrow escapes, but they made it back to the hospital without being arrested.

Edmund Arpin was in the army for two years. He was one of 4,791,172 Americans who served in the army, navy, and marines. He was one of the 2 million who went overseas and one of the 230,074 who were wounded. Some of his friends were among the 48,909 who were killed. When he was mustered out of the army in March 1919, he felt lost and confused. Being a civilian was not nearly as exciting as being in the army and visiting new and exotic places.

In time, Arpin settled down. He became a successful businessman, married, and raised a family. A member of the American Legion, he periodically went to conventions and reminisced with men from his division about their escapades in France. Although the war changed their lives in many ways, most would never again feel the same sense of common purpose and adventure. "I don't suppose any of us felt, before or since, so necessary to God and man," one veteran recalled.

For Edmund P. Arpin, Jr., the Great War was the most important event of a lifetime. Just as war changed his life, so, too, did it alter the lives of most Americans. Trends begun during the progressive era accelerated. The power and influence of the federal government increased. Not only did the war promote woman suffrage, prohibition, and public housing, but it also helped create an administrative bureaucracy that blurred the lines between public and private, between government and business—a trend that continued into the twenty-first century.

In this chapter, we examine the complicated circumstances that led the United States into the war and share the wartime experiences of American men and women overseas and at home. We will study not only military actions but also the impact of the war on domestic policies and on the lives of ordinary Americans, including the migration of African Americans into northern cities. The war cut off immigration from Europe and led to a policy of immigrant restriction in the next decade. The war left a legacy of prejudice and hate and raised the basic question, could the tenets of American democracy, such as freedom of speech, survive participation in a major war? The chapter concludes with a look at idealistic efforts to promote peace at the end of the war and the disillusion that followed. Woodrow Wilson's foreign policy, which sought to make the world safe for democracy, marked a watershed in the relationship of the United States to the world. The Great War was global war in every sense, and it thrust the United States into the role of world leadership as an interventionist savior of democratic values. Many Americans were reluctant to accept that role. But whether they liked it or not, the world was a different place in 1919 than it had been in 1914, and that would have a profound influence on American lives.

The Early War Years

Few Americans expected the Great War that erupted in Europe in the summer of 1914 to affect their lives or alter their comfortable world. When a Serbian student terrorist assassinated Archduke Franz Ferdinand of Austria-Hungary in Sarajevo, the capital of the province of Bosnia, a place most Americans had never heard of, the act precipitated a series of events leading to the most destructive war the world had ever known.

The Causes of War

The Great War, as everyone called it at the time, seemed to begin accidentally, but its root causes reached back many years and involved intense rivalry over trade, empire, and military strength. The Great War, which would cost at least 10 million lives and profoundly influence every aspect of culture and society, did not seem inevitable in 1914. There had been wars throughout the nineteenth century, including the Boer War, the Franco-Prussian War, and the American Civil War, but these wars, though bloody, were mostly local. There had not been a major global conflict since the end of the Napoleonic Wars in 1815. In fact, there were many signs of international cooperation, with agreements on telegraphs in 1865, postage in 1875, and copyright in 1880. Most nations had even agreed on international time zones by the 1890s. An international conference at The Hague in the Netherlands in 1899 had set up a World Court to

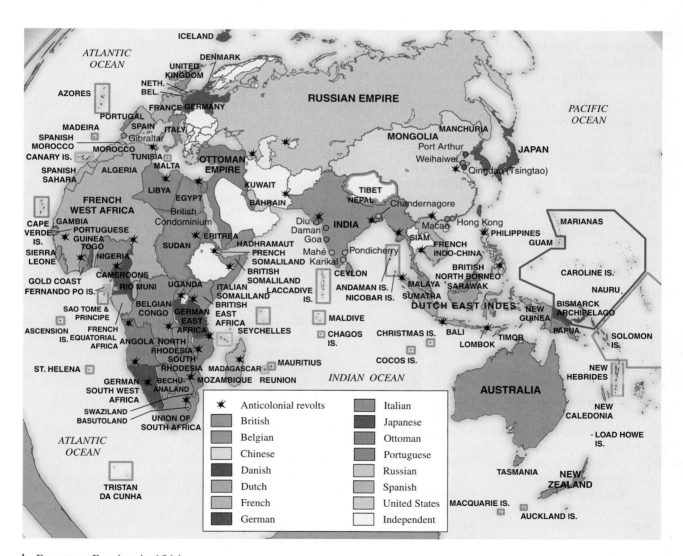

European Empires in 1914

In 1914, European countries had colonies or "spheres of influence" in all parts of the world. Although the United States got into the imperialism game late, it also had an empire and an interest in global trade. European imperialism and competition over trade was very much a factor in the origins of World War I. The war would alter the economic and political map of the world. Which European nations were most powerful in Asia and Africa in 1914? How has this map changed today?

settle disputes before they led to war. Peace advocates and politicians alike promoted disarmament conferences and predicted that better technology and improved communication would lead to permanent peace. "It looks as though we are going to be the age of treaties rather than the age of wars, the century of reason rather than the century of force," a leader of the American peace movement announced.

However, the same forces of improved technology and communication that seemed to bring nations closer together also helped create a rising tide of nationalism—a pride in being French or English or German. In Europe, nations competed over trade, colonies, and spheres of influence in Africa and Asia. Theodore Roosevelt tried to arbitrate differences among Germany, France, and Great Britain over trade at a conference in Morocco in 1905 and 1906, but tension and disagreements remained. At the same time, Austria and Russia clashed over territory and influence in the Balkans, where there was a rising sense of Slavic nationalism. Modern Germany, created from a number of small states in 1871, emerged as a powerful industrial giant. About 1900, Germany began to build a navy large enough to compete with the British fleet, the most powerful in the world. Great Britain, in turn, built even more battleships. As European nations armed, they drew up a complex series of treaties. Austria-Hungary and Germany (the Central Powers) became military allies, and Britain, France, and Russia (the Allied Powers) agreed to assist one another in case of attack. Despite peace conferences and international agreements, many promoted by the United States, the European balance of power rested precariously on layers of treaties that barely obscured years of jealousy and distrust.

The incident in Sarajevo destroyed that balance. The leaders of Austria-Hungary were determined to punish Serbia for the assassination. Russia mobilized to aid Serbia. Germany, supporting Austria-Hungary, declared war on Russia and France. Britain hesitated, but when Germany invaded Belgium to attack France, Britain declared war on Germany. Within a few months, the Ottoman Empire (Turkey) and Bulgaria joined the Central Powers. Italy joined the Allies after being secretly promised additional territory after the war. Japan declared war on Germany not because of an interest in the European struggle but in order to acquire German rights in China's Shantung province and a number of Pacific Islands. Spain, Switzerland, the Netherlands, Denmark, Norway, Sweden, and initially the United States, remained neutral. In August 1914, as Europe rushed toward war, British foreign secretary Sir Edward Grey remarked: "The lamps are going out all over Europe. We shall not see them lit again in our lifetime." His prediction proved to be deadly accurate.

When news of the German invasion of Belgium and reports of the first bloody battles began to reach the United States in late summer, most Americans believed that madness had replaced reason. Europeans "have reverted to the condition of savage tribes roaming the forests and falling upon each other in a fury of blood and carnage," the *New York Times* announced. Woodrow Wilson's official proclamation of neutrality on August 4, 1914, reinforced the belief that the United States had no major stake in the outcome of the war. The president was preoccupied with his own personal tragedy. His wife, Ellen Axson Wilson, died of Bright's disease the day after his proclamation. Two weeks later, still engulfed by grief, he urged all Americans to "be neutral in fact as well as in name,…impartial in thought as well as in action." The United States, he argued, must preserve itself "fit and free" to do what "is honest and disinterested…for the peace of the world." But remaining uninvolved, at least emotionally, was going to be difficult.

American Reactions

Although many Americans worked to promote world peace and a few sought to end the war through mediation, others could hardly wait to take part in the great adventure. Hundreds of young American men, most of them students or recent college graduates, volunteered to join ambulance units in order to take part in the war effort without actually fighting. Among these men were Ernest Hemingway, John Dos Passos, and E. E. Cummings, who later turned their wartime adventures into literary masterpieces. Others volunteered for service with the French Foreign Legion or joined the Lafayette Escadrille, a unit of pilots made up of well-to-do American volunteers attached to the French army. Many of these young men were inspired by an older generation who pictured war as a romantic and manly adventure. One college president talked of the chastening and purifying effect of armed conflict, and Theodore Roosevelt projected an image of war that was something like a football game in which red-blooded American men could test their idealism and manhood.

Many Americans visualized war as a romantic struggle for honor and glory because the only conflict they remembered was the "splendid little war" of 1898. For them, war meant Theodore Roosevelt leading the charge in Cuba and Commodore Dewey destroying the Spanish fleet in Manila harbor with no loss of American life. Many older Americans recalled the Civil War, but the horrors of those years had faded, leaving only the memory of heroic triumphs. As Oliver Wendell Holmes, the Supreme Court justice who had been wounded in the Civil War, remarked, "War, when you are at it, is horrible and dull. It is only when time has passed that you see that its message was divine."

Early reports from the battlefields should have indicated that the message was anything but divine. This would be a modern war in which men died by the thousands, cut down by an improved and efficient technology of killing.

The New Military Technology

Military planners had not anticipated the stalemate that quickly developed. The German Schlieffen plan called for a rapid strike through Belgium to attack Paris and the French army from the rear. However, the French stopped the German advance at the Battle of the Marne in September 1914, and the fighting soon bogged down in a costly and bloody routine. Soldiers on both sides dug miles of trenches and strung out barbed wire. Hundreds of thousands died in battles that gained only a few yards or nothing at all. Rapid-firing rifles, improved explosives, incendiary shells, and tracer bullets all added to the destruction. Most devastating of all, however, was the improved artillery that could fire over the horizon and hit targets many miles behind the lines. Machine guns neutralized frontal assaults, but generals on both sides continued to order their men to charge to almost certain deaths.

The war was both a traditional and a revolutionary struggle. It was the last war in which cavalry was used and the first to employ a new generation of military technologies. By 1918, airplanes, initially used only for observation, were dropping bombs and creating terror below. Tanks first appeared in 1916, but only in the last days of the war did this new offensive weapon begin to neutralize the machine gun. In the spring of 1915, the Germans introduced a terrible new weapon—poison gas. Chlorine gas blinded its victims, caused acid burns on the skin, and consumed the lungs. Gas masks provided some protection but were never entirely effective. Poison gas attacks, used by both sides after 1915, were one of the most terrifying aspects of trench warfare.

For most Americans, the western front, which stretched from Belgium through France, was the most important battleground of the war. But along the eastern front, Russian troops engaged German and Austrian armies in bitter fighting. After Italy joined the conflict in 1915, a third front developed along the northern Italian and Austrian border, while submarines and battleships carried the fight around the world.

The Great War was truly a global struggle. Soldiers from the British Empire, New Zealand, Australia, Canada, and India fought on the western front alongside French-speaking black Africans. The British and the French battled in Africa to capture Germany's African colonies, and the struggle continued until 1918, especially in East Africa. The British, who initially thought they were only going to support the French on the western front, found themselves in the Middle East, in Mesopotamia (Iraq), and fighting Turks in the Dardanelles between the Aegean and the Black Sea. In one of the great disasters of the war, the British attacked Gallipoli, first with battleships and then with hundreds of thousands of men. After losing one-third of their fleet and more than a quarter of a million men, many of them Australians and New Zealanders, the British withdrew. Reports of carnage, on and off the battlefield, poured in. In one of the worst acts of genocide in the world's history, the Turks systematically massacred an estimated 800,000 Armenians. Yet the United States and European countries stood by and did nothing.

Some Americans could hardly wait to join the fighting. Theodore Roosevelt and his friend Leonard Wood, the army chief of staff, led a movement to prepare American men for war. In 1913, Wood established a camp for college men at Plattsburgh, New York, to give them some experience with military life, order, discipline, and command. The young men learned to shoot rifles and to endure long marches and field exercises. Gathered around the campfire at night, they heard veterans tell of winning glory and honor on the battlefield. In their minds at least, they were already leading a bayonet charge against Germany.

Difficulties of Neutrality

Not all Americans were so eager to enter the fray, but many sympathized with one side or the other. Some Americans favored the Central Powers. About 8 million Austrian Americans and German Americans lived in the United States. Some supported their homeland. They viewed Kaiser Wilhelm II's Germany as a progressive parliamentary democracy. The anti-British sentiment of some Irish Americans led them to take sides not so much for Germany as against England. A number of American scholars, physicians, and intellectuals fondly remembered studying in Germany, and they admired its culture and progressive social planning. After all, did not the English-speaking people of the world have special bonds and special responsibilities to promote civilization and ensure justice in the world? American connections with the French were not so close, but they were sentimental. The French, everyone remembered, had supported the American Revolution, and the French people had given the United States the Statue of Liberty, the very symbol of American opportunity and democracy.

Other reasons made real neutrality nearly impossible. U.S. trade with the Allies was much more important than with the Central Powers. Wilson's advisers openly supported the French and the British. Most newspaper owners and editors had close ethnic, cultural, and sometimes economic ties to the British and the French. The newspapers were quick to picture the

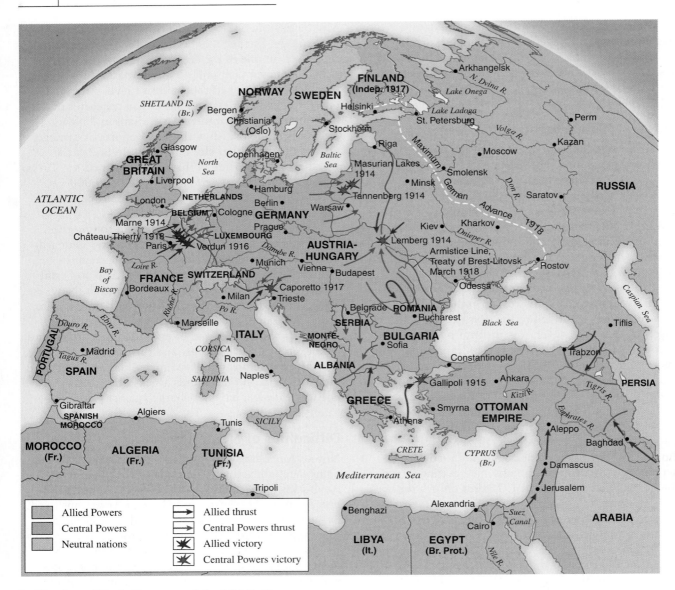

The Great War in Europe and the Middle East
The Great War had an impact not only on Europe but also on North Africa and the Middle East. Even the countries that remained neutral felt the influence of global war. For most Americans, the war was in France on the western front. Where else were major battles fought?

Germans as barbaric Huns and to accept and embellish atrocity stories from the front, some of them planted by British propaganda experts. Gradually for Wilson, and probably for most Americans, the perception that England and France were fighting to preserve civilization from the forces of Prussian evil replaced the idea that all Europeans were barbaric and decadent. But the American people were not yet willing to go to war to save civilization. Let France and England do that.

Woodrow Wilson also sympathized with the Allies for practical and idealistic reasons. He wanted to keep the United States out of the war, but he did not object to using force to promote diplomatic ends. He believed that by keeping the United States out of the war, he might control the peace. The war, he hoped, would show the futility of imperialism and would usher in a world of free trade in products and ideas. Remaining neutral while maintaining trade with the belligerents became increasingly difficult. Remaining neutral while speaking out about the peace eventually became impossible. The need to trade and the desire to control the peace finally led the United States into the Great War.

World Trade and Neutrality Rights

The United States was part of an international economic community in 1914 and the outbreak of war caused an immediate economic panic. On July 31, 1914, the

Wilson administration closed the stock exchange to prevent the unloading of European securities and panic selling. It also adopted a policy discouraging loans by American banks to belligerent nations. Most difficult was the matter of neutral trade. Wilson insisted on the rights of Americans to trade with both the Allies and the Central Powers, but Great Britain instituted an illegal naval blockade, mined the North Sea, and began seizing American ships, even those carrying food and raw materials to Italy, the Netherlands, and other neutral nations. The first crisis that Wilson faced was whether to accept the illicit British blockade. To do so would be to surrender one of the rights he supported most ardently, the right of free trade.

Wilson eventually accepted British control of the sea. His conviction that the destinies of the United States and Great Britain were intertwined outweighed his idealistic belief in free trade and caused him to react more harshly to German violations of international law than he did to British violators. Consequently, American trade with the Central Powers declined between 1914 and 1916 from $169 million to just over $1 million, whereas trade with the Allies increased during the same period from $825 million to more than $3 billion. At the same time, the U.S. government eased restrictions on private loans to belligerents. With dollars as well as sentiments, the United States gradually ceased to be neutral.

Germany retaliated against British control of the seas with submarine warfare, using its new weapon, the U-boat (Unterseeboot). International law required a belligerent warship to warn a passenger or merchant ship before attacking, but a U-boat rising to the surface to issue a warning would have meant being blown out of the water by an armed merchant ship. On February 4, 1915, Germany announced a submarine blockade of the British Isles. Until Britain gave up its campaign to starve the German population, the Germans would sink even neutral ships. Wilson warned Germany that it would be held to "strict accountability" for illegal destruction of American ships or lives.

In March 1915, a German U-boat sank a British liner en route to Africa, killing 103 people, including one American. How should the United States respond? Wilson's advisers could not agree. Robert Lansing, a legal counsel at the State Department, urged the president to issue a strong protest, charging a breach of international law. William Jennings Bryan, the secretary of state, argued that an American traveling on a British ship was guilty of "contributory negligence" and urged Wilson to prohibit Americans from traveling on belligerent ships in the war zone. Wilson never did settle the dispute, for on May 7, 1915, a greater crisis erupted. A German U-boat torpedoed the British luxury liner *Lusitania* off the Irish coast. The liner, which was not armed but was carrying war supplies,

sank in 18 minutes. Nearly 1,200 people, including many women and children, drowned. Among the dead were 128 Americans. Suddenly Americans confronted the horror of total war fought with modern weapons, a war that killed civilians, including women and children, just as easily as it killed soldiers.

Wilson and most Americans had no idea of going to war in the spring of 1915, but the president refused to take Bryan's advice and prevent further loss of American lives by simply prohibiting all Americans from traveling on belligerent ships. Instead, he sent a series of protest notes demanding reparation for the loss of American lives and a pledge from Germany that it would cease attacking ocean liners without warning.

Bryan resigned as secretary of state over the tone of the notes and charged that the United States was not being truly neutral. The president replaced Bryan with Robert Lansing, who was much more eager than Bryan to oppose Germany, even at the risk of war.

The tense situation eased late in 1915. After a German U-boat sank the British steamer *Arabic*, which claimed two American lives, the German ambassador promised that Germany would not attack ocean liners without warning (the *Arabic* pledge). The *Lusitania* crisis caused an outpouring of books and articles urging the nation to prepare for war. However, a group of progressive reformers also formed the American Union Against Militarism. They feared that those urging preparedness were deliberately setting out to destroy social reform at home and to promote imperialism abroad.

Wilson sympathized with the preparedness groups to the extent of asking Congress on November 4, 1915, for an enlarged and reorganized army. The bill met with great opposition, especially from southern and western congressmen, but the Army Reorganization Bill that Wilson signed in June 1916 increased the regular army to just over 200,000 and integrated the National Guard into the defense structure. Few Americans expected those young men to go to war. Even before American soldiers arrived in France, however, Wilson used the army and the marines in Mexico and Central America.

Intervening in Mexico and Central America

Wilson envisioned a world purged of imperialism, a world of free trade, but a world where American ideas and products would find their way. Combining the zeal of a Christian missionary with the conviction of a college professor, he spoke of "releasing the intelligence of America for the service of mankind." Although Wilson denounced the "big stick" and "dollar diplomacy" of the Roosevelt and Taft years, Wilson's administration used force more systematically than did his predecessors. The rhetoric was different, yet just as much as Roosevelt, Wilson tried to maintain stability in countries to the south in order to promote American economic and strategic interests.

At first, Wilson's foreign policy seemed to reverse some of the most callous aspects of dollar diplomacy in Central America. Secretary of State Bryan signed a treaty with Colombia in 1913 in which the United States agreed to pay $5 million for the loss of Panama and virtually apologized for the Roosevelt administration's treatment of Colombia. The Senate, not so willing to admit that the United States had been wrong, refused to ratify the treaty.

The change in spirit proved illusory. After a disastrous civil war in the Dominican Republic, the United States offered in 1915 to take over the country's finances and police force. When the Dominican leaders rejected a treaty making their country virtually a protectorate of the United States, Wilson ordered in the marines. They took control of the government in May 1916. Although Americans built roads, schools, and hospitals, people resented their presence. The United States intervened in Haiti with similar results. In Nicaragua, the Wilson administration kept the marines sent by Taft in 1912 to prop up a pro-American regime and acquired the right, through treaty, to intervene at any time to preserve order and protect American property. Except for a brief period in the mid-1920s, the marines remained until 1933.

Wilson's policy of intervention ran into greatest difficulty in Mexico, a country that had been ruled by dictator Porfirio Díaz, who had long welcomed American investors. By 1910, more than 40,000 American citizens lived in Mexico, and more than $1 billion of American money was invested there. In 1911, however, Francisco Madero, a reformer who wanted to destroy the privileges of the upper classes, overthrew Díaz. Two years later, Madero was deposed and murdered by order of Victoriano Huerta, the head of the army.

Wilson refused to recognize the Huerta government. Everyone admitted that Huerta was a ruthless dictator, but diplomatic recognition, the exchange of ambassadors, and the regulation of trade and communication had never meant approval. In the world of business and diplomacy, it merely meant that a particular government was in power. But Wilson set out to remove what he called a "government of butchers."

At first, Wilson applied diplomatic pressure. Then, using a minor incident as an excuse, he asked Congress for power to involve American troops if necessary. Few Mexicans liked Huerta, but they liked the idea of North American interference even less, and they rallied around the dictator. The United States landed troops at Veracruz, Mexico. Wilson's action outraged many Europeans and Latin Americans as well as Americans.

Wilson's military intervention drove Huerta out of office, but a civil war between forces led by Venustiano Carranza and those led by General Francisco "Pancho" Villa ensued. The United States sent arms to Carranza, who was considered less radical than Villa, and Carranza's soldiers defeated Villa's. When an angry Villa led what was left of his army in a raid on Columbus, New Mexico, in March 1916, Wilson sent an expedition commanded by Brigadier General John Pershing to track down Villa and his men. The strange and comic scene developed of an American army charging 300 miles into Mexico unable to catch the retreating villain. The Mexicans feared that Pershing's army was planning to occupy northern Mexico. Carranza shot off a bitter note to Wilson, accusing him of threatening war, but Wilson refused to withdraw the troops. Tensions rose. An American patrol attacked a Mexican garrison, with loss of life on both sides. In January 1917, just as war seemed inevitable, Wilson agreed to recall the troops and to recognize the Carranza government. Had it not been for the growing crisis in Europe, it is likely that war with Mexico would have resulted.

The United States Enters the War

A significant minority of Americans opposed joining the European war in 1917, and that decision would remain controversial when it was reexamined in the 1930s. But once involved, the government and the American people made the war into a patriotic crusade that influenced all aspects of American life.

The Election of 1916

American political campaigns do not stop even in times of international crisis. As 1915 turned to 1916, Wilson had to think of reelection as well as of preparedness, submarine warfare, and the Mexican campaign. At first glance, the president's chances of reelection seemed poor. If supporters of the Progressives in 1912 returned to the Republican fold, Wilson's chances were slim indeed. Because the Progressive party had done very badly in the 1914 congressional elections, Roosevelt seemed ready to seek the Republican nomination.

Wilson was aware that he had to win over voters who had favored Roosevelt in 1912. In January 1916, he appointed Louis D. Brandeis to the Supreme Court. The first Jew ever to sit on the Court, Brandeis was confirmed over the strong opposition of many legal organizations. His appointment pleased the social justice progressives because he had always championed reform causes. They made it clear to Wilson that the real test for them was whether he supported the anti–child labor and workers' compensation bills pending in Congress.

Within a few months, Wilson reversed his earlier New Freedom doctrines, which called for limited government, and aligned the federal government on the side of reform. In August 1916, Wilson pushed through Congress the Worker's Compensation Bill, which gave some protection to federal employees, and the Keatings–Owen Child Labor Bill, which barred from interstate commerce goods produced by children under age 14 and in some cases under 16. This bill, later declared unconstitutional, was a far-reaching proposal that for the first time used federal control over interstate commerce to dictate the conditions under which businesspeople could manufacture products.

To attract farm support, Wilson pushed for passage of the Federal Farm Loan Act, which created 12 Federal Farm Loan banks to extend long-term credit to farmers. Urged on by organized labor as well as by many progressives, he supported the Adamson Act, which established an eight-hour workday for all interstate railway workers. The flurry of legislation early in 1916 provided one triumph for the progressive movement. The strategy seemed to work, for progressives of all kinds enthusiastically endorsed the president.

The election of 1916, however, turned as much on foreign affairs as on domestic policy. The Republicans ignored Theodore Roosevelt and nominated instead the staid and respectable Charles Evans Hughes, a former governor of New York and future Supreme Court justice. Their platform called for "straight and honest neutrality" and "adequate preparedness." In a bitter campaign, Hughes attacked Wilson for not promoting American rights in Mexico more vigorously and for giving in to the unreasonable demands of labor. Wilson implied that electing Hughes would guarantee war with Mexico and Germany and that his opponents were somehow not "100 percent Americans." As the campaign progressed, the peace issue became more and more important, and the cry "He kept us out of war" echoed through every Democratic rally. The slogan would soon seem strangely ironic.

The election was extremely close. In fact, Wilson went to bed on election night thinking he had lost the presidency. The election was not finally decided until the Democrats carried California (by fewer than 4,000 votes). Wilson won by carrying the West as well as the South.

Deciding for War

Wilson's victory in 1916 seemed to be a mandate for staying out of the European war. Those who supported Wilson as a peace candidate applauded in January 1917 when he went before the Senate to clarify the American position on a negotiated settlement of the war. The German government had earlier indicated that it might be willing to go to the conference table.

Wilson outlined a plan for a negotiated peace without indemnities and annexations. The agreement Wilson outlined contained his idealistic vision of the postwar world as an open marketplace, and it could have worked only if Germany and the Allies were willing to settle for a draw. But neither side was interested in such a conclusion after years of bitter and costly conflict.

The German government refused to accept a peace without victory, probably because early in 1917, the German leaders thought they could win. On January 31, 1917, the Germans announced that they would sink on sight any ship, belligerent or neutral, sailing toward England or France. A few days later, in retaliation, the United States broke diplomatic relations with Germany. An intercepted telegram from the German foreign secretary, Arthur Zimmermann, to the German minister in Mexico increased anti-German feeling. If war broke out, the German minister was to offer Mexico the territory it had lost in Texas, New Mexico, and Arizona in 1848. In return, Mexico would join Germany in a war against the United States. When the Zimmermann note was released to the press on March 1, 1917, many Americans demanded war against Germany. Wilson still hesitated.

As the country waited on the brink of war, news of revolution in Russia reached Washington. That event proved as important as the war itself. The March 1917 revolution in Russia was a spontaneous uprising of workers, housewives, and soldiers against the government of Czar Nicholas II and its conduct of the war. The army had suffered staggering losses at the front. The civilian population was in desperate condition. Food was scarce, and the railroads and industry had nearly collapsed. At first, Wilson and other Americans were enthusiastic about the new republic led by Alexander Kerensky, which promised to continue the struggle against Germany. But on November 6, 1917, the revolution took a more extreme turn. Vladimir Ilyich Ulyanov, known as Lenin, returned from exile in Switzerland and led the radical Bolsheviks to victory over the Kerensky regime. He immediately signed an armistice with Germany that released thousands of German troops, who had been fighting the Russians, to join the battle against the Allies on the western front.

Lenin, a brilliant lawyer and revolutionary tactician, was a follower of Karl Marx (1818–1883). Marx was a German intellectual and radical philosopher who had described the alienation of the working class under capitalism and predicted a growing split between the proletariat (the unpropertied workers) and the capitalists. Lenin extended Marx's ideas and argued that capitalist nations eventually would be forced to go to war over raw materials and markets. Believing that capitalism and imperialism went hand in hand, Lenin argued that the only way to end imperialism was to end capitalism. Communism, Lenin predicted, would eventually dominate the globe, and the new Soviet Union, not the United States, would be the model for the rest of the world to follow. The Russian Revolution threatened Wilson's vision of the world and his plan to bring the United States into the war "to make the world safe for democracy."

More disturbing than the revolution in Russia, however, was the situation in the North Atlantic, where German U-boats sank five American ships between March 12 and March 21, 1917. Wilson no longer hesitated. On April 2, he urged Congress to declare war. His words conveyed a sense of mission about the country's entry into the war, but Wilson's voice was low and somber. "It is a fearful thing," he concluded, "to lead this great, peaceful people into war, into the most terrible and disastrous of all wars." The war resolution swept the Senate 82 to 6 and the House of Representatives 373 to 50.

Once war was declared, most Americans forgot their doubts. Young men rushed to enlist; women volunteered to become nurses or to serve in other ways. Towns were united by patriotism.

A Patriotic Crusade

Not all Americans applauded the declaration of war. Some pacifists and socialists and a few others opposed America's entry into the war. "To whom does war bring prosperity?" Senator George Norris of Nebraska asked on the Senate floor. "Not to the soldier,...not to the broken hearted widow,...not to the mother who weeps at the death of her brave boy....I feel that we are about to put the dollar sign on the American flag."

For most Americans in the spring of 1917, the war seemed remote. A few days after war was declared, a Senate committee listened to a member of the War Department staff list the vast quantities of materials needed to supply an American army in France. One of the senators, jolted awake, exclaimed, "Good Lord! You're not going to send soldiers over there, are you?"

To convince senators and citizens alike that the war was real and that American participation was just, Wilson appointed a Committee on Public Information, headed by George Creel, a muckraking journalist from Denver. The Creel Committee launched a gigantic propaganda campaign to persuade the American public that the United States had gone to war to promote the cause of freedom and democracy and to prevent the barbarous hordes from overrunning Europe and eventually the Western Hemisphere.

The patriotic crusade soon became stridently anti-German and anti-immigrant. Most school districts banned the teaching of German. Sauerkraut

was renamed "liberty cabbage," and German measles became "liberty measles." Many families Americanized their German surnames. Several cities banned music by German composers from symphony concerts. South Dakota prohibited the use of German on the telephone. Occasionally, the patriotic fever led to violence. The most notorious incident occurred in East St. Louis, Illinois, which had a large German population. A mob seized Robert Prager, a young German American, in April 1918, stripped off his clothes, dressed him in an American flag, marched him through the streets, and lynched him. The eventual trial acquitted the ringleaders on the ground that the lynching was a "patriotic murder."

The Wilson administration did not condone domestic violence and murder, but heated patriotism led to irrational hatreds and fears. Suspect were not only German Americans but also radicals, pacifists, and anyone who raised doubts about the American war efforts or the government's policies. The Los Angeles police ignored complaints that Mexicans were being harassed, because after learning of the Zimmermann telegram they believed that all Mexicans were pro-German. In Wisconsin, Senator Robert La Follette, who had voted against the war resolution, was burned in effigy and censured by the faculty of the University of Wisconsin. At a number of universities, professors were dismissed, some for as little as questioning the morality or the necessity of America's participation in the war.

On June 15, 1917, Congress, at Wilson's behest, passed the Espionage Act, which provided imprisonment of up to 20 years or a fine of up to $10,000, or both, for people who aided the enemy or who "willfully cause...insubordination, disloyalty, mutiny or refusal of duty in the military...forces of the United States." The act also authorized the postmaster general to prohibit from the mails any matter he thought advocated treason or forcible resistance to U.S. laws. The act was used to stamp out dissent, even to discipline anyone who questioned the administration's policies.

Congress later added the Trading with the Enemy Act and a Sedition Act. The latter prohibited disloyal, profane, scurrilous, and abusive remarks about the form of government, flag, or uniform of the United States. It even prohibited citizens from opposing the purchase of war bonds. For delivering a speech denouncing capitalism and the war, Socialist party leader Eugene Debs was convicted of violating the Sedition Act and sentenced to 10 years in prison. In 1919, the Supreme Court upheld the conviction, even though Debs had not explicitly urged violation of the draft laws. While still in prison, Debs polled close to 1 million votes in the presidential election of 1920.

Army Medical Examiner: "At last a perfect soldier!"

"At Last a Perfect Soldier"

This antiwar, antimilitary cartoon appeared in the American radical magazine *The Masses* in July 1916. *The Masses* was an irreverent journal that for a few years published important articles and illustrations by leading artists. It was shut down as subversive during the war by the U.S. government. How does this image contrast to the usual depiction of the soldier as hero? Do you agree with this image of the soldier today?

(*The Masses*, 8, July 1916, [back cover]/The Tamiment Institute Library, New York University)

Ultimately, the government prosecuted 2,168 people under the Espionage and Sedition Acts and convicted about half of them. These figures do not include thousands who were informally persecuted and deprived of their liberties and their right of free speech.

One woman was sentenced to prison for writing, "I am for the people and the government is for the profiteers." Ricardo Flores Magon, a leading Mexican American labor organizer and radical in the Southwest, was sentenced to 20 years in prison for criticizing Wilson's Mexican policy and violating the Neutrality Acts. The attorney general of the United States, speaking of critics, said, "May God have mercy on them for they need expect none from an outraged people and an avenging government."

The Civil Liberties Bureau, an outgrowth of the American Union Against Militarism, protested the blatant abridgment of freedom of speech during the war, but the protests fell on deaf ears at the Justice Department and in the White House. Rights and freedoms have been reduced or suspended during all wars, but the massive disregard for basic rights was greater during World War I than during the Civil War. This was ironic because Wilson had often written and spoken of the need to preserve freedom of speech and civil liberties. During the war, however, he tolerated the vigilante tactics of his own Justice Department, offering no more than feeble protest. Wilson was so convinced his cause was just that he ignored the rights of those who opposed him.

Raising an Army

Debate over a volunteer army versus the draft had been going on for several years before the United States entered the war. People who favored some form of universal military service argued that college graduates, farmers, and young men from the slums of eastern cities could learn from one another as they trained together. Opponents of a draft pointed out that people making such claims were most often the college graduates, who assumed they would command the boys from the slums. The draft was not democratic, they argued, but the tool of an imperialist power bent on ending dissent. Memories of massive draft riots during the Civil War also led some to fear a draft.

Wilson and his secretary of war, Newton Baker, both initially opposed the draft. In the end, both concluded that it was the most efficient way to organize military personnel. Ironically, it was Theodore Roosevelt who tipped Wilson in favor of the draft. Even though his health was failing and he was blind in one eye, the old Rough Rider was determined to recruit a volunteer division and lead it personally against the Germans. The thought of his old enemy Theodore Roosevelt blustering about Europe so frightened Wilson that he supported the Selective Service Act in part, at least, to prevent such volunteer outfits as Roosevelt planned. Congress argued over the bill, the House insisting that the minimum age for draftees should be 21, not 18. On June 5, 1917, some 9.5 million men between ages 21 and 31 registered, with little protest. In August 1918, Congress extended the act to men between ages 18 and 45. In all, more than 24 million men registered and more than 2.8 million were inducted, making up more than 75 percent of soldiers who served in the war.

The draft worked well, but it was not quite the perfect system that Wilson claimed. Draft protests erupted in a few places, the largest in Oklahoma, where a group of tenant farmers planned a march on Washington to take over the government and end the "rich man's war." But the Green Corn Rebellion, as it came to be called, died before it got started. A local posse arrested about 900 rebels and took them off to jail.

Some men escaped the draft. Some were deferred because of war-related jobs, and others resisted by claiming exemption for reasons of conscience. The Selective Service Act did exempt men who belonged to religious groups that forbade members from engaging in war, but religious motivation was often difficult to define, and nonreligious conscientious objection was even more complicated. Thousands of conscientious objectors were inducted. Some served in noncombat positions; others went to prison.

The Military Experience

Family albums in millions of American homes contain photographs of those who were drafted or volunteered: young men in uniform, some of them stiff and formal, some of them candid shots of soldiers on leave in Paris or Washington or Chicago. These photographs testify to the importance of the war to a generation of Americans. For some, the war was a tragic event, as they saw the horrors of the battlefield firsthand. For others, it was a liberating experience and the most exciting period of their lives.

The American Soldier

The typical soldier, according to the U.S. Medical Department, stood 5 feet 7½ inches tall, weighed 141½ pounds, and was 22 years old. He took a physical exam, an intelligence test, and a psychological test, and he probably watched a movie called *Fit to Fight,* which warned him about the dangers of venereal disease. The majority of American soldiers had not attended high school. The median level of education for native whites was 6.9 years, 4.7 years for immigrants, and just 2.6 years for southern blacks. As many as 31 percent of the recruits were declared illiterate, but the intelligence tests were so primitive that they probably tested social class more than anything else. Fully 29 percent of recruits were rejected as physically unfit for service, a finding that shocked health experts.

Most World War I soldiers were ill-educated and unsophisticated young men from farms, small towns, and urban neighborhoods. They came from all social classes and ethnic groups. The military experience changed the lives and often the attitudes of many young men and some women. Women contributed to the war effort as telephone operators and clerk typists in the navy and the marines. Some went overseas as army and navy nurses. Others volunteered with the Red Cross, the Salvation Army, or the YMCA. Yet the military experience in World War I was predominantly male. Even going to training camp was a new and often frightening experience. A leave in Paris or London, or even in New York or New Orleans, was an adventure to remember for a lifetime. Many soldiers saw their first movie in the army or had their first contact with trucks and cars. Military service changed the shaving habits of a generation because the new safety razor was standard issue. The war also led to the growing popularity of cigarettes rather than pipes or cigars because a pack of cigarettes fit into a shirt pocket and a cigarette could be smoked during a short break. The war experience also caused many men to abandon the pocket watch for the more convenient wristwatch, which had been considered effeminate before the war.

The Black Soldier

Blacks had served in all American wars, and many fought valiantly in the Civil War and the Spanish-American War. Yet black soldiers had most often performed menial work and belonged to segregated units. Most black leaders supported American participation in the war. W. E. B. Du Bois, editor of *The Crisis,* predicted that the war experience would cause the "walls of prejudice" to crumble gradually before the "onslaught of common sense." But the walls did not crumble, and the black soldier never received equal or fair treatment during the war.

The Selective Service Act made no mention of race, and African Americans in most cases registered without protest. Many whites, especially in the South, feared having too many blacks trained in the use of arms. In some areas, draft boards exempted single white men but drafted black fathers. Most southern whites found it difficult to imagine a black man in the uniform of the U.S. Army.

White attitudes toward African Americans sometimes led to conflict. In August 1917, violence erupted in Houston, Texas, involving soldiers from the regular army's all-black Twenty-Fourth Infantry Division. Harassed by the Jim Crow laws, which had been tightened for their benefit, a group of soldiers went on a rampage, killing 17 white civilians. More than 100 soldiers were court-martialed; 13 were condemned to death. Those convicted were hanged three days later before any appeals could be filed.

This violence, coming only a month after the race riot in East St. Louis, Illinois, brought on in part by the migration of southern blacks to the area, caused great concern about the handling of African American soldiers. Secretary of War Baker made it clear that the army had no intention of upsetting the status quo. The basic government policy was complete segregation and careful distribution of black units throughout the country.

African Americans were prohibited from joining the marines and restricted to menial jobs in the navy. Some African Americans were trained as junior

GOVERNMENT PROPAGANDA

All governments produce propaganda. Especially in time of war, governments try to convince their citizens that the cause is important and worthwhile even if it means sacrifice. Before the United States entered World War I, both Great Britain and Germany presented their side of the conflict through stories planted in newspapers, photographs, and other devices. Some historians argue that the British propaganda depicting the Germans as barbaric Huns who killed little boys and Catholic nuns played a large role in convincing Americans of the righteousness of the Allied cause.

When the United States entered the war, a special committee under the direction of George Creel did its best to persuade Americans that the war was a crusade against evil. The committee organized a national network of "four-minute men," local citizens with the proper political views who could be used to whip up a crowd into a patriotic frenzy. These local rallies, enlivened by bands and parades, urged people of all ages to support the war effort and buy war bonds. The Creel Committee also produced literature for the schools, much of it prepared by college professors who volunteered their services. One pamphlet, titled *Why America Fights Germany,* described in lurid detail a possible German invasion of the United States. The committee also used the new technology of motion pictures, which proved to be the most effective propaganda device of all.

There is a narrow line between education and propaganda. As early as 1910, Thomas Edison made films instructing the public about the dangers of tuberculosis, and others produced movies that demonstrated how to avoid everything from typhoid to tooth decay. However, during the war, the government quickly realized the power of the new medium and adopted it to train soldiers, instill patriotism, and help the troops avoid the temptations of alcohol and sex.

After the United States entered World War I, the Commission of Training Camp Activities made a film called *Fit to Fight* that was shown to almost all male servicemen. It was an hour-long drama following the careers of five young recruits. Four of them, by associating with the wrong people and through lack of willpower, caught venereal disease. The film interspersed a simplistic plot with grotesque shots of men with various kinds of venereal disease. The film also glorified athletics, especially football and boxing, as a substitute for sex. It emphasized the importance of patriotism and purity for America's fighting force. In one scene, Bill Hale, the only soldier in the film to remain pure, breaks up a peace rally and beats up the speaker. "It serves you right," the pacifist's sister remarks, "I'm glad Billy punched you."

Liberty Bond propaganda

(The Granger Collection, New York)

Fit to Fight was so successful that the government commissioned another film, *The End of the Road,* to be shown to women who lived near military bases. The film is the story of Vera and Mary. Although still reflecting progressive attitudes, the film's message is somewhat different from that of *Fit to Fight.* Vera's strict mother tells her daughter that sex is dirty, leaving Vera to pick up "distorted and obscene" information about sex on the street. She falls victim to the first man who comes along and contracts a venereal disease. Mary, in contrast, has an enlightened mother who explains where babies come from. When Mary grows up, she rejects marriage and becomes a professional woman, a nurse. In the end, she falls in love with a doctor and gets married. *The End of the Road* has a number of subplots and many frightening shots of syphilitic sores. Several illustrations show the dangers of indiscriminate sex. Among other things, the

Anti-VD poster issued by the U.S. Commission on Training Camp Activities

(Army Educational Commission)

Scene from *Fit to Fight*

(War Department, Commission on Training Camps)

film preached the importance of science and sex education and the need for self-control.

Reflecting on the Past What do the anti-VD films tell us about the attitudes, ideas, and prejudices of the World War I period? What images do they project about men, women, and gender roles? Would you find the same kind of moralism, patriotism, and fear of VD today? How have attitudes toward sex changed? Were you shown sex education films in school? Were they like these? Who sponsored them? What can historians learn from such films? Does the government produce propaganda today? ▪

officers in the army, but they were assigned to the all-black Ninety-Second Division, where the high-ranking officers were white. Most of the black soldiers, including about 80 percent of those sent to France, worked as stevedores and common laborers under the supervision of white, noncommissioned officers. "Everyone who has handled colored labor knows that the gang bosses must be white if any work is to be done," remarked Lieutenant Colonel U. S. Grant, the grandson of the Civil War general. Other black soldiers acted as servants, drivers, and porters for the white officers. It was a demeaning and ironic policy for a government that advertised itself as standing for justice, honor, and democracy.

Over There

The conflict that Wilson called the war "to make the world safe for democracy" had become a contest of stalemate and slaughter. To this ghastly war, Americans made important contributions. In fact, without their help, the Allies might have lost. But the American contribution was most significant only in the war's final months. When the United States entered the conflict in the spring of 1917, the fighting had dragged on for nearly three years. After a few rapid advances and retreats, the war in western Europe had settled down to a tactical and bloody stalemate. The human costs of trench warfare were horrifying. In one battle in 1916, a total of 60,000 British soldiers were killed or wounded

Entertaining Black Servicemen

Assigned to segregated units, black soldiers were also excluded from white recreation facilities. Here black women from Newark, New Jersey, aided by white social workers, entertain black servicemen. How do you think black men felt about fighting for freedom in a segregated army?

(National Archives)

in a single day, yet the battle lines did not move an inch. By the spring of 1917, the British and French armies were down to their last reserves. Italy's army had nearly collapsed. In the East, the Russians were engaged in a bitter internal struggle, and in November, the Bolshevik Revolution would cause them to sue for a separate peace, freeing the German divisions on the eastern front to join in one final assault in the West. The Allies desperately needed fresh American troops, but those troops had to be trained, equipped, and transported to the front. That took time.

A few token American regiments arrived in France in the summer of 1917 under the command of General John J. "Black Jack" Pershing, a tall, serious, Missouri-born graduate of West Point. He had fought in the Spanish-American War and led the expedition to track down Pancho Villa in Mexico in 1916. When the first troops marched in a parade in Paris on July 4, 1917, the emotional French crowd shouted, *"Vive les Américains"* and showered them with flowers, hugs, and kisses. But the American commanders worried that many of their soldiers were so inexperienced they did not even know how to march, let alone fight. The first Americans saw action near Verdun in October 1917. By March 1918, more than 300,000 American soldiers had reached France, and by November 1918, more than 2 million.

One reason that the U.S. forces were slow to see combat was Pershing's insistence that they be kept separate from the French and British divisions. An exception was made for four regiments of black

soldiers who were assigned to the French army. These soldiers fought so well that the French later awarded three of the regiments the Croix de Guerre, their highest unit citation.

In the spring of 1918, with Russia out of the war and the British blockade becoming more and more effective, the Germans launched an all-out, desperate offensive to win the war before full American military and industrial power became a factor. By late May, the Germans had pushed to within 50 miles of Paris. American troops were thrown into the line and helped stem the German advance at Château-Thierry, Belleau Wood, and Cantigny, place names that proud survivors would later endow with almost sacred significance. Americans also took part in the Allied offensive led by General Ferdinand Foch of France in the summer of 1918.

In September, more than half a million American troops fought near St. Mihiel; this was the first battle in which large numbers of Americans were pressed into action. One enlisted man remembered that he "saw a sight which I shall never forget. It was zero hour and in one instant the entire front as far as the eye could reach in either direction was a sheet of flame, while the heavy artillery made the earth quake." The Americans suffered more than 7,000 casualties, but they captured more than 16,000 German soldiers. The victory, even if it came against exhausted and retreating German troops, seemed to vindicate Pershing's insistence on a separate American army. British and French commanders were critical of

Deadly Weapons of the Great War
New technology made the Great War more horrible in some ways than past wars. British soldiers wearing primitive gas masks operate a Vickers machine gun. The machine gun effectively neutralized the tactic of massive infantry charges, while poison gas attacks increased the number of soldiers with "shell shock" or mental illness. How has war changed since 1918? Is mental illness still a factor among soldiers in time of war?

(Imperial War Museum, London)

what they considered the disorganized, inexperienced, and ill-equipped American forces.

In the fall of 1918, the combined British, French, and American armies drove the Germans back. Faced with low morale among the German soldiers, the mutiny of the German fleet, and the surrender of Austria, Kaiser Wilhelm II abdicated on November 8, and the armistice was signed on November 11. More than 1 million American soldiers took part in the final Allied offensive near the Meuse River and the Argonne forest. Many of the men were inexperienced, and some, who had been rushed through training as "90-day wonders," had never handled a rifle before arriving in France. There were many disastrous mistakes and bungled situations. The most famous blunder was the "lost battalion." An American unit advanced beyond its support and was cut off and surrounded. The battalion suffered 70 percent casualties before being rescued.

The performance of the all-black Ninety-Second Division was also controversial. The Ninety-Second had been deliberately dispersed around the United States and had never trained as a unit. Its higher officers were white, and they repeatedly asked to be transferred. Many of its men were only partly trained and poorly equipped, and they were continually being called away from their military duties to work as stevedores and common laborers. At the last minute during the Meuse-Argonne offensive, the Ninety-Second was assigned to a particularly difficult position on the line. They had no maps and no wire-cutting equipment. Battalion commanders lost contact with their men, and on several occasions, the men broke and ran in the face

of enemy fire. The division was withdrawn in disgrace, and for years politicians and military leaders used this incident to point out that black soldiers would never make good fighting men, ignoring the difficulties under which the Ninety-Second fought and the valor shown by black troops assigned to the French army.

The war produced a few American heroes. Joseph Oklahombie, a Choctaw, overran several German

---

WORLD WAR I LOSSES

The total cost of the war was estimated at more than $330 billion. The cost in human life was even more horrible. The number of known dead was placed at about 10 million men and the wounded at about 20 million, distributed among chief combatants as follows (round numbers). Which countries bore the brunt of the dead and wounded? How did this influence the peace settlement?

	Dead	Wounded	Prisoner
Great Britain	947,000	2,122,000	192,000
France	1,385,000	3,044,000	446,000
Russia	1,700,000	4,950,000	500,000
Italy	460,000	947,000	530,000
United States	115,000	206,000	4,500
Germany	1,808,000	4,247,000	618,000
Austria-Hungary	1,200,000	3,620,000	200,000
Turkey	325,000	400,000	—

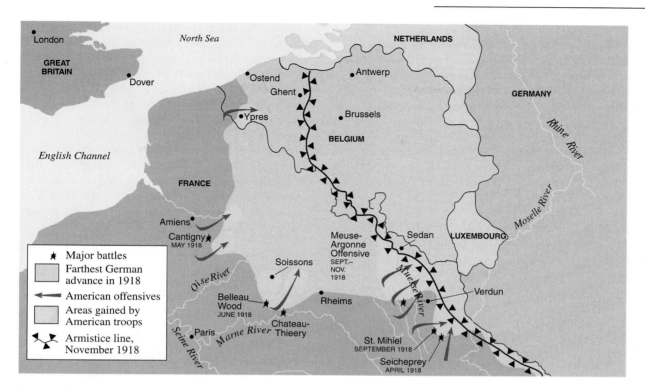

Western Front of the Great War, 1918

For more than three years, the war settled down to a bloody stalemate on the western front. But in 1918, American soldiers played important roles in the Allied offensive that finally ended the war. What can you learn about tactics and strategy during the Great War from studying this map?

machine gun nests and captured more than 100 German soldiers. Sergeant Alvin York, a former conscientious objector from Tennessee, single-handedly killed or captured 160 Germans using only his rifle and pistol. The press made him a celebrity, but his heroics were not typical. Artillery, machine guns, and, near the end, tanks, trucks, and airplanes won the war.

With few exceptions, the Americans fought hard and well. Although the French and British criticized American inexperience and disarray, they admired their exuberance, their "pep," and their ability to move large numbers of men and equipment efficiently. Sometimes Americans simply overwhelmed the enemy with their numbers. They suffered more than 120,000 casualties in the Meuse-Argonne campaign alone. One officer estimated that he lost 10 soldiers for every German his men killed in the final offensive.

The United States entered the war late but still lost more than 48,000 service personnel and had many more wounded. Disease claimed 15 of every 1,000 soldiers each year (compared with 65 per 1,000 in the Civil War). But American losses were tiny compared to those suffered by the European armies. The British lost 900,000 men, the French 1.4 million, and the Russians 1.7 million. Nor was the financial burden as costly for the United States as for its Allies. American units fired French artillery pieces; American soldiers were usually transported in British ships and wore helmets and other equipment modeled after the British. The United States purchased clothing and blankets, even horses, in Europe. American fliers, including heroes such as Eddie Rickenbacker, flew French and British planes. The United States contributed huge amounts of men and supplies in the last months of the war, and that finally tipped the balance. But it had entered late and sacrificed little compared with France and England. That would influence the peace settlement.

A Global Pandemic

The end of the Great War brought relief and joy to many, but in the fall of 1918 an influenza pandemic swept around the world, killing an estimated 50 million people, with 675,000 deaths in the United States in a little more than a year. The Spanish Flu, as it was called (although there is no evidence that it originated in Spain), seems to have started at about the same time in Europe, Asia, America, and even in remote Eskimo villages. Only a small percentage of those who caught the disease died from it, but unlike most epidemics, it hit hardest among young adults. More than 43,000 American servicemen died from the flu (almost as many as died on the battlefield). Early in the epidemic, rumors blamed German germ warfare for the disease, but the

German army was infected as well. No antibiotics or shots could prevent or cure the disease, and the surgical masks required in some cities did no good. Even President Wilson came near death from the disease in the spring of 1919. The flu of 1918–1919 killed more people in a short time than any event in human history, perhaps 20 million worldwide. The speed with which the disease spread around the world was another reminder of how the modern world was interconnected and isolation was impossible.

Domestic Impact of the War

For at least 30 years before the United States entered the Great War, a debate raged over the proper role of the federal government in regulating industry and protecting people who could not protect themselves. Controversy also centered on the question of how much power the federal government should have to tax and control individuals and corporations and the proper relation of the federal government to state and local governments. The war and the problems it raised increased the power of the federal government in a variety of ways. The wartime experience did not end the debate, but the United States emerged from the war a more modern nation, with more power residing in Washington.

Financing the War

The war, by one calculation, cost the United States more than $33 billion. Interest and veterans' benefits bring the total to nearly $112 billion. Early on, when an economist suggested that the war might cost the United States $10 billion, everyone laughed. Yet many in the Wilson administration knew the war was going to be expensive, and they set out to raise the money by borrowing and by increasing taxes.

Secretary of the Treasury William McAdoo was in charge of financing the war. Studying the policies that treasury secretary Salmon Chase had followed during the Civil War, he decided that Chase had made a mistake in not appealing to the emotions of the people. A war must be a "kind of crusade," he remarked. He also learned from the British, French, and German propaganda campaigns. McAdoo's campaign to sell liberty bonds to ordinary American citizens at a very low interest rate appealed to American loyalty. "Lick a Stamp and Lick the Kaiser," one poster urged. Celebrities such as film stars Mary Pickford and Douglas Fairbanks promoted the bonds, and McAdoo employed the Boy Scouts to sell them.

The public responded enthusiastically, but they discovered after the war that their bonds had dropped to about 80 percent of face value. Because the interest on the bonds was tax exempt, well-to-do citizens profited more from buying the bonds than did ordinary men, women, and children. But the wealthy were not as pleased with McAdoo's other plan to finance the war: raising taxes. The War Revenue Act of 1917 boosted the tax rate sharply, levied a tax on excess profits, and increased estate taxes. The next year, another bill raised the tax on the largest incomes to 77 percent. The wealthy protested, but a number of progressives were just as unhappy with the bill, for they wanted to confiscate all income over $100,000 a year. Despite taxes and liberty bonds, however, World War I, like the Civil War, was financed in large part by inflation. Food prices, for example, nearly doubled between 1917 and 1919.

Increasing Federal Power

The major wars of the twentieth century made huge demands on the nations that fought them and helped transform their governments. At first, Wilson tried to work through a variety of state agencies to mobilize the nation's resources. The need for more centralized control and authority soon led Wilson to create a series of federal agencies to deal with the war emergency. The first crisis was food. Poor grain crops for two years and an increasing demand for American food in Europe caused shortages. Wilson appointed Herbert Hoover, a young engineer who had won great prestige as head of the Commission for Relief of Belgium, to direct the Food Administration. Hoover instituted a series of "wheatless" and "meatless" days and urged housewives to cooperate. Women emerged during the war as the most important group of consumers. The government urged them to save, just as later it would urge them to buy.

The Wilson administration used the authority of the federal government to organize resources for the war effort. The War Industries Board, led by Bernard Baruch, a shrewd Wall Street broker, used the power of the government to control scarce materials and, on occasion, to set prices and priorities. Cooperation among government, business, and university scientists to promote research and develop new products was one legacy of the war. The government itself went into the shipbuilding business and ran the railroads. When a severe winter and a lack of coordination brought the rail system near collapse in December 1917, Wilson put all the nation's railroads under the control of the United Railway Administration. The government spent more than $500 million to improve the rails and equipment, and in 1918, the railroads did run more efficiently than they had under private control. Some businessmen complained of "war socialism" and of increased rules and regulations. Like it or not, the war increased the influence of the federal government.

War Workers

The Wilson administration sought to protect and extend the rights of organized labor during the war, while mobilizing the workers necessary to keep the factories running. The National War Labor Board insisted on adequate wages and reduced hours, and it tried to prevent exploitation of women and children working under government contracts. On one occasion, when a munitions plant refused to accept the War Labor Board's decision, the government simply took over the factory. When workers threatened to strike for better wages or hours or for greater control over the workplace, the board often ruled that they either work or be drafted into the army.

The Wilson administration favored the conservative labor movement of Samuel Gompers and the AFL, and the Justice Department put the radical Industrial Workers of the World "out of business." Beginning in September 1917, federal agents conducted massive raids on IWW offices and arrested most of its leaders.

Gompers took advantage of the crisis to strengthen the AFL's position to speak for labor. He supported the administration policies by making it clear that he opposed the IWW as well as socialists and communists. Convincing Wilson that it was important to protect the rights of organized labor during wartime, he announced that "no other policy is compatible with the spirit and methods of democracy." As the AFL won a voice in home-front policy, its membership increased from 2.7 million in 1916 to more than 4 million in 1917. Organized labor's wartime gains, however, would prove only temporary.

The war opened up industrial employment opportunities for black men. With 4 million men in the armed forces and the flow of immigrants interrupted by the war, American manufacturers for the first time hired African Americans in large numbers. In Chicago before the war, only 3,000 black men held factory jobs; in 1920, more than 15,000 did.

Northern labor agents and the railroads actively recruited southern blacks, but the news of jobs in northern cities spread by word of mouth as well. By 1920, more than 300,000 blacks had joined the "great migration" north. This massive movement of people, which continued into the 1920s, had a permanent impact on the South as well as on the northern cities. Like African Americans, thousands of Mexicans

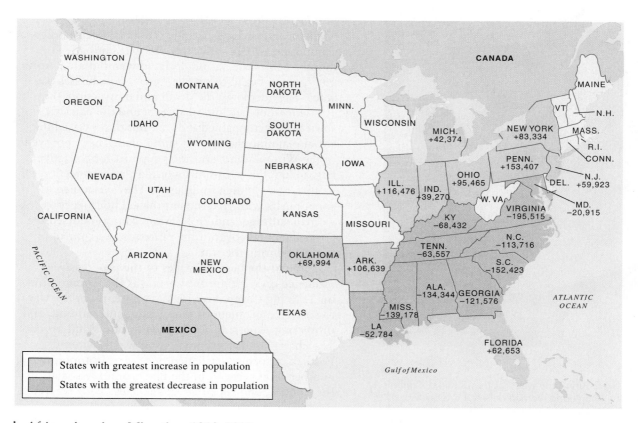

African American Migration, 1910–1920

This map illustrates the massive migration of African Americans from the South to the North during the Great War. Most moved to find better jobs, but in the process they changed the dynamics of race relations in the country. What other changes resulted from this migration?

headed north into the United States, as immigration officials relaxed the regulations because of the need for labor in the farms and factories of the Southwest.

The war also created new employment opportunities for women. Posters and patriotic speeches urged women to do their duty for the war effort. One poster showed a woman at her typewriter, the shadow of a soldier in the background, with the message: "STENOGRAPHERS, WASHINGTON NEEDS YOU." Women responded to these appeals out of patriotism, as well as out of a need to increase their earnings and to make up for inflation, which diminished real wages. Women went into every kind of industry. They labored in brickyards and in heavy industry, became conductors on the railroad, and turned out shells in munitions plants. They even organized the Woman's Land Army to mobilize female labor for the farms. They demonstrated that women could do any kind of job, whatever the physical or intellectual demands. Black women left domestic service for jobs in textile mills, even in the stockyards. However, racial discrimination, even in the North, prevented them from moving too far up the occupational ladder.

Even though women demonstrated that they could take over jobs once thought suitable only for men, their progress during the war proved temporary. Only about 5 percent of the women employed during the war were new to the workforce, and almost all of them were unmarried. For most, it meant a shift of occupations or a move up to a better-paying position. Moreover, the war accelerated trends already underway. It increased the need for telephone operators, sales personnel, secretaries, and other white-collar workers, and in these occupations, women soon became a majority. Telephone operator, for example, became an almost exclusively female job. By 1917, women represented 99 percent of all operators as the telephone network spanned the nation.

The war provided limited opportunities for some women, but it did not change the dominant perception that a woman's place was in the home. After the war was over, the men returned, and the gains made by women almost disappeared. There were 8 million women in the workforce in 1910 but only 8.5 million in 1920.

Icewomen
Women proved during the war that they could do "men's work." These two young women deliver ice, a backbreaking task, but one that was necessary in the days before electric refrigerators. Despite women like these, the war did not change the American ideal that women's proper place was in the home. Has that ideal changed since 1918?

(National Archives)

The Climax of Progressivism

Many progressives, especially the social justice progressives, opposed U.S. entry into the war until a few months before the nation declared war. But after April 1917, many began to see the "social possibilities of war." They deplored the death and destruction, the abridgment of freedom of speech, and the patriotic spirit that accompanied the war. But they praised the social planning the conflict stimulated. They approved of the Wilson administration's support for collective bargaining, the eight-hour workday, and protection for women and children in industry. They welcomed the experiments with government-owned housing projects, woman suffrage, and Prohibition. Many endorsed the government takeover of the railroads and control of business during the war.

One of the best examples of the progressives' influence on wartime activities was the Commission on Training Camp Activities, set up early in the war to solve the problem of mobilizing, entertaining, and protecting American servicemen at home and abroad. The chairman of the commission was Raymond Fosdick, a former settlement worker. He appointed a number of experts from the Playground Association, the YMCA, and social work agencies. They set out to organize community singing and baseball, establish post exchanges and theaters, and even provide university extension lectures to educate the servicemen. The overriding assumption was that the military experience would help produce citizens who would be ready to vote for social reform once they returned to civilian life.

The Commission on Training Camp Activities also incorporated the progressive crusades against alcohol and prostitution. The Military Draft Act prohibited the sale of liquor to men in uniform and gave the president power to establish zones around military bases where prostitution and alcohol would be prohibited. Some military commanders protested, and at least one city official argued that prostitutes were "God-provided means for the prevention of the violation of innocent girls, by men who are exercising their 'God-given passions.'" Yet the commission, with the full cooperation of the Wilson administration, set out to wipe out sin, or at least to put it out of the reach of servicemen. "Fit to fight" became the motto. It was a typical progressive effort combining moral indignation with the use of the latest scientific prophylaxis. The commissioners prided themselves on having eliminated all the red-light districts near the training camps by 1918. When the boys go to France, the secretary of war remarked, "I want them to have invisible armour to take with them. I want them to have armour made up of a set of social habits replacing those of their homes and communities."

France tested the "invisible armour." The government, despite hundreds of letters of protest from American mothers, decided that it could not prevent the soldiers from drinking wine in France, but it could forbid them to buy or accept as gifts anything but light wine and beer.

Sex was even more difficult to regulate in France than liquor. Both the British and the French armies had tried to solve the problem of venereal disease by licensing and inspecting prostitutes. Georges Clemenceau, the French premier, accused the Americans of spreading disease throughout the French civilian population and offered to provide the Americans with licensed prostitutes. When Clemenceau's letter reached Baker, the secretary of war said, "For God's sake…don't show this to the President or he'll stop the war." The Americans never accepted Clemenceau's offer, and he continued to be baffled by the American progressive mentality.

Suffrage for Women

In the fall of 1918, while American soldiers were mobilizing for the final offensive in France and hundreds of thousands of women were working in factories and serving as Red Cross and Salvation Army volunteers near the army bases, Woodrow Wilson asked the Senate to support extending the vote to women. He argued that woman suffrage was "vital to the winning of the war." Although Wilson had earlier opposed the vote for women and his positive statement at this late date was not necessary, his voice was a welcome addition to a rising chorus of support for an amendment to the Constitution that would permit the female half of the population to vote.

Many still opposed woman suffrage. Some argued that the vote would make women less feminine, more worldly, and less able to perform their primary tasks as wives and mothers. The National Association Opposed to Woman Suffrage protested that only radicals wanted the vote and declared that woman suffrage, socialism, and feminism were "three branches of the same Social Revolution."

Carrie Chapman Catt, an efficient administrator and tireless organizer, devised the strategy that finally secured the vote for women. Catt, who grew up in Iowa, joined the Iowa Woman Suffrage Association at age 28 shortly after her first husband died. Before remarrying, she insisted on a legal agreement giving her four months a year away from her husband to work for the suffrage cause. In 1915, she became president of the National American Woman Suffrage Association (NAWSA), the organization founded in 1890 and based in part on the society organized by Elizabeth Cady Stanton and Susan B. Anthony in 1869.

Catt coordinated the state campaigns with the office in Washington, directing a growing army of dedicated workers. This began to produce results, but a group of more militant reformers, impatient with the slow progress, broke off from NAWSA to form the National Women's Party (NWP) in 1916. This group was led by Alice Paul, a Quaker from New Jersey, who had participated in some of the suffrage battles in England. Paul and her group, using tactics borrowed from the militant British suffragettes, picketed the White House, chained themselves to the fence, and blocked the streets. They carried banners that asked, "MR. PRESIDENT, HOW LONG MUST WOMEN WAIT FOR LIBERTY?" In the summer of 1917, the government arrested more than 200 women and charged them with "obstructing the sidewalk." That was just the kind of publicity the militants sought, and they made the most of it. Wilson, fearing even more embarrassment, began to cooperate with the more moderate reformers.

The careful organizing of NAWSA and the more militant tactics of the NWP both contributed to the final success of the woman suffrage crusade. The war did not cause the passage of the Nineteenth Amendment, but it did accelerate the process. Fourteen state legislatures petitioned Congress in 1917 and 26 in 1919, urging the enactment of the amendment. Early in 1919, the House of Representatives passed the suffrage amendment 304 to 90, and the Senate approved by a vote of 56 to 25. Fourteen months later, the required 36 states had ratified the amendment, and women at last had the vote. "We are no longer petitioners," Catt announced in celebration. "We are not wards of the nation, but free and equal citizens." But the achievement of votes for women would not prove the triumph of feminism, nor the signal for the beginning of a new reform movement that the women leaders expected to occur.

Planning for Peace

Woodrow Wilson turned U.S. participation in the war into a religious crusade to change the nature of international relations. It was a war to make the world safe for democracy—and more. On January 8, 1918, in part to counteract the Bolshevik charge that the war was merely a struggle among imperialist powers, he announced his plan to organize the peace. Called the Fourteen Points, it argued for "open covenants of peace openly arrived at," freedom of the seas, equality of trade, and the self-determination of all peoples. But his most important point, the fourteenth, called for an international organization, a "league of nations," to preserve peace. The victorious Allies, who had suffered grievously in the conflict, had less idealistic goals than did Wilson for peacemaking.

The Versailles Peace Conference

Late in 1918, Wilson announced that he would head the American delegation at Versailles, near Paris, symbolizing his belief that he alone could overcome the forces of greed and imperialism in Europe and bring peace to the world. Wilson and his entourage of college professors, technical experts, and advisers set sail for Paris on the *George Washington* on December 4, 1918. Secretary of State Lansing, Edward House, and a number of other advisers were there; conspicuously missing, however, was Henry Cabot Lodge, chairman of the Senate Foreign Relations Committee and the most powerful man in the Senate, or any other Republican senator.

Lodge's absence would prove a serious blunder, for the Republican-controlled Senate would have to approve any treaty negotiated in Paris. It is difficult to explain Wilson's lack of political insight, except that he disliked Lodge intensely and hated political bargaining and compromise. Preferring to announce great principles, he had supreme confidence in his ability to persuade and to get his way by appealing to the people.

Wilson's self-confidence grew during a triumphant tour through Europe before the conference. The ordinary people greeted him as a savior who had ended the tragic war. But the American president had greater difficulty convincing the political leaders at the peace conference of his genius. In Paris, he faced the reality of European power politics and ambitions

and the personalities of David Lloyd George of Great Britain, Vittorio Orlando of Italy, and Georges Clemenceau of France.

Though Wilson was more naive and idealistic than his European counterparts, he was a clever negotiator who won many concessions at the peace table, sometimes by threatening to go home if his counterparts would not compromise. The European leaders were determined to punish Germany and enlarge their empires. Wilson, however, pressed for a new kind of international relations based on his Fourteen Points. He achieved limited acceptance of the idea of self-determination, his dream that each national group could have its own country and that the people should decide in what country they wanted to live.

From what had been the Austro-Hungarian and Ottoman empires, the peacemakers carved the new countries of Austria, Hungary, Yugoslavia, and Turkey. In addition, they created Poland, Czechoslovakia, Finland, Estonia, Latvia, and Lithuania, in part to help contain the threat of bolshevism in eastern Europe. France was to occupy the industrial Saar region of Germany for 15 years, after which a plebiscite would then determine whether the people wanted to become a part of Germany or France. Italy gained the port city of Trieste, but not the neighboring city of Fiume, with its largely Italian-speaking population. Dividing up the map of Europe was difficult at best, but perhaps the biggest mistake that Wilson and other major leaders made was to give the small nations little power at the negotiating table and to exclude Soviet Russia entirely.

While Wilson won some points at the peace negotiations, he also had to make major concessions. He was forced to give in to the Allied demand that Germany pay reparations (later set at $56 billion), lose much of its oil- and coal-rich territory, and admit to its war guilt. He accepted a mandate system, to be supervised by the League of Nations, that allowed France and Britain to take over portions of the Middle East and Japan to occupy Germany's colonies in the Pacific as well as China's Shantung province. And he acquiesced when the Allies turned Germany's African colonies into "mandate possessions" because they did not want to allow self-determination of blacks in areas they had colonized.

Although Wilson yielded to the Allies on the fate of Germany's former colonies in Africa, he did not envision a reordering of global race relations. He opposed and finally defeated a measure introduced by Japan to include a clause in the league covenant to support racial equality in all parts of the world. W. E. B. Du Bois, who was in Paris as part of the American delegation at the first Pan-African Congress, supported the Japanese resolution for racial equality. He also spoke against colonialism and criticized "white civilization" for

Europe and the Near East After World War I

Led in part by President Wilson's goal to promote the self-determination of people and in part by a desire to block the expansion of Germany and the Soviet Union, the diplomats meeting at Versailles reconfigured the map of Europe and the Near East. Redrawing the map, however, was easier than solving the problems of nationalism and ethnic conflict. How has the map of Europe and the Middle East changed since 1919?

subjugating blacks in various parts of the world. He hoped that the Pan-African movement would become a global effort to unite people of color around the world. But Wilson and the other leaders at Versailles ignored Du Bois.

The Versailles treaty did not represent "peace without victory," as Wilson hoped. The German people felt betrayed. Japan, which had expected to play a larger role in the peace conference, felt slighted. The Italians were angry because they received less territory than they expected. These resentments would later have

grave consequences. Wilson also did not win approval for freedom of the seas or the abolition of trade barriers, but he did gain endorsement for the League of Nations, the organization he hoped would prevent all future wars. The league consisted of a council of the five great powers, elected delegates from the smaller countries, and a World Court to settle disputes. But the key to collective security was contained in Article 10 of the league covenant, which pledged all members "to respect and preserve against external aggression the territorial integrity" of all other members.

Wilson's Failed Dream

While the statesmen met at Versailles to sign the peace treaty hammered out in Paris and to divide up Europe, a group of prominent and successful women met in Zurich, Switzerland. Jane Addams led the American delegation that included Jeannette Rankin, a congresswoman from Montana (one of the few states where women could vote). They formed the Women's International League for Peace and Freedom. Electing Addams president of the new organization, they denounced the harsh peace terms, which called for disarmament of only one side and exacted great economic penalties against the Central Powers.

Hate and intolerance were legacies of the war. They were present at the Versailles peace conference, where Clemenceau especially wanted to humiliate Germany for the destruction of French lives and property. Also hanging over the conference was the

Timeline	
1914	Archduke Ferdinand assassinated; World War I begins
	United States declares neutrality
	American troops invade Mexico and occupy Veracruz
1915	Germany announces submarine blockade of Great Britain
	Lusitania sunk
	Arabic pledge
	Marines land in Haiti
1916	Army Reorganization Bill
	Expedition into Mexico
	Wilson reelected
	Workmen's Compensation Bill
	Keatings–Owen Child Labor Bill
	Federal Farm Loan Act
	National Women's Party (NWP) founded
1917	Germany resumes unrestricted submarine warfare
	United States breaks relations with Germany
	Zimmermann telegram
	Russian Revolution
	United States declares war on Germany
	War Revenue Act
	Espionage Act
	Committee on Public Information established
	Trading with the Enemy Act
	Selective Service Act
	War Industries Board formed
1918	Sedition Act
	Flu epidemic sweeps nation
	Wilson's Fourteen Points
	American troops intervene in Russian Revolution
1919	Paris peace conference
	Eighteenth Amendment prohibits alcoholic beverages
	Senate rejects Treaty of Versailles
1920	Nineteenth Amendment grants suffrage for women

Bolshevik success in Russia. The threat of revolution seemed so great that Wilson and the Allies sent American and Japanese troops into Siberia in 1919 to attempt to defeat the Bolsheviks and create a moderate republic. But by 1920, the troops had failed in their mission. They withdrew, but the Soviet Union never forgot the American intervention and the threat of bolshevism remained.

Most Americans supported the concept of the League of Nations in the summer of 1919. A few, such as former senator Albert Beveridge of Indiana, an ardent nationalist, denounced the league as the work of "amiable old male grannies who, over their afternoon tea, are planning to denationalize America and denationalize the nation's manhood." But 33 governors endorsed the plan. In the end, however, the Senate refused to accept American membership in the league. The League of Nations treaty, one commentator has suggested, was killed by its friends and not by its enemies.

First there was Lodge, who had earlier endorsed the idea of some kind of international peacekeeping organization but who objected to Article 10, which obligated all members to come to the defense of the others in case of attack. He claimed that it would force Americans to fight the wars of foreigners. A Republican senator since 1893, he had great faith in the power and prestige of the Senate. He disliked all Democrats, especially Wilson, whose idealism and missionary zeal infuriated him.

Then there was Wilson, whose only hope of passage of the treaty in the Senate was a compromise to bring moderate senators to his side. But Wilson refused to compromise or to modify Article 10 to allow Congress the opportunity to decide whether the United States would support the league in time of crisis. Angry at his opponents, who were exploiting the disagreement for political advantage, he stumped the country to convince the American people of the rightness of his plan. The people did not need to be convinced. They greeted Wilson much the way the people of France had. Traveling by train, he gave 37 speeches in 29 cities in the space of three weeks. When he described the graves of American soldiers in France and announced that American boys would never again die in a foreign war, the people responded with applause.

After one dramatic speech in Pueblo, Colorado, Wilson collapsed. His health had been failing for some months, and the strain of the trip was too much. He was rushed back to Washington, where a few days later he suffered a massive stroke. For the next year and a half, the president was incapable of running the government. Protected by his second wife and his closest advisers, Wilson was partially paralyzed, depressed, and unable to lead a fight for the league.

For a year and a half, the country limped along without a president.

After many votes and much maneuvering, the Senate finally killed the league treaty in March 1920. Had the United States joined the League of Nations, it probably would have made little difference in the international events of the 1920s and 1930s. Nor would American participation in the league have prevented World War II. The United States did not resign from the world of diplomacy or trade, nor did the United States become isolated from the rest of the world by refusing to join the league. But the rejection of the league treaty was symbolic of the refusal of many Americans to admit that the world and America's place in it had changed dramatically since 1914.

Conclusion
THE DIVIDED LEGACY OF THE GREAT WAR

For Edmund Arpin and many of his friends, who left small towns and urban neighborhoods to join the military forces, the war was a great adventure. For the next decades at American Legion conventions and Armistice Day parades, they continued to celebrate their days of glory. For others who served, the war's results were more tragic. Many died. Some came home injured, disabled by poison gas, or unable to cope with the complex world that had opened up to them.

In a larger sense, the war was both a triumph and a tragedy for the American people. The war created opportunities for blacks who migrated to the North, for women who found more rewarding jobs, and for farmers who suddenly discovered a demand for their products. But much of the promise and the hope proved temporary.

The war proved to be a turning point for the progressive movement. The passage of the woman suffrage amendment and the use of federal power in a variety of ways to promote justice and order pleased reformers, who had been working toward these ends for many decades. But the results were often disappointing. Once the war ended, much federal legislation was dismantled or reduced in effectiveness and woman suffrage had little initial impact on social legislation. Yet the power of the federal government did increase during the war in a variety of ways. From taking control of the railroads to building ships and public housing, to regulating the economy, the government took an active role. Much of that role would diminish in the next decade, but a strong, active government during the war would become a model during the 1930s for those who tried to solve the problem of a major depression.

The Great War marked the coming of age of the United States as a world power. At the end of the war, the United States was the world's largest creditor and an important factor in international trade and diplomacy. But the country seemed reluctant to accept the new responsibility. The war and the settlement were at least in part responsible for the global depression of the 1930s, and the problems created by the war led directly to another global war, thus causing the next generation to label the conflict of 1914–1918 World War I. The war stimulated patriotism and pride in the country, but it also increased intolerance, cut off immigration from Europe, and led to disillusionment. With this mixed legacy from the war, the country entered the new era of the 1920s.

QUESTIONS FOR REVIEW AND REFLECTION

1. Why did the United States, so determined to stay out of the Great War in 1914, join the Allied cause enthusiastically in 1917?
2. Why did the war lead to hate, prejudice, and the abridgment of civil liberties?
3. How did the war affect women and minorities in the United States?
4. Why did Wilson's idealistic peace plan fail?
5. What were the long-range consequences of World War I? For the United States? For the world?

CHAPTER 23

Affluence and Anxiety

John Steuart Curry, *Baptism in Kansas*

Curry was one of the 1920s regionalist painters who found inspiration in the American heartland. In this painting, he depicts a religious ritual that underscores the conflict between rural and urban values. Is there still a religious split today between urban and rural America? Or is the cultural divide defined differently today?

(John Steuart Curry, (1897–1946), "Baptism in Kansas". 1928. Oil on canvas. 40" × 50". Collection of the Whitney Museum of American Art, New York.)

American Stories

A Black Sharecropper and His Family Move North

John and Lizzie Parker were black sharecroppers who lived in a "stubborn, ageless hut squatted on a little hill" in central Alabama. They had two daughters—one age 6, the other already married. The whole family worked hard in the cotton fields, but they had little to show for their labor. One day in 1917, Lizzie straightened her shoulders and declared, "I'm through. I've picked my last sack of cotton. I've cleared my last field." Like many southern African Americans, the Parkers sought opportunity and a better life in the North. World War I cut off the flow of immigrants from Europe, and suddenly there was a shortage of workers. Some companies sent special trains into the South to recruit African Americans. John Parker signed up with a mining company in West Virginia. The company offered free transportation for his family. "You will be allowed to get your food at the company store and there are houses awaiting for you," the agent promised.

The sound of the train whistle seemed to promise better days ahead for her family as Lizzie gathered her possessions and headed north. But it turned out that the houses in the company town in West Virginia were little better than those they left in Alabama. After deducting for rent and for supplies from the company store, almost no money was left at the end of the week. John hated the dirty and dangerous work in the mine and realized that he would never get ahead by staying there. But instead of venting his anger on his white boss, he ran away, leaving his family in West Virginia.

John drifted to Detroit, where he got a job with the American Car and Foundry Company. It was 1918, and the pay was good, more than he had ever made before. After a few weeks, he rented an apartment and sent for his family. For the first time, Lizzie had a gas stove and an indoor toilet, and Sally, who was now 7, started school. It seemed as if their dream had come true.

Detroit was not quite the dream, however. It was crowded with all kinds of migrants, many attracted by the wartime jobs at the Ford Motor Company and other factories. The new arrivals increased the racial tension already present in the city. Sally was beaten up by a gang of white youths at school. Even in their neighborhood, which had been solidly Jewish before their arrival, the shopkeepers and the old residents made it clear that they did not like blacks moving into their community. The Ku Klux Klan, which gained many new members in Detroit, also made life uncomfortable for the blacks who had moved north to seek jobs and opportunity.

Suddenly the war ended, and almost immediately John lost his job. Then the landlord raised the rent, and the Parkers were forced to leave their apartment for

housing in a section just outside the city near Eight Mile Road. The surrounding suburbs had paved streets, wide lawns, and elegant houses, but this black ghetto had dirt streets and shacks that reminded the Parkers of the company town where they had lived in West Virginia. Lizzie had to get along without her bathroom, for here there was no indoor plumbing and no electricity, only a pump in the yard and an outhouse.

The recession winter of 1921–1922 was particularly difficult. The auto industry and other companies laid off most of their workers. John could find only part-time employment, while Lizzie worked as a domestic servant for white families. Because no bus route connected the black community to surrounding suburbs, she often had to trek miles through the snow. The shack they called home was freezing cold, and it was cramped because their married daughter and her husband had joined them in Detroit.

Lizzie did not give up her dream, however. With strength, determination, and a sense of humor, she kept the family together. In 1924, Sally entered high school. By the end of the decade, Sally had graduated from high school, and the Parkers finally had electricity and indoor plumbing in the house, though the streets were still unpaved. Those unpaved streets stood as a symbol of their unfulfilled dream. The Parkers, like most of the African Americans who moved north in the decade after World War I, had improved their lot, but they still lived outside Detroit—and, in many ways, outside America.

Like most Americans in the 1920s, the Parkers pursued the American dream of success. For them, a comfortable house and a steady job, a new bathroom, and an education for their younger daughter constituted that dream. For others during the decade, the symbol of success might be owning a new automobile or a new suburban house, or perhaps making a killing on the stock market. The Parkers, like all Americans, whether they realized it or not, were influenced by a global market beyond their control. The 1920s, the decade between the end of World War I and the stock market crash, has often been referred to as the "jazz age," a time when the American people had one long party complete with flappers, speakeasies, illegal bathtub gin, and young people dancing the Charleston late into the night. This frivolous interpretation has some basis in fact, but most Americans did not share in the party, for they were too busy struggling to make a living.

In this chapter, we will explore some of the conflicting trends of an exciting decade. First, we will examine the currents of intolerance that influenced almost all the events and social movements of the time. We will also look at some developments in technology, especially the automobile, which changed life for almost everyone and created the illusion of prosperity for all. We will then focus on groups—women, blacks, industrial workers, and farmers—who had their hopes and dreams raised but not always fulfilled during the decade. We will conclude by looking at the way business, politics, and foreign policy were intertwined during the age of Harding, Coolidge, and Hoover.

Postwar Problems

Enthusiasm for social progress evaporated in 1919. Public housing, social insurance, government ownership of railroads, and many other experiments quickly ended. The sense of progress and purpose that the war had fostered withered. The year after the war was marked by strikes and violence and by fear that Bolsheviks, blacks, foreigners, and others were destroying the American way of life. Some of the fear and intolerance resulted from wartime patriotism, while some arose from the postwar economic and political turmoil that forced Americans to deal with new and immensely troubling situations.

The Red Scare

Americans have often feared radicals and other groups that seem to be conspiring to overthrow the American way of life. In the 1840s, in the 1890s, and at other times in the past, Catholics, Mormons, Populists, immigrants, and holders of many political views have all been attacked as dangerous and "un-American." Before 1917, anarchists seemed to pose the worst threat. The Russian Revolution changed that. *Bolshevik* suddenly became the most dangerous and devious radical, while *Communist* was transformed from a member of a utopian community to a dreaded, threatening subversive. For some Americans, *Bolshevik* and *German* became somehow mixed together, especially after the Treaty of Brest–Litovsk in 1918 removed the new Soviet state from the war. In the spring of 1919, with the Russian announcement of a policy of worldwide revolution and with Communist uprisings in Hungary and Bavaria, many Americans feared that Communists planned to take over the United States.

Immediately after the war, there were perhaps 25,000 American Communists, but they never threatened the United States. Some were idealists, such as John Reed, the son of a wealthy businessman, who had been converted to socialism in New York's Greenwich Village. Appalled by the carnage in what he considered a capitalistic war, Reed went to Russia as a journalist, just in time to witness the bloody Bolshevik takeover. His eyewitness account, *Ten Days That Shook the World*, optimistically predicted worldwide revolution. Seeing little hope for that revolution in postwar America, he returned to Moscow, where he died in 1920, disillusioned by the new regime's authoritarian nature.

The "Red Menace" and the Palmer Raids

Reed was one of the romantic American intellectuals who saw great hope for the future in the Russian Revolution. His mentor Lincoln Steffens, the muckraking journalist, remarked after a visit to the Soviet Union a few years later, "I have been over into the future and it works." But relatively few Americans, even among those who had been Socialists, and fewer still among the workers, joined the Communist party. The threat to the American system of government was very slight. But in 1919, the Communists seemed to be a threat, particularly as a series of devastating strikes erupted. Workers in the United States had suffered from wartime inflation, which had almost doubled prices between 1914 and 1919, while most wages remained the same. During 1919, more than 4 million workers took part in 4,000 strikes. Few wanted to overthrow the government; rather, they demanded higher wages, shorter hours, and in some cases more control over the workplace.

On January 21, 1919, some 35,000 shipyard workers went on strike in Seattle, Washington. Within a few days, a general strike paralyzed the city; transportation and business stopped. The mayor called for federal troops. Within five days, using strong-arm tactics, the mayor put down the strike and was hailed as a "red-blooded patriot."

Yet strikes continued elsewhere. In September 1919, all 343,000 employees of U.S. Steel walked out in an attempt to win an eight-hour workday and an "American living wage." The average workweek in the steel industry in 1919 was 68.7 hours; the unskilled worker averaged $1,400 per year, while the minimum subsistence for a family of five was estimated at $1,575. Within days, the strike spread to Bethlehem Steel.

Owners blamed the strikes on the Bolsheviks. They imported strikebreakers, provoked riots, broke up union meetings, and finally used police and soldiers to end the strike. Eighteen strikers were killed. Because most people believed that the Communists had inspired the strike, the issue of long hours and poor pay got lost, and eventually the union surrendered.

To many Americans, strikes were bad enough, but bombs were even worse. On April 28, 1919, a bomb was discovered in a package delivered to the home of the mayor of Seattle. The next day, the maid of a former senator from Georgia opened a package, and a bomb blew her hands off. Other bombings occurred in June, including one that shattered the front of Attorney General A. Mitchell Palmer's home in Washington. The bombings seem to have been the work of misguided radicals who thought they might spark a genuine revolution in America. But their effect was to provide evidence that revolution could be around the corner, even though most American workers wanted only shorter hours, better working conditions, and a chance to realize the American dream.

No one was more convinced than A. Mitchell Palmer. In the summer of 1919, he determined to find and destroy the Red network. He organized a special antiradical division within the Justice Department and put a young man named J. Edgar Hoover in charge of coordinating information on domestic radical activities.

Obsessed with the "Red Menace," Palmer instituted a series of raids, beginning in November 1919. Simultaneously, in several cities, his men rounded up 250 members of the Union of Russian Workers, many of whom were beaten in the process. In December, 249 aliens, including the famous anarchist Emma Goldman, were deported, although very few were Communists and even fewer had any desire to overthrow the government. Palmer's men arrested 500 people in Detroit and 800 in Boston.

The Palmer raids, one of the most massive violations of civil liberties in American history to that time, found few dangerous radicals but did fan the flames of fear and intolerance. In Indiana, a jury quickly acquitted a man who had killed an alien for yelling, "To hell with the United States." Billy Sunday, a Christian evangelist, suggested that the best solution was to shoot aliens rather than to deport them.

Palmer became a national hero, but in the end, only about 600 were deported out of more than 5,000 arrested. The worst of the "Red Scare" was over by the end of 1920, but fear of radicals and emotional patriotism survived to color almost every aspect of politics, daily life, and social legislation.

The Red Scare strengthened many patriotic organizations and societies determined to eliminate Communism from American life. The best known was the American Legion, but there were also the American Defense Society, the Sentinels of the Republic, the United States Flag Association, and the Daughters of the American Revolution. Such groups provided a sense of purpose and a feeling of belonging in a rapidly changing America. But often they were united by obsessive fear of Communists and radicals.

The Ku Klux Klan

Among the superpatriotic organizations claiming to protect the American way of life, the Ku Klux Klan (KKK) was the most extreme. The Klan was organized in Georgia by William J. Simmons, a lay preacher, salesman, and member of many fraternal organizations. He adopted the name and white-sheet uniform of the old antiblack Reconstruction organization that was glorified in 1915 in the immensely popular but racist feature film *Birth of a Nation*. Simmons appointed himself head ("Imperial Wizard") of the new Klan.

Women of the Ku Klux Klan

The Klan, with its elaborate rituals and uniforms, exploited the fear of blacks, Jews, liberals, and Catholics while preaching "traditional" values. The appeal of the Klan was not limited to the South, and many women joined. This is a photo of women Klan members marching in an America First Parade in Binghamton, New York. Why did so many women join the Klan? Is there anything like it today?

(Bettmann/CORBIS)

Unlike the original organization, which took almost anyone who was white, the new Klan was thoroughly Protestant and explicitly antiforeign, anti-Semitic, and anti-Catholic. The Klan declared that "America is Protestant and so it must remain." It opposed the teaching of evolution; glorified old-time religion; supported immigration restriction; denounced short skirts, petting, and "demon rum"; and upheld patriotism and the purity of women. The Klan was also militantly antiblack and its members took as their special mission the task of keeping blacks in their "proper place." If peaceful measures failed, they resorted to violence, kidnapping, and lynching.

The Klan flourished in small towns and rural areas in the South, where it set out to keep returning black soldiers in their "proper place," but it soon spread throughout the country; at least half the members came from urban areas. The Klan was especially strong in the working-class neighborhoods of Detroit, Indianapolis, Atlanta, and Chicago, where the migration of African Americans and other ethnic groups increased fear of everything "un-American." At the peak of its power, the Klan had several million members, many of them from the middle class. In some states, especially Indiana, Colorado, Oregon, Oklahoma, Louisiana, and Texas, it influenced politics. The Klan's power declined after 1925 because of a series of internal power struggles and several scandals. The Klan survived in some areas into the 1930s, but it had all but disappeared by the outbreak of World War II. Yet the end of the Klan did not mean the end of prejudice.

Ethnic and Religious Intolerance

One result of the Red Scare and the unreasoned fear of foreigners and radicals, which dragged on through much of the decade, was the conviction and sentencing of two Italian anarchists, Nicola Sacco and Bartolomeo Vanzetti. Arrested in 1920 for allegedly murdering a guard during a robbery of the shoe factory in South Braintree, Massachusetts, the two were convicted and sentenced to die in the summer of 1921 on what many liberals considered circumstantial and flimsy evidence. Indeed, it seemed to many that the two Italians, who spoke in broken English and were admitted anarchists, were punished because of their radicalism and their foreign appearance.

The case took on symbolic significance as many intellectuals in Europe and America rallied to their defense and to the defense of civil liberties. Appeal after appeal failed, but finally the governor of Massachusetts appointed a commission to reexamine the evidence. The commission reaffirmed the verdict, and the two were executed in the electric chair on August 23, 1927, despite massive protests and midnight vigils around the country. Recent evidence, including ballistic tests, suggests that they may have been guilty, but the trial and its aftermath nevertheless pointed to the ethnic prejudice and divisions in American society.

The KKK and well-publicized cases such as Sacco–Vanzetti touched relatively few people, but intolerance permeated the decade and influenced the lives of millions. In Dearborn, Michigan, Henry Ford published anti-Semitic diatribes in the *Dearborn Independent,* and many country clubs and resort hotels prohibited Jews from even entering. Jews built their own in the Catskills in New York State, Long Branch in New Jersey, and other areas. Many colleges, private academies, and medical schools had Jewish quotas, some openly and others informally, and many suburbs explicitly limited residents to "Christians." Few Catholics even tried to enroll in the elite colleges. There had always been a great deal of prejudice and intolerance in the United States, but during the decade of the 1920s, much of that intolerance became more fixed and formal.

A Prospering Economy

A time of intolerance and anxiety for many Americans, the decade after World War I also was a time of industrial expansion and widespread prosperity for numerous others. Recovering from a postwar depression in 1921 and 1922, the economy soared. Fueled by new technology, more efficient planning and management, and innovative advertising, industrial production almost doubled during the decade, and the gross national product rose by an astonishing 40 percent. A construction boom created new suburbs around American cities, and a new generation of skyscrapers transformed the cities themselves. However, the benefits of prosperity fell unevenly on the many social groups that formed American society.

While the American economy boomed, much of the rest of the world suffered in the aftermath of the war. Germany, wracked by inflation so great that it took millions of marks to buy a loaf of bread, sank into depression and was unable to make reparations payments. Great Britain and France recovered slowly from the war's devastation. The United States was part of a global economy and eventually would be affected by the economic difficulties of the rest of the world.

The Rising Standard of Living

Signs of the new prosperity abounded. Millions of homes and apartments were built and equipped with the latest conveniences. The number of telephones installed nearly doubled between 1915 and 1930.

Plastics, rayon, and cellophane altered American habits, and new products, such as cigarette lighters, reinforced concrete, dry ice, and Pyrex glass, created demands unheard of a decade before.

Perhaps the most tangible sign of the new prosperity was the modern American bathroom. Hotels and the urban upper class began to install cast-iron bathtubs and primitive flush toilets in the late nineteenth century, but not until the early 1920s did the enameled tub, toilet, and washbasin become standard. By 1925, American factories turned out 5 million enameled bathroom fixtures annually. The bathroom, with unlimited hot water, privacy, and clean white fixtures, symbolized American affluence.

In sharp contrast to people in European countries, middle-class Americans had more leisure time, a shorter workweek, and more paid vacation time. The American diet also improved during the decade. Health improved and life expectancy increased. Educational opportunities also expanded. In 1900, only 1 in 10 young people of high-school age remained in school; by 1930, that number had grown to 6 in 10, and much of the increase came in the 1920s. In 1900, only 1 college-age person in 33 attended an institution of higher learning; by 1930, the ratio was 1 in 7, and more than a million people were enrolled in the nation's colleges.

The Rise of the Modern Corporation

The structure and practice of American business were transformed in the 1920s. Mergers increased during the decade at a rate greater than at any time since the end of the 1890s—there were more than 1,200 mergers in 1929 alone—creating such giants as General Electric, General Motors, Sears Roebuck, Du Pont, and U.S. Rubber. These were not monopolies but oligopolies (industry domination spread among a few large firms). By 1930, the 200 largest corporations controlled almost half the corporate wealth.

Perhaps the most important business trend of the decade was the emergence of a new kind of manager. The prototype was Alfred P. Sloan, Jr., an engineer who reorganized General Motors. Sloan divided the company into components, freeing top managers to concentrate on planning new products, controlling inventory, and integrating the whole operation. Marketing and advertising became as important as production, and many businesses began to spend more money on research.

The new managers tried to keep employees working efficiently, but they used more than the stopwatch and the assembly line. They introduced pensions, recreation facilities, cafeterias, and, in some cases, paid vacations and profit-sharing plans. The managers were not being altruistic; rather, "welfare capitalism" was designed to reduce worker discontent and to discourage labor unions.

Planning was the key to the new corporate structure, and planning often meant continuing the business–government cooperation developed during World War I. All the planning and the new managerial authority failed to prevent the economic collapse of 1929, but the modern corporation survived the depression to exert a growing influence on American life in the 1930s and after.

Electrification

The 1920s marked the climax of the "second Industrial Revolution," powered by electricity and producing a growing array of consumer goods. By 1929, electrical generators provided 80 percent of the power used in industry. Fewer than one of every ten American homes had electricity in 1907; by 1919 more than two-thirds did.

Electricity brought dozens of gadgets and labor-saving devices into the home. Washing machines and electric irons gradually reduced the drudgery of washday for women, and vacuum cleaners, electric toasters, and sewing machines lightened housework. But the new machines still needed human direction and did not reduce the time the average housewife spent doing housework. For many poor urban and rural women, the traditional female tasks of carrying, pushing, pulling, and lifting went on as they had for centuries. In many ways, the electric revolution increased the contrast in American life. The "great white ways" of the cities, lit by electric lights, symbolized progress, but they also made the darkness of slums and hamlets seem even more forbidding.

A Global Automobile Culture

Automobile manufacturing, like electrification, underwent spectacular growth in the 1920s. The automobile was one major factor in the postwar economic boom. It stimulated and transformed the petroleum, steel, and rubber industries. The auto forced the construction and improvement of streets and highways and led to millions of dollars of expenditures on labor and concrete.

The auto created new suburbs and allowed families to live farther from work. The filling station, the diner, and the overnight cabin became familiar and eventually standardized objects on the American scene. Traffic lights, stop signs, billboards, and parking lots appeared. Hitching posts and watering troughs became rarer, and gradually the garage replaced the livery stable. The auto changed the look of the American landscape and threatened the environment as well. Oil and gasoline contaminated streams, and piles of old tires and rusting hulks of discarded cars became a familiar eyesore along highways. Emissions from thousands and then millions of internal combustion engines polluted the air. The increasing use of nonrenewable fossil fuels was already apparent in the 1920s, and the trend continued.

The auto changed American life in other ways. It led to the decline of the small crossroads store as well as many small churches because the rural family could now drive to the larger city or town. Tractors and trucks changed the methods of farming. Buses began to eliminate the one-room schoolhouse, because it was now possible to transport students to larger schools. The automobile allowed young people for the first time to escape the chaperoning of parents.

Gradually, as the decade progressed, the automobile became not just transportation but a sign of status. Advertising helped create the impression that it was the symbol of the good life, of sex, freedom, and speed. The auto in turn transformed advertising and design. It even altered the way products were purchased. By 1926, three-fourths of the cars sold were bought on some kind of deferred-payment plan. Installment credit, first tried by a group of businessmen in Toledo, Ohio, in 1915 to sell more autos, was soon used to promote sewing machines, refrigerators, and other consumer products. "Buy now, pay later" became the American way.

The United States had a love affair with the auto from the beginning. There were 8,000 motor vehicles registered in the country in 1900, and nearly a million in 1912. But only in the 1920s did the auto come within the reach of middle-class consumers. In 1929, Americans purchased 4.5 million cars, and by the end of that year, nearly 27 million were registered.

In part because of Henry Ford and the development of the inexpensive car, and because the United States had a much larger middle class who could afford a car, the ownership of automobiles expanded rapidly in the United States. This differed from Europe, where most autos were custom-made. The most important British company, Morris Motors, did not adopt the assembly line method of production until 1934. France, Germany, and England all subsidized auto manufacture for military purposes, further delaying the development of an inexpensive car. But because of their strong central governments, European countries adopted safety standards and required national licenses for vehicles and drivers before such measures were adopted in the United States.

In the United States, the states created the rules, and in the beginning it was assumed that anyone could drive a car. The world agreed on time zones, postage regulations, and other things, but not on which side of the road to drive on. In Great Britain, Japan, and all parts of the British empire, cars were driven on the left side, while in the United States and most of Europe, driving on the right side was the proper thing to do. Eventually most of the world, following the American lead, was transformed by automobile culture, but in many countries, that did not happen until after World War II.

Henry Ford

Many men contributed to the development and production of the auto—William Durant organized General Motors; Charles Kettering, an engineering genius, developed the electric self-starter; and Ransom E. Olds built the first mass-produced, moderately priced, light car. Above all the others loomed a name that became synonymous with the automobile itself—Henry Ford.

Ford had the reputation of being a progressive industrial leader and a champion of the common people. As with all men and women who take on symbolic significance, the truth is less dramatic than the stories. For example, Ford is often credited with inventing the assembly line. What he actually did (along with a team of engineers) was adapt the assembly line and the concept of interchangeable parts to the production of autos. Introduced in 1913, the new method reduced the time it took to produce a car from 14 hours to an hour and a half. The product of the carefully planned system, the Model T, was the prototype of the inexpensive family car.

In 1914, Ford startled the country by announcing that he was increasing the minimum pay of the Ford assembly-line worker to $5 a day (almost twice the national average pay for factory workers). Ford was not a humanitarian. He wanted a dependable workforce and realized that skilled workers were less likely to quit if they received good pay. Ford was one of the first to recognize that workers were consumers as well as producers and that they might buy Model T Fords. But work in the Ford factory had its disadvantages. The assembly line was repetitious and numbing. "You could drop over dead," one worker recalled, "and they wouldn't stop the line." And when the line closed down, as it did periodically, workers were released without compensation.

The Model T, which cost $600 in 1912, was reduced gradually in price until it sold for only $290 in 1924. The "Tin Lizzie," as it was affectionately called, was light and easily repaired. Some owners claimed all one needed were a pair of pliers and some baling wire to keep it running. If it got stuck on bad roads, as it often did, a reasonably healthy man could lift it. Replacement parts were standardized and widely available.

The Model T did not change from year to year, nor did it deviate from its one color, black. Except for adding a self-starter, offering a closed model, and making a few minor face-lift changes, Ford kept the Model T in 1927 much as he had introduced it in 1909. By that time, its popularity had declined as

The Model A, introduced in 1927, did not dominate the market as the Model T had done, but the gigantic River Rouge factory, spreading over a thousand acres in Dearborn, Michigan, was built especially to produce the new model. It became the symbol of mass production in the new era. The auto industry, like most American business, went through a period of consolidation in the 1920s. In 1908, more than 250 companies produced cars in the United States. By 1929, only 44 remained.

The Exploding Metropolis

The automobile transformed the city and led to the gradual decline of the streetcar and the interurban trolley. In the late nineteenth century, railroads and streetcars had created suburbs near the major cities, but the great expansion of suburban population occurred in the 1920s. Shaker Heights, a Cleveland suburb, was in some ways a typical development. Built on the site of a former Shaker community, the new suburb was planned and developed by two businessmen. They controlled the size and style of the homes and restricted buyers. No blacks were allowed. Curving roads led off the main auto boulevards, and landscaping and natural areas contributed to a parklike atmosphere. The suburb increased in population from 1,700 in 1919 to more than 15,000 in 1929, and the price of lots multiplied by 10 during the decade.

Other suburbs grew in an equally spectacular manner. Beverly Hills, near Los Angeles, increased in population by 2,485 percent during the decade.

Automobile Assembly Line

The automobile changed life in the United States in many ways. In 1929, 27 million cars were registered in the United States, up from 1 million in 1900. Hundreds of thousands of people were employed in the auto industry, in manufacturing, sales, and service. The assembly line, first used by Henry Ford in 1913, transformed not only the auto industry, but also the way other products were manufactured. In addition, it changed the nature of work and altered the lives of those who worked on the line. Can you imagine working in a factory like this? In what other ways did the auto change life for Americans in the 1920s?

(From the Collections of The Henry Ford Museum & Greenfield Village)

many people traded up to sleeker, more colorful, and, they thought, more prestigious autos from Ford's competitors; as a result, wages at Ford dipped below the industry average.

TEN LARGEST CITIES IN 1900 AND 1930*

What trends are revealed by this chart? Why are some cities growing faster than others?

1900		1930	
1. New York	4,023,000	1. New York	9,423,000
2. Chicago	1,768,000	2. Chicago	3,870,000
3. Philadelphia	1,458,000	3. Philadelphia	2,399,000
4. Boston	905,000	4. Detroit	1,837,000
5. Pittsburgh	622,000	5. Los Angeles	1,778,000
6. St. Louis	612,000	6. Boston	1,545,000
7. Baltimore	543,000	7. Pittsburgh	1,312,000
8. San Francisco	444,000	8. San Francisco	1,104,000
9. Cincinnati	414,000	9. St. Louis	1,094,000
10. Cleveland	402,000	10. Cleveland	1,048,000

*Figures are for the entire metropolitan areas, including suburbs.

Source: U.S. Bureau of the Census.

Grosse Point Park, near Detroit, grew by 725 percent, and Elmwood Park, near Chicago, increased by 716 percent. The automobile also allowed industry to move to the suburbs. The number of employees in manufacturing establishments in the suburbs of the 11 largest cities increased from 365,000 in 1919 to 1.2 million in 1937.

The biggest land boom of all occurred in Florida, where Miami mushroomed from 30,000 in 1920 to 75,000 in 1925. One plot of land in West Palm Beach sold for $800,000 in 1923; two years later, it was worth $4 million. A hurricane in 1926 ended the Florida land boom temporarily, but most cities and their suburbs continued to grow during the decade.

The most spectacular growth took place in two cities that the auto virtually created. Detroit grew from 300,000 in 1900 to 1,837,000 in 1930, and Los Angeles expanded from 114,000 in 1900 to 1,778,000 in 1930. With sprawling subdivisions connected by a growing network of roads, Los Angeles was the city of the future.

Cities expanded horizontally during the 1920s, sprawling into the countryside, but city centers grew vertically. A building boom that peaked near the end of the decade created new skylines for most urban centers. Even cities such as Tulsa, Dallas, Kansas City, Memphis, and Syracuse built skyscrapers. The most famous skyscraper of all, the Empire State Building in New York, towering 102 stories, was finished in 1931 but not completely occupied until after World War II.

A Communications Revolution

Changing communications altered the way many Americans lived as well as the way they conducted business. The telephone was first demonstrated in 1876. By 1899, more than 1 million phones were in operation. During the 1920s, the number of homes with phones increased from 9 million to 13 million. Still, by the end of the decade, more than half of American homes were without phones.

Even more than the telephone, the radio symbolized the technological and communicational changes of the 1920s. Department stores quickly began to stock radios, or crystal sets as they were called, but many Americans in the 1920s built their own receivers. The first station to begin commercial broadcasting was WWJ in Detroit in the summer of 1920. When WWJ and KDKA in Pittsburgh broadcast election returns in 1920, they ushered in a new era in politics. The next year, WJZ of Newark, New Jersey, broadcast the World Series, beginning a process that would transform baseball and eventually football and basketball as well. In 1922, a radio station in New York broadcast the first commercial, an indication that the airways would be used to increase the demand for the goods the factories were producing.

Much early broadcasting consisted of classical music, but soon came news analysis and coverage of presidential inaugurals and important events. Some stations produced live dramas, but more than any other programs serials such as *Amos 'n' Andy* made radio a national medium. Millions of people scattered across the country could sit in their living rooms (and after 1927, in their cars) listening to the same program. The record industry grew just as rapidly. By the end of the decade, people in all sections of the country hummed the same popular songs. Actors and announcers became celebrities. The radio, even more than the automobile, marked the end of silence and, to a certain extent, the end of privacy.

Even more dramatic was the phenomenon of the movies. Forty million viewers a week went to the movies in 1922, and by 1929 that number exceeded 100 million. Early movies were made in New York, Chicago, and a few other cities, but by the mid-1920s, the village of Hollywood, near Los Angeles, had become the movie capital of the world. Giant firms such as Metro-Goldwyn-Mayer, created in 1924, dominated the industry. Men, women, and children flocked to small theaters in the towns and to movie palaces in the cities, where they could dream of romance or adventure. Charlie Chaplin, Rudolph Valentino, Lillian Gish, and Greta Garbo were more famous and more important to millions of Americans than were most government officials. The motion pictures, which before the war had attracted mostly the working class, now seemed to appeal across class, regional, and generational lines.

The movies had the power to influence attitudes and ideas. In the 1920s, many parents feared that the movies would dictate ideas about sex and life. One young college woman remembered, "One day I went to see Viola Dana in *The Five Dollar Baby*. The scenes which showed her as a baby fascinated me so that I stayed to see it over four times. I forgot home, dinner and everything. About eight o'clock mother came after me." She also admitted that the movies taught her how to smoke, and in some of the movies "there were some lovely scenes which just got me all hot 'n' bothered."

Just as famous as the movie stars were sports figures such as Babe Ruth, Bobby Jones, Jack Dempsey, and Red Grange. The great spectator sports of the decade owed much to the increase in leisure time and to the automobile, the radio, and the mass-circulation newspaper. Thousands drove to college towns to watch football heroes perform. Millions listened for scores or read about the results the next day.

The year 1927 seemed to mark the beginning of the new age of mechanization and progress. That year, Henry Ford produced his 15 millionth car and introduced the Model A. Radio-telephone service was established between San Francisco and Manila. The

ADVERTISING

Have you ever noticed that television commercials can often be more interesting and creative than the programs? One authority has suggested that the best way for a foreign visitor to understand the American character and popular culture is to study television commercials. Television advertising, the thesis goes, appeals to basic cultural assumptions. The nature of advertising not only reveals for historians the prejudices, fears, values, and aspirations of a people but also makes an impact on historical development itself, influencing patterns of taste and purchasing habits. One modern critic calls advertising a "peculiarly American force that now compares with such long-standing institutions

Automobile advertisement (1929)

(CORBIS)

"...and Jane, dear... Jack just raved about my teeth."

"I just smiled my prettiest smile... and let him rave. I could have said 'Of course I have beautiful teeth ... I've used Colgate's all my life'. But I didn't want Jack to think I was a living advertisement for Colgate's tooth paste."

* * * * *

Beautiful teeth glisten gloriously. They compel the admiration of all who see them. And there is health as well as beauty in gleaming teeth, for when they are scrupulously kept clean, germs and poisons of decay can't lurk and breed around them.

Remove Those Causes of Decay

Save yourself the embarrassment so often caused by poor teeth. Fight the germs of tooth decay.

Colgate's will keep your teeth scrupulously clean. It reaches all the hard-to-get-at places between the teeth and around the edges of the gums, and so removes causes of tooth decay. It is the dependable tooth paste for you to use.

Washes—Polishes—Protects

The principal ingredients of Colgate's are mild soap and fine chalk, the two

things that dental authorities say a safe dental cream should contain. The combined action of these ingredients washes, polishes and protects the delicate enamel of your teeth.

Use Colgate's Regularly

Just remember that beautiful, healthy teeth are more a matter of good care than of good luck. Use Colgate's after meals and at bedtime. It will keep your teeth clean and gloriously attractive.

And you'll like its taste...even children love to use it regularly.

Priced right too! Large tube 25c.

Colgate's

Toothpaste advertisement

as the school and church in the magnitude of its social impact."

As long as manufacturing was local and limited, there was no need to advertise. Before the Civil War, for example, the local area could usually absorb all that was produced; therefore, a simple announcement in a local paper was sufficient to let people know that a particular product was available. But when factories began producing more than the local market could ordinarily consume, advertising came into play to create a larger demand.

Although national advertising began with the emergence of "name brands" in the late nineteenth century, it did not achieve the importance it now holds until the 1920s. In 1918, the total gross advertising revenue in magazines was $58.5 million. By 1920, it had more than doubled to $129.5 million, and by 1929, it was nearly $200 million. These

For Clean-up King
I Nominate...

by LOU GEHRIG

**New York Yankees' Clean-up Ace Makes
Novel Choice for All-Time Honor**

I DON'T need to tell baseball fans how important the "clean-up" (number four) man is in the batting line-up. With three reliable hitters batting ahead of him, it is his wallops that bring in the runs.

In my thirteen years of big league baseball I have watched some of the most famous "clean-up" men in the history of the game. But the other day in Boston I had the pleasure of seeing the "clean-up" king that gets my vote for the "all-time" honors. Strangely enough, this "clean-up" king isn't a slugger at all. Instead of cleaning up the bases, this one's specialty is cleaning up faces.

Here's how it happened. While in Boston playing the Red Sox, I made an inspection trip through the Gillette Safety Razor factory. There I discovered that what is true of baseball is also true of Gillette Blades. In baseball, the pick of the raw material is tried out, tested, and trained for the big league teams. At the Gillette factory I found that they buy only the finest steel, and put it through gruelling tests before it is made into Gillette Blades.

For instance, like a rookie baseball player, Gillette Blade steel has to be hardened and tempered.

To do this, Gillette uses electric furnaces, each one controlled by a device which can tell in an instant if the steel passing through the furnaces requires more heat or less heat. Faster than a speedball, the signal is flashed from the box to a great battery of switches, and the heat is raised or lowered accordingly. Then to make doubly sure that there is no possibility of error, they X-ray the steel with an electro-magnetic tester to detect hidden flaws.

A good ball player has to have precision and accuracy, too . . . and that's where Gillette chalks up a winning score. Grinding machines, adjustable to 1/10,000 of an inch give Gillette Blades shaving edges so keen you can't see them, even with the most powerful microscope.

These are some of the reasons why I nominate the Gillette Blade for all-time Clean-up King. For when it comes to cleaning up on stubborn bristles—with the greatest of ease and comfort—Gillette hits a home run with the bases loaded. Yes, Sir!—if baseball could only train players as accurately and efficiently as Gillette makes razor blades, we'd all find it easy to bat 1000.

With these important facts before you, why let anyone deprive you of shaving comfort by selling you a substitute! Ask for Gillette Blades and be sure to get them.

GILLETTE SAFETY RAZOR COMPANY, BOSTON, MASS.

| Razor blade advertisement

---

figures should not be surprising in a decade that often equated advertising with religion. The biblical Moses was called the "ad-writer for the Deity," and in a best-selling book, Bruce Barton, a Madison Avenue advertiser, reinterpreted Jesus, the "man nobody knows," as a master salesman. Wrote Barton: "He would be a national advertiser today."

The designers of ads began to study psychology to determine what motives, conscious or unconscious, influenced consumers. One psychologist concluded that the appeal to the human instinct for "gaining social prestige" would sell the most goods. Another way to sell products, many learned, was to create anxiety in the mind of the consumer over body odor, bad breath, oily hair, dandruff, pimples, and other embarrassing ailments. In 1921, the Lambert Company used the term *halitosis* for bad breath in an ad for Listerine. Within six years, sales of Listerine had increased from a little more than 100,000 bottles a year to more than 4 million.

The appeal to sex also sold products, advertisers soon found, as did the desire for the latest style or invention. But perhaps the most important thing advertisers marketed was youth. "We are going to sell every artificial thing there is," a cosmetics salesman wrote in 1926, "and above all it is going to be young-young-young! We make women feel young." A great portion of the ads were aimed at women. As one trade journal announced: "The proper study of mankind is man . . . , but the proper study of markets is woman."

Reflecting on the Past Look at the accompanying advertisements carefully. What do they tell you about American culture in the 1920s? What do they suggest about attitudes toward women? Do they reveal any special anxieties? How are they similar to and different from advertising today?

---

first radio network was organized (CBS), and the first talking movie (*The Jazz Singer*) was released. The Holland Tunnel, the first underwater vehicular roadway, connected New York and New Jersey, and Charles Lindbergh flew from New York to Paris in his single-engine plane in 33 1/2 hours. He was young and handsome, and his feat seemed to represent not only the triumph of an individual but also the triumph of the machine. When Americans cheered Lindbergh, they were reaffirming their belief in the American dream and their faith in individual initiative as well as in technology.

Hopes Raised, Promises Deferred

The 1920s was a time when it seemed all kinds of hopes could be realized. "Don't envy successful salesmen—be one!" one advertisement screamed. Buy a car. Build a house. Start a career. Invest in land. Invest in stocks. Make a fortune.

Not all Americans, of course, dreamed of making a stock-market killing or expected to win a huge fortune. Some merely wished to retain traditional values in a society that seemed to question them. Others wanted a steady job and a little respect. Still others hungered for the new appliances so alluringly described in ads and on the radio. Many discovered, however, that even their modest hopes lay tantalizingly out of reach.

Clash of Values

During the 1920s, radio, movies, advertising, and mass-circulation magazines promoted a national, secular culture. But this new culture, which emphasized consumption, pleasure, upward mobility, and even sex, clashed with traditional values of hard work, thrift, church, family, and home. Although it would be easy to see these cultural differences as a reflection of an urban–rural conflict, in fact, many people clinging to the old ways had moved into the cities. Still, many Americans feared that new cultural values, scientific breakthroughs, and new ideas such as bolshevism, relativism, Freudianism, and biblical criticism threatened their familiar way of life. A trial over the teaching of evolutionary ideas in high school in the little town of Dayton, Tennessee, symbolized, even as it exaggerated, the clash of the old versus the new, the traditional versus the modern, the city versus the country.

The scientific community and most educated people had long accepted the basic concepts of evolution, if not all the details of Charles Darwin's theories. But many Christians, especially those from Protestant evangelical churches, accepted the Bible as the literal truth. They believed that faith in the Gospel message was crucial to living a virtuous life on earth and, more important, going to heaven. Many of these faithful saw a major spiritual crisis in the dramatic changes of the 1920s. Resistance to the concept of evolution resulted in legislative efforts in several states to forbid its teaching.

John Scopes, a young biology teacher, broke the law by teaching evolutionary theory to his class, and the state of Tennessee brought him to trial. The American Civil Liberties Union hired Clarence Darrow, perhaps the country's most famous defense lawyer, to defend Scopes; the World Christian Fundamentalist Association engaged William Jennings Bryan, former presidential candidate and secretary of state, to assist

the prosecution. Bryan was old and tired (he died only a few days after the trial), but he was still an eloquent and deeply religious man. In cross-examination, Darrow reduced Bryan's statements to intellectual rubble and also revealed that Bryan was at a loss to explain much of the Bible. Nevertheless, the jury declared Scopes guilty, for he had clearly broken the law.

The national press covered the trial and upheld science and academic freedom. Journalists such as H. L. Mencken had a field day poking fun at Bryan and the fundamentalists. "Heave an egg out a Pullman window," Mencken wrote, "and you will hit a Fundamentalist almost anywhere in the United States today.... They are everywhere where learning is too heavy a burden for mortal minds to carry."

Religious Fundamentalism

Religious fundamentalism continued to survive in a world fast becoming urban, modern, and sophisticated. Fundamentalism cut across many denominations and covered over many differences, but all fundamentalists believed in the literal interpretation and the infallibility of the Bible and that Jesus Christ was the only road to salvation. They rejected secularism, liberal theology, pluralism, the Social Gospel, and any sense that reform on earth could lead to perfection. They had an unshakable faith in what they believed was the truth.

Throughout the 1920s and the 1930s, attendance at Christian colleges and the circulation of fundamentalist periodicals and newspapers increased dramatically, and evangelical ministers reached large audiences. One of the most popular and flamboyant of the ministers was Billy Sunday, a former baseball player who jumped about the stage as he pitched his brand of Christianity. Another popular preacher was Aimee Semple McPherson, a faith healer who founded her own church, the International Church of the Four Square Gospel, in Los Angeles in 1927. Dressed as a University of Southern California football player, she ran across the stage "carrying the ball for Christ"; wielding a pitchfork, she drove the devil out of the auditorium.

Radio dramatically extended the reach of the fundamentalist preachers. McPherson was the first woman to hold a radio license, and she had the second most popular radio show in Los Angeles in the late 1920s. For many, the period between the wars was a time when people drifted away from organized religion, an age of technological marvels, and modernism in all fields, but for many others, fundamentalist religion and old-fashioned values not only survived but also prospered. Yet many fundamentalist sects succeeded in winning numerous converts because their leaders were skilled at using modern technology.

Immigration and Migration

Immigrants and anyone else perceived as "un-American" seemed to threaten the old ways. A movement to restrict immigration had existed for decades. An act passed in 1882 prohibited the entry of criminals, paupers, and the insane, and special agreements between 1880 and 1908 restricted both Chinese and Japanese immigration. But the fear and intolerance of the war years and the period right after the war resulted in major restrictive legislation.

The first strongly restrictive immigration law passed in 1917 over President Wilson's veto. It required a literacy test for the first time (an immigrant had to read a passage in one of a number of languages). The bill also prohibited the immigration of certain political radicals. However, the literacy test did not stop the more than 1 million immigrants who poured into the country in 1920 and 1921.

In 1921, Congress limited European immigration in any one year to 3 percent of the number of each nationality present in the country in 1910. In order to limit immigration from southern and eastern Europe

and to ban all immigration from Asia, Congress in 1924 changed the quota to 2 percent of those in the country in 1890. The National Origins Act of 1927 set an overall limit of 150,000 European immigrants a year, with more than 60 percent coming from Great Britain and Germany, but fewer than 4 percent from Italy.

Ethnicity increasingly became a factor in political alignments. Restrictive immigration laws, sponsored by Republicans, helped drive American Jews, Italians, and Poles to the Democratic party. By 1924, the Democratic party was so evenly divided between northern urban Catholics and southern rural Protestants that the party voted, by a very small margin, to condemn the Ku Klux Klan.

The immigration acts of 1921, 1924, and 1927 sharply limited European immigration and virtually banned Asian immigrants. The 1924 law contained a provision prohibiting the entry of aliens ineligible for citizenship. This provision was aimed directly at the Japanese, for the Chinese had already been excluded; but even without this provision, only a small number

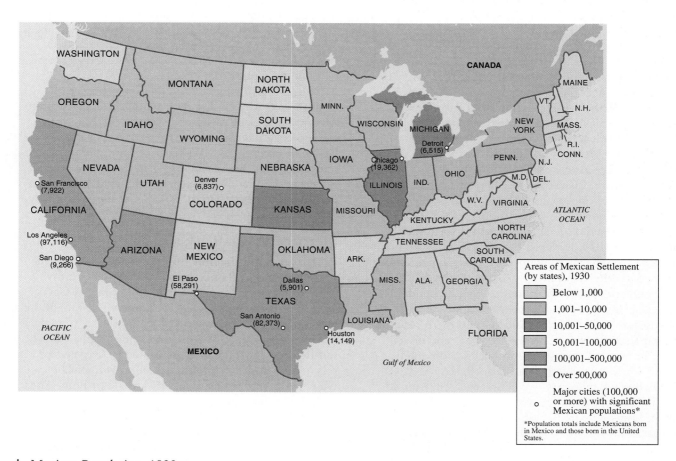

Mexican Population, 1930

Mexicans migrated across the border in great numbers in the 1920s; by 1930, they constituted a significant Spanish-speaking minority, especially in Texas, California, and Arizona. How did immigration laws of the 1920s shape ethnic cultures and communities in the United States?

could have entered the United States. "We try hard to be American," one California resident remarked, "But Americans always say you always Japanese." Denied both citizenship and the right to own land, the first-generation issei placed all of their hope in their children, but the second-generation nisei often felt trapped between the land of their parents and the America they lived in, and they still were treated as second-class citizens.

The immigration laws of the 1920s cut off the streams of cheap labor that had provided muscle for an industrializing country since the early nineteenth century. At the same time, by exempting immigrants from the Western Hemisphere, the new laws opened the country to Mexican laborers eager to escape poverty in their own land and to work in the fields and farms of California and the Southwest. Though they never matched the flood of eastern and southern Europeans who entered the country before World War I, Mexican immigrants soon became the country's largest first-generation immigrant group. Nearly half a million arrived in the 1920s, in contrast to only 31,000 in the first decade of the century. Mexican farm workers often lived in primitive camps, where conditions were unsanitary and health care was nonexistent.

Mexicans also migrated to industrial cities such as Detroit, St. Louis, and Kansas City. Northern companies recruited them and paid their transportation. During the 1920s, the population of El Paso, Texas, became more than 50 percent Mexican, and that of San Antonio a little less than 50 percent Mexican. In California, the Mexican population reached 368,000 in 1929, and in Los Angeles, the population was about 20 percent Mexican. Like African Americans, the Mexicans found opportunity by migrating, but they did not escape prejudice or hardship.

African Americans migrated north in great numbers from 1915 to 1920. Reduced European immigration and industrial growth caused many northern companies to recruit southern blacks. Trains stopped at the depots in small southern towns, sometimes picking up hundreds of blacks in a single day. Lured by editorials and advertisements placed by industries in northern black newspapers such as the Chicago *Defender* and driven out of the South by an agricultural depression, many African Americans eagerly headed north.

Most black migrants were unskilled. They found work in the huge meatpacking plants of Chicago, East St. Louis, Omaha, and Kansas City and in the shipyards and steel mills. Only 50 African Americans worked for the Ford Motor Company in 1916, but 2,500 worked there in 1920 and 10,000 in 1926. The black population of Chicago increased from 44,000 in 1910 to 234,000 by 1930. Cleveland's black population grew eightfold between 1910 and 1930.

African Americans unquestionably improved their lives by moving north. But most were like the Parkers, whom we met at the beginning of this chapter—their dreams were only partly fulfilled. Most crowded into segregated housing and faced prejudice and hate.

Often the young black men moved first, and only later brought their wives and children, putting great pressure on many black families. Some young men, like John Parker, restrained their anger, but others like Richard Wright's fictional Bigger Thomas, portrayed movingly in *Native Son* (1940), struck out violently against white society. The presence of more African Americans in the industrial cities of the North led to the development of black ghettos and increased the racial tension that occasionally flared into violence.

One of the worst race riots took place in Chicago in 1919. The riot began at a beach on a hot July day. A black youth drowned in a white swimming area. Blacks claimed he had been hit by stones, but the police refused to arrest any of the white men. A group of African Americans attacked the police, and the riot was on. It lasted four days. White youths drove through the black sections of the city, shooting blacks from car windows. Blacks returned the fire. Several dozen were killed, and hundreds were wounded. The tension between the races did not die when the riot was over. In the early 1920s, few cities escaped racial tension and violence.

The wave of violence and racism angered and disillusioned W. E. B. Du Bois, who had urged African Americans to close ranks and support the American cause during the war. In an angry editorial for *The Crisis*, he announced: "We return from fighting. We return fighting. Make way for Democracy; we saved it in France, and by the Great Jehovah, we will save it in the United States of America, or know the reason why."

Marcus Garvey: Black Messiah

Du Bois was not the only militant black leader in the postwar years. A flamboyant Jamaican fed a growing sense of black pride during that time. Marcus Garvey arrived in New York at age 29. Largely self-taught, he was an admirer of Booker T. Washington. Although he never abandoned Washington's philosophy of self-help, he thoroughly transformed it. Garvey saw self-help as a means of political empowerment by which African peoples would reclaim their homelands from European powers.

In Jamaica, Garvey had founded the Universal Negro Improvement Association. By 1919, he had established 30 branches in the United States and the Caribbean. He also set up the newspaper *The Negro World*, the Black Cross Nurses, and a chain of grocery stores, millinery shops, and restaurants. His biggest project was the Black Star Line, a steamship company that was to be owned and operated by African Americans. Advocating the return of blacks to Africa, he declared himself the "provisional president of Africa," a title he adopted from Eamon De Valera, the first "provisional president of Ireland." Garvey glorified the African past and preached that God and Jesus were black.

Garvey won converts, mostly among lower-middle-class blacks, through the force of his oratory and the power of his personality, but especially through his message that blacks should be proud of being black. "Up you mighty race, you can accomplish what you will," Garvey thundered. Thousands of blacks cheered as his Universal African Legions, dressed in blue and red uniforms, marched by. They waved the red, black, and green flag and sang "Ethiopia, the Land of Our Fathers," while thousands invested their money in the Black Star Line. The line soon collapsed, however, in part because white entrepreneurs sold Garvey inferior ships and equipment. Garvey was arrested for using

Black Messiah

Marcus Garvey (second from the right), shown dressed in his favorite uniform, became a hero for many black Americans. How did his appeal differ from that of other African American leaders?

(Hulton Archive/Getty Images)

the mails to defraud shareholders and was sentenced to five years in prison. Although President Coolidge commuted the sentence, Garvey was ordered deported as an undesirable alien and left America in 1927. Despite his failures, he convinced thousands of black Americans, especially the poor and discouraged, that they could join together and accomplish something and that they should feel pride in their heritage and their future.

The Harlem Renaissance

A group of black writers, artists, and intellectuals who settled in Harlem after the war led a movement related in some ways to Garvey's black nationalism crusade. It was less flamboyant but in the end more important. They studied anthropology, art, history, and music, and they wrote novels and poetry that explored the ambivalent role of blacks in America. Like Garvey, they expressed their pride in being black and sought their African roots and the folk tradition of blacks in America. But unlike Garvey, they had no desire to go back to Africa; instead, they sought a way to be both black and American.

Alain Locke, the first black Rhodes scholar, was in one sense the father of the movement called the Harlem Renaissance. His collection of essays and art, *The New Negro* (1925), announced the movement to the outside world. Langston Hughes, a poet and novelist, wrote bitter but humorous poems, using black vernacular to describe the pathos and the pride of African Americans. In *Weary Blues*, he adapted the rhythm and beat of black jazz and the blues to his poetry.

Jazz was an important force in Harlem in the 1920s, and many prosperous whites came from downtown to listen to Louis Armstrong, Fletcher Henderson, Duke Ellington, and other black musicians. The promise of expressing primitive emotions, the erotic atmosphere, the music, and the illegal sex, drugs, and liquor made Harlem an intriguing place for many brought up in Victorian white America.

Harlem jazz was also exported to Europe, especially to Paris. Returning black servicemen reported that African Americans were treated without prejudice in France, and black musicians began to drift to the Montmartre section of Paris, where American jazz and jazz singers such as the seductive Josephine Baker, star of *Revue Nègre,* became the toast of the town. Ironically, many American tourists in the 1920s first heard an African American jazz band in Paris. Many Europeans criticized the United States for its materialism and for its innocent exuberance. They were not impressed with American literature or American art, but they loved American jazz. It was the beginning of the export of American popular culture that would impress most of the rest of the world in the decades after World War II.

The Jamaican Claude McKay, who came to Harlem by way of Tuskegee and Kansas, wrote about the underside of life in Harlem in *Home to Harlem* (1925), one of the most popular of the "new Negro" novels. McKay portrayed two black men—one, named Jake, who has deserted the white man's army and finds a life of simple and erotic pleasure in Harlem's cabarets, the other an intellectual who is unable to make such an easy choice. "My damned white education has robbed me of much of the primitive vitality, the pure stamina, the simple unswaggering strength of the Jakes of the negro race," he laments.

This was the dilemma of many of the Harlem writers: how to be both black and intellectual. They worried that they depended on white patrons, who introduced them to writers and artists in Greenwich Village and made contacts for them at New York publishing houses. Many of the white patrons pressured the black writers to conform to the white elite idea of black authenticity. The black writers resented this intrusion, but it was their only hope to be recognized.

Many African American writers felt alienated from American society. They tried living in Paris or in Greenwich Village, but most felt drawn to Harlem, which in the 1920s was rapidly becoming the center of black population in New York City. More than 117,000 white people left the neighborhood during the decade, while more than 87,000 blacks moved in. Countee Cullen, the only writer in the group actually born in New York, remarked, "In spite of myself I find that I am activated by a strong sense of race consciousness." So, too, was Zora Neale Hurston activated. Born in Florida, she went to New York to study at Barnard College, earned an advanced degree in anthropology from Columbia University, and used her interest in folklore to write stories of robust and passionate rural blacks. Many Harlem writers reached a limited audience, but they were rediscovered in the 1960s by another generation of young black intellectuals struggling with the dilemma of how to be both black and American.

The Lost Generation

Many white intellectuals, writers, and artists also felt alienated from what they perceived as the materialism, conformity, and provincial prejudice that dominated American life. Many writers, including F. Scott Fitzgerald, Ernest Hemingway, E. E. Cummings, and T. S. Eliot, moved to Europe. Like so many American intellectuals in all periods, they had a love–hate relationship with their country.

For many writers, the disillusionment began with the war itself. Hemingway eagerly volunteered to go to Europe as an ambulance driver. But when he was wounded on the Italian front, he reevaluated the purpose of the war and the meaning of all the slaughter. His novel *The Sun Also Rises* (1926) is the story of the purposeless European wanderings of a group of Americans. But it is also the story of Jake Barnes, who was made impotent by a war injury. His "unreasonable wound" is a symbol of the futility of life in the postwar period.

F. Scott Fitzgerald, who loved to frequent the cafés and parties in Paris, became a celebrity during the 1920s. He epitomized some of the despair of his generation, which had "grown up to find all Gods dead, all wars fought, all faiths in man shaken." His best novel, *The Great Gatsby* (1925), was a critique of the American success myth.

It was not necessary to live in France to criticize American society. Sherwood Anderson, born in Camden, Ohio, created a fictional midwestern town in *Winesburg, Ohio* (1919) as a way to describe the dull, narrow, warped lives that seemed to provide a metaphor for American culture. Sinclair Lewis, another midwesterner, created scathing parodies of middle-class, small-town life in *Main Street* (1920) and *Babbitt* (1922). The "hero" of the latter novel is a salesman from the town of Zenith. He is a "he-man," a "regular guy" who distrusts "red professors," foreign-born people, and anyone from New York.

No one had more fun laughing at the American middle class than H. L. Mencken, who edited the *American Mercury* in Baltimore and denounced what he called the "booboisie." He labeled Woodrow Wilson a "self-bamboozled Presbyterian" and poked fun at Warren Harding's prose, which he said reminded him of "a string of wet sponges, . . . of stale bean soup, of college yells, of dogs barking idiotically through endless nights."

Ironically, while intellectuals despaired over American society and complained that art could not survive in a business-dominated civilization, literature flourished. The novels of Hemingway, Fitzgerald, Lewis, William Faulkner, and Gertrude Stein; the plays of Eugene O'Neill and Maxwell Anderson; the poetry of T. S. Eliot, Hart Crane, E. E. Cummings, and Marianne Moore; and the work of many black writers, such as Langston Hughes, Claude McKay, and Zora Neale Hurston, marked the 1920s as one of the most creative decades in American literature.

Women Struggle for Equality

Any mention of the role of women in the 1920s brings to mind the image of the flapper—a young woman with a short skirt, bobbed hair, and a boyish figure dancing the Charleston, smoking, drinking, and enjoying sexual encounters. F. Scott Fitzgerald's heroines in novels such as *This Side of Paradise* (1920) and *The Great Gatsby* (1925) provided the role models for young people to imitate, and movie stars such as Clara Bow and Gloria Swanson, aggressively seductive on the screen, supplied even more dramatic examples of provocative behavior.

Without question, women acquired more sexual freedom in the 1920s. "None of the Victorian mothers had any idea how casually their daughters were accustomed to being kissed," F. Scott Fitzgerald wrote. However, it is difficult, if not impossible, to know how accustomed those daughters (and their mothers) were to kissing and enjoying other sexual activity. Contraceptives, especially the diaphragm, became more readily available during the decade, and Margaret Sanger, who had been indicted for sending birth control information through the mail in 1914, organized the first American birth control conference in 1921. Still, most states made the selling or prescribing of birth control devices illegal, and federal laws prohibited sending literature discussing birth control through the mail.

Family size declined during the decade (from 3.6 children in 1900 to 2.5 in 1930), and young people were apparently more inclined to marry for love than for security. More women expected sexual satisfaction in marriage (nearly 60 percent in one poll) and felt that divorce was the best solution for an unhappy marriage. In another poll, nearly 85 percent approved of sexual intercourse as an expression of love and affection and not simply for procreation. But the polls were hardly scientific and tended to be biased toward the attitudes of the urban middle class. Despite more freedom for women, the double standard persisted.

Women's lives were shaped by other innovations of the 1920s. Electricity, running water, washing machines, vacuum cleaners, and other labor-saving devices made housework easier for the middle class. Yet these developments did not touch large numbers of rural and urban working-class women. Even middle-class women discovered that new appliances did not reduce time spent doing housework. Standards of cleanliness rose, and women were urged to make their houses more spotless than any nineteenth-century housekeeper would have felt necessary. At the same time, magazines and newspapers bombarded women with advertising urging them to buy products to make themselves better housekeepers yet still be beautiful. It must have been frustrating for those who could not afford the magic new products or whose hands and teeth and skin failed to look youthful despite all their efforts. The ads also promoted new dress styles, shorter skirts, and no corsets. The young adopted them quickly, and they also learned to swim (and to display more of their bodies on the beach), to play tennis (but only if they belonged to a tennis club), and to ride a bicycle.

More women worked outside the home. Whereas in 1890, only 17 percent of women were employed, by 1933, some 22 percent were. But their share of manufacturing jobs fell from 19 percent to 16 percent between 1900 and 1930. The greatest expansion of jobs was in white-collar occupations that were being feminized—for example, secretary, bookkeeper, clerk, and telephone operator. In 1930, fully 96 percent of stenographers were women. Although more married women had jobs (an increase of 25 percent during the decade), most of them held low-paying jobs, and most single women assumed that marriage would terminate their employment.

For some working women—secretaries and teachers, for example—marriage often led to dismissal. Married women are "very unstable in their work; their first claim is to home and children," a businessman concluded. Although women might not be able to work after their weddings (in one poll of college men, only one in nine said he would allow his wife to work after

WOMEN IN THE LABOR FORCE, 1900–1930

Why is the percentage of women working gradually increasing between 1900 and 1930? Why are more married women working?

Year	Women in Labor Force	Percentage of Women in Total Labor Force	Percentage of Total Women of Working Age	Single	Married	Widowed
1900	4,997,000	18.1	20.6	66.2	15.4	18.4
1910*	7,640,000	NA	25.4	60.2	24.7	15.0
1920	8,347,000	20.4	23.7	77.0†	23.0	—†
1930	10,632,000	21.9	24.8	53.9	28.9	17.2

*Data not comparable with other censuses due to a difference in the basis of enumeration.

† Single includes widowed and divorced.

Source: U.S. Bureau of the Census.

marriage), a job as a secretary could be good prepara-tion for marriage. A business office was a good place to meet eligible men, but more than that, a secretary learned endurance, self-effacement, and obedience, traits that would make her a good wife. Considering these attitudes, it is not surprising that the disparity between male and female wages widened during the decade. By 1930, women earned only 57 percent of what men were paid.

The image of the flapper in the 1920s promised more freedom and equality for women than they actually achieved. The flapper was young, white, slender, and upper class (Fitzgerald fixed her ideal age at 19), and most women did not fit those cate-gories. The flapper was frivolous and daring, not professional and competent. Although the proportion of women lawyers and bankers increased slightly dur-ing the decade, the rate of growth declined, and the number of women doctors and scientists dropped. In the 1920s, women acquired some sexual freedom and a limited amount of opportunity outside the home, but the promise of the prewar feminist move-ment and the hopes that accompanied the suffrage amendment remained unfulfilled.

Winning the vote for women did not ensure equality. Women could vote, but often they could not serve on juries. In some states, women could not hold office, own a business, or sign a contract without their husbands' permission. Women were usually held responsible for an illegitimate birth, and divorce laws almost always favored men. Many women leaders were disappointed in the small turnout of women in the presidential election of 1920. To educate women in the reality of politics, they organized the National League of Women Voters to "finish the fight."

Alice Paul, who had led the militant National Women's Party in 1916, chained herself to the White House fence once again to promote an equal rights amendment to the Constitution. The amendment got support in Wisconsin and in several other states, but many women opposed it on the grounds that such an amendment would cancel the special legislation to pro-tect women in industry that had taken so long to enact in the two preceding decades. Feminists disagreed in the 1920s on the proper way to promote equality and rights for women, but the political and social climate was not conducive to feminist causes.

Rural America in the 1920s

Most farmers did not share in the prosperity of the 1920s. Responding to worldwide demands and rising prices for wheat, cotton, and other products, many farmers invested in additional land, tractors, and farm equipment during the war. Then prices tumbled. By

1921, the price of wheat had dropped 40 percent, corn 32 percent, and hogs 50 percent. Total farm income fell from $10 million to $4 million in the postwar depression. Many farmers could not make payments on their tractors. Because the value of land fell, they often lost both mortgage and land and still owed the bank money.

The changing nature of farming was part of the problem. Chemical fertilizers and new hybrid seeds increased the yield per acre. By 1930, some 920,000 tractors and 900,000 trucks were in use on American farms. They not only made farming more efficient, but they also allowed land formerly used to raise feed for horses and mules to be planted in cash crops. Production increased at the very time that worldwide demand for American farm products declined. In 1929, the United States shipped abroad only one-third the wheat it had exported in 1919, and only one-ninth the meat. Farmers, especially in North America and Europe, had prospered during the war because of the great demand for food. Expecting the demand to continue, many farmers borrowed to purchase new equipment and to increase the number of acres they cultivated. But the demand for produce did not last, leading to a worldwide decline in prices and making debts difficult to repay.

Victims not only of the global marketplace, American farmers were also vulnerable to the power of nature. This became apparent in the spring of 1927 when the worst flood in the nation's history devastated the Mississippi River valley, flooding more than 27,000 square miles of land and making a million people homeless.

Not all farmers suffered. Large commercial opera-tions, using mechanized equipment, produced most of the cash crops. At the same time, many small farmers found themselves unable to compete with agribusiness. Some of them, along with many farm laborers, solved the problem of declining rural profitability by leaving the farms. In 1900, fully 40 percent of the labor force worked on farms; by 1930, only 21 percent earned their living from the land.

Few farmers could afford the products of the new technology. Although many middle-class urban families were more prosperous than they had ever been—buying new cars, radios, and bathrooms—only one farm family in ten had electricity in the 1920s. The lot of the farm wife had not changed for centuries. She ran a domestic factory, did all the household chores, and helped on the farm as well.

Farmers tried to improve their position by support-ing legislation in the state capitals and in Washington. Most of their efforts went into the McNary–Haugen Farm Relief Bill, which would have provided govern-ment price support for key agricultural products. The bill was introduced a number of times between 1924 and 1928 without success, but farm organizations in all parts of the country learned how to work together to influence Congress. That would have important ramifications for the future.

The Workers' Share of Prosperity

Hundreds of thousands of workers improved their standard of living in the 1920s, yet inequality grew. Real wages increased 21 percent between 1923 and 1929, but corporate dividends went up by nearly two-thirds in the same period. The workers did not profit from the increased production they helped create, and that boded ill for the future. The richest 5 percent of the population increased their share of the wealth from a quarter to a third, and the wealthiest 1 percent controlled a whopping 19 percent of all income.

Even among workers there was great disparity. Those employed on the auto assembly lines or in the new factories producing radios saw their wages go up, and many saw their hours decline. Yet the majority of American working-class families did not earn enough to move them much beyond subsistence level. One study suggested that a family needed $2,000 to $2,400 in 1924 to maintain an "American standard of living." But in that year, 16 million families earned less than $2,000.

Organized labor fell on hard times in the 1920s. Labor union membership fell from about 5 million in 1921 to less than 3.5 million in 1929. The National Association of Manufacturers and individual businesses carried on a vigorous campaign to restore the open shop. The leadership of the AFL became increasingly conservative during the decade and had little interest in launching movements to organize laborers in the large industries.

The more aggressive unions such as the United Mine Workers, led by the flamboyant John L. Lewis, also encountered difficulties. The union's attempt to organize miners in West Virginia had led to violent clashes between union members and imported guards. President Harding called out troops in 1921 to put down an "army organized by the strikers." The next year, Lewis called the greatest coal strike in history and further violence erupted, especially in Williamson County, Illinois. Internal strife also weakened the union, and Lewis had to accept wage reductions in the negotiations of 1927.

Organized labor, like so many other groups, struggled desperately during the decade to take advantage of the prosperity. It won some victories, and it made some progress. But American affluence was beyond the reach of many groups during the decade. Eventually, the inequality would lead to disaster.

The Business of Politics

"Among the nations of the earth today America stands for one idea: *Business*," a popular writer announced in 1921. "Through business, properly conceived, managed and conducted, the human race is finally to be redeemed." Bruce Barton, the head of the largest advertising firm in the country, was the author of one of the most popular nonfiction books of the decade. In *The Man Nobody Knows* (1925), he depicted Christ as "the founder of modern business." He took 12 men from the bottom ranks of society and forged them into a successful organization.

Business, especially big business, prospered in the 1920s, and the image of businessmen, enhanced by their important role in World War I, rose further. The government reduced regulation, lowered taxes, and cooperated to aid business expansion at home and abroad. Business and politics, always intertwined, were especially allied during the decade. Wealthy financiers such as Andrew Mellon and Charles Dawes participated in formulating both domestic and foreign policy. Even more significant, a new kind of businessman was elected president in 1928. Herbert Hoover, international engineer and efficiency expert, was the very symbol of the modern techniques and practices that many people confidently expected to transform the United States and the world. Business leaders wielded power in other countries, but in no country were business and politics so closely intertwined as in the United States.

Harding and Coolidge

The Republicans, almost assured of victory in 1920 because of bitter reaction against Woodrow Wilson, might have preferred nominating their old standard-bearer, Theodore Roosevelt, but he had died the year before. Warren G. Harding, a former newspaper editor from Ohio, captured the nomination after meeting late at night with some of the party's most powerful men in a hotel room in Chicago. No one ever discovered what Harding promised, but the meeting in the "smoke-filled room" became legendary. To balance the ticket, the Republicans chose as their vice presidential candidate Calvin Coolidge of Massachusetts, who had gained attention by his firm stand during the Boston police strike. The Democrats seemed equally unimaginative. After 44 roll calls, they finally nominated Governor James Cox of Ohio and picked Franklin D. Roosevelt, a young politician from New York, to run as vice president. Roosevelt had been the assistant secretary of the navy but otherwise had not distinguished himself.

Harding won in a landslide. His 60.4 percent of the vote was the widest margin yet recorded in a presidential election. More significant, fewer than 50 percent of the eligible voters went to the polls.

The newly enfranchised women, especially in working-class neighborhoods, stayed away from the voting booths. So did large numbers of men. To many people, it did not seem to matter who was president.

In contrast to the reform-minded presidents Roosevelt and Wilson, Harding reflected the conservatism of the 1920s. He was a jovial man who brought many Ohio friends to Washington and placed them in positions of power. A visitor to the White House described Harding and his cohorts discussing the problems of the day, with "the air heavy with tobacco smoke, trays with bottles containing every imaginable brand of whiskey" near at hand.

At a little house a few blocks from the White House on K Street, Harry Daugherty, Harding's attorney general and longtime associate, held forth with a group of friends. Amid bootleg liquor and the atmosphere of a brothel, they did a brisk business in selling favors, taking bribes, and organizing illegal schemes. Harding, however, was not personally corrupt, and the nation's leading businessmen approved of his policies of higher tariffs and lower taxes. Nor did Harding spend all his time drinking with his cronies. He called a conference on disarmament and another to deal with the problems of unemployment, and he pardoned Eugene Debs, who had been in prison since the war. Harding once remarked that he could never be considered one of the great presidents, but he thought perhaps he might be "one of the best loved." He was probably right. When he died suddenly in August 1923, the American people genuinely mourned him.

Only after Calvin Coolidge became president did the full extent of the corruption and scandals of the Harding administration come to light. A Senate committee discovered that the secretary of the interior, Albert Fall, had illegally leased government-owned oil reserves in the Teapot Dome section of Wyoming to private business interests in return for over $300,000 in bribes. Illegal activities were also discovered in the Veterans Administration and elsewhere in government. Daugherty resigned in disgrace, the secretary of the navy barely avoided prison, two of Harding's advisers committed suicide, and Fall was sentenced to jail.

Though dour and taciturn, Coolidge was honest. Born in a little town in Vermont, he was sworn in as president by his father, a justice of the peace, in a ceremony conducted by the light of kerosene lamps at his ancestral home. To many, Coolidge represented old-fashioned rural values, simple religious faith, and personal integrity—a world fast disappearing in the 1920s.

Coolidge ran for reelection in 1924 with the financier Charles Dawes as his running mate. There was little question that he would win. The Democrats were so equally divided between northern urban Catholics and southern rural Protestants that it took 103 ballots before they nominated John Davis, an affable corporate lawyer with little national following.

A group of dissidents, mostly representing the farmers and the laborers dissatisfied with both nominees, formed a new Progressive party. They adopted the name, but little else, from Theodore Roosevelt's party of 1912. Nominating Robert La Follette of Wisconsin for president, they drafted a platform calling for government ownership of railroads and ratification of the child labor amendment. La Follette attacked the "control of government and industry by private monopoly." He received nearly 5 million votes, only 3.5 million short of Davis's total. But Coolidge and prosperity won easily.

Like Harding, Coolidge was a popular president. Symbolizing his administration was his wealthy secretary of the treasury, Andrew Mellon, who set out to lower individual and corporate taxes. In 1922, Congress, with Mellon's endorsement, repealed the wartime excess profits tax. Although it raised some taxes slightly, it exempted most families from any tax at all by giving everyone a $2,500 exemption, plus $400 for each dependent. In 1926, the rate was lowered to 5 percent and the maximum surtax to 40 percent. Only families with incomes above $3,500 paid any taxes at all. In 1928, Congress reduced taxes further, removed most excise taxes, and lowered the corporate tax rate. The 200 largest corporations increased their assets during the decade from $43 to $81 billion.

"The chief business of the American people is business," Coolidge announced. "The man who builds a factory builds a temple.... The man who works there worships there." Coolidge's idea of the proper role of the federal government was to have as little as possible to do with the functioning of business and the lives of the people. Not everyone approved of his policies, or his personality. "No other president in my time slept so much," a White House usher remembered. But most Americans approved of his inactivity.

Herbert Hoover

One bright light in the lackluster Harding and Coolidge administrations was Herbert Hoover. Born in Iowa, raised in Oregon, and educated in California, he served as secretary of commerce under both presidents. Hoover had made a fortune as an international mining engineer before 1914 and then earned a reputation as a great humanitarian for his work managing the Belgian Relief Committee and directing the Food Administration during World War I. He was mentioned as a candidate for president in 1920, when he had the support of such progressives as Jane Addams, Louis Brandeis, and Walter Lippmann.

Businessmen and the President

Beginning in 1920, Henry Ford, Thomas Edison, and Harvey Firestone went on auto trips together in part to celebrate the new automobile culture. In the summer of 1924, they stopped in Plymouth, Vermont, to visit with President Calvin Coolidge, who was vacationing at the family homestead. A local photographer took this photograph and made it into a postcard, which he sold as a souvenir. The president is autographing a sap bucket to be placed in Henry Ford's new museum near Detroit. From left to right: Harvey Firestone, President Coolidge, Henry Ford, Thomas Edison, Russell Firestone, Grace Coolidge, and John Coolidge, the president's father. Coolidge often pretended he was a simple Vermonter, but actually he was much more comfortable around the corporate elite than he was dealing with ordinary Americans. What was the danger of the close relationship between the presidents and business leaders in the 1920s? Does that close relationship still exist?

(Allen F. Davis Collection)

Hoover was a dynamo of energy and efficiency. He expanded his department to control and regulate the airlines, radio, and other new industries. By directing the Bureau of Standards to work with the trade associations and with individual businesses, Hoover managed to standardize the size of almost everything manufactured in the United States, from nuts and bolts and bottles to automobile tires, mattresses, and electric fixtures. He supported zoning codes, the eight-hour workday in major industries, better nutrition for children, and the conservation of national resources. He pushed through the Pollution Act of 1924, which represented the first attempt to control oil pollution along the American coastline.

As secretary of commerce, Hoover used the force of the federal government to regulate, stimulate, and promote, but he believed first of all in free enterprise and local volunteer action to solve problems. In 1921, he convinced Harding of the need to do something about unemployment during the postwar recession. The president's conference on unemployment, convened in September 1921, marked the first time the national government had admitted any responsibility to the unemployed. The result of the conference (the first of many on a variety of topics that Hoover was to organize) was a flood of publicity, pamphlets, and advice from experts. Most of all, the conference urged state and local governments and businesses to cooperate on a volunteer basis to solve the problem. The primary responsibility of the federal government, Hoover believed, was to educate and promote. With all his activity and his organizing, Hoover earned a reputation during the Harding and Coolidge years as an efficient and progressive administrator and as a humanitarian who could organize flood relief. He became one of the most popular figures in government service.

Global Expansion

The decade of the 1920s is often remembered as a time of isolation, when the United States rejected the League of Nations treaty and turned its back on the rest of the world. It is true that many Americans had little interest in what was going on in Paris, Moscow, or Rio de Janeiro, and it is also true that a bloc of congressmen was determined that the United States would never again enter another European war. But the United States remained involved—indeed, increased its involvement—in international affairs during the decade. Although the United States never joined the League of Nations, and a few dedicated isolationists, led by Senator William Borah, blocked membership in the World Court, the United States cooperated with many league agencies and conferences and took the lead in trying to reduce naval armaments and to solve the problems of international finance caused in part by the war.

There were ominous clouds on the horizon. Great Britain and France were slow to recover from the war, while Germany was mired in economic and political chaos. Japan and Italy were unhappy with the peace settlement. Germany's African colonies had been split between France and Great Britain, but imperialism and colonial empires had not diminished. Fascism was establishing a foothold in Spain and Italy, while Soviet communism was becoming more firmly entrenched in Russia. The collapse of the Ottoman Empire had led to the establishment of a new Turkish republic in 1923, but the rest of the Middle East was fragmented both economically and politically and presented problems that would persist for the rest of the twentieth century and beyond.

Business, trade, and finance marked the decade as one of international expansion for the United States. With American corporate investments overseas growing sevenfold during the decade, the United States was transformed from a debtor to a creditor nation. The continued involvement of the United States in the affairs of South and Central American countries also indicated that the country had growing interests beyond its national boundaries. The United States also increased its international position in cable communication, wireless telegraphy, news services, and motion pictures. In some areas, such as film, the United States led the world. In 1925, 95 percent of the films shown in Great Britain and Canada and 70 percent of those shown in France were American made.

Despite growing global expansion in many areas, the U.S. government took up its role of international power reluctantly and with a number of contradictory and disastrous results. "We seek no part in directing the destiny of the world," Harding announced in his inaugural address, but even Harding discovered that international problems would not disappear. One that required immediate attention was the naval arms race.

The United States called the first international conference to discuss disarmament. At the Washington Conference on Naval Disarmament, which convened in November 1921, Secretary of State Charles Evans Hughes startled the delegates by proposing a 10-year "holiday" on the construction of warships and by offering to sink or scrap 845,000 tons of American

ships, including 30 battleships. He urged Britain and Japan to do the same. The delegates greeted Hughes's speech with enthusiastic cheering and applause, and they set about the task of sinking more ships than the admirals of all their countries had managed to do in a century.

The conference participants ultimately agreed to fix the tonnage of capital ships at a ratio of the United States and Great Britain, 5; Japan, 3; and France and Italy, 1.67. Japan agreed only reluctantly, but when the United States promised not to fortify its Pacific Island possessions, Japan yielded. In light of what happened in 1941, the Washington Naval Conference has often been criticized, but in 1921, it was appropriately hailed as the first time in history that the major nations of the world had agreed to disarm. The conference did not cause World War II; neither, as it turned out, did it prevent it. But it was a creative start to reducing tensions and to meeting the challenges of the modern arms race. And it was the United States that took the lead by offering to be the first to scrap its battleships.

American foreign policy in the 1920s tried to reduce the risk of international conflict, resist revolution, and make the world safe for trade and investment. In its dealings with Latin America, the United States continued its policy of intervention. By the end of the decade, the United States controlled the financial affairs of 10 Latin American nations. The marines were withdrawn from the Dominican Republic in 1924, but that country remained a virtual protectorate of the United States until 1941. The government ordered the marines out of Nicaragua in 1925 but sent them back the next year when a liberal insurrection threatened the conservative government. But the U.S. Marines, and the Nicaraguan troops they had trained, had a difficult time containing a guerrilla band led by Augusto Sandino, a charismatic leader and one of Latin America's greatest heroes. The Sandinistas, supported by the great majority of peasants, came out of the hills to attack the politicians and their American supporters. In 1934, Sandino was murdered by General Anastasio Somoza, a ruthless leader supported by the United States. For more than 40 years, Somoza and his two sons ruled Nicaragua as a private fiefdom, a legacy not yet resolved in that strife-torn country.

Mexico frightened American businessmen in the mid-1920s by beginning to nationalize foreign holdings in oil and mineral rights. Fearing that further military activity would "injure American interests," businessmen and bankers urged Coolidge not to send marines but to negotiate instead. Coolidge appointed Dwight W. Morrow of the J. P. Morgan Company as ambassador, and his conciliatory attitude led to agreements protecting American investments. Throughout the decade, the goal of U.S. policy toward Central and South America, whether in the form of negotiations or intervention, was to maintain a special sphere of influence.

The U.S. policy of promoting peace, stability, and trade was not always consistent or carefully thought out, and this was especially true in its relationships with Europe. At the end of the war, European countries owed the United States more than $10 billion, with Great Britain and France responsible for about three-fourths of that amount. Both countries, mired in postwar economic problems, suggested that the United States forgive the debts, arguing that they had paid for the war in lives and property destroyed. But the United States, although adjusting the interest and the payment schedule, refused to forget the debt. "They hired the money, didn't they?" Coolidge supposedly remarked.

The only way European nations could repay the United States was by exporting products, but in a series of tariff acts, especially the Fordney–McCumber Tariff of 1922, Congress erected a protective barrier to trade. This act also gave the president power to lower or raise individual rates; in almost every case, both Harding and Coolidge used the power to raise them. Finally, in 1930, the Hawley–Smoot Tariff raised rates even further, despite the protests of many economists. American policy of high tariffs (a counterproductive policy for a creditor nation) caused retaliation and restrictions on American trade, which American corporations were trying to increase.

The inability of the European countries to export products to the United States and to repay their loans was intertwined with the reparations agreement made with Germany. Germany's economy was in disarray after the war, with inflation raging and its industrial plant throttled by the peace treaty. By 1921, Germany was defaulting on its payments. The United States, which believed a healthy Germany important to European stability and world trade, instituted a plan engineered by Charles Dawes whereby the German debt would be renegotiated and spread over a longer period. In the meantime, American bankers and the American government lent Germany hundreds of millions of dollars. In the end, the United States lent money to Germany so it could make payments to Britain and France so that those countries could continue their payments to the United States.

The United States had replaced Great Britain as the dominant force in international finance, but the nation in the 1920s was a reluctant and inconsistent world leader. The United States had stayed out of the League of Nations and was hesitant to get involved in multinational agreements. However, some agreements seemed proper to sign; the most idealistic of all was the Kellogg–Briand pact to outlaw war. The French foreign minister, Aristide Briand, suggested a treaty between the United States and France in large part to commemorate long years of friendship between the two countries, but secretary of state Frank B. Kellogg in 1928 expanded the idea to a multinational treaty to outlaw war. Fourteen nations agreed to sign the treaty, and eventually 62 nations signed, but the only power behind the treaty was moral force rather than economic or military sanctions.

The Survival of Progressivism

The decade of the 1920s was a time of reaction against reform, but progressivism did not simply die. It survived in many forms through the period that Jane Addams called a time of "political and social sag."

The greatest success of the social justice movement was the 1921 Sheppard–Towner Maternity Act, one of the first pieces of federal social welfare legislation and the product of long progressive agitation. A study conducted by the Children's Bureau discovered that more than 3,000 mothers died in childbirth in 1918 and that more than 250,000 infants also died. The United States ranked eighteenth out of 20 countries in maternal mortality and eleventh in infant deaths. The low rank of the United States was caused in part by the poor conditions in urban slums and by rural poverty, especially among southern blacks. But it was also the result of the lack of government intervention to improve health care while many European countries provided health insurance and government-supported medical clinics.

The maternity bill called for $1 million a year to assist the states in providing medical aid and visiting nurses to teach expectant mothers how to care for themselves and their babies. The bill was controversial from the beginning. The American Medical Association, which had supported pure food and drug legislation and laws to protect against health quacks and to enforce standards for medical schools, attacked this bill as leading to socialism and interfering with the relationship between doctor and patient.

Despite the opposition, the bill passed Congress and was signed by President Harding in 1921. The appropriation for the bill was for only six years, and the opposition, again raising the specter of a feminist-Socialist-Communist plot, succeeded in repealing the law in 1929. Yet the Sheppard–Towner Act, promoted and fought for by a group of progressive women, indicated that concern for social justice was not dead in the age of Harding and Coolidge.

PRESIDENTIAL ELECTIONS, 1920–1928

What political trends are revealed in this chart?

Year	Candidate	Party	Popular Vote	Electoral Vote
1920	WARREN G. HARDING	Republican	16,152,200 (60.4%)	404
	James M. Cox	Democratic	9,147,353 (34.2%)	127
	Eugene V. Debs	Socialist	919,799 (3.4%)	0
1924	CALVIN COOLIDGE	Republican	15,725,016 (54.0%)	382
	John W. Davis	Democratic	8,385,586 (28.8%)	136
	Robert M. La Follette	Progressive	4,822,856 (16.6%)	13
1928	HERBERT C. HOOVER	Republican	21,392,190 (58.2%)	444
	Alfred E. Smith	Democratic	15,016,443 (40.9%)	87

Note: Winners' names appear in capital letters.

Temperance Triumphant

For one large group of progressives, Prohibition, like child labor reform and maternity benefits, was an important effort to conserve human resources. By 1918, more than three-fourths of the people in the country lived in dry states or counties, but it was the war that allowed the antisaloon advocates to associate Prohibition with patriotism. "We have German enemies across the water," one prohibitionist announced. "We have German enemies in this country too. And the worst of all our German enemies, the most treacherous, the most menacing are Pabst, Schlitz, Blatz and Miller." In 1919, Congress passed the Volstead Act, banning the brewing and selling of beverages containing more than one-half of one percent alcohol. In June 1919, the thirty-sixth state ratified the Eighteenth Amendment, prohibiting the manufacture, sale, and transport of intoxicating liquors. But the country had, for all practical purposes, been dry since 1917.

The Prohibition experiment probably did reduce the total consumption of alcohol in the country, especially in rural areas and urban working-class neighborhoods. Fewer arrests for drunkenness occurred, and deaths from alcoholism declined. But the legislation showed the difficulty of using law to promote moral reform. Most people who wanted to drink during the "noble experiment" found a way. Speakeasies replaced saloons, and people consumed bathtub gin, home brew, and many strange and dangerous concoctions. Bartenders invented the cocktail to disguise the poor quality of liquor, and women, at least middle- and upper-class women, began to drink in public for the first time.

Prohibition also created great bootlegging rings, which were tied to organized crime in many cities. Al Capone of Chicago was the most famous underworld figure whose power and wealth were based on the sale of illegal alcohol. His organization alone grossed an estimated $60 million in 1927; ironically, most of the profit came from distributing beer. Many supporters of Prohibition slowly came to favor its repeal, some because it reduced the power of the states, others because it stimulated too much illegal activity and because it did not seem to be worth the social and political costs.

The Election of 1928

On August 2, 1927, President Coolidge announced simply, "I do not choose to run for President in 1928." Hoover immediately became the logical Republican candidate. Hoover and Coolidge were not especially close. Coolidge resented what he considered Hoover's spendthrift ways. "That man has offered me unsolicited advice for six years, all of it bad," Coolidge once remarked. Though lacking an enthusiastic endorsement from the president and opposed by some Republicans who thought him to be too progressive, Hoover easily won the nomination. In a year when the country was buoyant with optimism and when prosperity seemed as if it would go on forever, few doubted that Hoover would be elected.

The Democrats nominated Alfred Smith, a Catholic Irish American from New York. With his New York accent, his opposition to Prohibition, and his flamboyant style, he contrasted sharply with the more sedate Hoover. On one level, it was a bitter contest between Catholic "wets" and Protestant "drys," between the urban, ethnic Tammany politician and former governor of New York against the rural-born but sophisticated secretary of commerce. Religious prejudice, especially a persistent anti-Catholicism, played an important role in the campaign. But looked at more closely, the two candidates differed little. Both

Timeline

1900–1930	Electricity powers the "second Industrial Revolution"
1917	Race riot in East St. Louis, Illinois
1918	World War I ends
1919	Treaty of Versailles
	Strikes in Seattle, Boston, and elsewhere
	Red Scare and Palmer raids
	Race riots in Chicago and other cities
	Marcus Garvey's Universal Negro Improvement Association spreads
1920	Warren Harding elected president
	Women vote in national elections
	First commercial radio broadcast
	Sacco and Vanzetti arrested
	Sinclair Lewis, *Main Street*
1921	Immigration Quota Law
	Naval Disarmament Conference
	First birth control conference
	Sheppard–Towner Maternity Act
1921–1922	Postwar depression
1922	Fordney–McCumber Tariff
	Sinclair Lewis, *Babbitt*
1923	Harding dies; Calvin Coolidge becomes president
	Teapot Dome scandal
1924	Coolidge reelected president
	Peak of Ku Klux Klan activity
	Immigration Quota Law
1925	Scopes trial in Dayton, Tennessee
	F. Scott Fitzgerald, *The Great Gatsby*
	Bruce Barton, *The Man Nobody Knows*
	Alain Locke, *The New Negro*
	Claude McKay, *Home to Harlem*
	5 million enameled bathroom fixtures produced
1926	Ernest Hemingway, *The Sun Also Rises*
1927	National Origins Act
	McNary–Haugen Farm Relief Bill
	Sacco and Vanzetti executed
	Lindbergh flies solo from New York to Paris
	First talking movie, *The Jazz Singer*
	Henry Ford produces 15 millionth car
1928	Herbert Hoover elected president
	Kellogg–Briand Treaty
	Stock market soars
1929	27 million registered autos in country
	10 million households own radios
	100 million people attend movies
	Stock market crash

were self-made men, both were "progressives." Social justice reformers campaigned for each candidate. Both candidates tried to attract women voters, both were favorable to organized labor, both defended capitalism, and both had millionaires and corporate executives among their advisers.

Hoover won in a landslide, 444 electoral votes to 76 for Smith, who carried only Massachusetts and Rhode Island outside the Deep South. But the 1928 campaign revitalized the Democratic party. Smith polled nearly twice as many votes as the Democratic candidate in 1924, and for the first time, the Democrats carried the 12 largest cities.

Stock Market Crash

Hoover, as it turned out, had only six months to apply his progressive and efficient methods to running the country; in the fall of 1929, the prosperity that seemed endless suddenly came to a halt. In 1928 and 1929,

rampant speculation made the stock market boom. Money could be made everywhere—in real estate and business ventures, but especially in the stock market. "Everybody ought to be Rich," Al Smith's campaign manager argued in an article in *Ladies' Home Journal* early in 1929. Just save $15 a month and buy good common stock with it, and that money would turn into $80,000 in 20 years (a considerable fortune in 1929). Good common stock seemed to be easy to find in 1929.

Only a small percentage of the American people invested in the stock market, for many had no way of saving even $15 a month. But a large number got into the game in the late 1920s because it seemed a safe and sure way to make money. For many, the stock market came to represent the American economy, and the economy was booming. The *New York Times* index of 25 industrial stocks reached 100 in 1924, moved up to 181 in 1925, dropped a bit in 1926, and rose again to 245 by the end of 1927.

Then the orgy started. During 1928, the market rose to 331. Many investors and speculators began to buy on margin (borrowing to invest). Businessmen and others began to invest in the market money that would ordinarily have gone into houses, cars, and other goods. Yet even at the peak of the boom, probably only about 1.5 million Americans owned stock.

In early September 1929, the *New York Times* index peaked at 452 and then began to drift downward. On October 23, the market lost 31 points. The next day ("Black Thursday"), it first seemed that everyone was trying to sell, but at the end of the day, the panic appeared to be over. It was not. By mid-November, the market had plummeted to 224, about half what it had been two months before. This represented a loss on paper of over $26 billion. Still, a month later, the chairman of the board of Bethlehem Steel could announce, "Never before has American business been as firmly entrenched for prosperity as it is today." Some businessmen even got back into the market, thinking that it had reached its low point. But it continued to go down. Tens of thousands of investors lost everything. Those who had bought on margin had to keep coming up with money to pay off their loans as the value of their holdings declined. There was panic and despair, but the legendary stories of executives jumping out of windows were grossly exaggerated.

The stock market crash was more symptom than cause of the economic collapse. Weak banking systems in both Europe and America, the rise of protectionism, the drop in farm prices, and the decline of purchasing power all foreshadowed the economic disaster that would follow the stock market debacle.

Conclusion

A NEW ERA OF PROSPERITY AND PROBLEMS

The stock market crash ended the decade of prosperity. The crash did not cause the Depression, but the stock market debacle revealed the weakness of the economy. The fruits of economic expansion had been unevenly distributed. The Parker family, introduced at the beginning of this chapter, and many other families in both rural and urban America did not share in the prosperity. Not enough people could afford to buy the autos, refrigerators, and other products pouring from American factories. Prosperity had been built on a shaky foundation. When that foundation crumbled in 1929, the nation slid into a major depression. But the Depression was related to global financial trends and to economic problems created by World War I and the peace settlement. High tariffs and reparations that wrecked the German economy and a weakened banking system all contributed to the economic collapse. Looking back from the vantage point of the 1930s or later, the 1920s seemed a golden era—an age of flappers, bootleg gin, constant parties, literary masterpieces, sports heroes, and easy wealth. The truth is much more complicated. More than most decades, the 1920s was a time of paradox and contradictions.

The 1920s was a time of prosperity, yet a great many people, including farmers, blacks, and other ordinary Americans, did not prosper. The 1920s was a time of modernization, but only about 10 percent of rural families had electricity. It was a time when women achieved more sexual freedom, but the feminist movement declined. It was a time of Prohibition, but many Americans increased their consumption of alcohol. It was a time of reaction against reform, yet progressivism survived. It was a time when intellectuals felt disillusioned with America, yet it was one of the most creative and innovative periods for American writers. It was a time of flamboyant heroes, yet the American people elected the lackluster Harding and Coolidge as their presidents. It was a time of progress, when almost every year saw a new technological breakthrough, but it was also a decade of hate and intolerance. The complex and contradictory legacy of the 1920s continues to fascinate and to influence our time.

QUESTIONS FOR REVIEW AND REFLECTION

1. What was the Harlem Renaissance?
2. Did the Prohibition experiment succeed or fail?
3. In foreign policy during the 1920s did the United States try to isolate itself from the rest of the world?
4. What groups did not share in the prosperity of the decade?
5. Why are Harding and Coolidge often considered among our worst presidents?

CHAPTER 24

The Great Depression and the New Deal

The American Dream

Margaret Bourke-White, one of the outstanding documentary photographers of the 1930s, captured the disjunction between the ideal and the real in the Depression era. This photograph, depicting African American flood victims lining up for food in Louisville, Kentucky, underneath a propaganda billboard erected by the National Association of Manufacturers, contrasts the American Dream with the reality of racism and poverty. Does this famous photograph depict the contrast in American life unfairly?

(Margaret Bourke-White, *The Louisville Flood*, 1937. Photograph Copyright © 1966: Whitney Museum of American Art, New York, Gift of Sean Callahan [92.58])

American Stories

Coming of Age and Riding the Rails During the Depression

Flickering in a Seattle movie theater in the depths of the Great Depression, the Hollywood production *Wild Boys of the Road* captivated 13-year-old Robert Symmonds. The film, released in 1933, told the story of boys hitching rides on trains and tramping around the country. It was supposed to warn teenagers of the dangers of rail riding, but for some it had the opposite effect. Robert, a boy from a middle-class home, already had a fascination with hobos. He had watched his mother give sandwiches to the transient men who sometimes knocked on the back door. He had taken to hanging around the "Hooverville" shantytown south of the King Street railroad station, where he would sit next to the fires and listen to the rail riders' stories. Stoked for adventure, when school let out in 1934, Robert and a school friend hopped onto a moving boxcar on a train headed out of town. Hands reached out to pull them aboard the car, which already held 20 men. The two boys journeyed as far as Vancouver, Washington, and home to Seattle again. It was frightening, and exhilarating.

In 1938, under the weight of the Depression, the Symmonds family's security business failed. Years later, Robert recalled the effects on his father: "It hurt him bad when he went broke and all his friends deserted him. He did the best he could but never recovered his self-esteem and his pride." The loss of income forced Robert's family to accept a relative's offer of shelter in a three-room mountain cabin without electricity. Because of the move, Robert could no longer attend high school in Seattle. Once again, this time out of necessity, he turned to the rails, leaving his parents and three sisters behind.

Robert faced a personal challenge of surviving difficult times, but he also was part of a looming problem that troubled the administration of Franklin D. Roosevelt. Thousands of young people were graduating from high school or leaving school early, with very few jobs open to them. An estimated 250,000 young people were among the drifters who resorted to the often dangerous practice of hitching rides on trains around the country. Robert rode the rails during summers to find work harvesting fruit up and down the West Coast. In 1939, his travels took him to Montana, where he encountered the Roosevelt administration's solution for the "youth problem": the Civilian Conservation Corps (CCC). When he enlisted in the CCC, Robert became one of nearly 3 million young men age 17 and older who found work in government-sponsored conservation projects between 1933 and 1942. CCC workers earned $25 a month for their families back home plus $5 a month spending money for themselves.

The CCC was known as Roosevelt's "tree army" because the corps planted trees covering more than 2 million acres, improved more than 4 million acres of existing forest, and fought forest fires. In addition, the CCC worked on a wide variety of conservation-related projects in a nation suffering from deforestation, erosion, drought, dust storms, and other environmental problems. They improved parks and recreation areas and even Civil War historic sites, including the notorious Andersonville prison camp in Georgia. In many ways, the CCC operated like a military organization, with workers wearing surplus World War I uniforms and following a fixed regimen of work and recreation that began with a bugler's call at 6 A.M.

One historian has called the CCC the greatest peacetime mobilization in U.S. history, and it set the stage for the wartime mobilization that followed. Like many CCC veterans, Robert Symmonds's next stop in life was military service. He joined the navy and after the war became a merchant seaman. In later years, like many Americans of his generation, Robert remembered his experiences of the Great Depression grimly, but with some nostalgia. He even returned to hopping rides on railroad cars again during his retirement years, out of a sense of adventure rather than necessity. "It's something that got into my blood years ago," he explained. "I guess it is a freedom thing."

The Great Depression changed the lives of all Americans, separating that generation from the one that followed. An exaggerated need for security, the fear of failure, a nagging sense of guilt, and a real sense that it might happen all over again divided the Depression generation from everyone born after 1940. Like Robert Symmonds, they never forgot those bleak years.

This chapter explores the causes and consequences of the Great Depression, which had an impact around the world. We will look at Herbert Hoover and his efforts to combat the Depression and then turn to Franklin Roosevelt, the dominant personality of the 1930s. We will examine the New Deal and Roosevelt's program to bring relief, recovery, and reform to the nation. The New Deal legislation, some of which continued reforms started during the progressive era, did not end the Depression. But this legislation was based on the idea that the federal government had some responsibility for the economy and for promoting the welfare of all the people. We will also look at the other side of the 1930s, for the decade did not consist only of crippling unemployment and New Deal agencies. It was also a time of great strides in technology, when innovative developments in radio, movies, and the automobile affected the lives of most Americans.

The Great Depression

There had been recessions and depressions in American history, notably in the 1830s, 1870s, and 1890s, but nothing compared with the devastating economic collapse of the 1930s. The Great Depression was all the more shocking because it came after a decade of unprecedented prosperity, when most experts assumed that the United States was immune to a downturn in the business cycle. The Great Depression had an impact on all areas of American life; perhaps most important, it destroyed American confidence in the future.

The Depression Begins

Few people anticipated the stock market crash in the fall of 1929. But even after the collapse of the stock market, few expected the entire economy to go into a tailspin. General Electric stock, selling for 396 in 1929, fell to 34 in 1932; U.S. Steel declined from 261 to 21. By 1932, the median income had plunged to half of what it had been in 1929. Construction spending fell to one-sixth of the 1929 level. By 1932, at least one of every four American breadwinners was out of work, and industrial production had almost ground to a halt.

Why did the nation sink deeper and deeper into depression? The answer is complex, but it appears in retrospect that the prosperity of the 1920s was superficial. Farmers and coal and textile workers had suffered all through the 1920s from low prices, and the farmers were the first group in the 1930s to plunge into depression. But other aspects of the economy also lurched out of balance. Two percent of the population received about 28 percent of the national income, but the lower 60 percent got only 24 percent. Businesses increased profits while holding down wages and the prices of raw materials. This pattern depressed consumer purchasing power. American workers, like American farmers, did not have the money to buy the goods they helped to produce. There was a relative decline in purchasing power in the late 1920s, unemployment was high in some industries, and the housing and automobile industries were already beginning to slacken before the crash.

Well-to-do Americans were speculating a significant portion of their money in the stock market. Their illusion of permanent prosperity helped fire the boom of the 1920s, just as their pessimism and lack of confidence helped exaggerate the Depression in 1931 and 1932.

Other factors were also involved. The stock market crash revealed serious structural weaknesses in the financial and banking systems (7,000 banks had failed during the 1920s). The Federal Reserve Board, fearing inflation, tightened credit—exactly the opposite of the action it should have taken to fight a slowdown in purchasing. But the Depression was also caused by global economic problems created by World War I and the peace settlement. Large reparations exacted against Germany had led to the collapse of the German economy, and high tariffs had reduced international trade. When American investment in Europe slowed in 1928 and 1929, European economies declined. Americans purchased fewer European goods, and Europeans got along without American products. As the European financial situation worsened, the American economy spiraled downward.

The federal government might have prevented the stock market crash and the Depression by more careful regulation of business and the stock market. Central planning might have ensured a more equitable distribution of income. But that kind of policy would have taken more foresight than most people had in the 1920s. It certainly would have required different people to be in power, and it is unlikely that the Democrats, had they been in control, would have altered the government's policies in fundamental ways.

Hoover and the Great Depression

Initial business and government reactions to the stock market crash were optimistic. "All the evidence indicates that the worst effects of the crash upon unemployment will have been passed during the next sixty days," Herbert Hoover reported. Hoover, the great planner and progressive efficiency expert, did not sit idly by and watch the country drift toward disorder. His upbeat first statements were calculated to prevent further panic.

Hoover acted aggressively to stem the economic collapse. More than any president before him, he used the power of the federal government and the office of the president to deal with an economic crisis. Nobody called it a depression for the first year at least, for the economic problems seemed very much like earlier cyclic recessions. Hoover called conferences of businessmen and labor leaders. He met with mayors and governors and encouraged them to speed up public works projects. He created agencies and boards, such as the National Credit Corporation and the Emergency Committee for Employment, to obtain voluntary action to solve the problem. Hoover even supported a tax cut, which Congress enacted in December 1929, but it did little to stimulate spending.

Economic Decline

Voluntary action and psychological campaigns could not stop the Depression. The stock market, after appearing to bottom out in the winter of 1930–1931, continued its decline, responding in part to the European economic collapse that undermined international finance and trade. Of course, not everyone lost money in the market. William Danforth, founder of

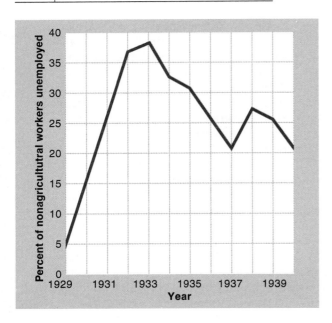

Unemployment Rate, 1929–1940

Although the unemployment rate declined during the New Deal years, the number still unemployed remained tragically high until World War II brought full employment.

Source: U.S. Bureau of the Census.

Ralston Purina, and Joseph Kennedy, film magnate, entrepreneur, and the father of a future president, were among those who made millions of dollars by selling short as the market went down.

More than a collapsing market afflicted the economy; an additional 1,300 banks failed in 1930. Despite Hoover's pleas, many factories cut back on production, and some simply closed. U.S. Steel announced a 10 percent wage cut in 1931. As the auto industry laid off workers, the unemployment rate rose to more than 40 percent in Detroit. More than 4 million Americans were out of work in 1930, and at least 12 million were unemployed by 1932. Foreclosures and evictions created thousands of personal tragedies. While the middle class watched in horror as their life savings and their dreams disappeared, the rich were increasingly concerned as the price of government bonds (the symbol of safety and security) dropped. They began to hoard gold and fear revolution.

There was never any real danger of revolution. Some farmers organized to dump their milk to protest low prices, and when a neighbor's farm was sold, they gathered to hold a penny auction, bidding only a few cents for equipment and returning it to their dispossessed neighbor. But everywhere, people despaired as the Depression deepened in 1931 and 1932. For unemployed blacks and for many tenant farmers, the Depression had little immediate effect because their lives were already so depressed. Most Americans (the 98 percent who did not own stock) hardly noticed

the stock market crash; for them, the Depression meant the loss of a job or a bank foreclosure. For Robert Symmonds it meant the failure of his father's business and being forced to drop out of high school. For some farmers, it was burning corn rather than coal because the price of corn had fallen so low that it was not worth marketing. Not everyone went hungry, stood in bread lines, or lost jobs during the Depression, but almost everyone was affected, and many tended to blame themselves.

The Depression probably disrupted women's lives less than men's. When men lost their jobs, their identity and sense of purpose as the family breadwinner were shattered. Some helped out with family chores, but usually with bitterness and resentment. For women, however, even when money was short, there was still cooking, cleaning, and mending, and women were still in command of their households. Yet many women were forced to do extra work. They took in laundry, found room for a boarder, and made the clothes they formerly would have bought. Women also bore the psychological burden of unemployed husbands, hungry children, and unpaid bills. The Depression altered patterns of family life, and many families were forced to move in with relatives. The marriage rate, the divorce rate, and the birthrate all dropped during the decade. Many of these changes created tension that statistics cannot capture.

A Global Depression

Hoover reacted to growing despair by urging more voluntary action. He insisted on maintaining the gold standard, believing it to be the only responsible currency, and a balanced budget. He blamed the Depression on international economic problems, and he was at least partly right. The legacy of the war and the global economic policies of the 1920s had been one cause of the economic downturn in the United States, and as the United States sank into depression, the world followed. In May 1931, the leading Austrian bank collapsed; by June, the German financial system, which had gone from hyperinflation to false stability, was in chaos. In September, England abandoned the gold standard, precipitating a decline in international lending and trade. Soon most of the industrialized world, including Argentina, Brazil, and Japan, was caught in the Great Depression. In some countries, the social safety net of health and unemployment insurance helped, but there were hungry and unemployed people in much of the world. That a stock market crash in the United States triggered a worldwide depression indicated that by 1930 the United States was an economic world power, but that was little solace as the global depression extended and heightened the Depression at home.

Despite the worldwide depression, Americans began to blame Hoover for some of the disaster. The president became isolated and bitter. The shanties that grew near all the large cities were called "Hoovervilles," and the privies "Hoover villas." Unable to admit mistakes and to take a new tack, he could not communicate personal empathy for the poor and the unemployed.

Hoover did try innovative schemes. More public works projects were built during his administration than in the previous 30 years. In the summer of 1931, he attempted to organize a pool of private money to rescue banks and businesses that were near failure. When the private effort failed, he turned reluctantly to Congress, which passed a bill early in 1932 authorizing the Reconstruction Finance Corporation. The RFC lent money to banks, insurance companies, farm mortgage companies, and railroads. Some critics charged that it was simply another trickle-down measure whereby businessmen and bankers would be given aid while the unemployed were ignored. Hoover, however, correctly understood the immense costs to individuals and to communities when a bank or mortgage company failed. The RFC did help shore up a number of shaky financial institutions and remained the major government finance agency until World War II. But it became much more effective under Roosevelt because it lent directly to industry.

Hoover also asked Congress for a Home Financing Corporation to make mortgages more readily available. The Federal Home Loan Bank Act of 1932 became the basis for the Federal Housing Administration of the New Deal years. He supported the passage of the Glass–Steagall Banking Act of 1932, which expanded credit to make more loans available to businesses and individuals. But Hoover rejected calls for the federal government to restrict production in hopes of raising farm prices—that, he believed, was too much government intervention. He maintained that the federal government should promote cooperation and even create public works. But he firmly believed in loans, not direct subsidies, and he thought it was the responsibility of state and local governments, as well as of private charity, to provide direct relief to the unemployed and the needy.

The Bonus Army

Many World War I veterans lost their jobs during the Great Depression, and beginning in 1930, they lobbied for the payment of their veterans' bonuses, which were not due until 1945. In May 1932, about 17,000 veterans marched on Washington. Some took up residence in an outlying shantytown called Bonus City.

In mid-June, the Senate defeated the bonus bill, and most of the veterans, disappointed but resigned, accepted a free railroad ticket home. Several thousand

remained, however, along with some wives and children, in the unsanitary shacks during the steaming summer heat. Among them were a small group of committed Communists and other radicals. Hoover, who exaggerated the subversive elements among those still camped out in Washington, refused to talk to the leaders and finally called out the U.S. army.

General Douglas MacArthur, the army chief of staff, ordered the army to disperse the veterans. He described the Bonus marchers as a "mob...animated by the essence of revolution." With tanks, guns, and tear gas, the army routed veterans who 15 years before had worn the same uniform as their attackers. Two Bonus marchers were killed, and several others were injured. The army was not attacking revolutionaries in the streets of Washington but was routing bewildered, confused, unemployed men who had seen their American dream collapse.

The Bonus army fiasco, bread lines, and Hoovervilles became the symbols of Hoover's presidency. He deserved better because he tried to use the power of the federal government to solve growing and increasingly complex economic problems. But in the end, his personality and background limited him. He could not understand why army veterans marched on Washington to ask for a handout when he thought they should all be back home working hard, practicing self-reliance, and cooperating "to avert the terrible situation in which we are today." He believed that the greatest problem besetting Americans was a lack of confidence. Yet he could not communicate with these people or inspire their confidence. Willing to use the federal government to support business, he could not accept federal aid for the unemployed. He feared an unbalanced budget and a large federal bureaucracy that would interfere with the "American way." Ironically, his actions and his inactions led in the next years to a massive increase in federal power and in the federal bureaucracy.

Roosevelt and the First New Deal

The first New Deal, lasting from 1933 to early 1935, focused mainly on recovery from the Depression and relief for the poor and unemployed. Some of the programs were borrowed from the Hoover administration, and some had their origin in the progressive period. Others were inspired by the nation's experiences in mobilizing for World War I. No single ideological position united all the legislation, for Franklin Roosevelt was a pragmatist who was willing to try a variety of programs. More than Hoover, however, he believed in economic planning and in government spending to help the poor.

Roosevelt's caution and conservatism shaped the first New Deal. He did not promote socialism or suggest nationalizing the banks. He was even careful in authorizing public works projects to stimulate the economy. The New Deal was based on the assumption that it was possible to create a just society by superimposing a welfare state on the capitalist system, leaving the profit motive undisturbed. While the progressives believed in voluntary action and only reluctantly concluded that the federal government needed to intervene to promote a just society, the New Dealers, from the beginning, believed in an active role for the government. Roosevelt was confident he could achieve his goals through cooperation with the business community. Later he would move more toward reform, but at first his primary concern was simply relief and recovery.

The Election of 1932

The Republicans nominated Herbert Hoover for a second term, but in the summer of 1932, the Depression and Hoover's unpopularity opened the way for the Democrats. After a shrewd campaign, Franklin D. Roosevelt, governor of New York, won the nomination. Distantly related to Theodore Roosevelt, FDR had served as an assistant secretary of the navy during World War I and had been the Democratic vice presidential candidate in 1920. Crippled by polio not long after, he had recovered enough to serve as governor of New York for two terms, although he was not especially well-known by the general public in 1932.

As governor, Roosevelt had promoted cheaper electric power, conservation, and old-age pensions. He became the first governor to support state aid for the unemployed, "not as a matter of charity, but as a matter of social duty." But it was difficult to tell during the presidential campaign exactly what he stood for. He did announce that the government must do something for the "forgotten man at the bottom of the economic pyramid," yet he also mentioned the need for balancing the budget and maintaining the gold standard. Ambiguity was probably the best strategy in 1932, but the truth was that Roosevelt did not have a master plan to save the country. He won the election overwhelmingly, carrying more than 57 percent of the popular vote.

During the campaign, Roosevelt had promised a "new deal for the American people." But the New Deal had to wait for four months because the Constitution provided that the new president be inaugurated on March 4 (this was changed to January 20 by the Twentieth Amendment, ratified in 1933). During the long interregnum, the state of the nation deteriorated badly. The banking system seemed near collapse, and the hardship increased. Hoover tried to cooperate with the president-elect and with a hostile Congress, but he could accomplish little. Everyone waited for the new president to take office and to act.

The Disabled President

This is a rare photograph of Franklin Roosevelt in his wheelchair taken in a private moment with his dog, Fala, and a young friend. Usually FDR's advisers carefully arranged to have the president photographed only when he was seated or propped up behind a podium. Despite being paralyzed from the waist down, the president gave the impression of health and vitality until near the end of his life. Did his physical disability restrict his ability to be president?

(Margaret Suckley Collection, Franklin Delano Roosevelt Library)

In his inaugural address, Roosevelt announced confidently, "The only thing we have to fear is fear itself." This, of course, was not true, for the country faced the worst crisis since the Civil War, but Roosevelt's confidence and his ability to communicate with ordinary Americans were obvious early in his presidency. He had clever speechwriters, a sense of pace and rhythm in his speeches, and an ability, when he spoke on the radio, to convince listeners that he was speaking directly to them. Recognizing the possibilities of the new media, he instituted a series of radio "fireside chats" to explain to the American people what he was doing to solve the nation's problems. When he said "my friends," millions believed that he meant it.

Roosevelt's Advisers

During the interregnum, Roosevelt surrounded himself with intelligent and innovative advisers. His cabinet was made up of a mixture of people from different backgrounds who often did not agree with one another. Harold Ickes, the secretary of the interior, was a Republican lawyer from Chicago and a one-time supporter of Theodore Roosevelt. Another Republican, Henry Wallace of Iowa, a plant geneticist and agricultural statistician, became the secretary of agriculture. Frances Perkins, the first woman ever appointed to a cabinet post, became the secretary of labor. A disciple of Jane Addams and Florence Kelley, she had been a settlement resident, secretary of the New York Consumers League, and an adviser to Al Smith.

In addition to the formal cabinet, Roosevelt appointed an informal "Brain Trust," including Adolph Berle, Jr., a young expert on corporation law, and Rexford Tugwell, a Columbia University authority on agricultural economics and a committed national planner. Roosevelt also appointed Raymond Moley, another Columbia professor, who later became one of the president's severest critics, and Harry Hopkins, a nervous, energetic man whose concern for the poor and unemployed would play a large role in the formulation of New Deal policy.

Eleanor Roosevelt was a controversial first lady. She wrote a newspaper column, made speeches and radio broadcasts, traveled widely, and listened to the concerns of women, minorities, and ordinary Americans. Attacked by critics who thought she had too much power and mocked for her protruding front teeth, her awkward ways, and her upper-class accent, she courageously took stands on issues of social justice and civil rights. She helped push the president toward social reform.

Roosevelt proved to be an adept politician. He was not well read, especially on economic matters, but he had the ability to learn from his advisers and yet not be dominated by them. He took ideas, plans, and suggestions from conflicting sources and combined them. He had a "flypaper mind," one of his advisers decided. There was no overall plan, no master strategy. An improviser and a pragmatist who once likened himself to a football quarterback who called one play and if it did not work called a different one, Roosevelt was an optimist by nature. And he believed in action.

One Hundred Days

Because Roosevelt took office in the middle of a major crisis, a cooperative Congress was willing to pass almost any legislation that he put before it. In three months, numerous bills were rushed through. Some of them were not well thought out, and some contradicted other legislation. But many of the laws passed during Roosevelt's first 100 days would have far-reaching implications for the relationship of government to society. Roosevelt was an opportunist, but unlike Hoover,

he was willing to use direct government action to solve the problems of depression and unemployment. As it turned out, none of the bills passed during the first 100 days cured the Depression, but taken together, the legislation constituted one of the most innovative periods in American political history.

The Banking Crisis

The most immediate problem Roosevelt faced was the condition of the banks. Many had closed, and American citizens, no longer trusting the financial institutions, were hoarding money and putting their assets into gold. Roosevelt immediately declared a four-day bank holiday. Three days later, an emergency session of Congress approved his action and within hours gave the president broad powers over financial transactions, prohibited the hoarding of gold, and allowed for the reopening of sound banks, sometimes with loans from the Reconstruction Finance Corporation.

Within the next few years, Congress passed additional legislation that gave the federal government more regulatory power over the stock market and over the process by which corporations issued stock. It also passed the Banking Act of 1933, which strengthened the Federal Reserve System, established the Federal Deposit Insurance Corporation (FDIC), and insured individual deposits up to $5,000. Although the American Bankers Association opposed the plan as "unsound, unscientific, unjust and dangerous," banks were soon attracting depositors by advertising that they were protected by government insurance.

The Democratic platform in 1932 called for reduced government spending and an end to Prohibition. Roosevelt moved quickly on both. The Economy Act, which passed Congress easily, called for a 15 percent reduction in government salaries as well as a reorganization of federal agencies to save money. The bill also cut veterans' pensions, despite their protests. However, the Economy Act's small savings were dwarfed by other bills passed the same week, which called for increased spending. The Beer-Wine Revenue Act legalized beer that had an alcohol content of 3.2 percent and light wines and levied a tax on both. The Twenty-First Amendment, ratified on December 5, 1933, repealed the Eighteenth Amendment and ended Prohibition.

Congress granted Roosevelt great power to devalue the dollar and to manipulate inflation. Some members argued for the old Populist solution of free and unlimited coinage of silver, while others called for issuing billions of dollars in paper currency. Bankers and businessmen feared inflation, but farmers and debtors favored an inflationary policy as a way to raise prices and put more money in their pockets. Roosevelt rejected the more extreme inflationary plans supported by many congressmen from the agricultural states, but he did take the country off the gold standard. No longer would paper currency be redeemable in gold. The action terrified some conservative businessmen, who argued that it would lead to "uncontrolled inflation and complete chaos." Even Roosevelt's director of the budget announced solemnly that going off the gold standard "meant the end of Western Civilization."

Devaluation did not end Western civilization, but neither did it lead to instant recovery. After experimenting with pushing the price of gold up by buying it in the open market, Roosevelt and his advisers fixed the price at $35 an ounce in January 1934 (against the old price of $20.63). This inflated the dollar by about 40 percent. Roosevelt also tried briefly to induce inflation through the purchase of silver, but soon the country settled down to a slightly inflated currency and a dollar based on both gold and silver.

Relief Measures

Roosevelt believed in economy in government and in a balanced budget, but he also wanted to help the unemployed and the homeless. One survey estimated in 1933 that 1.5 million Americans were homeless. One man with a wife and six children from Latrobe, Pennsylvania, who was being evicted wrote, "I have 10 days to get another house, no job, no means of paying rent, can you advise me as to which would be the most humane way to dispose of myself and family, as this is about the only thing that I see left to do."

Roosevelt's answer was the Federal Emergency Relief Administration (FERA), which Congress authorized with an appropriation of $500 million in direct grants to cities and states. A few months later, Roosevelt created a Civil Works Administration (CWA) to put more than 4 million people to work on various state, municipal, and federal projects. Hopkins, who ran both agencies, had experimented with work relief programs in New York. Like most social workers, he believed it was much better to pay people to work than to give them charity. An accountant working on a road project said, "I'd rather stay out here in that ditch the rest of my life than take one cent of direct relief."

The CWA was not always effective, but in just over a year, the agency built or restored half a million miles of roads and constructed 40,000 schools and 1,000 airports. It hired 50,000 teachers to keep rural schools open and others to teach adult education courses in the cities. It also put more than a billion dollars of purchasing power into the economy. Roosevelt, who later would be accused of deficit spending, feared that the program was costing too much and might create a permanent class of relief recipients. In the spring of 1934, he ordered the CWA closed down.

The Public Works Administration (PWA), directed by Harold Ickes, in some respects overlapped the work of the CWA, but it lasted longer. Between 1933 and 1939, the PWA built hospitals, courthouses, and school buildings. It helped construct projects as diverse as the port of Brownsville, Texas, two aircraft carriers, and low-cost housing for slum dwellers.

One purpose of the PWA was economic pump priming—the stimulation of the economy and consumer spending through the investment of government funds. Afraid that there might be scandals in the agency, Ickes spent money slowly and carefully. Thus, during the first years, PWA projects, worthwhile as most of them were, did little to stimulate the economy.

Agricultural Adjustment Act

In 1933, most farmers were desperate, as mounting surpluses and falling prices drastically cut their incomes. Some in the Midwest talked of open rebellion, even of revolution. But most observers saw only hopelessness and despair in farmers who had worked hard but were still losing their farms.

Congress passed a number of bills in 1933 and 1934 to deal with the agricultural crisis. But the New Deal's principal solution to the farm problem was the Agricultural Adjustment Act (AAA), which sought to control the overproduction of basic commodities so that farmers might regain the purchasing power they had enjoyed before World War I. To guarantee these "parity prices" (the average prices in the years 1909–1914), the production of major agricultural staples—wheat, cotton, corn, hogs, rice, tobacco, and milk—would be controlled by paying the farmers to reduce their acreage under cultivation. The AAA levied a tax at the processing stage to pay for the program.

The act aroused great disagreement among farm leaders and economists, but the controversy was nothing compared with the outcry from the public over the initial action of the AAA in the summer of 1933. To prevent a glut on the cotton and pork markets, the agency ordered 10 million acres of cotton plowed up and 6 million young pigs slaughtered. It seemed unnatural, even immoral, to kill pigs and plow up cotton when millions of people were underfed and in need of clothes.

The Agricultural Adjustment Act did raise the prices of some agricultural products. But it helped the larger farmers more than the small operators, and it was often disastrous for the tenant farmers and sharecroppers. Landowners often discharged tenant families when they reduced the acres under cultivation. Many sharecroppers were simply cast out on the road with a few possessions and nowhere to go. Large farmers cultivated their fewer acres more intensely, so that the total crop was little reduced. In the end, the prolonged drought that hit the Southwest in 1934 did more than the AAA to limit production and raise agricultural prices. But the long-range significance of the AAA, which was later declared unconstitutional, was the establishment of the idea that the government should subsidize farmers for limiting production.

Industrial Recovery

The legislation during the first days of the Roosevelt administration contained something for almost every group. The National Industrial Recovery Act (NIRA) was designed to help business, raise prices, control production, and put people back to work. The act established the National Recovery Administration (NRA), with the power to set fair competition codes in all industries. For a time, everyone forgot about antitrust laws and talked of cooperation and planning rather than competition. There were parades and rallies, even a postage stamp, and industries that cooperated could display a blue eagle, the symbol of the NRA, designed to symbolize patriotic cooperation. "We Do Our Part," the posters and banners proclaimed, but the results were somewhat less than the promise.

Section 7a of the NIRA, included at the insistence of organized labor, guaranteed labor's right to organize and to bargain collectively and established the National Labor Board to see that their rights were respected. But the board, usually dominated by businesspeople, often interpreted the labor provisions of the contracts loosely. In addition, small-business owners complained that the NIRA was unfair to their interests. Any attempt to set prices led to controversy.

Many consumers suspected that the codes and contracts were raising prices, while others feared the return of monopoly in some industries. When the Supreme Court declared the NIRA unconstitutional in 1935, few people complained. Still, the NIRA was an ambitious attempt to bring some order into a confused business situation, and the labor provisions of the act were picked up later by the National Labor Relations Act.

Civilian Conservation Corps

One of the most popular and successful of the New Deal programs, the Civilian Conservation Corps (CCC), combined work relief with the preservation of natural resources. It put young unemployed white men, such as Robert Symmonds, between ages 17 and 25 to work on reforestation, road and park construction, flood control, and other projects. There were a few carefully segregated black units. The men lived in work camps (more than 1,500 camps in all) and

earned $30 a month, $25 of which had to be sent home to their families. Some complained that the CCC camps, run by the U.S. army, were too military, and one woman wrote from Minnesota to point out that all the best young men were at CCC camps when they ought to be home looking for real jobs and finding brides. Others complained that the CCC did nothing for unemployed young women, so a few special camps were organized for them, but only 8,000 women took part in a program that by 1941 had nearly 3 million participants. Overall, the CCC was one of the most successful and least controversial of all the New Deal programs.

Tennessee Valley Authority

Franklin Roosevelt, like his distant Republican relative Theodore, believed in conservation. He promoted flood-control projects and added millions of acres to the country's national forests, wildlife refuges, and fish and game sanctuaries. But the most important New Deal conservation project, the Tennessee Valley Authority (TVA), owed more to Republican George Norris, a progressive senator from Nebraska, than to Roosevelt.

During World War I, the federal government had built a hydroelectric plant and two munitions factories at Muscle Shoals, on the Tennessee River in Alabama. The government tried unsuccessfully to sell these facilities to private industry, but all through the 1920s, Norris campaigned to have the federal government operate them for the benefit of the valley's residents. Twice Republican presidents vetoed bills that would have allowed federal operation, but Roosevelt endorsed Norris's idea and expanded it into a regional development plan.

Congress authorized the TVA as an independent public corporation with the power to sell electricity and fertilizer and to promote flood control and land reclamation. The TVA built nine major dams and many minor ones between 1933 and 1944, affecting parts of Virginia, North Carolina, Georgia, Alabama, Mississippi, Tennessee, and Kentucky. Some private utility companies claimed that the TVA offered unfair competition to private industry, but it was an imaginative experiment in regional planning. It promoted everything from flood control to library bookmobiles. For residents of the valley, it meant cheaper electricity and changed lifestyles. The TVA meant radios, electric irons, washing machines, and other appliances for the first time. The largest federal construction project ever launched, it also created jobs for many thousands who helped build the dams. But government officials and businessmen who feared that the experiment would lead to socialism curbed the regional planning possibilities of the TVA.

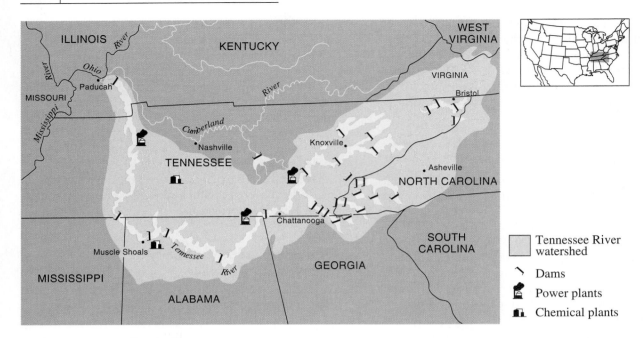

The Tennessee Valley Authority

The TVA transformed the way the Tennessee valley looked; it replaced a wild river with a series of flood-control and hydroelectric dams and created a series of lakes behind the dams. It stopped short of the coordinated regional planning that some people wanted, but it was one of the most important New Deal projects. How did electricity change the lives of everyday people in the Tennessee Valley?

Critics of the New Deal

The furious legislative activity during the first 100 days of the New Deal helped alleviate the pessimism and despair hanging over the country. Stock market prices rose slightly, and industrial production was up 11 percent at the end of 1933. Still, the country remained locked in depression, and nearly 12 million Americans were without jobs. Roosevelt captured the imagination of ordinary Americans everywhere. But conservatives were not so sure that Roosevelt was a savior; in fact, many businesspeople, after being impressed with Roosevelt's early economy measures and approving programs such as the NIRA, began to fear that the president was leading the country toward socialism.

The conservative revolt against Roosevelt surfaced in the summer of 1934 as the congressional elections approached. A group of disgruntled politicians and businesspeople formed the Liberty League. The league supported conservative or at least anti–New Deal candidates for Congress, but it had little influence. In the election of 1934, the Democrats increased their majority from 310 to 319 in the House and from 60 to 69 in the Senate (only the second time in the twentieth century that the party in power had increased its control of Congress in the midterm election). A few people were learning to hate Roosevelt, but it was obvious that most Americans approved of what he was doing.

While some thought the New Deal was too radical, others maintained that the government had not done enough to help the poor. One source of criticism was the Communist party. Attracting supporters from all walks of life during a time when capitalism seemed to have failed, the Communist party increased its membership from 7,500 in 1930 to 75,000 in 1938. The Communists organized protest marches and tried to reach out to the oppressed and unemployed. While a majority who joined the party came from the working class, communism had a special appeal to writers, intellectuals, and some college students during a decade when the American dream had turned into a nightmare.

Many Americans, however, were influenced by other movements promising easy solutions to poverty and unemployment. In Minnesota, Governor Floyd Olson, elected on a Farm–Labor ticket, accused capitalism of causing the Depression and startled some listeners when he thundered, "I hope the present system of government goes right to hell." In California, Upton Sinclair, the muckraking socialist and author of *The Jungle,* ran for governor on the platform "End Poverty in California." He promised to pay everyone over age 60 a pension of $50 a month using higher income and inheritance taxes to finance the program. He won in the primary but lost the election, and his program collapsed.

California also produced Dr. Francis E. Townsend, who claimed he had a national following of more than 5 million people. His supporters backed the Townsend Old Age Revolving Pension Plan, which promised $200

The Radio Priest

Father Charles E. Coughlin from Royal Oak, Michigan, was a flamboyant Catholic priest who was just as much the master of the radio as the president himself. At first he supported Roosevelt, but in 1935 he became one of FDR's most caustic critics. His impassioned anti-Semitic remarks finally caused the Catholic church to take him off the air. In what other ways was the radio important in the 1920s and 1930s?

(Library of Congress [LC-USZ6-2-111027])

a month to all unemployed citizens over age 60 on the condition that they spend it in the same month they received it. Economists laughed, but followers organized thousands of Townsend Pension Clubs.

More threatening to Roosevelt and the New Deal were the protest movements led by Father Charles E. Coughlin and Senator Huey P. Long. Father Coughlin, a Roman Catholic priest from a Detroit suburb, attracted an audience of 30 million to 45 million to his national radio show. At first, he supported Roosevelt's policies, but later he savagely attacked the New Deal as excessively probusiness. Mixing religious commentary with visions of a society operating without bankers and big businessmen, he roused his audience with blatantly anti-Semitic appeals.

Like Coughlin, Huey Long had a charisma that won support from the millions still trying to survive in a country where the continuing depression made day-to-day existence a struggle. Elected governor of Louisiana in 1928, Long promoted a "Share the Wealth" program. He taxed the oil refineries and built hospitals, schools, and thousands of miles of new highways. By 1934, he was the virtual dictator of his state, personally controlling the police and the courts. Long talked about a guaranteed $2,000 to $3,000 income for all American families (18.3 million families earned less than $1,000 per year in 1936) and promised pensions for the elderly and college educations for the young. He would pay for

these programs by taxing the rich and liquidating the great fortunes. Had not an assassin's bullet cut Long down in September 1935, he might have mounted a third-party challenge to Roosevelt.

The Second New Deal

Responding in part to the discontent of the lower middle class but also to the threat of various utopian schemes, Roosevelt moved his programs in 1935 toward the goals of social reform and social justice. At the same time, he departed from attempts to cooperate with the business community. "We find our population suffering from old inequalities," Roosevelt announced in his annual message to Congress in January 1935. "In spite of our efforts and in spite of our talk, we have not weeded out the overprivileged and we have not effectively lifted up the underprivileged."

Work Relief and Social Security

The Works Progress Administration (WPA), authorized by Congress in April 1935, was the first massive attempt to deal with unemployment and its demoralizing effect on millions of Americans. The WPA employed about 3 million people a year on a variety of socially useful projects. The WPA workers, who earned wages lower than private industry paid, built bridges, airports, libraries, roads, and golf courses. Nearly 85 percent of the funds went directly into salaries and wages. A minor but important part of the WPA funding supported writers, artists, actors, and musicians.

Only one member of a family could qualify for a WPA job, and first choice always went to the man. A woman could qualify only if she headed the household. But eventually more than 13 percent of the people who worked for the WPA were women, although their most common employment was in the sewing room, where old clothes were made over. "For unskilled men we have the shovel. For unskilled women we have only the needle," one official remarked.

The WPA was controversial from the beginning. The initials WPA, some wags charged, stood for "We Pay for All" or "We Putter Around." Yet for all the criticism, the WPA did useful work; the program built nearly 6,000 schools, more than 2,500 hospitals, and 13,000 playgrounds. More important, it restored the morale of millions of unemployed Americans.

The National Youth Administration (NYA) supplemented the work of the WPA and assisted young men and women between ages 16 and 25, many of them students. A young law student named Richard Nixon earned 35 cents an hour working for the NYA while he was at Duke University, and Lyndon Johnson began his political career as director of the Texas NYA.

By far the most enduring reform came with the passage of the Social Security Act of 1935. Since the progressive period, social workers and reformers had argued for a national system of health insurance, old-age pensions, and unemployment insurance. By the 1930s, the United States remained the only major industrial country without such programs. Within the Roosevelt circle, Frances Perkins argued most strongly for social insurance, but the popularity of the Townsend Plan and other schemes to aid the elderly helped convince Roosevelt to act. The number of people over age 65 in the country increased from 5.7 million in 1925 to 7.8 million in 1935, and that group demanded action.

The Social Security Act of 1935 was a compromise. Congress quickly dropped a plan for federal health insurance because of opposition from the medical profession. The most important provision of the act was old-age and survivor insurance to be paid for by a tax of 1 percent on both employers and employees. The benefits initially ranged from $10 to $85 a month. The act also established a cooperative federal–state system of unemployment compensation. Other provisions authorized federal grants to the states to help care for the disabled and the blind. Finally, the Social Security Act provided some aid to dependent children. This provision would eventually expand to become the largest federal welfare program.

The National Association of Manufacturers denounced social security as a program that would regiment the people and destroy individual self-reliance. Yet in no other country was social insurance paid for in part by a regressive tax on workers' wages. "We put those payroll contributions there so as to give the contributors a legal, moral, and political right to collect their pensions and unemployment benefits," Roosevelt later explained. "With those taxes in there, no damn politician can ever scrap my social security program." It was never intended as a traditional pension program, but rather as a social contract whereby one generation helped to pay for the previous generation's retirement. But the law also excluded many people, such as farm laborers and domestic servants. It discriminated against married women wage earners, and it failed to protect against sickness. Yet for all its weaknesses, it was one of the most important New Deal measures. A landmark in American social legislation, it marked the beginning of the welfare state that would expand significantly after World War II.

Aiding the Farmers

The Social Security Act and the Works Progress Administration were only two signs of Roosevelt's greater concern for social reform. The flurry of legislation in 1935 and early 1936, often called the "second New Deal," also included an effort to help American farmers. More than 1.7 million farm families had annual incomes of less than $500 in 1935, and 42 percent of all those who lived on farms were tenants. The Resettlement Administration (RA), motivated in part by a Jeffersonian ideal of yeoman farmers working their own land, set out to relocate tenant farmers on land purchased by the government. Lack of funds and fears that the Roosevelt administration was trying to establish Soviet-style collective farms limited the effectiveness of the RA program.

Much more important in improving the lives of farm families was the Rural Electrification Administration (REA), authorized in 1935 to lend money to cooperatives to generate and distribute electricity in isolated rural areas not served by private utilities. Only 10 percent of the nation's farms had electricity in 1936. When the REA's lines were finally attached, they dramatically changed the lives of millions of farm families who had been able only to dream about the radios, washing machines, and farm equipment advertised in magazines.

In the hill country west of Austin, Texas, for example, there was no electricity until the end of the 1930s. Houses were illuminated by kerosene lamps, whose wicks had to be trimmed just right or the lamp smoked or went out, but even with perfect adjustment, it was difficult to read by them. There were no bathrooms,

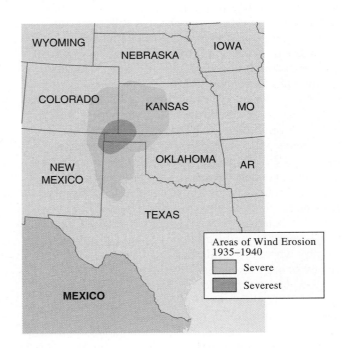

The Dust Bowl

This map depicts the wide extent of damage caused by high winds and drought, the worst in the history of the country, according to the U.S. Weather Bureau. What options are open to residents of areas hit by such natural disasters?

because bathrooms required running water, and running water depended on an electric pump.

It was memory of life in the hill country and personal knowledge of how hard his mother and grandmother toiled that inspired a young congressman from Texas, Lyndon Johnson, to work to bring rural electrification to the area. In November 1939, the lights finally came on in the hill country, plugging the area into the twentieth century.

The Dust Bowl: An Ecological Disaster

Those who tried to farm on the Great Plains fell victim to years of drought and dust storms. Record heat waves and below-average rainfall in the 1930s turned an area from the Oklahoma panhandle to western Kansas into a giant dust bowl. A single storm on May 11, 1934, removed 300 million tons of topsoil and turned day into night. Between 1932 and 1939, there was an average of 50 storms a year. Cities kept their streetlights on for 24 hours a day. Dust covered everything from food to bedspreads and piled up in dunes in city streets and barnyards. Overall 10,000 farm homes were abandoned to the elements, and 9 million acres of farmland were reduced to a wasteland. By the end of the decade, 3.5 million people abandoned their farms and joined a massive migration to find better lives. Many tenant farmers and hired hands were evicted, their plight immortalized by John Steinbeck in his novel *The Grapes of Wrath* (1939).

The dust bowl was a natural disaster, but it was aided and exaggerated by human actions and inactions. The semiarid plains west of the ninety-eighth meridian were not suitable for intensive agriculture.

Overgrazing, too much plowing, and indiscriminate planting over a period of 60 years exposed the thin soil to the elements. When the winds came in the 1930s, much of the land simply blew away. In the end, it was a matter of too little government planning and regulation and too many farmers using new technology to exploit natural resources for their own gain.

The Roosevelt administration did try to deal with the problem. The Taylor Grazing Act of 1934 restricted the use of the public range in an attempt to prevent overgrazing, and it ended an era of unregulated use of natural resources in the West. Before 1934, anyone could use public land, but the 1934 act required a permit and a fee. The Taylor Act established the principle that the remaining public domain was under federal control and not for sale. The Civilian Conservation Corps and other New Deal agencies planted trees, and the Soil Conservation Service promoted drought-resistant crops and contour plowing, but it was too little and too late. Even worse, according to some authorities, government measures applied after the disaster of 1930 encouraged farmers to return to raising wheat and other inappropriate crops, leading to more dust bowl crises in the 1950s and 1970s.

The New Deal and the West

The New Deal probably aided the West more than any other region. The CCC, AAA, drought relief measures, and various federal agencies helped the region to an extent that was out of proportion to the people who lived there. In fact, the top 14 states in per capita expenditure by federal agencies during the 1930s were all in the West. Most important were the large-scale

Dust Bowl Family

Thousands of families fled the dust bowl in old cars and headed for California. With no place to sleep, they used sheets and blankets to turn their cars into tents. John Steinbeck wrote about these migrants in *The Grapes of Wrath*. Do the dust bowl migrants represent a failure of the American dream?

(Courtesy Franklin D. Roosevelt Library [53227(575)])

water projects. The Boulder Dam (later renamed the Hoover Dam) on the Colorado River not only provided massive amounts of hydroelectric power but, with the construction of a 259-mile aqueduct, also provided the water that caused the city of Los Angeles to boom.

The largest power project of all was the Grand Coulee Dam on the Columbia River northwest of Spokane, Washington. Employing tens of thousands of men and pouring millions of dollars into the economy, the dam, finally completed in 1941, provided cheap electricity for the Pacific Northwest and eventually irrigated more than a million acres of arid land.

Despite all the federal aid to the region, many westerners, holding fast to the myth of frontier individualism, bitterly criticized the regulation and the bureaucracy that went with the grants. Cattlemen in Wyoming, Colorado, and Montana desperately needed the help of the federal government, but even as they accepted the aid, they denounced Roosevelt and the New Deal.

Controlling Corporate Power and Taxing the Wealthy

In the summer of 1935, Roosevelt set out to control the large corporations, and he even toyed with radical plans to tax the well-to-do heavily and redistribute wealth in the United States. The Public Utility Holding Company Act, passed in 1935, attempted to restrict the

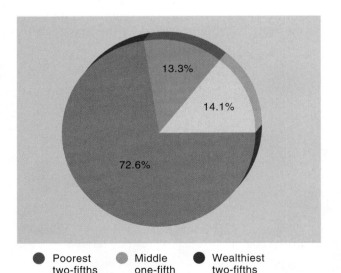

● Poorest two-fifths   ● Middle one-fifth   ● Wealthiest two-fifths

Distribution of Income, 1935–1936

Roosevelt and the New Deal never sought consistently to redistribute wealth in America, and a great disparity in income and assets remained. Why didn't Roosevelt and his advisers try to redistribute wealth?

Source: U.S. Bureau of the Census.

power of the giant utility companies, the 12 largest of which controlled more than half the country's power. The act gave various government commissions the authority to regulate and control the power companies and included a "death sentence" clause that gave each company five years to demonstrate that its services were efficient. If it could not demonstrate this, the government could dissolve the company. This was one of the most radical attempts to control corporate power in American history.

In his message to Congress in 1935, Roosevelt also pointed out that the federal revenue laws had "done little to prevent an unjust concentration of wealth and economic power." He suggested steeper income taxes for wealthy groups and a much larger inheritance tax. When Congress dropped the inheritance tax provision, however, Roosevelt did not fight to have it restored. Even the weakened bill, increasing estate and gift taxes and raising the income tax rates at the top, angered many in the business community who thought that Roosevelt had sold out to Huey Long's "Share the Wealth" scheme.

The New Deal for Labor

Like many progressive reformers, Roosevelt was more interested in improving the lot of working people by passing social legislation than by strengthening the bargaining position of organized labor. Yet he saw labor as an important balance to the power of industry, and he listened to his advisers, especially Frances Perkins and Senator Robert Wagner of New York, who persistently brought up the needs of organized labor.

Roosevelt supported the National Labor Relations Act. Passed in 1935, it outlawed blacklisting and a number of other practices and reasserted labor's right to organize and to bargain collectively. The act also established a Labor Relations Board with the power to certify a properly elected bargaining unit. The act did not require workers to join unions, but it made the federal government a regulator, or at least a neutral force, in management–labor relations. That alone made the National Labor Relations Act one of the most important New Deal reform measures.

The Roosevelt administration's friendly attitude toward organized labor helped increase union membership from less than 3 million in 1933 to 4.5 million by 1935. Many groups, however, were left out, including farm laborers, unskilled workers, and women. Only about 3 percent of working women belonged to unions, and women earned only about 60 percent of wages paid to men for equivalent work. Still, many people resented that women were employed at all. The Brotherhood of Railway and Steamship Clerks ruled that no married woman whose husband could support her was eligible for a job.

The American Federation of Labor (AFL) had little interest in organizing unskilled workers, but a new group of committed and militant labor leaders emerged in the 1930s to take up that task. John L. Lewis, the eloquent head of the United Mine Workers, was the most aggressive. He was joined by David Dubinsky of the International Ladies' Garment Workers, and Sidney Hillman, president of the Amalgamated Clothing Workers. Dubinsky and Hillman were socialists who believed in economic planning, but both had worked closely with social justice progressives. These new progressive labor leaders formed the Committee of Industrial Organization (CIO) within the AFL and set out to organize workers in the steel, auto, and rubber industries. Rather than separating workers by skill or craft as the AFL preferred, they organized everyone into an industry-wide union much as the Knights of Labor had done in the 1880s. They also used new and aggressive tactics.

In 1936, the workers at three rubber plants in Akron, Ohio, went on unauthorized strikes. Instead of picketing outside the factory, they occupied the buildings and took them over, preventing the owners from running the factory with non-union workers. The "sit-down strike" became a new protest technique. Sometimes the workers occupied a factory for a week or more. After sit-down strikes against General Motors plants in Atlanta, Georgia, and Flint, Michigan, General Motors finally accepted the United Auto Workers (UAW) as their employees' bargaining agent. The General Motors strike was the most important event in a critical period of labor upheaval. Labor's voice now began to be heard in the decision-making process in major industries in which labor had long been denied any role. The strikes at General Motors also helped raise the status of organized labor in the eyes of many Americans.

Violence spread along with the sit-down strike. Chrysler capitulated, but the Ford Motor Company used hired gunmen to discourage the strikers. A bloody struggle ensued before Ford agreed to accept the UAW as the bargaining agent. Even U.S. Steel, which had been militantly anti-union, signed an agreement with the Steel Workers Organizing Committee calling for a 40-hour workweek and an eight-hour workday. But other steel companies refused to go along. In Chicago on Memorial Day in 1937, a confrontation between the police and peaceful picketers at the Republic Steel plant resulted in 10 deaths. In the "Memorial Day Massacre," as it came to be called, the police fired without provocation into a crowd of workers and their families, who had gathered near the plant in a holiday mood. All 10 of the dead were shot in the back.

The CIO's aggressive tactics gained many new members, to the horror of AFL leaders. They expelled the CIO leaders from the AFL, only to see them form a separate Congress of Industrial Organization (the initials stayed the same). By accepting unskilled workers, African Americans, and others who had never belonged to a union before, the CIO infused the labor movement with a new spirit.

America's Minorities in the 1930s

Half a million African Americans joined unions through the CIO during the 1930s, and many blacks were aided by various New Deal agencies. Yet the familiar pattern of discrimination, low-paying jobs, and intimidation through violence persisted. Lynchings in the South actually increased in the New Deal years, rising from 8 in 1932 to 28 in 1933 and 20 in 1935.

One particular case came to symbolize and dramatize discrimination against African Americans in the 1930s. On March 25, 1931, in Scottsboro, Alabama, two young white women accused nine black men of raping them in a railroad boxcar as they all hitched a free ride. A jury of white men found all nine blacks guilty, and the court sentenced eight to die. The U.S. Supreme Court ordered new trials in 1933, on the grounds that the accused rapists had not received proper legal counsel. The case garnered much publicity in the United States and abroad. The youth of the defendants, their quick trial, and the harsh sentences made the "Scottsboro boys" a popular cause for many northern liberals and especially the Communist party.

For many southerners, however, it was a matter of defending the honor of white women. As one observer remarked of one of the accusers, she "might be a fallen woman, but by God she is a white woman." However, evidence supporting the alleged rapes was never presented, and eventually one of the women recanted. Yet the case dragged on. In new trials, five of the young men were convicted and given long prison terms. Charges against the other four were dropped in 1937. Four of the remaining five were paroled by 1946, and the fifth escaped to Michigan.

African Americans did not have to be accused of rape to want to flee to the North, however, and the migration of blacks to northern cities, which had accelerated during World War I, continued during the 1930s. The collapse of cotton prices forced black farmers and farm laborers to flee north for survival. But since most were poorly educated, they soon became trapped in northern ghettos, where they were eligible for only the most menial jobs. The black unemployment rate was triple that of whites, and blacks often received less per person in welfare payments.

Black leaders attacked the Roosevelt administration for supporting or allowing segregation in government-sponsored facilities. Roosevelt, fearing that he might antagonize southern congressmen whose backing he needed, refused to support the two major civil rights

Sharecroppers

Despite the black migration North during World War I and the 1920s, more than 80 percent of African Americans lived in the South during the 1930s. Most were sharecroppers, tenant farmers who often were in debt to the landlord. They were trapped by prejudice, unable to vote, and oppressed by poverty. The New Deal policies often made their situation worse. Many were kicked off the land and became homeless drifters. Can you imagine what it was like to be a sharecropper? Why did the nation tolerate such inequality?

(Library of Congress, LC-USF34T01–9575)

bills of the era, an antilynching bill and a bill to abolish the poll tax. Yet Harold Ickes and Harry Hopkins worked to ensure that blacks were given opportunities in New Deal agencies. By 1941, black federal employees totaled 150,000, more than three times the number during the Hoover administration. Most worked in the lower ranks, but some were lawyers, architects, office managers, and engineers.

Partly responsible for the presence of more black employees was the "black cabinet," a group of more than 50 young blacks who had appointments in various New Deal agencies and were led by Mary McLeod Bethune, the daughter of a sharecropper. She had founded a black primary school in Florida and then transformed it into Bethune-Cookman College. In the 1920s, she had organized the National Council of Negro Women. In 1934, Harry Hopkins, following the advice of Eleanor Roosevelt, appointed her to the advisory committee of the National Youth Administration. Bethune had some impact on New Deal policy and on the black cabinet. She spoke out forcefully, she picketed and protested, and she intervened shrewdly to obtain civil rights and more jobs for African Americans, but in the end the gains for blacks during the New Deal were very limited.

Although Roosevelt appointed a number of blacks to government positions, he was never particularly committed to civil rights. That was not true of Eleanor Roosevelt, who was educated in part by Mary McLeod Bethune. In 1939, when the Daughters of the American Revolution refused to allow Marian Anderson, a black concert singer, to use their stage, Mrs. Roosevelt publicly protested and resigned her membership in the DAR. She also arranged for Anderson to sing from the steps of the Lincoln Memorial, where 75,000 people gathered to listen and to support civil rights for all black citizens.

Hundreds of thousands of Mexicans, brought to the United States to work in the 1920s, lost their jobs in the Depression. Drifting to the Southwest or settling in the urban *barrios* and the small towns and farms in the Southwest, they met signs such as "Only White Labor Employed" and "No Niggers, Mexicans, or Dogs Allowed." Some New Deal agencies helped destitute Mexicans. A few worked for the CCC and the WPA, but to be employed, an applicant had to qualify for state relief, and that eliminated most migrants. The primary solution was not to provide aid for Mexicans but to ship them back to Mexico. In Los Angeles and other cities, the police and immigration authorities rounded up aliens and held them illegally. A trainload of repatriates left Los Angeles every month during 1933, and officials deported thousands from other cities. One estimate placed the number sent back in 1932 at 200,000, including some American citizens.

Not all the Mexicans were repatriated, however, and some who remained adopted militant tactics to obtain fair treatment. Mexican strawberry pickers went on strike in El Monte, California, and 18,000 cotton pickers walked away from their jobs in the San Joaquin valley in 1933. On August 31, 1939, during a record-breaking heat wave, nearly all of the 430 workers, most of them Mexican American women, staged a massive walkout at one of the largest food processing plants in Los Angeles.

Asians (Chinese, Japanese, and a smaller number of Koreans and Asian Indians) also suffered during the Depression. Most lived in ethnic enclaves, lost their jobs, and were treated as foreigners—not quite black, but not white either. Asians, especially the second generation who were automatically citizens if they were born in the United States, were troubled by a "twoness." They were both Chinese or Japanese and American. At least their parents wanted them to retain ties to the old country and the old culture. One young Chinese student from San Francisco had to go to Chinese school after her regular school. "We never became proficient in reading or writing Chinese," she recalled, "probably because we never thought of ourselves as needing Chinese. After all, weren't we Americans?" Most other Americans treated all Asians as aliens, and they had great difficulty distinguishing a Chinese from a Japanese from a Korean.

Native Americans also experienced alienation, disease, and despair during the Depression, and their plight was compounded by years of exploitation. Since the Dawes Act of 1887 (described in Chapter 17), government policy had sought to make the Indian into a property-owning farmer and to limit tribal rights. Native Americans lost more than 60 percent of the 138 million acres granted them in 1887. The government declared some of the land surplus and encouraged individuals to settle on 160 acres and adopt the "habits of civilized life." Few Native Americans profited from this system, but many whites did.

Just as other progressives sought the quick assimilation of immigrants, the progressive-era Indian commissioners sped up the allotment process to increase Indian detribalization. But many Native Americans who remained on the reservations were not even citizens. Finally, in 1924, Congress granted citizenship to all Indians born in the United States. The original Americans became U.S. citizens, but that did not end their suffering.

Franklin Roosevelt brought a new spirit to Indian policy by appointing John Collier as commissioner of Indian affairs. Collier was primarily responsible for the passage of the Indian Reorganization Act of 1934, which sought to restore the political independence of the tribes and to end the allotment policy of the Dawes Act. The bill also sought to promote the "study of Indian civilization" and to "preserve and develop the special cultural contributions and achievements of such civilization, including Indian arts, crafts, skills and traditions."

Not all Indians agreed with the new policies. Some chose to become members of the dominant culture, and many voted to reject the Reorganization Act because it required written tribal constitutions, which they viewed as inflexible or unnecessary. Some Americans charged that the act was inspired by communism. Others argued that its principal result would be to increase government bureaucracy, while missionaries claimed that the government was promoting paganism by allowing the Indians to practice their native religions.

The paradox and contradictions of U.S. policy toward the Indians can be illustrated by Collier's attempt to solve the Navajo problem. The Navajo lands, like most of the West, were overgrazed, and soil erosion threatened to fill the new lake behind the Hoover Dam with silt. By supporting a policy of reducing the herds of sheep and goats on Indian land and by promoting soil conservation, Collier contributed to the change in the Navajo lifestyle and to the end of their self-sufficiency, something he wanted to support.

Women and the New Deal

Women made some gains during the 1930s, and more women occupied high government positions than in any previous administration. Besides Frances Perkins, the secretary of labor, there was Molly Dewson, a social worker with the Massachusetts Girls Parole Department and the National Consumers League before becoming head of the Women's Division of the Democratic Committee and then an adviser to Roosevelt. Working closely with Eleanor Roosevelt to promote women's causes, she helped achieve a number of firsts: two women appointed ambassadors, a judge on the U.S. Court of Appeals, the director of the mint, and many women in government agencies.

Despite some gains, the early New Deal programs did nothing for an estimated 140,000 homeless women, or the 2 million to 4 million unemployed women. Married women often were fired from their jobs on the grounds that they should be home caring for their families rather than depriving men of employment. Single, divorced, and widowed women were usually ignored. Eleanor Roosevelt was genuinely concerned over the plight of poor women. She sponsored a White House Conference in November 1933 on the Emergency Needs of Women. She also advocated including more women in the CCC, the WPA, and other programs, but in the end the New Deal did little for poor women.

The Third New Deal

The New Deal was neither a consistent nor a well-organized effort to end the Depression and restructure society. Roosevelt was a politician and a pragmatist, unconcerned about ideological or programmatic consistency. The first New Deal of 1933–1934 concentrated on relief and recovery, while the legislation passed in 1935 and 1936 was more involved with social reform. In many ways, the election of 1936 marked the high point of Roosevelt's power and influence. After 1937, in part because of the growing threat of war but also because of increasing opposition in Congress, the pace of social legislation slowed. Yet several measures passed in 1937 and 1938 had such far-reaching significance that some historians refer to a third New Deal. Among the new measures were bills that provided for a minimum wage and for housing reform.

The Election of 1936

The Republicans in 1936 nominated a moderate, Governor Alfred Landon of Kansas. Although he attacked the New Deal, charging that new government programs were wasteful and created a dangerous

FDR'S SUCCESSFUL PRESIDENTIAL CAMPAIGNS, 1932–1944

Year	Candidate	Party	Popular Vote	Electoral Vote
1932	FRANKLIN D. ROOSEVELT	Democratic	22,809,638 (57.4%)	472
	Herbert C. Hoover	Republican	15,758,901 (39.7%)	59
	Norman Thomas	Socialist	881,951 (2.2%)	0
1936	FRANKLIN D. ROOSEVELT	Democratic	27,751,612 (60.8%)	523
	Alfred M. Landon	Republican	16,681,913 (36.5%)	8
	William Lemke	Union	891,858 (1.9%)	0
1940	FRANKLIN D. ROOSEVELT	Democratic	27,243,466 (54.8%)	449
	Wendell L. Willkie	Republican	22,304,755 (44.8%)	82
1944	FRANKLIN D. ROOSEVELT	Democratic	25,602,505 (53.5%)	432
	Thomas E. Dewey	Republican	22,006,278 (46.0%)	99

Note: Winners' names appear in capital letters.

federal bureaucracy, Landon only promised to do the same thing more cheaply and efficiently. Two-thirds of the newspapers in the country supported him, and the *Literary Digest* predicted his victory on the basis of a "scientific" telephone poll.

Roosevelt, helped by signs that the economy was recovering and supported by a coalition of the Democratic South, organized labor, farmers, and urban voters, won easily. A majority of African Americans for the first time deserted the party of Lincoln, not because of Roosevelt's interest in civil rights for blacks but because New Deal relief programs assisted many poor blacks. A viable candidate to the left of the New Deal failed to materialize. In fact, the Socialist party candidate, Norman Thomas, polled fewer than 200,000 votes. Roosevelt won by more than 10 million votes, carrying every state except Maine and Vermont. Even the traditionally Republican states of Pennsylvania, Delaware, and Connecticut, which had voted Republican in almost every election since 1856, went for Roosevelt.

The Battle of the Supreme Court

"I see one-third of a nation ill-housed, ill-clad, ill-nourished," Roosevelt declared in his second inaugural address, and he vowed to alter that situation. But the president's first action in 1937 did not call for legislation to alleviate poverty. Instead, he announced a plan to reform the Supreme Court and the judicial system. The Court had invalidated not only a number of New Deal measures—including the NIRA and the first version of the AAA—but other measures as well.

Increasingly angry at the "nine old men" who seemed to be destroying New Deal initiatives and defying Congress's will, Roosevelt determined to create a more sympathetic Court. He hoped to gain power to appoint an extra justice for each justice over age 70, of whom there were six. His plan also called for modernizing the court system at all levels, but that plan got lost in the public outcry over the Court-packing scheme.

Roosevelt's plan to nullify the influence of the older and more reactionary justices foundered. Republicans accused him of being a dictator and of subverting the Constitution. Many congressmen from his own party refused to support him. Led by Vice President John Nance Garner of Texas, a number of southern Democrats broke with the president and formed a coalition with conservative Republicans that lasted for more than 30 years. After months of controversy, Roosevelt withdrew the legislation and admitted defeat. He had perhaps misunderstood his mandate, and he certainly underestimated the respect, even the reverence, that most Americans felt for the Supreme Court.

Ironically, though he lost the battle of the Supreme Court, Roosevelt won the war. By the spring of 1937, the Court began to reverse its position and in a 5–4 decision upheld the National Labor Relations Act. When Justice Willis Van Devanter retired, Roosevelt was able to make his first Supreme Court appointment, thus ensuring at least a shaky liberal majority on the Court. After 1937 a series of court cases established the principle that Congress and federal power trumped states' rights and local control. But Roosevelt triumphed at great cost. His attempt to reorganize the Court dissipated energy and slowed the momentum of his legislative program. Seen as the most unpopular action he took as president, it made him vulnerable to criticism from opponents of the New Deal, and even some of his supporters were dismayed by what they regarded as an attack on the principle of separation of powers.

The economy improved in late 1936 and early 1937, but in August, the fragile prosperity collapsed.

Unemployment shot back up, industrial production fell, and the stock market plummeted. Facing an embarrassing economic slump that evoked charges that the New Deal had failed, Roosevelt resorted to "deficit spending," as recommended by John Maynard Keynes, the British economist. Keynes argued that to get out of a depression, the government must spend massive amounts of money on goods and services to increase demand and revive production. The economy responded slowly but never fully recovered until wartime expenditures, beginning in 1940, stimulated it, reduced unemployment, and ended the Depression.

Completing the New Deal

Despite increasing hostility, Congress passed a number of important bills in 1937 and 1938 that completed the New Deal reform legislation. The Bankhead–Jones Farm Tenancy Act of 1937 created the Farm Security

KEY 1930s REFORM LEGISLATION

Year	Legislation	Provisions
1932	Reconstruction Finance Corporation (RFC)	Granted emergency loans to banks, life insurance companies, and railroads (passed during Hoover administration)
1933	Civilian Conservation Corps (CCC)	Employed young men (and a few women) in reforestation, road construction, and flood control projects
1933	Agricultural Adjustment Act (AAA)	Granted farmers direct payments for reducing production of certain products; funds for payments provided by a processing tax, which was later declared unconstitutional
1933	Tennessee Valley Authority (TVA)	Created independent public corporation to construct dams and power projects and to develop the economy of a nine-state area in the Tennessee River valley
1933	National Industrial Recovery Act (NIRA)	Sought to revive business through a series of fair-competition codes; Section 7a guaranteed labor's right to organize (later declared unconstitutional)
1933	Public Works Administration (PWA)	Sought to increase employment and business activity through construction of roads, buildings, and other projects
1934	National Housing Act—created Federal Housing Administration (FHA)	Insured loans made by banks for construction of new homes and repair of old homes
1935	Emergency Relief Appropriation Act—created Works Progress Administration (WPA)	Employed more than 8 million people to repair roads, build bridges, and work on other projects; also hired artists and writers
1935	Social Security Act	Established unemployment compensation and old-age and survivors' insurance paid for by a joint tax on employers and employees
1935	National Labor Relations Act (Wagner–Connery Act)	Recognized the right of employees to join labor unions and to bargain collectively; created a National Labor Relations Board to supervise elections and to prevent unfair labor practices
1935	Public Utility Holding Act	Outlawed pyramiding of gas and electric companies through the use of holding companies and restricted these companies to activity in one area; a "death sentence" clause gave companies five years to prove local, useful, and efficient operation or be dissolved
1937	National Housing Act (Wagner–Steagall Act)	Authorized low-rent public housing projects
1938	Agricultural Adjustment Act (AAA)	Continued price supports and payments to farmers to limit production, as in 1933 act, but replaced processing tax with direct federal payment
1938	Fair Labor Standards Act	Established minimum wage of 40 cents an hour and maximum workweek of 40 hours in enterprises engaged in interstate commerce

Administration (FSA) to aid tenant farmers, sharecroppers, and farm owners who had lost their farms. The FSA, which provided loans to grain collectives, also set up camps for migratory workers. Some people saw such policies as the first step toward Communist collectives, but the FSA in fact never had enough money to make a real difference.

Congress passed a new Agricultural Adjustment Act in 1938 that tried to solve the problem of farm surpluses, which persisted even after hundreds of thousands of farmers had lost their farms. The new act replaced the processing tax (which the Supreme Court had declared unconstitutional) with direct payments from the federal treasury to farmers; added a soil conservation program; and provided for the marketing of surplus crops. Like its predecessor, the new act tried to stabilize farm prices by controlling production. But only the outbreak of World War II would end the problem of farm surplus, and then only temporarily.

In the cities, housing continued to be a problem. Progressive reformers had dreamed of providing better housing for the urban poor. They had campaigned for city ordinances and state laws and had built model tenements, but the first experiment with federal housing occurred during World War I. That brief experience encouraged a number of social reformers, who later became advisers to Roosevelt. They convinced him that federal low-cost housing should be part of New Deal reform.

The Reconstruction Finance Corporation made low-interest loans to housing projects, and the Public Works Administration constructed some apartment buildings. But not until the National Housing Act of 1937 did Roosevelt and his advisers try to develop a comprehensive housing policy for the poor. The act provided federal funds for slum clearance projects and for the construction of low-cost housing. By 1939, however, only 117,000 units had been built.

In the long run, New Deal housing legislation had a greater impact on middle-class housing policies and patterns. During the first 100 days of the New Deal, at Roosevelt's urging, Congress passed a bill creating the Home Owners Loan Corporation (HOLC), which over the next two years made more than $3 billion in low-interest loans and helped more than a million people save their homes from foreclosure. The HOLC also had a strong impact on housing policy by introducing the first long-term, fixed-rate mortgages. Formerly, all mortgages were for periods of no more than five years and were subject to frequent renegotiation.

The HOLC also introduced a uniform system of real estate appraisal that tended to undervalue urban property, especially in neighborhoods that were old, crowded, and ethnically mixed. The system gave the highest ratings to suburban developments where, according to the HOLC, there had been no "infiltration of Jews" or other undesirable groups. This was the beginning of the practice later called "redlining," in which lending agencies drew lines around neighborhoods and made it nearly impossible for prospective home buyers of certain ethnic or racial backgrounds to obtain a mortgage.

The Federal Housing Administration (FHA), created in 1934 by the National Housing Act, expanded and extended many of these HOLC policies. The FHA insured mortgages, many of them for 25 or 30 years; reduced the down payment required from 30 percent to less than 10 percent; and allowed more than 11 million families to buy homes between 1934 and 1972. The system, however, tended to favor purchasing new suburban homes rather than repairing older urban residences. New Deal housing policies helped make the suburban home with the long FHA mortgage part of the American way of life, but the policies also contributed to the decline of many urban neighborhoods.

Just as important as housing legislation was the Fair Labor Standards Act, which Congress passed in June 1938. Roosevelt's bill proposed for all industries engaged in interstate commerce a minimum wage of 25 cents an hour, to rise in two years to 40 cents an hour, and a maximum workweek of 44 hours, to be reduced to 40 hours. The act covered only 20 percent of the labor force and only 14 percent of working women. Nevertheless, when it went into effect, 750,000 workers immediately received raises, and by 1940, some 12 million had received pay increases. The law also prohibited child labor in interstate commerce, making it the first permanent federal law to prohibit youngsters under age 16 from working. And without emphasizing the matter, the law made no distinction between men and women, thus diminishing, if not completely ending, the need for special legislation for women.

The Fair Labor Standards Act was the last New Deal measure passed. The New Deal had many weaknesses, but it did dramatically increase government support for the needy. In 1913, local, state, and federal governments spent $21 million on public assistance. By 1932, that had risen to $218 million; by 1939, it was $4.9 billion.

The Other Side of the 1930s

The Great Depression and the New Deal so dominate the history of the 1930s that it is easy to conclude that nothing else happened, that there were only bread lines and relief agencies. But there is another side of the decade, for a communications revolution changed the lives of middle-class Americans. The sale of radios and attendance at movies increased during the 1930s, and literature flourished. Americans were fascinated by technology, especially automobiles. Many people traveled during the decade; they stayed in motor courts and looked ahead to a brighter future dominated by streamlined appliances and gadgets that would mean an easier life.

Taking to the Road

"People give up everything in the world but their car," a banker in Muncie, Indiana, remarked during the Depression, and that seems to have been true all over the country. Although automobile production dropped off after 1929 and did not recover until the end of the 1930s, the number of motor vehicles registered, which declined from 26.7 million in 1930 to just over 24 million in 1933, increased to more than 32 million by 1940. People who could not afford new cars drove used ones. Even the "Okies" fleeing the dust bowl of the Southwest traveled in cars. They were secondhand, run-down cars to be sure, but the fact that even many poor Americans owned cars shocked visitors from Europe, where automobiles were still only for the rich.

The American middle class traveled at an increasing rate after the low point of 1932 and 1933. In 1938, the tourist industry was the third largest in the United States, behind only steel and automobile production. More than 4 million Americans traveled every year, and four out of five went by car.

The Electric Home

If the 1920s was the age of the bathroom, the 1930s was the era of the modern kitchen. The sale of electrical appliances increased throughout the decade, with

Wash Day

Although the washing machine dates from the mid-nineteenth century, it did not end the drudgery of wash day; even the introduction of electric washers did not eliminate the constant wringing and rinsing that made wash day (usually Monday) a day to dread. The first automatic washing machines were introduced in the late 1930s but did not become commonplace until after World War II. This advertisement promotes the convenience of a machine that will spin-dry as well as wash. Notice the gender roles in the advertisement. The husband appreciates the saving but apparently does not put the clothes in the machine. "The Bendix" was a great improvement, but it was not until the 1950s that electric and gas dryers finally ended the task of hanging clothes on the line. How do you do your laundry today? Have things changed much since the 1930s?

(Bendix Home Appliances, Inc.)

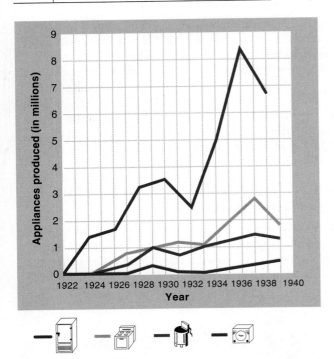

Household Appliance Production, 1922–1939
Electric appliances altered the lives of many American middle-class families during the 1930s. The replacement of the icebox with the electric refrigerator was especially dramatic. How did these appliances change the lifestyle of those who purchased them?

Source: U.S. Bureau of the Census.

refrigerators leading the way. In 1930, the number of refrigerators produced exceeded the number of iceboxes for the first time. Refrigerator production continued to rise throughout the decade, reaching a peak of 2.3 million in 1937. At first, the refrigerator was boxy and looked very much like an icebox with a motor sitting on top. In 1935, however, the refrigerator, like most other appliances, became streamlined. The Sears Coldspot, which quickly influenced the look of all other models, was designed by Raymond Loewy, one of a group of industrial designers who emphasized sweeping horizontal lines, rounded corners, and a slick modern look. They hoped modern design would stimulate an optimistic attitude and, of course, increase sales. At the end of the decade, in 1939, the World's Fair in New York glorified the theme of a streamlined future, carefully planned and based on new technology.

Ironically, despite these new conveniences, a great many middle-class families maintained their standard of living during the 1930s only because the women in the family learned to stretch and save and make do, and most wives spent as much time on housework as before. Some also took jobs outside the home to maintain their level of consumption. The number of married women who worked increased substantially during the decade.

The Age of Leisure

During the Depression, many middle-class people found themselves with time on their hands and sought out ways of spending it. The 1920s had been a time of spectator sports, of football and baseball heroes, of huge crowds that turned out to see boxing matches. Those sports continued during the Depression decade, although attendance suffered. Softball and miniature golf, which were cheap forms of entertainment and did not require expensive travel, also became popular. But leisure in the 1930s actually grew to be a problem, and professionals published some 450 new books on the subject. Leisure was mechanized; millions put their nickels in a slot and listened to a record played on a jukebox. Millions more played a pinball machine, a mechanized device that had no practical use other than entertainment and could end the game with one word: "Tilt."

Many popular games of the period had elaborate rules and directions. Contract bridge swept the country during the decade, and Monopoly was the most popular game of all. Produced by Parker Brothers, Monopoly was a fantasy of real estate speculation in which chance, luck, and the roll of the dice determined the winner. But one still had to obey the rules: "Go Directly to Jail. Do Not Pass Go. Do Not Collect $200." During a depression brought on in part by frenzied speculation, Americans were fascinated by a game whose purpose was to obtain real estate and utility monopolies and drive one's opponents into bankruptcy.

The 1930s was also a time of fads and instant celebrities, created by radio, newsreels, and businesspeople ready to turn almost anything to commercial advantage. The leading box office attraction between 1935 and 1938 was Shirley Temple, a blond and adorable child star. She inspired dolls, dishes, books, and clothes. Even stranger was the excitement created by the birth of five girl babies to a couple in northern Ontario in 1934. The Dionne quintuplets appeared on dozens of magazine covers and endorsed every imaginable product. Millions of people waited eagerly for the latest news about the babies, and more than 3 million traveled to see their home in Canada. The crazes over Shirley Temple and the Dionne quintuplets were products of the new technology, especially radio and the movies.

Literary Reflections of the 1930s

Though much of the literature of the 1930s reflected the decade's troubled currents, reading continued to be a popular and cheap entertainment. John Steinbeck, whose later novel *The Grapes of Wrath* (1939) followed the fortunes of the Joad family, described the plight of Mexican migrant workers in *Tortilla Flat* (1935). His novels

THE MOVIES

Just as some historians have used fiction to help define the cultural history of a decade, others in the twentieth century have turned to film to describe the "spirit of an age." On an elementary level, the movies help us appreciate changing styles in dress, furniture, and automobiles. We can even get some sense of how a particular time defined a beautiful woman or a handsome man, and we can learn about ethnic and racial stereotypes and assumptions about gender and class.

The decade of the 1930s is sometimes called the "golden age of the movies." Careful selection among the 500 or so feature films Hollywood produced each year during the decade—ranging from gangster and cowboy movies to Marx Brothers comedies, from historical romances to Busby Berkeley musical extravaganzas—could support a number of interpretations about the special myths and assumptions of the era. But one historian has argued that, especially after 1934, "not only did the movies amuse and entertain the nation through its most severe economic and social disorder, holding it together by their capacity to create unifying myths and dreams, but movie culture in the 1930s became a dominant culture for many Americans, providing new values and social ideals to replace shattered old traditions."

The year 1934 was a dividing line for two reasons. The motion picture industry, like all other industries, had suffered during the Depression; 1933 marked the low point in attendance, with more than one-third of the theaters in the country shut down. The next year, however, attendance

picked up, heralding a revival that lasted until 1946. Also in 1934, the movie industry adopted a code for which the Catholic Legion of Decency and other religious groups had lobbied. The new code prohibited the depiction of "sex perversion, interracial sex, abortion, incest, drugs and profanity." Even married couples could not be shown together in a double bed. Although a movie could depict immoral behavior, sin always had to be punished. "Evil and good should never be confused," the code announced.

Before the code, Hollywood had indeed produced graphic films, such as *The Public Enemy* (1931) and *Scarface* (1932), with a considerable amount of violence; musicals, such as *Gold Diggers of 1933,* filled with scantily clad young women; films featuring prostitutes, such as Jean Harlow in *Red Dust* (1932) and Marlene Dietrich in *Blond Venus* (1930); and other films that confronted the problems of real life. But after 1934, Hollywood concentrated on movies that created a mythical world in which evil was always punished, family moral values won out in the end, and patriotism and American democracy were never questioned. Although the code was modified from time to time, it was not abandoned until 1966, when it was replaced by a rating system.

It Happened One Night (1934) and *Drums Along the Mohawk* (1939), two films out of thousands, illustrate some of the myths the movies created and sustained. Frank Capra, one of Hollywood's masters at entertaining without disturbing, directed *It Happened One Night,* a comedy-romance. A rich girl (played by Claudette Colbert) dives from her father's yacht off the coast of Florida and takes a bus for

A scene from *It Happened One Night,* 1934

(Photofest)

A scene from *Drums Along the Mohawk*, 1939

(20th Century Fox/The Kobal Collection)

New York. She meets a newspaper reporter (Clark Gable), and they have a series of madcap adventures and fall in love. But mix-ups and misunderstandings make it appear that she will marry her old boyfriend. In the end, however, they are reunited and marry in an elaborate outdoor ceremony. Afterward, they presumably live happily ever after. The movie is funny and entertaining and presents a variation on the poor-boy-marries-rich-girl theme. Like so many movies of the time, this one suggests that life is fulfilled for a woman only if she can find the right man to marry.

Claudette Colbert also stars in *Drums Along the Mohawk*, this time with Henry Fonda. Based on a 1936 novel by Walter Edmonds, *Drums* is a sentimental story about a man who builds a house in the wilderness, marries a pretty girl, fights off the Indians, and works with the simple country folk to create a satisfying life in the very year the American colonies rebel against Great Britain. *Drums* was one of a number of films based on historical themes that Hollywood released just before World War II. *The Howards of Virginia*

(1940), *Northwest Passage* (1939), and, most popular of all, *Gone with the Wind* (1939) were others in the same genre. Historical themes had been popular before, but with the world on the brink of war, the story of men and women in the wilderness struggling for family and country against Native Americans (stereotyped as savages) proved comforting as well as entertaining.

Reflecting on the Past Can a historian use movies to describe the values and myths of a particular time, or are the complexities and exaggerations too great? Are the most popular or most critically acclaimed films more useful than others in getting at the "spirit of an age"? Which films that are popular today tell us the most about our time and culture? Is there too much sex and violence in movies today? Should the government control the language, themes, and values depicted in movies? Are movies as important today as they were in the 1930s in defining and influencing the country's myths and values? ■

expressed his belief that there was in American life a "crime . . . that goes beyond denunciation." He warned, "In the eyes of the hungry there is a growing wrath."

Other writers also questioned the American dream. John Dos Passos's trilogy *U.S.A.* (1930–1936) conveyed a deep pessimism about American capitalism that many other intellectuals shared. Less political were

the novels of Thomas Wolfe and William Faulkner, who more sympathetically portrayed Americans caught up in the web of local life and facing the complex problems of the modern era. Faulkner's fictional Yoknapatawpha County, brought to life in *The Sound and the Fury, As I Lay Dying, Sanctuary,* and *Light in August* (1929–1932), documented the South's racial

Timeline

1929	Stock market crashes
1930	Depression worsens
1932	Reconstruction Finance Corporation established
	Federal Home Loan Bank Act
	Glass–Steagall Banking Act
	Federal Emergency Relief Act
	Bonus march on Washington
	Franklin D. Roosevelt elected president
1933	Emergency Banking Relief Act
	Home Owners Loan Corporation
	Twenty-first Amendment repeals Eighteenth Amendment, ending Prohibition
	Agricultural Adjustment Act
	National Industrial Recovery Act
	Civilian Conservation Corps
	Tennessee Valley Authority established
	Public Works Administration established
1934	Unemployment peaks
	Federal Housing Administration established
	Indian Reorganization Act
1935	Second New Deal begins
	Works Progress Administration established
	Social Security Act
	Rural Electrification Act
	National Labor Relations Act
	Public Utility Holding Company Act
	Committee of Industrial Organization (CIO) formed
1936	United Auto Workers hold sit-down strikes against General Motors
	Roosevelt reelected president
	Economy begins to rebound
	Margaret Mitchell, *Gone with the Wind*
1937	Attempt to expand the Supreme Court
	Economic collapse
	Farm Security Administration established
	National Housing Act
1938	Fair Labor Standards Act
	Agricultural Adjustment Act
1939	John Steinbeck, *The Grapes of Wrath*

problems and its poverty as well as its stubborn pride. But the book about the South that became one of the decade's best-sellers was far more optimistic and far less complex than Faulkner's work—Margaret Mitchell's *Gone with the Wind* (1936). Its success suggested that many Americans read to escape, not to explore their problems.

Radio's Finest Hour

The number of radios purchased increased steadily during the decade. In 1929, slightly more than 10 million households owned radios; by 1939, more than 27.5 million households had radios. Not just a source of music and news, the radio was a focal point of the living room. In many homes, the top of the radio became the symbolic mantel where cherished photos were displayed. Families gathered around the radio at night to listen to and laugh at Jack Benny or Edgar Bergen and Charlie McCarthy or to try to solve a murder mystery with Mr. and Mrs. North. *The Lone Ranger,* another popular program, had 20 million listeners by 1939.

During the day there were soap operas. After school, teenagers and younger children argued over whether to listen to *Jack Armstrong, the All-American Boy* and *Captain Midnight* or *Stella Dallas* and *The Young Widder Brown.* Radio allowed many people to feel connected to distant places and to believe they knew the radio performers personally. Radio was also responsible for one of the most widespread episodes of mass hysteria of all time. On October 31, 1938, Orson Welles broadcast *The War of the Worlds* so realistically that thousands of listeners really believed that Martians had landed in New Jersey. If anyone needed proof, that single program demonstrated the power of the radio.

The Silver Screen

The 1930s were the golden decade of the movies. Between 60 million and 90 million Americans went to the movies every week. The medium was not entirely Depression-proof, but talking films had replaced the silent variety in the late 1920s, and attendance soared. Though it fell off slightly in the early 1930s, by 1934 movie viewing was climbing again. For many families, even in the depth of the Depression, movie money was almost as important as food money.

In the cities, one could go to an elaborate movie palace and live in a fantasy world far removed from the reality of Depression America. In small towns across the country, for 25 cents (10 cents for those under age 12) one could go to at least four movies during the week. Sometimes a double feature played, and there were always short subjects, a cartoon, and a newsreel. On Saturday, there was usually a serial that

left the heroine or hero in such a dire predicament that one just had to come back the next week to see how she or he survived.

The animated cartoons of Walt Disney, one of the true geniuses of the movie industry, were so popular that Mickey Mouse was more famous and familiar than most human celebrities. In May 1933, halfway into Roosevelt's first 100 days, Disney released *The Three Little Pigs,* whose theme song "Who's Afraid of the Big Bad Wolf?" became a national hit overnight. Some people felt it boosted the nation's morale as much as New Deal legislation. One critic suggested that the moral of the story, as retold by Disney, was that the little pig survived because he was conservative, diligent, and hardworking; others felt that it was the pig who used modern tools and planned ahead who won out.

Conclusion
THE MIXED LEGACY OF THE GREAT DEPRESSION AND THE NEW DEAL

The New Deal, despite its great variety of legislation, did not end the Depression, nor did it solve the problem of unemployment. For many Americans looking back on the decade of the 1930s, the most vivid memory was the shame and guilt of being unemployed, the despair and fear that came from losing a business or being evicted from a home or an apartment. For Robert Symmonds's generation, the experience of the Depression would influence their lives and their attitude toward money for the rest of their lives. Parents who lived through the decade urged their children to find a secure job, to get married, and to settle down. "Every time I've encountered the Depression it has been used as a barrier and a club," one daughter of Depression parents remembered; "older people use it to explain to me that I can't understand anything: I didn't live through the Depression."

New Deal legislation did not solve the country's problems, but it did strengthen the federal government, especially the executive branch. Federal agencies such as the Federal Deposit Insurance Corporation and programs such as social security influenced the daily lives of most Americans, and rural electrification, the WPA, and the CCC changed the lives of millions. The New Deal also established the principle of federal responsibility for the health of the economy, initiated the concept of the welfare state, and dramatically increased government spending to help the poor. Federally subsidized housing, minimum-wage laws, and a policy for paying farmers to limit production, all aspects of these principles, had far-reaching implications. The shift of responsibility for the nation's welfare to Washington marked the New Deal as a landmark in the continuing story of the relationship of government to society.

The New Deal was as important for what it did not do as for what it did. It did not promote socialism or redistribute income or property. It promoted social justice and social reform, but it provided little for people at the bottom of American society, and less for African Americans and other minorities. The New Deal did not prevent business consolidation, and, in the end, it probably strengthened corporate capitalism.

Roosevelt, with his colorful personality and his dramatic response to the nation's crisis, dominated his times in a way few presidents have done. Yet for some people who lived through the decade, neither Roosevelt nor bread lines but a new streamlined refrigerator or a Walt Disney movie symbolized the Depression decade. It is easy to study the United States in the 1930s without reference to what was going on in the rest of the world. But the United States was influenced by international economic and political trends during the decade. The Depression was global in its impact, and it was at least in part responsible for the rise of Hitler in Germany, for economic and military expansionism in Japan, and for encouraging Mussolini to undertake foreign adventures. Great Britain, France, the United States, and other countries, faced with economic disaster, passed high tariffs that in turn increased international tensions and led to aggressive nationalism. These global trends would eventually involve the United States in World War II.

QUESTIONS FOR REVIEW AND REFLECTION

1. Explain the origins of the Great Depression. How was the Depression in the United States related to global economic factors?
2. Explain the two major phases of the New Deal. What programs were enacted in each phase, and what did they seek to accomplish?
3. Who criticized the New Deal and why?
4. How did communication technologies and popular culture change during the 1930s?
5. Why are the Depression and the New Deal considered to have a mixed legacy?

CHAPTER 25

World War II

"Rosie the Riveter"

Many African Americans moved north, lured by jobs in war industries. Prejudice remained even in the North, and some blacks were denied employment or were given the most menial tasks. Others, like these welders, found good jobs, improved their lives, and helped change the dynamics of race relations in the United States. What other developments resulted from the wartime employment of women and minorities?

(Library of Congress, [LCUSW3–34282-CC])

American Stories

A Native American Boy Plays at War

N. Scott Momaday, a Kiowa Indian born in Lawton, Oklahoma, in 1934, grew up on Navajo, Apache, and Pueblo reservations. He was only 11 years old when World War II ended, yet the war had changed his life. Shortly after the United States entered the war, Momaday's parents moved to New Mexico, where his father got a job with an oil company and his mother worked in the civilian personnel office at an army air force base. Like many couples, they had struggled through the hard times of the Depression. The war meant jobs.

Momaday's best friend was Billy Don Johnson, a "reddish, robust boy of great good humor and intense loyalty." Together they played war, digging trenches and dragging themselves through imaginary minefields. They hurled grenades and fired endless rounds from their imaginary machine guns, pausing only to drink Kool-Aid from their canteens. At school, they were taught history and math and also how to hate the enemy and be proud of America. They recited the Pledge of Allegiance to the flag and sang "God Bless America," "The Star-Spangled Banner," and "Remember Pearl Harbor." Like most Americans, they believed that World War II was a good war fought against evil empires. The United States was always right, the enemy always wrong. It was an attitude that would influence Momaday and his generation for the rest of their lives.

Momaday's only difficulty was that his Native American face was often mistaken for that of an Asian. Almost every day on the playground, someone would yell, "Hi ya, Jap," and a fight was on. Billy Don always came to his friend's defense, but it was disconcerting to be taken for the enemy. His father read old Kiowa tales to Momaday, who was proud to be an Indian but prouder still to be an American. On Saturday, he and his friends would go to the local theater to cheer as they watched a Japanese Zero or a German ME-109 go down in flames. They pretended that they were P-40 pilots. "The whole field of vision shuddered with our fire: the 50-caliber tracers curved out, fixing brilliant arcs upon the span, and struck; then there was a black burst of smoke, and the target went spinning down to death."

Near the end of the war, his family moved again, as so many families did, so that his father might get a better job. This time they lived right next door to an air force base, and Momaday fell in love with the B-17 "Flying Fortress," the bomber that military strategists thought would win the war in the Pacific and in Europe. He felt a real sense of resentment and loss when the B-17 was replaced by the larger but not nearly so glamorous B-29.

Looking back on his early years, Momaday reflected on the importance of the war in his growing up. "I see now that one experiences easily the ordinary things of life," he decided, "the things which cast familiar shadows upon the sheer, transparent panels of time, and he perceives his experience in the only way he can, according to his age." Though Momaday's life during the war differed from the lives of boys old enough to join the armed forces, the war was no less real for him. Though his youth was affected by the fact that he was male, was an Indian, and lived in the Southwest, the most important influence was that he was an American growing up during the war. Ironically, his parents had been made U.S. citizens by an act of Congress in 1924, but like all Native Americans living in Arizona and New Mexico, they were denied the right to vote by state law.

The Momadays fared better than most Native Americans, who found prejudice against them undiminished and jobs, even in wartime, hard to find. Native American servicemen returning from the war discovered that they were still treated like "Indians." They were prohibited from buying liquor in many states, and those who returned to the reservations learned that they were ineligible for veterans' benefits. Still, Momaday thought of himself not so much as an Indian as an American, and that too was a product of his generation. But as he grew to maturity, he became a successful writer and spokesman for his people. In 1969, he won the Pulitzer Prize for his novel *House Made of Dawn*. He also recorded his experiences and memories in a book called *The Names* (1976). In his writing, he stresses the Native American's close identification with the land. Writing about his grandmother, he says: "The immense landscape of the continental interior lay like memory in her blood."

Momaday was just a child during World War II, but it had a profound effect on his life as it did on all of those who remembered the conflict. His generation would judge the global events of the rest of the twentieth century in terms of their sense of patriotism and valor acquired during the war. Although no American cities were bombed and the mainland was never invaded, World War II influenced almost every aspect of American life. The war ended the Depression. Industrial jobs were plentiful, and even though prejudice and discrimination did not disappear, blacks, Hispanics, women, and other minorities had new opportunities. Like World War I, the second war expanded cooperation between government and industry and increased the influence of government in all areas of American life. The war also ended the last remnants of American isolationism. The United States emerged from the war in 1945 as the most powerful and prosperous nation in the world.

This chapter traces the gradual involvement of the United States in the international events during the 1930s that finally led to participation in the most devastating war the world had seen. It recounts the diplomatic and military struggles of the war and the search for a secure peace. It also seeks to explain the impact of the war on ordinary people and on American attitudes about the world, as well as its effect on patriotism and the American way of life. Even those, like N. Scott Momaday, who grew up during the war and were too young to fight, were influenced by the war—and the sense of moral certainty that the war inspired—for the rest of their lives. The war brought prosperity to some as it brought death to others. It left the American people the most affluent in the world and the United States the most powerful nation.

The Twisting Road to War

Looking back on the events between 1933 and 1941 that eventually led to American involvement in World War II, it is easy either to be critical of decisions made or actions not taken or to see everything that happened during the period as inevitable. Historical events are never inevitable, and leaders who must make decisions never have the advantage of retrospective vision; they have to deal with situations as they find them, and they never have all the facts.

Foreign Policy in a Global Age

In March 1933, Roosevelt faced not only overwhelming domestic difficulties but also an international crisis. The worldwide depression had caused near financial disaster in Europe. Germany had defaulted on its reparations installments, and most European countries were unable to keep up the payments on their debts to the United States.

Roosevelt had no master plan in foreign policy, just as he had none in the domestic sphere. In the first days of his administration, he gave conflicting signals as he groped to respond to the international situation. At first, it seemed that the president would cooperate in some kind of international economic agreement on tariffs and currency. But then he undercut the American delegation in London by refusing to go along with any international agreement. Solving the American domestic economic crisis seemed more important to Roosevelt in 1933 than international economic cooperation. His actions signaled a decision to go it alone in foreign policy.

Roosevelt did, however, alter some of the foreign policy decisions of previous administrations. He recognized the Soviet government, hoping to gain a market for surplus American grain. Although the expected trade bonanza never materialized, the Soviet Union agreed to pay the old debts and to extend rights to American citizens living in the Soviet Union. Diplomatic recognition opened communications between the two emerging world powers.

The United States continued to support dictators, especially in Central America, because they promised to promote stability and preserve American economic interests. But Roosevelt completed the removal of American military forces from Haiti and Nicaragua in 1934, and in a series of pan-American conferences, he joined in pledging that no country in the hemisphere would intervene in the "internal or external affairs" of any other.

The first test case came in Cuba, where a revolution threatened American investments of more than $1 billion. But the United States did not send troops. Instead, Roosevelt dispatched special envoys to work out a conciliatory agreement with the revolutionary government. A short time later, when a coup led by Fulgencio Batista overthrew the revolutionary government, the United States not only recognized the Batista government but also offered a large loan and agreed to abrogate the Platt Amendment (which made Cuba a virtual protectorate of the United States) in return for the rights to the Guantanamo naval base.

The Trade Agreements Act of 1934 gave the president power to lower tariff rates by as much as 50 percent. Using this act, the Roosevelt administration negotiated a series of agreements that improved trade. By 1935, half of American cotton exports and a large proportion of other products were going to Latin America. The Good Neighbor policy was good business for the United States, but increased trade did not solve the economic problems for either the United States or Latin America.

Another test of Latin American policy came in 1938 when Mexico nationalized the property of a number of American oil companies. Instead of intervening, as many businessmen urged, the State Department patiently worked out an agreement that included some compensation for the companies. The American government might have acted differently, however, if the threat of war in Europe in 1938 had not suggested that all the Western Hemisphere nations would have to cooperate to resist the growing power of Germany and Italy. At a pan-American conference held that year, the United States and most Latin American countries agreed to resist all foreign intervention in the hemisphere.

Europe on the Brink of War

Around the time that Roosevelt was first elected president, Adolf Hitler came to power in Germany. Born in Austria in 1889, Hitler had served as a corporal in the German army during World War I. Like many other Germans, he was angered by the Treaty of Versailles, and he blamed Germany's defeat on the Communists and the Jews. World War II in Europe was caused by World War I and by Germany's attempt to reverse the peace settlement.

Hitler became the leader of the National Socialist party of the German workers (*Nazi* is short for the German National Sozialist), and in 1923, after leading an unsuccessful coup, he was sentenced to prison. While in jail he wrote *Mein Kampf* ("My Struggle"), a long, rambling book spelling out his theories of racial purity, his hopes for Germany, and his venomous hatred of the Jews. After his release from prison, Hitler's following grew. He had a charismatic style and a plan. On January 30, 1933, he became chancellor of Germany, and within months the Reichstag (parliament) suspended the constitution, making Hitler Fuehrer (leader) and dictator. His Fascist regime concentrated political and economic power in a centralized state. He intended to conquer Europe and to make the German Third Reich (empire) the center of a new civilization.

In 1934, Hitler announced a program of German rearmament, violating the Versailles Treaty of 1919. Meanwhile, in Italy, the Fascist dictator Benito Mussolini was building a powerful military force; in 1934, he threatened to invade the East African country of Ethiopia. These ominous rumblings in Europe frightened Americans at the very time they were reexamining American entry into the Great War and vowing that they would never again get involved in a European conflict.

Senator Gerald P. Nye of North Dakota, who had helped expose the Teapot Dome scandal in 1924, turned to an investigation of the connection between corporate profits and American participation in World War I. His committee's public hearings revealed that many American businessmen had close relationships with the War Department. Businesses producing war materials had made huge profits. Though the committee failed to prove a conspiracy, it was easy to conclude that the United States had been tricked into going to war by the people who profited the most from it.

On many college campuses, students demonstrated against war. Students joined organizations such as Veterans of Future Wars and Future Gold Star Mothers and protested the presence of the Reserve Officers Training Corps (ROTC) on their campuses. Many were determined never again to support a foreign war. But in Europe, Asia, and Africa, there were already rumblings of another great international conflict.

Ethiopia and Spain

In May 1935, Italy invaded Ethiopia after rejecting the League of Nations' offer to mediate the difficulties between the two countries. Italian dive bombers and machine guns made quick work of the small and poorly equipped Ethiopian army. The Ethiopian war, remote as it seemed, frightened Congress, which passed a Neutrality Act authorizing the president to prohibit all arms shipments to nations at war and to advise all U.S. citizens not to travel on belligerents' ships except at their own risk. Remembering the process that had led the United States into World War I, Congress was determined that it would not happen again.

The League of Nations condemned Italy as the aggressor in the war, and Great Britain moved its fleet to the Mediterranean. Roosevelt used the authority of the Neutrality Act of 1935 to impose an arms embargo. But, in the midst of depression, neither Britain nor the United States wanted to stop shipments of oil to Italy or to commit its own soldiers to the fight. The embargo on arms had little impact on Italy, but it was disastrous for Ethiopia.

"We shun political commitments which might entangle us in foreign war," Roosevelt announced in 1936. But isolation became more difficult when a civil war broke out in Spain in 1936. General Francisco Franco, supported by the Catholic church and large landowners, revolted against the republican government. Mussolini had joined forces with Germany to form the Rome–Berlin Axis in 1936, and Germany and Italy aided Franco, sending planes and other weapons, while the Soviet Union came to the support of the anti-Franco Loyalists.

The war in Spain polarized the United States. Most Catholics and many anti-Communists sided with Franco. But many American radicals, even those opposed to all war a few months before, found the Loyalist cause worth fighting and dying for. More than 3,000 Americans joined the Abraham Lincoln Brigade, and hundreds were killed fighting fascism in Spain. "If this were a Spanish matter, I'd let it alone," Sam Levenger, a student at Ohio State, wrote. "But the rebellion would not last a week if it weren't for the Germans and the Italians. And if Hitler and Mussolini can send troops to Spain to attack the government elected by the people, why can't they do so in France? And after France?" Levenger was killed in Spain in 1937 at age 20.

Picasso's *Guernica*

On April 26, 1937, German airplanes supporting Franco's soldiers bombed and machine-gunned the historic Basque capital city of Guernica, killing more than 1,600 people and foreshadowing the massive destruction of civilians during World War II. Pablo Picasso, probably the most famous artist of the twentieth century, painted this black-and-white mural to denounce the attack. After the defeat of the Republican forces in Spain, Picasso refused to allow the painting to be displayed in the country. Only in 1975, after the end of the Franco regime, did the painting return to Madrid. What kind of symbols and images can you find in the painting?

(Pablo Picasso (1881–1973), "Guernica," 1937. Oil on canvas, 350 × 782 cm. Museo Nacional Centro de Arte Reina Sofia, Madrid, Spain. Copyright John Bigelow Taylor/Art Resource, NY. © 2008 Estate of Pablo Picasso/Artists Rights Society (ARS), New York.)

The U.S. government tried to stay neutral and to ship arms and equipment to neither side. While the United States, along with Britain and France, carefully protected its neutrality, Franco consolidated his dictatorship with the active aid of Germany and Italy. Meanwhile, Congress in 1937 passed another Neutrality Act, this time making it illegal for American citizens to travel on belligerents' ships. The act extended the embargo on arms and made even nonmilitary items available to belligerents only on a cash-and-carry basis.

In a variety of ways, the United States tried to avoid repeating the mistakes that had led it into World War I. Unfortunately, World War II, which moved closer each day, would be a different kind of war, and the lessons of the first war would be of little use.

War in Europe

Roosevelt was by no means an isolationist, but he wanted to keep the United States out of the European conflagration. When he announced, "I hate war," he was expressing a deep personal belief that wars solve few problems. Unlike his distant cousin Theodore Roosevelt, he did not view war as a test of one's manhood. In foreign policy, just as in domestic affairs, FDR responded to events, but he moved reluctantly toward greater American involvement.

In March 1938, Hitler's Germany annexed Austria and then in September, as a result of the Munich Conference, occupied the Sudetenland, a part of Czechoslovakia. Within six months, Hitler's armies had overrun the rest of Czechoslovakia. Little protest came from the United States. Most Americans sympathized with the victims of Hitler's aggression, and at first, almost everyone hoped that compromises could be worked out and that Europe could settle its own problems. But that notion was destroyed on August 23, 1939, by the news of a Nazi–Soviet pact. Fascism and communism were political philosophies supposedly in deadly opposition. Many Americans had secretly hoped that Nazi Germany and Soviet Russia would fight it out, neutralizing each other. Now they had signed a nonaggression pact. A week later, Hitler's army attacked Poland, marking the official beginning of World War II. Britain and France honored their treaties and came to Poland's defense. "This nation will remain a neutral nation," Roosevelt announced, "but I cannot ask that every American remain neutral in thought as well."

Roosevelt asked for a repeal of the embargo section of the Neutrality Act and for the approval of the sale of arms on a cash-and-carry basis to France and Britain. Yet Roosevelt did take some secret risks. In August 1939, Albert Einstein, a Jewish refugee from Nazi Germany, and other distinguished scientists warned the president that German researchers were at work on an atomic bomb. Fearing the consequences of a powerful new weapon in Hitler's hands, Roosevelt authorized funds for a top-secret project to build an American bomb first. Only a few advisers and key members of Congress knew of the project, which was officially organized in 1941 and would ultimately change the course of human history.

The war in Poland ended quickly. With Germany attacking from the west and the Soviet Union from the east, the Poles were overwhelmed in a month. The fall of Poland in September 1939 brought a lull in the fighting.

Great Britain sent several divisions to aid the French against the expected German attack, but for months nothing happened. This interlude, sometimes called the "phony war," dramatically ended on April 9, 1940, when Germany attacked Norway and Denmark with a furious air and sea assault. A few weeks later, using armored vehicles supported by massive air strikes, the German *Blitzkrieg* ("lightning war") swept through Belgium, Luxembourg, and the Netherlands. A week later, the Germans stormed into France.

The famed Maginot line, a series of fortifications designed to repulse a German invasion, was useless, as German mechanized forces swept around the end of the line and attacked from the rear. The French guns, solidly fixed in concrete and pointing toward Germany, were never fired. France surrendered in June as the British army fled back across the English Channel from Dunkirk.

How should the United States respond to the new and desperate situation in Europe? William Allen White, journalist and editor, and other concerned Americans organized the Committee to Defend America by Aiding the Allies, but others, including Charles Lindbergh, the hero of the 1920s, supported a group called America First. They argued that the United States should forget about England and concentrate on defending America. Roosevelt steered a cautious course. He approved the shipment to Britain of 50 overage American destroyers. In return, the United States received the right to establish naval and air bases on British territory from Newfoundland to Bermuda and British Guiana.

Winston Churchill, prime minister of Great Britain, asked for much more, but Roosevelt hesitated. In July 1940, the president did sign a measure authorizing $4 billion to increase the number of American naval warships. In September, Congress passed the Selective Service Act, which provided for the first peacetime draft in the history of the United States. More than a million men were to serve in the army for one year, but only in the Western Hemisphere.

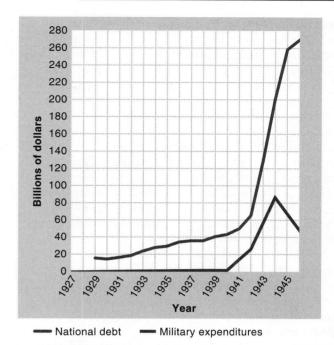

Military Expenditures and the National Debt, 1929–1945

Increased taxes, the sale of war bonds, and price controls kept inflation under relative control during the war. Still, the war industry not only stimulated the economy but also increased the national debt. In what other ways do wars influence the economy?

Source: U.S. Bureau of the Census.

The Election of 1940

Part of Roosevelt's reluctance to aid Great Britain more energetically came from his genuine desire to keep the United States out of the war, but it was also related to the presidential campaign waged during the crisis months of the summer and fall of 1940. Roosevelt broke a long tradition by seeking a third term. He marked the increasing support he was drawing from the liberal wing of the Democratic party by selecting liberal farm economist Henry Wallace of Iowa as his running mate.

The Republicans nominated Wendell Willkie of Indiana. Despite his big-business ties, Willkie approved of most New Deal legislation and supported aid to Great Britain. Energetic and attractive, Willkie was the most persuasive and exciting Republican candidate since Theodore Roosevelt. Yet in an atmosphere of international crisis, most voters chose to stay with Roosevelt. He won, 27 million to 22 million, and carried 38 of 48 states.

Lend-Lease

After the election, Roosevelt invented a scheme for sending aid to Britain without demanding payment. He called it "lend-lease." He compared the situation to lending a garden hose to a neighbor whose house was on fire. Senator Robert Taft of Ohio, however, thought the idea of lending military equipment and expecting it back was absurd. He decided it was more like lending chewing gum to a friend: "Once it had been used you did not want it back."

The Lend-Lease Act, which Congress passed in March 1941, destroyed the fiction of neutrality. By that time, German submarines were sinking half a million tons of shipping each month in the Atlantic. In June, Roosevelt proclaimed a national emergency and ordered the closing of German and Italian consulates in the United States. On June 22, Germany suddenly attacked the Soviet Union. It was one of Hitler's biggest blunders of the war, forcing his armies to fight on two fronts.

When Roosevelt extended lend-lease aid to Russia in November 1941, most Americans accepted the Soviet Union as a friend and ally. By the autumn of 1941, the United States was virtually at war with Germany in the Atlantic. On September 11, Roosevelt issued a "shoot on sight" order for all American ships operating in the Atlantic, and on October 30, a German submarine sank an American destroyer off the coast of Newfoundland. The war in the Atlantic, however, was undeclared. Eventually, the sinking of enough American ships or another crisis would probably have provided the excuse for a formal declaration of war against Germany. It was not Germany, however, but Japan that catapulted the United States into World War II.

The Path to Pearl Harbor

Japan, controlled by ambitious military leaders, was the aggressor in the Far East as Hitler's Germany was in Europe. Intent on becoming a major world power yet desperately needing natural resources, especially oil, Japan was willing to risk war with China, the Soviet Union, and even the United States to get those resources. Japan invaded Manchuria in 1931 and launched an all-out assault on China in 1937. This was the beginning of what the Japanese would call "the Pacific War." The Japanese leaders assumed that at some point the United States would go to war if Japan tried to take the Philippines, but the Japanese attempted to delay that moment as long as possible by diplomatic means. The United States feared a two-front war and was willing to delay the confrontation with Japan until it had dealt with the German threat. Thus, between 1938 and 1941, the United States and Japan engaged in a kind of diplomatic shadow boxing.

The United States began to apply economic pressure in July 1939, giving Japan the required six months' notice regarding cancellation of the 1911 commercial agreement between the two countries. In September 1940, the Roosevelt administration forbade the shipment of airplane fuel and scrap metal to Japan. Other items were added to the embargo until by the spring of 1941, the United States allowed only oil to be shipped to Japan, hoping that the threat of cutting off this important resource would lead to negotiations and avert a crisis. Japan did open negotiations with the United States, but there was little to discuss. Japan would not withdraw from China as the United States demanded. Indeed, Japan, taking advantage of the situation in Europe, occupied French Indochina in 1940 and 1941. In July 1941, Roosevelt froze all Japanese assets in the United States, effectively embargoing trade with Japan.

Roosevelt had an advantage in the negotiations with Japan, for the United States had broken the Japanese secret diplomatic code. But Japanese intentions were hard to decipher from the intercepted messages. American leaders knew that Japan planned to attack, but they didn't know where. In September 1941, the Japanese decided to strike sometime after November unless the United States offered real concessions.

On the morning of December 7, 1941, Japanese airplanes launched from aircraft carriers attacked the U.S. fleet at Pearl Harbor in Hawaii. The surprise attack destroyed or disabled 19 ships (including 5 battleships) and 150 planes and killed 2,335 soldiers and sailors and 68 civilians. On the same day, the Japanese launched attacks on the Philippines, Guam, and the Midway Islands, as well as on the British colonies of Hong Kong and Malaya. The next day, with only one dissenting vote, Congress declared war on Japan.

December 7, 1941, was a date that would "live in infamy," in the words of Franklin Roosevelt. It was also a day that would have far-reaching implications for American foreign policy and for American attitudes toward the world. The surprise attack united the country as nothing else could have. Even isolationists and America First advocates quickly rallied behind the war effort.

After the shock and anger subsided, Americans searched for a villain. Someone must have blundered, someone must have betrayed the country to have allowed the "inferior" Japanese to have carried out such a successful and devastating attack. A myth persists to this day that the villain was Roosevelt, who, the story goes, knew of the Japanese attack but failed to warn the military commanders so that the American people might unite behind the war effort against Germany. But Roosevelt did not know. There was no specific warning that the attack was coming against Pearl Harbor, and the American ability to read the Japanese coded messages was of no help because the fleet kept radio silence.

The irony was that the Americans, partly because of racial prejudice against the Japanese, underestimated their ability. They ignored many warning signals because they did not believe that the Japanese could launch an attack on a target as far away as Hawaii. Most of the experts, including Roosevelt, expected the Japanese to attack the Philippines or perhaps Thailand. Many people blundered, but there was no conspiracy.

More important in the long run than the way the attack on Pearl Harbor united the American people was its effect on a generation of military and political leaders. Pearl Harbor became the symbol of unpreparedness. For a generation that experienced the anger and frustration of the attack on Pearl Harbor by an unscrupulous enemy, the lesson was to be prepared and ready to stop an aggressor before it had a chance to strike. The smoldering remains of the sinking battleships at Pearl Harbor on the morning of December 7, 1941, and the history lesson learned there would influence American policy not only during World War II but also in Korea, Vietnam, and beyond.

The Home Front

Too often wars are described in terms of presidents and generals, emperors and kings, in terms of grand strategy and elaborate campaigns. But wars affect the lives of all people—the soldiers who fight and the women and children and men who stay home. World War II especially had an impact on all aspects of society—the economy, the movies and radio, even attitudes toward women and blacks. For many people, the war represented opportunity and the end of the Depression. For others, the excitement of faraway places meant that they could never return home again. For still others, the war left lasting scars.

Mobilizing for War

Converting American industry to war production was a complex task. Shortly after Pearl Harbor, Roosevelt created the War Production Board (WPB) and appointed Donald Nelson, executive vice president of Sears, Roebuck, to mobilize the nation's resources for an all-out war effort. The Roosevelt administration tried hard to gain the cooperation of businesspeople, many of them alienated by New Deal policies. The president appointed many business leaders to key positions and abandoned antitrust actions in any industry that was remotely related to the war effort. The policy worked. Industrial production and net corporate profits nearly doubled during the war. Large commercial farmers also profited. The war years accelerated the mechanization of the farm and dramatically increased the use of fertilizer, but between 1940 and 1945 the farm population declined by 17 percent.

Many government agencies in addition to the War Production Board helped monitor the war effort. The Office of Price Administration (OPA) set prices and rationed products—and because it affected so many lives so disagreeably, many Americans regarded it as oppressive. The National War Labor Board (NWLB) had the authority to set wages and hours and to regulate working conditions, and it could seize factories whose owners refused to cooperate.

Union membership grew rapidly during the war, from 10.5 million in 1941 to 14.7 million in 1945. In return for a "no-strike pledge," the NWLB allowed agreements that required workers to retain their union membership through the life of a contract. Labor leaders, however, complained about increased government regulations and argued that wage controls coupled with wartime inflation

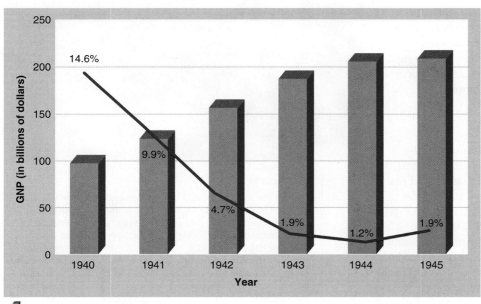

Gross National Product and Unemployment, 1940–1945

The war economy virtually wiped out unemployment and increased production to unprecedented levels. How would these changes affect everyday life in the United States?

Source: U.S. Bureau of the Census.

were unfair. The NWLB finally allowed a 15 percent cost-of-living increase on some contracts, but that did not apply to overtime pay, which helped drive up wages in some industries during the war by about 70 percent.

Besides wage and price controls and rationing, the government tried to reduce inflation by selling war bonds and by increasing taxes. The Revenue Act of 1942 raised tax rates, broadened the tax base, increased corporate taxes to 40 percent, and raised the excess-profits tax to 90 percent. In addition, the government initiated a payroll deduction for income taxes. The war made the income tax a reality for most Americans for the first time.

Despite some unfairness and much confusion, the American economy responded to the wartime crisis and produced the equipment and supplies that eventually won the war. American industries built 300,000 airplanes, 88,140 tanks, and 3,000 merchant ships. In 1944 alone, American factories produced 800,000 tons of synthetic rubber to replace the supply of natural rubber captured by the Japanese. Although the national debt grew from about $143 billion in 1943 to $260 billion in 1945, the government policy of taxation paid for about 40 percent of the war's cost. At the same time, full employment and the increase in two-income families, together with forced savings, helped provide capital for postwar expansion. In a limited way, the tax policy also tended to redistribute wealth, which the New Deal had failed to do. The top 5 percent income bracket, which controlled 23 percent of the disposable income in 1939, accounted for only 17 percent in 1945.

The war stimulated the growth of the federal bureaucracy and accelerated the trend, begun during World War I and extended in the 1920s and 1930s, toward the government's central role in the economy. The war also increased the cooperation between industry and government, creating what would later be called a military-industrial complex. But for most Americans, despite anger at the OPA and the income tax, the war meant the end of the Depression.

Patriotic Fervor

The war, so horrible elsewhere, was remote in the United States—except for the families that received the official telegram informing them that a loved one had been killed. The government tried to keep the conflict alive in the minds of Americans and to keep the country united behind the war effort. The Office of War Information controlled the news the American public received about the war and promoted patriotism. The government also sold war bonds, not only to help pay for the war and reduce inflation but also to sell the war to the American people. Schoolchildren purchased war stamps and faithfully pasted them in an album until they

had accumulated stamps worth $18.75, enough to buy a $25 bond (redeemable 10 years later). Their bonds, they were told, would purchase bullets or a part for an airplane to kill "Japs" and Germans and defend the American way of life. "For Freedom's Sake, Buy War Bonds," one poster announced. Working men and women purchased bonds through payroll deduction plans and looked forward to spending the money on consumer goods after the war. In the end, the government sold more than $135 billion in war bonds. While the bond drives did help control inflation, they were most important in making millions of Americans feel that they were contributing to the war effort.

The Enemy

During the war American magazines and newspapers often depicted the Japanese as monkeys, insects, or rodents. Germans were rarely pictured this way. This December 12, 1942, issue of *Collier's* magazine pictures Japanese prime minister Hideki Tojo as a vampire bat carrying a bomb to drop on the United States. The Japanese, on the other hand, often pictured Americans and British as bloated capitalists and imperialists. What effect, do you suppose, did these caricatures have on attitudes and actions during the war?

(akg-images)

Those too old or too young to join the armed forces became air raid wardens or civilian defense and Red Cross volunteers. They raised victory gardens and took part in scrap drives. Even small children could join the war effort by collecting old rubber, wastepaper, and kitchen fats. Some items, including gasoline, sugar, butter, and meat, were rationed, but few people complained. Even horsemeat hamburgers seemed edible if they helped win the war. Newspaper and magazine advertising characterized ordinary actions as either speeding victory or impeding the war effort.

Internment of Japanese Americans

Wartime campaigns not only stimulated patriotism but also promoted hatred for the enemy. The Nazis, especially Hitler and his Gestapo, had become synonymous with evil even before 1941. At the beginning of the war there was little animosity toward the German people, but before long most Americans ceased to make distinctions. All Germans seemed evil, although the anti-German hysteria that had swept the country during World War I never developed.

The Japanese were easier to hate than the Germans. The attack on Pearl Harbor created a special animosity toward the Japanese, but the depiction of the Japanese as warlike and subhuman owed something to a long tradition of fear of the so-called yellow peril and a distrust of all Asians. Two weeks after Pearl Harbor, *Time* magazine explained to Americans how they could distinguish our Asian friends the Chinese "from the Japs": "The Chinese expression is likely to be more kindly, placid, open; the Japanese more positive, dogmatic, arrogant."

The racial stereotype of the Japanese played a role in the treatment of Japanese Americans during the war. Some prejudice was shown against German and Italian Americans and some were relocated, but Japanese Americans were the only group confined in concentration camps in large numbers and for the duration of the war. It was the greatest mass abridgment of civil liberties in American history.

At the time of Pearl Harbor, about 127,000 Japanese Americans lived in the United States, most on the West Coast. About 80,000 were *nisei* (Japanese born in the United States and holding American citizenship) and *sansei* (the sons and daughters of nisei); the rest were *issei* (aliens born in Japan who were ineligible for U.S. citizenship). The Japanese had long suffered from racial discrimination and prejudice in the United States. They were barred from intermarriage with other groups and excluded from many clubs, restaurants, and recreation facilities. Many worked as tenant farmers, fishermen, and small-business owners. Others made up a small professional class of lawyers, teachers, and doctors and a large number of landowning farmers.

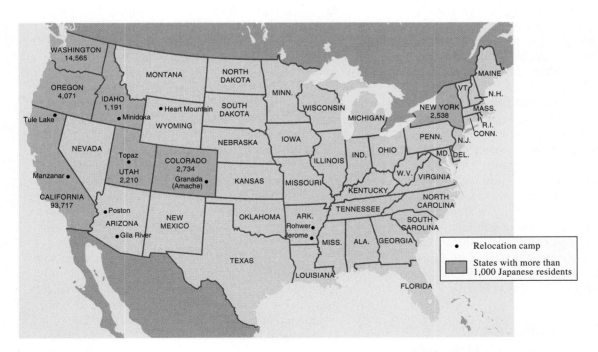

Relocation Camps

Early in 1942, responding to the hysterical fear that Japanese Americans living on the West Coast might engage in sabotage, the government ordered more than 100,000 Japanese Americans (many of them citizens) into relocation camps. A larger group of Japanese Americans living in Hawaii did not have their lives disrupted or their property confiscated. How do you explain the pattern of Japanese relocation?

Although many retained cultural and linguistic ties to Japan, they posed no more threat to the country than did the much larger groups of Italian Americans and German Americans. But their appearance made them stand out. After Pearl Harbor, an anti-Japanese panic seized the West Coast.

West Coast politicians and ordinary citizens urged the War Department and the president to evacuate the Japanese. The president capitulated and issued Executive Order 9066 authorizing the evacuation in February 1942. "The continued pressure of a largely unassimilated, tightly knit racial group, bound to an enemy nation by strong ties of race, culture, custom and religion, constituted a menace which had to be dealt with," General John De Witt argued, justifying the removal on military grounds. But racial fear and animosity, not military necessity, stood behind the order.

Eventually, the government built the "relocation centers" in remote, often arid, sections of the West. "The Japs live like rats, breed like rats, and act like rats. We don't want them," the governor of Idaho announced. The camps were primitive and unattractive. "When I first entered our room, I became sick to my stomach," a Japanese American woman remembered. "There were seven beds in the room and no furniture nor any partitions to separate the males and the females of the family. I just sat on the bed, staring at the bare wall."

The government evacuated about 110,000 Japanese, including about 60,000 American citizens. The Japanese Americans lost their worldly possessions, and something more—their pride and respect. One 6-year-old kept asking his mother to "take him back to America." He thought his relocation center was in Japan.

The evacuation was unjustified. Even in Hawaii, where a much larger Japanese population existed, the government evacuated only a few (in part because the Japanese were so vital to the economy of the Islands), and no sabotage and little disloyalty occurred. The government allowed Japanese American men to volunteer for military service, and many served bravely in Europe. The 442nd Infantry Combat Team, made up entirely of *nisei*, became the most decorated unit in all the military service—another indication of the loyalty and patriotism of most Japanese Americans. In 1988, Congress belatedly voted limited compensation for the Japanese Americans relocated during World War II.

Asian, African, and Hispanic Americans at War

The Pacific War made China an ally of the United States, but Congress did not repeal the Chinese Exclusion Act until 1943, and then only 105 Chinese a year were allowed to enter the United States legally. Despite this, Chinese communities in the United States joined the war effort enthusiastically. They bought war bonds, collected scrap metal, and in other ways tried to show that they were loyal citizens. The Korean, Filipino, and Asian Indian population also contributed to the war effort, even though they still faced prejudice and were often denied service in restaurants or refused admittance to theaters. Many Americans hated the Japanese; to them, all Asians looked like the enemy.

Even in much of the North, the United States remained a segregated society in 1941. African Americans could not live, eat, travel, work, or go to school with the same freedom that whites enjoyed. Black Americans profited little from the revival of prosperity and the expansion of jobs early in the war. Those who joined the military were usually assigned to menial jobs as cooks or laborers and were always assigned to segregated units with whites as the high-ranking officers. The myth persisted that black soldiers had failed to perform well in World War I. "Leadership is not embedded in the negro race yet," Secretary of War Henry Stimson wrote, "and to try to make commissioned officers . . . lead men into battle—colored men—is only to work a disaster to both."

Some black leaders found it especially ironic that as the country prepared to fight Hitler and his racist policies, the United States persisted in its own brand of racism. "A jim crow Army cannot fight for a free world," announced *The Crisis*, the journal of the NAACP. A. Philip Randolph decided to act rather than talk. Randolph had worked with the first wave of African Americans migrating from the South to the northern cities during and just after World War I. He spent years trying "to carry the gospel of unionism to the colored world." He organized and led the Brotherhood of Sleeping Car Porters, and in 1937, he finally won grudging recognition of the union from the Pullman Company.

Admired by black leaders of all political persuasions, Randolph convinced many of them in 1941 to join him in a march on Washington to demand equal rights. The threat of as many as 100,000 African Americans marching in protest in the nation's capital alarmed Roosevelt. He talked to Randolph and struck a bargain. Roosevelt refused to desegregate the armed forces, but in return for Randolph's calling off the march, the president issued Executive Order 8802, which stated that it was the policy of the United States that "there shall be no discrimination in the employment of workers in defense industries or government because of race, creed, color or national origin." He also established the Fair Employment Practices Commission (FEPC) to enforce the order.

By threatening militant action, the black leaders wrested a major concession from the president. But the executive order did not end prejudice, and the FEPC, which its chairman described as the "most hated agency in Washington," had limited success in erasing the color line. Many black soldiers were angered and humiliated throughout the war by being made to sit in the back of buses and being barred from hotels and restaurants. Years later, one former black soldier recalled being refused service in a restaurant in Salina, Kansas, while the same restaurant served German prisoners from a camp nearby. "We continued to stare," he recalled. "This was really happening. . . . The people of Salina would serve these enemy soldiers and turn away black American G.I.'s."

Jobs in war industries helped many African Americans improve their economic conditions. Continuing the migration that had begun during World War I, about 1 million southern blacks moved to northern and western cities. The new arrivals increased pressure on overcrowded housing, aggravating tension among all hard-pressed groups. In Detroit, a race riot broke out in the summer of 1943 after Polish Americans protested a public housing development that promised to bring blacks into the neighborhood. Before federal and state troops could restore order, 25 blacks and 9 whites had been killed and more than $2 million worth of property was destroyed. Groups of white men roamed the city attacking blacks, overturning cars and setting fires. Other riots broke out in Mobile, Los Angeles, New York, and Beaumont, Texas. In all these cities, and in others, the legacy of hate lasted long after the war.

Mexican Americans, like most minority groups, profited during the war from the increased job opportunities provided by wartime industry, but they, too, faced racial prejudice. In California and in many parts of the Southwest, Mexicans could not use public swimming pools. Often lumped together with blacks, they were excluded from certain restaurants. Usually they were limited to menial jobs and were constantly harassed by the police, picked up for minor offenses, and jailed on the smallest excuse.

In Los Angeles, anti-Mexican prejudice flared into violence. The increased migration of Mexicans into the city as well as old hatreds created a volatile situation. Most of the hostility and anger focused on Mexican gang members, or *pachucos,* especially those wearing zoot suits. The suits consisted of long, loose coats with padded shoulders, ballooned pants pegged at the ankles, and a wide-brimmed hat. A watch chain and a ducktail haircut completed the uniform. The zoot suit had originated in the black sections of northern cities and became a national craze during the war. It was a look some teenage males adopted to call attention to themselves and shock conventional society.

The zoot-suiters especially angered soldiers and sailors who were stationed in or on leave in Los Angeles. After a number of provocative incidents, violence broke out between the Mexican American youths and the servicemen in the spring of 1943. The servicemen, joined by others, beat up the Mexicans, stripped them of their offensive clothes, and then gave them haircuts. The police, both civilian and military, looked the other way, and when they did move in, they arrested the victims rather than their attackers.

Social Impact of the War

Modern wars have been incredibly destructive of human lives and property, but they have social results as well. World War II altered patterns of work, leisure, education, and family life; caused a massive migration of people; created jobs; and changed lifestyles. It is difficult to overemphasize the impact of the war on the generation that lived through it.

Wartime Opportunities

More than 15 million American civilians moved during the war. Like the Momadays, many left home to find better jobs. In fact, for many Native Americans, wartime opportunities led to a migration from rural areas and reservations into cities. Americans moved off farms and away from small towns, flocking to cities, where defense jobs were readily available. World War II migrants poured into industrial centers: 200,000 came to the Detroit area, nearly half a million to Los Angeles, and about 100,000 to Mobile, Alabama.

Nowhere was the change more dramatic than in the West, and especially in California, where the wartime boom transformed the region more dramatically than any development since the nineteenth-century economic revolution created by the railroads and mining. The federal government spent more than $70 billion in the state (one-tenth of the total for the entire country) to build army bases, shipyards, supply depots, and testing sites. In addition, private industry constructed so many facilities that the region became the center of a growing military-industrial complex. San Diego, for example, was transformed from a sleepy port and naval base into a sprawling metropolis.

This spectacular growth created housing shortages and overwhelmed schools, hospitals, and municipal services. Crime and prostitution increased as did racial tensions. Some migrants had never lived in a city and were homesick. On one occasion in a Willow Grove, Michigan, school, the children were all instructed to sing "Michigan, My Michigan"; no one knew the words because they all came from other states.

For the first time in years, many families had money to spend, but they had nothing to spend it on. The last new car rolled off the assembly line in February 1942. There were no washing machines, refrigerators, or radios in the stores, no gasoline and no tires to permit weekend trips. Even when people had time off, they tended to stay at home or in the neighborhood.

The war required major adjustments in American family life. With several million men in the service and others far away working at defense jobs, the number of households headed by a woman increased dramatically. The number of marriages also rose sharply. Early in the war, a young man could be deferred if he had a dependent, and a wife qualified as a dependent. Later, many servicemen got married, often to women they barely knew, because they wanted a little excitement and perhaps someone to come home to. The birthrate also began to rise in 1940, as young couples started families as fast as they could. The number of births outside marriage also rose, and from the outset of the war, the divorce rate began to climb sharply. Yet most of the wartime marriages survived, and many of the women left at home looked ahead to a time after the war when they could settle down to a normal life.

Women Workers for Victory

Thousands of women took jobs in heavy industry that formerly would have been considered unladylike. They built tanks, airplanes, and ships, but they still earned less than men. At first, women were rarely hired because as the war in Europe pulled American industry out of its long slump, unemployed men snapped up the newly available positions. But by 1943, with many men drafted and male unemployment virtually nonexistent, the government was quick to suggest that it was women's patriotic duty to take their place on the assembly line. Nearly 3 million women served in the Women's Land Army to replace farm laborers who were in the army, but it was the woman factory worker who captured the public's imagination. A popular song was "Rosie the Riveter," who was "making history working for victory." She also helped her marine boyfriend by "working overtime on the riveting machine."

At the end of the war, the labor force included 19.5 million women, but three-fourths of them had been working before the conflict, and some of the additional ones might have sought work in normal times. The new women war workers tended to be older, and they were more often married than single. Some worked for patriotic reasons. "Every time I test a batch of rubber, I know it's going to help bring my three sons home quicker," a woman worker in a rubber plant remarked. But others worked for the money or to have something useful to do. Yet in 1944, women's weekly wages averaged $31.21, compared with $54.65 for men, reflecting women's more menial tasks and their low seniority as well as outright discrimination. Still, many women enjoyed factory work.

Black women faced the most difficult situation during the war, and often when they applied for work, they were told, "We have not yet installed separate toilet facilities" or "We can't put a Negro in the front office." Not until 1944 did the telephone company in New York City hire a black telephone operator. Still, some black women moved during the war from domestic jobs to higher-paying factory work. Married women with young children also found it difficult to obtain work. There were few day-care facilities, and women were often informed that they should be home with their children.

Many women war workers quickly left their jobs after the war ended. Some left by choice, but dismissals ran twice as high for women as for men. The war had barely shaken the notion that a woman's place was at home. Some women would have preferred to keep working. But most women, and an even larger percentage of men, agreed at the end of the war that women did not deserve an "equal chance with men" for jobs. For most Americans, a woman's place was still in the home.

Entertaining the People

According to one survey, Americans listened to the radio an average of $4\frac{1}{2}$ hours a day during the war. The major networks increased their news programs from less than 4 percent to nearly 30 percent of broadcasting time. Americans heard Edward R. Murrow broadcasting from London during the German air blitz with the sound of the air raid sirens in the background. They listened to Eric Sevareid cover the battle of Burma and describe the sensation of jumping out of an airplane. Often the signal faded out and the static made listening difficult, but the live broadcasts had drama and authenticity never before possible.

The war also intruded on almost all programming. Music, which took up a large proportion of radio programming, also conveyed a war theme. There were "Goodbye, Mama (I'm Off to Yokohama)" and "Praise the Lord and Pass the Ammunition," but more numerous were songs of romance and love, songs about separation and hope for a better time after the war. The danceable tunes of Glenn Miller and Tommy Dorsey became just as much a part of wartime memories as ration books and far-off battlefields.

For many Americans, the motion picture became the most important leisure activity and a part of their fantasy life during the war. Attendance at the movies averaged about 100 million viewers a week. There might not be gasoline for weekend trips or Sunday drives, but the whole family could go to the movies. Even those in the military service could watch American movies on board ship or at a remote outpost.

"Pinup" photographs of Hollywood stars decorated the barracks and even tanks and planes wherever American troops were stationed.

The war engulfed Hollywood. Newsreels that offered a visual synopsis of the war news, always with an upbeat message and a touch of human interest, preceded most movies. Their theme was that the Americans were winning the war, even if early in the conflict there was little evidence to that effect. Many feature films also had a wartime theme, picturing the war in the Pacific complete with grinning, vicious Japanese villains (usually played by Chinese or Korean character actors). In the beginning of these films, the Japanese were always victorious, but in the end, they always got "what they deserved."

The movies set in Europe differed from those depicting the Far Eastern war. British and Americans, sometimes spies, sometimes downed airmen, could dress up like Germans and get away with it. They outwitted the Germans at every turn, sabotaging important installations, and made daring escapes from prison camps. Many wartime movies featured a multicultural platoon led by a veteran sergeant with a Protestant, a Catholic, a Jew, a black, a farmer, and a city resident. In several movies, the army was integrated, but in the real army, blacks served in segregated platoons.

Religion in Time of War

One of the four freedoms threatened by German and Japanese aggression was the "freedom to worship," and Roosevelt continually emphasized that the enemy was opposed to all religion. According to one estimate in 1940, 65 million Americans belonged to 250,000 churches and other religious institutions. There were about 23 million Catholics and 5 million Jews, and most of the rest were of one Protestant denomination or another. Most Americans thought of the United States as a Christian nation, and by that they usually meant a Protestant nation. While the war did lead to a measure of religious tolerance, anti-Semitism and anti-Catholicism did not disappear. According to one poll, although 18 percent of Americans never went to church, more than 30 percent said that the war had strengthened their religious faith.

Those who joined the armed forces were given three choices under religion: They were asked to check Protestant, Catholic, or Jew, and their "dog tags" were marked *P, C,* or *H* (for *Hebrew*). There was no room for Hindu, Buddhist, Muslim, or atheist. Some men refused to fight on religious grounds. During World War I, only members of the traditional peace churches (Quaker, Brethren, and Mennonite) were deferred from military service as conscientious objectors. In World War II, the criterion was broadened to include those who opposed war because of "religious training and belief." More than 70,000 claimed exemption on those grounds, and the government honored about half those claims. Twenty-five thousand were assigned to noncombat military service.

A few clergymen remained pacifists and opposed the war, but far fewer than in World War I. A great many more volunteered to serve as chaplains, and like the men, they were categorized as Protestant, Catholic, or Jew. One of the most influential of the ministers who supported the use of force to combat evil was the Protestant theologian and clergyman Reinhold Niebuhr. In a series of books including *Moral Man and Immoral Society* (1932) and *Children of Light and Children of Darkness* (1944), he struck out against what he saw as a naive faith in the goodness of men, a faith that permeated the Social Gospel movement, the Progressive movement, and the New Deal. In a world gone mad, he interpreted all men as sinful, and he stressed the "evil that good men do." He argued for the use of force against evil. Niebuhr's Christian Realism had little impact on most Americans, but he influenced the continuing debate in the 1930s, 1940s, and 1950s over the proper American response to evil around the world.

The GIs' War

GI, the abbreviation for *government issue,* became the affectionate designation for the ordinary soldier in World War II. The GIs came from every background and ethnic group. Some served reluctantly, some eagerly. A few became genuine heroes. All were turned into heroes by the press and the public, who seemed to believe that one American could easily defeat at least 20 Japanese or Germans. Ernie Pyle, one of the war correspondents who chronicled the authentic story of the ordinary GI, wrote of soldiers "just toiling from day to day in a world full of insecurity, discomfort, homesickness, and a dulled sense of danger."

In the midst of battle, the war was no fun, but only one soldier in eight who served ever saw combat, and even for many of those, the war was a great adventure (just as World War I had been). "When World War II broke out I was delighted," Mario Puzo, author of *The Godfather,* remembered. "There is no other word, terrible as it may sound. My country called. I was delivered from my mother, my family, and delivered *without guilt.*" World War II catapulted young men and women out of their small towns and urban neighborhoods into exotic places, where they met new people and did new things.

Mexican Americans were drafted and volunteered in great numbers. One-third of a million served in all branches of the military, a larger percentage than for many other ethnic groups. Although they encountered prejudice, they probably found less in the armed forces than they had at home, and many returned to civilian life with new ambitions and a new sense of self-esteem.

Many Native Americans also served. In fact, many were recruited for special service in the Marine Signal Corps. One group of Navajo completely befuddled the Japanese with a code based on their native language. But the Navajo code talkers and all other Native Americans who chose to return to the reservations after the war were ineligible for veterans' loans, hospitalization, and other benefits. They lived on federal land, and that, according to the law, canceled all the advantages that other veterans enjoyed after the war.

For African Americans, who served throughout the war in segregated units and faced prejudice wherever they went, the military experience also had much to teach. Fewer blacks were sent overseas (about 79,000 of 504,000 blacks in the service in 1943), and fewer were in combat outfits, so the percentage of black soldiers killed and wounded was low. Many illiterate blacks, especially from the South, learned to read and write in the service. Blacks who went overseas began to realize that not everyone viewed them as inferior. One black army officer said, "What the hell do we want to fight the Japs for anyhow? They couldn't possibly treat us any worse than these 'crackers' right here at home." Most realized the paradox of fighting for freedom when they themselves had little freedom; they hoped things would improve after the war.

Because the war lasted longer than World War I, its impact was greater. In all, more than 16 million men and women served in some branch of the military service. About 322,000 were killed in the war, and more than 800,000 were wounded. The 12,000 listed as missing just disappeared. The war claimed many more lives than World War I and was the nation's costliest after the Civil War. But because of penicillin, blood plasma, sulfa drugs, and rapid battlefield evacuation, the wounded in World War II were twice as likely to survive as those wounded in World War I. Penicillin also minimized the threat of venereal disease, but all men who served saw an anti-VD film, just as their predecessors had in World War I.

American Dead
More than 300,000 American servicemen died during the war, but the government tried to protect the American people from learning the real cost of the battles. This photograph, published in 1943, was the first to show dead American soldiers. Why did the government protect the American people from seeing dead American soldiers?

(Time/Life Pictures/Getty Images)

Women in Uniform

Women had served in all wars as nurses and cooks and in other support capacities, and during World War II many continued in these traditional roles. A few nurses landed in France just days after the Normandy invasion. Nurses served with the army and the marines in the Pacific. They dug their own foxholes and treated men under enemy fire. Sixty-six nurses spent the entire war in the Philippines as prisoners of the Japanese. Most nurses, however, served far behind the lines tending the sick and wounded.

Though nobody objected to women's serving as nurses, not until April 1943 did women physicians win the right to join the Army and Navy Medical Corps. Some people questioned whether it was right for women to serve in other capacities, but Congress authorized full military participation for women (except for combat) because of the military emergency and the argument that women could free men for combat duty. About 350,000 women joined the military service, most in the Women's Army Corps (WAC) and the women's branch of the Navy (WAVES), but others served in the coast guard and the marines. More than 1,000 women trained as pilots. As members of Women's Airforce Service Pilots (WASP), they flew bombers from the factories to landing fields in Great Britain.

Still, men and women were not treated equally. Women were explicitly kept out of combat situations and were often underused by male officers who found it difficult to view women in nontraditional roles. Men were informed about contraceptives and encouraged to use them, but information about birth control was explicitly prohibited for women. Rumors charged many servicewomen with sexual promiscuity. On one occasion, the secretary of war defended the morality and the loyalty of the women in the service, but the rumors continued, spread apparently by men made uncomfortable by women's invasion of the male military domain. One cause for immediate discharge was pregnancy; yet the pregnancy rate for both married and unmarried women remained low.

Thus, despite difficulties, women played important roles during the war, and when they left the service (unlike the women who had served in other wars), they had the same rights and privileges as the male veterans. The women in the service did not permanently alter the military or the public's perception of women's proper role, but they did change a few minds, and many of the women who served had their lives changed and their horizons broadened.

A War of Diplomats and Generals

Pearl Harbor catapulted the country into war with Japan, and on December 11, 1941, Hitler declared war on the United States. Why he did so has never been fully explained; he was perhaps impressed by the apparent weakness of America that was demonstrated at Pearl Harbor. He was not required by his treaty with Japan to go to war with the United States, and without his declaration, the United States might have concentrated on the war against Japan. But Hitler forced the United States into the war against the Axis powers in both Europe and Asia.

War Aims

Why was the United States fighting the war? What did it hope to accomplish in a peace settlement once the war was over? Roosevelt and the other American leaders never really decided. In a speech before Congress in January 1941, Roosevelt had mentioned the four freedoms: freedom of speech and expression, freedom of worship, freedom from want, and freedom from fear. For many Americans, especially after Norman Rockwell expressed those freedoms in four sentimental paintings, this was what they were fighting

for. Roosevelt spoke vaguely of the need to extend democracy and to establish a peacekeeping organization, but in direct contrast to Woodrow Wilson's Fourteen Points, he never spelled out in any detail the political purposes for fighting. There were some other implied reasons for going to war. Henry Luce, the editor of *Life* magazine, made those reasons explicit in an editorial written nine months before Pearl Harbor. He called his essay "The American Century," and he argued that the United States had the responsibility to spread the American way of life around the world.

Roosevelt and his advisers, realizing that it would be impossible to mount an all-out war against both Japan and Germany, decided to fight a holding action in the Pacific while concentrating efforts against Hitler in Europe, where the immediate danger seemed greater. But the United States was not fighting alone. It joined the Soviet Union and Great Britain in what became a difficult, but ultimately effective alliance to defeat Nazi Germany. Churchill and Roosevelt got along well, although they often disagreed on strategy and tactics. Roosevelt's relationship with Stalin was much more strained, but he often agreed with the Russian leader about the way to fight the war. Stalin, a ruthless leader who had maintained his position of power only after eliminating hundreds of thousands of opponents, distrusted both the British and the Americans, but he needed them, just as they depended on him. Without the tremendous sacrifices of the Russian army and the Russian people in 1941 and 1942, Germany would have won the war before the vast American military and industrial might could be mobilized.

A Year of Disaster

The first half of 1942 was disastrous for the Allies. The Japanese captured the Dutch East Indies, swept into Burma, took Wake Island and Guam, and invaded the Aleutian Islands of Alaska. They pushed the American garrison on the Philippines onto the Bataan peninsula and finally onto the tiny island of Corregidor, where U.S. General Jonathan Wainwright surrendered more than 11,000 men to the Japanese. American reporters tried to play down the disasters, concentrating their stories on the few American victories and tales of American heroism against overwhelming odds.

In Europe, the Germans pushed deep into Russia, threatening to capture all the industrial centers and the valuable oil fields. For a time, it appeared that they would even take Moscow. In North Africa, General Erwin Rommel and his mechanized divisions, the Afrika Korps, drove the British forces almost to Cairo in Egypt and threatened the Suez Canal. In the Atlantic, German submarines sank British and American ships more rapidly than they could be replaced. For a few dark months in 1942, it seemed that the Berlin–Tokyo Axis would win the war before the United States was ready to fight.

The Allies could not agree on the proper military strategy in Europe. Churchill advocated tightening the ring around Germany, using bombing raids to weaken the enemy and encouraging resistance among the occupied countries but avoiding any direct assault on the continent until success was ensured. Remembering the vast loss of British lives during World War I, he was determined to avoid similar casualties in this conflict. Stalin demanded a second front, an invasion of Europe in 1942, to relieve the pressure on the Russian army, which faced 200 German divisions along a 2,000-mile front. Roosevelt agreed to an offensive in 1942. But in the end, the invasion in 1942 came not in France but in North Africa. The decision was probably right from a military point of view, but Stalin never forgave Churchill and Roosevelt for not coming to the aid of the beleaguered Soviet troops.

Attacking in North Africa in November 1942, American and British troops tried to link up with a beleaguered British army. The American army, enthusiastic but inexperienced, met little resistance in the beginning. At Kasserine Pass in Tunisia, the Germans counterattacked and destroyed a large American force, inflicting 5,000 casualties. Roosevelt, who launched the invasion in part to give the American people a victory to relieve the dreary news from the Far East, learned that victories often came with long casualty lists.

He also learned the necessity of political compromise. To gain a cease-fire in conquered French territory in North Africa, the United States recognized Admiral Jean Darlan as head of its provisional government. Darlan persecuted the Jews, exploited the Arabs, imprisoned his opponents, and collaborated with the Nazis. He seemed diametrically opposed to the principles the Americans said they were fighting for. Did the Darlan deal mean the United States would negotiate with Mussolini? Or with Hitler? The Darlan compromise reinforced Soviet distrust of the Americans and angered many Americans as well.

Roosevelt never compromised or made a deal with Hitler, but he did aid General Francisco Franco, the Fascist dictator in Spain, in return for safe passage of American shipping into the Mediterranean. But the United States did not aid only right-wing dictators. It also supplied arms to the left-wing resistance in France, to the Communist Tito in Yugoslavia, and to Ho Chi Minh, the anti-French resistance leader in Indochina. Roosevelt also authorized large-scale lend-lease aid to the Soviet Union. Although liberals criticized his support of dictators, Roosevelt was willing to do almost anything to win the war. Military expediency often dictated his political decisions.

Even on one of the most sensitive issues of the war, the plight of the Jews in occupied Europe, Roosevelt's solution was to win the war as quickly as possible. By November 1942, confirmed information had reached the United States that the Nazis were systematically exterminating Jews, but that evidence got little attention

Buchenwald

Only at the end of the war did most Americans learn about the horrors of Nazi concentration camps and gas chambers. Senator Alben Barkley of Kentucky looks in disbelief at dead Jews stacked like wood at Buchenwald on April 24, 1945. Why didn't Americans learn about the Holocaust sooner?

(National Archives [RG-111-SC-204745, Box 63])

in the United States. The Roosevelt administration did nothing for more than a year, and even then it did scandalously little to rescue European Jews from the gas chambers. Only 21,000 refugees were allowed to enter the United States over a period of $3\frac{1}{2}$ years, just 10 percent of those who could have been admitted under immigration quotas.

The U.S. War Department rejected suggestions that the gas chambers and railway lines be bombed. That might not have worked, but anti-Semitic feelings in the United States in the 1940s and the fear of massive Jewish immigration help explain the failure of the Roosevelt administration to act. The fact that the mass media, Christian leaders, and even American Jews failed to mount effective pressure on the government does not excuse the president for his indifference to the systematic murder of millions of people. Roosevelt could not have prevented the Holocaust, but vigorous action on his part might have saved many thousands of lives during the war.

A Strategy for Ending the War

The commanding general of the Allied armies in the North African campaign emerged as a genuine leader. Born in Texas, Dwight D. Eisenhower spent his boyhood in Abilene, Kansas. His small-town background made it easy for biographers and newspaper reporters to make him into an American hero. Eisenhower, however, had not come to hero status easily. In World War I, he trained soldiers in Texas and never got to France. He was only a lieutenant colonel when World War II erupted. George Marshall, the army's top general, had discovered Eisenhower's talents even before the war began. Eisenhower was quickly promoted to general and achieved a reputation as an expert planner and organizer. Gregarious and outgoing, he had a broad smile that made most people like him instantly. He was not a brilliant field commander and made many mistakes in the African campaign, but he had the ability to get diverse people to work together, which was crucial in situations in which British and American units had to cooperate.

The American army moved slowly across North Africa, linked up with the British, invaded Sicily in July 1943, and finally stormed ashore in Italy in September. The Italian campaign proved long and bitter. Although the Italians overthrew Mussolini and surrendered in September 1943, the Germans occupied the peninsula and gave ground only after bloody fighting. The whole American army seemed bogged down for months. The Allies did not reach Rome until June 1944, and they never controlled all of Italy.

Despite the decision to make the war in Europe the first priority, American ships and planes halted the Japanese advance in the spring of 1942. In the Battle of Coral Sea in May 1942, American carrier-based planes inflicted heavy damage on the Japanese fleet and prevented the invasion of the southern tip of New Guinea and probably of Australia as well. It was the first naval battle in history in which no guns were fired from one surface ship against another; airplanes caused all the damage. In World War II, the aircraft carrier proved more important than the battleship. A month later, at the Battle of Midway, American planes sank four Japanese aircraft carriers and destroyed nearly 300 planes. This was the first major Japanese defeat; it restored some balance of power in the Pacific and ended the threat to Hawaii.

In 1943, the American sea and land forces leapfrogged from island to island, gradually retaking territory from the Japanese and building bases to attack the Philippines and eventually Japan itself. Progress often had terrible costs. In November 1943, about 5,000 marines landed on the coral beaches of the tiny island of Tarawa. Despite heavy naval bombardment and the support of hundreds of planes, the marines met fierce opposition. The four-day battle left more than 1,000 Americans dead and more than 3,000 wounded.

The Pacific War was often brutal and dehumanizing. American soldiers often collected Japanese ears, skulls, and other body parts as souvenirs, something unheard of on the European battlegrounds. "In Europe we felt that our enemies, horrible and deadly as they were, were still people," Ernie Pyle, the American war correspondent, remarked. "But out here I soon gathered that the Japanese were looked upon as something subhuman or repulsive, the way some people feel about cockroaches or mice."

The Invasion of France

Operation Overlord, the code name for the largest amphibious invasion in history, the invasion Stalin had wanted in 1942, finally began on June 6, 1944. It was, according to Churchill, "the most difficult and complicated operation that has ever taken place." The initial assault along a 60-mile stretch of the Normandy coast was conducted with 175,000 men supported by 600 warships and 11,000 planes. It cost 2,245 killed and 1,670 wounded to secure the beachhead. Within a month, more than a million troops and more than 170,000 vehicles had landed. Such an invasion would have been impossible during World War I.

For months before the invasion, American and British planes had bombed German transportation lines, industrial plants, and even cities. In all, more than 1.5 million tons of bombs were dropped on Europe. The massive bombing raids helped make the invasion a success, but evidence gathered after the war suggests that the bombs did not disrupt German war production as seriously as Allied strategists believed at

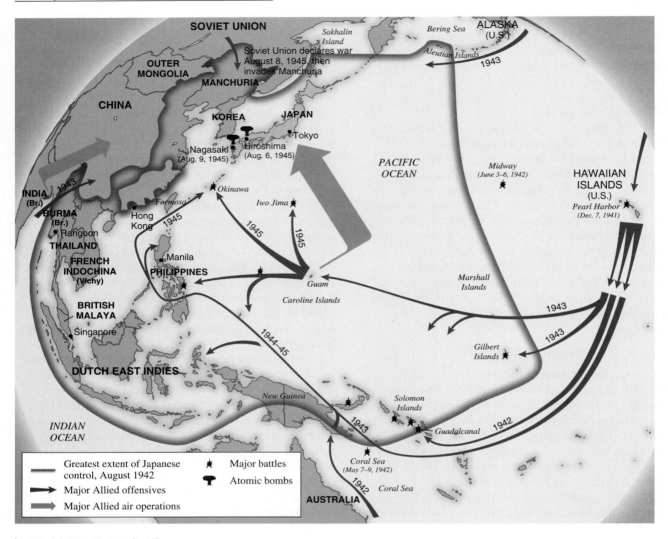

World War II: Pacific Theater

After the surprise attack on Pearl Harbor, the Japanese extended their control in the Pacific from Burma to the Aleutian Islands and almost to Australia. But after American naval and air victories at Coral Sea and Midway in 1942, the Japanese were increasingly on the defensive. How did the great distances in the Pacific influence military plans for both sides? Why was the aircraft carrier more important than the battleship in the Pacific War? Was there any alternative to the American strategy of moving slowly from one Japanese-occupied island to another? Why did China play such a crucial role in the war against Japan?

the time. Often a factory or a rail center would be back in operation within a matter of days, sometimes within hours, after an attack. In the end, the bombing of the cities, rather than destroying morale, may have strengthened the resolve of the German people to fight to the bitter end. And the destruction of German cities did not come cheaply. German fighters and antiaircraft guns shot down 22 of 60 B-17s on June 23, 1943, and in July 1943, 100 planes and 1,000 airmen were lost and an additional 75 men had mental breakdowns.

The most destructive bombing raid of the war, carried out against Dresden on the nights of February 13 and 14, 1945, had no strategic purpose. It was launched by the British and Americans to help demonstrate to Stalin that they were aiding the Russian

offensive. Dresden, a city of 630,000, was a communications center. Three waves of 1,200 planes dropped more than 4,000 tons of bombs, causing a firestorm that swept over eight square miles, destroyed everything in its path, and killed an estimated 25,000 to 40,000 civilians. The fire-bombing of Tokyo on March 9, 1945, also killed an estimated 100,000 people. The massive "strategic" bombing of European and Asian cities for the purpose of breaking the morale of the civilian population introduced terror as a strategy and eventually made the decision to drop the atomic bomb on two Japanese cities easier.

With eccentric General George Patton leading the charge and the more staid General Omar Bradley in command, the American army broke out of the Normandy beachhead in July 1944. Led by the tank

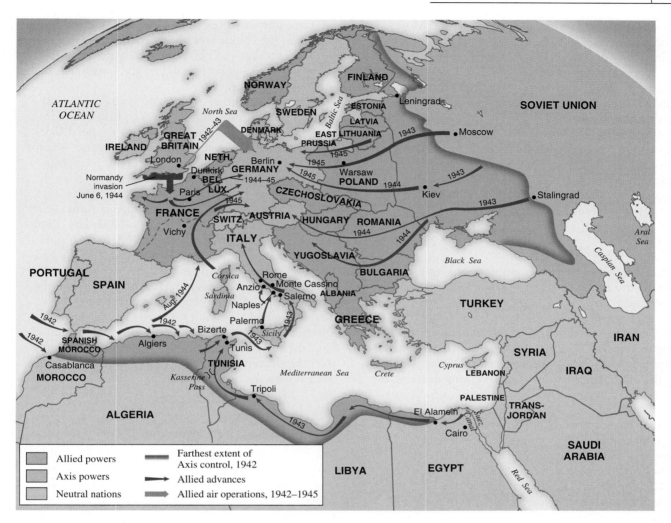

World War II: European and North African Theaters

The German war machine swept across Europe and North Africa and almost captured Cairo and Moscow, but after major defeats at Stalingrad and El Alamein in 1943, the Axis powers were in retreat. Many lives were lost on both sides before the Allied victory in 1945. How was the African campaign important to the Allies' strategy to defeat Germany and Italy? Why was the invasion of France necessary even after the capture of North Africa and a portion of Italy? Why was the Soviet Union crucial to the war in Europe? Why was the war in Europe very different from the war in the Pacific?

battalions, it swept across France. American productive capacity and the ability to supply a mobile and motorized army eventually brought victory. But not all American equipment was superior. The American fighter plane, the P-40, could not compete early in the war with the German ME-109. The United States was also far behind Germany in the development of rockets, but that was not as important in the actual fighting as was the inability of the United States, until the end of the war, to develop a tank that could compete in armament or firepower with the German tanks. But the American army made up for the deficiency of its tanks in part by having superior artillery. Perhaps even more important, most of the American soldiers had grown up tinkering with cars and radios. Children of the machine age, they managed to make repairs and

to keep tanks, trucks, and guns functioning under difficult circumstances. They helped give the American army the superior mobility that eventually led to the defeat of Germany.

By late 1944, the American and British armies had swept across France, while the Russians had pushed the German forces out of much of eastern Europe. The war seemed nearly over. However, just before Christmas in 1944, the Germans launched a massive counterattack along an 80-mile front, much of it held by thinly dispersed and inexperienced American troops. The Germans drove 50 miles inside the American lines before they were checked. During the Battle of the Bulge, as it was called, Eisenhower was so desperate for additional infantry that he offered to pardon any military prisoners in Europe who would take up a rifle and go into battle. Most of the prisoners, who were serving short sentences, declined the opportunity to clear their record. Eisenhower also promised any black soldiers in the service and supply outfits an opportunity to become infantrymen in the white units, though usually with a lower rank. However, his chief of staff pointed out that this was against War Department regulations and was the "most dangerous thing I have seen in regard to race relations." Eisenhower recanted, not wishing to start a social revolution. Black soldiers who volunteered to join the battle fought in segregated platoons commanded by white officers.

The Politics of Victory

As the American and British armies assaulted Germany in the winter and spring of 1945, the political and diplomatic aspects of the war began to overshadow military concerns. It became a matter not only of defeating Germany but also of determining who was going to control Germany and the rest of Europe once Hitler fell. The relationship between the Soviet Union and the other Allies had been badly strained during the war; with victory in sight, the tension became even greater. Although the American press pictured Stalin as a wise and democratic leader and the Russian people as quaint and heroic, a number of high-level American diplomats and presidential advisers distrusted the Russians and looked ahead to a confrontation with Soviet communism after the war. They urged Roosevelt to make military decisions with the postwar political situation in mind.

The most pressing concern in the spring of 1945 was who should capture Berlin. The British wanted to beat the Russians to the capital city. Eisenhower, however, fearing that the Germans might barricade themselves in the Austrian Alps and hold out indefinitely, ordered the armies south rather than toward Berlin. He also wanted to avoid unnecessary American casualties, and he planned to meet the Russian army at an easily marked spot to avoid any unfortunate incidents. The British and American forces could probably not have arrived in Berlin before the Russians in any case, but Eisenhower's decision generated controversy after the war. Russian and American troops met on April 25, 1945, at the Elbe River. On May 2, the Russians took Berlin. Hitler committed suicide. The long war in Europe finally came to an end on May 8, 1945.

Meanwhile, the United States continued to tighten the noose on Japan. American long-range B-29 bombers began sustained strikes on the Japanese mainland in June 1944. In a series of naval and air engagements, especially at the Battle of Leyte Gulf, American planes destroyed most of the remaining Japanese navy. By the end of 1944, an American victory in the Pacific was all but ensured. American forces recaptured the Philippines early the next year, yet it might take years to conquer the Japanese on their home islands.

While the military campaigns reached a critical stage in both Europe and the Pacific, Roosevelt ran for an unprecedented fourth term. He dropped Vice President Henry Wallace from the ticket because some thought him too radical and impetuous. To replace him, the Democratic convention selected a relatively unknown senator from Missouri. Harry S Truman, a World War I veteran, had been a judge in Kansas City before being elected to the Senate in 1934. His only fame came when, as chairman of the Senate Committee to Investigate the National Defense Program, he had insisted on honesty and efficiency in war contracts.

The Republicans nominated Thomas Dewey, the colorless and politically moderate governor of New York, who had a difficult time criticizing Roosevelt without appearing unpatriotic. Roosevelt seemed haggard and ill during much of the campaign, but he won the election easily. He would need all his strength to deal with the difficult political problems of ending the war and constructing a peace settlement.

The Big Three at Yalta

Roosevelt, Churchill, and Stalin, together with many of their advisers, met at Yalta in the Crimea in February 1945 to discuss the problems of the peace settlements. Most of the agreements reached at Yalta were secret, and in the atmosphere of the subsequent Cold War, many would become controversial. Roosevelt wanted Soviet help in ending the Pacific war, to avoid the slaughter of American men in an invasion of the Japanese mainland. In return for a promise to enter the war within three months after the war in Europe was over, the Soviet Union was granted the Kurile Islands, the southern half of Sakhalin, and railroads and port facilities in North Korea, Manchuria, and Outer Mongolia. Later that seemed like a heavy price to pay for the promise, but realistically the Soviet Union controlled most of this territory and could not have been dislodged short of going to war.

When the provisions of the secret treaties were revealed much later, many people accused Roosevelt of trusting the Russians too much. But Roosevelt wanted to retain a working relationship with the Soviet Union. Moreover, Roosevelt hoped to get the Soviet Union's agreement to cooperate with a new peace-preserving United Nations organization after the war.

The European section of the Yalta agreement proved even more controversial. The diplomats decided to partition Germany and to divide the city of Berlin.

The Polish agreements were even more difficult to swallow. The Polish government-in-exile in London was militantly anti-Communist and looked forward to returning to Poland after the war. Stalin demanded that the eastern half of Poland be given to the Soviet Union. Churchill and Roosevelt finally agreed to the Russian demands with the proviso that Poland be compensated with German territory on its western border. Stalin also agreed to include some members of the London-based Polish group in the new Polish government. He also promised to carry out "free and unfettered elections as soon as possible."

The Polish settlement would prove divisive after the war, and it quickly became clear that what the British and Americans wanted in eastern Europe contrasted with what the Soviet Union intended. Yet at the time it seemed imperative that Russia enter the war in the Pacific, and the reality was that in 1945 the Soviet army occupied most of eastern Europe.

The most potentially valuable accomplishment at Yalta was Stalin's agreement to join Roosevelt and Churchill in calling a conference in San Francisco in April 1945 to draft a United Nations charter. The charter gave primary responsibility for keeping global peace to the Security Council, composed of five permanent members (the United States, the Soviet Union, Great Britain, France, and China) and six other nations elected for two-year terms.

Perhaps just as important as Yalta for structuring the postwar world was the Bretton Woods Conference, held at a resort hotel in New Hampshire in the summer of 1944 and attended by delegates from 44 nations (the Soviet Union refused to participate). The economists and politicians established a Bank for Reconstruction and Development (the World Bank) and the International Monetary Fund. They also decided on a fixed rate of exchange among the world's currencies using the dollar rather than the pound as the standard. The Bretton Woods agreement lasted for 25 years and established that the United States, not Great Britain, would be the dominant economic power in the postwar world.

The Atomic Age Begins

Two months after Yalta, on April 12, 1945, Roosevelt died suddenly of a massive cerebral hemorrhage. Hated and loved to the end, he was replaced by Harry Truman, who was both more difficult to hate and harder to love. In the beginning, Truman seemed tentative and unsure of himself. Yet it fell to the new president to make some of the most difficult decisions of all time. The most momentous of all was the decision to drop the atomic bomb.

The Manhattan Project, first organized in 1941, was one of the best-kept secrets of the war. A distinguished group of scientists, whose work on the project was centered in Los Alamos, New Mexico, set out to perfect and manufacture an atomic bomb before Germany did. But by the time the bomb was successfully tested in the New Mexico desert on July 16, 1945, the war in Europe had ended. The scientists working on the bomb assumed that they were perfecting a military weapon. Yet when they saw the ghastly power of that first bomb, J. Robert Oppenheimer, a leading scientist on the project, remembered that "some wept, a few cheered. Most stood silently." Some opposed the military use of the bomb. They realized its revolutionary power and worried about the future reputation of the United States if it unleashed this new force. But a presidential committee made up of scientists, military leaders, and politicians recommended that it be used on a military target in Japan as soon as possible.

"The final decision of where and when to use the atomic bomb was up to me," Truman later remembered. "Let there be no doubt about it. I regarded the bomb as a military weapon and never had any doubt that it should be used." But the decision had both military and political ramifications. Even though Japan had lost most of its empire by the summer of 1945, it still had a military force of several million men and thousands of kamikaze planes that had already wreaked havoc on the American fleet. The kamikaze pilots gave up their own lives to make sure that their planes, heavily laden with bombs, crashed on American ships. In the Battle of Okinawa, kamikaze pilots destroyed or disabled 28 American ships and killed 5,000 American sailors. There was little defense against such fanaticism.

Even with the Russian promise to enter the war, it appeared that an amphibious landing on the Japanese mainland would be necessary to end the war. The month-long battle for Iwo Jima, only 750 miles from Tokyo, had resulted in more than 4,000 American dead and 15,000 wounded, and the battle for Okinawa was even more costly. An invasion of the Japanese mainland would presumably be even more expensive in human lives. The bomb, many thought, could end the war without an invasion. But some people involved in the decision wanted to retaliate for Pearl Harbor, and still others needed to justify spending more than $2 billion on the project in the first place. To some historians, the timing of the first bomb indicates that the decision was intended to impress the Russians and ensure that they had little to do with the peace settlement in the Far East.

Historians debate whether the use of the atomic bomb on the Japanese cities was necessary to end the war, but for the hundreds of thousands of American troops waiting on board ships and on island bases (even in Europe) to invade the Japanese mainland, there was no question about the rightness of the decision. They believed that the bombs ended the war and saved their lives. On August 6, 1945, two days before the Soviet Union had promised to enter the war

Recovering the Past

HISTORY, MEMORY, AND MONUMENTS

In recent years, historians have been studying collective memory—the stories people tell about the past. Collective memory is closely related to national regional identity and is often associated with patriotism and war. But memory is usually selective and often contested. The generation that lived through World War II is getting older, and often these people fear that few remember or care about their war. One veteran of the Italian campaign recently remarked: "Today they don't even know what Anzio was. Most people aren't interested." The collective memory of World War II may include letters, photos, old uniforms, and stories told to grandchildren (oral history), but the collective memory of war often includes monuments as well.

Almost every small town and city in the Northeast, the Midwest, and the South has a monument to the soldiers who fought and died in the Civil War; often it is a statue of a common soldier with rifle at rest. In the South, a statue of Robert E. Lee on horseback came to symbolize the "Lost Cause." Usually monuments to war symbolize triumph or fighting for a just cause, even in defeat.

A large monument to World War II veterans finally opened on the mall in Washington in 2004 after years of controversy. There have been many other attempts to honor the World War II generation. The Air and Space Museum of the Smithsonian Institution in Washington, D.C., planned a major exhibit for 1995 to commemorate the fiftieth anniversary of the dropping of the first atomic bomb on Hiroshima and the end of World War II. The *Enola Gay,* the B-29 that dropped the bomb, was to be the centerpiece of the exhibit, but the historians and curators who organized the exhibit also planned to raise a number of questions that historians had been debating for years. Would the war have ended in days or weeks without the bomb? How was the decision to drop the bomb made? Was there a racial component to the decision? Would the United States have dropped the bomb on Germany? Was the bomb dropped more to impress the Soviet Union than to force the Japanese to surrender? What was the impact of the bomb on the ground? What implications did dropping the bomb have on the world after 1945?

The exhibit (except in greatly modified form) never took place. Many veterans of World War II and other Americans denounced it as traitorous and un-American. For these critics the decision to drop the bomb was not something to debate. For them, World War II was a contest between good and evil, and the bomb was simply a way to defeat the evil empire and save American lives. The controversy over the *Enola Gay* exhibit demonstrated that 50 years later, memory and history were at odds and that the memory of the war was still contested. The main reason the exhibit did not satisfy those who remembered the war was that it did not commemorate triumph but instead seemed to question the motives of those who fought and died.

The Vietnam Veterans Memorial erected in Washington in 1982 was initially controversial for similar reasons.

Dedication of the Iwo Jima Memorial Monument in Washington, D.C., November 10, 1954

(National Archives [127-GRA-A409861])

Designed by Maya Lin, a young artist and sculptor, it consists of a wall of polished granite inscribed with the names of 58,000 dead. There are no soldiers on horseback; in fact, there are no figures at all, not even a flag. Critics called it a "black gash of shame." Even the addition of a sculpture of three "fighting men" did not satisfy many. But to almost everyone's surprise, hundreds of thousands of veterans and friends of veterans found the monument deeply moving, and they left photos, flowers, poems, and other objects. For them, the memorial successfully represented collective memory. Still the critics were dissatisfied; they wanted something more like the Iwo Jima monument.

Iwo Jima was a tiny, desolate island 640 miles from Tokyo, important only because it was a base for Japanese fighters to attack American bombers on their way to the Japanese mainland. The Fourth and Fifth Marine Divisions invaded the island on February 17, 1945. After bitter fighting, the marines captured Mt. Suribachi, the highest point on the island, on February 23 and completed the conquest of the island on March 17. But it was a costly victory—there were 6,832 Americans killed, more than 20,000 wounded, and 419 missing.

Associated Press photographer Joe Rosenthal was one of several journalists who went ashore with the marines and one of three photographers assigned to record the raising of the American flag on top of Mt. Suribachi. A group of marines raised the flag twice so the photographers could get their pictures. It was Rosenthal's photograph of the second flag raising that became famous. On February 25, 1945, his photograph of the five marines and a navy corpsman raising the flag was on the front page of Sunday newspapers across the country. "Stars and Stripes on Iwo," "Old Glory over Volcano," the captions read. Within months, the image of the flag raising appeared on a War Bond poster with the caption: "Now All Together" and also on a postage stamp. Three of the six flag raisers were killed in the battle for Iwo Jima, but those who survived became heroes, and their images were used to sell war bonds. Clearly, the flag-raising image had touched American emotions and quickly became part of the collective memory of the war, a symbol of the country pulling together to defeat the enemy.

In November 1954, a giant statue of the flag raising, designed by Felix De Weldon, was dedicated as a memorial to the U.S. Marine Corps on the edge of Arlington National Cemetery. Vice President Richard Nixon, speaking at the dedication, said that the statue symbolized "the hopes and

Official poster for the 1945 war bond drive using the image of the Iwo Jima flag raising

(Courtesy of the Virginia War Museum)

dreams of the American people and the real purpose of our foreign policy." The flag-raising image played an important role in two movies: *The Sands of Iwo Jima* (1949), starring John Wayne, and *The Outsider* (1960), starring Tony Curtis. During the 1988 presidential campaign, George H. W. Bush chose to make a speech in front of the marine monument urging a constitutional amendment to ban the desecration of the flag. The image of the flag raising in photograph, drawing, film, and cartoon remains part of the collective memory of World War II.

Reflecting on the Past Why did the Iwo Jima monument mean so much to the World War II generation? Was the monument more important than the photograph? What makes a monument meaningful? Is it the size? The accuracy? The ability to arouse emotion? Why do some monuments and symbols become part of collective memory, while others become controversial or forgotten? There are more than 15,000 outdoor sculptures and monuments in the country, most created since the Civil War. What monuments can you locate in your community? What collective memory do they symbolize? ■

Timeline

1931–1932	Japan seizes Manchuria
1933	Hitler becomes German chancellor
	United States recognizes the Soviet Union
	Roosevelt extends Good Neighbor policy
1934	Germany begins rearmament
1935	Italy invades Ethiopia
	First Neutrality Act
1936	Spanish civil war begins
	Second Neutrality Act
	Roosevelt reelected
1938	Hitler annexes Austria, occupies Sudetenland
	German persecution of Jews intensifies
1939	Nazi–Soviet Pact
	German invasion of Poland; World War II begins
1940	Roosevelt elected for a third term
	Selective Service Act
1941	FDR's "Four Freedoms" speech
	Proposed black march on Washington
	Executive Order 8802 outlaws discrimination in defense industries
	Lend-Lease Act
	Germany attacks Russia
	Japanese assets in United States frozen
	Japanese attack Pearl Harbor; United States declares war on Japan
	Germany declares war on United States
1942	Internment of Japanese Americans
	Second Allied front in Africa launched
1943	Invasion of Sicily
	Italian campaign; Italy surrenders
	Race riots in Detroit and other cities
1944	Normandy invasion (Operation Overlord)
	Roosevelt elected for a fourth term
1945	Yalta Conference
	Roosevelt dies; Harry Truman becomes president
	Germany surrenders
	Successful test of atomic bomb
	Hiroshima and Nagasaki bombed; Japan surrenders

against Japan, a B-29 bomber, the *Enola Gay*, dropped a single atomic bomb over Hiroshima. It killed or severely wounded 160,000 civilians and destroyed four square miles of the city. One of the men on the plane saw the thick cloud of smoke and thought that they had missed their target. "It looked like it had landed on a forest. I didn't see any sign of the city." The Soviet Union entered the war on August 8. When Japan refused to surrender, a bomb was dropped on Nagasaki on August 9. The Japanese surrendered five days later. The war was finally over. The problems of the atomic age and the postwar world were just beginning.

Conclusion

PEACE, PROSPERITY, AND INTERNATIONAL RESPONSIBILITIES

The United States emerged from World War II with an enhanced reputation as the world's most powerful industrial and military nation. The war had finally ended the Great Depression and brought prosperity to most Americans. Even N. Scott Momaday's family secured better jobs because of the war, but, like many Americans, they had to move to take those jobs. The war also increased the power of the federal government. The payroll deduction of federal income taxes, begun during the war, symbolized the growth of a federal bureaucracy that affected the lives of all Americans. Ironically the war to preserve liberty and freedom was fought with segregated armed forces, and some American citizens, including many Japanese Americans, were deprived of their freedom. The war had also ended American isolationism and made the United States into the dominant global power. Of all the nations that fought in the war, the United States had suffered the least. No bombs were dropped on American factories, and no cities were destroyed. Although more than 300,000 Americans lost their lives, even this carnage seemed minimal when compared with more than 20 million Russian soldiers and civilians who died or the 6 million Jews and millions of others systematically exterminated by Hitler.

Americans greeted the end of the war with joy and relief. But those who lived through the war years, even those too young to fight, like N. Scott Momaday, recalled the war as a time when all Americans were united to achieve victory. They looked forward to the peace and prosperity for which they had fought. Yet within two years, the peace would be jeopardized by the Cold War, and the United States would be rearming its former enemies, Japan and Germany, to oppose its former friend, the Soviet Union. The irony of that situation reduced the joy of the hard-won peace and made the American people more suspicious of their government and its foreign policy. Yet the memory of World War II and the perception that the country was united against evil enemies, indeed that World War II was a "good war," would have an impact on American foreign policy, and even on Americans' perception of themselves, for decades to come.

QUESTIONS FOR REVIEW AND REFLECTION

1. Trace the series of international events that led to the United States' entry into World War II. Could the United States have stayed neutral?
2. Explain why and how the United States interned Japanese Americans in the aftermath of the attack on Pearl Harbor. Was the internment justified?
3. How did the war change the lives of women, African Americans, and Hispanic Americans?
4. What were the war aims of the United States, and how were they achieved?
5. What led the United States to develop the atomic bomb? What were the consequences of this new weapon for the Japanese, for Americans, and for the outcome of World War II?

CHAPTER 26

Postwar America at Home, 1945–1960

McDonald's provided a model for other franchisers in the 1950s and the years that followed. The golden arches, shown here in an early version, were virtually the same wherever they appeared and became a symbol for the age.

American Stories

An Entrepreneur Franchises the American Dream

Ray Kroc, an ambitious salesman, headed toward San Bernardino, California, on a business trip in 1954. For more than a decade he had been selling "multimixers"—stainless steel machines that could make six milkshakes at once—to restaurants and soda shops around the United States. On this trip, he was particularly interested in checking out a hamburger stand run by Richard and Maurice McDonald, who had bought eight of his "contraptions" and could therefore make 48 shakes at the same time.

Always eager to increase sales, Kroc wanted to see the McDonalds' operation for himself. The 52-year-old son of Bohemian parents had sold everything from real estate to radio time to paper cups before peddling the multimixers but had enjoyed no stunning success. Yet he was still on the alert for the key to the fortune that was part of the American dream. As he watched the lines of people at the San Bernardino McDonald's restaurant, the answer seemed at hand.

The McDonald brothers sold only standard hamburgers, french fries, and milkshakes, but they had developed a system that was fast, efficient, and clean. It drew on the automobile traffic that moved along Route 66. And it was profitable indeed. Sensing the possibilities, Kroc proposed that the two owners open other establishments as well. When they balked, he negotiated a 99-year contract that allowed him to sell the fast-food idea and the name—and their golden arches design—wherever he could.

On April 15, 1955, Kroc opened his first McDonald's restaurant in Des Plaines, a suburb of Chicago. Three months later, he sold his first franchise in Fresno, California. Others soon followed. Kroc scouted out new locations, almost always on highway "strips"; persuaded people to put up the capital; and provided them with specifications guaranteed to ensure future success. For his efforts, he received a percentage of the gross take.

From the start, Kroc insisted on standardization. Every McDonald's restaurant was the same—from the two functional arches supporting the glass enclosure that housed the kitchen and take-out window to the single arch near the road bearing a sign indicating how many 15-cent hamburgers had already been sold. All menus and prices were exactly the same, and Kroc demanded that everything from hamburger size to cooking time be constant. He insisted, too, that the establishments be clean. No pinball games or cigarette machines were permitted; the premium was on a good, inexpensive hamburger, quickly served, at a nice place.

McDonald's, of course, was an enormous success. In 1962, total sales exceeded $76 million. In 1964,

before the company had been in operation for 10 years, it had sold more than 400 million hamburgers and 120 million pounds of french fries. By the end of the next year, there were 710 McDonald's stands in 44 states. In 1974, only 20 years after Kroc's vision of the hamburger's future, McDonald's did $2 billion worth of business. When Kroc died in 1984, a total of 45 billion burgers had been sold at 7,500 outlets in 32 countries. Ronald McDonald, the clown who came to represent the company, became known to children around the globe after his Washington, D.C., debut in November 1963. When McDonald's began to advertise, it became the country's first restaurant to buy television time. Musical slogans such as "You deserve a break today" and "We do it all for you" became better known than some popular songs.

The success of McDonald's provides an example of the development of new economic and technological trends—and their cultural implications—in the United States in the post–World War II years. Ray Kroc capitalized on the changes of the automobile age. He understood that a restaurant had a better chance of success not in the city but along the highways, where it could draw on heavier traffic. Kroc understood, too, that the franchise notion provided the key to rapid economic growth. Finally, he sensed the importance of standardization and uniformity. He understood the mood of the time—the quiet conformity of people searching for the key to the American dream of prosperity and stability. The McDonald's image may have been monotonous, but that was part of its appeal. Customers always knew what they would get wherever they found the golden arches. If the atmosphere was "bland," that too was deliberate. As Kroc said, "Our theme is kind of synonymous with Sunday school, the Girl Scouts and the YMCA. McDonald's is clean and wholesome." It was a symbol of the age.

This chapter describes the economic, political, and cultural changes in American society in the 25 years following World War II. Even as the nation became involved in the global confrontations of the Cold War with the Soviet Union (a story taken up in Chapter 27), Americans were preoccupied with the shifts in social and structural patterns that were taking place. This chapter examines how economic growth, spurred by technological advances, transformed the patterns of work and daily life in the United States. In a prosperous time, most people gained a level of material comfort previously unknown. Comforted by a renewed commitment to organized religion that involved people of all persuasions, they felt confident in the patterns of their lives. The political world reflected the prosperity and affluence that followed years of depression and war. Building on the impact of the New Deal and the American role as the "arsenal of democracy" in World War II, government was larger and more involved in people's lives than ever before, despite Republican resistance in the 1950s. Political commitments in the decade and a half after the war laid the groundwork for the welfare state that emerged in the 1960s.

But even as the nation prospered, it experienced serious social and economic divisions among its diverse peoples. This chapter also shows the enormous gaps that existed between rich and poor, even in the best of times. It shows the continuing presence of what one critic eloquently called "the other America" and documents the considerable income disparity and persistent prejudice that African Americans (like members of other minority groups) encountered in their efforts to share in postwar prosperity and democratic dreams. The frustrations they experienced highlighted the limits of the American dream and led to the reform movements that changed American society.

Economic Boom

Most Americans were optimistic after 1945. As servicemen returned home from fighting in World War II, their very presence caused a change in family patterns. A baby boom brought unprecedented population growth. The simultaneous and unexpected economic boom had an even greater impact. Large corporations increasingly dominated the business world, but unions grew as well, and most workers improved their lives. Technology appeared triumphant, with new products flooding the market and finding their way into most American homes. Prosperity convinced the growing middle class that all was well in the United States.

The Thriving Peacetime Economy

The wartime return of prosperity after the Great Depression continued in the postwar years, relieving fears of another depression. The United States solidified its position as the richest nation in the world with a sustained economic expansion. Other nations struggled with the aftereffects of World War II. Yet in the United States, prosperity was the norm.

The statistical evidence of economic success was impressive. The gross national product (GNP) jumped dramatically between 1945 and 1960, while per capita personal income likewise rose—from $1,087 in 1945 to $2,026 in 1960. Almost 60 percent of all families in the country were now part of the middle class, a dramatic change from the class structure in the nineteenth and early twentieth centuries.

Personal resources fueled economic growth. During World War II, American consumers had been unable to spend all they earned because factories were producing for war. With accumulated savings of $140 billion at the end of the struggle, consumers were ready to buy whatever they could. Equally important was the 22 percent rise in real purchasing power between 1946 and 1960. Families now had far more discretionary income—money to satisfy wants as well as needs—than before. At the end of the Great Depression, fewer than one-quarter of all households had any discretionary income; in 1960, three of every five did.

This new consumer power, in contrast to the underconsumption of the 1920s and 1930s, spurred the economy. Most homes now had an automobile, a television set, a refrigerator, a washing machine, and a vacuum cleaner. But consumers could also indulge themselves with electric can openers, electric pencil sharpeners, electric toothbrushes, aerosol cans, and automatic transmissions for their cars.

The automobile industry played a key part in the boom. Just as cars and roads transformed America in the 1920s when mass production came of age, so they contributed to the equally great transformation three decades later. Limited to the production of military vehicles during World War II, the auto industry expanded dramatically in the postwar period. Seventy thousand cars were made in 1945; 8 million were manufactured in 1955; and not quite 7 million were produced in 1960. Customers now chose from a wide variety of engines,

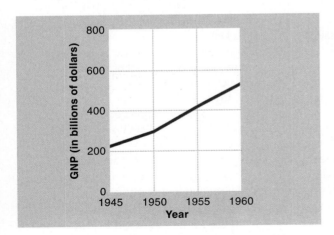

Increase in GNP, 1945–1960

The gross national product (GNP) rose steadily in the decade and a half after World War II as the United States enjoyed an unprecedented period of prosperity.

Source: National Income and Product Accounts, 1929–1994.

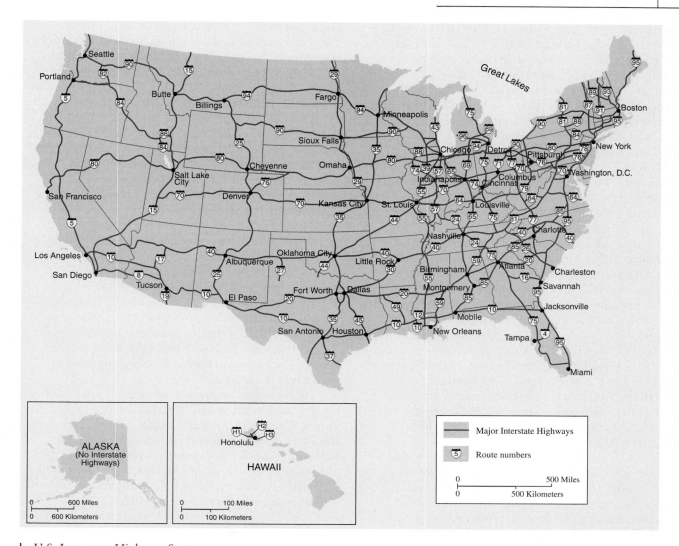

U.S. Interstate Highway System

The interstate highway system, established by legislative action in 1956, created an extensive network of roads that changed the landscape and living patterns of people throughout the United States. While the network was most extensive in the East, it extended throughout the entire country.

colors, and optional accessories. The development of a massive interstate highway system also stimulated auto production and so contributed to prosperity. Through the Interstate Highway Act of 1956, the Eisenhower administration poured $26 billion, the largest public works expenditure in American history, into building more than 40,000 miles of federal highways, linking all parts of the United States. Federal officials claimed the system would make evacuation quicker in the event of nuclear attack. President Dwight D. Eisenhower boasted that "the amount of concrete poured to form these roadways would build…six sidewalks to the moon.…More than any single action by the government since the end of the war, this one would change the face of America." Significantly, this massive effort helped create a nation dependent on oil.

A housing boom also fed economic growth as home-ownership rates rose from 53 percent in 1945 to 62 percent in 1960. Much of the stimulus came from the GI Bill of 1944. In addition to giving returning servicemen priority for many jobs and providing educational benefits, it offered low-interest home mortgages. Millions of former servicemen from all social classes eagerly purchased their share of the American dream.

The government's increasingly active economic role both stimulated and sustained the expansion. Businesses were allowed to buy almost 80 percent of the factories built by the government during the war for much less than they cost. Even more important was the dramatic rise in defense spending as the Cold War escalated. In 1947, Congress passed the National

Security Act creating the Department of Defense and authorized an initial budget of $13 billion. With the onset of the Korean War, the defense budget rose to $22 billion in 1951 and to about $47 billion in 1953. Approximately half of the total federal budget went to the armed forces. This spending, in turn, helped stimulate the aircraft and electronic industries. Close business–government ties of World War II grew stronger.

Most citizens welcomed the huge expenditures, not only because they supported the American stance in the struggle against communism but also because they understood the economic impact of military spending. Columnist David Lawrence noted in 1950, "Government planners figure they have found the magic formula for almost endless good times. Cold war is an automatic pump primer. Turn a spigot, and the public clamors for more arms spending."

Postwar American growth avoided some of the major problems that often bedevil periods of economic expansion—inflation and the enrichment of a few at the expense of the many. Inflation, a problem in the immediate postwar period, slowed from an average of 7 percent per year in the 1940s to a gentle 2 to 3 percent per year in the 1950s. And though the concentration of income remained the same—the bottom half of the population still earned less than the top tenth—the ranks of middle-class Americans grew.

American products were sold around the world. People in other countries had developed a taste for Coca-Cola during the war. Now numerous other goods became available overseas. American books, magazines, movies, and records promoted the spread of American culture and provided still more profits for American entrepreneurs.

A major economic transformation had occurred in the United States. Peaceful, prosperous, and productive, the nation had became what economist John Kenneth Galbraith called the "affluent society."

Postwar Growth Around the World

Elsewhere in the world, postwar reconstruction began but affluence took longer to arrive. Both European and Asian countries had suffered greater casualties than the United States, and some nations, even those on the winning side, had to deal with enormous devastation.

Great Britain was ravaged by the war. Rationing, necessary to provide the equitable distribution of scarce resources, lasted until the early 1950s. British factories, which had been the first to industrialize, were now inefficient and outdated. The automobile industry, for example, yielded part of its share of the world market to other nations, such as Germany, which introduced the inexpensive and reliable Volkswagen Beetle that was soon sold around the globe. Meanwhile, Britain lagged behind other European nations in developing a modern superhighway system that could spur industrial development.

In the general election of 1945, British voters ousted Winston Churchill and the Conservative party in favor of the Labour party, which was committed to social change. It took over the coal and railroad industries and began to nationalize the steel industry. While owners were compensated, some critics argued that the government's actions stifled industrial progress. Nevertheless, Great Britain began an economic and social recovery. It even provided a system of socialized medicine far in advance of anything in the United States.

While France was on the winning side of the war, it had suffered the indignity of occupation. It, too, experienced recovery, thanks in part to a rising birthrate, which was also occurring in the United States. At the same time, France, like Britain, was struggling with the demands of its colonial empire to be free. Brutal struggles in Indochina and Algeria caused financial instability and helped undermine economic development until France pulled out of both areas in the 1950s.

Defeated nations showed the most dramatic development of all. As the United States decided that a strong West Germany was necessary as a buffer against the Soviet Union, it helped cause what came to be known as "the German miracle." Because much of German industrial capacity had been destroyed by the war, new factories could be built with modern technological equipment. In the early 1950s, the West German rate of growth reached 10 percent a year, while the gross national product rose from $23 billion in 1950 to $103 billion in 1964.

Japan likewise revived quickly. Like Germany, it suffered tremendous wartime destruction, due to both conventional bombing and to the new atomic bombs that devastated Hiroshima and Nagasaki in 1945. Under the direction of General Douglas MacArthur, the United States directed the reconstruction effort. A new constitution created a democratic framework and led to the signing of a peace treaty in 1952. As political change occurred, the economy grew rapidly, and Japan overtook France and West Germany, soon ranking third in the world behind the United States and the Soviet Union.

So too did the Soviet Union rebuild. Reparations from West Germany and industrial extractions from Eastern Europe helped promote the reconstruction effort. The totalitarian structure of the Soviet state eliminated public debate about the allocation of resources, and the nation embarked on a series of initiatives that led to the development of a Soviet atomic bomb and an increase in the size of collective farms.

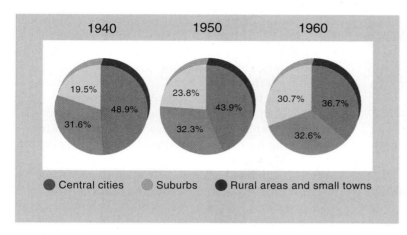

1940   1950   1960

1940: 19.5%, 48.9%, 31.6%
1950: 23.8%, 43.9%, 32.3%
1960: 30.7%, 36.7%, 32.6%

● Central cities   Suburbs   ● Rural areas and small towns

Shifts in Population Distribution, 1940–1960

These graphs show the progressive decline in rural population and the corresponding increase in suburban population between 1940 and 1960.

Source: U.S. Bureau of the Census.

forests were now divided into tiny standardized squares, each bearing a small house with a two-car garage and a manicured lawn. Folksinger Malvina Reynolds described the new developments she saw:

Little boxes on the hillside
Little boxes made of ticky tacky
Little boxes on the hillside
Little boxes all the same.
There's a green one and a pink one
And a blue one and a yellow one
And they're all made out of ticky tacky
And they all look just the same.

Mass production was the key. Individually designed houses were a thing of the past, he believed. "The reason we have it so good in this country," he said, "is that we can produce lots of things at low prices through mass production." Houses were among them. Working on a careful schedule, Levitt's team brought precut and preassembled materials to each site, put them together, and then moved on to the next location.

Levitt proved that his system worked. Construction costs at Levittown, New York, a new community of 17,000 homes built in the late 1940s, were only $10 per square foot, compared with the $12 to $15 common elsewhere. The next Levittown appeared in Bucks County, Pennsylvania, several years after the first, and another went up in Willingboro, New Jersey, at the end of the 1950s. Levitt's success provided a model for other developers.

Levitt argued that his homes helped underscore American values. "No man who owns his own house and lot can be a Communist," he once said. "He has too much to do." Levitt also helped perpetuate segregation by refusing to sell homes to blacks. "We can solve a housing problem, or we can try to solve a racial problem but we cannot combine the two," he declared in the early 1950s.

Government-insured mortgages, especially for veterans, fueled the housing boom. So did fairly low postwar interest rates. With many American families vividly remembering the Depression and saving significant parts of their paychecks, the nation had a pool of savings large enough to keep mortgage interest rates in the affordable 5 percent range.

Suburbanization transformed the American landscape. Huge tracts of former fields, pastures, and

As suburbs flourished, businesses followed their customers out of the cities. Shopping centers led the way. At the end of World War II, there were eight, but the number multiplied rapidly in the 1950s. In a single three-month period in 1957, 17 new centers opened; by

Levittown

Step-by-step mass production, with units completed in assembly line fashion, was the key to William Levitt's approach to housing. But the suburban developments he and others created were marked by street after street of houses that all looked the same. The Levittown in this picture was built on 1,200 acres of potato fields on Long Island in New York. How did the pattern you see here reflect the overall culture of the 1950s?

(Cornell Capa/Magnum Photos, Inc.)

1960, there were 3,840 in the United States. Shopping centers allowed suburban shoppers to avoid the cities entirely and further eroded urban health.

The Environmental Impact

Suburbanization had environmental consequences. Rapid expansion often took place without extensive planning and encroached on some of the nation's most attractive rural areas. Before long, virtually every American city was ringed by an ugly highway sporting garish neon signs. Billboard advertisements filled whatever space was not yet developed.

Responding to the increasingly cluttered terrain, architect Peter Blake ruthlessly attacked the practices of the 1950s in his muckraking book *God's Own Junkyard: The Planned Deterioration of America's Landscape,* published in 1964. As he deplored the unconscionable desecration of the American landscape, he wrote:

> Our suburbs are interminable wastelands dotted with millions of monotonous little houses on monotonous little lots and crisscrossed by highways lined with billboards, jazzed-up diners, used-car lots, drive-in movies, beflagged gas stations, and garish motels. Even the relatively unspoiled countryside beyond these suburban fringes has begun to sprout more telephone poles than trees, more trailer camps than national parks.

Despite occasional protests, there was little real consciousness of environmental issues in the early post–World War II years. The term *environment* itself was hardly used prior to the war. Yet the very prosperity that created the dismal highway strips in the late 1940s and 1950s was leading more and more Americans to appreciate natural environments as treasured parts of their rising standard of living. The shorter workweek provided more free time, and many Americans now had the means for longer vacations. They began to explore mountains and rivers and ocean shores and to ponder how to protect them. In 1958, Congress established the National Outdoor Recreation Review Commission, a first step toward consideration of environmental issues that became far more common in the next decade. Americans also began to recognize the need for open space in their communities in order to compensate for the urban overdevelopment.

Technology Supreme

A technological revolution transformed postwar America. Some developments—the use of atomic energy, for example—flowed directly from war research. Federal support for scientific activity increased dramatically, as the pattern of wartime collaboration continued. The government established the National Institutes of Health in 1948 to coordinate medical research and the National Science Foundation in 1950 to fund basic scientific research.

The advent of the Cold War led to ever-greater government involvement. The Atomic Energy Commission, created in 1946, and the Department of Defense, established in 1949, provided rapidly increasing funding for research and development. Support for the Los Alamos Scientific Laboratory, where the atomic bomb had been assembled, continued, while the government contracted with the University of California to open the new Livermore Laboratory near San Francisco. Money went to other large research universities as well and fueled their growth. Scientists engaged in both basic and applied research and helped develop nuclear weapons, jet planes, satellites, and consumer goods that were often the side products of military research. Computers both reflected and assisted the process of technological development. Prior to World War II, Vannevar Bush, an electrical engineer at the Massachusetts Institute of Technology, had built a machine filled with gears and shafts, along with electronic tubes in place of some mechanical parts, to solve differential equations. Wartime advances brought large but workable calculators, such as the Mark I electromechanical computer developed by engineer Howard Aiken and installed by IBM at Harvard in 1944. It was huge—55 feet long and 8 feet high—and had a million components.

Even more complicated was the Electronic Numerical Integrator and Calculator, called ENIAC, built in 1946 at the University of Pennsylvania. Like the Mark I, it was large, containing 18,000 electronic tubes and requiring tremendous amounts of electricity and special cooling procedures. It also needed to be "debugged" to remove insects attracted to the heat and light, giving rise to the term still used today by computer scientists for fixing software glitches. ENIAC performed impressively for the time, but at a snail's pace by modern standards. A key breakthrough in making computers faster and more reliable was the development of the transistor by three scientists at Bell Laboratories in 1948. They helped computers transform American society as surely as industrialization had changed it a century before. Computer programmers and operators were in increasing demand as computers contributed dramatically to the centralization and interdependence of American life.

Computers were essential for space exploration. They helped scientists perform the mathematical calculations that let astronauts venture beyond the confines of the earth. In the postwar years, increasingly sophisticated forms of space flight became possible. Rocketry had developed during World War II but came of age after the war. Rockets could deliver nuclear weapons but could also launch satellites and provide the means to venture millions of miles into outer space.

Computer advances also powered a wide variety of new appliances and gadgets designed for personal use. A transistorized miniature hearing aid, for example, could fit into the frame of a pair of eyeglasses. Stereophonic high-fidelity systems, using new transistor components, provided better sound.

An ominous technological trend related to computerization was the advent of automation. Mechanization was not new, but now it became far more widespread, threatening both skilled and unskilled workers. In 1952, the Ford Motor Company began using automatic drilling machines in an engine plant and found that now 41 workers could do a job that had previously required 117 workers. The implications of falling purchasing power as machines replaced workers were serious for an economy dependent on consumer demand.

The Consumer Culture

Americans maintained an ardent love affair with the machines, appliances, and gadgets produced by modern technology. By the end of the 1950s, most families had at least one automobile, often two or more, particularly as commuting from the suburbs became more common, and cars grew bigger and fancier than ever before. More powerful engines were the norm, while tailfins sometimes looked like airplane wings.

Television became a major influence on American life after World War II. Developed in the 1930s, prior to the war, the government deferred production and to allow for increased attention to radio to support the military effort. In 1946, there were fewer than 17,000 television sets, but by 1960, three-quarters of all American families owned at least one set. In 1955, the average American family tuned in four to five hours each day. Some studies predicted that an American student, on graduating from high school, would have spent 11,000 hours in class and 15,000 hours before the "tube." Young Americans grew up to the strains of "Winky Dink and You," "The Mickey Mouse Club," and "Howdy Doody Time" in the 1950s. Older viewers watched situation comedies such as *I Love Lucy* and *Father Knows Best* and live dramas such as *Playhouse 90*.

Television highlighted the rock-and-roll music that developed in the 1950s. Americans watched Elvis Presley play his guitar and sing, gyrating his hips in a sexually suggestive way that terrified parents, who worried about the influence of this new music, based on black rhythm and blues songs, on their children. Young people eagerly watched their counterparts dance to the music of Bill Haley and the Comets, Little Richard, Chuck Berry, and Elvis himself on *American Bandstand* every afternoon.

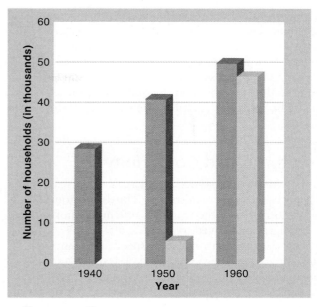

Households Owning Radios and Televisions, 1940–1960

Radio became increasingly popular in the postwar years, but observe the astronomical increase in the number of households owning television sets in the decade after 1950.

Source: U.S. Bureau of the Census.

Consumption, increasingly a pillar of the American economy, required a vast expansion of consumer credit. Installment plans facilitated buying a new car, while credit cards encouraged the purchase of smaller items such as television sets and household appliances. Eating out became easier when meals could be charged on a card. The first of the consumer credit cards—the Diner's Club card—appeared in 1950, followed at the end of the decade by the American Express card and the BankAmericard (later renamed Visa). By the end of the 1960s, about 50 million credit cards of all kinds were in use in the United States. Consumer credit—total private indebtedness—increased from $8.4 billion in 1946 to nearly $45 billion in 1958.

For consumers momentarily unsure about new purchases, a revitalized advertising industry was ready to persuade them to go ahead and buy. Advertising had come of age in the 1920s, as businesses persuaded customers that buying new products brought status and satisfaction. It had faltered when the economy collapsed in the 1930s but began to revive during the war, as firms kept the public aware of consumer goods, even those in short supply. With the postwar boom, advertisers again began to hawk their wares, this time even more aggressively than before.

Having weathered the poverty and unemployment of the 1930s and made sacrifices during a long war,

Americans now regarded abundance and leisure as their due, sometimes neglecting to look beyond the immediate objects of their desire. As journalist William Shannon wrote, the decade was one of "self-satisfaction and gross materialism. . . . The loudest sound in the land has been the oink and grunt of private hoggishness. . . . It has been the age of the slob."

Consensus and Conformity

As the economy expanded, an increasing sense of sameness pervaded American society. Third- and fourth-generation ethnic Americans became much more alike. As immigration slowed to a trickle after 1924, ties to Europe weakened, assimilation speeded up, and interethnic marriage skyrocketed. Television gave young and old a shared, visually seductive experience. Escaping the homogenizing tendencies was difficult.

Contours of Religious Life

Postwar Americans discovered a common religious sense and returned to their churches in record numbers. By the end of the 1950s, fully 95 percent of all Americans identified with some religious denomination.

Ecumenical activities—worldwide efforts on the part of different Christian churches—promoted greater religious involvement. Within the United States, evangelical revivalism, led by Southern Baptist Billy Graham and others, became increasingly popular.

Catholicism also sought to broaden its appeal. This effort succeeded as Pope John XXIII convened the Vatican Ecumenical Council in 1962 to make the Catholic church's traditions and practices more accessible—for example, substituting modern languages for Latin in the liturgy. Judaism likewise broadened its appeal. As assimilation occurred, quotas that had kept many out of more exclusive universities and other institutions began to disappear. Jews, like others, relied on the GI Bill to move to the suburbs, where they bought new homes and built new synagogues, most of which followed the more casual patterns of Reform or Conservative, rather than Orthodox, Judaism. Across all faiths, religion reinforced the importance of family life, for, according to one slogan, "The family that prays together stays together."

President Dwight D. Eisenhower reflected the national mood when he observed that "our government makes no sense unless it is founded in a deeply felt religious faith—and I don't care what it is." In 1954, Congress added the words "under God" to the pledge to the flag and the next year voted to require the phrase "In God We Trust" on all U.S. currency. Yet the revival sometimes seemed to rest on a shallow base of religious knowledge. In one public opinion poll, 80 percent of the respondents indicated that the Bible was God's revealed word, but only 35 percent were able to name the four Gospels and more than half were unable to name even one.

A challenge to religious conformity came from members of the so-called Beat Generation who embraced Buddhism. They helped promote the Buddhist vogue that emerged in the 1950s and 1960s, with Zen centers opening in Los Angeles in 1956, San Francisco in 1959, and New York in 1966. Zen stressed Buddha's emphasis on meditation that led to his enlightenment.

Traditional Roles for Men and Women

World War II had interrupted traditional patterns of behavior for both men and women. As servicemen went overseas, women left their homes to work. After 1945, women faced tremendous pressure to leave their jobs and to conform to accepted prewar gender patterns, even though, paradoxically, more women entered the workforce than ever before.

Men and women had different postwar expectations. Most men expected to go to school and then find jobs to support their families as the primary breadwinners. For women, the situation was more complex. While they wanted to resume patterns of family life that had been disrupted by the war, many had enjoyed working in the military plants and were reluctant to retreat to the home, despite pressure to do so.

In 1947, *Life* magazine ran a long photo essay called "The American Woman's Dilemma" that summed up the problem. The essay observed that women were caught in a conflict between the traditional expectation to stay home and the desire to have a paid job. A 1946 *Fortune* magazine poll also captured the discontent of some women. Asked whether they would prefer to be born again as men or as women, 25 percent of the women interviewed said they would prefer to be men. That dissatisfaction was strongest among white, well-educated, middle-class women, for black and lower-class white women often had no choice but to continue working outside the home.

By the 1950s, middle-class doubts and questions had largely receded. The baby boom increased average family size and made the decision to remain home easier. The flight to the suburbs gave women more to do, and they settled into the routines of redecorating their homes and gardens and transporting children to and from activities and schools.

Marriage and home became the most important priorities. Many women went to college to find husbands—and dropped out if they succeeded. Almost two-thirds of the women in college, but less than half the men, left before completing a degree. Women were expected to marry young, have children early, and

Recovering the Past

CLOTHING

Clothing can be an important source of information about the past. The clothes people wear often announce their age, gender, and class and frequently transmit some sense of their origin, occupation, and even their politics. The vocabulary of dress includes more than garments alone: hairstyles, jewelry, and makeup all contribute to the way people choose to present themselves. Clothing can signal strong emotions; a torn, unbuttoned shirt, for example, can indicate that a person who seldom dresses that way is really upset. Bright colors can demonstrate a daring sense and a willingness to make a strong statement. By examining clothing styles in a number of different decades, we can begin to understand something of the changing patterns of people's lives.

In the 1920s, flappers and other women often dressed like children, with loose dresses usually in pastel colors ending just below the knee. Large trimmings, such as huge artificial flowers, accentuated the effect. A "boyish" figure was considered most attractive. The clothes conveyed a feeling of playfulness and a willingness to embrace the freedom of the young. Men's suits in the same period were now made out of lighter materials and looked less padded than before. As the tall, stiff collar of an earlier age disappeared and trousers became more high-waisted, men too had a more youthful look.

The Great Depression of the 1930s brought a change in style. Flappers now looked silly, especially as millions of people were starving. Advertisements and films promoted a new maturity and sophistication, more appropriate to hard times. Men's suits became heavier and darker, as if symbolically to provide protection in a bread line. Trousers were wider, and jackets were frequently double-breasted. Overcoats became longer. Women's clothes were likewise made out of heavier fabrics and used darker colors. Skirts fell almost to the ankles on occasion and were covered by longer coats. Clothes indicated that there was no place for the playfulness of the decade before.

As conditions improved during and after World War II, styles changed once more. In the 1940s, young teenage girls frequently wore bobby socks rolled down to their ankles. Working women wore overalls, but with their own adornments to maintain their femininity. Rosie the Riveter, drawn by noted artist Norman Rockwell, wore her overalls proudly as she sat with a riveting gun in her lap and an attractive scarf around her hair. In the postwar years, the "Man in the Gray Flannel Suit" looked serious, sober, and well tailored, ready to go work for corporate America. His female partner wanted to look equally worldly and sophisticated and wore carefully tailored adult clothing, with the waist drawn in (often by a girdle) and heels as tall as three inches, when going out. The fashion industry helped define the decorative role women were supposed to play in supporting men as they advanced their business careers.

Harlem women in the 1920s

(Photographs and Prints Division, Schomburg Center for Research in Black Culture, The New York Public Library, Astor, Lenox and Tilden Foundations/Art Resources, NY)

Frances Perkins with laborers in the 1930s

(Brown Brothers)

World War II women at work

(Oregon Historical Society, OrHi 37401)

A woman and child in the 1950s

(© The Dorothea Lange Collection, The Oakland Museum of California, City of Oakland, Gift of Paul S. Taylor)

Then came the 1960s and an entirely new look. Casual clothing became a kind of uniform. The counterculture was a movement of the young, and clothing took on an increasingly youthful look. Skirts rose above the knee in 1963 and a few years later climbed to mid-thigh. Women began to wear pants and trouser suits. Men and women both favored jeans and informal shirts and let their hair grow longer. Men broke away from the gray suits of the preceding decade and indulged themselves in bright colors in what has been called the "peacock revolution."

Reflecting on the Past Look carefully at the pictures on these pages. They show fashions from different periods and can tell us a good deal about how these people defined themselves. Examine first the photo of the three black women from the 1920s. What kinds of adornments do you notice? What impression do these women convey?

Look at the photograph of Frances Perkins, secretary of labor in the 1930s. What kind of dress is she wearing? How do her clothes differ from those of the women in the 1920s? In the picture, she is talking to a number of working men. What do their clothes tell you about the kind of work they might be doing?

In the picture of two drill press operators during World War II, the women are dressed to handle the heavy machinery. Are their clothes different from those of the laborers in the preceding picture? How have the women accommodated themselves to their work, while still maintaining their individuality?

Countercultural dress in the 1960s

(Ken Heyman/Woodfin Camp & Associates)

Now look at the picture of a woman in the 1950s. What kind of work might she do? What kind of flexibility do these clothes give her? What do the stylistic touches convey? Finally, examine the photograph of the man and woman at an outdoor music festival in the 1960s. What does their clothing remind you of? Where might it come from? What impression are these people trying to create by their dress? ▪

encourage their husbands' careers. An article in *Esquire* magazine in 1954 called working wives a "menace."

Adlai Stevenson, Democratic presidential candidate in 1952 and 1956, defined the female role in politics. "The assignment for you, as wives and mothers," he told a group of young women, "you can do in the living room with a baby in your lap or in the kitchen with a can opener in your hand." They were "to influence man and boy" in the "humble role of housewife" and mother.

Pediatrician Benjamin Spock agreed. In 1946 he published *Baby and Child Care,* the book most responsible for the child-rearing patterns of the postwar generation. In it, he advised mothers to stay at home if they wanted to raise stable and secure youngsters. Working outside the home might jeopardize their children's mental and emotional health.

Popular culture highlighted the stereotype of the woman concerned only about marriage and family. Author Betty Friedan described these patterns in her explosive 1963 critique, *The Feminine Mystique.* Women "could desire no greater destiny than to glory in their own femininity.... All they had to do was to devote their lives from earliest girlhood to finding a husband and bearing children." Their role was clear. "It was unquestioned gospel," she wrote, "that women could identify with *nothing* beyond the home—not politics, not art, not science, not events large or small, war or peace, in the United States or the world, unless it could be approached through female experience as a wife or mother or translated into domestic detail."

The family was all-important in this scenario. Fewer than 10 percent of all Americans felt that an unmarried person could be happy. In a pattern endlessly reiterated by popular television programs, the family was meant to provide all satisfaction and contentment. The single-story ranch house that became so popular in this period reflected the focus on the family as the source of recreation and fun. No longer were kitchen and den private, as they had been earlier in a reflection of the notion of separate spheres. Now houses, with far more shared and open space, stressed livability and family comfort.

Sexuality was a troublesome if compelling postwar concern. In 1948, Alfred C. Kinsey published *Sexual Behavior in the Human Male.* Kinsey was an Indiana University zoologist who had previously studied the gall wasp. When asked to teach a course on marriage problems, he found little published material about human sexual activity and decided to collect his own. He compiled case histories of 5,300 white males and recorded patterns of sexual behavior.

Kinsey shocked the country with his statistics on premarital, extramarital, and otherwise illicit sexual acts. Among males who went to college, he concluded, 67 percent had engaged in sexual intercourse before marriage, as had 84 percent of those who went to high school but not beyond. Thirty-seven percent of the total male population had experienced some kind of overt homosexual activity. Five years later, Kinsey published a companion volume, *Sexual Behavior in the Human Female,* which detailed many of the same sexual patterns. Although critics denounced Kinsey for what they considered his unscientific methodology and challenged his results, both books sold widely, for they opened the door to a subject previously considered taboo.

Interest in sexuality was reflected in the fascination with sex goddesses such as Marilyn Monroe. With her blond hair, breathy voice, and raw sexuality, she personified the forbidden side of the good life and became one of Hollywood's most popular stars. The images of such film goddesses corresponded to male fantasies of women, visible in *Playboy* magazine, which first appeared in 1953 and soon achieved a huge readership. As for men's wives, they were expected to manage their suburban homes and to be cheerful and willing objects of their husbands' desire.

Despite reaffirming the old ideology that a woman's place was in the home, the 1950s were years

Biologist Alfred Kinsey interviewed thousands of men and women about their sex lives. Here he is conducting an interview with a young woman. How did his manner encourage people to talk?

of unnoticed but important change. Because the supply of single women workers fell as a result of the low birthrate of the Depression years and increased schooling and early marriage, older married women continued the pattern begun during the war and entered the labor force in larger numbers than before. In 1940, only 15 percent of American wives had jobs. By 1950, 21 percent were employed, and 10 years later, the figure had risen to 30 percent. Moreover, more than half of all working women were married, a dramatic reversal of pre–World War II patterns. While many working women were poor, divorced, or widowed, many others worked to acquire the desirable new products that were badges of middle-class status. They stepped into the new jobs created by economic expansion, clustering in office, sales, and service positions, occupations already defined as female. They and their employers considered their work subordinate to their primary role as wives and mothers. The conviction that women's main role was homemaking justified low wages and the denial of promotions. Comparatively few women entered professions where they would have challenged traditional notions of a woman's place.

African American women worked as always but often lost the jobs they had held during the war. Bernice McCannon, an African American employee at a Virginia military base, observed, "I have always done domestic work for families. When war came, I made the same move many domestics did. I took a higher paying job in a government cafeteria as a junior baker. If domestic work offers a good living, I see no reason why most of us will not return to our old jobs. We will have no alternative." In the 1950s, the employment picture improved somewhat. African American women succeeded both in moving into white-collar positions and in increasing their income. By 1960, more than one-third of all black women held clerical, sales, service, or professional jobs. The income gap between white women and black women holding similar jobs dropped from about 50 percent in 1940 to about 30 percent in 1960.

Cultural Rebels

Not all Americans fit the 1950s stereotypes. Some were alienated from the culture and rebelled against its values. Many were intrigued by Holden Caulfield, the main figure in J. D. Salinger's popular novel *The Catcher in the Rye* (1951), who rebelled against the "phonies" around him who threatened his individuality and independence.

Writers of the "Beat Generation" espoused unconventional values in their stories and poems. Challenging the apathy and conformity of the period, they stressed spontaneity and spirituality and claimed that intuition was more important than reason, Eastern mysticism (with its Buddhist influence) more valuable than Western faith. The "Beats" deliberately outraged respectability by sneering at materialism, flaunting unconventional sex lives, and smoking marijuana.

Their literary work reflected their approach to life. Finding conventional academic forms confining, they rejected them. Jack Kerouac typed his best-selling novel *On the Road* (1957), describing freewheeling trips across country, on a 250-foot roll of paper. Dispensing with conventional punctuation and paragraphing, the book was a song of praise to the free lifestyle the "Beats" espoused.

Rock-and-Roll Star Elvis Presley

Elvis Presley, a truck driver from Memphis, Tennessee, turned rock and roll into a kind of teenage religion. In appearances such as this one at a state fair in Memphis, Tennessee, in 1956, his fans worked themselves into a frenzy. How did Elvis's popularity help a new youth culture develop?

(Getty Images)

Poet Allen Ginsberg, who, like Kerouac, was a Columbia University dropout, became equally well known for his poem "Howl." Written during a wild weekend in 1955, the poem was a scathing critique of modern, mechanized culture. The powerful poem, which began with the line "I saw the best minds of my generation destroyed by madness, starving hysterical naked," became a cult piece, particularly after the police seized it on the grounds that it was obscene. When the work survived a court test, national acclaim followed for Ginsberg. He and the other "Beats" furnished a model for rebellion in the 1960s.

The signs of cultural rebellion also appeared in popular music. Parents recoiled as their children flocked to hear a young Tennessee singer named Elvis Presley belt out rock-and-roll songs. Presley's sexy voice, gyrating hips, and other techniques borrowed from black singers made him the undisputed "king of rock and roll." A multimedia blitz of movies, television, and radio helped make songs such as "Heartbreak Hotel," "Don't Be Cruel," and "Hound Dog" smash singles. Eighteen Presley hits sold more than a million copies in the last four years of the 1950s. His black leather jacket and duck-tail haircut became standard dress for rebellious male teenagers.

American painters, shucking off European influences that had shaped American artists for two centuries, also became a part of the cultural rebellion. Led by Jackson Pollock and the "New York school," some artists discarded the easel, laid gigantic canvases on the floor, and then used trowels, putty knives, and sticks to apply paint, glass shards, sand, and other materials in wild explosions of color. Known as abstract expressionists, these painters regarded the unconscious as the source of their artistic creations. Like much of the literature of rebellion, abstract expressionism reflected the artist's alienation from a world filled with nuclear threats, computerization, and materialism.

Origins of the Welfare State

The modern American welfare state originated in the New Deal. Franklin D. Roosevelt's efforts to deal with the ravages of the Great Depression and protect Americans from the problems stemming from industrial capitalism provided the basis for subsequent efforts to commit the government to help those who could not help themselves, even in prosperous times. Harry Truman's Fair Deal built squarely on Roosevelt's New Deal. Truman's Republican successor, Dwight Eisenhower, sought to scale down spending but made no effort to roll back the most important initiatives of the welfare state.

Harry S Truman

Harry S Truman, America's first postwar president, was an unpretentious man who took a straightforward approach to public affairs. He was, however, ill prepared for the office he assumed in the final months of World War II. His three months as vice president had done little to school him in the complexity of postwar issues. Nor had Franklin Roosevelt confided in Truman. It was no wonder that the new president felt insecure. To a former colleague in the Senate, he groaned, "I'm not big enough for this job." Critics agreed.

Yet Truman matured rapidly. A sign on the president's White House desk read, "The Buck Stops Here," and he was willing to make quick decisions on issues, even if associates sometimes wondered whether he understood all the implications.

Truman took the same feisty approach to public policy that characterized his conduct of foreign affairs (see Chapter 27). Believing in plain speaking, he seldom hesitated to let others know exactly where he stood. He attacked his political enemies vigorously when they resisted his initiatives and often took his case to the American people. He was, in many ways, an old-style Democratic politician who hoped to use his authority to benefit the middle-class and working-class Americans who made up his political base.

Truman's Struggles with a Conservative Congress

Like Roosevelt, Harry Truman believed that the federal government had the responsibility for ensuring the social welfare of all Americans. He shared his predecessor's commitment to assisting less-prosperous inhabitants of the country in a systematic, rational way. Truman wanted his administration to embrace and act on a series of carefully defined social and economic goals to extend New Deal initiatives even further.

Less than a week after the end of World War II, Truman called on Congress to pass a 21-point program. He wanted housing assistance, a higher minimum wage, more unemployment compensation, and a national commitment to maintaining full employment. During the next 10 weeks, Truman sent blueprints of further proposals to Congress, including health insurance and atomic energy legislation. But this liberal program soon ran into fierce political opposition.

The debate surrounding the Employment Act of 1946 hinted at the fate of Truman's proposals. This measure was a deliberate effort to apply the theory of English economist John Maynard Keynes who argued that aggressive spending could head off another depression and maintain economic equilibrium. While liberals and labor leaders hailed the initial bill, which committed the government to maintaining full employment by monitoring the economy and taking remedial action in case of decline, business groups such as the National Association of Manufacturers condemned it. They claimed that government intervention would undermine free enterprise and promote socialism. Responding to the business community, Congress cut the proposal to bits. As finally passed, the act created a Council of Economic Advisers to make recommendations to the president, but it stopped short of committing the government to using fiscal tools to maintain full employment when economic indicators turned downward.

As the midterm elections of 1946 approached, Truman knew he was vulnerable. As more and more people questioned his competence as president, his support dropped from 87 percent of those polled after he assumed the office to 32 percent in November 1946. Gleeful Republicans asked the voters, "Had enough?" They had. Republicans won majorities in both houses of Congress for the first time since the 1928 elections and gained a majority of the governorships as well.

After the 1946 elections, Truman faced an unsympathetic Eightieth Congress. Republicans and conservative Democrats, dominating both houses, planned to reverse the liberal policies of the Roosevelt years. Hoping to reestablish congressional authority and cut the power of the executive branch, they insisted on less government intervention in business and private affairs. They also demanded tax cuts and curtailment of the privileged position they felt labor had come to enjoy.

When the new Congress met, it slashed federal spending and taxes. In 1947, Congress twice passed tax-cut measures, which Truman vetoed. In 1948, another election year, Congress overrode the veto.

Congress also struck at Democratic labor policies. Angry at the gains won by labor in the 1930s and 1940s, Republicans wanted to check unions and to circumscribe their right to engage in the kind of disruptive strikes that had occurred immediately after the war. Early in Truman's presidency, Congress had passed a bill requiring notice for strikes as well as a cooling-off period if a strike occurred. Truman vetoed it. But in 1947, commanding more votes, the Republicans passed the Taft–Hartley Act, which sought to limit the power of unions by restricting the weapons they could employ. It spelled out unfair labor practices (such as preventing nonunion workers from working if they wished) and outlawed the closed shop, whereby an employee had to join a union before getting a job. The law likewise allowed states to prohibit the union shop, which forced workers to join the union after they had been hired. It gave the president the right to call for an 80-day cooling-off period in strikes affecting national security and required union officials to sign non-Communist oaths.

Union leaders and members were furious. They called the measure a "slave-labor law" and argued vigorously that it eliminated many of their hard-won rights and left labor–management relations the way they had been in pre–New Deal days. Vetoing the measure, Truman claimed that it was unworkable and unfair and went on nationwide radio to seek public approval. This move regained him some of the support he had lost earlier when he had sought to force strikers to go back to work immediately after the war. Congress, however, passed the Taft–Hartley measure over Truman's veto.

The Fair Deal and Its Fate

In 1948, Truman wanted a chance to consolidate a liberal program and decided to seek the presidency in his own right. Aware that he was an accidental occupant of the White House, he won what most people thought was a worthless nomination. Not only was his own popularity waning, but the Democratic party itself seemed to be falling apart.

The civil rights issue split the Democrats. When liberals defeated a moderate platform proposal and pressed for a stronger commitment to African American rights, angry delegates from Mississippi and Alabama stormed out of the convention. They later formed the States' Rights, or Dixiecrat, party. At their own convention, delegates from 13 states nominated Governor J. Strom Thurmond of South Carolina as their presidential candidate and affirmed their support for continued racial segregation.

Meanwhile, Henry A. Wallace, first secretary of agriculture, longtime member of the government until Truman fired him for advocating a more moderate approach to the Soviet Union, mounted his own challenge, becoming the presidential candidate of the Progressive party. In that fragmented state, the Democrats took on the Republicans, who coveted the White House after 16 years out of power. Once again, the GOP nominated New York Governor Thomas E. Dewey, the unsuccessful candidate in 1944. Even though he was stiff and egocentric, the polls uniformly picked the Republicans to win. Dewey saw little value in brawling with his opponent and campaigned, in the words of one commentator, "with the humorless calculation of a Certified Public Accountant in pursuit of the Holy Grail."

Truman, as the underdog, conducted a two-fisted campaign. He appealed to ordinary Americans as an unpretentious man engaged in an uphill fight. Believing that everyone was against him but the people, he addressed Americans in familiar language. He called the Republicans a "bunch of old mossbacks" out to destroy the New Deal as he attacked the "do nothing" Eightieth Congress. Speaking informally in his choppy,

Harry Truman Celebrating His Unexpected Victory

In one of the nation's most extraordinary political upsets, Harry Truman beat Thomas E. Dewey in 1948. Here an exuberant Truman holds a newspaper headline printed while he slept, before the vote turned his way. Why is Truman so gleeful?

(Bettmann/CORBIS)

aggressive style, he appealed to crowds yelling, "Give 'em hell, Harry!" He did.

The pollsters predicting a Republican victory were wrong. On election day, disproving the bold headline "Dewey Defeats Truman" in the *Chicago Daily Tribune*, the incumbent president scored one of the most unexpected political upsets in American history, winning 303–189 in the Electoral College. Democrats also swept both houses of Congress.

Truman won primarily because he was able to revive the major elements of the Democratic coalition that Franklin Roosevelt had constructed more than a decade before. Despite the rocky days of 1946,

Truman managed to hold on to labor, farm, and black votes. Labor's support was crucial. Working men and women had been irritated by his response to the strikes in the immediate postwar period but had been buoyed by his veto, even though unsuccessful, of the Taft–Hartley Act. In the end, wary of Wallace, they backed Truman.

With the election behind him, Truman pursued his liberal program. In his 1949 State of the Union message, he declared, "Every segment of our population and every individual has a right to expect from our Government a fair deal." While parts of Truman's Fair Deal worked, others did not. Lawmakers raised

PRESIDENTIAL ELECTIONS, 1948–1956

Year	Candidate	Party	Popular Vote	Electoral Vote
1948	HARRY S TRUMAN	Democratic	24,105,812 (49.5%)	303
	Thomas E. Dewey	Republican	21,970,065 (45.1%)	189
	J. Strom Thurmond	States' Rights	1,169,063 (12.4%)	39
	Henry A. Wallace	Progressive	1,157,172 (12.4%)	0
1952	DWIGHT D. EISENHOWER	Republican	33,936,234 (55.1%)	442
	Adlai E. Stevenson	Democratic	27,314,992 (44.4%)	89
1956	DWIGHT D. EISENHOWER	Republican	35,590,472 (57.4%)	457
	Adlai E. Stevenson	Democratic	26,022,752 (42.0%)	73

Note: Winners' names appear in capital letters.

the minimum wage and expanded social security programs. A housing program brought modest gains but did not really meet housing needs. A farm program, aimed at providing income support to farmers if prices fell, never made it through Congress. Although he desegregated the military, other parts of his civil rights program failed to win congressional support. The American Medical Association undermined the effort to provide national health insurance, and Congress rejected a measure to provide federal aid to education.

The mixed record was not entirely Truman's fault. Conservative legislators were largely responsible for sabotaging his efforts. At the same time, critics charged correctly that Truman was often unpragmatic and shrill in his struggles with an unsympathetic Congress. They argued that he sometimes seemed to provoke the confrontations that became a hallmark of his presidency. They also claimed that he was most concerned with foreign policy as he strove to secure bipartisan support for Cold War initiatives (see Chapter 27) and allowed his domestic program to suffer. Rising defense expenditures meant less money for projects at home.

Still, Truman kept the liberal vision alive. The Fair Deal ratified many of the initiatives begun during the New Deal and led Americans to take programs such as social security for granted. Truman had not achieved everything he wanted—he had not even come close—but the nation had taken another step toward endorsing liberal goals.

The Election of Ike

Acceptance of the liberal state continued in the 1950s, even as the Republicans took control. By 1952, Truman's popularity had plummeted to 23 percent of the American people, and all indicators pointed to a political shift. The Democrats nominated Adlai Stevenson, Illinois's articulate and moderately liberal governor. The Republicans turned to Dwight Eisenhower, the World War II hero known as Ike.

While Stevenson approached political issues in intellectual terms, the Republicans focused on communism, corruption, and Korea as major priorities. They called the Democrats "soft on communism," condemned scandals involving Truman's cronies and friends, and promised to end the unpopular Korean War. Eisenhower proved to be a highly effective campaigner. He had a natural talent for taking his case to the American people, speaking in simple, reassuring terms they could understand. He struck a grandfatherly pose, unified the various wings of his party, and went on to victory at the polls. He received 55 percent of the vote and carried 41 states. The new president took office with a Republican Congress as well and had little difficulty winning a second term in 1956.

Dwight D. Eisenhower

Eisenhower stood in stark contrast to Truman. His easy manner and warm smile made him widely popular. As British field marshal Bernard Montgomery observed, "He has the power of drawing the hearts of men towards him as a magnet attracts bits of metal."

Eisenhower had not taken the typical route to the presidency. After World War II, he served successively as army chief of staff, president of Columbia University, and head of the North Atlantic Treaty Organization (NATO). Despite his lack of formal political background, he had a real ability to get people to compromise and work together.

Ike's limited experience with everyday politics conditioned his sense of the presidential role. Whereas Truman loved political infighting and wanted to take charge, Eisenhower was more restrained. The presidency for him was no "bully pulpit," as it had been for Theodore Roosevelt and even FDR. "I am not one of those desk-pounding types that likes to stick out his jaw and look like he is bossing the show," he said. "You do not lead by hitting people over the head. Any damn fool can do that, but it's usually called 'assault'— not 'leadership.' "

"Modern Republicanism"

Eisenhower wanted to limit the presidential role. He was uncomfortable with the growth of the executive office over the past 20 years. Like the Republicans in Congress with whom Truman had tangled, he wanted to restore the balance between the branches of government and to reduce the authority of the national government. He recognized, however, that it was impossible to scale back federal power to the limited levels of the 1920s, and he wanted to preserve social gains that even Republicans now accepted. Eisenhower sometimes termed his approach "dynamic conservatism" or "modern Republicanism," which, he explained, meant "conservative when it comes to money, liberal when it comes to human beings." Liberals quipped that his approach meant endorsing social projects and then failing to authorize the funds.

Economic concerns dominated the Eisenhower years. The president and his chief aides wanted desperately to preserve the value of the dollar, pare down levels of funding, cut taxes, and balance the budget after years of deficit spending. Eisenhower's administration also supported business interests. This orientation became obvious when defense secretary Charles E. Wilson, former president of General Motors, declared at his confirmation hearing, "What is good for our country is good for General Motors, and vice versa."

Eisenhower fulfilled his promise to reduce government's economic role. The administration sought to circumscribe federal activity in the electric power field. Eisenhower favored private rather than public development of power, and once said about the Tennessee Valley Authority (TVA), the extensive public power and development project begun during the New Deal, "I'd like to see us sell the whole thing, but I suppose we can't go that far." He opposed a TVA proposal for expansion to provide power to the Atomic Energy Commission and instead authorized a private group to build a plant in Arkansas for that purpose. Later, when charges of scandal arose, the administration canceled the agreement, but the basic preference for private development remained.

Committed to supporting business interests, the administration sometimes saw its program backfire. As a result of Eisenhower's reluctance to stimulate the economy too much, the annual rate of economic growth declined from 4.3 percent between 1947 and 1952 to 2.5 percent between 1953 and 1960. The economy was still growing, but more slowly than before. The country also suffered three recessions—in 1953–1954, 1957–1958, and 1960–1961—in Eisenhower's eight years. During the slumps, tax revenues fell and the deficits that Eisenhower so wanted to avoid increased.

Eisenhower's understated approach led to a legislative stalemate, particularly when the Democrats regained control of Congress in 1954. Opponents gibed at Ike's restrained stance and laughed about limited White House leadership. One observed that Eisenhower proved that the country did not "need" a president. Another spoke of the Eisenhower doll—you wound it up and it did nothing for eight years.

Yet Eisenhower understood just what he was doing; he had a better grasp of public policy than his critics realized. Beneath his casual approach lay real shrewdness. "Don't worry," he once assured his aides as they briefed him for a press conference. "If that question comes up, I'll just confuse them." He worked quietly to create the consensus that he believed was necessary for legislative progress and practiced what later observers called a "hidden hand" presidency, unobtrusively orchestrating support for his own ends.

Even more important was his role in ratifying the welfare state. By 1960, the government had become a major factor in ordinary people's lives. It had grown enormously, employing close to 2.5 million people throughout the 1950s. Federal expenditures, which had stood at $3.5 billion in 1927, rose to $97 billion in 1960. The White House now took the lead in initiating legislation and in steering bills through Congress. Individuals had come to expect old-age pensions, unemployment payments, and a minimum wage. By accepting the fundamental features of the national state that the Democrats had created, Eisenhower ensured its survival.

A Popular and Personable President
Dwight Eisenhower provided a reassuring presence in the White House in the 1950s. His very presence conveyed the impression that everything was going to be all right. How did his wide smile, pictured here, make Americans feel good about themselves and their country?

(Hulton Archive/Getty Images)

For all the jokes at his expense, Eisenhower remained popular with the voters. He accomplished most of his goals, and he was one of the few presidents to leave office as highly regarded by the people as when he entered it. He was the kind of leader Americans wanted in prosperous times.

The Other America

Not all Americans shared postwar middle-class affluence. African Americans, uprooted from rural patterns and transplanted into urban slums, were among the hardest hit. But members of other minority groups, as well as less fortunate whites, suffered similar dislocations, unknown to the middle class.

Poverty amid Affluence

Many people in the "affluent society" lived in poverty. Although the popular "trickle-down" theory argued that economic expansion benefited all classes, little wealth reached the citizens at the bottom. In 1960, the Federal Bureau of Labor Statistics reported that 40 million people (almost one-quarter of the population) lived below what it defined as the poverty level, with nearly the same number only marginally above the line.

Michael Harrington, socialist author and critic, shocked the country with his 1962 study *The Other America*. The poor, Harrington showed, were everywhere. He described New York City's "economic underworld," where "Puerto Ricans and Negroes, alcoholics, drifters, and disturbed people" haunted employment agencies for temporary positions as "dishwashers and day workers, the fly-by-night jobs." In the afternoon, he continued, "the jobs have all been handed out, yet the people still mill around."

Despite the prosperity that surrounded them, the mountain folk of Appalachia, the tenant farmers of Mississippi, and the migrant farmers of Florida, Texas, and California were all caught in poverty's relentless cycle.

Hard Times for African Americans

African Americans were among the postwar nation's least prosperous citizens. In the South, agricultural workers continued to fall victim to foreign competition, mechanization, and eviction as white farmers turned to less labor-intensive crops such as soybeans and peanuts.

The southern agricultural population declined dramatically as millions of blacks moved to southern cities, where they found better jobs, better schooling, and freedom from landlords. Some achieved middle-class status; many more did not. They remained poor, with even less of a support system than they had known before.

Millions of African Americans also headed for northern cities after 1940. In the 1950s, Detroit's black population increased from 16 percent to 29 percent, Chicago's from 14 percent to 23 percent. At one point in this decade, Chicago's black population rose by more than 2,200 people each week. The new arrivals congregated in urban slums, where the growth of social services failed to keep pace with population growth.

The experiences of African Americans in the cities often proved different from what they had expected. As author Claude Brown recalled, blacks were told that in the North, "Negroes lived in houses with bathrooms, electricity, running water, and indoor toilets. To them, this was the 'promised land' that Mammy had been singing about in the cotton fields for many years." But no one had told them "about one of the most important aspects of the promised land: it was a slum ghetto.... There were too many people full of hate and bitterness crowded into a dirty, stinky, uncared-for closet-size section of a great city." The constant slights that accompanied segregation in both the North and the South in the midst of such conditions took a heavy toll.

Still, the black community remained intact. Chicago's South Side neighborhood was a vibrant place, replacing New York's Harlem as black America's cultural capital in the 1950s. This section of the city included such figures as boxing champion Joe Louis, gospel singer Mahalia Jackson, and Representative William Dawson, one of the few African American members of Congress.

The black church played an important role in sustaining African American life. Blacks moving into the cities retained churchgoing habits and a commitment to religious institutions from their rural days. The churches offered more than religious sustenance alone. Many provided day-care facilities, ran Boy Scout and Girl Scout troops, and sponsored a variety of other social services.

The growth of the black urban population fostered the increased growth of businesses catering to the African American community. Black newspapers now provided a more regional, rather than a national, focus, but magazines such as *Jet*, a pocket-size weekly with a large, countrywide circulation, filled the void. Black-owned and black-operated banks and other financial institutions increased in number.

Yet most African Americans remained second-class citizens. Escape from the slums was difficult for many and impossible for most. Persistent poverty remained a dismal fact of life.

African American Gains

African Americans had made significant gains during World War II. Black servicemen returning from the war vowed to reject second-class citizenship and helped mobilize a grassroots movement to counter discrimination. In the postwar years, African struggles for independence, such as the Kenyan Mau Mau revolt against the British, inspired African American leaders who now saw the quest for black equality in a broader context. They took enormous pride in the achievement of independence by a number of African nations and demanded comparable change at home.

The racial question received dramatic attention in 1947 when Jackie Robinson broke the color line and began playing major league baseball with the Brooklyn Dodgers. Sometimes teammates were hostile, sometimes opponents crashed into him with spikes high, but Robinson kept his frustrations to himself. A splendid first season helped ease the way and resulted in his selection as Rookie of the Year. African Americans flocked to the ballpark and followed his exploits on the radio. As Charles Jones of Charlotte, North Carolina, noted, "Robinson was knocking a ball everywhere on a *white man's* baseball field." After Robinson's trailblazing effort, other blacks, formerly confined to the old Negro leagues, moved into the major leagues in baseball and then into other sports.

Somewhat reluctantly, Truman supported the civil rights movement. A moderate on questions of

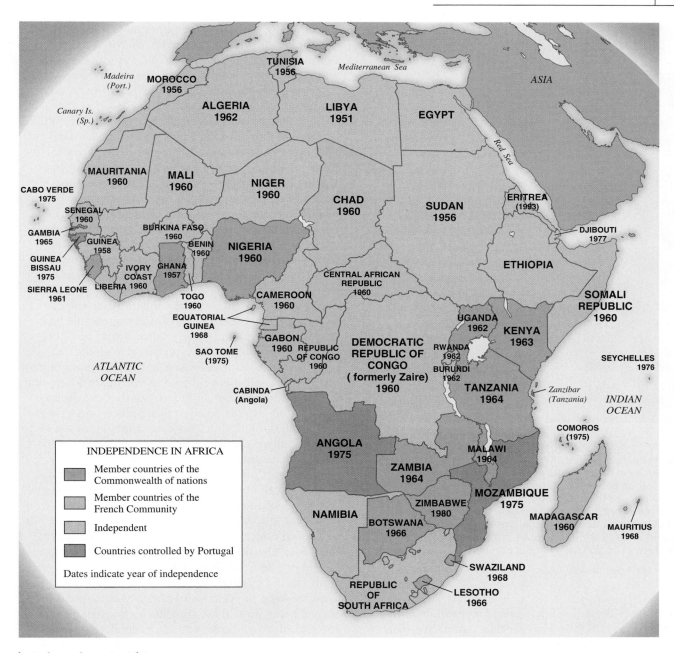

Independence in Africa

In the 1950s and 1960s, most African nations threw off their colonial rulers and achieved independence. During which decade did more nations become free? How did attaining independence change social and economic patterns in the African nations? What effect did it have on the patterns of the Cold War? What effect did it have on the civil rights struggle in the United States?

race, who believed in political, not social, equality, he responded to the growing strength of the African American vote. In 1946, he appointed a Committee on Civil Rights to investigate the problem of lynching and other brutalities against blacks and recommend remedies. The committee's report, released in October 1947, showed that black Americans remained second-class citizens in every area of American life and called for change. In February

1948, he sent a 10-point civil rights program to Congress, the first presidential civil rights plan since Reconstruction. Then he moved forward even more aggressively. First he issued an executive order barring discrimination in the federal establishment. Then he ordered equality of treatment in the military services. Personnel needs in the Korean War broke down the last restrictions, particularly when the army found that integrated units performed well.

Baseball Superstar Jackie Robinson
Jackie Robinson's electrifying play as the first African American in the major leagues led to acceptance of the integration of baseball. A spectacular rookie season in 1947 opened the way for other African Americans who had earlier been limited to the Negro leagues. In this photo, taken at Ebbets Field in Brooklyn during the 1957 World Series, Robinson is about to steal home. What impression do you have of Robinson here?

(Time Life Pictures/Getty Images)

As the civil rights struggle gained momentum during the 1950s, the judicial system played a crucial role. The National Association for the Advancement of Colored People (NAACP) was determined to overturn the 1896 Supreme Court decision *Plessy* v. *Ferguson,* in which the Court had declared that segregation of the black and white races was constitutional if the facilities used by each were "separate but equal." The decree had been used for generations to sanction rigid segregation, primarily in the South, even though separate facilities were seldom, if ever, equal. A series of cases chipped away at the ruling.

Then in 1951, Oliver Brown, the father of 8-year-old Linda Brown, sued the school board of Topeka, Kansas, to allow his daughter to attend a school for white children that she passed as she walked to the bus that carried her to a black school farther away. The case reached the Supreme Court, which grouped several school segregation cases together.

On May 17, 1954, the Supreme Court released its bombshell ruling in *Brown* v. *Board of Education.* For more than a decade, Supreme Court decisions had gradually expanded black civil rights. Now the Court unanimously decreed that "separate facilities are inherently unequal" and concluded that the "separate but equal" doctrine had no place in public education. African Americans were elated. "The Supreme Court decision is the greatest victory for the Negro people since the Emancipation Proclamation," Harlem's *Amsterdam News* proclaimed. Author Ralph Ellison observed, "What a wonderful world of possibilities are unfolded for the children." A year later, the Court turned to the question of implementation and declared that local school boards, acting with the guidance of lower courts, should move "with all deliberate speed" to desegregate their facilities.

President Eisenhower had the ultimate responsibility for executing the law. Doubting that simple legislative changes could improve race relations, he once observed, "I don't believe you can change the hearts of men with laws or decisions." While he thought privately that the *Brown* ruling was wrong, he knew that it was his constitutional duty to see that the decision was carried out. He acted immediately to desegregate the Washington, D.C., schools as a model for the rest of the country. He also ordered desegregation in navy yards and veterans' hospitals.

The South resisted. The crucial confrontation came in Little Rock, Arkansas, in 1957. A desegregation plan, beginning with the token admission of a few black students to Central High School, was ready to go into effect. Just before the school year began, Governor Orval Faubus declared on television that it would not be possible to maintain order if integration took place. National Guardsmen, posted by the governor to keep the peace and armed with bayonets, turned away nine black students as they tried to enter the school. After three weeks, a federal court ordered the troops to leave. When the black children entered the building, the white students, spurred on by their elders, belligerently opposed them, chanting such slogans as "Two, four, six, eight, we ain't gonna integrate." In the face of hostile mobs, the black children left the school.

With the lines drawn, Ike knew that such resistance could not be tolerated, and he finally took the one action he had earlier called unthinkable. For the first time since the end of Reconstruction, an American president called out federal troops to protect the rights of black citizens. Eisenhower ordered paratroopers to Little Rock and placed National Guardsmen under federal command. The black children entered the school and attended classes with the military protecting their rights. Thus desegregation began.

Meanwhile, African Americans, encouraged by their churches, began organizing themselves to take direct action, and their efforts significantly advanced the civil rights movement. All were horrified by the brutal murder of Emmett Till, a 14-year-old boy from Chicago visiting Mississippi, who offended a white woman at a country store. Pictures of his mangled body in an open casket helped energize the effort to promote racial equality.

The catalyzing event occurred in Montgomery, Alabama, in December 1955. Rosa Parks, a 42-year-old black seamstress who was also secretary of the Montgomery branch of the NAACP, sat down in the front of a bus in a section reserved by custom for whites. When ordered to move back, the longtime activist refused to budge. The bus driver called the police at the next stop, and Parks was arrested for violating the segregation laws. E. D. Nixon, state NAACP president, told Parks, "This is the case we've been looking for. We can break this situation on the bus with your case." Fifty black leaders met to discuss the case and decided to organize a massive boycott of the bus system.

Martin Luther King, Jr., the 27-year-old minister of the Baptist church where the meeting was held, soon emerged as the preeminent spokesman of the protest. King was an impressive figure and an inspiring speaker. "There comes a time when people get tired . . . of being kicked about by the brutal feet of oppression," he declared. It was time to be more assertive, to cease being "patient with anything less than freedom and justice."

Although King, like others, was arrested on the trumped-up charge of speeding and jailed, grassroots support bubbled up. In Montgomery, 50,000 African Americans walked or formed car pools to avoid the transit system. Their actions cut gross revenue on city buses by 65 percent. Almost a year later, the Supreme Court ruled that bus segregation, like school segregation, violated the Constitution, and the boycott ended. But the mood it fostered continued, as ordinary black men and women challenged the racial status quo and forced both white and black leaders to respond.

Meanwhile, a concerted effort developed to guarantee black voting rights. The provisions of the Fifteenth Amendment notwithstanding, many states had circumvented the law for decades. Some states required a poll tax or a literacy test or an examination of constitutional understanding. Blacks often found themselves excluded from the polls.

Largely because of the legislative genius of Senate majority leader Lyndon B. Johnson of Texas, a civil rights bill, the first since Reconstruction, moved toward passage. Paring the bill down to the provisions he felt would pass, Johnson pushed the measure through.

The Civil Rights Act of 1957 created a Civil Rights Commission and empowered the Justice Department to

Civil Rights Leaders Martin Luther King, Jr., and Ralph Abernathy

Baptist minister Martin Luther King, Jr., emerged as the black spokesman in the Montgomery, Alabama, bus boycott and soon became the most eloquent African American leader of the entire civil rights movement. He was often jailed for his efforts, as shown in this picture of him sharing a cell with Ralph Abernathy, another civil rights leader. What effect did the jailing of King have on the larger movement?

(Bettmann/CORBIS)

go to court in cases in which blacks were denied the right to vote. The bill was a compromise measure, yet it was the first successful effort to protect civil rights in 82 years.

Again led by Johnson, Congress passed the Civil Rights Act of 1960. This new measure set stiffer penalties for people who interfered with the right to vote but again stopped short of authorizing federal registrars to register blacks to vote and so, like its predecessor, was generally ineffective.

Latinos on the Fringe

Latinos, like other groups, had similar difficulties in the postwar United States. Latino immigrants from Cuba, Puerto Rico, Mexico, and Central America, often unskilled and illiterate, followed other less fortunate Americans to the cities. The conditions they encountered there were similar to those faced by blacks. Author Piri Thomas, born of Puerto Rican and Cuban parents in New York City's Spanish Harlem, described standing "on the rooftop of my broken-down building at night," seeing "the stark naked truth of garbage-lepered streets." Despite those conditions, Spanish-speaking groups maintained a strong sense of group identity. The urban *barrios* where they settled preserved a sense of community and close-knit cohesive culture, even in the midst of pervasive poverty. The ties fostered in these communities provided a strong base for a growing political consciousness.

Chicanos, or Mexican Americans, were the most numerous of the newcomers and faced peculiar difficulties. During World War II, as the country experienced a labor shortage at home, American farmers sought Mexican *braceros* (helping hands) to harvest their crops. A program to encourage the seasonal immigration of farm workers continued after the war when the government signed a Migratory Labor Agreement with Mexico. Between 1948 and 1964, some 4.5 million Mexicans were brought to the United States for temporary work. *Braceros* were expected to return to Mexico at the end of their labor contract, but often they stayed. Joining them were millions more who entered the country illegally.

Conditions were harsh for the *braceros* in the best of times, but in periods of economic difficulty, troubles worsened. During a serious recession in 1953–1954, the government mounted Operation Wetback to deport illegal entrants and *braceros* who had remained in the country illegally and expelled 1.1 million. As immigration officials searched out illegal workers, all Chicanos found themselves vulnerable.

Operation Wetback did not end the reliance on poor Mexican farm laborers. A coalition of southern Democrats and conservative Republicans, mostly representing farm states, extended the Migratory Labor Agreement with Mexico, for the legislators wanted to continue to take advantage of the cheap labor. Two years after the massive deportations of 1954, a record 445,000 *braceros* crossed the border.

Puerto Ricans were numerous in other parts of the country. A steady stream of immigrants had been coming to New York from Puerto Rico since the 1920s. As the island's sugarcane economy became more mechanized, nearly 40 percent of the inhabitants left their homes. By the end of the 1960s, New York City had more Puerto Ricans than San Juan, the island's capital. El Barrio, in East Harlem, became the center of Puerto Rican activity, the home of *salsa* music and small *bodegas,* grocery stores that served the neighborhood. Author Guillermo Cotto-Thorner described the place fondly in his autobiographical novel, *Trópico en Manhattan,* through the words of Antonio, an older resident.

This . . . is our neighborhood, El Barrio. . . . It's said that we Latins run things here. . . . While the Americans take most of the money that circulates around here, we consider this part of the city to be ours. . . . The stores, barbershops, restaurants, butcher shops, churches, funeral parlors, greasy spoons, pool halls, everything is all Latino.

Puerto Ricans, like many other immigrants, hoped to earn money in America and then return home. Some did; others stayed. Like countless Latinos, most failed to enjoy the promise of the American dream.

Like African Americans, Latinos fought for their own rights. The roots of the Latino struggle dated back to the pre-World War II years. Chicanos established the American GI Forum because a Texas funeral home refused to bury a Mexican American casualty of World War II. When the group's protest led to a burial in Arlington National Cemetery, the possibilities of concerted action became clear. In the waning months of the war, a court case challenged Mexican American segregation in the schools. Gonzalo Méndez, an asparagus grower and a U.S. citizen who had lived in Orange County, California, for 25 years, filed suit to permit his children to attend the school reserved for Anglo-Americans, which was far more attractive than the Mexican one to which they had been assigned. A federal district court upheld his claim in the spring of 1945, and two years later, the circuit court affirmed the original ruling. With the favorable decision, other communities filed similar suits and began to press for integration of their schools. New organizations arose to struggle for equal rights. The Community Service Organization mobilized Chicanos against discrimination, as did the more radical Associación Nacional México-Americana. And the League of United Latin American Citizens continued reform efforts.

Confrontations continued. Los Angeles, with its large number of Chicanos, was the scene of numerous unsavory racial episodes. In mid-1951, on receiving a complaint about a loud record player, police officers raided a baptismal gathering at the home of Simon Fuentes. Breaking into the house without a warrant, they assaulted the members of the party. In the "Bloody Christmas" case at the end of the year, officers removed seven Mexican Americans from jail cells and beat them severely.

Chicano activism in the 1950s was fragmented. Some Mexican Americans considered their situation hopeless. More effective mobilization had to await another day.

The Native American Struggle

Native Americans likewise remained outsiders in the postwar years. Years of persistent discrimination made it even harder to cope with the changes they faced. As power lines reached their reservations, Indians purchased televisions, refrigerators, washing machines, and automobiles. As they partook of the consumer culture, old patterns inevitably changed. Reservation life lost its cohesiveness, and alcohol became a major problem. With good jobs unavailable on the reservations, more and more Indians gravitated to the cities. Bennie Bearskin, a Winnebago, left home for Chicago in 1947, explaining: "The most important reason was that I could at least feel confident that [I could get] perhaps fifty paychecks a year here.... Even though it might be more pleasant to be back home, for instance, Nebraska." But Indians who moved to the cities often had difficulty adjusting to urban life and frequently faced hostility from white Americans.

Native Americans, like Latinos, began their own struggle for equality. They achieved an important victory just after the end of World War II when Congress established the Indian Claims Commission. Hundreds of tribal suits charging that ancestral lands had been illegally seized could now be filed against the government in federal courts. Many of them led to large settlements of cash—a form of reparation for past injustices—and sometimes the return of long-lost lands.

In the 1950s, federal Indian policy shifted course. As part of its effort to limit the role of the national government, the Eisenhower administration turned

Troubles for Native American Veterans

After returning home at the end of World War II, many Native American veterans found it difficult to fit into either Native American or white society. Alcoholism—which sometimes led to confrontations with the law—became a problem, as reflected in this sketch by Native American artist Aaron Yava, who drew what he saw in what he called the "border towns of the Navajo Nation." What might have caused such confrontations?

(Courtesy of the family of Aaron Yava)

away from the New Deal policy of government support for tribal autonomy. In 1953, instead of trying to encourage Native American self-government, the administration adopted a new approach, known as "termination." The government proposed settling all outstanding claims and eliminating reservations as legitimate political entities. To encourage their assimilation into mainstream society, families who would leave the reservations and move to cities were offered small subsidies by the government.

The new policy infuriated Native Americans. Earl Old Person, a Blackfoot elder, declared: "It is important to note that in our Indian language the only translation for termination is to 'wipe out' or 'kill off'... How can we plan our future when the Indian Bureau threatens to wipe us out as a race? It is like trying to cook a meal in your tipi when someone is standing outside trying to burn the tipi down." With their lands no longer federally protected and their members deprived of treaty rights, many tribes became unwitting victims of people who wanted to seize their land. Though promising more freedom, the new policy caused great disruption as the government terminated tribes such as the Klamath in Oregon, the Menominee in Wisconsin, the Alabama and Coushatta in Texas, and bands of Paiute in Utah.

The policy increased Indian activism. The National Congress of American Indians mobilized opposition to the federal program. A Seminole petition to the president in 1954 summed up a general view:

> We do not say that we are superior or inferior to the White Man and we do not say that the White Man is superior or inferior to us. We do say that we are not White Men but Indians, do not wish to become White Men but wish to remain Indians, and have an outlook on all things different from the outlook of the White Man.

Not only did the termination policy foster a sense of Indian identity, but it also sparked a dawning awareness among whites of the Indians' right to maintain their heritage. In 1958, the Eisenhower administration changed the policy of termination so that it required a tribe's consent. The policy continued to have the force of law, but implementation ceased.

Asian American Advances

For Asian Americans, conditions improved somewhat in the aftermath of World War II. The war against Nazism eroded the racism that proclaimed a commitment to white superiority. Japanese Americans, ravaged by their devastating internment during the war, fought back after the struggle. In 1946, a measure supporting a wartime law confiscating Japanese American

Timeline

1946	4.6 million workers on strike
	ENIAC computer built
	Benjamin Spock, *Baby and Child Care*
	Employment Act
1947	Defense budget of $13 billion
	Taft–Hartley Act
	Jackie Robinson breaks the color line in major league baseball
1948	GM offers UAW cost-of-living adjustment
	Transistor developed at Bell Laboratories
	Alfred C. Kinsey, *Sexual Behavior in the Human Male*
	"Dixiecrat" party formed
	Truman defeats Dewey
1949	Truman launches Fair Deal
1950s	Each year a million farmers leave farms
1950	Diner's Club card inaugurated
	Associación Nacional México-Americana formed
1951	J. D. Salinger, *The Catcher in the Rye*
1952	Dwight D. Eisenhower elected president
1953	Defense budget of $47 billion
	Operation Wetback begins
	Submerged Lands Act
1954	Congress adds "under God" to pledge to flag
	Brown v. *Board of Education*
1955	First McDonald's opens in Illinois
	Merger of AFL and CIO
	Congress adds "In God We Trust" to currency
	Montgomery, Alabama, bus boycott begins
	Allen Ginsberg, "Howl"—written and read
1956	Interstate Highway Act
	Majority of U.S. workers hold white-collar jobs
	Eisenhower reelected
1957	Baby boom peaks
	Jack Kerouac, *On the Road*
	Little Rock, Arkansas, school integration crisis
	Civil Rights Act
1960	Three-quarters of all American families own a TV set
	Civil Rights Act
1962	Michael Harrington, *The Other America*
1963	California passes New York as most populous state
	Betty Friedan, *The Feminine Mystique*
1964	Peter Blake, *God's Own Junkyard*

property appeared on the ballot in California. But a spirited campaign by the Japanese American Citizens League reminding voters of the contributions of Japanese American soldiers during the war led to the measure's overwhelming defeat. Two years later, the Supreme Court, noting that the law itself, still on the books was "nothing more than outright racial discrimination," declared it unconstitutional.

In 1952, the Immigration and Nationality Act, also known as the McCarran–Walter Act, eased immigration quotas. Although the basic framework of the National Origins Act of 1924 remained intact, it removed the longstanding ban on Japanese immigration and made first-generation Japanese immigrants eligible for citizenship. It also established a quota of 100 immigrants a year from each Asian country. While that number was tiny compared to those admitted annually from northern and western Europe, the measure was a first step in ending the discriminatory exclusion of the past.

By the 1950s, many second- and third-generation Chinese, Japanese, and Koreans had moved into white-collar work. Promoting education for their children, they became part of the growing middle class, hoping like others to enjoy the benefits of the American dream.

Conclusion

QUALMS AMID AFFLUENCE

In general, the United States during the decade and a half after World War II was stable and secure. Structural adjustments caused occasional moments of friction but were seldom visible in prosperous times. Recessions occurred periodically, but the economy righted itself after short downturns. For the most part, business boomed. The standard of living for many of the nation's citizens reached new heights, especially compared with standards in other parts of the world. Millions of middle-class Americans joined the ranks of suburban property owners, enjoying the benefits of shopping centers, fast-food establishments, and other

material manifestations of what they considered the good life. Workers found themselves savoring the materialistic advantages of the era. The political world reflected prosperous times.

Some Americans did not share in the prosperity, but they were not visible in the affluent suburbs. Many African Americans and members of other minority groups were seriously disadvantaged, although they still believed they could share in the American dream and remained confident that deeply rooted patterns of discrimination could be changed. Even when they began to mobilize, their protest was peaceful at first.

Beneath the calm surface, though, there were signs of discontent. The seeds for the protest movements of the 1960s had already been sown. Disquieting signs were likewise evident on other fronts. The divorce rate increased as one-third of all marriages in the 1950s broke apart. Americans increasingly used newly developed tranquilizers in an effort to cope with problems in their lives. Some Americans began to criticize the materialism that seemed to undermine American efforts in the Cold War. Such criticisms in turn legitimized challenges by other groups, in the continuing struggle to make the realities of American life match the nation's ideals.

Criticisms and anxieties notwithstanding, the United States—for most whites and for some people of color—continued to develop according to Ray Kroc's dreams as he first envisioned McDonald's establishments across the land. Healthy and comfortable, upper- and middle-class Americans expected prosperity and growth to continue in the years ahead.

QUESTIONS FOR REVIEW AND REFLECTION

1. What were the sources of American prosperity?
2. Who prospered most in the postwar United States?
3. Who was left out?
4. To what degree did conformity become the norm in the postwar United States?
5. How would you characterize the broad social and economic changes that took place in America in the years after World War II?

CHAPTER 27

Chills and Fever During the Cold War, 1945–1960

The Cold War was closely connected to the nuclear arms race. The spectacular mushroom cloud, like the one created by this hydrogen blast at Eniwetok in the Pacific in 1952, was beautiful but frightening at the same time.

(National Archives)

American Stories

A Government Employee Confronts the Anti-Communist Crusade

Val Lorwin was in France in November 1950 when he learned of the charges against him. A State Department employee on leave of absence after 16 years of government service, he was in Paris working on a book. Now he had to return to the United States to defend himself against the accusation that he was a member of the Communist party and thus a loyalty and security risk. It seemed to him a tasteless joke. Yet communism was no laughing matter in the United States. Suspicions of the Soviet Union had escalated after 1945, and a wave of paranoia swept through the United States.

Lorwin was an unlikely candidate to be caught up in the fallout of the Cold War. He had begun to work for the government in 1935, serving in a number of New Deal agencies, then in the Labor Department and on the War Production Board before he was drafted during World War II. While in the army, he was assigned to the Office of Strategic Services, an early intelligence agency, and he was frequently granted security clearances.

Lorwin, however, did have a left-wing past as an active socialist in the 1930s. His social life then had revolved around Socialist party causes, particularly the unionization of southern tenant farmers and the provision of aid to the unemployed. He and his wife, Madge, drafted statements and stuffed envelopes to support their goals. But that activity was wholly open and legal, and Lorwin had from the start been aggressively anti-Communist in political affairs.

Suddenly, Lorwin, like others in the period, faced a nightmare. Despite his spotless record, Lorwin was told that an unnamed accuser had identified him as a Communist. The burden of proof was entirely on him, and the chance of clearing his name was slim. He was entitled to a hearing if he chose, or he could resign.

Lorwin requested a hearing, and one was held late in 1950. Still struck by the absurdity of the situation, he refuted all accusations but made little effort to cite his own positive achievements. At the conclusion, he was informed that the government no longer doubted his loyalty but considered him a security risk, likewise grounds for dismissal from his job.

When he appealed the judgment, Lorwin was again denied access to the identity of his accuser. This time, however, he thoroughly prepared his defense. At the hearing, 97 witnesses either spoke under oath on Lorwin's behalf or left sworn written depositions testifying to his good character and meritorious service.

The issues in the hearings might have been considered comic in view of Lorwin's record, had not a man's reputation been at stake. The accuser had once lived with the Lorwins in Washington, D.C. Fifteen years later, he claimed that in 1935 Lorwin had revealed that he was holding a Communist party meeting in his home and had even shown him a party card.

Lorwin proved all the charges groundless. He also showed that in 1935 the Socialist party card was red, the color the accuser reported seeing, while the Communist party card was black. In March 1952, Lorwin was finally cleared for both loyalty and security.

Lorwin's troubles were not yet over. His name appeared on one of the lists produced by Senator Joseph McCarthy of Wisconsin, the most aggressive anti-Communist of the era, and the next year, Lorwin was indicted for making false statements to the State Department Loyalty-Security Board. The charges this time proved as specious as before. Finally, in May 1954, admitting that its special prosecutor had deliberately lied to the grand jury and had no legitimate case, the Justice Department asked for dismissal of the indictment. Cleared at last, Lorwin went on to become a distinguished labor historian.

Val Lorwin was more fortunate than some victims of the anti-Communist crusade. Caught up in a global conflict that engulfed most of the world, he managed to weather a catastrophe that threatened to shatter his life. People rallied around him and gave him valuable support. Despite considerable emotional cost, he survived the witch hunt of the early 1950s, but his case still reflected vividly the ugly domestic consequences of the breakdown in relations between the Soviet Union and the United States.

The Cold War, which unfolded soon after the end of World War II and lasted for nearly 50 years, powerfully affected all aspects of American life. Rejecting for good the isolationist impulse that had governed foreign policy in the 1920s and 1930s, the United States began to play a major role in the world in the postwar years. Doubts about intervention in other lands faded as the nation acknowledged its dominant international position and resolved to do whatever was necessary to maintain it. The same sense of mission that had infused the United States in the Spanish-American War, World War I, and World War II now appeared in a revived evangelical faith and committed most Americans to the struggle against communism at home and abroad.

This chapter explores that continuing sense of mission and its consequences. It examines the roots of the Cold War both in the idealistic aim to keep the world safe for democracy and in the pursuit of economic self-interest that had long fueled American capitalism. It records how the determination to prevent the spread of communism led American policymakers to consider vast parts of the world as pivotal to American security and to act accordingly, particularly in Korea and Vietnam. It notes the impact on economic development, particularly in the West, where the mighty defense industry flourished. And it considers the tragic consequences of the effort to promote ideological unity in a rigid and doctrinaire version of the American dream that led to excesses threatening the principles of democracy itself.

Origins of the Cold War

The Cold War developed by degrees. It stemmed from divergent views about dominance of the post–World War II world as the colonial empires in Asia, Africa, and the Middle East began to crumble. The United States, strong and secure, was intent on spreading its vision of freedom and free trade around the world to maintain its economic hegemony. The Soviet Union, concerned about security after a devastating war, demanded politically sympathetic neighbors on its borders to preserve its own autonomy. Suppressed during World War II, these differences now surfaced in a virulent Soviet–American confrontation.

The American Stance

The United States emerged from World War II more powerful than any nation ever before, and it sought to use that might to achieve a world order that could sustain American aims. American policymakers, following in Woodrow Wilson's footsteps, hoped to spread the values—liberty, equality, and democracy—underpinning the American dream. They did not always recognize that what they considered universal truths were rooted in specific historical circumstances in their own country and might not flourish elsewhere.

At the same time, American leaders sought a world where economic enterprise could thrive. With the American economy operating at full speed as a result of the war, world markets were needed once the fighting stopped. Government officials wanted to eliminate trade barriers—imposed by the Soviet Union and other nations—to provide outlets for industrial products and for surplus farm commodities such as wheat, cotton, and tobacco. As the largest source of goods for world markets, with exports totaling $14 billion in 1947, the United States required open channels for growth to continue. Americans assumed that their prosperity would benefit the rest of the world, even when other nations disagreed.

Soviet Aims

The Soviet Union formulated its own goals after World War II. Russia had usually been governed in the past by a strongly centralized, sometimes autocratic, government, and that tradition—as much as Communist ideology, with its stress on class struggle and the inevitable triumph of a proletarian state—guided Soviet policy.

During the war, the Russians had played down talk of world revolution, which they knew their allies found threatening, and had mobilized domestic support with nationalistic appeals. As the struggle drew to a close, the Soviets still said little about world conquest, emphasizing socialism within the nation itself.

Rebuilding was the first priority. Devastated by the war, Soviet agriculture and industry lay in shambles. But revival required internal security. At the same time, the Russians felt vulnerable along their western flank. Such anxieties had a historical basis, for in the early nineteenth century, Napoleon had reached the gates of Moscow. Twice in the twentieth century, invasions had come from the west, most recently when Hitler had attacked in 1941. Haunted by fears of a quick German recovery, the Soviets demanded defensible borders and neighboring regimes sympathetic to Russian aims. They insisted on military and political stability in the regions nearby.

Early Cold War Leadership

Both the United States and the Soviet Union had strong leadership in the early years of the Cold War. On the American side, presidents Harry Truman and Dwight Eisenhower accepted the centralization of authority Franklin Roosevelt had begun, as the executive branch became increasingly powerful in guiding foreign policy. In the Soviet Union, first Joseph Stalin, then Nikita Khrushchev provided equally forceful direction.

Truman and Eisenhower paid close attention to the Cold War struggle with the Soviet Union. Both subscribed to traditional American attitudes about self-determination and the superiority of American political institutions and values. Both were determined to stand firm in the face of the Soviet threat.

As World War II drew to an end, Truman grew increasingly hostile to Soviet actions. Viewing collaboration as a wartime necessity, he was uncomfortable with what he felt were Soviet designs in Eastern Europe and Asia as the struggle wound down. It was now time, he said, "to stand up to the

Soviet Propaganda

Joseph Stalin's autocratic approach to foreign and domestic affairs affronted American sensibilities. The Russian caption on this Soviet propaganda poster reads: "Under the Leadership of the Great Stalin—Forward to Communism!" What image does Stalin convey in this image?

(Hoover Institution Archives, Stanford, CA Russian & Soviet Poster Collection)

ПОД ВОДИТЕЛЬСТВОМ ВЕЛИКОГО СТАЛИНА—ВПЕРЕД К КОММУНИЗМУ!

Russians" before they solidified positions in various parts of the world.

Like Truman, Eisenhower saw communism as a monolithic force struggling for world supremacy and agreed that the Kremlin in Moscow was orchestrating subversive activity around the globe. Yet Eisenhower was more willing than Truman to practice accommodation when it served his ends.

Joseph Stalin, the Soviet leader at war's end, possessed almost absolute powers. He looked, in the words of one American diplomat, like "an old battle-scarred tiger." He had presided over ruthless purges against his opponents in the 1930s. Now he was determined to do whatever was necessary to rebuild Soviet society, if possible with Western assistance, and to keep Eastern Europe within the Russian sphere of influence.

Stalin's death in March 1953 left a power vacuum in Soviet political affairs that was eventually filled by Nikita Khrushchev, who by 1958 held the offices of both prime minister and party secretary. A crude man, Khrushchev once used his shoe to pound a table at the United Nations. During Khrushchev's regime, the Cold War continued, but for brief periods of time Soviet–American relations became less hostile.

Disillusionment with the USSR

American support for the Soviet Union faded quickly after the war. In September 1945, 54 percent of a national sample trusted the Russians to cooperate with the Americans in the postwar years. Two months later, the figure dropped to 44 percent, and by February 1946, to 35 percent.

As Americans soured on Russia, they began to equate the Nazi and Soviet systems. Just as they had in the 1930s, authors, journalists, and public officials pointed to similarities, some of them legitimate, between the regimes. Both states, they contended, maintained total control over communications and could eliminate political opposition. Both states used terror to silence dissidents, and Stalin's labor camps in Siberia could be compared with Hitler's concentration camps. After the U.S. publication in 1949 of George Orwell's frightening novel *1984*, *Life* magazine noted in an editorial that the ominous figure Big Brother was but a "mating" of Hitler and Stalin. Truman spoke for many Americans when he said in 1950 that "there isn't any difference between the totalitarian Russian government and the Hitler government. . . . They are all alike."

The lingering sense that the nation had not been quick enough to resist totalitarian aggression in the 1930s heightened American fears. Many people believed that the free world had not responded promptly when the Germans, Italians, and Japanese first caused international trouble and were determined never to repeat the same mistake.

The Troublesome Polish Question

The first clash between East and West came, even before the war ended, over Poland. Soviet demands for a government willing to accept Russian influence clashed with American hopes for a more representative structure patterned after the Western model. The Yalta Conference of February 1945 provided a loosely worded and correspondingly imprecise agreement (see Chapter 25), and when Truman assumed office, the Polish situation remained unresolved.

Truman's unbending stance on Poland was made clear in an April 1945 meeting with Soviet foreign minister Vyacheslav Molotov. Concerned that the Russians were breaking the Yalta agreements, fluid as they were, the American leader demanded a new democratic government there. Though Molotov appeared conciliatory, Truman insisted on Russian acquiescence. Truman later recalled that when Molotov protested, "I have never been talked to like that in my life," he himself retorted bluntly, "Carry out your agreements and you won't get talked to like that." Such bluntness contributed to the deterioration of Soviet–American relations.

Truman and Stalin met face-to-face for the first (and last) time at the Potsdam Conference in July 1945, the final wartime meeting of the United States, the Soviet Union, and Great Britain. There, outside devastated Berlin, the U.S. and Soviet leaders sized each other up as they considered the Russian–Polish boundary, the fate of Germany, and the American desire to obtain an unconditional surrender from Japan. It was Truman's first exposure to international diplomacy at the highest level, and it left him confident of his abilities. When he learned during the meeting of the first successful atomic bomb test in New Mexico, he became even more determined to insist that the Soviets behave in the ways he wished.

Economic Pressure on the USSR

One major source of controversy in the last stages of World War II was the question of U.S. aid to its allies. Responding to congressional pressure at home to limit foreign assistance as hostilities ended, Truman acted impulsively. Six days after V-E Day signaled the end of the European war in May 1945, he issued an executive order cutting off lend-lease supplies to the Allies. Ships heading for allied ports had to turn back in mid-ocean. Though the policy affected all nations receiving aid, it hurt the Soviet Union most of all.

The United States intended to use economic pressure in other ways as well. The USSR desperately needed financial assistance to rebuild after the war and, in January 1945, had requested a $6 billion loan. Roosevelt hedged, hoping to win concessions in return. In August, four months after FDR's death, the Russians renewed their application, but this time for only $1 billion. Truman dragged his heels, seeking to use the loan as a lever to gain access to markets in areas traditionally dominated by the Soviet Union. The United States first claimed to have lost the Soviet request, then in March 1946 indicated a willingness to consider the matter—but only if Russia pledged "nondiscrimination in world commerce." Stalin refused the offer and launched his own five-year plan instead.

Declaring the Cold War

As Soviet–American relations deteriorated, both sides stepped up their rhetorical attacks. In 1946, Stalin spoke out first, arguing that capitalism and communism were on a collision course, that a series of cataclysmic disturbances would tear the capitalist world apart, and that the Soviet system would inevitably triumph. Stalin's speech was a stark and ominous statement that worried the West. Supreme Court justice William O. Douglas called it the "declaration of World War III."

The response to Stalin's speech came not from an American but from England's former prime minister, Winston Churchill. Speaking in Fulton, Missouri, in 1946, with Truman on the platform during the address, Churchill declared that "from Stettin in the Baltic to Trieste in the Adriatic, an iron curtain has descended across the Continent." To counter the threat, he urged that a vigilant association of English-speaking peoples work to contain Soviet designs.

Containing the Soviet Union

Containment formed the basis of postwar American policy. While the fledgling United Nations, established in 1945, might have provided a forum to ease tensions, both the United States and the Soviet Union acted unilaterally, and with the aid of allies, in pursuit of their own ends.

Containment Defined

George F. Kennan, chargé d'affaires at the American embassy in the Soviet Union and an expert on Soviet matters, was primarily responsible for defining the new policy of containment. After Stalin's speech in February 1946, Kennan sent an 8,000-word telegram to the State Department. In it he argued that Soviet hostility stemmed from the "Kremlin's neurotic view of world affairs," which in turn came from the "traditional and instinctive Russian sense of insecurity." The stiff Soviet stance was not so much a response to American actions as a reflection of the Russian leaders' own efforts to maintain their autocratic rule. Russian fanaticism would not soften, regardless of how accommodating American policy became. Therefore, it had to be opposed at every turn.

Kennan's "long telegram" struck a resonant chord in Washington. Soon he published an extended analysis, under the pseudonym "Mr. X," in the prominent journal *Foreign Affairs*. "The whole Soviet governmental machine, including the mechanism of diplomacy," he wrote, "moves inexorably along the prescribed path, like a persistent toy automobile wound up and headed in a given direction, stopping only when it meets with some unanswerable force."

Many Americans agreed with Kennan that Soviet pressure had to "be contained by the adroit and vigilant application of counter-force at a series of constantly shifting geographical and political points." The concept of containment provided the philosophical justification for the hard-line stance the United States adopted.

The First Step: The Truman Doctrine

The Truman Doctrine represented the first major application of containment policy. The Soviet Union was pressuring Turkey for joint control of the Dardanelles, the passage between the Black Sea and the Mediterranean. Meanwhile, a civil war in Greece pitted Communist elements against the ruling English-aided right-wing monarchy. Revolutionary pressures threatened to topple the Greek government.

In February 1947, Britain, still reeling from the war, informed the State Department that it could no longer give Greece and Turkey economic and military aid. Truman administration officials willing to move into the void knew they needed bipartisan support to accomplish such a major policy shift. A conservative Congress wanted smaller budgets and lower taxes rather than massive and expensive aid programs. Senator Arthur Vandenberg of Michigan, a key Republican, aware of the need for bipartisanship, told top policymakers that they had to begin "scaring hell out of the country" if they wanted support for a bold new containment policy.

Undersecretary of State Dean Acheson took the lead. Meeting with congressional leaders, he declared that "like apples in a barrel infected by one rotten one, the corruption of Greece would infect Iran and all to the east." He warned ominously that a Communist victory would "open three continents to Soviet penetration." The major powers were now "met at Armageddon," as the Soviet Union pressed forward. Only the United States had the power to resist.

On March 12, 1947, Truman told Congress, in a statement that came to be known as the Truman Doctrine, "I believe that it must be the policy of the United States to support free peoples who are resisting subjugation by armed minorities or by outside pressures." Unless the United States acted, the free world might not survive. To avert that calamity, he urged Congress to appropriate $400 million for military and economic aid to Turkey and Greece.

Not everyone approved of Truman's request. Autocratic regimes controlled Greece and Turkey, some observers pointed out. And where was the proof that Stalin had a hand in the Greek conflict? Others warned that the United States could not by itself stop communist encroachment in all parts of the world. Nonetheless, Congress passed Truman's foreign aid bill. In assuming that Americans could police the globe, the Truman Doctrine was a major step in the advent of the Cold War.

The Next Steps: The Marshall Plan, NATO, and NSC-68

The next step for American policymakers involved sending extensive economic aid for postwar recovery in Western Europe. At the war's end, most of Europe was economically and politically unstable, thereby offering inviting opportunities for communism to take hold. In

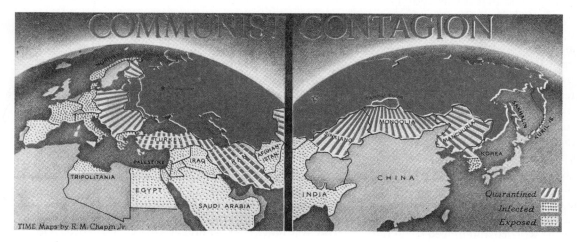

The Contagion of Communism

Americans in the early postwar years were afraid that communism was a contagious disease spreading around the globe. In this picture from the spring of 1946, *Time* magazine pictured the relentless spread of an infection that would need to be contained. Why would such a map seem frightening to people who looked at it?

(© 1946 Time, Inc. Reprinted by permission.) (The Art Archive)

France and Italy, large Communist parties grew stronger and refused to cooperate with established governments. In such circumstances, U.S. officials believed, the Soviet Union might easily intervene. Decisive action was needed, for as the new secretary of state, George Marshall, declared, "The patient is sinking while the doctors deliberate." Bolstering the European economy to provide markets for American goods provided another motive for action. Excellent customers earlier, Western Europeans in the aftermath of the war were able to purchase less at a time when the United States was producing more.

Marshall revealed the administration's willingness to assist European recovery in a Harvard University commencement address in June 1947. He asked all troubled European nations to draw up an aid program that the United States could support, a program "directed not against any country or doctrine but against hunger, poverty, desperation, and chaos." Soviet-bloc countries were welcome to participate, Marshall announced, aware that their involvement was unlikely since they would have to disclose economic records to join.

The proposed program would assist the ravaged nations, provide the United States with needed markets, and advance the nation's ideological aims. The Marshall Plan and the Truman Doctrine, Truman noted, were "two halves of the same walnut."

Responding quickly to Marshall's invitation, the Western European nations worked out the details of massive requests. In early 1948, Congress committed $13 billion over a period of four years to 16 cooperating nations. But not all Americans supported the Marshall Plan. Henry A. Wallace, former vice president and secretary of agriculture, called the scheme the "Martial Plan" and argued that it was another step toward war. Some members of Congress feared spreading American resources too thin. But most legislators approved, and the containment policy moved forward another step.

Closely related to the Marshall Plan was a concerted Western effort to integrate a rebuilt Germany into a reviving Europe. At the war's end, Allied leaders had agreed to divide the defeated Nazi nation and its capital, Berlin, into four occupation zones (Soviet, American, British, and French). Allied leaders intended the division of both Germany and Berlin to be temporary, until a permanent peace treaty could be signed, but the lines of demarcation became rigid. With the onset of the Cold War and the growing Soviet domination of Eastern Europe, the West became worried and moved to fill the vacuum in Central Europe to counter the Russian threat. In late 1946, the Americans and British merged their zones for economic purposes and began assigning administrative duties to Germans. By mid-1947, despite French fears of a resurgent Germany, the process of rebuilding German industry in the combined Western

sector was underway. Meanwhile, increasingly rigid separation divided Berlin into two separate cities.

The Soviet Union was furious at what it regarded as a violation of the wartime agreement to act together. In mid-1948, the Soviets became irritated at an effort to introduce a new currency for the combined Western zones, a first step toward the creation of a separate West German nation, that would include the western part of divided Berlin, located within the Soviet-controlled eastern part of Germany. A crisis erupted when the Soviets attempted to force the Western powers out of Berlin by refusing to allow them land access to their part of the city and banning all shipments through eastern Germany. In what became known as the Berlin airlift, the United States and the British Royal Air Force flew supplies to the beleaguered Berliners. Over the next year, more than 200,000 flights provided 13,000 tons daily of food, fuel, and other necessary materials. The airlift proved to be a public relations disaster for the Soviet Union, a triumph for the West. The Soviets finally ended the blockade, but Berlin remained a focal point of conflict, and there were now two separate German states: the Federal Republic of Germany, or West Germany, and the German Democratic Republic, or East Germany.

The next major link in the containment strategy was the creation of a military alliance in Europe in 1949 to complement the economic program. After the Soviets tightened their control of Hungary and Czechoslovakia, the United States took the lead in establishing the North Atlantic Treaty Organization (NATO). Twelve nations formed the alliance, vowing that an attack against any one member would be considered an attack against all, to be met by appropriate armed force.

The Senate, long opposed to such military pacts, approved this time. In his presidential farewell address in 1796, George Washington had warned against "entangling alliances," and the United States had long heeded his warning. Now the nation established its first military treaty ties with Europe since the American Revolution. Congress also voted military aid for its NATO allies. The Cold War had softened long-standing American reluctance to become closely involved in European affairs.

Two dramatic events in 1949—the Communist victory in the Chinese civil war and the Russian detonation of an atomic device—shocked the United States. The Communist victory in China was frightening enough, but the erosion of the American atomic monopoly was horrifying. Although American scientists had understood that, once the secret of the atom had been unlocked, the Soviets would be able to create a bomb of their own in several years, many top policymakers believed it would take the less technologically advanced Russians at least a decade and a half to do so. President Truman thought they might never be able to accomplish such a feat at all. In September 1949, an air force reconnaissance plane picked up air samples with a radioactivity content that revealed the Soviets had tested their own bomb, just four years after the United States had ushered in the atomic age. Now a nuclear arms race beckoned. Truman requested a full-fledged review of U.S. foreign and defense policy. The National Security Council, organized in 1947 to provide policy coordination, produced a document called NSC-68, which shaped U.S. policy for the next 20 years.

NSC-68 built on the Cold War rhetoric of the Truman Doctrine, describing challenges facing the United States in cataclysmic terms. "The issues that face us are momentous," the paper said, "involving the fulfillment or destruction not only of this Republic but of civilization itself." Conflict between East and West, the document assumed, was unavoidable, for amoral Soviet objectives ran totally counter to U.S. aims. Negotiation was useless, for the Soviets could never be trusted to bargain in good faith.

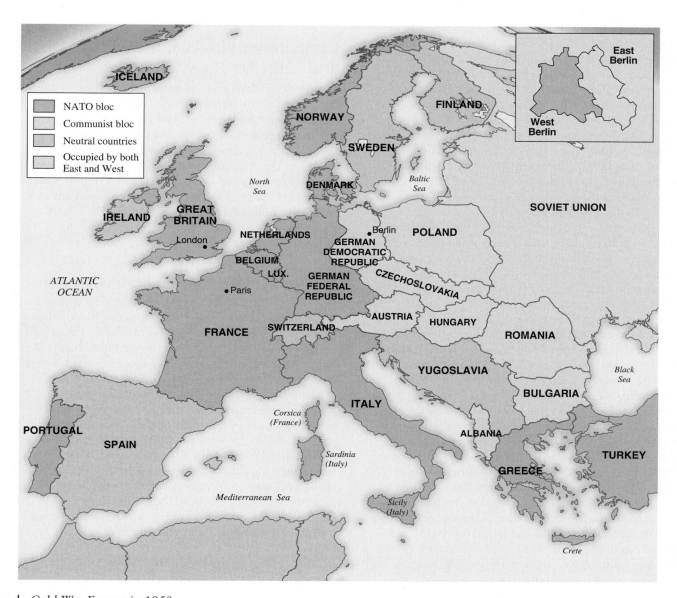

Cold War Europe in 1950

This map shows the rigid demarcation between East and West during the Cold War. Although there were a number of neutral countries in Europe, the other nations found themselves in a standoff, as each side tried to contain the possible advances of the other. The small insert map in the upper right-hand corner shows the division of Berlin that paralleled the division of Germany itself after World War II. How widespread was the policy of neutrality in Cold War Europe? How powerful was the NATO bloc? How easily could one side move against the other in divided Europe?

NSC-68 then argued that if the United States hoped to meet the Soviet challenge, it must increase defense spending from the $13 billion set for 1950 to as much as $50 billion per year and increase the percentage of its budget allotted to defense from 5 percent to 20 percent. The costs were huge but necessary if the free world was to survive.

Containment in the 1950s

Containment, the keystone of American policy throughout the Truman years, was the rationale for the Truman Doctrine, the Marshall Plan, NATO, and NSC-68. Because this policy required detailed and up-to-date information about Communist moves, the government relied increasingly on the Central Intelligence Agency (CIA). Established by the National Security Act of 1947, the CIA conducted espionage in foreign lands, some of it visible, more of it secret. With President Eisenhower's approval, by 1957, 80 percent of the CIA's budget went toward covert activities. More and more, Eisenhower relied on clandestine CIA actions to undermine foreign governments, subsidize friendly newspapers in distant lands, and assist those who supported the U.S. stance in the Cold War.

The civil rights movement that was gaining momentum in the 1950s also affected Cold War policy. American policymakers were aware of the impact of stories about racial discrimination in other nations, particularly nations moving toward independence in sub-Saharan Africa. In propaganda aimed abroad, U.S. leaders sought to portray the domestic civil rights movement in the best possible light.

At the same time, the administration reassessed the impact of the containment policy itself, especially in light of criticism that it was too cautious to counter the threat of communism. For most of Eisenhower's two terms, John Foster Dulles was secretary of state. A devout Presbyterian, he sought to move beyond containment and to counter the "Godless terrorism" of communism with a holy crusade to promote democracy and to free the countries under Soviet domination. Instead of advocating containment, the United States should make it "publicly known that it wants and expects liberation to occur." Dulles also advocated immediate retaliation in the face of hostile Soviet ventures: "There is one solution and only one: that is for the free world to develop the will and organize the means to retaliate instantly against open aggression by Red armies, so that, if it occurred anywhere, we could and would strike back where it hurts, by means of our own choosing."

Eisenhower's own rhetoric was equally strong. In his 1953 inaugural address, he declared, "Forces of good and evil are massed and armed and opposed as rarely before in history. Freedom is pitted against slavery, lightness against the dark." Yet he was more conciliatory than Dulles and recognized the impossibility of changing the governments of the USSR's satellites. In mid-1953, when East Germans mounted anti-Soviet demonstrations, in a challenge that foreshadowed the revolt against communism three and a half decades later, the United States maintained its distance. In 1956, when Hungarian "freedom fighters" rose up against Russian domination, the United States again stood back as Soviet forces smashed the rebels. Because Western action could have precipitated a more general conflict, Eisenhower refused to translate rhetoric into action. Throughout the 1950s, the policy of containment remained in effect.

Containment in Asia, the Middle East, and Latin America

In a dramatic departure from its history of noninvolvement, the United States extended the policy of containment to meet challenges around the globe. Colonial empires were disintegrating, and countries seeking and attaining their independence now found themselves caught in the midst of the superpower struggle. In Asia, the Middle East, and Latin America, the United States discovered the tremendous appeal of communism as a social and political system in emerging nations and found that ever-greater efforts were required to advance American aims.

The Shock of the Chinese Revolution

The Communist victory in the Chinese civil war in 1949 strengthened the U.S. commitment to global containment. An ally during World War II, China had struggled against the Japanese, while simultaneously fighting a bitter civil war deeply rooted in the Chinese past—in widespread poverty, disease, oppression by the landlord class, and national humiliation at the hands of foreign powers. Mao Zedong (Mao Tse-tung)*, founder of a branch of the Communist party, gathered followers who wished to reshape China in a distinctive Marxist mold. Opposing the Communists were the Nationalists, led by Jiang Jieshi (Chiang Kai-shek) who wanted to preserve their power and governmental leadership. By the early 1940s, Jiang's inefficient and corrupt regime was exhausted. Mao's movement, meanwhile, grew stronger during the Second World War as Mao opposed the Japanese invaders and won the loyalty of Chinese peasants. Mao finally prevailed, as Jiang fled in 1949 to the island of Taiwan (Formosa).

---

*Chinese names are rendered in their modern *pinyin* spelling. At first occurrence, the older but perhaps more familiar spelling (usually Wade-Giles) is given in parentheses.

PUBLIC OPINION POLLS

In recent years, historians have used a new source of evidence: the public opinion poll. People have always been concerned with what others think, and leaders have often sought to frame their behavior according to the preferences of the populace. As techniques of assessing the mind of the public have become more sophisticated, the poll has emerged as an integral part of the analysis of social and political life. Polls now measure opinion on many questions—social, cultural, intellectual, political, and diplomatic. Because of polls' increasing importance, it is useful to know how to use them in an effort to understand and recover the past.

The principle of polling is not new. In 1824, the *Harrisburg Pennsylvanian* sought to predict the winner of that year's presidential race, and in the 1880s, the *Boston Globe* sent reporters to selected precincts on election night to forecast final returns. In 1916, *Literary Digest* began conducting postcard polls to predict political results. By the 1930s, Elmo Roper and George Gallup had further developed the field of market research and public opinion polling. Notwithstanding an embarrassing mistake by *Literary Digest* in predicting a Landon victory over FDR in 1936, polling had become a scientific enterprise by World War II.

According to Gallup, a poll is not magic but "merely an instrument for gauging public opinion," especially the views of those often unheard. As Elmo Roper said, the poll is "one of the few ways through which the so-called common man can be articulate." Polling, therefore, is a valuable way to recover the attitudes, beliefs, and voices of ordinary people.

Yet certain cautions should be observed. Like all instruments of human activity, polls are imperfect and may even be dangerous. Historians using information from polls need to be aware of how large the samples were, when the interviewing was done, and how opinions might have been molded by the form of the poll itself. Questions can be poorly phrased. Some hint at the desirable answer or plant ideas in the minds of those interviewed. Polls sometimes provide ambiguous responses that can be interpreted many ways. More seriously, some critics worry that human freedom itself is threatened by the pollsters' manipulative and increasingly accurate predictive techniques.

Despite these limitations, polls have become an ever-present part of American life. In the late 1940s and early 1950s, Americans were polled frequently about topics ranging from foreign aid, the United Nations, and the

Foreign Policy Polls

DECEMBER 2, 1949—ATOM BOMB
Now that Russia has the atom bomb, do you think another war is more likely or less likely?

More likely	45%
Less likely	28%
Will make no difference	17%
No opinion	10%

BY EDUCATION
College

More likely	36%
Will make no difference	23%
Less likely	35%
No opinion	6%

High School

More likely	44%
Will make no difference	19%
Less likely	28%
No opinion	9%

Grade School

More likely	50%
Will make no difference	12%
Less likely	26%
No opinion	12%

MAY 1, 1950—NATIONAL DEFENSE
Do you think United States Government spending on national defense should be increased, decreased, or remain about the same?

Increased	63%
Same	24%
Decreased	7%
No opinion	6%

SEPTEMBER 18, 1953—INDOCHINA
The United States is now sending war materials to help the French fight the Communists in Indochina. Would you approve or disapprove of sending United States soldiers to take part in the fighting there?

Approve	8%
Disapprove	85%
No opinion	7%

JANUARY 11, 1950—RUSSIA
As you hear and read about Russia these days, do you believe Russia is trying to build herself up to be the ruling power of the world—or is Russia just building up protection against being attacked in another war?

Rule the world	70%
Protect herself	18%
No opinion	12%

BY EDUCATION
College

Rule the world	73%
Protect herself	21%
No opinion	6%

High School

Rule the world	72%
Protect herself	18%
No opinion	10%

Grade School

Rule the world	67%
Protect herself	17%
No opinion	16%

FEBRUARY 12, 1951—ATOMIC WARFARE
If the United States gets into an all-out war with Russia, do you think we should drop atom bombs on Russia first—or do you think we should use the atom bomb only if it is used on us?

Drop A-bomb first	66%
Only if used on us	19%
No opinion	15%

The greatest difference was between men and women—72% of the men questioned favored our dropping the bomb first, compared to 61% of the women.

OCTOBER 29, 1949—WOMEN IN POLITICS

If the party whose candidate you most often support nominated a woman for President of the United States, would you vote for her if she seemed qualified for the job?

Yes	48%
No	48%
No opinion	4%

BY SEX
Men

Yes	45%
No	50%
No opinion	5%

Women

Yes	51%
No	46%
No opinion	3%

BY POLITICAL AFFILIATION
Democrats

Yes	50%
No	48%
No opinion	2%

Republicans

Yes	46%
No	50%
No opinion	4%

Would you vote for a woman for Vice President of the United States if she seemed qualified for the job?

Yes	53%
No	43%
No opinion	4%

MAY 5, 1950—MOST IMPORTANT PROBLEM

What do you think is the most important problem facing the entire country today?

War, threat of war	40%
Atomic bomb control	6%
Economic problems, living costs, inflation, taxes	15%
Strikes and labor troubles	4%
Corruption in government	3%
Unemployment	10%
Housing	3%
Communism	8%
Others	11%

JULY 12, 1950—PROFESSIONS

Suppose a young man came to you and asked your advice about taking up a profession. Assuming that he was qualified to enter any of these professions, which one of them would you first recommend to him?

Doctor of medicine	29%
Government worker	6%
Engineer, builder	16%
Professor, teacher	5%
Business executive	8%
Banker	4%
Clergyman	8%
Dentist	4%
Lawyer	8%
Veterinarian	3%
None, don't know	9%

JULY 15, 1950—PROFESSIONS

Suppose a young girl came to you and asked your advice about taking up a profession. Assuming that she was qualified to enter any of these professions, which one of them would you first recommend?

CHOICE OF WOMEN

Nurse	33%
Teacher	15%
Secretary	8%
Social service worker	8%
Dietitian	7%
Dressmaker	4%
Beautician	4%
Airline stewardess	3%
Actress	3%
Journalist	2%
Musician	2%
Model	2%
Librarian	2%
Medical, dental technician	1%
Others	2%
Don't know	4%

The views of men on this subject were nearly identical with those of women.

---

occupation of Germany and Japan to labor legislation, child punishment, and whether women should wear slacks in public (39 percent of men said no, as did 49 percent of women). Such topics as the first use of nuclear arms, presidential popularity, national defense, and U.S. troop intervention in a troubled area of the world remain as pertinent today as they were then.

Reflecting on the Past A number of the polls included here deal with foreign policy during the Cold War in the early 1950s. How did people respond to Soviet nuclear capability? How did they regard Russian intentions and the appropriate American response? How do you analyze the results of these polls? What do you think is the significance of rating responses by levels of education? In what ways are the questions "loaded"? How might the results of these polls influence American foreign policy? What do you think is significant about the Indochina poll? These polls show the challenge-and-response nature of the Cold War. How do you think Americans would respond today to these questions?

Polls also shed light on domestic issues. Consider the poll on professions for young men and women taken in 1950. What does it tell us about the attitudes of the pollster on appropriate careers for men and women? Why do you think both men and women had nearly identical views on this subject? How do you think people today would answer these questions? Would they be presented in the same way? Also observe the poll on women in politics. To what extent have attitudes on this issue changed in the intervening years? ■

A New Chinese Leader

Mao Zedong, chairman of the Chinese Communist party, was a powerful and popular leader who drove Jiang Jieshi from power in 1949 and established a stronghold over the People's Republic of China he created at that time. How was Mao able to defeat his opponents and win the revolutionary war?

(Bettmann/CORBIS)

The United States failed to understand issues that were part of the long internal conflict in China or the immense popular support Mao had garnered. As the Communist army moved toward victory, the *New York Times* termed Mao's party a "nauseous force," a "compact little oligarchy dominated by Moscow's nominees." Mao's proclamation of the People's Republic of China on October 1, 1949, fanned fears of Russian domination, for he had already announced his regime's support for the Soviet Union against the "imperialist" United States.

Events in China caused near hysteria in America. Even before Mao's victory, the State Department issued a 1,000-page document entitled *The China White Paper,* which outlined the background of the struggle and argued that the United States was powerless to alter the results. "The unfortunate but inescapable fact is that the ominous result of the civil war in China was beyond the control of the government of the United States," the *White Paper* declared. Staunch anti-Communists nonetheless argued that Truman and the United States were to blame for the Nationalist defeat because they failed to provide Jiang

with sufficient support. Four senators called the *White Paper* a "whitewash of a wishful, do-nothing policy which has succeeded only in placing Asia in danger of Soviet conquest with its ultimate threat to the peace of the world and our own national security." Secretary of State Dean Acheson briefly considered granting diplomatic recognition to the new Chinese government but backed off after the Communists seized American property, harassed American citizens, and openly allied China with the USSR. Like other Americans, Acheson mistakenly viewed the Chinese as Soviet puppets.

Tension with China increased during the Korean War (1950–1953) and again in 1954 when Mao's government began shelling Nationalist positions on the offshore islands of Quemoy and Matsu. Eisenhower, elected U.S. president in 1952, was committed to defending the Nationalists on Taiwan from a Communist attack, but he was unwilling to risk war over the islands.

Stalemate in the Korean War

The Korean War highlighted growing U.S. concern about Asia. The conflict in Korea stemmed from tensions lingering after World War II. Korea, long under Japanese control, hoped for independence after Japan's defeat. But after the atomic bombs dropped on Japan, the Allies, seeking to bring a rapid end to the Pacific struggle and expedite the transition to peace, temporarily divided Korea along the 38th parallel. The Soviet–American line, initially intended as a matter of military convenience, hardened after 1945, just as a similar division became rigid in Germany. In time, the Soviets set up a Korean government in the north and the Americans a second Korean government in the south. Though the major powers left Korea by the end of the decade, they continued to support the regimes they had created. Each Korean government hoped to reunify the country on its own terms.

North Korea moved first. On June 25, 1950, North Korean forces crossed the 38th parallel and invaded South Korea. While the North Koreans used Soviet-built tanks, they operated on their own initiative. Kim Il Sung, the North Korean leader, had visited Moscow earlier and gained Soviet acquiescence in the idea of an attack, but both the planning and the implementation occurred in Korea.

Taken by surprise and certain that Russia had masterminded the North Korean offensive to test the U.S. containment policy, Truman told the American public that "the attack upon Korea makes it plain beyond all doubt that communism has passed beyond the use of subversion to conquer independent nations and will now use armed invasion and war." He later reflected in his memoirs: "If this was allowed to go unchallenged it would mean a third world war, just

General MacArthur

General Douglas MacArthur was a superb tactician but a supremely egotistical commander of UN forces in Korea, where this picture was taken in the first year of the Korean War. Eventually his arrogance led him to challenge Truman's policy, whereupon the president relieved him of his command. How does this image convey MacArthur's strong-willed approach?

(Time Life Pictures/Getty Images)

as similar incidents had brought on the second world war."

Truman directed General Douglas MacArthur, head of the American occupation forces in Japan, to supply South Korea. The United States also went to the United Nations Security Council and secured a unanimous resolution branding North Korea an aggressor, then another resolution calling on members of the organization to assist South Korea in repelling aggression and restoring peace. MacArthur became leader of all UN forces in this largest UN operation to date. The United States and South Korea provided more than 90 percent of the personnel, but 15 other nations participated in the UN effort.

Air and naval forces, then ground forces, went into battle south of the 38th parallel. Following a daring amphibious invasion that pushed the North Koreans back to the former boundary line, UN troops crossed

the 38th parallel, hoping to reunify Korea under an American-backed government. Despite Chinese signals that this movement toward their border threatened their security, the UN troops pressed on. In October, Chinese troops appeared briefly in battle, then disappeared. The next month, the Chinese mounted a full-fledged counterattack, which pushed the UN forces back below the dividing line.

The resulting stalemate provoked a bitter struggle between MacArthur and Truman. The brilliant but arrogant general called for retaliatory air strikes against China. He faced opposition from General Omar Bradley, chairman of the Joint Chiefs of Staff, who declared, "Frankly, in the opinion of the Joint Chiefs of Staff, this strategy would involve us in the wrong war, at the wrong place, at the wrong time, with the wrong enemy," and from President Truman, who remained committed to conducting a limited war. MacArthur finally went too far. In April 1951, he argued that the American approach in Korea was wrong and asserted publicly that "there is no substitute for victory." Truman had no choice but to relieve the general for insubordination. The decision outraged many Americans. After the stunning victories of World War II, limited war was frustrating and difficult to understand.

The Korean War dragged on into Eisenhower's presidency. Campaigning in 1952, Ike promised to go to Korea, and three weeks after his election, he did so. When UN truce talks bogged down in May 1953, the new administration privately threatened the Chinese with the use of atomic weapons. This threat prompted the renewal of negotiations, and on July 27, 1953, an armistice was signed. After three long years, the unpopular war ended.

American involvement carried a heavy price: more than 33,000 Americans killed in action with more than 142,000 American casualties in all. The other 15 UN nations involved in the struggle accounted for another 17,000 casualties. But those figures paled in comparison to Korean casualties: as many as 2 million Koreans dead and countless others wounded and maimed.

The war significantly changed American attitudes and institutions. For the first time, American forces fought in racially integrated units. As commander in chief, Truman had ordered the integration of the armed forces in 1948, over the opposition of many generals, and African Americans became part of all military units. Their successful performance led to acceptance of military integration.

During the Korean War military expenditures soared from $13 billion in 1950 to about $47 billion three years later, as defense spending followed the guidelines proposed in NSC-68. In the process, the United States accepted the demands of permanent

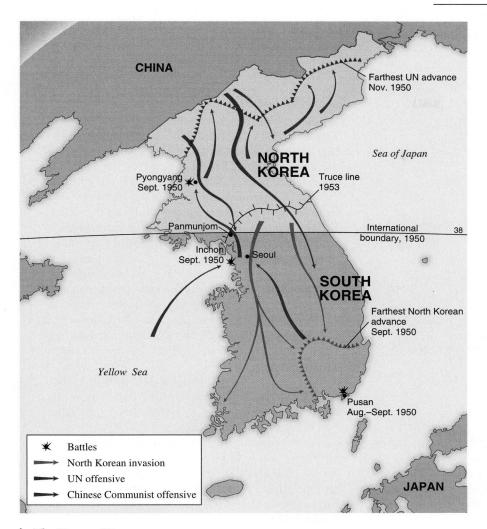

The Korean War

This map shows the ebb and flow of the Korean War. North Korea crossed the thirty-eighth parallel first, then the UN offensive drove the North Koreans close to the Chinese border, and finally the Chinese Communists entered the war and drove the UN forces back below the thirty-eighth parallel. The armistice signed at Panmunjom in 1953 provided a dividing line very close to the prewar line. How far did both North Korea and South Korea penetrate into the territory of the other nation? What role did China play in the Korean War?

mobilization. Whereas the military absorbed less than one-third of the federal budget in 1950, a decade later, it took half. More than a million military personnel were stationed around the world. At home, an increasingly powerful military establishment became closely tied to corporate and scientific communities and created a military–industrial complex that employed 3.5 million Americans by 1960.

The Korean War had significant political effects as well. In September 1951, the United States signed a peace treaty with Japan and came to rely on the Japanese to maintain the balance of power in the Pacific. At the same time, the struggle poisoned relations with the People's Republic of China, which

remained unrecognized by the United States, and ensured a diplomatic standoff that lasted more than 20 years.

Vietnam: The Roots of Conflict

The commitment to stopping the spread of communism led to the massive U.S. involvement in Vietnam. That struggle tore the United States apart, wrought enormous damage in Southeast Asia, and finally forced a reevaluation of U.S. Cold War policies.

The roots of the war extended far back in the past. Indochina—the part of Southeast Asia that included Vietnam, Laos, and Cambodia—had been a

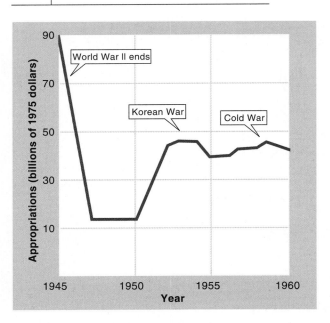

Defense Expenditures, 1945–1960

Defense spending plummeted after World War II, only to quadruple with the onset of the Korean War. After that increase, spending levels never dropped dramatically, even after the end of the war.

Source: U.S. Bureau of the Census.

French colony since the mid-nineteenth century. During World War II, Japan occupied the region but an independence movement, led by the Communist organizer and revolutionary Ho Chi Minh, sought to expel the Japanese conquerors from Vietnam. In 1945, the Allied powers faced the decision of how to deal with Ho and his nationalist crusade.

France was determined to regain its colony as a way of preserving its status as a great power. Meanwhile, Ho established the Democratic Republic of Vietnam in 1945. The new government's declaration of independence echoed its American counterpart, declaring: "All men are created equal. They are endowed by their Creator with certain inalienable rights, among these are Life, Liberty and the pursuit of Happiness." Despite widespread popular support, the United States refused to recognize the new government.

A long, bitter struggle broke out between French and Vietnamese forces, which became entangled with the larger Cold War. President Truman was less concerned than Franklin Roosevelt had been about ending colonialism but he was intent on checking Soviet power. He needed France to balance the Soviets in Europe, where he wanted French support for America's policy in Germany and as a member of NATO, and that meant cooperating with France in Vietnam.

Although Ho did not have close ties to the Soviet Union and was committed to his independent nationalist effort, Truman and his advisers, who saw communism

as a monolithic force, assumed wrongly that Ho took orders from Moscow. Hence, in 1950, the United States formally recognized the French puppet government in Vietnam, and by 1954, the United States was paying more than three-quarters of the cost of France's Indochina war.

After Eisenhower took office, France's position in Southeast Asia deteriorated. Secretary of State Dulles was eager to assist the French, and the chairman of the Joint Chiefs of Staff even contemplated using nuclear weapons, but Eisenhower refused to intervene directly. He understood the lack of American support for intervention in that far-off land. Senator John F. Kennedy spoke for many of his congressional colleagues when he declared in 1954: "I am frankly of the belief that no amount of American military assistance in Indochina can conquer an enemy which is everywhere and at the same time nowhere, 'an enemy of the people' which has the sympathy and covert support of the people." As a French fortress at Dien Bien Phu in the north of Vietnam finally fell to Ho's forces, an international conference in Geneva sought to prevent Ho Chi Minh from gaining control of the entire country. The final declaration of the conference divided Vietnam along the 17th parallel, with elections promised in 1956 to unify the country and determine its political fate.

Two separate Vietnamese states emerged. Ho Chi Minh held power in the north, while in the south, Ngo Dinh Diem, a fierce anti-Communist who had been in exile in the United States, returned to form a government. Diem enjoyed the full support of the United States, which saw him as a way of securing stability in Southeast Asia and avoiding further communist incursions. When he decided not to hold the elections mandated in the Geneva accord, the United States backed him in that decision. In the next few years, American aid increased and military advisers—675 by the time Eisenhower left office—began to assist the South Vietnamese. The United States had taken its first steps toward direct involvement in a ruinous war halfway around the world that would escalate out of control.

The Creation of Israel and Its Impact on the Middle East

The creation of the state of Israel became intertwined with larger Cold War issues. Jews had longed for a homeland for years, and the Zionist movement had sought a place in Palestine, in the Middle East, since the latter part of the nineteenth century. Jewish settlers who began to gravitate to Palestine were not welcomed by the Turks, who dominated the region, or by the British, who exercised control after World War I.

Father Ho

Ho Chi Minh waged a long struggle first against France, then Japan, and finally the United States for the independence of Vietnam. The Vietnamese people viewed him as the father of the country. How does this picture of him with children contribute to that impression?

(Library of Congress [LC-USZ62–126864])

Then the Holocaust—and the slaughter of 6 million Jews—during World War II created new pressure for a Jewish state. The unwillingness—and inability—of the Western powers to intervene in time to stop the Nazi genocide created a groundswell of support, particularly among American Jews, for a Jewish homeland in the Arab-dominated Middle East.

In 1948, the fledgling United Nations attempted to partition Palestine into an Arab state and a Jewish state. Truman officially recognized the new state of Israel 15 minutes after it was proclaimed. But bitter animosities persisted between Arabs, who believed they had been robbed of their territory, and Jews, who felt they had finally regained a homeland after the horrors of the Holocaust. As Americans looked on, Arab forces invaded Israel, in the first of a series of conflicts that continues to the present day. The Israelis, fighting for the survival of their new nation, won the war with a truce mediated by African American diplomat Ralph Bunche, and added territory

to what the UN had given them. But struggles erupted in 1967 and again in 1973 with adversaries who did not recognize Israel's right to exist.

While sympathetic to Israel, the United States tried at the same time to maintain stability in the rest of the region. The Middle East had tremendous strategic importance as the supplier of oil for industrialized nations. In 1953, the CIA helped the Iranian army overthrow the government of Mohammed Mossadegh, which had nationalized oil wells formerly under British control, and placed the shah of Iran securely on the throne. After the coup, British and American companies regained command of the wells.

As it cultivated close ties with Israel, the United States also tried to maintain the friendship of oil-rich Arab states or, at the very least, to prevent them from falling into the Soviet orbit. In Egypt, the policy ran into trouble when Arab nationalist General Gamal Abdel Nasser planned a huge dam on the Nile River to produce electric power and proclaimed his country's neutrality in the Cold War. Although Secretary of State Dulles offered U.S. financial support for the Aswan Dam project, Nasser also began discussions with the Soviet Union. A furious Dulles, who believed that neutralism was immoral, withdrew the American offer. Left without funds for the dam, in July 1956, Nasser seized and nationalized the British-controlled Suez Canal and closed it to Israeli ships. Now Great Britain was enraged and Europe worried about a continuing supply of oil.

In the fall, Israeli, British, and French military forces invaded Egypt. Eisenhower, who had not been consulted, was irate. When told that paratroopers were about to land near the canal, he said, "I think it's the biggest error of our time, outside of losing China." Realizing that the attack might push Nasser into Moscow's arms, the United States sponsored a UN resolution condemning the attack and Dulles persuaded other nations not to send petroleum to England and France. These actions persuaded the invaders to withdraw.

Before long, the United States again intervened in the Middle East. Concerned about the region's stability, the president declared in 1957, in what came to be called the Eisenhower Doctrine, that "the existing vacuum in the Middle East must be filled by the United States before it is filled by Russia." A year later, he authorized the landing of 14,000 soldiers in Lebanon to prop up a right-wing government challenged from within.

Restricting Revolt in Latin America

The Cold War also led to intervention in Latin America. In 1954, Dulles sniffed Communist activity in Guatemala, and Eisenhower ordered CIA support for a coup aimed at ousting the elected government of reform-minded Colonel Jacobo Arbenz Guzmán. It trained and equipped Guatemalans to overthrow the legitimate regime, which had appropriated property of the American-owned United Fruit Company. The right-wing takeover succeeded, established a military dictatorship that responded to U.S. wishes, and restored the property of the United Fruit Company. These actions demonstrated again the shortsighted American commitment to stability and private investment, whatever the internal effect or ultimate cost. The interference in Guatemala fed anti-American sentiment throughout Latin America.

In 1959, when Fidel Castro overthrew the dictatorship of Fulgencio Batista in Cuba, the shortsightedness of American policy became even clearer. Nationalism and the thrust for social reform were powerful forces in Latin America, as in the rest of the developing world formerly dominated by European powers. As Milton Eisenhower, Ike's brother and adviser, pointed out: "Revolution is inevitable in Latin America. The people are angry. They are shackled to the past with bonds of ignorance, injustice, and poverty. And they no longer accept as universal or inevitable the oppressive prevailing order." But when Castro confiscated American property in Cuba, the Eisenhower administration cut off exports and severed diplomatic ties. In response, Cuba turned to the Soviet Union for support.

Atomic Weapons and the Cold War

Throughout the Cold War, the atomic bomb cast an ominous cloud over all diplomatic discussions and military initiatives. Atomic weapons were destructive enough, but the development of hydrogen bombs in both the United States and the Soviet Union ushered in an age of overkill.

Sharing the Secret of the Bomb

The United States, with British aid, had built the first atomic bomb and attempted to conceal the project from its wartime ally, the Soviet Union. Soviet spies, however, discovered that the Americans were working on the bomb, and, even before the war was over, the Soviets had initiated a program to create a bomb of their own.

The United States briefly considered sharing the atomic secret. Just before he retired, Secretary of War Henry L. Stimson pushed for cooperating with the Soviet Union rather than acting unilaterally. Recognizing the futility of trying to cajole the Russians while "having this weapon ostentatiously on our hip," he warned that "their suspicions and their distrust of our purposes and motives will increase." Only mutual accommodation could bring international cooperation.

Yet as negotiations to develop an international arms control system broke down, the United States gave up on the idea of sharing atomic secrets. Intent on retaining the technological advantage until the creation of a "foolproof method of control," Truman endorsed the Atomic Energy Act, passed by Congress in 1946. It established the Atomic Energy Commission (AEC) to supervise all atomic energy development in the United States and, under the tightest security, to regulate all nuclear activity in the nation at large. It also opened the way to a nuclear arms race once Russia developed its own bomb.

Nuclear Proliferation

As the atomic bomb found its way into popular culture, Americans at first showed more excitement than fear. In Los Angeles, the "Atombomb Dancers" wiggled at the Burbank Burlesque Theater. In 1946, the Buchanan Brothers released a record called "Atomic Power," noting the brimstone fire from heaven that was "given by the mighty hand of God." David E. Lilienthal, first chairman of the AEC, recalled that the atom "had us bewitched.... It would either destroy us all or it would bring about the millennium."

Anxiety lurking beneath the exuberance did not surface dramatically as long as the United States held a nuclear monopoly. Then, in September 1949, when Americans learned that the Soviet Union had tested its own bomb, the security of being the world's only atomic power vanished. People wondered whether the Soviet test foreshadowed a nuclear attack and speculated when it might come. The editors of the *Bulletin of the Atomic Scientists,* the nation's foremost publication dealing with nuclear affairs, moved the minute hand of the "doomsday clock" on the journal's cover from seven minutes before midnight to three minutes before midnight to reflect their fear of proliferation.

In early 1950, Truman authorized the development of a new hydrogen superbomb, potentially far more devastating than the atomic bomb. By 1953, both the United States and the Soviet Union had unlocked the secret of fusion—joining atoms together in a reaction like that on the surface of the sun. A far more powerful reaction could do far more damage. After the 1954 BRAVO test, AEC chairman Lewis Strauss admitted that "an H-bomb can be made...large enough to take out a city," even New York. Then, in 1957, shortly after the news that the Soviets had successfully tested their first intercontinental ballistic missile (ICBM), Americans learned that the Soviets had launched into outer space *Sputnik,* the first artificial satellite—with a rocket that could also deliver a hydrogen bomb.

The discovery of radioactive fallout added another dimension to the nuclear dilemma. Fallout became publicly known after the BRAVO blast in 1954 showered Japanese fishermen on a ship called the *Lucky Dragon* 85 miles away with radioactive dust. They became ill with radiation sickness, and several months later, one of the seamen died. The Japanese, who had been the first to experience the effects of atomic weapons, were outraged and alarmed to be the first victims of the hydrogen bomb. Everywhere people began to realize the terrible consequences of nuclear proliferation. Fallout became a serious international problem—in the words of physicist Ralph Lapp, "a peril to humanity."

Authors in both the scientific and the popular press focused attention on radioactive fallout. Radiation, Lapp observed, "cannot be felt and possesses all the terror of the unknown. It is something which evokes revulsion and helplessness—like a bubonic plague." Nevil Shute's best-selling 1957 novel *On the Beach*, and the film that followed, also sparked public awareness and fear. The story described a war that released so much radioactive waste that all life in the Northern Hemisphere disappeared, while the Southern Hemisphere awaited the same deadly fate. In 1959, when *Consumer Reports*, the popular magazine that tested and compared various products, warned of the contamination of milk with the radioactive isotope strontium-90, the public grew even more alarmed.

The discovery of fallout initiated a shelter craze. Bob Russell, a Michigan sheriff, declared that "to build a new home in this day and age without including such an obvious necessity as a fallout shelter would be like leaving out the bathroom 20 years ago." *Good Housekeeping* magazine carried a full-page editorial in November 1958 urging the construction of family shelters. More and more companies advertised ready-made shelters. *Life* magazine in 1955 featured an "H-Bomb Hideaway" for $3,000. By late 1960, the Office of Civil and Defense Mobilization estimated that a million family shelters had been built.

The Nuclear West

The bomb stimulated more than just shelter building. It sparked an enormous increase in defense spending and created a huge nuclear industry, particularly in the West. Contractors liked the region because of its anti-union attitudes; labor stability, they argued, would make it easier to meet government deadlines.

During World War II, a number of the Manhattan Project's major centers were located in the West. The plant at Hanford, Washington, was one of the most important producers of fissionable material, and the first atomic weapon had been produced at Los Alamos, New Mexico. Development in this area expanded after the war. Hanford continued to produce plutonium, a facility outside Denver made plutonium triggers for thermonuclear bombs, the new Sandia National

Laboratory in Albuquerque provided the production engineering of nuclear bombs, and the Los Alamos laboratory remained a major atomic research center. In 1951, the United States opened the Nevada Test Site, 65 miles north of Las Vegas, and the facility had a major impact on the city. The Chamber of Commerce offered schedules of test shots, and the mushroom cloud became the logo for the Southern Nevada telephone directory. Satirist and songwriter Tom Lehrer highlighted the West in the song "The Wild West Is Where I Want to Be" in his first album in 1953. The first verse went:

> *Along the trail you'll find me lopin'*
> *Where the spaces are wide open,*
> *In the land of the old A.E.C.*
> *Where the scenery's attractive,*
> *And the air is radioactive,*
> *Oh, the wild west is where I want to be.*

Defense spending promoted other development as well. Naval commands had headquarters in Seattle, San Francisco, San Diego, and Honolulu. Radar sites, aimed at tracking incoming missiles, stretched all the way up to Alaska. The Boeing Company, located in Seattle, stimulated tremendous development in that city as it produced B-47 and B-52 airplanes that were the U.S. Air Force's main delivery vehicles for nuclear bombs.

"Massive Retaliation"

As Americans grappled with the implications of nuclear weapons, government policy came to depend increasingly on an atomic shield. Truman authorized the development of a nuclear arsenal but also stressed conventional forms of defense. Eisenhower was concerned with controlling the budget and cutting taxes, and his administration decided to rely on atomic weapons rather than combat forces as the key to American defense.

Secretary of State Dulles developed the policy of threatening "massive retaliation." The United States, he declared, was willing and ready to use nuclear weapons against Communist aggression on whatever targets it chose. The policy allowed troop cutbacks and promised to be cost-effective by giving "more bang for the buck."

Massive retaliation provided for an all-or-nothing response, leaving no middle course, no alternatives between nuclear war and retreat. Critics called the policy "brinkmanship" and wondered what would happen if the line was crossed in the new atomic age. Eisenhower himself was horrified when he saw reports indicating that a coordinated atomic attack could leave a nation "a smoking, radiating ruin at the end of two hours." With characteristic caution, he did his best to ensure that the rhetoric of massive retaliation did not lead to war.

Atomic Protest

As the arms race spiraled, critics demanded that it end. In 1956, Democratic presidential candidate Adlai Stevenson pointed to "the danger of poisoning the atmosphere" and called for a halt to nuclear tests. Eisenhower did not respond, but Vice President Richard Nixon called Stevenson's suggestion "catastrophic nonsense," while Dulles minimized the hazards of radiation by arguing, "From a health standpoint, there is greater danger from wearing a wrist watch with a luminous dial."

In 1957, activists organized SANE, the National Committee for a Sane Nuclear Policy. One of its most effective advertisements featured internationally known pediatrician Benjamin Spock, looking down at a little girl with a frown on his face. "Dr. Spock is worried," the caption read, and the text below amplified on his concern. "I *am* worried," he said, "not so much about

the effect of past tests but at the prospect of endless future ones. As the tests multiply, so will the damage to children—here and around the world."

Several years later, women who had worked with SANE took the protest movement a step further. To challenge continued testing, which dropped lethal radiation on all inhabitants of the globe, the protesters called on women throughout the country to suspend normal activities for a day and strike for peace. An estimated 50,000 women marched in 60 communities around the nation. Their slogans proclaimed "Let the Children Grow" and "End the Arms Race—Not the Human Race."

Pressure from many groups produced a political breakthrough and sustained it for a time. The superpowers began a voluntary moratorium on testing in the fall of 1958. It lasted until the Soviet Union resumed testing in September 1961 and the United States began again the following March.

Dr. Spock is worried.

Worrying About the Future

SANE tried to get the United States, and the rest of the world, to stop testing nuclear weapons and dumping huge amounts of fallout in the atmosphere. This newspaper advertisement, which appeared in 1962, was part of the larger effort to make the world a safer place. How does this picture of noted pediatrician Dr. Benjamin Spock underscore a sense of fear?

(Records of SANE, Inc., Swarthmore College Peace Collection)

The Cold War at Home

The Cold War also affected domestic affairs and led to the creation of an internal loyalty program that seriously violated civil liberties. Fears of radical subversion made the Soviet Union appear increasingly ominous. Maps showed half the world colored red to dramatize the spread of communism. As Americans began to suspect Communist infiltration at home, some determined to root out all traces of communism inside the United States.

Truman's Loyalty Program

In mobilizing support for its containment program, the Truman administration used increasingly shrill rhetoric. For Truman, the issue confronting the world was one of "tyranny or freedom." Attorney general J. Howard McGrath spoke of "many Communists in America," each bearing the "germ of death for society."

When administration officials discovered classified documents in the offices of the allegedly pro-Communist *Amerasia* magazine, Truman appointed a Temporary Commission on Employee Loyalty to head off Republican charges that the Democrats were "soft on communism."

On the basis of its report, Truman established a new Federal Employee Loyalty Program in 1947. In the same week that he announced his containment policy, he ordered the FBI to check its files for evidence of subversive activity and to bring suspects before a new Civil Service Commission Loyalty Review Board. Initially, the program included safeguards and assumed that a challenged employee was innocent until proven guilty. But as the Loyalty Review Board assumed more power, it ignored individual rights, and suspects had little chance to fight back. Val Lorwin, whose story started this chapter, was just one of many victims.

The Truman loyalty program examined several million employees but found grounds for dismissing only several hundred. Nonetheless, it bred the unwarranted fear of subversion, led to the assumption that absolute loyalty could be achieved, and legitimated investigative tactics that were used irresponsibly to harm innocent individuals.

The Congressional Loyalty Program

At the same time, Congress launched its own program. In the early years of the Cold War, the law became increasingly explicit about what was illegal in the United States. The requirement that members of Communist organizations had to register with the attorney general led to the decline of the American Communist party. Membership, numbering about 80,000 in 1947, fell to 55,000 in 1950 and to 25,000 in 1954.

The investigations of the House Un-American Activities Committee (HUAC) contributed to that decline. Intent on rooting out subversion, HUAC probed the motion picture industry in 1947, claiming that left-wing sympathies of writers, actors, directors, and producers were corrupting the American public. A frequent refrain in congressional hearings was "Are you now or have you ever been a member of the Communist party?" Altogether, HUAC called

19 Hollywood figures to testify. When 10 of them—including noted writers Ring Lardner, Jr., and Dalton Trumbo—refused to answer such accusatory questions by invoking their constitutional right to remain silent, Congress issued contempt citations. Members of the "Hollywood Ten" served prison sentences ranging from six months to one year. At that point, the movie industry knuckled under and blacklisted anyone with even a marginally questionable past. Hollywood executives issued a statement that declared: "We will not knowingly employ a Communist nor a member of any party or groups which advocates the overthrow of the Government of the United States by force or by illegal or unconstitutional means." No one on the blacklist could find a job at the studios, although some managed to work secretly under other names.

Congress made a greater splash with the Hiss–Chambers case. Whittaker Chambers, a former Communist who had broken with the party in 1938 and had become a successful editor of *Time* magazine, charged that Alger Hiss had been a Communist in the 1930s. Hiss was a distinguished New Dealer who had served in the Agriculture Department before becoming assistant secretary of state. Now out of the government, he was president of the Carnegie Endowment for International Peace. He denied Chambers's charge, and the matter might have died there had not freshman congressman Richard Nixon taken up the case. Nixon finally extracted from Hiss an admission that he had

An Anti-Communist Message from Hollywood

As Hollywood implemented its blacklist of anyone deemed sympathetic to communism, filmmakers also began to make a number of anti-Communist films, such as *The Red Menace* in 1949, to show their own loyalty. How does this poster highlight the problems facing the United States?

(Michael Barson Collection)

once known Chambers, though by a different name. Hiss then sued Chambers for libel, whereupon Chambers changed his story and charged that Hiss was a Soviet spy. Hiss was indicted for perjury for lying under oath about his former relationship with Chambers, for the statute of limitations prevented prosecution for espionage. The sensational case made front-page news around the nation. Millions of Americans read about it at around the same time they learned of Russia's first atomic explosion and the final victory of the Communist revolution in China. Chambers appeared unstable, but Hiss seemed contradictory in his testimony and never adequately explained how he had such close ties with members of the Communist party or how some copies of stolen State Department documents had been typed on his typewriter. The first trial ended in a hung jury; the second trial, in January 1950, sent Hiss to prison for almost four years. He continued to assert his innocence for the remainder of his life, although later evidence makes his involvement clear.

For many Americans, the Hiss case proved that a Communist threat indeed existed in the United States. It "forcibly demonstrated to the American people that domestic Communism was a real and present danger to the security of the nation," Richard Nixon declared as he used the case to win a Senate seat from California. It helped justify the even worse witch hunts that followed.

Congress also charged that homosexuals posed a security risk. The issue surfaced in February 1950, when Undersecretary of State John Peurifoy mentioned in testimony before the Senate Appropriations Committee that most of the 91 employees the State Department had dismissed for reasons of "moral turpitude" were homosexuals. Then, in December, the Senate released a report that painted a threatening picture of the problems of homosexuals in the civil service. They lacked moral and emotional stability, the report suggested, and were therefore likely candidates for blackmail, which threatened national security.

Senator Joe McCarthy

The key anti-Communist warrior in the 1950s was Joseph R. McCarthy, Republican senator from Wisconsin. He capitalized on the fear sparked by congressional and executive investigations and made the entire country cognizant of the Communist threat.

McCarthy came to the Communist issue almost accidentally. Elected to the U.S. Senate in 1946, McCarthy had an undistinguished career for much of his first term. He first gained national attention with a speech before the Wheeling, West Virginia, Women's Club in February 1950, not long after the conviction of Alger Hiss. In that address, McCarthy brandished in his hand what he said was a list of 205 known Communists in the State Department. Pressed for details, McCarthy first said that he would release his list only to the president, then reduced the number of names to 57.

Early reactions to McCarthy were mixed. A subcommittee of the Senate Foreign Relations Committee, after investigating, called his charge a "fraud and a hoax." As his support grew, however, Republicans realized his partisan value and egged him on. Senator John Bricker of Ohio allegedly told him, "Joe, you're a dirty s.o.b., but there are times when you've got to have an s.o.b. around, and this is one of them."

McCarthy selected assorted targets in his crusade to wipe out communism. He called Dean Acheson the "Red Dean of the State Department" and slandered George C. Marshall, the architect of victory in World

McCarthy's Anti-Communist Campaign

Senator Joseph McCarthy's spurious charges inflamed anti-Communist sentiment in the 1950s. Here he uses a chart of Communist party organization in the United States to suggest that the nation would be at risk unless subversives were rooted out. How does the chart contribute to the impression McCarthy wanted to convey?

(Bettmann/CORBIS)

War II and the Marshall Plan for European recovery, as a "man steeped in falsehood . . . who has recourse to the lie whenever it suits his convenience."

A demagogue throughout his career, McCarthy gained visibility through extensive press and television coverage. He knew how to issue press releases just before newspaper deadlines and to provide reporters with leaks that became the basis for stories. Playing on his tough reputation, he did not mind appearing disheveled, unshaven, and half sober. He used obscenity and vulgarity freely in lashing out against his "vile and scurrilous" enemies as part of his effort to appear as an ordinary man of the people.

McCarthy's tactics worked because of public alarm about the Communist threat. The Korean War revealed the aggressiveness of Communists in Asia. The arrest in 1950 of Julius and Ethel Rosenberg fed fears of internal subversion. The Rosenbergs, a seemingly ordinary American couple with two small children, were charged with stealing and transmitting atomic secrets to the Russians. To many Americans, it was inconceivable that the Soviets could have developed the bomb on their own. Treachery helped explain the Soviet explosion of an atomic device.

The next year, the Rosenbergs were found guilty of espionage. Judge Irving Kaufman expressed the rage of an insecure nation as he sentenced them to death. "I consider your crime worse than murder," he said. "Your conduct in putting into the hands of the Russians the A-bomb years before our best scientists predicted Russia would perfect the bomb has already caused, in my opinion, the Communist aggression in Korea...." Their execution in the electric chair after numerous appeals reflected a national commitment to respond to the Communist threat. For years, supporters of the Rosenbergs claimed that they were innocent victims of the anti-Communist crusade. More recent evidence indicates that Julius was guilty. Ethel, cognizant of his activities but not involved herself, was arrested, convicted, and executed in a futile government attempt to make Julius talk.

When the Republicans won control of the Senate in 1952, McCarthy's power grew. He became chairman of

MAJOR EVENTS OF THE COLD WAR

Year	Event	Effect
1946	Winston Churchill's "Iron Curtain" speech	First Western "declaration" of the Cold War
	George F. Kennan's long telegram	Spoke of Soviet insecurity and the need for containment
1947	George F. Kennan's article signed "Mr. X"	Elaborated on arguments in the telegram
	Truman Doctrine	Provided economic and military aid to Greece and Turkey
	Federal Employee Loyalty Program	Sought to root out subversion in the U.S. government
	HUAC investigation of the motion picture industry	Sought to expose Communist influences in the movies
1948	Marshall Plan	Provided massive American economic aid in rebuilding postwar Europe
	Berlin airlift	Brought in supplies when USSR closed off land access to the divided city
1949	NATO	Created a military alliance to withstand a possible Soviet attack
	First Soviet atomic bomb	Ended the American nuclear monopoly
	Communist victory in China	Made Americans fear the worldwide spread of communism
1950	Conviction of Alger Hiss	Seemed to bear out Communist danger at home
	Joseph McCarthy's first charges	Launched aggressive anti-Communist campaign in the United States
	NSC-68	Called for vigilance and increased military spending to counter the Communist threat
	Outbreak of the Korean War	North Korean invasion of South Korea viewed as part of Soviet conspiracy
1953	Armistice in Korea	Brought little change after years of bitter fighting
1954	Vietnamese victory over French at Dien Bien Phu	Early triumph for nationalism in Southeast Asia
	Army–McCarthy hearings	Brought downfall of Joseph McCarthy

Timeline

1945	Yalta Conference
	Roosevelt dies; Harry Truman becomes president
	Potsdam Conference
1946	American plan for control of atomic energy fails
	Atomic Energy Act
	Iran crisis in which U.S. forces USSR to leave
	Churchill's "Iron Curtain" speech
1947	Truman Doctrine
	Federal Employee Loyalty Program
	House Un-American Activities Committee (HUAC) investigates the movie industry
1948	Marshall Plan launched
	Berlin airlift
	Israel created by the United Nations
	Hiss–Chambers case
	Truman elected president
1949	Soviet Union tests atomic bomb
	North Atlantic Treaty Organization (NATO) established
	George Orwell, *1984*
	Mao Zedong's forces win Chinese civil war; Jiang Jieshi flees to Taiwan
1950	Truman authorizes development of the hydrogen bomb
	Alger Hiss convicted
	Joseph McCarthy's Wheeling (W. Va.) speech on subversion
	NSC-68
1950–1953	Korean War
1951	Japanese–American treaty
1952	Dwight D. Eisenhower elected president
	McCarthy heads Senate Permanent Investigations Subcommittee
1953	Stalin dies; Khrushchev consolidates power
	East Germans stage anti-Soviet demonstrations
	Shah of Iran returns to power in CIA-supported coup
1954	Fall of Dien Bien Phu ends French control of Indochina
	Geneva Conference on Vietnam
	Guatemalan government overthrown with CIA help
	Mao's forces shell Quemoy and Matsu
	Army–McCarthy hearings
1956	Suez incident
	Hungarian "freedom fighters" suppressed
	Eisenhower reelected
1957	Russians launch *Sputnik* satellite
1958	U.S. troops sent to support Lebanese government
1959	Castro deposes Batista in Cuba

the Government Operations Committee and head of its Permanent Investigations Subcommittee. He now had a stronger base and two dedicated assistants, Roy Cohn and G. David Schine, who helped keep attention focused on the ostensible Communist threat. They assisted him in his domestic investigations and even traveled abroad, ripping books off the shelves of American embassy libraries that they deemed subversive. The lists of suspects, including Val Lorwin (introduced at the start of this chapter), grew ever larger.

McCarthy finally pushed too far. In 1953, after the army drafted Schine and then refused to allow preferential treatment, McCarthy began to investigate army security and even top-level army leaders. When the army charged that McCarthy was going too far, the Senate investigated the complaint.

The Army–McCarthy hearings began in April 1954 and lasted 36 days. Beamed to a captivated nationwide audience, they demonstrated the power of television to shape people's opinions. Americans saw McCarthy's savage tactics on screen. He came across to viewers as irresponsible and destructive, particularly in contrast to Boston lawyer Joseph Welch, who argued the army's case with quiet eloquence and showed McCarthy as the demagogue he was. At a climactic point in the hearings, when McCarthy accused a member of Welch's staff of being involved with an organization sympathetic to the Communist party, despite an earlier agreement not to raise the issue, Welch exploded dramatically, "Have you no sense of decency, sir, at long last? Have you left no sense of decency?"

The hearings shattered McCarthy's mystical appeal. In broad daylight, before a national television audience, his ruthless tactics offended millions. The Senate, which had earlier backed off confronting McCarthy, finally censured him for his conduct. Although McCarthy remained in office, his influence disappeared. Three years later, at age 48, he died a broken man.

Yet for a time he had exerted a powerful hold in the United States. "To many Americans," radio commentator Fulton Lewis, Jr., said, "McCarthyism is Americanism." Seizing on the frustrations and anxieties of the Cold War, McCarthy struck a resonant chord. As his appeal grew, he put together a following that included both lower-class ethnic groups, who responded to the charges against established elites, and conservative midwestern Republicans. But his real power base was the Senate, where conservative Republicans saw McCarthy as a means of reasserting their own authority.

The Casualties of Fear

The anti-Communist campaign kindled pervasive suspicion in American society. In the late 1940s and early 1950s, dissent no longer seemed safe. Civil servants, government workers, academics, and actors all came under attack and found that the right of due process often evaporated amid the Cold War Red Scare.

This paranoia affected American life in countless ways. In New York, subway workers were fired when they refused to answer questions about their own political activities and beliefs. In Seattle, a fire department officer who denied current membership in the Communist party but refused to speak of his past was dismissed just 40 days before he reached the 25 years of service that would have qualified him for retirement benefits. Navajos in Arizona and New Mexico, facing starvation in the bitter winter of 1947–1948, were denied government relief because of charges that their communal way of life was communistic and therefore un-American. Racism became intertwined with the anti-Communist crusade when African American actor Paul Robeson was accused of Communist leanings for criticizing American foreign policy and denied opportunities to perform. Black author W. E. B. Du Bois, who joined the Communist party, faced even more virulent attacks. Latino laborers faced deportation for membership in unions with left-wing sympathies. In 1949, the Congress of Industrial Organizations (CIO) expelled 11 unions with a total membership of more than 1 million for alleged domination by Communists. Val Lorwin weathered the storm of malicious accusations and was finally vindicated, but others were less lucky. They were the unfortunate victims as the United States became consumed by the passions of the Cold War.

Conclusion
THE COLD WAR IN PERSPECTIVE

The Cold War dominated international relations in the post–World War II years. Tensions grew after 1945 as the United States and the Soviet Union found themselves engaged in a bitter standoff that affected all diplomatic exchanges, encouraged an expensive arms race, and limited the resources available for reform at home. For the United States, it was a first experience with the fiercely competitive international relations that had long plagued the nations of Europe. And while there was seldom actual shooting, the struggle required warlike measures and imposed costs on all countries involved.

What caused the Cold War? Historians have long argued over the question of where responsibility should be placed. In the early years after the Second World War, policymakers and commentators who supported their actions justified the American stance as a bold and courageous effort to meet the Communist threat. Later, particularly in the 1960s, as the war in Vietnam eroded confidence in American foreign policy, revisionist historians began to argue that American actions were misguided, insensitive to Soviet needs, and at least partially responsible for escalating friction. As with most historical questions, there are no easy answers, but both sides must be weighed.

The Cold War stemmed from a competition for international influence between the two great world powers. After World War II, the U.S. goal was to exercise economic and political leadership in the world and thus to establish capitalist economies and democratic political institutions throughout Europe and in nations emerging from colonial rule. But these goals put the United States on a collision course with nations such as the Soviet Union that had a different vision of what the postwar world should be like and with anticolonial movements in emerging countries around the globe. Perceiving threats from the Soviet Union, China, and other Communist countries, the United States clung

to its deep-rooted sense of mission and embarked on an increasingly aggressive effort at containment, based on its reading of the lessons of the past. American efforts culminated in the ill-fated war in Vietnam as the Communist nations of the world defended their own interests with equal force. The Cold War, with its profound effects at home and abroad, was the unfortunate result.

QUESTIONS FOR REVIEW AND REFLECTION

1. What were the roots of the Cold War conflict?
2. Why did the United States and Soviet Union find it so difficult to get along in the years after World War II?
3. How did American Cold War policy change in the late 1940s?
4. What impact did the Cold War have on American society at home?
5. Could the Cold War have been avoided?

CHAPTER 28

Reform and Rebellion in the Turbulent Sixties, 1960–1969

The United States was comfortable and confident as the 1960s began. There was a basic consensus about the responsibility of the government to help those who could not help themselves. Then that consensus fragmented in the turbulence that accompanied the Vietnam War.

(Romare Bearden (1914–1988), "The Dove". 1964. Cut-and-pasted photoreproductions and papers, gouache, pencil and colored pencil on cardboard. 13 3/8 x 18 3/4". Blanchette Rockefeller Fund. (377.1971). The Museum of Modern Art/Licensed by Scala-Art Resource, NY. Art © Romare Bearden Foundation/Licensed by VAGA, NY)

American Stories

A Young Liberal Questions the Welfare State

Paul Cowan was an idealist in the 1960s. Like many students who came of age in these years, he believed in the possibility of social change and plunged into the struggle for liberal reform. He shared the hopes and dreams of other members of his generation, who felt that their government could make a difference in people's lives.

Cowan's commitment had developed slowly. He was a child of the 1950s, when most Americans were caught up in the consumer culture and paid little attention to the problems of people less fortunate than themselves. His grandfather had sold used cement bags in Chicago, but his father had become an executive at CBS television, and Cowan grew up in comfortable surroundings. He graduated from the Choate School (where John Kennedy had gone) in 1958, and then from Harvard University (where Kennedy had also been a student) in 1963.

When he entered college, Cowan was interested in politically conscious writers such as John Dos Passos, John Steinbeck, and James Agee and folk singers such as Pete Seeger and Woody Guthrie. They offered him entrance, he later recalled, into a "nation that seemed to be filled with energy and decency," one that lurked "beneath the dull, conformist facade of the Eisenhower years." While at Harvard, he was excited by antinuclear campaigns in New England and civil rights demonstrations in the South.

After college, he made good on his commitment to civil rights by going to Mississippi to work in the Freedom Summer project of 1964. He was inspired by the example of John Kennedy, the liberal president whose administration promised "a new kind of politics" that could make the nation, and the world, a better place. During that summer, he wrote, "it was possible to believe that by changing ourselves we could change, and redeem, our America."

The Peace Corps came next. Paul and his wife, Rachel, were convinced that this organization, the idea of the young president, "really was a unique government agency, permanently protected by the lingering magic of John F. Kennedy's name." They were assigned to the city of Guayaquil, in Ecuador, in South America. Their task was to serve as mediators between administrators of the city hall and residents of the slums. They wanted to try to raise the standard of living by encouraging local governments to provide basic services such as garbage disposal and clean water.

But the work proved more frustrating than they had imagined. They bristled at the restrictions imposed by the Peace Corps bureaucracy. They despaired at the inadequate resources local government officials had to accomplish their aims. They wondered whether they were simply new imperialists, trying to impose their values on others who had priorities of their own. "From the day we moved into the *barrio*," Cowan later recalled, "the question we were most frequently asked by the people we were supposed to be organizing was whether we would leave them our clothes when we returned to the States."

Cowan came home disillusioned. "I saw that even the liberals I had wanted to emulate, men who seemed to be devoting their lives to fighting injustice, were unable to accept people from alien cultures on any terms but their own." He called his account of his own odyssey *The Making of an Un-American.*

Paul Cowan's passage through the 1960s mirrored the passage of American society as a whole. Millions of Americans shared his views of the possibilities of democracy as the period began. Mostly comfortable and confident, they supported the liberal agenda advanced by the Democratic party of John Kennedy and Lyndon Johnson. They endorsed the proposition that the government had responsibility for the welfare of all its citizens and accepted the need for a more active government role to help those of its diverse peoples who were unable to help themselves. That commitment lay behind the legislative achievements of the "Great Society," the last wave of twentieth-century reform that built on the gains of the Progressive era and the New Deal years before.

Then political reaction set in as the nation was torn apart by the ravages of the Vietnam War. The escalation of the war, which led to charges that the United States was engaging in an imperialistic crusade like those of other nations in the past, sent more than half a million American soldiers to fight in a far-off land and provoked a protest movement that ripped apart the society. Young Americans, espousing different values and a different version of the American dream, challenged the priorities of their parents. At the same time, they paraded their sexuality more openly, experimented with different forms of mystical religious faith, and enjoyed readily available drugs. In the end, their challenges helped reverse the course of the war. But in the process, liberal assumptions eroded as conservatives argued that an activist approach was responsible for the social and political chaos that consumed the country.

This chapter describes both the climax of twentieth-century liberalism and the turbulence that led to its decline. It focuses on the effort of the government, begun in the New Deal of Franklin Roosevelt, to help those caught short by the advances of industrial capitalism. It first examines the democratic commitment in the 1960s to provide necessary assistance to the less fortunate members of American society and then describes the turmoil that undermined the possibility of such aid. In pondering the possibilities of reform, this chapter outlines the various attempts to devise an effective political response to the major structural changes in the post–World War II economy described in Chapter 26. And then it shows how the Cold War assumptions outlined in Chapter 27 led to the rifts that ripped the nation apart and tarnished the United States in the eyes of the world.

John F. Kennedy: The Camelot Years

The commitment to an American welfare state reached its high-water point in the 1960s. As the left-wing Labour Party in Great Britain played a more and more influential role and occasionally assumed power, and social democratic coalitions were equally active in other European nations, Americans took note. Democrats wanted to follow their example and broaden the role of government even further than Franklin D. Roosevelt and Harry S Truman had done in the 1930s and 1940s, in an effort to address the problems of poverty, unemployment, and racism. John F. Kennedy, a senator from Massachusetts, demanded that the United States move in the direction of what he called a "New Frontier."

The Election of 1960

In the 1960 presidential campaign, Kennedy ran against Vice President Richard Nixon, who clearly had more executive experience. Kennedy argued that the government in general, and the president in particular, had to play an even more active role than they had in the Eisenhower years. He charged that the country had become lazy as it reveled in the prosperity of the 1950s. There were, in fact, serious problems that needed to be solved.

Seventy million Americans tuned in to watch the two men square off against one another in the first televised presidential debate. Kennedy appeared tanned and rested. Nixon, who had recently been hospitalized with an infection, looked tired and gaunt. Even worse, the makeup he applied to hide his heavy beard growth only accentuated it and gave him a swarthy complexion on screen. The debates made a major difference in the campaign (see the "Recovering the Past" essay, pp.(697–698). Kennedy himself admitted, "It was TV more than anything else that turned the tide." Kennedy overcame seemingly insuperable odds to become the first Catholic in the White House. Yet Kennedy's victory was razor-thin. The electoral margin of 303 to 219 concealed the close popular tally, in which he triumphed by fewer than 120,000 of 68 million votes cast. While Kennedy had Democratic majorities in Congress, many members of his party came from the South and were less sympathetic to liberal causes.

JFK

John Kennedy served as a symbol of the early 1960s. He was far younger than his predecessor; at age 43, he was the youngest man ever elected to the presidency. He came from an Irish Catholic family from Massachusetts that saw politics as a means of acceptance in Protestant America. Raised in comfort, he graduated from Harvard University and went on to serve heroically in the navy during World War II. He was elected first to the House of Representatives in 1946, then to the Senate in 1952, and was reelected six years later by the largest majority in the history of the state.

The new president had a charismatic public presence. He was able to voice his aims in eloquent yet understandable language that motivated his followers. During the campaign, he pointed to challenges at home and abroad, observing that "the New Frontier is here whether we seek it or not." He made the same point even more movingly in his inaugural address: "The torch has been passed to a new generation of Americans—born in this century, tempered by war, disciplined by a hard and bitter peace, proud of our ancient heritage." Many Americans, like Paul Cowan, whom we met at the start of the chapter, were inspired by Kennedy's ringing call to action: "And so, my fellow Americans: Ask not what your country can do for you—ask what you can do for your country."

For Kennedy, strong leadership was all-important. Viewing himself as "tough-minded" and "hard-nosed," he was determined to provide firm direction and play a leading role in creating the national agenda, just as Franklin Roosevelt had done. To that end, he surrounded himself with talented assistants. On his staff were 15 Rhodes scholars and several famous authors. The secretary of state was Dean Rusk, a former member of the State Department who had then served as president of the Rockefeller Foundation. The secretary of defense was Robert S. McNamara, the highly successful president of the Ford Motor Company.

An Energetic Young Leader

John Kennedy's energy and enthusiasm captured the imagination of Americans and people around the world, though few were aware of the physical ailments that affected him. He was fond of using this rocking chair in the White House, which he found comfortable for his ailing back. How did Kennedy's appearance contribute to his popularity and appeal?

(Bettmann/CORBIS)

Further contributing to Kennedy's attractive image were his glamorous wife, Jacqueline, and the glittering social occasions the couple hosted. Nobel Prize winners, musicians, and artists attended White House dinners. Energy, exuberance, and excitement filled the air. The administration seemed like the Camelot of King Arthur's day, popularized in a Broadway musical in 1960.

The New Frontier in Action

In office, Kennedy sought to bolster the economy and to enlarge the welfare state. On the economic front, he wanted to end the lingering recession that began in Eisenhower's last year by working with the business community while controlling price inflation.

These two goals conflicted when, in the spring of 1962, the large steel companies decided on a major price increase after steel unions had accepted a modest wage package. The angry president termed the price increases unjustifiable and pressed for executive and congressional action to force the steel companies to back down. The large companies capitulated, but they disliked Kennedy's heavy-handed approach and decided that this Democratic administration, like all others, was hostile to business. Six weeks after the steel crisis, the stock market plunged in the greatest drop since the Great Crash of 1929. Kennedy received the blame. It now seemed doubly urgent to end the recession. Earlier a proponent of a balanced budget, Kennedy began to listen to his liberal advisers who proposed a Keynesian approach to economic growth. Budget deficits had promoted prosperity during the Second World War and might work in the same way in peacetime, too. A tax cut could put money in people's pockets, and their spending could stimulate the economy. In early 1963, the president called for a $13.5 billion cut in corporate taxes over the next three years. While that cut would cause a large deficit, it would also provide capital that business leaders could spend to revive the economy and ultimately increase tax revenues.

Opposition mounted. Conservatives refused to accept the basic premise that deficits would stimulate economic growth and argued, in Eisenhower's words, that "no family, no business, no nation can spend itself into prosperity." Some liberals claimed that it would be better to stimulate the economy by spending money to improve society rather than by cutting taxes and putting money in people's pockets. What good would it do, economist John Kenneth Galbraith wondered, to have "a few more dollars to spend if the air is too dirty to breathe, the water is . . . too polluted to drink, the commuters are losing out in the struggle to get in and out of cities, the streets are filthy, and the schools are so bad that the young, perhaps wisely, stay away?" Congress pigeonholed the proposal in committee, and there it remained.

On other issues on the liberal agenda, Kennedy met similar resistance. Though he proposed legislation increasing the minimum wage and providing for federal aid for education, medical care for the elderly, housing subsidies, and urban renewal, the results were meager. His new minimum-wage measure passed Congress in pared-down form, but Kennedy did not have the votes in Congress to achieve most of his legislative program.

His inability to win necessary congressional support was most evident in the struggle to aid public education. Soon after taking office, Kennedy proposed a $2.3 billion program of grants to the states over a three-year period to help build schools and raise teachers' salaries. Immediately, a series of prickly questions emerged. Was it appropriate to spend large sums of money for social

Recovering the Past

TELEVISION

In the last 50 years, television has played an increasingly important part in American life, providing historians with another source of evidence about American culture and society in the recent past. Television's popularity by the 1950s was the result of decades of experimentation dating back to the nineteenth century. In the 1930s, NBC installed a television station in the new Empire State Building in New York. Wearing green makeup and purple lipstick to provide better visual contrast, actors began to perform before live cameras in studios. At the end of the decade, *Amos 'n' Andy,* a popular radio show, was telecast, and as the 1940s began, Franklin D. Roosevelt became the first president to appear on television. World War II interrupted the development of television, and Americans relied on radio to bring them news. After the war, however, the commercial development of television quickly resumed. Assembly lines that had made electronic implements of war were now converted to consumer production, and thousands of new sets appeared on the market. The opening of Congress could be seen live in 1947; baseball coverage improved that same year owing to the zoom lens; children's shows such as *Howdy Doody* made their debut; and *Meet the Press,* a radio interview program, made the transition to television.

Although sports programs, variety shows hosted by Ed Sullivan and Milton Berle, TV dramas, and episodic series (*I Love Lucy* and *Gunsmoke,* for example) dominated TV broadcasting in the 1950s, television soon became entwined with politics and public affairs. Americans saw Senator Joseph McCarthy for themselves in the televised Army–McCarthy hearings in 1954; his malevolent behavior on camera contributed to his downfall. The 1948 presidential nominating conventions were the first to be televised, but the use of TV to enhance the public image of politicians was most thoroughly developed by the fatherly Dwight D. Eisenhower and the charismatic John F. Kennedy.

In November 1963, people throughout the United States shared the tragedy of John Kennedy's assassination, sitting for hours before their sets trying to understand the events of his fateful Texas trip. The shock and sorrow of the American people was repeated in the spring of 1968 as they gazed in disbelief at the funerals of Martin Luther King, Jr., and Robert Kennedy. A year later, a quarter of the world's population watched as Neil Armstrong became the first man to set foot on the moon. In that same era, television played an important part in shaping impressions of the war in Vietnam. More and more Americans began to understand the nature and impact of the conflict from what they saw on TV.

This combination of visual entertainment and enlightenment made owning a television set virtually a necessity. By 1970, fully 95 percent of American households owned a TV set, a staggering increase from the 9 percent only 20 years earlier. In fact, fewer families owned refrigerators or indoor toilets.

Reflecting on the Past The implications of the impact of television on American society are of obvious interest to

The candidates squaring off in their debate
(AP/Wide World Photos)

historians. How has television affected other communications and entertainment industries, such as radio, newspapers, and movies? Look at the "Television Tonight" listings shown here. What does the content of TV programming tell us about the values, interests, and tastes of the American people?

Perhaps most significant, what impact has TV had on the course of historical events like presidential campaigns, human relations, and wars? The pictures shown here are from the Kennedy–Nixon debates in the presidential campaign of 1960. The first picture shows the two candidates in the studio. The second picture shows a relaxed and energetic Kennedy staring directly into the TV camera. The third picture shows a taut and tense Nixon challenging the points made by his opponent. Which candidate seems to be speaking directly to the American people? Which candidate makes the better impression? Why? Polls of radio listeners taken after the first debate showed Nixon the winner; surveys of television viewers placed Kennedy in front. How do you account for this discrepancy? ■

John Kennedy (above) and Richard Nixon (right)

(AP/Wide World Photos)

Television Tonight

6:00—WTTV 4: *Leave It to Beaver.* Beaver tries to help a friend who has run away from home. Repeat.

6:30—WLW-I 13: *Cheyenne* has a Laramie adventure in which Slim, Jess, and Jonesy work on a cattle drive. Repeat.

7:30—WTTV 4: *The Untouchables.* Eliot Ness tries to deal with a late gangster's niece who has a record of the murdered hood's career. Repeat.

7:30—WLW-I 13: *Voyage to the Bottom of the Sea* presents "Mutiny," in which Admiral Nelson shows signs of a mental breakdown during the search for a giant jellyfish which supposedly consumed a submarine.

7:30—WFBM-TV 6: Members of the Indianapolis Rotary Club discuss the 1965 business outlook with former U.S. Sen. Homer Capehart.

8:00—WFBM-TV 6: *The Man from UNCLE* is in at a new time and night. Thrush agents try to recapture one of their leaders before Napoleon Solo can deliver him to the Central Intelligence Agency. Ralph Taeger is guest star.

8:00—WISH-TV 8: *I've Got a Secret* welcomes the panel from To Tell the Truth: Tom Poston, Peggy Cass, Kitty Carlisle, and Orson Bean.

8:30—WLW-I 13: Basketball, I.U. vs. Iowa.

8:30—WISH-TV 8: *Andy Griffith's* comedy involves Goober's attempts to fill in at the sheriff's office.

9:00—WFBM-TV 6: *Andy Williams* is visited by composer Henry Mancini, Bobby Darin, and Vic Damone. Musical selections include "Charade," "Hello Dolly," and "Moon River."

9:00—WTTV 4: *Lloyd Thaxton* welcomes vocal group Herman's Hermits.

9:30—WISH-TV 8: *Many Happy Returns.* Walter's plan for currying favor with the store's boss hits a snag.

10:00—WFBM-TV 6: *Alfred Hitchcock* presents Margaret Leighton as a spinster who goes mad when she cannot cope with the strain of rearing an orphaned niece in "Where the Woodbine Twineth."

10:00—WLW-I 13: *Ben Casey* gets help in diagnosing a boy's illness from an Australian veterinarian with terminal leukemia. The vet's knowledge of bats provides the key.

10:00—WISH-TV 8: "Viet Nam: How We Got In—Can We Get Out?" is the topic of CBS Reports.

Source: Indianapolis News, January 11, 1965.

goals? Would federal aid bring federal control of school policies and curriculum? Should assistance go to segregated schools? Should it go to parochial schools? In the end, compromise on these issues proved impossible and the school aid measure died in committee.

Kennedy was more successful in securing funding for the exploration of space. The space program was caught up in the competition of the Cold War, and with the Soviet launching of *Sputnik* and the first manned flights, the USSR clearly had the lead. In response, Kennedy proposed that the United States commit itself to landing a man on the moon and returning him to earth before the end of the decade. Congress assented and increased funding of the National Aeronautics and Space Administration (NASA).

Kennedy also established the Peace Corps, which sent young men and women overseas to assist developing countries by working with people at a grassroots level. Paul Cowan, introduced at the start of this chapter, was one of thousands of volunteers who hoped to share their liberal dreams.

If Kennedy's successes were modest, he had at least made commitments that could be broadened later. He had reaffirmed the importance of executive leadership in the effort to extend the boundaries of the welfare state. And he had committed himself to using modern economics to maintain fiscal stability. The nation was poised to achieve liberal goals.

Civil Rights and Kennedy's Response

So it was with civil rights. The pressures that had mounted in the decade and a half after World War II had brought significant change in eliminating segregation in American society. As the effort continued, a spectrum of organizations carried the fight forward. The NAACP, founded in 1910, remained committed to overturning the legal bases for segregation in the aftermath of its victory in the *Brown* v. *Board of Education* case of 1954 (see Chapter 26). The Congress of Racial Equality (CORE), an interracial group established in 1942, promoted change through peaceful confrontation. In 1957, after their victory in the bus boycott in Montgomery, Alabama, Martin Luther King, Jr., and others formed the Southern Christian Leadership Conference (SCLC), an organization of southern black clergy. Far more militant was the Student Nonviolent Coordinating Committee (SNCC, pronounced "snick"), which began to operate in 1960 and recruited young Americans not previously involved.

Confrontations continued in the 1960s. On January 31, 1960, four black college students from the Agricultural and Technical College in Greensboro, North Carolina, frustrated that they were permitted to shop but not to eat at a Woolworth's, a popular department store chain, sat down at the lunch counter and refused to leave. When a reporter inquired how long they had been planning the protest, the students responded, "All our lives!" The next day more students showed up, and the following day still more. The sit-ins, which spread to other cities, captured media attention and eventually included as many as 70,000 participants. Those protesting often met with a brutal response. John Lewis, an African American activist who participated in a sit-in in Nashville, Tennessee, described how "a group of young white men came in and they started pulling and beating primarily the young women. They put lighted cigarettes down their

Sitting-In

In violation of southern law, black college students refused to leave a lunch counter, launching a new campaign in the struggle for civil rights. Here the students wait patiently for service, or forcible eviction, as a way of dramatizing their determination to end segregation. What did the students hope to achieve by their actions?

(Bruce Roberts/Photo Researchers)

back, in their hair, and they were really beating people." And then the black protesters were arrested for disturbing the peace.

The following year, sit-ins gave rise to freedom rides, aimed at testing southern transportation facilities that recently had been desegregated by a Supreme Court decision. Organized initially by CORE and aided by SNCC, the program sent groups of blacks and whites together on buses heading south and stopping at terminals along the way. The riders, peaceful themselves, anticipated confrontations that would publicize their cause and generate political support, and they frequently ended up in jail. The civil rights movement became the most powerful moral campaign since the abolitionist crusade before the Civil War. Anne Moody, who grew up in a small town in Mississippi, personified the awakening of black consciousness. As a child, she had watched the murder of friends and acquaintances who had somehow transgressed the limits set for blacks. Overcoming the hardships of growing up poor and black in the rural South, Moody became the first member of her family to go to college and later joined the NAACP and became involved in the activities of SNCC and CORE. Slowly, she noted, "I could feel myself beginning to change. For the first time I began to think something would be done about whites killing, beating, and misusing Negroes. I knew I was going to be a part of whatever happened." Participating in sit-ins, where she was thrashed and jailed for her activities, she remained deeply involved in the movement.

Many whites also joined the movement in the South. Mimi Feingold, a white student at Swarthmore College in Pennsylvania, helped picket the Woolworth's nearby. After her sophomore year, she headed south to join the freedom rides sponsored by CORE. Like many others, Feingold found herself in the midst of often-violent confrontations and went to jail as an act of conscience.

In 1962, the civil rights movement accelerated. James Meredith, a black air force veteran and student at Jackson State College, applied to the all-white University of Mississippi, only to be rejected on racial grounds. Although the Supreme Court affirmed his right to attend, Governor Ross Barnett, an adamant racist, announced defiantly that Meredith would not be admitted, and on one occasion personally blocked the way. A major riot followed; tear gas covered the university grounds; and by the riot's end, two men lay dead and hundreds were hurt.

Other governors were equally aggressive. In his 1963 inaugural address, George C. Wallace of Alabama declared boldly, "Segregation now! Segregation tomorrow! Segregation forever!" as he voiced his opposition to integration.

Alabama became a national focus that year as a violent confrontation unfolded in Birmingham. Local black leaders encouraged Martin Luther King, Jr., to launch another attack on southern segregation in the city. Though the demonstrations were nonviolent, the responses were not. City officials declared that protest

Attacks on Demonstrators in Birmingham

In Birmingham, city officials responded to peaceful demonstrators with brutal force. Here city police use trained dogs to drive marchers back. Televised nationally, the police response appalled the American public. As newsman Eric Sevareid observed, "A newspaper or television picture of a snarling police dog set upon a human being is recorded on the permanent photoelectric file of every human brain." What did the Birmingham authorities hope to achieve by use of these dogs?

(Charles Moore/Black Star)

marches violated city regulations against parading without a license, and, over a five-week period, they arrested 2,200 blacks, some of them schoolchildren. Police Commissioner Eugene "Bull" Connor used high-pressure fire hoses, electric cattle prods, and trained police dogs to force the protesters back. As the media recorded the events, Americans watching television and reading newspapers were horrified.

Kennedy claimed to be sickened by the pictures from Birmingham but insisted that he could do nothing, even though he had sought and won black support in 1960. The narrowness of his electoral victory made him reluctant to press white southerners on civil rights when he needed their votes on other issues. Events finally forced Kennedy to act more boldly. In the James Meredith confrontation, the president, like his predecessor in the Little Rock crisis, had to send federal troops to restore control and to guarantee Meredith's right to attend the university. The administration also forced the desegregation of the University of Alabama and helped arrange a compromise that eased discrimination in Birmingham's municipal facilities and hiring practices. And when white bombings aimed at eliminating black leaders in Birmingham caused thousands of blacks to abandon nonviolence and rampage through the streets, Kennedy readied federal troops to intervene.

He also spoke out more forcefully than before. In a nationally televised address, he called the quest for equal rights a "moral issue" and asked, "Are we to say to the world, and, much more importantly, to each other that this is a land of the free except for the Negroes?" Just hours after the president spoke, assassins killed Medgar Evers, a black NAACP official, in his own driveway in Jackson, Mississippi.

Kennedy sent Congress a new and stronger civil rights bill, outlawing segregation in public places, banning discrimination wherever federal money was involved, and advancing the process of school integration. Polls showed that 63 percent of the nation supported his stand.

To lobby for passage of this measure, civil rights leaders, pressed from below by black activists, arranged a massive march on Washington in August 1963. More than 200,000 people—black and white, common folk and celebrities—gathered from across the country. The folk music artists of the early 1960s were there as well. Joan Baez, Bob Dylan, and Peter, Paul, and Mary led the crowd in songs associated with the movement, such as "Blowin' in the Wind" and "We Shall Overcome."

The high point of the day was the address by Martin Luther King, Jr., who by now was the nation's preeminent spokesman for civil rights and proponent of nonviolent protest. King proclaimed his faith in the decency of his fellow citizens and in their ability to extend the promises of the Constitution and the Declaration of Independence to every American. With all the power of a southern preacher, he implored his audience to share his faith.

"I have a dream," King declared, "that one day this nation will rise up and live out the true meaning of its creed: 'We hold these truths to be self-evident, that all men are created equal.' I have a dream that one day on the red hills of Georgia, the sons of former slaves and the sons of former slave-owners will be able to sit together at the table of brotherhood." Each time King used the refrain "I have a dream," thousands of blacks and whites roared together. King concluded by quoting from an old hymn: "Free at last! Free at last! Thank God almighty, we are free at last!"

Not all were moved. Anne Moody, who had come up from her activist work in Mississippi to attend the event, sat on the grass by the Lincoln Memorial as the speaker's words rang out. "Martin Luther King went on and on talking about his dream," she said. "I sat there thinking that... we never had time to sleep, much less dream." Nor was Congress prompted to do much. Despite large Democratic majorities, strong white southern resistance to the cause of civil rights continued, and the bill was bottled up in committee.

Lyndon B. Johnson and the Great Society

Kennedy knew he faced a difficult reelection battle in 1964. He wanted not only to win the presidency for a second term but also to increase liberal Democratic strength in Congress. Instead, an assassin's attack took his life and brought a new leader to the helm.

Change of Command

In November 1963, Kennedy traveled to Texas, where he hoped to unite the state's Democratic party for the upcoming election. Dallas, one of the stops on the trip, was reputed to be hostile to the administration. Entering the city in an open car, the president encountered friendly crowds. Suddenly shots rang out, and Kennedy slumped forward as bullets ripped through his head and throat. Mortally wounded, he died a short time later at a Dallas hospital. Lee Harvey Oswald, the accused assassin, was shot and killed a few days later by a minor underworld figure as he was being moved within the jail.

Americans were stunned. For days, people stayed at home and watched endless television replays of the assassination and its aftermath. The images of the handsome president felled by bullets, the funeral cortege, and the president's young son saluting his father's casket as it rolled by on the way to final burial at Arlington National Cemetery were all imprinted on people's minds. Vice President Lyndon Johnson succeeded Kennedy as president. Though less polished, Johnson was a more effective political leader than Kennedy and brought his own special skills and vision to the presidency.

LBJ

Johnson had taken a different road to the White House and came from a far more humble background than Kennedy. He had begun his public career as a legislative assistant in the House of Representatives in Washington, D.C., then served as a New Deal official in Texas. He won election first to the House in 1937 and then to the Senate in 1948. Eager to be president, he accepted the vice presidential nomination when it became clear in 1960 that Kennedy was going to win the nomination for president.

Johnson was a man of elemental force. Always manipulative, he was often difficult to like. There was a streak of vulgarity that contributed to his earthy appeal but was frequently offensive. Those qualities notwithstanding, he was successful in the passion of his life—politics—and was the most able legislator of the postwar years. As Senate majority leader, he became famous for his ability to get things done. Ceaseless in his search for information, tireless in his attention to detail, he could flatter and cajole, and became famous for what came to be called the "Johnson treatment." According to columnists Rowland Evans, Jr., and Robert Novak, he zeroed in, "his face a scant millimeter from his target, his eyes widening and narrowing, his eyebrows rising and falling." He grabbed people by

the lapels, made them listen, and usually got his way (see the series of illustrations).

As vice president, Johnson went into a state of eclipse. He felt useless and stifled in his new role without his power base in the Senate and was uncomfortable with the Kennedy crowd. Despite his own ambivalence about Kennedy, Johnson sensed the profound shock that gripped the United States after the assassination and was determined to utilize Kennedy's memory to achieve legislative success. Even more than Kennedy, he was willing to wield presidential power aggressively and to use the media to shape public opinion in pursuit of his vision of a society in which the comforts of life would be more widely shared and poverty would be eliminated.

The Great Society in Action

Lyndon Johnson had an expansive vision of the possibilities of reform. Using his considerable political skills, he succeeded in pushing through Congress the most extensive reform program in American history.

Johnson began to develop the support he needed the day he took office. In his first public address, delivered to Congress and televised nationwide, he sought to dispel the image of impostor as he embraced Kennedy's liberal program. He began, in a measured tone, with the words, "All I have, I would have given gladly not to be standing here today." He asked members of Congress to work with him, and he underscored the theme "Let us continue."

As a first step, Johnson resolved to secure the measures Kennedy had been unable to extract from Congress. Bills to reduce taxes and ensure civil rights were his first and most pressing priorities,

Lyndon Johnson in Action
Lyndon Johnson kept tight control of the Senate in the 1950s and was known for his ability to get his way. Here he is shown giving the famous "Johnson treatment" to Senator Theodore Francis Green in 1957. Note the way Green is bending backward in an unsuccessful effort to keep his distance from LBJ. Why do you think LBJ usually got his way?

(George Tames/The New York Times)

but he was interested too in aiding public education, providing medical care for the aged, and eliminating poverty. By the spring of 1964, he began to use the phrase "Great Society" to describe his expansive reform program.

Johnson's landslide victory over conservative Republican challenger Barry Goldwater of Arizona in the 1964 election validated his approach. This was the first time in recent history that a conservative had gained the Republican nomination. Goldwater, however, frightened even members of his own party by proclaiming that "extremism in the defense of liberty is no vice," and by speaking out against such popular programs as social security. LBJ received 61 percent of the popular vote and 486 electoral votes to Goldwater's 52 and gained Democratic majorities in both the Senate and the House. Goldwater's candidacy drove moderate Republicans to vote for the Democratic party this time and gave Johnson a far more impressive mandate than Kennedy had ever enjoyed.

Civil rights reform was LBJ's first legislative priority and an integral part of the Great Society program, but other measures were equally important. Following Kennedy's lead, Johnson pressed for a tax cut. He accepted the Keynesian theory that deficits, properly managed, could promote prosperity. If people had more money to spend, then their purchases could stimulate the economy. Soon the tax bill passed.

With the tax cut in hand, the president pressed for the antipoverty program that Kennedy had begun to plan. Such an effort was bold and unprecedented in the United States, even though social democracy had a long history in European nations and other countries around the world. During the Progressive era at the turn of the century, some legislation had attempted to alleviate conditions associated with poverty. During the New Deal, Franklin Roosevelt had proposed programs to assist people who could not help themselves. Now Johnson took a step that no president had taken before; in his 1964 State of the Union message, he declared an "unconditional war on poverty in America."

The center of this expansive effort to eradicate poverty was the Economic Opportunity Act of 1964. It created an Office of Economic Opportunity (OEO) to provide education and training through programs such as the Job Corps for unskilled young people trapped in the poverty cycle. VISTA (Volunteers in Service to America), patterned after the Peace Corps, offered assistance to the poor at home, while Head Start tried to give disadvantaged children a chance to succeed in school. Assorted community action programs gave the poor a voice in improving housing, health, and education. Two agencies responded to

Native American pressure by allowing Indians to devise programs and budgets and then administer programs themselves.

Aware of the escalating costs of medical care, Johnson also proposed a medical assistance plan. Both Truman and Kennedy had supported such an initiative but had failed to win congressional approval. Johnson succeeded. To head off conservative attacks, the administration tied the Medicare measure to the social security system and limited the program to the elderly. The complementary Medicaid program met the needs of those on welfare and certain other groups who could not afford private insurance. The Medicare–Medicaid initiative was the most important extension of federally directed social benefits since the Social Security Act of 1935. Johnson was similarly successful in his effort to provide aid for elementary and secondary schools. His legislation allocated education money to the states based on the number of children from low-income families. Those funds would then be distributed to assist deprived children in public as well as private schools.

In LBJ's optimistic vision, the federal government would ensure that everyone shared in the promise of American life. Under his prodding, Congress passed a new housing act to give rent supplements to the poor and created a Cabinet Department of Housing and Urban Development.

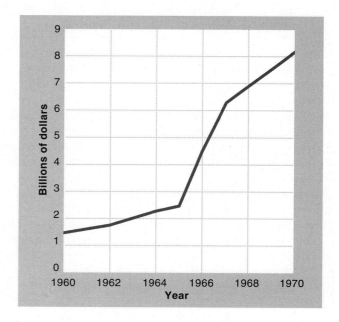

Federal Aid to Education in the 1960s

Passage of a bill to provide federal aid to education in 1965 led to rapidly increasing government support at all levels for the remainder of the decade.

Source: U.S. Bureau of the Census.

The federal government provided new forms of aid, such as legal assistance for the poor and allocated additional funds for higher education. Congress also provided artists and scholars with assistance through the National Endowments for the Arts and Humanities, created in 1965. At the same time, Johnson's administration provided much-needed immigration reform. The Immigration Act of 1965 replaced previously restrictive policy, in place since 1924, with a measure that vastly increased the ceiling on immigration and opened the door to immigrants from Asia and Latin America. By the late 1960s, some 350,000 immigrants were entering the United States annually, compared to the average of 47,000 per year between 1931 and 1945. This new stream of immigration created a population more diverse than it had been since the early decades of the twentieth century. The Great Society also reflected the stirring of the environmental movement. In 1962, naturalist Rachel Carson alerted the public to the dangers of pesticide poisoning and environmental pollution in her book *Silent Spring*. She took aim at chemical pesticides, especially DDT, which had increased crop yields but had brought disastrous side effects:

> The most alarming of all man's assaults upon the rivers, and sea with dangerous and even lethal materials. This pollution is for the most part irrecoverable; the chain of evil it initiates not only in the world that must support life but in living tissues is for the most part irreversible. In this now universal contamination of the environment, chemicals are the sinister and little-recognized partners of radiation in changing the very nature of the world—the very nature of its life.

Johnson was determined to address such problems and to provide protection for wildlife. The National Wilderness Preservation Act of 1964 set aside 9.1 million acres of wilderness, and Congress passed other measures to limit air and water pollution. In addition, Lady Bird Johnson, the president's wife, led a beautification campaign to eliminate unsightly billboards and junkyards along the nation's highways.

Roots of Selected Great Society Programs

Progressive Period	New Deal	Great Society
Settlement house activity of Jane Addams and others	Relief efforts to ease unemployment (FERA, WPA)	Poverty programs (OEO)
Efforts to clean up slums (tenement house laws)	Housing program	Rehabilitation of slums through Model Cities program
Progressive party platform calling for federal accident, old-age, and unemployment insurance	Social security system providing unemployment compensation and old-age pensions	Medical care for the aged through social security (Medicare)
Activity to break up monopolies and regulate business	Regulation of utility companies	Regulation of highway safety and transportation
Efforts to regulate working conditions and benefits	Establishment of standards for working conditions and minimum wage	Raising of minimum wage
Efforts to increase literacy and spread education at all levels	Efforts to keep college students in school through NYA	Assistance to elementary, secondary, and higher education
Theodore Roosevelt's efforts at wilderness preservation	Conservation efforts (CCC, TVA planning)	Safeguarding of wilderness lands
Establishment of federal income tax	Tax reform to close loopholes and increase taxes for the wealthy	Tax cut to stimulate business activity
Theodore Roosevelt's overtures to Booker T. Washington	Discussion (but not passage) of antilynching legislation	Civil rights measures to ban discrimination in public accommodations and to guarantee right to vote

Achievements and Challenges in Civil Rights

Lyndon Johnson was enormously successful in advancing the cause of civil rights. Seizing the opportunity provided by Kennedy's assassination, Johnson told Congress, "No memorial oration or eulogy could more eloquently honor President Kennedy's memory than the earliest possible passage of the civil rights bill." Heading off a Senate filibuster, he pushed the bill through Congress.

The Civil Rights Act of 1964 outlawed racial discrimination in all public accommodations and authorized the Justice Department to act with greater authority in school and voting matters. In addition, an equal-opportunity provision prohibited discriminatory hiring on grounds of race, gender, religion, or national origin in firms with more than 25 employees. Although the law was one of the great achievements of the 1960s, widespread discrimination still existed in American society and African Americans in large areas of the South still found it difficult to vote. Freedom Summer,

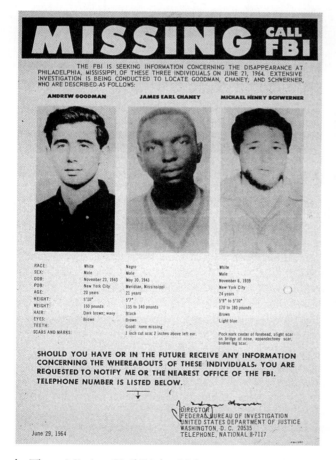

Three Missing Civil Rights Volunteers

This poster shows pictures of the three civil rights workers who were missing soon after their arrival in Mississippi in the summer of 1964. What do the pictures tell you about the volunteers? What do you think people at the time would have thought when they saw this poster?

(Getty Images)

sponsored by SNCC and other civil rights groups in 1964, focused attention on the problem by sending black and white students to Mississippi to work for black rights. Early in the summer, two whites, Michael Schwerner and Andrew Goodman, and one black, James Chaney, were murdered. By the end of the summer, 80 workers had been beaten, 1,000 arrests had been made, and 37 churches had been bombed. In the face of such resistance, Johnson asked Congress for a voting bill that would close the loopholes of the previous two acts.

The Voting Rights Act of 1965 was perhaps the most important law of the decade. It singled out the South for its restrictive practices and authorized the U.S. attorney general to appoint federal examiners to register voters where local officials were obstructing the registration of blacks. In the year after passage of the act, 400,000 blacks registered to vote in the Deep South; by 1968, the number reached 1 million.

Despite passage of the Civil Rights Act of 1964 and the Voting Rights Act of 1965, racial discrimination remained throughout the country. Still-segregated schools, wretched housing, and inadequate job opportunities were continuing problems. As the struggle for civil rights moved north, dramatic divisions within the movement emerged.

Initially, the civil rights campaign had been integrated and nonviolent. Its acknowledged leader was Martin Luther King, Jr. But now tensions between blacks and whites flared within organizations, and younger black leaders began to challenge King's nonviolent approach. They were tired of beatings, jailings, church bombings, and the slow pace of change when dependent on white liberal support and government action. Anne Moody, the stalwart activist in Mississippi, voiced the doubts so many blacks harbored about the possibility of real change. Discouraged after months of struggle, she boarded a bus taking civil rights workers north to testify about the abuses that still remained. As she listened to the others singing the movement's songs, she was overwhelmed by the suffering she had so often seen. "We Shall Overcome" reverberated around her, but all she could think was, "I wonder. I really wonder."

One episode that contributed to many blacks' suspicion of white liberals occurred at the Democratic national convention of 1964 in Atlantic City. SNCC, active in the Freedom Summer project in Mississippi, had founded the Freedom Democratic party as an alternative to the all-white delegation that was to represent the state. Testifying before the credentials committee, black activist Fannie Lou Hamer reported that she had been beaten, jailed, and denied the right to vote. Yet the committee's final compromise, pressed by President Johnson, who worried about losing southern support in the coming election, was that the white delegation would still be seated, with two members of the protest organization offered seats at large. That response hardly satisfied those who had risked their lives and families to try to vote in Mississippi. SNCC, once a religious, integrated organization, began to change into an all-black cadre that could mobilize poor blacks for militant action. Malcolm X was perhaps the leader most responsible for channeling black frustration into a new set of goals and tactics. Born Malcolm Little and reared in ghettos from Detroit to New York, he hustled gambling numbers and prostitutes in the big cities. Arrested and imprisoned, he became a convert to the Nation of Islam and a disciple of black leader Elijah Muhammad. He began to preach that the white man was responsible for the black man's condition and that blacks had to help themselves.

Malcolm was impatient with the moderate civil rights movement. He grew tired of hearing "all of this nonviolent, begging-the-white-man kind of dying... all of this sitting-in, sliding-in, wading-in, eating-in, diving-in, and all the rest." Espousing black separatism and black nationalism for most of his public career, he argued for black control of black communities, preached an international perspective embracing African peoples in diaspora, and appealed to blacks to fight racism "by any means necessary."

Malcolm X became the most dynamic spokesman for poor northern blacks since Marcus Garvey in the 1920s. Though he was assassinated by black antagonists in 1965, his African-centered, uncompromising perspective helped shape the struggle against racism.

One man influenced by Malcolm's message was Stokely Carmichael. Born in Trinidad, he came to the United States at the age of 11, where he grew up with an interest in political affairs and black protest. Frustrated with the strategy of civil disobedience as he became active in SNCC, he urged fieldworkers to carry weapons for self-defense. It was time for blacks to cease depending on whites, he argued, and to make SNCC into a black organization. His election as head of the student group reflected SNCC's growing radicalism.

The split in the black movement was dramatized in June 1966 when Carmichael's followers challenged those of Martin Luther King, Jr., during a march in Mississippi. King still adhered to nonviolence and interracial cooperation. Just out of jail after being arrested for his protest activities, Carmichael jumped onto a flatbed truck to address the group. "This is the twenty-seventh time I have been arrested—and I ain't going to jail no more!" he shouted. "The only way we gonna stop them white men from whippin' us is to take over. We been saying freedom for six years and we ain't got nothing. What we gonna start saying now is Black Power!" Carmichael had the audience in his hand as he repeated, and the crowd shouted back, "We...want...Black...Power!"

Malcolm X at the Lectern
"The day of nonviolence is over," Malcolm X proclaimed, as many African Americans listened enthusiastically. A compelling speaker, Malcolm made a powerful case for a more aggressive campaign for black rights. What image does Malcolm X convey in this photograph?

(Bettmann/CORBIS)

Black Power was a call to build independent institutions in the African American community and it fostered a powerful sense of black pride. The movement included a wide variety of different figures, ranging from cultural nationalists to revolutionaries to advocates of black capitalism. Its most enduring legacy was political and cultural mobilization at the grassroots level, even if it only partially realized its goals.

Black Power led to demands for more drastic action. The Black Panthers, radical activists who organized first in Oakland, California, and then in other cities, formed a militant organization that vowed to eradicate not only racial discrimination but capitalism as well. H. Rap Brown, who succeeded Carmichael as head of SNCC, became known for his statement that "violence is as American as cherry pie."

Violence accompanied the more militant calls for reform and showed that racial injustice was not a southern problem but an American one. Riots erupted in Rochester, New York City, and several New Jersey cities in 1964. In 1965, in the Watts neighborhood of Los Angeles, a massive uprising lasting five days left

34 dead, more than 1,000 injured, and hundreds of structures burned to the ground. Violence broke out again in other cities in 1966, 1967, and 1968.

A Sympathetic Supreme Court

With the addition of four new liberal justices appointed by Kennedy and Johnson, the Supreme Court supported and promoted the liberal agenda. Under the leadership of chief justice Earl Warren, the Court followed the lead it had taken in *Brown* v. *Board of Education* outlawing school segregation by moving against Jim Crow practices in other public establishments.

The Court also supported civil liberties by beginning to protect the rights of individuals with radical political views. Similarly, the Court sought to protect accused suspects from police harassment. In *Gideon* v. *Wainwright* (1963), the justices decided that poor defendants in serious cases had the right to free legal counsel. In *Escobedo* v. *Illinois* (1964), they ruled that a suspect had to be given access to an attorney during questioning. In *Miranda* v. *Arizona* (1966), they argued that offenders had to be warned that statements extracted by the police could be used against them and that they could remain silent.

Other decisions similarly broke new ground. *Baker* v. *Carr* (1962) opened the way to reapportionment of state legislative bodies according to the standard, defined a year later in Justice William O. Douglas's words, of "one person, one vote." This crucial ruling helped break the political control of lightly populated rural districts in many state assemblies and made the U.S. House of Representatives much more responsive to urban and suburban issues. Meanwhile, the Court outraged conservatives by ruling that prayer could not be required in the public schools and that obscenity laws could no longer restrict allegedly pornographic material that might have some "redeeming social value."

The Great Society Under Attack

Supported by healthy economic growth, the Great Society worked for a few years as Johnson had hoped. The tax cut proved effective, and the consumer and business spending that it promoted led to a steady increase in the gross national product (GNP) of 7.1 percent in 1964, 8.1 percent in 1965, and 9.5 percent in 1966. As the economy improved, the budget deficit dropped just as predicted. Unemployment fell, and inflation remained under control. Medical programs provided basic security for the old and the poor. Education flourished as schools were built, and teachers' salaries increased as a result of the influx of federal aid.

Yet Johnson's dream of the Great Society proved illusory. Some programs promised too much; others were simply ill conceived or were underfunded. Factionalism was also a problem. Lyndon Johnson had reconstituted the old Democratic coalition in his triumph in 1964, with urban Catholics and southern whites joining organized labor, the black electorate, and the middle class. But conservative white southerners and blue-collar white northerners felt threatened by the government's support of civil rights. Local urban bosses, long the backbone of the Democratic party, objected to grassroots participation of the urban poor, which threatened their own political control.

Criticisms of the Great Society and its liberal underpinnings came from across the political spectrum. Conservatives disliked the centralization of authority and the government's increased role in defining the national welfare. They also questioned involving the poor in reform programs, arguing that poor people lacked a broad vision of the nation's needs. Even middle-class Americans, generally supportive of liberal goals, sometimes grumbled that the government was paying too much attention to the underprivileged and neglecting the needs of the middle class. Radicals, meanwhile, attacked the Great Society for not going far enough. With its assumption that the American system was basically sound, they argued, the Great Society made no real effort to redistribute income and thereby transform American life.

The Vietnam War (discussed later in this chapter) dealt the Great Society a fatal blow. LBJ wanted to maintain both the war and his treasured domestic reform programs, but his effort to pursue these goals simultaneously produced serious inflation. The economy was already booming as a result of the tax cut and the spending for reform. As military expenditures increased, the productive system of the country could not keep up with demand. When Johnson refused to raise taxes, in an effort to hide the costs of the war, inflation spiraled out of control. Congress finally slashed Great Society programs, deciding the country could no longer afford such extensive social reform.

Continuing Confrontations with Communists

The Cold War continued throughout the 1960s. Presidents John F. Kennedy and Lyndon B. Johnson were both aggressive cold warriors who subscribed to the policies of their predecessors. Their commitment to stopping the spread of communism kept the nation locked in the same bitter conflict that had dominated foreign policy in the 1950s and led to continuing global confrontations that sometimes threatened the stability of the entire world.

The Bay of Pigs Fiasco and Its Consequences

Kennedy was intensely interested in foreign affairs. In his ringing inaugural address, he eloquently described the dangers and challenges the United States faced in the Cold War. "In the long history of the world," he cried out, "only a few generations have been granted the role of defending freedom in its hour of maximum danger." The United States would "pay any price, bear any burden, meet any hardship, support any friend, oppose any foe, to assure the survival and success of liberty."

Kennedy perceived direct challenges from the Soviet Union almost from the beginning of his presidency. The first came at the Bay of Pigs in Cuba in the spring of 1961. Cuban–American relations had been strained since Fidel Castro's revolutionary army had seized power in 1959. A radical regime in Cuba, leaning toward the Soviet Union, could provide a model for upheaval elsewhere in Latin America and threaten the venerable Monroe Doctrine. One initiative to counter the Communist threat was the Alliance for Progress, which provided social and economic assistance to the less-developed nations of the hemisphere. But other, more aggressive, responses were deemed necessary as well.

Just before Kennedy assumed office, the United States broke diplomatic relations with Cuba. The CIA, meanwhile, was covertly training anti-Castro exiles to storm the Cuban coast at the Bay of Pigs. The American planners assumed the invasion would lead to an uprising of the Cuban people against Castro. While some top officials resisted the scheme, Kennedy approved the plan.

The invasion, which took place on April 17, 1961, was an unmitigated disaster. When an early air strike failed to destroy Cuban air power, Castro was able to hold off the troops coming ashore. Urged to use American planes for air cover, Kennedy refused, for by that time failure was clear. Rather than supporting the exiles, the Cubans had followed Castro instead, and the predicted popular uprising never materialized. The United States stood exposed to the world, attempting to overthrow a sovereign government. It had broken agreements not to interfere in the internal affairs of hemispheric neighbors and had intervened clumsily and unsuccessfully.

Although chastened by the debacle at the Bay of Pigs, Kennedy remained determined to deal sternly with the perceived Communist threat. Germany became the next battleground. For more than a decade, the nation had been divided (see Chapter 27). The Western powers had promoted the industrial development of West Germany, which was prospering and which stood in stark contrast to the drab, Soviet-controlled East Germany. Berlin, likewise divided, remained an irritant to the Russians, particularly since some 2.6 million East Germans had fled to West Germany, many of them making their escape through the city. Following a hostile meeting with Soviet leader Nikita Khrushchev in Vienna in June 1961, Kennedy reacted aggressively. He asked Congress for $3 billion more in defense appropriations, for more personnel in the armed forces, and for funds for a civil defense fallout-shelter program, explicitly warning of the threat of nuclear war. The USSR responded in August by erecting a wall in Berlin to seal off its section of the city entirely. The concrete structure, topped by barbed wire, was 96 miles long and an average of 11.8 feet high. Menacing machine-gun emplacements made escape difficult. People who were caught scaling the wall were shot. Families were separated as the wall became a dramatic symbol of the division between East and West.

The Cuban Missile Face-Off

The next year, a new crisis arose. American aerial photographs taken in October 1962 revealed that the USSR had begun to place what Kennedy considered offensive missiles on Cuban soil, although Cuba insisted they were defensive. The missiles did not change the strategic balance significantly, for the Soviets could still wreak untold damage on American targets from more distant bases. But with Russian weapons installed just 90 miles from American shores, appearance was more important than reality. This time Kennedy was determined to win a confrontation with the Soviet Union over Cuba.

Top administration officials discussed various alternatives. Some members of the Executive Committee of the National Security Council wanted an air strike to knock out the sites; others, including Attorney General Robert Kennedy, the president's brother, opposed such a move. Still, the United States moved to a state of full alert. Bombers and missiles were armed with nuclear weapons and readied to go. The fleet prepared to move toward Cuba, and troops geared up to invade the island.

Kennedy went on nationwide television to tell the American people about the missiles and to demand their removal. He declared that the United States would not shrink from the risk of nuclear war and announced what he had decided to do: impose a naval "quarantine"—not a blockade, which would have been an act of war—around Cuba to prevent Soviet ships from bringing in additional missiles.

As the Soviet ships steamed toward the blockade, the nations stood "eyeball to eyeball" at the brink. Before they reached the quarantine line, Khrushchev called the Soviet ships back. Khrushchev then sent a long letter, transmitted by teletype, pledging to remove the missiles if the United States lifted the quarantine and promised to stay out of Cuba altogether. A second letter demanded that America remove its own missiles from Turkey as well. The United States agreed to the

Israeli Conquests in 1967

The Six-Day War of 1967 ended in huge Israeli territorial gains, both in the Sinai and on the West Bank of the Jordan River. How did the new territory compare with the size of the state of Israel prior to 1967? What effect did the Israeli victory have on the stability of the Middle East? How would the Arab nations have responded to the defeat?

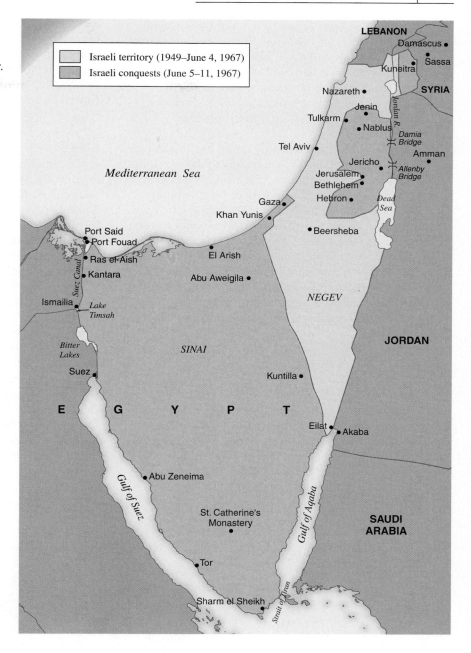

Israeli territory (1949–June 4, 1967)
Israeli conquests (June 5–11, 1967)

first letter, ignored the second, and said nothing about its intention, already voiced, of removing its missiles from Turkey. With that, the crisis ended. Secretary of State Dean Rusk observed, "We have won a considerable victory. You and I are still alive."

The Cuban missile crisis was the most terrifying confrontation of the Cold War. The world was closer than it had ever been to nuclear war. Yet the president emerged from it as a hero who had stood firm. His reputation was enhanced, and his party benefited a few weeks later in the congressional elections. As the relief began to fade, however, critics charged that what Kennedy saw as his finest hour was in fact an unnecessary crisis. One consequence of the affair was the installation of a Soviet–American hotline to avoid similar episodes in the future. Another consequence was the USSR's determination to increase its nuclear arsenal so that it would never again be exposed as inferior to the United States. Despite the Limited Test Ban Treaty of 1963, which prohibited atmospheric testing, the nuclear arms race continued.

Confrontation and Containment Under Johnson

Johnson shared many of Kennedy's assumptions about the threat of communism. His understanding of the onset of World War II led him to believe that aggressors had to be stopped cold. Like Eisenhower and Kennedy, Johnson believed in the domino theory: if one country in a region fell, others were bound to follow. He assumed he could treat foreign adversaries just as he treated political opponents in the United States, and he was frustrated with what he called "piddly little piss-ant" countries that caused trouble.

In 1965, Johnson acted hastily in the Caribbean. He dispatched more than 20,000 troops to the Dominican Republic to counter "Castro-type elements" that were, in fact, engaged in a democratic revolution. His credibility suffered badly from the episode.

In the Middle East, the United States sought to use its influence to temper the violence that erupted in the area. In 1967, Israeli forces defeated the Egyptian army in the Six-Day War and seized the West Bank and Jerusalem, the Golan Heights, and the Sinai Peninsula. Americans pressed for a quick end to the fighting to maintain regional equilibrium and uninterrupted supplies of oil.

War in Vietnam and Turmoil at Home

The commitment to stopping the spread of communism led to the massive U.S. involvement in Vietnam. The roots of the conflict, described in Chapter 26, extended back to the early post–World War II years, but American participation remained relatively limited

until Kennedy took office. Then the United States became increasingly engaged in the effort to resist a Communist takeover. That struggle wrought enormous damage in Southeast Asia, tore the United States apart, and finally forced a full-fledged reevaluation of America's Cold War policies.

Escalation in Vietnam

JFK's commitment to Cold War victory led him to expand the American role in Vietnam, the country he once called the "cornerstone of the free world in Southeast Asia." During the Kennedy administration, the number of advisers rose from 675 to more than 16,000, and American soldiers began to lose their lives.

Despite American backing, South Vietnamese leader Ngo Dinh Diem, a Catholic, was rapidly losing support in his own country. Buddhist priests burned themselves alive in the capital of Saigon to protest the corruption and arbitrariness of Diem's regime. With American approval, South Vietnamese military leaders assassinated Diem and seized the government. While Kennedy understood the importance of popular support for the South Vietnamese government, he was reluctant to withdraw and let the Vietnamese solve their own problems.

Lyndon Johnson shared the same reservations. Soon after assuming the presidency, he made a fundamental decision that guided policy for the next four years. Guerrillas, known as Viet Cong, challenged the

A Protest in Vietnam

In 1963, Buddhist priests in Vietnam burned themselves to death in Saigon to dramatize their opposition to the Diem government. Photographs in American newspapers horrified readers and created suspicion that South Vietnam was led by a corrupt and autocratic leader. Why would this photograph have affected people who saw it so strongly?

(Bettmann/CORBIS)

The Vietnam War

This map shows the major campaigns of the Vietnam War. The North Vietnamese Tet offensive of early 1968, pictured with red arrows, turned the tide against U.S. participation in the war and led to peace talks. The U.S. invasion of Cambodia in 1970, pictured with blue arrows, provoked serious opposition. What role did North Vietnam play in the war? How far did American air power penetrate? Why did the United States and South Vietnam attack neighboring nations, such as Cambodia?

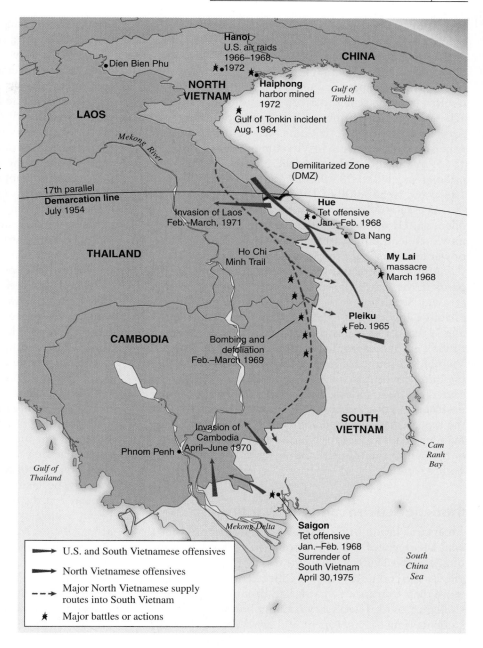

regime, sometimes covertly and sometimes through the National Liberation Front, their political arm. Aided by Ho Chi Minh and the North Vietnamese, the insurgent Viet Cong slowly gained ground. Johnson chose to stand firm and resist them. "I am not going to lose Vietnam," he said. "I am not going to be the President who saw Southeast Asia go the way China went."

In the 1964 election campaign, Johnson posed as a man of peace. "We don't want our American boys to do the fighting for Asian boys," he declared. But secretly he was planning to escalate the American role.

In August 1964, Johnson cleverly obtained congressional authorization for war. He charged that North Vietnamese torpedo boats had made unprovoked attacks on American destroyers in the international waters of the Gulf of Tonkin, 30 miles from North Vietnam. While there had been initial conflict, in fact the attacks Johnson highlighted never occurred. But before the real nature of the engagement became clear, LBJ used the episode to obtain from Congress a resolution giving him authority to "take all necessary measures to repel any armed attack against the forces of the United States and to prevent further aggression." The Gulf of Tonkin resolution gave Johnson the leverage he sought. As he noted, it was "like grandma's nightshirt—it covered everything."

Military escalation began in earnest in February 1965, after Johnson's landslide electoral victory.

When Viet Cong forces killed 7 Americans and wounded 109 in an attack on an American base at Pleiku, Johnson responded by authorizing retaliatory bombing of North Vietnam to cut off the flow of supplies and to ease pressure on South Vietnam. A few months later, he sent American ground troops into action. This marked the crucial turning point in the Americanization of the Vietnam War. Only 25,000 American soldiers were in Vietnam at the start of 1965; by the end of the year, there were 184,000. The number swelled to 385,000 in 1966, to 485,000 in 1967, and to 543,000 in 1968.

As escalation occurred, Johnson recognized his dilemma. He understood that the war was probably unwinnable, but he feared the loss of both American power and personal prestige if he pulled out.

And so American forces became direct participants in the fight to prop up a dictatorial regime in faraway South Vietnam. Although a somewhat more effective government headed by Nguyen Van Thieu and Nguyen Cao Ky was finally established, the level of violence increased. Saturation bombing of North Vietnam continued. Fragmentation bombs, killing and maiming countless civilians, and napalm, which seared off human flesh, were used extensively. Similar destruction wracked South Vietnam. And still, despite the repeatedly expressed contention of military commander William Westmoreland that there was "light at the end of the tunnel," the violence continued without pause.

Student Activism and Antiwar Protest

Americans began to protest U.S. involvement in the war. Members of the baby boom generation who came of age in the 1960s were in the forefront of the struggle. By the end of the 1960s, college enrollment was more than four times what it had been in the 1940s. College provided necessary training but also gave students time to experiment and grow before they had to make a living. Some students joined the struggle for civil rights. Hopeful at first, they gradually became discouraged by the gap between Kennedy's New Frontier rhetoric and the government's actual commitment.

Out of that disillusionment arose the radical spirit of the New Left. Civil rights activists were among those who in 1960 organized Students for a Democratic Society (SDS). In 1962, SDS issued a manifesto, the *Port Huron Statement,* written largely by Tom Hayden of the University of Michigan, which outlined both complaints and goals for a participatory democracy. "We are people of this generation, bred in at least modest comfort, housed now in universities, looking uncomfortably at the world we inherit," it began. It went on to deplore the vast social and economic

distances separating people from each other and to condemn the estrangement of modern life.

The first blow of the growing student rebellion came at the University of California in Berkeley. There, civil rights activists became involved in a confrontation soon known as the Free Speech Movement. When the university refused to allow students to distribute protest material outside the main campus gate, they asserted their constitutional rights. After police arrested one of the leaders, students surrounded the police car and kept it from moving all night. The university regents brought charges against the student leaders, and when the regents refused to drop the charges, the students occupied the administration building. Police stormed in and arrested the students. A strike, with faculty aid, mobilized wider support for the right to free speech.

The Free Speech Movement at Berkeley was basically a plea for traditional liberal reform. Students sought only the reaffirmation of the long-standing right to express themselves as they chose, and they aimed their attacks at the university, not at society as a whole. Later, in other institutions, the attack broadened. Students sought greater involvement in university affairs, argued for curriculum reform, and demanded admission of more minority students. The mounting protest against the escalation of the Vietnam War fueled and refocused the youth movement. The first teach-in took place in March 1965 at the University of Michigan. Others soon followed. Initially, both supporters and opponents of the war appeared at the teach-ins, but quickly the sessions became more like antiwar rallies than instructional affairs. Boxer Muhammad Ali legitimated draft resistance when he declared, "I ain't got no quarrel with them Viet Cong," and refused military induction. Working through SDS and other organizations, radical activists campaigned against the draft, attacked ROTC units on campus, and sought to discredit firms that produced the destructive tools of war. "Make love, not war," students proclaimed. As the antiwar movement expanded, students became even more shrill. "Hey, hey, LBJ. How many kids did you kill today?" they chanted as they marched in protest. Women Strike for Peace, the most forceful women's antiwar organization, mobilized support by saying, "Stop! Don't drench the jungles of Asia with the blood of our sons. Don't force our sons to kill women and children whose only crime is to live in a country ripped by civil war." In 1967, some 300,000 people demonstrated in New York City. In Washington, D.C., 100,000 tried to close down the Pentagon.

Working-class and middle-class Americans began to sour on the war at the time of the Tet offensive, celebrating the lunar new year, in early 1968. The North Vietnamese mounted massive attacks across South

Vietnam. In Saigon, they struck the American embassy, Tan Son Nhut air base, and the presidential palace. Though beaten back, they won a psychological victory. American audiences saw images of burning huts and wounded soldiers each evening on television as they ate dinner. During the Tet offensive, American television networks showed scenes of a kind never screened before. One such clip, from NBC News, appears here in still photograph form (below). Viewers who watched the television clip saw the corpse drop to the ground, blood spurting from his head. Gazing at such graphic representations of death and destruction, many Americans wondered about their nation's purposes and actions.

Protest became a way of life. Between January 1 and June 15, 1968, hundreds of thousands of students staged 221 major demonstrations at more than 100 educational institutions. One of the most dramatic episodes came in April 1968 at Columbia University, where the issues of civil rights and war were tightly intertwined. A strong SDS chapter urged the university to break ties with the Institute of Defense Analysis, which specialized in military research. The Students' Afro-American Society tried to stop the building of a new gymnasium, which it claimed encroached on the Harlem community and disrupted life there. Whites occupied one building, blacks another. Finally, the president of the university called in the police. Hundreds of students were arrested; many were hurt. A student sympathy strike followed, and Columbia closed for the summer several weeks early.

The student protests in the United States were part of a worldwide wave of student activism. French students demonstrated in the streets of Paris. In Germany, young radicals were equally vocal in challenging conventional norms. In Japan, students waged armed battles with police.

The Counterculture

Cultural change accompanied political upheaval. Many Americans—some politically active, some not—found new ways to assert their individuality and independence. As in the political sphere, the young led the way, often drawing on the example of the Beats of the 1950s as they sought new means of self-gratification and self-expression.

Surface appearances were most visible and, to older Americans, most troubling. The "hippies" of the 1960s carried themselves in different ways. Men let their hair grow and sprouted beards; men and women both donned jeans, muslin shirts, and other simple garments. Stressing spontaneity above all else, some rejected traditional marital customs and gravitated to communal living groups. Sexual norms underwent a revolution as more people separated sex from its traditional ties to family life. A generation of young women came of age with access to "the pill"—an oral contraceptive that was effortless to use and freed sexual experimentation from the threat of pregnancy. In 1960, the Food and Drug Administration approved Enovid, the first oral contraceptive available on the market. Within three years of its introduction, more than 2 million women

Death of a Viet Cong Suspect

In this picture, General Nguyen Ngoc Loan, the chief of the South Vietnamese National Police, looks at a Viet Cong prisoner, lifts his gun, and calmly blows out the captive's brains. This prize-winning photograph captured the horror of the war for many Americans. What impressions do you think this picture conveyed to people who saw it?

(AP/Wide World Photos)

were on the pill, and as the cost dropped, millions more began to use it.

Americans of all social classes became more open to exploring, and enjoying, their sexuality. Scholarly findings supported natural inclinations. Author and editor Nora Ephron summed up the sexual changes in the 1960s as she reflected on her own experiences. Initially she had "a hangover from the whole Fifties virgin thing," she recalled. "The first man I went to bed with, I was in love with and wanted to marry. The second one I was in love with, but I didn't have to marry him. With the third one, I thought I might fall in love."

The arts reflected the sexual revolution. Federal courts ruled that books like D. H. Lawrence's *Lady Chatterley's Lover* and other suppressed works could not be banned. Nudity became more common on stage and screen. In *Hair,* a rock musical, one scene featured the disrobing of performers of both genders in the course of an erotic celebration.

Paintings reflected both the mood of dissent and the urge to innovate, apparent in the larger society. "Op" artists painted sharply defined geometric figures in clear, vibrant colors, starkly different from the flowing, chaotic work of the abstract expressionists. "Pop" artists such as Andy Warhol, Roy Lichtenstein, and Jasper Johns made ironic comments on American materialism and taste with their representations of everyday objects such as soup cans, comic strips, and pictures of Marilyn Monroe.

Hallucinogenic drugs also became a part of the counterculture. One prophet of the drug scene was Timothy Leary, a scientific researcher experimenting with LSD at Harvard University. Fired for violating a pledge not to use undergraduates as subjects, Leary aggressively asserted that drugs were necessary to free the mind. Working through his group, the League for Spiritual Discovery, he dressed in long robes and preached his message, "Tune in, turn on, drop out."

Another apostle of life with drugs was Ken Kesey. While writing his first novel, *One Flew Over the Cuckoo's Nest,* he began participating in medical experiments at a hospital where he was introduced to LSD. With the profits from his novel, Kesey established a commune of "Merry Pranksters" near Palo Alto, California. In 1964, the group headed east in a converted school bus painted in psychedelic Day-Glo colors, wired for sound, and stocked with enough orange juice and "acid" (LSD) to sustain the Pranksters across the continent.

Drug use was no longer confined to urban subcultures. Soldiers brought experience with drugs back from Vietnam. Taking a "tab" of LSD became part of the coming-of-age ritual for many middle-class college students. Marijuana became phenomenally popular in the 1960s. "Joints" of "grass" were passed around at high school, neighborhood, and college parties as readily as cans of beer had been in the previous generation.

Music became intimately connected with these cultural changes. The rock and roll of the 1950s and the gentle strains of folk music gave way to a new kind of rock that swept the country—and the world (see the "Recovering the Past" essay in Chapter 29, pp. 726–727, for a discussion of the music of the 1960s).

Rock festivals became popular throughout the decade. On an August weekend in 1969, some 400,000 people gathered in a large pasture in upstate New York for the Woodstock rock festival. This exuberant celebration, which featured earsplitting, around-the-clock entertainment and endlessly available marijuana, went off without a hitch. Another festival four months later at a stock car raceway in Altamont, California, was less fortunate. Four people died when audience members clashed with members of Hell's Angels, a motorcycle gang hired to provide security for the Rolling Stones.

The underside of the counterculture was most visible in the Haight-Ashbury section of San Francisco, where runaway "flower children" mingled with "burned-out" drug users and radical activists. For all the spontaneity and excitement, the counterculture had a darker side.

An Age of Assassination

In 1968, American society seemed to be tearing apart. The so called "generation gap" caused major rifts between parents and children. Political protest was growing increasingly violent. Yet there was still a basic confidence that the democratic process could bring meaningful change. John Kennedy had fallen to an assassin's bullet five years before and the nation had survived that trauma. Then two more killings of highly prominent figures undermined any sense of hope.

Martin Luther King, Jr., was the most visible spokesman for African Americans in the years after 1955. By the mid-1960s, he had broadened his crusade to attack poverty and economic injustice and had also begun to speak out against the war in Vietnam, which included a disproportionate number of black soldiers serving in combat roles and losing their lives.

King knew he was a target. On April 3, 1968, he spoke eloquently at a church service, making reference to threats on his life. "We've got some difficult days ahead," he said. "But it doesn't matter with me now, because I've been to the mountain top . . . and I've seen the promised land." The next day, as King stood on the balcony of his motel in Memphis, Tennessee, a bullet from a high-powered rifle ripped through his jaw and killed him. King's assassination sparked a wave of violence throughout the United States. In a spontaneous outburst of rage, African Americans in 124 cities rioted, setting fires and looting stores. For all Americans, King's death eroded faith in the possibility of nonviolent change.

Several months later, Robert F. Kennedy likewise lost his life. Bobby had won election to the Senate from New York after his brother's death and was running for the 1968 Democratic presidential nomination. Kennedy had spoken out eloquently to the poor and had persuaded antiwar activists that he could bring the Vietnam conflict to an end. In June, he won an important victory in the California primary. That evening, after his victory speech, he too was shot by an assassin. Kennedy's death, like King's, shattered hopes for reconciliation or reform.

The Chaotic Election of 1968

The turbulent Democratic convention undermined any final hopes the party had for victory. Chicago Mayor Richard Daley was outraged that radicals and hippies were coming to his city to protest and ordered law enforcement officers to clear out the demonstrators. They did so in front of television cameras as the country watched Hubert Humphrey, Johnson's vice president, running for the Democratic nomination after Johnson declined to seek reelection, win a tainted victory.

Humphrey faced former vice president Richard Nixon. He had failed in his first bid in 1960 and later lost a race for governor of California. Written off by most politicians, he staged a comeback after the Goldwater debacle of 1964, and by 1968, he seemed to have a good shot at the presidency again.

Governor George C. Wallace of Alabama, a third-party candidate, exploited social and racial tensions in his campaign. Appealing to northern working-class voters as well as southern whites, Wallace characterized those who wanted to reform American life as "left-wing theoreticians, briefcase-totin' bureaucrats, ivory-tower guideline writers, bearded anarchists, smart-aleck editorial writers and pointy-headed professors." He hoped to ride into office on blue-collar resentment of social disorder and liberal aims.

Nixon addressed the same constituency, calling it the "silent majority." Capitalizing on the dismay these Americans felt over campus disruptions and inner-city riots and appealing to latent racism, he promised law and order if elected. He also called the Great Society a costly mistake. Nixon received 43 percent of the popular vote, not quite 1 percent more than Humphrey, with Wallace capturing the rest. But it was enough to give the Republicans a majority in the Electoral College and Nixon the presidency at last.

Continuing Protest

Meanwhile, protests continued. The next year, in October 1969, the Weathermen, a militant fringe group of SDS, that took its name from a line in a Bob Dylan song—"You don't need a weatherman to know which way the wind blows"—descended on Chicago and rampaged through the streets for four days in an armed battle with police.

Why had the Weathermen launched their attack? "The status quo meant to us war, poverty, inequality, ignorance, famine and disease in most of the world," Bo Burlingham, a participant from Ohio, reflected. "To accept it was to condone and help perpetuate it. We felt like miners trapped in a terrible poisonous shaft with no light to guide us out. We resolved to destroy the tunnel even if we risked destroying ourselves in the process." The rationale of the Chicago "national action" may have been clear to the participants, but it infuriated citizens around the country.

PRESIDENTIAL ELECTIONS OF THE 1960S				
Year	Candidate	Party	Popular Vote	Electoral Vote
1960	JOHN F. KENNEDY	Democratic	34,227,096 (49.9%)	303
	Richard M. Nixon	Republican	34,108,546 (49.6%)	219
	Harry F. Byrd	Independent	501,643 (0.7%)	15
1964	LYNDON B. JOHNSON	Democratic	43,126,584 (61.1%)	486
	Barry M. Goldwater	Republican	27,177,838 (38.5%)	52
1968	RICHARD M. NIXON	Republican	31,783,783 (43.4%)	301
	Hubert M. Humphrey	Democratic	31,271,839 (42.7%)	191
	George C. Wallace	American Independent	9,899,557 (13.5%)	46

Note: Winners' names appear in capital letters.

Timeline

1960	John F. Kennedy elected president	**1965**	Department of Housing and Urban Development established
	Birth control pill becomes available		Elementary and Secondary Education Act
	Sit-ins begin		Medicare established
	Students for a Democratic Society (SDS) founded		Medicaid established
1961	Freedom rides		Martin Luther King, Jr., leads march from Selma to Montgomery
	Joseph Heller, *Catch-22*		Voting Rights Act
	Ken Kesey, *One Flew Over the Cuckoo's Nest*		United Farm Workers grape boycott
	Bay of Pigs invasion fails		Malcolm X assassinated
	Khrushchev and Kennedy meet in Berlin		Riot in Watts section of Los Angeles
	Berlin Wall constructed		Ralph Nader, *Unsafe at Any Speed*
	JFK confronts steel companies		Vietnam conflict escalates
1962	Cuban missile crisis		Marines sent to Dominican Republic
	James Meredith crisis at the University of Mississippi	**1966**	Stokely Carmichael becomes head of SNCC and calls for "Black Power"
	SDS's *Port Huron Statement*		Black Panthers founded
	Rachel Carson, *Silent Spring*	**1967**	Urban riots in 22 cities
1963	Buddhist demonstrations in Vietnam	**1967–1968**	Antiwar demonstrations
	Birmingham demonstration	**1968**	Student demonstrations at Columbia University and elsewhere
	Civil rights march on Washington		Tet offensive in Vietnam
	Kennedy assassinated; Lyndon B. Johnson becomes president		Martin Luther King, Jr., assassinated
	Betty Friedan, *The Feminine Mystique*		Robert F. Kennedy assassinated
1964	Economic Opportunity Act initiates War on Poverty		Police and protesters clash at Democratic national convention
	Gulf of Tonkin resolution		Richard Nixon elected president
	Johnson elected president	**1969**	Woodstock and Altamont rock festivals
	Civil Rights Act		Weathermen's "Days of Rage" in Chicago
	Free Speech Movement, Berkeley		
	Tax Cut passed		

Conclusion

POLITICAL AND SOCIAL UPHEAVAL

The 1960s were turbulent years. In the first part of the decade, the United States was relatively calm. Liberal Democrats went even further than Franklin Roosevelt and Harry Truman as they pressed for large-scale government intervention to meet the social and economic problems that accompanied the modern industrial age. They were inspired by John Kennedy's rhetoric and saw the triumph of their approach in Lyndon Johnson's Great Society, as the nation strengthened its commitment to a capitalist welfare state. Then the Democratic party became impaled on the Vietnam War, and opposition to the conflict created more turbulence than the nation had known since the Civil War.

American society was in a state of upheaval. Young radicals challenged basic assumptions about how the government worked. They railed against social injustice at home, and they protested a foreign policy that they regarded as wrong. Their efforts faltered at first but then succeeded when they seized on the war in Vietnam as a primary focus and began to attack the Cold War policy that led to massive American military involvement in that faraway land. Student leaders soon found hundreds of thousands of followers who joined in the marches and demonstrations that finally forced the nation to reconsider its aims. Meanwhile, members of the counterculture promoted their own more fluid values, challenged the patterns of conformity so important in the 1950s, and led millions of other Americans, some politically active, some not, to dress and act differently than in the past. The two strands of political activism and countercultural action were independent but intertwined, and they left the nation at the end of the decade very different than it had been before.

Most Americans, like Paul Cowan (introduced at the start of this chapter), embraced the message of John Kennedy and the New Frontier in the early 1960s and endorsed the liberal approach. But over time, they began to question the tenets of liberalism as the economy faltered, as hard economic choices had to be made, and as the country became mired in an unwinnable war in Vietnam. Conservatives deplored the chaos, while disillusioned liberals like Paul Cowan wondered if their approach could ever succeed.

QUESTIONS FOR REVIEW AND REFLECTION

1. How did John F. Kennedy represent the hopes and ideals of Americans in the early 1960s?
2. How successful was Lyndon Johnson's Great Society?
3. What impact did the war in Vietnam have on protest at home?
4. What were the most important changes experienced by the United States in the late 1960s?
5. What was the lasting impact of the protest that rocked America in the 1960s?

CHAPTER 29

Disorder and Discontent, 1969–1980

Latinos, like women and members of other groups, worked to mobilize their communities behind the campaign for equal rights. This mural in an East Los Angeles housing project helped foster a sense of Chicano pride.

(Craig Aurness/Woodfin Camp & Associates)

American Stories

An Older Woman Returns to School

Ann Clarke—as she chooses to call herself now—always wanted to go to college. But girls from Italian families rarely did when she was growing up. Her mother, a Sicilian immigrant and widow, asked her brother for advice: "Should Antonina go to college?" "What's the point?" he replied. "She's just going to get married."

Life had not been easy for Antonina Rose Rumore. As a child in the 1920s, her Italian-speaking grandmother cared for her while her mother worked to support the family, first in the sweatshops, then as a seamstress. Even as she dreamed about the future, Ann accommodated her culture's demands for dutiful daughters. Responsive to family needs, Ann finished the high school commercial course in three years. She struggled with ethnic prejudice as a legal secretary on Wall Street but still believed in the American dream and the Puritan work ethic. She was proud of her ability to bring money home to her family.

When World War II began, Ann wanted to join the WACs. "Better you should be a prostitute," her mother said. Ann went off to California instead, where she worked at a number of resorts. When she left California, she vowed to return to that land of freedom and opportunity.

After the war, Ann married Gerard Clarke, a college man with an English background. Her children would grow up accepted with Anglo-Saxon names. Over the next 15 years, Ann devoted herself to her family. She was a mother first and foremost, and that took all her time. But she still waited for her own chance. "I had this hunger to learn, this curiosity," she later recalled. By the early 1960s, her three children were all in school. Promising her husband to have dinner on the table every night at six, she enrolled at Pasadena City College. It was not easy, for family still came first, but Ann proved creative in finding time to study. When doing dishes or cleaning house, she memorized lists of dates, historical events, and other material for school. Holidays, however, complicated her efforts to complete assignments. Ann occasionally felt compelled to give everything up "to make Christmas." Forgetting about a whole semester's work two weeks before finals one year, she sewed nightgowns instead of writing her art history paper.

Her conflict over her studies was intensified by her position as one of the first older women to go back to college. "Sometimes I felt like I wanted to hide in the woodwork," she admitted. Often her teachers were younger than she was. It took four years to complete the two-year program. But she was not yet done, for she really wanted a bachelor's degree. Back she went, this time to California State College at Los Angeles.

As the years passed and the credits piled up, Ann became an honors student. Her children, now in college themselves, were proud and supportive; dinners became arguments over Faulkner and foreign policy. Even so, Ann still felt caught between her world at home and the world outside. Since she was at the top of her class, graduation should have been a special occasion. But she was only embarrassed when a letter from the school invited her parents to attend the final ceremonies. Ann could not bring herself to go.

With a college degree in hand, Ann returned to school for a teaching credential. Receiving her certificate at age 50, she faced the irony of social change. Once denied opportunities, Italians had assimilated into American society. Now she was just another Anglo in Los Angeles, caught in a changing immigration wave; now the city sought Latinos and other minorities to teach in the schools. Jobs in education were scarce, and she was close to retirement age, so she became a substitute teacher in Mexican American areas for the next 10 years, specializing in bilingual education.

Meanwhile, Ann was troubled by the Vietnam War. "For every boy that died, one of us should lie down," she told fellow workers. She was not an activist, but rather one of the millions of quieter Americans who ultimately helped bring about change. The social adjustments caused by the war affected her. Her son grew long hair and a beard and attended protest rallies. She worried that he would antagonize the ladies in Pasadena. Her daughter came home from college in boots and a leather miniskirt designed to shock. Ann accepted her children's changes as relatively superficial, confident in their fundamental values; they were "good kids," she knew. She trusted them, even as she worried about them.

Ann Clarke's experience paralleled that of millions of women in the post–World War II years. Caught up in traditional patterns of family life, these women began to recognize their need for something more against a backdrop of continuing political turbulence that sometimes seemed to undermine the nation's stability. They worried about both the global and the domestic consequences of the war in Vietnam and the constitutional issues in the Watergate scandal that threatened the American democratic system and eventually brought President Richard Nixon down. Meanwhile, American women, like blacks, Latinos and Latinas, Native Americans, and members of other groups, struggled to transform the conditions of their lives and the rights they enjoyed within American society. Building on the successes of the past several decades, these diverse groups demanded their own right to equality and equitable treatment in fulfillment of their own American dreams. In the course of their struggle, they changed the nation itself.

This chapter describes the continuing upheaval that shook American society in the 1970s. It shows the ongoing impact of global events as the Nixon administration struggled to find a way of ending the devastating struggle in Vietnam. Its effort to extricate American soldiers eased domestic protest, but then its decision to widen the war with incursions into other parts of Southeast Asia created further chaos in the United States. The chapter chronicles the most serious political scandal in American history, which led the president to resign. It records the growing agitation of environmental and consumer activists as they learned how to make their voices heard. And it describes the ongoing effort to provide liberty and equality in racial, gender, and social relations. While political challenges came from middle-class activists, social complaints came from often marginalized Americans who finally spoke out in an attempt to make the nation live up to its professed values. This chapter highlights the diverse voices that continued to echo throughout the 1970s in a heated debate about the distribution of social, political, and economic power in the United States.

The Decline of Liberalism

After eight years of Democratic rule, many Americans were frustrated with the liberal approach. They questioned the liberal agenda and the government's ability to solve social problems. As the war in Vietnam polarized the country, critics argued that the government was trying to do too much. Capitalizing on the alienation sparked by the war, the Republican administration of Richard Nixon resolved to scale down the commitment to social change. Like Dwight Eisenhower a decade and a half before, Nixon accepted some social programs as necessary but still wanted to trim the federal bureaucracy. Furthermore, he and his political colleagues were determined to pay more attention to the needs of white, middle-class Americans who disliked the social disorder they saw as a consequence of rapid social change and resented the government's perceived favoritism toward the poor and dispossessed.

Richard Nixon and His Team

In and out of office, Nixon was a complex, remote man who carefully concealed his private self. Born poor, he was determined to be successful and accomplished that aim in the political sphere. Yet he constantly appeared to be scheming or conniving. There was, one of his aides noted, "a mean side to his nature" that he sought to keep from public view. Physically awkward and humorless, he was most comfortable alone or with a few wealthy friends. Even at work he insulated himself, preferring written contacts to personal ones.

Nixon was keenly aware of the psychology of politics in the electronic age. He believed that "in the modern presidency, concern for image must rank with concern for substance." Thus, he posed in public as the defender of American morality, though in private he was frequently coarse and profane. Earlier in his career he had been labeled "Tricky Dick" for his apparent willingness to do anything to advance his career. In subsequent years, he had tried to create the appearance of a "new Nixon," but to many he still appeared to be a mechanical man, always calculating his next step. As author and columnist Garry Wills pointed out, "He is the least 'authentic' man alive,... A survivor. There is one Nixon only, though there seem to be new ones all the time—he will try to be what people want."

Richard Nixon

Speaking to the "silent majority," Nixon promised to reinstitute traditional values and restore law and order. A private man, Nixon tried to insulate himself from the public and present a carefully crafted image through the national media. What impression does Nixon convey in this photograph? How does his body language communicate his intentions?

(Hiroji Kubota/Magnum Photos)

Philosophically, Nixon disagreed with the liberal faith in federal planning and wanted to decentralize social policy. But he agreed with his liberal predecessors that the presidency ought to be the engine of the political system. Faced with a Congress dominated by Democrats and their allocations of money for programs he opposed, he simply impounded (refused to spend) funds authorized by Congress. Later commentators saw the Nixon years as the height of what they came to call the "imperial presidency."

Nixon's cabinet appointees were white, male Republicans. For the most part, however, the president worked around his cabinet, relying on other White House staff members. In domestic affairs, Arthur Burns, a former chairman of the Council of Economic Advisers, and Daniel Patrick Moynihan, a Harvard professor of government (and a Democrat) were the most important. In foreign affairs, the talented and ambitious Henry A. Kissinger, another Harvard government professor, directed the National Security Council staff and later became secretary of state.

Another tier of White House officials—none with public-policy experience but all intensely loyal—insulated the president from the outside world and carried out his commands. Advertising executive H. R. Haldeman, a tireless Nixon campaigner, became chief of staff. Working with Haldeman was lawyer John Ehrlichman. Starting as a legal counselor, he rose to the post of chief domestic adviser. Haldeman and Ehrlichman came to be called the "Berlin Wall" for the way they guarded the president's privacy. John Mitchell was known as "El Supremo" by the staff, as the "Big Enchilada" by Ehrlichman. A tough, successful lawyer, Mitchell became a fast friend and managed Nixon's 1968 campaign. In the new administration, he became attorney general and gave the president daily advice.

The Republican Agenda at Home

Although Nixon had come to political maturity in Republican circles, he understood that it was impossible to roll back the government's expanded role altogether. He sought instead to systematize and scale back the programs of the welfare state, "to reverse the flow of power and resources" away from the federal government and channel them to state and local governments, where he believed they belonged.

Despite initial reservations, Nixon proved willing to use economic tools to maintain stability. The economy was faltering when he assumed office. As inflation rose, largely as a result of the Vietnam War, Nixon reduced government spending and pressed the Federal Reserve Board to raise interest rates. Although parts of the conservative plan worked, a mild recession occurred in 1969–1970, and inflation continued to rise. Realizing the political dangers of pursuing this policy, Nixon shifted course, imposed wage and price controls to stop inflation, and used monetary and fiscal policies to stimulate the economy. After his reelection in 1972, however, he lifted wage and price controls, and inflation resumed.

A number of factors besides the Vietnam War contributed to the troubling price spiral. Eager to court the farm vote, the administration made a large wheat sale to Russia in 1972. With insufficient wheat left for the American market, grain prices shot up. Between 1971 and 1974, farm prices rose 66 percent, as agricultural inflation accompanied industrial inflation.

The most critical factor in disrupting the economy, though, was the Arab oil embargo. American economic expansion had rested on cheap energy, just as American patterns of life had depended on inexpensive gasoline. Turbulence in the Middle East intruded on the economic stability of the Western world.

The Six-Day War in 1967 made it clear that the Middle East was still a battleground. In 1967, anticipating an attack and launching a preemptive strike, Israeli forces defeated the Egyptian army and seized the West Bank and the Golan Heights, as well as the Arab sector of Jerusalem, which was reunited with the Israeli part of the city for the first time since 1948.

In the aftermath of the Six-Day War, the Organization of Petroleum Exporting Countries (OPEC) slowly raised oil prices in the early 1970s. Another Arab-Israeli war in 1973—the Yom Kippur War—came as Jews celebrated their holiest holiday—the Day of Atonement—and took them by surprise. The war pitted Israel against Egypt, Syria, Iraq, and Jordan. Initially Egypt, in the Sinai peninsula, and Syria, in the Golan Heights, were successful, but then the Israelis fought back. In the end, after several weeks of fighting, ceasefires went into effect, leaving Egypt and Syria with modest gains but the Israelis largely in control.

Meanwhile, in the midst of the fighting, Saudi Arabia, an economic leader of the Arab nations, imposed an embargo on oil shipped to Israel's ally, the United States. Other OPEC nations continued to supply oil but quadrupled their prices. Dependent Americans faced shortages and skyrocketing prices. When the embargo ended in 1974, prices remained high. Even though oil prices around the world increased, the United States was hardest hit because of the huge amounts of oil it used.

The oil crisis affected all aspects of American economic life. Manufacturers, farmers, homeowners—all were touched by high energy prices. A loaf of bread that had cost 28 cents in the early 1970s jumped to 89 cents, and automobiles cost 72 percent more in 1978 than they had in 1973. Accustomed to filling up their cars' tanks for only a few dollars, Americans were shocked at paying 65 cents a gallon. In 1974, inflation reached 11 percent. But then, as higher energy prices encouraged consumers to cut back on their purchases, the nation entered a recession as well. Unemployment climbed to 9 percent for several months in 1975, the highest level since the 1930s.

The United States faced fierce economic competition from abroad. The auto industry found itself challenged by smaller Japanese imports such as Hondas, Toyotas, and Datsuns (later called Nissans) that were

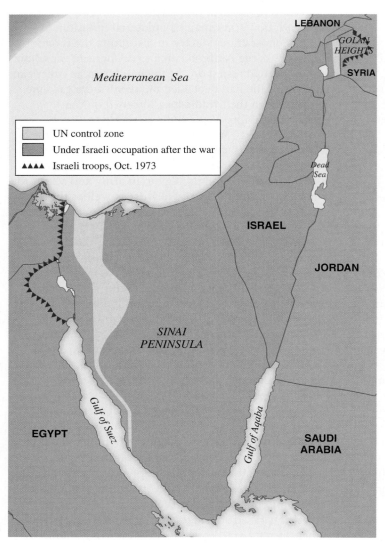

The Yom Kippur War of 1973

The Arab attack during the Yom Kippur observance took Israel by surprise. Initially, Egypt and Syria regained some of their lost territory, but then the Israeli counterattack cut back many of the gains. In the end, UN troops were stationed on borders of the Sinai Peninsula and Golan Heights to help stabilize those regions. How had the map of the Middle East changed in the years after the establishment of the state of Israel in 1948? Who was the victor in the 1973 Yom Kippur War? Why could UN forces help maintain stability?

far more fuel-efficient. As economic growth and stability eluded the nation, Nixon also tried to reorganize rapidly expanding and expensive welfare programs. Critics claimed that welfare was inefficient and that benefits discouraged people from seeking work. Nixon faced a political dilemma. He recognized the conservative tide growing in the Sun Belt regions of the country from Florida to Texas to California, where many voters wanted cutbacks in what they viewed as excessive government programs. At the same time, he wanted to win over traditionally Democratic blue-collar workers with reassurances that the Republicans would not dismantle the parts of the welfare state on which they relied.

Nixon endorsed the Family Assistance Plan, which would have guaranteed a minimum yearly stipend of $1,600 to a family of four, with food stamps providing about $800 more. The program, aiming to cut "welfare cheaters" who took unfair advantage of the system and to encourage recipients to work, was promising but it was attacked by both liberals, who felt it was too limited, and conservatives, who claimed it tried to do too much. It died in the Senate.

Nixon irritated liberals still further in his effort to restore "law and order." Political protest, rising crime rates, increased drug use, and more permissive attitudes toward sex all created a growing backlash among working-class and many middle-class Americans. Nixon decided to use government power to silence disruption and thereby strengthen his conservative political constituency.

Part of the administration's campaign involved denouncing disruptive elements. Nixon lashed out at demonstrators, but more and more he relied on his vice president to play the part of hatchet man. Spiro Agnew branded opposition elements, students in particular, as "ideological eunuchs" who made up an "effete corps of impudent snobs." At the same time, Nixon and Agnew attacked the communications industry, which they believed voiced the views of the hostile "Eastern establishment."

The strongest part of Nixon's plan to circumscribe the liberal approach was Attorney General Mitchell's campaign on crime, sometimes waged at the expense of individuals' constitutional rights. Mitchell's plan included reshaping the Supreme Court, which had rendered increasingly liberal decisions in the past decade and a half. During his first term, Nixon had the opportunity to name four judges to the Court, and he nominated men who shared his views. His first choice was Warren E. Burger as chief justice and he was confirmed quickly. Other appointments, however, were more partisan and reflected Nixon's aggressively conservative approach.

Intent on appealing to white southerners, he first selected Clement Haynesworth of South Carolina, then G. Harold Carswell of Florida. Both men on examination showed such racial biases or limitations that the Senate refused to confirm them. Nixon then appointed Harry Blackmun, Lewis F. Powell, Jr., and William Rehnquist, all able and qualified, and all inclined to tilt the Court in a more conservative direction.

Not surprisingly, the Court gradually shifted to the right. It narrowed defendants' rights in an attempt to ease the burden of the prosecution in its cases and slowed liberalizing of pornography laws. It supported Nixon's assault on the media by ruling that journalists did not have the right to refuse to answer questions for a grand jury, even if they had promised sources confidentiality. On other questions, however, the Court did not always act as the president had hoped. In the controversial 1973 *Roe* v. *Wade* decision, the Court legalized abortion, stating that women's rights included the right to control their own bodies.

Continuing Confrontations in Civil Rights

Richard Nixon was less sympathetic to the cause of civil rights than his predecessors. In 1968, the Republicans won only 12 percent of the black vote, leading Nixon to embark on a "southern strategy" based on the conclusion that any effort to woo the black electorate would endanger the effort to obtain white southern support.

From the start, the Nixon administration sought to scale back the federal commitment to civil rights. It first moved to reduce appropriations for fair-housing enforcement, then tried to block an extension of the Voting Rights Act of 1965. Although Congress approved the extension, the administration's position on racial issues was clear. When South Carolina senator Strom Thurmond and others tried to suspend federal school desegregation guidelines, the Justice Department lent support by urging a delay in meeting desegregation deadlines in 33 of Mississippi's school districts. While a unanimous Supreme Court rebuffed the effort, the president disagreed publicly with the decision.

Nixon also faced the growing controversy over busing as a means of desegregation, a highly charged issue in the 1970s. Transporting students from one area to another to attend school was nothing new. By 1970, more than 18 million students, almost 40 percent of those in the United States, rode buses to school. Yet when busing became tangled with the question of integration, it inflamed passions.

In the South, before the Supreme Court endorsed integration, busing had long been used to maintain segregated schools. Now, however, busing was a means of breaking down racial barriers. In 1971, the Supreme Court ruled that district courts had broad authority to order the desegregation of school systems—by busing, if necessary.

In response, Nixon proposed a moratorium or even a restriction on busing and went on television to denounce it. Although Congress did not accede to his request, southerners knew where the president stood. So did northerners, for the issue became a national one. Schools in many of the nation's largest northern cities were as rigidly segregated as those in the South, largely because of residential patterns. This segregation was called *de facto* to differentiate it from the *de jure*, or legal, segregation that had existed in the South. Court decisions now ordered many northern cities to end such *de facto* segregation and to desegregate their schools.

For many younger students, attendance at different elementary schools went smoothly. Reassigned high school students were less fortunate. A white boycott at South Boston High in Massachusetts cut attendance from the anticipated 1,500 to fewer than 100 on the first day. Buses bringing in black students were stoned, and some children were injured. White, working-class South Bostonians felt that they were being asked to carry the burden of middle-class liberals' racial views. Some white families either enrolled their children in private schools or fled the city.

The Republicans managed to slow down the school desegregation movement. Nixon openly catered to his conservative constituents and demonstrated he was on their side. His successor, Gerald Ford, never came out squarely against civil rights, but his lukewarm approach to desegregation demonstrated a further weakening of the federal commitment.

Integration at the postsecondary level came easier. Federal affirmative action guidelines seeking to provide opportunities for groups discriminated against in the past brought more blacks into colleges and universities. Black enrollment in colleges reached 9.3 percent of the college population in 1976, then dropped back slightly.

As blacks struggled on the educational and occupational fronts, some whites protested that gains came at their expense and amounted to "reverse discrimination." In 1973 and 1974, for example, Allan Bakke, a white, applied to the medical school at the University of California at Davis. Twice rejected, he sued on the grounds that a racial quota reserving 16 of 100 places for minority-group applicants was a form of reverse discrimination that violated the Civil Rights Act of 1964. In 1978, the Supreme Court ordered Bakke's admission to the medical school, but in a complex ruling including six separate opinions, the Court allowed "consideration" of race in admissions policies, though not quotas.

The civil rights movement underscored the democratic values on which the nation was based, but the gap between rhetoric and reality remained. In an era

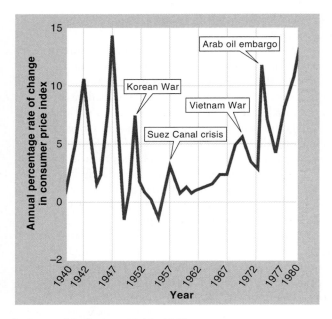

Rate of Inflation, 1940–1980

Inflation often accompanied military spending in the postwar years. In the early 1970s, the Arab oil embargo contributed to an even higher rate.

Source: U.S. Bureau of the Census.

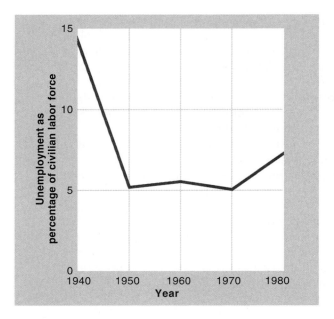

Unemployment Rate, 1940–1980

The unemployment rate fell dramatically during World War II, remained relatively constant from 1950–1969, and rose as inflation increased in the 1970s.

Source: U.S. Bureau of Labor Statistics.

when industrial and farming employment declined and rents rose at a highly inflationary rate, most black families remained poor. African American income was substantially lower than white income. After early optimism in the years when the movement made its greatest strides, black Americans and sympathetic whites were troubled by the wavering national commitment to reform in the 1970s.

The Ongoing Effort in Vietnam

The war in Vietnam continued into the 1970s. When Nixon assumed office in 1969, he understood the need to heal the rifts that the struggle created in American society. During the campaign, he had spoken about a plan to end involvement in the war without specifying details. Once in office, he embarked on an effort to bring American troops home as a way of defusing opposition to the struggle. Unfortunately, his decision to try to avoid losing the war led to even further chaos at home.

Vietnamization—Bringing the Soldiers Home

Nixon gave top priority to extricating the United States from Vietnam while still seeking a way to win the war. To that end, he announced the Nixon Doctrine, which asserted that the United States would aid friends and

allies but would not undertake the full burden of troop defense. The policy of Vietnamization entailed removing American forces and replacing them with Vietnamese troops. Between 1968 and 1972, American troop strength dropped from 543,000 to 39,000, and the reduction won political support for Nixon at home. Yet as the transition occurred, the South Vietnamese steadily lost ground to the Viet Cong.

At the same time, Americans launched ferocious air attacks on North Vietnam. "Let's blow the hell out of them," Nixon instructed the Joint Chiefs of Staff. Nixon used the bombing campaign to portray himself to the North Vietnamese as an anti-Communist zealot with his hand on the nuclear trigger, assuming that fear of annihilation would bring the enemy to the peace table.

But peace proved elusive, and war protests multiplied in 1969 and 1970. In November 1969, as a massive protest demonstration took place in Washington, D.C., stories surfaced about a horrifying massacre of civilians in My Lai, a small village in South Vietnam, the year before. An American infantry company was helicoptered in to clear out the Viet Cong. Instead of troops, it found women, children, and old men. Perhaps confused by the sometimes fuzzy distinction between combatants and civilians in a guerrilla war, the American forces lost control and mowed down hundreds of civilians in cold blood. Stories of the massacre at My Lai underscored the senseless violence associated with the war and increased pressure for the United States to get out of Vietnam.

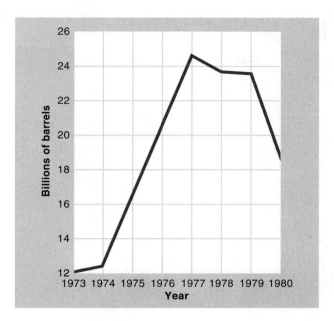

Oil Imports, 1973–1980

American reliance on foreign oil increased in the mid-1970s, until the United States tried to respond to price increases by reducing reliance on imports.

Source: U.S. Energy Information Administration.

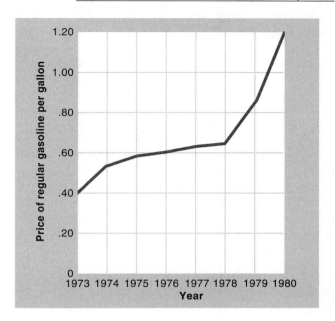

Gasoline Prices, 1973–1980

Gasoline prices rose steadily in the years following the Arab oil embargo and affected the entire American economy.

Source: U.S. Energy Information Administration.

Widening the War

As much as Nixon wanted to defuse opposition to the war, he was determined not to lose the struggle either. Realizing that the Vietnamese relied on supplies funneled through Cambodia, Nixon announced in mid-1970 that American and Vietnamese troops were invading that country to clear out Communist enclaves. The United States, he said, would not stand by as a "pitiful helpless giant" when there were actions it could take to stem the Communist advance.

Nixon's invasion of Cambodia brought renewed demonstrations on college campuses, some with tragic results. At Kent State University in Ohio, the antiwar response was fierce. Two days after the president announced his move, disgruntled students protested by setting the ROTC building on fire and watched it burn to the ground.

Governor James Rhodes of Ohio ordered the National Guard to the university. Tension grew, and finally the situation exploded as the guardsmen fired without provocation on the students. When the shooting stopped, four students lay dead, nine wounded. Two of the dead had been demonstrators who were more than 250 feet away when shot. The other two were innocent bystanders, almost 400 feet from the troops.

Students around the country, as well as other Americans, were outraged by the attack. Many were equally disturbed about a similar attack at Jackson State University in Mississippi, where a few students taunted police and National Guardsmen. The troops responded without warning by firing 460 rounds of automatic-weapon fire into a women's dormitory. When the gunfire ceased, two people were dead, more wounded. The dead, however, were black students at a black institution, and white America paid less attention to this attack.

In 1971, the Vietnam War made major headlines once more. The *New York Times* began publishing the Pentagon Papers, a secret Department of Defense account of American involvement that gave Americans a firsthand look at the fabrications and faulty assumptions that had guided the war. Even though the study stopped with the Johnson years, the Nixon administration was furious and tried, without success, to block publication.

The End of the War and Détente

Vietnam remained a political football as Nixon ran for reelection in 1972. Negotiations led Secretary of State Henry Kissinger to announce, "Peace is at hand." When South Vietnam seemed to balk at the proposed settlement, the administration responded with the most intensive bombing campaign of the war that included Hanoi, the capital of North Vietnam. Only in the new year was a ceasefire finally signed.

The conflict in Vietnam lingered on into the spring of 1975. When the North Vietnamese finally consolidated their control over the entire country,

Recovering the Past

POPULAR MUSIC

One way to recover the past is through music. Popular songs not only provide insight into attitudes and beliefs but also quickly convey the mood and feelings of an era. Through their lyrics, songwriters express the hopes and fears of a people and the emotional tone of an age. Consider, for example, the powerful message conveyed in the Democratic party adoption of "Happy Days Are Here Again" as a campaign theme during the Great Depression. The decline of pop music and the rise of rock and roll in the 1950s tell historians a great deal about the mood of that period. Similarly, the popularity of both folk music and rock in the 1960s provides another way of following social change in that turbulent decade.

The music of the 1960s and 1970s moved beyond the syrupy ballads of the early 1950s and the rock-and-roll movement that Elvis Presley helped launch in the middle of the decade. As the United States confronted the challenges of the counterculture and the crosscurrents of political and social reform, new kinds of music began to be played.

Folk music took off at the start of the period. Building on a tradition launched by Woody Guthrie, Pete Seeger, and the Weavers, Joan Baez was one of the first folk singers to become popular. Accompanying herself on a guitar as she performed at coffee shops in Harvard Square and at the Newport Folk Festival, she soon overwhelmed audiences with her crystal-clear voice. She sang ballads, laments, and spirituals such as "We Shall Overcome" and became caught up in the protest activities of the period.

Equally active was Bob Dylan, who grew up playing rock and roll in high school, then folk music in college at the University of Minnesota. Disheveled and gravelly voiced, he wrote remarkable songs such as "Blowin' in the Wind" that were soon sung by other artists such as Peter, Paul, and

Bob Dylan

(AP/Wide World Photos)

Mary as well. His song "The Times They Are A-Changin'" (excerpted here) captured the inexorable force of the student protest movement best of all. Dylan, who alienated some of his folk music fans when he began playing the electric guitar, continued performing for decades.

The Times They Are A-Changin'

BY BOB DYLAN

Come mothers and fathers
Throughout the land
And don't criticize
What you can't understand
Your sons and your daughters
Are beyond your command
Your old road is
Rapidly agin'.
Please get out of the new one
If you can't lend your hand
For the times they are a-changin'.

But these years were marked by far more than folk music alone. In the early part of the decade, an English group from Liverpool began to build a following in Great Britain.

Joan Baez

(John Launois/Stockphoto)

The Beatles
(Getty Images)

The Supremes
(Brown Brothers)

At the start of 1964, the Beatles released "I Want to Hold Your Hand" in the United States and appeared on the popular Ed Sullivan television show. Within weeks, Beatles songs held the first, second, third, fourth, and fifth positions on the *Billboard* singles chart, and *Meet the Beatles* became the best-selling LP record to date. With the release of *Sergeant Pepper's Lonely Hearts Club Band* a few years later, the Beatles branched out in new musical directions and reflected the influence of the counterculture with songs such as "Lucy in the Sky with Diamonds" (which some people said referred to the hallucinogenic drug LSD).

Mick Jagger and the Rolling Stones followed at the end of the 1960s. Another English group that changed the nature of American music, the Stones played a blues-based rock music that proclaimed a commitment to drugs, sex, and a decadent life of social upheaval. Jagger was an aggressive, sometimes violent showman on stage, whose androgynous style showed his contempt for conventional sexual norms. Other artists, such as Jim Morrison of the Doors and Janis Joplin, reflected the same intensity of the new rock world, and both died from drug overdoses. This music too continued into the 1970s.

Meanwhile, other groups were setting off in different directions. On the pop scene, Motown Records in Detroit popularized a new kind of black rhythm and blues. By 1960, the gospel-pop-soul fusion was gaining followers. By the late 1960s, Motown Records was one of the largest black-owned companies in America and one of the most successful independent recording ventures in the business. Stevie Wonder, the Temptations, and the Supremes were among the groups who became enormously popular. The Supremes, led by Diana Ross, epitomized the Motown sound with such hits as "Where Did Our Love Go."

Reflecting on the Past What songs come to your mind when you think of the 1960s and 1970s? How is the music different from that of the 1950s? What do the lyrics tell you about the period?

Look at the verse from "The Times They Are A-Changin' " that is reprinted here. What does it tell you about the turbulence of the time? What, if anything, do these lyrics imply can be done about the changes in the air? What other songs can you think of that give you a similar handle on these turbulent years? ■

Gerald Ford, Nixon's successor as president, called for another $1 billion in aid, but Congress refused. The long conflict had enormous consequences. Disillusionment with the war undermined assumptions about America's role in world affairs. In the longest war in its history, the United States lost almost 58,000 men, with far more wounded or maimed. Blacks and Latinos suffered more than whites since they were disproportionately represented in combat units. In 1965, 24 percent of all soldiers killed in Vietnam were African American—a figure far higher than their percentage of the population as a whole. Financially, the nation spent more than $150 billion on the unsuccessful war. Domestic reform slowed, then stopped. Cynicism about the government increased, and American society was deeply divided.

If the Republicans' Vietnam policy was a questionable success, accomplishments in other areas were impressive. Nixon, the consummate Red-baiter of the past, dealt imaginatively and successfully with the major Communist powers, reversing the direction of American policy since World War II.

Nixon's most dramatic step was establishing better relations with the People's Republic of China. In the two decades since Mao Zedong's victory in the Chinese revolution in 1949, the United States had refused to recognize the Communist government on the mainland, insisting that Jiang Jieshi's rump regime on Taiwan was the rightful government. In 1971, with an eye on the upcoming elections, Nixon began softening his administration's rigid stance by announcing that he intended to visit China the following year. He suspected that he could use Chinese friendship as a bargaining chip in dealing with the Soviet Union. He acknowledged what most nations already knew: Communism was not monolithic. Nixon also recognized that the press and television coverage of a dramatic trip could boost his image.

Nixon went to China in February 1972. He met with Chinese leaders Mao Zedong and Zou Enlai (Chou En-lai), talked about international problems, exchanged toasts, and saw the Great Wall and other major sights. Wherever he went, American television cameras followed, helping introduce to the American public a nation about which it knew little. Though formal diplomatic relations were not yet restored, détente between the two countries had begun.

Seeking to play one Communist state against the other, Nixon also visited Russia, where he was likewise warmly welcomed. At a cordial summit meeting, the president and Soviet premier Leonid Brezhnev signed the first Strategic Arms Limitation Treaty (SALT I), which included a five-year agreement setting ceilings on intercontinental and other ballistic missiles, and an antiballistic missile treaty restricting the number of systems each nation could develop and deploy. At the same time, the two nations agreed to cooperate in space and to ease long-standing restrictions on trade. Business applauded the new approach, and most Americans approved of détente.

Nixon also recognized the need to promote peace in the Middle East. Henry Kissinger engaged in shuttle diplomacy—moving from one nation to another—to help arrange a ceasefire in the Yom Kippur War. In the aftermath of the struggle, recognizing the need for oil, Nixon and Kissinger worked to establish better relations with the Arab nations, even if they intruded on American support of Israel.

When Gerald Ford assumed office, he followed the policies begun under Nixon. He continued the strategic arms limitation talks that provided hope for eventual nuclear disarmament and culminated in the even more comprehensive SALT II agreement, signed but never ratified during Jimmy Carter's presidency.

Constitutional Conflict and Its Consequences

As he dealt with chaos at home and abroad, Nixon worried about maintaining his political base. In his quest for reelection, he went too far and embroiled himself in a devastating political scandal that undermined his administration.

The Watergate Affair

Faced with a solidly Democratic Congress, the Nixon administration found many of its legislative initiatives blocked. Nixon was determined to end the stalemate by winning a second term and sweeping Republican majorities into both houses of Congress in 1972.

Nixon's reelection campaign was even better organized than the effort four years earlier. His fiercely loyal aides were prepared to do anything to win. Special counsel Charles W. Colson described himself as a "flag-waving, kick-'em-in-the-nuts, anti-press, anti-liberal Nixon fanatic." White House counsel John Dean defined his task as finding a way to "use the available federal machinery to screw our political enemies." One way was by authorizing tax audits of political opponents. Active in carrying out commands were E. Howard Hunt, a former CIA agent and a specialist in "dirty tricks," and G. Gordon Liddy, a onetime member of the FBI, with a flamboyant streak.

The Committee to Re-Elect the President (CREEP), headed by John Mitchell, who resigned as attorney general, launched a massive fundraising drive, aimed at collecting as much money as it could before a new campaign-finance law took effect. That money could be used for any purpose, including payments for the performance of dirty tricks aimed at disrupting the opposition's campaign. Other funds financed an intelligence branch within CREEP.

Early in 1972, Liddy and his lieutenants proposed an elaborate scheme to wiretap the phones of various Democrats and to disrupt their nominating convention. Twice Mitchell refused to go along, arguing that the proposal was too risky and expensive. Finally, he approved a modified version of the plan to tap the phones of the Democratic National Committee at its headquarters in the Watergate apartment complex in Washington, D.C. The wiretapping attempt took place on the evening of June 16, 1972, and ended with the arrest of those involved. Nixon's aides played down the matter and used federal resources to head off any investigation. When the FBI traced the money carried by the burglars to CREEP, the president authorized the CIA to call off the FBI on the grounds that national security was at stake. Though not involved in the planning of the break-in, the president was now party to the cover-up. In the succeeding months, he authorized

DOONESBURY

by Garry Trudeau

A Cartoonist Comments on Watergate

Although Nixon steadfastly denied his complicity in the Watergate affair, his tape recordings of White House conversations told a different story. In this classic *Doonesbury* cartoon from September 17, 1973, Garry Trudeau notes Nixon's efforts to head off the investigation. What do you think the cartoonist is trying to say here?

payment of hush money to silence the burglars. Members of the administration, including Mitchell, perjured themselves in court to shield the top officials who were involved.

Nixon trounced Democrat George McGovern in the election of 1972, receiving 61 percent of the popular vote. In a clear indication of the collapse of the Democratic coalition, 70 percent of southern voters cast their ballots for Nixon. The president, however, failed to gain the congressional majorities he sought.

The Watergate burglars pleaded guilty and were sentenced to jail, but the case refused to die. The evidence indicated that others had played a part and the investigation of two zealous reporters, Bob Woodward and Carl Bernstein of the *Washington Post,* uncovered many of those involved. Meanwhile, the Senate Select Committee on Presidential Campaign Activities undertook its own investigation, and one of the convicted burglars testified that the White House had been involved in the episode. Newspaper stories generated further leads, and the Senate hearings in turn provided new material for the press. Faced with rumors that the White House was actively involved, Nixon decided that he had to release Haldeman and Ehrlichman, his two closest aides, to save his own neck, claiming on nationwide television, "there can be no whitewash at the White House."

In May 1973, the Senate committee began televised public hearings, reminiscent of the McCarthy hearings of the 1950s. As millions of Americans watched, the drama built. John Dean, seeking to save himself, testified that Nixon knew about the cover-up, and other staffers revealed a host of illegal activities undertaken at the White House: money had been paid to the burglars to silence them; State Department documents had been forged to smear a previous administration; wiretaps had been used to prevent top-level leaks. The most electrifying moment was the disclosure by another aide that the president had installed a secret taping system in his office that recorded all conversations. Tapes could verify or disprove the growing rumors that Nixon had in fact been party to the cover-up all along.

To show his own honesty, Nixon appointed Harvard law professor Archibald Cox as a special

Year	Candidate	Party	Popular Vote	Electoral Vote
1972	RICHARD M. NIXON	Republican	45,767,218 (60.7%)	520
	George S. McGovern	Democratic	28,357,668 (37.5%)	17
1976	JIMMY CARTER	Democratic	40,830,763 (50.0%)	297
	Gerald R. Ford	Republican	39,147,793 (48.0%)	240

PRESIDENTIAL ELECTIONS OF THE 1970S

Note: Winners' names appear in capital letters.

prosecutor in the Department of Justice. But when Cox tried to gain access to the tapes, Nixon resisted and finally fired him. Nixon's own popularity plummeted, and even the appointment of another special prosecutor, Leon Jaworski, did not help. More and more Americans now believed that the president had played at least some part in the cover-up and should take responsibility for his acts. *Time* magazine ran an editorial headlined, "The President Should Resign," and Congress considered impeachment.

The first steps, in accordance with constitutional mandate, took place in the House of Representatives. The House Judiciary Committee, made up of 21 Democrats and 17 Republicans, began to debate the impeachment case in late July 1974. By sizable tallies, it voted to impeach the president on the grounds of obstruction of justice, abuse of power, and refusal to obey a congressional subpoena to turn over his tapes. The full House of Representatives still had to vote, and the Senate would have to preside over a trial and convict the president of the charges before he could be removed from office. But for Nixon, the handwriting was on the wall.

After a brief delay, on August 5, Nixon obeyed a Supreme Court ruling and released the tapes. Despite a suspicious 18½ minute silence, they contained the "smoking gun"—clear evidence of his complicity in the cover-up. His ultimate resignation became but a matter of time. Four days later, on August 9, 1974, the extraordinary episode came to an end, as Nixon became the first American president ever to resign.

The Watergate affair provided disturbing evidence that the appropriate balance of power in the federal government had disappeared. Many began to question the centralization of power in the American political system. Others simply lost faith in the presidency altogether. A 1974 survey showed that trust in the presidency had declined by 50 percent in a two-year period. Coming on the heels of Lyndon Johnson's lying to the American people about involvement in Vietnam, the Watergate affair contributed to the cumulative disillusionment with politics in Washington and to the steady decrease in political participation. Barely half of those eligible to vote bothered to go to the polls in the presidential elections of 1976, 1980, and 1984.

Gerald Ford: Caretaker President

Gerald Ford succeeded Nixon as president. An unpretentious, middle-American Republican who believed in traditional virtues, Ford had been appointed vice president in 1973 when Spiro Agnew resigned in disgrace for accepting bribes. Although he was an able congressman, there was significant doubt that Ford was qualified to be chief executive. The new president acknowledged his own limitations, declaring, "I am a Ford, not a Lincoln."

More important than his limitations were his views about public policy. In the House of Representatives, Ford had opposed federal aid to education, the poverty program, and mass transit. He had voted for civil rights measures only when weaker substitutes he had favored had gone down to defeat. Like his predecessor, he was determined to stop the liberal advances promoted by the Democrats in the 1960s.

Ford faced a daunting task. After Watergate, Americans wondered whether any politician could be trusted to guide public affairs. Ford worked quickly to restore trust in the presidency. He emphasized conciliation and compromise, and he promised to cooperate both with Congress and with American citizens. The nation responded gratefully. *Time* magazine pointed to a "mood of good feeling and even exhilaration in Washington that the city had not experienced for many years."

The new feeling did not last long. Ford weakened his base of support by pardoning Richard Nixon barely a month after his resignation. Ford's decidedly conservative bent in domestic policy often threw him into confrontation with a Democratic Congress. Economic problems proved most pressing in 1974, as inflation, fueled by oil price increases, hit 11 percent, unemployment reached 6.6 percent at the end of the year, and

A President by Appointment

Gerald Ford, a genial man, sought to reestablish confidence in the government after succeeding Nixon as president. Far different from his predecessor, he served just over two years, as his bid for election to the presidency in 1976 ended in defeat. What mood dose this picture convey?

(Bettmann/CORBIS)

GNP declined. Home construction slackened and interest rates rose, while stock prices fell. Nixon, preoccupied with the Watergate crisis, had been unable to curb rising inflation and unemployment. Not since Franklin Roosevelt took office in the depths of the Great Depression had a new president faced economic difficulties so severe.

Like Herbert Hoover 45 years before, the conservative Ford hoped to restore confidence and persuade the public that conditions would improve with patience and goodwill. But his campaign to cajole Americans to "Whip Inflation Now" voluntarily failed dismally. At last convinced of the need for strong government action, the administration introduced a tight-money policy as a means of curbing inflation. It led to the most severe recession since the Great Depression, with unemployment peaking at 9 percent in early 1975. In response, Congress pushed for an antirecession spending program. Recognizing political reality, Ford endorsed a multibillion-dollar tax cut coupled with higher unemployment benefits. The economy made a modest recovery, although inflation and unemployment remained high, and federal budget deficits soared.

The Carter Interlude

In the election of 1976, the nation's bicentennial year, Ford faced Jimmy Carter, former governor of Georgia. Carter, appealing to voters distrustful of political leadership, portrayed himself as an outsider. He stressed that he was not from Washington and observed that, unlike many of those mired in recent scandals, he was not a lawyer. Assisted by public relations experts, he effectively utilized the media, especially television, which allowed him to bypass party machines and establish a direct electronic relationship with voters.

In the election, most elements of the old Democratic coalition came together once again, as the Democrats profited from the fallout of the Watergate affair. Carter won a 50-to-48-percent majority of the popular vote and a 297-to-240 tally in the Electoral College. He did well with members of the working class, African Americans, and Catholics. He won most of the South, heartening to the Democrats after Nixon's gains there. Racial voting differences continued, however, as Carter attracted less than half of all white voters but an overwhelming majority of black voters.

Carter stood in stark contrast to his recent predecessors in the White House. Rooted in the rural South, he was a peanut farmer who shared the values of the region. He was also a graduate of the Naval Academy, trained as a manager and an engineer. A modest man, he was uncomfortable with the pomp and incessant political activity in Washington. He hoped to take a more restrained approach to the presidency and thereby defuse its imperial stamp.

Initially, voters saw Carter as a reform Democrat committed to his party's liberal goals, but he was hardly the old-line liberal some had expected. Though he called himself a populist, his political philosophy and priorities were never clear. Critics charged that he had no legislative strategy. Rather, they said with some truth, he responded to problems in a haphazard way and failed to provide firm direction. His status as an outsider led him to ignore traditional political channels. He also seemed to become mired in detail and to lose sight of larger issues. Like Herbert Hoover, he was a technocrat in the White House when liberals wanted a visionary to help them overcome hard times.

Celebrating a Triumph at Camp David
One of Jimmy Carter's greatest achievements was taking the first steps toward peace in the Middle East. Here he celebrates the Camp David Agreement of September 1978, in which Anwar al-Sadat of Egypt, on the left, and Menachem Begin, on the right, shook hands and agreed to work together. What do the faces of these three leaders convey about the moment captured in this photograph?

(Black Star)

In economic affairs, Carter gave liberals some hope at first as he accepted deficit spending. But when record deficits brought inflation to about 10 percent a year, Carter slowed down the economy by reducing spending and cutting the deficit slightly. These budget cuts fell largely on social programs and distanced Carter from reform-minded Democrats who had supported him before. Yet even that effort to arrest growing deficits was not enough. When the budget released in early 1980 still showed high spending levels, the financial community reacted strongly. Bond prices fell, and interest rates rose dramatically.

Similarly, Carter disappointed liberals by failing to construct an effective energy policy. OPEC's increase of oil prices led many Americans to resent their dependence on foreign oil and to clamor for energy self-sufficiency. Carter responded in April 1977 with a comprehensive energy program, which he called the "moral equivalent of war." Critics seized on the acronym of that expression, MEOW, to ridicule the plan and had a field day attacking the president. Never an effective leader in working with the legislative branch, Carter watched his proposals bog down in Congress for 26 months. Eventually, the program committed the nation to move from oil dependence to reliance on coal, possibly even on sun and wind, and established a new synthetic-fuel corporation. Nuclear power, another alternative, seemed less attractive as costs rose and accidents occurred.

Carter further upset liberals by beginning deregulation—the removal of government controls in economic life. Arguing that certain restrictions established over the past century stifled competition and increased consumer costs, he supported decontrol of oil and natural gas prices to spur production. He also deregulated the railroad, trucking, and airline industries.

One of the high points in Carter's administration came with his involvement in the ever-turbulent Middle East. In the aftermath of the Yom Kippur War, Egyptian leader Anwar al-Sadat was disappointed in the ultimate failure of the struggle and flew to Israel in a gesture of peace. At that point, Carter intervened and invited Sadat and Israeli leader Menachem Begin to come to a retreat at Camp David, in Maryland (not far from Washington, D.C.), where he helped the two leaders work out an accord in September 1978. It led to a formal peace treaty the next March. Egypt recognized Israel—and the Israeli right to exist—for the first time, and the Israelis gave up part of the occupied Sinai Peninsula. The United States promised substantial military aid to both parties, which led to a closer relationship with Egypt that has continued ever since. As the United States superseded the Soviet Union as an ally of Egypt, the Russians countered by arming the radical Palestine Liberation Organization (PLO) and helped encourage leader Yasir Arafat in the ongoing guerrilla war.

Carter puzzled people overseas by his passionate commitment to human rights. It became a hallmark of his administration, especially when he ordered the United States to pull out of the Olympics in Moscow in 1980 in protest of the Soviet invasion of neighboring Afghanistan. Some Americans wondered how this commitment squared with the long-standing American approach of supporting dictators and overlooking human rights abuses in countries whose support the United States wanted in the Cold War.

As the 1970s ended, liberals were disappointed. Their hopes for a stronger commitment to a welfare state had been dashed, and conservatives had the upper hand. Despite a tenuous Democratic hold on the presidency at the end of the decade, liberalism was in trouble. And the turbulence that had marked the beginning of the decade had not disappeared.

The Continuing Quest for Social Reform

A struggle for social reform was one more factor contributing to the turbulence of the 1970s. The black struggle for equality in the 1950s and 1960s helped spark a women's movement that soon developed a life of its own. This struggle, like the struggles of Latinos and Native Americans, employed the confrontational approach and the insistent vocabulary of the civil rights movement to create pressure for change. In time, other groups appropriated the same strategies and kept reform efforts alive. While these movements had preexisting roots and usually began in the 1960s, they came of age in the 1970s, and in these years achieved their greatest gains.

Attacking the Feminine Mystique

Although the civil rights movement helped spark the women's movement, broad social changes provided the preconditions. During the 1950s and 1960s, increasing numbers of married women entered the labor force (see Chapter 26). Equally important, many more young women were attending college. By 1970, women earned 41 percent of all B.A. degrees awarded, in comparison with only 25 percent in 1950. These educated young women held high hopes for themselves, even if they were often treated as second-class citizens and earned substantially less than men.

The women's movement, which came into its own in the 1970s, depended on reform legislation. Title VII of the 1964 Civil Rights bill, as originally drafted, prohibited discrimination on the grounds of race. During legislative debate, conservatives opposed to black civil rights seized on an amendment to include discrimination

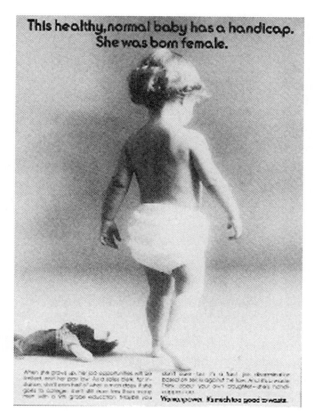

**This healthy, normal baby has a handicap.
She was born female.**

A Message from NOW on Gender Discrimination
Awareness of racial discrimination led women to speak out against discrimination based on gender, as shown in this pointed advertisement sponsored by the National Organization for Women. What is the tone of the message? What does it imply should be done?

(Sponsored by Legal Momentum [then known as NOW Legal Defense and Education Fund])

discrimination. Jo Freeman, a radical activist, observed, "Women's liberation does not mean equality with men . . . [because] equality in an unjust society is meaningless." These feminists tried, through the technique of consciousness raising, to help women understand the extent of their oppression and to analyze their experience as a political phenomenon. They wanted to demonstrate, in their phrase, that the personal was political.

The radicals gained mass-media attention at the Miss America pageant in Atlantic City, New Jersey, in September 1968. On the boardwalk, a hundred women nominated a sheep as their candidate for Miss America. They also set up a "freedom trash can" and placed in it "instruments of torture": bras, girdles, hair curlers, high heels, and copies of *Playboy* and *Cosmopolitan* magazines. In the pageant hall, they chanted "Freedom for Women" and unfurled banners reading "Women's Liberation." The women's movement hit its stride in the 1970s. In 1971, Helen Reddy expressed the energy of the movement in a song called "I Am Woman" that reflected a new militancy and sense of self-confidence:

I am woman, hear me roar
In numbers too big to ignore
And I know too much to go back and pretend
'Cause I've heard it all before
And I've been down there on the floor,
No one's ever gonna keep me down again.
Oh, yes, I am wise
But it's wisdom born of pain.
Yes, I've paid the price
But look how much I gained
If I have to
I can do anything.
I am strong,
I am invincible,
I am woman.

on the basis of gender, in the hope of defeating the entire bill. But the amendment passed, and then the full measure was approved, giving women a legal tool for attacking discrimination.

Women's organizations played an important role in bringing about change in the 1970s. In 1966, a group of 28 professional women, including author Betty Friedan, established the National Organization for Women (NOW) "to take action to bring American women into full participation in the mainstream of American society now." NOW pushed for fair pay and equal opportunity in the workforce and also attacked the "false image of women . . . in the media." By 1967, some 1,000 women had joined the organization; four years later its membership reached 15,000.

NOW was a pressure group that sought to reform American society by promoting equal opportunity for women. To radical feminists, who had come up through the civil rights movement, NOW's agenda failed to confront adequately the problem of gender

Real changes were underway. A 1970 survey of first-year college students showed that men interested in such fields as business, medicine, engineering, and law outnumbered women eight to one; by 1975, the ratio had dropped to three to one. The proportion of women beginning law school quadrupled between 1969 and 1973. Women gained access to the military academies and entered senior officer ranks, although they were still restricted from combat command ranks. According to the Census Bureau, 45 percent of mothers with preschool children held jobs outside the home in 1980. That figure was four times as high as it had been 30 years before. Legal changes brought women more benefits and opportunities. Title IX of the Education Amendments of 1972 broadened the provisions of the Civil Rights Act of 1964. The new legislation, which barred gender bias in federally assisted educational activities and programs, made easier the admission of women to colleges and changed the nature of intercollegiate athletics by requiring schools to fund sports teams for women. By 1980, fully 30 percent of the participants in intercollegiate sports were women, compared with 15 percent before Title IX became law.

A flurry of publications spread the principles of the women's movement. In 1972, journalist Gloria Steinem and several other women founded a new magazine, *Ms.*, which attracted almost 200,000 subscribers by the next year. *Our Bodies, Ourselves,* a handbook published by a women's health collective, encouraged women to understand and control their bodies; it sold 850,000 copies between 1971 and 1976. Unlike older women's magazines, these publications dealt with abortion, employment, discrimination, and other feminist issues.

Women both in and out of NOW worked for congressional passage, then ratification, of the Equal Rights Amendment (ERA) to the Constitution. Passed by Congress in 1972, with ratification seemingly assured, it stated simply, "Equality of rights under the law shall not be denied or abridged by the United States or by any State on account of sex."

Feminism was not monolithic. More radical feminists insisted that legal changes were not sufficient. Traditional gender and family roles would have to be discarded to end social exploitation. Socialist feminists claimed that it was not enough to strike out at male domination, for capitalist society itself was responsible for women's plight. Only through revolution could women be free.

Black women frequently viewed the women's movement with ambivalence. Some, like attorney Pauli Murray, became feminists. She worked closely with bureaucrats and legislators in Washington on legal measures to end gender discrimination. Others felt that the struggle for racial equality took precedence, and they were reluctant to divert energy and attention from it. Members of NOW and similar organizations, they claimed, "suffered little more than boredom, gentle repression, and dishpan hands" and were hardly confronting the most important issues when they burned their bras and insisted on using the title Ms. rather than Mrs. or Miss.

Not all women were feminists. Many felt the women's movement was contemptuous of women who stayed at home to perform traditional tasks. Marabel Morgan was one who still insisted that a woman had a place at home by her husband's side. She argued that "it is only when a woman surrenders her life to her husband, reveres and worships him, and is willing to serve him, that she becomes really beautiful to him."

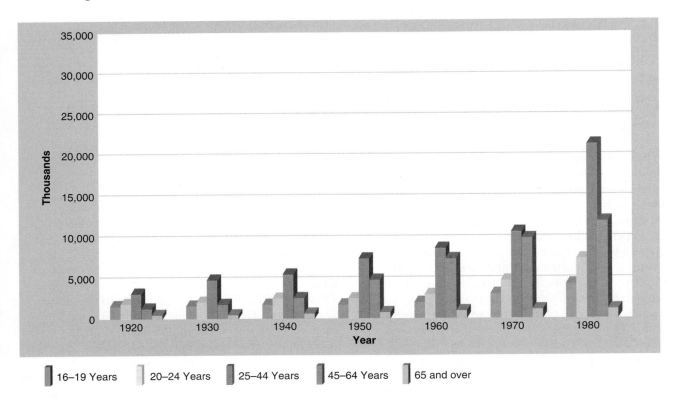

Women in the Workforce, 1920–1980

This graph shows the dramatic increase in the number of women in the workforce over the years. Note particularly the rise in the number of working women 25–44 years old in the 1970s.

Source: U.S. Bureau of the Census.

In her book *The Total Woman* (1973), she counseled others to follow the 4A approach: accept, admire, adapt, appreciate. As of 1975, some 500,000 copies of the hardcover volume had been sold.

In politics, Phyllis Schlafly headed a nationwide campaign to block ratification of the ERA. "It won't do anything to help women," she said, "and it will take away from women the rights they already have, such as the right of a wife to be supported by her husband, the right of a woman to be exempted from military combat, and the right, if you wanted it, to go to a single-sex college." The ERA, she predicted, would lead to the establishment of coed bathrooms, the elimination of alimony, and the legalization of homosexual marriage.

Schlafly and her allies had their way. Within a few years after passage of the ERA, 35 states had agreed to the measure, but then the momentum disappeared. Even with an extension of the deadline granted in 1979, the amendment could not win support of the necessary 38 states. By mid-1982, the ERA was dead.

Despite the counterattacks, the women's movement flourished in the late 1960s and 1970s. In the tenth-anniversary issue of *Ms.* magazine in 1982, Gloria Steinem noted the differences a decade had made. "Now, we are becoming the men we wanted to marry," she said. "Ten years ago, we were trained to marry a doctor, not be one."

Latino Mobilization

Latinos, like women, profited from the example of blacks in their struggle for equality that came of age in the 1970s. Long denied equal access to the American dream, they became more vocal and confrontational as their numbers increased dramatically in the postwar years. In 1970, some 9 million residents of the United States declared they were of Spanish origin; in 1980, the figure was 14.6 million. But median household income remained less than three-fourths that of Anglos, and inferior education and political weakness reinforced social and cultural separation. Latinos included Puerto Ricans in the Northeast, Cubans in Florida, and Chicanos—Mexican Americans—in the West and Southwest. Though "Hispanic" remained an acceptable term, "Latino" was now more commonly used. Chicanos took the lead in the protest struggle, though all groups developed a heightened sense of solidarity and group pride as they began to assert their own rights.

In the 1960s and 1970s, Mexican Americans became more active politically. In 1960, Chicanos supported Kennedy, helping him win Texas, and began to see the benefits of such support. In 1961, Henry B. González was elected to Congress from San Antonio. Three years later, Elizo ("Kika") de la Garza of Texas won election to the House and Joseph Montoya of New Mexico went to the Senate. Chicanos were gaining a political voice.

An Advocate for Migrant Workers

César Chávez organized the United Farm Workers to give migrant Mexican workers representation in their struggle for better wages and working conditions. Here he works with laborers in his tireless campaign for their support. What kind of a leader do you think Chávez was on the basis of his appearance in this picture?

(Bob Fitch/Take Stock/Black Star)

More important than political representation, which came only slowly, was direct action, which triumphed in the 1970s. César Chávez, founder of the United Farm Workers, proved what could be done by organizing one of the most exploited and ignored groups of laboring people in the country, the migrant farm workers of the West. Chávez concentrated on migrant Mexican field hands, who worked long hours for meager pay. By 1965, his organization had recruited 1,700 people and was beginning to attract volunteer help.

Latina women played an important part in the organizing effort. Dolores Huerta, a third-generation Mexican American, who became vice president of the United Farm Workers, observed how entire families were involved:

Excluding women, protecting them, keeping women at home, that's the middle-class way. Poor people's movements have always had whole families on the line, ready to move at a moment's notice, with more courage because that's all we had. It's a class not an ethnic thing.

Chávez first took on the grape growers of California. Calling the grape workers out on strike, the union demanded better pay and working conditions as well as recognition of the union. When the growers resisted, Chávez launched a nationwide consumer boycott of their products that was ultimately successful. Similar boycotts of lettuce and other products harvested by exploited labor also ended in success. In 1975, César Chávez's long struggle for farmworkers won passage in California of a measure that required growers to bargain collectively with the elected representatives of the workers. Farmworkers now had achieved the legal basis for representation that could help bring higher wages and improved working conditions. And Chávez had become a national figure.

Meanwhile, Mexican Americans pressed for reform in other areas. In the West and Southwest, Mexican American studies programs flourished. Colleges and universities offered degrees, built library collections, and gave Chicanos access to their own past. The campuses also provided a network linking students together and mobilizing them for political action.

Beginning in 1968, Mexican American students began to protest conditions in secondary schools. They pointed to overcrowded and run-down institutions and to the 50 percent dropout rate that came from expulsion, transfer, or failure because students had never been taught to read. School walkouts took place in Colorado, Texas, and other parts of California and led to successful demands for Latino teachers, counselors, and courses as well as better facilities.

At the same time, new organizations emerged. Young Citizens for Community Action, founded by teenager David Sánchez and four Chicanos in East Los Angeles, began as a service club to assist the neighborhood. Later, the organization adopted a paramilitary stance and evolved into a defensive patrol, now known as Young Chicanos for Community Action, which tried to protect local residents. Its members became identified as the Brown Berets and formed chapters throughout the Midwest and Southwest.

Other Latinos followed a more political path. In Texas, José Angel Gutiérrez formed a citizens' organization that developed into the La Raza Unida political party and successfully promoted Mexican American candidates for political offices. Throughout the 1970s, it gained strength in the West and Southwest.

Among the new Chicano leaders was the charismatic Reies López Tijerina, or "El Tigre." A preacher, he became interested in land-grant issues and argued that the U.S. government had fraudulently deprived Chicanos of village lands. He formed an organization, La Alianza Federal de Mercedes (the Federal Alliance of Land Grants), which marched on the New Mexico state capital and occupied a number of national forests. Arrested, he stood trial and eventually served time in prison, where he became a symbol of political repression.

Rodolfo "Corky" Gonzáles was another such leader. A Golden Gloves boxing champion as a youth, he later served as a district captain for the Democratic party in Denver. He helped direct Denver poverty programs until he was fired for being overly zealous in his support of the Chicano community. Eloquently he described the despair many Chicanos felt:

> I am Joaquin,
> lost in a world of confusion,
> caught up in the whirl of a gringo society,
> confused by the rules,
> scorned by attitudes,
> suppressed by manipulation
> and destroyed by modern society.

Gonzáles founded the Crusade for Justice to advance the Chicano cause through community organization. Like Tijerina, he was arrested for his part in a demonstration but was subsequently acquitted.

Latinos made a particular point of protesting the Vietnam War. Because the draft drew most heavily from the poorer segments of society, the Latino casualty rate was far higher than that of the population at large. In 1969, the National Chicano Moratorium Committee demonstrated against what it argued was a racial war, with black and brown Americans being used against their third-world compatriots. Aware of the growing numbers and growing demands of Latinos, the Nixon administration sought to defuse their anger and win their support. Cuban American refugees, strongly opposed to communism, shifted toward the Republican party, which they assumed was more likely eventually to intervene against Fidel Castro. Meanwhile, Nixon courted Chicanos by dangling political positions, government jobs, and promises of better programs for Mexican Americans. The effort paid off; Nixon received 31 percent of the Latino vote in 1972. Despite occasional gains in the 1970s, Latinos from all groups faced continuing problems. Discrimination persisted in housing, education, and employment. Activists had laid the groundwork for a campaign for equal rights, but the struggle had just begun.

Native American Protest

Like Latinos, Native Americans continued to suffer second-class status in the 1960s and 1970s. But, partly inspired by the confrontational tactics of other groups, they became more aggressive in their efforts to claim their rights and improve their living and working conditions. Their soaring numbers—the census put them at 550,000 in 1960 and 1,480,000 in 1980—gave them greater visibility and political clout.

In the 1960s, Native Americans had begun to assert themselves even more. Several hundred Indians meeting together in 1961 asked the government for the right to help make decisions about programs and budgets for the tribes. A group of college-educated Indians at the conference formed a National Indian Youth Council aimed at reestablishing national pride. Over the next several decades, the council helped change the attitudes of tribal leaders, who were frequently called "Uncle Tomahawks" and "apples" (red outside, white inside) for their willingness to sacrifice their people's needs to white demands.

American Indians learned from the examples of protest they saw around them in the rising nationalism of the developing world and, even more important, in the civil rights revolution. They too came to understand the place of interest-group politics in a diverse society. Finally, they were chastened by the excesses of the Vietnam War. They recognized a pattern of killing people of color that connected Indian–white relations to the excesses in the Philippines at the turn of the century and to atrocities in Korea and Vietnam.

Indians in the late 1960s and 1970s successfully promoted their own values and designs. Indian fashions became more common, museums and galleries displayed Indian art, and Indian jewelry found a new market. In 1968, N. Scott Momaday won the Pulitzer Prize for his book *House Made of Dawn*. Vine Deloria, Jr.'s, *Custer Died for Your Sins* (1969) had even wider readership. Meanwhile, popular films such as *Little Big Man* (1970) provided sympathetic portrayals of Indian history. Indian-studies programs developed in colleges and universities. Organizations like the American Indian Historical Society protested traditional textbook treatment of Indians and demanded more honest portrayals.

At the same time, Native Americans became more confrontational. Like other groups, they worked through the courts when they could but also challenged authority more aggressively when necessary.

Led by a new generation of leaders, American Indians tried to protect what was left of their tribal lands. For generations, federal and state governments had steadily encroached on Native American territory. That intrusion had to cease. The protest spirit was apparent on the Seneca Nation's Allegany reservation in New York State. When state authorities tried to condemn a section of Seneca land to build a superhighway to run through part of the Allegany reservation, the Indians went to court. In 1981, the state finally agreed to an exchange: state land elsewhere in addition to a cash settlement in return for an easement through the reservation. That decision encouraged tribal efforts in Montana, Wyoming, Utah, New Mexico, and Arizona to resist similar incursions on reservation lands.

The Occupation at Wounded Knee
The Native American movement's armed occupation of Wounded Knee, South Dakota, the site of a late-nineteenth-century massacre of the Sioux, resulted in bloodshed that dramatized unfair government treatment of Native Americans. What elements of this scene convey the determination behind this episode?

(AP/Wide World Photos)

Native American leaders found that lawsuits charging violations of treaty rights could give them powerful leverage. In 1967, in the first of many subsequent decisions upholding the Indian side, the U.S. Court of Claims ruled that the government in 1823 had forced the Seminole in Florida to cede their land for an unreasonably low price. The court directed the government to pay additional funds 144 years later. American Indians also vigorously and successfully protested new assaults on their long-abused water and fishing rights.

Urban Indian activism became highly visible in 1968 when George Mitchell and Dennis Banks, Chippewa living in Minneapolis, founded the activist American Indian Movement (AIM). AIM got Office of Economic Opportunity funds channeled to Indian–controlled organizations. It also established patrols to protect drunken Indians from harassment by the police. As its successes became known, chapters formed in other cities.

An incident in November 1969 dramatized Native American militancy. A landing party of 78 Indians seized Alcatraz Island in San Francisco Bay in an effort to protest symbolically the inability of the Bureau of Indian Affairs to "deal practically" with questions of Indian welfare. The Indians converted the island, with its defunct federal prison, into a cultural and educational center. In 1971, federal officials removed the Indians from Alcatraz.

Similar protests followed. In 1972, militants launched the Broken Treaties Caravan to Washington. For six days, insurgents occupied the Bureau of Indian Affairs. In 1973, AIM took over the South Dakota village of Wounded Knee, where in 1890 the U.S. Seventh Cavalry had massacred the Sioux. The reservation surrounding the town was mired in poverty. Half the families were on welfare, alcoholism was widespread, and 81 percent of the student population had dropped out of school. The occupation was meant to dramatize these conditions and to draw attention to the 371 treaties AIM leaders claimed the government had broken. Federal officials responded by encircling the area and, when AIM tried to bring in supplies, killed one Indian and wounded another. The confrontation ended with a government agreement to reexamine the treaty rights of the Indians, although little changed.

Meanwhile, Native Americans devoted increasing attention to providing education and developing legal skills. Because roughly half of the Indian population continued to live on reservations, many tribal communities founded their own colleges. In 1971, the Oglala Sioux established Oglala Lakota College on the Pine Ridge Reservation in South Dakota. The motto "Wa Wo Ici Ya" ("We can do it ourselves") revealed the college's goal. Nearby Sinte Gleska College on the Rosebud Reservation was the first to offer accredited four-year and graduate programs. The number of Indians in college increased from a few hundred in the early 1960s to tens of thousands by 1980. Many of these graduates studied law and acted as legal advocates for their own people in the court cases they filed.

Indian protest brought results. The outcry against termination in the 1950s (see Chapter 26) had led the Kennedy and Johnson administrations in the 1960s to steer a middle course, neither endorsing nor disavowing the policy. Instead, they tried to bolster reservation economies and raise standards of living by persuading private industries to locate on reservations and by promoting the leasing of reservation lands to energy and development corporations. In the 1970s, the Navajo, Northern Cheyenne, Crow, and other tribes tried to cancel or renegotiate such leases, fearing "termination by corporation." At the same time, the Menominee of

Wisconsin confronted the hated policy head on. Activist Ada Deer became a major figure in the effort to restore reservation status. She and others organized new protest groups, secured political support from the state's senators, and in 1973 had the satisfaction of seeing President Richard Nixon sign the Menominee Restoration Act.

Legislation likewise disavowed the termination policy. In 1975, Congress passed an Indian Self-Determination Act. An Education Assistance Act that same year involved subcontracting federal services to tribal groups. Both laws reflected the government's decision to respond to Indian pressure and created a framework to guide federal policy in the decades ahead.

Gay and Lesbian Rights

Closely tied to the revolution in sexual norms that affected sexual relations, marriage, and family life was a fast-growing and increasingly militant gay liberation movement. Because American society as a whole was unsympathetic, many homosexuals kept their orientation to themselves. The climate of the 1970s encouraged gays to "come out of the closet." A nightlong riot in 1969, in response to a police raid on the Stonewall Inn, a homosexual bar in Greenwich Village in New York, helped spark a new consciousness and a movement for gay rights. Throughout the 1970s, homosexuals successfully fought the most blatant forms of discrimination. In 1973, the American Psychiatric Association ruled that homosexuality should no longer be classified as a mental illness, and that decision was overwhelmingly supported in a vote by the membership the next year. In 1975, the U.S. Civil Service Commission lifted its ban on employment of homosexuals.

In this new climate of acceptance, many gay men who had hidden or suppressed their sexuality revealed their secret. Women, too, became more open about their sexual orientation and demanded not to be penalized for choosing other females as partners. A lesbian movement developed, sometimes involving women active in the more radical wing of the women's movement. But many Americans and some churches remained unsympathetic—occasionally vehemently so—to anyone who challenged traditional sexual norms.

Environmental and Consumer Agitation

Although many of the social movements of the 1960s and 1970s were defined by race, gender, and sexual orientation, one cut across all boundaries. Emerging in the early 1960s but not flourishing until the 1970s, a powerful movement of Americans concerned with the environment began to revive issues raised in the Progressive era and to push them further.

The modern environmental movement stemmed in part from post–World War II yearnings for a better "quality of life." Many Americans began to recognize that clear air, unpolluted waters, and unspoiled wilderness were indispensable to a decent existence. They worried about threats to their natural surroundings, particularly after naturalist Rachel Carson published her brilliant book *Silent Spring* in 1962 (see Chapter 28). By 1970, 53 percent of the population considered air and water pollution to be one of the major national problems.

Public concern focused on a variety of targets. In 1969, Americans were troubled to learn that thermal pollution from nuclear power plants was killing fish in both eastern and western rivers. A massive oil spill off the coast of southern California turned white beaches black and wiped out much of the marine life in the immediate area. In 1978, the public became alarmed about the lethal effects of toxic chemicals dumped in the Love Canal neighborhood of Niagara Falls, New York. A few years later, attention focused on the deadly substance dioxin, which appeared in the Love Canal and elsewhere.

Equally frightening was the potential environmental damage from a nuclear accident. Such a calamity occurred in 1979 at Three Mile Island near Harrisburg, Pennsylvania. Human error compounded a mechanical problem and part of the nuclear core began to disintegrate. An explosion releasing radioactivity into the atmosphere appeared possible, and thousands of area residents fled. The scenario of nuclear disaster depicted in the film *The China Syndrome* (1979) seemed frighteningly real. The worst never occurred and the danger period passed, but the plant remained shut down, filled with radioactive debris, a monument to a form of energy Americans feared.

The threat of a nuclear catastrophe underscored the arguments of grassroots environmental activists. Groups such as the Clamshell Alliance in New Hampshire and the Abalone Alliance in northern California campaigned aggressively against licensing new nuclear plants at Seabrook, New Hampshire, and Diablo Canyon, California. While activist tactics did not always succeed in their immediate goals, they mobilized opinion sufficiently so that no new plants were authorized after 1978. This pattern was at variance with the pattern in many other countries around the world, which continued to rely on nuclear power.

Western environmentalists were particularly worried about excessive use of water. The American West, one critic observed, had become "the greatest hydraulic society ever built in history." Massive irrigation systems had boosted the nation's use of water from 40 billion gallons a day in 1900 to 393 billion gallons by 1975, though the population had only tripled. Americans used three times as much water per capita

as the world's average, and far more than other industrialized societies.

One serious source of concern was the Ogallala aquifer in the Great Plains. The drawing of enormous amounts of water in the 1950s and 1960s to make arid areas productive for farming had by the mid-1970s dramatically depleted the water stored in the aquifer. Conservation measures might delay, but not prevent, the day of reckoning.

California was particularly vulnerable. Because the state was naturally dry, its prosperity rested on massive irrigation projects, and in the late 1970s, it had 1,251 major reservoirs. Virtually every large river had at least one dam. Almost as much water was pumped from the ground, with little natural replenishment and even less regulation. Pointing to the destruction of the nation's rivers and streams and the severe lowering of the water table in many areas, environmentalists argued that something needed to be done. Critic Marc Reisner later noted, "Forty years ago, only a handful of heretics, howling at wilderness, challenged the notion that the West needed hundreds of new dams. Today they are almost vindicated."

Environmental agitation produced legislative results in the 1960s and 1970s. Lyndon Johnson's Great Society was responsible for basic legislation to halt the depletion of the country's natural resources. In the next few years, environmentalists went further, pressuring legislative and administrative bodies to regulate polluters. During Richard Nixon's presidency, Congress passed the Clean Air Act, the Water Quality Improvement Act, and the Resource Recovery Act and mandated a new Environmental Protection Agency (EPA) to spearhead the effort to control abuses. Initially, these measures aimed at controlling the toxic by-products of the modern industrial order. In subsequent years, environmentalists broadened the effort to include occupational health and social justice issues.

One such effort developed into an extraordinarily bitter economic and ecological debate. The Endangered Species Act of 1973 prohibited the federal government from supporting any projects that might jeopardize species threatened with extinction. It ran into direct conflict with commercial imperatives in the Pacific Northwest. Loggers in the Olympic Peninsula had long exploited the land by clear-cutting (cutting down all trees in a region, without leaving any standing). Environmentalists claimed that the forests they cut provided the last refuge for the spotted owl. Scientists and members of the U.S. Forest Service pushed to set aside timberland so that the owl could survive. Loggers protested that this action jeopardized their livelihood. As the issue wound its way through the courts, logging fell off drastically.

Another protest against regulation in the late 1970s and early 1980s came to be called the Sagebrush

Rebellion. Critics argued that large federal landholdings in the West put that region at a disadvantage in economic competition with the East. They demanded that the national government cede the lands to states, which could sell or lease them for local gain. Conservative state legislatures in the Rocky Mountain states supported the scheme. Ranchers applauded the notion. In the end, it went nowhere, though the agitation did persuade federal authorities to endorse a less restrictive policy on grazing.

Related to the environmental movement was a consumer movement. As Americans bought fashionable clothes, house furnishings, and electrical and electronic gadgets, they began to worry about unscrupulous sellers, just as they had earlier in the twentieth century during the Progressive era. Over the years, Congress had established a variety of regulatory efforts as it started to safeguard citizens from marketplace abuse. In the 1970s, a stronger consumer movement developed, aimed at protecting the interests of the purchasing public and making business more responsible to consumers.

Ralph Nader, a onetime Department of Labor consultant, led the movement. His book *Unsafe at Any*

Timeline

1968	Richard Nixon elected president
1969	Native Americans seize Alcatraz
	La Raza Unida founded
1970	U.S. invasion of Cambodia
	Shootings at Kent State and Jackson State Universities
1971	*New York Times* publishes Pentagon Papers
1971–1975	School busing controversies in North and South
1972	Nixon visits People's Republic of China
	Nixon reelected
	SALT I agreement on nuclear arms
	Ms. magazine founded
	Congress passes Equal Rights Amendment
1973	Vietnam ceasefire agreement
	Watergate hearings in Congress
	Spiro Agnew resigns as vice president
	AIM occupies Wounded Knee, South Dakota
1974	OPEC price increases
	Inflation hits 11 percent
	Nixon resigns; Gerald Ford becomes president
	Ford pardons Nixon
1975	South Vietnam falls to the Communists
	End of the Vietnam War
	Unemployment reaches 9 percent
	Farmworkers win right to bargain collectively with growers
	Indian Self-Determination and Education Assistance Acts
1976	Jimmy Carter elected president
1977	Carter energy program
1978	*Bakke* v. *Regents of the University of California*
1979	Accident at Three Mile Island nuclear power plant
	SALT II agreement signed
1982	Ratification of ERA fails

Speed: The Designed-In Dangers of the American Automobile (1965) argued that many cars were coffins on wheels. Head-on collisions, even at low speeds, could easily kill, for cosmetic bumpers could not withstand modest shocks. His efforts paved the way for the National Traffic and Motor Vehicle Safety Act of 1966, which set minimum safety standards for vehicles on public highways, provided for inspection to ensure compliance, and created a National Motor Vehicle Safety Advisory Council.

The consumer movement developed into a full-fledged campaign in the 1970s. Nader's efforts attracted scores of volunteers, called "Nader's Raiders." They turned out critiques and reports and, more important, inspired consumers to become more vocal in defending their rights.

Conclusion
SORTING OUT THE PIECES

The late 1960s and 1970s were turbulent years. The chaos that seemed to reach a peak in 1968 continued, even as American participation in the war in Vietnam wound down. Richard Nixon recognized that he could contain the protest movement by bringing American soldiers home. He understood too the growing frustration with liberal reform and the wish of some Americans to dispense with the excesses they attributed to the young. For a time, he managed to silence protest and to promote a measure of harmony by his policy of Vietnamization, which cut back on the number of Americans dying in battle. But his desire to avoid losing the war led him to expand the conflict into neighboring parts of Indochina, and that move sparked even greater opposition than before.

Meanwhile, his own overarching ambition and need for electoral support led to the worst political scandal in American history. At just the time that the nation was trying to pick up the pieces from the unpopular war, he found himself embroiled in the Watergate affair, which threatened the United States with a real constitutional crisis that ended only when the president resigned.

During this entire time, disadvantaged groups demanded that the nation expand the meaning of equality. Building on the accomplishments of the civil rights movement in the 1950s and 1960s, women such as Ann Clarke, introduced at the start of the chapter, returned to school in ever-increasing numbers and found jobs and sometimes independence after years of being told that their place was at home. Native Americans and Latinos mobilized too and could see the stirrings of change. Gay rights activists made their voices heard. Environmentalists created a new awareness of the global dangers the nation and the world faced. Slowly, reformers succeeded in pressuring the government to help the nation fulfill its promise and ensure the realization of the ideals of American life.

But the course of change was ragged. Reform efforts suffered from the disillusionment with liberalism. Some movements were circumscribed by the changing political climate; others simply ran out of steam. Still, the various efforts left a legacy of ferment that could help spark further change in future years.

QUESTIONS FOR REVIEW AND REFLECTION

1. What were Richard Nixon's social and political priorities in the presidency?
2. How did Nixon propose to end the war in Vietnam?
3. What impact did the Watergate crisis have on American political life?
4. What advances did the women's movement make in the 1970s?
5. How successful was the quest for social reform in the 1970s?

CHAPTER 30

The Revival of Conservatism, 1980–1992

Ronald Reagan appealed to millions of Americans with his vision of a heroic national past. Working closely with his wife, Nancy, he helped revive conservatism and created a new political consensus in the United States.

(Bettmann/CORBIS)

American Stories

A Young Woman Embraces Republican Values

Leslie Maeby, a Republican political staffer in New York State in the 1980s, came from an immigrant family that had long been sympathetic to the Democratic party. Her great-grandfather, Aleksander Obrycki, had come to Baltimore from Poland in 1895. A common laborer who became a naturalized citizen in 1907, he worked for the Democratic party, meeting new immigrants on their arrival and introducing them to Democrats who could help them.

Leslie's grandfather Joe Obrycki became a numbers runner, collecting bets for local gamblers. More successful than his father, he survived the Great Depression of the 1930s with little difficulty. He too was a member of the Democratic party, a cog in the machine. As New Deal programs undermined machine rule, Joe, a ward heeler and professional gambler, ran for city council but lost. Defeat notwithstanding, he remained a loyal Democrat.

Leslie's mother, Vilma, was likewise a Democrat. Leslie's father, Jack Maeby, came from a working-class background in Baltimore and was raised as a Democrat. But as his football exploits took him to college at Bucknell University in Pennsylvania, he began to see the possibility of upward mobility. His own father, a factory worker, counseled him to "use this," pointing to his head, "instead of these," looking at his hands. Turning down an offer to go to graduate school, he entered a management training program with Montgomery Ward. The Maebys moved to Chicago first, then to the Albany, New York, area, where they settled in the suburb of Colonie. While Albany, like most big cities, voted Democratic, Colonie was Republican.

Leslie Maeby was raised in the 1950s in a home where her mother remained Democratic, though frustrated with the Albany machine, and her father was Republican. The suburb, in the midst of a housing boom, developed quickly, as whites fled the larger city— and its black population—and sought safety in the standardized tract houses that were going up everywhere. Nelson Rockefeller, the liberal Republican governor of New York, garnered the support of both of Leslie's parents and many of their neighbors. Yet besides voting, neither Jack nor Vilma was very active politically.

Leslie drifted into politics in 1968, at age 15, without thinking about it. A cheerleader, she was drafted into a congressional campaign by the wife of Fred Field, the Republican candidate, who wanted her to wave pom-poms for her husband and greet supporters. Like the other "Field Girls," she dressed in a blue felt skirt, a white blouse, and suspenders that were striped like the flag. Several nights a week, the group rang doorbells and passed out campaign literature to voters. Leslie often made the first overtures in a household, to be followed by the candidate himself. She found the experience intoxicating, even more so when Fred Field won.

Leslie had followed an increasingly common course into the Republican fold. In a second-grade classroom, she had supported Republican presidential candidate Richard Nixon in 1960. In a mock presidential debate in 1964, she had represented conservative Republican presidential nominee Barry Goldwater. And even though Leslie talked about current events with her mother, a liberal Democrat, she was also influenced by her increasingly conservative Republican father as well as by the Republican community in which she lived. She followed her father's political inclinations and became Republican, as she put it, "almost by default." Race riots, first in Detroit, later in Albany and other American cities, troubled her and others. The chaos in Vietnam led to the rifts in the nation that helped elect Richard Nixon—along with Fred Field—in 1968. By the time she went to the State University of New York at Albany in 1971, she was a solid Republican.

In college, she joined a sorority, where she found women of a similar personal and political bent. Her group drank beer, rather than smoking pot, and wore evening gowns to formal dances, rather than wearing tattered jeans to a rock concert. A sorority sister recommended her for a position as a page in the State Senate in Albany, and Leslie found herself immersed in the political world.

Leslie saw firsthand the underside of politics, including the ways those in power manipulated issues to their own advantage. Yet she decided to set aside her idealism and to work within the system. She rose quickly, serving in 1974 on the state platform committee. She worked for John Dunne, a Republican state senator, after graduating from college in 1975, and attended the Republican National Convention as a delegate at large in 1976. When Dunne sought the office of executive of Nassau County, Leslie ran his campaign. He lost and Leslie left the United States and backpacked through Europe. Yet everywhere she went, she was interested in what she could find about American politics. She wanted to be part of the process as the United States—under the leadership of Ronald Reagan—moved away from the welfare state.

Returning to the United States, in 1984 Leslie took the job of salvaging the reelection campaign of a Republican state senator. She succeeded in that effort, served for four years as executive assistant to the Republican state comptroller, and in 1989 became finance director of the state Republican party.

Leslie was a rock-ribbed Republican, who, like many Americans, reacted with frustration to chaos in national life and moved right as the party moved right. "It's like if you decide to be a nurse when you're eighteen, and stay one for twenty years," she said. "It becomes who you are. How you read the paper. How you watch the news. Your whole outlook."

The experience of Leslie Maeby mirrored that of countless Americans in the 1980s who left the Democratic party and supported the Republican agenda instead. At a time when people were disturbed by continuing racial conflict, troubled by changes in the welfare state that seemed to help disadvantaged citizens at the expense of middle- and upper-class Americans, and upset at the chaos caused by the Vietnam War, they began to reassess priorities within the democratic political system. In a time of flux, the Republican party seized the initiative and consolidated its own political power. In a process that began in the 1960s (as Jack Maeby left his Democratic roots and became a Republican), a new majority emerged in the United States. Millions of Americans, including members of groups who had long considered themselves Democrats, voiced their frustration by voting Republican, some for the first time. Relying on a fervent religious faith, they succeeded in transforming their vision of the American dream into national policy, and in the 1980s and early 1990s, they watched the economy improve, though often to the benefit of the most affluent Americans. At the same time, members of a variety of minority groups continued to have difficulty finding jobs, the national debt skyrocketed, and finally, the stock market crashed. Meanwhile, harsh Cold War rhetoric led to fears that the continuing confrontation on the global stage between the Soviet Union and the United States might end in nuclear war.

This chapter describes the enormous changes that occurred in the 1980s and early 1990s. It highlights the role of people like Leslie Maeby in bringing to power a new political force that altered the landscape of the United States. It describes the economic and technological shifts that affected the daily lives of millions of Americans, bringing unprecedented prosperity to people at the top of the economic pyramid but leaving millions of less fortunate Americans behind. It explores the efforts of the Republican administrations of Ronald Reagan and George Bush to redefine—and limit—the government's role in the economy, and it assesses the impact such constriction had on ordinary Americans. And finally, it examines how foreign policy initiatives brought a successful end to the long and costly Cold War.

The Conservative Transformation

In the 1980s and early 1990s, the Republican party reestablished itself as the dominant force in national politics. The Republican ascendancy that had begun in the Nixon era was now largely complete. The liberal agenda that had governed national affairs ever since the New Deal of Franklin Roosevelt gave way to a new Republican coalition determined to scale back the welfare state and prevent what it perceived as the erosion of the nation's moral values. Firmly in control of the presidency, sometimes in control of the Senate and later the whole Congress, the Republican party set the new national agenda.

The New Politics

Conservatism gained respect in the 1980s, not just in the United States but in other parts of the world as well. In Great Britain, for example, problems with both inflation and unemployment plagued the welfare state policies of the Labour Party, which had gained power in the latter part of the 1960s, and by the 1980s, the Conservative party was back in power, with Margaret Thatcher as prime minister. Elsewhere in the late 1980s, particularly as communism began to crumble in Eastern and Central Europe, moderately conservative Christian Democratic movements became increasingly popular. As socialism deteriorated, they seemed a more viable alternative.

In the United States, conservatism attracted countless new adherents after the turbulence of the 1960s and the backlash of the Vietnam War. Innovative advertising and fund-raising techniques capitalized on national disaffection with liberal solutions to continuing social problems and made the conservative movement almost unstoppable.

Conservatives seized on Thomas Jefferson's maxim: "That government is best which governs least." The dramatic economic growth of the 1960s and 1970s, they believed, left a legacy of rising inflation, falling productivity, enormous waste, and out-of-control entitlements. The liberal solution of "throwing money at social problems" no longer worked, conservatives argued. Therefore, they sought to downsize government, reduce taxes, and roll back regulations that they claimed hampered business competition. They wanted to restore the focus on individual initiative and private enterprise.

The conservative philosophy had tremendous appeal. It promised profitability to those who worked hard and showed initiative. It attracted middle-class Americans, who were troubled that they were being forgotten in the commitment to assist minorities and the poor. It also offered hope for the revival of basic social and religious values that many citizens worried had been eaten away by rising divorce rates, legalized abortion, homosexuality, and media preoccupation with violence and sex.

The new conservative coalition covered a broad spectrum. Some followers embraced the economic doctrines of University of Chicago economist Milton Friedman, who promoted the free play of market forces and a sharp restriction of governmental control. Others applauded the social and political conservatism of North Carolina senator Jesse Helms, a tireless foe of anything he deemed pornographic and a fervent campaigner for a limited federal role. Still others flocked to the Republican fold because of their conviction that civil rights activists and "bleeding-heart liberals" practiced "reverse racism" with affirmative action, job quotas, and busing to promote equal opportunity.

The conservative coalition also drew deeply from religious fundamentalists who advocated a literal interpretation of Scriptures. Millions—devout Catholics, orthodox Jews, evangelical Protestants—demanded a return to stricter standards of morality. Muslims, relying on the Qur'an, took an equally fundamentalist approach. All groups worried about sexual permissiveness, gay rights, drugs, crime, and women working outside the home, a practice they believed eroded family life. In short, fundamentalists objected to liberalizing tendencies and sought to refashion society by reaffirming scriptural morality and the centrality of religion in American life.

Many of these activists belonged to the so-called Moral Majority. The Reverend Jerry Falwell of Virginia and other television evangelists who focused on the concerns of religious fundamentalism attracted large followings in the 1980s. Emulating Father Charles E. Coughlin, the radio priest of the 1930s, they used electronic means to preach fiery sermons to enormous audiences and focused their television congregations on specific political ends. They also used their fund-raising ability to support candidates sympathetic to their cause. Moral Majority money began to fund politicians who demanded reinstituting school prayer, ending legalized abortion, and defeating the Equal Rights Amendment. Later a group calling itself the Christian Coalition became even more powerful in supporting—and electing—candidates who met its litmus test on conservative values. The Christian Coalition and other similar groups believed strongly that "to proclaim Christ's lordship in politics means evaluating political candidates by their commitment to biblical principles, rather than by their pragmatism, patriotism, or personality."

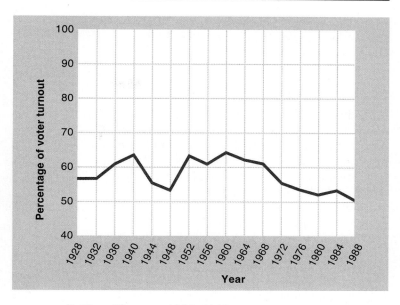

Voter Turnout, 1928–1988
Voter turnout was far lower in the twentieth century than it had been in the nineteenth century. The fact that barely 50 percent of the electorate voted in the 1980s reflects a pervasive sense of disillusionment with the political process.

Source: Data from Historical Statistics of the United States and Statistical Abstract of the United States.

Conservatives from all camps capitalized on changing political techniques more successfully than their liberal opponents. They understood the value of polling to assess and polish a candidate's image and the importance of television in providing instant access to the American public. Politicians became increasingly adept at using "sound bites," often lasting no more than 15 or 30 seconds, to state their views. They also relied on new electronic systems such as e-mail, fax machines, and the Internet to mobilize their followers.

Similarly, conservatives outdid liberals in using negative political advertising. Mudslinging has always been a part of the American political tradition, but now carefully crafted television ads concentrated not so much on conveying a positive image of a candidate's platform but on subtly attacking an opponent's character in order to create fundamental doubt in a voter's mind. Conservatives also were most successful in raising unprecedented sums of money for their campaigns. Richard Viguerie, the New Right mastermind, understood how to tap the huge conservative constituency for political ends and developed direct-mail appeals that assisted conservative candidates around the country.

At the same time, conservatives understood the need to provide an intellectual grounding for their positions. Conservative scholars worked in "think tanks" and other research organizations, such as the Hoover Institution at Stanford University and the American Enterprise Institute in Washington, D.C., that gave conservatism a solid institutional base. Their books, articles, and reports helped elect Ronald Reagan and other conservative politicians.

Conservative Leadership

More than any other Republican, Ronald Reagan was responsible for the success of the conservative cause. An actor turned politician, he had been a radio broadcaster in his native Midwest, then gravitated to California, where he began a movie career. Initially drawn to the Democratic party and impressed with the accomplishments of Franklin D. Roosevelt's New Deal, he was also sympathetic to union causes and served as president of the Screen Actors Guild in Hollywood. But his success on the silver screen affected his political inclinations, and he changed his affiliation from Democrat to Republican in the early 1960s. He went to work as a public spokesman for General Electric, where his visibility and ability to articulate corporate values attracted the attention of conservatives who recognized his political potential and helped him win election as governor of California in 1966. He failed in his first bid for the presidency in 1976 but consolidated his strength over the next four years. By 1980, he had the firm support of the growing Right, which applauded his promise to reduce the size of the federal government but bolster military might.

Running against incumbent Jimmy Carter in 1980, Reagan scored a landslide victory, gaining a popular vote of 51 to 41 percent and a 489 to 49 Electoral College advantage. He also led the Republican party to control of the Senate for the first time since 1955. In 1984, he was reelected by an even larger margin. He received 59 percent of the popular vote and swamped Democratic candidate Walter Mondale in the Electoral College 525 to 13, losing only Minnesota, Mondale's home state, and the District of Columbia. The Democrats, however, netted two additional seats in the Senate and maintained superiority in the House of Representatives.

Reagan had a pleasing manner and a special skill as a media communicator. Relying on his acting experience, he used television as Franklin D. Roosevelt had used radio in the 1930s. He was a gifted storyteller who loved using anecdotes and one-liners to make his point.

He spoke of the United States as "the last best hope of man on earth." Echoing John Winthrop's sermon to Puritans coming to the New World in 1630, he referred to America as a "shining city on a hill." He was fond of invoking images of Pilgrims coming ashore in New England, American prisoners of war returning from Vietnam, and astronauts landing on the moon, and he argued that history still had a place for the nation and its ideals. In response to those who spoke of a "national malaise," he retorted, "I find nothing wrong with the American people."

Ronald Reagan

Ronald Reagan was fond of projecting an old-fashioned cowboy image. This picture captured the sense of rugged individualism he valued and appeared on the covers of both *Time* and *Newsweek* magazines when he died in 2004. What qualities seem to come across in this photograph? Why did this image have such a powerful appeal?

(Courtesy Ronald Reagan Library)

Throughout his eight years in office, Reagan enjoyed enormous popularity. People talked about a "Teflon" presidency, making a comparison with nonstick frying pans, for even serious criticisms failed to stick and disagreements over policy never diminished his personal-approval ratings. When he left the White House, an overwhelming 68 percent of the American public approved of his performance.

But Reagan had a number of liabilities that surfaced over time. As the oldest president the nation had ever had, his attention often drifted, and he occasionally fell asleep during meetings, including one with the pope. While he could speak eloquently with a script in front of him, he was frequently unsure about what was being asked in press conferences. Uninterested in governing, he delegated a great deal of authority, even if that left him unclear about policy decisions. Worst of all, he suffered from charges of "sleaze" in his administration,

George H. W. Bush

George H. W. Bush capitalized on his position as vice president under Ronald Reagan and won a resounding victory in the election of 1988. Even so, he did not have the solid conservative mandate that Reagan enjoyed. How does the flag contribute to the impression Bush hoped to convey?

(CORBIS)

prospered in the Texas oil industry, then served in Congress, as top envoy to China, and as head of the CIA. Termed a preppy wimp by the press, he became a pit bull who ran a mudslinging campaign against his Democratic opponent, Governor Michael Dukakis of Massachusetts. On election day, Bush swamped Dukakis, winning a 54–46 percent popular-vote majority and carrying 40 states. But conservatives who admired Reagan were suspicious of Bush, and he did not have the kind of mandate Reagan had enjoyed. Even worse from the Republican point of view, Democrats controlled both houses of Congress.

Bush quickly put his own imprint on the presidency. Despite his upper-crust background, he was an unpretentious man who made a point of trying to appear down-to-earth. More than a year and a half into his term, he was still on his political honeymoon, with a personal approval rating of 67 percent. Support grew even stronger as he presided over the Persian Gulf War in 1991. Then, as the economy faltered and the results of the war seemed suspect, approval levels began to drop, and he failed in his bid for reelection in 1992.

Republican Policies at Home

Republicans in the 1980s and early 1990s aimed to reverse the economic stagnation of the Carter years and to provide new opportunities for business to prosper. The United States, like industrialized nations around the world, had suffered from the Arab oil embargo of 1973 (see Chapter 29). As the cost of driving cars and heating homes skyrocketed, the entire economy faltered. In an increasingly globalized economy, in which multinational firms had interests around the world, a downturn in one area—or one country—affected business efforts around the globe. Republicans wanted to provide American business interests with the ability to prosper at home and wherever else they operated.

with several aides and even his attorney general forced from office for improprieties ranging from perjury to influence peddling.

In 1988, Republican George H. W. Bush, who served eight years as Reagan's vice president, ran for the presidency. Though a New Englander, he had

PRESIDENTIAL ELECTIONS, 1980–1988				
Year	Candidate	Party	Popular Vote	Electoral Vote
1980	RONALD REAGAN	Republican	43,899,248 (50.8%)	489
	Jimmy Carter	Democratic	36,481,435 (41.0%)	49
	John B. Anderson	Independent	5,719,437 (6.6%)	0
1984	RONALD REAGAN	Republican	53,428,357 (58.7%)	525
	Walter F. Mondale	Democratic	36,930,923 (40.6%)	13
1988	GEORGE BUSH	Republican	47,946,422 (53.9%)	426
	Michael Dukakis	Democratic	41,016,429 (46.1%)	112

Note: Winners' names appear in capital letters.

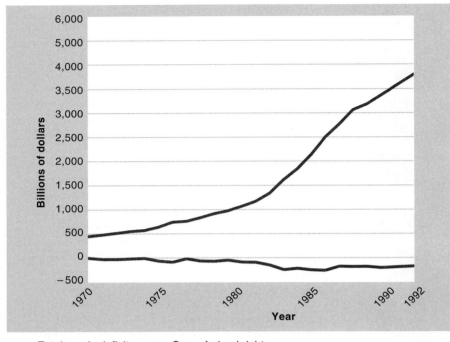

Federal Budget Deficits and the National Debt, 1970–1992

In the 1970s, 1980s, and early 1990s, the yearly federal budget deficit grew steadily larger, and the gross federal debt skyrocketed. In this economy, deficits and debt affected spending priorities.

Source: Data from *Statistical Abstract of the United States.*

━━ Total yearly deficit   ━━ Gross federal debt

To that end, Reagan proposed and implemented an economic recovery program that rested on the theory of supply-side economics. According to this much-criticized theory, reduction of taxes would encourage business expansion, which in turn would lead to a larger supply of goods to help stimulate the system as a whole. Even George Bush, during his brief run for the Republican nomination in 1980, was critical, charging that Reagan was promoting "voodoo economics." Despite such criticism, Republicans endorsed "Reaganomics." One early initiative involved tax reductions. A 5 percent cut in the tax rate was enacted to go into effect on October 1, 1981, followed by 10 percent cuts in 1982 and 1983. Although all taxpayers received some tax relief, the rich gained far more than middle- and lower-income Americans. Poverty-level Americans did not benefit at all. Tax cuts and enormous defense expenditures increased the budget deficit. From $74 billion in 1980, it jumped to $290 billion in 1992. Such massive deficits drove the gross federal debt—the total national indebtedness—upward from $909 billion in 1980 to $4.4 trillion in 1992. When Reagan assumed office, the per capita national debt was $4,035; 10 years later, in 1990, it was about $12,400.

Faced with the need to raise more money and rectify an increasingly skewed tax code, in 1986 Congress passed and Reagan signed the most sweeping tax reform since the federal income tax began in 1913. It lowered rates, consolidated brackets, and closed loopholes. Though it ended up neither increasing nor

decreasing the government's tax take, the measure was an important step toward treating low-income Americans more equitably. Still, most of the benefits went to the richest 5 percent of Americans.

At the same time, Reagan followed Carter in a major deregulation effort that included agencies such as the Environmental Protection Agency (EPA), the Consumer Product Safety Commission, and the Occupational Safety and Health Administration (OSHA). The Republican administration argued that regulations pertaining to the consumer, the workplace, and the environment were inefficient, paternalistic, excessively expensive, and impeded business growth.

The Federal Communications Commission (FCC), which had effectively regulated the airwaves in the public interest, now assumed a business posture. The head of the agency under Reagan scoffed at the idea that television had a public-service role. "Television is just another appliance," he declared. "It's just a toaster with pictures." The FCC increased the amount of time allotted to commercials and eliminated the rule that some programming had to be in the area of public-service broadcasts.

Meanwhile, Reagan challenged the New Deal consensus that the federal government should monitor the economy and assist the least fortunate citizens. He had played by the rules of the system and had succeeded. Others could do the same. He charged that government intruded too deeply into American life. It was time to eliminate "waste, fraud, and abuse" by cutting unnecessary programs.

Reagan needed to curtail social programs both because of sizable tax cuts and because of enormous military expenditures. Committed to a massive arms buildup, over a five-year period the administration sought an unprecedented military budget of $1.5 trillion. By 1985, the United States was spending half a million dollars a minute on defense and four times as much as at the height of the Vietnam War.

The huge cuts in social programs reversed the approach of liberals over the past 50 years. Republicans and conservative Democrats eliminated public-service jobs and reduced other aid to the cities, where the poor congregated. They cut back unemployment compensation and required Medicare patients to pay more for treatment. They slashed legal assistance for the poor. They lowered welfare benefits and food stamp allocations. Spending on human resources fell by $101 billion between 1980 and 1982. The process continued even after Reagan left office. Between 1981 and 1992, federal spending (adjusted for inflation) fell 82 percent for subsidized housing, 63 percent for job training and employment services, and 40 percent for community services. Middle-class Americans, benefiting from the tax cuts, were not hurt by the slashes in social programs. But the administration's approach caused real suffering for the nation's poorest citizens.

Ironically, despite the huge cuts, overall federal spending for social welfare rose from $313 billion in 1980 to $533 billion in 1988. The increase came about because of growth in the payments of entitlement programs such as social security and Medicare, which provided benefits automatically to citizens in need. Even the most aggressive efforts of the Republicans could not wholly dismantle the welfare state.

Distrustful of centralized government, Reagan wanted to place more power in the hands of state and local governments. His "New Federalism" attempted to shift responsibilities from the federal to the state level. By eliminating federal funding and instead making grants to the states, which could spend the money as they saw fit, he hoped to fortify local initiative. Critics charged that the proposal was merely a way of moving programs from one place to another while eliminating federal funding. When a prolonged recession began in 1990, the administration's policy contributed to the near-bankruptcy of a number of states and municipalities, which now bore responsibility for programs formerly funded in Washington.

Reagan took a conservative approach to social issues as well. Accepting the support of the New Right, he strongly endorsed conservative social goals. To avoid compromising his economic program, however, he provided only symbolic support at first. He spoke out for public prayer in the schools without expending political capital in Congress to support the issue. In the same way, he showed his opposition to abortion by making sure that the first nongovernmental group to receive an audience at the White House was an antiabortion March for Life contingent.

George Bush faithfully adhered to Reagan's general economic policy. Running for president in 1988, he promised "no new taxes," although he later backed down from that pledge to join a bipartisan effort to bring the budget deficit under control.

Like Reagan, Bush wanted deep cuts in social programs. Tireless in his criticism of the Democratic majorities in the Senate and House of Representatives, he vetoed measure after measure to assist those caught in the ravages of a troubling recession that sent unemployment rates up to 8 percent and left one of every four urban children living in poverty.

Bush was more outspoken than Reagan in his support of conservative social goals. At the start of the 1980s, conservatives had questioned Bush's commitment to their social agenda, and, indeed, Bush had been sympathetic to a woman's right to choice on the abortion issue. As president, however, he firmly opposed abortion, and his Supreme Court appointments, like Reagan's, guaranteed that the effort to roll back or overturn *Roe* v. *Wade* would continue.

The Republican philosophy under Reagan and Bush dramatically reversed the nation's domestic agenda. Liberalism in the 1960s had reached a high-water mark in a time of steady growth, but in the 1980s decisions about social programs became more difficult, and millions of Americans like Leslie Maeby, introduced at the start of the chapter, came to believe that most of the Great Society programs had failed to conquer poverty and in fact had created lifelong welfare dependency. Conservatism offered a more attractive answer, particularly to Americans in the middle and upper classes who were already comfortable.

But the transformation was accompanied by a number of serious problems that emerged in the early 1990s. Bush faced a bankruptcy crisis in the savings and loan industry, which had taken advantage of the Republican deregulation policy to make unwise, high-risk investments that led to tremendous losses. Congress approved a $166 billion rescue plan (that soon reached more than $250 billion) to bail out the industry.

Republican policy also widened the gap between rich and poor. Tax breaks for the wealthy, deregulation initiatives, high interest rates for investors, permissiveness toward mergers, and enormous growth in the salaries of top business executives all contributed to the disparity.

The 1980s, it became clear, produced "a decade of money fever," as author Tom Wolfe put it. The concentration of capital—an amassing of wealth at the top levels—produced dekamillionaires, centimillionaires, half-billionaires, and billionaires.

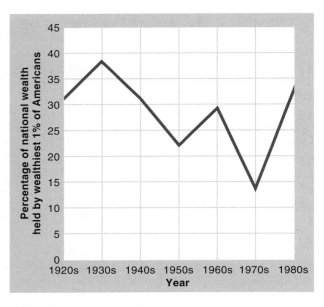

The Wealthiest Americans

During the 1980s, the percentage of national wealth held by the richest 1 percent of Americans reached the highest level since the 1930s.

Source: New York Times, August 16, 1992.

According to one study, the share of national wealth of the richest 1 percent of the nation rose from about 18 percent in 1976 to 36 percent in 1989.

Meanwhile, less-fortunate Americans suffered more than they had since the Great Depression. In 1987, one out of every five American children lived in poverty, up 24 percent since 1979. And millions of people, ranging from foreclosed farmers to laid-off industrial workers, were struggling to make ends meet.

An End to Social Reform

The Republican attack on the welfare state included an effort to limit the commitment to social reform. Enough had been done already, conservatives argued, and gains for less fortunate Americans came at the expense of the middle class. It was time to end federal "intrusion" in this area.

Slowdown in the Struggle for Civil Rights

Republican policies slowed the civil rights movement. Reagan opposed busing to achieve racial balance, and his attorney general worked to dismantle affirmative action programs. Initially reluctant to support extension of the enormously successful Voting Rights Act of 1965, Reagan relented only after severe bipartisan criticism. He also launched an assault on the Civil Rights Commission and hampered its effectiveness by appointing members who did not support its main goals.

The courts similarly weakened commitments to equal rights. As a result of judicial appointments, federal courts stopped pushing for school integration. The Supreme Court's *Freeman* v. *Pitts* decision in 1992 granted a suburban Atlanta school board relief from a desegregation order on the grounds that it was not possible to counteract massive demographic shifts.

Yet African Americans kept the struggle alive. The Reverend Jesse Jackson, a longtime civil rights activist, established what he called the Rainbow Coalition in 1984 and ran for the presidency. Though he lost his bid for the Democratic nomination, he had the support of nearly 400 delegates, and in a nationally televised speech at the convention, he vowed not to forget his constituency of "the desperate, the damned, the disinherited, the disrespected, and the despised."

Jesse Jackson

Jesse Jackson demonstrated that an African American could attract a substantial level of support as he ran for president in 1984 and 1988. Here he is shown on the campaign trail in Chicago in 1988. Why were Jackson's campaigns so important? Who do you think his strongest supporters were?

(Marc Pokempner)

All Americans, he went on, needed to work together for a common cause: "Our flag is red, white and blue, but our nation is a rainbow—red, yellow, brown, black and white—and we're all precious in God's sight." Four years later, in 1988, he sought the Democratic nomination again, this time with the support of 1,200 delegates at the convention, before falling short of his goal once more.

Despite significant victories in mayoral elections in major cities and other electoral gains, black–white relations remained tense. A riot in Los Angeles in 1992 revealed the continuing racial polarization. The year before, Americans had watched a videotaped, savage beating of black motorist Rodney King by white police officers, the most dramatic of a long string of incidents involving police brutality. When a California jury that did not include any African Americans acquitted the policemen, many people throughout the country became convinced that people of color could not obtain equal justice under the law. In Los Angeles, thousands reacted with uncontrolled fury, targeting supermarkets, drug stores, Korean businesses, restaurants, and mini-malls. Much of the chaos was orchestrated by gang members, but it also involved hundreds of ordinary citizens who acted irresponsibly, yet with a sense that the social contract had been broken by politicians and the rich who were unresponsive to their plight. After the riot had run its course, 51 people (most of them black and Hispanic) lay dead, 2,000 were injured, and $1 billion in damage had been done to the city. It was the worst riot in decades and served notice that racial injustice, social inequality, and poverty could no longer be ignored.

Obstacles to Women's Rights

Women, too, made significant electoral gains at the local, state, and national levels. In 1981, President Reagan named Sandra Day O'Connor as the first woman Supreme Court justice, and in 1984 Democrat Geraldine Ferraro became the first major-party female vice presidential nominee. The women's movement also became racially inclusive.

Yet women still faced problems that were compounded by conservative social policies. Access to new positions did not change their concentration in lower-paying jobs. In 1985, most working women were still secretaries, cashiers, bookkeepers, registered nurses, and waitresses—the same jobs most frequently held 10 years before. Even when women moved into positions traditionally held by men, their progress often stopped at the lower and middle levels, at what came to be called a "glass ceiling," and wage differentials continued to exist. In 1985, full-time working women still earned only 59 cents for every dollar earned by men.

Sandra Day O'Connor

Sandra Day O'Connor became the first woman justice to sit on the U.S. Supreme Court. Her pre-Court career was similar to that of many other women, as she was denied numerous jobs when she emerged from law school. A decade later, Ruth Bader Ginsburg joined O'Connor on the nation's highest court. Here O'Connor testified at her confirmation hearings. What impression does she convey as she answered senators' questions?

(Getty Images)

Conservatives also waged a dedicated campaign against the right to legal abortion. Despite the 1973 Supreme Court decision legalizing abortion, the issue remained very much alive. The number of abortions increased dramatically in the decade after the decision. In response, "pro-life" forces mobilized. Opponents lobbied to cut off federal funds that allowed the poor to obtain the abortions that the better-off could pay for themselves; they insisted that abortions should be performed in hospitals and not in less-expensive clinics; and they worked to reverse the original decision itself.

Though the Supreme Court underscored its judgment in 1983, the pro-life movement was not deterred. In 1989, a solidifying conservative majority on the Court ruled in *Webster* v. *Reproductive Health*

Services that while women's right to abortion remained intact, state legislatures could impose limitations if they chose. In 1992, in *Planned Parenthood v. Casey*, the Supreme Court reaffirmed what it termed the essence of the right to abortion, while permitting further state restrictions. It declared that a 24-hour waiting period for women seeking abortions was acceptable and required teenage girls to secure the permission of a parent (or a judge) before ending a pregnancy. The ruling made an abortion harder to obtain, particularly for poor women and young women.

Women and men became more sensitive to the issue of sexual harassment. The dramatic confrontation between Supreme Court nominee Clarence Thomas and lawyer Anita Hill during confirmation hearings in 1991 dramatized both racial questions and the problem of sexual harassment. After the retirement of Thurgood Marshall, the only African American on the Supreme Court, President Bush sought to replace him with the much more conservative Clarence Thomas, putting African Americans, who wanted one of their own on the court, in a political bind. Then, during nationally televised confirmation hearings, Anita Hill accused Thomas of harassing her when she had worked for him earlier. Despite powerful opposition, the Bush administration managed to garner the necessary votes for confirmation. In the aftermath of the turbulent confirmation hearings, Americans in Congress, in the business community, and in the larger workplace all became more aware of inappropriate behavior that could no longer be tolerated.

The Limited Commitment to Latino Rights

Latinos likewise faced continuing concerns in the 1980s and early 1990s as the commitment to reform eroded. The Latino population increased substantially as a result of immigration reform during the Great Society of the 1960s (see Chapter 28). In the 1980s, 47 percent of all legal American immigration came from Mexico, the Caribbean, and Latin America. Many other immigrants arrived illegally. As the populations of Latin American nations soared and economic conditions deteriorated, more and more people looked to the United States for relief.

Many of the new arrivals were skilled workers or professionals, who still had to retool after arriving in the United States. But even more prevalent were laborers, service sector workers, and semiskilled employees, who needed the benefit of social services at just the time they were being cut back.

Spanish-speaking students often found it difficult to finish school. In 1987, 40 percent of all Latino high school students did not graduate, and only 31 percent of Latino seniors were enrolled in college-preparatory courses; those who were in such classes frequently received little help from guidance counselors. Like other groups, Latinos slowly extended their political gains. In the 1980s, Henry Cisneros became mayor of San Antonio and Federico Peña was elected mayor of Denver. In New Mexico, Governor Toney Anaya called himself the nation's highest-elected Hispanic. The number of Latinos holding elective offices nationwide increased 3.5 percent between 1986 and 1987, and the number of Latina women in such offices increased 20 percent in that time. The number of Latino public officials nationwide increased 73 percent between 1985 and 1994, and Lauro Cavazos became the first Latino Cabinet official when he was appointed secretary of education in 1988.

Latino workers, however, continued to have a hard time in the employment market. Even as the nation's overall unemployment rate dropped, the rate for the 12 million Latino workers barely budged—and worsened in relation to the rate for African Americans.

Continuing Problems for Native Americans

Native Americans likewise experienced the waning commitment to reform, but they made some gains as a result of their own efforts. Some tribal communities developed business skills, although traditional Indian attitudes hardly fostered the capitalist perspective. As Dale Old Horn, an MIT graduate and department head at Little Big Horn College in Crow Agency, Montana, explained:

> The Crow Indian child is taught that he is part of a harmonious circle of kin relations, clans and nature. The white child is taught that he is the center of the circle. The Crow believe in sharing wealth, and whites believe in accumulating wealth.

Some Indian groups did adapt to the capitalist ethos. The Choctaw in Mississippi were among the most successful. Before they began a drive toward self-sufficiency in 1979, their unemployment rate was 50 percent. By the middle of the 1980s, Choctaw owned all or part of three businesses on the reservation, employed 1,000 people, generated $30 million in work annually, and cut the unemployment rate in half. After Congress approved Native American gambling in 1988, an increasing number of tribes became involved in this industry. Despite entrepreneurial gains, Indians still remained (as the 1990 census showed) the nation's poorest group. As Ben Nighthorse Campbell, Republican senator from Colorado, noted in 1995, average Indian household income fell by 5 percent in the 1980s, while it rose for all other ethnic and racial groups. According to the 1990 census, median Indian household income was less than $20,000 a year.

Asian American Gains

Asian Americans climbed the social and economic ladder one rung at a time. The Asian American population increased dramatically with the influx of refugees at the end of the Vietnam War, with more than half a million arriving after 1975. In the 1980s, 37 percent of all immigrants to the United States came from Asia. In Los Angeles and other cities, Samoans, Taiwanese, Koreans, Vietnamese, Filipinos, and Cambodians competed for jobs and apartments with Mexicans, African Americans, and Anglos, just as newcomers had contended with one another in New York City a century earlier.

Immigrants from India, the Philippines, China, and Korea often brought skills and professional expertise, although Southeast Asian refugees were frequently less well-off when they arrived. Many of these unskilled immigrants provided the labor for the rapidly expanding West Coast electronics industry, though Indians contributed impressive engineering and scientific talent. Asian immigrants, following a pattern established decades before, sought better and better opportunities for their children, and in California they became the largest group of entering students at a number of college campuses.

Sometimes the media highlighted the successes of Asian immigrants, particularly in contrast to the problems encountered by other groups. In 1986, *U.S. News & World Report* noted Asian American advances in a cover story, while *Newsweek* ran a lead article on "Asian Americans: A 'Model Minority,'" and *Fortune* called them "America's Super Minority." Asian Americans were proud of the exposure but pointed out that many members of the working class still struggled for a foothold. In the Chinatowns of San Francisco and Los Angeles, 40 to 50 percent of the workers were employed in the ill-paid service sector or garment industry; in New York's Chinatown, the figure was close to 70 percent. Chinese immigrant women, in particular, often had little choice but to work as seamstresses.

Professionals from some countries had a hard time. One Vietnamese physician who resettled in Oklahoma noted, "When I come here, I am told that I must be a beginner again and serve like an apprentice for two years. I have no choice, so I will do it, but I have been wronged to be asked to do this." Professionals from other nations, with programs recognized in the United States, made the transition more easily.

Violent episodes sometimes highlighted discrimination. In 1982, in Detroit, Chinese American Vincent Chin was about to get married. At a strip club with friends the week before his wedding, he encountered two auto workers who thought that Chin was Japanese, and they regarded Japan as responsible for the crisis in the American auto industry as Japanese cars flooded the market. They followed Chin out the door and killed him with a baseball bat. In response to a guilty plea, both murderers received three years probation and $3,780 in fines. Detroit's Asian Americans were incensed but were reluctant to jeopardize what they considered their already vulnerable role in America.

Pressures on the Environmental Movement

Environmentalists, too, were discouraged by the direction of public policy in the 1980s and early 1990s. Activists found that they faced fierce opposition in the Republican years. Reagan systematically restrained the EPA in his avowed effort to promote economic growth. Under the leadership of James Watt of Colorado, the Department of the Interior opened forest lands, wilderness areas, and coastal waters to economic development, with no concern for preserving the natural environment. When asked whether he believed it was important to protect the environment for future generations, Watt, a devout Christian, responded that he did not know how many generations there were before the Second Coming. Bush initially proved more sympathetic to environmental causes and delighted environmentalists by signing new clean-air legislation. Later, as the economy faltered, he was less willing to support environmental action that he claimed might slow economic growth. In 1992, he accommodated business by easing clean-air restrictions. That same year, at a United Nations–sponsored Earth Summit in Rio de Janeiro, Brazil, with 100 other heads of state, Bush stood alone in his refusal to sign a biological diversity treaty framed to conserve plant and animal species.

Economic and Demographic Change

Republicans sought to reorganize the government against the backdrop of an economy that was volatile in the 1980s and early 1990s and left millions of workers struggling to survive the shocks. Under Republican supply-side economics, the business cycle moved from recession to boom and back to recession again. When Reagan took office in 1980, the economy was reeling under the impact of declining productivity, galloping inflation, oil shortages, and high unemployment. It revived in the early 1980s, then gave way to a deep recession that lasted from 1990 to 1992, underscoring the need for renewed productivity, full employment, and a more equitable distribution of wealth.

Recovering the Past

THE INTERNET AND THE WORLD WIDE WEB

The Internet has become an integral part of our daily lives. More and more people use e-mail to communicate quickly with friends and colleagues around the world. Many Americans use the World Wide Web to make purchases ranging from books to automobiles. Others buy stocks online and rely on the Web to manage their portfolios. Historians and other scholars have come to depend on huge databases on the Web that are accessible from computers anywhere around the world.

The Internet has become an important tool for historical research. Historians can acquire census data on the Web. They can find essential statistical files, from both government offices and the private sector. They can examine huge collections of historical images. They can read the text of vital speeches. They can look at moving-picture clips from the Spanish-American War and listen to songs of the 1960s. But they need to be cautious in what they do. While the Internet provides access to a huge amount of material, the historian must evaluate it as if it was a more traditional source. But with that caution, it can be an extraordinarily useful tool.

While the Internet has only recently become an important source of historical information, it is not new. Its roots extend back 30 years, to the mid-1960s, when Americans were worried about the nuclear arms race with the Soviet Union at the height of the Cold War. After the Russians launched their *Sputnik* satellite in 1957 with a rocket that demonstrated the ability to send atomic weapons from one continent to another, American scientists dedicated themselves to catching up with and then surpassing the Soviets in space. To do so, they needed to develop their computer technology.

Scientists were also interested in figuring out how to maintain communication in the aftermath of a nuclear attack. As both the United States and the Soviet Union developed bigger and better atomic bombs and then in the 1950s began to create even more potent hydrogen weapons, it became clear that a full-scale nuclear war could wipe out a nation's ability to communicate with its distant military bases. The Department of Defense wanted to create a decentralized communication system that could continue to function even if part of it was wiped out.

In the early 1960s, scientists at the Massachusetts Institute of Technology developed the concept of timesharing, in which different users at widely separated sites could use the same central computer at the same time. Another step forward came in the mid-1960s with the development of "packet-switching" technology, which broke down data into small, discrete packets that could be transmitted over telephone lines, using modems to connect the computers to the phone lines, and then reassembled when received by another computer at the other end.

Building on those steps, the Department of Defense established the Advanced Research Projects Agency Network, known as ARPANET, in 1969. It linked the computers of four institutions—the University of California campuses at Los Angeles and Santa Barbara, the Stanford Research Institute, and the University of Utah. Two years later, the system had expanded to include 23 universities and research centers around the country.

The system was hardly user-friendly in these early days. In an age before the advent of personal computers at home, or even office computers at work, only computer professionals, engineers, and other scientists mastered the intricacies of what were very complex systems. Once they did, however, they were able to communicate with one another through what became known as electronic mail, or e-mail.

The term *Internet* was first used to describe this decentralized network in 1982, and in 1986 the National Science Foundation created a network called NSFNET with a better-organized backbone for the entire system. This new infrastructure had different *domains,* each marked by a different suffix at the end of an e-mail address, such as "edu" for educational establishments, "com" for commercial enterprises, and "gov" for government offices.

But even with improvements, the Internet remained hard to use. While computer experts could find all kinds of information, others found it difficult to access what they wanted. Then, in 1991, the University of Minnesota developed a system for finding information by accessing a huge number of databases, and they named it after the university mascot—the golden gopher.

At about the same time, another development made an even greater impact on Internet use. In 1989, Tim Berners-Lee and others at the European Laboratory for Particle Physics (known as CERN) in Geneva, Switzerland, developed a new system for information distribution. It was based on the concept of hypertext, which involved embedding links to other documents or pieces of information in the text of a document itself. While reading an article or essay on the computer, you could simply move to another document by selecting the appropriate link. This system became the basis for what came to be called the World Wide Web in 1991; over the next few years, it supplanted the gophers as the easiest way to maneuver the masses of information in cyberspace. In 1993, Mark Andreessen and others at the National Center for Superconducting Applications at the University of Illinois at Champaign–Urbana went a step further when they developed what they called Mosaic, which was a graphical Web browser. It was an easy-to-use piece of computer software that enabled the user to click the mouse on graphics or icons as well as text in a document to move to another document or Web site. Andreessen and others then formed the Netscape Communications Corporation, a private company, which marketed Netscape Navigator to browse the Web. Microsoft's Internet Explorer provides another browser.

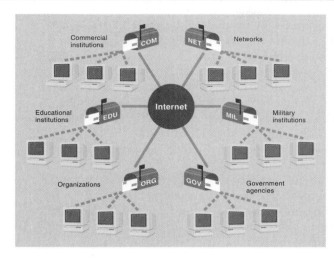

Internet and World Wide Web addresses are organized into domains, each indicated by a different three-letter suffix. Colleges and universities, for example, all use the "edu" designation.

The next step made searching for information on the Web even easier. In 1996, Larry Page and Sergey Brin, two doctoral students at Stanford University, developed a new search engine to help access Web sites that might be most helpful. They incorporated their concept in 1998 under the name Google, and two years later began selling advertising on the site to help generate revenue. While

other new Internet corporations sometimes floundered, Google grew and grew, and the name itself found its way into dictionaries as a verb meaning using this search engine to find relevant information.

Reflecting on the Past Today, the World Wide Web is more accessible than ever before. But as more and more adults and children use the Web, legal issues remain to be resolved. What kinds of censorship are acceptable on the Web? How can writers, artists, and musicians maintain copyright protection for their work when the materials they produce are frequently instantly accessible on the Web? How can high-speed connections be made available to people with limited resources? How can systems be protected from "hackers" who use their ingenuity to break into commercial or government computer systems and disrupt the flow of information?

What kind of historical research might you do on the Web? How can you assess the veracity of the material you find on the Internet? What cautions are essential if you are to make the best use of Web sources?

To find more about Ronald Reagan, go to the Google search box on your computer and type in his name and see what you find. Locate audio clips of his speeches. Then go to "You Tube," another popular site, by typing in that name in the Google search box, and locate videos of his "Morning in America" advertisement as he ran for reelection and other film clips about his life and presidency. ■

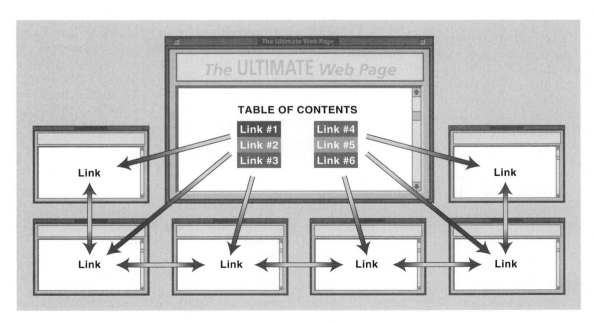

The World Wide Web links numerous Web pages together. By clicking the computer mouse on a highlighted item, a user can move easily from one linked page to another.

The Changing Nature of Work

Automation and other technological advances had a powerful impact on the American workplace. The *New York Times* reported in 1990 that "Some factories look as if they have been hit by a kind of economic neutron bomb, which left assembly lines running at full speed but eliminated most of the people who worked on them." Formerly profitable jobs disappeared. One pulp-mill worker voiced gloom about the future: "I think the country has a problem. The managers want everything run by computers. But if no one has a job, no one will know how to do anything anymore. Who will pay the taxes? What kind of society will it be when people have lost their knowledge and depend on computers for everything?"

In human terms, the introduction of the computer had other consequences as well. Workers who sat for hours before their screens complained about a feeling of "floating in space" as they worked, or of being "lost behind the screen." Others worried about radiation from the monitor or muscular fatigue from sitting at a keyboard all day. Still others complained that they could no longer touch their work. As more Americans began to use computers, people who did not work with them complained about a growing "digital divide" that further increased the gap between rich and poor. Members of the middle and upper classes had easy access to computer technology, while less fortunate individuals, many of whom belonged to minority groups, found themselves left behind.

Yet even as the nature of work changed, people seemed to be working more. In past decades, leisure time had seemed to expand, and there was talk of a four-day workweek in the 1950s. In subsequent years, however, the amount of time Americans worked steadily rose so that in the mid-1990s, American employees worked many more hours each year than their counterparts in Germany or France. The effort to juggle the pressures between employment and family life led to increasing stress. Problems were particularly severe for women, still trying to cope with the pressures of a double load, as they maintained responsibility for the home even when working outside. Marriages came under significant strain.

The Shift to a Service Economy

The scarcity of good jobs stemmed in part from the restructuring of the economy that occurred in the 1980s. In a trend that had been underway for more than half a century, the United States continued its shift from an industrial base, in which most workers actually produced things, to a service base, in which most provided expertise or service to others in the workforce. By the mid-1980s, three-fourths of the 113 million employees in the country worked in the service sector as fast-food workers, clerks, computer programmers, doctors, lawyers, bankers, teachers, and bureaucrats. That shift, in turn, had its roots in the decline of the country's industrial sector. The United States had been the world's industrial leader since the late nineteenth century. By the 1980s and early 1990s, productivity had slowed in virtually all American industries.

The causes of this decline in productivity were complex. The most important factor was a widespread failure on the part of the United States to invest sufficiently in its basic productive capacity. During the Reagan years, capital investment in real plants and equipment within the United States gave way to speculation, mergers, and spending abroad. At the end of the 1980s, domestic investment was down—5.7 percent in 1990 and 9.5 percent in 1991. The energy crisis and rising oil prices also contributed to the industrial decline. Finally, the war in Vietnam diverted federal funds from research and development with consequences that continued even after the conflict ended.

While American industry became less productive, other industrial nations moved forward. German and Japanese industries, rebuilt after World War II with U.S. aid and aggressively modernized thereafter, reached new heights of efficiency. As a result, the United States began to lose its share of the world market for industrial goods. In 1946, the country had provided 60 percent of the world's iron and steel; in 1978, it provided a mere 16 percent. By 1980, Japanese car manufacturers had captured nearly one-quarter of the American automobile market. The auto industry, which had been a mainstay of economic growth for much of the twentieth century, suffered plant shutdowns and massive layoffs. In 1991, its worst year ever, Ford lost a staggering $2.3 billion.

Workers in Transition

In the 1980s and early 1990s, American labor struggled to hold on to the gains realized by the post–World War II generation of blue-collar workers. The shift to a service economy, while providing new jobs, was difficult for many American workers. Millions of men and women who lost positions as a result of mergers, plant closings, and permanent economic contractions now found themselves in low-paying jobs with few opportunities for advancement.

Entry-level posts were seldom located in the central cities, where most of the poor lived. Even when new jobs were created in the cities, minority residents often lacked the skills to get them.

Meanwhile, the trade union movement faltered as the economy moved from an industrial to a service base. Unions had been most successful in organizing the nation's industrial workers in the years since the 1930s, and the United States emerged from World War II with unions strong. In the years that followed, the percentage of workers belonging to unions dropped, from just over 25 percent in 1980 to barely over 16 percent a decade later. As the total number of wage and salary workers rose substantially between 1983 and 1993, the overall number of union members dropped from 17.7 million to 16.6 million.

Union membership declined for a number of reasons. The shift from blue-collar to white-collar work contributed to the contraction. The increase in the workforce in the numbers of women and young people (groups that have historically been difficult to organize) was another factor, as was the more forceful opposition to unions by managers applying the provisions of the Taft–Hartley Act of 1947, which restricted labor's tactics. At the same time, union organizing efforts fell off significantly.

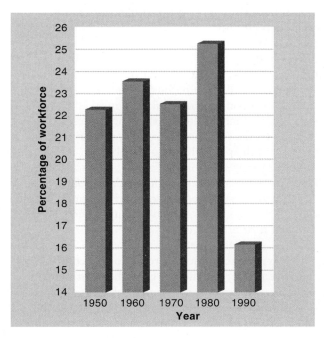

Union Membership, 1950–1990

The percentage of workers belonging to unions dropped dramatically after 1980 and continued to fall in the 1990s.

Source: U.S. Bureau of Labor Statistics.

Union vulnerability was visible early in Reagan's first term, when members of the Professional Air Traffic Controllers Organization (PATCO) went on strike. Charging that the strike violated the law, the president—who had once been a union leader himself—fired the strikers, decertified the union, and ordered the training of new controllers at a cost of $1.3 billion. The message was clear: government employees could not challenge the public interest.

Anti-union sentiments reverberated throughout the nongovernment sector as well, as many companies across the nation—confronted by falling prices and losses in revenue—sought to dissolve union agreements about hiring, wages, and benefits. Workers who kept their jobs found that their unions could not get favorable contracts. For example, in 1984 the United Auto Workers (UAW) ended a strike at General Motors by trading a pledge that GM would guarantee up to 70 percent of the production workers' lifetime jobs for a smaller wage increase than the union sought and a modification of the cost-of-living allowance that had been a part of UAW contracts since 1948.

Farmers also had to adjust as the larger workforce changed. Continuing a trend that began in the early twentieth century, the number of farms and farmers declined steadily. When Franklin Roosevelt took office in 1933, some 6.7 million farms covered the American landscape. Fifty years later, there were only 2.4 million. As family farms disappeared, farming income became more concentrated in the hands of the largest operators. In 1983, the top 1 percent of the nation's farmers produced 30 percent of all farm products, while the top 12 percent generated 90 percent of all farm income. The top 1 percent of the growers in the United States had average annual incomes of $572,000, but the small and medium-sized farmers who were being forced off the land frequently had incomes below the official government poverty line.

The extraordinary productivity of the most successful American farmers derived in part from the use of chemical fertilizers, irrigation, pesticides, and scientific management. Government price-support programs helped, too. Yet that very productivity caused unexpected setbacks. In the 1970s, food shortages abroad made the United States the "bread-basket of the world." Farmers increased their output to meet multibillion-bushel grain export orders and profited handsomely from high prices in India, China, Russia, and other countries. To increase production, farmers often borrowed heavily at high interest rates. When a worldwide economic slump began in 1980, overseas demand for American farm products declined sharply and farm prices dropped.

Thousands of farmers, caught in the cycle of over-production, heavy indebtedness, and falling prices, watched helplessly as banks and federal agencies foreclosed on their mortgages and drove them out of business.

The Roller-Coaster Economy

The economy shifted back and forth during the 1980s and early 1990s. The Reagan years began with a recession that lasted for several years. An economic boom between 1983 and 1990 gave way to a punishing recession as the new decade began. It appeared that the United States had embarked on another unsettling boom-and-bust cycle.

The recession of 1980 to 1982 began during the Carter administration, when the Federal Reserve Board tried to deal with mounting deficits by increasing the money supply. Program cuts to counter inflation brought substantial unemployment in the workforce. During Reagan's first year, the job situation deteriorated further, and by the end of 1982, the unemployment rate had climbed to 10.8 percent (and over 20 percent among African Americans). Nearly one-third of the nation's industrial capacity lay idle, and 12 million Americans were out of work.

Inflation, accompanied by heavy unemployment, continued to be a problem. The inflation rate, which reached 12.4 percent a year under Carter in 1980, fell after Reagan assumed office, to 8.9 percent in his first year and to about 5 percent during the remainder of his first term. But even the lower rate eroded the purchasing power of people already in difficulty.

The recession of 1980–1982 afflicted every region of the country. Business failures proliferated in every city and state, as large and small businesses closed their doors and fired employees. In 1982, business bankruptcies rose 50 percent from the previous year. In auto-making Detroit, Japanese competition and high interest rates sent car sales plummeting. The Detroit unemployment rate rose to more than 19 percent and affected the entire city.

Even the Sun Belt—the vast southern region stretching from coast to coast—showed the effects of the recession. It had enjoyed economic growth fostered by the availability of cheap, nonunion labor, tax advantages that state governments offered corporations willing to locate plants there, and a favorable climate. Now it, too, began to suffer economic problems, and large areas began to stagnate. Overexpansion in the oil industry led to a collapse in prices that disrupted the economy in Texas, Oklahoma, Louisiana, and other oil-producing regions. Worldwide gluts of some minerals, copper for example, added to unemployment elsewhere in the Southwest.

Economic conditions improved in late 1983 and early 1984, particularly for Americans in the middle- and upper-income ranges. The federal tax cut Reagan pushed through encouraged consumer spending, and huge defense expenditures had a stimulating effect. The Republican effort to reduce restrictions and cut waste sparked business confidence. A voluntary Japanese quota on car exports assisted the ailing automobile industry. The stock market climbed as it reflected the optimistic buying spree. Inflation remained low, about 3 to 4 percent annually from 1982 to 1988. Interest rates likewise fell from 16.5 percent to 10.5 percent in the same period. The unemployment rate at the end of the 1980s fell to below 6 percent nationally (though many of the new jobs that were created paid less than $13,000 per year). Between the start of the recovery and 1988, real GNP grew at an annual rate of 4.2 percent.

But the economic upswing masked a number of problems. Millions of Americans remained poor. Many families continued to earn a middle-class income, but only by having two full-time income earners. They also went deeply into debt. To buy homes, young people accepted vastly higher mortgage interest rates than their parents had. Stiff credit card debts, often at 20 percent interest, were common. Under such circumstances, some young families struggled to remain in the middle class. Blue-collar workers had to accept lower standards of living. Single mothers were hit hardest of all.

The huge and growing budget deficits reflected the fundamental economic instability. Those deficits provoked doubts that resulted in the stock market crash of 1987. Six weeks of falling prices culminated with a 22.6 percent drop on Monday, October 19, almost double the plunge of "Black Tuesday," October 29, 1929. The deficits, negative trade balances, and exposures of Wall Street fraud all combined to puncture the bubble. The stock market revived, but the crash foreshadowed further problems.

Those problems surfaced in the early 1990s, as the country experienced another recession. A combination of massive military spending, growth of entitlement programs, and tax cuts sent budget deficits skyward. As bond traders in the 1980s speculated recklessly and pocketed huge profits, the basic productive structure of the country continued to decline. The huge increase in the national debt eroded business confidence, and this time the effects were felt not simply in the stock market but in the economy as a whole.

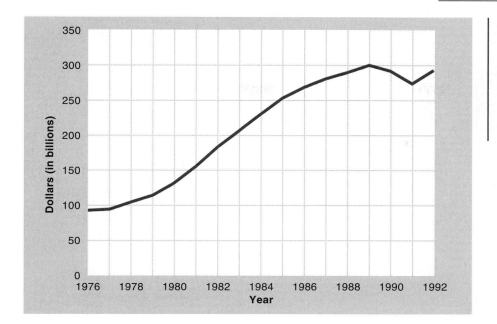

Federal Defense Spending, 1976–1992

Federal defense spending rose dramatically during the presidencies of Ronald Reagan and George Bush. The enormous expenditures on the military led to the huge deficits that threw the economy out of kilter.

Source: Statistical Abstract of the United States.

American firms suffered a serious decline, and to cope with shrinking profits and decreased consumer demand, companies scaled back dramatically. In late 1991, General Motors announced that it would close 21 plants, lay off 9,000 white-collar employees the next year, and eliminate more than 70,000 jobs in the next several years. Hundreds of other companies did the same thing. As a result, the unemployment rate rose once again, and by mid-1991, it reached 7 percent, the highest level in nearly five years.

Around the nation, state governments found it impossible to balance their budgets without resorting to massive spending cuts. Reagan's efforts to move programs from the federal to the state level worked as long as funding lasted, but as national support dropped and state tax revenues declined, states found themselves in a budgetary gridlock. Most had constitutional prohibitions against running deficits, and so they had to slash spending for social services and education.

After a number of false starts, the economy began to recover in mid-1992. The unemployment rate dropped, the productivity index rose, and a concerted effort began to bring the federal deficit down.

Population Shifts

As the American people dealt with the swings of the economy, demographic patterns changed significantly. The nation's population increased from 228 million to approximately 250 million between 1980 and 1990—a rise of 9.6 percent (as opposed to 11.5 percent in the 1970s) that was one of the lowest rates of growth in American history. At the same time, the complexion of the country changed. In 1992, the country's nonwhite population—African Americans, Latinos, Asians, and Native Americans—stood at an all-time high of 25 percent, the result of increased immigration and of minority birthrates significantly above the white birthrate.

The population shifted geographically as well. American cities increasingly filled with members of the nation's minorities. White families continued to leave for the steadily growing suburbs, which by 1990 contained almost half the population, more than ever before. In 15 of the nation's 28 largest cities—New York, Chicago, and Houston among them—minorities made up at least half the population. Minority representation varied by urban region. In Detroit, Washington, New Orleans, and Chicago, African Americans were the largest minority; in Phoenix, El Paso, San Antonio, and Los Angeles, Latinos held that position; in San Francisco, Asians outnumbered other groups. The cities also grew steadily poorer. As had been the case since World War II, commuters from the suburbs took the better-paying jobs, while people living in the cities held lower-paying positions.

At the same time, the population was moving west. In 1900, the Mountain and Pacific states contained about 5 percent of the nation's population. By 1990, that figure stood at 21 percent. The population of the nation as a whole rose by less than

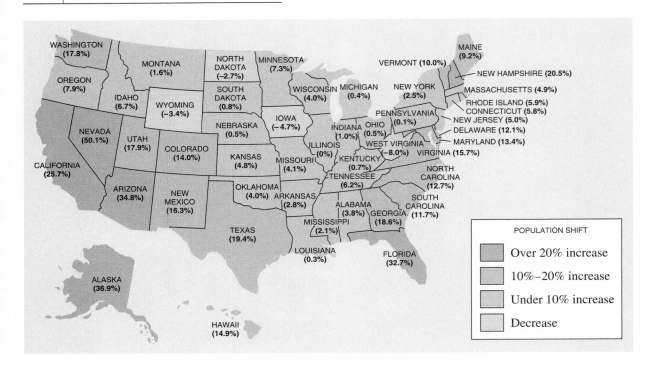

Population Shifts, 1980–1990
This map shows the population shifts between 1980 and 1990. Note the substantial increases in western regions of the country and the much smaller increases along the Atlantic seaboard.

10 percent in the 1980s, but the population of the West increased by 22 percent.

That population was becoming much more urbanized. In the 50 years following 1940, the six largest metropolitan areas in the West grew by 380 percent; the six largest in the East expanded by only 64 percent.

With its urban development, the West became a pacesetter for the rest of the country. If the New England village was a symbol of the eighteenth century and the midwestern town was a similar symbol of the nineteenth century, then the western metropolis had special symbolic importance in the late twentieth century. Western cities were unbounded, open-ended, and sprawling in all directions. They seemed capable of expanding indefinitely. Horizontal, low-slung homes made western neighborhoods look very different from those in the Northeast. Tourism became a dynamic industry, with the West in the forefront. The motel, a western invention, made automobile travel easier.

California was the nation's fastest-growing state, its population increasing in the 1980s by nearly 26 percent. Responding to a question about California's impact on the rest of the country, writer Wallace Stegner replied, "We *are* the national culture, at its most energetic end." Los Angeles became the most dynamic example of American vitality and creativity. The motion picture industry exerted a worldwide impact. The city became a capital of consumption and served as a symbol of a dynamic national life.

Foreign Policy and the End of the Cold War

In the early 1990s, the United States emerged triumphant in the Cold War that had dominated international politics since the end of World War II. In one of the most momentous turns in modern world history, communism collapsed in Eastern Europe and in the Soviet Union, and the various republics in the Soviet orbit moved toward capitalism and democracy. Other regions—the Middle East and Africa—experienced equally breathtaking change.

Reagan, Bush, and the Soviet Union

The Cold War was very much alive when Ronald Reagan assumed power in 1981. Like most of his compatriots, Reagan believed in large defense budgets and a militant approach toward the Soviet Union. He wanted to cripple the USSR economically by forcing it to spend more than it could afford on defense.

The Last Premier of the Soviet Union
Mikhail Gorbachev was the Soviet leader who initiated the process that helped ease tensions with the United States and ultimately ended the Cold War. Gorbachev's policies provided for major readjustments in Soviet society, but those eventually tore the Soviet Union apart. Why was Gorbachev willing to work with the United States? What image does he convey in this photograph?

(AP/Wide World Photos)

Viewing the Soviet Union as an "evil empire" in his first term, Reagan promoted a larger atomic arsenal by arguing that a nuclear war could be fought and won. The administration dropped efforts to obtain Senate ratification of SALT II, the arms reduction plan negotiated under Carter, although it observed the pact's restrictions. Then Reagan proposed the enormously expensive and bitterly criticized Strategic Defense Initiative, popularly known as "Star Wars" after a 1977 movie, to intercept Soviet missiles in outer space.

In his second term, Reagan softened his belligerence. Mikhail Gorbachev, the new Soviet leader, watching his own economy collapse under the pressure of the superheated arms race, realized the need for greater accommodation with the West. He understood that the only way the Soviet Union could survive was through arms negotiations with the United States. He therefore proposed a policy of *perestroika* (restructuring the economy) and *glasnost* (political openness to encourage personal initiative). His overtures opened the way to better relations with the United States.

Concerned with his own place in history, Reagan met with Gorbachev, and the two developed a close working relationship. Summit meetings led to an Intermediate-Range Nuclear Forces Treaty in 1987 that provided for the withdrawal and destruction of 2,500 Soviet and American nuclear missiles in Europe.

George Bush maintained Reagan's comfortable relationship with Gorbachev. At several summit meetings in 1989 and 1990, the two leaders signed agreements reducing the number of long-range nuclear weapons, ending the manufacture of chemical weapons, and easing trade restrictions. The Strategic Arms Reduction Treaty (START) signed in 1991 dramatically cut stockpiles of long-range weapons.

The End of the Cold War

The Cold War ended with astonishing speed. Gorbachev's efforts to restructure Soviet society and to work with the United States brought him acclaim around the world but led to trouble at home. In mid-1991, he faced an old-guard Communist coup, led by those who opposed *glasnost* and *perestroika*. He survived this right-wing challenge, but he could not resist those who wanted to go even further to

President of a New Russia
Boris Yeltsin, president of Russia, the largest of the republics in what had been the Soviet Union, became the most influential leader after Gorbachev's fall. But Yeltsin's efforts at economic reform met with serious opposition and led to his resignation as the century came to an end. How is Yeltsin conveying his confidence in this picture? What did he hope to achieve?

(Reuters/CORBIS)

establish democracy and capitalism. The forces he had unleashed finally destroyed the Soviet system and tore the USSR apart.

Boris Yeltsin, president of Russia, the strongest and largest of the Soviet republics, emerged as the dominant leader, but even he could not contain the forces of disintegration. Movements in the tiny Baltic republics of Latvia, Lithuania, and Estonia, culminating with independence in 1991, began the dismantling of the Soviet Union. The once-powerful superpower was now a collection of separate states. Although the republics coalesced loosely in a Commonwealth of Independent States, led by Russia, they retained their autonomy—and independent leadership—in domestic and foreign affairs.

Meanwhile, Communist regimes throughout Europe collapsed. The most dramatic chapter in this story unfolded in Germany in November 1989. Responding to Gorbachev's softening stance toward the West, East Germany's Communist party boss announced unexpectedly that citizens of his country would be free to leave East Germany. Within hours, thousands of people gathered on both sides of the 28-mile Berlin Wall—the symbol of the Cold War that divided Berlin into East and West sectors. As the border guards stepped aside, East Germans flooded into West Berlin amid dancing, shouting, and fireworks. Within days, sledgehammer-wielding Germans pulverized the Berlin Wall, and soon the Communist government itself came tumbling down. By October 1990, the two Germanys were reunited.

The fall of the Berlin Wall reverberated all over Eastern Europe. In Poland, the 10-year-old Solidarity movement led by Lech Walesa triumphed in its long struggle against Soviet domination and found itself in power in December 1990, with Walesa as president. In Czechoslovakia, two decades after Soviet tanks had rolled into the streets of Prague to suppress a policy of liberalization, the forces of freedom were likewise victorious. Like Poland, Czechoslovakia sought and received aid from the United States. But not even economic assistance could keep the nation intact, as turbulence led to the creation of separate and independent Czech and Slovak republics. The same forces that culminated in the independence of Czechoslovakia brought new regimes in Bulgaria, Hungary, Romania, and Albania.

Yugoslavia, held together by a Communist dictatorship since 1945, proved to be the extreme case of ethnic hostility resurging amid collapsing central authority. In 1991, Yugoslavia splintered into its ethnic components. In Bosnia, the decision of the Muslim and Croatian majority to secede from Serbian-dominated Yugoslavia led Bosnian Serbs, backed by the Serbian republic, to embark on a brutal siege of the city of Sarajevo and an even more ruthless "ethnic cleansing" campaign to liquidate opponents. The United States remained out of the conflict, unsure about what to do.

Early in 1992, Bush and Yeltsin proclaimed a new era of "friendship and partnership" and formally declared an end to the Cold War. After half a century of confrontation, the United States had won. It then extended aid to the former Soviet republics, which needed help in reorganizing their economies as free enterprise systems.

Dismantling the Berlin Wall
The destruction of the Berlin Wall in November 1989 was a symbolic blow to the entire Cold War structure that had solidified in Europe in the postwar years. People grabbed hammers and joined together in tearing down the hated wall. Joyous celebrations marked the reunification of a city that had been divided for decades. How does this dramatic picture convey the exuberant mood of the time?

(Alexandria Avakian/Woodfin Camp & Associates)

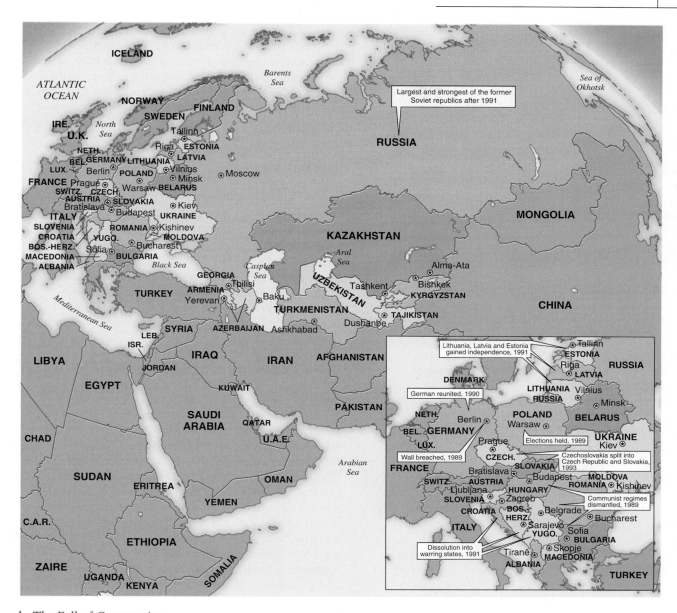

The Fall of Communism

In the late 1980s and early 1990s, the Soviet Union fragmented and lost control of its satellites in Eastern Europe. As many countries shown here declared their independence, Czechoslovakia broke into two nations, while Yugoslavia ruptured into a group of feuding states. How widespread was the turbulence that led to the fall of communism? How quickly did the process take place? How did events in one country influence events in another country?

American Involvement Overseas

As the United States struggled to keep abreast of the momentous changes in Eastern Europe, it was equally involved with events in the rest of the world. Here again the nation sought to preserve stability as the Cold War drew to an end.

In Latin America, the United States intervened frequently as it had in the past, hoping to impose order on the volatile region. Viewing Central America as a Cold War battlefield early in his presidency, Reagan openly opposed left-wing guerrillas in El Salvador who fought to overthrow a repressive right-wing regime. The United States increased its assistance to the anti-revolutionary Salvadoran government, heedless of a similar course followed years before in Vietnam. Efforts to destroy the radical forces failed, but in 1989, a far-right faction won the Salvadoran elections and polarized the country.

Nicaragua became an even bloodier battleground. In 1979, revolutionaries calling themselves Sandinistas (after César Sandino, who fought in the 1920s against U.S. occupation troops) overthrew the repressive

Nelson Mandela

Nelson Mandela served as a source of inspiration to black South Africans, as the long struggle against apartheid finally brought that system of rigid segregation to an end and led to the setting up of a biracial democracy with Mandela himself as president. How did Mandela manage to convey his own sense of confidence, commitment, and reconciliation?

(AP/Wide World Photos)

Somoza family, which had ruled for three decades. Republicans in their 1980 platform pledged to replace the Sandinistas with a "free and independent" government. Once in office, Reagan circumvented congressional opposition to his efforts to defeat the revolutionary reformers and signed a National Security directive in November 1981 authorizing the CIA to arm and train counterrevolutionaries known as *contras* as Nicaragua became enmeshed in a bitter civil war. Upon discovering the secret CIA missions, Congress cut off military aid to the *contras*. Peaceful elections in early 1990 finally drove the Sandinistas out and brought the fighting to an end. Though the economy remained in desperate straits, the new regime seemed to offer the best hope of healing the wounds of the bloody conflict.

Reagan found it easier to maintain stability on the tiny Caribbean island of Grenada. The president ordered marines there in October 1983 after a coup installed a government sympathetic to Fidel Castro's Cuba. Concerned about the construction of a large airfield, 2,000 marines invaded the island, rescued a number of American medical students, and claimed triumph. Though the United Nations condemned it, Americans cheered what the administration called its "rescue mission."

Middle Eastern and Central American concerns became entangled in the Iran–*contra* affair. In 1987, Congress learned that the National Security Council had launched an effort to free American hostages in the Middle East by selling arms to Iran and then using the funds to aid the *contras,* in direct violation of both the law and congressional will. The trial of Oliver North, the National Security Council official responsible for the policy, focused on his distortions and falsifications before congressional committees and on his destruction of official documents that could have substantiated charges of wrongdoing by top officials. Convicted in 1989, North received a light sentence requiring no time in prison from a judge who recognized that North was not acting entirely on his own.

Bush, too, was involved in a variety of episodes abroad. Despite memories of past imperialism, the United States invaded Panama in 1989; the reasons it gave were to protect the canal, defend American citizens, and stop drug traffic. The campaign resulted in the capture of military leader Manuel Noriega, notorious for his involvement in the drug trade. Noriega was brought to the United States, tried, and convicted of drug-trafficking charges.

In South Africa, the United States supported the long and ultimately successful struggle against apartheid. This policy, whereby the white minority (only 15 percent of the population) segregated, suppressed, and denied basic human rights to the black majority, was part of South African law. A resistance movement, spearheaded by the African National Congress (ANC) sought to end apartheid. While the United States had long expressed its dislike of this ruthless system of segregation, economic and political ties to South Africa kept the United States from taking steps to weaken it. Then, in 1986, bowing to increased domestic pressure, Congress imposed sanctions, including a rule prohibiting new American investments. The economic pressure damaged the South African economy and persuaded more than half of the 300 American firms doing business there to leave.

The final blow to apartheid came from the efforts of Nelson Mandela. The black ANC activist, who had become a symbol of the militant resistant movement during his 27 years in prison, steered his nation through a stunning transformation. In 1990, during Bush's presidency, South African prime minister Frederik W. de Klerk succumbed to pressure from the United States and the rest of the world and freed Mandela. Talks between the white government and the ANC produced a smooth transition to a biracial democracy and led to peaceful elections in 1994, in which blacks voted for the first time. The African National Congress assumed power and Mandela himself became president. American aid provided support in transitional times.

Elsewhere in Africa, U.S. policymakers had greater difficulty in maintaining post–Cold War stability. Somalia, an impoverished East African nation, suffered from a devastating famine, compounded by struggles between warlords that led to an almost total disintegration of order. In 1992, Bush sent U.S. troops to assist a UN effort to relieve the starvation and stabilize the country, but those efforts proved unsuccessful in a struggle that continued into the twenty-first century.

A dramatic crisis occurred in the Middle East in 1990 when Saddam Hussein, the dictator of Iraq, invaded and annexed oil-rich neighboring Kuwait. President Bush reacted vigorously. Working through the UN, as Harry Truman had done in Korea, the United States persuaded the Security Council to vote unanimously to condemn the attack and impose an embargo on Iraq. After Hussein refused to relinquish Kuwait, in mid-January 1991 a 28-nation coalition struck at Iraq with an American-led multinational army of nearly half a million troops. In Operation Desert Storm, the coalition forces' sophisticated

missiles, aircraft, and tanks swiftly overwhelmed the Iraqis. Americans were initially jubilant. Then the euphoria faded as Saddam turned his remaining military power against minorities in Iraq. Bush's unwillingness to become bogged down in an Iraqi civil war and his eagerness to return U.S. troops home left the conflict unfinished. A year after his defeat, Hussein was as strongly entrenched as ever.

Meanwhile, the United States was involved in a larger, and ultimately more important, effort to bring peace to the Middle East. In the early 1990s, Secretary of State James Baker finally secured agreement from the major parties in the region to speak to one another face to face. A victory in the Israeli parliamentary elections in mid-1992 for Yitzhak Rabin, a soldier who recognized the need for peace and was ready to compromise, offered further hope for the talks.

Timeline

1980	Ronald Reagan elected president
1980–1982	Recession
1981	Reagan breaks air controllers' strike
	AIDS (acquired immune deficiency syndrome) discovered
1981–1983	Tax cuts; deficit spending increases
1983	Reagan proposes Strategic Defense Initiative ("Star Wars")
1984	Reagan reelected
1986	Tax reform measure passed
	Immigration Reform and Control Act
1987	Iran–*contra* affair becomes public
	Stock market crashes
	Intermediate-Range Nuclear Forces Treaty signed
1988	George H. W. Bush elected president
1989	Federal bailout of savings and loan industry
	Fall of the Berlin Wall
1990	National debt reaches $3.1 trillion
	Sandinistas driven from power in Nicaragua
	Nelson Mandela freed in South Africa
	U.S. population reaches 250 million
1990–1992	Recession
1991	Persian Gulf War
	Failed coup in Soviet Union
	Disintegration of the Soviet Union
	Strategic Arms Reduction Treaty (START) signed
	Ethnic turbulence in fragmented former Yugoslavia
1992	Declaration of the end of the Cold War

Conclusion

CONSERVATISM IN CONTEXT

In the 1980s and early 1990s, the United States witnessed the resurgence of conservatism. The assault on the welfare state, dubbed the "Reagan Revolution," created a less-regulated economy, whatever the implications for less-fortunate Americans. The policies of Ronald Reagan and George Bush continued the trend begun by Richard Nixon in the 1970s. They reshaped the political agenda and reversed the liberal approach that had held sway since the New Deal of Franklin Roosevelt in the 1930s. In foreign affairs, Republican administrations likewise shifted course. Reagan first assumed a steel-ribbed posture toward the Soviet Union, then moved toward détente, and watched as his successor declared victory in the Cold War.

To be sure, there were limits to the transformation. Such fundamental programs as social security and Medicare remained securely in place, accepted by all but the most implacable splinter groups. Even the most conservative presidents of the past half century could not return to an imagined era of unbridled individualism and puny federal government. On the international front, despite the end of the Cold War, the nation's defense budget remained far higher than many Americans wished, and the nuclear arsenal continued to pose a threat to the human race.

Nor was the transformation beneficial to everyone. Periods of deep recession wrought havoc on the lives of blue-collar and white-collar workers alike. Working-class Americans were caught in the spiral of downward mobility that made them question the ability of the nation's economy to reward hard work. Liberals and conservatives both worried about the mounting national debt and the capacity of the economy to compete with Japan, South Korea, Germany, and other countries. Countless Americans fretted about the growing gaps between rich and poor. They fought with one another over what rules should govern a woman's right to an abortion. For the first time in American history, many children could not hope to do better than their parents had done. Reluctantly they tried to prepare themselves to accept a scaled-down version of the American dream.

QUESTIONS FOR REVIEW AND REFLECTION

1. How did the conservative movement become a major force in American life?
2. How successful was Reagan in implementing his conservative program?
3. What was the fate of social reform movements in the 1980s?
4. How did economic issues affect American life in the 1980s?
5. How did the Cold War finally come to an end?

The Post–Cold War World, 1992–2008

American society became more and more aware of its multicultural past and present in the 1990s. Different groups competed with each other for positions in the marketplace and other public spaces as the gap between rich and poor continued to grow greater.

(Billy Morrow Jackson, *Station,* 1981–1982, Beloit College Collection, Beloit, WI)

American Stories

An Immigrant Family Struggles as the Economy Improves

In 1997, Marlene Garrett bundled up her three sleepy children—ages 4, 3, and 1—and took them to the babysitter's home every morning at 5 A.M. "Mama has to go to work so she can buy you shoes," she told them as she left for a job behind the counter at a bagel café in Fort Lauderdale, Florida, that began at 6 A.M. This was a new position and she did not want to be late.

Marlene had come to the United States from Jamaica eight years earlier. She and her husband, Rod, had high hopes for a better life in the United States, and they were fortunate enough to be employed. But both of them held entry-level jobs and had to struggle to make ends meet. Rod worked in a factory making hospital curtains and brought home about $250 a week. Marlene had just left a $5.25-an-hour job selling sneakers for her $6-an-hour job at the bagel café. With the $200 she earned weekly she could pay the monthly rent of $400 and buy groceries. With luck, they could repair or replace the car, which had recently died, and perhaps begin to pay off their $5,000 debt from medical bills. They had no health insurance and could only hope that no one got sick.

Marlene was not happy about her babysitting arrangements. Her real preference was to stay at home. "Who's a better caretaker than mom?" she asked. But remaining at home was out of the question. Welfare might have been a possibility in the past, but the United States was in the process of cutting back drastically on its welfare rolls, and, in any event, Marlene was not comfortable with that alternative. "I don't want to plant that seed in my children," she said. "I want to work."

Marlene had few day-care options. She would have liked to have taken Scherrod, Angelique, and Hasia to the Holy Temple Christian Academy—her church's day-care center and preschool—but it cost $180 a week for three children and was beyond reach. Several months before, when she had been earning $8 an hour as a home health aide for the elderly, she had thought she could afford the church center and had even put money down for school uniforms for the kids. Then her car gave out and made it impossible to continue that job.

Instead of the Holy Temple Christian Academy, Marlene took the children to the home of Vivienne, a woman from the Bahamas who worked nights at the self-service laundry where Marlene did her wash. Vivienne's apartment was simple and clean but had no toys or books anywhere in sight. Most days, the children watched television during the 10 hours that Marlene was away.

The Garretts knew how important it was to stimulate their children. Reflecting longingly on the church center

and what it offered, Marlene said, "The children play games. They go on field trips. They teach them, they train them. My children are bright. You would be amazed at what they would acquire in a year." But instead of a stimulating center, the Garretts had to settle for a place that was simply safe.

At a time when the administration of Bill Clinton was trying to reconfigure the welfare system, people like the Garretts found themselves left out. Florida, like many states, budgeted most of its child-care money for families moving off welfare to jobs. People who had never been on welfare received nothing. As the executive director of a Florida child-care referral agency observed, "Many of these parents have no choice but to leave their children in substandard arrangements that are rotting their brains, and jeopardizing their futures."

Marlene refused to give up hope. Her children were on a waiting list for help from the state that might make the Holy Temple Christian Academy accessible. Meanwhile, she took a second job working nights at the local Marriott Hotel. She had to pay Vivienne more money for the extra hours, and she worried even more about the additional time away from the children, but felt she had no choice. "It is temporary," she said. "I am doing what I have to do."

Marlene and Rod Garrett were like millions of poor Americans who found themselves left out of the prosperity that returned to the United States in the mid-1990s. Despite rosy economic indicators, more than 35 million Americans still lived below the federally defined poverty line. Life was hardly easy for the Garretts or for other families who found themselves on the bottom side of the line. Then, soon after George W. Bush succeeded Bill Clinton as president in 2001, the economy faltered. Now even more Americans found themselves in the same straits as the Garretts.

The Garretts' struggle to care for their children—and for themselves—unfolded against the backdrop of the longest period of economic growth in American history. As a deep recession in the early 1990s lifted, the economy went on a tear. American corporations, increasingly operating in a multinational context, dominated the global economy. Taking advantage of remarkable advances in communications technology, corporations found it easy to do business in a world smaller than ever before. The easy availability of money encouraged middle- and upper-class Americans to invest in the stock market and mutual funds, often enabling them to realize large gains, at least on paper. The troubling budget deficit that had soared in the Reagan administration disappeared as the government, guided by Democratic president Bill Clinton, ran a surplus for the first time in years. The unemployment level dropped, yet for Americans at the bottom of the economic ladder, some of them immigrants from abroad, conditions remained difficult. Many of the jobs now available as a result of the relentless shift toward a service economy paid little more than the minimum wage, and people like the Garretts, who dreamed of a better life, still found themselves struggling to survive.

Meanwhile, the global scene shifted abruptly. The cataclysmic events in Europe that ended nearly a half century of Cold War required the United States to redefine its international role. This led to substantial debate as both Republicans, who controlled Congress for most of the 1990s, and Democrats, who controlled the White House for the same period, voiced reservations about playing an interventionist, and potentially expensive, role abroad. Then, as the new decade began, the United States confronted the menace of

terrorism on a scale never known before. The attacks that destroyed the World Trade Center towers in New York City and left a gaping hole in the Pentagon in Washington, D.C., led to a war on terrorism and a fundamental reconfiguration of American foreign policy.

This chapter describes demographic shifts, reflected in the census of 2000, that changed the face of the American people. It highlights the revival of the economy that brought unprecedented prosperity for many but still failed to accommodate the needs of less fortunate Americans like the Garretts, and then records the even greater suffering as the economy fell apart. It examines the political struggle between Democrats and Republicans that led to a debate about democratic values and brought the second presidential impeachment in American history. It notes the bitterly contested national election of 2000 and its conservative aftermath. Finally, it explores the continuing effort to define the American role in the turbulent and terrorist-dominated post–Cold War world.

The Changing Face of the American People

The United States changed dramatically in the 1990s, as the continuing influx of new immigrants reshaped demographic patterns. The overall population, as reported in the census of 2000, grew more rapidly than it had in the past several decades and reflected the steady increase in the number of nonwhite Americans.

The New Pilgrims

The second great wave of immigrants in the twentieth century changed the face of America. The number of immigrants to the United States in the 20-year period from 1981 to 2000 was approximately 17.5 million, making it the most voluminous period of immigration in American history. In the decade of the 1990s, close to 10 million immigrants were counted, just less than the 10.1 million immigrants recorded in the 10 years from 1905 to 1914, which stands as the all-time record for that span of time. The increase continued in the first five years of the twenty-first century, and in 2005, immigrants made up 12.4 percent of America's population, compared to 11.2 percent in 2000.

Patterns of immigrant settlement changed. Whereas most immigrants around the turn of the preceding century remained near the East Coast, or in contiguous states, in 2000, 39.9 percent of the foreign born settled in western states, with only 22.6 percent of the foreign born living in the Northeast. The shift was a result of larger

demographic shifts in the United States. As the twentieth century began, the Northeast still dominated the economic and cultural life of the nation. A hundred years later, the West was increasingly dominant. California had surpassed New York as the most populous state, and Los Angeles International Airport, known as LAX, had replaced Ellis Island as the port of entry for many immigrants.

The sources of recent immigration were similar to those of the 1970s and 1980s. In 2000, just over one-third of all immigrants—legal and illegal—came from Central America, and just over one-quarter came from Asia. Over the next 6 years, the total Latino population increased by 24 percent, while the Asian population grew by almost 28 percent. Immigrants everywhere, often living on the fringe, looked toward the United States, just as they had done in the past.

Illegal immigration remained a problem. Of the 33.5 million foreigners that the Census Bureau estimated lived in America in 2004, about a third, perhaps even more, were illegal entrants. After 2000, about 850,000 unauthorized immigrants arrived each year. People talked about the nation's "broken borders" as record numbers of immigrants lost their lives in the desert while trying to cross into the United States from Mexico.

The influx of new arrivals was spurred by the Immigration Act of 1965 (see Chapter 28). Part of Lyndon Johnson's Great Society program, this act authorized the impartial acceptance of immigrants from all parts of the world and was directly responsible for

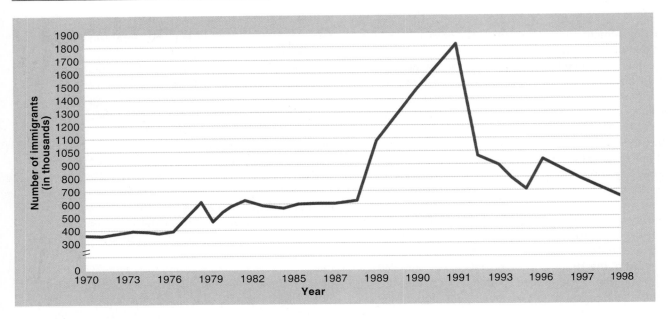

Immigration, 1970–1998

This chart shows the significant rise in immigration after 1970, as the tightly restricted quotas in force from the 1920s to 1965 were liberalized. The steady rise in the 1970s and 1980s reflected the arrival of Asian and Latin Americans, while the spike in the early 1990s occurred because of the amnesty that legalized the status of many illegal immigrants who were now officially counted.

Source: Data from *Statistical Abstract of the United States.*

the greater numbers of Asians and Latin Americans. In 1986, Congress passed the Immigration Reform and Control Act, aimed at curbing illegal immigration while offering amnesty to aliens living in the United States. The Immigration Act of 1990 opened the doors wider, raising immigration quotas while cutting back on restrictions that had limited entry in the past. It also provided for swift deportation of aliens who committed crimes. Two other measures in 1992 expanded eligibility slightly. In 2001, the United States and Mexico began to talk about how to ease the plight of Mexican immigrants and permit illegal arrivals to stay.

The rise in the number of immigrants fueled anti-immigrant feeling in some quarters that resembled similar resistance in Europe. In the 1970s and 1980s, America's efforts to help immigrants coincided with still-intact social-assistance programs of the liberal welfare state. Multiculturalism, stressing the different values that made up a larger American identity, became a dominant theme. Yet those efforts to assist immigrants brought increasing resistance from Americans facing a scarcity of good jobs. There was also a cultural backlash, as opponents of immigration worried about the challenge to America's character posed by new arrivals with their own social patterns.

That opposition, which echoed the anti-immigrant feeling of the past, included strenuous efforts to restrict illegal immigration. Resistance came to a head in 1994 in California, where voters passed Proposition

187, denying illegal aliens access to public education and medical clinics. Within days of the vote, a federal judge issued a preliminary injunction to prevent implementation of the measure, which she made permanent several years later. Yet Proposition 187 provided a model for other states to follow and caught the attention of congressional members, especially Republicans, who gained control of Congress that same year. Two years later, Congress passed legislation barring legal immigrants (who were not yet citizens) from receiving food stamps and disability assistance from the federal government. Toward the end of the decade, California ended its support for bilingual education.

Economic improvement, and the move toward full employment in the latter part of the 1990s, brought a political shift in the immigration debate. In 2000, pressure mounted to increase the number of visas for high-tech workers for businesses and to admit more unskilled workers for the service sector, where there were unfilled jobs. Political considerations also played a part in the shift as both Democrats and Republicans recognized the voting power of Latinos in particular.

Immigration issues became headline news at the end of the 1990s in the highly publicized case of six-year-old Elián Gonzales. In November 1999, he was miraculously pulled out of the water near Florida when a group of Cuban boat people trying to reach the United States drowned. His father, still back in

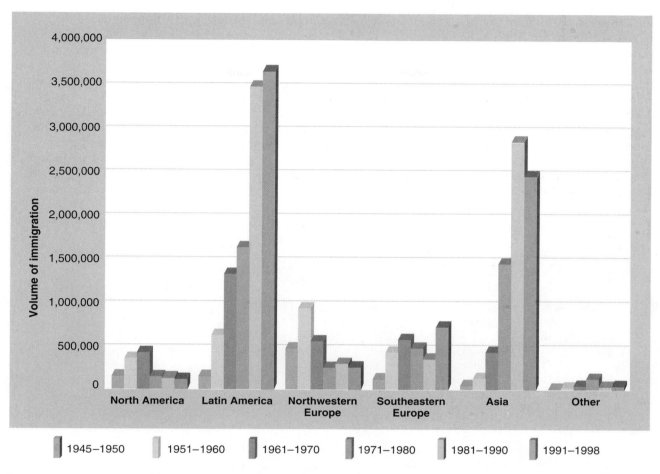

Immigration: Volume and Sources, 1945–1998

This chart shows the shifting patterns of American immigration in the postwar years. In particular, note the large increase in Asian and Latin American immigration in the past several decades.

Source: Data from U.S. Bureau of the Census.

Cuba, had not given permission for the boy to leave and wanted him back. The Miami Cuban community, which hated Fidel Castro and his Communist regime, wanted the boy to receive asylum and stay in the United States. Others, including the Immigration and Naturalization Service (INS), argued that the boy should be returned to his father in Cuba. In the end, the INS seized the boy and returned him to Cuba.

The INS, already unpopular, attracted fierce criticism in the face of the terrorist attacks of September 11, 2001. It had allowed into the country immigrants from Saudi Arabia and elsewhere who had orchestrated the airplane hijackings that shocked the world. Now Americans began to look askance at Arabs or Muslims throughout the country and to condemn the INS for its laxity in screening out potential terrorists.

Meanwhile, in the years after 2000, as the number of illegal immigrants swelled, Americans became increasingly agitated. Congress passed a measure to prevent illegal aliens from obtaining state drivers' licenses. Volunteers patrolled the border between Mexico and Arizona to keep people away. The federal government tried—and failed—in 2006 to enact legislation to tighten border security while making it easier for illegal immigrants to gain citizenship.

The Census of 2000

The 2000 census reported a 13 percent increase in the nation's population, as the United States gained 32.7 million people in the 1990s to reach a total of 281.4 million inhabitants. This expansion surpassed the record 10-year increase of 28 million people in the 1950s, in the midst of the baby boom after World War II. The rate of growth, which had slowed down over the next three decades, accelerated in the 1990s as a result of both increased immigration and longer life expectancy. By 2008, the total population of the United States reached the 303 million mark.

While every state had a net increase in population, growth was greatest in the West, an increasingly important area in the nation's economic, social, and cultural life. Altogether, the West as a whole gained 10.4 million people and expanded by 19 percent. The United States remained about 69 percent white, with a 12 percent African American and 11 percent Latino population. Latinos continued to flock to southern California, the Texas border region, and the south of Florida, and they also began to congregate in increasing numbers in such places as Chicago and Denver. Overall, their numbers increased by 38.8 percent. African Americans maintained their dominance in older cities such as Detroit and Washington, D.C., while continuing to move into metropolitan suburbs.

Nationally, the Asian and Pacific Islander population increased by 43 percent. In California, Asians showed the largest increase of any group. They now comprised nearly 13 percent of the state population and maintained their position as the third-largest population group, after whites and Latinos. Much of the Asian population growth occurred in the suburbs, where the more affluent moved, though large pockets

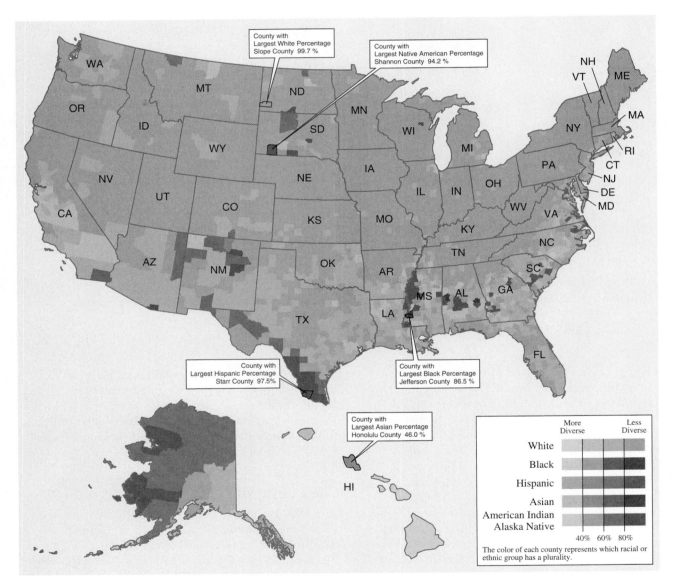

Portrait of a Nation

The 2000 census documented changing population patterns and reported where different groups resided in the United States. Note the concentration of African Americans in the Southeast and the concentration of Hispanics in the Southwest. The Asian American population was greatest in the West, while Native Americans, who had once roamed the continent, were now confined to a number of much smaller western areas. Where are the densest American Indian areas? Why are they so widely dispersed?

Source: "Portrait of a Nation," *New York Times,* April 1, 2001. Copyright © 2001 by The New York Times Co. Reprinted with permission.

of the poor remained in Chinatown in Los Angeles and Little Phnom Penh in Long Beach.

The 2000 census revealed that the combination of Latinos, African Americans, and Asians now outnumbered whites in California. This was the first time since 1860, when California began to provide accurate census data, that whites did not have a majority. State politics already began to reflect the shift. In 1998, Cruz Bustamante became the first Latino elected to statewide office in California since 1871, when he became lieutenant governor. The United States, founded as a white man's country, had now developed into a nation where people of color were increasingly numerous and influential.

One new feature of the 2000 census revealed the desire of large numbers of Americans to identify themselves as part of more than one racial or ethnic group. Nationwide, 2.4 percent of the American people identified themselves as multiracial. In Hawaii, 21 percent of all residents traced their heritage to two or more racial or ethnic groups.

Economic and Social Change

The American economy improved dramatically in the 1990s. Yet despite the revival, millions of Americans remained poor, and homelessness became an increasingly visible problem. Meanwhile, groups pushing for equality made significant gains, but they still faced resistance in their long, continuing struggle for fair treatment in the United States.

Boom and Bust

American economic recovery began in mid-1992, even as other parts of the world found themselves facing industrial problems. In reunified Germany, where extraordinary economic growth had occurred in the post–World War II years, the economy—the largest in Europe—faltered. The Japanese economy, the second-largest in the world after the U.S. economy, likewise encountered trouble.

Against that backdrop, the American revival was even more remarkable. The promotion of big business in the Reagan era spurred investment and led to significant economic expansion. The lowering of interest rates by the Federal Reserve Board revived confidence and promoted consumer spending. Productivity rose steadily throughout the decade, though not quite as quickly as it had in the 1950s and 1960s. Similarly, the national economic growth rate began to rise again. Growth, like productivity, was not as dramatic as it had sometimes been in the golden years of industrial development, but it was sustained in what became the longest expansion in American history. Inflation fell to

a 30-year low. The unemployment rate also declined, dropping from 7.8 percent in 1992 to 4.6 percent in 1997. Taking credit for the recovery, President Bill Clinton declared that the drop in unemployment was "the latest evidence that our economy is growing, steady and strong, that the American dream is in fact alive and well."

One reflection of the return of prosperity was the soaring stock market. The decade of the 1990s was marked by a dramatic increase in the number of investors, reaching approximately 50 percent of the population in 2000. Some purchased stocks for themselves, often working on their own computers, without using a stockbroker. Much of the investment was in the high-tech area, in which people poured billions of dollars into start-up companies not yet making a profit, in the hope that they would take off. The market soared, with the Dow Jones average topping the once-unimaginable 10,000 barrier in 1999 and quickly moving past the 11,000 mark. An even more important sign of economic health was the dramatic reduction in the budget deficit. A Democratic effort to preempt a Republican issue and hold down spending paid off, particularly as low interest rates encouraged economic expansion. In 1998, the United States finished with a budget surplus for the first time in 29 years. With $70 billion—the largest surplus ever—left over at the end of the fiscal year, Democrats and Republicans began arguing about how the money should be used. Most Democrats favored using funds to bolster the social security system, while Republicans, who controlled Congress, preferred a politically attractive tax cut. Forgotten in the euphoria was the fact that the national debt—the total of all past deficits—remained over $5.4 trillion.

In these prosperous times, American companies embarked on a wave of mergers like those around the turn of the century that created the great oil and steel corporations. In 1997, a record $1 trillion in mergers involving American companies took place as huge conglomerates swallowed up smaller competitors in the interests of efficiency and ever-larger profits. One consequence of the mergers, however, was layoffs of workers who duplicated tasks and seemed superfluous. The jobs available to those looking for other work were often low-paying positions such as those held by Marlene Garrett and her husband, introduced earlier in this chapter.

Then, all too quickly, the economy faltered. Alan Greenspan, chairman of the Federal Reserve Board, cautioned in 1996 against "irrational exuberance" in the market, but most investors, especially those making millions of dollars, ignored the warning. In 2000, the stock market began to slide, as investors realized that many of the financial gains did not reflect commensurate gains in productivity. The year ended with the major stock indexes—the Dow Jones Industrial Average and the Nasdaq Composite—showing their worst performance in decades, and in 2001 and 2002, the market continued to fall, wiping out the paper gains of millions of large and small investors.

The nation's overall growth rate began to slow as investment declined. Lack of confidence in the market, particularly in the high-tech area that had fueled the boom, led to a corresponding lack of confidence in the economy. As a recession began in 2000, a tax cut further undermined the stability of the economy. Promoted by Republican George W. Bush after his victory in the 2000 presidential election, the tax cut was skewed in favor of wealthy Americans and not only failed to provide a necessary stimulus but contributed to the decline.

By early 2001, it was clear that the economy was slumping. In February, manufacturing fell to its lowest point in 10 years. Unemployment rolls increased and applications for state unemployment benefits surged. Outsourcing—moving jobs overseas and thereby displacing American workers—increased at an alarming rate. Confidence in the economy was further eroded by growing reports of corporate greed and managerial fraud. Emboldened by deregulation in the 1980s, many corporations had taken advantage of lax oversight practices and made huge—and sometimes illegal—profits. Toward the end of 2001, the Enron Corporation, a company that bought and sold energy, admitted that it had filed five years of misleading reports and declared bankruptcy. As the scandal grew, it became clear that the Arthur Andersen accounting firm had participated in providing cover for financial irregularities and faced an indictment for its role in the process. As the corporate empire began to tumble, the top executives cashed in their stock and made millions of dollars, while the company's workers, unaware of the looming catastrophe and prohibited from unloading stock, lost not just their jobs but their life savings as well.

Some people argued that the Enron case was an anomaly—a bad apple in the barrel—and contended that the rest of corporate America was in good shape. As 2002 unfolded, it became clear that many other companies, such as WorldCom, had been falsifying their books.

The economy became increasingly fragile in the next few years. In 2007, the national debt—the sum of all yearly deficits—reached $9 trillion for the first time. As the housing market collapsed that year, with risky mortgages leading to foreclosure, ordinary working Americans saw the erosion of their dreams of becoming part of the middle class.

Meanwhile overall union membership continued to fall. The AFL–CIO, which had about 16.6 million members in 1993, had only 13 million members a decade later. In 2006, only 12 percent of all workers belonged to a union, down from 12.5 percent in 2005 and 20.1 percent in 1983. One important shift, however, was the increase in membership in public employee unions. That figure, only 400,000 in the mid-1950s, soared to more than 4 million in the 1970s and continued to increase even as unions in the private sector lost members. In the 1990s, the National Educational Association, which was not affiliated with the AFL–CIO, was the largest union in the nation, with about 2 million members. These shifts reflected the changing nature of the workforce and the continuing effort to look out for the interests of the working population.

Poverty and Homelessness

Poverty was a problem even in boom times. The Census Bureau reported in 1997 that 35.6 million people in the United States—the richest country in the world—still lived below what was defined as the poverty line of about $16,000 a year for a family of four. The percentage—13.3 percent—had fallen slightly in each of the previous few years, but it was still sizable, especially considering that it included one out of every three *working* Americans. Worse still was the fact that in 1998, there were 900,000 more Americans living below the poverty line than in 1990. Nor did the situation improve in the new century. In 2004, the Department of Agriculture reported that more than 12 million American families struggled—sometimes without success—to feed themselves. Meanwhile, record levels of Americans lacked health insurance. A Census Bureau report in 2004 showed a figure of 45 million in 2003, which increased to 47 million—or 16 percent of the population—two years later.

Poverty in the United States was different than in other parts of the world, to be sure. People in American slums had more material benefits than many of the residents of Soweto, the huge slum just outside Johannesburg in South Africa. But the poverty was still corrosive.

Urban Americans had the toughest time of all. Even as population shifts led more and more people to live in cities, government programs often failed to provide fully for urban needs. As cities lost population to the suburbs in the last half of the twentieth century, they lost their tax base at the same time and could not easily meet the demand for services. The gap between rich and poor increased significantly in the last two decades of the twentieth century. The efforts of the Reagan and Bush administrations in the 1980s and early 1990s to cut back on government spending and eliminate social programs that had provided services for the poor contributed to the growing gap. Tax records from 2005 revealed that there was greater income inequality in America than in any period since the Great Depression of the 1930s.

Homeless in America
The homeless became far more visible in the 1990s. Here a man lies sleeping under a thin sheet of plastic, serving as his blanket, right in front of the White House in Washington, D.C. What impression does the proximity to the White House convey?

(Bettmann/CORBIS)

As always, minorities fared worse than whites. The net worth of a typical white household at the beginning of the 1990s was 12 times greater than the net worth of a typical black household and 8 times greater than the net worth of a typical Latino household. Minorities and women continued to lose ground faster than the rest of the population as the decade unfolded. That trend continued in the first years of the new century. Even as the Internal Revenue Service was reporting that overall income fell between 2000 and 2002, the wealthy increased their share, so that a white household now had a net worth 14 times that of a black household and 11 times that of a Latino household. A 2007 study indicated that the gap between blacks and whites continued to grow.

Just as the United States rediscovered its poor in the 1960s, so it rediscovered its homeless in the 1980s and 1990s. Even as unemployment dropped in the 1980s, the number of homeless quadrupled. Numbers were hard to ascertain, for the homeless had no fixed addresses, but one estimate in 1990 calculated that 6 million to 7 million people had been homeless at some point in the past five years. A federal report in 2000 noted that approximately 3.5 million people would become homeless at least once during the year, with 1.35 million of those children.

People became homeless for a variety of reasons. Some started life in disturbed families. Others fell prey to alcohol and drugs. Still others had health or learning problems that eroded the possibility of a stable life. For millions of working Americans, homelessness was just a serious and unaffordable illness away.

Aging and Illness

The American population was older than ever before as the century came to an end. Between 1900 and 1994, when the population of the country tripled, the number of people over age 65 rose elevenfold and continued to rise in the next decade, reaching 33 million, or just about 12 percent of the population, in 2001. Underlying the rapid increase was the steady advance in medical care, which in the twentieth century had increased life expectancy in the United States from 47 to 74 years as the elderly were healthier than ever before. People once considered themselves old when they reached age 65; now, many Americans in their 80s continued to lead productive lives—participating in activities such as writing books, teaching classes, and consulting with corporate clients.

One component of the aging revolution was Viagra, a new drug designed to help men suffering from impotence that came on the market in the 1990s. Whether sexual dysfunction was a result of prostate illness, common among older males, or emotional distress, Viagra helped ailing men enjoy normal sex lives. Americans, including the elderly, now talked frankly about erectile dysfunction, just as they had talked openly about birth control when the birth control pill was introduced three and a half decades before. *Newsweek* magazine noted in 1998 that Viagra was the fastest-selling drug in history.

The elderly raised new issues in a nation suffering periodic recessions. Many wanted to continue working and opposed mandatory retirement rules that drove

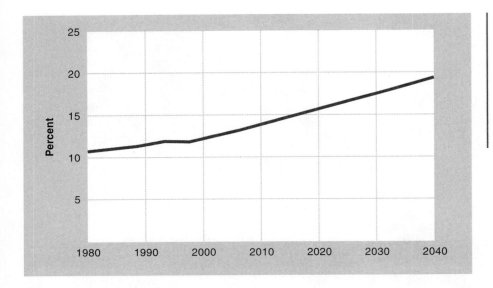

American Population Age 65 or Older, 1980–2040

The percentage of the American population age 65 and older increased as the baby boom population began to age. This graph shows the steady increase up to 2000 and the projected increase for the next 40 years.

Source: Statistical Abstract of the United States, 1997.

them from their jobs. Legislation in 1978 that raised the mandatory retirement age from 65 to 70 helped older workers but decreased employment opportunities for younger workers seeking jobs. In 1986, federal legislation amending the Age Discrimination in Employment Act prohibited mandatory retirement on the basis of age for virtually all workers and created continuing problems for younger employees in the 1990s. A Supreme Court ruling in 2005 held that a worker suing to reverse age discrimination did not need to prove that the employer had acted intentionally. The political power of the elderly became increasingly visible.

Generational resentment over jobs was compounded by the knotty problems faced by the social security system, which had been established a half century earlier. Other parts of the world—Scandinavia, for example—provided social services out of general revenues and took such expenditures for granted. However, in the United States, contributions to the system were necessary to keep it solvent, and as more and more Americans retired, the system could not generate sufficient funds without assistance from general revenues. In the early 1980s, it appeared that the entire system might collapse. A government solution involving higher taxes for those still employed and a later age for qualifying for benefits rescued the fund for a time, but many Americans in the 1990s and early years of the twenty-first century wondered whether social security would survive. Meanwhile, millions of elderly people wondered how they could afford the rapidly increasing cost of prescription drugs, even with a drug benefit plan passed in 2003 that seemed to help people in only a limited way at a huge cost to the government.

As Americans lived longer, they suffered increasingly from Alzheimer's disease, an affliction that gradually destroys a patient's memory and ability to function mentally or physically. Diagnosis is difficult, and there is no treatment to reverse the ailment's course. The illness gained exposure in 1995 when the family of Ronald Reagan disclosed that the former president was suffering from the incurable disease.

Other illnesses affected old and young alike. The discovery of AIDS (acquired immune deficiency syndrome) in 1981 marked the start of one of the most serious diseases in the history of the United States—and the world. Some nations found themselves decimated by AIDS. In China, for example, entire villages were infected with HIV (the human immunodeficiency virus that causes AIDS) as a result of unsterile practices in blood stations. Africa was hit even harder. In 2005, the United Nations estimated that 40 million people around the world were living with the HIV virus. One million of those were in America, while a huge percentage were in Africa. In Zimbabwe, estimates of life expectancy were expected to fall from age 61 in 2005 to age 33 in 2010. The good news was that in late 2007, the UN reported a decline in the number of new HIV infections, giving rise to the hope that perhaps the epidemic could be brought under control.

While health conditions in the United States were better than those in many parts of the world, AIDS still had a devastating effect. The sexual revolution of the 1960s had brought a major change in sexual patterns, particularly among the young, but now sexual experimentation was threatened by this deadly new disease. Although it seemed to strike intravenous drug users and homosexuals with numerous partners more than other groups at first, it soon spread to the heterosexual population as well. AIDS became the leading cause of death in Americans between ages 25 and 44. The growing number of deaths—approximately

550,000 in 2005—was horrifying, even as more and more people learned how to survive with the disease. New drugs, taken in combination, extended the life span of those with the HIV virus and reduced the death rate in the 1990s, but AIDS remained a lethal, and ultimately fatal, disease. Despite medical advances, a cure remained elusive.

Recognizing the devastating worldwide impact of the disease, President Bush announced a major new effort in 2003. He committed the United States to triple its commitment to $15 billion over the next five years to try to counter AIDS in Africa. It was a bold attempt both to head off new infections and to care for those already experiencing the effects of the virus in one of the hardest-hit areas of the globe.

Minorities and Women Face the Twenty-First Century

Americans fighting for equality made gains in the 1990s. But efforts at reform often encountered resistance.

AFRICAN AMERICANS For African Americans, home ownership and employment figures rose. The numbers of murders and other violent crimes that involved blacks dropped. A record 40 percent of African Americans attended college in 1997, up from 32 percent in 1991. Yet incremental improvements often failed to erode racist ideas that still permeated American society. Fifty years after the landmark *Brown* v. *Board of Education* decision of 1954, two-thirds of the public school students in the Cincinnati, Ohio, area attended schools that were at least 90 percent black or 90 percent white. Incidents such as the beating of black motorist Rodney King in Los Angeles in 1991 and the rioting that occurred the next year made many people wonder just how much progress the civil rights movement had made. A survey in San Diego noted that the police there stopped African American and Latino motorists more than whites and Asian Americans—a pattern that was common around the country. The 2000 census revealed that the nation was more racially and ethnically diverse than ever before, yet it pointed out that many people still lived in neighborhoods inhabited by people like themselves.

Affirmative action led to a backlash. Energized by their political victories in 1994, conservatives launched a powerful attack on the policy of giving preferential treatment to groups that had suffered discrimination in the past. They pushed ballot initiatives and pressured public agencies to bring the practice to an end. The most visible of those was Proposition 209 in California, approved by voters in the election of 1996, which prohibited the use of gender or race in awarding state government contracts or admitting students to state colleges and universities. The increasingly conservative Supreme Court in 1995 let stand a lower court ruling prohibiting colleges and universities from awarding special scholarships to African Americans or other minorities. In 1996, it declined to hear an appeal of a U.S. District Court decision two years before in *Hopwood* v. *Texas* that prohibited the use of affirmative action in higher education. In late 2003, the Supreme Court ruled in two cases involving the University of Michigan that affirmative action was acceptable, even as it rejected a point system the university used in carrying out the policy in undergraduate admissions. Around the country, states sought to find ways to maintain diversity without violating the rulings of the Court.

Then, in 2007, an even more conservative Supreme Court, bolstered by two Bush appointees, ruled that public schools could not promote integration through measures taking account of a student's race. After more than 50 years, it appeared that *Brown* v. *Board of Education* had run its course.

The booming job market in the late 1990s helped foster better race relations for a time. It provided new opportunities for people who had been unable to find work. A survey in 1999 reported that young black men in particular were moving back into the economic mainstream at a faster rate than their white counterparts, and crime levels were falling in areas where joblessness was declining. The jobless rate for young black men was still twice that for young white men, but the improvement was encouraging. But then, midway through the first decade of the twenty-first century, it was apparent that the dream for blacks was in decline. The drop in union membership hit them particularly hard. And the gap in income levels between blacks and whites was growing.

Tensions that had existed throughout the twentieth century persisted. Issues stemming from continuing discrimination in finding jobs and persistent antagonism by the police erupted in the spring of 2001 in Cincinnati, Ohio. When a white policeman killed an unarmed black youth, confrontations around the city provided a bitter reminder of riots in the past. In early 2002, African American television correspondent Ed Bradley pointed to changes he had seen in the course of his career. "When asked about progress," he said, "I'm often reminded of the old lady sitting in the church who says, 'It ain't what it ought to be, but thank God it ain't what it used to be.'" Bradley was right, but many African Americans wondered when further change would come.

WOMEN Women likewise made steady progress in the 1990s. They were increasingly involved in academic programs and professions that had been closed to them several decades earlier. In 2001, for example, women made up 49.4 percent of all first-year law students, compared to 10 percent in 1970; that pattern was reflected in other segments of society as well. At the same time there was still continuing resistance to inclusion at the top. Women started to become the heads of major firms as the glass ceiling, preventing women from rising to the top of the corporate ladder, began to crack in the 1990s, yet most leaders were still men. In 2005, only about 17 percent of the partners at major law firms were women.

Abortion remained a polarizing issue, particularly as antiabortion activists sought to disrupt abortion clinics. They launched around-the-clock pickets, aimed at frightening away women seeking abortions. Physicians performing abortions found their lives at risk; Barnet Slepian, a Buffalo doctor, was killed in 1998 in his own home by a sniper shooting through a window. Abortion opponents also took aim at a seldom used, late-term procedure they called "partial birth abortion." Congress passed a measure banning the procedure, but President Clinton vetoed it twice. Then in 2003 President Bush signed a new version of the measure, which the Supreme Court upheld in 2007. Meanwhile, the Food and Drug Administration finally approved a drug known as RU-486, the so-called "morning-after" pill, whereupon abortion opponents jumped into the controversy and sought—unsuccessfully—to attach conditions that would effectively eliminate its use.

The abortion debate was just one measure that created a backlash against the feminist label, even as men and women both accepted the changes brought by the women's movement. Women hesitated to be associated with what they still considered a radical fringe, and that affected how they identified themselves. In 1998, only 26 percent of working women said, "To me, a career is as important as being a wife and mother," down from 36 percent in 1979. While young women took for granted the gains fought for and won by their mothers and grandmothers, fewer wanted to call themselves feminists.

Though the feminist movement persisted, serious problems remained. The 2000 census revealed that the number of families headed by single mothers had risen to 7.5 million, an increase of 25 percent since 1990. A report based on census figures noted that in 2005, only 51 percent of all American women were living with a spouse. Meanwhile, the gender pay gap ceased narrowing. In 2005, women earned about 75 cents for every dollar paid to men.

LATINOS   Latinos likewise pushed for greater equality and had demographic change on their side. The 2000 census and subsequent studies based on the data provided noted that the Latino population spread farther and faster than any previous immigrant wave, even exceeding the influx of eastern Europeans in the early twentieth century. The Latino population increase of 38 percent since 1990 dwarfed the national rise. In 2005, there were 40 million Latinos in the United States, compared to 500,000 in 1900. In 2000, 46 percent of all Latinos owned their own homes, compared to 42 percent a decade before, though that figure still lagged behind the national number of 66 percent. In 2003, Latinos edged past African Americans and became the nation's largest minority group, and experts predicted that by 2100, one in three Americans would be Latino.

The emergence of a sturdy middle class gave Latinos a greater voice in social and political affairs. As more and more of them voted, they played an increasingly influential public role. In 1993, Henry Cisneros became secretary of housing and urban development, and Federico Peña became secretary of transportation in Bill Clinton's administration. At the end of the decade, Latino political figures became even more numerous and visible. In California, for example, both the lieutenant governor and the speaker of the assembly were Chicano, as was the mayor of San Jose. Democrat Loretta Sanchez, who defeated eight-term congressman Robert Dornan in Orange County, served in the U.S. House of Representatives. In the George W. Bush administration, White House counsel Alberto Gonzales played a major role in advising the president during the first term and became attorney general in the second.

As the nation's overall unemployment rate dropped in the mid-1990s, the rate for the 12 million Latino workers likewise fell—from 9.8 percent in 1992 to 7.3 percent in 1997. Then it rose again during the recession that hit in the early part of the new century, moving to about 8.5 percent in 2002, with only 40 percent of the 1.26 million unemployed Latinos eligible for unemployment benefits. Meanwhile, median Latino household income fell, even as it rose for every other ethnic and racial group. Some Mexican immigrants feared that they would become members of a permanent underclass. Latinos nevertheless had a growing impact on American culture. Merengue music could often be heard in music stores or on the radio. Argentine steakhouses could be found in many cities. Use of the Spanish language became more and more common around the country. President George W. Bush himself used Spanish in appealing to this important electoral bloc.

NATIVE AMERICANS   Native Americans found they had less influence, in part because of their smaller numbers. In the 2000 census, only 4.1 million people, or 1.5 percent of the population, identified themselves as American Indian or Alaska Native. Yet Indians still managed to keep the causes that concerned them before the public.

Indians continued their legal efforts to regain lost land. In 1999, the federal government joined the

Oneida Indians in a lawsuit demanding restitution for the 270,000 acres of land in central New York that they claimed state and local governments had illegally acquired from them in the late eighteenth and early nineteenth centuries, and arguing that restitution was warranted. In early 2000, the federal government returned 84,000 acres in northern Utah that it had taken from the Ute in 1916 when it sought to secure the rights to valuable reserves of oil shale. "We're trying to do the right thing, returning land to its rightful owners," energy secretary Bill Richardson declared.

Indians also pressed successfully for the return of their ancestors' skeletal remains, removed by white scientists and museum officials over the course of the last century. With passage of the Native American Graves Protection and Repatriation Act of 1990, skeletons and sacred objects flowed back to the tribes where they belonged. In 1997, Harvard's Peabody Museum sent back the bones of nearly 2,000 Pueblo Indians in the largest single return of these remains.

Native American women became increasingly active in the larger reform effort. Ada Deer, who had successfully fought the government's termination policy in the 1970s, served as assistant secretary of the interior in the 1990s. Winona LaDuke, an environmental activist, directed the Honor the Earth Fund and the White Earth Land Recovery Project, fought needless hydroelectric development, and was singled out by *Time* magazine as one of the nation's 50 most promising leaders under age 40. In 2000, she served as Ralph Nader's vice presidential running mate on the small Green party ticket.

Many Indians still felt a sense of dislocation, captured by novelist Sherman Alexie in 1993. In one of the stories in *The Lone Ranger and Tonto Fistfight in Heaven*, he wrote: "Sometimes I still feel like half of me is lost in the city, with its foot wedged into a steam grate or something. Stuck in one of those revolving doors, going round and round while all the white people are laughing."

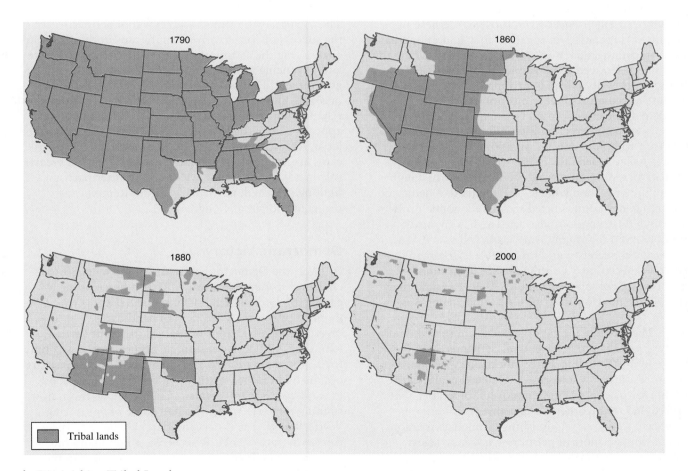

Diminishing Tribal Lands

While Native Americans steadily lost their territory over a period of 200 years, in the 1990s, Indians field lawsuits to regain tribal lands and were successful in some of their claims. How would you characterize the changing patterns of Indian land ownership?

Source: "Mending a Trail of Broken Treaties," *The Nation, New York Times,* June 25, 2002. Copyright © 2002 by The New York Times Co. Reprinted with permission.

An important symbolic gesture occurred in the last months of the Clinton administration. As the Bureau of Indian Affairs celebrated its 175th anniversary, Kevin Gover, head of the agency, reversed the pattern that had been so predominant in the past when he apologized for the nation's repressive treatment of Native Americans. "In truth, this is no occasion for celebration," he said. It was, rather, a time "for sorrowful truths to be spoken, a time for contrition." He spoke of "the decimation of the mighty bison herds, the use of the poison alcohol to destroy minds and body, and the cowardly killing of women and children." The suffering inflicted on the Indians "made for tragedy on a scale so ghastly that it cannot be dismissed as merely the inevitable consequence of the clash of competing cultures."

ASIAN AMERICANS   Asian Americans enjoyed real success in the 1990s. With about 11 million people—approximately 4 percent of the national population—of Asian descent in the United States in 2000, there was now a critical mass. They came from a variety of cultures, to be sure, and Filipinos often had different experiences from those of Chinese or Koreans or Japanese, yet together they had an increasingly important impact on American society. Many of the children enjoyed remarkable educational achievements, making up a disproportionate share of the students at the most prestigious universities. In 2000, President Clinton appointed Norman Y. Mineta as secretary of commerce, making him the first Asian American to hold a cabinet position.

Yet Asian Americans in the 1990s found themselves in an ambiguous position. While they had higher median incomes than whites, due in part to a dedicated work ethic, newcomers faced serious economic problems. Older assumptions also persisted. A report in 2000 observed that many Americans still saw Asian Americans as secretive and inscrutable. "Too many people in this country continue to see us in simple stereotypes," complained Paul M. Ong, a social policy professor at the University of California at Los Angeles.

GAYS   The struggle for gay rights also continued, and slowly gays began to achieve their demands. In a major change in 2000, the Big Three automakers—General Motors, Ford, and Chrysler—announced health-care benefits for partners of gay employees, in a move that covered 465,000 workers. That same year, Vermont recognized same-sex relationships through civil unions, though stopped short of permitting gay marriages. In 2002, the American Academy of Pediatricians announced its support of the right of gay men and women to adopt the children of their partners. Gay activism helped broaden the definition of family. As the gay rights movement celebrated the 30-year anniversary of the gay rights movement in a parade commemorating

the 1969 riot at the Stonewall Inn in Greenwich Village that had sparked gay resistance, proponents noted that the event had changed from a protest to a party. As the *New York Times* observed, "that in itself is a sign of success."

Yet resistance to gays playing a more visible role in American society persisted. In 1998, 21-year-old University of Wyoming student Matthew Shepard died after being brutally beaten and tortured by two men troubled by his lifestyle. While most American cities had thriving gay communities, there was still deep-seated resistance to gays living openly in some quarters.

Resistance became more open in the election of 2004. As Massachusetts courts ruled that gay marriage was constitutional, and San Francisco permitted gay couples to marry there, a backlash helped mobilize conservatives around the country, and voters in a number of states approved constitutional bans on gay marriage.

Democratic Revival

The 1990s saw a Democratic revival in politics. After the success of conservative Republicans in the 1980s in challenging the assumptions of the liberal welfare state and advancing a more limited conception of the role of government, Democrats regrouped, reformulated their message, and followed the lead of the Republicans in relying on new forms of media to broadcast political appeals. The pattern in the United States reflected similar shifts in the rest of the world as more liberal politicians asserted that government needed to play a greater role in advancing public welfare. But bitter partisan fighting persisted, particularly as the Republicans regained control of Congress.

Democratic Victory

In 1992, the Democratic party mounted an aggressive challenge to Republican rule. After a fierce primary campaign, Governor Bill Clinton of Arkansas triumphed over a crowded field of candidates. Overcoming allegations of marital instability, marijuana use, and draft evasion, he argued that it was time for a new generation to take command. Forty-six years old, he had reached maturity in the 1960s and stood in stark contrast to President George H. W. Bush, now running for reelection, who had come of age during World War II. The third candidate in what became a three-way race was H. Ross Perot, a billionaire businessman from Texas who had made a fortune in the computer data-processing field.

This campaign, more than any in the past, was fought on television. In addition to three televised presidential debates, the candidates appeared on talk shows and interview programs. Perot energized his campaign

Recovering the Past

AUTOBIOGRAPHY

As we reach our own time, the historical past perhaps most worth recovering is our own. Our own story is as valid a part of the story of American history as the tale of Revolutionary War soldiers, frontier women, reform politicians, and immigrant grandparents. In this computerized age, the person we need to recover is ourself, a self that has been formed, at least in part, by the entire American experience we have been studying.

Autobiography is the form of writing in which people tell their own life's history. Although written autobiographies are at least as old as the literature of the early Christians (for example, *The Confessions of St. Augustine*), the word *autobiography* dates from the late eighteenth century, around the time of the French and American revolutions. That is no accident. These momentous events represented the triumph of individual liberty and the sovereignty of the self. *The Autobiography of Benjamin Franklin,* written

between 1771 and Franklin's death in 1790 (and excerpted here), is a classic celebration of the American success story. Franklin's work set the standard for one autobiographical form, the memoir of one's public achievements and success. The other brief autobiographical memoir, from the reminiscences of Elizabeth Cady Stanton, also reflects the tone and range of this tradition.

Not all autobiographies are written late in life to celebrate one's accomplishments. The confessional autobiography, unlike most memoirs, explores the author's interior life, acknowledging flaws and failures as well as successes; it may be written at any age. The purpose of this type of autobiography is not just to reconstruct one's past to preserve it for posterity, but to find from one's past an identity in order to know better how to live one's future. The story of religious confessions and conversions is an obvious example. This form also includes secular self-examinations such as those

---

Autobiographical Memoirs

Benjamin Franklin

DEAR SON,

I have ever had a pleasure in obtaining any little anecdotes of my ancestors. You may remember the enquiries I made among the remains of my relations when you were with me in England and the journey I undertook for that purpose. Imagining it may be equally agreeable to you to know the circumstances of my life—many of which you are yet unacquainted with—and expecting a week's uninterrupted leisure in my present country retirement, I sit down to write them for you. Besides, there are some other inducements that excite me to this undertaking. From the poverty and obscurity in which I was born and in which I passed my earliest years, I have raised myself to a state of affluence and some degree of celebrity in the world. As constant good fortune has accompanied me even to an advanced period of life, my posterity will perhaps be desirous of learning the means, which I employed, and which, thanks to Providence, so well succeeded with me. They may also deem them fit to be imitated, should any of them find themselves in similar circumstances.

Source: The Autobiography of Benjamin Franklin (1771).

Elizabeth Cady Stanton

Elizabeth Cady Stanton

It was 'mid such exhilarating scenes that Miss Anthony and I wrote addresses for temperance, anti-slavery, educational and woman's rights conventions. Here we forged resolutions, protests, appeals, petitions, agricultural reports, and constitutional arguments; for we made it a matter of conscience to accept every invitation to speak on every question, in order to maintain woman's right to do so. To this end we took turns on the domestic watchtowers, directing amusements, settling disputes, protecting the weak against the strong, and trying to secure equal rights to all in the home as well as the nation.

It is often said, by those who know Miss Anthony best, that she has been my good angel, always pushing and goading me to work, and that but for her pertinacity I should never have accomplished the little I have. On the other hand it has been said that I forged the thunderbolts and she fired them. Perhaps all this is, in a measure, true. With the cares of a large family I might, in time, like too many women, have become wholly absorbed in a narrow family selfishness, had not my friend been continually exploring new fields for missionary labors. Her description of a body of men on any platform, complacently deciding questions in which women had an equal interest, without an equal voice, readily aroused me to a determination to throw a firebrand into the midst of their assembly.

Source: Elizabeth Cady Stanton, Eighty Years and More: Reminiscences, 1815–1897 (1898).

Confessional Autobiographies

Black Elk

And so it was all over.

I did not know then how much was ended. When I look back now from this high hill of my old age, I can still see the butchered women and children lying heaped and scattered all along the crooked gulch as plain as when I saw them with eyes still young. And I can see that something else died there in the bloody mud, and was buried in the blizzard. A people's dream died there. It was a beautiful dream.

And I, to whom so great a vision was given in my youth,—you see me now a pitiful old man who has done nothing, for the nation's hoop is broken and scattered. There is no center any longer, and the sacred tree is dead.

Source: Black Elk Speaks, as told through John G. Neihardt (1932).

Malcolm X

I want to say before I go on that I have never previously told anyone my sordid past in detail. I haven't done it now to sound as though I might be proud of how bad, how evil, I was.

But people are always speculating—why am I as I am? To understand that of any person, his whole life, from birth, must be reviewed. All of our experiences fuse into our personality. Everything that ever happened to us is an ingredient.

Today, when everything that I do has an urgency, I would not spend one hour in the preparation of a book which has the ambition to perhaps titillate some readers. But I am spending many hours because the full story is the best way that I know to have it seen, and understood, that I had sunk to the very bottom of the American white man's society when—soon now, in prison—I found Allah and the religion of Islam and it completely transformed my life.

Source: The Autobiography of Malcolm X, with the assistance of Alex Haley (1964).

---

by Maxine Hong Kingston in *The Woman Warrior* (1976), Piri Thomas in *Down These Mean Streets* (1967), or Maya Angelou in a series of five autobiographical sketches beginning with *I Know Why the Caged Bird Sings* (1969). The other two excerpts presented here are among the finest examples of confessional autobiography and suggest its variety.

These examples hardly convey the full range of the autobiographical form or how available to all people is the opportunity to tell the story of one's life. In 1909, William Dean Howells called autobiography the "most democratic province in the republic of letters." A recent critic agrees, pointing out:

To this genre have been drawn public and private figures: poets, philosophers, prizefighters; actresses, artists, political activists; statesmen and penitentiary prisoners; financiers and football players; Quakers and Black Muslims; immigrants and Indians. The range of personality, experience, and profession reflected in the forms of American autobiography is as varied as American life itself.

Your story, too, is a legitimate part of American history. But writing an autobiography, while open to all, is deceptively difficult. Like historians, autobiographers face problems of sources, selection, interpretation, and style. As in the writing of any history, the account of one's past must be objective, not only in the verifiable accuracy of details but also in the honest selection of representative events to be described. Moreover, in fiction as well as history, the autobiographer must provide a structured form, an organizing principle, literary merit, and thematic coherence to the story. Many other challenges face the would-be autobiographer, such as finding a balance between one's public life and the private self and handling problems of memory, ego (should one, for example, use the first or third person?), and death.

Reflecting on the Past To get an idea of the difficulties of writing an autobiography, try writing your own. Limit yourself to 1,000 words. Good luck. ■

The "Hip" Candidate

Bill Clinton was an exuberant campaigner who used his musical talent to attract support when he ran for president in 1992. Here he plays his saxophone on nationwide television on *The Arsenio Hall Show* in Los Angeles. What kind of image was Clinton trying to convey in this photograph?

(AP/Wide World Photos)

with appearances on *Larry King Live*. Bill Clinton used a post–Super Bowl appearance on *60 Minutes* to answer charges questioning his character and later played his saxophone on *The Arsenio Hall Show* and appeared on MTV. On election day, Clinton won 43 percent of the popular vote to 38 percent for Bush and 19 percent for Perot. The electoral vote margin was even larger: 357 for Clinton, 168 for Bush, 0 for Perot. The Democrats retained control of both houses of Congress, with more women and minority members than ever before.

The president-elect wanted to check the cynicism that was poisoning political life. In 1964, three-quarters of the American public trusted the government to do the right thing most of the time. Three decades later, after the deception of leaders in the Vietnam War and the Watergate affair, the number was closer to one-quarter. Clinton sought to shift the nation's course after 12 years of Republican rule with Cabinet nominations that included four women, four African Americans, and two Latinos. He held a televised "economic summit" to explore national options and demonstrated a keen grasp of the details of policy. In his inaugural address, Clinton declared that "a new season of American renewal has begun."

Clinton soon found his hands full at home. Although the economy finally began to improve, the public gave the president little credit for the upturn. He gained Senate ratification of the North American Free Trade Agreement (NAFTA)—aimed at promoting free trade between Canada, Mexico, and the United States—in November 1993 after a bitter battle in which opponents argued that American workers would lose their jobs to less well-paid Mexicans. He secured passage of a crime bill banning the manufacture, sale, or possession of assault weapons. But he failed to win approval of his major legislative initiative: health-care reform. The United States lagged behind most other industrialized countries in the way it provided for public health. Medicare took care of the elderly, and Medicaid provided some relief for the poor, but both were limited when compared to the coverage provided by other nations. Particularly troublesome were escalating costs and the lack of universal medical care, which left 35 million Americans with no medical insurance. Clinton's complicated proposal provoked intense opposition from the health-care and insurance industries and from politicians with plans of their own. In the end, he was unable to persuade Congress either to accept his approach or adopt a workable alternative.

Republican Resurgence

Voters demonstrated their dissatisfaction in the midterm elections of 1994. Republicans argued that government regulations were hampering business and costing too much. They challenged the notion that the federal government was primarily responsible for health care and other such services. Capitalizing on the continuing appeal of the leadership of Ronald Reagan in the 1980s, they demanded a scaled-down role for the government. Republicans swept control of both the Senate and the House of Representatives for the first time in more than 40 years. At the state level, Republicans picked up 12 governorships and took control in seven of the eight largest states.

The election marked the end of the commitment to the welfare state. The 104th Congress moved aggressively to make good on its promises—outlined during the campaign in the Republicans' Contract with America—to scale back the role of the federal government, eliminate environmental regulations, cut funding for educational programs such as Head Start, reduce taxes, and balance the budget. Under the leadership of Newt Gingrich, the new speaker of the House of Representatives, Congress launched a frontal attack on the budget, proposing massive cuts in virtually all social services. It demanded eliminating three Cabinet departments and insisted on gutting the National Endowment for the Humanities, the National Endowment for the Arts, and the Public

Broadcasting System. When, at the end of 1995, President Clinton and Speaker Gingrich tangled with one another on the size of the cuts and refused to compromise on a budget, the government shut down and 800,000 federal employees found themselves temporarily "furloughed."

While the House of Representatives passed most of the measures proposed in the Contract with America, only a few of them became law. The Senate balked at some; the president vetoed others. After all the attention it received, voters lost interest in the Contract with America. As the election of 1996 approached, Newt Gingrich found himself out of favor, as millions of Americans began to realize that they would suffer from the cuts more aggressive Republicans sought.

A Second Term for Clinton

As Bill Clinton sought a second term in 1996, the Republicans nominated Senate minority leader Robert Dole as their presidential candidate. The 73-year-old Dole ran a lackluster campaign. His pledge to push through a sweeping 15 percent tax reduction failed to excite voter interest. Even supporters wondered how he would balance the budget at the same time. Stung by Democratic congressional defeats two years before, Clinton co-opted Republican issues, pledging to balance the budget himself and enraging liberal supporters by signing a welfare reform bill that slashed benefits and removed millions of people from the rolls. At the same time, he posed as the protector of Medicare and other programs that were threatened by proposed Republican cuts.

Clinton's strategy worked. On election day, he won a resounding victory over Dole. He received 49 percent of the popular vote to 41 percent for Dole and 8 percent for H. Ross Perot, who ran again, though this time less successfully. In the electoral tally, Clinton received 379 votes to 159 for Dole. Yet the Republicans kept control of Congress. In the House of Representatives, they lost a number of seats but retained a majority. In the Senate, they added two seats to what they had won in 1994. Voters seemed willing to support Clinton, but not to give him the mandate he sought.

Partisan Politics and Impeachment

Democrats made small gains in the midterm elections of 1998. They worried about their prospects as election day approached, for Clinton had been accused by an independent prosecutor, appointed by the Justice Department, of having engaged in an improper sexual relationship with Monica Lewinsky, a White House intern. While Clinton denied the relationship at first, the lengthy report presented to Congress left little

doubt that such a connection existed, and Clinton finally admitted to the relationship in a nationally televised address.

As Republicans in Congress began to consider impeachment, Americans outside Washington felt differently. Disturbed at what Clinton had done in his personal life, they nonetheless approved overwhelmingly of the job he was doing as president; in fact, his approval ratings were higher than any of his presidential predecessors in the recent past.

Those sentiments were reflected in the 1998 midterm election. Republicans maintained their 55–45 margin in the Senate, but lost five seats in the House of Representatives, ending up with a 223–211 margin that made it even more difficult to pursue their own agenda.

Despite that clear signal from the voters, House Republicans continued their efforts to remove the president. Just weeks after the election, a majority impeached him on counts of perjury and obstruction of justice. At the start of 1999, the case moved to the Senate for a trial, in which Clinton fought to retain his office, just as Andrew Johnson had done 131 years before. In the Senate, presided over by the chief justice of the Supreme Court, a two-thirds vote was necessary to find the president guilty and remove him from office. After weeks of testimony, despite universal condemnation of Clinton's personal behavior, the Senate voted for acquittal. Democrats, joined by a number of Republicans, stood by the president, and with that coalition, neither charge managed to muster even a majority. The count of perjury was decided by a 45–55 vote, while the count of obstruction of justice failed on a 50–50 vote. At long last, the ordeal was over, and the country could once again turn its attention to more pressing issues.

Clinton was an enormously successful politician. Not only had he escaped conviction in the highly visible—and embarrassing—impeachment case, but he also managed to co-opt Republican issues and seize the political center. He quietly advanced liberal goals, with incremental appropriations, even when he was unable to push major programs, such as his medical insurance scheme, through Congress. Suits against the nation's tobacco companies for deliberately misleading advertising in the face of known health risks were popular with the public, and led in 1997 to a landmark $368 billion settlement to cover liability claims and reimburse the states for medical costs related to smoking.

Throughout both terms, Clinton remained popular, despite personal flaws. Overall, in the words of the New York Times, Clinton demonstrated "striking strengths, glaring shortcomings." He came into office wanting to be a Roosevelt-like figure, with dreams of reconfiguring the role of government, but ended up instead quietly endorsing and implementing a variety of more modest causes. He faced powerful criticism from opponents, yet he brought some of his troubles on himself and paid a heavy price for his misdeeds.

The Second Bush Presidency

Republicans regained control of the White House in the election of 2000. Unable to oust Bill Clinton from the presidency by impeachment, they were determined to win back what they considered to be rightfully theirs in the conservative resurgence of the past 20 years. Texas governor George W. Bush (son of former president George H. W. Bush—the first father–son combination since John Adams and John Quincy Adams) vowed to return morality and respect to the White House and appealed to those disturbed by Clinton's behavior.

The Election of 2000

The election of 2000 promised to be close. The strong economy gave Vice President Al Gore, the Democratic nominee, an initial advantage. Yet the Republicans, led by the younger Bush, insisted the country needed a change. The campaign revolved around what the government should do with the federal budget surplus, with Republicans arguing that much of the money should be returned to the public in the form of a tax cut and Democrats countering that the surplus should be used to bolster the ailing social security program and to pay down the national debt. In the weeks before the election, polls showed that the race was virtually tied.

On election night, as the returns trickled in, neither Bush nor Gore had captured the 270 electoral votes necessary to win the presidency. The electoral vote in Florida, one of the undecided states, was large enough to give the winner a victory. A recount, required by law, began, and Florida became a battleground as lawyers for both sides swarmed to the state to monitor the counting. Democrats and Republicans argued bitterly, in court and in the media, about how the recount should proceed. Democrats also contended that in certain African American precincts, voters had been turned away from the polls. That charge was all the more significant because black voters around the country favored Gore by a 9–1 margin.

In December, more than five weeks after the election, after suits and countersuits by both sides, the case reached the Supreme Court. In *Bush* v. *Gore,* the justices overturned a Florida Supreme Court decision allowing the recount to proceed, and ruled, by a 5–4 vote, with the most conservative justices voting in a bloc, that the recount should be curtailed, leaving Bush the winner. Although Gore won the popular vote by

about 450,000 votes, Bush triumphed in the Electoral College by a 271–266 majority. Ill feelings persisted as a result of the partisan ruling. Supreme Court justice John Paul Stevens wrote a scathing dissent, in which he argued: "Although we may never know with complete certainty the identity of the winner of this year's presidential election, the identity of the loser is perfectly clear. It is the nation's confidence in the judge as an impartial guardian of the law."

The voting in congressional races was equally close. The new Senate was evenly split, with each party holding 50 seats. Republicans organized the chamber and gained all committee chairs, because Vice President Dick Cheney broke the tie. Yet five months after the new session began, Senator James Jeffords of Vermont, frustrated with the approach of the Bush administration, left the Republican party, giving control to the Democrats. Republicans also lost seats in the House of Representatives, leaving them with but a nine-vote majority.

The New Leader

George W. Bush had enjoyed an eclectic career before becoming president. Born into a political family, he had shown little interest in politics himself, gravitating into the Texas oil business and then gaining part ownership of a professional baseball team before running successfully for governor of Texas.

Bush was very different from Clinton. Whereas his predecessor was interested in the details of public policy, Bush saw himself as a corporate chief executive officer (CEO) who established the broad outlines of policy but then left the details to others. Ronald Reagan had taken that approach, and while Bush lacked Reagan's communication skills, he had a dogged tenacity that served him well. Author Gail Sheehy observed that "the blind drive to win is a hallmark of the Bush family clan." The new president, she said "has to win, he absolutely has to win and if he thinks he's going to lose, he will change the rules or extend the play. Or if it really is bad he'll take his bat and ball and go home." Bush often seemed to ignore criticism and to push ahead with a resolute persistence, no matter what. His religious faith gave him the support he needed, and when once asked if he relied on his father in hard times, he responded that his father "is the wrong father to appeal to in terms of strength. There is a higher father that I appeal to."

Promoting the Private Sector

As president, Bush had the interests of corporate America at heart. During the campaign, he talked about a tax cut, and this became his first priority. Supply-side economists, who argued successfully in the

Looking for a Place in History?

George Bush paid close attention to the image conveyed to the American people, and photographers constantly captured him in ways that underscored his importance. Here he stands in front of Mt. Rushmore, with its famous rock sculptures of several of America's best-known presidents. What impression does the juxtaposition in this photograph convey to you?

(AP/World Wide Photos)

1980s that lower tax rates were necessary to promote economic growth, became more influential in his administration.

By mid-2001, the tax cut became law. It lowered tax rates for everyone, allowed more tax-free saving for education, and reduced estate taxes. The measure promised to save every taxpayer at least several hundred dollars a year, though it was heavily skewed in favor of the wealthy. Meanwhile, the economy continued to falter as the growth rate slowed and a full-blown recession ensued.

Like his father and Reagan, Bush wanted to reduce the size of government and squelch its intrusions into private affairs, but at the same time, he sought to bolster the military. His first budget, for example, proposed deep cuts in health programs for people without access to health insurance. But his proposals for defense called for far greater spending, even before the terrorist attacks of September 11, 2001. Military spending increased dramatically in the years that followed, providing the administration already dealing with smaller revenue as a result of the tax cut with an even stronger argument to cut back social programs that conservatives had never liked.

Bush infuriated environmentalists. Quietly, the new administration moved to allow road building in national forests and made it easier for mining companies to dig for gold, zinc, and copper on public lands. Under pressure from real estate interests, the administration sought to shrink legal protection of endangered species. And, catering to the interests of oil companies, the administration fought to promote drilling in the protected Arctic National

PRESIDENTIAL ELECTIONS, 1992–2004

Year	Candidate	Party	Popular Vote		Electoral Vote
1992	BILL CLINTON	Democratic	43,728,275	(43.2%)	357
	George Bush	Republican	38,167,416	(37.7%)	168
	H. Ross Perot	Independent	19,237,245	(19.0%)	0
1996	BILL CLINTON	Democratic	47,401,185	(49.2%)	379
	Robert Dole	Republican	39,197,469	(40.7%)	159
	H. Ross Perot	Reform	8,085,294	(8.4%)	0
2000	GEORGE W. BUSH	Republican	50,546,002	(47.87%)	271
	Albert Gore	Democratic	50,999,897	(48.38%)	266
	Ralph Nader	Green	2,882,955	(2.74%)	0
2004	GEORGE W. BUSH	Republican	60,934,251	(51%)	286
	John F. Kerry	Democratic	57,765,291	(48%)	252
	Ralph Nader	Independent	405,933	(0%)	0

Note: Winners' names appear in capital letters.

Wildlife Refuge, even in the face of estimates that very little oil was there to be found. When his own Environmental Protection Agency (EPA) issued a report in mid-2002 linking the use of fossil fuel (such as coal and oil) to global warming, Bush dismissed the study. Gone was the commitment to the public interest that had increased over the course of the twentieth century.

A Second Term for Bush

The election of 2004 was bitter and contentious. Running for reelection, Bush faced Massachusetts senator John Kerry, a Vietnam War hero who attacked Republican efforts in the foreign policy sphere, questioned the administration's ability to protect the nation from terrorist attacks, and charged that tax cuts had done little to revive a still-sluggish economy. Both candidates raised huge amounts of money, far more than had been solicited in the past, and both parties ended up running attack ads that questioned the integrity of the other candidate. Republican groups tore into Kerry's service record; Democratic groups called attention to Bush's successful effort to avoid the war in Vietnam by serving in the National Guard. Civility sometimes seemed to disappear. But even though Bush seemed vulnerable, Kerry failed to arouse the interest of voters. He seemed to be, according to *The Economist* magazine, "the political equivalent of Valium." In a race that remained close to the end, Bush prevailed with 51 percent of the popular vote and a modest Electoral College majority. Republicans added to their majorities in both the Senate and the House of Representatives, as voters in the heartland of American agreed with the Republican party's conservative moral values.

At the start of his second term, Bush moved quickly to demand reform of social security. The program, which had run surpluses in the past, faced increasing pressures as the baby boom generation born just after World War II approached retirement. Experts disagreed on just when the system would run short of money, but it was clear that problems were imminent in the next few decades. Bush called for an overhaul that would allow workers to invest part of their contributions in private retirement accounts that would depend on gains in the stock market. Critics charged that the new proposal would undermine the policy of guaranteed pensions and could make millions of workers vulnerable if the market dropped, as it had just a few years before. They argued that the system could be made more secure by increasing payroll taxes, raising the amount on which such taxes were levied, or mandating that workers retire a year or two later. Even as Bush pushed ahead, members of both political parties resisted the effort.

The budget that Bush submitted to Congress in early 2005 reflected the administration's priorities. As the surplus of the Clinton years turned into an ever-larger deficit under Bush—estimated to be almost $400 billion in the year ahead—the budget still contained tax cuts of $100 billion over the next five years. Critics charged that the underlying intention was to make it impossible to support programs aimed at assisting poor people like Rod and Marlene Garrett, met at the start of the chapter. They also noted the irony that this budget was the largest ever in the nation's history and pointed out that an administration that claimed to want to scale down big government was playing an ever-increasing role when it came to regulation of social issues through faith-based initiatives and resistance to abortion. The proposed budget for 2007 reflected similar priorities. Meanwhile, the president asked for record levels of defense spending.

By the time of the 2006 midterm Congressional elections, many Americans were disturbed by the violence of the war in Iraq (see next section) and troubled by a conflict that seemed to be spiraling out of control. They were also frustrated by a series of scandals on Capitol Hill and by the insensitive response of the administration to the devastation caused by Hurricane Katrina in New Orleans in September 2005. Voter discontent shifted control of Congress. Democrats won a substantial majority in the House of Representatives and a narrow margin in the Senate.

Bush seemed to be on the wrong side of many public policy issues. His veto in 2007 of a measure to provide increased funding for children without health insurance aroused tremendous opposition. His failure to take aggressive steps to combat global warning stood in bold relief to the Academy Award defeated presidential candidate Al Gore won and the Nobel Peace Prize he shared for his eloquent work in this arena.

During his last two lame duck years in the White House, Bush faced more serious problems than ever before. Public support eroded, leaving him with a dismal 30 percent approval rating. Republican presidential candidates distanced themselves from him and his administration. People commented casually about how he might well be judged one of the least competent presidents in American history.

Foreign Policy in the Post–Cold War World

As the Cold War ended, the United States had to examine its own assumptions about its international role. The world was now a different place. With extraordinary communications advances, it was more closely linked than ever before. Violence and upheaval in one part of the globe now had an almost immediate impact on other areas. In this setting, new questions arose: What kind of leadership would the United States exert as the one remaining superpower on the globe? How involved would it become in peacekeeping missions in violence-wracked lands? What kind of assistance would it extend to developing nations now that the competition with the Soviet Union that had fueled foreign aid was over? How would it deal with the threat of terrorism? These questions, asked in different forms over the course of past centuries, helped shape foreign policy in transitional times.

The Balkan Crisis

In the Balkans, in Eastern Europe, ethnic and religious violence worsened in the mid-1990s. Yugoslavia—a collection of different ethnic constituencies held together by a Communist dictatorship—had collapsed in 1991. Muslims and Croats had fought bitterly with Serbs in the province of Bosnia (see Chapter 30). The world watched the Bosnian Serbs liquidate opponents in a process that came to be called "ethnic cleansing" during the siege of the city of Sarajevo. As the region became increasingly volatile, the United States remained out of the conflict, while the United Nations proved unable to bring about peace. In mid-1995, a North Atlantic Treaty Organization (NATO) bombing campaign forced the Bosnian Serbs into negotiations, and a peace conference held in Dayton, Ohio, led to the commitment of American troops, along with soldiers from other countries, to stabilize the region.

In 1999, a smoldering conflict in Kosovo, another of the provinces of the former Yugoslavia, led to war.

In an effort to stop Slobodan Milosevic, the Serbian leader responsible for the devastation of Bosnia, from squelching a movement for autonomy in Kosovo, NATO launched an American-led bombing campaign. Milosevic responded with an even more violent "ethnic cleansing" campaign that drove hundreds of thousands of Kosovars from their homes.

Milosevic finally succumbed. After refusing to recognize the election victory of the opposition leader in 2000, he was arrested in 2001 and brought to the Netherlands to stand trial for crimes against humanity at the International Court of Justice in The Hague.

The Middle East in Flames

In the Middle East, Clinton tried to play the part of peacemaker, just as Jimmy Carter had done 15 years before. On September 13, 1993, in a dramatic ceremony on the White House lawn, Palestine Liberation Organization leader Yasir Arafat and Israeli Prime Minister Yitzhak Rabin took the first public step toward ending years of conflict as they shook hands and signed a peace agreement that led to Palestinian self-rule in the Gaza strip. In 1995, Israel and the PLO signed a further agreement, and the Israelis handed over control of the West Bank of the Jordan River to the Palestinians. A treaty between Jordan and Israel brought peace on still another border. While extremists tried to destroy the peace process by assassinating Rabin, the effort to heal old animosities continued. As Clinton prepared to leave office, he sought to seal a final agreement between the Israelis and the Palestinians, but this time he was not successful, as the Palestinians rejected a generous settlement offer,

A Historic Handshake

President Bill Clinton helped orchestrate this famous handshake between Israeli prime minister Yitzhak Rabin and Palestine Liberation Organization chairman Yasir Arafat in 1993. Though the two men had long been adversaries, they now began to work together to settle the bitter conflicts in the Middle East. How do Clinton's actions in the picture give a sense of his role? How do the two longtime adversaries appear to react to one another?

(AP/Wide World Photos)

and the smoldering Middle Eastern tensions burst once more in flames that threatened to engulf the entire region.

The level of Mideast violence in the early twenty-first century was worse than it had ever been before. The shortsighted Israeli policy of building settlements in occupied Arab land, and the Palestinian unwillingness to compromise at the negotiating table, culminated in a horrifying escalation of suicide bombings and other bloody attacks following an Israeli visit to a holy Palestinian religious site in Jerusalem, a city claimed by both sides. Bush was at first reluctant to intervene. Eventually, as the killing cycle continued, he moved from inattention to intermittent attention, becoming increasingly sympathetic to Israel as the suicide attacks continued. He lashed out at Yasir Arafat for not speaking out against the bombings, but was unable to bring the adversaries to the negotiating table. Nor could he do anything about separation fences the Israelis built both in the West Bank and the Gaza Strip to protect settlements there. Meanwhile, many of the European nations, feeling that only the United States could help bring peace to the region, voiced dismay at American policy.

At the end of 2007, at the urging of Secretary of State Condoleezza Rice, Bush became more engaged. Perhaps recognizing that only with American assistance might a peace settlement emerge, he convened a conference of Israeli and Palestinian participants to see if they might get back on track for what all agreed would be a long and extended process.

African Struggles

Africa also remained a source of concern to American policymakers who struggled to deal with a series of never-ending crises. Left behind as other parts of the world industrialized and moved ahead, the continent was also ravaged by the AIDS epidemic, which infected and killed far more people than in other parts of the world. Meanwhile, most other nations paid little attention to the region. During the Cold War, the United States and the Soviet Union had competed for the allegiance of African nations, but with the end of the conflict, that focus faded. Bill Clinton made a highly publicized visit to Africa, as he sought to dramatize international responsibility for assisting the continent, and he watched with satisfaction as Nelson Mandela handed over power in South Africa to his successor in a peaceful transition. But other areas proved more problematical. Six months after Clinton became president, a firefight with one faction in war-ravaged Somalia, in East Africa, resulted in several dozen American casualties. The shooting prompted some Americans, still haunted by the memory of Vietnam, to demand withdrawal. Reluctant to

back down as he groped to define his policy, Clinton first increased the number of U.S. troops, then in 1993, recalled the soldiers without having restored order.

The United States was similarly baffled by a crisis in Rwanda, in central Africa. There a fragile balance of power between two ethnic groups—the Tutsis and the Hutus—broke down and hard-line Hutus embarked on a massive genocidal campaign that resulted in the slaughter of hundreds of thousands of innocent Tutsis and moderate Hutus. The United States, like many European nations, debated the possibility of intervention on humanitarian grounds but decided to do nothing. Eventually the killing stopped, although the friction between the rival groups remained.

George W. Bush was much less interested in Africa than his predecessor. He chose not to attend a conference on sustainable development held in South Africa in the summer of 2002, which gave a clear signal that the United States was more interested in its own business interests than in the economic problems of the less-developed world. In 2003, he visited five African nations, but it was a whirlwind trip aimed at supporting areas sympathetic to the United States.

Relations with Russia

In the area that formerly had been the Soviet Union, the United States continued to try to promote both democracy and free-market capitalism. It worked closely with Boris Yeltsin in Russia, and then with his successor, Vladimir Putin, who assumed power on the last day of the twentieth century and was then elected president in his own right in 2001. But Russia remained unstable, still caught up in the complications of a huge political, social, and economic transformation.

Bush recognized the need to cooperate with Putin. In a series of meetings, both in Russia and in the United States, the two men developed a close working relationship that helped maintain European stability. The Soviet Union had ceased to exist, but the component parts still remained important in the larger international scene.

Terror on September 11

On September 11, 2001, three hijacked airplanes slammed into the World Trade Center towers in New York City and the Pentagon in Washington, D.C. The fires in New York from exploding jet fuel caused the towers to crumble, altering the skyline forever. Altogether about 3,000 people died in the terrorist attacks. A fourth plane, probably headed for either the White House or the Capitol, crashed in

An Indelible Image of September 11, 2001
The World Trade Center towers in New York City once dominated the skyline on the Hudson River. As two hijacked commercial airplanes crashed into the tall structures on September 11, 2001, both towers burst into flames and later collapsed, killing most of the people who were still inside. What impression does this photograph of the burning towers convey?

(Steve Ludlum/The New York Times)

unprovoked strikes, President Bush vowed to find and punish the terrorists. Like his father in the Gulf War a decade earlier, he put together a worldwide coalition to assist the United States, and he quickly launched a bombing campaign to smoke out Osama bin Laden and his network. Although the bombing, followed by attacks by ground troops in Afghanistan, defeated the Taliban and drove its members from power, the campaign failed to find Osama bin Laden, who remained at large. As Bush's approval ratings soared to over 90 percent, he vowed a lengthy campaign to root out terrorism wherever it surfaced in the world. He embarked on a massive governmental reorganization to create a new Department of Homeland Security to help prevent future attacks. In the Patriot Act, he invoked terrorism as a reason to allow the government to encroach on individual liberties—in the interest of security—more extensively than in the past. Ironically, a president dedicated to smaller government now found himself in the forefront of an effort to give government a much larger role.

American Muslims were often the victims. Some faced attacks by Americans angry at the terrorist strikes. Others were taken into custody, often without being charged with a crime, on the suspicion that they were somehow involved, as the government instituted new security measures.

The antiterrorism campaign escalated. In early 2002, Bush spoke out forcefully against what he called an "axis of evil," as he referred to Iraq, Iran, and North Korea. He was particularly intent on driving Iraqi leader Saddam Hussein from power. Hussein had launched the attack on Kuwait that had led to the Gulf War during the administration of Bush's father. Now, 11 years later, Bush argued that Hussein was creating weapons of mass destruction and vowed to bring about a regime change. Within the Bush administration, Secretary of State Colin Powell, inclined to a more restrained foreign policy, fought against Secretary of Defense Donald Rumsfeld and Vice President Dick Cheney, who enthusiastically supported an attack. Bush's argument that he could invade Iraq even without the support of Congress aroused a firestorm of protest both in the United States and around the world.

The war in Iraq, fought with British but not United Nations support, began in March 2003. American forces were successful, and just a month and a half later, Bush declared that the major phase of combat operations was over. In December, U.S. soldiers captured Saddam Hussein hiding in a hole in the ground. But even the capture of the Iraqi dictator could not quell increasing opposition to the American occupation, which led to fierce fighting in the months

Pennsylvania when passengers fought back against the attackers.

The hijackers were Muslim extremists, most from Saudi Arabia, trained at flight schools in the United States, who belonged to the al Qaeda network headed by Saudi exile Osama bin Laden. Bin Laden and his organization were headquartered in Afghanistan, where the extremely conservative Muslim Taliban group had imposed the law of the Qur'an, the Muslim holy book, on civil society. Bin Laden and his associates hated the United States for its Middle Eastern policy of support for Israel, and they also hated its affluent and materialistic values that often conflicted with their religious values.

The terrorist attacks shattered America's sense of security within its own borders. Irate at the

Timeline

1991–1999	Ethnic turbulence in fragmented former Yugoslavia
1992	Bill Clinton elected president
	Czechoslovakia splits into separate Czech and Slovak Republics
	Riots erupt in Los Angeles
1993	North American Free Trade Agreement (NAFTA) ratified
	Palestine Liberation Organization and Israel sign peace treaty
1994	Nelson Mandela elected president of South Africa
1996	Bill Clinton reelected
1998	Budget surplus announced
	Bill Clinton impeached by the House of Representatives
1999	Bill Clinton acquitted by the Senate
	Stock market soars as Dow Jones average passes 10,000
2000	George W. Bush elected president
2001	Economy falters
	Stock market dips below 10,000
	Tax cut passed
	Terrorists strike New York City and Washington, D.C.
2002	Recession continues and Dow Jones average drops below 8,000
2003	U.S. and coalition forces invade Iraq
2004	George W. Bush reelected
2005	Bush calls for a major overhaul of social security
2006	Democrats regain control of both houses of Congress

that followed. As the deadline for handing sovereignty over to Iraq in mid-2004 approached, Sunnis, Shiites, and Kurds fought with each other for a share of power, but were united in their opposition to the continuing American presence. Insurgent attacks against American troops and Iraqis in new official positions continued as Iraq descended into civil war. Photographs of American abuse of prisoners in the notorious Abu Ghraib prison aroused resentment in the Middle East and among people around the world. By early 2008, the American death toll in Iraq passed 4,000 and significantly exceeded the number killed in the terrorist attacks of 9/11, with another 30,000 Americans wounded. As the Iraqi government demonstrated its inability to maintain order in the face of mounting sectarian conflict, more and more Americans demanded an end to involvement in what they perceived as serious, and perhaps intractable, problems.

Bush responded in early 2007 by increasing the number of American troops, in what he called a "surge" to quell violence in Baghdad. But pressure, particularly from Democrats, to bring troops home persisted.

Conclusion
THE RECENT PAST IN PERSPECTIVE

In the 1990s, the United States prospered in a period of economic growth longer than any in its history. After weathering a recession at the start of the decade, the economy began to boom, and the boom continued for the next 10 years. Most middle- and upper-class Americans prospered. The budget deficit disappeared, and the government ran a sizable surplus. Yet not all Americans shared in the prosperity. Despite the drop in the unemployment level, many of the available jobs paid little more than the minimum wage, and people like Marlene and Rod Garrett, met at the start of the chapter, had trouble making ends meet. Members of minority groups, whose numbers grew throughout the decade, had the toughest time of all.

Meanwhile, Americans worried about their role in the outside world. As they enjoyed their newfound prosperity, some were reluctant to spend money in an activist role abroad. They debated what to do about the defense establishment, which had begun to deteriorate, and were hesitant to become deeply involved in foreign conflicts where they had trouble ascertaining American interests. Then, in 2001, the brutal terrorist attacks on New York City and Washington, D.C., mobilized the nation. Recognizing at long last that terrorism threatened the entire globe, including the United States, they prepared themselves for an extended effort to try to bring it under control and to make the world a safer place. As they had in years past, in both World War I and World War II, the United States again sought to protect the democratic way of life for the American people and for people elsewhere as well.

QUESTIONS FOR REVIEW AND REFLECTION

1. What were the major economic developments in the 1990s, and how did they affect political action?
2. How were the Democrats able to regain power in 1992 after more than a decade of Republican rule?
3. How successful was Bill Clinton's presidency?
4. What did the closeness of the elections of 2000 and 2004 indicate about divisions in American society?
5. How did the terrorist attacks of September 11, 2001, affect the course of American foreign policy?

APPENDIX

The Declaration of Independence in Congress, July 4, 1776

THE UNANIMOUS DECLARATION OF THE THIRTEEN UNITED STATES OF AMERICA

When, in the course of human events, it becomes necessary for one people to dissolve the political bonds which have connected them with another, and to assume, among the powers of the earth, the separate and equal station to which the laws of nature and of nature's God entitle them, a decent respect to the opinions of mankind requires that they should declare the causes which impel them to the separation.

We hold these truths to be self-evident: That all men are created equal; that they are endowed by their Creator with certain unalienable rights; that among these are life, liberty, and the pursuit of happiness; that, to secure these rights, governments are instituted among men, deriving their just powers from the consent of the governed; that whenever any form of government becomes destructive of these ends, it is the right of the people to alter or to abolish it, and to institute new government, laying its foundation on such principles, and organizing its powers in such form, as to them shall seem most likely to effect their safety and happiness. Prudence, indeed, will dictate that governments long established should not be changed for light and transient causes; and accordingly all experience hath shown that mankind are more disposed to suffer, while evils are sufferable, than to right themselves by abolishing the forms to which they are accustomed. But when a long train of abuses and usurpations, pursuing invariably the same object, evinces a design to reduce them under absolute despotism, it is their right, it is their duty, to throw off such government, and to provide new guards for their future security. Such has been the patient sufferance of these colonies; and such is now the necessity which constrains them to alter their former systems of government. The history of the present King of Great Britain is a history of repeated injuries and usurpations, all having in direct object the establishment of an absolute tyranny over these states. To prove this, let facts be submitted to a candid world.

He has refused his assent to laws, the most wholesome and necessary for the public good.

He has forbidden his governors to pass laws of immediate and pressing importance, unless suspended in their operation till his assent should be obtained; and, when so suspended, he has utterly neglected to attend to them.

He has refused to pass other laws for the accommodation of large districts of people, unless those people would relinquish the right of representation in the legislature, a right inestimable to them, and formidable to tyrants only.

He has called together legislative bodies at places unusual, uncomfortable, and distant from the depository of their public records, for the sole purpose of fatiguing them into compliance with his measures.

He has dissolved representative houses repeatedly, for opposing, with manly firmness, his invasions on the rights of the people.

He has refused for a long time, after such dissolutions, to cause others to be elected; whereby the legislative powers, incapable of annihilation, have returned to the people at large for their exercise; the state remaining, in the mean time, exposed to all the dangers of invasions from without and convulsions within.

He has endeavored to prevent the population of these states; for that purpose obstructing the laws for naturalization of foreigners; refusing to pass others to encourage their migration hither, and raising the conditions of new appropriations of lands.

He has obstructed the administration of justice, by refusing his assent to laws for establishing judiciary powers.

He has made judges dependent on his will alone, for the tenure of their offices, and the amount and payment of their salaries.

He has erected a multitude of new offices, and sent hither swarms of officers to harass our people and eat out their substance.

He has kept among us, in times of peace, standing armies, without the consent of our legislatures.

He has affected to render the military independent of, and superior to, the civil power.

He has combined with others to subject us to a jurisdiction foreign to our constitution, and unacknowledged by our laws, giving his assent to their acts of pretended legislation:

For quartering large bodies of armed troops among us;

For protecting them, by a mock trial, from punishment for any murder which they should commit on the inhabitants of these states;

For cutting off our trade with all parts of the world;

For imposing taxes on us without our consent;

For depriving us, in many cases, of the benefits of trial by jury;

For transporting us beyond seas, to be tried for pretended offenses;

For abolishing the free system of English laws in a neighboring province, establishing therein an arbitrary government, and enlarging its boundaries, so as to render it at once an example and fit instrument for introducing the same absolute rule into these colonies;

For taking away our charters abolishing our most valuable laws, and altering fundamentally the forms of our governments;

For suspending our own legislatures, and declaring themselves invested with power to legislate for us in all cases whatsoever.

He has abdicated government here, by declaring us out of his protection and waging war against us.

He has plundered our seas, ravaged our coasts, burned our towns, and destroyed the lives of our people.

He is at this time transporting large armies of foreign mercenaries to complete the works of death, desolation, and tyranny already begun with circumstances of cruelty and perfidy scarcely paralleled in the most barbarous ages, and totally unworthy the head of a civilized nation.

He has constrained our fellow-citizens, taken captive on the high seas, to bear arms against their country, to become the executioners of their friends and brethren, or to fall themselves by their hands.

He has excited domestic insurrection among us, and has endeavored to bring on the inhabitants of our frontiers the merciless Indian savages, whose known rule of warfare is an undistinguished destruction of all ages, sexes, and conditions.

In every stage of these oppressions we have petitioned for redress in the most humble terms; our repeated petitions have been answered only by repeated injury. A prince, whose character is thus marked by every act which may define a tyrant, is unfit to be the ruler of a free people.

Nor have we been wanting in our attentions to our British brethren. We have warned them, from time to time, of attempts by their legislature to extend an unwarrantable jurisdiction over us. We have reminded them of the circumstances of our emigration and settlement here. We have appealed to their native justice and magnanimity; and we have conjured them, by the ties of our common kindred, to disavow these usurpations, which would inevitably interrupt our connections and correspondence. They, too, have been deaf to the voice of justice and of consanguinity. We must, therefore, acquiesce in the necessity which denounces our separation, and hold them, as we hold the rest of mankind, enemies in war, in peace friends.

We, therefore, the representatives of the United States of America, in General Congress assembled, appealing to the Supreme Judge of the world for the rectitude of our intentions, do, in the name and by the authority of the good people of these colonies, solemnly publish and declare, that these United Colonies are, and of right, ought to be, FREE AND INDEPENDENT STATES; that they are absolved from all allegiance to the British crown, and that all political connection between them and the state of Great Britain is, and ought to be, totally dissolved; and that, as free and independent states, they have full power to levy war, conclude peace, contract alliances, establish commerce, and do all other acts and things which independent states may of right do. And for the support of this declaration, with a firm reliance on the protection of Devine Providence, we mutually pledge to each other our lives, our fortunes, and our sacred honor. ■

JOHN HANCOCK

BUTTON GWENNETT
LYMAN HALL
GEO. WALTON
WM. HOOPER
JOSEPH HEWES
JOHN PENN
EDWARD RUTLEDGE
THOS. HEYWARD, JUNR.
THOMAS LYNCH, JUNR.
ARTHUR MIDDLETON
SAMUEL CHASE
WM. PACA
THOS. STONE
CHARLES CARROLL OF CARROLLTON
GEORGE WYTHE
RICHARD HENRY LEE
TH. JEFFERSON
BENJA. HARRISON
THS. NELSON, JR.

FRANCIS LIGHTFOOT LEE
CARTER BRAXTON
ROBT. MORRIS
BENJAMIN RUSH
BENJA. FRANKLIN
JOHN MORTON
GEO. CLYMER
JAS. SMITH
GEO. TAYLOR
JAMES WILSON
GEO. ROSS
CAESAR RODNEY
GEO. READ
THO. MíKEAN
WM. FLOYD
PHIL. LIVINGSTON
FRANS. LEWIS
LEWIS MORRIS
RICHD. STOCKTON

JNO. WITHERSPOON
FRAS. HOPKINSON
JOHN HART
ABRA. CLARK
JOSIAH BARTLETT
WM. WHIPPLE
SAML. ADAMS
JOHN ADAMS
ROBT. TREAT PAINE
ELBRIDGE GERRY
STEP. HOPKINS
WILLIAM ELLERY
ROGER SHERMAN
SAMíEL. HUNTINGTON
WM. WILLIAMS
OLIVER WOLCOTT
MATHEW THORNTON

The Constitution of the United States of America

PREAMBLE

We the People of the United States, in Order to form a more perfect Union, establish Justice, insure domestic Tranquility, provide for the common defence, promote the general Welfare, and secure the Blessings of Liberty to ourselves and our Posterity, do ordain and establish this Constitution for the United States of America.

ARTICLE I.

Section 1   All legislative Powers herein granted shall be vested in a Congress of the United States, which shall consist of a Senate and House of Representatives.

Section 2   The House of Representatives shall be composed of Members chosen every second Year by the People of the several States, and the Electors in each State shall have the Qualifications requisite for Electors of the most numerous Branch of the State Legislature.

No Person shall be a Representative who shall not have attained to the Age of twenty five Years, and been seven Years a Citizen of the United States, and who shall not, when elected, be an Inhabitant of that State in which he shall be chosen.

Representatives and direct Taxes shall be apportioned among the several States which may be included within this Union, according to their respective Numbers, *which shall be determined by adding to the whole Number of free Persons, including those bound to Service for a Term of Years, and excluding Indians not taxed, three fifths of all other Persons.* The actual Enumeration shall be made within three Years after the first Meeting of the Congress of the United States, and within every subsequent Term of ten Years, in such Manner as they shall by Law direct. The Number of Representatives shall not exceed one for every thirty Thousand, but each State shall have at Least one Representative; *and until such enumeration shall be made, the State of New Hampshire shall be entitled to chuse three, Massachusetts eight, Rhode-Island and Providence Plantations one, Connecticut five, New-York six, New Jersey four, Pennsylvania eight, Delaware one, Maryland six, Virginia ten, North Carolina five, South Carolina five, and Georgia three.*

When vacancies happen in the Representation from any State, the Executive Authority thereof shall issue Writs of Election to fill such Vacancies.

The House of Representatives shall chuse their Speaker and other Officers; and shall have the sole Power of Impeachment.

Section 3   The Senate of the United States shall be composed of two Senators from each State, chosen by the Legislature thereof, for six Years; and each Senator shall have one Vote.

Immediately after they shall be assembled in Consequence of the first Election, they shall be divided as equally as may be into three Classes. The Seats of the Senators of the first Class shall be vacated at the Expiration of the second Year, of the second Class at the Expiration of the fourth Year, and of the third Class at the Expiration of the sixth Year, so that one third may be chosen every second Year; and if Vacancies happen by Resignation, or otherwise, during the Recess of the Legislature of any State, the Executive thereof may make temporary Appointments until the next Meeting of the Legislature, which shall then fill such Vacancies.

No Person shall be a Senator who shall not have attained to the Age of thirty Years, and been nine Years a Citizen of the United States, and who shall not, when elected, be an Inhabitant of that State for which he shall be chosen.

The Vice President of the United States shall be President of the Senate, but shall have no Vote, unless they be equally divided.

The Senate shall choose their other Officers, and also a President *pro tempore,* in the Absence of the Vice President, or when he shall exercise the Office of President of the United States.

The Senate shall have the sole Power to try all Impeachments. When sitting for that Purpose, they shall be on Oath or Affirmation. When the President of the United States is tried the Chief Justice shall preside: And no Person shall be convicted without the Concurrence of two thirds of the Members present.

Judgment in Cases of Impeachment shall not extend further than to removal from Office, and disqualification to hold and enjoy any Office of honor, Trust or Profit under the United States: but the Party convicted shall nevertheless be liable and subject to Indictment, Trial, Judgment and Punishment, according to Law.

Section 4   The Times, Places and Manner of holding Elections for Senators and Representatives, shall be prescribed in each State by the Legislature thereof; but the Congress may at any time by Law make or alter such Regulations, except as to the Places of chusing Senators.

The Congress shall assemble at least once in every Year, and such Meeting *shall be on the first Monday in December, unless they shall by Law appoint a different Day.*

Section 5   Each House shall be the Judge of the Elections, Returns and Qualifications of its own Members, and a Majority of each shall constitute a Quorum to do Business; but a smaller Number may adjourn from day to day, and may be authorized to compel the Attendance of absent Members, in such Manner, and under such Penalties as each House may provide.

Each House may determine the Rules of its Proceedings, punish its Members for disorderly Behaviour, and, with the Concurrence of two thirds, expel a Member.

---

* The Constitution became effective March 4, 1789. Any portion of the text that has been amended is printed in italics.

Each House shall keep a Journal of its Proceedings, and from time to time publish the same, excepting such Parts as may in their Judgment require Secrecy; and the Yeas and Nays of the Members of either House on any question shall, at the Desire of one fifth of those Present, be entered on the Journal.

Neither House, during the Session of Congress, shall, without the Consent of the other, adjourn for more than three days, nor to any other Place than that in which the two Houses shall be sitting.

Section 6   The Senators and Representatives shall receive a Compensation for their Services, to be ascertained by Law, and paid out of the Treasury of the United States. They shall in all Cases, except Treason, Felony and Breach of the Peace, be privileged from Arrest during their Attendance at the Session of their respective Houses, and in going to and returning from the same; and for any Speech or Debate in either House, they shall not be questioned in any other Place.

No Senator or Representative shall, during the Time for which he was elected, be appointed to any civil Office under the Authority of the United States, which shall have been created, or the Emoluments whereof shall have been encreased during such time; and no Person holding any Office under the United States, shall be a Member of either House during his Continuance in Office.

Section 7   All Bills for raising Revenue shall originate in the House of Representatives; but the Senate may propose or concur with Amendments as on other Bills.

Every Bill which shall have passed the House of Representatives and the Senate, shall, before it become a Law, be presented to the President of the United States; If he approve he shall sign it, but if not he shall return it, with his Objections to that House in which it shall have originated, who shall enter the Objections at large on their Journal, and proceed to reconsider it. If after such Reconsideration two thirds of that House shall agree to pass the Bill, it shall be sent, together with the Objections, to the other House, by which it shall likewise be reconsidered, and if approved by two thirds of that House, it shall become a Law. But in all such Cases the Votes of both Houses shall be determined by yeas and Nays, and the Names of the Persons voting for and against the Bill shall be entered on the Journal of each House respectively. If any Bill shall not be returned by the President within ten Days (Sundays excepted) after it shall have been presented to him, the Same shall be a Law, in like Manner as if he had signed it, unless the Congress by their Adjournment prevent its Return, in which Case it shall not be a Law.

Every Order, Resolution, or Vote to which the Concurrence of the Senate and House of Representatives may be necessary (except on a question of Adjournment) shall be presented to the President of the United States; and before the Same shall take Effect, shall be approved by him, or being disapproved by him, shall be repassed by two thirds of the Senate and House of Representatives, according to the Rules and Limitations prescribed in the Case of a Bill.

Section 8   The Congress shall have Power:

To lay and collect Taxes, Duties, Imposts and Excises, to pay the Debts and provide for the common Defence and general Welfare of the United States; but all Duties, Imposts and Excises shall be uniform throughout the United States;

To borrow Money on the credit of the United States;

To regulate Commerce with foreign Nations, and among the several States, and with the Indian Tribes;

To establish an uniform Rule of Naturalization, and uniform Laws on the subject of Bankruptcies throughout the United States;

To coin Money, regulate the Value thereof, and of foreign Coin, and fix the Standard of Weights and Measures;

To provide for the Punishment of counterfeiting the Securities and current Coin of the United States;

To establish Post Offices and post Roads;

To promote the Progress of Science and useful Arts, by securing for limited Times to Authors and Inventors the exclusive Right to their respective Writings and Discoveries;

To constitute Tribunals inferior to the supreme Court;

To define and punish Piracies and Felonies committed on the high Seas, and Offences against the Law of Nations;

To declare War, grant Letters of Marque and Reprisal, and make Rules concerning Captures on Land and Water;

To raise and support Armies, but no Appropriation of Money to that Use shall be for a longer Term than two Years;

To provide and maintain a Navy;

To make Rules for the Government and Regulation of the land and naval Forces;

To provide for calling forth the Militia to execute the Laws of the Union, suppress Insurrections and repel Invasions;

To provide for organizing, arming, and disciplining, the Militia, and for governing such Part of them as may be employed in the Service of the United States, reserving to the States respectively, the Appointment of the Officers, and the Authority of training the Militia according to the discipline prescribed by Congress;

To exercise exclusive Legislation in all Cases whatsoever, over such District (not exceeding ten Miles square) as may, by Cession of particular States, and the Acceptance of Congress, become the Seat of the Government of the United States, and to exercise like Authority over all Places purchased by the Consent of the Legislature of the State in which the Same shall be, for the Erection of Forts, Magazines, Arsenals, dock-Yards, and other needful Buildings;

To make all Laws which shall be necessary and proper for carrying into Execution the foregoing Powers, and all other Powers vested by this Constitution in the Government of the United States, or in any Department or Officer thereof.

Section 9 *The Migration or Importation of such Persons as any of the States now existing shall think proper to admit, shall not be prohibited by the Congress prior to the Year one thousand eight hundred and eight, but a Tax or duty may be imposed on such Importation, not exceeding ten dollars for each Person.*

The Privilege of the Writ of Habeas Corpus shall not be suspended, unless when in Cases of Rebellion or Invasion the public Safety may require it.

No Bill of Attainder or ex post facto Law shall be passed.

No Capitation, or other direct, Tax shall be laid, unless in Proportion to the Census or Enumeration herein before directed to be taken.

No Tax or Duty shall be laid on Articles exported from any State.

No Preference shall be given by any Regulation of Commerce or Revenue to the Ports of one State over those of another: nor shall Vessels bound to, or from, one State, be obliged to enter, clear, or pay Duties in another.

No Money shall be drawn from the Treasury, but in Consequence of Appropriations made by Law; and a regular Statement and Account of the Receipts and Expenditures of all public Money shall be published from time to time.

No Title of Nobility shall be granted by the United States: And no Person holding any Office of Profit or Trust under them, shall, without the Consent of the Congress, accept of any present, Emolument, Office, or Title, of any kind whatever, from any King, Prince, or foreign State.

Section 10 No State shall enter into any Treaty, Alliance, or Confederation; grant Letters of Marque and Reprisal; coin Money; emit Bills of Credit; make any Thing but gold and silver Coin a Tender in Payment of Debts; pass any Bill of Attainder, ex post facto Law, or Law impairing the Obligation of Contracts, or grant any Title of Nobility.

No State shall, without the Consent of the Congress, lay any Imposts or Duties on Imports or Exports, except what may be absolutely necessary for executing it's inspection Laws: and the net Produce of all Duties and Imposts, laid by any State on Imports or Exports, shall be for the Use of the Treasury of the United States; and all such Laws shall be subject to the Revision and Controul of the Congress.

No State shall, without the Consent of Congress, lay any Duty of Tonnage, keep Troops, or Ships of War in time of Peace, enter into any Agreement or Compact with another State, or with a foreign Power, or engage in War, unless actually invaded, or in such imminent Danger as will not admit of delay.

ARTICLE II.

Section 1 The executive Power shall be vested in a President of the United States of America. He shall hold his Office during the Term of four Years, and, together with the Vice President, chosen for the same Term, be elected, as follows

Each State shall appoint, in such Manner as the Legislature thereof may direct, a Number of Electors, equal to the whole Number of Senators and Representatives to which the State may be entitled in the Congress: but no Senator or Representative, or Person holding an Office of Trust or Profit under the United States, shall be appointed an Elector.

The Electors shall meet in their respective States, and vote by Ballot for two Persons, of whom one at least shall not be an Inhabitant of the same State with themselves. And they shall make a List of all the Persons voted for, and of the Number of Votes for each; which List they shall sign and certify, and transmit sealed to the Seat of Government of the United States, directed to the President of the Senate. The President of the Senate shall, in the Presence of the Senate and House of Representatives, open all the Certificates, and the Votes shall then be counted. The Person having the greatest Number of Votes shall be the President, if such Number be a Majority of the whole Number of Electors appointed; and if there be more than one who have such Majority, and have an equal Number of Votes, then the House of Representatives shall immediately chuse by Ballot one of them for President; and if no Person have a Majority, then from the five highest on the List the said House shall in like Manner chuse the President. But in chusing the President, the Votes shall be taken by States, the Representation from each State having one Vote; A quorum for this Purpose shall consist of a Member or Members from two thirds of the States, and a Majority of all the States shall be necessary to a Choice. In every Case, after the Choice of the President, the Person having the greatest Number of Votes of the Electors shall be the Vice President. But if there should remain two or more who have equal Votes, the Senate shall chuse from them by Ballot the Vice President. The Congress may determine the Time of chusing the Electors, and the Day on which they shall give their Votes; which Day shall be the same throughout the United States.

No Person except a natural born Citizen, *or a Citizen of the United States, at the time of the Adoption of this Constitution,* shall be eligible to the Office of President; neither shall any Person be eligible to that Office who shall not have attained to the Age of thirty five Years, and been fourteen Years a Resident within the United States.

In Case of the Removal of the President from Office, or of his Death, Resignation, or Inability to discharge the Powers and Duties of the said Office, the Same shall devolve on the Vice President, and the Congress may by Law provide for the Case of Removal, Death, Resignation or Inability, both of the President and Vice President declaring what Officer shall then act as President, and such Officer shall act accordingly, until the Disability be removed, or a President shall be elected.

The President shall, at stated Times, receive for his Services, a Compensation, which shall neither be increased nor diminished during the Period for which he shall have been elected, and he shall not receive within that Period any other Emolument from the United States, or any of them.

Before he enter on the Execution of his Office, he shall take the following Oath or Affirmation: "I do solemnly swear (or affirm) that I will faithfully execute the Office of President of the United States, and will to the best of my Ability, preserve, protect and defend the Constitution of the United States."

Section 2 The President shall be Commander in Chief of the Army and Navy of the United States, and of the Militia of the several States, when called into the actual Service of the United States; he may require the Opinion, in writing, of the principal Officer in each of the executive Departments, upon any Subject relating to the Duties of their respective Offices, and he shall have Power to grant Reprieves and Pardons for Offences against the United States, except in Cases of Impeachment.

He shall have Power, by and with the Advice and Consent of the Senate, to make Treaties, provided two thirds of the Senators present concur; and he shall nominate, and by and with the Advice and Consent of the Senate, shall appoint Ambassadors, other public Ministers and Consuls, Judges of the supreme Court, and all other Officers of the United States, whose Appointments are not herein otherwise provided for, and which shall be established by Law: but the Congress may by Law vest the Appointment of such inferior Officers, as they think proper, in the President alone, in the Courts of Law, or in the Heads of Departments.

The President shall have Power to fill up all Vacancies that may happen during the Recess of the Senate, by granting Commissions which shall expire at the End of their next Session.

Section 3 He shall from time to time give to the Congress Information of the State of the Union, and recommend to their Consideration such Measures as he shall judge necessary and expedient; he may, on extraordinary Occasions, convene both Houses, or either of them, and in Case of Disagreement between them, with Respect to the Time of Adjournment, he may adjourn them to such Time as he shall think proper; he shall receive Ambassadors and other public Ministers; he shall take Care that the Laws be faithfully executed, and shall Commission all the Officers of the United States.

Section 4 The President, Vice President and all civil Officers of the United States, shall be removed from Office on Impeachment for, and Conviction of, Treason, Bribery, or other high Crimes and Misdemeanors.

ARTICLE III.

Section 1 The judicial Power of the United States, shall be vested in one supreme Court, and in such inferior Courts as the Congress may from time to time ordain and establish. The Judges, both of the supreme and inferior Courts, shall hold their Offices during good Behaviour, and shall, at stated Times, receive for their Services, a Compensation which shall not be diminished during their Continuance in Office.

Section 2 The judicial Power shall extend to all Cases, in Law and Equity, arising under this Constitution, the Laws of the United States, and Treaties made, or which shall be made, under their Authority;—to all Cases affecting Ambassadors, other public Ministers and Consuls;—to all Cases of admiralty and maritime Jurisdiction;—to Controversies to which the United States shall be a Party;—to Controversies between two or more States;—*between a State and Citizens of another State;*—between Citizens of different States;—between Citizens of the same State claiming Lands under Grants of different States, and between a State, or the Citizens thereof, and foreign States, Citizens or Subjects.

In all Cases affecting Ambassadors, other public Ministers and Consuls, and those in which a State shall be Party, the supreme Court shall have original Jurisdiction. In all the other Cases before mentioned, the supreme Court shall have appellate Jurisdiction, both as to Law and Fact, with such Exceptions, and under such Regulations as the Congress shall make.

The Trial of all Crimes, except in Cases of Impeachment, shall be by Jury; and such Trial shall be held in the State where the said Crimes shall have been committed; but when not committed within any State, the Trial shall be at such Place or Places as the Congress may by Law have directed.

Section 3 Treason against the United States, shall consist only in levying War against them, or in adhering to their Enemies, giving them Aid and Comfort. No Person shall be convicted of Treason unless on the Testimony of two Witnesses to the same overt Act, or on Confession in open Court.

The Congress shall have Power to declare the Punishment of Treason, but no Attainder of Treason shall work Corruption of Blood, or Forfeiture except during the Life of the Person attainted.

ARTICLE IV.

Section 1 Full Faith and Credit shall be given in each State to the public Acts, Records, and judicial Proceedings of every other State. And the Congress may by general Laws prescribe the Manner in which such Acts, Records and Proceedings shall be proved, and the Effect thereof.

Section 2 The Citizens of each State shall be entitled to all Privileges and Immunities of Citizens in the several States.

A Person charged in any State with Treason, Felony, or other Crime, who shall flee from Justice, and be found in another State, shall on Demand of the executive Authority of the State from which he fled, be delivered up, to be removed to the State having Jurisdiction of the Crime.

No Person held to Service or Labour in one State, under the Laws thereof, escaping into another, shall, in Consequence of any Law or Regulation therein, be discharged from such Service or Labour, but shall be delivered up on Claim of the Party to whom such Service or Labour may be due.

Section 3 New States may be admitted by the Congress into this Union; but no new State shall be formed or erected within the Jurisdiction of any other State; nor any State be formed by the Junction of two or more States, or Parts of States, without the Consent of the Legislatures of the States concerned as well as of the Congress.

The Congress shall have Power to dispose of and make all needful Rules and Regulations respecting the Territory or other Property belonging to the United States; and nothing in this Constitution shall be so construed as to Prejudice any Claims of the United States, or of any particular State.

Section 4 The United States shall guarantee to every State in this Union a Republican Form of Government, and shall protect each of them against Invasion; and on Application of the Legislature, or of the Executive (when the Legislature cannot be convened) against domestic Violence.

ARTICLE V.

The Congress, whenever two thirds of both Houses shall deem it necessary, shall propose Amendments to this Constitution, or, on the Application of the Legislatures of two thirds of the several States, shall call a Convention for proposing Amendments, which, in either Case, shall be valid to all Intents and Purposes, as Part of this Constitution, when ratified by the Legislatures of three fourths of the several States, or by Conventions in three fourths thereof, as the one or the other Mode of Ratification may be proposed by the Congress; Provided that *no Amendment which may be made prior to the Year One thousand eight hundred and eight shall in any Manner affect the first and fourth Clauses in the Ninth Section of the first Article; and* that no State, without its Consent, shall be deprived of its equal Suffrage in the Senate.

ARTICLE VI.

All Debts contracted and Engagements entered into, before the Adoption of this Constitution, shall be as valid against the United States under this Constitution, as under the Confederation.

This Constitution, and the Laws of the United States which shall be made in Pursuance thereof; and all Treaties made or which shall be made, under the Authority of the United States, shall be the supreme Law of the Land; and the Judges in every State shall be bound thereby, any Thing in the Constitution or Laws of any State to the Contrary notwithstanding.

The Senators and Representatives before mentioned, and the Members of the several State Legislatures, and all executive and judicial Officers, both of the United States and of the several States, shall be bound by Oath or Affirmation, to support this Constitution; but no religious Test shall ever be required as a Qualification to any Office or public Trust under the United States.

ARTICLE VII.

The Ratification of the Conventions of nine States, shall be sufficient for the Establishment of this Constitution between the States so ratifying the Same.

Done in Convention by the Unanimous Consent of the States present the Seventeenth Day of September in the Year of our Lord one thousand seven hundred and Eighty seven and of the Independence of the United States of America the Twelfth IN WITNESS whereof We have hereunto subscribed our Names, ■

GEORGE WASHINGTON,
President and Deputy from Virginia

North Carolina
WILLIAM BLOUNT
RICHARD DOBBS SPRAIGHT
HU WILLIAMSON

Pennsylvania
BENJAMIN FRANKLIN
THOMAS MIFFLIN
ROBERT MORRIS
GEORGE CLYMER
THOMAS FITZSIMONS
JARED INGERSOLL
JAMES WILSON
GOUVERNEUR MORRIS

Delaware
GEORGE READ
GUNNING BEDFORD, JR.
JOHN DICKINSON
RICHARD BASSETT
JACOB BROOM

South Carolina
J. RUTLEDGE
CHARLES C. PINCKNEY
PIERCE BUTLER

Virginia
JOHN BLAIR
JAMES MADISON, JR.

New Jersey
WILLIAM LIVINGSTON
DAVID BREARLEY
WILLIAM PATERSON
JONATHAN DAYTON

Maryland
JAMES MCHENRY
DANIEL OF ST. THOMAS JENIFER
DANIEL CARROLL

Massachusetts
NATHANIEL GORHAM
RUFUS KING

Connecticut
WILLIAM S. JOHNSON
ROGER SHERMAN

New York
ALEXANDER HAMILTON

New Hampshire
JOHN LANGDON
NICHOLAS GILMAN

Georgia
WILLIAM FEW
ABRAHAM BALDWIN

Amendments to the Constitution

AMENDMENT I

Congress shall make no law respecting an establishment of religion, or prohibiting the free exercise thereof; or abridging the freedom of speech, or of the press; or the right of the people peaceably to assemble, and to petition the Government for a redress of grievances.

AMENDMENT II

A well regulated Militia, being necessary to the security of a free State, the right of the people to keep and bear Arms, shall not be infringed.

AMENDMENT III

No Soldier shall, in time of peace be quartered in any house, without the consent of the Owner, nor in time of war, but in a manner to be prescribed by law.

AMENDMENT IV

The right of the people to be secure in their persons, houses, papers, and effects, against unreasonable searches and seizures, shall not be violated, and no Warrants shall issue, but upon probable cause, supported by Oath or affirmation, and particularly describing the place to be searched, and the persons or things to be seized.

AMENDMENT V

No person shall be held to answer for a capital, or otherwise infamous crime, unless on a presentment or indictment of a Grand Jury, except in cases arising in the land or naval forces, or in the Militia, when in actual service in time of War or public danger; nor shall any person be subject for the same offence to be twice put in jeopardy of life or limb; nor shall be compelled in any criminal case to be a witness against himself, nor be deprived of life, liberty, or property, without due process of law; nor shall private property be taken for public use, without just compensation.

AMENDMENT VI

In all criminal prosecutions, the accused shall enjoy the right to a speedy and public trial, by an impartial jury of the State and district wherein the crime shall have been committed, which district shall have been previously ascertained by law, and to be informed of the nature and cause of the accusation; to be confronted with the witnesses against him; to have compulsory process for obtaining witnesses in his favor, and to have the Assistance of Counsel for his defence.

AMENDMENT VII

In Suits at common law, where the value in controversy shall exceed twenty dollars, the right of trial by jury shall be preserved, and no fact tried by a jury, shall be otherwise re-examined in any Court of the United States, than according to the rules of the common law.

AMENDMENT VIII

Excessive bail shall not be required, nor excessive fines imposed, nor cruel and unusual punishments inflicted.

AMENDMENT IX

The enumeration in the Constitution, of certain rights, shall not be construed to deny or disparage others retained by the people.

AMENDMENT X

The powers not delegated to the United States by the Constitution, nor prohibited by it to the States, are reserved to the States respectively, or to the people.

AMENDMENT XI [ADOPTED 1798]

The Judicial power of the United States shall not be construed to extend to any suit in law or equity, commenced or prosecuted against one of the United States by Citizens of another State, or by Citizens or Subjects of any Foreign State.

AMENDMENT XII [ADOPTED 1804]

The Electors shall meet in their respective states, and vote by ballot for President and Vice-President, one of whom, at least, shall not be an inhabitant of the same state with themselves; they shall name in their ballots the person voted for as President, and in distinct ballots the person voted for as Vice-President, and they shall make distinct lists of all persons voted for as President, and of all persons voted for as Vice-President, and of the number of votes for each, which list they shall sign and certify, and transmit sealed to the seat of the government of the United States, directed to the President of the Senate;—The President of the Senate shall, in the presence of the Senate and House of Representatives, open all the certificates and the votes shall then be counted;—The person having the greatest number of votes for President, shall be the President, if such number be a majority of the whole number of Electors appointed; and if no person have such majority, then from the persons having the highest numbers not exceeding three on the list of those voted for as President, the House of Representatives shall choose immediately, by ballot, the President. But in choosing the President, the votes shall be taken by states, the representation from each state having one vote; a quorum for this purpose shall consist of a member or members from two thirds of the states, and a majority of all the states shall be necessary to a choice. And if the House of Representatives shall not choose a President whenever the right of choice shall devolve upon them, before the *fourth day of March* next following, then the Vice-President shall act as President, as in the case of the death or other constitutional disability of the President.

The person having the greatest number of votes as Vice-President, shall be the Vice-President, if such number be a majority of the whole number of Electors appointed, and if no person have a majority, then from the two highest numbers on the list, the Senate shall choose the Vice-President; a quorum for the purpose shall consist of two thirds of the whole number of Senators, and a majority of the whole number shall be necessary to a choice. But no person constitutionally ineligible to the office of President shall be eligible to that of Vice-President of the United States.

AMENDMENT XIII [ADOPTED 1865]

Section 1 Neither slavery nor involuntary servitude, except as a punishment for crime whereof the party shall have been duly convicted, shall exist within the United States, or any place subject to their jurisdiction.

Section 2 Congress shall have power to enforce this article by appropriate legislation.

AMENDMENT XIV [ADOPTED 1868]

Section 1 All persons born or naturalized in the United States, and subject to the jurisdiction thereof, are citizens of the United States and of the State wherein they reside. No State shall make or enforce any law which shall abridge the privileges or immunities of citizens of the United States; nor shall any State deprive any person of life, liberty, or property, without due process of law; nor deny to any person within its jurisdiction the equal protection of the laws.

Section 2 Representatives shall be apportioned among the several States according to their respective numbers, counting the whole number of persons in each State, excluding Indians not taxed. But when the right to vote at any election for the choice of electors for President and Vice-President of the United States, Representatives in Congress, the Executive and Judicial officers of a State, or the members of the Legislature thereof, is denied to any of the male inhabitants of such State, being twenty-one years of age, and citizens of the United States, or in any way abridged, except for participation in rebellion, or other crime, the basis of representation therein shall be reduced in the proportion which the number of such male citizens shall bear to the whole number of male citizens twenty-one years of age in such State.

Section 3 No person shall be a Senator or Representative in Congress, or elector of President and Vice-President, or hold any office, civil or military, under the United States, or under any State, who, having previously taken an oath, as a member of Congress, or as an officer of the United States, or as a member of any State legislature, or as an executive or judicial officer of any State, to support the Constitution of the United States, shall have engaged in insurrection or rebellion against the same, or given aid or comfort to the enemies thereof. But Congress may by a vote of two thirds of each House, remove such disability.

Section 4 The validity of the public debt of the United States, authorized by law, including debts incurred for payment of pensions and bounties for services in suppressing insurrection or rebellion, shall not be questioned. But neither the United States nor any State shall assume or pay any debt or obligation incurred in aid of insurrection or rebellion against the United States, or any claim for the loss or emancipation of any slave; but all such debts, obligations and claims shall be held illegal and void.

Section 5 The Congress shall have power to enforce, by appropriate legislation, the provisions of this article.

AMENDMENT XV [ADOPTED 1870]

Section 1 The right of citizens of the United States to vote shall not be denied or abridged by the United States or by any State on account of race, color, or previous condition of servitude.

Section 2 The Congress shall have power to enforce this article by appropriate legislation.

AMENDMENT XVI [ADOPTED 1913]

The Congress shall have power to lay and collect taxes on incomes, from whatever source derived, without apportionment among the several States, and without regard to any census or enumeration.

AMENDMENT XVII [ADOPTED 1913]

The Senate of the United States shall be composed of two Senators from each State, elected by the people thereof, for six years; and each Senator shall have one vote. The electors in each State shall have the qualifications requisite for electors of the most numerous branch of the State legislatures.

When vacancies happen in the representation of any State in the Senate, the executive authority of such State shall issue writs of election to fill such vacancies: *Provided,* That the legislature of any State may empower the executive thereof to make temporary appointments until the people fill the vacancies by election as the legislature may direct.

This amendment shall not be so construed as to affect the election or term of any Senator chosen before it becomes valid as part of the Constitution.

AMENDMENT XVIII [ADOPTED 1919; REPEALED 1933]

Section 1 After one year from the ratification of this article the manufacture, sale, or transportation of intoxicating liquors within, the importation thereof into, or the exportation thereof from the United States and all territory subject to the jurisdiction thereof for beverage purposes is hereby prohibited.

Section 2 The Congress and the several States shall have concurrent power to enforce this article by appropriate legislation.

Section 3 This article shall be inoperative unless it shall have been ratified as an amendment to the Constitution by the legislatures of the several States, as provided in the Constitution, within seven years from the date of the submission hereof to the States by the Congress.

AMENDMENT XIX [ADOPTED 1920]

Section 1 The right of citizens of the United States to vote shall not be denied or abridged by the United States or by any State on account of sex.

Section 2 Congress shall have power to enforce this article by appropriate legislation.

AMENDMENT XX [ADOPTED 1933]

Section 1 The terms of the President and Vice-President shall end at noon on the 20th day of January, and the terms of Senators and Representatives at noon on the third day of January, of the years in which such terms would have ended if this article had not been ratified; and the terms of their successors shall then begin.

Section 2 The Congress shall assemble at least once in every year, and such meeting shall begin at noon on the third day of January, unless they shall by law appoint a different day.

Section 3 If, at the time fixed for the beginning of the term of the President, the President elect shall have died, the Vice-President elect shall become President. If a President shall not have been chosen before the time fixed for the beginning of his term, or if the President elect shall have failed to qualify, then the Vice-President elect shall act as President until a President shall have qualified; and the Congress may by law provide for the case wherein neither a President elect nor a Vice-President elect shall have qualified, declaring who shall then act as President, or the manner in which one who is to act shall be selected, and such person shall act accordingly until a President or Vice-President shall have qualified.

Section 4 The Congress may by law provide for the case of the death of any of the persons from whom the House of Representatives may choose a President whenever the right of choice shall have devolved upon them, and for the case of the death of any of the persons from whom the Senate may choose a Vice-President whenever the right of choice shall have devolved upon them.

Section 5 Sections 1 and 2 shall take effect on the 15th day of October following the ratification of this article.

Section 6 This article shall be inoperative unless it shall have been ratified as an amendment to the Constitution by the legislatures of three fourths of the several States within seven years from the date of its submission.

AMENDMENT XXI [ADOPTED 1933]

Section 1 The eighteenth article of amendment to the Constitution of the United States is hereby repealed.

Section 2 The transportation or importation into any State, Territory, or possession of the United States for delivery or use therein of intoxicating liquors, in violation of the laws thereof, is hereby prohibited.

Section 3 This article shall be inoperative unless it shall have been ratified as an amendment to the Constitution by conventions in the several States, as provided in the Constitution, within seven years from the date of the submission hereof to the States by the Congress.

AMENDMENT XXII [ADOPTED 1951]

Section 1 No person shall be elected to the office of the President more than twice, and no person who has held the office of President, or acted as President, for more than two years of a term to which some other person was elected President shall be elected to the office of the President more than once. But this Article shall not apply to any person holding the office of President when this Article was proposed by the Congress, and shall not prevent any person who may be holding the office of President, or acting as President, during the term within which this Article becomes operative from holding the office of President or acting as President during the remainder of such term.

Section 2 This article shall be inoperative unless it shall have been ratified as an amendment to the Constitution by the legislatures of three fourths of the several States within seven years from the date of its submission to the States by the Congress.

AMENDMENT XXIII [ADOPTED 1961]

Section 1 The District constituting the seat of Government of the United States shall appoint in such manner as the Congress may direct:

A number of electors of President and Vice-President equal to the whole number of Senators and Representatives in Congress to which the District would be entitled if it were a State, but in no event more than the least populous State; they shall be in addition to those appointed by the States, but they shall be considered, for the purposes of the election of President and Vice-President, to be electors appointed by a State; and they shall meet in the District and perform such duties as provided by the twelfth article of amendment.

Section 2 The Congress shall have power to enforce this article by appropriate legislation.

AMENDMENT XXIV [ADOPTED 1964]

Section 1 The right of citizens of the United States to vote in any primary or other election for President or Vice-President, for electors for President or Vice-President, or for Senator or Representative in Congress, shall not be denied or abridged by the United States or any State by reason of failure to pay any poll tax or other tax.

Section 2 The Congress shall have power to enforce this article by appropriate legislation.

AMENDMENT XXV [ADOPTED 1967]

Section 1 In case of the removal of the President from office or his death or resignation, the Vice-President shall become President.

Section 2 Whenever there is a vacancy in the office of the Vice-President, the President shall nominate a Vice-President who shall take the office upon confirmation by a majority vote of both houses of Congress.

Section 3   Whenever the President transmits to the President pro tempore of the Senate and the Speaker of the House of Representatives his written declaration that he is unable to discharge the powers and duties of his office, and until he transmits to them a written declaration to the contrary, such powers and duties shall be discharged by the Vice-President as Acting President.

Section 4   Whenever the Vice-President and a majority of either the principal officers of the executive departments, or of such other body as Congress may by law provide, transmit to the President pro tempore of the Senate and the Speaker of the House of Representatives their written declaration that the President is unable to discharge the powers and duties of his office, the Vice-President shall immediately assume the powers and duties of the office as Acting President.

Thereafter, when the President transmits to the President pro tempore of the Senate and the Speaker of the House of Representatives his written declaration that no inability exists, he shall resume the powers and duties of his office unless the Vice-President and a majority of either the principal officers of the executive department, or of such other body as Congress may by law provide, transmit within four days to the President pro tempore of the Senate and the Speaker of the House of Representatives their written declaration that the President is unable to discharge the powers and duties of his office. Thereupon Congress shall decide the issue, assembling within 48 hours for that purpose if not in session. If the Congress, within 21 days after receipt of the latter written declaration, or, if Congress is not in session, within 21 days after Congress is required to assemble, determines by two-thirds vote of both houses that the President is unable to discharge the powers and duties of his office, the Vice-President shall continue to discharge the same as Acting President; otherwise, the President shall resume the powers and duties of his office.

AMENDMENT XXVI [ADOPTED 1971]

Section 1   The right of citizens of the United States, who are eighteen years of age or older, to vote shall not be denied or abridged by the United States or any state on account of age.

Section 2   The Congress shall have power to enforce this article by appropriate legislation.

AMENDMENT XXVII [ADOPTED 1992]

No law, varying the compensation for the services of Senators and Representatives, shall take effect until an election of Representatives have intervened. ■

Year	Candidates	Parties	Popular Vote	Electoral Vote	Voter Participation
1789	GEORGE WASHINGTON		*	69	
	John Adams			34	
	Others			35	
1792	GEORGE WASHINGTON		*	132	
	John Adams			77	
	George Clinton			50	
	Others			5	
1796	JOHN ADAMS	Federalist	*	71	
	Thomas Jefferson	Democratic-Republican		68	
	Thomas Pinckney	Federalist		59	
	Aaron Burr	Dem.-Rep.		30	
	Others			48	
1800	THOMAS JEFFERSON	Dem.-Rep.	*	73	
	Aaron Burr	Dem.-Rep.		73	
	C. C. Pinckney	Federalist		64	
	John Jay	Federalist		1	
1804	THOMAS JEFFERSON	Dem.-Rep.	*	122	
	C. C. Pinckney	Federalist		14	
1808	JAMES MADISON	Dem.-Rep.	*	122	
	C. C. Pinckney	Federalist		47	
	George Clinton	Dem.-Rep.		6	
1812	JAMES MADISON	Dem.-Rep.	*	128	
	De Witt Clinton	Federalist		89	
1816	JAMES MONROE	Dem.-Rep.	*	183	
	Rufus King	Federalist		34	
1820	JAMES MONROE	Dem.-Rep.	*	231	
	John Quincy Adams	Dem.-Rep.		1	
1824	JOHN Q. ADAMS	Dem.-Rep.	108,740 (10.5%)	84	26.9%
	Andrew Jackson	Dem.-Rep.	153,544 (43.1%)	99	
	William H. Crawford	Dem.-Rep.	46,618 (13.1%)	41	
	Henry Clay	Dem.-Rep.	47,136 (13.2%)	37	
1828	ANDREW JACKSON	Democratic	647,286 (56.0%)	178	57.6%
	John Quincy Adams	National Republican	508,064 (44.0%)	83	
1832	ANDREW JACKSON	Democratic	687,502 (55.0%)	219	55.4%
	Henry Clay	National Republican	530,189 (42.4%)	49	
	John Floyd	Independent		11	
	William Wirt	Anti-Mason	33,108 (2.6%)	7	
1836	MARTIN VAN BUREN	Democratic	765,483 (50.9%)	170	57.8%
	W. H. Harrison	Whig		73	

*Electors elected by state legislators.

Year	Candidates	Parties	Popular Vote	Electoral Vote	Voter Participation
	Hugh L. White	Whig	739,795 (49.1%)	26	
	Daniel Webster	Whig		14	
	W. P. Magnum	Independent		11	
1840	WILLIAM H. HARRISON	Whig	1,274,624 (53.1%)	234	80.2%
	Martin Van Buren	Democratic	1,127,781 (46.9%)	60	
	J. G. Birney	Liberty	7,069	—	
1844	JAMES K. POLK	Democratic	1,338,464 (49.6%)	170	78.9%
	Henry Clay	Whig	1,300,097 (48.1%)	105	
	J. G. Birney	Liberty	62,300 (2.3%)	—	
1848	ZACHARY TAYLOR	Whig	1,360,967 (47.4%)	163	72.7%
	Lewis Cass	Democratic	1,222,342 (42.5%)	127	
	Martin Van Buren	Free-Soil	291,263 (10.1%)	—	
1852	FRANKLIN PIERCE	Democratic	1,601,117 (50.9%)	254	69.6%
	Winfield Scott	Whig	1,385,453 (44.1%)	42	
	John P. Hale	Free-Soil	155,825 (5.0%)	—	
1856	JAMES BUCHANAN	Democratic	1,832,955 (45.3%)	174	78.9%
	John C. Fremont	Republican	1,339,932 (33.1%)	114	
	Millard Fillmore	American	871,731 (21.6%)	8	
1860	ABRAHAM LINCOLN	Republican	1,865,593 (39.8%)	180	81.2%
	Stephen A. Douglas	Democratic	1,382,713 (29.5%)	12	
	John C. Breckinridge	Democratic	848,356 (18.1%)	72	
	John Bell	Union	592,906 (12.6%)	39	
1864	ABRAHAM LINCOLN	Republican	2,213,655 (55.0%)	212	73.8%
	George B. McClellan	Democratic	1,805,237 (45.0%)	21	
1868	ULYSSES S. GRANT	Republican	3,012,833 (52.7%)	214	78.1%
	Horatio Seymour	Democratic	2,703,249 (47.3%)	80	
1872	ULYSSES S. GRANT	Republican	3,597,132 (55.6%)	286	71.3%
	Horace Greeley	Democratic; Liberal Republican	2,834,125 (43.9%)	66	
1876	RUTHERFORD B. HAYES	Republican	4,036,298 (48.0%)	185	81.8%
	Samuel J. Tilden	Democratic	4,300,590 (51.0%)	184	
1880	JAMES A. GARFIELD	Republican	4,454,416 (48.5%)	214	79.4%
	Winfield S. Hancock	Democratic	4,444,952 (48.1%)	155	
1884	GROVER CLEVELAND	Democratic	4,874,986 (48.5%)	219	77.5%
	James G. Blaine	Republican	4,851,981 (48.2%)	182	
1888	BENJAMIN HARRISON	Republican	5,439,853 (47.9%)	233	79.3%
	Grover Cleveland	Democratic	5,540,309 (48.6%)	168	
1892	GROVER CLEVELAND	Democratic	5,556,918 (46.1%)	277	74.7%
	Benjamin Harrison	Republican	5,176,108 (43.0%)	145	
	James B. Weaver	People's	1,041,028 (8.5%)	22	

Year	Candidates	Parties	Popular Vote	Electoral Vote	Voter Participation
1896	WILLIAM McKINLEY	Republican	7,104,779 (51.1%)	271	79.3%
	William J. Bryan	Democratic People's	6,502,925 (47.7%)	176	
1900	WILLIAM McKINLEY	Republican	7,207,923 (51.7%)	292	73.2%
	William J. Bryan	Dem.-Populist	6,358,133 (45.5%)	155	
1904	THEODORE ROOSEVELT	Republican	7,623,486 (57.9%)	336	65.2%
	Alton B. Parker	Democratic	5,077,911 (37.6%)	140	
	Eugene V. Debs	Socialist	402,283 (3.0%)	—	
1908	WILLIAM H. TAFT	Republican	7,678,908 (51.6%)	321	65.4%
	William J. Bryan	Democratic	6,409,104 (43.1%)	162	
	Eugene V. Debs	Socialist	420,793 (2.8%)	—	
1912	WOODROW WILSON	Democratic	6,293,454 (41.9%)	435	58.8%
	Theodore Roosevelt	Progressive	4,119,538 (27.4%)	88	
	William H. Taft	Republican	3,484,980 (23.2%)	8	
	Eugene V. Debs	Socialist	900,672 (6.0%)	—	
1916	WOODROW WILSON	Democratic	9,129,606 (49.4%)	277	61.6%
	Charles E. Hughes	Republican	8,538,221 (46.2%)	254	
	A. L. Benson	Socialist	585,113 (3.2%)	—	
1920	WARREN G. HARDING	Republican	16,152,200 (60.4%)	404	49.2%
	James M. Cox	Democratic	9,147,353 (34.2%)	127	
	Eugene V. Debs	Socialist	919,799 (3.4%)	—	
1924	CALVIN COOLIDGE	Republican	15,725,016 (54.0%)	382	48.9%
	John W. Davis	Democratic	8,386,503 (28.8%)	136	
	Robert M. La Follette	Progressive	4,822,856 (16.6%)	13	
1928	HERBERT HOOVER	Republican	21,391,381 (58.2%)	444	56.9%
	Alfred E. Smith	Democratic	15,016,443 (40.9%)	87	
	Norman Thomas	Socialist	267,835 (0.7%)	—	
1932	FRANKLIN D. ROOSEVELT	Democratic	22,821,857 (57.4%)	472	56.9%
	Herbert Hoover	Republican	15,761,841 (39.7%)	59	
	Norman Thomas	Socialist	881,951 (2.2%)	—	
1936	FRANKLIN D. ROOSEVELT	Democratic	27,751,597 (60.8%)	523	61.0%
	Alfred M. Landon	Republican	16,679,583 (36.5%)	8	
	William Lemke	Union	882,479 (1.9%)	—	
1940	FRANKLIN D. ROOSEVELT	Democratic	27,244,160 (54.8%)	449	62.5%
	Wendell L. Willkie	Republican	22,305,198 (44.8%)	82	
1944	FRANKLIN D. ROOSEVELT	Democrat	25,602,504 (53.5%)	432	55.9%
	Thomas E. Dewey	Republican	22,006,285 (46.0%)	99	
1948	HARRY S TRUMAN	Democratic	24,105,695 (49.5%)	304	53.0%
	Thomas E. Dewey	Republican	21,969,170 (45.1%)	189	
	J. Strom Thurmond	State-Rights Democratic	1,169,021 (2.4%)	38	
	Henry A. Wallace	Progressive	1,156,103 (2.4%)	—	
1952	DWIGHT D. EISENHOWER	Republican	33,936,252 (55.1%)	442	63.3%
	Adlai E. Stevenson	Democratic	27,314,992 (44.4%)	89	

Year	Candidates	Parties	Popular Vote	Electoral Vote	Voter Participation
1956	DWIGHT D. EISENHOWER	Republican	35,575,420 (57.6%)	457	60.5%
	Adlai E. Stevenson	Democratic	26,033,066 (42.1%)	73	
	Other	—	—	1	
1960	JOHN F. KENNEDY	Democratic	34,227,096 (49.9%)	303	62.8%
	Richard M. Nixon	Republican	34,108,546 (49.6%)	219	
	Other	—	—	15	
1964	LYNDON B. JOHNSON	Democratic	43,126,506 (61.1%)	486	61.7%
	Barry M. Goldwater	Republican	27,176,799 (38.5%)	52	
1968	RICHARD M. NIXON	Republican	31,770,237 (43.4.%)	301	60.6%
	Hubert H. Humphrey	Democratic	31,270,633 (42.7%)	191	
	George Wallace	American Indep.	9,906,141 (13.5%)	46	
1972	RICHARD M. NIXON	Republican	47,169,911 (60.7%)	520	55.2%
	George S. McGovern	Democratic	29,170,383 (37.5%)	17	
	Other	—	—	1	
1976	JIMMY CARTER	Democratic	40,828,587 (50.0%)	297	53.5%
	Gerald R. Ford	Republican	39,147,613 (47.9%)	241	
	Other	—	1,575,459 (2.1%)	—	
1980	RONALD REAGAN	Republican	43,901,812 (50.7%)	489	52.6%
	Jimmy Carter	Democratic	35,483,820 (41.0%)	49	
	John B. Anderson	Independent	5,719,722 (6.6%)	—	
	Ed Clark	Libertarian	921,188 (1.1%)	—	
1984	RONALD REAGAN	Republican	54,455,075 (59.0%)	525	53.3%
	Walter Mondale	Democratic	37,577,185 (41.0%)	13	
1988	GEORGE H. W. BUSH	Republican	48,886,000 (45.6%)	426	57.4%
	Michael S. Dukakis	Democratic	41,809,000 (45.6%)	111	
1992	WILLIAM J. CLINTON	Democratic	43,728,375 (43%)	370	55.0%
	George H. W. Bush	Republican	38,167,416 (38%)	168	
	Ross Perot	—	19,237,247 (19%)	—	
1996	WILLIAM J. CLINTON	Democratic	45,590,703 (50%)	379	48.8%
	Robert Dole	Republican	37,816,307 (41%)	159	
	Ross Perot	Independent	7,866,284 (9%)		
2000	GEORGE W. BUSH	Republican	50,456,062 (47%)	271	51.0%
	Albert Gore	Democratic	50,996,582 (49%)	267	
	Ralph Nader	Independent	2,858,843 (3%)	—	
2004	GEORGE W. BUSH	Republican	60,934,251 (51%)	286	
	John F. Kerry	Democrat	57,765,291 (48%)	252	
	Ralph Nader	Independent	405,933 (0%)	—	

States of the United States

State	Date of Admission	State	Date of Admission
Delaware	December 7, 1787	Michigan	January 16, 1837
Pennsylvania	December 12, 1787	Florida	March 3, 1845
New Jersey	December 18, 1787	Texas	December 29, 1845
Georgia	January 2, 1788	Iowa	December 28, 1846
Connecticut	January 9, 1788	Wisconsin	May 29, 1848
Massachusetts	February 6, 1788	California	September 9, 1850
Maryland	April 28, 1788	Minnesota	May 11, 1858
South Carolina	May 23, 1788	Oregon	February 14, 1859
New Hampshire	June 21, 1788	Kansas	January 29, 1861
Virginia	June 25, 1788	West Virginia	June 19, 1863
New York	July 26, 1788	Nevada	October 31, 1864
North Carolina	November 21, 1789	Nebraska	March 1, 1867
Rhode Island	May 29, 1790	Colorado	August 1, 1876
Vermont	March 4, 1791	North Dakota	November 2, 1889
Kentucky	June 1, 1792	South Dakota	November 2, 1889
Tennessee	June 1, 1796	Montana	November 8, 1889
Ohio	March 1, 1803	Washington	November 11, 1889
Louisiana	April 30, 1812	Idaho	July 3, 1890
Indiana	December 11, 1816	Wyoming	July 10, 1890
Mississippi	December 10, 1817	Utah	January 4, 1896
Illinois	December 3, 1818	Oklahoma	November 16, 1907
Alabama	December 14, 1819	New Mexico	January 6, 1912
Maine	March 15, 1820	Arizona	February 14, 1912
Missouri	August 10, 1821	Alaska	January 3, 1959
Arkansas	June 15, 1836	Hawaii	August 21, 1959

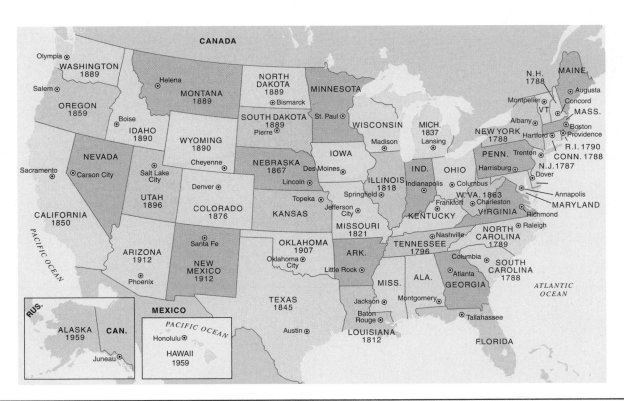

Population of the United States

Year	Number of States	Population	Percent Increase	Population per Square Mile
1790	13	3,929,214		4.5
1800	16	5,308,483	35.1	6.1
1810	17	7,239,881	36.4	4.3
1820	23	9,638,453	33.1	5.5
1830	24	12,866,020	33.5	7.4
1840	26	17,069,453	32.7	9.8
1850	31	23,191,876	35.9	7.9
1860	33	31,443,321	35.6	10.6
1870	37	39,818,449	26.6	13.4
1880	38	50,155,783	26.0	16.9
1890	44	62,947,714	25.5	21.2
1900	45	75,994,575	20.7	25.6
1910	46	91,972,266	21.0	31.0
1920	48	105,710,620	14.9	35.6
1930	48	122,775,046	16.1	41.2
1940	48	131,669,275	7.2	44.2
1950	48	150,697,361	14.5	50.7
1960	50	179,323,175	19.0	50.6
1970	50	203,235,298	13.3	57.5
1980	50	226,545,805	11.5	64.1
1990	50	248,709,873	9.8	70.3
2000	50	281,421,906	13.0	77.0

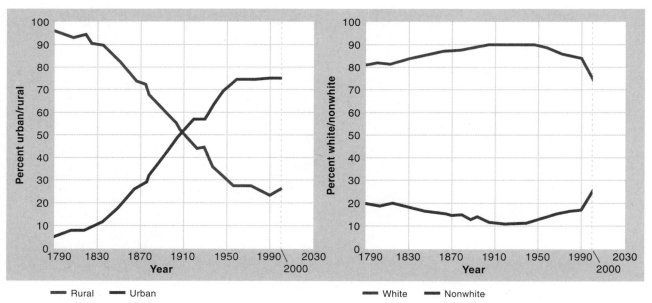

Source: U.S. Bureau of the Census estimates